Fodor's 2019

ESSENTIAL
SPAIN

WELCOME TO SPAIN

Spain conjures images of flamenco dancers, café-lined plazas, white hillside villages, and soaring cathedrals. Beyond these traditional associations, this modern country offers top-notch art museums, inventive cuisine, and exciting nightlife. From the Pyrenees to the coast, its landscapes and varied cultures are worth exploring. Especially enticing is the national insistence on enjoying everyday pleasures. The Spanish live life to its fullest whether they are strolling in the park, pausing for a siesta, lingering over lunch, or dancing until dawn.

TOP REASONS TO GO

★ **Cool Cities:** Barcelona, Madrid, Seville, Granada, Valencia, Bilbao, San Sebastián, and Salamanca.

★ **Amazing Architecture:** From the Moorish Alhambra to Gaudí's eclectic Sagrada Família.

★ **History:** From Segovia's Roman aqueduct to Córdoba's Mezquita, history comes alive.

★ **Superlative Art:** Masterpieces by Goya, El Greco, Picasso, Dalí, and Miró thrill.

★ **Tapas and Wine:** Spain's justly famed small bites pair perfectly with its Riojas.

★ **Beautiful Beaches:** From Barcelona's city beaches to Ibiza's celebrated strands.

1 Park Güell

A sweeping view of Barcelona awaits you at this architectural park, Gaudí's pièce de résistance in urban planning. Peer out from the mosaic benches over gingerbread-like houses and fountains guarded by giant tiled lizards. *(Ch. 7)*

2 Picos de Europa

A national park where you can hike between lakes, meadows, and snowy peaks, this mountain range on Spain's northern coast is a choice adventure for outdoorsy types. *(Ch. 4)*

3 Gorgeous Cathedrals

Towering temples in cities including Sevilla, León, and Burgos have been presided over by bishops for centuries and are some of the greatest marvels in Spain. *(Ch. 3)*

4 Food tours

Take a delicious dive into Spanish culture by trying dishes like tortilla española (Spanish potato omelet) and paella with a local guide who knows the best haunts. *(Ch. 1)*

5 Guggenheim Bilbao

Thought-provoking works by artists like Mark Rothko and Andy Warhol will entrance you at Bilbao's riverfront museum, a titanium work of art itself. *(Ch. 5)*

6 Beaches

You can't go wrong on the Iberian Peninsula, where you can choose between the sun-drenched beaches of the Mediterranean and the wild, brisk shores of the Atlantic. *(Ch. 7, 9. 10, 11)*

7 Flamenco

A foot-stomping whirlwind of click-clacking castanets, guitar solos, and gut-wrenching vocals will have you shouting "¡Olé!" at the tablaos (flamenco venues) of Sevilla. *(Ch. 10)*

8 El Escorial

A leisurely day trip from the hustle and bustle of Madrid, this medieval town's main attraction is a gargantuan royal residence set high on a hill. *(Ch. 2)*

9 Córdoba Mosque

The ancient Mezquita's engraved columns and candy cane-striped double arches are an enchanting reminder of Andalusia's 10th century Islamic grandeur. *(Ch. 10)*

10 Barri Gòtic

Barcelona's most ancient quarter is a maze of cobblestone streets and stone arcades that empty into medieval plaças. It also boasts some of the city's chicest boutiques. *(Ch. 7)*

11 Rioja wine caves

Don't miss the bodegas in Haro, in the heart of Rioja Alta, for their centuries of history and mysterious cellars, draped with penicillin mold and cobwebs, or calados. *(Ch. 5)*

12 Mérida

Tour the remnants of an ancient Roman city, home to one of the best-preserved stone amphitheaters in Europe. The UNESCO site is the largest of its kind in Spain. *(Ch. 3)*

13 Canary Islands volcanoes

The tallest mountain in Spain is also an active volcano—and you can climb it. Make it to the peak of 12,000-foot El Teide, and you'll be rewarded with bird's-eye views.

14 Alhambra

Nothing epitomizes the Moors' power and ingenuity like this sprawling centuries-old fortress. Set aside a few hours to take in arched courtyards and intricate Arabesques. *(Ch. 10)*

15 Sagrada Família

Gaudí's iconic church is a soaring fantasy world of vivid stained glass and zoomorphic motifs. It is slated for completion in 2026 after 150 years of construction. *(Ch. 7)*

16 Toledo

When Toledo was the ancient capital of Spain, Muslims, Jews, and Christians cohabitated in harmony—hence the city's nickname, "City of Three Cultures." *(Ch. 3)*

17 Skiing

Some of the best slopes in western Europe (with reasonable ticket prices, no less) can be found in the Pyrenees, the mountain range Spain shares with France and Andorra. *(Ch. 6)*

18 Retiro Park

The tree-shaded trails, cafés, and French gardens here are an oasis right in Madrid's city center. Find the Palacio de Cristal, an impressive iron-and glass greenhouse. *(Ch. 2)*

19 Feria!

Vibrant ferias, or fairs, are some of the country's wildest parties, complete with traditional dance performances, carnival rides, street food, and makeshift discotecas. *(Ch. 10)*

20 Paradores

Want to hole up in a property with personality and a true sense of place? Look to Paradores, a state-run network of accommodations housed in historic buildings. *(Ch. 5)*

21 Cuenca's hanging houses

It doesn't get much more picturesque than these buildings perched on a cliffside overlooking the Huécar River. They seem to defy gravity as they jut over the ravine. *(Ch. 10)*

22 Museums in Madrid

Madrid's Golden Triangle is home to three world-class museums within blocks of each other. Don't miss Guernica at Museo Reina Sofia. *(Ch. 2)*

23 Segovia aqueduct

This work of Roman engineering has stood for more than 2,000 years—mind-boggling, considering that mortar is entirely absent from construction. *(Ch. 3)*

24 Pueblos blancos

Road trip through these stark white villages on Andalusian hilltops, one of southern Spain's most postcard-perfect attractions. *(Ch. 10)*

25 Santiago de Compostela

The best way to reach the Galician capital is the Walk of St. James, a thousand-year-old Christian pilgrimage—but you don't have to be religious to appreciate the hike. *(Ch. 4)*

Fodor's ESSENTIAL SPAIN 2019

Editorial: Douglas Stallings, *Editorial Director*; Margaret Kelly, Jacinta O'Halloran, *Senior Editors*; Kayla Becker, Alexis Kelly, Amanda Sadlowski, *Editors*; Teddy Minford, *Content Editor*; Rachael Roth, *Content Manager*

Design: Tina Malaney, *Design and Production Director*; Jessica Gonzalez, *Production Designer*

Photography: Jill Krueger, *Senior Photo Editor*

Maps: Rebecca Baer, *Senior Map Editor*; Mark Stroud (Moon Street Cartography), David Lindroth, *Cartographers*

Production: Jennifer DePrima, *Editorial Production Manager*; Carrie Parker, *Senior Production Editor*; Elyse Rozelle, *Production Editor*

Business & Operations: Chuck Hoover, *Chief Marketing Officer*; Joy Lai, *Vice President and General Manager*; Stephen Horowitz, *Director of Business Development and Revenue Operations*; Tara McCrillis, *Director of Publishing Operations*

Public Relations and Marketing: Joe Ewaskiw, *Manager;* Esther Su, *Marketing Manager*

Writers: Lauren Frayer, Benjamin Kemper, Malia Politzer, Elizabeth Prosser, Joanna Styles, Steven Tallantyre

Editors: Jacinta O'Halloran, Kayla Becker, Linda Cabasin

Production Editor: Jennifer DePrima

ISBN 978-1-64097-076-2

ISSN 2471–920X

Library of Congress Control Number 2018950374

All details in this book are based on information supplied to us at press time. Always confirm information when it matters, especially if you're making a detour to visit a specific place. Fodor's expressly disclaims any liability, loss, or risk, personal or otherwise, that is incurred as a consequence of the use of any of the contents of this book.

SPECIAL SALES

This book is available at special discounts for bulk purchases for sales promotions or premiums. For more information, e-mail SpecialMarkets@fodors.com.

PRINTED IN THE UNITED STATES OF AMERICA

10 9 8 7 6 5 4 3 2 1

CONTENTS

Fodor's Features

CONTENTS

CONTENTS

MAPS

CONTENTS

ABOUT
THIS GUIDE

Fodor's Recommendations

Everything in this guide is worth doing—we don't cover what isn't—but exceptional sights, hotels, and restaurants are recognized with additional accolades. Fodor'sChoice★ indicates our top recommendations. Care to nominate a new place? Visit Fodors.com/contact-us.

Trip Costs

We list prices wherever possible to help you budget well. Hotel and restaurant price categories from $ to $$$$ are noted alongside each recommendation. For hotels, we include the lowest cost of a standard double room in high season. For restaurants, we cite the average price of a main course at dinner or, if dinner isn't served, at lunch. For attractions, we always list adult admission fees; discounts are usually available for children, students, and senior citizens.

Hotels

Our local writers vet every hotel to recommend the best overnights in each price category, from budget to expensive. Unless otherwise specified, you can expect private bath, phone, and TV in your room. For expanded hotel reviews, facilities, and deals visit Fodors.com.

Top Picks	Hotels &
★ Fodor'sChoice	**Restaurants**
	🏨 Hotel
Listings	⤵ Number of
✉ Address	rooms
✉ Branch address	⫼ Meal plans
☎ Telephone	✕ Restaurant
🖷 Fax	⤢ Reservations
⊕ Website	🏛 Dress code
✍ E-mail	▭ No credit cards
🎫 Admission fee	$ Price
⊙ Open/closed	
times	**Other**
Ⓜ Subway	⇨ See also
✛ Directions or	☞ Take note
Map coordinates	🏌 Golf facilities

Restaurants

Unless we state otherwise, restaurants are open for lunch and dinner daily. We mention dress code only when there's a specific requirement and reservations only when they're essential or not accepted. To make restaurant reservations, visit Fodors.com.

Credit Cards

The hotels and restaurants in this guide typically accept credit cards. If not, we'll say so.

EUGENE FODOR

Hungarian-born Eugene Fodor (1905–91) began his travel career as an interpreter on a French cruise ship. The experience inspired him to write *On the Continent* (1936), the first guidebook to receive annual updates and discuss a country's way of life as well as its sights. Fodor later joined the U.S. Army and worked for the OSS in World War II. After the war, he kept up his intelligence work while expanding his guidebook series. During the Cold War, many guides were written by fellow agents who understood the value of insider information. Today's guides continue Fodor's legacy by providing travelers with timely coverage, insider tips, and cultural context.

EXPERIENCE SPAIN

WHAT'S WHERE

1 Madrid. Its boundless energy creates sights and sounds larger than life. The Prado, Reina Sofía, and Thyssen-Bornemisza museums make one of the greatest repositories of Western art in the world. The manicured gardens of Buen Retiro Park offer a respite from the busy porticoes of the cobblestoned Plaza Mayor, and the buzzing wine bars in the nearby Cava Baja and Plaza Santa Ana. Sunday's crowded flea market in El Rastro is thick with overpriced oddities.

2 Toledo and Trips from Madrid. From Madrid there are several important excursions, notably Toledo, as well as Segovia and Salamanca. Other cities in Castile–La Mancha and Castile–León worth visiting include León, Burgos, Soria, Sigüenza, Ávila, and Cuenca. Extremadura, Spain's remote borderland with Portugal, is often overlooked, but has some intriguing places to discover. Highlights include Cáceres, packed with medieval and Renaissance churches and palaces; Trujillo, lined with mansions of Spain's imperial age; Mérida, Spain's richest trove of Roman remains; and the Jerte Valley, which turns white in late March with a million cherry-tree blossoms.

3 Galicia and Asturias. On the way to Galicia to pay homage to St. James, pilgrims once crossed Europe to this corner of Spain so remote it was called *finis terrae* ("world's end"), and today Santiago de Compostela still resonates with mystic importance. In nearby Asturias, villages nestle in green highlands, backed by the snowcapped Picos de Europa mountains, while sandy beaches stretch out along the Atlantic. Farther east, in Cantabria, is the Belle Époque beach resort of Santander.

4 The Basque Country, Navarra, and La Rioja. The Basque region is a country within a country, proud of its own language and culture as well as the wild, dramatic coast of the Bay of Biscay. Nearby Navarra and La Rioja are famous for the running of the bulls in Pamplona and for excellent wines, respectively.

5 The Pyrenees. Cut by some 23 steep north–south valleys on the Spanish side alone, with four independent geographical entities—the valleys of Camprodón, Cerdanya, Aran, and Baztán— the Pyrenees have a wealth of areas to explore, with different cultures and languages, as well as world-class ski resorts.

Bay of Biscay

**BASQUE COUNTRY
(EUSKADI)**

Santander

*PIOS DE
EUROPA* **CANTABRIA**

San
Sebastián

Bilbao

FRANCE

Trevino

Pamplona

NAVARRA

ANDORRA

Burgos

Logroño

PYRENEES

Girona

Palencia

LA RIOJA

Huesca

CATALONIA

Soria

*COSTA
BRAVA*

Valladolid *Duero*

Zaragoza

Lleida

CASTILE–LEÓN

ARAGON

Barcelona

Segovia

Siguenza

Tarragona

Ávila

Tortosa *COSTA
DORADA*

MADRID

Tajo

Teruel

*Balearic
Sea*

Menorca

Toledo

Cuenca

Castellón
de la Plana

Aranjuez

COSTA DEL AZAHAR

**CASTILE–
LA MANCHA**

Alcázar
de San Juan

Requena

Valencia

Mallorca

*BALEARIC
ISLANDS*

Guadiana Ciudad Real

Jucar

VALENCIA

Ibiza

Valdepeñas

Albacete

Formentera

Segura

Alicante

COSTA BLANCA

Córdoba

MURCIA

Jaén

Murcia

Lorca

Cartagena

*Mediterranean
Sea*

ANDALUSIA

Granada

Antequera

Málaga

Almería

*COSTA DE
ALMERÍA*

COSTA DEL SOL

Melilla

MOROCCO

0   100 miles

0   150 km

WHAT'S WHERE

6 Barcelona. La Rambla, in the heart of the Ciutat Vella, is packed day and night with strollers, artists, street entertainers, vendors, and vamps, all preparing you for Barcelona's startling architectural landmarks. But treasures lie beyond the tourist path, including Antoni Gaudí's sinuous Casa Milà and unique Sagrada Família church, masterpieces of the Moderniste oeuvre.

7 Catalonia, Valencia, and the Costa Blanca. A cultural connection with France and Europe defines Catalonia. The mountain-backed plain of the Levante is dotted with Christian and Moorish landmarks and Roman ruins. Valencia's signature paella fortifies visitors touring the city's medieval masterpieces and modern architecture. The Costa Blanca has party-'til-dawn resort towns like Benidorm as well as villages that seem suspended in time. The rice paddies and orange groves of the Costa Blanca lead to the palm-fringed port city of Alicante.

8 Ibiza and the Balearic Islands. Ibiza still generates buzz as a summer playground for clubbers from all over, but even this isle has its quiet coves. Alternatively, much of Ibiza's rave-all-night crowd choose neighboring

Formentera as their chill-out daytime destination. Mallorca has some heavily touristed pockets, along with pristine mountain vistas in the island's interior. On serene Menorca, the two cities of Ciutadella and Mahón have different histories, cultures, and points of view.

9 Andalusia. Eight provinces—five of which are coastal (Huelva, Cádiz, Málaga, Granada, and Almería) and three of which are landlocked (Seville, Córdoba, and Jaén)— make up this southern autonomous community known for its Moorish influences. Highlights include the haunting Mezquita of Córdoba, Granada's romantic Alhambra, and seductive Seville. Andalusia is home to what's quintessentially Spanish: tapas and flamenco music.

10 Costa del Sol and Costa de Almería. With more than 320 days of sunshine a year, the costas are popular with Northern Europeans eager for a break from the cold. As a result, vast holiday resorts occupy much of the Mediterranean coast, although there are respites: Málaga is a vibrant city with world-class art museums; Marbella has a pristine Andalusian old quarter; and villages such as Casares seem immune to the goings-on along the water.

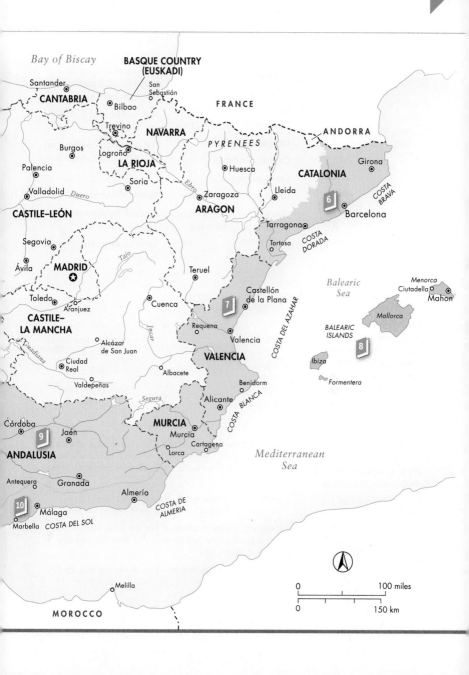

NEED TO KNOW

Bay of Biscay

Madrid

SPAIN

Mediterranean Sea

AT A GLANCE

Capital: Madrid

Population: 48,958,159

Currency: Euro

Money: ATMs are common, credit cards widely accepted

Language: Spanish

Country Code: 34

Emergencies: 112

Driving: On the right

Electricity: 220v/50 cycles; electrical plugs have two round prongs

Time: Six hours ahead of New York

Documents: Up to 90 days with valid passport; Schengen rules apply

Mobile Phones: GSM (900 and 1800 bands)

Major Mobile Companies: Movistar, Orange, Vodafone

WEBSITES

Spain: ⊕ www.spain.info

Spanish Paradores: ⊕ www.parador.es

Spanish Airports: ⊕ www.aena.es

GETTING AROUND

✈ **Air Travel:** The major airports for trans-Atlantic flights are Madrid and Barcelona, but many low-cost European flights head directly to coastal airports in Málaga, Alicante, Reus, and Girona.

🚌 **Bus Travel:** The best and cheapest way to get around, but beware of complicated journeys if you're traveling off the main tourist trail.

🚆 **Train Travel:** Fast AVE trains link Madrid with major cities like Barcelona, Toledo, Segovia, Valencia, Seville, Córdoba, and Málaga, but book early for the best fares. Slower, cheaper trains connect to Cáceres, Ávila, Granada, and Cádiz.

PLAN YOUR BUDGET

	HOTEL ROOM	MEAL	ATTRACTIONS
Low Budget	€60	€15	Centro de Arte Reina Sofía, €10
Mid Budget	€150	€30	Alhambra, €14
High Budget	€250	€100	Barça football match, €80

WAYS TO SAVE

Lunch on the *menú del día* . Take advantage of daily prix-fixe menus (which usually include a drink) offered at many bars and restaurants. Go off the tourist trail for the best values.

Book a rental apartment. For space and a kitchen, consider a furnished rental—a good bet for families.

Book rail tickets in advance. For the cheapest AVE rail fares, book online without a fee 90 days before travel (⊕ www.renfe.com).

Look for free museums. Many museums are free, and even those that aren't may be free at certain times of the week.

Hassle Factor	Low. Flights to Madrid are frequent, and the AVE takes you to most big cities quickly.
3 days	You can get a good feel for Madrid or Barcelona, and perhaps take a day trip out to Toledo or Bilbao.
1 week	Combine two or three days in Madrid with a trip to Andalusia to take in Seville and Granada, plus a day trip to Toledo.
2 weeks	You have time to center on Madrid and Barcelona for a few days each. In between, include a trip in Andalusia to soak up Spain's Moorish roots and take in the southern highlights, including the Alhambra and Córdoba's mosque.

WHEN TO GO

High Season: June through mid-September is the most expensive and popular time to visit the coast and islands; July and August are especially crowded. Inland cities are quieter but hot, and many businesses close for August. Sunshine is guaranteed almost everywhere, except in the north where weather is changeable.

Low Season: Winter offers the least appealing weather, though it's the best time for airfares and hotel deals. The Mediterranean coast can be balmy during the daytime, even in December—and there are no crowds—but nighttime temperatures drop.

Value Season: May, June, and September are lovely with warm weather, saner airfares, and good hotel offers. You can hang with the locals without the tourist crowds. October still has great weather, though temperatures start to fall by November. Bring an umbrella in March and April.

BIG EVENTS

February/March: Second only to Rio, Spain celebrates Carnival before Lent. Highlights are Santa Cruz de Tenerife and Cádiz.

March/April: Holy Week events range from solemn processions to enactments of the Passion throughout Spain.

April: Celebrations at Seville's Feria de Abril are a week of dance, song, and joie de vivre.

October: October 12 is the national day honoring Spain's patron, the Virgen del Pilar.

READ THIS

■ *For Whom the Bell Tolls,* Ernest Hemingway. A classic fictional account of the Spanish Civil War.

■ *Driving Over Lemons,* Chris Stewart. Humorous memoir by ex-drummer for the rock band Genesis, about buying a farm in Andalusia's Alpujarras mountains.

■ *The New Spaniards,* John Hooper. A portrait of modern Spain.

WATCH THIS

■ *Volver.* Rural and urban family feuds as seen by Pedro Almodóvar.

■ *Welcome, Mr. Marshall!* Luis García Berlanga's comedy about Spanish and American cultural misconceptions.

■ *Belle Époque.* Rural Spain in the liberal 1930s.

EAT THIS

■ *Churros*: deep-fried batter sticks great for dipping in hot chocolate

■ *Cocido*: a winter classic stew of pork, vegetables, and garbanzo beans

■ *Paella*: rice with meat (chicken, pork, or rabbit), fish, or shellfish

■ *Tortilla española*: potato (and often onion) omelet—it's a nationwide staple

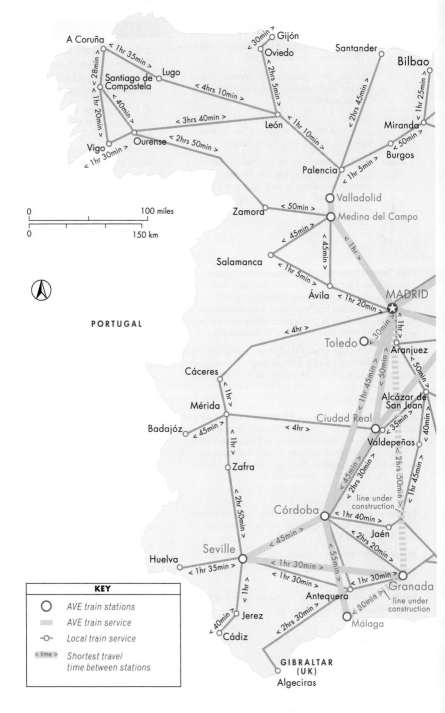

Travel Times by Train

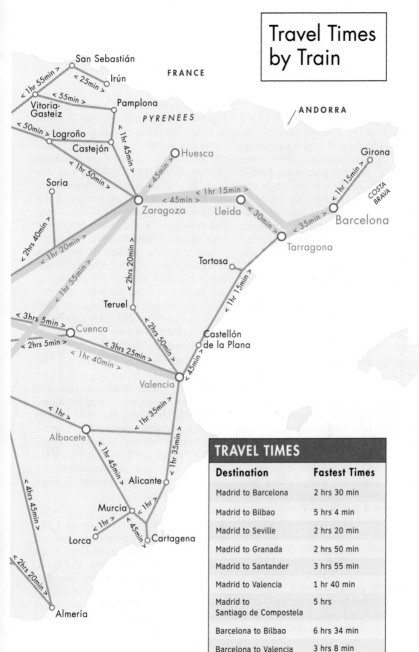

San Sebastián

< 25min > Irún

< 1hr 55min >

FRANCE

Vitoria-Gasteiz

< 55min > Pamplona

PYRENEES

ANDORRA

< 50min > Logroño

Castejón

< 1hr 50min >

< 1hr 45min >

Soria

Huesca

< 45min >

Girona

< 1hr 15min >

COSTA BRAVA

< 1hr 15min >

< 45min > Lleida

Zaragoza

< 30min >

< 35min > Barcelona

< 2hrs 40min >

< 1hr 20min >

Tarragona

< 1hr 55min >

Tortosa

< 2hrs 20min >

< 1hr 15min >

Teruel

< 3hrs 5min > Cuenca

< 2hrs 50min >

Castellón de la Plana

< 2hrs 5min >

< 3hrs 25min >

< 45min >

< 1hr 40min >

Valencia

< 1hr >

< 1hr 35min >

Albacete

< 1hr 35min >

< 1hr 45min >

Alicante

< 4hrs 45min >

Murcia

< 1hr >

< 1hr >

< 45min > Cartagena

Lorca

< 2hrs 20min >

Almería

TRAVEL TIMES	
Destination	**Fastest Times**
Madrid to Barcelona	2 hrs 30 min
Madrid to Bilbao	5 hrs 4 min
Madrid to Seville	2 hrs 20 min
Madrid to Granada	2 hrs 50 min
Madrid to Santander	3 hrs 55 min
Madrid to Valencia	1 hr 40 min
Madrid to Santiago de Compostela	5 hrs
Barcelona to Bilbao	6 hrs 34 min
Barcelona to Valencia	3 hrs 8 min
Seville to Granada	3 hr 15 min

SPAIN TODAY

Politics

Since the advent of democracy in 1978 and until 2014, Spanish politics was dominated by the two largest parties: the socialist Partido Socialista Obrero Español (PSOE) and the right-wing Partido Popular (PP). In 2011, at the height of a punishing economic crisis, the PSOE—in power since 2004—was handed widespread defeats, giving the PP opposition outright majorities in 8 of the 13 regions, and, nationally, installing Mariano Rajoy as prime minister.

In 2014, however, as Spain continued to battle an economic crisis and as some high-profile scandals came to light, the political scenario changed. "Renovation" became the watchword, and Spaniards clamored for more ethical behavior from public figures. On the back of this, two parties have become forces to be reckoned with in the political arena: Podemos (We Can), a far-left grassroots party whose policies are loosely based on demands from the *indignados* (the "indignant ones" who carried out Occupy Wall Street–style protests against cutbacks in major cities in 2012); and Ciudadanos (Citizens), a centrist Catalan-led party whose policies focus on political regeneration. Both parties gained seats in the European elections in 2014 and the Andalusian regional elections in March 2015. The national elections held in December 2015 left all parties well short of the required 175-seat majority. General elections in June 2016 renewed the deadlock with a near rerun of the December vote. Recent polls show Ciudadanos could overtake the PP in the next general election, scheduled for early 2020.

Meanwhile, a push for Catalan independence, led by separatist parties that hold a slim majority in the Catalan regional legislature, has nearly brought Spain to its knees. On October 1, 2017, separatist politicians presided over an independence referendum (similar to the one celebrated in Scotland in 2014), which had been outlawed by Spanish courts. The Spanish central government sent national police and civil guards into Catalonia to halt voting, and newspapers worldwide were splashed with images of police beating unarmed voters at polling stations. To punish its renegade region, Madrid imposed emergency rule on Catalonia, suspending its autonomy and firing top regional politicians. Catalonia repeated regional elections in December 2017, with the same result: a slim majority for separatists, and a stalemate with Madrid.

Throughout the spring of 2018, the Catalan capital Barcelona filled with street protesters. Flights were canceled and schools and businesses closed for a general strike. The unrest prompted tourists to cancel vacations, thousands of companies changed their tax residency to neighboring regions, and the Catalan economy slumped. The region remains safe to visit today, but visitors are advised to avoid large demonstrations.

The Economy

After Spain entered recession in 2008, stringent financial measures were imposed by the European Union and the IMF. Spain struggled to find its economic feet again, particularly as unemployment soared to 26%, and youth unemployment reached double that. Since 2014, the economy has shown signs of recovery: GDP growth for 2017 was 3.1%, one of the highest rates in Europe. While tourism to Catalonia briefly slumped in the fall of 2017, it has surged in the rest of the country. In

2017, Spain surpassed the United States to become the world's second-most-visited country, after France.

Religion

The state-funded Catholic Church, closely tied to the right-wing PP and with the national Cadena Cope radio station as its voice, continues to hold considerable social and political influence in Spain, with members of secretive groups such as Opus Dei and the Legionarios de Cristo holding key government and industry positions.

Despite the church's influence, at street level Spain has become a secular country, as demonstrated by the fact that 70% of Spaniards supported the decidedly un-Catholic law allowing gay marriage. And although more than 75% of the population claims to be Catholic, less than 20% go to church on a regular basis.

More than 1 million Muslims reside in Spain, making Islam the country's second-largest religion.

The Arts

Spain's devotion to the arts is clearly shown by the attention, both national and international, paid to its annual Princesa de Asturias prize, where Princess Leonor hands out accolades to international high achievers such as Frank Gehry, Francis Ford Coppola, and Bob Dylan, and to homegrown talent such as the writer Antonio Muñoz Molina, who has taught at the City University of New York.

Film is at the forefront of the Spanish arts scene. Spain's most acclaimed director, Pedro Almodóvar, is still at it, most recently with a 2016 film, *Julieta,* based on three short stories by Alice Munro. *The Bookshop,* an English-language film directed and produced by Spaniards, won Best Film and Best Director awards at the 2018 Goya Awards, Spain's version of the Oscars.

While authors such as Miguel Delibes, Rosa Montero, and Maruja Torres flourish in Spain, few break onto the international scene, with the exception of Arturo Pérez Reverte, whose books include *Captain Alatriste* and *The Fencing Master,* and Carlos Ruiz Zafón, author of the acclaimed *Shadow of the Wind, The Angel's Game,* and *Prisoner of Heaven.* Spain's contribution to the fine arts is still dominated by three names: the Mallorca-born artist Miquel Barceló; the Basque sculptor Eduardo Chillida, who died in 2002; and the Catalan abstract painter Antoni Tàpies, who died in 2012.

Sports

With Real Madrid and FC Barcelona firmly established as international brands, and with La Liga recognized as one of the world's most exciting leagues, soccer remains the nation's favorite sport. The national soccer team, known as La Roja (The Red One), won the World Cup in 2010, and has won the European Cup three times—a record tied only by Germany. In other sports, national heroes include: Rafael Nadal, the first tennis player to hold Grand Slam titles on clay, grass, and hard court; Garbiñe Muguruza, the 2017 Wimbledon champion; brothers Pau and Marc Gasol, who play for the San Antonio Spurs and the Memphis Grizzlies, respectively; Anna Cruz, who plays for the Minnesota Lynx; and Javier Fernández, the 2018 Olympic bronze medalist in figure skating.

IF YOU LIKE

Fairy-tale Castles

Ever dream of spending the night in a hilltop monastery or a fairy-tale castle? You can fulfill that dream in some of Spain's nearly 100 *paradores* (state-run hotels). They've all got one thing in common: heritage status. More often than not they also have killer views. Lodging is generally equivalent to a four-star hotel and occasionally a five-star, and all have modern amenities amidst their historic splendor.

Parador de Cangas de Onis. This beautiful former monastery is in the mountainous Picos de Europa.

Parador de Granada. Within the walls of the Alhambra, this former monastery is Spain's most popular (and most expensive) parador.

Parador de Hondarribia. This 10th-century castle-cum-fortress in the heart of Hondarribia looks severe from the outside but is elegant and lovely inside, with sweeping views of the French coastline.

Parador de León. Pure luxury sums up this five-star monastery, with arguably the best restaurant in the parador network.

Parador de Plasencia. This Gothic convent lies in the heart of Plasencia's beautiful old quarters.

Parador de Santiago de Compostela. This 15th-century hospital is one of the most luxurious and beautiful of the parador chain.

Parador de Santillana Gil Blas. Santillana del Mar may be one of the most beautiful towns in Spain; this parador puts you in the heart of the village.

Parador de Sigüenza. This sprawling 12th-century Moorish citadel is arguably the finest architectural example of all the parador castles.

Art Museums

In the Golden Age of Empire (1580–1680), Spanish monarchs used Madrid's wealth not only to finance wars and civil projects but also to collect and commission great works of art. This national patrimony, since greatly expanded, makes Spain a museum-lover's paradise.

Centro de Arte Reina Sofía, Madrid. The modern collection focuses on Spain's three great modern masters: Picasso, Dalí, and Miró. The centerpiece is Picasso's monumental *Guernica*.

City of Arts and Sciences, Valencia. An aquarium, opera house, botanical garden, and science museum are all housed in this ultramodern complex. It's Valencia's most popular attraction.

Fundació Miró, Barcelona. Designed by Miró's friend and collaborator, architect Lluís Sert, this museum houses some 11,000 of Miró's works.

Museo de Bellas Artes, Valencia. One of the finest smaller collections in Spain, the MBA showcases masterworks by Ribalta, Velázquez, Ribera, Goya, and 19th-century Valencian painter Joaquin Sorolla.

Museo del Prado, Madrid. In a magnificent neoclassical building, the Prado, with its collection of Spanish and European masterpieces, is frequently compared to the Louvre.

Museo Guggenheim, Bilbao. Frank Gehry's building is a work of art in its own right, while inside, the galleries showcase international and Spanish art by modern and contemporary painters and sculptors.

Museu Nacional d'Art de Catalunya, Barcelona. MNAC has the finest collection of Romanesque frescoes and devotional sculpture in the world, most rescued from abandoned chapels in the Pyrenees.

Museu Picasso, Barcelona. Five elegant medieval and early-Renaissance palaces in the Barri Gòtic (the Gothic Quarter) house this collection of some 3,600 works by Picasso.

Beaches

Spain has some excellent beaches and is an increasingly popular destination for water sports. Among the best city beaches are **La Concha** (San Sebastián), **Playa de la Victoria** (Cádiz), **La Barceloneta** (Barcelona), and **El Cabanyal** (Valencia). Some of the best beaches outside the cities include:

Cabo de Gata. The southeast corner of Andalusia is a protected nature reserve, and a paradise of hidden and unspoiled sandy and rocky coves.

Es Pujols. Rated one of the best beaches in the Balearic Islands, this white sandy cove on the island of Formentera is half a mile long and family-friendly.

Islas Cies. This string of three protected islands off the Galician coast, each with lovely (and quiet) sandy coves, can only be reached by ferry.

Tamariu. A pretty cove on the Costa Brava, backed by pines, has a family-friendly vibe.

Tarifa. Here there are long stretches of Atlantic sands with perfect conditions for windsurfing and kitesurfing.

Mountains

After Switzerland, Spain is the most mountainous country in Europe. Some of the most scenic and easily accessible include:

Los Gredos. The best kept-secret within two hours of Madrid, these mountains offer plunge pools for wild swimming in summer. The southern foothills comprise a microclimate with palm trees, and cherry blossoms in spring.

Los Picos de Europa. Literally, the "peaks of Europe," this range stretches across northern Spain, parallel to the Atlantic coast and dotted with ancient cheese makers and *sidrerías* (cider houses).

Pyrenees. The serrated frontier between France and Spain offers some of Europe's best hiking and downhill skiing, without the crowds in the Alps. Hop onto sections of the GR-11 hiking trail and sleep at *refugios*—mountain huts—along the way.

Sierra Guadarrama. Public transit makes Madrid's peaks easily accessible for daytrippers with bicycles, hiking boots—even skis. Hop on a train for less than an hour and get off at the foot of an 8,000-foot mountain.

Sierra Nevada. These are the peaks you see from the terrace of the Alhambra Palace, and also from the beaches of Andalusia. In a single day you can hike or ski the slopes and swim in the Mediterranean Sea.

Picturesque Towns

From the stone-walled settlements of the north to the whitewashed villages in the south, there are picture-postcard visions in every province. Spain's most picturesque towns include:

Altea (Alicante). Whitewashed facades and blue-tiled domes make up this seaside town.

Cangas de Onís (Asturias). Stone walls and a historic river bridge are the highlights of this mountain village.

La Guardia (La Rioja). A walled fortress is home to excellent wineries.

Ronda (Malaga). Here you'll find Andalusian architecture atop a river gorge.

Vejer de la Frontera (Cádiz). Brilliant-white houses give way to a castle on a hill.

HISTORY YOU CAN SEE

Ancient Spain

The story of Spain, a romance-tinged tale of counts, caliphs, crusaders, and kings, begins long before written history. The Basques were among the first here, fiercely defending the green mountain valleys of the Pyrenees. Then came the Iberians, apparently crossing the Mediterranean from North Africa around 3000 BC. The Celts arrived from the north about a thousand years later. The seafaring Phoenicians founded Gadir (now Cádiz) and several coastal cities in the south three millennia ago. The parade continued with the Greeks, who settled parts of the east coast, and then the Carthaginians, who founded Cartagena around 225 BC and dubbed the then-wild, forested, and game-rich country "Ispania," after their word for rabbit: *span*.

What to See: Near Barcelona, on the Costa Brava, rocket yourself back almost 3,000 years at **Ullastret**, a settlement occupied by an Iberian people known as the Indiketas. On a tour, actors guide groups through the homes and fortifications of some of the peninsula's earliest inhabitants, the defensive walls attesting to the constant threat of attack and the bits of pottery evidence of the settlement's early ceramic industry. Not far away in **Empúries** are ruins of the Greek colony established in the 6th century BC. At the **Museo de Cádiz** in Andalusia, you can view sarcophagi dating back to the 1100 BC founding of the city.

In Madrid, the outstanding, newly renovated **National Archaeological Museum** displays more than 1 million years of artifacts unearthed in what is now Spain: from Paleolithic tools found in Madrid's Manzanares River basin to 19th-century textiles and musical instruments.

The Roman Epoch

Modern civilization in Iberia began with the Romans, who expelled the Carthaginians and turned the peninsula into three imperial provinces. It took the Romans 200 years to subdue the fiercely resisting Iberians, but their influence is seen today in the fortifications, amphitheaters, aqueducts, and other ruins in cities across Spain, as well as in the country's legal system and in the Latin base of Spain's Romance languages and dialects.

What to See: Segovia's nearly 3,000-foot-long **Acueducto Romano** is a marvel of Roman engineering. Mérida's Roman ruins are some of Spain's finest, including its **bridge, theater,** and **outdoor amphitheater.**

1100 BC	Earliest Phoenician colonies are formed, including Cádiz, Villaricos, Almuñecar, and Málaga. Natives include Basques in the Pyrenees, Iberians in the south, and Celts in the northwest.
237 BC	Carthaginians land in Spain.
206 BC	Romans expel Carthaginians from Spain and gradually conquer peninsula.
AD 74	Roman citizenship extended to all Spaniards.
419	Visigothic kingdom established in central and northern Spain, with capital at Toledo.
711–12	Visigothic kingdom overthrown by invading Muslims (Moors), who create an emirate, with the capital at Córdoba.
813	Discovery of remains of St. James; the cathedral of Santiago de Compostela is built and becomes a major pilgrimage site.
1085–1270	Main years of the Reconquest.
1478	Spanish Inquisition begins.

Tarragona was Rome's most important city in Catalonia, as the **walls, circus,** and **amphitheater** bear witness, while Zaragoza boasts a **Roman amphitheater** and a **Roman fluvial port** that dispatched flat-bottom riverboats loaded with wine and olive oil down the Ebro.

The Visigoths and Moors

In the early 5th century, invading tribes crossed the Pyrenees to attack the weakening Roman Empire. The Visigoths became the dominant force in central and northern Spain by AD 419, establishing their kingdom at Toledo and eventually adopting Christianity. But the Visigoths, too, were to fall before a wave of invaders. The Moors, an Arab-led Berber force, crossed the Strait of Gibraltar in AD 711 and swept through Spain in an astonishingly short time, launching almost eight centuries of Muslim rule. The Moorish architecture and Mudejar Moorish-inspired Gothic decorative details found throughout most of Spain tell much about the splendor of the Islamic culture that flourished here.

What to See: Moorish culture is most spectacularly evident in Andalusia, derived from the Arabic name for the Moorish reign on the Iberian Peninsula, al-Andalus,

HIDDEN MEANINGS

What's *not* there in Spain can be just as revealing as what is. For example, there are no Roman ruins in Madrid, as it was founded as a Moorish outpost in the late 10th century and was not the capital of Spain until 1560, a recent date in Spanish history. Likewise, Barcelona has no Moorish architecture—the Moors sacked Barcelona but never established themselves there, testifying to Catalonia's medieval past as part of Charlemagne's Frankish empire. Al-Andalus, the 781-year Moorish sojourn on the peninsula, was farther south and west.

which meant "western lands." The fairy-tale **Alhambra** palace overlooking Granada captures the refinement of the Moorish aesthetic, while the earlier 9th-century **Mezquita** at Córdoba bears witness to the power of Islam in al-Andalus.

Spain's Golden Age

By 1085, Alfonso VI of Castile had captured Toledo, giving the Christians a firm grip on the north. In the 13th century, Valencia, Seville, and finally Córdoba—the capital of the Muslim caliphate in Spain—fell to Christian forces, leaving only Granada in Moorish hands. Nearly

1479–1504	Isabella and Ferdinand rule jointly.	ca. 1520 –1700	Spain's Golden Age.
1492	Granada, the last Moorish outpost, falls. Christopher Columbus, under Isabella's sponsorship, discovers the islands of the Caribbean, setting off a wave of Spanish exploration. Ferdinand and Isabella expel Jews and Muslims from Spain.	1605	Miguel de Cervantes publishes the first part of *Don Quixote de la Mancha*.
		1618–1648	Thirty Years' War: a dynastic struggle between Habsburgs and Bourbons.
1516	Ferdinand dies. His grandson Carlos I inaugurates the Habsburg dynasty.	1701–14	War of the Spanish Succession. Claimant to the throne are Louis XIV of France, Holy Roman Emperor Leopold I, and electoral prince Joseph Ferdinand of Bavaria.
1519 –22	First circumnavigation of the world by Ferdinand Magellan's ships.	1756–63	Seven Years' War: Spain and France versus Great Britain.

200 years later, the so-called Catholic Monarchs—Ferdinand of Aragón and Isabella of Castile—were joined in a marriage that would change the world. Finally, on January 2, 1492—244 years after the fall of Córdoba—Granada surrendered and the Moorish reign was over.

The year 1492 was the beginning of the nation's political golden age: Christian forces conquered Granada and unified all of present-day Spain as a single kingdom; in what was, at the time, viewed as a measure promoting national unity, Jews and Muslims who did not convert to Christianity were expelled from the country. The departure of educated Muslims and Jews was a blow to the nation's agriculture, science, and economy from which it would take nearly 500 years to recover. The Catholic Monarchs and their centralizing successors maintained Spain's unity, but they sacrificed the spirit of international free trade that was bringing prosperity to other parts of Europe. Carlos V weakened Spain with his penchant for waging war, and his son, Felipe II, followed in the same expensive path, defeating the Turks in 1571 but losing the "Invincible Spanish Armada" in the English Channel in 1588.

What to See: Celebrate Columbus's voyage to America with **festivities in Seville, Huelva, Granada, Cádiz, and Barcelona,** all of which display venues where "the Discoverer" was commissioned, was confirmed, set out from, returned to, or was buried. Wander through the somber **Escorial,** a monastery northwest of Madrid commissioned by Felipe II in 1557 and finished in 1584, the final resting place of most of the Habsburg and Bourbon kings of Spain ever since.

War of the Spanish Succession

The War of the Spanish Succession (1700–14) ended with the fall of Barcelona, which sided with the Habsburg Archduke Carlos against the Bourbon Prince Felipe V. El Born market, completed in 1876, covered the buried remains of the Ribera neighborhood, where the decisive battle took place. Ribera citizens were required to tear down a thousand houses to clear space for the Ciutadella fortress, from which fields of fire were directed, quite naturally, toward the city the Spanish and French forces had taken a year to subdue. The leveled neighborhood, then about a third of Barcelona, was plowed under and forgotten by the victors, though never by barcelonins.

What to See: In Barcelona, the **Fossar de les Moreres cemetery,** next to the Santa

1808	Napoléon takes Madrid.
1809 –14	The Spanish War of Independence: Napoleonic armies thrown out of Spain.
1834 –39	First Carlist War: Don Carlos contests the crown; an era of upheaval begins.
1873	First Spanish Republic declared. Three-year Second Carlist War begins.
1898	Spanish-American War: Spain loses Cuba, Puerto Rico, and the Philippines.
1936 –39	Spanish Civil War; more than 600,000 die. General Francisco Franco wins and rules Spain for the next 36 years.
1977 –78	First democratic election in 40 years; new constitution restores civil liberties and freedom of the press.
1992	Olympic Games held in Barcelona.
2000	Juan Carlos celebrates 25 years as Spain's king.
2002	Spain bids farewell to the peseta, adopts the euro.
2004	Terrorist bombs on Madrid trains claim almost 200 lives; the conservative Partido Popular loses the general election and the socialist PSOE under Prime Minister José Luis Zapatero comes to power.

María del Mar basilica, remains a powerful symbol for Catalan nationalists who gather there every September 11, Catalonia's National Day, to commemorate the fall of the city in 1714.

Spanish Civil War

Spain's early-19th-century War of Independence required five years of bitter guerrilla fighting to rid the peninsula of Napoleonic troops. Later, the Carlist wars set the stage for the Spanish Civil War (1936–39), which claimed more than half a million lives. Intellectuals and leftists sympathized with the elected government; the International Brigades, with many American, British, and Canadian volunteers, took part in some of the worst fighting, including the storied defense of Madrid. But General Francisco Franco, backed by the Catholic Church, got far more help from Nazi Germany, whose Condor legions destroyed the Basque town of Gernika (in a horror made infamous by Picasso's monumental painting *Guernica*), and from Fascist Italy. For three years, European governments stood by as Franco's armies ground their way to victory. After the fall of Barcelona in January 1939, the Republican cause became hopeless. Franco's Nationalist forces entered Madrid on March 27, 1939, and thus began nearly

40 years of dictatorship under Franco. This dark period in recent Spanish history ended on November 20, 1975, when Franco died.

What to See: Snap a shot of **Madrid's Plaza Dos de Mayo,** in the Malasaña neighborhood, where officers Daoiz and Velarde held their ground against the superior French forces at the start of the popular uprising against Napoléon. The archway in the square is all that remains of the armory Daoiz and Velarde defended to the death. Trace the shrapnel marks on the wall of the **Sant Felip Neri church** in Barcelona, evidence of the 1938 bombing of the city by Italian warplanes under Franco's orders. East of Zaragoza, **Belchite** was the scene of bloody fighting during the decisive Battle of the Ebro. The town has been left exactly as it appeared on September 7, 1937, the day the battle ended.

Return to Democracy

After Franco's death, Spain began the complex process of national reconciliation and a return to democracy. Despite opposition from radical right-wing factions and an attempted coup d'etat in February 1981, Spain celebrated the first general elections for 40 years in 1977 and approved a democratic constitution in 1978.

2005	Parliament legalizes gay marriage, grants adoption and inheritance rights to same-sex couples.
2007	Parliament passes a bill formally denouncing Franco's rule, and ordering Franco-era statues and plaques removed from streets and buildings.
2009	Spain enters recession for the first time since 1993; unemployment hits 19.4%, with nearly 5 million people jobless.
2010	Spain wins the FIFA soccer World Cup.
2011	PP wins in a landslide parliamentary election; Mariano Rajoy becomes prime minister.
2012	Spain continues in recession with unemployment at an all-time high of 26%. Economic recovery isn't forecast until 2015 at the earliest.
2014	Economic recovery appears on the horizon, and Spain receives a record 65 million tourists. Juan Carlos abdicates in favor of his son, Felipe.

SPANISH TAPAS

Tapas with a *caña* (a 4- to 6-ounce beer) or glass of wine are part and parcel of daily life in Spain, at both lunch and dinner time. From the lowly (but delicious) potato omelet to the relatively expensive (but really exquisite) jamón ibérico; from simple home-cooked stew to sophisticated gourmet creations; and from individual *pinchos* (tapas on bread) to *raciones* (small plates) shared among several people, this free-wheeling and spontaneous approach to food and socializing is at the heart of the Spanish experience. Eating tapas is such a way of life that a verb had to be created for it: *tapear* (to eat tapas) or *ir a tapeo* (to go eat tapas).

ORIGIN OF TAPAS

The origin of tapas is the stuff of heated tapas-bar debates. Various reports cloud the history of when and how it started. Some credit Alfonso X's diet and his delicate stomach. However, the most commonly accepted explanation is that a flat object (be it a slice of bread or a flat card with some nuts or sunflower seeds) was used to cover the rim of wine glasses to keep dive-bombing fruit flies out. (To cover something up is *tapar* in Spanish.)

TAPAS TO TRY

Andalusia: Known for the warmth of its climate and its people, Andalusian bars tend to be very generous with their tapas. Seafood is extremely popular in Andalusia, and you will find tapas ranging from sizzling prawns to small anchovies soaked in vinegar or olive oil. *Pescado frito* (fried fish) and *albóndigas* (meatballs) are two common tapas in the region, and it's worth grazing multiple bars to try the different preparations. The fish usually includes squid, anchovies, and other tiny fish, deep fried and served as is. Since the bones are very small, they are not removed and considered fine for digestion; if this idea bothers you, sip some more wine. The saffron-almond sauce (*salsa de almendras y azafrán*) that accompanies the meatballs might very well make your eyes roll with pleasure. Not incidentally, Spain's biggest export, olives, grows in Andalusia, so you can expect many varieties among the tapas served with your drinks.

Basque Country: More than any other community in Spain, the Basque Country is known for its culinary originality. The tapas, like the region itself, tend to be more expensive and inventive. And since the Basques insist on doing things their way, they call their unbelievable bites *pintxos* (or *pinchos* in Spanish) rather than tapas. The *gilda,* probably the most ordered pintxo in the Basque Country, is a simple toothpick skewer comprising a special green pepper (*guindilla vasca*), an anchovy, and a pitted olive. *Pimientos rellenos de bacalao* (roasted red peppers stuffed with cod) are another Basque delicacy.

Madrid: It is often difficult to qualify what is authentically from Madrid and what has been gastronomically cribbed from other regions, thanks to Madrid's melting-pot status for people and customs all over Spain. *Patatas bravas* and *calamares* can be found in almost any restaurant in Madrid. The popular *patatas* are a very simple mixture of fried or roasted potatoes with a *brava* sauce that is as spicy as the cook's recipe makes it. The *calamares,* fried in olive oil, can be served alone or with alioli sauce, mayonnaise, or—and you're reading this correctly—in a sandwich.

1

MENU VOCABULARY

Tapas Terms

bocadillo, bocata: large hot or cold sandwich on crusty baguette

media-ración: half-size portion of tapas

montadito: small open-face sandwich, or tapa mounted on small baguette slice

pincho, pintxo: small bite on baguette slice and secured with a toothpick

pulga, pulguita: smaller sandwich on baguette

ración: large portion of tapas, usually to share

sandwich: smaller sandwich on sliced white bread

tapa: small plate

Method of Cooking/Preparation

a la plancha: grilled

a la parilla: barbecued

a leña: cooked slowly over wood fire

al horno: baked

brocheta: on a kebab stick

en vinagre: marinated in vinegar brine (usually uncooked)

frito: fried (usually in olive oil, breaded)

surtido de ...: an assortment

Typical Tapas

aceitunas: olives

albóndigas: meatballs

almendras: almonds, usually fried or roasted

banderilla: small kebab of vegetables

boquerones: anchovies, in vinegar or fried

caracoles: small snails

champiñones, setas: mushrooms; wild mushrooms

chipirones: baby squid (sometimes called *calamaritos* or *chopitos*)

croquetas: breaded, fried croquettes with béchamel, frequently stuffed with jamón or fish

embutidos: cured meats

empanadas, empanadillas: pastry stuffed with meat, fish, or vegetables

ensalada rusa: cold potato salad with mayonnaise, peas, and carrots

gambas al ajillo: shrimp sautéed with garlic

judias: beans

morcilla: blood sausage

morros: pig snout

patatas mixta: fried potatoes with half spicy red sauce, half garlic sauce

pimientos de Padrón: fried and salted green peppers from Padrón, usually sweet with the occasional hot one

pincho de tortilla: slice of potato (and sometimes onion) omelet

rabo de toro: stew made from bull's tail (sometimes fresh from the bull ring)

Asking for Help

What would you recommend? *¿Qué recomienda?*

What's in that dish? *¿Qué lleva ese plato?*

I don't eat meat. *No como carne.*

I'm allergic to ... *Tengo alergia a* ...

Places

bar: bar, which nearly always serves food

tasca: neighborhood dive bar

taverna: informal restaurant serving tapas

marisquería: seafood restaurant

vinoteca: wine bar or wine store

SPANISH WINE

After years of being in the shadows of other European wines, Spanish wines are now finally in the spotlight. A generation of young, ambitious winemakers has jolted dormant areas awake, and even the most established regions have undergone makeovers in order to compete in the global market. As a result, Spanish wines frequently receive top international accolades.

THEN AND NOW

Spain has a long wine history dating back to the time when the Phoenicians introduced viticulture to the peninsula, over 3,000 years ago. True expansion of the wine trade came in the 16th century, with the Spanish Empire, and again during the 19th century, when Vega Sicilia (Spain's most revered winery) was set up in Castile; the famous Tío Pepe brand was established; the Marqués de Murrieta and Marqués de Riscal wineries opened, creating the modern Rioja region; and *cava*—Spain's white or pink sparkling wine—was created in Catalonia. Then a succession of phylloxera infestations, civil war, and a long dictatorship left the country's wine scene dominated by sherry, Rioja, cava, and loads of cheap, watered-down wines made by local cooperatives. This continued until the 1970s, when a wave of innovation spread from La Rioja and emergent regions like Ribera del Duero and Penedés to cover practically the entire country. This veritable wine revolution continues today with more and more labels joining the long list of excellent Spanish wines. Aside from tempranillo, other native varietals—such as albariño, godello, and verdejo (whites), and callet, cariñena, garnacha, graciano, mandó, manto negro, mencía, and monastrell (reds)—have been rediscovered, joining the ranks of reputable wines.

TERMINOLOGY

One unique feature of Spanish wines is the indication of aging process on wine labels. Denominación de Origen (Appellation of Origin, abbreviated "D.O.") wines show this on mandatory back panels. Aging requirements are longer for reds, but also apply to white, rosé, and sparkling wines. For reds, the rules are as follows:

Crianza: A wine aged for at least 24 months, six of which are in barrels (12 in La Rioja, Ribera del Duero, and Navarra).

Gran Reserva: Traditionally the top of the Spanish wine hierarchy, and the pride of the historic Rioja wineries. A red wine aged for at least 24 months in oak, followed by 36 months in the bottle before release.

Reserva: A wine aged for a minimum of 36 months, at least 12 of which in oak.

Vino Joven: A young wine that may or may not have spent some time aging in oak barrels before it was bottled.

SPAIN'S DOMINANT VARIETALS

Spain has more than 60 Denominaciones de Origen which are tightly regulated to protect the integrity and characteristics of the wines produced there. Beyond international varieties like cabernet sauvignon and chardonnay, the country is home to several high-quality varietals, both indigenous and imported.

Reds

Garnacha: The Spanish name for France's grenache, this grape produces a spicy, full-bodied red wine, sometimes mixed with tempranillo

Tempranillo: This is an early-ripening grape that blends and ages well, and the dominant variety in Spanish wine.

Whites

Albariño or Rueda: These grapes are used in the most popular white wines made in Galicia and Rueda; they are light and aromatic.

Verdejo: This sharper-tasting grape produces a full-bodied wine.

Wine Regions

Andalusia: In sun-drenched Andalusia, where the white albariza limestone soils reflect the powerful sunlight while trapping the scant humidity, the fortified Jerez (sherry) and Montilla-Moriles emerge. In all their different incarnations, from dry finos, manzanillas, amontillados, palo cortados, and olorosos, to sweet creams and Pedro Ximénez, they are the most original wines of Spain.

Bierzo: In the Bierzo DO, the mencía grape distills the essence of the schist slopes, where it grows into minerally infused red wines.

Catalonia: Catalonia is best known as the heartland of cava, the typically dry, sparkling wine made from three indigenous Spanish varietals: parellada, xarel-lo, and macabeo. The climatically varied **Penedès** produces full-bodied reds like garnacha on coastal plains, and cool-climate varietals like riesling and sauvignon blanc in the mountains. Innovative **Priorat** winemakers blend traditional grapes like garnacha and cariñena with cabernet sauvignon and syrah to produce rich, concentrated reds with powerful tannins.

Duero: In the iron-rich riverbanks of the Duero, tempranillo grapes produce complex and ageworthy Ribera del Duero reds (now internationally acclaimed and on a par with those from La Rioja) and hefty Toro wines. Close by, the Rueda D.O. adds aromatic and grassy whites from local verdejo and adopted sauvignon blanc.

La Mancha: In the central plateau south of Madrid, modernization and replanting is resulting in medium bodied, easy drinking, and fairly priced wines made with tempranillo (here called *cencíbel*), cabernet, syrah, and even petit verdot.

Navarra: Navarra and three small D.O.'s in Aragón deliver great wines made with the local garnacha and tempranillo grapes, as well as international varieties.

Rías Baixas: The green and more humid areas of the northwest deliver crisp, floral white albariños in Galicia's Rías Baixas.

Rioja: The Rioja region is a winemaker's paradise. Here a mild, nearly perfect vine-growing climate marries limestone and clay soils with tempranillo, Spain's most noble grape. Tempranillo-based Riojas evolve from a young cherry color and aromas of strawberries and red fruits, to a brick hue, infused with scents of tobacco and leather.

Valencia: The region of Valencia is south of Catalonia on the Mediterranean coast. The wines of this area have improved markedly in recent years, with red wines from Jumilla and other appellations finding their way onto the international market. A local specialty of the area is Moscatel de Valencia, a highly aromatic sweet white wine.

GREAT ITINERARIES

MADRID TO THE ALHAMBRA, 10-DAY ITINERARY

This trip takes in the best of vibrant Madrid and its world-class art museums and showcases some of Castile's historic gems before whisking you to the Moorish south where Córdoba's majestic mosque, Seville's fragrant orange blossoms, and Granada's "heaven on earth" await.

Days 1–3: Madrid

Start the day with a visit to either the **Prado**, the **Museo Thyssen-Bornemisza**, or the **Centro de Arte Reina Sofía**. Then head to the elegant **Plaza Mayor**—a perfect jumping-off point for a tour of the Spanish capital. To the west, see the **Plaza de la Villa**, **Palacio Real** (the Royal Palace), **Teatro Real** (Royal Theater), and the royal convents; to the south, wander around the maze of streets of **La Latina** and **El Rastro** and try some local tapas.

On Day 2, visit the sprawling **Barrio de las Letras,** centered on the Plaza de Santa Ana. This was the favorite neighborhood of writers during the Spanish golden literary age in the 17th century (Cervantes lies buried under a convent nearby), and it's still crammed with theaters, cafés, and good tapas bars. It borders the Paseo del Prado on the east, allowing you to comfortably walk to any of the art museums in the area. If the weather is pleasant, take an afternoon stroll in the **Parque del Buen Retiro.**

For your third day in the capital, wander in **Chueca** and **Malasaña,** the two funky hipster neighborhoods most favored by young madrileños. Fuencarral, a landmark pedestrianized street that serves as the border between the two, is one of the city's trendiest shopping enclaves.

From there you can walk to the **Parque del Oeste** and the **Templo de Debod**—the best spot from which to see the city's sunset. Among the lesser-known museums, consider visiting the captivating **Museo Sorolla,** Goya's frescoes and tomb at the **Ermita de San Antonio de la Florida,** or the **Real Academia de Bellas Artes de San Fernando** for classic painting. People-watch at any of the terrace bars in either Plaza de Chueca or Plaza 2 de Mayo in Malasaña.

Logistics: If you're traveling light, the subway (Metro Línea 8) or the bus (No. 203 during the day and N27 at night) will take you from the airport to the city for €5. The train costs €2.60 and a taxi is a fixed price of €30. Once in the center consider walking or taking the subway rather than cabbing it in gridlock traffic.

Days 4 and 5: Castilian Cities

There are several excellent options for half- or full-day side trips from Madrid to occupy Days 4 and 5. **Toledo** and **Segovia** are two of the oldest Castilian cities—both have delightful old quarters dating back to the Romans. There's also **El Escorial,** which houses the massive monastery built by Felipe II. Two other nearby towns also worth visiting are **Aranjuez** and **Alcalá de Henares.**

Logistics: Toledo and Segovia are stops on the high-speed train line (AVE), so you can get to either of them in a half hour from Madrid. To reach the old quarters of both cities, take a bus or cab from the train station or take the bus from Madrid. Buses and trains both go to El Escorial. Reach Aranjuez and Alcalá de Henares via the intercity train system.

Day 6: Córdoba or Extremadura

Córdoba, the capital of both Roman and Moorish Spain, was the center of Western art and culture between the 8th and 11th

centuries. The city's breathtaking **Mezquita** (mosque), which is now a cathedral, and the medieval **Jewish Quarter** bear witness to the city's brilliant past. From Madrid you could also rent a car and visit the lesser-known cities in the north of **Extremadura**, such as **Guadalupe** and **Trujillo**, and overnight in **Cáceres**, a UNESCO World Heritage Site, then return to Madrid the next day.

Logistics: The AVE will take you to Córdoba from Madrid in less than two hours. One alternative is to stay in Toledo, also on the route heading south, and then head to Córdoba the next day, although you need to return to Madrid by train first. Once in Córdoba, take a taxi for a visit out to the summer palace at Medina Azahara.

Days 7 and 8: Seville

Seville's **Cathedral**, with its tower La Giralda, **Plaza de Toros Real Maestranza**, and **Barrio de Santa Cruz** are visual feasts. Forty minutes south by train, you can sip the world-famous sherries of **Jerez de la Frontera**, then munch jumbo shrimp on the beach at **Sanlúcar de Barrameda.**

Logistics: From Seville's AVE station, take a taxi to your hotel. After that, walking and hailing the occasional taxi are the best ways to explore the city. A rental car is the best option to reach towns beyond Seville, except for Jerez de la Frontera, where the

TIP

Spain's modern freeways and toll highways are as good as any in the world—with the exception of the signs, which are often tiny and hard to decipher as you sweep past them at the routine speed of 120 kph (74 mph).

train station is an architectural gem in its own right.

Days 9 and 10: Granada

The hilltop **Alhambra** palace, Spain's most visited attraction, was conceived by the Moorish caliphs as heaven on earth. Try any of the city's famous tapas bars and tea shops, and make sure to roam the magical, steep streets of the **Albayzín**, the ancient Moorish quarter.

Logistics: The Seville–Granada leg of this trip is best accomplished by renting a car; Antequera makes a good quick stop on the way. However, the Seville–Granada trains (four daily, about 3½ hours, €30) are one alternative. Another idea is to head first from Madrid to Granada, and then from Granada to Seville via Córdoba.

GREAT ITINERARIES

BARCELONA, THE NORTH COAST, AND GALICIA, 16-DAY ITINERARY

Dive into happening Barcelona, with its unique blend of Gothic and Gaudí architecture, colorful markets, and long city beaches. Then head to the verdant north for culinary sophistication in San Sebastián and to check out the Guggenheim in chic Bilbao. Next, wind your way along the wild, rugged coastline, taking in the mountains, fishing ports, bagpipes, and Europe's best seafood along the way.

Days 1–3: Barcelona

To get a feel for Barcelona, begin with **La Rambla** and the **Boquería** market. Then set off for the **Gothic Quarter** to see the **Catedral de la Seu, Plaça del Rei,** and the Catalan and Barcelona government palaces in **Plaça Sant Jaume.** Next, cross Via Laietana to the **Born-Ribera** (waterfront neighborhood) for the Gothic **Santa Maria del Mar** and nearby **Museu Picasso.**

Make Day 2 a Gaudí day: visit the **Temple Expiatori de la Sagrada Família,** then **Park Güell.** In the afternoon see the **Casa Milà** and **Casa Batlló,** part of the Manzana de la Discòrdia on Passeig de Gràcia. **Palau Güell,** off the lower Rambla, is probably too much Gaudí for one day, but don't miss it.

On Day 3, climb **Montjuïc** for the **Museu Nacional d'Art de Catalunya,** in the hulking **Palau Nacional.** Investigate the **Fundació Miró, Estadi Olímpic,** the **Mies van der Rohe Pavilion,** and **CaixaForum** exhibition center. At lunchtime, take the cable car across the port for seafood in **Barceloneta** and then stroll along the beach.

Logistics: In Barcelona, walking or taking the subway is better than cabbing it.

Day 4: San Sebastián

San Sebastián is one of Spain's most beautiful—and delicious—cities. Belle Époque buildings nearly encircle the tiny bay, and tapas bars flourish in the old quarter. Not far from San Sebastián is historic **Pasajes (Pasaia) de San Juan.**

Logistics: Take the train from Barcelona to San Sebastián (5 hours 30 minutes) first thing in the morning. You don't need a car in San Sebastián proper, but visits to cider houses in Astigarraga, Chillida Leku on the outskirts of town, and many of the finest restaurants around San Sebastián are possible only with your own transportation or a taxi (the latter with the advantage that you won't get lost). The freeway west to Bilbao is beautiful and fast, but the coastal road is recommended at least as far as Zumaia.

Days 5 and 6: The Basque Coast

The Basque coast between San Sebastián and Bilbao has a succession of fine beaches, rocky cliffs, and picture-perfect fishing ports. The wide beach at **Zarautz,** the fishermen's village of **Getaria,** the **Zuloaga Museum in Zumaia,** and **Bermeo's** port and fishing museum should all be near the top of your list.

Days 7 and 8: Bilbao

Bilbao's **Guggenheim Museum** is worth a trip for the building itself, and the **Museo de Bellas Artes** has an impressive collection of Basque and Spanish paintings. Restaurants and tapas bars are famously good in Bilbao.

Logistics: In Bilbao, use the subway or the Euskotram, which runs up and down the Nervión estuary.

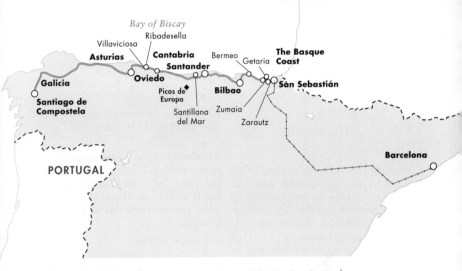

Bay of Biscay
Ribadesella
Villaviciosa
Asturias   **Cantabria**   Bermeo   **The Basque**
Oviedo   **Santander**   Getaria   **Coast**
Galicia   Picos de   **Bilbao**   **San Sebastián**
Europa
Santiago de   Santillana   Zumaia
Compostela   del Mar   Zarautz
Barcelona
PORTUGAL

Days 9 and 10: Santander and Cantabria

The elegant beach town of **Santander** has an excellent summer music festival every August. Nearby, **Santillana del Mar** is one of Spain's best Renaissance towns, and the museum of the **Altamira Caves** displays reproductions of the famous underground Neolithic rock paintings discovered here. Exploring the **Picos de Europa** will take you through some of the peninsula's wildest reaches, and the port towns along the coast provide some of Spain's most pristine beaches.

Days 11–13: Oviedo and Asturias

The coast road through **Ribadesella** and the cider capital **Villaviciosa** to **Oviedo** is scenic and punctuated with tempting beaches. Oviedo, its **cathedral,** and the simplicity of its pre-Romanesque churches are worlds away from the richness of Córdoba's Mezquita and Granada's Alhambra.

Logistics: The A8 coastal freeway gets you quickly and comfortably to Gijón, then hop on the A-66 to Oviedo. From there, head back to the A-8 and go west through Avilés and into Galicia via the coastal N634—a slow but scenic route to Santiago.

Days 14–16: Santiago de Compostela and Galicia

Spain's northwest corner, with **Santiago de Compostela** at its spiritual and geographic center, is a green land of bagpipes and apple orchards. The albariño wine country, along the Río Miño border with Portugal, and the *rías* (estuaries), full of delicious seafood, will keep you steeped in *enxebre*—Gallego for "local specialties and atmosphere."

Logistics: The four-lane freeways AP9 and A6 whisk you from Lugo and Castro to Santiago de Compostela and to the Rías Baixas. By car is the only way to tour Galicia. The AC862 route around the upper northwest corner and the Rías Altas turns into the AP9 coming back into Santiago.

GREAT ITINERARIES

MADRID AND BARCELONA, 6-DAY ITINERARY

Combining Spain's two largest and greatest cities on a six-day itinerary gives you the chance to take in the contrasts of Imperial Madrid and Moderniste Barcelona. Both cities are vibrant, energetic cultural centers showcasing some of Europe's greatest art and architecture as well as Spanish gastronomy at its best. You can also get a taste for Spain's late-night fun, sample its colorful markets, and stay at some of the country's best lodgings. However, Madrid and Barcelona feel very different, and you'll find huge contrasts in their landscapes, culture, and ambience. By visiting them both you'll get a good idea of the many facets that make up Spain.

For what to do on your days in Madrid, see the "Madrid to the Alhambra" itinerary above. For Barcelona, see the "Barcelona, the North Coast, and Galicia" itinerary above.

Logistics: Take the high-speed train (AVE) from Madrid to Barcelona (2 hours 30 minutes). For the return journey, fly from Barcelona to Madrid Barajas Airport in time to catch your flight home.

ANDALUSIA 7-DAY ITINERARY

Head south to a land of fiery flamenco passion, unique Moorish treasures, impossibly white villages, and delicious sherry and tapas. As you make your way from Córdoba to Granada via Seville, Jerez de la Frontera, and Málaga, prepare yourself to see some of Europe's finest

monuments, prettiest villages, and loveliest—albeit most sweltering—landscapes.

Day 1: Córdoba

Córdoba's breathtaking **Mezquita** (mosque), now a cathedral, is an Andalusian highlight, and the medieval **Jewish Quarter** is lovely to explore. If you're here during May, visit the **Festival de los Patios** (Patio Festival).

Days 2–3: Seville

The city that launched Christopher Columbus to the New World, **Seville** is a treasure trove of sights. Start with the **cathedral** and climb La Giralda for great views of the city. Move on to the richly decorated **Alcázar,** still an official royal residence, with its many beautiful patios, and where, more recently, much of the Game of Thrones epic was filmed. The **Jewish Quarter** in Santa Cruz is a charming labyrinth of alleyways and squares. In the afternoon, cross to **Triana** over the Guadalquivir River and lose yourself in the quiet streets, which are the birthplace of many a flamenco artist.

Logistics: Take the high-speed train (AVE) to Seville from Córdoba (45 minutes). Seville is a compact city and easy to navigate so it's best to explore on foot—or pick up a municipal bicycle at one of the hundreds of Sevici bike stations spread out across the city

Day 4: Jerez de la Frontera and Ronda via Arcos de la Frontera

Jerez de la Frontera is the world's sherry headquarters and home to some of the greatest bodegas. Visit Domecq, Harvey, or Sandeman, and, if you have time, watch the world's finest dancing horses at the prestigious Royal Andalusian School of Equestrian Art. The lovely cliff-top village of **Arcos de la Frontera,** one of Andalusia's prettiest *pueblos blancos* (white villages),

PORTUGAL

ANDALUSIA

Córdoba
Seville
Arcos de la Frontera
Granada
Jerez de la Frontera
Ronda
Málaga
COSTA DEL SOL

Mediterranean Sea

makes a great stop on the way to **Ronda.** One of the oldest towns in Spain, Ronda is famed for its spectacular position and views; get the best photo from the Juan Peña El Lebrijano Bridge.

Logistics: Rent a car in Seville and take the highway to Jerez de la Frontera before making your way to Ronda via Arcos de la Frontera. If you have time, stop off in the lovely village of Grazalema.

Day 5: Málaga

Start your exploration of the capital of the **Costa del Sol, Málaga,** with the **Roman theater,** Moorish **Alcazaba,** and Gothic **cathedral.** Stroll down to the Muelle Uno on the port for views of the city skyline and **Gibralfaro** castle before returning to the center to visit the **Museo Picasso** and browse the shops in Larios and surrounding streets.

Logistics: Leave Ronda early and enjoy the scenic drive to Málaga via the A367 and A357. In Málaga, explore on foot, leaving your car in a central lot or at your hotel.

Days 6–7: Granada

Allow a good half day to visit the hilltop **Alhambra** palace and Generalife gardens. From there, walk down to the city center to the **cathedral** and **Capilla Real,** the shrine of Isabella of Castile and Ferdinand of Aragón. Finish your day with some tapas

TIP

Rent a car with a GPS navigation system to help you find your way from one Andalusian city to the next. Help with navigating is also useful in the cities themselves.

at one of the many famous tapas bars. On Day 7, walk up to the Albayzín, the ancient Moorish quarter, for a leisurely wander around the narrow streets. Take your time in the Plaza de San Nicolás and admire the magnificent views of the Alhambra and Sierra Nevada before you leave.

Logistics: The drive to Granada from Málaga takes about 1 hour 30 minutes. Granada is best explored on foot, so leave your car at the hotel.

SPAIN MADE EASY

Do I need to book hotels beforehand, or can I just improvise once I'm in Spain? In big cities or popular tourist areas it's best to reserve well ahead. In smaller towns and rural areas, you can usually find something on the spot, except when local fiestas are on—for those dates you may have to book months in advance.

What are my lodging musts in Spain? For a slice of Spanish culture, stay in a parador: some are modern resorts, and the rest are splendid restorations—of ducal palaces, hilltop castles, monasteries and convents, and Arab fortresses. The historic paradores make wonderful romantic getaways, but they can also be surprisingly family-friendly stopovers. To indulge your pastoral fantasies, try a *casa rural* (country house), Spain's version of a bed-and-breakfast.

Will I get by with my High School Spanish? You don't need to be fluent to make yourself understood pretty much anywhere in Spain, but you might be surprised to hear different languages spoken. For example, Barcelonans speak Catalan, a Latin-based language that has similarities to Spanish, French, and Italian. Same goes for Galicia, whose language Gallego resembles both Portuguese and Spanish. And then in San Sebastian you'll hear Euskera, the Basque language, which is considered one of the most unique languages in the world.

Do shops really close for siesta? In general, shops close 2–5 pm, particularly in small towns and villages. The exceptions are supermarkets and large department stores, which tend to be open 9 am–9 pm in the center of Madrid and Barcelona, and stores at major resorts, which often stay open all day.

Can I get dinner at 7 pm, or do I really have to wait until the Spanish eat at 9 pm? If you really can't wait, head for the most touristy part of town; there you should be able to find bars and cafés that will serve meals at any time of day. But it won't be nearly as good as the food the Spaniards are eating a couple of hours later. You might be better off just dining on tapas.

If I only have time for one city, should I choose Barcelona or Madrid? It depends on what you're looking for. Madrid will give you world-class art and much more of a sense of a workaday Spanish city, while cosmopolitan Barcelona has Gaudí, Catalan cuisine, and its special Mediterranean atmosphere.

How easy is it to cross the border from Spain into neighboring countries? Spain, Portugal, and France are members of the EU's Schengen zone, so borders are open. Overnight trains connect Madrid and Lisbon (11 hours, from about €85), and Madrid and Paris (10–12 hours, depending on stops, from about €250). American citizens need only a valid passport to enter Morocco; ferries run regularly to Tangier from Tarifa (€37 one-way, €200 with a car) and Algeciras (€37 one-way, €130 with a car).

Can I bring home the famous ibérico ham, Spanish olives, almonds, or baby eels? Products you can legally bring into the United States include olive oil, cheese, olives, almonds, wood-smoked paprika, and saffron. These products must be declared at customs. Ibérico ham, even vacuum sealed, is not legal, so you may not get past customs agents and their canine associates. If caught, you risk confiscation and fines. And don't even think about trying to bring back *angulas* (eels).

For more help on trip planning, see the Travel Smart Spain chapter.

MADRID

WELCOME TO MADRID

TOP REASONS TO GO

★ **Hit the Centro Histórico:** The Plaza Mayor, on any late night when it's almost empty, is the place that best evokes the glory of Spain's Golden Age.

★ **Stroll down museum row:** Find a pleasant mix of art and architecture in the Prado, the Reina Sofía, and the Thyssen-Bornemisza, all of which display extensive and impressive collections.

★ **Nibble tapas into the night:** Indulge in a madrileño way of socializing. Learn about the art of tapas and sample local wines while wandering among the bars of Cava Baja and Calle Ponzano.

★ **Relax in the Retiro gardens:** Visit on a Sunday morning, when it's at its most boisterous, to unwind and enjoy some primo people-watching.

★ **Burn the midnight oil:** As other Europeans tuck themselves in, madrileños swarm to the bars of the liveliest neighborhoods—Malasaña, Chueca, Lavapiés, Barrio de las Letras, and more—and stretch the party out until dawn.

Madrid comprises 21 districts, each broken down into several neighborhoods. The most central district is called just that: Centro. Here you'll find all of Madrid's oldest neighborhoods: Palacio, Sol, La Latina, Lavapiés, Barrio de las Letras, Malasaña, and Chueca. Other well-known districts, which we'll call neighborhoods for the sake of convenience, are Salamanca, Retiro, Chamberí (north of Centro), Moncloa (east of Chamberí), and Chamartín.

The first written mentions of Madrid date to the 9th century, making it a relatively new city by Spanish standards. It blossomed into the busy metropolis we know today in the mid-19th century, when an urban planner knocked down the city walls built in 1625 and charted new neighborhoods in what were formerly the outskirts. Today Madrid is the third-most-populated city in Europe (after London and Berlin) with 3.2 million residents spread over a a sprawling metropolitan area—though the walkable historic center continues to harbor most of the city's main attractions.

1 Palacio, La Latina, and Sol. Palacio and La Latina have the city's highest concentration of aristocratic buildings and elegant yet affordable bars and restaurants, and Sol has some of the city's busiest streets and oldest shops.

2 Barrio de las Letras.
This area is where many of Spain's great writers eventually settled, and it still has good nightlife and trendy hotels.

3 Chueca and Malasaña.
These newly gentrified neighborhoods offer eclectic, hip restaurants, designer boutiques, and cafés where an international crowd sips flat whites.

4 Embajadores. The two areas in the Embajadores neighborhood, El Rastro and Lavapiés, are full of winding streets and a popular flea market; Lavapiés is the city's hottest new neighborhood.

5 Salamanca, Retiro, and Chamberí. Retiro, so called for its proximity to the park, holds some of the city's most regal buildings. Salamanca has long been

the upper-middle-class's favorite enclave and has elegant if staid shops and restaurants. Chamberí, farther north, is largely residential, with spacious plazas and rootsy tapas bars.

6 Chamartín and Tetuán.
These northerly neighborhoods are international, tourist-free, and ripe for discovery.

EATING AND DRINKING WELL IN MADRID

Spain's capital draws the finest cuisine—from seafood to rice dishes and more—from all over the Iberian Peninsula, but the most quintessential local fare is akin to Castilian cuisine, which revolves around roasted meats and stewed legumes.

(top left) A selection of tapas, including smoked ham and roasted peppers (top right) A hearty clam and beans stew (bottom left) Ingredients for a classic cocido madrileño

With a climate sometimes described as *nueve meses de invierno y tres de infierno* (nine months of winter and three of hell), it's no surprise that classic Madrid cuisine is essentially comfort food. Garlic soup, stewed chickpeas, and roast suckling pig and lamb are standard components of Madrid feasts, as are baby goat and deeply flavored beef from Ávila and the Sierra de Guadarrama. *Cocido madrileño* (a meat-packed winter stew) and *callos a la madrileña* (stewed tripe) are favored local specialties, while *jamón ibérico de bellota* (acorn-fed Ibérico ham)—a specialty from *las dehesas*, the rolling oak forests of Extremadura and Andalusia—is a staple on special occasions. Summer fare hinges on minimally manipulated fruits and vegetables, while contemporary restaurants frequently offer lighter dishes.

TAPAS

Itinerant grazing from tavern to tavern is especially popular in Madrid, beneficiary of tapas traditions from every corner of Spain. The areas around Plaza Santa Ana, Plaza Mayor, Calle Ponzano, and Cava Baja buzz with excitement as crowds drink beer and wine while devouring platefuls of *boquerones* (pickled anchovies), *calamares a la romana* (fried squid), or *albóndigas* (meatballs).

2

SOUPS

Sopa de ajo (garlic soup), also known as *sopa castellana,* is a homey soup that starts with an unapologetically garlicky ham-bone stock. Stale bread is then torn in to thicken it up, followed by a cracked egg—a final enriching flourish. *Caldo* (hot chicken or beef broth), a Madrid favorite on wet winter days, is often offered free of charge in traditional bars and cafés with an order of anything else.

STEWS

Cocido madrileño is Madrid's ultimate comfort food, a boiled dinner of garbanzo beans, vegetables, potatoes, sausages, pork, and hen simmered for hours in earthenware crocks over coals and presented in multiple courses. It is usually served in an earthenware casserole to keep the stew piping hot. *Estofado de judiones de La Granja* (broad-bean stew) is another soul-satisfying favorite: pork, quail, ham, or whatever meat is available simmers with onions, tomatoes, carrots, and luxuriously creamy broad beans from the Segovian town of La Granja de San Ildefonso.

ROASTS

Asadores (restaurants specializing in roasts) are an institution in and around Madrid, where the *cochinillo asado,* or roast suckling pig, is the crown jewel. Whether you taste this culinary specialty at Casa Botín in Madrid or Mesón de

Cándido in Segovia or Adolfo Restaurant in Toledo, the preparation is largely the same: milk-fed piglets are roasted in oak-burning wood ovens and emerge shatteringly crisp yet tender enough to carve using the edge of a plate. *Lechazo,* or milk-fed lamb, is another asador stalwart that emerges from wood ovens accompanied by the aromas of oak and Castile's wide meseta: thistle, rosemary, and thyme..

WINES

The traditional Madrid house wine, a coarse Valdepeñas from La Mancha, south of the capital, has fallen out of favor as better-quality cuvées from Rioja and Ribera del Duero (for reds) and Rueda and Rías Baixas (for whites) have become more readily available. Deep-pink *rosados*, the best of which hail from Rioja, Catalonia, and Navarra, are increasingly popular in the summer.

Updated by Benjamin Kemper

Madrid, the Spanish capital since 1561, is Europe's city that never sleeps. A vibrant and increasingly international metropolis, Madrid has an infectious appetite for art, music, and epicurean pleasures yet remains steadfast in its age-old traditions.

The modern city spreads east into the 19th-century grid of the Barrio de Salamanca and sprawls north through the neighborhoods of Chamberí and Chamartín, but the part of Madrid that draws visitors the world over is its historic center, situated between the Palacio Real and the city's green lung, the Parque del Buen Retiro. A conglomeration of Belle Époque buildings with intricate facades, terra-cotta-roofed residences and redbrick Mudejar Revival churches, Madrid is a stately stunner, but the city's most memorable aspect may be its culture of being outdoors as much as possible: restaurant patios, flea markets, and parks and plazas are always abuzz with madrileños.

Then there are the paintings—the artistic legacy of one of the most important global empires ever assembled. King Carlos I (1500–58), who later became Emperor Carlos V (or Charles V), set out to collect the best specimens from all European schools of art, many of which found their way to Spain's palaces and, later, to the Prado Museum. Between the classical Prado, the contemporary Reina Sofía, the wide-ranging Thyssen-Bornemisza, and Madrid's smaller artistic repositories—the Real Academia de Bellas Artes de San Fernando, the Convento de las Descalzas Reales, the Sorolla Museum, the Lázaro Galdiano Museum, and the CaixaForum, to name a few—there are more paintings here than you could admire in a lifetime.

Not all of the city's most memorable attractions are centuries old. The CaixaForum arts center is an architectural triumph by Jacques Herzog and Pierre de Meuron. Futuristic towers by Norman Foster and César Pelli have changed the city's northern landscape. Other newly finished projects include Madrid Río, which has added nearly 20 miles of green space along the banks of the Manzanares River, and the Conde Duque cultural center, a multidisciplinary haven that hosts film screenings, dance nights, poetry readings, and more.

PLANNING

WHEN TO GO

Madrid is hot and dry in summer—with temperatures reaching 40°C (105°F) in July and August—and chilly and damp in winter, with minimum temperatures around 1°C (in the low 30s), though snow in the city is rare. The most pleasant time to visit is spring, especially May, when the city honors its patron saint with street fairs and celebrations. June and September–December are also fine times to visit.

If you can, avoid Madrid in July and August—especially August, even though fares are better and there are plenty of concerts and open-air activities; locals flee the punishing heat and head to the coast or to the mountains, so many restaurants, bars, and shops are closed. Winter is a pleasant time to visit, if you don't mind bundling up a bit in the evenings.

PLANNING YOUR TIME

Madrid's most valuable art treasures are all on display within a few blocks of Paseo del Prado. This area is home to the Museo del Prado, whose collection amasses masterworks by Velázquez, Goya, El Greco, and others; the Centro de Arte Reina Sofía, whose eclectic contemporary art pieces include Picasso's *Guernica*; and the Museo Thyssen-Bornemisza, whose collection stretches from the Renaissance to the 21st century. Each can take hours to explore, so it's best to alternate museum visits with less overwhelming attractions. If you're running short on time and want to pack everything in, recharge at any of the tapas bars or restaurants in the Barrio de las Letras (behind the Paseo del Prado, across from the Prado).

Any visit to Madrid should include a walk through the historic area between Puerta del Sol and the Palacio Real. Leave the map in your back pocket and wander through the Plaza Mayor, Plaza de la Villa, Plaza de Oriente, pausing to marvel at some of the city's oldest churches and convents.

GETTING HERE AND AROUND

AIR TRAVEL

Madrid's Adolfo Suárez Madrid–Barajas Airport is Europe's sixth-busiest. Terminal 4 (T4) handles flights from 22 carriers, including American Airlines, British Airways, and Iberia. All other U.S. airlines use Terminal 1 (T1).

AIRPORT TRANSFERS Airport terminals are connected by bus service and also to Línea 8 of the metro, which reaches the city center in 30–45 minutes for around €5 (€1.50–€2 plus a €3 airport supplement). For €5 there are also convenient buses (Nos. 203 and 203 Exprés) to the Atocha train station (with stops on Calle de O'Donnell and Plaza de Cibeles) and to Avenida de América (note that bus drivers don't take bills greater than €20), where you can catch the metro or a taxi to your hotel. Taxis charge a flat fee of €30 from the airport to anywhere in the city center.

BIKE TRAVEL

Bicimad (⊕ *www.bicimad.com*) is Madrid's public bike-share service with almost 200 docks scattered around the city center. The bikes are electric, meaning you hardly have to pedal, and are an excellent alternative to the metro and buses, provided the weather is good and you're comfortable riding in traffic (separate bike lanes are virtually nonexistent). Locals can purchase a yearly membership, but visitors can pay per ride, buying a ticket at each service station. The bikes can be borrowed from, and returned to, any station in the system. Occasional users pay €2 for the first half hour and €4 for each successive half hour.

BUS TRAVEL

Buses are generally less popular than trains, though they're sometimes faster and cheaper. Madrid has no central bus station: most of southern and eastern Spain (including Toledo) is serviced by the Estación del Sur, while Intercambiador de Moncloa and Estación de Avenida de América service northern destinations. All have eponymous metro stops (except for Estación del Sur, serviced by Méndez Álvaro).

Blue city buses (€1.50 one-way) run about 6 am–11:30 pm. Less frequent night buses run through the night on heavily trafficked routes.

Bus Stations **Estación de Avenida de América.** ⊠ *Av. de América 9, Salamanca* 🕾 *90/242–2242 for ALSA Bus Company* ⊕ *www.crtm.es/tu-transporte-publico/intercambiadores.aspx* Ⓜ *Av. de América.* **Estación del Sur.** ⊠ *Calle Méndez Álvaro s/n, Atocha* 🕾 *91/468–4200* ⊕ *www.estaciondeautobuses.com* Ⓜ *Méndez Álvaro.* **Intercambiador de Moncloa.** ⊠ *Princesa 89, Moncloa* 🕾 *012 for Madrid city hotline* ⊕ *www.crtm.es* Ⓜ *Moncloa.*

CAR TRAVEL

Driving in Madrid is best avoided, because parking is a nightmare and traffic is challenging, but many of the nation's highways radiate from Madrid, including the A6 (Segovia, Salamanca, Galicia); the A1 (Burgos and the Basque Country); the A2 (Guadalajara, Barcelona, France); the A3 (Cuenca, Valencia, the Mediterranean coast); the A4 (Aranjuez, La Mancha, Granada, Seville); the A42 (Toledo); and the A5 (Talavera de la Reina, Portugal). The city is surrounded by ring roads (M30, M40, and M50), from which most of these highways are easily picked up. There are also toll highways (marked R2, R3, R4, and R5) that bypass major highways, and the A41, a toll highway connecting Madrid and Toledo.

Blablacar is Spain's leading rideshare app in intercity travel with more global users than Uber. Its free platform allows you to book ahead using a credit card, and message with the driver to set meeting and drop-off points. Blablacar is the most affordable way to travel to Madrid's outlying cities and beyond as drivers aren't allowed to make a profit (you essentially help the driver offset the price of gas and tolls).

SUBWAY TRAVEL

The metro costs €1.50–€2, depending on how far you're traveling within the city; you can also buy a 10-ride Metrobus ticket (€12.20). The **Abono Turístico** (Tourist Pass) allows unlimited use of public buses and the subway for one day (€8.40 for Zone A, €17 for Zone T) to seven days (€35.40 for Zone A, €70.80 for Zone T); buy it at tourist offices, metro stations, or select newsstands. The metro runs 6 am–1:30 am, though a few entrances close earlier. *(See the metro map in this chapter.)*

Subway Information Metro Madrid. ☎ *90/244-4403* ⊕ *www.metromadrid.es.*

TAXI TRAVEL

Taxis work under several tariff schemes. Tariff 1 is for the city center 7 am–9 pm; meters start at €2.40. There is a fixed taxi fare of €30 to or from the airport from the city center. Supplements include €3 to or from bus and train stations. Tariff 2 is for the city center 9 pm–7 am on weekdays (and 7 am–9 pm on weekends and holidays); the meter starts at €2.90 and charges more per kilometer. Besides reserving a taxi by phone, you can also do it through mobile app MyTaxi, which works with local official taxi drivers. As of mid-2018, Uber and Cabify are back in operation after a hiatus due to legal restrictions; in 2017, UberONE, Uber's premium service, added 50 Teslas to its Madrid fleet.

Taxi Services **Radio Taxi Gremial.** ☎ *91/447–3232, 91/447–5180* ⊕ *www. radiotaxigremial.com.* **Radioteléfono Taxi.** ☎ *91/547–8200* ⊕ *www.radiotele-fono-taxi.com.* **Tele-Taxi.** ☎ *91/371–2131* ⊕ *www.tele-taxi.es.*

TRAIN TRAVEL

Madrid is the geographical center of Spain, and all major train lines depart from one of its two main train stations (Chamartín and Atocha) or pass through Madrid. Though train travel is comfortable, for some destinations buses run more frequently and make fewer stops; this is true for Segovia and Toledo, unless you take the more expensive high-speed train.

Commuter trains to El Escorial, Aranjuez, and Alcalá de Henares run frequently. The best way to get a ticket for such trains is to use one of the automated reservation terminals at the station. You can reach Segovia and Toledo from Atocha station in a half hour on the high-speed Alvia and Avant lines; if you book ahead, the ticket may cost less than €25. Train stations in Toledo and Segovia are outside the city, meaning once there you'll have to take a bus or a taxi into the center.

The high-speed AVE can get you to Barcelona in less than three hours. If you buy the ticket ahead online (with discounts up to 60% off the official fare), you may pay less than €40 each way for (often nonrefundable) tickets. Otherwise expect to pay between €60 and €100 each way—the higher price is for nonstop service.

⇨ *For more information about buying train tickets, see the Travel Smart chapter.*

Train Information **Estación Chamartín.** ✉ *Calle Agustín de Foxá s/n, Chamartín* ☎ *91/232–0320* ⊕ *www.adif.es* Ⓜ *Chamartín.* **Estación de Atocha.** ✉ *Glorieta del Emperador Carlos V, Atocha* ☎ *91/232–0320* ⊕ *www.adif. es* Ⓜ *Atocha.* **Estación de Príncipe Pío (Norte).** ✉ *Paseo de la Florida s/n, Moncloa* ☎ *90/210–9804* Ⓜ *Príncipe Pío.*

TOURS
BIKE TOURS

Biking in Madrid can be a white-knuckle experience for those unaccustomed to biking in traffic, but for leisurely sightseeing through parks and along the river, bike tours can be a pleasant activity.

BravoBike. BravoBike offers guided bike tours in English (from €35 for three hours). It also offers multiday guided and self-guided bike tours near Madrid, in Toledo, Aranjuez, Chinchón, and Segovia, as well as tours along the pilgrimage route to Santiago de Compostela and Andalusia, among others. ⊠ *Calle Juan Álvarez Mendizábal 19, Moncloa* ☏ *91/758–2945, 60/744–8440 for WhatsApp* ⊕ *www.bravobike.com* ⊠ *From €35.*

BUS TOURS

Madrid City Tours. These ubiquitous red double-decker tourist buses make 1½-hour circuits of the city, allowing you to get on and off at various attractions (there is a Historic Madrid tour and a Modern Madrid tour, plus a Night Tour June 16–September 15) with recorded English commentary. There are one- and two-day passes. ☏ *90/202–4758* ⊕ *www.madrid.city-tour.com* ⊠ *From €19.*

Plaza Mayor tourist office. Madrid's main tourist office, open 365 days a year, is a treasure trove of maps and resources and will happily recommend popular bus, segway, cycling, and walking tours to meet your needs. ⊠ *Pl. Mayor 27, Sol* ☏ *91/531–0074* ⊕ *www.esmadrid.com.*

WALKING TOURS

Asociación Nacional de Guías de Turismo (APIT). This tour operator offers custom history and art walks by government-certified travel guides. ⊠ *Calle Jacometrezo 4, 9º 13, Sol* ☏ *91/542–1214* ⊕ *www.apit.es.*

Carpetania Madrid. This company offers niche, brainy tours and literary walks on topics like "Women of Malasaña" and "Almodóvar's Madrid." (Spanish only.) ⊠ *Calle Jesús del Valle 11, Malasaña* ☏ *91/531–1418* ⊕ *www.carpetaniamadrid.com* ⊠ *From €10.*

FAMILY
Fodor's Choice
★

Devour Madrid. A hip, young tour company catering to foodie travelers of all interests and ages (custom and kids' tours are available), Devour Madrid hosts walks that run the gamut from a "Tapas Like a Local" neighborhood crawl to a "Prado Museum Tour" that culminates in a lunch at Botín, Madrid's oldest restaurant. ⊠ *Calle de la Torrecilla del Leal 10, Cortes* ☏ *69/511–1832* ⊕ *www.madridfoodtour.com* ⊠ *From €49.*

EXPLORING

You won't find the soul of Madrid on the tourist-packed arteries of the Gran Vía and the Paseo de la Castellana; look instead on the quiet, residential streets and squares that give the city its signature charm. Duck into the warren of villagelike byways in the downtown area between the Palacio Real and the Parque del Buen Retiro, or get lost in the more alternative neighborhoods between Plaza de Lavapiés and the Glorieta de Bilbao. Broad *avenidas*, twisting medieval alleys, grand museums, stately gardens, and boisterous taverns are all jumbled together, creating an urban texture so rich that walking is the best way to soak it in.

Madrid Metro

KEY

- **1** *Metro Terminals*
- ○ *Metro Stations*
- ■ *Transfer Stations*
- —•— *Railway Lines*
- • *Train Stations*

PALACIO, LA LATINA, AND SOL

Madrid's historic center, a mishmash of centuries-old buildings and newfangled shops, winds from the Palacio through La Latina neighborhood and ends at the Puerta del Sol, the city's busiest square. Madrid may not be as spellbindingly ancient as nearby Toledo or Segovia, but what the city lacks in antiquity it makes up for with charm and panache.

Just beyond the Palacio Real, Moncloa boasts large swaths of green space in the Parque del Oeste, which houses Templo de Debod and connects with Madrid Río and Casa de Campo.

PALACIO

Madrid's oldest neighborhood, Palacio is the home of the imposing Palacio Real. This is where Muhammad I established the city's first military post in the 9th century, essentially founding the city. The quarter, bounded by the Plaza Mayor to the east, is a maze of cobblestone streets lined with homey restaurants and old-school cafés and shops.

Monasterio de la Encarnación (*Monastery of the Incarnation*). Once connected to the Palacio Real by an underground passageway, this Augustinian convent now houses fewer than a dozen nuns. Founded in 1611 by Queen Margarita de Austria, the wife of Felipe III, it has several artistic treasures, including a reliquary where a vial with the dried blood of St. Pantaleón is said to liquefy every July 27. The ornate church has superb acoustics for medieval and Renaissance choral concerts. ⊠ *Pl. de la Encarnación 1, Palacio* ☎ *91/454–8800 for tourist office* ✆ *From €6* ⊘ *Closed Mon.* Ⓜ *Ópera.*

Monasterio de las Descalzas Reales (*Monastery of the Royal Discalced, or Barefoot, Nuns*). This 16th-century building was restricted for 200 years to women of royal blood. Its plain, brick-and-stone facade begets an opulent interior strewn with paintings by Francisco de Zurbarán, Titian, and Pieter Brueghel the Elder—all part of the dowry that novices had to provide when they joined the monastery—as well as a hall of sumptuous tapestries crafted from drawings by Peter Paul Rubens. The convent was founded in 1559 by Juana of Austria, one of Felipe II's sisters, who ruled Spain while he was in England and the Netherlands. It houses 33 different chapels—the age of Christ when he died and the maximum number of nuns allowed to live at the monastery—and more than 100 sculptures of Jesus as a baby. About 30 nuns (not necessarily of royal blood) still live here and grow vegetables in the convent's garden. ■ TIP→ **You must take a (Spanish-only) tour in order to visit the convent.** ⊠ *Pl. de las Descalzas Reales 3, Palacio* ☎ *91/454–8800* ✆ *From €6* ⊘ *Closed Mon.* Ⓜ *Sol.*

▮ **NEED A BREAK**

✕ **Chocolatería Valor.** Despite what the ads say, Madrid is not always sunny. If you hit a rainy or chilly day, walk along the western side of the Monasterio de las Descalzas Reales until you reach Chocolatería Valor, an ideal spot to indulge in piping-hot churros dipped in thick hot chocolate. ⊠ *Calle Postigo de San Martín 7, Palacio* ⊕ *www.valor.es* Ⓜ *Callao.*

★ **Palacio Real.** Emblematic of the oldest part of the city, the Royal Palace awes visitors with its sheer size and monumental presence. The palace was commissioned in the early 18th century by the first of Spain's Bourbon rulers, Felipe V. Outside, you can see the classical French architecture on the graceful Patio de Armas; inside, 2,800 rooms compete with each other for over-the-top opulence. A two-hour guided tour in English points out highlights including the Salón de Gasparini, King Carlos III's private apartments; the Salón del Trono, a grand throne room; and the banquet hall, which seats up to 140 people for state dinners. Also worth visiting are the Museo de Música (Music Museum), the world's largest collection of five-stringed instruments by Antonio Stradivari; the Painting Gallery, with works by Spanish, Flemish, and Italian artists; the Armería Real (Royal Armory), with suits of armor and medieval torture implements; and the Real Oficina de Farmacía (Royal Pharmacy). ✉ *Calle Bailén s/n, Palacio* 🕾 *91/454–8800* 💲 *From €5* Ⓜ *Ópera.*

Plaza de la Villa. Madrid's town council met in the medieval-looking complex here from the Middle Ages until 2009, when it moved to the new city hall headquarters in the Palacio de Cibeles. It now houses municipal offices. The oldest building on the plaza is the **Casa de los Lujanes**—it's the one with the Mudejar tower. Built as a private home in the late 15th century, the house carries the Lujanes crest over the main doorway. Also on the plaza's east end is the brick-and-stone **Casa de la Villa,** built in 1629, a classic example of Madrid design, with clean lines and spire-topped corner towers. Connected by an overhead walkway, the **Casa de Cisneros** was commissioned in 1537 by the nephew of Cardinal Cisneros. It's one of Madrid's rare examples of the flamboyant plateresque style, which has been likened to splashed water. Sadly, none of these landmarks are open to the public. ✉ *Palacio* Ⓜ *Sol, Ópera.*

Plaza de Oriente. This stately plaza, in front of the Palacio Real, is surrounded by massive statues of Spanish monarchs. They were meant to be mounted on the railing on top of the palace, but Queen Isabel of Farnesio, one of the first royals to live in the palace, had them removed because she was afraid their enormous weight would bring the roof down. (At least that's the *official* reason; according to local lore, the queen wanted the statues removed because her own likeness had not been placed front and center.) A Velázquez drawing of King Felipe IV is the inspiration for the statue in the plaza's center. It's the first equestrian bronze ever cast with a rearing horse. The sculptor, Italian artist Pietro de Tacca, enlisted Galileo Galilei's help in configuring the statue's weight so it wouldn't tip over. ✉ *Palacio* Ⓜ *Ópera.*

LA LATINA

Officially part of the Palacio neighborhood, this bustling area bordered by Calle de Segovia to the north; Calle Toledo to the east; Plaza de la Cebada to the south; and Calle Bailén, with its imposing Basílica de San Francisco, to the west, houses some of the city's oldest buildings, plenty of sloping streets, and an array of unmissable tapas spots—especially on Cava Baja and Cava Alta, and in the area around Plaza de la Paja.

Cava Baja. The epicenter of the fashionable and historic La Latina neighborhood—a maze of narrow streets that extend south of Plaza

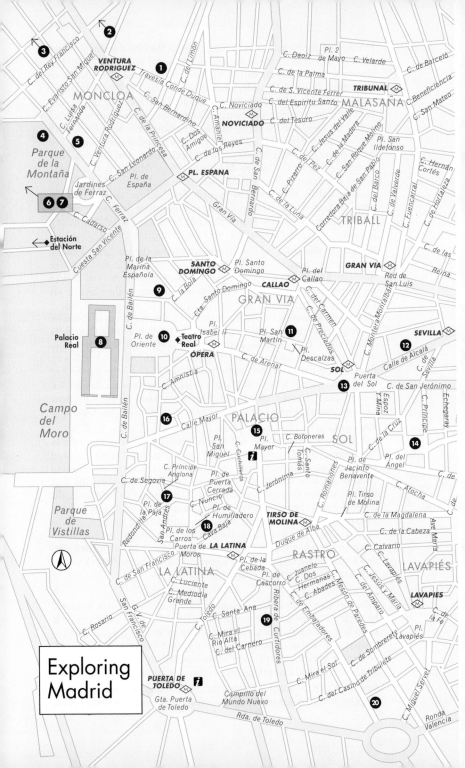

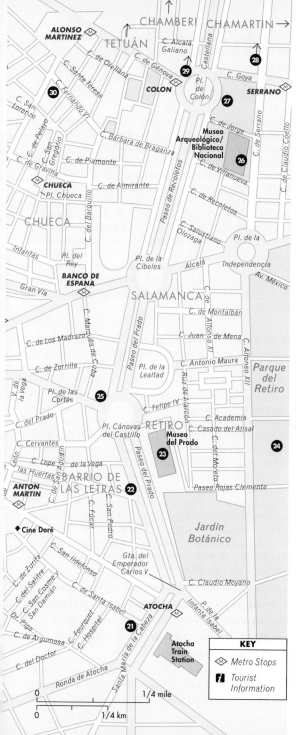

Mayor and across Calle Segovia—this is a diagonal street crowded with excellent (if overpriced) tapas bars and traditional tabernas. Its lively atmosphere spills over onto nearby streets and squares including Almendro, Cava Alta, Plaza del Humilladero, and Plaza de la Paja. ✉ *La Latina* Ⓜ *La Latina.*

Plaza de la Paja. At the top of the hill, on Costanilla San Andrés, sits the most important square in medieval Madrid. The plaza's jewel is the **Capilla del Obispo** (Bishop's Chapel), built between 1520 and 1530, where peasants deposited their tithes, called *diezmas*—one-tenth of their crop. Architecturally the chapel embodies the transition from the blocky Gothic period, which gave the structure its basic shape, to the Renaissance, the source of its decorations. It houses an intricately carved polychrome altarpiece by Francisco Giralta with scenes from the life of Christ. To visit the chapel (*Tuesday 9:30–12:30, Thursday 4–5:30*) reserve in advance (*91/559–2874* or *reservascapilladelobispo@ archimadrid.es*). The chapel is part of the complex of the domed church of San Andrés, one of Madrid's oldest. For centuries the church held the remains of Madrid's male patron saint, San Isidro Labrador; he was thought to have ended a drought on fields belonging to the Vargas family, whose 16th-century Vargas Palace forms the eastern side of the plaza. ✉ *La Latina* Ⓜ *La Latina.*

SOL

This small neighborhood, built in the 16th century around the Puerta del Sol, used to mark the city's geographic center, which today sits a tad to its east. Sol encompasses, among other sites, the monumental Plaza Mayor and the popular pedestrian shopping area around Callao.

Plaza Mayor. Austere, grand, and often surprisingly quiet compared to other plazas in the city, this public square, finished in 1619 under Felipe III—whose equestrian statue stands in the center—is one of the largest in Europe, measuring 360 feet by 300 feet. It's seen it all: autos-da-fé (public burnings of heretics); the canonization of saints; criminal executions; royal marriages; bullfights (until 1847); masked balls; and all manner of other events. This space was once occupied by a city market, and many of the surrounding streets retain names of the trades and foods once headquartered there (e.g., Knifemakers' Street, Lettuce Street). The plaza's oldest building, Casa de la Panadería (Bakery House), has brightly painted murals and gray spires; it is now the tourist office. Opposite sits Casa de la Carnicería (Butcher Shop), now a police station. The plaza is closed to motorized traffic, making it a pleasant if touristy spot to enjoy a cup of coffee. ✉ *Sol* Ⓜ *Sol.*

QUICK BITES

Mercado de San Miguel. Adjacent to the Plaza Mayor, this "gastronomic market" is a feast for the senses. Its bustling interior—a mixture of tapas spots and immaculately arranged grocery stalls—sits beneath a fin-de-siècle glass dome reinforced by elaborate wrought iron. ✉ *Pl. de San Miguel s/n, Sol* ⊕ *www.mercadodesanmiguel.es* Ⓜ *Ópera.*

Puerta del Sol. Crowded with people, hawkers, and street performers, the Puerta del Sol is the nerve center of Madrid. The city's main metro interchange, the largest in the world, is below. A brass plaque in the

sidewalk on the south side of the plaza marks Kilometer 0, the point from which all distances in Spain are measured. The restored 1756 French-neoclassical building near the marker now houses the offices of the regional government, but during Franco's reign, it was the headquarters of his secret police and is still known colloquially as the Casa de los Gritos (House of Screams). Across the square are a bronze statue of Madrid's official symbol, a bear with a *madroño* (strawberry tree), and a statue of King-Mayor Carlos III on horseback. ⊠ *Sol* Ⓜ *Sol.*

QUICK BITES

Gourmet Experience Callao. On the rooftop of El Corte Inglés, Spain's largest department store, there's a gourmet food court with some of the best views in the city. Grab a couple of tapas and a glass of wine here after perusing the shops around Callao. ⊠ *Pl. de Callao 1, Sol* ✛ *Take second entrance to El Corte Inglés as you're walking down Callao on Calle Carmen and across from Fnac* Ⓜ *Sol.*

Real Academia de Bellas Artes de San Fernando (*St. Ferdinand Royal Academy of Fine Arts*). Designed by José Benito de Churriguera in the waning baroque years of the early 18th century, this museum showcases 500 years of Spanish painting, from José Ribera and Bartolomé Esteban Murillo to Joaquín Sorolla and Ignacio Zuloaga. The tapestries along the stairways are stunning. The gallery displays paintings up to the 18th century, including some by Goya. Worthwhile guided tours are available on Tuesday, Thursday, and Friday at 11, except during August. The same building houses the **Instituto de Calcografía** (Prints Institute), which sells limited-edition prints from original plates engraved by Spanish artists. Check the website for classical concerts and literary events in the small upstairs hall. ⊠ *Calle de Alcalá 13, Sol* ☎ *91/524–0864* ⊕ *www.realacademiabellasartessanfernando.com* 🎫 *€8 (free Wed.)* 🕓 *Closed Mon.* Ⓜ *Sol.*

MONCLOA

A large neighborhood extending to the northwest of Madrid, Moncloa includes high-class residential areas, such as Puerta de Hierro and Aravaca; more urban ones such as Argüelles, teeming with college students and budget bars; and wonderfully scenic parks including Casa de Campo, Parque del Oeste (with the Templo de Debod gardens), and Dehesa de la Villa.

Ermita de San Antonio de la Florida (Goya's tomb). Built between 1792 and 1798 by the Italian architect Francisco Fontana, this neoclassical church was financed by King Carlos IV, who also commissioned Goya to paint the vaults and the main dome: it took him 120 days to fully depict events of the 13th century (St. Anthony of Padua resurrecting a dead man) as if they had happened five centuries later, with naturalistic images never used before to paint religious scenes. Opposite the image of the frightening dead man on the main dome, Goya painted himself as a man covered with a black cloak. The frescoes' third restoration phase ended in 2005, and visitors can now admire them in their full splendor. Goya, who died in Bordeaux in 1828, is buried here (without his head, because it was stolen in France) under an unadorned gravestone. ⊠ *Glorieta de*

The Puerta del Sol, Madrid's central transportation hub, is sure to be passed through by every visitor to the city.

San Antonio de la Florida 5, Moncloa ☎ *91/542–0722* ⊕ *www.sanantoniodelaflorida.es* ✉ *Free* ⊗ *Closed Mon.* Ⓜ *Príncipe Pío.*

Faro de Moncloa. This UFO-like tower, reopened in 2017 after a temporary closing due to fire damage, is 360 feet tall and an excellent viewpoint from which to gaze at some of the city's most outstanding buildings including the Palacio Real, Palacio de Cibeles (city hall), the four skyscrapers to the north, and up to 50 landmarks for which you'll find descriptions in English and Spanish. ⊠ *Av. Arco de la Victoria 2, Moncloa* ⊕ *www.esmadrid.com/en* ✉ *€3* Ⓜ *Moncloa.*

Museo del Traje (*Costume Museum*). This museum traces the evolution of dress in Spain, from old royal burial garments (very few of which remain) to French fashion pieces of Felipe V's reign to the haute couture creations of Balenciaga and Pertegaz. Explanatory notes are in English, and the museum has a superb restaurant overlooking the gardens that specializes in modern Spanish fare. ⊠ *Av. Juan de Herrera 2, Moncloa* ☎ *91/550–4700* ⊕ *museodeltraje.mcu.es* ✉ *€3 (free Sat. after 2:30 and Sun.)* ⊗ *Closed Mon.* Ⓜ *Ciudad Universitaria.*

FAMILY **Teleférico.** Kids and adults alike appreciate the sweeping views from this retro cable car, which takes you from the Rosaleda gardens in the Parque del Oeste to the center of Casa de Campo in about 10 minutes. If you're feeling active, take the (very) challenging hike to the top and ride the car down, or you can find hiking trails and horseback riding opportunities at the top. ■ TIP→ **This is not the best way to get to the zoo and theme park, located approximately 2 km (1 mile) from the drop-off point in Casa de Campo. You're better off riding the Teléferico out and back, then taking the bus to the zoo.** ⊠ *Estación Terminal Teleférico, Paseo* *de Pintor Rosales, at C. Marqués de Urquijo, Moncloa* ☎ *91/541–1118* ⊕ *www.telefericomadrid.es* 🎫 *From €5* 🕐 *Closed Oct.–Mar. and week-days* Ⓜ *Arguelles.*

Templo de Debod. It's not every day that you can marvel at a fully recon-structed ancient Egyptian temple from the 4th century BC, but thanks to the Egyptian government, which bequeathed the edifice to the Span-ish government in 1968 for its assistance with the construction of the Aswan Dam, it's free for the public to appreciate. Visit at sunset and watch as the day's last light radiates off the timeworn stones. The interior of the temple is closed until further notice. ✉ *Paseo del Pintor Rosales, Moncloa* ☎ *91/765–1008* 🎫 *Free* Ⓜ *Pl. de España, Ventura Rodríguez.*

FAMILY **Zoo-Aquarium.** Madrid's zoo-aquarium houses one of Europe's largest variety of animals (including rarities such as an albino tiger) that are grouped according to their geographical origin. It also has a dolphinar-ium and a wild bird sanctuary that hold entertaining exhibitions twice a day on weekdays and more often on weekends—check times on arrival and show up early to get a good seat. ■TIP➔ Reduced ticket prices are available by booking online. The zoo is in the Casa de Campo, a large park right outside the western part of the city. Although the nearest metro stop is Casa de Campo, it's best reached via the Príncipe Pío stop, then Bus No. 33. ✉ *Casa de Campo s/n, Moncloa* ☎ *91/154–7479* ⊕ *www.zoomadrid.com* 🎫 *€24* Ⓜ *Casa de Campo; Príncipe Pío, then Bus No. 33.*

BARRIO DE LAS LETRAS

The Barrio de las Letras, long favored by tourists for its charming build-ings and mix of historic and trendy bars and restaurants, is named for the many writers and playwrights from the Spanish Golden Age (16th and 17th centuries) who set up house within a few blocks of Plaza de Santa Ana. Once a shelter to *los madrileños castizos*—the word *cas-tizo* means "authentic"—it is now the favored living area of Spanish and international yuppies. Calle de las Huertas (full of bars and clubs) is pedestrian-only, making the neighborhood even more attractive for walking around and socializing.

CaixaForum. Swiss architects Jacques Herzog and Pierre de Meuron, who transformed a former London power station into that city's Tate Modern, performed a similar feat here. Their conversion of this early-20th-century power station has created a stunning arts complex fit to become the fourth point in Madrid's former triangle of great art institutions—the Prado, the Reina Sofía, and the Thyssen-Bornemisza museums. Belonging to one of the country's wealthiest foundations (La Caixa), the structure seems to float on the sloped public plaza, with a tall vertical garden designed by French botanist Patrick Blanc on its northern side contrasting with a geometric rust-color roof. Inside, the huge exhibition halls display ancient as well as contemporary art, including a sample of La Caixa's own collection. The restaurant on the fourth floor has good views. ✉ *Paseo del Prado 36, Barrio de las Letras* ☎ *91/330–7300* ⊕ *www.caixaforum.es* 🎫 *€4* Ⓜ *Atocha.*

The vertical outdoor garden is a stunning element of the CaixaForum cultural center. The sculpture in front of the building is changed periodically.

Fodor's Choice
★ **Museo Thyssen-Bornemisza.** Opened in 1992, the Thyssen occupies the spacious salmon-painted galleries of the late-18th-century Villahermosa Palace. Its ambitious collection of almost 1,000 paintings traces the history of Western art with examples from every important movement, from the 13th-century Italian Gothic through 20th-century American pop art. The works were gathered from the 1920s to the 1980s by Swiss industrialist Baron Hans Heinrich Thyssen-Bornemisza and his father. The baron donated the entire collection to Spain in 1993, and a renovation in 2004 increased the number of paintings on display to include the baroness's personal collection (considered of lesser quality). Critics have described the museum's paintings as the minor works of major artists and the major works of minor artists, but the collection still traces the development of Western humanism as no other in the world. It includes works by Hans Holbein, Gilbert Stuart, many impressionists and postimpressionists, and a number of German expressionist paintings. ✉ *Paseo del Prado 8, Barrio de las Letras* ☎ *91/369–0151* ⊕ *www.museothyssen.org* ☛ *From €12* Ⓜ *Banco de España.*

Plaza de Santa Ana. This plaza was the heart of the theater district in the 17th century—the Golden Age of Spanish literature—and is now one of Madrid's many thumping nightlife centers. A statue of 17th-century playwright Pedro Calderón de la Barca faces the **Teatro Español,** where playwrights such as Lope de Vega, Tirso de Molina, Pedro Calderón de la Barca, and Ramón del Valle-Inclán released some of their plays. Opposite the theater, beside the ME by Meliá hotel, is the diminutive **Plaza del Ángel,** with one of Madrid's best jazz clubs, **Café Central. Cervecería**

Alemana, a favorite haunt of Hemingway, is on Plaza Santa Ana and is still catnip to writers and poets. ⊠ *Barrio de las Letras* Ⓜ *Sevilla.*

CHUECA AND MALASAÑA

Once known primarily for thumping nightlife and dodgy streets, these two Madrid neighborhoods have changed significantly in the past 20 years. Money from city hall and private investors was used to renovate buildings and public zones, thereby drawing prosperous businesses and many professional and young inhabitants. The triangular area bounded by Fuencarral, Gran Vía, and Corredera Baja is one of the city's trendiest and is known colloquially as triBall.

CHUECA

Chueca is Madrid's "gayborhood." Noisy bars and overcrowded nightclubs are still a trademark of the area, but it now also makes for pleasant daytime walks and has many inexpensive restaurants, hip shops, great cultural life, and inviting summer terraces.

QUICK BITES

Cisne Azul. You may wonder why bland-looking Cisne Azul is crowded with locals in this style-obsessed neighborhood. The reason is simple: wild mushrooms. ⊠ *Calle Gravina 19, Chueca* ☎ *91/521–3799* Ⓜ *Chueca.*

Mercado de San Antón. Following the successful transformation of the Mercado de San Miguel, near the Plaza Mayor, the city completely refurbished this old neighborhood market into a more cosmopolitan enclave. Above the traditional market, join madrileños for booze and international food—think sushi, Greek, Italian—and tapas (seafood options are particularly noteworthy). ⊠ *Calle Augusto Figueroa 24, Chueca* ☎ *913/300730* ⊕ *www.mercadosananton.com* Ⓜ *Chueca.*

MALASAÑA

Famous for being the epicenter of La Movida, the countercultural movement that united rockers, punks, artists and other creative tribes in the 1980s, this neighborhood maintains the same bubbling and transgressive spirit despite its heavy gentrification. There are lots of bars, terraces, and shops, mostly by young designers, and happening squares such as Plaza del Dos de Mayo, Plaza de las Comendadoras, and Plaza de San Ildefonso, whose neighboring discotecas offer some of the city's best nightlife.

Centro Cultural de Conde Duque. Built by Pedro de Ribera in 1717–30 to accommodate the Regiment of the Royal Guard, this imposing building (the facade is 750 feet long) was used as a military academy and an astronomical observatory in the 19th century. It is now a cultural and arts center with a contemporary art museum and temporary art exhibitions in some of its spaces, including the public and historical libraries. Local history professors offer free tours (in Spanish) of the building every Friday at 5 pm. In summer, concerts are held outside in the main plaza. ⊠ *Calle Conde Duque 9 and 11, Malasaña* ☎ *91/588–5834* ⊕ *www.condeduquemadrid.es* ⊗ *Closed Mon.* Ⓜ *San Bernardo.*

NEED A BREAK

✕ **Federal Café.** A favorite hangout among expats and trendsters, Federal Café is a third-wave coffee house known for its international-inflected brunches and pleasant laptop zone with unrestricted Wi-Fi. Another Federal outpost (with more outdoor seating) opened in May 2017 on Plaza de Conde de Barajas, just downhill from the Plaza Mayor. **Known for:** iced coffee; pet-friendly dining; expat clientele. ⊠ *Pl. de las Comendadoras 9, Malasaña* ☎ *91/532–8424* ⊕ *www.federalcafe.es.*

EMBAJADORES

Bordering the old city wall (torn down in the mid-19th century) to the south, Embajadores included most of Madrid's old industrial areas in the 17th and 18th centuries, when it housed, among others, beer, glass, and car factories. That industrial past is long gone and now it's a residential area with some historical buildings and some of the city's liveliest areas, such as El Rastro and Lavapiés. Purse-snatching and petty crime are not uncommon in these two areas, so be alert.

EL RASTRO

The Rastro area in Embajadores traces back to the last third of the 16th century, when it marked the lower part of the old city's wall. The old slaughterhouses of this quarter (and all the other businesses related to that trade) are the origins of today's flea market, which spreads all over the neighborhood on Sunday. It gets quite busy on the weekends, especially on Sunday morning.

Fodor'sChoice
★

El Rastro. Named for the *arrastre* (dragging) of animals in and out of the slaughterhouse that once stood here and, specifically, the *rastro* (blood trail) left behind, this site explodes into a rollicking flea market every Sunday 9–3 with dozens and dozens of street vendors with truly bizarre bric-a-brac ranging from costume earrings to mailed postcards to thrown-out love letters. There are also more formal shops, where it's easy to turn up treasures such as old iron grillwork, a marble tabletop, or a gilt picture frame. The shops (not the vendors) are open during the week, allowing for quieter and more serious bargaining. Even so, people-watching on Sunday is the best part. ⊠ *Calle de la Ribera de los Curtidores s/n, Embajadores* Ⓜ *La Latina, Puerta de Toledo.*

LAVAPIÉS

Lavapiés, which has overtaken Malasaña and La Latina as Madrid's trendiest neighborhood, has the city's highest concentration of immigrants—mostly Chinese, Indian, and North and West African—and as a result the area has plenty of international markets and inexpensive restaurants. The area also has the highest number of extant *corralas*—a type of building (now protected by the city after many years of abandonment) popular in Madrid in the 17th century. In the corralas, all the apartments are connected to a central patio, which serves as the community's social hub.

Fodor'sChoice
★

Centro de Arte Reina Sofía (*Queen Sofía Art Center*). Madrid's premier museum of modern art, housed in a historic hospital building, features more than 1,000 works on four floors. Painting is the focus here, but photography and cinema are also represented. The new collection contextualizes the works of the great modern masters—Picasso, Miró, and Salvador Dalí—and of other famed artists, such as Juan Gris, Jorge Oteiza, Pablo Gargallo, Julio Gonzalez, Eduardo Chillida, and Antoni Tàpies, into broader narratives that attempt to better explain the evolution of modern art. This means, for instance, that the Dalís are not all displayed together in a single area, but scattered around the 38 rooms. The museum's showpiece is Picasso's *Guernica,* in Room No. 206 on the second floor. The huge black-and-white canvas depicts the horror of the Nazi Condor Legion's bombing of the ancient Basque town of Gernika in 1937 during the Spanish Civil War. Check out the rooftop area for scenic city views. ✉ *Calle de Santa Isabel 52, Embajadores* ☎ *91/467–5062* ⊕ *www.museoreinasofia.es* ⬚ *€10; free admission Mon. and Wed.–Sat. after 7 pm, Sun. 1:30–7* ⊙ *Closed Tues.* Ⓜ *Atocha.*

Tabacalera (*Tabacalera Art Promotion*). This cultural center, which occupies an 18th-century cigarette factory, is divided in two parts: on the building's northwest corner, there's the city-funded exhibition and event space (called Espacio Promoción del Arte), a hub of contemporary art, while at its southwest corner is an entrance to the city's most famous art squat. Both venues are worth visiting, but the latter (with no official opening schedule) is truly unique with its thought-provoking graffiti and sculptural art. ✉ *Calle de Embajadores 51, Lavapiés* ☎ *91/701–7045* ⬚ *Free* ⊙ *Closed Mon.*

SALAMANCA, RETIRO, AND CHAMBERÍ

By the mid-19th century, city officials decided to expand Madrid beyond the 1625 wall erected by Felipe IV. The result was a handful of new, well-laid-out neighborhoods.

SALAMANCA

The Salamanca neighborhood, one of the new areas included in the program of city expansions which started in the second half of the 19th century, was originally supposed to provide shelter for the working classes. However, it soon became a favorite location for the bourgeois, the upper class, and the aristocracy. Currently it draws a more mixed crowd but still houses most of the city's expensive restaurants and luxury shops.

Museo Arqueológico Nacional (*Museum of Archaeology*). This museum boasts three large floors filled with Spanish relics, artifacts, and treasures ranging from ancient history to the 19th century. Among the highlights are *La Dama de Elche* , the bust of a wealthy 5th-century-BC Iberian woman (notice that her headgear vaguely resembles the mantillas and hair combs still associated with traditional Spanish dress); the ancient Visigothic votive crowns discovered in 1859 near Toledo, believed to date back to the 7th century; and the medieval ivory crucifix of Ferdinand and Sancha. There is also a replica of the early cave paintings in Altamira (access to the real thing, in Cantabria Province, is highly restricted). ■ TIP→ **Consider getting the multimedia guide offering select itineraries to make your visit more manageable.** ✉ *Calle de*

You can rent rowboats at the lake in the Parque del Buen Retiro; it's a great way to cool off in the summer.

Serrano 13, Salamanca ☎ *91/577–7912* ⊕ *www.man.es* ✉ *€3; free Sat. after 2 pm and Sun. before 2 pm* ⊗ *Closed Mon.* Ⓜ *Colón.*

Museo Lázaro Galdiano. This stately mansion of writer and editor José Lázaro Galdiano (1862–1947), a 10-minute walk across the Castellana from the Museo Sorolla, has decorative items and paintings by Bosch, El Greco, Murillo, and Goya, among others. The remarkable collection comprises five centuries of Spanish, Flemish, English, and Italian art. Bosch's *St. John the Baptist* and the many Goyas are the stars of the show, with El Greco's *San Francisco de Assisi* and Zurbarán's *San Diego de Alcalá* close behind. ✉ *Calle de Serrano 122, Salamanca* ☎ *91/561–6084* ⊕ *www.flg.es* ✉ *€6 (free last hr)* ⊗ *Closed Mon.* Ⓜ *Gregorio Marañón.*

Plaza Colón. Named for Christopher Columbus, this plaza has a statue of the explorer (identical to the one in Barcelona's port) looking west from a high tower in the middle of the square. Behind Plaza Colón is **Calle de Serrano,** the city's premier shopping street (think Gucci, Prada, and Loewe). Stroll in either direction on Serrano for some window-shopping. ✉ *Salamanca* Ⓜ *Colón.*

RETIRO

The Retiro holds the city's best-known park, Parque del Buen Retiro, and the neighborhood's borders extend to its east and west. The area between the western side of the park and the Paseo del Prado showcases some of the city's most exclusive and expensive real estate. The area on the opposite side of the park is livelier and more casual with plentiful tapas bars and mom-and-pop restaurants.

Continued on page 83

EL PRADO:
MADRID'S BRUSH WITH GREATNESS

One of the world's top museums, the Prado is to Madrid what the Louvre is to Paris, or the Uffizi to Florence: a majestic city landmark and premiere art institution that merits the attention of every traveler who visits the city.

Approaching its 200th anniversary, the Prado, with its unparalleled collection of Spanish paintings (from the Romanesque period to the 19th century—don't expect to find Picassos here), is one of the most visited museums in the world. Foreign artists are also well represented—the collection includes masterpieces of European painting such as Hieronymus Bosch's *Garden of Earthly Delights*, *The Annunciation* by Fra Angelico, *Christ Washing the Disciples' Feet* by Tintoretto, and *The Three Graces* by Rubens—but the Prado is best known as home to more paintings by Diego Velázquez and Francisco de Goya than anywhere else.

Originally meant by King Charles III to become a museum of natural history, the Prado nevertheless opened, in 1819, as a sculpture and painting museum under the patronage of his grandchild, King Philip VII. For the first bewildered *madrileños* who crossed the museum's entrance back then, there were only about 300 paintings on display. Today there are more than 3 million visitors a year and 2,000-plus paintings are on display (the whole collection is estimated at about 8,000 canvases, plus 1,000 sculptures).

WHEN TO GO
The best time to visit the Prado is during lunch time, from 1-3, to beat the rush.

HUNGRY?
If your stomach rumbles during your visit, check out the café/restaurant in the foyer of the new building.

CONTACT INFORMATION
✉ Paseo del Prado s/n, 28014 Madrid
☎ (+34) 91 330 2800.
⊕ www.museodelprado.es
Ⓜ Banco de España, Atocha

HOURS OF OPERATION
🕐 Mon.–Sat. 10 AM–8 PM, Sun. 10 AM–7 PM, Closed New Year's Day, Fiesta del Trabajo (May 1), and Christmas.

ADMISSION
🎟 €15. Free Mon. to Sat. 6 PM–8 PM, Sun. 5PM-7PM. To avoid lines, buy tickets in advance online.

The Trinity by El Greco, 1577. Oil on canvas.

THE COLLECTION

With works from the Middle Ages to the 19th century, the Prado's painting collection—though smaller than that of the Louvre and St. Petersburg's Hermitage—may arguably be the world's most captivating for the quality of the masterworks it features.

The Prado's origins can be traced back to the royal collections put together by the successive Hapsburg kings, who were not all equally adept at governing but who all had a penchant for the arts. Throughout the 16th and 17th centuries they amassed troves of paintings from Spanish and foreign painters and spread them among their many palaces. This meant that the bulk of the Prado's collection grew out of the rulers' whim and therefore doesn't offer, like some of its peers, an uninterrupted vision of the history of painting. This shortcoming turned into a blessing, though, as the kings' artistic "obsessions" are the reason you'll find such extensive collections of paintings by Velázquez, Titian, and Rubens (in the latter case, it was Phillip IV who, when Rubens died, sent repre-

(top) A Velázquez statue graces the museum's old entrance. (bottom) Visitors now enter via a new $202 million wing, designed by Rafael Moneo.

sentatives to Antwerp to bid for the artist's best works).

The collection starts with the Spanish Romanesque (12th and 13th century), and features important Italian (Veronese, Tintoretto, Titian), Flemish (Van Dyck, Rubens), and Dutch (Bosch, Rembrandt) collections, as well as scores of works by the great Spanish masters (Velázquez, Goya, Ribera, Zurbarán, Murillo, and others). The Jerónimos building made it possible to add some new works from 19th-century Spanish painters (Rosales, Fortuny, Madrazo, and more).

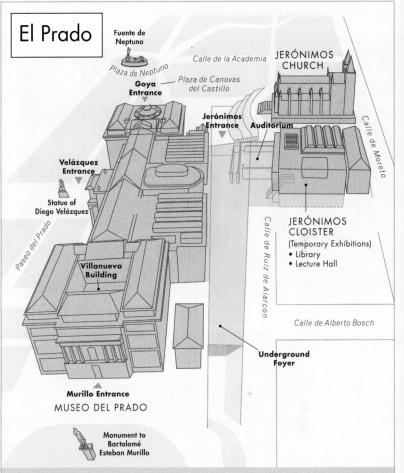

El Prado

Fuente de Neptuno

Calle de la Academia

JERÓNIMOS CHURCH

Plaza de Neptuno

Goya Entrance

Plaza de Canovas del Castillo

Jerónimos Entrance

Auditorium

Calle de Moreto

Velázquez Entrance

Statue of Diego Velázquez

Paseo del Prado

Villanueva Building

Calle de Ruiz de Alarcon

JERÓNIMOS CLOISTER
(Temporary Exhibitions)
• Library
• Lecture Hall

Calle de Alberto Bosch

Underground Foyer

Murillo Entrance

MUSEO DEL PRADO

Monument to Bartolomé Esteban Murillo

GETTING IN

The museum has two ticket-selling points and four entrance points. **The best thing to do is buy your tickets online**: you'll avoid the usually long lines; you can also reserve an audio guide (pick it up in the main foyer in the Jerónimos building) at the same time. If you don't buy tickets online, **another time-saving option is the two vending machines** outside the Goya entrance.

All in-person ticket sales are at the Goya entrance, on the north side of the museum, either at the main entrance at street level, or on the upper level: street level is ticket sales for temporary exhibitions and where you collect tickets bought online if you didn't print them out at home; the upper level gives access to the permanent collection. If you've purchased tickets for the temporary exhibition, you must access the museum through the Jerónimos entrance. **With online tickets printed at home, or a Museum Pass, you can enter at the Goya or Jerónimos entrances.**

HOW TO SEE THE ESSENTIALS

Inside the Jerónimos cloister.

Don't let the Prado's immense size intimidate you. You can't see it all in a day, but if you zero in on some of the museum's masterpieces, you can have a rich experience without collapsing.

With 2,000 paintings distributed among dozens of galleries, the question immediately arises: what should I see? Let's face it: while the Prado has sculptures, drawings, and other treasures spanning centuries, its "why-go"—its "must-go"—is its paintings. Most of the attention, all of it deserved, goes to the Spanish historical headliners: Diego Velázquez, El Greco, and Francisco de Goya, and on a lesser scale, Pedro Ribera, Bartolomé Murillo, and Francisco de Zurbarán. Most of these artists' works are on display on the first floor of the Villanueva building.

A QUICK TOUR

If you want to focus on the essentials—which will take about an hour and a half—enter the museum through the Goya entrance on the upper level: to the left and right, after you enter, are the galleries devoted to Renaissance and Baroque Italian painting (Titian, Tintoretto, Veronés, and Caravaggio). From there move onto Rubens (gallery 24), then on to the long spinal gallery (rooms 25 to 29) that accommodates the works of Ribera and Murillo. Make a required detour to the adjacent

THE JERÓNIMOS CLOISTER

On the second floor of the new addition is the restored cloister of San Jerónimo el Real, the medieval church now adjacent to the museum. There, in one of the quietest corners of the Prado, you'll find a collection of 16th-century sculptures by Milanese bronze artists Leone and Pompeo Leoni. While you take it all in, ponder the fact that during Rafael Moneo's expansion, the 3,000 blocks of stone that make up this cloister had to be dismantled, restored, and reassembled in their original positions.

galleries (rooms 9A-10A) on the east side to admire the elongated spiritual figures of El Greco, and the folkloric characters and penetrating self-portraits of Rembrandt (room 7). Head back to the main corridor, where you'll find 46 of Velázquez's masterful works, and which will also take you past Gallery 12, home to the museum's most famous canvas: Velázquez's *Las Meninas*. Make sure, also, to see Goya's two *Majas*—one fully dressed, the other nude—displayed next to each other in Gallery 36, and his famous subtle royal composition *The Family of Charles IV* (Gallery 32). Then head down to the ground floor to see some of Goya's best known works (*Second of May, 1808* and *Third of May 1808*, as well as *Saturn Devouring One of His Sons*, and the gory Black Paintings (all in rooms 64-67).

Once you exit the Goya galleries downstairs you'll be facing the 12 new galleries (60 to 75) devoted to the 19th-century Spanish painters: if you're curious about Joaquín Sorolla and haven't had a chance to visit the museum dedicated to his work, stop at galleries 60 and 60A to see some of his colorful art. Otherwise, cross the main foyer and stop at gallery 56 to take in Hieronymus Bosch's triptych *The Garden of Earthly Delights,* before heading toward the Velázquez exit or toward the Jerónimos building and its small but bustling café/restaurant for a well-deserved break.

THE PRADO ONLINE

The Prado has followed the example many other big-name museums and enhanced its website in an attempt to make the collection more accessible, even if you can't be there in person. The site includes an online gallery of more than 1,000 paintings (3,000 if you speak Spanish), and offers audio commentary and in-depth analysis of

The airy upper-level galleries.

some paintings, among other things. The Museo del Prado Official Guide app allows you to explore all of the museum's masterpieces and plan your visit in advance. If you're hungry for more, check out the 14 paintings scanned and displayed in super-high definition on Google Earth—search for Prado 3D, activate the tag "3D Buildings," and enjoy the technological feat!

MONEO'S DAZZLING EXPANSION

In 2007 Spanish architect Rafael Moneo's gleaming new addition to the Prado opened, bringing the museum into a new era. Moneo's red stucco "cube" envelopes the Cloister of the Jerónimos behind the old Villanueva building, but the bulk of the new premises are under the street in a vast steel-and-glass wedge-shape foyer that houses the temporary exhibitions plus some state-of-the-art add-ons: a café/restaurant, a bookshop with print-on-demand services, and a 400-seat auditorium. The building has enabled the Prado to double its exhibition space to a total of 16,000 square meters (52,800 square feet) and to showcase more than 400 hundred new paintings—mostly from the Romanesque and the 19th century—that until the addition had laid hidden on huge steel shelves in the museum's underground vaults.

THREE GREAT MASTERS

FRANCISCO DE GOYA 1746–1828

Goya's work spans a staggering range of tone, from bucolic to horrific, his idyllic paintings of Spaniards at play and portraits of the family of King Carlos IV contrasting with his dark, disturbing "black paintings." Goya's attraction to the macabre assured him a place in posterity, an ironic statement at the end of a long career in which he served as the official court painter to a succession of Spanish kings, bringing the art of royal portraiture to unknown heights.

Francisco de Goya

Goya found fame in his day as a portraitist, but he is admired by modern audiences for his depictions of the bizarre and the morbid. Beginning as a painter of decorative Rococo figures, he evolved into an artist of great depth in the employ of King Charles IV. The push-pull between Goya's love for his country and his disdain for the enemies of Spain yielded such masterpieces as *Third of May 1808*, painted after the French occupation ended. In the early 19th century, Goya's scandalous *The Naked Maja* brought him before the Spanish Inquisition, whose judgment was to end his tenure as a court painter.

DIEGO VELÁZQUEZ 1599–1660

A native of Seville, Velázquez gained fame at age 24 as court painter to King Philip IV. He developed a lifelike approach to religious art in which both saints and sinners were specific people rather than generic types. The supple brushwork of his ambitious history paintings and portraits was unsurpassed. Several visits to Rome, and his friendship with Rubens, made him the quintessential baroque painter with an international purview.

Diego Velázquez

DOMENIKOS THEOTOKOPOULOS (AKA "EL GRECO") 1541–1614

El Greco's art was one of rapture and devotion, but beyond that his style is almost impossible to categorize. "The Greek" found his way from his native Crete to Spain through Venice; he spent most of his life in Toledo. His twisted, elongated figures imbue both his religious subjects and portraits with a sense of otherworldliness. While his palette and brushstrokes were inspired by Italian Mannerism, his approach to painting was uniquely his own. His inimitable style left few followers.

Domenikos Theotokopoulos

SIX PAINTINGS TO SEE

SATURN DEVOURING ONE OF HIS SONS (1819)
FRANCISCO DE GOYA Y LUCIENTES

In one of fourteen nightmarish "black paintings" executed by Goya to decorate the walls of his home in the later years of his life, the mythological God Kronos, or Saturn, cannibalizes one of his children in order to derail a prophecy that one of them would take over his throne. *Mural transferred to canvas.*

Saturn Devouring One of His Sons

THE GARDEN OF DELIGHTS OR LA PINTURA DEL MADROÑO (1500)
HIËRONYMUS BOSCH

Very little about the small-town environment of the Low Countries where the Roman Catholic Bosch lived in the late Middle Ages can explain his thought-provoking, and downright bizarre, paintings. His depictions of mankind's sins and virtues, and the heavenly rewards or demonic punishments that await us all, have fascinated many generations of viewers. The devout painter has been called a "heretic," and compared to Salvador Dalí for his disturbingly twisted renderings. In this three-panel painting, Adam and Eve are created, mankind celebrates its humanity, and hell awaits the wicked, all within a journey of 152 inches! *Wooden Triptych.*

The Garden of Delights

LAS MENINAS (THE MAIDS OF HONOR) (1656-57)
DIEGO VELÁZQUEZ DE SILVA

Velázquez's masterpiece of spatial perspective occupies pride-of-place in the center of the Spanish baroque galleries. In this complex visual game, *you* are the king and queen of Spain, reflected in a distant hazy mirror as the court painter (Velázquez) pauses in front of his easel to observe your features. The actual subject is the Princess Margarita, heir to the throne in 1656. *Oil on canvas.*

Las Meninas

STILL LIFE (17th Century; no date)
FRANCISCO DE ZURBARÁN

Best known as a painter of contemplative saints, Zurbarán, a native of Extremadura who found success working with Velázquez in Seville, was a peerless observer of beauty in the everyday. His rendering of the surfaces of these homely objects elevates them to the stature of holy relics, urging the viewer to touch them. But the overriding mood is one of serenity and order. *Oil on canvas.*

Still Life

DAVID VICTORIOUS OVER GOLIATH (1599)
MICHELANGELO MERISI (CARAVAGGIO)

Caravaggio used intense contrasts between his dark and light passages (called *chiaroscuro* in Italian) to create drama in his bold baroque paintings. Here, a surprisingly childlike David calmly ties up the severed head of the giant Philistine Goliath, gruesomely featured in the foreground plane of the picture. The astonishing realism of the Italian painter, who was as well known for his tempestuous personal life as for his deftness with a paint brush, had a profound influence on 17th century Spanish art. *Oil on canvas.*

David Victorious over Goliath

THE TRINITY (1577)
DOMENIKOS THEOTOKOPOULOS (EL GRECO)

Soon after arriving in Spain, Domenikos Theotokopoulos created this view of Christ ascending into heaven supported by angels, God the Father, and the Holy Spirit. It was commissioned for the altar of a convent in Toledo. The acid colors recall the Mannerist paintings of Venice, where El Greco was trained, and the distortions of the upward-floating bodies show more gracefulness than the anatomical contortions that characterize his later works. *Oil on canvas.*

The Trinity

PICASSO AND THE PRADO

The Prado contains no modern art, but one of the greatest artists of the 20th century had an important history with the museum. **Pablo Picasso** (1891–1973) served as the director of the Prado during the Spanish civil war, from 1936 to 1939. The Prado was a "phantom museum" in that period, Picasso once noted, since it was closed for most of the war and its collections hidden elsewhere for safety.

Picasso with his wife
Jacqueline Roque

Later that century, the abstract artist's enormous *Guernica* hung briefly on the Prado's walls, returning to Spain from the Museum of Modern Art in 1981. Picasso had stipulated that MoMA give up his anti-war masterpiece after the death of fascist dictator Francisco Franco, and it was displayed at the Prado and the Casón del Buen Retiro until the nearby Reina Sofía was built to house it in 1992.

Picasso in his atelier

CLOSE UP

The Art Walk (Paseo del Prado)

2

Any visit to Madrid should include a stroll along Paseo del Prado, lined with world-class museums housed in majestic old buildings. You can tour the area in about two hours (longer if you visit the Prado).

■ TIP➜ **The Paseo del Arte (Art Walk) pass allows you to visit the Prado, the Reina Sofía, and the Thyssen-Bornemisza for €31.90. You can buy it at any of the three museums, and you don't have to visit all of them on the same day.**

The Paseo del Prado stretches from the Plaza de Cibeles to Plaza del Emperador Carlos V (also known as Plaza de Atocha) and is home to Madrid's three main art museums—the Prado, the Reina Sofía, and the Thyssen-Bornemisza—as well as the CaixaForum, an art institution with fabulous temporary exhibitions. In earlier times the Paseo marked the eastern boundary of the city, and in the 17th century it was given a cleaner neoclassical look. A century later, King Carlos III designed a leafy nature walk with glorious fountains and a botanical garden to provide respite to madrileños during the scorching summers.

Start your walk on Plaza Cánovas del Castillo, with its Fuente de Neptuno (Fountain of Neptune); on the northwestern corner is the **Museo Thyssen-Bornemisza.** To your left, across from the plaza, is the elegant Ritz hotel (under renovation as of 2018), alongside the obelisk dedicated

to those who have died for Spain, and across from it on the right is the **Museo del Prado,** the best example of neoclassical architecture in the city and one of the world's best-known museums. It was enlarged in 2007 with the addition of what's widely known as "Moneo's cube," architect Rafael Moneo's steel-and-glass building that now encloses the cloister of the old Monasterio de los Jerónimos. The monastery, by far the oldest building in this part of town (built in 1503), is dwarfed by the museum. It once sat at the core of the **Parque del Buen Retiro** (the park stretched as far as the Paseo del Prado until the 19th century, when Queen Isabel II sold a third of its terrain to the state) and is the reason for the park's name: the monastery is where the Habsburg kings would temporarily "retire" from their state affairs. The park, always bustling, is a great place to unwind after sightseeing.

To the right of the Prado, across from the Murillo Gate, is the **Jardín Botánico,** also a wonderful place to relax with a book or to sketch in the shade of an exotic tree. Across the street is a sloping plaza that leads to the **CaixaForum.**

The Paseo del Prado ends by the **Estación de Atocha,** a train station resembling the overturned hull of a ship. To its west, across from Calle Atocha, lies the **Centro de Arte Reina Sofía,** Madrid's modern art museum and the home of Picasso's *Guernica.*

Museo del Prado *(Prado Museum).* See feature in this chapter. ⊠ *Paseo del Prado s/n Madrid, Retiro* Ⓜ *Banco de España, Atocha* ☎ *91/330– 2800* ⊕ *www.museodelprado.es* ⊠ *€15 (permanent collection free Mon.–Sat. 6–8 pm, Sun 5–7 pm).*

FAMILY
Fodor's Choice
★
Parque del Buen Retiro *(The Retreat).* Once the private playground of royalty, Madrid's crowning park is a vast expanse of green encompassing formal gardens, fountains, lakes, exhibition halls, children's play areas, outdoor cafés, and a puppet theater. Shows take place on Saturday at 1 and on Sunday at 1, 6, and 7. The park, especially lively on weekends, also holds a book fair in May and occasional flamenco concerts in summer. From the entrance at the Puerta de Alcalá, head straight toward the center to find the Estanque (lake), presided over by a grandiose equestrian statue of King Alfonso XII. The 19th-century Palacio de Cristal (Crystal Palace) was built to house exotic plants from the Philippines; the Rosaleda (Rose Garden) is bursting with color and heavy with floral scents for most of the summer. Madrileños claim that a statue called the *Ángel Caído (Fallen Angel)* is the only one in the world depicting the Prince of Darkness before his fall from grace. ⊠ *Puerta de Alcalá, Retiro* ⊠ *Free* Ⓜ *Retiro.*

CHAMBERÍ

Chamberí is a large area to the north of Salamanca. It's mostly residential but has a few lively spots, especially the streets around Plaza de Olavide.

Fodor's Choice
★
Museo Sorolla. See the world through the exceptional eye of Spain's most famous impressionist painter, Joaquín Sorolla (1863–1923), who lived and worked most of his life at the home and garden he designed. Every corner is filled with exquisite artwork—including plenty of original Sorollas—and impeccably selected furnishings, which pop against brightly colored walls that evoke the Mediterranean coast, where the painter was born. This museum can be seen as part of the Abono Cinco Palacios, a €12 pass that grants access to five mansion-museums. ⊠ *Paseo del General Martinez Campos 37, Chamberí* ☎ *91/310–1584* ⊕ *museosorolla.mcu.es* ⊠ *€3 (free after 2 pm Sat. and all day Sun.)* ⊘ *Closed Mon.* Ⓜ *Rubén Darío, Gregorio Marañón.*

WHERE TO EAT

Spain is an essential foodie pilgrimage, and no city holds a candle to Madrid when it comes to variety of national and international cuisines. Its cutting-edge restaurants helmed by celebrated chefs make the city one of Europe's most renowned dining capitals.

When it comes to dining, younger madrileños gravitate toward trendy neighborhoods like bearded-and-bunned Malasaña, gay-friendly Chueca, rootsy La Latina, and multicultural Lavapiés for their boisterous and affordable restaurants and bars. Dressier travelers, and those visiting with kids, will feel more at home in the quieter, more buttoned-up restaurants of Salamanca, Chamartín, and Retiro. Of course, these are broad-brush generalizations, and there are plenty of exceptions.

The house wine in old-timey Madrid restaurants is often a sturdy, uncomplicated Valdepeñas from La Mancha. A plummy Rioja or a gutsy Ribera del Duero—the latter from northern Castile—are the usual choices for reds by the glass in chicer establishments, while popular whites include fruity Verdejo varietals from Rueda and slatey albariños from Galicia After dinner, try the anise-flavored liqueur (*anís*), produced outside the nearby village of Chinchón, or a fruitier *patxaran*, a digestif made with sloe berries.

Use the coordinate (⊕ B2) at the end of each listing to locate a site on the corresponding map.

WHAT IT COSTS IN EUROS

	$	$$	$$$	$$$$
RESTAURANTS	under €16	€16–€22	€23–€29	over €29

Prices in the reviews are the average cost of a main course or equivalent combination of smaller dishes at dinner or, if dinner is not served, at lunch.

PALACIO, LA LATINA, AND SOL

PALACIO

$$ CHINESE FAMILY

🍴 **Casa Lafu.** Madrid has a vibrant Chinese community, which means there are noodles to slurp and dumplings to dunk all around town. Casa Lafu stands out for its expertly prepared repertoire of dishes, a veritable taste tour of the enormous country, from Sichuan-style *má là* plates to Shanghainese wine-cooked meats to Cantonese dim sum. **Known for:** hot pot; white-tablecloth Chinese cuisine; rare regional specialties. [$] *Average main: €17* ✉ *Calle Flor Baja 1, Palacio* ☎ *91/548–7096* 🌐 *www.casalafu.com* ⊕ *C2.*

$$ SPANISH

🍴 **La Bola.** La Bola is renowned for its cocido madrileño, a soul-satisfying chickpea and meat stew, and for its decor, which has hardly changed a lick since 1868, when the restaurant was founded. Originally, La Bola served three types of cocido: a simple rendition at noon for blue-collar workers and employees, a chicken-only version at 1 for students, and a multimeat extravaganza at 2 for politicians and journalists. **Known for:** cocido madrileño; 19th-century decor; palace-side dining. [$] *Average main: €22* ✉ *Calle La Bola 5, Palacio* ☎ *91/547–6930* 🌐 *www.labola.es* 💳 *No credit cards* 🕒 *No dinner Sun.* [M] *Ópera* ⊕ *B3.*

$$ SPANISH

🍴 **Taberneros.** Wine lovers unite at Taberneros, a cozy restaurant whose cuisine is as eclectic as its far-reaching wine list. In a dining room lined with wine racks and decanters, complement your vino with ibérico ham *croquetas*, fried squid with miso, or an Italian-inflected artichoke salad. **Known for:** unique wines; nueva cocina tapas; personable chef who greets diners. [$] *Average main: €19* ✉ *Calle Santiago 9, Palacio* ☎ *91/542–2460* 🕒 *No dinner Mon.* [M] *Ópera* ⊕ *C4.*

A typical evening scene: beer and tapas on the terrace of one of Madrid's many tapas bars

LA LATINA

$$$ SPANISH

🍴 **Casa Botín.** According to *Guinness World Records*, Madrid is home to the world's oldest restaurant, Botín, established in 1725 and a favorite of Ernest Hemingway (the final scene of *The Sun Also Rises* is set in this very place). A menu must, by all accounts, is the cochinillo asado (suckling pig), which is stuffed with aromatics, doused with wine, and crisped in the original wood-burning oven. **Known for:** world's oldest restaurant; roast lamb and suckling pig; roving traditional musical groups. [$] *Average main: €25* ✉ *Calle Cuchilleros 17, La Latina* ☎ *91/366–4217* 🌐 *www.botin.es* [M] *Tirso de Molina* ✥ *C5.*

$$ SPANISH

🍴 **Casa Lucas.** Quieter than its boisterous neighbors, this small, quaint bar with just a few tables offers a short yet varied selection of local wines and homemade tapas. Top dishes include the squid-ink cannelloni filled with fried seafood and farmer's cheese and *huevos a la Macarena,* eggs in puff pastry topped with wild mushrooms and fried artichokes bound with béchamel. **Known for:** locals-only spot; standout seafood tapas; unusual wine selection. [$] *Average main: €19* ✉ *Calle Cava Baja 30, La Latina* ☎ *91/365–0804* 🌐 *www.casalucas.es* 🕒 *No lunch Wed.* [M] *La Latina* ✥ *C5.*

$$$ STEAKHOUSE Fodor's Choice ★

🍴 **Casa Paco.** Packed with madrileños downing Valdepeñas wine, this Castilian tavern, with its zinc-top bar and tiled walls, wouldn't have looked out of place a century ago. Warm up with the city's best rendition of sopa de ajo, garlic soup crowned with a poached egg, and then feast on thick slabs of Spanish beef, served medium rare and sizzling. **Known for:** ornate wooden zinc-topped bar; rustic Valdepeñas wine; city's best garlic soup. [$] *Average main: €23* ✉ *Pl. Puerta Cerrada 11,*

La Latina ☎ *91/366–3166* ⊕ *www.casapaco1933.es* ⊗ *Closed Mon. No dinner Sun.* Ⓜ *Tirso de Molina* ✛ *C5.*

$ ✗ **Casa Revuelta.** There's a cod war in Madrid between Casa Lavra and
SPANISH   Casa Revulta: both claim to make the city's best *pincho de bacalao*, or battered salt cod. As locals will tell you, Revuelta's rendition is far and away the superior choice—provided you're successful at elbowing your way to the 1930s-era bar. **Known for:** battered salt cod canapés; midmorning vermú (vermouth) rush; time-warp decor. Ⓢ *Average main: €5* ⊠ *Calle Latoneros 3, La Latina* ☎ *91/366–3332* ⊗ *Closed Mon. No dinner Sun.* ⊟ *No credit cards* ✛ *C5.*

$$$ ✗ **El Landó.** This *castizo* ("rootsy") restaurant, with dark wood-paneled
SPANISH   walls lined with bottles of wine, serves classic Spanish food like *huevos estrellados* (fried eggs with potatoes and sausage), grilled meats, a good selection of fish (sea bass, haddock, grouper) with many different sauces, and steak tartare. Check out the pictures of famous celebrities who've eaten at this typically noisy landmark; they line the staircase that leads to the main dining area. **Known for:** castizo ambience; huevos estrellados; impeccably cooked seafood. Ⓢ *Average main: €26* ⊠ *Pl. Gabriel Miró 8, La Latina* ☎ *91/366–7681* ⊗ *No dinner Sun.* Ⓜ *La Latina* ✛ *B5.*

$ ✗ **Taberna Almendro 13.** Getting a weekend seat in this rustic old favor-
TAPAS   ite is a feat, but drop by any other time and you'll be served ample, stick-to-your-ribs *raciones* such as *roscas* (hot bread rounds filled with cured meats), *huevos rotos* (fried eggs over homemade potato chips), and *revueltos* (scrambled eggs; opt for the habanero with fava beans and black pudding). **Known for:** roscas sandwiches; greasy-spoon tapas (in the best way); old-timey decor. Ⓢ *Average main: €13* ⊠ *Calle del Almendro 13, La Latina* ☎ *91/365–4252* ⊕ *www.almendro13.com* ⊟ *No credit cards* Ⓜ *La Latina* ✛ *C5.*

$$ ✗ **Txirimiri.** This perennially packed Basque tapas spot, one of four
TAPAS   branches in a local chain, is famous for its Unai slider, fried in tempura and topped with a boletus sauce, and more traditional Spanish omelet, one of the city's best. Arrive early and you may be lucky enough to get one of the tables in the back. **Known for:** tortilla española; nueva cocina tapas; sardine-can digs. Ⓢ *Average main: €18* ⊠ *Calle Humilladero 6, La Latina* ☎ *91/364–1196* ⊕ *www.txirimiri.es* ⊟ *No credit cards* Ⓜ *La Latina* ✛ *C5.*

SOL

$$ ✗ **La Hojaldrería.** A veritable temple of all things flaky and buttery
CAFÉ   (*hojaldre* is Spanish for "puff pastry") this new concept café by Javier Bonet (the brains behind the buzzy Sala de Despiece and Muta) is a sophisticated spot to enjoy a fancy pastry and a well-made cappuccino at breakfast or innovative bistro fare at lunch and dinner. **Known for:** best croissants in town; throwback rococo decor; gourmet sandwiches. Ⓢ *Average main: €16* ⊠ *Calle Virgen de los Peligros 8, Sol* ☎ *91/059–5193* ⊕ *www.hojaldreria.com* ⊗ *No dinner Sun.* ✛ *E3.*

$$$$ ✗ **La Terraza del Casino de Madrid.** This award-winning restaurant by chef
ECLECTIC   Paco Roncero is in an aerie above one of Madrid's oldest, most exclusive gentlemen's clubs. Awaken your palate with mousses, foams, and liquid jellies, or indulge in gustatory experiments in flavor, texture, and

temperature such as the hake with lilacs and codium or the mushroom with marrow and pine essence. **Known for:** "thousand-year-old" olive oil; awards and stars; foams, jellies, and tweezed garnishes. [$] *Average main: €38* ✉ *Calle Alcalá 15, Sol* ☎ *91/521–8700* 🌐 *www.casinodemadrid.es* ⏲ *Closed Sun. and Mon.* 👔 *Jacket required* [M] *Sol* ✥ *E3.*

$ SPANISH 🍴 **Lambuzo.** This laid-back Andalusian tavern, one of three locations in the city, embodies the soul and joyful spirit of that sunny region. Let cheerful waiters help guide you through the extensive menu, which includes fried-fish dishes, unconventional croquetas (flecked with garlicky shrimp, for instance), and more filling dishes like cuttlefish meatballs and seared Barbate tuna loin. **Known for:** sunny Andalusian vibe; an ocean's worth of seafood dishes; chatty owners. [$] *Average main: €12* ✉ *Calle de las Conchas 9, Sol* ☎ *91/143–4862* 🌐 *www.barlambuzo.com* ⏲ *Closed Mon. No dinner Sun.* [M] *Ópera* ✥ *C3.*

BARRIO DE LAS LETRAS

$$$ SPANISH 🍴 **Askuabarra.** This austere yet polished restaurant, with about 10 tables, has a meat-focused menu with highlights like roasted bone marrow with cilantro salad, grilled lamb sweetbreads, and an outstanding steak tartare. **Known for:** smooth steak tartare; eclectic offal dishes; cozy digs. [$] *Average main: €23* ✉ *Calle Arlabán 7, Barrio de las Letras* ☎ *91/593–7507* 🌐 *www.askuabarra.com* ⏲ *Closed Sun.* [M] *Sevilla* ✥ *E3.*

$ TAPAS 🍴 **Cervecería Cervantes.** Cervecería Cervantes is an improbably down-to-earth neighborhood bar—the type where you throw your olive pits and napkins right onto the floor—among the glut of underwhelming, tourist-oriented eateries in the area. Most patrons come for the ice-cold *cañas* (half pints), but if you're peckish, there's a fine menu of Spanish standbys including *pulpo a la gallega* (octopus with potatoes, olive oil, and paprika), *empanada* (tuna-stuffed pastry), stuffed piquillo peppers, and more. **Known for:** free tapa with beer; diamond in the touristy rough; generous portions of Galician-style octopus. [$] *Average main: €13* ✉ *Pl. de Jesús 7, Barrio de las Letras* ☎ *91/429–6093* ⏲ *No dinner Sun.* [M] *Antón Martín* ✥ *F4.*

$$$ SPANISH 🍴 **Gofio.** Savor a rare taste of Canary Islands cuisine—with quite a few twists—at this envelope-pushing restaurant helmed by Canarian chef Safe Cruz. Dinner might start with olives marinated in green mojo, a garlicky cilantro-and-parsley sauce ground in a mortar, and continue with crispy goat tacos or Gomero cheese (smoked tableside) before finishing with gofio ice cream, made with the Canarian corn flour from which the restaurant takes its name. **Known for:** Canarian "fusion" cuisine; smoky volcanic wines; gorgeous, uncontrived plating. [$] *Average main: €23* ✉ *Calle Lope de Vega 9, Barrio de las Letras* ☎ *91/599–4404* 🌐 *www.gofiomadrid.com* ⏲ *Closed Mon.* ✥ *E5.*

$ TAPAS 🍴 **Taberna de la Dolores.** A lively corner bar with a colorful tiled facade, this is a solid spot for a cold beer and a quick bite after visiting the nearby museums. Try the *matrimonio* ("marriage") tapa, which weds a pickled and a cured anchovy on a crusty baguette. **Known for:** affordable, no-nonsense tapas; ice-cold cañas; mixed crowd of expats and locals. [$] *Average main: €12* ✉ *Pl. de Jesús 4, Barrio de las Letras* ☎ *91/429–2243* 💳 *No credit cards* [M] *Antón Martín* ✥ *F5.*

$$ TAPAS
🍴 **TriCiclo.** A Spanish-style bistro, TriCiclo serves inventive tapas—think surf-and-turf livers and ibérico pork tartare—in an environment where you don't have to throw elbows to place your order. This may be the only restaurant in town that serves raciones in one-third portions as well as half and full ones—ideal for creating your own tasting menu. **Known for:** traditional and modern tapas; tranquil ambience; excellent service. [$] *Average main: €19* ✉ *Calle Santa María 28, Barrio de las Letras* ☎ *91/024–4798* 🌐 *www.eltriciclo.es* 🕒 *Closed Sun.* [M] *Antón Martín* ✣ *F5.*

2

CHUECA AND MALASAÑA

CHUECA

$$ SPANISH FAMILY Fodor's Choice ★
🍴 **Casa Hortensia Restaurante & Sidrería.** Approximate a vacation to the north of Spain by dining at this true-blue Asturian restaurant (or at the more casual *sidrería,* located in the bar area), where that region's unsung comfort-food dishes—such as *fabada* (pork and bean stew), Cabrales cheese, and *cachopo* (cheese-stuffed beef cutlets)—take center stage. The obligatory tipple is *sidra,* bone-dry Asturian cider that's aerated using a battery-powered gadget designed for this task. **Known for:** authentic fabada; cider bottles with DIY aerators; locals-only crowd. [$] *Average main: €19* ✉ *Calle Farmacia 2, 2nd and 3rd fl., Chueca* ✣ *Situated in what appears to be an apartment building* ☎ *91/539–0090* 🌐 *www.casahortensia.com* 🕒 *Closed Mon. No dinner Sun.* ✣ *E2.*

$ TAPAS FAMILY
🍴 **Celso y Manolo.** Named after the brothers who founded the restaurant, this place has around a dozen tables and an extensive, eclectic menu geared toward sharing that hinges on natural products—game meats, seafood, cheeses—from the mountainous northerly region of Cantabria. Natural and often organic wines sourced from around the country make for spot-on pairings. **Known for:** market-driven cuisine; Cantabrian specialties; organic wines. [$] *Average main: €14* ✉ *Calle Libertad 1, Chueca* ☎ *91/531–8079* 🌐 *www.celsoymanolo.es* [M] *Chueca* ✣ *F3.*

$$ LATIN AMERICAN
🍴 **La Candelita.** Let this elevated Peruvian–Venezuelan restaurant whisk you away to the tropics with its Cuban rum cocktails, zippy ceviches and *tiraditos,* and fresh-off-the-griddle arepas. Sunday brunches are a blast. **Known for:** refreshing tiraditos and ceviches; trendy Peruvian–Venezuelan fare; terrific Sunday brunch. [$] *Average main: €22* ✉ *Calle Barquillo 30, Chueca* ☎ *91/523–8553* 🕒 *Closed Mon.* ✣ *F2.*

$ SPANISH
🍴 **La Tita Rivera.** This place—specializing in hot stuffed bread rolls (called *casis*) and flavored hard cider—has an industrial vibe, thanks to exposed pipes, high ceilings, and a semiopen kitchen. But the bar's most exceptional asset is its interior patio area, a well-kept secret among madrileños living in the area. **Known for:** stuffed bread rolls; hidden interior patio; flavored draft ciders. [$] *Average main: €11* ✉ *Calle Pérez Galdós 4, Chueca* ☎ *91/522–1890* 🌐 *www.latitarivera.com* [M] *Chueca* ✣ *E2.*

$$ TAPAS
🍴 **Mercado de la Reina.** This might be the only worthwhile tapas restaurant on Gran Vía, Madrid's main commercial artery. Dishes here—from croquetas to grilled vegetables to tossed salads—are market-driven and inexpensive, and they can be enjoyed in the casual bar area, slightly more formal dining room, or outdoor patio. **Known for:** inexpensive

eats; only decent spot on Gran Via; lounge bar downstairs. [$] *Average main: €17* ✉ *Calle Gran Vía 12, Chueca* ☎ *91/521–3198* 🌐 *www.grupomercadodelareina.com* [M] *Banco de España* ✥ *E3.*

$ ITALIAN FAMILY 🍴 **Pulcinella.** When Enrico Bosco arrived in Madrid from Italy in the early '90s, he couldn't find a decent Italian restaurant—so he decided to open one. Always bustling and frequented by families and young couples, this trattoria seems like a direct transplant from Naples with its superb fresh pastas, pizzas, and focaccias. (The branch across the street, Cantina di Pulcinella, is under the same ownership and serves the same food.) **Known for:** affordable down-home Italian fare; family-friendly vibe; excellent fresh pastas. [$] *Average main: €14* ✉ *Calle de Regueros 7, Chueca* ☎ *91/319–7363* 🌐 *www.gruppopulcinella.com* [M] *Chueca* ✥ *F1.*

MALASAÑA

$ SPANISH Fodor's Choice ★ 🍴 **Bodega de la Ardosa.** A 19th-century bodega, with barrel tables and dusty gewgaws hanging from the walls, Bodega de a Ardosa is an anachronism in Malasaña, an unapologetically gentrified neighborhood. La Ardosa pours refreshing vermouth and draft beers, but the bar's claim to fame—and the dish madrileños make special trips for—is its award-winning tortilla española, or Spanish omelet, always served warm with a gooey center. **Known for:** 100-plus years of history; award-winning tortilla española; draft vermú and unfiltered fino sherry. [$] *Average main: €13* ✉ *Calle Colón 13, Malasaña* ☎ *91/521–4979* 🌐 *www.laardosa.es* 💳 *No credit cards* [M] *Tribunal* ✥ *E2.*

$$ SPANISH Fodor's Choice ★ 🍴 **Café Comercial.** When this centenary café—one of the oldest in Madrid—shuttered in 2015, ostensibly for good, the public outcry was so great that it inspired Grupo El Escondite (of Lady Madonna, Barbara Ann, and El Escondite) to buy the property and give it a much-needed revamp in 2017. In a dining room that combines original design elements (huge mirrors, carved wooden columns) with new cutting-edge fixtures, feast on a menu that's a dance between Café Comercial *clásicos* and novel creations by chef Pepe Roch. **Known for:** one of Madrid's first literary cafés; modern menus by Pepe Roch; outstanding seafood rice. [$] *Average main: €18* ✉ *Glorieta de Bilbao 7, Malasaña* ☎ *91/088–2525* 🌐 *www.cafecomercialmadrid.com* ✥ *E1.*

LAVAPIÉS

$ AFRICAN 🍴 **Baobab.** Get a taste of Lavapiés's vibrant Senegalese community at Baobab, an indoor-outdoor restaurant on Plaza de Nelson Mandela that serves up €7 *thiéboudienne,* a rich fish-and-vegetable braise ladled over *fonio* (a West African "super grain"). The fountain beside the restaurant, called Fuente de Cabestreros, displays one of the city's only remaining references to "La República" that survived Franco's anti-Republican propaganda campaign following the Spanish Civil War. **Known for:** feast for under €10; real-deal thiéboudienne; primo people-watching. [$] *Average main: €8* ✉ *Calle de Cabestreros 1, Lavapiés* ☎ *63/211–5681* ⏲ *Closed Tues.* ✥ *D6.*

2

$ ✕ **Hola Coffee.** Spaniards love their morning *cafés con leche* and after-
CAFÉ   noon *cortados*, but it's never been easy to find a great-quality cup of
Fodor'sChoice   jo in Madrid—until now: Hola Coffee, a pocket coffee shop that pulls
★   complex-tasting third-wave espressos and cappuccinos using beans they
roast themselves. Larger groups should head to Mision Café, Hola's
shiny new outpost in Malasaña. **Known for:** third-wave coffees; expat
staff and clientele; terrific cold brew. $ *Average main: €5* ⊠ *Calle del
Dr. Fourquet 33, Lavapiés* ☎ *91/056–8263* ⊕ *www.hola.coffee* ✛ *E6.*

$ ✕ **Melo's.** This old-timey Galician bar serves eight simple dishes, and
SPANISH   they're infallible. Come for the ultracreamy croquetas, blistered padrón
peppers, and football-sized *zapatilla* sandwiches; stay for the dressed-
down conviviality and the *cuncos* (ceramic bowls) overflowing with
slatey albariño. **Known for:** old-school Galician bar food; oversize ham
croquetas; cheap, good albariño. $ *Average main: €8* ⊠ *Calle del Ave
María 44, Lavapiés* ☎ *91/527–5054* ◷ *Closed Sun. and Mon.* ▭ *No
credit cards* ✛ *E6.*

$$ ✕ **Taberna de Antonio Sánchez.** A Lavapiés landmark opened in 1786, this
SPANISH   taberna's regulars have included realist painter Ignacio Zuloaga, count-
Fodor'sChoice   less champion bullfighters, and King Alfonso XIII. Sip on a sudsy caña,
★   or half pint, in the creaky bar area, and nibble on house specialties like
cazón en adobo (fried shark bites with cumin) and *torrijas* (custardy
fried bread dusted with cinnamon). **Known for:** centuries-old decor;
museum-grade bullfighting paraphernalia; cazón (fried shark). $ *Aver-
age main: €16* ⊠ *Calle del Mesón de Paredes, Lavapiés* ☎ *91/539–7826*
⊕ *www.tabernaantoniosanchez.com* ◷ *No dinner Sun.* ✛ *D6.*

SALAMANCA, RETIRO, AND CHAMBERÍ

SALAMANCA

$$$ ✕ **Álbora.** The owners of this sleek award-winning restaurant also pro-
TAPAS   duce cured hams and top-notch canned foods, and these quality ingre-
dients are included in a menu that manages to be both traditional and
creative. There's an avant-garde tapas bar on the street level, ideal for
cocktails and quick bites, and a more refined restaurant on the second
floor, perfect for impressing a client or a date. **Known for:** top-quality
charcutería; experimental Spanish cuisine; well-heeled clientele. $ *Aver-
age main: €25* ⊠ *Calle de Jorge Juan 33, Salamanca* ☎ *91/781–6197*
⊕ *www.restaurantealbora.com* ◷ *No dinner Sun.* Ⓜ *Velázquez* ✛ *H1.*

$ ✕ **Casa Dani.** Hidden in a back corner of Mercado de la Paz, the neigh-
SPANISH   borhood's famed traditional market, Casa Dani is a no-frills bar that
Fodor'sChoice   happens to serve one of the best Spanish omelets in town; each hefty
★   wedge is packed with caramelized onions and served hot and slightly
runny (adventurous eaters should opt for the *con callos* version, topped
with braised tripe). The €10 prix fixe, which hinges on market ingredients, is the best lunch deal in the area. **Known for:** top-notch tortilla española; €10 prix-fixe lunch; local crowd. $ *Average main: €10*
⊠ *Calle de Ayala 28, Salamanca* ☎ *91/575–5925* ⊕ *www.casadanima-
drid.blogspot.com* ◷ *Closed Sun. No dinner* ✛ *H1.*

$$$ ✕ **El Pescador.** Owned by the proprietors of the best fish market in
SEAFOOD   town, this seafood restaurant with a warm modern interior welcomes

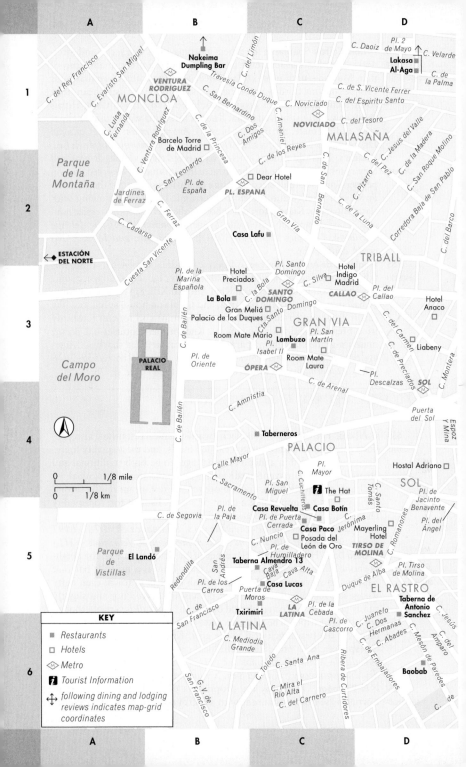

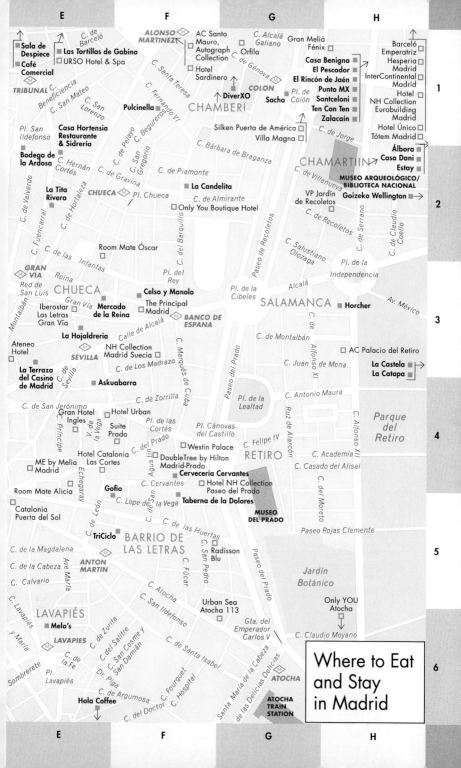

Where to Eat and Stay in Madrid

guests with an impressive window display of fresh seafood—red and white prawns, Kumamoto oysters, goose barnacles, and the renowned Galician Carril clams are just some of what you might see. Fish (including turbot, sole, grouper, and sea bass) is cooked to each customer's liking in the oven, on the grill, in a pan with garlic, or battered and fried. **Known for:** extravagant seafood displays; dayboat fish; crisp albariño. $ *Average main: €25* ⊠ *Calle de José Ortega y Gasset 75, Salamanca* 🕾 *91/402–1290* ⊕ *www.marisqueriaelpescador.net* 🕙 *Closed Sun.* Ⓜ *Lista, Núñez de Balboa* ✛ *H1.*

<table><tr><td>$$</td></tr><tr><td>SPANISH</td></tr><tr><td>FAMILY</td></tr></table>

✕ **El Rincón de Jaén.** An Andalusian-style taberna, El Rincón de Jaén evokes the raucous energy and down-home cuisine of that sunny region. Start with the *pescaíto frito,* a mix of seafood that's lightly fried and served with lemon halves, before moving onto more substantial dishes like the peeled tomato salad topped with oil-cured tuna belly (easily one of the best salads in town) and whole roasted fish and braised meats. **Known for:** Andalusian joie de vivre; tomato and tuna salad; complimentary tapas with drinks. $ *Average main: €22* ⊠ *Calle Don Ramón de la Cruz 88, Salamanca* 🕾 *91/401–6334* ⊕ *www.elrincondejaen.es* ✛ *H1.*

$$ | SPANISH

✕ **Estay.** A spacious, tranquil place presided over by white-jacketed waitstaff that makes fine breakfasts (choose from *pan con tomate,* toast with jam, or a griddled all-butter croissant plus coffee) for less than €3—this is the quintessential Salamanca restaurant. The interiors got a makeover in 2016, but the unassuming elegance of Estay was retained. **Known for:** runny tortilla española; weekday prix fixe; classic Salamanca atmosphere. $ *Average main: €20* ⊠ *Calle de Hermosilla 46, Salamanca* 🕾 *91/578–0470* 🕙 *Closed Sun.* Ⓜ *Velázquez* ✛ *H1.*

$$$ | SPANISH

✕ **Goizeko Wellington.** Aware of the sophisticated palate of Spain's new generation of diners, the owners of Goizeko Kabi (a terrific restaurant in its own right) opened this more modern restaurant, which shares the virtues of its kin but none of its stuffiness. Think neutral tones, bright wood paneling, and personable service. **Known for:** elevated Basque cuisine; simply perfect seafood; elegant atmosphere. $ *Average main: €27* ⊠ *Hotel Wellington, Calle de Villanueva 34, Salamanca* 🕾 *91/577–6026* ⊕ *www.goizekogaztelupe.com* 🕙 *Closed Sun.* Ⓜ *Retiro, Príncipe de Vergara* ✛ *H2.*

$$$$ | MEXICAN | Fodor's Choice ★

✕ **Punto MX.** The first Mexican restaurant in Europe to land a Michelin star, Punto MX, helmed by Roberto Ruiz, draws on Spanish ingredients and international techniques to redefine Mexican food with dishes like nopal "ceviche," ibérico pork tacos, and squab mole. If you can't snag a reservation in the dining room, book a more casual experience in the Mezcal Lab bar area. **Known for:** award-winning Mexican restaurant; real-deal Oaxacan moles; Spanish twists on Mexican classics. $ *Average*

2

main: €38 ✉ Calle de General Pardiñas 40, Salamanca ☎ 91/402–2226 🌐 www.puntomx.es ⏲ Closed Sun. and Mon. ✥ H1.

$$$ SPANISH 🍴 **Ten Con Ten.** One of the "gin bars" that started the Spanish *gin-tónic* craze of the late aughts, though perhaps not as trendy as it once was, the quality of food and drinks at Ten Con Ten is consistently excellent. Grab a cocktail at one of the wooden high-tops in the bar area, or sit down for a soup-to-nuts dinner in the classy dining room at the back. **Known for:** expertly made gin-tónics; fancy bar snacks; hand-cut jamón ibérico. [$] *Average main: €24 ✉ Calle de Ayala 6, Salamanca ☎ 91/575–9254 🌐 www.restaurantetenconten.com [M] Serrano ✥ H1.*

$$$$ BASQUE Fodor's Choice ★ 🍴 **Zalacaín.** This newly renovated restaurant, which in its heyday held three Michelin stars, introduced nouvelle Basque cuisine to Spain in the 1970s and has since become a Madrid classic. It's particularly known for using the best and freshest seasonal products available in signature dishes like steak tartare with pommes soufflés prepared tableside. **Known for:** old-guard Spanish fine dining; revamped interiors and menus; unbeatable "materia prima.". [$] *Average main: €34 ✉ Calle Álvarez de Baena 4, Salamanca ☎ 91/561–4840 🌐 www.restaurantezalacain.com ⏲ Closed Sun., Easter wk, and Aug. No lunch Sat. 👔 Jacket and tie [M] Gregorio Marañón ✥ H1.*

RETIRO

$$$$ GERMAN 🍴 **Horcher.** A beacon of old-world Spanish hospitality, Horcher is a Madrid classic with German influences. Wild game—boar, venison, partridge, and duck—is the centerpiece of the menu, which also includes comfort-food classics like ox Stroganoff with a Pommery mustard sauce and pork chops with sauerkraut. **Known for:** wild game dishes; German-inflected wine list; to-die-for baumkuchen (a German-style spit cake). [$] *Average main: €37 ✉ Calle de Alfonso XII 6, Retiro ☎ 91/522–0731 🌐 www.restaurantehorcher.com ⏲ Closed Sun. No lunch Sat. 👔 Jacket and tie [M] Retiro ✥ H3.*

$$ TAPAS 🍴 **La Castela.** Traditional taverns with tin-top bars, vermouth on tap, and no-nonsense waiters are a dying breed in Madrid, but this one, just a couple of blocks from the Parque del Buen Retiro, has stood the test of time. It's always busy with locals clamoring over plates of sautéed wild mushrooms, anchovies served with a cucumber and tomato salad (*pipirrana*), and clams in white wine. **Known for:** fresh seafood and fish; vintage bar; local crowd. [$] *Average main: €18 ✉ Calle Doctor Castelo 22, Retiro ☎ 91/574–0015 🌐 www.lacastela.com ⏲ No dinner Sun. [M] Ibiza ✥ H3.*

$$ SPANISH 🍴 **La Catapa.** La Catapa's tapas are classic but never old hat, inventive but never pretentious. The burst-in-your-mouth croquetas and garlicky razor clams may lure the crowds, but the hidden gems are in the vegetable section: it's hard to decide between the artichoke confit "flowers" with crunchy salt, peeled tomatoes dressed with olive oil, and umami-packed seared mushrooms. **Known for:** elevated tapas; market-driven specials; eclectic wines. [$] *Average main: €16 ✉ Calle Menorca 14, Retiro ☎ 68/614–3823 ⏲ Closed Sun. and Mon. ✥ H3.*

CHAMBERÍ

$$$
SPANISH

✕ **Lakasa.** Basque chef César Martín has a devoted local following for his hyperseasonal menus that show a sincere dedication to food sustainability. Lakasa may have moved into a bigger, more modern space, but Martín's specialties haven't wavered: be sure to indulge in the Idiazabal fritters, crisp orbs redolent of smoky sheep's cheese. **Known for:** experimental Basque cuisine; Idiazabal fritters; pristine seafood. $ *Average main: €24* ⊠ *Calle Santa Engracia 120, Chamberí* ☎ *91/533–8715* ⊕ *www.lakasa.es* ☯ *Closed Sun. and Mon.* Ⓜ *Cuatro Caminos* ✛ *D1.*

$$
TAPAS

✕ **Las Tortillas de Gabino.** At this lively restaurant you'll find crowds of Spaniards gobbling up one of the city's finest, most upmarket renditions of the tortilla española with unconventional add-ins like octopus, potato chips, and truffles. Travelers with tortilla fatigue can rest easy knowing that the menu includes plenty of equally succulent non-egg choices (the rice dishes in particular stand out). **Known for:** fancy tortillas; date-night ambience; carefully selected wines. $ *Average main: €16* ⊠ *Calle Rafael Calvo 20, Chamberí* ☎ *91/319–7505* ⊕ *www.lastortillasdegabino.com* ☯ *Closed Sun.* Ⓜ *Rubén Darío* ✛ *E1.*

$$
ASIAN FUSION

✕ **Nakeima Dumpling Bar.** Good thing the *baos*, dumplings, and nigiris are out-of-this-world spectacular at Nakeima—if not, no one would wait the hour (on average) it takes to get in. Dishes here are "Asian freestyle" (their term) and bridge the gap between East and West with dishes like Thai-spiced tripe and a squab "Kit Kat." **Known for:** Spanish-Asian fusion cuisine; eclectic dumplings and baos; lines out the door. $ *Average main: €22* ⊠ *Calle de Meléndez Valdés 54, Chamberí* ☎ *62/070–9399* ☯ *Closed Sun. and Mon.* ✛ *B1.*

$$
SPANISH
Fodor's Choice
★

✕ **Sala de Despiece.** The opening of this ultratrendy butcher-shop-themed restaurant spurred the revival of Calle Ponzano as Madrid's most exciting tapas street. Feast on eye-catching, impeccably prepared dishes like carpaccio-truffle roll-ups and grilled octopus slathered in chimichurri. **Known for:** local celebrity chef; playful industrial decor; see-and-be-seen crowd. $ *Average main: €19* ⊠ *Calle de Ponzano 11, Chamberí* ☎ *91/752–6106* ⊕ *www.saladedespiece.com* ✛ *E1.*

$$$$
MEDITERRANEAN

✕ **Santceloni.** Chef Óscar Velasco delivers exquisite combinations of Mediterranean ingredients accompanied by a comprehensive and unusual wine list. Go with an appetite and lots of time (a minimum of three hours), because a meal here is ceremonious. **Known for:** wide cocktail and wine menu; highly orchestrated tasting menus; standout cheese course. $ *Average main: €50* ⊠ *Hotel Hesperia, Paseo de la Castellana 57, Chamberí* ☎ *91/210–8840* ⊕ *www.restaurantesantceloni. com* ☯ *Closed Sun. No lunch Sat.* Ⓜ *Gregorio Marañón* ✛ *H1.*

CHAMARTÍN AND TETUÁN

CHAMARTÍN

$$$
SPANISH
Fodor's Choice
★

✕ **Casa Benigna.** Owner Don Norberto, a quirky, jolly gent, offers a health-conscious menu with painstakingly selected wines to match at this snug, book-lined restaurant. Rice dishes are the house specialty, and they're cooked in extra-flat paella pans specially manufactured for the restaurant. **Known for:** city's best paella; larger-than-life owner; homey atmosphere. $ *Average main: €26* ✉ *Calle de Benigno Soto 9, Chamartín* ☎ *91/416–9357* ◷ *No dinner Sun. and Mon.* Ⓜ *Concha Espina, Prosperidad* ✛ *H1.*

$$$$ ✕ **DiverXO.** When you ask a madrileño about a remarkable food experi-
ECLECTIC ence—something that stirs the senses beyond feeding one's appetite—
Fodor'sChoice David Muñoz's bombastic venue is often the first name you'll hear.
★ Nothing is offered à la carte; the restaurant serves tasting menus (called
"canvases") only, running €195–€250. **Known for:** punk-rock fine din-
ing; courses that use the whole table as a canvas; hard-to-get reserva-
tions. $ *Average main: €200* ✉ *NH Hotel Eurobuilding , Calle Padre
Damian 23, Chamartín* ☎ *91/570–0766* ⊕ *www.diverxo.com* ◷ *Closed
Sun. and Mon.* Ⓜ *Cuzco* ✛ *G1.*

$$$ ✕ **Sacha.** Settle into a unhurried feast at Sacha, a cozy bistro with soul-
SPANISH satisfying food and hand-selected wines, and you might never want to
leave—especially if you strike up a conversation with Sacha himself,
who's quite the character. The cuisine is regional Spanish—think buti-
farra sausages with sautéed mushrooms or razor clams with black garlic
emulsion—with just enough imagination to make you wonder why the
restaurant isn't better known. **Known for:** Spanish bistro fare; impeccable steak tartare; hard-to-find wines. $ *Average main: €24* ✉ *Calle
Juan Hurtado de Mendoza 11, Chamartín* ☎ *91/345–5952* ◷ *Closed
Sun.* Ⓜ *Cuzco* ✛ *G1.*

TETUÁN

$ ✕ **Al-Aga.** Madrileños love kebabs, and the smoky, juicy version served
MIDDLE EASTERN at Al-Aga is far and away the city's best. Opened by a family of
refugees fleeing Syria's civil war, Al-Aga draws on recipes handed
down to the chef and owner, Labib, who cooks with care and attention to detail: meat is ground by hand for each order, and all the
sauces are homemade. **Known for:** flame-grilled kebabs; grab and go;
Syrian specialties. $ *Average main: €5* ✉ *Calle Villaamil 52, Tetuán*
☎ *91/070–3115* ✛ *D1.*

WHERE TO STAY

Spain overtook the United States as the world's second-most-visited
country in 2018, so it's no surprise that Madrid is in the throes
of a hotel construction boom, the first the city has seen since the
economic crisis hit in 2008. The Old Guard of hotels is shaking
in its boots as newcomers offer modern-day amenities (Bluetooth
speakers, international power outlets, bedside thermostats, etc.) at
affordable prices: the Westin Palace is in the midst of a seemingly
never-ending remodel, while the Ritz Madrid will remain closed for
massive renovations until late 2019. The last couple of years have
also ushered in several cutting-edge boutique and designer properties, the likes of which the city has never seen, such as Barceló Torre
de Madrid, Tótem, and Only You Atocha. And Madrid can finally
lay claim to a chic, immaculately clean hostel in The Hat.

*Use the coordinate (✛ B2) at the end of each listing to locate a site on
the corresponding map.*

WHAT IT COSTS IN EUROS				
	$	**$$**	**$$$**	**$$$$**
HOTELS	under €125	€125–€174	€175–€225	over €225

Prices are for two people in a standard double room in high season.

2

PALACIO, MONCLOA, LA LATINA, AND SOL

PALACIO

$$$$
HOTEL
Fodor'sChoice
★

Gran Meliá Palacio de Los Duques. Spanish-art lovers will geek out at the new Gran Meliá Palacio de los Duques, a luxury hotel tucked behind Gran Vía where reproductions of famous Diego Velázquez paintings feature in every room. **Pros:** one of the city's best hotel restaurants; underfloor heating and deep-soak tubs; rooftop pool and bar. **Cons:** rooms are distinctly less attractive than public areas; rooftop often off-limits because of private events; no great views from rooms. $ *Rooms from: €350* ⊠ *Cuesta Santo Domingo 5, Palacio* ☎ *91/276–4747* ⊕ *www.melia.com* ⇗ *180 rooms* ❙❍❙ *No meals* ✛ *C3.*

$$
HOTEL

Hotel Índigo Madrid. A hip, vibrant hotel off the bustling Gran Vía thoroughfare, Hotel Índigo is best known for its stunning rooftop lounge and outdoor infinity pool, rare features in Madrid. **Pros:** sceney rooftop infinity pool; restaurant that punches above its weight; surprisingly well-equipped gym. **Cons:** interior rooms get little natural light; loses much of its vitality in cold-weather months; decor borders on gaudy. $ *Rooms from: €170* ⊠ *Calle de Silva 6, Palacio* ☎ *91/200–8585* ⊕ *www.indigomadrid.com* ⇗ *85 rooms* ❙❍❙ *No meals* ✛ *C3.*

$$$
HOTEL

Room Mate Laura. A quirky, clubby hotel located overlooking Plaza de San Martín near the Royal Theater and Palace, Room Mate Laura feels like a time warp to an IKEA catalog of the early aughts. **Pros:** free portable Wi-Fi gadgets; kitchenettes; clean and comfortable. **Cons:** only the best rooms have views of the convent; no restaurant; some bathrooms need to be revamped. $ *Rooms from: €190* ⊠ *Travesía de Trujillos 3, Palacio* ☎ *91/701–1670* ⊕ *www.room-matehotels.com* ⇗ *36 rooms* ❙❍❙ *No meals* Ⓜ *Ópera* ✛ *C3.*

$$
HOTEL

Room Mate Mario. In the city center, steps from the Royal Palace and Teatro Real, Mario is small with limited services, but a welcome alternative to Madrid's traditional hotel options, at a good price. **Pros:** centrally located; good breakfast served until noon; it's the cheapest of the chain. **Cons:** no restaurant; cramped entry-level rooms; unremarkable views compared to other Room Mate hotels. $ *Rooms from: €140* ⊠ *Calle Campomanes 4, Palacio* ☎ *91/548–8548* ⊕ *www.room-matehotels.com* ⇗ *57 rooms* ❙❍❙ *Free Breakfast* Ⓜ *Ópera* ✛ *C3.*

MONCLOA

$$$
HOTEL
Fodor'sChoice
★

Barceló Torre de Madrid. A jewel box of glowing lights, harlequin furniture, and gilded mirrors, the soaring Barceló Torre de Madrid is the trendiest hotel in town—and one of the newest, opened in February 2017. **Pros:** cutting-edge design by local artists; offers experiences with local influencers; excellent Somos restaurant. **Cons:** certain bathrooms

WHERE SHOULD I STAY?

	Neighborhood Vibe	Pros	Cons
Palacio, Moncloa, La Latina, and Sol	Anchored by the Plaza Mayor, this historic quarter is full of narrow streets and taverns.	Has the most traditional feel of Madrid neighborhoods; varied lodging and dining including many inexpensive (though usually undistinguished) hostals and old-flavor taverns.	Can be tough to navigate; many tourist traps.
Barrio de las Letras (including Carrera de San Jerónimo and Paseo del Prado)	A magnet for tourists, this classic literary nest has several pedestrian-only streets.	Renovated Plaza Santa Ana and Plaza del Ángel; posh hotels and restaurants; conveniently located between the oldest part of the city and all the major art museums.	Noisy, especially around Plaza Santa Ana; some bars and restaurants overpriced due to the tourists.
Chueca and Malasaña	Vibrant and bustling, this is where you want to be if you're past your twenties but still don't want to be in bed before midnight.	These barrios burst with a bit of everything: busy nightlife, alternative shops, charming cafés, and fancy and inexpensive local and international restaurants.	Extremely loud, especially on the weekends; dirtier than some other neighborhoods.
Salamanca, Retiro, and Chamberí	Swanky, posh, and safe, these are the neighborhoods many high-end hotels and restaurants call home.	Quiet at day's end; plenty of good restaurants; home to the upscale shopping (Salamanca) and residential (Salamanca and the eastern side of Retiro) areas.	Bland and culturally homogeneous; restaurant staff and locals can be snooty; expensive.

offer questionable privacy; some minor technical foibles; ironing out kinks in service. $ *Rooms from: €210* ⊠ *Pl. de España 18, Moncloa* ☎ *91/524–2339* ⊕ *www.barcelo.com* ⟳ *256 rooms* ❑ *No meals* ✛ *B2.*

$$
HOTEL

❑ **Dear Hotel.** On Gran Vía overlooking the tree-lined Plaza de España, Dear Hotel is a sleek urban property designed by Tarruella Trenchs Studio, the firm behind such lauded projects as H10 La Mimosa hotel in Barcelona and La Bien Aparecida restaurant in Madrid. **Pros:** all rooms face out; swanky rooftop bar; minimalist decor. **Cons:** lilliputian pool; no gym or spa; cramped lobby. $ *Rooms from: €135* ⊠ *Gran Vía 80, Moncloa* ☎ *91/412–3200* ⊕ *www.dearhotelmadrid.com* ⟳ *162 rooms* ❑ *No meals* ✛ *C2.*

LA LATINA

$
HOTEL
Fodor's Choice
★

❑ **The Hat.** The Hat epitomizes the fast-growing category of "designer hostels": affordable properties geared toward the millennial set that boast sleek multiperson rooms, bumping weekend events, and generous breakfasts. **Pros:** rooftop bar; steps from the Plaza Mayor; bountiful breakfasts. **Cons:** hotel guests not prioritized on rooftop, which fills up fast; some rooms are dark; location means tourists are everywhere.

[$] *Rooms from: €45* ✉ *Calle Imperial 9, La Latina* ☎ *91/772–8572* 🌐 *www.thehatmadrid.com* 🛏 *42 rooms* 🍴 *Free Breakfast* ⊕ *C3.*

$$ HOTEL **Posada del León de Oro.** More like a village guesthouse than a metropolitan hotel, this refurbished late-19th-century property was built atop the remains of a stone wall that encircled the city in the 12th century, which you can see through glass floor panels at the hotel entrance and in the restaurant. **Pros:** unbeatable location; restaurant with over 300 Spanish wines; high ceilings with exposed wood beams. **Cons:** rooms facing the courtyard are quite small; late-night noise on weekends; cramped entry-level rooms. [$] *Rooms from: €160* ✉ *Calle Cava Baja 12, La Latina* ☎ *91/119–1494* 🌐 *www.posadadelleondeoro.com* 🛏 *27 rooms* 🍴 *No meals* [M] *La Latina* ⊕ *C5.*

SOL

$ HOTEL **Ateneo Hotel.** This clean and economical property is set in an 18th-century building that was once home to the Ateneo, a club founded in 1835 to promote freedom of thought. **Pros:** sizeable rooms; triple and quadruple rooms available; some rooms have skylights and balconies. **Cons:** safe yet slightly sketchy street; noisy area; dated decor. [$] *Rooms from: €120* ✉ *Calle de la Montera 22, Sol* ☎ *91/521–2012* 🌐 *www.hotel-ateneo.com* 🛏 *44 rooms* 🍴 *Free Breakfast* [M] *Gran Vía, Sol* ⊕ *E3.*

$ HOTEL **Hostal Adriano.** On a street with dozens of bland competitors a couple of blocks from Sol, this budget hotel stands out for its price and quality. **Pros:** friendly service; good value; charming touches. **Cons:** shares the building with other hostales; reception desk not staffed 24 hours; street noise. [$] *Rooms from: €72* ✉ *Calle de la Cruz 26, 4th fl., Sol* ☎ *91/521–1339* 🌐 *www.hostaladriano.com* 🛏 *22 rooms* 🍴 *No meals* [M] *Sol* ⊕ *D4.*

$$ HOTEL **Hotel Preciados.** In a 19th-century building on the quieter edge of one of Madrid's main shopping districts, Preciados is a charming midrange hotel ideal for travelers who value space and comfort. **Pros:** conveniently located; complimentary minibar (you read that correctly!); valet parking a steal at €19.50 per day. **Cons:** expensive breakfast; chaotic street; dated decor. [$] *Rooms from: €165* ✉ *Calle Preciados 37, Sol* ☎ *91/454–4400* 🌐 *www.preciadoshotel.com* 🛏 *101 rooms* 🍴 *No meals* [M] *Callao* ⊕ *B3.*

$$ HOTEL Fodor's Choice ★ **Iberostar Las Letras Gran Vía.** A modern, reasonably priced hotel on the stately avenue of Gran Vía, Iberostar Las Letras is a welcoming oasis from the area's constant hubbub of tourists and shoppers. **Pros:** state-of-the-art gym; many rooms have balconies; happening rooftop bar. **Cons:** finicky air-conditioning; no spa; awkward bathroom design. [$] *Rooms from: €142* ✉ *Gran Vía 11, Sol* ☎ *91/523–7980* 🌐 *www.hoteldelasletras.com* 🛏 *110 rooms* 🍴 *No meals* [M] *Banco de España* ⊕ *E3.*

$$ HOTEL **Liabeny.** This classically decorated hotel situated between Gran Vía and Puerta del Sol has large, comfortable carpeted rooms with striped fabrics and big windows. **Pros:** spacious bathrooms; near Princesa shopping area; upscale Castilian restaurant. **Cons:** small rooms; crowded, noisy neighborhood; stairs to access public areas. [$] *Rooms from: €130* ✉ *Calle de la Salud 3, Sol* ☎ *91/531–9000* 🌐 *www.liabeny.es* 🛏 *220 rooms* ⊕ *D3.*

$ **Mayerling Hotel.** Sleek minimalism at just the right value can be found
HOTEL   in this former textile wholesaler's premises, now a 22-room boutique
hotel, just a few blocks off Plaza Mayor and Plaza Santa Ana. Serene
(if slightly clinical) white rooms come in three sizes—standard, superior, and triple—and are decorated with colorful headboards, charcoal
valances, and small open closets. **Pros:** some rooms accommodate up
to three people; 24-hour "help yourself" bar with coffee, snacks, and
juices; prime location. **Cons:** rooms are smallish by U.S. standards;
white walls show smudges; no restaurant or gym. $ *Rooms from: €110*
✉ *Calle del Conde de Romanones 6, Sol* ☎ *91/420–1580* ⊕ *www.may-
erlinghotel.com/en* ⪢ *22 rooms* ⦿ *Free Breakfast* Ⓜ *Tirso de Molina*
✛ *D5.*

BARRIO DE LAS LETRAS

$$ **Catalonia Puerta del Sol.** The regal cobblestone corridor leading to the
HOTEL   reception desk, the atrium with walls made partly of original granite
blocks, and the magnificent main wooden staircase (presided over by
a lion statue) reveal this building's 18th-century origins. **Pros:** grand,
quiet building; spacious rooms; room service. **Cons:** street looks a bit
scruffy; rooms and common areas lack character; smoking permitted
in the courtyard. $ *Rooms from: €130* ✉ *Calle de Atocha 23, Barrio
de las Letras* ☎ *91/369–7171* ⊕ *www.hoteles-catalonia.es* ⪢ *63 rooms*
⦿ *No meals* Ⓜ *Tirso de Molina* ✛ *E5.*

$$$$ **DoubleTree by Hilton Madrid-Prado.** Opened in January 2017, this
HOTEL   DoubleTree is a sparkling, immaculately designed hotel two blocks
from the Prado Museum. **Pros:** relaxing earth-tone accents; excellent
in-room amenities; arguably the city's best Japanese restaurant. **Cons:**
no valet parking; dull bar; no sense of place. $ *Rooms from: €270*
✉ *Calle de San Agustín 3, Barrio de las Letras* ☎ *91/360–0820* ⊕ *www.
doubletree3.hilton.com* ⪢ *61 rooms* ⦿ *No meals* ✛ *F4.*

$$$$ **Gran Hotel Inglés.** This grand hotel, opened in 1853, is the oldest in
HOTEL   Madrid—and after a long renovation, it reopened in 2018 to great
fanfare. **Pros:** one of the city's most historic hotels; impeccable design;
all rooms at least 280 square feet. **Cons:** pricey food and beverages;
stairs to get to some rooms; occasional weekend street noise. $ *Rooms
from: €315* ✉ *Calle Echegaray 8, Barrio de las Letras* ☎ *91/360–0001*
⊕ *www.granhotelingles.com* ⪢ *48 rooms* ⦿ *No meals* ✛ *E4.*

$$$ **Hotel Catalonia Las Cortes.** A late-18th-century palace formerly owned
HOTEL   by the Duke of Noblejas, this hotel, situated a few yards from Plaza
Santa Ana, still bears traces of opulence and grandeur. **Pros:** tastefully decorated rooms; big walk-in showers; gorgeous architectural
details. **Cons:** common areas are rather dull; no gym, pool, or spa; no
bar. $ *Rooms from: €200* ✉ *Calle del Prado 6, Barrio de las Letras*
☎ *91/389–6051* ⊕ *www.hoteles-catalonia.com* ⪢ *74 rooms* ⦿ *No
meals* Ⓜ *Sevilla, Antón Martín* ✛ *E4.*

$$$ **Hotel NH Collection Paseo del Prado.** In a turn-of-the-20th-century
HOTEL   palace overlooking Plaza de Neptuno, this hotel preserves the build-
ing's erstwhile grandeur with canopy beds, gold-framed mirrors, and
wing chairs. **Pros:** within the Golden Triangle of museums; gym with
panoramic views; "lazy Sunday checkout" at 3 pm. **Cons:** need to

CLOSE UP

Lodging Alternatives

If you want a home base that's roomy enough for a family and comes with cooking facilities, consider a furnished rental. Apartment rentals are increasingly popular in Madrid, and they can save you money, too. Prices run €50–€250 per person per night, and perfectly acceptable lodging for four can be found for around €150 per night. These are just a few of the apartment rental agencies that Fodorites are using these days: ⊕ *www.airbnb.com;* ⊕ *www.niumba. com;* ⊕ *www.homeclub.com;* ⊕ *www. habitatapartments.com/madrid-apart- ments;* ⊕ *www.idealista.com;* ⊕ *www. apartinmadrid.com.*

---

upgrade to get good views; inconsistent food at Estado Puro; dated decor. $ *Rooms from: €200* ⊠ *Pl. Cánovas del Castillo 4, Barrio de las Letras* ☏ *91/330–2400* ⊕ *www.nh-hoteles.es* ⌖ *115 rooms* ⦵ *No meals* Ⓜ *Banco de España* ✛ *F4.*

$$$$ 🏨 **Hotel Urban.** A five-minute walk from Puerta del Sol, Hotel Urban
HOTEL conveys Madrid's cosmopolitan spirit with its stylish mix of Papua New
Fodor'sChoice Guinean artifacts and rare designer wares. **Pros:** eclectic, internationally
★ sourced art; rooftop swimming pool; flamboyant public spaces. **Cons:** some rooms are small; rooms near the elevator can be noisy; no coffeemakers in entry-level rooms. $ *Rooms from: €250* ⊠ *Carrera de San Jerónimo 34, Barrio de las Letras* ☏ *91/787–7770* ⊕ *www.derbyhotels. com* ⌖ *103 rooms* ⦵ *No meals* Ⓜ *Sevilla* ✛ *E4.*

$$$$ 🏨 **ME by Meliá Madrid.** In an unbeatable location, this ultramodern hotel
HOTEL bears a few reminders of the era when bullfighters would convene here before setting off to Las Ventas—a few bulls' heads hang in the lounge and some abstract pictures of bullfighting are scattered around, but the old flair has been superseded by cutting-edge amenities. **Pros:** cool, clubby vibe; popular restaurant; rooftop bar boasts great views of city. **Cons:** some rooms are cramped; plaza-facing rooms can be noisy; key cards demagnetize easily. $ *Rooms from: €280* ⊠ *Pl. Santa Ana 14, Barrio de las Letras* ☏ *91/531–4500* ⊕ *www.melia.com* ⌖ *191 rooms* ⦵ *No meals* Ⓜ *Sol* ✛ *E4.*

$$$$ 🏨 **NH Collection Madrid Suecia.** The 1956 building the NH Collection
HOTEL Madrid Suecia occupies was once home to Ernest Hemingway and Che Guevara; today's guests are decidedly tamer, but the retro aesthetic lives on in the hotel's brown velvet couches, towering tropical plants, and suave concierges. **Pros:** renovated in 2016; rooftop bar with great views; stylish rooms. **Cons:** robes and slippers not provided in entry-level rooms; windowless gym; overpriced restaurant. $ *Rooms from: €230* ⊠ *Calle del Marqués de Casa Riera 4, Barrio de las Letras* ☏ *91/200– 0570* ⊕ *www.nh-hotels.com* ⌖ *123 rooms* ⦵ *No meals* ✛ *F3.*

$$ ⛨ **Only You Atocha.** Arguably the hottest hotel in town, the newly opened
HOTEL Only YOU Atocha is a stunner with its swanky lobby, rooftop restau-
Fodor's Choice rant, and well-appointed, industrial-chic accommodations. **Pros:** sceney
★ rooftop brunch; interesting pop-ups in the lobby; cutting-edge design.
Cons: exterior-facing rooms can be noisy; food quality could be better in
both restaurants; ugly views of major intersection. ⓢ *Rooms from: €170*
✉ *Paseo de la Infanta Isabel 13, Barrio de las Letras* ☎ *91/409–7876*
⊕ *www.onlyyouhotels.com* ⤳ *205 rooms* ⓞ *No meals* ✛ *H6.*

$$$ ⛨ **Radisson Blu.** Surprisingly "boutique" for a Radisson Blu, this hotel
HOTEL has an intimate, urban feel that suits its middle-of-it-all location. **Pros:**
pool and spa access; great location; breakfast from 6:30 am. **Cons:**
some standard rooms are rather small; pricey breakfast; middling restaurant. ⓢ *Rooms from: €190* ✉ *Calle de Moratín 52, Barrio de las
Letras* ☎ *91/524–2626* ⊕ *www.radissonblu.com* ⤳ *54 rooms* ⓞ *No
meals* Ⓜ *Atocha* ✛ *F5.*

$$ ⛨ **Room Mate Alicia.** The all-white lobby, with curving walls, backlit ceil-
HOTEL ing panels, and gilded columns, may have looked trendy 10 years ago,
when the hotel opened, but today it verges on tacky, so it's a good thing,
then, that Room Mate Alicia's prime location and competitive rates
continue to make it a worthwhile contender. **Pros:** good value; brightly
colored rooms; laid-back atmosphere. **Cons:** standard rooms are small;
zero-privacy bathroom spaces; no restaurant or gym. ⓢ *Rooms from:
€165* ✉ *Calle Prado 2, Barrio de las Letras* ☎ *91/389–6095* ⊕ *www.
room-matehoteles.com* ⤳ *34 rooms* ⓞ *No meals* Ⓜ *Sevilla* ✛ *E4.*

$$ ⛨ **Suite Prado.** Popular with Americans, this basic yet comfortable
HOTEL apartment hotel is situated a few steps from the Prado, the Thyssen-
Bornemisza, and the Plaza Santa Ana tapas area. **Pros:** variety of room
options; great for families and longer stays; complimentary room-
service breakfasts. **Cons:** a bit noisy; dated decor; low ceilings on the
top floor. ⓢ *Rooms from: €160* ✉ *Calle Manuel Fernández y González
10, Barrio de las Letras* ☎ *91/420–2318* ⊕ *www.suiteprado.com* ⤳ *18
apartments* ⓞ *Free Breakfast* Ⓜ *Sevilla* ✛ *F4.*

$ ⛨ **Urban Sea Atocha 113.** A metropolitan outpost of the Blue Sea resort
HOTEL chain, Urban Sea Atocha 113 is a no-frills 36-room hotel just north of
the eponymous railway station. **Pros:** equidistant between Barrio de las
Letras and Lavapiés; rooftop terrace with gorgeous views; single rooms
ideal for solo travelers. **Cons:** bare-bones services; in-room sinks; exterior rooms facing Calle Atocha are pricey. ⓢ *Rooms from: €100* ✉ *Calle
Atocha 113, Barrio de las Letras* ☎ *91/369–2895* ⊕ *www.blueseahotels.
com* ⤳ *36 rooms* ⓞ *No meals* Ⓜ *Atocha* ✛ *F6.*

$$$$ ⛨ **Westin Palace.** An iconic hotel situated inside the "Golden Triangle"
HOTEL (the district connecting the Prado, Reina Sofía, and Thyssen museums), the Westin Palace is known for its unbeatable location, stately
facade, and classical decor. **Pros:** historic grand hotel; 24-hour gym with
adjoining roof deck; spacious bathrooms. **Cons:** standard rooms face a
backstreet; daily turndown only provided on request; some renovation
choices in poor taste. ⓢ *Rooms from: €350* ✉ *Pl. de las Cortés 7, Barrio
de las Letras* ☎ *91/360–8000* ⊕ *www.palacemadrid.com* ⤳ *467 rooms*
ⓞ *No meals* Ⓜ *Banco de España, Sevilla* ✛ *F4.*

CHUECA

$$$$ HOTEL Fodor's Choice ★ 🏨 **Only You Boutique Hotel.** The Ibizan owners of this hotel bring that island's mix of glamour, energy, and cutting-edge music and design to one of Madrid's most happening neighborhoods. **Pros:** location among trendy cafés and shops; stylish and state-of-the art; late check-out. **Cons:** sleeping area is a bit cramped; rooms with views of Calle Barquillo are pricey; scant storage space for suitcases. [$] *Rooms from: €260* ✉ *Calle Barquillo 21, Chueca* ☎ *91/005–2222* 🌐 *www.onlyyouhotels.com/en* 🛏 *70 rooms* 🍴 *No meals* ⊕ *F2.*

$$$$ HOTEL 🏨 **The Principal Madrid.** Dozens of hotels flank Gran Vía, Madrid's main artery, but only the Principal can claim five stars. **Pros:** hotel rooftop with best views in Madrid; Ramón Freixa–helmed restaurant; luxury feel with personal touches. **Cons:** rooms not properly soundproofed; rooftop pool is tiny; gym doesn't open until 10 am. [$] *Rooms from: €300* ✉ *Calle Marqués de Valdeiglesias 1, Chueca* ☎ *91/521–8743* 🌐 *www.theprincipalmadridhotel.com* 🛏 *76 rooms* 🍴 *No meals* ⊕ *F3.*

$$$ HOTEL Fodor's Choice ★ 🏨 **Room Mate Óscar.** Boasting one of the swankiest rooftop pools in the heart of Chueca, Madrid's "gayborhood," Room Mate Óscar caters to an artsy crowd. **Pros:** playful design accents; see-and-be-seen clientele; rooftop pool and lounge. **Cons:** noisy street and rooftop; might be too happening for some; pool only open in summer. [$] *Rooms from: €175* ✉ *Pl. Vázquez de Mella 12, Chueca* ☎ *91/701–1173* 🌐 *www.room-matehotels.com* 🛏 *69 rooms* 🍴 *Free Breakfast* [M] *Chueca* ⊕ *E2.*

$$$ HOTEL Fodor's Choice ★ 🏨 **URSO Hotel & Spa.** Housed in a regal turn-of-the-20th-century municipal building, this luxury hotel and spa boasts old-world luxury and avant-garde design to satisfy alternative types and jet-setters alike. **Pros:** stunning facade; Natura Bissé spa with 7-meter hydromassage pool; sanctuarylike rooms. **Cons:** bar closes at midnight; construction next door; smallish gym. [$] *Rooms from: €210* ✉ *Calle de Mejía Lequerica 8, Chueca* ☎ *91/444–4458* 🌐 *www.hotelurso.com* 🛏 *78 rooms* 🍴 *No meals* ⊕ *E1.*

SALAMANCA, RETIRO, AND CHAMBERÍ

SALAMANCA

$$$ HOTEL 🏨 **Barceló Emperatriz.** Worthy of an empress, as its name implies, this swanky property on a tree-shaded block opened in 2016 and offers knowledgeable concierge services, healthy breakfast options, and an extensive pillow menu. **Pros:** private terraces; king-size beds and in-room hot tubs; portable Wi-Fi hot spot. **Cons:** cramped lobby; 10-minute taxi from center of town; small pool and gym. [$] *Rooms from: €210* ✉ *Calle de López de Hoyos 4, Salamanca* ☎ *91/342–2490* 🌐 *www.barcelo.com* 🛏 *146 rooms* 🍴 *No meals* ⊕ *H1.*

$$$$ HOTEL 🏨 **Gran Meliá Fénix.** A Madrid institution that has played host to the likes of the Beatles, Cary Grant, and Rita Hayworth, this hotel is a mere hop from the posh shops of Calle Serrano. **Pros:** close to shopping; great breakfast buffet; opulent, spacious rooms. **Cons:** small bathrooms; below-average restaurant; elitist VIP policy that excludes standard-room guests from certain areas. [$] *Rooms from: €230* ✉ *Calle*

de Hermosilla 2, Salamanca ☎ *91/431–6700* 🌐 *www.melia.com* 🛏 *225 rooms* 🍴 *No meals* [M] *Colón* ✣ *H1.*

$$$$ HOTEL 🏨 **Hotel Único.** Situated on a quiet side street in the posh, tree-lined district of Salamanca, Hotel Único is a boutique property suited to travelers seeking a relaxing, cosmopolitan vacation. **Pros:** pleasant, bright breakfast area; quaint street views from exterior rooms; Ramón Freixa restaurant. **Cons:** rooms facing the street can be noisy; fewer facilities than some of the larger hotels; lobby and rooms could use a design refresh. [$] *Rooms from: €350* ✉ *Calle de Claudio Coello 67, Salamanca* ☎ *91/781–0173* 🌐 *www.unicohotelmadrid.com* 🛏 *44 rooms* 🍴 *No meals* [M] *Serrano* ✣ *H1.*

$$$ HOTEL Fodor's Choice ★ 🏨 **Tótem Madrid.** A breath of fresh air on the Madrid hotel scene, particularly in this notoriously stuffy part of town, Tótem checks all the boxes: genial service, state-of-the-art design, sought-after location, terrific food and cocktails—you name it, they've got it. **Pros:** charming neighborhood; excellent cocktail bar and restaurant; stylish and modern. **Cons:** main attractions not within walking distance; slightly stodgy neighborhood; interior rooms not as pleasant. [$] *Rooms from: €200* ✉ *Calle Hermosilla 23, Salamanca* ☎ *91/426–0035* 🌐 *www.totem-madrid.com* 🛏 *64 rooms* 🍴 *No meals* ✣ *H1.*

$$$$ HOTEL Fodor's Choice ★ 🏨 **Villa Magna.** If the Ritz caters to old-money Madrid, then Villa Magna, located on the shady Castellana mall, is its low-profile, new-money counterpart, frequented by celebrities, foreign financiers, and other high-society types. **Pros:** exceptional service; arguably the best breakfast in Madrid; in-room perks and family-friendly touches. **Cons:** expensive room service; the exterior is a little dull; attempts at trendiness can come across as corny. [$] *Rooms from: €500* ✉ *Paseo de la Castellana 22, Salamanca* ☎ *91/587–1234* 🌐 *www.mythahotels.com* 🛏 *150 rooms* 🍴 *No meals* [M] *Rubén Darío* ✣ *G1.*

$$$ HOTEL FAMILY 🏨 **VP Jardín de Recoletos.** This boutique apartment hotel offers great value on a quiet street just a couple of blocks from Retiro Park, the Prado, and Madrid's main shopping area. **Pros:** spacious rooms with kitchens; good restaurant; periodic deals on the hotel's website. **Cons:** the garden closes at midnight and, when crowded, can be noisy; design is a bit outmoded; breakfast not served in the garden. [$] *Rooms from: €190* ✉ *Calle Gil de Santivañes 6, Salamanca* ☎ *91/781–1640* 🌐 *www.recoletos-hotel.com* 🛏 *43 rooms* 🍴 *No meals* [M] *Colón* ✣ *H2.*

RETIRO

$$$$ HOTEL Fodor's Choice ★ 🏨 **AC Palacio del Retiro.** A palatial early-20th-century building, once owned by a noble family with extravagant habits (the elevator carried their horses up and down from the rooftop exercise ring), this spectacular hotel shows that mixing classical and modern decor can work when done right. **Pros:** spacious, stylish rooms; within walking distance of the Prado; bathrooms stocked with all sorts of complimentary products. **Cons:** pricey breakfast; lower rooms facing the park can get noisy; cumbersome room keys. [$] *Rooms from: €300* ✉ *Calle de Alfonso XII 14, Retiro* ☎ *91/523–7460* 🌐 *www.ac-hotels.com* 🛏 *58 rooms* 🍴 *No meals* [M] *Retiro* ✣ *H3.*

2

CHAMBERÍ

$$$$ HOTEL Fodor's Choice ★ **AC Santo Mauro, Autograph Collection.** This fin-de-siècle palace in the Chamberí district, first a duke's residence and later the Canadian embassy, is now an intimate luxury hotel (managed by Marriott), an oasis of calm removed from the city center. **Pros:** a world away from the city's hustle and bustle; cloudlike beds; fine restaurant. **Cons:** pricey breakfast; not in the historic center; some rooms on the smaller side. [$] *Rooms from: €320* ✉ *Calle Zurbano 36, Chamberí* ☎ *91/319–6900* 🌐 *www.ac-hotels.com* 🛏 *51 rooms* 🍴 *No meals* [M] *Alonso Martínez, Rubén Darío* ✥ *F1.*

$$ HOTEL **Hotel Sardinero.** Steps from the trendy Malasaña and gay-friendly Chueca districts, and slightly off the tourist track, Hotel Sardinero opened in May 2017 in a turn-of-the-century palace previously occupied by Innside Génova. **Pros:** mellow earth-tone interiors; two rooftop terraces; gorgeous neoclassical facade. **Cons:** gym could be bigger; no restaurant; kettles and coffeemakers only available upon request. [$] *Rooms from: €130* ✉ *Pl. Alonso Martínez 3, Chamberí* ☎ *91/206–2160* 🌐 *www.hotelsardineromadrid.com* 🛏 *63 rooms* 🍴 *No meals* ✥ *F1.*

$$$$ HOTEL **Intercontinental Madrid.** Chauffeur-driven town cars snake around the block day and night at the Intercontinental Madrid, a classically decorated hotel frequented by dignitaries, diplomats, and other international bigwigs. **Pros:** starchy, dependable elegance; newly refurbished 24-hour gym; excellent business facilities. **Cons:** cookie-cutter business hotel decor; removed from the center; street-facing rooms can be noisy. [$] *Rooms from: €250* ✉ *Paseo de la Castellana 49, Chamberí* ☎ *91/700–7300* 🌐 *www.ihg.com* 🛏 *302 rooms* 🍴 *No meals* ✥ *H1.*

$$$$ HOTEL **Orfila.** On a leafy residential street not far from Plaza Colón and the gallery-lined Chueca district, this elegant 1886 town house boasts every comfort of larger five-star Madrid hotels—sans the stuffy corporate vibes. **Pros:** quiet street; refined, classic interiors; attentive service. **Cons:** decidedly unhip decor; no gym; low-key neighborhood without much nightlife. [$] *Rooms from: €400* ✉ *Calle Orfila 6, Chamberí* ☎ *91/702–7770* 🌐 *www.hotelorfila.com* 🛏 *32 rooms* 🍴 *No meals* [M] *Alonso Martínez* ✥ *G1.*

CHAMARTÍN

$$$ HOTEL **Hesperia Madrid.** A five-star hotel geared toward the business traveler, Hesperia Madrid is located in the city's financial district, miles away from the tourist hubbub and within walking distance of Bernabéu Stadium and the National Museum of Natural Sciences. **Pros:** open-air gym; award-winning restaurant; 24-hour room service. **Cons:** interior rooms can be dark; stuffy, corporate feel; miles from the center. [$] *Rooms from: €200* ✉ *Paseo de la Castellana 57, Chamartín* ☎ *91/210–8800* 🌐 *www.hesperia-madrid.com* 🛏 *170 rooms* 🍴 *No meals* ✥ *H1.*

$$$$ HOTEL Fodor's Choice ★ **Hotel NH Collection Madrid Eurobuilding.** The towering NH Collection Madrid Eurobuilding, located blocks from Real Madrid's home stadium, is a state-of-the-art luxury property with large, airy rooms, and an enormous pool and gym complex. **Pros:** 180-degree views from some rooms; excellent gym and spa; one of Madrid's top restaurants.

Cons: inconsistent service; hotel can't secure bookings at DiverXO; area dies at night. $ *Rooms from: €270* ✉ *Calle de Padre Damián 23, Chamartín* ☎ *91/353-7300* ⊕ *www.nh-hotels.com* ⌦ *440 rooms* ⦿ *No meals* ✛ *H1.*

$$
HOTEL

▦ **Silken Puerta de América.** Inspired by Paul Eluard's *La Liberté*, whose verses are written across the facade, the owners of this hotel granted an unlimited budget to 19 of the world's top architects and designers. **Pros:** an architect's dreamland; top-notch restaurant and bars; candlelit pool and steam room area. **Cons:** miles from the center; interiors doesn't always get the required maintenance; design impractical in places. $ *Rooms from: €130* ✉ *Av. de América 41, Chamartín* ☎ *91/744-5400* ⊕ *www.hotelpuertamerica.com* ⌦ *315 rooms* ⦿ *No meals* Ⓜ *Av. de América* ✛ *G1.*

NIGHTLIFE

Nightlife, or *la marcha,* is often drawn out past 6 am in Madrid, and visitors always wonder how locals can get by on (what appears to be) so little shut-eye. Unlike in other European cities, where partying is a pastime geared only toward the young, there are plenty of bars and discotecas with mixed-age crowds, and it's not uncommon for children to play on the sidewalks past midnight while multigenerational families and friends convene over coffee or cocktails at an outdoor café. For those in their thirties, forties, and up who don't plan on staying out until sunrise, the best options are the bars along the Cava Alta and Cava Baja, Calle Huertas near Plaza de Santa Ana, and Calle Moratín near Antón Martín. Those who want to stay out till the wee hours have more options: Calle Príncipe and Calle De la Cruz, lined with sardine-can bars lined with locals, and the scruffier streets that snake down toward Plaza de Lavapiés. But the neighborhood most synonymous with *la vida nocturna* is Malasaña, which has plenty of trendy hangouts along Calle San Vicente Ferrer, Calle La Palma, and all around Plaza de Dos de Mayo. Another major nightlife contender is is Chueca, where tattoo parlors and street-chic boutiques sit between LGBT+ (yet hetero-friendly) bars bars, dance clubs, and after-hours clubs.

In general, cafés in Madrid can be classified into two groups: those that have been around for many years (La Pecera del Círculo, Café de Oriente), where writers, singers, poets, and discussion groups still meet and where conversations are usually more important than the coffee itself, and Nordic-style third-wave venues (Hanso, Toma Café, Hola Coffee, Federal Café) tailored to hip and hurried urbanites that tend to have a wider product selection, modern interiors, and Wi-Fi.

PALACIO, LA LATINA, AND SOL

PALACIO

DANCE CLUBS

Cool. This gritty, Berlin-style underground club hosts techno-driven dance parties on weekend nights for a primarily LGBT+ clientele. The younger set shouldn't miss the more pop-centric "Stardust" parties, which happen every week or two. ⊠ *Calle Isabel la Católica 6, Palacio.*

Velvet. Magical and chameleonlike thanks to the use of LED lighting and the undulating shapes of the columns and walls, this is the place to go if you want a late-night drink—it opens at 11 and closes at 5:30 am—without the thunder of a full-blown DJ. ⊠ *Calle Jacometrezo 6, Palacio* ☎ *63/341–4887* ⊕ *www.velvetdisco.es* Ⓜ *Callao.*

MUSIC CLUBS

Fodor'sChoice **Café Berlin.** For a space so small, Café Berlin packs quite the acoustic
★ punch and draws an international, eclectic crowd. Before midnight, catch nightly live music acts in a panoply of styles (flamenco, swing, soul, and more); from around 1 am on, drop in for the disco-inflected DJ sets that ooze good vibes until 6 am. ⊠ *Costanilla de los Ángeles 20, Palacio* ☎ *91/559–7429* ⊕ *www.berlincafe.es.*

El Amante. Blocks from Plaza Mayor, this might be the closest thing you'll find in Madrid to a posh private New York club. Its creative and lush spaces, two winding floors filled with nooks, host the city's trendiest crowds. There's a tough door policy, so be sure to dress to impress. Get here before 1:30 am or be ready to wait in line. ⊠ *Calle Santiago 3, Palacio* ☎ *91/755–4460* ⊕ *www.amantelifestyle.com* Ⓜ *Ópera.*

Marula. Popular for its quiet summer terrace under the Puente de Segovia arches, its unbeatable electro-funk mixes, and for staying open into the wee hours, this is a cleverly designed narrow space with lots of illuminated wall art. There's a branch in Barcelona, too. Check the website for concert listings. Live music usually begins at 11 pm. ⊠ *Calle Caños Viejos 3, Palacio* ☎ *91/366–1596* ⊕ *www.marulacafe.com* Ⓜ *La Latina.*

LA LATINA

BARS AND CAFÉS

Delic. This warm, inviting café is an all-hours hangout for Madrid's trendy crowd. Homesick travelers will find comfort in Delic's carrot cake, brownies, and pumpkin pie (seasonal), while low-key revelers will appreciate the bar's coziness and late hours (open until 2:30 on weekends). ⊠ *Costanilla de San Andrés 14, Pl. de la Paja, La Latina* ☎ *91/364–5450* ⊕ *www.delic.es* ☾ *Closed Mon.* Ⓜ *La Latina.*

El Viajero. You can get food here, but this place is better known among madrileños for its middle-floor bar, which fills up with a cocktail-drinking after-work crowd. There's also a shady, semihidden terrace that tends to be packed; beware of the 10% surcharge that comes with outdoor dining. ⊠ *Pl. de la Cebada 11, La Latina* ☎ *91/366–9064* ⊕ *www. elviajeromadrid.com* ☾ *Closed Sun. night and Mon.* Ⓜ *La Latina.*

Palacio de Anglona (*Anglona Palace*). This clubby restaurant and bar in La Latina is situated in the basement of a 17th-century palace and decorated with black-and-white photos of the building through the centuries. The lounge bar (open until 3 am on weekends) serves mojitos and often hosts live jazz and bossa nova concerts. ⊠ *Calle Segovia 13, La Latina* ☎ *91/365–3153* ⊕ *www.palaciodeanglona.com* ⊘ *Closed Mon.* Ⓜ *La Latina.*

DANCE CLUBS

Marula Café. Remixed soul and funk are the genres du jour at this intimate, colorfully (yet dimly) lit venue that attracts a local crowd. Strong cocktails—think Negronis, caipirinhas, and tequila sours—are sure to loosen you up. ⊠ *Cuesta Canos Viejos 3, La Latina* ☎ *91/366–1596* ⊕ *www.marulacafe.com.*

SOL

CAFÉS

Café del Círculo (*La Pecera*). Spacious and elegant with large velvet curtains, marble columns, hardwood floors, painted ceilings, and sculptures, this venue inside the famous art center Círculo de Bellas Artes feels more like a private club than a café. Stop in for a midmorning coffee or a midafternoon *merienda* rather than a full meal; the food is nothing to write home about. ⊠ *Círculo de Bellas Artes, Marqués de Casa Riera 2, Sol* ☎ *91/522–5092* ⊕ *www.lapeceradelcirculo.com* Ⓜ *Banco de España, Sevilla.*

Fodor'sChoice
★ **Chocolatería San Ginés.** San Ginés is to Madrid what Café du Monde is to New Orleans. A national sensation, for generations this 19th-century café has been frying spirals of piping-hot churros and *porras* (a churro's larger cousin—try them) day and night. You may see other patrons dunking their breakfast in café con leche or Cola Cao (Spanish chocolate milk); pay them no mind and spring instead for the age-old sidekick, a mug filled with melted dark chocolate thicker than oatmeal. ⊠ *Pasadizo de San Ginés, enter by Arenal 11, Sol* ☎ *91/365–6546* ⊕ *www.chocolateriasangines.com* Ⓜ *Sol.*

DANCE CLUBS

Cocó Madrid. This club, with its wild color palette, huge dance floor, and better-than-average cocktails, is best known for its Mondo Disko nights (Thursday and Saturday), which rage until dawn with house and electronic music often by international DJs. ⊠ *Calle Alcalá 20, Sol* ☎ *91/445–7938* ⊕ *www.web-mondo.com* ⊘ *Closed Mon.–Wed.* Ⓜ *Sevilla.*

El Sol. Madrid's oldest dance club continues to win over its patrons with all-night dancing to live music (around midnight Thursday–Saturday) and DJ sets. ⊠ *Calle Jardines 3, Sol* ☎ *91/532–6490* ⊕ *www.elsolmad. com* ⊘ *Closed Mon.* Ⓜ *Gran Vía.*

Joy Eslava. A downtown club in a converted theater, this is a long-established standby that attracts a varied, somewhat bourgeois crowd of locals and tourists. ⊠ *Calle del Arenal 11, Sol* ☎ *91/366–3733* ⊕ *www. joy-eslava.com* Ⓜ *Sol.*

MUSIC CLUBS

Costello. A multiuse space that combines a café and a lounge, this place caters to a relaxed, conversational crowd; the bottom floor is suited to partygoers, with the latest in live and club music. On weekdays, there are theater and stand-up comedy shows. Check the website for events

and ticket prices. ⊠ *Calle Caballero de Gracia 10, Sol* ☎ *91/522–1815* ⊕ *www.costelloclub.com* Ⓜ *Gran Vía.*

BARRIO DE LAS LETRAS

BARS AND CAFÉS

Radio. This bar in the ME Madrid Reina Victoria is split between a bottom-floor lounge, ideal for after-work martinis, and a more exclusive rooftop terrace with 360-degree views—a boon to chic summer revelers. ⊠ *ME Madrid Reina Victoria, Pl. Santa Ana 14, Barrio de las Letras* ☎ *91/445–6886* ⊕ *www.melia.com* Ⓜ *Antón Martín.*

DANCE CLUBS

Azúcar. Salsa has become a fixture in Madrid; check out the most spectacular moves here. Check the website for occasional promotions. ⊠ *Calle de Atocha 107, Barrio de las Letras* ☎ *91/429–6208* ⊙ *Closed Sun.–Wed.* Ⓜ *Atocha.*

Fodor's Choice ★ **Teatro Kapital.** Easily Madrid's most famous nightclub, Kapital has seven floors—each of which plays a different type of music (spun by the city's top DJs, of course)—plus a small movie theater and rooftop terrace. Dress to impress for this one: no sneakers, shorts, or tanks allowed. ⊠ *Calle Atocha 125, Barrio de las Letras* ☎ *91/420–2906* ⊕ *www. grupo-kapital.com.*

MUSIC CLUB

Fodor's Choice ★ **Café Central.** Madrid's best-known jazz venue is chic, and the musicians are often internationally known. Performances are usually 9–11 nightly. ⊠ *Pl. de Ángel 10, Barrio de las Letras* ☎ *91/369–4143* ⊕ *www.cafe-centralmadrid.com* Ⓜ *Antón Martín.*

CHUECA AND MALASAÑA

CHUECA

BARS AND CAFÉS

Bar Cock. Resembling a gentlemen's club, this classic bar (est. 1921)—with dark-wood interiors and cathedral-like ceilings—serves a variety of cocktails (hence the name) to an older, businessy crowd. ⊠ *Calle de la Reina 16, Chueca* ☎ *91/532–2826* ⊕ *www.cargocollective.com/ barcock* Ⓜ *Gran Vía.*

Café Belén. The handful of tables here are rarely empty on weekends, thanks to the candlelit, cozy atmosphere—it attracts a young, mixed postdinner crowd. Weeknights are more mellow. ⊠ *Calle Belén 5, Chueca* ☎ *91/308–2747* ⊕ *www.elcafebelen.com* Ⓜ *Chueca.*

Del Diego. Arguably Madrid's most renowned cocktail bar, this family-owned landmark is frequented by a varied, and sometimes celebrity, clientele. ⊠ *Calle de la Reina 12, Chueca* ☎ *91/523–3106* ⊕ *www.deldiego.com* ⊙ *Closed Sun.* Ⓜ *Gran Vía.*

Fodor's Choice ★ **Macera TallerBar.** The most novel cocktail bar in Madrid, Macera foregoes brand-name liquor in favor of house-macerated spirits flavored with fruits, aromatics, and herbs. You might, for instance, opt for a Manhattan made with almond- and cherry-infused whiskey or a margarita shaken with cilantro-scented tequila. ⊠ *Calle San Mateo 21, Chueca* ☎ *91/011–5810* ⊕ *www.maceradrinks.com.*

Fodor's Choice
★ **Vinoteca Vides.** This dressed-down wine bar is a great spot to sample rare, boutique bottles at a terrific price. There's a particularly deep selection of grippy Monastrels from the black-horse wine region of Yecla, in Murcia province. ⊠ *Calle Libertad 12, Chueca* ☎ *91/531–8444* ⊕ *www. vinotecavides.es.*

MUSIC CLUBS

El Intruso. Easy to miss (it's tucked inside a building just a block off Fuencarral), this is one of Chueca's best lounge-bars. There are live DJs and funk and jazz bands almost every night playing for a mostly thirtysomething crowd starting at 9 pm. ⊠ *Calle Augusto Figueroa 3, Chueca* ⊕ *www.intrusobar.com* ☉ *Closed Mon.* Ⓜ *Chueca.*

Libertad 8 Café. Almost every famous madrileño songwriter, musician, and poet has passed through this timeworn evenings-only hangout (it opens at 4 pm and entertainment starts at 9 pm). Acoustic guitar concerts are fantastic—and virtually tourist-free. ⊠ *Calle de la Libertad 8, Chueca* ☎ *91/532–1150* ⊕ *www.libertad8cafe.com* Ⓜ *Chueca.*

Museo Chicote. This landmark cocktail bar–lounge is said to have been one of Hemingway's haunts. Much of the interior can be traced back to the 1930s, but modern elements (like the in-house DJ and hordes of international visitors) keep this spot firmly in the present. ⊠ *Gran Vía 12, Chueca* ☎ *91/532–6737* ⊕ *www.grupomercadodelareina.com* ☉ *Closed Sun.* Ⓜ *Gran Vía.*

DANCE CLUB

DLRO Live (*Delirio Party*). This unpretentious, unapologetically campy bar attracts a motley crew of LGBT+ (but primarily gay male) revelers of all ages and nationalities with its pop and reggaeton music. ⊠ *Calle Pelayo 59, Chueca* ☎ *91/319–5302* ⊕ *www.deliriochueca.com.*

MALASAÑA
BARS AND CAFÉS

Cazador. You may as well be in Williamsburg or Kreuzberg at this popular and unflamboyant gay bar where a bearded-and-bunned clientele sips cañas and cocktails before heading out to the discoteca. ⊠ *Calle Pozas 7, Malasaña* ☎ *63/997–0916.*

De Vinos. A snug, casual wine bar situated in the artsy Conde Duque area of Malasaña, De Vinos pours hard-to-find wines from regions like Bierzo, Somontano, and—*claro que sí*—Madrid. Cured sausages and Spanish cheeses make fine accompaniments. ⊠ *Calle de la Palma 76, Malasaña* ☎ *91/182–3499.*

Fodor's Choice
★ **1862 Dry Bar.** Madrid's swankiest and most skilled coctelería, 1862 Dry Bar shakes and stirs meticulously prepared cocktails that incorporate sherries and unconventional aromatics. The only snag: on busy nights, drinks take forever to arrive. ⊠ *Calle Pez 27, Malasaña* ☎ *60/953–1151* ⊕ *www.1862drybar.com.*

Fábrica Maravillas. This is Madrid's only city-center brewpub; taste fun and funky beers that were fermented in the "beer lab" just feet from your barstool. ⊠ *Calle de Valverde 29, Malasaña* ☎ *91/521–8753* ⊕ *www.fmaravillas.com.*

Lolina Café. Diverging in spirit from the stuffier baroque-style cafés of the neighborhood, this romantic spot with mismatched vintage furniture attracts an artsy crowd with its free Wi-Fi and assortment of teas, booze, and baked goods. ⊠ *Calle del Espíritu Santo 9, Malasaña* ☎ *91/523–5859* ⊕ *www.lolinacafe.com* Ⓜ *Tribunal.*

Santamaría. This space mixes vintage design with artsy touches and caters to a chic, bohemian crowd. Choose from a variety of cocktails including one bearing the club's name, made with mixed-berry juice and vodka or gin. ⊠ *Calle de la Ballesta 6, Malasaña* ☎ *91/166–0511* Ⓜ *Gran Vía.*

DANCE CLUBS

Fodor'sChoice ★ **BarCo.** One of Madrid's most popular nightclubs, for both its live shows (funk, jazz, and more) and late-night DJ sets, Barco is a guaranteed good time. Acoustics here are top-notch. ⊠ *Calle del Barco 34, Malasaña* ☎ *91/531–7754* ⊕ *www.barcobar.com.*

Ocho y Medio. If you like booze-fueled pop and techno parties that peak at 3 am, then Ocho y Medio is for you. Arrive before 1 am to avoid slow, snaking lines. ⊠ *Calle Barceló 11, Malasaña* ☎ *91/541–3500* ⊕ *www.ochoymedioclub.com* ☉ *Closed Mon.–Wed.* Ⓜ *Tribunal.*

Teatro Barceló. A landmark discoteca that until 2013 was called Pachá, Teatro Barceló has been bumping for more than three decades. Dress shoes or ultratrendy kicks are required at this preppy venue geared toward twentysomethings. ⊠ *Calle Barceló 11, Malasaña* ☎ *91/447–0128* ⊕ *www.teatrobarcelo.com* ☉ *Closed Sun.–Wed.* Ⓜ *Tribunal.*

MUSIC CLUBS

Café la Palma. There are four different spaces in this divey local favorite: a bar in front, a music venue for intimate concerts (pop, rock, electronic, hip-hop), a chill-out room in the back, and a café in the center room. ⊠ *Calle de La Palma 62, Malasaña* ☎ *91/522–5031* ⊕ *www.cafelapalma.com* Ⓜ *Noviciado.*

EMBAJADORES

LAVAPIÉS

BARS AND CAFÉS

Bendito Vinos y Vinillos. This unassuming stall inside Mercado de San Fernando, a wine-industry hangout, is one of the city's top spots for sampling hard-to-find natural and biodynamic wines from Spain and beyond. Pair one with Bendito's hand-selected cheeses and charcuterie. ⊠ *Mercado de San Fernando, Calle de Embajadores 41, Lavapiés* ☎ *66/175–0061.*

La Fisna. An ideal date spot, this understated yet elegant vinoteca pours over 50 wines by the glass and serves a delectable if overpriced menu of market-driven tapas. ⊠ *Calle Amparo 91, Lavapiés* ☎ *91/539–5615.*

MUSIC AND DANCE CLUBS

Club 33. This intimate nightclub caters to a local, alternative crowd and has quickly become a stalwart on the lesbian party circuit. ⊠ *Calle de la Cabeza 33, Lavapiés* ☎ *91/369–3302* ⊕ *www.club33madrid.es.*

Medias Puri. A decades-old, exclusive underground party made public in 2017, Medias Puri is the brainchild of Puri, an ageless Madrid socialite who rolled with Ava Gardner and Lola Flores back in the day. It's one of the hottest venues in town. ⊠ *Pl. Tirso de Molina 1, Lavapiés* ☎ *91/521–6911* ⊕ *www.mediaspuri.com.*

Fodor's Choice ★ **Sala Juglar.** Sala Juglar is proof that nontouristy, affordable, and skillful flamenco still exists in Madrid. Tropical-inflected dance parties are another draw. ⊠ *Calle de Lavapiés 37, Lavapiés* ☎ *91/528–4381* ⊕ *www.salajuglar.com.*

SALAMANCA, RETIRO, AND CHAMBERÍ

SALAMANCA

DANCE CLUB

Bling Bling. This glitzy nightclub (opened in 2018 by the owners of equally exclusive Opium Madrid) attracts a well-heeled local crowd. Dress to impress: this isn't an easy door. ⊠ *Calle Génova 28, Salamanca* ☎ *91/064–4479.*

CHAMBERÍ

MUSIC CLUB

Clamores. Hear good jazz concerts and world music until 5:30 am on weekdays and 6 am on weekends. Check the website for performance listings and to buy tickets. ⊠ *Albuquerque 14, Chamberí* ☎ *91/445–5480* ⊕ *www.salaclamores.es* ☉ *Closes at 11 pm Sun.*

CHAMARTÍN AND TETUÁN

CHAMARTÍN

CAFÉ

Domo Cocktail. The NH hotel chain is building a top-notch food-and-drink stronghold north of the city around its Eurobuilding property. Besides DiverXO and Domo restaurants there's now a cocktail bar with an enclosed terrace, run by Diego Cabrera, the city's top name when it comes to creating drink experiences. There are all-time classic cocktails and original creations. ⊠ *Calle de Padre Damián 23, Chamartín* ☎ *91/353–7300* ⊕ *www.nh-hotels.com* Ⓜ *Cuzco.*

TETUÁN

DANCE CLUB

New Garamond. At this hopping venue, popular among Latino locals, you'll find plenty of space to dance (under the gaze of go-go girls), and also quieter nooks where you can chat and sip a drink. It's open nights Tuesday–Saturday. ⊠ *Calle Rosario Pino 14, Tetuán* ☎ *62/053–2656* ⊕ *www.newgaramondmadrid.es* ☉ *Closed Sun.–Wed.* Ⓜ *Cuzco.*

PERFORMING ARTS

As Madrid's reputation as a vibrant, contemporary arts center has grown, artists and performers have been arriving in droves. Consult the daily listings and Friday city-guide supplements in any of the leading newspapers—*El País, El Mundo,* or *ABC*—all of which are fairly easy to understand, even if you don't read much Spanish. Websites such as ⊕ *www.guiadelocio.com* and ⊕ *www.timeout.es* are also useful.

TICKETS

El Corte Inglés. You can buy tickets for major concerts online. ☎ 90/240–0222 ⊕ *www.elcorteingles.es/entradas.*

Entradas.com. This website sells tickets for musicals and big-name concerts. ☎ 90/222–1622 ⊕ *www.entradas.com.*

Ticketea. ☎ 90/204–4226 ⊕ *www.ticketea.com.*

DANCE AND MUSIC PERFORMANCES

In addition to concert halls listed here, the Convento de la Encarnación and the Real Academia de Bellas Artes de San Fernando museum *(see Exploring)* hold concerts.

Auditorio Nacional de Música. This is Madrid's main concert hall, with spaces for both symphonic and chamber music. ⊠ *Calle del Príncipe de Vergara 146, Salamanca* ☎ 91/337–0140 ⊕ *www.auditorionacional. mcu.es* Ⓜ *Cruz del Rayo.*

Centro Cultural de Conde Duque. This massive venue is best known for its summer live music concerts (flamenco, jazz, pop) and also has free and often interesting exhibitions, lectures, and theater performances. ⊠ *Calle Conde Duque 11, Centro* ☎ 91/588–5834 ⊕ *www.condeduque-madrid.es* Ⓜ *Ventura Rodríguez.*

Círculo de Bellas Artes. Concerts, theater, dance performances, art exhibitions, and events are all part of the calendar here. There is also an extremely popular café and a rooftop restaurant-bar with great views of the city. ⊠ *Calle del Marqués de Casa Riera 2, Centro* ☎ 90/242–2442 ⊕ *www.circulobellasartes.com* Ⓜ *Banco de España.*

La Casa Encendida. Film festivals, alternative art shows, dance performances, and weekend events for children are held here. ⊠ *Ronda de Valencia 2, Lavapiés* ☎ 91/506–3875 ⊕ *www.lacasaencendida.com* Ⓜ *Embajadores, Lavapiés.*

Matadero Madrid. The city's newest and biggest arts center is in the city's old slaughterhouse—a massive early-20th-century neo-Mudejar compound of 13 buildings—and has a theater, multiple exhibition spaces, workshops, and a lively bar. ⊠ *Paseo de la Chopera 14, Legazpi* ☎ 91/517–7309 ⊕ *www.mataderomadrid.org* Ⓜ *Legazpi.*

Teatro Real. This resplendent theater is the venue for opera and dance performances. Built in 1850, this neoclassical theater was long a cultural center for madrileño high society. A major restoration project endowed it with golden balconies, plush seats, and state-of-the-art stage equipment. ⊠ *Pl. de Isabel II, Palacio* ☎ *91/516–0660* ⊕ *www.teatro-real.com* Ⓜ *Ópera.*

FILM

Most of Madrid's movie theaters show films with original soundtracks and Spanish dubbing. For audio in the original language, seek out *versión original* films, listed in newspapers and on websites under *v.o.*

Cine Doré. A rare example of Art Nouveau architecture in Madrid, the hip Cine Doré shows movies from the Spanish National Film Archives and eclectic foreign films for €2.50 per session (you frequently get a short film or two in addition to a feature). Showtimes are listed in newspapers under "Filmoteca." The pink neon-trimmed lobby has a sleek café-bar and a bookshop. ⊠ *Calle de Santa Isabel 3, Lavapiés* ☎ *91/369–1125* Ⓜ *Antón Martín.*

Ideal Yelmo Cineplex. This is your best bet for new releases. ⊠ *Calle del Doctor Cortezo 6, Centro* ☎ *90/222–0922* ⊕ *www.yelmocines.es* Ⓜ *Tirso de Molina.*

Fodor's Choice
★ **Sala Equis.** Madrid trendsters and film geeks unite at Sala Equis, a multipurpose movie theater that hosts a wide range of events and screens independent and alternative films in an industrial, ultramodern hall. There's an ample outdoor terrace serving light bites. ⊠ *Calle del Duque de Alba 4, Lavapiés* ☎ *91/429–6686* ⊕ *www.salaequis.es.*

FLAMENCO

Although the best place in Spain to find flamenco is Andalusia, there are a few venues in Madrid. Note that *tablaos* (flamenco venues) charge around €40–€55 for the show only (with a complimentary drink included), so save money by dining elsewhere. If you want to dine at the tablaos anyway, note that three of them—Carboneras, Corral de la Morería, and Café de Chinitas—also offer a show-plus-fixed-menu option that's worth considering.

Café de Chinitas. This touristy spot fills up fast. Make reservations, because shows often sell out. The restaurant opens at 8 and there are performances Monday–Saturday at 8:15 and 10:30. ⊠ *Calle Torija 7, Palacio* ☎ *91/559–5135* ⊕ *www.chinitas.com* Ⓜ *Santo Domingo.*

Casa Patas. Along with tapas, this well-known space offers good, authentic flamenco. Prices are more reasonable than elsewhere. Shows are at 10:30 pm Monday–Thursday, and at 9 pm and midnight on Friday and Saturday. ⊠ *Calle Canizares 10, Lavapiés* ☎ *91/369–0496* ⊕ *www.casapatas.com* Ⓜ *Antón Martín.*

Corral de la Morería. Dinner à la carte and well-known visiting flamenco stars accompany the resident dance troupe here. Since Morería opened its doors in 1956, celebrities such as Frank Sinatra and Ava Gardner have left their autographed photos for the walls. Shows last for about an hour and a half and begin at 8:30 and 10:20 nightly. ⊠ *Calle de la Morería 17, on Calle de Bailén, La Latina* ✛ *Cross bridge over Calle* *de Segovia and turn right* ☎ *91/365–8446* ⊕ *www.corraldelamoreria. com* Ⓜ *La Latina.*

Las Carboneras. A prime flamenco showcase, this venue rivals Corral de la Morería as the best option in terms of quality and price. Performers here include both the young, less commercial artists and more established stars on tour. The show is staged at 8:30 and 10:30 Monday–Thursday and at 8:30 and 11 Friday and Saturday. ✉ *Pl. del Conde de Miranda 1, Centro* ☎ *91/542–8677* ⊕ *www.tablaolascarboneras.com* ☻ *Closed Sun.* Ⓜ *La Latina, Ópera.*

SPORTS AND THE OUTDOORS

GOLF

Golf Olivar de la Hinojosa. Golf Olivar de la Hinojosa, in Campo de las Naciones, is open to the public, with two courses (18 holes and 9 holes) and golf lessons. Reservations (essential on weekends) can be made up to one week in advance. ✉ *Av. Dublín s/n, Barajas* ☎ *91/721–1889* ⊕ *www.golfolivar.com.*

La Herrería Club. La Herrería Club, in San Lorenzo de El Escorial, is also open to the public. Check the website for green fees. Weekends are usually reserved for members. Playing golf at La Herrería Club's 18-hole course, in the shadow of the monolithic Monastery of San Lorenzo del Escorial, is one of Spain's great golfing experiences. ✉ *Ctra. Robledo de Chavela s/n, San Lorenzo de El Escorial* ☎ *91/890–5111* ⊕ *www. golflaherreria.com.*

RUNNING

Madrid's best running spots are the Parque del Buen Retiro, where the main path circles the park (approximately 2½ miles) and others weave under trees and through gardens, and the Parque del Oeste, with more uneven terrain but fewer people. The Casa de Campo, six times the area of New York's Central Park, is crisscrossed by numerous hilly trails.

SOCCER

Fútbol is Spain's number one sport, and Madrid has four teams: Real Madrid, Atlético Madrid, Rayo Vallecano, and Getafe. The two major teams are Real Madrid and Atlético Madrid. For tickets, book online or call a week in advance to reserve and pick them up at the stadium—or, if the match isn't sold out, stand in line at the stadium of your choice.

Santiago Bernabéu Stadium. Home to Real Madrid, this stadium seats 85,400 and offers daytime tours of the facilities. ✉ *Paseo de la Castellana 140, Chamartín* ☎ *91/398–4300* ⊕ *www.realmadrid.es* Ⓜ *Santiago Bernabeu.*

Wanda Metropolitano. Since 2017, Atlético Madrid has called this stadium in the San Blas–Canillejas district home. ✉ *Av. de Luis Aragones 4* ☎ *90/226–0403* ⊕ *www.atleticomadrid.com.*

TENNIS

Instalación Deportiva Municipal Casa de Campo. There are public courts at the Instalación Deportiva Municipal Casa de Campo. To get there, take the metro (Línea 10) to Lago, then walk for about five minutes. Make sure you keep the big lake on your right. ⊠ *Camino Principe 2, Casa de Campo* ☎ *91/464–9617.*

SHOPPING

Madrid is a world design center. You'll have no trouble finding traditional crafts, such as ceramics, woven baskets, guitars, and leather goods, as well as a wealth of contemporary art and fashion pieces. Small, family-run shops and boutiques generally close during lunch hours, on Saturday afternoon, and on Sunday.

Madrid has three main shopping areas. The first stretches from Callao to Puerta del Sol (Calle Preciados, Gran Vía on both sides of Callao, and the streets around the Puerta del Sol) and includes the major department stores (El Corte Inglés and the French music, book, and electronics chain FNAC) and popular brands such as H&M and Zara.

The second area, far more elegant and expensive, is in the eastern Salamanca district, bounded roughly by Serrano, Juan Bravo, Jorge Juan (and its mews), and Velázquez; the shops on Goya extend as far as Alcalá. The streets just off the Plaza de Colón, particularly Calle Serrano and Calle Ortega y Gasset, have the widest selection of designer goods—think Prada, Loewe, Armani, and Louis Vuitton—as well as other mainstream and popular local designers (Purificación García, Pedro del Hierro, Adolfo Domínguez, Roberto Verino). Calle Jorge Juan, Calle Lagasca, and Calle Claudio Coello hold the widest selection of smart boutiques from renowned Spanish designers such as Sybilla, DelPozo, and Dolores Promesas.

Finally, for hipper clothes, Chueca, Malasaña, and the streets around the Conde Duque cultural center are your best bets. Calle Fuencarral, between Gran Vía and Tribunal, has the most shops in this area with outposts from Diesel, Adidas, and Footlocker, but also local brands such as El Ganso, Adolfo Domínguez U (selling the Galician designer's younger collection), and Custo as well as some cosmetics stores (Madame B and M.A.C). Less mainstream and sometimes more exciting is the selection you can find on nearby Calles Hortaleza, Almirante, and Piamonte and around the Conde Duque cultural center.

PALACIO AND SOL

PALACIO

CERAMICS

Fodor's Choice ★ **Antigua Casa Talavera.** This is the best of Madrid's many ceramics shops. Despite the name, the finest wares sold here are from Manises, near Valencia, but the blue-and-yellow Talavera ceramics are also excellent. ⊠ *Calle de Isabel la Católica 2, Palacio* ☎ *91/547–3417* ⊕ *www.antiguacasatalavera.com* Ⓜ *Santo Domingo.*

The bustling Rastro flea market takes place every Sunday 10–2; you never know what kind of treasures you might find.

SPECIALTY STORE

Alambique. Amateur and professional cooks will love this terrific little shop (est. 1978) that sells everything from paella pans to earthenware cazuelas to olive-wood cheese boards. Cooking classes (in Spanish) are also available. ✉ *Pl. de la Encarnación 2, Palacio* ☎ *91/547–4220* ⊕ *www.alambique.com.*

SPORTING GOODS

Toxic World Boardshop. Madrid may be hours from the nearest beach, but that doesn't keep the scruffy young set from flocking to this trendster shop to buy the latest surfing and skating gear. ✉ *Calle de Segovia 67, Palacio* ☎ *91/245–7444* ⊕ *www.toxicworldboardshop.com.*

SOL

BOOKS

Casa del Libro. At this shop not far from the Puerta del Sol you'll find an impressive collection of English-language books, including translated Spanish classics. It's also a good source for maps. ✉ *Calle Gran Vía 29, Sol* ☎ *90/202–6402* ⊕ *www.casadellibro.com* Ⓜ *Gran Vía.*

BOUTIQUES AND FASHION

Capas Seseña. Since the turn of the 20th century, this boutique has outfitted international celebrities in traditional wool and velvet capes, some lined with red satin. ✉ *Calle de la Cruz 23, Sol* ☎ *91/531–6840* ⊕ *www.sesena.com* Ⓜ *Puerta del Sol.*

2

CRAFTS AND DESIGN

El Arco Artesanía. El Arco has contemporary handicrafts from all over Spain, including modern ceramics, handblown glassware, jewelry, and leather items. ✉ *Pl. Mayor 9, Centro* ☎ *91/365–2680* ⊕ *www.artesaniaelarco.com.*

DEPARTMENT STORES

El Corte Inglés. Spain's largest department store carries everything from groceries to electronics, lingerie, and designer fashions. It also sells tickets for sporting and arts events and has its own travel agency, a restaurant (usually the building's top floor), and Club Gourmet specialty food store. Madrid's biggest branch is on the corner of Calle Raimundo Fernández Villaverde and Castellana, which is not a central location. Try instead the one at Sol–Callao (split into three separate buildings) or those at Serrano or Goya (each with two independent buildings). ✉ *Calle Preciados 1, 2, and 3, Sol* ☎ *91/379–8000, 90/112–2122 for info, 90/240–0222 for event tickets* ⊕ *www.elcorteingles.es* Ⓜ *Puerta del Sol* ✉ *Calle Goya 76 and 85, Salamanca* ☎ *91/432–9300* Ⓜ *Goya* ✉ *Calle de la Princesa 41, 47, and 56, Moncloa* ☎ *91/454–6000* Ⓜ *Argüelles* ✉ *Calle de Serrano 47, Salamanca* ☎ *91/432–5490* Ⓜ *Rubén Darío* ✉ *Pl. del Callao 2, Sol* ☎ *91/379–8000* Ⓜ *Santo Domingo* ✉ *Calle de Raimundo Fernández Villaverde 79, Cuatro Caminos* ☎ *91/418–8800* Ⓜ *Nuevos Ministerios.*

MUSIC

José Ramírez. This company has sold guitars since 1882, and its store includes a museum of antique instruments. Prices for new models run €122–€227 for children and €153–€2,200 for adults, though some of the top concert models easily break the €10,000 mark. ✉ *Calle de la Paz 8, Sol* ☎ *91/531–4229* ⊕ *www.guitarrasramirez.com* Ⓜ *Puerta del Sol.*

BARRIO DE LAS LETRAS

BOUTIQUES AND FASHION

Eduardo Rivera. A block off Plaza de Santa Ana, this is the flagship store of a young Spanish designer with clothes and accessories for both men and women. ✉ *Pl. del Ángel 4, Barrio de las Letras* ☎ *91/843–5852* ⊕ *www.eduardorivera.es* Ⓜ *Puerta del Sol.*

FLEA MARKETS

El Rastro. On Sunday morning, Calle de Ribera de Curtidores is closed to traffic and jammed with outdoor booths selling everything under the sun—this is its weekly transformation into the Rastro flea market. Crowds get so thick that it takes a while just to advance a few feet amid the hawkers and gawkers. (Be careful of pickpockets.) The flea market sprawls into the surrounding streets with certain areas specializing in particular products. Find everything from antique furniture to rare vinyls of flamenco music to keychains emblazoned with "CNT," Spain's old anarchist trade union. Practice your Spanish by bargaining with vendors over paintings, heraldic iron gates, new and used clothes, and even hashish pipes. Plaza General Vara del Rey has some of El Rastro's best antiques, and the streets beyond—Calles Mira el Río Alta and Mira el Río Baja—boast all sorts of miscellany and bric-a-brac. The market shuts down shortly after 2 pm, in time for a street party to start in the area known as La Latina, centered on the bar El Viajero in Plaza Humilladero. Off the Ribera are two *galerías,* courtyards with higher-quality, higher-price antiques shops. All the shops (except for the street vendors) are open during the week. ⊠ *Calle de Ribera de Curtidores, Barrio de las Letras* Ⓜ *Puerta de Toledo.*

FOOD AND WINE

Casa González. This food store (est. 1931) contains a cozy bar where you can sample most of its fare including canned asparagus, charcuterie, smoked anchovies, and a good selection of Spanish cheeses and wines. It also serves good, inexpensive breakfasts. ⊠ *Calle León 12, Barrio de las Letras* ☎ *91/429–5618* ⊕ *www.casagonzalez.es* Ⓜ *Antón Martín.*

María Cabello. Named after the current owner, this charming 150-year-old liquor and wine store looks like a warehouse rather than a shop, but María knows what she's selling. Find a good selection of Rioja wines (some dating as far back as 1920) and liqueurs including anisettes and *pacharán,* a fruity digestif infused with sloe berries. ⊠ *Calle Echegaray 19, Barrio de las Letras* ☎ *91/429–6088* Ⓜ *Antón Martín, Sevilla.*

CHUECA AND MALASAÑA

CHUECA

BOUTIQUES AND FASHION

Lemoniez. After more than 20 years in the fashion industry, Basque designer Fernando Lemoniez finally took the plunge and opened his own boutique, in what used to be a fruit shop. Women of all ages can be found browsing the feminine silk and chiffon dresses and gathering insight from Lemoniez himself, who often drops by the store on Saturday morning. ⊠ *Calle Argensola 17, Chueca* ☎ *91/308–4821* ⊕ *www.lemoniez.com* Ⓜ *Alonso Martínez.*

Pez. A favorite among fashion-magazine editors, this store has two branches—one dedicated to high-end women's wear and another to furniture and decor—on the same street. ⊠ *Calle de Regueros 2 and 15, Chueca* ☎ *91/308–6677* ⊕ *www.pez-pez.es* Ⓜ *Chueca.*

Próxima Parada. The bubbly owner of this store culls daring garments from Spanish designers for her devoted clientele. ⊠ *Calle Conde de Xiquena 9, Chueca* ☎ *91/523–1929* ⊕ *www.proximaparadamadrid.com* Ⓜ *Chueca.*

Roberto Torretta. This Argentine designer, with a celebrity following, makes sophisticated and elegant women's wear. There's no browsing here; it's so exclusive, you have to make an appointment to shop. ⊠ *Calle Fereluz 17, Chueca* ☎ *91/319–5920* ⊕ *www.robertotorretta.com* Ⓜ *Chueca.*

Zara. Zara is no longer a dressed-up version of H&M; in recent years its fashion lines have skewed younger with more street appeal. The Spanish chain is the world's biggest fashion retailer, and its founder, Amancio Ortega, is Europe's richest billionaire. Zara is considerably cheaper in Spain than in other countries, and for deal hunters, there are several outlet stores in Madrid called Lefties. ⊠ *Calle Gran Vía 34, Chueca* ☎ *91/521–1283* ⊕ *www.zara.com* Ⓜ *Callao.*

FOOD AND WINE

Poncelet Cheese Bar. At this gourmet cheese bar and shop, you can find more than 120 different cheeses from all over Spain as well as some 300 others from France, Portugal, Italy, and the Netherlands. Marmalades, wines, and other assorted cheese accompaniments are available. ⊠ *Calle José Abascal 61, Chamberí* ☎ *91/399–2550* ⊕ *www.ponceletcheesebar. es* Ⓜ *Gregorio Marañón.*

MALASAÑA

ART AND DESIGN

El Paracaidista. This ultratrendy hybrid space is an art gallery, boutique cinema, performance venue, rooftop bar, and furniture showroom all at once. Visit to get a sense of Malasaña's artsy pulse. ⊠ *Calle de la Palma 10, Malasaña* ☎ *91/445–1913* ⊕ *www.elparacaidista.es.*

La Fiambrera. The polar opposite of your standard stuffy gallery, La Fiambrera sells colorful pop art at affordable prices. There's a small bookshop and café, should your feet need a rest. ⊠ *Calle del Pez 7, Malasaña* ☎ *91/704–6030* ⊕ *www.lafiambrera.net.*

BOOKS

J&J. A block off San Bernardo, this is a charming café and bookstore with a good selection of used books in English. They sell bagels, too—a rarity in Madrid. ⊠ *Calle del Espíritu Santo 47, Malasaña* ☎ *91/521–8576* ⊕ *www.jandjbooksandcoffee.com* Ⓜ *Noviciado.*

BOUTIQUES AND FASHION

Duke. This pocket-size men's footwear store always has the trendiest limited-release kicks. ⊠ *Calle Conde Duque 18, Malasaña* ☎ *91/542–4849.*

Magpie Vintage. A fashion temple that screams "Movida Madrileña," the '80s countercultural movement that ushered Madrid into the modern era, this vintage store is decked out with wildly patterned skirts and dresses and fluorescent track jackets. ⊠ *Calle Velarde 3, Malasaña* ☎ *91/448–3104* ⊕ *www.magpie.es.*

Mango. The Turkish brothers Isaac and Nahman Andic opened their first store in Barcelona in 1984. Today, Mango has stores all over the world, and the brand rivals Zara as Spain's most successful fashion venture. ⊠ *Calle Fuencarral 70, Malasaña* ☎ *91/523–0412* ⊕ *www.mango. com* Ⓜ *Tribunal* ⊠ *Calle Arenal 24, Sol* ☎ *91/547–8246* ⊠ *Calle de Goya 79, Salamanca* ☎ *91/435–3435* Ⓜ *Goya* ⊠ *Gran Vía 32, Centro* ☎ *91/576–8303* Ⓜ *Gran Vía.*

Fodor'sChoice ★ **Sportivo.** This is the best menswear boutique in the city with two floors of hand-picked garments by the buzziest designers out of Spain, France, Japan, and beyond. ⊠ *Calle Conde Duque 20, Malasaña* ☎ *91/542–5661* ⊕ *www.sportivostore.com.*

FOOD

Fodor'sChoice ★ **Quesería Cultivo.** This sleek *quesería*, which opened in 2014, is easily one of the city's top three cheese shops. Seek out rare treasures like Torrejón, a raw ashed-rind sheep's cheese from Castile. ⊠ *Calle Conde Duque 15, Malasaña* ☎ *91/127–3126* ⊕ *www.queseriacultivo.com.*

JEWELRY

Uno de 50. This is a good place for original and inexpensive (less than €200) costume jewelry—mostly made from leather and a silver-plated tin alloy—and accessories by Spanish designer Concha Díaz del Río. ⊠ *Calle Fuencarral 17, Malasaña* ☎ *91/523–9975* ⊕ *www.unode50. com* Ⓜ *Gran Vía* ⊠ *Calle de Serrano 54, Salamanca* ☎ *91/576–9878* Ⓜ *Serrano.*

EMBAJADORES

LAVAPIÉS

BOOKS

La Casquería. This stall in Mercado de San Fernando sells used (mostly Spanish) books by the pound. ⊠ *Mercado de San Fernando, Calle de Embajadores 41, Lavapiés* ☎ *91/527–2512* ⊕ *www.lacasqueria.com.*

MUSIC

Percusión Campos. This percussion shop and workshop—where Canarian Pedro Navarro crafts his own *cajones flamencos,* or flamenco box drums—is hard to find, but his pieces are greatly appreciated among professionals. Prices run €90–€220 and vary according to the quality of woods used. ⊠ *Calle Olivar 36, Lavapiés* ☎ *91/539–2178* ⊕ *www. percusioncampos.com* Ⓜ *Lavapiés.*

▌QUICK BITES

Bar Santurce. This *abuelo* bar near the top of the Rastro is famous for grilled sardines, blistered Padrón peppers, and fried calamari. ⊠ *Pl. General Vara del Rey 14, Lavapiés* ☎ *64/623–8303* ⊕ *www.barsanturce. com* Ⓜ *La Latina.*

SALAMANCA, RETIRO, AND CHAMBERÍ

SALAMANCA

BOUTIQUES AND FASHION

Salamanca is Madrid's quintessential shopping district with a high concentration of large and small shops and boutiques on Calles Claudio Coello, Lagasca, and the first few blocks of Serrano.

Adolfo Domínguez. This popular Galician designer creates simple, sober, and elegant lines for both men and women. Of the numerous locations around the city, the flagship at Calle Serrano 5 is the most varied. There's also a large store at Madrid–Barajas Airport. ⊠ *Calle de Serrano 5, Salamanca* ☎ *91/436–2600* ⊕ *www.adolfodominguez.com* Ⓜ *Serrano.*

Delpozo. Jesús del Pozo, the prominent designer behind this renowned fashion house, died in 2011, and it's now Josep Font who extends its creative legacy with modern clothes for both sexes. It's an excellent, if pricey, place to try on some classic Spanish style. ⊠ *Calle de Lagasca 19, Salamanca* ☎ *91/219–4038* ⊕ *www.delpozo.com* Ⓜ *Serrano.*

Intropia. Intropia's fashion lines are consistently subtle, gossamer, and flowy. (Note that this brand used to be called Hoss.) ⊠ *Calle de Serrano 18, Salamanca* ☎ *91/781–0612* ⊕ *www.intropia.com* Ⓜ *Serrano* ⊠ *Calle Fuencarral 16, Chueca* ☎ *91/524–1728* ⊕ *www.intropia.com* Ⓜ *Gran Vía.*

Loewe. This sumptuous store carries high-quality designer purses, accessories, and clothing made of butter-soft leather in gorgeous jewel tones. The store at Serrano 26 displays the women's collection; men's items are a block away, at Serrano 34. ⊠ *Calle de Serrano 26 and 34, Salamanca* ☎ *91/577–6056* ⊕ *www.loewe.com* Ⓜ *Serrano* ⊠ *Calle Gran Vía 8, Chueca* ☎ *91/522–6815* Ⓜ *Banco de España.*

Pedro del Hierro. This madrileño designer has a solid reputation for his sophisticated but uncomplicated clothes for both sexes. ⊠ *Calle de Serrano 24, 29, and 40, Salamanca* ☎ *91/575–6906* ⊕ *www.pedrodel-hierro.com* Ⓜ *Serrano.*

Purificación García. For women and men searching for contemporary all-day wear, this store delivers. There's another branch at Claudio Coello 95. ⊠ *Calle de Serrano 28, Salamanca* ☎ *91/435–8013* ⊕ *www.purificaciongarcia.com* Ⓜ *Serrano.*

CERAMICS

Cerámica El Alfar. You'll find pottery from all over Spain here. ⊠ *Calle de Claudio Coello 112, Salamanca* ☎ *91/411–3587* ⊕ *www.ceramicaelalfar.com* Ⓜ *Núñez de Balboa.*

FOOD AND WINE

Lavinia. This is one of the largest wine stores in Europe, with a large selection of bottles, books, and bar accessories as well as a restaurant and tasting bar. ⊠ *Calle de José Ortega y Gasset 16, Salamanca* ☎ *91/426–0604* ⊕ *www.lavinia.es* Ⓜ *Núñez de Balboa.*

Mantequerías Bravo. In the heart of Salamanca's shopping area, this store sells Spanish wines, olive oils, cheeses, and hams. ⊠ *Calle de Ayala 24, Salamanca* ☎ *91/576–7641* ⊕ *www.mantequeriasbravo.com* Ⓜ *Serrano.*

SHOPPING MALLS

Centro Comercial ABC. Named for the daily newspaper founded on these premises in the 19th century, Madrid's newest mall is a quadruple-decker. The building has an ornate tile facade; inside, a large café is surrounded by shops, including leather stores and hairdressers. The fourth-floor restaurant has a rooftop terrace. ⊠ *Paseo de la Castellana 34, at Calle de Serrano 61, Salamanca* ⊕ *www.abcserrano.com* Ⓜ *Rubén Darío.*

El Jardín de Serrano. This is a smaller mall with an exclusive selection of high-end brands that include jewelry, fashions for men and women, and shoes. ⊠ *Calle de Goya 6–8, next to Prada, Salamanca* ⊕ *www.jardindeserrano.es* Ⓜ *Velázquez.*

CHAMBERÍ

BOOKS

Booksellers. Just across from the Alonso Cano subway exit, Booksellers has a large selection of books in English; there's another branch nearby at Fernández de la Hoz 40. ⊠ *Calle de Santa Engracia 115, Chamberí* ☎ *91/702–7944* ⊕ *www.booksellers.es* Ⓜ *Alonso Cano.*

BOUTIQUES AND FASHION

Nac. You'll find a good selection of European designer brands (like Bergamot, Forte Forte, Pomandere, Babo) at Nac. The store on Calle Génova is the biggest of the six in Madrid. ⊠ *Calle de Génova 18, Chamberí* ☎ *91/310–6050* ⊕ *www.nac.es* Ⓜ *Colón, Alonso Martínez.*

TOLEDO AND TRIPS FROM MADRID

WELCOME TO
TOLEDO AND TRIPS FROM MADRID

TOP REASONS TO GO

★ **See El Greco's Toledo:** Tour the Renaissance painter's home and studio on an El Greco–themed tourist trail in the stunning city that the Greek-born painter called home.

★ **Be mesmerized by Cuenca's "hanging houses":** Las Casas Colgadas seem to defy gravity, clinging to a cliff side with views over Castile–La Mancha's parched plains.

★ **See Salamanca's old and new cathedrals:** The cathedrals are a fascinating dichotomy—the intricate detail of the new contrasts with the simplicity of the old.

★ **Visit Segovia's aqueduct:** Amazingly well preserved, this still-functioning 2,000-year-old Roman aqueduct is unforgettable.

★ **Get stuck in a time warp:** The walled city of Cáceres is especially evocative at dusk, with its skyline of ancient spires, towers, and cupolas.

Castile–La Mancha and Castile and León are like parentheses around Madrid, one north and one south. The name "Castile" refers to the great east–west line of castles and fortified towns built in the 12th century between Salamanca and Soria. Segovia's Alcázar, Ávila's fully intact city walls, and other bastions of Spain's regal past are among Castile's greatest monuments.

Extremadura, west of Madrid, covers 41,602 square km (16,063 square miles) and consists of two provinces: Cáceres to the north and Badajoz to the south, divided by the Toledo Mountains. The landlocked region is bordered by Portugal to the west, Andalusia to the south, Castile–La Mancha to the east.

1 Castile–La Mancha. Toledo, the pre-Madrid capital of Spain, is the main destination, though travelers willing to venture farther afield can explore Cuenca with its "hanging houses," Almagro with its green-and-white plaza and splendid parador, or Consuegra with its Don Quixote-esque windmills.

2 Castile and León. This region's crown jewel is Segovia with its famed Roman aqueduct and 12th-century Alcázar, though medieval Ávila is a close second. Farther north lie Salamanca, dominated by luminescent sandstone buildings, and the ancient capitals of Burgos and León. Burgos, an early outpost of Christianity, is said to have the most beautiful Gothic cathedral in Spain. León is a fun college town with some of its Roman walls still in place.

3 Extremadura. Green valleys and pristine mountain villages, along with dusty cities like Cáceres and Trujillo, are the main attractions in upper Extremadura, while the Jerte Valley has stunning natural settings with remote villages that seem to have stopped short of the 20th century. Southern Extremadura reveals the influence of Portugal and Andalusia, and the early Roman capital of Lusitania at Mérida is one of Iberia's finest compendiums of Roman ruins. The *dehesa*, southwestern Spain's rolling oak forest and meadowland, is prime habitat for the semiwild Iberian pig and covers much of southern Extremadura.

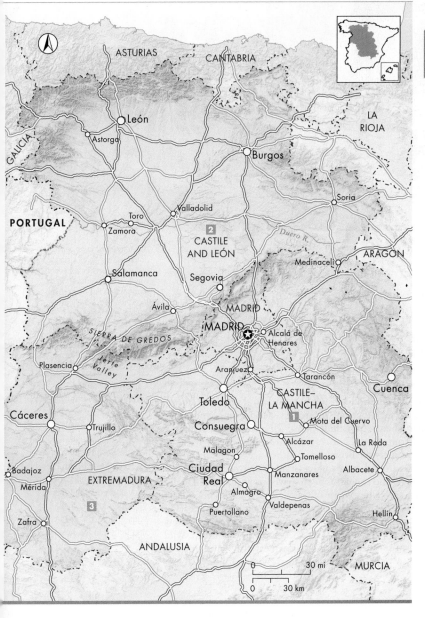

EATING AND DRINKING WELL IN CASTILE AND EXTREMADURA

In Spain's central *meseta,* an arid, high plateau, peasant cooking provides comfort and energy. Roast lamb, pork, and goat are staples, as are soups, stews, and dishes made from scraps, such as the classic *migas de pastor,* shepherd's bread crumbs.

(top left) Roast lamb with potatoes (top right) A simple dish of migas is an excellent way to use up leftover bread. (bottom left) Pisto manchego incorporates a variety of stewed vegetables.

Classic Castilian dishes are *cordero* (lamb) and *cochinillo* (suckling pig) roasted in wood ovens, and other prized entrées include *perdiz en escabeche* (marinated partridge) and *perdices a la toledana* (stewed partridge, Toledo-style). Broad-bean dishes are specialties in the areas around Ávila and La Granja (Segovia), while *trucha* (trout) and *cangrejos de río* (river crayfish) are Guadalajara specialties. Some of Castile's most surprising cuisine is found in Cuenca, where a Moorish influence appears in such dishes as *gazpacho pastor* (shepherd's stew), a stew made with several meats and a matzo-like flatbread. Wild mushrooms enhance aromas in meat dishes and stews or are served on their own in earthenware dishes.

DON QUIXOTE FOOD

Cervantine menus are favorites at taverns and inns throughout Quixote country southeast of Madrid. They usually feature *gachas manchegas* (a thick peasant porridge based on fried grass-pea flour and pork) and *duelos y quebrantos* (scrambled eggs and bacon), dishes mentioned in the novel.

LAMB

Roast lamb, *cordero asado,* is a favorite dish throughout Castile. *Lechazo,* or milk-fed lamb, is handled with great care and roasted slowly on low heat which renders a mild, ultratender meat that's a true delicacy.

PARTRIDGE

Perdices a la toledana, partridge prepared "Toledo style," is one of Castile–La Mancha's most sought-after dishes. Toldeo partridges are neither *estofadas* (stewed) nor *escabechadas* (marinated but, rather, cooked on low heat in wine with vinegar, olive oil, onions, garlic, and bay leaves until the sauce is thick and rich. October to February is the hunting season for partridge and the best time to try this local favorite.

VEGETABLE STEW

La Mancha, the mostly arid and windswept area southeast of Madrid, has moist vegetable-growing pockets along the Tajo River. *Pisto manchego,* a ratatouille-like vegetable stew with peppers, onions, ripe tomatoes, and zucchini, is a classic dish. Served in an earthenware vessel with a fried egg on top, it makes a wonderful light lunch.

MIGAS

Translated as "shepherd's bread crumbs," this ancient dish is made with stale bread that's been softened with water and fried in olive oil with lots of garlic and (sometimes) eggs, as well as

finely chopped bacon, chorizo, peppers, and potato.

GAZPACHO PASTOR (SHEPHERD'S STEW)

Andalusian gazpacho is a cold soup, but in La Mancha, especially in and around Cuenca, gazpacho is a thick, hot braise made with virtually everything in the barnyard, and served very hot. Partridge, hare, rabbit, hen, peppers, paprika, and *tortas gazpacheras* (flatbread made especially for this dish) complete the stew.

CASTILIAN WINES

In Toledo, Carlos Falcó (aka El Marqués de Griñón) has developed excellent Dominio de Valdepusa wines using petit verdot and syrah grapes. In Ribera del Duero, winemakers from Pingus and Protos to Pago de Carraovejas offer full-bodied wines using tempranillo, while Bierzo, northwest of León, has good values and earthy wines made with the local mencía grape.

Updated by
Benjamin
Kemper

Madrid, in the center of Spain, is an excellent jumping-off point for exploring, and the high-speed train puts many destinations within easy reach. The Castiles, which bracket Madrid to the north and south, and Extremadura, bordering Portugal, are filled with compelling destinations steeped in tradition.

For all the variety in the towns and countryside around Madrid, there's something of an underlying unity in Castile—the high, wide meseta of gray, bronze, and (briefly) green. This central Spanish steppe is divided into what was historically known as Old and New Castile, the former north of Madrid, the latter south (known as "new" because it was captured from the Moors a bit later), but nowadays people prefer Castilla y León, or Castile and León, for the area north of Madrid and Castilla–La Mancha, or Castile–La Mancha, for the area to the south.

Over the centuries, poets and others have characterized Castile as austere and melancholy. Gaunt mountain ranges frame the horizons; gorges and rocky outcrops break up flat expanses; and the fields around Ávila and Segovia are littered with giant boulders. Castilian villages are built predominantly of granite, and their solid, formidable look contrasts markedly with the whitewashed walls of most of southern Spain.

The very name Extremadura, literally "the far end of the Duero" (as in the Duero River), expresses the wild, isolated, and end-of-the-line character of the region bordering Portugal. With its poor soil and minimal industry, Extremadura hardly experienced the economic booms felt in other parts of Spain, and it's still the country's poorest province—but for the tourist, this otherworldly, lost-in-time feel is unforgettable. No other place in Spain has as many Roman monuments as Mérida, capital of the vast Roman province of Lusitania, which included most of the western half of the Iberian Peninsula. Mérida guarded the Vía de la Plata, the major Roman highway that crossed Extremadura from north to south, connecting Gijón with Seville. The economy and the arts declined after the Romans left, but the region revived in the 16th century when explorers and conquerors of the New World—from

Francisco Pizarro and Hernán Cortés to Francisco de Orellana, first navigator of the Amazon—returned to their birthplace. These men built the magnificent palaces that now glorify towns such as Cáceres and Trujillo, and they turned the remote monastery of Guadalupe into one of the great artistic repositories of Spain.

PLANNING

WHEN TO GO

July and August can be brutally hot, and November–February can get bitterly cold, especially in the Sierra de Guadarrama. May and October, when the weather is sunny but relatively cool, are the two best months to visit central Spain.

Spring is the ideal season in Extremadura, especially in the countryside, when the valleys and hills are covered with a dazzle of wildflowers. The stunning spectacle of cherry-blossom season in the Jerte Valley and La Vera takes place around mid-March. Fall is also a good time for Extremadura, though there may be rain starting in late October.

PLANNING YOUR TIME

Madrid is an excellent hub for venturing farther into Spain, but with so many choices, we've divided them into must-see stand-alone destinations and worthy stops en route to other parts of the country. Some are day trips; others are best overnight.

Must-see, short-trip destinations from Madrid are **Toledo, Segovia** (with **Sepúlveda,** if time allows), **Sigüenza,** and **Salamanca.** Salamanca should be an overnight trip, because it's farther and it has fun nightlife.

If you're traveling to other areas in Spain, we suggest the following stopover destinations:

If you're on your way to Salamanca, stop in **Ávila** (buses go direct to Salamanca without stopping, but most trains stop in Ávila).

If you're on your way to Santander, San Sebastián, or Bilbao, stop in **Burgos.**

If you're on your way to Asturias, stop in **León.**

If you're on your way to Lugo and A Coruña, in Galicia, stop in **Villafranca del Bierzo** or **Astorga.**

If you're on your way to Córdoba or Granada, stop in **Almagro.**

If you're on your way to Valencia, detour to **Cuenca.** Most trains, including the new high-speed AVE to Valencia, stop in Cuenca.

Extremadura is a neglected destination, even for Spanish tourists, but it's a beautiful part of the country with fascinating cities like Cáceres (a UNESCO World Heritage Site) and Trujillo, both of which have been used as filming locations for *Game of Thrones.* You can get a lightning impression of Extremadura in a day's drive from Madrid (or on a pit stop on the way to Lisbon), though overnighting is preferable. It's about 2½ hours from Madrid to **Jerte;** from there, take the A66 south to **Cáceres** before heading east to **Trujillo** on the N521. Split your time evenly between Cáceres and Trujillo. If you have more time, spend a day exploring the Roman monuments in Mérida and do some world-famous bird-watching in the **Parque Natural de Monfragüe**, near **Plasencia**. If you can, visit the **Monasterio de Yuste**, where Spain's founding emperor Carlos V died in 1558.

FESTIVALS

Central Spain is the land of festivals. Cuenca's Easter celebration and Toledo's Corpus Christi draw people from all over Spain, if not the world. During the pre-Lenten carnival, León and nearby Bañeza are popular party centers. Expect crowds and book accommodations in advance. Gastronomic festivals also abound.

Capeas. From early to mid-September the town fills with bullfighting aficionados from across the country for 12 days of bull-running and bullfighting events with young bulls—with a proviso that no harm should come to them (they are returned to their pastures when it's all over). ⊠ *Segura de León.*

Celebración del Cerdo y Vino. This September festival celebrates two of Spain's great triumphs, pork and wine, with innumerable pork products prepared in public demonstrations. ⊠ *Cáceres* ☎ *92/725–5765 for tourist office* ⊕ *www.ayto-caceres.es.*

FAMILY **Cherry Blossom Festival.** Beginning in March, Spain's prized cherry-growing region, the Jerte Valley, turns pink and white as more than a million cherry trees bloom in unison. Throughout the area, a series of live concerts, street markets, and gastronomic presentations accompany nature's show. ⊠ *Jaraíz de la Vera* ☎ *92/747–2558* ⊕ *www.turismov-alledeljerte.com.*

FAMILY **Feria del Queso.** Trujillo's cheese festival, in early May, brings together Spain's finest cheese makers with hundreds of varieties to taste and buy (don't pass up Pascualete, named the best cheese in Spain by the World Cheese Awards). The event is understandably popular with foodies. ⊠ *Trujillo* ☎ *92/732–1450* ⊕ *www.feriadelquesotrujillo.es.*

Festival de Teatro Clásico. In Mérida, the highlight of the cultural calendar is this annual festival, held in the Roman theater early July–mid-August. It features opera as well as classical drama and will celebrate its 65th year in 2019. ⊠ *Pl. Margarita Xirgu, Mérida* ☎ *92/400–9480* ⊕ *www.festivaldemerida.es.*

Fodor's Choice ★ **Fiesta de la Rosa del Azafrán** (*Consuegra Saffron Festival*). This festival, held in the last week of October since 1963, celebrates the annual saffron harvest, one of La Mancha's longest-standing traditions. Watch a saffron-plucking contest, savor locally-made manchego cheeses, and marvel at folk dance spectacles—all with a backdrop of Don Quixote-style windmills. ☎ *92/547–5731 Consuegra tourist office* ⊕ *www.consuegra.es/fiestas/fiesta-de-la-rosa-del-azafrán.*

Los Escobazos. On December 7, the city is filled with bonfires to celebrate this festival, dedicated to the Virgen de la Concepción, during which locals play-fight with torches made out of brooms. ⊠ *Jarandilla de la Vera* ☎ *92/756–0460 for tourist office* ⊕ *www.jarandilla.com.*

WOMAD Cáceres. The World of Music, Arts and Dance draws crowds of around 75,000 in early May. Main stages are set up in the magical surroundings of this ancient city's plazas for free concerts, and other events include shows staged in the Gran Teatro, children's events, and a grand procession. ⊠ *Calle San Antón 0, Cáceres* ☎ *92/701–0884* ⊕ *www.womad.org.*

GETTING HERE AND AROUND

AIR TRAVEL

The only international airport in Castile is Madrid's Barajas; Salamanca, León, and Valladolid have domestic airports, but the economic crisis has led to a reduction in traffic and they receive very few flights these days. Extremadura's only airport is Badajoz, which receives domestic flights from Madrid, Barcelona, and Bilbao.

Airport Contacts Adolfo Suárez Madrid–Barajas Airport. ⊠ *Barajas* ☎ *91/321–1000* ⊕ *www.aena.es.*

BUS TRAVEL

Bus connections between Madrid and Castile are frequent and cheap; there are several stations and stops in Madrid. Buses to Toledo (1 hour) leave every half hour from the southerly Plaza Elíptica, and buses to Segovia (1¼ hours) leave every hour from La Sepulvedana's headquarters, near Príncipe Pío. Jiménez Dorado sends buses to Ávila (1¾ hours) from the Estación del Sur. ALSA has service to León (4½ hours), Valladolid (2¼ hours) and Soria (3 hours). Auto-Res (aka Avanza) serves Cuenca (2¾ hours), Salamanca (3 hours), and Burgos (2½ hours).

From Burgos, buses head north to the Basque Country; from León, you can press on to Asturias. Service between towns is not as frequent as it is to and from Madrid, so you may find it quicker to return to Madrid and make your way from there. Reservations are rarely necessary.

Buses to Extremadura's main cities from Madrid are reliable. The first bus of the day on lesser routes often sets off early in the morning, so plan carefully to avoid getting stranded. Some examples of destinations from Madrid are: Cáceres (7 daily), Guadalupe (2 daily), Trujillo (12 daily), and Mérida (8 daily). For schedules and prices, check the tourist offices or contact the Auto-Res bus line. Note that it's best to avoid taking the bus at rush hour as journeys can be delayed by more than an hour.

■TIP→ **The easiest way to plan bus travel is on www.goeuro.com, a scheduling and purchasing site that allows you to view different prices and bus companies on one platform.**

Bus Contacts ALSA. ☎ *90/242–2242* ⊕ *www.alsa.es.* **Auto-Res** (*Avanza*). ☎ *91/272–2832* ⊕ *www.avanzabus.com.* **La Sepulvedana.** ☎ *90/211–9699* ⊕ *www.lasepulvedana.es.* **Larrea** (*Avanza*). ☎ *91/851–5592* ⊕ *www.autobuseslarrea.com.* **Movelia.** ☎ *90/264–6428* ⊕ *www.movelia.es.*

CAR TRAVEL

Major divided highways—the A1 through A6—radiate out from Madrid, making Spain's farthest corners no more than five- to six-hour drives, and the capital's outlying towns are only minutes away. If possible, avoid returning to Madrid on major highways at the end of a weekend or a holiday. The beginning and end of August are notorious for traffic jams, as is Semana Santa (Holy Week), which starts on Palm

Sunday and ends on Easter Sunday. National (toll-free) highways and back roads are slower but provide one of the great pleasures of driving around the Castilian countryside: surprise encounters with historical monuments and spectacular vistas.

If you're driving from Madrid to Extremadura, the main gateway, the six-lane A5, moves quickly. The A66, or Vía de la Plata, which crosses Extremadura from north to south, is also effective. The fastest way from Portugal is the (Portuguese) A6 from Lisbon to Badajoz (not to be confused with the Spanish A6, which runs northwest from Madrid to Galicia). Side roads—particularly those that cross the wilder mountainous districts, such as the Sierra de Guadalupe—differ in terms of upkeep but afford some of the most spectacular vistas in Extremadura.

Mileage from Madrid:

Madrid to Burgos is 243 km (151 miles).

Madrid to Cáceres is 299 km (186 miles).

Madrid to Cuenca is 168 km (104 miles).

Madrid to Granada is 428 km (266 miles).

Madrid to Léon is 334 km (208 miles).

Madrid to Salamanca is 212 km (132 miles).

Madrid to Segovia is 91 km (57 miles).

Madrid to Toledo is 88 km (55 miles).

Madrid to Ávila is 114 km (71 miles).

⇨ *The Travel Smart chapter has contact information for major car rental agencies.*

RIDESHARE TRAVEL

As right-lane-cruising buses and low-speed trains are often only transportation options for intercity travel in Castile, travelers of all ages are increasingly taking rideshares, the most popular of which is Blablacar, an app with more global users than Uber. Its free platform allows you to book ahead via credit card and message with the driver to set up pickup and drop-off points. It's not only the quickest way from A to B without a rental car but also often the cheapest, since drivers aren't allowed to make a profit on trips (the amount you pay only offsets costs for tolls and gas). Check ⊕ *www.blablacar.com* for details.

TRAIN TRAVEL

All the main towns in Castile and León and Castile–La Mancha are accessible by multiple daily trains from Madrid, with tickets running about €10–€30, depending on train speed (the high-speed AVE service costs more), the time of day, and the day of the week. Several towns make feasible day trips: there are commuter trains from Madrid to Segovia (30 minutes), Guadalajara (30 minutes), and Toledo (30 minutes). Trains to Toledo depart from Madrid's Atocha station; trains to Salamanca, Burgos, and León depart from Chamartín; and both stations serve Ávila, Segovia, El Escorial, and Sigüenza, though Chamartín has more frequent service. Trains from Segovia go only to Madrid, but you can change at Villalba for Ávila and Salamanca.

For Extremadura, (notoriously dingy and sluggish) trains from Madrid stop at Monfragüe, Plasencia, Cáceres, Mérida, Zafra, and Badajoz and run as often as six times daily. The journey from Madrid to Cáceres takes about four hours. Within the province there are services from Badajoz to Cáceres (three daily, 1 hour 55 minutes), to Mérida (five daily, 40 minutes), and to Plasencia (two daily, 2 hours 40 minutes); from Cáceres to Badajoz (three daily, 1 hour 55 minutes), to Mérida (five daily, 1 hour), to Plasencia (four daily, 1 hour 10 minutes), and to Zafra (two daily, 2 hours 10 minutes); from Plasencia to Badajoz (two daily, 3 hours), to Cáceres (four daily, 1 hour 10 minutes), and to Mérida (four daily, 2 hours 10 minutes). Several cities have separate train stations for normal versus AVE high-speed rail service; the newer AVE stations are often farther from town centers. ⚠ **As of summer 2018, expect delays and schedule changes as the government implements a €20 million project to update the Extremaduran train network.**

Train Contacts RENFE. ☎ *90/232-0320* ⊕ *www.renfe.com.*

RESTAURANTS

This is Spain's rugged heartland, bereft of touristy hamburger joints and filled instead with the country's most traditional *tavernas,* which attract Spanish foodies from across the country. Some of the most renowned restaurants in this region are small and family run, while a few new avant-garde spots in Extremadura serve up modern architecture as well as experimental fusion dishes.

HOTELS

Many of the oldest and most attractive paradores (⊕ *www.paradores. es*) in Castile are in quiet towns such as Almagro, Ávila, Cuenca, and Sigüenza. Those in Toledo, Segovia, and Salamanca are modern buildings with magnificent views and, in the case of Segovia, have wonderful indoor and outdoor swimming pools. There are plenty of pleasant alternatives to paradores, too, such as Segovia's Hotel Infanta Isabel, Salamanca's Hotel Rector, and Cuenca's Posada de San José, a 16th-century convent. In Extremadura the paradores occupy buildings of great historic or architectural interest.

The Extremaduran government runs a few *hospederías,* regional versions of the parador chain; some have historic quarters in scenic areas. Most other high-end hotels, with a few exceptions, are modern boxes with little character. Extremadura's countryside boasts a number of charming, underrated *hoteles rurales* (bed-and-breakfast inns) and 135 *casas rurales* (guesthouses).

⇨ *Hotel reviews have been shortened. For full information, visit Fodors.com.*

WHAT IT COSTS IN EUROS			
	$	**$$**	**$$$**	**$$$$**
Restaurants	under €12	€12–€17	€18–€22	over €22
Hotels	under €90	€90–€125	€126–€180	over €180

Restaurant prices are the average cost of a main course or equivalent combination of smaller dishes at dinner. Hotel prices are the lowest cost of a standard double room in high season.

TOURS

In summer the tourist offices of Segovia, Toledo, and Sigüenza organize Trenes Turísticos (miniature tourist trains) that glide past all the major sights; contact local tourist offices for schedules.

A great way to really get to know Extremadura is by bike (in any season but scorching summer), and you can essentially forego all maps by following the ancient Roman road, the Vía de la Plata: it runs through Extremadura from north to south along A66, dividing it in two, and passes by such villages as Plasencia, Cáceres, Mérida, and Zafra. Note that the region north of the province of Cáceres, including the Jerte Valley, La Vera, and the area surrounding Guadalupe, is mountainous and uneven: be prepared for a bumpy and exhausting ride. The regional government has also opened a Vía Verde, or "green way" path, along disused railroads; it goes from Logrosán (a couple of miles southwest of Guadalupe) to Villanueva de la Serena (east of Mérida and near Don Benito). This path is a roughly cleared track, more like a nature trail for hikers and bikers, and closed to motor vehicles. Check ⊕ *www. viasverdes.com* for maps of this and other trails.

FAMILY **Equiberia.** Horseback tours, ranging 1–10 days, offer a unique way to experience the gorges, fields, and forests of the Sierra de Guadarrama, Segovia, Ávila, and beyond. ⊠ *Navarredonda de Gredos, Ávila* ☎ 68/934–3974 ⊕ *www.equiberia.com* ✉ *From €150.*

FAMILY **Valle Aventura.** Hiking, horseback riding, cycling, and kayaking trips in the Jerte Valley can be organized with this company. Prices may not include meals. ☎ 63/663–1182 ⊕ *www.valleaventura.com* ✉ *From €180.*

CASTILE–LA MANCHA

Castile–La Mancha is the land of Don Quixote, Miguel de Cervantes's chivalrous hero. Some of Spain's oldest and noblest cities are found here, steeped in culture and legend, though many are run-down in a charming sort of way. In 2016, these mostly untouristed cities marked the 400th anniversary of the death of Cervantes, who died within days of his contemporary, William Shakespeare. The architecture of Toledo and Cuenca are definite highlights, but the dusty villages and stark plains (a rarity in Western Europe) are also enchanting.

TOLEDO

88 km (55 miles) southwest of Madrid.

The spiritual capital of Spain, Toledo is perched atop a rocky mount with steep golden hills rising on either side and bound on three sides by the Río Tajo (Tagus River). When the Romans arrived here in 192 BC, they built their fortress (the Alcázar) on the highest point of the rock. Later, the Visigoths remodeled the stronghold.

In the 8th century, the Moors arrived and strengthened Toledo's reputation as a center of religion and learning. Unusual tolerance was extended to those who practiced Christianity (the Mozarabs) and to the city's exceptionally large Jewish population. Today, the Moorish legacy is evident in Toledo's strong crafts tradition, the mazelike streets, and the predominance of brick construction (rather than the stone of many of Spain's historical cities). For the Moors, beauty was to be savored from within rather than displayed on the surface. Even Toledo's cathedral—one of the most richly endowed in Spain—is hard to see from the outside, largely obscured by the warren of houses around it.

Alfonso VI, aided by El Cid ("Lord Conqueror"), captured the city in 1085 and dubbed himself emperor of Toledo. Under the Christians, the town's strong intellectual life was maintained, and Toledo became famous for its school of translators, who taught Arab medicine, law, culture, and philosophy. Religious tolerance continued, and during the rule of Pedro the Cruel (so named because he allegedly had members of his own family murdered to advance his position), a Jewish banker, Samuel Levi, became the royal treasurer and one of the wealthiest men in the booming city. By the late 1400s, however, hostility toward Jews and Arabs had grown as Toledo developed into a bastion of the Catholic Church.

Under Toledo's long line of cardinals—most notably Mendoza, Tavera, and Cisneros—Renaissance Toledo emerged as a center of the humanities. Economically and politically, however, Toledo began to decline at the end of the 15th century. The expulsion of the Jews from Spain in 1492, as part of the Spanish Inquisition, eroded Toledo's economic and intellectual prowess. When Madrid became the permanent center of the Spanish court in 1561, Toledo lost its political importance, and the expulsion from Spain of the converted Arabs (Moriscos) in 1601 meant the departure of most of the city's artisans. The years the painter El Greco spent in Toledo—from 1572 to his death in 1614—were those of the city's decline, which is greatly reflected in his works. In the late 19th century, after hundreds of years of neglect, the works of El Greco came to be widely appreciated, and Toledo was transformed into a major tourist destination. Today, Toledo is conservative, prosperous, proud—and a bit provincial. Its winding streets and steep hills can be exasperating, especially when you're searching for a specific sight. Take a full day (or three) to absorb the town's medieval trappings—and expect to get a little lost.

GETTING HERE AND AROUND

The best way to get to Toledo from Madrid is the high-speed AVE train, which leaves from Madrid at least nine times daily from Atocha station and gets you there in 30 minutes.

ALSA buses leave every half hour from Plaza Elíptica and take 1¼ hours.

TOURS

Cuéntame Toledo. The name translates as "Tell me about Toledo," and that's what they do. The company offers free tours (in English and Spanish) of Toledo's historic center at 5 pm daily, plus a range of other paid tours of the city's monuments, best-kept secrets, underground passageways, and urban legends. There are also El Greco–themed tours, nighttime ghost tours, and other routes that include visits to ancient Arab baths. ☒ *Corral de Don Diego 5* ☏ *92/521–0767, 60/893–5856* ⊕ *www.cuentametoledo.com* ☒ *Historic center tour free, other tours from €12.*

Fodor'sChoice ★ **Toledo de la Mano.** These private tours, led by Toledophile Adolfo Ferrero (who has written a 200-page guidebook on the town), delve far deeper than those run by competitors, touching on the city's history of multiculturalism and its significance in medieval Europe. Groups of up to 55 people can be accommodated. ☒ *Calle Nuncio Viejo 10* ☏ *62/917–7810* ⊕ *www.toledodelamano.com* ☒ *From €140.*

Fodor'sChoice ★ **Toledo Tours.** General and customized guided tours cater to those interested in the city's gastronomy, art, history, and wildlife with full- or half-day options. Tour prices include admission to various museums and landmarks—you can pick and choose which to visit. If you're interested in art or El Greco, ask for Inma Sánchez, a local art historian who speaks English well. Prices depend on the number of people and the length of the tour. ☒ *Toledo* ☏ *92/582–6616* ⊕ *www.toledoturismo. org* ☒ *From €15.*

FAMILY **Toledo Train Vision.** This unabashedly touristy "train" chugs past many of Toledo's main sights, departing from the Plaza de Zocodover every hour on the hour during the week, and every 30 minutes on weekends. The tour takes 45–50 minutes and has recorded information in 13 languages (including English, Spanish, and French) plus children's versions in those three languages, too. Buy tickets at the kiosk in Plaza de Zocodover. ☒ *Pl. de Zocodover* ☏ *62/530–1890* ☒ *€6.*

ESSENTIALS

Visitor Information Provincial Tourist Office. ☒ *Paseo Merchán, s/n* ☏ *92/524-8232* ⊕ *www.diputoledo.es.* **Toledo Tourist Office.** ☒ *Pl. de Zocodover 8* ☏ *92/526-7666, 68/785-4965, 925/239121* ⊕ *www.turismo.toledo.es.*

EXPLORING

Alcázar. Originally a Moorish citadel (*alcázar* is Arabic for "fortress") and occupied from the 10th century until the Reconquest, Toledo's Alcázar is on a hill just outside the walled city, dominating the horizon. The south facade—the building's most severe—is the work of Juan de Herrera, of Escorial fame, while the east facade incorporates a large section of battlements. The finest facade is the northern, one of many

Sinagoga de Santa María La Blanca. Founded in 1203, Toledo's second synagogue—situated in the heart of the Jewish Quarter—is nearly two centuries older than the more elaborate Tránsito, just down the street. Santa María's white interior has a forest of columns supporting capitals with fine filigree work. ✉ *Calle de los Reyes Católicos 4* ☎ *92/522–7257* 🎫 *€3.*

Fodor's Choice ★ **Sinagoga del Tránsito** (*Museo Sefardí, Sephardic Museum*). This 14th-century synagogue's plain exterior belies sumptuous interior walls embellished with colorful Mudejar decoration. There are inscriptions in Hebrew and Arabic glorifying God, Peter the Cruel, and Samuel Levi (the original patron). It's a rare example of architecture reflecting Arabic as the lingua franca of medieval Spanish Jews. It's said that Levi imported cedars from Lebanon for the building's construction, à la Solomon when he built the First Temple in Jerusalem. This is one of only three synagogues still fully standing in Spain (two in Toledo, one in Córdoba), from an era when there were hundreds—though more are in the process of being excavated. Adjoining the main hall is the **Museo Sefardí,** a small but informative museum of Jewish culture in Spain. ✉ *Calle Samuel Levi 2* ☎ *92/522–3665* 🌐 *www.mecd.gob.es/msefardi/home.html* 🎫 *€3 (free Sat. afternoon and Sun.).*

WHERE TO EAT

$$$$ SPANISH Fodor's Choice ★ 🍴 **Adolfo Restaurant.** Visit this white-tablecloth restaurant, situated steps from the cathedral, for traditional Toledan recipes with fine-dining twists, complemented by a 2,800-bottle-deep wine list. Don't pass up the hearty partridge stew, deemed the best in Spain by the former Spanish king Juan Carlos I; it sings alongside a glass of Adolfo's proprietary red wine. **Known for:** chef's menu; historic building; game dishes. [$] *Average main: €50* ✉ *Calle del Hombre de Palo 7* ☎ *92/522–7321* 🌐 *www.grupoadolfo.com* 🕒 *No dinner Sun.*

$$ SPANISH 🍴 **Bar Ludeña.** Locals and visitors come together at this old-timey tapas bar for steaming cauldrons of *carcamusas,* a traditional Toledan meat stew studded with peas and chorizo. (The rest of the menu is nothing special.) **Known for:** hearty carcamusas stew; free tapa with every drink; rustic ambience. [$] *Average main: €12* ✉ *Pl. de la Magdalena 10* ☎ *92/522–3384* 🕒 *Closed Wed.*

$$ SPANISH Fodor's Choice ★ 🍴 **Cervecería El Trébol.** You can't leave Toledo without indulging in one of El Trébol's famous *bombas,* fried fist-sized spheres of mashed potato stuffed with spiced meat and anointed with alioli. They're best enjoyed on the twinkly outdoor patio with a locally brewed beer in hand. **Known for:** to-die-for bombas; most pleasant patio in town; local craft beers. [$] *Average main: €15* ✉ *Calle de Santa Fe 1* ☎ *92/528–1297* 🌐 *www.cerveceriatrebol.com.*

$$$ SPANISH 🍴 **La Flor de la Esquina.** The most coveted seats at this charming restaurant are the patio tables on the Plaza del Padre, which boast views of Toledo's cathedral spires. Three-course lunch menus are a great value at €9.90, and there are tapas menus for those looking to sample a bit of everything (don't pass up the charcuterie boards). **Known for:** steal prix-fixe menu; cathedral views; top-quality cured meats. [$] *Average main: €20* ✉ *Pl. del Padre Juan de Mariana 2* ☎ *62/794–5020.*

3

Toledo's Santa María La Blanca synagogue is a fascinating symbol of cultural cooperation: built by Islamic architects, in a Christian land, for Jewish use.

WHERE TO STAY

$$
HOTEL
Fodor'sChoice
★

Antídoto Rooms. Antídoto is a breath of fresh air in Toledo's mostly staid hotel scene: expect turquoise beamed ceilings, poured-concrete floors, and designer light fixtures. **Pros:** highly Instagrammable rooms; in the heart of the Old Town; friendly staff. **Cons:** awkward room layout; in-room bathrooms with no curtains and transparent doors; poor-quality sheets. [$] *Rooms from: €110* ⊠ *Calle Recoletos 2* ☎ *92/522–8851* ⊕ *www.antidotorooms.com* ⤻ *10 rooms* ⦿ *No meals.*

$$
HOTEL

Hacienda del Cardenal. Once a summer palace for Cardinal Lorenzana, who lived in the 1700s, this serene three-star hotel on the outskirts of the Old Town hits the sweet spot between rustic and refined. **Pros:** lovely courtyard; convenient dining; spacious rooms. **Cons:** restaurant often full; parking is pricey; stairs inconvenient for those with heavy luggage. [$] *Rooms from: €100* ⊠ *Paseo de Recaredo 24* ☎ *92/522–4900* ⊕ *www.hostaldelcardenal.com* ⤻ *27 rooms* ⦿ *No meals.*

$$
HOTEL

Hotel Pintor El Greco Sercotel. Next door to the painter's house, this former 17th-century bakery is now a chic, contemporary hotel managed by the Sercotel chain. **Pros:** parking garage adjacent; cozy decor; complimentary wine and olives. **Cons:** street noise in most rooms; elevator goes to the second floor only; bar area sometimes closed for private events. [$] *Rooms from: €100* ⊠ *Alamillos del Tránsito 13* ☎ *92/528–5191* ⊕ *www.hotelpintorelgreco.com* ⤻ *60 rooms* ⦿ *Free Breakfast.*

$$$
HOTEL
FAMILY

Parador de Toledo. This modern building with Mudejar-style touches on Toledo's outskirts has an unbeatable panorama of the town from the rooms' terraces and adjacent swimming pool, where you can sit and watch the sunset. **Pros:** outdoor swimming pool; gorgeous views; fine breakfasts. **Cons:** long walk from the city center; swimming pool only open June 15–September 15; not in a historic building like other para-dores. $] *Rooms from: €180* ⊠ *Cerro del Emperador* ☎ *92/522–1850, 90/254–7979 for reservations* ⊕ *www.parador.es* ⤴ *77 rooms* ⏺ *Free Breakfast.*

SHOPPING

The Moors established silverwork, damascene (metalwork inlaid with gold or silver), pottery, embroidery, and marzipan traditions here. A turn-of-the-20th-century art school next to the Monasterio de San Juan de los Reyes keeps some of these crafts alive. For inexpensive pottery, stop at the large stores on the outskirts of town, on the main road to Madrid.

El Baúl de la Piker. There's no shortage of vintage treasures at this inde-pendently owned vintage shop specializing in women's wear. Keep an eye out for retro leather pieces—Toledo has long been known for its fine leather artisanship. ⊠ *Calle Trastámara 17* ☎ *92/567–2083* ⊕ *www. elbauldelapiker.com.*

La Encina de Ortega. This is a one-stop-shop for local wines, olive oil, manchego cheese, and—most notably—*ibérico* pork products (ham, chorizo, dry-cured sausages) made from pigs raised on the family farm. ⊠ *Calle La Plata 22* ☎ *92/510–2072* ⊕ *www.laencinadeortega.com.*

Santo Tomé Marzipan. Since 1856, Santo Tomé has been Spain's most famous maker of marzipan, a Spanish confection made from sugar, honey, and almond paste. Visit the main shop on the Plaza de Zocodover, or take a tour of the old convent-turned-factory where it's actually made on Calle Santo Tomé 3 (advance booking required). ⊠ *Pl. de Zocodover 7* ☎ *92/522–1168, 92/522–3763* ⊕ *www.mazapan.com.*

ALMAGRO

215 km (134 miles) south of Madrid.

The center of this noble town contains the only preserved medieval theater in Europe, which stands beside the ancient Plaza Mayor, where 85 Roman columns form two colonnades supporting green-frame 16th-century buildings. Enjoy casual tapas (such as pickled baby eggplant, an Almagro specialty known the country over) and rustic local wines in the unfussy bars lining the square. Near the plaza are granite man-sions emblazoned with the heraldic shields of their former owners and a splendid parador in a restored 17th-century convent.

GETTING HERE AND AROUND

Almagro can be reached by train from Madrid, with one scheduled departure per day departing from Atocha or Chamartín stations for the 2½-hour journey, but it's probably best to rent a car or book a Blablacar rideshare. The drive south from the capital takes you across the plains of La Mancha, where Don Quixote's adventures unfolded.

ESSENTIALS

Visitor Information Almagro. ⊠ *Pl. Mayor 1* ☎ *92/686–0717* ⊕ *www.ciudad-almagro.com.*

EXPLORING

Fodor's Choice
★

Corral de Comedias. Appearing almost as it did in 1628 when it was built, this theater has wooden balconies on four sides and the stage at one end of the open patio. During the golden age of Spanish theater—the time of playwrights Pedro Calderón de la Barca, Cervantes, and Lope de Vega—touring actors came to Almagro, once a burgeoning urban center for its mercury mines and lace industry. Forego the tourist-oriented spectacles unless you're a Spanish theater buff: poor acoustics and archaic Spanish scripts make it difficult to understand what's going on. ✉ *Pl. Mayor 18* ☎ *92/686–1539* ⊕ *www.corraldecomedias.com* 🎟 *From €4.*

Fodor's Choice
★

Museo Etnográfico Campo de Calatrava. For a window into what agrarian life was like in this area in centuries past, pop into this tiny museum presided over by the passionate historian who amassed the (mostly obsolete) curiosities on display. A guided tour, in Spanish, takes a little under an hour and is well worth it. ✉ *Calle Chile 6* ☎ *65/701–0077* ⊕ *www.museodealmagro.com* 🎟 *€5.*

Museo Nacional del Teatro. This museum displays models of the Roman amphitheaters in Mérida (Extremadura) and Sagunto (near Valencia), both still in use, as well as costumes, pictures, and documents relating to the history of Spanish theater. ✉ *Calle del Gran Maestre 2*

☎ *92/626–1014, 92/626–1018* 🌐 *museoteatro.mcu.es* 🎟 *€3 (free Sat. afternoon and Sun. morning)* ⏱ *Closed Mon.*

WHERE TO STAY

$$$ HOTEL Fodor's Choice ★ 🏨 **Parador de Almagro.** Five minutes from the Plaza Mayor of Almagro, this parador is a finely restored 16th-century Franciscan convent with cells, cloisters, and patios. **Pros:** pretty indoor courtyards; outdoor pool; ample parking. **Cons:** untidy public areas; double-bed rooms smaller than normal rooms; inconsistent restaurant. [$] *Rooms from: €135* ✉ *Ronda de San Francisco 31* ☎ *92/686–0100* 🌐 *www.parador.es* 🛏 *54 rooms* 🍴 *Free Breakfast.*

CUENCA

168 km (105 miles) southeast of Madrid, 150 km (93 miles) northwest of Valencia.

Fodor's Choice ★ The delightful old town of Cuenca is one of the most surreal looking in Spain, built on a sloping rock with precipitous sides that plunge to the gorges of the Huécar and Júcar rivers. Because the town ran out of room to expand, some medieval houses dangle right over the abyss and are now a unique architectural attraction, the Casas Colgadas (Hanging Houses). The old town's dramatic setting grants spectacular views of the surrounding countryside, and its cobblestone streets, cathedral, churches, and taverns contrast starkly with the modern town, which sprawls beyond the river gorges. Though somewhat isolated, Cuenca makes a good overnight stop if you're traveling between Madrid and Valencia, or even a worthwhile detour between Madrid and Barcelona.

GETTING HERE AND AROUND

From Madrid, buses leave for Cuenca about every two hours from Conde de Casal. From Valencia, four buses leave every four–six hours, starting at 8:30 am. A high-speed AVE train leaves Madrid approximately every hour and stops in Cuenca (after about 55 minutes) on its way to Valencia. Slower, cheaper trains also run several times daily between Cuenca and Valencia, Madrid, Albacete, and Alicante, on the coast. Rideshares (via Blablacar) to and from the city are plentiful.

ESSENTIALS

Visitor Information Cuenca. ✉ *Av. Cruz Roja 1* ☎ *96/924–1050.*

EXPLORING

Cuenca has more than a dozen churches and two cathedrals, but visitors are allowed inside only about half of them. The best views of the city are from the square in front of a small palace at the very top of Cuenca, where the town tapers out to the narrowest of ledges. Here, gorges flank the precipice, and old houses sweep down toward a distant plateau. The lower half of the old town is a maze of tiny streets, any of which will take you up to the Plaza del Carmen. From here the town narrows and a single street, Calle Alfonso VIII, continues the ascent to the Plaza Mayor, which passes under the arch of the town hall.

Fodor's Choice ★ **Casas Colgadas** (*Hanging Houses*). As if Cuenca's famous Casas Colgadas, suspended impossibly over the cliffs below, were not eye-popping enough, they also house one of Spain's finest and most curious

Cuenca's precarious Casas Colgadas (Hanging Houses) are also home to the well-regarded Museum of Abstract Art.

museums, the **Museo de Arte Abstracto Español** (Museum of Spanish Abstract Art)—not to be confused with the adjacent Museo Municipal de Arte Moderno. Projecting over the town's eastern precipice, these houses originally formed a 15th-century palace, which later served as a town hall before falling into disrepair in the 19th century. In 1927 the cantilevered balconies that had once hung over the gorge were rebuilt, and in 1966 the painter Fernando Zóbel decided to create (inside the houses) the world's first museum devoted exclusively to abstract art. The works he gathered—by such renowned names as Carlos Saura, Eduardo Chillida, Lucio Muñoz, and Antoni Tàpies—are primarily by exiled Spanish artists who grew up under Franco's regime. The museum has free smartphone audio guides that can be downloaded from the website. ⊠ *Calle de los Canónigos* ☎ *96/921–2983* ⊕ *www.march.es/ arte/cuenca* ⊠ *Free.*

Cathedral of Santa María La Mayor. This cathedral looms large and casts an enormous shadow in the evening throughout the adjacent Plaza Mayor. Built during the Gothic era in the 12th century atop ruins of a conquered mosque, the cathedral's massive triptych facade lost its Gothic character in the Renaissance. Inside are the tombs of the cathedral's founding bishops, an impressive portico of the Apostles, and a Byzantine reliquary. ⊠ *Pl. Mayor* ☎ *96/922–4626* ⊕ *www.catedralcuenca.es* ⊠ *From €5 (free 1st Mon. of month).*

Fodor's Choice
★

Puente de San Pablo. The 16th-century stone footbridge over the Huécar gorge was fortified with iron in 1903 for the convenience of the Dominican monks of San Pablo, who lived on the other side. If you don't have a fear of heights, cross the narrow bridge to take in the vertiginous view of the river and equally thrilling panorama of the Casas Colgadas. It's by far the best view of the city. If you've read the popular English novel *Winter in Madrid,* you'll recognize this bridge from the book's final scene. ✉ *Cuenca.*

WHERE TO EAT

Much of Cuenca's cuisine is based on wild game, and partridge, lamb, rabbit, and hen are ubiquitous on menus. *Trucha* (trout) from the adjacent river is the fish of choice, and it turns up in entrées and soups. In almost every town restaurant, you can find *morteruelo,* Cuenca's pâté of *jabalí* (wild boar), rabbit, partridge, hen, liver, pork loin, and spices, as well as *galianos,* a thick stew served on wheat cake. For dessert, try the almond-based confection called *alajú,* which is enriched with honey, nuts, and lemon, and *torrijas,* bread dipped in milk, fried until custardy, and sprinkled with powdered sugar.

$$$$ SPANISH 🍴 **El Figón de Huécar.** This family-run tavern serves updated Castilian classics in an airy dining room set within a medieval stone house with sweeping views of the city (ask for an outdoor table when booking). Specialty dishes include Manchegan migas (bread crumbs fried with chorizo and garlic) and "old wine," veal with potatoes *al montón* (fried with garlic). **Known for:** breathtaking views; scrumptious desserts; elegant dining room. [$] *Average main: €35* ✉ *Ronda de Julián Romero 6* ☎ *96/924–0062, 62/906–3366* 🌐 *www.figondelhuecar.es* 🕑 *Closed Mon. No dinner Sun.*

$$ TAPAS Fodor's Choice ★ 🍴 **La Ponderosa.** La Ponderosa is a quintessential yet elevated Castilian bar where locals mingle at high volume while tossing back local wine and munching on well-priced seasonal delicacies like griddled wild asparagus, suckling lamb chops, and seared wild mushrooms. It's a standing-room-only joint, so if you want to sit, you'll have to come early and find a place on the terrace. **Known for:** hidden-gem local wines; simple and delicious vegetable dishes; buzzy atmosphere. [$] *Average main: €15* ✉ *Calle de San Francisco 20* ☎ *96/921–3214* 🕑 *Closed Sun., and July.*

$$$$ SPANISH 🍴 **Trivio.** The punchy, artfully presented dishes at Trivio—think wild game tartare and house-pickled vegetables—are an anomaly in a region known for its stick-to-your-ribs country fare. Choose from three well-priced tasting menus in the dining room, or opt for a more casual experience in the Bistró-Bar. **Known for:** bold tasting menus; award-winning croquetas; pretty plating. [$] *Average main: €30* ✉ *Calle Colón 25* ☎ *96/903–0593* 🌐 *www.restaurantetrivio.com* 🕑 *Closed Mon., no dinner Sun.*

WHERE TO STAY

$ HOTEL FAMILY 🏨 **Cueva del Fraile.** Surrounded by dramatic landscapes, this family-friendly three-star lodging occupies a 16th-century building on the outskirts of town. **Pros:** beautiful interior garden terrace; outdoor swimming pool and tennis courts; good value. **Cons:** location 7 km (4½ miles) from town; no a/c in some rooms; some rooms have leaky showers. [$] *Rooms from: €50* ✉ *Ctra. Cuenca–Buenache, Km 7* ☎ *96/921–1571* 🌐 *www.hotelcuevadelfraile.com* 🕑 *Closed Jan.* 🛏 *75 rooms* 🍽 *No meals.*

$ B&B/INN **Hostal Cánovas.** Near Plaza España, in the heart of the new town, this is one of Cuenca's best bargains, and though the lobby's not impressive, the inviting rooms more than compensate. **Pros:** low prices even during high season; spacious digs; clean rooms. **Cons:** uphill trek to the old quarter; thin walls; uncomfortable beds. [$] *Rooms from: €55* ✉ *Calle Fray Luis de León 38* ☎ *96/921–3973* 🌐 *www.hostalcanovas.com* 🛏 *17 rooms* 🍴 *No meals.*

$$$$ HOTEL Fodor's Choice ★ **Parador de Cuenca.** The rooms are luxurious and serene at the exquisitely restored 16th-century convent of San Pablo, pitched on a precipice across a dramatic gorge from Cuenca's city center. **Pros:** great views of the hanging houses and gorge; spacious rooms; consistently good restaurant. **Cons:** expensive breakfast not always included in room rate; secure garage parking not always available; calls to reception sometimes go unanswered. [$] *Rooms from: €220* ✉ *Subida a San Pablo* ☎ *96/923–2320* 🌐 *www.parador.es* 🛏 *63 rooms* 🍴 *No meals.*

$ B&B/INN FAMILY Fodor's Choice ★ **Posada San José.** This family-friendly inn, housed in a centuries-old convent, clings to the top of the Huécar gorge in Cuenca's old town. **Pros:** cozy historical rooms; stunning views of the gorge; well-prepared local food. **Cons:** built to 17th-century proportions, some doorways are low; certain rooms are cramped; sloping floors can be vertiginous when lying in bed. [$] *Rooms from: €65* ✉ *Calle Julián Romero 4* ☎ *96/921–1300, 63/981–6825* 🌐 *www.posadasanjose.com* 🛏 *31 rooms* 🍴 *Free Breakfast.*

SIGÜENZA

132 km (82 miles) northeast of Madrid.

The ancient university town of Sigüenza dates back to Roman, Visigothic, and Moorish times and still has splendid architecture and one of the most beautifully preserved cathedrals in Castile. It's one of the rare Spanish towns that has not surrendered to modern development and sprawl. If you're coming from Madrid via the A2, the approach, through craggy hills and ravines, is dramatic. Sigüenza is an ideal base for exploring the countryside on foot or by bike, thanks to the Ruta de Don Quixote, a network of paths named for Cervantes's literary hero that passes through Sigüenza and nearby villages.

GETTING HERE AND AROUND

There are five train departures daily to Sigüenza from Madrid's Chamartín station, and the journey takes about 1½ hours. Sigüenza's train station is an easy walk from the historic walled center. Buses depart from Madrid's Avenida de América station once a day and take two hours. If you arrive by car, park near the train station to avoid the narrow cobblestone streets of the city center. Rideshares, such as Blablacar, are another option, provided there are trips that align with your schedule.

ESSENTIALS

BICYCLE RENTAL **Bicicletas del Olmo.** This company rents mountain bikes for €10 per day or €17 for two. Call ahead to reserve on busy holiday weekends. Note to parents: they don't have trailers or child seats. ✉ *Ctra. de Moratilla, nave 1* ☎ *94/939–0754, 60/578–7650.*

3

VISITOR
INFORMATION

Sigüenza Tourist Office. Guided tours depart daily from the tourist office in front of the cathedral at noon and 4:30, and at 5:15 May–September. A minimum of 10 people is required. ☒ *Calle Serrano Sanz 9* ☎ *94/934–7007* ⊕ *www.siguenza.es* ▧ *Tours €7.*

EXPLORING

FAMILY **Castillo de Sigüenza.** This enchanting castle overlooking wild, hilly countryside from above Sigüenza is now a parador. The structure was founded by the Romans and rebuilt at various later periods. Most of the current structure was erected in the 14th century, when it became a residence for the queen of Castile, Doña Blanca de Borbón, who was banished here by her husband, Pedro the Cruel. During the Spanish Civil War (1936–39), the castle was the scene of fierce battles, and much of the structure was destroyed. The parador's lobby has an exhibit on the subsequent restoration with photographs of the bomb damage. Nonguests can also visit the dining room and common areas. If you've got half an hour or so to spare, there's a lovely walking path around the hilltop castle with a 360-degree view of the city and countryside below. ☒ *Pl. de Castillo.*

Catedral de Sigüenza. Begun around 1150 and completed in the 16th century, Sigüenza's cathedral combines Spanish architecture dating from the Romanesque period to the Renaissance. Upon entering, ask the sacristan (the officer in charge of the care of the sacristy, which holds sacred vestments) to access the cathedral's wealth of ornamental and artistic masterpieces. From there, take a guided tour from the late-Gothic cloister to a room lined with 17th-century Flemish tapestries and onto the north transept, where the 15th-century plateresque sepulchre of Dom Fadrique of Portugal is housed. The Chapel of the Doncel (to the right of the sanctuary) contains Don Martín Vázquez de Arca's tomb, commissioned by Queen Isabella, to whom Don Martín served as *doncel* (page) before dying young (at 25) at the gates of Granada in 1486. Tours of the cathedral's catacombs, on weekends only, are run by the Museo Diocesano de Sigüenza. ☒ *Calle Serrano Sanz 2* ☎ *61/936–2715* ▧ *Free; €4 for tour of chapel, cloister, and tower.*

FAMILY **Museo Diocesano de Sigüenza** (*Diocesan Museum of Sacred Art*). In a refurbished early-19th-century house next to the cathedral's west facade, the small Diocesan Museum has a prehistoric section and mostly religious art from the 12th to 18th century. It also runs the tours of the burial chambers (catacombs) under the cathedral—a spooky favorite for kids. ☒ *Pl. Obispo Don Bernardo* ☎ *94/939–1023* ▧ *From €1 (free on 3rd Wed. of month).*

Plaza Mayor. The south side of the cathedral overlooks this harmonious, arcaded Renaissance square. The plaza hosts a medieval market on weekends. Legend has it, a group of American tycoons found the plaza so charming that they offered to buy it, in order to reconstruct it, piece by piece, stateside. ☒ *Sigüenza* ⊕ *www.siguenza.es.*

FAMILY **Tren Medieval.** Leaving from Madrid's Chamartín station, this delightful medieval-themed train service runs to Sigüenza mid-April–mid-November. The (otherwise thoroughly modern) train comes populated with minstrels, jugglers, and other entertainers, and it's a great activity for children. The ticket price includes round-trip fare, guided visit to Sigüenza, entry to all monuments and museums, and discounts at area restaurants. ✉ *Sigüenza* ☎ *90/232–0320* 🌐 *www.renfe.com/trenesturisticos/otros-trenes-renfe.html* 🎫 *€35 round-trip* 🕓 *Closed mid-Nov.–mid-Apr.*

WHERE TO EAT AND STAY

$$ TAPAS FAMILY Fodor's Choice ★

🍴 **Bar Alameda.** This family-run bar and restaurant punches above its weight with market-driven tapas that reflect a sense of place. Spring for the stuffed foraged mushrooms or seared Sigüenza-style blood sausage. **Known for:** thoughtfully prepared tapas; local wines by the glass; family-friendly atmosphere. [$] *Average main: €15* ✉ *Calle de la Alameda 2* ☎ *94/939–0553* 💳 *No credit cards* 🕓 *Closed Thurs.*

$$$ HOTEL FAMILY Fodor's Choice ★

🏨 **Parador de Sigüenza.** This fairy-tale 12th-century castle has hosted royalty for centuries, from Ferdinand and Isabella right up to Spain's present king, Felipe VI. **Pros:** excellent food; sense of history and place; plenty of parking. **Cons:** much of castle is a neo-medieval replica; bland, modern furniture that doesn't jibe with the space; occasionally surly service. [$] *Rooms from: €140* ✉ *Pl. del Castillo* ☎ *94/939–0100* 🌐 *www.parador.es* 🛏 *81 rooms* 🍽 *Free Breakfast.*

CASTILE AND LEÓN

This is Spain's dusty, rugged interior, stretching from the sweeping plains of Castile–La Mancha to the hilly vineyards of Ribera del Duero, and up to the foot of several mountain ranges: the Sierra de Gredos, Sierra de Francia, and northward toward the towering Picos de Europa. The area combines two of Spain's old kingdoms, Léon and Old Castile, each with their many treasures of palaces, castles, and cathedrals. Segovia and Salamanca are cultural highlights, and Ávila remains one of Europe's best-preserved medieval walled cities.

SEGOVIA

91 km (57 miles) north of Madrid.

Fodor's Choice ★

Medieval Segovia rises on a steep ridge that juts above a stark, undulating plain. It's defined by its ancient monuments, excellent cuisine, embroideries and textiles, and small-town charm. An important military town in Roman times, Segovia was later established by the Moors as a major textile center. Captured by the Christians in 1085, it was enriched by a royal residence, and in 1474 the half-sister of Henry IV, Isabella the Catholic (married to Ferdinand of Aragón), was crowned queen of Castile here. By that time Segovia was a bustling city of about 60,000 (its population is about 80,000 today), but its importance soon diminished as a result of its taking the losing side of the Comuneros in the popular revolt against Emperor Carlos V. Though the construction of a royal palace in nearby La Granja in the 18th century somewhat revived Segovia's fortunes, it never recovered its former vitality. Early in the 20th century, Segovia's sleepy charm came to be appreciated by artists and writers, among them painter Ignacio Zuloaga and poet Antonio

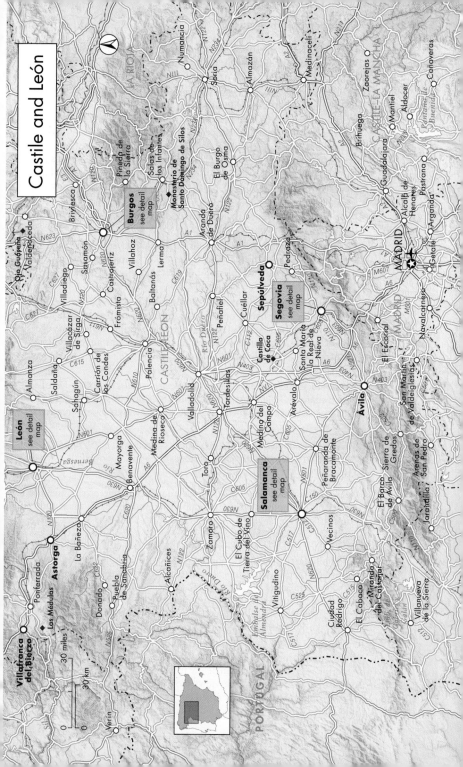

Castile and León

Machado. Today the streets swarm with day-trippers from Madrid—if you can, visit sometime other than in summer, and spend the night.

Tourists on a day trip from Madrid generally hit the triumvirate of basic sights: the aqueduct, the Alcázar, and the cathedral. If you have time, an overnight visit will allow you to sample Segovia's renowned food and nightlife in the Plaza Mayor, where you'll see Segovianos of all ages out until the early hours.

GETTING HERE AND AROUND

High-speed AVE trains from Madrid's Chamartín station—the fastest and costliest option—take 30 minutes and drop you at the Guiomar station, about 7 km (4 miles) outside Segovia's center. Bus Nos. 11 and 12 are timed to coincide with arriving trains. Bus No. 11 will take you to the foot of the aqueduct after about a 15-minute ride, and No. 12 drops you near the bus station.

La Sepulvedana buses depart Madrid (Moncloa station) for Segovia some 28 times a day. Direct routes take 55 minutes and cost €8 each way. There are also plentiful Blablacar options. (Check ⊕ *www. blablacar.com* or the app for details.)

Urbanos de Segovia operates the 13 inner-city bus lines and one tourist line, which are better options for getting around than struggling through the narrow streets (and problematic parking) with a car. Segovia's central bus station is a five-minute walk from the aqueduct along the car-free Paseo de Ezequiel González.

ESSENTIALS

Bus Contacts Bus Station. ⊠ *Paseo de Ezequiel González* ☎ *92/142–7705.* **La Sepulvedana.** ⊠ *Pl. la Estación de Autobuses* ☎ *90/211–9699* ⊕ *www.lasepulvedana.es.* **Urbanos de Segovia.** ☎ *90/233–0080* ⊕ *www.segovia.avanzagrupo.com.*

Visitor Information Segovia Tourist Office. ⊠ *Azoguejo 1* ☎ *92/146–6720, 92/146–6721* ⊕ *www.turismodesegovia.com.*

EXPLORING

Fodors Choice ★ **Acueducto Romano.** Segovia's Roman aqueduct is one of the greatest surviving examples of Roman engineering and the city's main sight. Stretching from the walls of the old town to the lower slopes of the Sierra de Guadarrama, it's about 2,952 feet long and rises in two tiers to a height of 115 feet. The raised section of stonework in the center originally carried an inscription, of which only the holes for the bronze letters remain. Neither mortar nor clamps hold the massive granite blocks together, but miraculously, the aqueduct has stood since the end of the 1st century AD. ⊠ *Pl. del Azoguejo.*

FAMILY Fodors Choice ★ **Alcázar.** Possibly dating to Roman times, this castle was considerably expanded in the 14th century, remodeled in the 15th, altered again toward the end of the 16th, and completely reconstructed after being gutted by a fire in 1862, when it was used as an artillery school. The exterior, especially when seen below from the Ruta Panorámica, is awe-inspiring, as are the superb views from the ramparts. Its crenellated towers appear to have been carved out of icing (it's widely believed that the Walt Disney logo is modeled after this castle's silhouette). Inside,

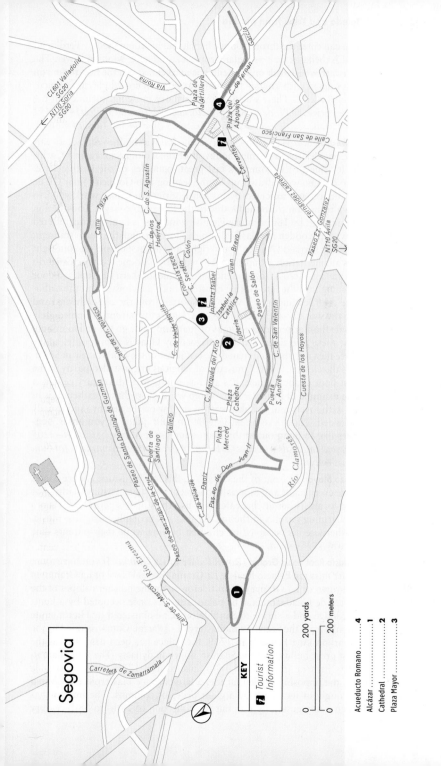

Segovia

KEY

i Tourist Information

| 0 | 200 yards |
| 0 | 200 meters |

Acueducto Romano **4**
Alcázar **1**
Cathedral **2**
Plaza Mayor **3**

you can enter the throne room, chapel, and bedroom used by Ferdinand and Isabella as well as a claustrophobia-inducing winding tower. The intricate woodwork on the ceiling is marvelous, and the first room you enter, lined with knights in shining armor, is a crowd pleaser, particularly for kids. There's also a small armory museum, included in the ticket price. ⊠ *Pl. de la Reina Victoria* ☎ *92/146–0759, 92/146–0452* ⊕ *www.alcazardesegovia.com* ✉ *From €3 (free on 3rd Tues. of month).*

Fodor's Choice **Cathedral.** Segovia's 16th-century cathedral was built to replace an ear-
★ lier one destroyed during the revolt of the Comuneros against Carlos V. It's one of the country's last great examples of the Gothic style. The designs were drawn up by the leading late-Gothicist Juan Gil de Hontañón and executed by his son Rodrigo, in whose work you can see a transition from the Gothic to the Renaissance style. The interior, illuminated by 16th-century Flemish windows, is light and uncluttered (save the wooden neoclassical choir). Enter through the north transept, which is marked "Museo"; turn right, and the first chapel on your right has a lamentation group carved in wood by baroque sculptor Gregorio Fernández. Across from the entrance, on the southern transept, is a door opening into the late-Gothic cloister—both the cloister and the elabo-rate door leading into it were transported from the old cathedral and are the work of architect Juan Guas. Under the pavement immediately inside the cloister are the tombs of Juan and Rodrigo Gil de Hontañón; that these two lie in a space designed by Guas is appropriate, as the three men together dominated the last phase of the Gothic style in Spain. Off the cloister, a small museum of religious art, installed partly in the first-floor chapter house, has a white-and-gold 17th-century ceiling, a late example of Mudejar *artesonado* work. At night the cathedral is lit up with lovely amber lights, casting a glow on the nearby (and usually crowded) Plaza Mayor. ■TIP➜ Be on your guard as you enter: beg-gars like to hang out at the main door. ⊠ *Pl. Mayor* ☎ *92/146–2205* ⊕ *www.catedralsegovia.es* ✉ *From €3 (free cathedral entrance for Sun. Mass only).*

Plaza Mayor. In front of the cathedral, this lovely historic square comes alive every night and especially on weekends, when visiting madrileños and locals gather at chic cafés that line the square's perimeter. There's a charming gazebo in the middle that occasionally hosts live music. (Otherwise it's occupied by children playing while their parents dine nearby.) ⊠ *Segovia.*

OFF THE BEATEN PATH

Palacio Real de La Granja (*Royal Palace of La Granja*). If you have a car, don't miss the Palacio Real de La Granja (Royal Palace of La Granja) in the town of La Granja de San Ildefonso, on the northern slopes of the Sierra de Guadarrama. The palace site was once occupied by a hunt-ing lodge and a shrine to San Ildefonso, administered by Hieronymite monks from the Segovian monastery of El Parral. Commissioned by the Bourbon king Felipe V in 1719, the palace has been described as the first great building of the Spanish Bourbon dynasty. The Italian archi-tects Juvarra and Sachetti, who finished it in 1739, were responsible for the imposing garden facade, a late-baroque masterpiece anchored throughout its length by a giant order of columns. The interior has been badly gutted by fire, but the collection of 15th- to 18th-century

Segovia's Roman aqueduct, built over 2,000 years ago, is remarkably well preserved.

tapestries warrants a visit. Even if you don't go into the palace, walk through the magnificent gardens: terraces, ornamental ponds, lakes, classical statuary, woods, and baroque fountains dot the mountainside. On Wednesday, Saturday, and Sunday evenings in the summer (April–August, 5:30–7 pm), the illuminated fountains are turned on, one by one, creating an effect to rival that of Versailles. The starting time has been known to change on a whim, so call ahead. ✉ *Pl. de España 15, about 11 km (7 miles) southeast of Segovia on N601, San Ildefonso* ☎ *92/147–0019, 92/147–0020* 🌐 *www.patrimonionacional.es* 🎫 *From €4.*

WHERE TO EAT

$$$$ SPANISH

🍴 **Casa Duque.** This is Segovia's oldest continuously operated restaurant, founded in 1895 and still run by the same family. The rustic interior, with wood beams and bric-a-brac hanging on the walls, suits the unfussy (if overpriced) cuisine, which features roast meats and stewed broad beans. **Known for:** ultratender cochinillo asado (roast suckling pig); tourist-friendly menus and service; historic setting. [$] *Average main: €30* ✉ *Calle Cervantes 12* ☎ *92/146–2487, 92/146–2486* 🌐 *www.restauranteduque.es.*

$$$ SPANISH Fodor's Choice ★

🍴 **El Fogón Sefardí.** This tavern in Segovia's historic Jewish quarter is owned by La Casa Mudejar Hospedería hotel and wins awards year after year for the region's best tapas. The menu is exquisite, featuring segoviano specialties like cochinillo as well as traditional Sephardic Jewish cuisine (though it's not a kosher kitchen), plus a variety of well-executed *raciones* (tapas). **Known for:** traditional Sephardic Jewish cuisine;

cochinillo; generous salads. $ *Average main: €20* ⊠ *Calle Judería Vieja 17* ☎ *92/146–6250* ⊕ *www.lacasamudejar.com* ▬ *No credit cards.*

$$$$ ✕**Mesón de Cándido.** Beginning life as an inn near the end of the 18th
SPANISH century, this restaurant beneath the aqueduct was declared a national monument in 1941. Amid the dark-wood beams and Castilian knick-knacks hang photos of celebrities who have dined here, among them Ernest Hemingway and Princess Grace. **Known for:** cochinillo; partridge stew; famous former patrons like Ernest Hemingway. $ *Average main: €30* ⊠ *Pl. de Azoguejo 5* ☎ *92/142–5911* ⊕ *www.mesondecandido.es.*

$$$$ ✕**Mesón de José María.** According to foodies, this old-timey mesón (tra-
SPANISH ditional tavern-restaurant) serves the most delectable cochinillo asado
Fodor's Choice (roast suckling pig) in town, but there are plenty of lighter, fresher dishes
★ to choose from as well. Expect a boisterous mix of locals and tourists. **Known for:** best cochinillo in town; beamed dining room; local crowd (a rarity in this touristy town). $ *Average main: €35* ⊠ *Calle Cronista Lecea 11, off Pl. Mayor* ☎ *92/146–1111, 92/146–6017* ⊕ *www.restaurantejosemaria.com.*

WHERE TO STAY

$$ ⊡**Infanta Isabel Hotel.** Perched on the corner of Plaza Mayor, this clas-
HOTEL sically appointed hotel boasts cathedral views in a bustling shopping area. **Pros:** lived-in, cozy ambience; central location; some rooms have balconies overlooking the plaza. **Cons:** some rooms are cramped and oddly shaped; rooms facing the plaza can be noisy on weekends; decidedly unhip decor. $ *Rooms from: €120* ⊠ *Pl. Mayor 12* ☎ *92/146–1300* ⊕ *www.hotelinfantaisabel.com* ⇗ *37 rooms* ⍥*No meals.*

$$ ⊡**La Casa Mudejar Hospedería.** Built in the 15th century as a Mudejar
HOTEL palace, this historical property has spacious rooms and a well-priced spa (€24 per person) that's extremely popular, even with nonguests. **Pros:** terrific restaurant serving rare Sephardic dishes; historic building with Roman ruins; affordable spa. **Cons:** forgettable interiors; no nearby parking; beds nothing special. $ *Rooms from: €100* ⊠ *Calle Isabel la Católica 8* ☎ *92/146–6250* ⊕ *www.lacasamudejar.com* ⇗ *40 rooms* ⍥*No meals.*

$$$ ⊡**Parador de Segovia.** From the large windows of this modern-style
HOTEL parador, 3 km (2 miles) from the old town, you can take in spectacular views of the cathedral and aqueduct. **Pros:** beautiful views of the city; sunny, picturesque pool area; spacious rooms. **Cons:** need a car to get here; uncozy, passé decor; lacks antique touches of more historic paradores. $ *Rooms from: €130* ⊠ *Crta. de Valladolid* ☎ *92/144–3737* ⊕ *www.parador.es* ⇗ *113 rooms* ⍥*No meals.*

SHOPPING

After Toledo, the province of Segovia is Castile's most important area for traditional artisanry. Glass and crystal are specialties of La Granja, and ironwork, lace, basketry, and embroidery are famous in Segovia. You can buy good lace from the Romani vendors in Segovia's Plaza del Alcázar, but be prepared for some strenuous bargaining, and never offer more than half the opening price. The area around Plaza San Martín is a good place to buy crafts.

Calle Daoíz. Leading to the Alcázar, this street overflows with locally made (if tourist-oriented) ceramics, textiles, and gift shops. ⊠ *Segovia.*

Plaza San Martín. Several excellent antique shops line this small plaza. ⊠ *Segovia.*

Salchicherías Briz. The city's best artisanal sausages—from chorizo to morcilla (blood sausage) to lomo (cured pork loin)—can be found at this 40-year-old butcher shop. The cured meats travel well and can be kept for months at a cool room temperature. ⊠ *Calle Fernández Ladreda 20, Segovia* ☎ *92/146–1755* ⊕ *www.salchicheriabriz.es.*

SEPÚLVEDA

58 km (36 miles) northeast of Segovia.

A walled village with a commanding position, Sepúlveda has a charming main square, but the main reasons to visit are its 11th-century Romanesque church and striking gorge with a scenic hiking trail.

GETTING HERE AND AROUND

Sepúlveda is about an hour north of Madrid on the A1. There are also several buses (and Blablacar rideshares) a day from both Segovia and Madrid. The city is perched atop a hill overlooking a ravine, so you'll likely want transportation to the top. Don't park or get off the bus too soon.

ESSENTIALS

Visitor Information Sepúlveda Tourist Office. ⊠ *Pl. del Trigo 6* ☎ *92/154–0237* ⊕ *www.sepulveda.es.*

EXPLORING

El Salvador. This 11th-century church is the oldest Romanesque church in Segovia Province. The carvings on its capitals, probably by a Moorish convert, are quite outlandish. ⊠ *Calle Subida a El Salvador 10.*

Fodor'sChoice ★ **San Frutos.** This 11th-century monastery is in ruins, but its location, on a peninsula jutting out into a bend 100 meters above the Duratón River, is extraordinary. You'll need a car to get there, about 15 minutes' drive west of Sepúlveda. Stay on the marked paths—the surrounding area is natural park and a protected nesting ground for rare vultures—and try to go at sunset, when the light enhances spectacular views of the sandstone monastery and river below. Inside the monastery, there's a small chapel and plaque describing the life of San Frutos, the patron saint of Segovia. An ancient pilgrimage route stretches 77 km (48 miles) from the monastery to Segovia's cathedral, and pilgrims still walk it each year. As an add-on to the trip, you can rent kayaks from **NaturalTur** (☎ *921/521727* ⊕ *www.naturaltur.com*) to paddle the river. ⊕ *www. caminodesanfrutos.org* 🎫 *Free.*

OFF THE BEATEN PATH

Castillo de Coca. Perhaps the most famous medieval sight near Segovia—worth the 52 km (32-mile) detour northwest of the city en route to Ávila or Valladolid—is the Castillo de Coca. Built in the 15th century for Archbishop Alonso de Fonseca I, the castle is a turreted Mudejar structure of plaster and red brick surrounded by a deep moat. Highly Instgrammable, it looks like a stage set for a fairy tale, and, indeed, it

Ávila's city walls, which still encircle the old city, have a perimeter of about 2.5 km (1½ miles).

was intended not as a fortress but as a place for the notoriously pleasure-loving archbishop to hold riotous parties. The interior, now occupied by a forestry school, has been modernized, with only fragments of the original decoration preserved. ⊠ *C. Antigua Cauca Romana, Coca* ☎ *92/158–6622, 61/757–3554* ⊕ *www.castillodecoca.com* ✉ *€3* ⊗ *Closed Jan.*

ÁVILA

114 km (71 miles) northwest of Madrid.

In the middle of a windy plateau littered with giant boulders, with the Sierra de Gredos in the background, Ávila is a walled fairy-tale town that wouldn't look out of place in *Game of Thrones*. Shortly after the town was reclaimed from the Moors in 1090, crenulated walls were erected in just nine years—thanks to the employment of an estimated 1,900 builders. The walls have nine gates and 88 cylindrical towers bunched together, making them unique to Spain in form—they're quite unlike the Moorish defense architecture that the Christians adapted elsewhere. They're most striking when seen from afar; for the best views (and photos), cross the Adaja River, turn right on the Carretera de Salamanca, and walk uphill about 250 yards to a monument of pilasters surrounding a cross known as the "Four Posts."

The walls reflect Ávila's strength during the Middle Ages. Populated during the reign of Alfonso VI by Christians, many of whom were nobles, the town came to be known as Ávila of the Knights. Decline set in at the beginning of the 15th century with the gradual departure of the nobility to the court of Carlos V in Toledo. Ávila's later fame was largely due to St. Teresa. Born here in 1515 to a noble family of Jewish origin, Teresa spent much of her life in Ávila, leaving a legacy of convents and the ubiquitous *yemas* (candied egg yolks), originally distributed free to the poor and now sold for high prices to tourists. Ávila is well preserved, but it can feel a tad sad and austere, particularly in the cold-weather months. Its quiet is dispelled, however, during the Fiestas de la Santa Teresa in October; the weeklong celebration includes lighted decorations, parades, singing in the streets, and religious observances.

GETTING HERE AND AROUND

Jiménez Dorado (⊕ *www.jimenezdorado.com*) and Avilabus (⊕ *www. avilabus.com*) serve Ávila and its surrounding villages. Twenty-three trains depart for Ávila each day from Chamartín station, and there are usually plentiful Blablacar rideshares available. The city itself is easily managed on foot.

ESSENTIALS

Visitor Information Ávila Tourist Office. ⊠ *Pl. de la Catedral, Av. de Madrid 39* ☎ *92/021–1387* ⊕ *www.avilaturismo.com.*

EXPLORING

Fodor'sChoice
★

Catedral de San Salvador. The battlement apse of Ávila's cathedral forms the most impressive part of the city's walls. Entering the town gate to the right of the apse, you can reach the sculpted north portal by turning left and walking a few steps. The west portal, flanked by 18th-century towers, is notable for the crude carvings of hairy male figures on each side. Known as "wild men," these figures appear in many Castilian palaces of this period. The Transitional Gothic structure, with its granite nave, is considered to be the first Gothic cathedral in Spain. The Lisbon earthquake of 1755 shattered its Flemish stained glass, so the main note of color appears in the yellow and red mottled stone in the apse. Plateresque choir stalls built in 1547 complement the soaring altar by painters Juan de Borgoña and Pedro Berruguete. On the ambulatory wall, look for the early-16th-century marble sepulchre of Bishop Alonso de Madrigal, a remarkably lifelike representation of the bishop seated at his writing table. Known as El Tostado (the Toasted One) for his swarthy complexion, the bishop was a tiny man of enormous intellect and author of 54 books. When on one occasion Pope Eugenius IV ordered him to stand—mistakenly thinking him to still be on his knees—the bishop pointed to the space between his eyebrows and hairline, and retorted, "A man's stature is to be measured from here to here!" ⊠ *Pl. de la Catedral s/n* ☎ *92/021–1641* ⊕ *catedralavila.es* 💶 *€6.*

Convento de Santa Teresa. This Carmelite convent was founded in the 17th century on the site of the saint's birthplace. Teresa's account of an ecstatic vision, in which an angel pierced her heart, inspired many baroque artists, most famously the Italian sculptor Giovanni Bernini. The convent has a small museum with relics including one of Teresa's fingers. You can also see the small and rather gloomy garden where she played as a child. ⊠ *Pl. de la Santa 2* ☎ *92/021–1030* ⊕ *www.santateresadejesus.com* 💶 *Church and reliquary free; museum €2.*

Mysticism Interpretation Center. The only such museum of its kind in Europe, this small modern museum is devoted to mysticism, the idea made famous by Ávila's native daughter, St. Teresa—one of Christianity's first female mystics. Exhibits explain the role of mysticism in Judaism, Christianity, and a number of Eastern religions. While the exterior of the building, a medieval house, is original, architects installed a giant prism ceiling that reflects light throughout the interior. ✉ *Paseo del Rastro s/n* ☎ *92/021–2154* 🌐 *www.avilamistica.es* 🎟 *€3.*

Real Monasterio de Santo Tomás. In a most unlikely location—among housing projects a good 10-minute walk from the walls—is one of the most important religious institutions in Castile. The monastery was founded by Ferdinand and Isabella with the financial assistance of the notorious Inquisitor-General Tomás de Torquemada, who is buried in the sacristy. Further funds were provided by the confiscated property of converted Jews who were dispossessed during the Inquisition. Three decorated cloisters lead to the church; inside, a masterful high altar (circa 1506) by Pedro Berruguete overlooks a serene marble tomb by the Italian artist Domenico Fancelli. One of the earliest examples of the Italian Renaissance style in Spain, this work was built for Prince Juan, the only son of Ferdinand and Isabella, who died at 19. After Juan's burial here, his heartbroken parents found themselves unable to return; in happier times, they attended mass here, seated in the upper choir behind a balustrade exquisitely carved with their coats of arms. There are free guided tours at 6 pm on weekends and holidays. The monastery also includes a quirky museum of Asian art collected by missionaries who traveled to the East. ✉ *Pl. de Granada 1* ☎ *92/022–0400* 🌐 *www.monasteriosantotomas.com* 🎟 *€4.*

WHERE TO EAT AND STAY

$$$ SPANISH 🍴 **Las Cancelas.** Locals flock to this little tavern for the tapas and fat, juicy steaks served in the boisterous barroom or white-tablecloth dining area, set in a covered courtyard. There are 14 hotel rooms available, too—simple, slightly ramshackle arrangements at moderate prices. **Known for:** chuletón de Ávila (gargantuan local steaks); quaint, romantic dining room; good value. [$] *Average main: €20* ✉ *Calle de la Cruz Vieja 6* ☎ *92/021–2249* 🌐 *www.lascancelas.com* 🕓 *Closed early Jan.–early Feb. No dinner Sun.*

$$$$ SPANISH FAMILY 🍴 **Restaurante El Molino de la Losa.** Sitting at the edge of the serene Adaja River, El Molino, housed in a 15th-century mill, enjoys one of the best views of the town walls. Lamb, the restaurant's specialty, is roasted in a medieval wood oven, and the beans from nearby El Barco de Ávila (*judías de El Barco*) are famous. **Known for:** succulent roast lamb; views of the river and city walls; refined cuisine. [$] *Average main: €30* ✉ *Calle Bajada de la Losa 12* ☎ *92/021–1101, 92/021–1102* 🌐 *www.elmolinodelalosa.com* 🕓 *No dinner Sun.*

$$$ HOTEL Fodor's Choice ★ 🏨 **Palacio de los Velada.** Ávila's top four-star hotel occupies a beautifully restored 16th-century palace in the heart of the city next to the cathedral, an ideal spot if you like to relax between sightseeing. **Pros:** gorgeous glass-covered patio; amiable service; bountiful breakfast buffet. **Cons:** some rooms don't have views because the windows are so high; expensive off-site parking; lack of power outlets. [$] *Rooms from:*

€150 ✉ *Pl. de la Catedral 10* ☎ *92/025–5100* 🌐 *www.veladahoteles.com* 🛏 *145 rooms* 🍴 *No meals.*

$$$ **HOTEL** **FAMILY** **Parador de Ávila.** This largely rebuilt 16th-century medieval castle is attached to the massive town walls, and a standout feature is its lush garden containing archaeological ruins. **Pros:** gorgeous garden and views; good restaurant; family-friendly rooms and services. **Cons:** long walk into town; interiors need a refresh; underwhelming breakfast. [$] *Rooms from: €160* ✉ *Marqués de Canales de Chozas 2* ☎ *92/021–1340* 🌐 *www.parador.es* 🛏 *61 rooms* 🍴 *No meals.*

SALAMANCA

212 km (132 miles) northwest of Madrid.

Fodor's Choice ★ Salamanca's radiant sandstone buildings, immense Plaza Mayor, and hilltop riverside perch make it one of the most majestic and beloved cities in Spain. Today, as it did centuries ago, the university imbues the city with an intellectual verve, a stimulating arts scene, and raging nightlife to match. You'll see more foreign students here per capita than anywhere else in Spain.

If you approach from Madrid or Ávila, your first glimpse of Salamanca will be of the city rising on the northern banks of the wide and winding Tormes River. In the foreground is its sturdy, 15-arch Roman bridge; soaring above it is the combined bulk of the old and new cathedrals. Piercing the skyline to the right is the Renaissance monastery and church of San Esteban. Behind San Esteban and the cathedrals, and largely out of sight from the river, extends a stunning series of palaces, convents, and university buildings that culminates in the Plaza Mayor. Despite enduring considerable damage over the centuries, Salamanca remains one of Spain's greatest cities architecturally, a showpiece of the Spanish Renaissance.

GETTING HERE AND AROUND

You'll probably feel rushed if you try to visit Salamanca from Toldeo in an out-and-back day trip: to take in its splendor, plan on an overnight. Approximately 13 trains depart Madrid for Salamanca daily, several of which are high-speed ALVIA itineraries that take just over an hour and a half. Avanza buses leave from the Estación Sur de Autobuses; Blablacar rideshares (about 2 hours and 15 minutes) are faster and more affordable.

Once in town, Salamanca de Transportes runs 64 municipal buses equipped with lifts for passengers with disabilities on routes throughout the city of Salamanca. You may opt to take a bus in order to reach the train and bus stations on the outskirts of the city.

Intracity Bus Contact **Salamanca de Transportes.** ☎ *92/319–0545* 🌐 *www.salamancadetransportes.com.*

ESSENTIALS

Visitor Information **Salamanca Municipal Tourist Office.** ✉ *Pl. Mayor 32* ☎ *92/321–8342* 🌐 *www.salamanca.es.* **Salamanca Regional Tourist Office.** ✉ *Rúa Mayor s/n* ☎ *92/326–8571, 90/220–3030* 🌐 *www.salamanca.es.*

EXPLORING

Fodor'sChoice
★ **Casa de Las Conchas** (*House of Shells*). This house, whose facade is covered in scallop shell carvings, was built around 1500 for Dr. Rodrigo Maldonado de Talavera, a chancellor of the Order of St. James, whose symbol is the shell. Among the playful plateresque details are the lions over the main entrance, engaged in a fearful tug-of-war with the Talavera crest. The interior has been converted into a public library. Duck into the charming courtyard, which has an intricately carved upper balustrade that imitates basketwork. ⊠ *Calle Compañía 2* ☎ *92/326–9317* 🖾 *Free.*

> ### FONSECA'S MARK
>
> Nearly all of Salamanca's outstanding Renaissance buildings bear the five-star crest of the all-powerful and ostentatious Fonseca family. The most famous of them, Alonso de Fonseca I, was the archbishop of Santiago and then of Seville; he was also a notorious womanizer and a patron of the Spanish Renaissance.

Fodor'sChoice
★ **Cathedrals.** For a complete exterior tour of Salamanca's old and new cathedrals, take a 10-minute walk around the complex. Nearest the river stands the **Catedral Vieja** (Old Cathedral), built in the late 12th century and one of the most interesting examples of the Spanish Romanesque. Because the dome of the crossing tower has strange, plumelike ribbing, it's known as the Torre del Gallo (Rooster's Tower). The two cathedrals are part of the same complex, though they have different visiting hours, and you need to enter the new one to get to the Old Cathedral.

The much larger **Catedral Nueva** (New Cathedral) was built between 1513 and 1526 under the late-Gothic architect Juan Gil de Hontañón. Take a moment to marvel at the west facade, dazzling in its sculptural complexity.

The interior of the New Cathedral is a harmonious baroque effusion designed by the Churriguera family with carvings of cherubim, foliage, and strange animals. The dome, Byzantine in form, achieves a remarkably airy effect, thanks to two tiers of arcaded openings. Not the least of the Old Cathedral's attractions are its furnishings, including sepulchres from the 12th and 13th centuries and a curved high altar comprising 53 colorful and delicate scenes by the mid-15th-century artist Nicolás Florentino. In the apse above, Florentino painted an astonishingly fresh Last Judgment fresco.

From the south transept of the Old Cathedral, a door leads into the cloister, which was begun in 1177. The ornate chair in front of the recumbent effigy of Bishop Juan Lucero is a relic of a time when theology scholars studied in the chapels around the cloister, between the 13th and 15th centuries. ⊠ *Pl. de Anaya and Calle Cardenal Pla y Deniel* ☎ *92/321–7476, 92/328–1123* ⊕ *www.catedralsalamanca.org* 🖾 *Catedral Nueva free, Catedral Vieja €5 (free Tues. 10–noon).*

Fodor'sChoice
★ **Convento de Las Dueñas** (*Convent of the Dames*). Founded in 1419, this convent hides a 16th-century cloister that is the most fantastically decorated in Salamanca, if not in all of Spain. The capitals of its two superimposed Salmantine arcades are crowded with a baffling

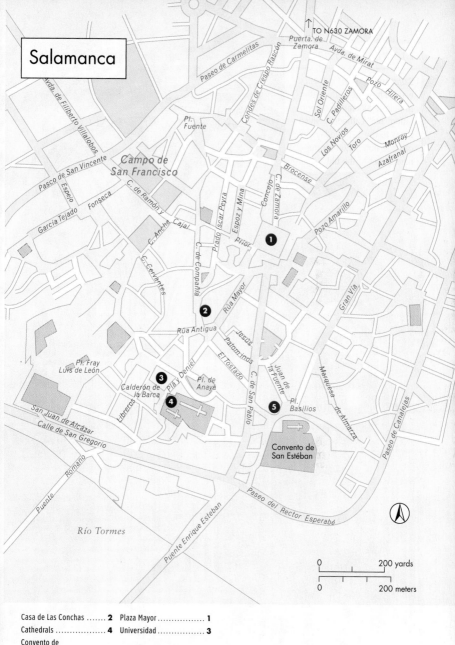

Salamanca

TO N630 ZAMORA

Puerta de Zamora

Avda. de Mirat

Paseo de Carmelitas

Condes de Crespo Rascón

Sol Oriente

C. Padilleros

Pozo Hilera

Los Novios

Toro

Monroy

Azafranal

C. de Zamora

Brocense

Pozo Amarillo

Avda. de Filiberto Villalobos

Pl. Fuente

Campo de San Francisco

Paseo de San Vincente

Espejo

Fonseca

C. de Ramón y Cajal

C. Ancha

Prado Iscar. Peyra

Espoz y Mina

Prior

Concejo

Gran Vía

García Tejado

C. Cervantes

C. de Compañía

Rúa Mayor

Rúa Antigua

Jesús

Palominos

El Tostado

C. de San Pablo

Juan de la Fuente

Marquesa de Almarza

Paseo de Canalejas

Pl. Fray Luis de León

Calderón de la Barca

Pl. y Dániel

Pl. de Anaya

Pl. Basilios

San Juan de Alcázar

Libreros

Convento de San Estéban

Calle de San Gregorio

Puente Romano

Puente Enrique Estéban

Paseo del Rector Esperabé

Río Tormes

0 — 200 yards

0 — 200 meters

Casa de Las Conchas .... **2** Plaza Mayor **1**

Cathedrals .... **4** Universidad **3**

Convento de
Las Dueñas **5**

profusion of grotesques that can absorb you for hours. Don't forget to look down: the interlocking diamond pattern on the ground floor of the cloister is decorated with the knobby vertebrae of goats and sheep. It's an eerie yet perfect accompaniment to all the grinning, disfigured heads sprouting from the capitals looming above you. The museum has a fascinating exhibit on Spain's little-known slavery industry. And don't leave without buying some sweets—the nuns are excellent bakers. ⊠ *Pl. del Concilio de Trento s/n* ☎ *92/321–5442* 🖭 *€2.*

Fodor's Choice ★ **Plaza Mayor.** Built in the 1730s by Alberto and Nicolás Churriguera, Salamanca's Plaza Mayor is one of the largest and most beautiful squares in Spain. The lavishly elegant, pinkish **ayuntamiento** (city hall) dominates its northern side. The square and its arcades are popular gathering spots for salmantinos of all ages, and its *terrazas* are the perfect spot for a coffee break. At night, the plaza swarms with students meeting "under the clock" on the plaza's north side. *Tunas* (strolling musicians in traditional garb) often meander among the cafés and crowds, playing for smiles and applause rather than tips. The plaza was in the news in 2017 when, after decades of controversy, the infamous medallion portraying Franco was removed from one of its capitals. ⊠ *Pl. Mayor.*

Universidad. Parts of the university's walls, like those of the cathedral and other structures in Salamanca, are covered with large ocher lettering recording the names of famous university graduates. The earliest names are said to have been written in the blood of the bulls killed to celebrate the successful completion of a doctorate (call it medieval graffiti). The elaborate facade of the **Escuelas Mayores** (Upper Schools) dates to the early 16th century; see if you can spy the "lucky" frog that's become the symbol of the city—legend has it that students who spot the frog on their first try will pass all their exams.

The interior of the **Escuelas Mayores,** drastically restored in parts, is disappointing after the splendor of the facade and not worth entering unless you're a diehard Spanish literature buff. But if you are, the *aula* (lecture hall) of Fray Luis de León, where Cervantes, Pedro Calderón de la Barca, and numerous other luminaries of Spain's golden age once sat, is of particular interest, as is the grand library. Whatever you do, don't miss the serene courtyard (free entry) of the Escuelas Menores (Lower Schools) that wraps around the patio in front of the Escuelas Mayores. ⊠ *Calle Libreros* ☎ *92/329–4400, 95/222–2998* ⊕ *www.usal.es* 🖭 *Free to view the facade; €10 to enter (free Mon. morning).*

Universidad Pontificia. The ornate, towering complex of the university features a lovely baroque courtyard, but the highlight here is the early-16th-century Escalera Noble (Noble Staircase). The bottom of each flight is decorated with portrayals of games, tournaments, and bullfighting on horseback. From below, it provides one of the best architectural views in Salamanca. Founded in the 13th century as part of the University of Salamanca, the Universidad Pontificia was closed in 1854 after the Spanish government dissolved the University of Salamanca's faculties of theology and canon law in 1854. Reopened in the 1940s, the university continues to teach theology, philosophy, and canon law. Take note of the chapel's slightly cracked dome—the Lisbon earthquake of 1755 is to blame. ⊠ *Calle Compañía 5* ☎ *92/327–7100* ⊕ *www.upsa. es* 🎫 *Guided tours €3.*

WHERE TO EAT

$$
**TAPAS
✕Bambú.** Bambú is two restaurants in one: there's a jovial basement tapas bar serving gargantuan tapas and beers to hungry locals, and then there's the far more sedate white-tablecloth dining room, whose nueva cocina menu is subtler, fussier, and more expensive. Both are worthwhile options; go with the vibe that suits you best. **Known for:** free tapas with every drink at the bar; sedate nueva cocina dining room; friendly collegiate ambience. Ⓢ *Average main: €12* ⊠ *Calle Prior 4* ☎ *92/326–0092* ⊕ *www.cafeteriabambu.com.*

$$$$
SPANISH
Fodor'sChoice
★
✕La Hoja 21. Just off the Plaza Mayor, this upscale restaurant has a glass facade, high ceilings, butter-yellow walls, and minimalist art—a welcome relief from the dime-a-dozen Castilian dining spots. Savor traditional fare with a twist, such as ibérico pork ravioli and langoustine-stuffed trotters at dinner, or spring for the €16 lunch prix fixe, an absolute steal served Tuesday–Thursday. **Known for:** nuanced yet unpretentious modern fare; phenomenally affordable menú del día; romantic, low-key atmosphere. Ⓢ *Average main: €30* ⊠ *Calle San Pablo 21* ☎ *92/326–4028* ⊕ *www.lahoja21.com* ☯ *Closed Mon. No dinner Sun.*

$$
TAPAS
Fodor'sChoice
★
✕Tapas 2.0. This tapas bar is decidedly modern, dependably delicious, and shockingly cheap. The cool *ensaladilla rusa* (potato salad mixed with tuna), a specialty, is one of the best in Spain; then there are more substantial dishes, like "Momofuku-style" fried chicken and saucy lamb meatballs, all complemented by a wine list featuring unexpected wines like German Riesling. **Known for:** ensaladilla rusa; uncommon wines; the best tapas in town. Ⓢ *Average main: €14* ⊠ *Calle Felipe Espino 10* ☎ *92/321–6448* ⊕ *www.tapastrespuntocero.es.*

$$$
SPANISH
Fodor'sChoice
★
✕Valencia. Despite its Mediterranean name, this traditional, family-run restaurant serves up Castilian specialties like garlic soup, partridge salad, local river trout, white asparagus, and suckling lamb. The tiny front bar is decorated with black-and-white photos of local bullfighters, and is usually packed with locals (as is the back room), but the most privileged place to dine is outdoors on the square under the awnings. **Known for:** hidden-gem local hangout; soul-warming Castilian fare; outdoor seating. Ⓢ *Average main: €20* ⊠ *Calle Concejo 15* ☎ *92/321–7868* ⊕ *www.restaurantevalencia.com* ☯ *Closed Mon. Nov., Tues. Sept.–May, and Sun. June–Aug.*

WHERE TO STAY

$$$$
HOTEL
🛏Don Gregorio. This upscale boutique hotel has spacious, contemporary rooms in a building with roots in the 15th century. **Pros:** chic, contemporary facilities; complimentary cava upon arrival; spa and in-room massages. **Cons:** restaurant is expensive—the more casual cafeteria is a better bet; no outdoor space for lounging; some receptionists speak poor English. Ⓢ *Rooms from: €220* ⊠ *Calle San Pablo 80–82* ☎ *92/321–7015* ⊕ *www.hoteldongregorio.com* 🛏 *17 rooms* ❍❘ *Free Breakfast.*

$$$ HOTEL Fodor's Choice ★ 🏨 **Hotel Rector.** From the stately entrance to the high-ceiling guest rooms, this lovely hotel offers a fairy-tale European experience. **Pros:** terrific value for a luxury hotel; personal service; good location. **Cons:** parking costs extra; no balconies; breakfast could be more ample. [$] *Rooms from: €160* ✉ *Paseo Rector Esperabé 10* ☎ *92/321–8482* 🌐 *www.hotel-rector.com* 🛏 *13 rooms* 🍴 *No meals.*

$$ B&B/INN Fodor's Choice ★ 🏨 **Microtel Placentinos.** This is a lovely B&B tucked down a quiet pedestrian street in Salamanca's historic center, near the Palacio de Congresos convention center and a short walk from the Plaza Mayor. **Pros:** some rooms have whirlpool baths; quirky decor; short walk to bus station. **Cons:** rooms by interior staircase can be noisy; some accommodations are cramped; boring breakfast buffet. [$] *Rooms from: €95* ✉ *Calle Placentinos 9* ☎ *92/328–1531* 🌐 *www.microtelplacentinos.com* 🛏 *9 rooms* 🍴 *Free Breakfast.*

$ HOTEL 🏨 **Revolutum Hostel.** Embodying the swiftly growing hotel category of "designer hostel," this is the best budget option in Salamanca. **Pros:** breakfast included; all rooms have private bathrooms; special rates for families and longer stays. **Cons:** deposit required for towels; you have to make your own bed in some rooms; small bathrooms in some rooms. [$] *Rooms from: €49* ✉ *Calle Sánchez Barbero 7* ☎ *92/321–7656* 🌐 *www.revolutumhostel.com* 🛏 *20 rooms* 🍴 *Free Breakfast.*

NIGHTLIFE AND PERFORMING ARTS

Particularly in summer, Salamanca sees the greatest influx of foreign students of any city in Spain: by day they study Spanish, and by night they fill Salamanca's bars and clubs.

NIGHTLIFE

BARS AND CAFÉS **Café Corrillo.** This lively (if unstylish) restaurant-bar-café is the main hangout for fans of live music, especially jazz, and solid tapas seal the deal. Check the website for the concert list and special events like craft beer nights. ✉ *Calle Meléndez 18* ☎ *92/327–1917* 🌐 *www.cafecorrillo.com.*

Fodor's Choice ★ **The Doctor Cocktail Bar.** This petite, unpretentious *coctelería* off the Plaza Mayor serves an enormous breadth of drinks, from colorful tiki numbers (some with pyrotechnics) to Prohibition-era classics until 1:30 am daily. ✉ *Calle Doctor Pinuela 5* ☎ *92/326–3151.*

Gran Café Moderno. After-hours types end the night here, snacking on churros with chocolate at daybreak. ✉ *Gran Vía 75–77* ☎ *63/753–8165, 92/326–0147.*

La Posada de las Animas. Bask in the romantic glow from stained-glass lamps at this preferred cocktail-and-conversation nightspot for stylish students boasting more than 30 types of gin and rum. Wrought-iron chandeliers hang from high wood-beam ceilings, harp-strumming angels top elegant pillars, and one entire wall of shelves showcases a somewhat bizarre collection of colorful dollhouses. ✉ *Pl. San Boal 7* ☎ *92/321–2631* 🌐 *www.laposadadelasanimas.es.*

DANCE CLUB **Camelot.** After 11, well-dressed twenty- and thirtysomethings come to dance at Camelot, an ancient stone-wall warehouse in one corner of the 16th-century Convento de Las Ursulas. Hours vary, but things generally get going around 1 am. There's a sister club called Cubic Club around the corner on Calle Iscar Peira. ⊠ *Calle de los Bordadores 3* ☎ *92/321–9091, 92/321–2182* ⊕ *www.camelot.es.*

PERFORMING ARTS

Teatro Liceo. This 732-seat theater, 40 yards from Plaza Mayor, got a face-lift in 2002, but traces of the old 19th-century theater, built over an 18th-century convent, remain. It hosts classic and modern performances of opera, dance, and flamenco as well as film festivals. ⊠ *Calle del Toro 23* ☎ *92/328–0619.*

SHOPPING

El Rastro. On Sunday, this flea market—named after the larger one in Madrid—is held just outside Salamanca's historic center. Buses leave from Plaza de España. ⊠ *Av. de Aldehuela.*

Isisa Duende. If you have a car, skip the souvenir shops in Salamanca's center and instead head 35 km (22 miles) through the countryside along the rural SA300 road to Isisa Duende, a wooden crafts workshop run by a charming husband-and-wife team. Their music boxes, photo frames, and other items are carved with local themes, from the *bailes charros,* Salamanca's regional dance, to the floral designs embroidered on the hems of provincial dresses. With limited hours, it's best to call ahead to schedule a free, personal tour; if you're pressed for time, you can buy some of their wares in the tourist office on the Plaza Mayor. ⊠ *Calle San Miguel 1, Ledesma* ☎ *62/651–0527, 62/533–6703* ⊕ *www.isisa-duende.es/donde-trabajamos.*

FAMILY **Mercado Central.** At Salamanca's most historic market you can stock up on local gourmet specialties—such as farinato sausages, jamón ibérico, and sheep's cheeses—and round out your shopping spree with a glass of wine at any of the market's traditional tapas counters. The 53 stalls are sure to keep any foodie occupied. ⊠ *Pl. del Mercado* ☎ *92/321–3000* ⊕ *www.mercadocentralsalamanca.com.*

BURGOS

243 km (151 miles) north of Madrid on A1.

On the banks of the Arlanzón River, this small city boasts some of Spain's most outstanding medieval architecture. If you approach on the A1 from Madrid, the spiky twin spires of Burgos's cathedral, rising above the main bridge, welcome you to the city. Burgos's second pride is its heritage as the city of El Cid, the part-historical, part-mythical hero of the Christian Reconquest of Spain. The city has been known for centuries as a center of both militarism and religion, and even today more nuns fill the streets than almost anywhere else in Spain. Burgos was born as a military camp—a fortress built in 884 on the orders of the Christian king Alfonso III, who was struggling to defend the upper reaches of Old Castile from the constant forays of the Arabs. It quickly became vital in the defense of Christian Spain, and its reputation as an early outpost of Christianity was cemented with the founding of the Royal Convent of Las Huelgas, in 1187. Burgos also became a place of rest and sustenance for Christian pilgrims on the Camino de Santiago.

The small city of Burgos is famous for its magnigicent Gothic cathedral.

These days, it's also a food town, known for its namesake white cheese and morcilla (blood sausage bound with rice).

GETTING HERE AND AROUND

Burgos can be reached by train from Madrid, with 13 departures daily from Chamartín (2½ hours on the fast ALVIA train and 4½ on the regional line) and by bus, with hourly service from various Madrid stations. There are usually several Blablacar rideshares available as well. Once there, municipal buses cover 45 routes throughout the city, many of them originating in Plaza de España.

ESSENTIALS

Visitor Information Burgos Tourist Office. ⊠ *Calle Nuño Rasura 7* ☎ *94/728-8874* ⊕ *www.turismoburgos.org.*

EXPLORING

Fodor'sChoice
★

Cathedral. Start your tour of the city with the cathedral, which contains such a wealth of art and other treasures that the local burghers lynched their civil governor in 1869 for trying to take an inventory of it: the proud citizens feared that the man was plotting to steal their riches. Just as opulent as what's inside is the sculpted Flamboyant Gothic facade. The cornerstone was laid in 1221, and the two 275-foot towers were completed by the middle of the 14th century, though the final chapel was not finished until 1731. There are 13 chapels, the most elaborate of which is the hexagonal Condestable Chapel. You'll find the **tomb of El Cid** (1026–99) and his wife, Ximena, under the transept. El Cid (whose real name was Rodrigo Díaz de Vivar) was a feudal warlord revered for his victories over the Moors; the medieval *Song of My Cid* transformed him into a Spanish national hero.

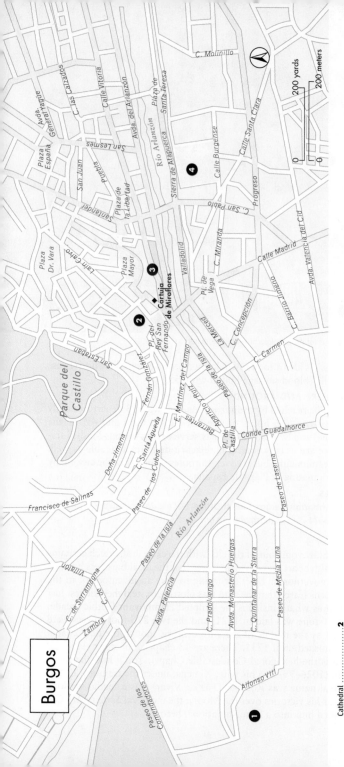

Burgos

At the other end of the cathedral, high above the West Door, is the **Reloj de Papamoscas** (Flycatcher Clock), so named for the sculptured bird that opens its mouth as the hands mark each hour. The grilles around the choir have some of the finest wrought-iron work in central Spain, and the choir itself has 103 delicately carved walnut stalls, no two alike. The 13th-century stained-glass windows that once shed a beautiful, filtered light were destroyed in 1813, one of many cultural casualties of Napoléon's retreating troops. ✉ *Pl. de Santa María* ☎ *94/720–4712* 🌐 *www.catedraldeburgos.es* 🎫 *€7.*

Espolón. The Arco de Santa María frames the city's loveliest promenade, the Espolón. Shaded with black poplars, it follows the riverbank. ✉ *Burgos.*

FAMILY Fodor's Choice ★ **Museo de la Evolución Humana.** This airy, modern complex is one of the best natural history museums in the world and traces human evolution from primate to the present day. There are life-size replicas of our ancient ancestors, plus hands-on exhibits and in-depth scientific explanations (in English) that will fascinate visitors of all ages. Pair with a museum-led visit to the Atapuerca archaeological site (inquire at reception or online to arrange). ✉ *Paseo Sierra de Atapuerca* ☎ *94/725–7103* 🌐 *www.museoevolucionhumana.com* 🎫 *€6* 🕒 *Closed Mon.*

Monasterio de Santa María La Real de Las Huelgas (*Monasterio de las Huelgas*). This convent on the outskirts of town, founded in 1187 by King Alfonso VIII, is still run by nuns. There's a small textile museum on-site, but the building's main attraction is its stained-glass panels, some of the oldest in Spain. Admission includes a guided tour of the monastery, but you can browse the museum at your own pace. ✉ *Calle de Los Compases s/n* ☎ *94/720–1630 Tues.–Sat. 10:30–1:30 and 4–6:30* 🌐 *www.patrimonionacional.es* 🎫 *From €6.*

WHERE TO EAT AND STAY

$$$$ SPANISH 🍴 **Casa Ojeda.** This centennial restaurant—a Castilian classic—is known for refined Burgos standbys, especially cochinillo and lamb straight from the 200-year-old wood oven. Wines by the glass are local and reasonable. **Known for:** fall-off-the-bone lamb; old-school waitstaff; tried-and-true Castilian cuisine. [$] *Average main: €32* ✉ *Calle Vitoria 5* ☎ *94/720–9052* 🌐 *www.restauranteojeda.com* 🕒 *No dinner Sun.*

$$$ HOTEL FAMILY 🏨 **Landa.** If you've ever dreamed of holing up in a luxurious castle, consider booking a room at Landa, a converted 14th-century palace some 5 km (3 miles) from the city center surrounded by lush gardens. **Pros:** stunning indoor-outdoor swimming pool; surprisingly affordable for level of luxury; beautiful lobby. **Cons:** roads to and from town are busy; you'll need your own transportation to get here; inconsistent food quality. [$] *Rooms from: €140* ✉ *Ctra. de Madrid–Irún, Km 235* ☎ *94/725–7777* 🌐 *www.landa.as* 🛏 *37 rooms* 🍽 *No meals.*

$ HOTEL 🏨 **Mesón del Cid.** Once home to a 15th-century printing press, this independently owned hotel and restaurant has been hosting travelers for generations in light, airy guest rooms (ask for one facing the cathedral). **Pros:** cathedral views from upgraded rooms; comfy, clean digs; central location. **Cons:** parking is a tight squeeze; could use a face-lift; some rooms noisy. [$] *Rooms from: €80* ✉ *Pl. Santa María 8* ☎ *94/720–8715* 🌐 *www.mesondelcid.es* 🛏 *55 rooms* 🍽 *No meals.*

NIGHTLIFE

Due to its student population, Burgos has a lively *vida nocturna* (nightlife) in **Las Llanas,** near the cathedral. House wines and *cañas* (small glasses of beer) flow freely through the crowded tapas bars along Calles Laín Calvo and San Juan, near the Plaza Mayor. Calle Puebla, a small, dark street off Calle San Juan, also gets constant revelers. When you order a drink at any Burgos bar, the bartender plunks down a free *pinchito* (small tapa)—a long-standing tradition.

> **EL CAMINO**
>
> West of Burgos, the N120 to León crosses the ancient Camino de Santiago, or Way of St. James, revealing lovely old churches, tiny hermitages, ruined monasteries, and medieval villages across rolling fields. West of León, you can follow the well-worn Camino pilgrimage route as it approaches the giant cathedral in Santiago de Compostela.

Bardeblás. You'll want to stay awhile at this intimate bar, open until 4:30 on the weekends, for both its strong and affordable drinks and catchy throwback jams. ⊠ *Calle de la Puebla 29* ☎ *94/720–1162.*

Fodor's Choice ★ **Cervecería Flandes.** With 13 beers on tap that run the gamut from Belgian ales to rare Castilian microbrews, Cervecería Flandes attracts a diverse crowd of students, travelers, and beer geeks. Just don't expect any fancy food here—potato chips, nachos, and other sundry snacks are the only grub available. ⊠ *Pl. Huerto del Rey 21* ☎ *65/993–4813* ⊕ *www.cerveceriaflandes.es.*

SHOPPING

Ribera del Duero wines, bottled south of the city along the eponymous river, might not be as well-known as those from Rioja, but they can be equally (if not more) sublime. You'll want to stock up on Burgos-style morcilla and local cheese, too. Beyond culinary finds, keep your eye out for small artisan shops specializing in ceramics and textiles.

Fodor's Choice ★ **Delicatessen Ojeda.** A food lover's paradise, this pristine, well-lit store carries all the Castilian delicacies you can imagine, from Burgos-style morcilla to roasted oil-packed peppers to top-quality dried beans and pulses. ⊠ *Calle de Vitoria 5* ☎ *94/720–4832* ⊕ *www.delicatessenojeda. com.*

Marietta Moda. Uncover fashionable treasures at this ladies-only boutique specializing in high-end secondhand apparel. Unlike most vintage shops, Marietta is bright, inviting, and organized. ⊠ *Calle del Almirante Bonifaz 20* ☎ *94/710–4449* ⊕ *www.mariettamoda.com.*

EN ROUTE

Monastery of Santo Domingo de Silos. For a sojourn with masters of the Gregorian chant, head to the monastery where 1994's triple-platinum album *Chant* was recorded in the 1970s and '80s. Located 58 km (36 miles) southeast of Burgos, the monastery has an impressive two-story cloister that's lined with intricate Romanesque carvings. Try to drop in for an evening vespers service. It's a unique experience that's well off the tourist path. Single men can stay here for up to eight days (€42 per night with full board). Guests are expected to be present for breakfast, lunch, and dinner but are otherwise left to their own devices. ⊠ *Calle Santo*

Domingo 2, Santo Domingo de Silos ☎ *94/739–0068, 94/739–0049* ⊕ *www.abadiadesilos.es* ✉ *€4* ⊗ *Closed Mon.*

FAMILY **Ojo Guareña.** If you have a day to spare or are traveling on to Cantabria, stop at this breathtaking hermitage hewn into a karst cliff side surrounded by leafy woodlands. It's estimated that the cave complex housing the religious structure stretches some 90 km (56 miles), and there's evidence that humans lived inside it as early as the Middle Paleolithic. A worthwhile guided tour of the hermitage lasts 45 minutes; far more scintillating is the tour of nearby Palomera Cave, one of the largest in the world (by appointment only). ✉ *Cueva Ermita de San Bernabé, Burgos* ☎ *94/713–8755 for San Bernabé hermitage, 94/713–8614 for Palomera Cave reservations* ⊕ *www.turismoburgos.org* ✉ *From €4* ⊗ *Closed Mon. and Tues.*

LEÓN

334 km (208 miles) northwest of Madrid, 184 km (114 miles) west of Burgos.

León, the ancient capital of Castile and León, sits on the banks of the Bernesga River in the high plains of Old Castile; today it's a wealthy and conservative provincial capital and prestigious university town. The wide avenues of western León are lined with boutiques, and the twisting alleys of the half-timber old town hide the bars, bookstores, and chocolaterías most popular with students.

Historians say that the city was not named for the proud lion that has been its emblem for centuries; rather, they assert that the name is a corruption of the Roman word *legio* (legion), from the fact that the city was founded as a permanent camp for the Roman legions in AD 70. The capital of Christian Spain was moved here from Oviedo in 914 as the Reconquest spread south, ushering in the city's richest era.

As you wander the old town, you can still see fragments of the 6-foot-thick ramparts that were once part of the Roman walls. Look down and you might notice small brass scallop shells set into the street. The scallop is the symbol of St. James; the town government installed them to mark the path for modern-day pilgrims heading north to Santiago de Compostela.

León was chosen as Spain's "Capital of Gastronomy" in 2018, which lured hordes of foodie tourists, inspired restaurants to up their game, and confirmed what those who've been to León already knew—that the city is a fantastic food town.

GETTING HERE AND AROUND

León can be reached by train from Madrid with 14 departures daily from Chamartín station; the journey takes two hours 15 minutes on the high-speed lines (ALVIA and AVE) and between three and four on trains making local stops. ALSA has several bus departures daily, and there are generally plentiful Blablacar rideshares available.

ESSENTIALS

Visitor Information León Tourist Office. ✉ *Pl. de San Marcelo 1* ☎ *98/787–8327* ⊕ *www.turismoleon.org.*

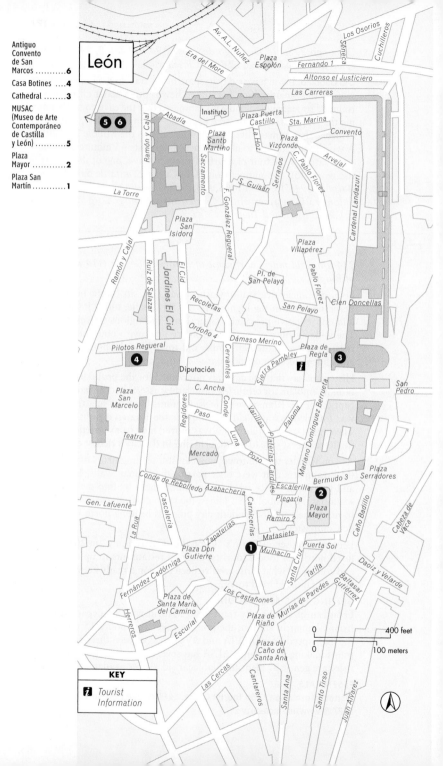

León

KEY

i Tourist Information

0   400 feet

0   100 meters

EXPLORING

Antiguo Convento de San Marcos. Fronted by an airy pedestrian plaza, this sumptuous building is now the Parador de León. Originally a home for knights of the Order of St. James, who patrolled the Camino de Santiago, the monastery was begun in 1513 by the head of the order, King Ferdinand. The plateresque facade is a majestic swath of small, intricate sculptures (many depicting knights and lords) and ornamentation—one of the most impressive Renaissance works in Spain. Inside, a cloister full of medieval statues leads you to the bar, which still has the original defensive arrow slits as windows. As the Anexo Monumental del Museo de León, the convent also displays historic paintings and artifacts. ⊠ *Pl. de San Marcos 7* ☎ *98/724–5061, 98/723–7300* ⊕ *www. parador.es* 🎫 *Museum €1* ⊗ *Closed Mon.*

Casa Botines. This Gaudí masterpiece, which previously housed a bank, was converted into an excellent museum dedicated to the Moderniste architect in April 2017. Under its conical spires and behind its fish-scale-patterned facade, you'll find over 5,000 works of art spanning eight centuries by such renowned masters as Sorolla, Madrazo, Gutiérrez, and Solana. Given that this is the largest of Gaudí's buildings to be opened as a museum, it's worth ponying up the extra few euros for a guided tour. ⊠ *Calle Legión VII 3* ⊕ *www.casabotines.es* 🎫 *From €5* ⊗ *Closed Wed. morning, Sun. afternoon.*

Fodor'sChoice ★ **Cathedral.** The pride of León is its soaring cathedral, begun in 1205, an outstanding example of Gothic architecture complete with gargoyles, flying buttresses, and pointed arches. Its 2,000 square yards of vivid stained-glass panels—second only, perhaps, to those in Chartres, France—depict biblical stories and Castilian landscapes. A glass door to the choir gives an unobstructed view of nave windows and the painted altarpiece, framed with gold leaf. The cathedral also contains the sculpted tomb of King Ordoño II, who moved the capital of Christian Spain to León. The museum's collection boasts giant medieval hymnals, textiles, sculptures, wood carvings, and paintings. Look for the carved-wood Mudejar archive, with a letter of the alphabet above each door—it's one of the world's oldest file cabinets. ■ TIP→ **In theory, the cathedral is closed to tourists during Sunday Mass; some foreigners have complained of being asked to pay an entrance fee to attend services.** ⊠ *Pl. de Regla s/n* ☎ *98/787–5770* ⊕ *www.catedraldeleon. org* 🎫 *From €5.*

MUSAC (Museo de Arte Contemporáneo de Castilla y León) (*Museum of Modern Art of Castilla y León*). It's worth a visit to this museum for its facade alone, a modern technicolor masterpiece by famed Spanish architects Mansilla + Tuñón. The endless rainbow of rectangles that encloses the building is an homage to the colorful stained glass of the cathedral. Inside, wander through rooms bearing the latest art and multimedia projects by locally and nationally acclaimed artists. Films and concerts are also shown throughout the year. ⊠ *Av. de los Reyes Leoneses 24* ☎ *98/709–0000* ⊕ *www.musac.es* 🎫 *€3 (free Sun. 5–9)* ⊗ *Closed Mon.*

The colorful panels on León's MUSAC, the Museum of Contemporary Art, were inspired by the rose window of the city's Gothic cathedral.

Plaza Mayor. This is the heart of the old town, and on Wednesday and Saturday mornings the arcaded plaza bustles with farmers selling produce and cheeses. ✉ *León.*

Plaza San Martín. Most of León's tapas bars are in this 12th-century square. The surrounding area is called the Barrio Húmedo, or "Wet Neighborhood," allegedly because of the large amount of wine spilled here late at night. ✉ *León.*

WHERE TO EAT AND STAY

$$$$ SPANISH 🍴 **Adonías del Pozo.** In this softly lit dining room furnished with rustic tables and colorful ceramics, feast on top-of-the-line cured ham, roasted peppers, and chorizo. Grilled sea bream is a treat for seafood lovers; banana pudding with chocolate sauce is a treat for just about everyone. **Known for:** well-priced menú del día; excellent sausages and roast meats; homey dining room. [$] *Average main: €30* ✉ *Calle Santa Nonia 16* ☎ *98/720–6768, 98/725–2665* ⏲ *Closed Sun.*

$ TAPAS 🍴 **El Rebote.** Though every drink comes with a complimentary croqueta at El Rebote, a pocket-size bar frequented by locals, the crisp, gooey orbs are so succulent that you'll want to order a few extra. Be sure to sample the smoky *cecina* rendition incorporating the Leonese air-cured beef delicacy. **Known for:** to-die-for croquetas; quirky local wines by the glass; sardine-can digs. [$] *Average main: €8* ✉ *Pl. San Martín 9* ☎ *987/213510* ⏲ *Closed Mon.*

$$$$ SPANISH 🍴 **LAV.** The most exciting nueva cocina restaurant on the León dining scene, LAV appeals to all the senses with unexpected flavor combinations, playful plating, and personable service. Tasting menus—a steal at €37—begin with "surprise sandwiches" at the bar and progress into the kitchen for a brief "show cooking" demo before winding up in the dining room. **Known for:** fine dining that doesn't take itself too seriously; terrific-value tasting menu; local ingredients used in ways you've never seen before. [$] *Average main: €37* ✉ *Av. del Padre Isla 1* ☎ *98/779–8190* 🌐 *www.restaurantelav.com* 🕒 *Closed Sun.*

$$$ SPANISH FAMILY Fodor's Choice ★ 🍴 **Restaurante Sorrento.** León is a cold, windy town for much of the year, so it's no surprise that the local version of cocido (boiled dinner) is heartier than usual with mounds of green cabbage, spoonable blood sausage, and some 10 types of meat (chorizo, beef shanks, pork belly, and chicken, to name a few). Sample the city's best rendition at this spartan yet inviting restaurant outside the historic center—and be sure to bring an appetite. **Known for:** soul-satisfying cocido leonés; warm service; local crowd. [$] *Average main: €19* ✉ *Calle Bernardo del Carpio 1* ☎ *98/707–3270* 🕒 *Closed Mon.*

$$$$ HOTEL 🏨 **Hotel Real Colegiata de San Isidoro.** Other hotels around town bill themselves as being steps from the main tourist attractions, but the Hotel Real Colegiata, which houses a Romanesque collegiate library and museum, is located within one. **Pros:** gorgeous historic building; modern Spanish restaurant; free tour of the grounds. **Cons:** no gym, pool, or spa; furnishings lack style; cleanliness can be inconsistent. [$] *Rooms from: €280* ✉ *Pl. Santo Martino 5* ☎ *98/787–5088* 🌐 *www.hotelrealcolegiata.com* 🛏 *32 rooms* 🍽 *Free Breakfast.*

$$$ HOTEL Fodor's Choice ★ 🏨 **NH Collection León Plaza Mayor.** This handsome hotel, housed in a palace overlooking the 17th-century Plaza Mayor, is awash with whites, dark woods, and neutral tones. **Pros:** subdued, elegant interiors; parking below building; varied breakfasts. **Cons:** some furniture could use replacing; maintenance a little inconsistent; parking is a tight squeeze. [$] *Rooms from: €170* ✉ *Pl. Mayor 15–17* ☎ *98/734–4357* 🌐 *www.nh-collection.com* 🛏 *51 rooms* 🍽 *No meals.*

NIGHTLIFE

León's most popular hangouts are clustered around the Plaza Mayor, frequented mainly by couples and families, and Plaza San Martín, where the college kids go. The surrounding streets (Calles Escalerilla, Plegaria, Ramiro 2, Matasiete, and Mulhacén) are packed with tapas bars. In the Plaza Mayor, you might want to start at **La Pañería, The Harley,** or **Mishiara.** In the Plaza San Martín, begin your evening with tapas and *cortitos* (local slang for two-gulp glasses of beer) at **Taberna Los Cazurros, El Rebote,** or **Mesón Jabugo.** Then, go clubbing at **Studio 54,** a *discoteca* housed in an old theater whose crowd gets progressively younger (and LGBT friendly) as the night goes on.

SHOPPING

Tasty regional treats include roasted red peppers, potent brandy-soaked cherries, and candied chestnuts—but León's most prized and artisinal product is cecina, air-dried beef that packs an umami punch similar to that of a dry-aged steak. You can buy all of these items in food shops around the city.

Prada a Tope. This restaurant, winery, and gourmet store has a huge estate in the countryside just outside León and operates a small café and shop in the city. Delicacies include chestnuts in syrup, bittersweet figs and pears in wine, jams, and liqueurs. Not enough room in your suitcase? You can also order by mail from its website. ⊠ *Calle Alfonso IX 9* ☎ *98/725–7221, 98/756–3366* ⊕ *www.pradaatope.es.*

YOWE. This high-end clothing boutique, with two stores in León and one in Santander, was opened by two fashion-obsessed twin sisters in 1984 and has remained relevant to the present day—no small feat in the fashion industry. Their chic new concept store carries lines by the likes of Bally, Dsquared2, Herno, Moncler, and Missoni. ⊠ *Calle Carmen 8, León* ☎ *63/858–3426* ⊕ *www.yowe.es.*

ASTORGA

46 km (29 miles) southwest of León.

Astorga, where the pilgrimage roads from France and Portugal merge, once had 22 hospitals to lodge and care for ailing travelers. Though the city is no longer the crossroads that it once was, plenty of travelers visit this charming town for its eye-popping Gaudí masterpiece, El Palacio Episcopal, and its famed *cocido maragato*, a stick-to-your-ribs stew. Astorga is in an area once known as La Maragatería, home to a community that once stood apart from its neighbors for its special dialect, elaborate dress, and distinctive folk music.

GETTING HERE AND AROUND
Several buses depart daily from León; the trip takes about 45 minutes. If you're driving yourself, there's ample parking, and the city is navigable on foot.

ESSENTIALS
Visitor Information Astorga Tourist Office. ⊠ *Pl. Eduardo de Castro 5* ☎ *98/761–8222* ⊕ *www.aytoastorga.es.*

EXPLORING
Museo de la Catedral. This museum displays 10th- and 12th-century chests, religious silverware, and paintings and sculptures by Astorgans through the ages. ⊠ *Pl. de la Catedral* ☎ *98/761–5820* 🎫 *€5.*

FAMILY

Fodor's Choice

★

Museo Romano (*Roman Museum*). This hidden-gem museum uses the archaeological record to show what life was like in Astorga during Roman times, when the city was called Asturica Augusta. The most memorable part of the experience is the **Ruta Romana,** a walking tour of Roman archaeological remains in Astorga (combined tickets can be bought at the museum). ⊠ *Pl. San Bartolomé 2* ☎ *98/761–6937* ⊕ *www.asturica.com* 🎫 *€5* 🕐 *Closed Mon.*

Palacio de Gaudí (*Palacio Episcopal*). Just opposite Astorga's cathedral is this fairy-tale neo-Gothic palace, designed for a Catalan cleric by Antoni Gaudí in 1889. Though the interiors pale in comparison to the eye-popping exteriors, those interested in local ecclesiastical history shouldn't miss visiting the **Museo de Los Caminos** (Museum of the Way). ⊠ *Glorieta Eduardo de Castro s/n, Pl. de la Catedral* ☎ *98/761–6882* ⊕ *www.palaciodegaudi.es* 🎫 *€5* 🕐 *Closed Mon.*

WHERE TO EAT AND STAY

$$$$ SPANISH 🍴 **Restaurante Serrano.** This local hangout serves Astorgan dishes that incorporate wild game, foraged mushrooms, and regional meats. For a break from carniverous Castilian cuisine, tuck into handmade pasta dishes or chickpeas stewed with fresh octopus, a house specialty. **Known for:** dishes using local "pico pardal" garbanzos; attentive old-school service; wild game. [$] *Average main: €35* ✉ *Calle Portería 2* ☎ *98/761–7866, 64/607–1736* 🌐 *www.restauranteserrano.es* 🕓 *Closed Mon.*

$ HOTEL 🏨 **Astur Plaza.** This cheap and cheerful hotel on Astorga's Plaza de España is a good value. **Pros:** reliable and well-priced hotel; quality restaurant; private, secure parking lot. **Cons:** drab decor; head-splitting church bells in the morning; beds aren't particularly comfortable. [$] *Rooms from: €85* ✉ *Pl. de España 2–3* ☎ *98/761–7665* 🌐 *www.hotelasturplaza.es* 🛏 *37 rooms* 🍽 *No meals.*

$$ HOTEL FAMILY Fodor's Choice ★ 🏨 **Hotel Vía de la Plata.** A giant slate terrace with views of the countryside is the main draw of this airy, modern hotel. **Pros:** great views and service; gorgeous terrace; free parking. **Cons:** wedding parties can be noisy; small breakfast area; spa not included in rate. [$] *Rooms from: €90* ✉ *Calle Padres Redentoristas 5* ☎ *98/761–9000 for hotel, 98/760–4165 for spa* 🌐 *www.hotelviadelaplata.com* 🛏 *38 rooms* 🍽 *No meals.*

VILLAFRANCA DEL BIERZO

135 km (84 miles) west of León.

After crossing León's grape-growing region, where the funky, floral Bierzo wines are produced, you'll arrive in this medieval village, dominated by a massive (and still-inhabited) feudal fortress. Visit the Romanesque church of Santiago to see the Puerta del Perdón (Door of Pardon), a sort of spiritual consolation prize for exhausted Camino pilgrims who couldn't make it over the mountains. Stroll the streets and seek out the onetime home of the infamous Grand Inquisitor Tomás de Torquemada. If you've made it all the way here, don't leave Bierzo without visiting the area's most famous archaeological site, Las Médulas, whose bizarre stone formations are the remnants of Roman gold mines.

GETTING HERE AND AROUND

Charter bus trips from León—or better yet, a rental car—remain the best ways to get to this rural region. You'll likely want your own transportation once you get here, to visit Las Medulas, which is several kilometers away. It's also possible to hike or get there by bicycle.

ESSENTIALS

Visitor Information **Villafranca del Bierzo Tourist Office.** ✉ *Av. Díaz Ovelar 10* ☎ *98/754–0028* 🌐 *www.villafrancadelbierzo.org.*

EXPLORING

FAMILY Fodor's Choice ★ **Las Médulas.** One of northern Spain's most impressive archaeological sites, this mountainous area of former Roman gold mines—located 24 km (15 miles) south of town—is now a UNESCO World Heritage Site. The landscape is the result of an ancient mining technique in which myriad water tunnels were burrowed into a mountain, causing it to collapse. Miners would then sift through the rubble for gold. What's left at Las Médulas are half-collapsed mountains of golden clay, with exposed tunnels, peeking through lush green forest. Take in the best panorama from the Orellán viewpoint. There are hiking paths, a small archaeology exhibit (open only on weekends), and a visitor center. You can pay to enter some of the tunnels or browse the larger area for free. The visitor center also organizes 3-km (2-mile) walking tours—call ahead to book. ✉ *Carucedo* ☎ *98/742–2848* 🌐 *www.espaciolasmedulas.es* 🎟 *Free; archaeology center €2, Orellán tunnel €2, guided walking tour €3.*

WHERE TO STAY

$ B&B/INN FAMILY Fodor's Choice ★ 🏨 **Casa do Louteiro.** This charming, rustic inn, in a tiny village near the archaeological site of Las Médulas, was lovingly converted from a series of medieval ruins. **Pros:** rustic details; friendly staff; fire pit on winter evenings. **Cons:** plenty of hiking and biking nearby, but you'll need a car to get here; disorganized front-desk management; no housekeeping service. [$] *Rooms from: €65* ✉ *Calle Louteiro 6, Orellán* ☎ *65/293–3419, 65/293–3971* 🛏 *3 cottages* 🍴 *No meals.*

$$ HOTEL FAMILY 🏨 **Parador de Villafranca del Bierzo.** This modern two-story hotel built with local stone looks out over the Bierzo valley. **Pros:** indoor and outdoor swimming pools; quiet surroundings; comfortable beds. **Cons:** lacks history of other paradores; some rooms overlook parking lot; noisy a/c in some rooms. [$] *Rooms from: €105* ✉ *Av. de Calvo Sotelo 28* ☎ *98/754–0175* 🌐 *www.parador.es* 🛏 *51 rooms* 🍴 *No meals.*

EXTREMADURA

Rugged Extremadura a nature lover's paradise, so bring your mountain bike (or plan on renting one), hiking boots, and binoculars. The lush Jerte Valley and the craggy peaks of the Sierra de Gredos mark Upper Extremadura's fertile landscape. South of the Jerte Valley is the historical town of Plasencia and the 15th-century Yuste Monastery. Don't miss medieval Cáceres—boasting one of the best-preserved old towns in Europe—and Mérida with its immaculately preserved Roman amphitheater. Extremadura's other main towns—Badajoz, Trujillo, Olivenza, and Zafra—are charming (if a tad provincial) and virtually tourist-free.

JERTE AND EL VALLE DEL JERTE (JERTE VALLEY)

220 km (137 miles) west of Madrid.

Every spring, the Jerte Valley in northern Extremadura becomes one of Spain's top attractions for its riot of cherry blossoms. Unsurprisingly, this is where Spain's biggest cherry harvest originates, backed by the snowcapped Gredos mountains. Book ahead for March and April—peak cherry blossom season.

GETTING HERE AND AROUND

You will need a car to get here and explore the valley. For a scenic route, follow N110 southwest from Ávila to Plasencia.

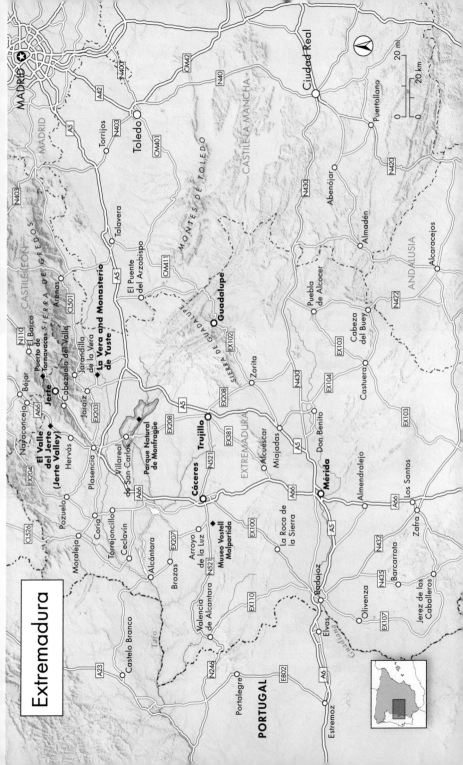

Cherry trees in blossom in the Jerte Valley

ESSENTIALS

Visitor Information **Valle del Jerte Tourist Office.** ⊠ *Paraje Virgen de Peñas Albas s/n (N110), Cabezuela del Valle* ☎ *92/747–2558* ⊕ *www.turismovall-edeljerte.com.*

EXPLORING

Cabezuela del Valle. Full of half-timber stone houses, this is one of the valley's best-preserved villages. Follow N110 to Plasencia, or, if you enjoy mountain scenery, detour from the village of Jerte to Hervás, traveling a narrow road that winds 35 km (22 miles) through forests of low-growing oak trees and over the Honduras Pass. ⊠ *Cabezuela del Valle.*

Puerto de Tornavacas (*Tornavacas Pass*). There's no more striking introduction to Extremadura than the Puerto de Tornavacas—literally, the "point where the cows turn back." Part of the N110 road northeast of Plasencia, the pass marks the border between Extremadura and the stark plateau of Castile. At 4,183 feet above sea level, it boasts a breathtaking view of the valley formed by the fast-flowing Jerte River. The valley's lower slopes are covered with a dense mantle of ash, chestnut, and cherry trees, whose richness contrasts with the granite cliffs of Castile's Sierra de Gredos. Cherries are the principal crop. To catch their brilliant blossoms, visit in spring. Camping is popular in this region, and even the most experienced hikers can find some challenging trails. ⊠ *Plasencia.*

WHERE TO EAT AND STAY

$$ **✕La Cabaña del Jerte.** This homey, sun-drenched restaurant serves
SPANISH honest Extremaduran fare at an excellent price. Unlike other dining
Fodor'sChoice options in the area, cooks here pay special attention to presentation and
★ ingredient quality—attributes on display in the not-too-greasy migas,
ultrajuicy Iberian pork dishes, and refreshing tomato salads. **Known
for:** home-cooked food; Iberian pork dishes; bright, casual dining room.
$ *Average main: €15* ✉ *Av. Ramón y Cajal 17, Jerte* ☎ *64/523–3953*
⊕ *www.restaurantelacabañajerte.es.*

$ **Hotel Rural Finca El Carpintero.** The best rooms in this restored
B&B/INN 150-year-old stone mill and farmhouse have fireplaces, sitting areas,
FAMILY and separate entrances, though entry-level rooms are perfectly pleas-
ant with canopy beds and hydromassage tubs. **Pros:** cozy atmosphere;
picturesque grounds with swimming pool; ideal country escape, espe-
cially in spring and fall. **Cons:** disparity in quality between rooms and
suites; need a car to get here; spent towels and small TVs. $ *Rooms
from: €76* ✉ *N110, Km 360.5, 9 km (5½ miles) northeast of Jerte,
Tornavacas* ☎ *92/717–7089, 65/932–8110* ⊕ *www.fincaelcarpintero.
com* ⌖ *5 rooms, 3 suites* ⦿ *Free Breakfast.*

$ **La Casería.** One of Extremadura's first rural guesthouses, this ram-
B&B/INN bling home 10 km (6 miles) southeast of Jerte, is on a spectacular
FAMILY 120-acre working farm, once a 16th-century Franciscan convent. **Pros:**
privacy in the cottages; outdoor activities; views of Jerte Valley. **Cons:**
main lodge often rented out to groups; need a car to get here; far from
all main sights and national parks. $ *Rooms from: €80* ✉ *N110, Km
378.5, Navaconcejo* ☎ *92/717–3141* ⊕ *www.lacaseria.es* ⌖ *6 rooms,
3 cottages* ⦿ *Free Breakfast.*

LA VERA AND MONASTERIO DE YUSTE

45 km (28 miles) east of Plasencia.

In northern Extremadura, the fertile La Vera region sits at the foot of
the Gredos mountains, which are usually snowcapped through June.
With its wildflowers, mountain vistas, and world-famous Yuste Mon-
astery, the area welcomes hordes of tourists, especially in spring, its
most beautiful season. One of the favourite souvenirs to take home is
La Vera's famous smoky paprika—*pimentón*, available in three types:
dulce (mild), *agridulce* (medium), and *picante* (hot). You're likely to
see strings of red peppers hanging out to dry on the windowsills of
area homes.

GETTING HERE AND AROUND

You'll need a car to get here. Turn left off the C501 at Cuacos and fol-
low signs for the monastery (1 km [½ mile]).

ESSENTIALS

Visitor Information Jaraíz de la Vera Tourist Office. ✉ *Calle Mérida 17*
☎ *92/717–0587.*

EXPLORING

Fodor's Choice ★ **Monasterio de Yuste** (*Yuste Monastery*). In the heart of La Vera—a region of steep ravines (*gargantas*), rushing rivers, and sleepy villages—lies the Monasterio de San Jerónimo de Yuste, founded by Hieronymite monks in the early 15th century. Badly damaged in the Peninsular War, it was left to decay after the suppression of Spain's monasteries in 1835, but it has since been restored by the Hieronymites. Today it's one of the most impressive monasteries in all of Spain. Carlos V (1500–58), founder of Spain's vast 16th-century empire, spent his last two years in the Royal Chambers, enabling the emperor to attend mass within a short stumble of his bed. The guided tour also covers the church, the crypt where Carlos V was buried before being moved to El Escorial (near Madrid), and a glimpse of the monastery's cloisters. ✉ *Carretera de Yuste s/n, Cuacos* ☎ *92/717–2197* 🌐 *www.patrimonionacional.es* 🎟 *From €7 (free Apr.–Sept., Wed. and Thurs. 5–8; Oct.–Mar., Wed. and Thurs. 3–6).*

Museo del Pimentón (*Paprika Museum*). Tucked away in a 17th-century row house, this quirky museum tells the history of the locally made paprika, dubbed "red gold," for which Jaraíz de la Vera is probably best known nationally. The three floors feature audiovisual presentations and examples of grinding tools and recipes. The museum is the centerpiece of the village's annual pepper festival, held in August. ✉ *Pl. Mayor 7, Jaraíz de la Vera* ☎ *92/746–0810* 🌐 *museodelpimenton.business.site* 🎟 *Free* 🕒 *Closed Sun. afternoon and Mon.*

WHERE TO STAY

$ B&B/INN FAMILY 🏨 **Camino Real.** In a village in the highest valley of the Vera, this former mansion has rustic guest rooms with exposed stone walls and wood-beam ceilings. **Pros:** sprawling terrace with gorgeous views over the valley; family activities organized; lavish breakfast buffet included. **Cons:** those great views of Extremadura's plains also make for windy, cold winters; few modern perks; no online bookings. [$] *Rooms from: €75* ✉ *Calle Monje 27, Guijo de Santa Bárbara* ☎ *92/756–1119* 🛏 *10 rooms* 🍴 *Free Breakfast.*

$$ B&B/INN FAMILY 🏨 **La Casona.** This rustic estate with spectacular views of the Gredos mountains has six cozy rooms in the main house and six log-cabin bungalows. **Pros:** great service; very family friendly; bevy of outdoor activities. **Cons:** need your own transportation; has gone downhill in recent years; hard to find because there's hardly any signage. [$] *Rooms from: €100* ✉ *Ctra. Navalmoral (EX392), Km 15, Jaraíz de la Vera* ☎ *92/719–4145, 62/964–5930* 🌐 *www.la-casona.es* 🛏 *6 rooms, 6 bungalows* 🍴 *Free Breakfast.*

SHOPPING

If you like to cook, pick up a tin or two of pimentón de La Vera (smoked sweet paprika), made from the region's prized red peppers, at a grocery shop in the area.

EN ROUTE **Parque Natural de Monfragüe.** At the junction of the rivers Tiétar and Tajo, 20 km (12 miles) south of Plasencia on the EX208, lies Extremadura's only national park. This rocky, mountainous wilderness is known for its diverse plant and animal life including lynxes, boars, deer, foxes, black storks, imperial eagles, and the world's largest colony of black vultures, attracting bird-watchers from around the world. Bring binoculars and head for the lookout point called Salto del Gitano (Gypsy's Leap), on the C524 just south of the Tajo River—vultures can often be spotted wheeling in the dozens at close range. The park's visitor center and main entrance is in the hamlet of Villareal de San Carlos. ⊠ *Ctra. EX208, Villareal de San Carlos* ☎ *92/719–9134, 92/711–6498* ⊕ *www. parquedemonfrague.com.*

CÁCERES

299 km (186 miles) west of Madrid, 125 km (78 miles) southwest of Monasterio de Yuste.

Fodor's Choice ★ The provincial capital and one of Spain's oldest cities, Cáceres is known for its UNESCO-protected old town and lively *tapeo* (tapas scene). The Roman colony called Norba Caesarina was founded in 35 BC, but when the Moors took over in the 8th century, they named the city Quazris, which eventually morphed into the Spanish Cáceres. Amazingly, some 22 Moorish towers survive in the historic center today. Ever since noble families helped Alfonso IX expel the Moors in 1229, the city has prospered; the pristine condition of the medieval and Renaissance quarter is the result of the families' continued occupancy of the palaces erected in the 15th century.

GETTING HERE AND AROUND

Trains from Madrid take about 2½ hours and are the cheapest and easiest way to get to Cáceres. Catch a city bus outside the train station, which takes you to Plaza Mayor in the historic quarter, or walk 15 minutes into town. From Madrid, Blablacar rideshares are an excellent option as well. The city center is navigable on foot. If you drive, park on the outskirts as the winding, narrow medieval streets are difficult for parking.

Train Station Cáceres. ⊠ *Av. Juan Pablo II 6* ☎ *92/723–5061, 90/224–0202* ⊕ *www.renfe.com.*

TOURS

FAMILY
Fodor's Choice ★ **Los Cuenta Trovas de Cordel.** One of the best ways to see Cáceres is by night. The energetic local guides Vicente and Patxi weave lots of knowledge about Cáceres folklore, legends and ghost stories into their multilingual weekend tours of Cáceres's old quarter, which they present in medieval costume. Call ahead to reserve, or book online. ⊠ *Pl. Mayor* ☎ *667/283187, 667/776205* ⊠ *From €10.*

ESSENTIALS

Visitor Information Cáceres. ⊠ *Pl. Mayor* ☎ *927/010834, 927/217237 for tours* ⊕ *turismo.ayto-caceres.es.*

EXPLORING

Ciudad Vieja de Cáceres (Old Cáceres), which begins just east of Plaza San Juan, is where all the action is.

The San Mateo church, with the Torre de las Cigüeñas (Tower of the Storks) in the background

Fodor's Choice **Ciudad Monumental.** Travel back a few centuries in Cáceres's Ciudad ★ Monumental (aka *casco antiguo* or *ciudad vieja*), one of the best-preserved medieval quarters in Europe. It's so convincingly ancient that *Game of Thrones* used it as a filming location in 2017: there isn't a single modern building to detract from its aura. It's virtually deserted in winter and occasionally dusted with a light coating of snow—quite a sight to behold. Most of the city's main sights are located here, but of Cáceres's approximately 100,000 residents, only 380 reside within this tiny enclave. ⊠ *Cáceres.*

Concatedral de Santa María. This Gothic church, built mainly in the 16th century, is now the cathedral and the city's most important religious site. The elegantly carved wooden reredos (dating to 1551), left unpainted according to Extremaduran custom, is barely visible in the gloom. Follow the lines of pilgrims to the statue of San Pedro de Alcántara in the corner; legend says that touching the stone figure's shoes brings luck. A small museum in the back displays religious artifacts. ⊠ *Pl. de Santa María s/n* 🕾 *92/721–5313* ⊕ *www.diocesiscoriacaceres.org* 🎟 *€4.*

Fundación Helga de Alvear (*Visual Arts Center Foundation Helga de Alvear*). After a day spent meandering through medieval passageways and marveling at ancient churches, this small contemporary art museum is a breath of fresh air. Highlights include sculptures by Ai Weiwei and Dan Graham and paintings by Josef Albers and John Baldessari. A much-anticipated renovation by Tuñón Arquitectos, which will add additional rooms and multimedia spaces, is underway and set to be completed by the end of 2018. ⊠ *Calle Pizarro 8* 🕾 *92/762–6414* ⊕ *www.fundacionhelgadealvear.es* 🎟 *Free* 𝄇 *Closed Mon.*

Fodor'sChoice **Museo de Cáceres.** The Casa de las Veletas (House of the Weather Vanes)
★ is a 12th-century Moorish mansion that is now used as the city's
museum. Filled with finds from the Paleolithic through Visigothic periods, the museum also includes an art section with works by El Greco,
Picasso, and Miró. The highlight is the superbly preserved Moorish
cistern—the *aljibe*—with horseshoe arches supported by mildewy stone
pillars. ⊠ *Pl. de las Veletas 1* ☎ *92/701–0877* ⊕ *museodecaceres.gobex.
es* ⊠ *€2 (free for EU residents)* ⊗ *Closed Mon.*

Fodor'sChoice **Museo Vostell Malpartida.** The first thing that grabs your attention at this
★ museum—located 14 km (9 miles) outside town—is the landscape that
surrounds it: the Los Barruecos nature reserve. Spanning 800 acres, the
park's otherworldly landscape comprises rolling grasslands, lakes, and
enormous, peculiarly shaped boulders, which you can explore on foot.
These curious natural forms inspired Wolf Vostell, a German artist of
the Fluxus and Happening movements (whose wife was extremeña),
to turn a defunct yarn factory located within the park into a museum.
Today you can still take in his bizarre, thought-provoking work—
including a Cadillac surrounded by dinner plates and a wall of rusty
Guardia Civil motorcycles—much as it was when he was alive. ⊠ *Calle
Los Barruecos s/n* ☎ *92/701–0812* ⊕ *www.museovostell.gobex.es* ⊠ *€3*
⊗ *Closed Mon.*

Palacio de Carvajal. This is the only palace in Cáceres you can visit,
aside from the one housing the Museo de Cáceres. There is an imposing
granite facade, arched doorway, and tower, and the interior has been
restored with period furnishings and art to look as it did when the
Carvajal family lived here in the 16th century. Legend has it that King
Ferdinand IV ordered the execution of two brothers from the Carvajal
family, whom he accused of killing one of his knights. Thirty days later,
the king was sued in the Court of God. Judgment was postponed until
after the king's death, when the Carvajal brothers were declared inno-
cent. ⊠ *Calle Amargura 1 at Pl. Santa María* ☎ *92/725–5597* ⊠ *Free.*

Plaza Mayor. On this long, inclined, arcaded plaza you'll find several
cafés, the tourist office, and—on breezy summer nights—nearly everyone in town. In the middle of the arcade opposite the old quarter is the
entrance to the lively Calle General Ezponda, lined with tapas bars,
student hangouts, and discotecas that keep the neighborhood awake
and moving until dawn. ⊠ *Cáceres.*

Santuario de la Virgen de la Montaña (*Sanctuary of the Virgin of the Mountain*). Overlooking Cáceres's Ciudad Monumental is this 18th-century
shrine dedicated to the city's patron saint. It's built on a mountain with
highly Instagrammable views of the old town, especially at sunset. The
panorama is worth the 15-minute drive—or even the grueling two-hour
walk past chalets and farms—despite the rather mundane interior of
the church (the golden baroque altar being the only exception). ⊠ *Ctra.
Santuario Virgin de la Montaña s/n* ⊠ *Free.*

WORTH NOTING

Iglesia de Santiago. The chief building of interest outside the walls of
Cáceres' old town, this church was rebuilt in the 16th century by
Rodrigo Gil de Hontañón, Spain's last great Gothic architect. The

easiest way to reach the church is by exiting the old town on the west side, through the Socorro gate. Inside the church, there is a single nave with ribbed vaults, and a choir stall in the back. The magnificent altarpiece was commissioned in 1557 and made by the Valladolid-based master Alonso de Berruguete. ⊠ *Pl. de Santiago.*

> ### VISIT THE STORKS
>
> Storks are common in the old quarter of Cáceres, and virtually every tower and spire is topped by nests of storks, considered since the Roman era to be sacred birds emblematic of home, the soul, maternity, spring, and well-being.

Museo Apple e Historia de la Computación. Medieval Cáceres is about the last place you'd expect to find an eclectic collection of more than 150 Apple computers through the ages, but in this pocket-sized space you can see (and sometimes play around with) museum curator Carlos's prehistoric-looking machines from the '80s, '90s, and early aughts. Tours take about an hour and are well worth the nominal fee. ⊠ *Pl. de San Juan 13* ☎ *92/731–6501* ⊕ *www.museoapple.com* ✉ *€5* ⊗ *Closed Mon.*

Palacio de los Golfines de Abajo. The stony severity of this palace on the Plaza Mayor seems appropriate when you consider it was once the headquarters of General Franco. The exterior is somewhat relieved by elaborate Mudejar and Renaissance decorative motifs. Some 400 years before Franco, the so-called Reyes Católicos purportedly slept here. Guided tours by appointment only. ⊠ *Pl. de los Golfines* ⊕ *www. palaciogolfinesdeabajo.com* ✉ *€2* ⊗ *Closed Mon.*

Palacio de los Golfines de Arriba. After you pass through the gate leading to the old quarter, you'll see this palace, dominated by a soaring tower dating to 1515. Only three of the four corner towers remain, adorned with various coats of arms of the families who once lived here. Inside, there are classical colonnaded courtyards with Renaissance details, but they're no longer open to the public. Still, the impressive building is worth a stop. ⊠ *C. de los Olmos 2.*

Palacio del Capitán Diego de Cáceres. The battlement tower of this palace is also known as the Torre de las Cigüeñas (Tower of the Storks) for obvious reasons. It's now a military residence, but some rooms are occasionally opened for exhibitions. ⊠ *Pl. San Mateo.*

San Mateo. Construction on this church began in the 14th century, purportedly over the ruins of a mosque, and took nearly 300 years to finish. The interior is austere, with a 16th-century choir and walls lined with the tombs of prominent Cáceres citizens. The church opens at 10 most mornings, but check with the tourist office in case of changes. ⊠ *Pl. de San Mateo* ☎ *92/724–6329* ✉ *Free.*

WHERE TO EAT

$$$$
SPANISH
Fodor's Choice
★

✕ **Atrio.** This elegant, award-winning restaurant (and drool-worthy boutique hotel with a rooftop pool), housed in a medieval building redesigned by starchitect firm Mansilla + Tuñón, is easily the best in Extremadura. It specializes in refined contemporary cooking, and the menu changes according to what's in season in chef Toño Pérez's private garden. **Known for:** affordable two-Michelin-star restaurant; stunning interiors with bespoke furniture and Warhols; tasting menu only. $ *Average main: €75* ✉ *Pl. de San Mateo 1* 🕾 *92/724–2928* ⊕ *www.restauranteatrio.com.*

$
EUROPEAN
FAMILY

✕ **Chocolat's.** This little coffee and pastry shop is the best place in town for breakfast, dessert, or a quick snack. **Known for:** homemade cakes; pleasant staff; dependably good breakfasts. $ *Average main: €6* ✉ *Calle Maestro Sanchez Garrido s/n* 🕾 *92/722–0158, 60/831–1204.*

$$$$
SPANISH

✕ **El Figón de Eustaquio.** A fixture on the quiet and pleasant Plaza San Juan, this restaurant has been run by the same family for 70 years and counting. In its jumble of old-fashioned dining rooms with wood-beam ceilings, feast on regional delicacies including *venado de montería* (wild venison) or *perdiz estofada* (partridge stew) complemented by bold local wines. **Known for:** old-school Extremaduran cooking; good selection of local wines; pleasant outdoor patio. $ *Average main: €30* ✉ *Pl. San Juan 12–14* 🕾 *92/724–4362, 92/724–8194* ⊕ *www.elfigondeeustaquio.com.*

$$
TAPAS
Fodor's Choice
★

✕ **La Tapería.** This tiny taverna, which serves some of the best tapas in town, is always packed with locals. Order a few *tostas* and raciones, and pair them with wines from local vineyards. **Known for:** fresh, filling tostas; local hangout; free tapa with every drink. $ *Average main: €12* ✉ *Calle Sánchez Garrido 1, bajo* 🕾 *92/722–5147* ▭ *No credit cards* ⊘ *Closed Mon.*

WHERE TO STAY

$
HOTEL
FAMILY

🛏 **Hotel Iberia Plaza Mayor.** Confusingly, this budget-friendly hotel isn't on the Plaza Mayor but rather 100 yards down a quiet side street. **Pros:** great value; generous breakfast buffet; great location. **Cons:** dated furniture; no on-site parking; soundproofing could be better. $ *Rooms from: €65* ✉ *Calle Pintores 2* 🕾 *92/724–7634* ⊕ *www.iberiahotel.com* 🛏 *38 rooms* ❙◎❙ *Free Breakfast.*

$$$
HOTEL
Fodor's Choice
★

🛏 **NH Collection Cáceres Palacio de Oquendo.** This 16th-century palace, which spans the length of Plaza San Juan on the edge of the old quarter, is now an impressive NH Collection hotel that rivals the town's parador— at much lower rates. **Pros:** excellent value; new design; quiet area close to Plaza Mayor. **Cons:** no parking; pricey breakfast and mediocre restaurant; some rooms have only skylights (no windows). $ *Rooms from: €135* ✉ *Pl. San Juan 11* 🕾 *92/721–5800* ⊕ *www.nh-hotels.com* 🛏 *86 rooms* ❙◎❙ *No meals.*

$$$$
HOTEL

🛏 **Parador de Cáceres.** This 14th-century palace in the old town boasts elegant public spaces filled with antiques. **Pros:** gorgeous old building; inviting outdoor dining area; spacious rooms. **Cons:** spartan decor; unattractive indoor dining room; some bathrooms need work. $ *Rooms from: €220* ✉ *Calle Ancha 6* 🕾 *92/721–1759* ⊕ *www.parador.es* 🛏 *39 rooms* ❙◎❙ *Free Breakfast.*

NIGHTLIFE

Bars in Cáceres stay busy until the wee hours. Nightlife centers on the **Plaza Mayor,** which fills after dinner with families out for a *paseo* (stroll), as well as students swigging *calimocho* (a mix of red wine and Coca-Cola) or *litronas* (liter bottles of beer). **Calle de Pizarro,** south of Plaza San Juan, is lined with cafés and bars.

El Corral de las Cigüeñas. There's a hopping nighttime music scene at this charming old-town café with an outdoor patio. In winter months, the club is open evenings Thursday–Sunday. Hours vary depending on events; call ahead or check concert schedules online. ⊠ *Cuesta de Aldana 6* ☎ *92/721–6425, 64/775–8245* ⊕ *www.elcorralcc.com.*

SHOPPING

Some of the best shopping in Cáceres is culinary: the city and surrounding countryside are renowned for producing unparalleled Iberian ham and chorizo, complex cheeses, grippy wines, and mouthwatering pastries. But there are also distinctive artisan crafts worth seeking out.

Centro de Artesanía Casa Palacio de los Moraga. Eschew the usual souvenir shops and instead drop by this art collective that sells wallets, purses, pins, toys, clothes, and other decorative elements in leather and ceramics made by local artisans. ⊠ *Calle Cuesta de Aldana 1, Cáceres* ☎ *92/722–7453* ⊕ *www.extremadurartesana.com.*

Pastelería Isa. The city's premier pastry shop since 1952, the year it opened, "La Isa" is best known for its *mojicón*, an oversized orange-scented muffin native to Extremadura that tastes best when dunked in café con leche. ⊠ *Pl. Mayor 25, Cáceres* ☎ *92/724–8185.*

Fodor's Choice ★ **Sierra de Montánchez.** Satisfy your jamón cravings at this gourmet shop specializing in acorn-fed pork products. There are usually baskets of terrific-quality La Dalia pimentón on sale as well; grab one or two tins here as they're hard to find outside Extremadura. ⊠ *Pl. de la Concepción 5, Cáceres* ☎ *62/547–1315* ⊕ *www.sierrademontanchez.es.*

TRUJILLO

45 km (28 miles) east of Cáceres, 256 km (159 miles) southwest of Madrid.

Trujillo rises up from the boulder-strewn fields like a great granite schooner under full sail. From above, the rooftops and towers are worn and medieval looking. At street level, Renaissance architecture flourishes in squares such as the Plaza Mayor, with its elegant San Martín church. As in Cáceres, storks' nests top many towers—the birds have become a symbol of Trujillo. With roots in Roman times, the city was captured from the Moors in 1232 and colonized by a number of leading military families.

GETTING HERE AND AROUND

There is no train service to Trujillo, but Avanza bus (⊕ *www.avanzabus. com*) offers several departures daily from Madrid's Estacion de Sur (3½ hours). There are usually several Blablacar rideshares available each day as well. Take in Trujillo on foot, as the streets are mostly cobbled or crudely paved with stone (suitable footwear needed; prepare for hills, too). The two main roads into Trujillo leave you at the unattractive bottom end of town. Things get progressively older the farther you climb, but even on the lower slopes—where most of the shops are concentrated—you need walk only a few yards to step into what seems like the Middle Ages.

Bus Contacts Avanza Bus. ☎ 91/272–2832 ⊕ www.avanzabus.com.

ESSENTIALS
Visitor Information Trujillo Tourist Office. ✉ Pl. Mayor ☎ 92/732–2677
⊕ www.turismotrujillo.com.

EXPLORING

Casa Museo de Pizarro. The Pizarro family residence is now a modest museum dedicated to the connection between Spain and Latin America. The first floor emulates a typical home from 15th-century Trujillo, and the second floor is divided into exhibits on Peru and Pizarro's life there. The museum explains the "Curse of the Pizarro," recounting how the conquistador and his brothers were killed in brutal battles with rivals; those who survived never again enjoyed the wealth they had achieved in Peru. ✉ Pl. de Santa María and Calle Merced s/n 🖾 €2.

Castillo. For spectacular views, climb this large fortress, built by the Moors in the 9th century over old Roman foundations. To the south are silos, warehouses, and residential neighborhoods. To the north are green fields and brilliant flowers, partitioned by a maze of nearly leveled Roman stone walls, and an ancient cistern. The castle's size underscores the historic importance of now-tiny Trujillo. ✉ Cerro Cabeza de Zorro 🖾 €2.

Iglesia de Santa María La Mayor. Attached to a Romanesque bell tower, this Gothic church is the most beautiful in Trujillo. It's only occasionally used for mass, and its interior has been virtually untouched since the 16th century. The upper choir has an exquisitely carved balustrade, and the coats of arms at each end indicate the seats Ferdinand and Isabella occupied when they came here to worship. Note the high altar, circa 1480, adorned with great 15th-century Spanish paintings. To see it properly illuminated, place a coin in the box next to the church entrance. Climb the tower for stunning views of the town and vast plains stretching toward Cáceres and the Sierra de Gredos. ✉ Pl. de Santa María 🖾 From €1.

Fodor's Choice ★ **La Villa.** This is Trujillo's oldest area, enclosed by restored stone walls. Follow them along Calle Almenas, which runs west from the Palacio de Orellana-Pizarro, beneath the **Alcázar de Los Chaves,** a castle-fortress that was converted into a guest lodge in the 15th century and hosted visiting dignitaries including Ferdinand and Isabella. Now a college, the building has seen better days. Passing the Alcázar, continue west along the wall to the **Puerta de San Andrés,** one of La Villa's four surviving gates (there were originally seven). Views from the hilltop are particularly memorable at sunset, when spotlights illuminate the old quarter. ✉ Trujillo.

Fodor's Choice ★ **Plaza Mayor.** One of the fines plazas in Spain, this superb Renaissance creation is dominated by a bronze equestrian statue of Francisco Pizarro—the work of an American sculptor, Charles Rumsey. Notice the Palacio del Marqués de la Conquista, the most dramatic building on the square with plateresque ornamentation and imaginative busts of the Pizarro family flanking its corner balcony. It was built by Francisco Pizarro's half-brother Hernando. ✉ Trujillo.

WORTH NOTING

Museo de la Coria (*Fundación Xavier de Salas*). Near the Puerta de la Coria and occupying a former Franciscan convent built in the 15th century, this museum's exhibits on the relationship between Spain and Latin America are similar to those in the Casa Museo de Pizarro but with an emphasis on the troops as well as other conquistadores who led missions across the water. The museum is worth visiting if only for a look inside the old convent's two-tier central cloister. ✉ *Pl. de Santa María* ☎ *92/765–9032, 92/732–1898* 🌐 *www.fundacionxavierdesalas.com* 🎫 *Free* ⏲ *Closed weekdays.*

Palacio de Orellana-Pizarro. The Palacio de Orellana-Pizarro, renovated by Juan Pizarro himself in the 16th century, now serves as a school and has one of the most elegant Renaissance courtyards in town. The ground floor, open to visitors, has a deep, arched front doorway; on the second story is an elaborate Renaissance balcony bearing the crest of the Pizarro family. Miguel de Cervantes, on his way to thank the Virgin of Guadalupe for his release from prison, spent time writing in the palace. ✉ *Behind Pl. Mayor* 🎫 *Free.*

WHERE TO EAT AND STAY

$$$ SPANISH
🍴 **Bizcocho.** A Trujillo institution conveniently located on the Plaza Mayor, Bizcocho specializes in (slightly overpriced) Extramaduran cuisine—think local jamón, queso, and migas—and the stone-and-tile dining room is cozy and cool even in the summer. Reservations are essential on holiday weekends. **Known for:** central location; excellent Iberian pork dishes; well-presented plates. [$] *Average main: €20* ✉ *Pl. Mayor 11* ☎ *92/732–2017* 🌐 *restaurantebizcochoplaza.com* 💳 *No credit cards.*

$$$ SPANISH Fodor's Choice ★
🍴 **El 7 de Sillerías.** Ask aTrujillo local for the best food in town, and many will point you here for fresh, reasonably priced tapas and mains including croquetas (try the wild mushroom rendition) and *secreto ibérico* (seared Iberian pork shoulder steak). For just €14, the weekday lunch menú del día—including three courses and wine—is a steal. **Known for:** pleasant patio out back; secreto ibérico, a specialty pork dish; prix-fixe weekday lunch deal. [$] *Average main: €20* ✉ *Calle Sillerías 7* ☎ *92/732–1856* 🌐 *www.el7desillerias.com.*

$ HOTEL FAMILY
🏨 **Izán Trujillo.** Once a 16th-century convent, this splendid four-star hotel is a short walk from the historic center. **Pros:** air of calm throughout the property; friendly and efficient staff; central location. **Cons:** small swimming pool; rooms vary in size; unpredictable food quality in restaurant. [$] *Rooms from: €77* ✉ *Pl. del Campillo 1* ☎ *92/745–8900* 🌐 *www.izanhoteles.es* 🛏 *78 rooms* 🍽 *No meals.*

$$$ HOTEL FAMILY Fodor's Choice ★
🏨 **Parador de Trujillo.** In another of the region's 16th-century convents, this parador is the essence of peace and tranquility, with rooms that are cozy and serene. **Pros:** peace and quiet in the heart of town; swimming pool; homey decor. **Cons:** somewhat overpriced; rooms are a bit like monastery quarters—on the small side; poor-quality bath products. [$] *Rooms from: €175* ✉ *Calle Santa Beatriz de Silva 1* ☎ *92/732–1350* 🌐 *www.parador.es* 🛏 *50 rooms* 🍽 *Free Breakfast.*

$ HOTEL Fodor's Choice ★
🏨 **Posada Dos Orillas.** This hotel occupies a 16th-century stagecoach inn on a quiet pedestrian street uphill from the Plaza Mayor. **Pros:** pleasant interiors; beautiful terrace; good weekend rates. **Cons:** no reserved

parking; beds a little basic; small TVs. [$] *Rooms from: €70* ✉ *Calle de los Cambrones 6* ☎ *92/765–9079* 🌐 *www.dosorillas.com* 🛏 *13 rooms* 🍴 *Free Breakfast.*

SHOPPING

Trujillo is a good place to shop for folk art. Look for multicolor rugs, blankets, and embroidery.

Eduardo Pablos Mateos. This workshop specializes in wood carvings, basketwork, and furniture. Call ahead to schedule a personal tour. ✉ *Calle de San Judas 3* ☎ *92/732–1066, 60/617–4382 mobile.*

3

Fodor's Choice ★ **La Despensa.** This gourmet shop on the corner of Plaza Mayor used to be the wine cellar of a 16th-century palace. Now it sells local products—including jamón, cheese, wine, and even locally made beer—at excellent prices ✉ *Cuesta de la Sangre s/n* ☎ *65/450–3419.*

GUADALUPE

200 km (125 miles) southwest of Madrid, 96 km (60 miles) east of Trujillo.

Guadalupe's monastery is one of the most inspiring sights in Extremadura, and its story begins around 1300, when a local shepherd uncovered a statue of the Virgin, supposedly carved by St. Luke. King Alfonso XI, who often hunted here, had a church built to house the statue and vowed to found a monastery should he defeat the Moors at the battle of Salado in 1340. After his victory, he kept his promise. The greatest period in the monastery's history was between the 15th and 18th centuries, when, under the rule of the Hieronymites, it was turned into a pilgrimage center rivaling Santiago de Compostela in importance. Pilgrims have been coming here since the 14th century and have been joined by a growing number of tourists. Yet the monastery's isolation—a good two-hour drive from the nearest town—has protected it from commercial excess. Documents authorizing Columbus's first voyage to the Western Hemisphere were signed here, which is why the Virgin of Guadalupe became the patroness of Latin America, honored by the dedication of thousands of churches and towns in the New World. The monastery's decline coincided with Spain's loss of overseas territories in the 19th century. Guadalupe is also known for its copperware, crafted here since the 16th century.

GETTING HERE AND AROUND

There's no train to Guadalupe, and bus service is sporadic. It's easiest if you have your own car and park on the outskirts of town. It's small enough to explore on foot but hilly with cobblestone streets, so wear comfortable shoes.

ESSENTIALS

Visitor Information Guadalupe Tourist Office. ✉ *Pl. Santa María de Guadalupe* ☎ *92/715–4128* 🌐 *www.turismoextremadura.com.*

EXPLORING

Plaza Mayor (*Plaza de Santa María de Guadalupe*). In the middle of this tiny, irregularly shaped plaza—which is transformed during festivals into a bullring—is a 15th-century fountain, where Columbus's two Native American servants were baptized in 1496. ✉ *Guadalupe.*

Fodor's Choice ★ **Real Monasterio de Santa María de Guadalupe** (*Royal Monastery of Our Lady of Guadalupe*). Looming in the background of the Plaza Mayor is the late-Gothic facade of Guadalupe's colossal **monastery church,** flanked by battlement towers. The (required) guided tour begins in the Mudejar cloister and continues on to the **chapter house,** with hymnals, vestments, and paintings including a series of small panels by Zurbarán. The ornate 17th-century **sacristy** has a series of eight Zurbarán paintings, from 1638–47. These austere representations of monks of the Hieronymite order and scenes from the life of St. Jerome are the artist's only significant paintings housed in the setting for which they were intended. The tour concludes in the garish, late-baroque **Camarín,** the chapel where the famous *Virgen Morena* (*Black Virgin*) is housed. The dark, mysterious wooden figure hides under a heavy veil and mantle of red and gold; painted panels tell her life's story. Each September 8, the virgin is brought down from the altarpiece and walked around the cloister in a procession with pilgrims following on their knees. Outside, the monastery's gardens have been restored to their original, geometric Moorish style. ✉ *Entrance on Pl. Mayor* ☎ *92/736–7000* 🌐 *www.monasterioguadalupe.com* 🎫 *€5.*

WHERE TO STAY

$ B&B/INN FAMILY 🏨 **Casa Rural la Abacería.** For a simple, inexpensive overnight stay, try this small, tidy guesthouse on a quiet side street near the center of the village, around the corner from the parador. **Pros:** private location; good for families; plenty of peace and quiet. **Cons:** individual rooms are a bit small; cold hallways in the winter; no Wi-Fi. [$] *Rooms from: €50* ✉ *Calle Marqués de la Romana* ☎ *92/715–4282, 65/020–8405* 🌐 *www.guadaluperural.com* 💳 *No credit cards* 🛏 *3 rooms* 🍴 *Free Breakfast.*

$ HOTEL Fodor's Choice ★ 🏨 **Hospedería del Real Monasterio.** An excellent and considerably cheaper alternative to the town parador, this inn was built around the 16th-century Gothic cloister of the monastery itself. **Pros:** guests get free monastery admission; excellent restaurant; helpful staff. **Cons:** the monastery's church bells chime around the clock; a bit pricey; uncomfortable beds. [$] *Rooms from: €75* ✉ *Pl. Juan Carlos I* ☎ *92/736–7000* 🌐 *www.hotelhospederiamonasterioguadalupe.com* ⏲ *Closed mid-Jan.–mid-Feb.* 🛏 *47 rooms* 🍴 *No meals.*

$$$ HOTEL 🏨 **Parador de Guadalupe.** This exquisite estate, once the 15th-century palace of the Marquis de la Romana, now houses one of Spain's finest paradores. **Pros:** stunning architecture; authentic extremeño cooking; idyllic balconies. **Cons:** tight parking; long hike from reception to the farthest rooms; old-world property with old-world amenities. [$] *Rooms from: €140* ✉ *Calle Marqués de la Romana 12* ☎ *92/736–7075* 🌐 *www.parador.es* 🛏 *41 rooms* 🍴 *Free Breakfast.*

Mérida's excellently preserved Roman amphitheater is the site of a drama festival every July.

MÉRIDA

76 km (47 miles) south of Cáceres, 191 km (119 miles) north of Seville, 347 km (216 miles) southwest of Madrid.

Mérida has some of the most impressive Roman ruins in Iberia. Founded by the Romans in 25 BC on the banks of the Río Guadiana, the city is strategically located at the junction of major Roman roads from León to Seville and Toledo to Lisbon. Augusta Emerita, as the Romans called it, quickly became the capital of the vast Roman province of Lusitania. A bishopric in Visigothic times, Mérida never regained the importance that it had under the Romans, and other than the Roman monuments, which pop up all over town, the city is rather plain.

The glass-and-steel bus station is in a modern district on the other side of the river from the town center. It commands a good view of the exceptionally long **Roman bridge**. On the bank opposite the ruins is the Alcazaba.

Other Roman sites nearby require a drive. Across the train tracks in a modern neighborhood is the **circo** (circus), where chariot races were held. Little remains of the grandstands, which seated 30,000, but the outline of the circus is clearly visible and impressive for its size: 1,312 feet long and 377 feet wide. Of the existing aqueduct remains, the most impressive is the **Acueducto de los Milagros** (Aqueduct of Miracles), north of the train station. It carried water from the Roman dam of Proserpina, still standing, 5 km (3 miles) away.

GETTING HERE AND AROUND
There are several buses daily to Mérida from Badajoz (1 hour), Sevilla (2½ hours), Cáceres (45 minutes), Trujillo (1½ hours), and Madrid (4½ hours). There are also several daily trains, which take about the same travel time but cost more. Check the RENFE website (⊕ *www. renfe.com*) or tourist office for schedules. Alternatively, there are usually several Blablacar rideshare departures from Madrid and Mérida's neighboring cities each day. Once in Mérida, the city center is navigable on foot or by tourist train.

ESSENTIALS
Visitor Information Mérida Tourist Office. ⊠ *Paseo José Álvarez Sáenz de Buruaga* ☎ *92/433–0722* ⊕ *www.turismomerida.org.*

TOURS **Tren Turístico.** Mérida is walkable, but this tourist train follows a 35-minute circular route past all the sites, starting at the tourist office in front of the Roman theater. Call ahead to book as service is sometimes canceled if there isn't a minimum number of passengers. ⊠ *Paseo José Álvarez Sáenz de Buruaga* ☎ *66/747–1907* 🎟 *€5.*

EXPLORING

Fodor'sChoice **Museo Nacional de Arte Romano** (*National Museum of Roman Art*).
★ Across the street from the entrance to the Roman sites and connected by an underground passageway is Mérida's superb Roman art museum, in a monumental building designed by the renowned Spanish architect Rafael Moneo. Walk through a series of passageways to the luminous, cathedral-like main exhibition hall, which is supported by arches the same proportion and size (50 feet) as the Roman arch in the center of Mérida, the Arco de Trajano (Trajan's Arch). The exhibits include mosaics, frescoes, jewelry, statues, pottery, household utensils, and other Roman works. Be sure to visit the **crypt** beneath the museum—it contains the remains of several homes and a necropolis that were uncovered while the museum was being built in 1981. ⊠ *Calle José Ramón Mélida s/n* ☎ *92/431–1690, 92/431–1912* ⊕ *www.mecd.gob. es/mnromano/home.html* 🎟 *€3* ⊗ *Closed Mon.*

Fodor'sChoice **Plaza de España.** Mérida's main square adjoins the northwestern corner
★ of the Alcazaba and is lively both day and night. The plaza's oldest building is a 16th-century palace, now the Mérida Palace hotel. Behind the palace stretches Mérida's most charming area with Andalusian-style white houses shaded by palms, in the midst of which stands the **Arco de Trajano,** part of a Roman city gate. This is a great place to people-watch over tapas at sunset. ⊠ *Mérida.*

FAMILY **Roman monuments.** Mérida's Roman **teatro** (theater) and **anfiteatro**
Fodor'sChoice (amphitheater) are set in a verdant park, and the theater—the best pre-
★ served in Spain—seats 6,000 and is used for a classical drama festival each July. The amphitheater, which holds 15,000 spectators, opened in 8 BC for gladiatorial contests. Next to the entrance to the ruins is the **main tourist office,** where you can pick up maps and brochures. You can buy a ticket to see only the Roman ruins or, for a slightly higher fee, an *entrada conjunta* (joint admission), which also grants access to the Basílica de Santa Eulalia and the Alcazaba. To reach the monuments by

car, follow signs to the "Museo de Arte Romano." Parking is usually easy to find. ✉ *Av. de los Estudiantes* ☎ *92/431–2530* 🎟 *From €12.*

WHERE TO EAT AND STAY

$$$$ SPANISH 🍴 **Gonzalo Valverde.** This kitchen turns out traditional extremeño classics executed with a modern (if slightly precious) flair such as Iberian pork mousse-filled spring rolls and roast venison loin. The prix-fixe menu del día is a great value at €30. **Known for:** creative extremeño cuisine; attentive service; riverside location. [$] *Average main: €35* ✉ *Av. Fernández López 7* ☎ *92/430–4512* 🌐 *www.gonzalovalverde.com* 🕒 *No dinner Sun. and Mon.*

$ TAPAS FAMILY 🍴 **La Despensa del Castúo.** One of the specialties at this local hangout, known for its cheap, thoughtfully prepared tapas, is morcilla de Guadalupe, blood sausage made in the nearby town of the same name. Note to diners with time constraints: the service is notoriously slow when the restaurant is packed. **Known for:** €10 menú del día; fall-off-the-bone stewed meats; worth-the-wait outdoor seating. [$] *Average main: €10* ✉ *Calle José Ramón Mélida 48* ☎ *92/430–2251* 💳 *No credit cards.*

$$ HOTEL FAMILY Fodor's Choice ★ 🏨 **Ilunion Mérida Palace.** Dominating the Plaza de España, this five-star luxury hotel has a rooftop pool deck, Moorish-themed design elements, and a twinkly central courtyard. **Pros:** outdoor pool, terrace, and solarium; gym facilities; excellent restaurant. **Cons:** some front rooms facing the Plaza de España can be noisy in summer; valet parking is expensive and alternatives are scarce; a bit far from the Roman ruins. [$] *Rooms from: €120* ✉ *Pl. de España 19* ☎ *92/438–3800* 🌐 *www.ilunionmeridapalace.com* 🛏 *76 rooms* 🍽 *No meals.*

$$$ HOTEL FAMILY 🏨 **Parador de Mérida** (*Parador Vía de la Plata*). This spacious hotel exudes Andalusian cheerfulness with hints at its Roman and Moorish past—it was built over the remains of a Roman temple, later became a baroque convent, and then served as a prison. **Pros:** central location; stunning interior courtyard; dazzling-white interior. **Cons:** expensive parking; erratic Wi-Fi; could use a revamp. [$] *Rooms from: €150* ✉ *Pl. de la Constitución and Calle Almendralejo 56* ☎ *92/431–3800* 🌐 *www.parador.es* 🛏 *81 rooms* 🍽 *No meals.*

GALICIA AND ASTURIAS

with Cantabria

WELCOME TO GALICIA AND ASTURIAS

TOP REASONS TO GO

★ **Experience gourmet heaven:** Beautiful Santiago de Compostela is said to contain more restaurants and bars per square mile than any other city in Spain.

★ **Go on rugged hikes:** Spend days in the spectacular Picos de Europa range getting lost in forgotten mountain villages.

★ **Get in on the grapevine:** The Ribeiro region yields Spain's finest white wines.

★ **Enjoy the waterfront activity:** Watch the oyster hawkers at work while dining on a fresh catch on Vigo's Rúa Pescadería.

★ **Discover Santander:** With its intoxicating schedule of live music, opera, and theater performances on the beach and in gardens and monasteries, the city's August festival of music and dance is the perfect backdrop for exploring this vibrant city.

The bewitching provinces of Galicia and Asturias lie in Spain's northwest; these rugged Atlantic regions hide a corner of Spain so remote it was once called *finis terrae* (the end of the earth). Galicia is famous for Santiago de Compostela, for centuries a destination for Christian pilgrims seeking to pay homage to St. James. As for Asturias, its verdant hills, sandy beaches, and the massive Picos de Europa mountain range are all part of its pull. To the east, Cantabria borders the Bay of Biscay.

1 Santiago de Compostela and Eastern Galicia. Books and movies have been written about it and millions have walked it, but you don't have to be a pilgrim to enjoy the Camino de Santiago. At the end of the path is Santiago itself, a vibrant university town embedded in hills around the soaring spires of one of Spain's most emblematic cathedrals.

2 The Costa da Morte and Rías Baixas. From the small fishing village of Malpica to Muros, from Fisterra (World's End) down to Vigo and the Portuguese border, this area takes in the peaceful seaside towns of

Cambados and Baiona, the exquisite beaches of Las Islas Cíes, and the beautifully preserved medieval streets of Pontevedra.

3 A Coruña and Rías Altas. Galicia has more coastline and unspoiled, nontouristy beaches than anywhere else in Spain. Opt for vast expanses of sand facing the Atlantic Ocean or tiny, tucked-away coves, but

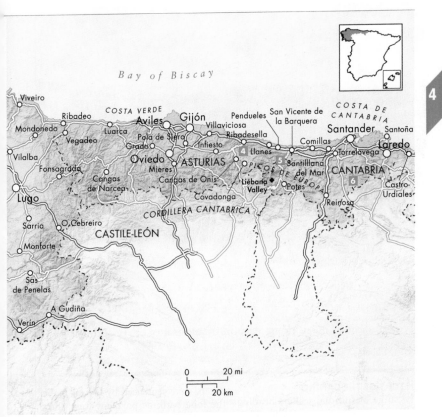

4

take note: the water is colder than the Mediterranean, and the weather is more unreliable.

4 Asturias. Also known as the Senda Costera (Coastal Way), this partly paved nature route between Pendueles and Llanes takes in some of Asturias's most spectacular coastal scenery, including noisy *bufones* (large waterspouts created naturally by erosion) and the Playa de Ballota.

5 The Picos de Europa. One of Spain's best-kept secrets, the "Peaks of Europe" lie across Asturias, Cantabria, and León. In addition to 8,910-foot peaks, the area has deep caves, excellent mountain refuges, and interesting wildlife. This region is also known for its fine cheeses.

6 Cantabria. Santander's wide beaches and summer music-and-dance festival are highlights of this mountain and maritime community. The Liébana Valley, the Renaissance town at Santillana del Mar, and ports and beaches like San Vicente de la Barquera all rank among northern Spain's finest treasures.

EL CAMINO DE SANTIAGO

Traversing meadows, mountains, and villages across Spain, about 100,000 travelers embark each year on a pilgrimage to Galicia's Santiago de Compostela, the sacred city of St. James—they're not all deeply religious these days, though a spiritual quest is generally the motivation.

HISTORY OF THE CAMINO

The surge of spiritual seekers heading to Spain's northwest coast began as early as the 9th century, when news spread that the apostle James's remains were there. By the middle of the 12th century, about 1 million pilgrims were arriving in Santiago de Compostela each year. An entire industry of food hawkers, hoteliers, and trinket sellers awaited their arrival. They even had the world's first travel guide, the Codex Calixtinus (published in the 1130s), to help them on their way. Some made the journey in response to their conscience, to do penance for their sins against God, while others were sentenced by law to make the long walk as payment for crimes against the state. Legend claims that St. James's body was transported secretly to the area by boat after his martyrdom in Jerusalem in AD 44. The idea picked up steam in 814, when a hermit claimed to see miraculous lights in the sky, accompanied by the sound of angels singing, on a wooded hillside near Padrón. Human bones were quickly discovered at the site, and immediately—and perhaps somewhat conveniently—declared to be those of the apostle (the bones may actually have belonged to Priscillian, the leader of a 4th-century Christian sect).

Word of this important find quickly spread across a relic-hungry Europe. Within a couple of centuries, the road to Santiago had become as popular as the other two major medieval pilgrimages, to Rome and to Jerusalem. After the 12th century, pilgrim numbers began to gradually decline, due to the dangers of robbery along the route, a growing skepticism about the genuineness of St. James's remains, and the popular rise of science in place of religion.

4

THE PILGRIMAGE TODAY

The pilgrims follow one of seven main routes, walking about 19 miles per day in a nearly 500-mile journey. Along the way, they encounter incredible local hospitality and trade stories with fellow adventurers. By the late 1980s, there were only about 3,000 pilgrims a year, but in 1993 the Galician government launched an initiative called the Xacobeo (i.e., Jacobean; the name James comes from the Hebrew word "Jacob") to increase the number of visitors to the region, and the popularity of the pilgrimage soared. Numbers increased exponentially, and there have been over 100,000 annually since 2006. In holy years, when St. James Day (July 25) falls on a Sunday, the number of pilgrims usually doubles.

WHO WAS ST. JAMES?

St. James the Great, brother of St. John the Evangelist (author of the Gospel of John and the Book of Revelation), was one of Jesus's first apostles. Sent by Jesus to preach that the kingdom of heaven had come, he crossed Europe and ended up in Spain. Along the way, he saved a knight from drowning in the sea. As legend goes, the knight resurfaced, covered in scallop shells: this is why Camino pilgrims carry this seashell on their journey. Legend has it that St. James was beheaded by King Herod Agrippa on his return to Judea in AD 44, but that he was rescued by angels and transported in a rudderless stone boat back to Spain, where his lifeless body was encased in a rock. James is said to have resurfaced to aid the Christians in the Reconquista Battle of Clavijo, gaining him the title of Matamoros, or Moor Killer. When the body of St. James was found, people came in droves to see his remains—the Spanish and Portuguese name for St. James is Santiago. The belief arose that sins would be cleansed through the penance of this long walk, an idea no doubt encouraged by the Church at the time.

THE PILGRIMAGE EXPERIENCE

Not everyone does the route in one trip. Some split it into manageable chunks and take years to complete the whole course. Most, however, walk an average of 30 km (19 miles) per day to arrive in Santiago after a monthlong trek. The Camino, which sometimes follows a mountain trail and other times passes through a village or across a

field, is generally so well marked that most travelers claim not to need a map (bringing one is highly recommended, however). Travelers simply follow the route markers—gold scallop-shell designs on blue backgrounds posted on buildings or painted on rocks and trail posts. Walking is not the only option: bicycles are common and will cut the time needed to complete the pilgrimage in half; horseback riding, or walking with a donkey in tow, carrying the bags, are also options. Every town along the route has an official Camino *albergue,* or hostel, often in an ancient monastery or original pilgrim's hospice. They generally accommodate 40–150 people. You can bunk for free—though a donation is expected—in the company of fellow walkers, but may only stay one night, unless severe Camino injuries prevent you from moving on. Be aware that these places can fill up fast. Walkers get first priority, followed by cyclists and those on horseback, with organized walking groups at the bottom of the pecking order. If there is no room at the official albergues, there are plenty of paid hostels along the route. Wherever you stay, get your Pilgrims' Passport, or *credencial,* stamped, as proof of how far you've walked.

A TYPICAL DAY

A typical day on the Camino involves walking hard through the morning to the next village in time to get a free bed. The afternoon is for catching up with fellow pilgrims, having a look around town, and doing a bit of washing. The Spanish people you meet along the way and the camaraderie with fellow pilgrims is a highlight of the trip for many. Some albergues serve a communal evening meal, but there is always a bar in town that offers a lively atmosphere and a cheap (€8–€10) Pilgrim's set menu (quality and fare varies; it consists of three courses plus bread and beverage). Sore feet are compared, local wine is consumed, and new walking partners are found for the following day's stage. Just make sure you get back to the albergue before curfew, around 10 or 11, or you may find a locked door.

THE FINISH LINE

Arriving at the end of the Camino de Santiago is an emotional experience. It is common to see small groups of pilgrims, hands clasped tightly together, tearfully approaching the moss- and lichen-covered Cathedral in Santiago's Plaza del Obradoiro. After entering the building through the Pilgrim's Door and hugging the statue of St. James, a special mass awaits them at midday, the highlight of which is seeing the *botafumeiro,* a giant incense-filled censer, swinging from the ceiling. Those that have covered more than 100 km (62 miles) on foot, or twice that distance on a bicycle—as shown by the stamped passport—can then collect their Compostela certificate from the Pilgrim's office (near the Cathedral, at Rúa do Vilar 1).

USEFUL WEBSITES

The modern pilgrim has technology at his or her fingertips. The official Xacabeo website (⊕ *www.xacobeo.es/en*) can not only help you plan your trip, with detailed route maps and hostel locations, it also has a Xacoblog where you can share videos, photos, and comments, as well as a forum for asking questions and getting feedback. A cell phone application helps you check routes, hostels, and sites to see while you're walking. Other websites include: ⊕ *www.caminodesantiago.me,* ⊕ *www. csj.org.uk,* ⊕ *www.caminoadventures. com,* ⊕ *www.caminosantiagodecompostela.com.*

CAMINO TIPS

The most popular of the seven main routes of the Camino de Santiago is the 791-km (480-mile) **Camino Francés** (French Way), which starts in France (in Saint-Jean-Pied-de-Port) and crosses the high meseta plains into Galicia. The **Camino Norte** (Northern Way), which runs through the woodlands of Spain's rugged north coast, is also gaining in popularity.

The busiest time on the Camino is in the summer months, June–September. That means crowded paths and problems finding a room at night, particularly if you start the Camino on the first few days of any month, plus hot temperatures. Consider starting in April, May, or September instead. Making the journey in winter is not advised.

The most important part of your equipment is your hiking boots, which should be as professional as your budget allows and well worn in before you hit the trail. Other essentials include a good-quality—and waterproof (it rains year-round in Galicia)—backpack, sleeping bag, sunscreen, and a medical kit, including Vaseline and blister remedies for sore feet. Don't forget a set of earplugs as well.

To get your credencial, contact one of the Camino confraternity groups. These are not-for-profit associations formed by previous pilgrims to help those who are thinking about doing the Camino (⊕ *www.csj.org.uk*). You can also pick up a passport at many of the common starting points, local churches, and Amigos del Camino de Santiago in villages throughout Spain. Many albergues throughout Spain also can provide you with a valid credencial for a small fee.

4

Updated by Elizabeth Prosser

Spain's westernmost region is en route to nowhere, an end in itself. This magical, remote area is sure to pull at your heartstrings, so be prepared to fall in love. In Gallego they call the feeling *morriña*, a powerful longing for a person or place you've left behind.

Stretching northwest from the lonesome Castilian plains to the rocky seacoast, Asturias and Galicia incorporate lush hills and vineyards, gorgeous *rías* (estuaries), and the country's wildest mountains, the Picos de Europa. Santander and the entire Cantabrian region are cool summer refuges with sandy beaches, high sierras (including part of the Picos de Europa), and tiny highland towns. Santander, once the main seaport for Old Castile on the Bay of Biscay, is in a mountainous zone wedged between the Basque Country and Asturias.

Northwestern Spain is a series of rainy landscapes, stretching from your feet to the horizon. Ancient granite buildings wear a blanket of moss, and even the stone *horreos* (granaries) are built on stilts above the damp ground. Swirling fog and heavy mist help keep local folktales of the supernatural alive. Rather than a guitar, you'll hear the *gaita* (bagpipe), a legacy of the Celts' settlements here in the 5th and 6th centuries BC. Spanish families flock to these cool northern beaches and mountains each summer. Santiago de Compostela, where the Cathedral holds the remains of the apostle James, has drawn pilgrims for 900 years, leaving churches, shrines, and former hospitals in their path. Asturias, north of the main pilgrim trail, has always maintained a separate identity, isolated by the rocky Picos de Europa. This and the Basque Country are the only parts of Spain never conquered by the Moors, so Asturian architecture shows little Moorish influence. It was from a mountain base at Covadonga that the Christians won their first decisive battle against the Moors and launched the Reconquest of Spain. Despite being very much its own region, Cantabria is in spirit much closer to Asturias—with which it shares the Picos de Europa, Castilian Spanish, and similar architecture—than its passionately independent neighbor, the Basque Country.

PLANNING

WHEN TO GO

Galicia can get very hot (more than 90°F [30°C]) June–September, although summer is the best time for swimming and water sports and for Celtic music festivals. Asturias, in the mountains, is cooler. Galicia can be rainy to the point of saturation—not for nothing is this region called Green Spain—so avoid the area in winter: the rain, wind, and freezing temperatures make driving an arduous experience. Spring and fall are ideal, as the weather is reasonable and crowds are few. At any time of year in Galicia, it is not unusual to experience all seasons in one day.

PLANNING YOUR TIME

You can fly into Santiago de Compostela, and a week should be long enough to cover the Santiago area and Galicia's south. From Santiago, you can drive down the PO550 to Cambados, stopping on the way at fishing villages along the Ría de Arousa. If you take the coastal road to Pontevedra, you can spend time there exploring the medieval streets and tapas bars and then drive down to Vigo for a lunch of oysters on Rúa Pescadería. Continue south and arrive before dark at the Baiona parador. Alternatively, travel to A Coruña, and from there head north to some of Spain's loveliest beaches and Viveiro. From here cross into Asturias and spend time in Luarca or Gijón. Another attractive option is getting lost in a small village in the Picos de Europa.

Heading farther east, Santillana del Mar's Renaissance architecture, the Altamira Caves, and the Sardinero Beach at Santander are top spots, while the fishing villages and beaches around Llanes in eastern Asturias, and San Vicente de la Barquera in Cantabria have charming ports and inlets. If you want to delve more deeply into the Picos de Europa and the region's pretty coastline, Asturias and Cantabria merit more than a week's exploration.

FESTIVALS

There's a full calendar of special events in Galicia, including international festivals, major national celebrations, saints' days, and unique local events, some in towns that don't otherwise have much to offer the average traveler.

Carnival. In February and March, on this first major fiesta of the year after Three Kings' Day (January 6), cities, towns, and villages across the region erupt with festive fun, including parades, parties, and wild costumes.

Corpus Christi. During this feast day in June, the town of Ponteareas celebrates flowers and the harvest by carpeting the streets throughout the night with an intricate weave of fresh flowers and leaves, over which a somber parade progresses the following day.

El Día de Santiago (*St. James's Day*). Because it's named for the saint, Santiago is a good place to be on his feast day, July 25, celebrated here with processions, street parties, and spectacular fireworks. It is also one of the few days of the year that the enormous botafumeiro (incense burner) is released and swung across the naves of Santiago's Cathedral.

On July 24, there's a huge fireworks display and a ritual burning of a large pyrotechnic castle, which represents the Gothic facade of the Cathedral.

Festa do Marisco (*Seafood Festival*). Galicia's famous culinary event, held in O Grove in October, draws crowds to feast on a stunning number of seafood delicacies. ⊕ *www.turismogrove.es.*

Festa do Viño Albariño (*Albariño Wine Festival*). On the first Sunday of August, the town of Cambados, capital of albariño country, draws thousands to witness its processions, concerts, cultural events, fireworks, and other revelry honoring local vineyards and wineries—including wine tastings from around 40 different Rías Baixas wineries. The festival has been held since the early 1950s. ⊕ *www.cambados.es.*

Festival Internacional Santander. The city of Santander's big event fills up almost all of August with world-class opera, ballet, classical concerts, and recitals, and attracts top international musicians and dancers. ☎ 942/210508, 902/106601 *for tickets* ⊕ *www.festivalsantander.com.*

Hogueras de San Juan (*San Juan Bonfires*). On the night of June 23, the skies of A Coruña are alight with hundreds of bonfires, notably along the beach, following a day of parades, colorful costumes, and traditional music and dance. ☎ 881/990321 ⊕ *www.hoguerassanjuan.com.*

Ortigueira Festival. This major Celtic music festival, which takes place in early or mid-July over four days in the coastal city of Ortigueira, attracts folk musicians from around the world. ☎ 981/422089 *for tourist office* ⊕ *www.festivaldeortigueira.com.*

Rapa das Bestas (*Taming of the Beasts*). The beasts that are tamed during this celebration, held in various locations around Galicia over the first weekend in July, are wild horses, which are grappled and subdued by local experts. ⊕ *www.rapadasbestas.gal.*

Semana Santa (*Holy Week*). Easter and the rest of Holy Week are observed throughout the region with religious services and colorful processions. Viveiro has a barefoot parade of flagellants illuminated by hundreds of candles. ⊕ *semanasanta.galiciadigital.com.*

GETTING HERE AND AROUND

AIR TRAVEL

The region's domestic airports are in Santander, A Coruña, Vigo, and near San Estéban de Pravia, 47 km (29 miles) north of Oviedo. Santiago de Compostela is a hub for both domestic and international flights. Airport shuttles usually take the form of ALSA buses from the city bus station. Iberia sometimes runs a private shuttle from its office to the airport; inquire when you book your ticket.

BIKE TRAVEL

Cycling the Camino de Santiago de Compostela is becoming increasingly popular every year, particularly with international visitors. The official *French Way by Bicycle* booklet, available from **Xacobeo** or from the Santiago tourist office, warns that the approximately 800-km (500-mile) route from the French border to Santiago is a very tough bike trip—bridle paths, dirt tracks, rough stones, and mountain passes. The best time of year to tackle it is late spring or early autumn. The Asturias tourist office's booklet, *Sus Rutas de Montaña y Costa,* available online (⊕ *www.asturias.es*), outlines additional routes. For something a little less arduous, try the final leg of the Camino Francés, from Sarria to Santiago.

BIKE ROUTES **CaminoWays.com.** This tour operator can help you bike the Camino with tailor-made packages for individuals and families, child-friendly accommodations if necessary, meals, luggage transfer, and bike rental. ⊠ *Calle Gomez Ulla 6, Santiago de Compostela* ☎ *1/525–2886* ⊕ *www. caminoways.com.*

Santiago bike route information. You'll find useful information including what kind of bicycle to take on the Camino, where to find bicycle rentals, advice on how to ship a bicycle to and from Europe, and suggested routes here. ⊕ *www.caminhodesantiago.com.br/index3.htm.*

Xacobeo. This is the definitive website for pilgrims embarking upon the Camino de Santiago, maintained by the Galicia's tourism department. ⊕ *www.xacobeo.es.*

BUS TRAVEL

ALSA runs daily buses from Madrid to Galicia and Asturias. Once here, there is good bus service between the larger destinations in the area, like Santiago, Vigo, Pontevedra, Lugo, A Coruña, Gijón, Oviedo, and Santander, though train travel is generally smoother, faster, and easier. Getting to the smaller towns by bus is more difficult. Galicia-based Monbus offers quick, inexpensive transportation between major cities like Santiago, A Coruña, Vigo, and Pontevedra, as well as smaller towns that may not be easily accessible by train.

Contacts ALSA. ☎ *902/422242* ⊕ *www.alsa.com.* **Monbus.** ☎ *902/292900* ⊕ *www.monbus.es.*

CAR TRAVEL

Driving is the best way to get around. The four-lane A6 expressway links the area with central Spain; it takes about 6½ hours to cover the 650 km (403 miles) from Madrid to Santiago, and from Madrid, it's 240 km (149 miles) on the N1 or the A1 toll road to Burgos, after which you can take the N623 to complete the 390 km (242 miles) to Santander.

The expressway north from León to Oviedo and Gijón is the fastest way to cross the Cantabrian Mountains. The AP9 north–south Galician ("Atlantic") expressway links A Coruña, Santiago, Pontevedra, and Vigo, and the A8 in Asturias links Santander to Luarca and beyond. Local roads along the coast or through the hills are more scenic but slower.

TRAIN TRAVEL

RENFE (⊕ *www.renfe.es*) runs several trains a day from Madrid to Santander (4½ hours), Oviedo (7 hours), and Gijón (8 hours), and a separate line serves Santiago (11 hours). Local RENFE trains connect the region's major cities with most of the surrounding small towns, but there may be dozens of stops on the way. Narrow-gauge FEVE trains clatter slowly across northern Spain, connecting Galicia and Asturias with Santander, Bilbao, and Irún, on the French border.

FEVE's Transcantábrico narrow-gauge train tour (⊕ *www.eltranscantabricogranlujo.com*) is an eight-day, 1,000-km (600-mile) journey through the Basque Country, Cantabria, Asturias, and Galicia. English-speaking guides narrate, and a private bus takes the group from train stations to natural attractions. Passengers sleep on the train in suites and dine on local specialties. Trains run April–October; the all-inclusive cost is €4,980 for seven nights per person in a suite.

HOTELS

Expect to feel at home in the region's classic inns: they're usually small, centuries-old, family-owned properties, with plenty that's pleasing, such as gardens, exposed stone walls, and genuinely friendly service. City hotels may not have the same country charm, but they make up for it with professional service, sparkling facilities, and spacious, comfortable rooms. Many big chain hotels may resemble their American counterparts, but you may not be able to assume that they also come with ample parking, big breakfasts, fitness rooms, or other amenities that are more-or-less standard back home. It's a very good idea to book ahead of time May–September, particularly if your stay includes a weekend.

Hotel reviews have been shortened. For full information, visit Fodors. com.

WHAT IT COSTS IN EUROS			
$	**$$**	**$$$**	**$$$$**
Restaurants	under €12	€12–€17	€18–€22	over €22
Hotels	under €90	€90–€125	€126–€180	over €180

Restaurant prices are the average cost of a main course or equivalent combination of smaller dishes at dinner. Hotel prices are the lowest cost of a standard double room in high season.

SANTIAGO DE COMPOSTELA AND EASTERN GALICIA

The main pilgrimage route of the Camino de Santiago, the Camino Francés, crosses the Pyrenees from France and heads west across northern Spain. If you drive into Galicia on the A6 expressway from Castile-León, you enter the homestretch, but many people fly into Santiago de Compostela and start exploring from here.

SANTIAGO DE COMPOSTELA

650 km (403 miles) northwest of Madrid.

Fodor's Choice   You don't need to be a pilgrim to enjoy this medieval city, which is one
★   of the most popular and beautiful in all of Galicia. Wander down the cobblestone streets of the picturesque old town, and admire the unique mix of Romanesque, Gothic, and baroque buildings. Or pop into an art gallery or one of the city's many chic literary cafés to catch some

poetry or local music. A large, lively university makes Santiago one of the most exciting cities in Spain, and its Cathedral makes it one of the most impressive. The building is opulent and awesome, yet its towers create a sense of harmony as a benign St. James, dressed in pilgrim's costume, looks down from his perch. Santiago de Compostela welcomes more than 4½ million visitors a year, with an extra million during Holy Years (the next will be in 2021), when St. James's Day (July 25) next falls on a Sunday.

GETTING HERE AND AROUND

Santiago is connected to Pontevedra (61 km [38 miles]) and A Coruña (57 km [35 miles]) via the AP9 tollway. The N550 is free, but slower. Parking anywhere in the city center can be difficult unless you use one of the numerous car parks around the outside edge of the historical quarter.

Bus service out of Santiago's station is plentiful, with eight daily buses to Madrid (7–9 hours) and hourly buses to A Coruña and to the Santiago Airport.

High-speed Talgo trains to Madrid take just over six hours; there is daily service to Irún, on the French border, via León and Santander. Trains depart every hour for Galicia's other major towns.

Santiago's center is very pedestrian-friendly, and the distances between attractions are relatively short, so walking is the best and often the only way around town.

Bus Station **Santiago de Compostela Bus Station.** ⊠ *Praza de Camilo Díaz Baliño s/n* ☎ *981/542416.*

Train Station **Santiago de Compostela Train Station.** ⊠ *Rúa do Hórreo 75 A* ☎ *912/320320 RENFE.*

VISITOR INFORMATION

Contacts **Santiago de Compostela Turismo.** ⊠ *Rúa do Vilar 63* ☎ *981/555129* ⊕ *www.santiagoturismo.com.*

TOURS

La Asociación Profesional de Guías Turísticos de Galicia. Santiago's association of well-informed guides, which is part of the tourist office, can arrange private walking tours of the city or tours to any place in Galicia. Tours start from €100 on weekdays (per group of up to nine people), €120 on weekends. ⊠ *Dársena de Xoan XXIII, Av. Xoan XXIII* ☎ *981/576698* ⊕ *www.guiasdegalicia.org* ☑ *From €100.*

EXPLORING

Fodor's Choice **Catedral de Santiago de Compostela** (*Cathedral of Santiago de Compostela*). Although the facade is baroque, the interior holds one of the finest Romanesque sculptures in the world, the **Pórtico de la Gloria.** Completed in 1188 by Maestro Mateo, this is the Cathedral's original entrance, its three arches carved with figures from the Apocalypse, the Last Judgment, and purgatory. Below Jesus is a serene St. James, poised on a carved column. Look carefully and you can see five smooth grooves, formed by the millions of pilgrims who have placed their hands

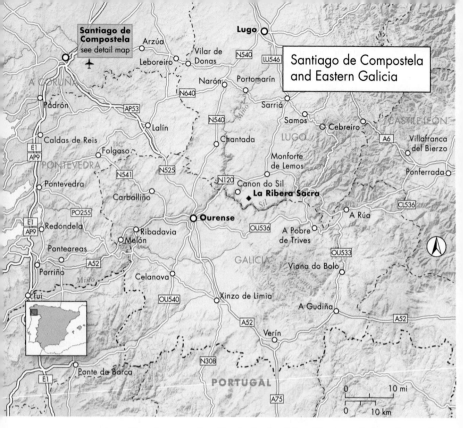

here over the centuries. On the back of the pillar, people lean forward to touch foreheads in the hope that his genius can be shared.

In his bejeweled cloak, St. James presides over the **high altar.** The stairs behind it are the Cathedral's focal point, surrounded by dazzling baroque decoration, sculpture, and drapery. Here, as the grand finale of their spiritual journey, pilgrims embrace St. James and kiss his cloak. In the crypt beneath the altar lie the remains of James and his disciples St. Theodore and St. Athenasius.

A pilgrims' Mass is celebrated every day at noon. On certain holidays, the botafumeiro (huge incense burner) is attached to the thick ropes hanging from the ceiling and, as small flames burn inside, swung in a massive semicircle across the apse. In earlier centuries, this rite served as an air freshener—by the time pilgrims reached Santiago, they were not, to put it mildly, at their freshest. A botafumeiro and other Cathedral treasures are on display in the **museums** downstairs and next door. On the right (south) side of the nave is the **Porta das Praterías** (Silversmiths' Door), the only purely Romanesque part of the Cathedral's facade. The double doorway opens onto the **Praza das Praterías,** named for the silversmiths' shops that once lined it. ⊠ *Praza do Obradoiro* ☎ *902/557812 for Cathedral* ⊕ *www.catedraldesantiago.es/en/liturgy* ⌑ *Cathedral free, museum €6.*

Fodor's Choice
★
Casco Antiguo (*Old Town*). The best way to spend your time in Santiago de Compostela is simply to walk around the casco antiguo, losing yourself in its maze of stone-paved narrow streets and little plazas. The streets hold many old *pazos* (manor houses), convents, and churches. The most beautiful pedestrian thoroughfares are Rúa do Vilar, Rúa do Franco, and Rúa Nova—portions of which are covered by arcaded walkways called *soportales,* designed to keep walkers out of the rain. Don't miss the Praza da Quintana, a small enclosed square surrounded by the majestic walls of the Cathedral and the 9th century Monastery of San Paio de Anteʼaltares, founded by Alfonso II—it's the haunt of young travelers and folk musicians in summer. The Porta Santa (Holy Door) here is open only during years when St. James's Day falls on a Sunday (the next is 2021). ⊠ *Santiago de Compostela.*

Hostal dos Reis Católicos (*Hostel of the Catholic Monarchs*). Facing the Cathedral from the left, the hostal was built in 1499 by Ferdinand and Isabella to house the pilgrims who slept on Santiago's streets every night. Having lodged and revived travelers for more than 500 years, it's the oldest refuge in the world; it was converted from a hospital to a parador in 1954. The facade bears two Castilian coats of arms along with Adam, Eve, and various saints; inside, the four arcaded patios have gargoyle rainspouts said to be caricatures of 16th-century townsfolk. Behind the lobby is the building's focal point, a Renaissance chapel in the shape of a cross. Thanks to the "Parador Museo" initiative, visitors (as opposed to just guests staying at the parador) can behold these architectural treasures on a guided tour (⊕ *https://freetoursantiago. com*) ⊠ *Praza do Obradoiro 1* ☎ *981/582200* ⊕ *www.santiagoturismo. com/actividades-santiago/tour-hostal-de-los-reyes-catolicos* 🎫 *€10.*

Fodor's Choice
★
Mercado de Abastos de Santiago (*Santiago City Market*). Built in 1941 and designed by architect Joaquín Vaquero Palacios, this charming stone building houses a lively and bustling market. Open from seven in the morning until about three in the afternoon, the market gets particularly busy around 11, when locals come to buy food in preparation for the traditional midday meal. Whether you want to buy local cheeses and tinned fish to take home, or merely ogle Galicia's bounty of shellfish and colorful fruits and vegetables, it's a destination not to be missed. ⊠ *Rúa Ameás s/n* ⊕ *www.mercadodeabastosdesantiago.com* ⊙ *Closed Sun.*

Praza do Obradoiro. This vast square is presided over by the intricate baroque facade of the Cathedral. Look out for the stone slab in the center, which indicates "kilometer zero" on the pilgrimage trail. It is also the setting for the spectacular fireworks display on July 24 (the eve of St. James's Day). Traffic free, and flanked on all sides by historical buildings—including the 16th century Hostal dos Reis Católicos—it is a unique place to soak up the city's atmosphere. ⊠ *Main square, Praza do Obradoiro.*

WHERE TO EAT

$$$$
TAPAS
Fodor's Choice
★
╳ **Abastos 2.0.** "From the market to the plate" is the philosophy here, where the chefs start and finish the day with an empty larder and a blank menu. Ingredients are handpicked at market each morning and crafted into impeccable dishes bursting with fresh flavors and new ideas. **Known for:** inventive tapas; market fresh ingredients; contemporary design.

4

Santiago de Compostela

KEY

i   *Tourist Information*

●1   *Exploring Sites*

①   *Hotels & Restaurants*

| 0 | 100 yards |
| 0 | 100 meters |

Exploring ▼

Casco Antiguo **4**

Catedral de
Santiago de Compostela ... **3**

Hostal dos Reis
Católicos **1**

Mercado de
Abastos de Santiago **5**

Praza do Obradoiro **2**

Restaurants ▼

Abastos 2.0 .... **8**

Adega Abrigadoiro **10**

Bierzo Enxebre **5**

La Bodeguilla de San Roque . **3**

O Curro da Parra **6**

Restaurant Filigrana **9**

Tafona Casa de Xantar **7**

Hotels ▼

Hotel Costa Vella **2**

Hotel Monumento
San Francisco **1**

Hotel Spa Relais & Châteaux
A Quinta Da Auga **11**

Parador de Santiago de
Compostela: Hostal dos
Reis Católicos **4**

[$] *Average main: €25* ✉ *Casetas 13–18, Pl. de Abastos s/n* ☎ *654/015937* 🌐 *www.abastosdouspuntocero.es* 💳 *No credit cards* 🕒 *Closed Sun.*

$$ TAPAS 🍴 **Adega Abrigadoiro.** This rustic stone-walled bodega serves up Galician delicacies in an authentic setting with a fully functioning waterwheel as its centerpiece. Lean up against a barrel or sit at one of the long wooden tables and feast on *embutidos* (cold cuts of meat) and cheeses, accompanied by a selection of wines by the glass or bottle. **Known for:** local cold cuts and cheeses; rustic stone-walled setting; proximity to Colexio San Xerome. [$] *Average main: €15* ✉ *Rúa da Carreira do Conde 5* ☎ *981/563163* 💳 *No credit cards.*

$$ SPANISH 🍴 **Bierzo Enxebre.** Tucked behind the Cathedral, this tapas bar specializes in products from El Bierzo, a comarca in Castile–León, either in the animated bar or in one of the stone-walled dining rooms. Visitors stopping in for a drink at the bar can expect a generous portion of free tapas, while the menu has a selection of grilled meats, *revueltos* (scrambled eggs with a variety of toppings), cold meats, and cheeses. **Known for:** food and wine from El Bierzo; good value prix-fixe lunch menu; grilled meat. [$] *Average main: €15* ✉ *Rúa La Troia 10* ☎ *981/581909* 🌐 *www.bierzoenxebre.es* 💳 *No credit cards* 🕒 *Closed Tues.*

$$ TAPAS 🍴 **La Bodeguilla de San Roque.** This is one of Santiago's favorite spots for *tapeo* (tapas grazing) and *chiquiteo* (wine sampling); it's just a five-minute walk from the Cathedral. The traditional bar area takes center stage, playing host to locals, pilgrims, and tourists alike, all gathering for wine, Iberian cured meats, cheeses, and seasonal dishes. **Known for:** tapas; wine; lively crowd. [$] *Average main: €15* ✉ *C. San Roque 13* ☎ *981/564379* 🌐 *www.labodeguilladesanroque.com* 💳 *No credit cards.*

$$ SPANISH 🍴 **O Curro da Parra.** Located directly across from the market, this lively, two-floor restaurant has exposed brick walls, wooden tables, and gastronomic delicacies such as *menestra crujiente de verduras y algas, pesto de cacahuete y mayonesa de wasabi* (Crunchy vegetables and seaweed warm salad, peanuts pesto sauce and wasabi mayo), *langostinos, pil-pil, jugo de sus cabezas, sal de ajo, jalapeños y cebollino* (king-prawns, pil-pil, its own juices, garlic salt, chili peppers and spring onion), and *croquetas de jamón ibérico* (croquettes made with Iberian ham). **Known for:** king prawns; pork belly; wine list. [$] *Average main: €17* ✉ *Rúa Travesa 20* ☎ *981/556059* 🌐 *www.ocurrodaparra.com* 🕒 *Closed Mon.*

$$$$ SPANISH Fodor's Choice ★ 🍴 **Restaurant Filigrana.** Although the cheery yellow walls, crystal chandeliers, and carefully chosen antique furniture may evoke a traditional French bistro, the food prepared by this restaurant attached to the Hotel Spa Relais & Châteaux A Quinta Da Auga is undeniably Galician. Try delicacies such as the sea urchin soup, served in its shell, fresh-caught merluza served on a bed of mashed potatoes alongside crunchy asparagus, drizzled with white-wine vinaigrette, or bay scallops roasted in their shells, with garlic parsley oil. **Known for:** one of the best restaurants in Galicia; good value lunch menu; exquisitely presented seafood. [$] *Average main: €25* ✉ *Hotel Spa Relais & Châteaux A Quinta Da Auga, Paseo da Amaia 23B* ☎ *981/534636* 🌐 *www.aquintadaauga.com.*

$$$ SPANISH 🍴 **Tafona Casa de Xantar.** Located a block away from the Mercado de Abastos, Santiago's premier food market, this excellent restaurant serves tapas and more substantial dishes made exclusively from seasonal,

Santiago de Compostela's Praza do Obradoiro

locally sourced ingredients. The chefs are relentlessly inventive, serving up traditional Galician specialties with an avant-garde touch in the modern, minimalist dining room with exposed stone walls. **Known for:** creative menu; traditional Galician specialties; garden tomatoes with tuna and figs. $ *Average main: €18* ⊠ *Virxe da Cerca 7* ☎ *981/562314* ⊕ *www.restauranteatafona.com* ⊘ *Closed Mon. No dinner Sun.*

WHERE TO STAY

$

B&B/INN

🏨 **Hotel Costa Vella.** At this classically Galician inn, there's a perfect little garden and views of red-tile rooftops, the baroque convent of San Francisco, and the green hills beyond (ask for a garden view). **Pros:** charming views; ideal location; warm, accommodating staff. **Cons:** creaky floors; thin walls; no elevator. $ *Rooms from: €83* ⊠ *Rúa Porta da Pena 17* ☎ *981/569530* ⊕ *www.costavella.com* ⇆ *14 rooms* ❏ *No meals.*

$$$

HOTEL

🏨 **Hotel Monumento San Francisco.** Contemporary stained-glass windows add a touch of pizzazz to the solemn interior of this converted 13th-century convent, adjoining the church of the same name. **Pros:** indoor swimming pool and Jacuzzi; easily accessible by car; very tidy. **Cons:** a bit too quiet at times; decor a bit dated; can get a bit chilly. $ *Rooms from: €140* ⊠ *Campillo San Francisco 3* ☎ *981/581634* ⊕ *www.sanfranciscohm.com* ⇆ *81 rooms* ❏ *No meals.*

$$$

HOTEL

Fodor'sChoice

★

🏨 **Hotel Spa Relais & Châteaux A Quinta Da Auga.** Tastefully converted from a 14th-century printing factory, this elegantly restored building is surrounded by manicured gardens, with a view of the burbling Río Sar. Adorned with French crystal chandeliers and carefully restored antique furniture—handpicked by the owner for each room—and managed with exquisite attention to detail, this illustrious hotel feels both classic and fresh at once. **Pros:** excellent restaurant; warm, professional, and attentive staff; luxurious accommodations; designer spa. **Cons:** a 10-minute car ride from the center of Santiago de Compostela; Wi-Fi spotty in some rooms. [$] *Rooms from: €154* ✉ *Paseo da Amaia 23B* ☎ *981/534636* 🌐 *www.aquintadaauga.com* 🛏 *61 rooms* 🍴 *Free Breakfast.*

IT'S GALLEGO TO ME

In the Gallego language, the Castilian Spanish *plaza* (town square) is *praza* and the Castilian *playa* (beach) is *praia*. Closer to Portuguese than to Castilian Spanish, Gallego is the language of nearly all road signs in Galicia.

$$$$ HOTEL Fodor's Choice ★ 🏨 **Parador de Santiago de Compostela: Hostal dos Reis Católicos.** One of the parador chain's most highly regarded hotels, this 15th-century masterpiece, once a royal hostel and hospital for sick pilgrims, has a mammoth baroque doorway that gives way to austere courtyards of box hedge and simple fountains, and to rooms furnished with antiques, some with canopy beds. **Pros:** views of Praza do Obradoiro; excellent cuisine; fascinating collection of antiques and paintings. **Cons:** confusing corridors; often filled with people on guided tours; pricey. [$] *Rooms from: €284* ✉ *Praza do Obradoiro 1* ☎ *981/582200* 🌐 *www.parador.es* 🛏 *137 rooms* 🍴 *Free Breakfast.*

$ B&B/INN 🏨 **Pazo Cibrán.** This comfortable 18th-century Galician manor house, 7 km (4 miles) from Santiago de Compostela, has an antiques-packed living room that overlooks gardens with camellias, magnolias, palms, vines, and a bamboo walk. **Pros:** personal hospitality; authentic and stately country house; delightful gardens. **Cons:** inaccessible without a car; poor local dining options; only open for groups November–March. [$] *Rooms from: €70* ✉ *San Xulián de Sales s/n, Vedra* ✣ *Take N525 toward Ourense from Santiago and turn right at Km 11, after gas station* ☎ *981/511515* 🌐 *www.pazocibran.com* 🛏 *11 rooms* 🍴 *No meals.*

NIGHTLIFE

Santiago's nightlife peaks on Thursday night, because many students spend weekends at home with their families. For up-to-date info on concerts, films, and clubs, pick up the monthly *Compostela Capital Cultural,* available at the main tourist office on Rúa do Vilar, or visit the official tourism website (🌐 *www.santiagoturismo.com*). Bars and seafood-themed tapas joints line the old streets south of the Cathedral, particularly **Rúa do Franco, Rúa da Raiña,** and **Rúa do Vilar.** A great first stop, especially if you haven't eaten dinner, is **Rúa de San Clemente,** off the Praza do Obradoiro, where several bars offer two or three plates of tapas free with each drink.

BARS

Casa das Crechas. Drink to Galicia's Celtic roots here, with live music and Celtic wood carvings hanging from thick stone walls, while dolls of playful Galician witches ride their brooms above the bar. ✉ *Vía Sacra 3* ☎ *981/560751.*

Modus Vivendi. Galicia's oldest pub is also one of its most unusual: Modus Vivendi is in a former stable. The old stone feeding trough is now a low table, and instead of stairs you walk on ridged stone inclines designed for the former occupants—horses and cattle. On weekends the bar hosts live music (jazz, ethnic, Celtic) and sometimes storytelling. ✉ *Praza Feixóo 1* ☎ *607/804140.*

CAFÉS

Santiago is a great city for coffee drinking and people-watching. Most of the cafés are clustered around the Cathedral, in the casco antiguo, especially on Rúa Calderería and Rúa do Vilar.

Café Casino. Upholstered armchairs, mirrors, and wood paneling make this atmospheric Art Nouveau café feel like an elegant and comfortable library. ✉ *Rúa do Vilar 35* ☎ *981/577503* ⊕ *www.cafecasino.gal.*

Cafe Literarios. Tranquil by day and lively at night, Cafe Literarios comes with colorful paintings, large windows, and a good supply of outdoor tables. It overlooks the plaza. ✉ *Praza da Quintana 1* ☎ *981/565630.*

Iacobus. Cozy Iacobus blends stone walls with contemporary wood trim and light fixtures; there's a glass cache of coffee beans in the floor. Another branch is located at Rúa Calderería 42. ✉ *Rúa da Senra 24* ☎ *981/585967.*

SHOPPING

Bolillos. In the fishing town of Camariñas, women fashion exquisite lace collars, scarves, and table linens. This is the best place to buy their work, and watch some of it being crafted. ✉ *Rúa Nova 40* ☎ *981/589776.*

Catrineta. This is a great place to buy locally produced gourmet preserves typical of the region, such as *bacalao a gallega "Los Peperetes"* (Galician cod), *bonito en aceite de oliva "La Pureza"* (bonito tuna fish in olive oil), *mejillones en escaveche* (mussels marinated in a vinegary pimiento sauce often used to preserve fish), and *calamares en su tinta* (squid in its ink). ✉ *Ruela Altamira 2-baixo* ☎ *981/577544* ⊕ *www. catrineta.com.*

Sargadelos. Galicia is known throughout Spain for its distinctive blue-and-white ceramics with bold modern designs, made in Sargadelos and O Castro. There is a wide selection at Sargadelos. It's often possible to watch artisans work (weekdays 8:30–2), but call ahead to confirm. ✉ *Rúa Nova 16* ☎ *981/581905.*

Vide, Vide! The definitive place to buy, taste, and learn about Galician wines, this shop is well stocked with a wide range of wine of various types and vintages from local bodegas across the region. ✉ *Rúa Fonte de Sano Antonio 10-baixo* ☎ *981/582911* ⊕ *www.videvide.net.*

OURENSE AND LA RIBEIRA SACRA

105 km (65 miles) southeast of Santiago de Compostela, 95 km (59 miles) east of Vigo.

Despite the uninspiring backdrop of Ourense's new town, Galicia's third-largest city has bubbling thermal springs and an attractive medieval quarter whose animated streets, tapas bars, and plazas come alive on weekends. A smattering of notable historical monuments includes the colossal arches of the Ponte Vella spanning the Río Miño and the 13th-century Cathedral of San Martino. Ourense is a good starting point for exploring the surrounding dramatic landscapes of the Ribeira Sacra (Sacred Riverbank) and Cañon do Sil (Sil River Canyon). This less explored region of interior Galicia is dotted with vineyards, Romanesque churches, and monasteries. Well worth a visit or a short stay is the Parador de Santo Estevo, converted from the Benedictine 10th-century Monasterio de Santo Estevo and perched high above the spectacular scenery of the Cañon do Sil.

GETTING HERE AND AROUND

RENFE and Monbus offer frequent services to Ourense from Santiago and Vigo in less than two hours. The A52 links Ourense to Vigo and Pontevedra, and the AG53 with Santiago.

WHERE TO STAY

$$ HOTEL **Hotel Carrís Cardenal Quevedo.** Offering stylish city-chic accommodations, this hotel is in a handy location for Ourense's shopping district, restaurants, and lively tapas scene, and is only a five-minute stroll from the historical quarter. **Pros:** well positioned for both shopping district and historical quarter; restaurant serves regional cuisine; modern and spotless. **Cons:** expensive breakfast; tight parking space; uninspiring views. *$ Rooms from: €105 ✉ Rúa Cardenal Quevedo 28–30 ☎ 988/375523, 902/105173 information and bookings 🌐 www.carrishoteles.com 💳 No credit cards 🛏 39 rooms 🍴 No meals.*

$$$ HOTEL Fodor's Choice ★ **Parador de Santo Estevo.** Clinging to the edge of the Cañon do Sil, this parador, carefully built into the colossal 12th-century Benedictine Monasterio de Santo Estevo, stands out for its atmospheric setting and spectacular vistas. **Pros:** magnificent setting with views; historical sanctuary surrounded by nature; spa on-site. **Cons:** mediocre food; can get booked up by wedding parties; remote. *$ Rooms from: €150 ✉ Monasterio de Santo Estevo, off CV323 beyond Luintra, 26 km (16 miles) northeast of Ourense ☎ 988/010110 🌐 www.parador.es 💳 No credit cards ⏲ Closed Dec.–Feb. 🛏 77 rooms 🍴 No meals.*

LUGO

102 km (63 miles) east of Santiago de Compostela.

Just off the A6 freeway, Galicia's oldest provincial capital is most notable for its 2-km (1½-mile) **Roman wall.** These beautifully preserved ramparts completely surround the streets of the old town. The walkway on top has good views. The baroque Ayuntamiento has a magnificent rococo facade overlooking the tree-lined **Praza Maior** (Plaza Mayor). There's a good view of the Río Miño valley from the **Parque Rosalía de Castro,** outside the Roman walls near the cathedral, which is a mixture of Romanesque, Gothic, baroque, and neoclassical styles.

GETTING HERE AND AROUND

RENFE runs eight trains per day to and from A Coruña, a journey of 1½–2 hours. Several daily ALSA buses connect Lugo to Santiago de Compostela, Oviedo, and Gijón.

Contacts Estación de Autobuses Lugo. ✉ *Prazo da Constitución s/n* ☎ *912/320320 RENFE.* **Estación de Tren Lugo.** ✉ *Pl. Conde de Fontao s/n* ☎ *912/320320 RENFE.*

VISITOR INFORMATION

Contacts Lugo Turismo. ✉ *Praza do Campo 11* ☎ *982/251658* 🌐 *www.lugo.gal.*

EXPLORING

City Walls. Declared a UNESCO World Heritage Site, the Roman walls encircling Lugo, built in the 3rd century, provide a picturesque 2-km (1 mile) walk and the best bird's-eye views of the town. Comprised of 85 towers and 10 gates, the walls have four staircases and two ramps providing access to the top. ✉ *Lugo.*

WHERE TO EAT AND STAY

$$$ SPANISH 🍴 **Mesón de Alberto.** A hundred meters from the cathedral, this cozy venue has excellent Galician fare and professional service. The bar and adjoining *bodega* (winery) serve plenty of cheap *raciónes* (appetizers). **Known for:** small restaurant so reservations recommended; authentic Galician food; local cheeses with quince jelly. [$] *Average main: €20* ✉ *C. de la Cruz 4* ☎ *982/228310* 🌐 *www.mesondealberto.com* 🕓 *Closed Sun. No dinner Tues.*

$ B&B/INN 🏨 **Casa Grande da Fervenza.** This graceful 17th- to 19th-century manor house, set in a forested area on the banks of the Río Miño 14 km (8 miles) south of Lugo, has rustic but comfortable rooms. **Pros:** intimate feel; excellent restaurant; great base for hiking. **Cons:** a bit out of town; rooms are dark and could stand to be refurbished. [$] *Rooms from: €76* ✉ *Ctra. Lugo–Paramo, Km 11, O Corgo* ☎ *982/150610* 🌐 *www.fervenza.com* 🛏 *9 rooms* 🍽 *No meals.*

THE COSTA DA MORTE AND RÍAS BAIXAS

West of Santiago de Compostela, the scenic C543 leads to the coast. It's windy, rocky, and treacherous—hence its eerie name, the "Coast of Death." Small villages and towns, often surrounded in mist, dot this dramatic stretch of coastline, each with its own collection of legends and traditions. In contrast, the series of wide, quiet estuaries south of here are called the Rías Baixas (Low Estuaries). The hilly drive takes you through a green countryside dappled with vineyards, tiny farms, and Galicia's trademark *hórreos* (Galician small stone or wood granery, raised on pillars), most with a cross at one or both ends. There is plenty to see and do along its coast. You can find Galicia's most popular holiday towns and beaches, and taste exceptional wine and some of Galicia's best food. At its heart lies the medieval charm of handsome Pontevedra; the striking natural port of Vigo dominates a large part of its coastline.

MUXIA

75 km (47 miles) northwest of Santiago de Compostela, 30 km (18 miles) north of Fisterra.

A small fishing village far off the beaten path, surrounded by the stunning rocky cliffs and virgin beaches of the Costa da Morte, close to great hiking trails and lush green forests, Muxia is the perfect destination for a rural getaway.

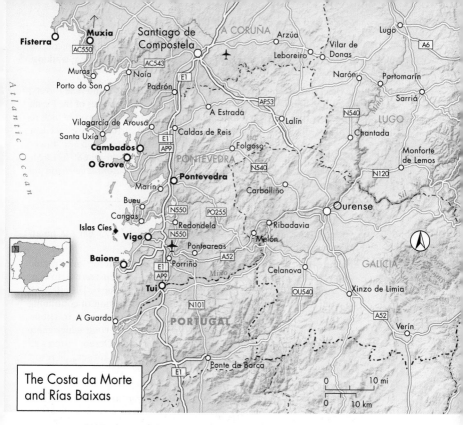

The Costa da Morte and Rías Baixas

EXPLORING

O Camino dos Faros (*Way of the Lighthouses*). For a pleasant excursion, the Faro de Cabo Turiñan, Faro Punto de Barca, and Faro de Cabo Vilán, three lighthouses in the region of Muxia, can all be visited by car within an hour and a half, and offer extraordinary views of the rocky cliffs and churning waters below that have earned this part of Galicia its nickname, the Costa da Morte. The lighthouses are part of a 200-km (124-mile) hiking route, the Way of the Lighthouses, that begins in Malpica and ends in Finiesterre. Start with the Faro de Cabo Turiñan, which guards a narrow peninsula that marks the westernmost point of continental Europe. Just a 20-minute drive away is the Faro Punto de Barca, a stone lighthouse built in 1926 alongside the 16th-century Sanctuario de Virxe da Barca (Sanctuary of the Virgin of the Boat). Finish with Faro de Cabo Vilán, a lighthouse with unique architecture that emerges seamlessly from the surrounding red rock; it was the first in Spain to run by electricity. ⊕ *www.caminodosfaros.com/en.*

BEACHES

Playa Nemiña. A favorite with surfers and sport fisherman, this virgin beach is buffered from the wind by the green forested hills on either side. Still relatively undiscovered by tourists, this semiprivate beach is an excellent place for a romantic stroll at sunset, or a midday picnic on the fine white sand. **Amenities:** showers. **Best for:** sunset; surfing; walking.

WHERE TO STAY

$ B&B/INN 🏨 **Hotel Rústico Fontequeiroso.** Surrounded by green hills and pine forests, just a five-minute drive from the stunning, pristine beaches of the Costa da Morte, this small bed-and-breakfast is the ideal base from which to explore Galicia's natural bounty. **Pros:** beautiful surroundings; excellent local fare; bicycles available for guests. **Cons:** remote; lunch and dinner must be prebooked; no amenities nearby. [$] *Rooms from: €80* ✉ *Lugar de Queiroso, Nemiña* ☎ *981/748946* 🌐 *www.casafontequeiroso.com* 🛏 *6 rooms* 🍴 *Free Breakfast* 💳 *No credit cards.*

FISTERRA

50 km (31 miles) west of Santiago de Compostela, 75 km (48 miles) southwest of A Coruña.

There was a time when this lonely, windswept outcrop over raging waters was thought to be the end of the earth—the *finis terrae*. In fact, the official westernmost point of Europe is in Portugal. Despite this, many Camino pilgrims choose to continue the tradition of continuing onto the "end of the earth" from Santiago de Compostela to triumphantly finish at Fisterra's windswept lighthouse, beyond which there is nothing but the boundless expanse of the Atlantic Ocean. Fisterra all but shuts down in winter, but in summer it's a pleasant seaside resort with an attractive harbor.

VISITOR INFORMATION

Contacts Fisterra Turismo. ✉ *Calle Real 2* ☎ *981/740781.*

EXPLORING

Santa María das Areas. Aside from legends, another draw in this tiny seaside town is its main plaza and the 12th-century church of Santa María das Areas. Romanesque, Gothic, and baroque elements combine in an impressive (but gloomy) facade. ✉ *Manuel Lago País s/n.*

WHERE TO STAY

$$ HOTEL 🏨 **Hotel Naturaleza & Playa Mar da Ardora.** Just a two-minute walk from Fisterra's Mar de Fora Beach, this small boutique hotel is surrounded by gardens, with stunning views of the beach. **Pros:** exquisite views of the sea; spa and wellness center; dinner on the terrace. **Cons:** expensive compared to other regional options; noise carries between the rooms; outside the town center. [$] *Rooms from: €110* ✉ *Playa de la Potiña 15* ☎ *667/641304* 🌐 *www.hotelmardaardora.com* 🛏 *6 rooms* 🍴 *No meals.*

CAMBADOS

34 km (21 miles) north of Pontevedra, 61 km (37 miles) southwest of Santiago de Compostela.

This breezy seaside town has a charming, almost entirely residential old quarter and is the center for the full-bodied and fruity albariño, one of Spain's best white wines. The impressive main square, **Praza de Fefiñanes,** is bordered by an imposing bodega.

Wine Tasting in Rías Baixas

ALBARIÑO WINE

The Rías Baixas region, in the southern part of Galicia, is the most important Denomination of Origin (D.O.) in the province, and is the largest global producer of albariño, a crisp, young, aromatic white wine that has earned international prestige. Albariño has been compared to Riesling for its pungent acidity, to Petit Manseng and Viognier for fruity qualities suggesting peach and apricot, and to Pinot Gris for its distinctive floral bouquet. Classically paired with Galician seafood dishes, albariño's ripe fruit flavor and relatively low alcohol content also make it an excellent complement to more exotic fare, such as Indian and Thai food.

The Rías Baixas vineyards and bodegas are spread throughout the Pontevedra region, with a particularly high density in Cambados, the capital of the albariño-producing region. With more than 6,500 growers and 20,000 individual vineyard plots in Rías Baixas, planning a wine trip to the region can feel overwhelming. **Ruta de Vino Rías Baixas** (⊕ *www.rutadelvinoriasbaixas.com/ en*) and **Rías Baixas Wines** (⊕ *www.*

riasbaixaswines.com/index.php) have information about wine tasting in the Rías Baixas region, including a detailed explanation of albariño, a list of wineries, and places to stay. Guiados Pontevedra and North West Iberia Wine Tours can arrange a tour, but you don't need to hire a guide to enjoy wine tasting in the region. Head to these bodegas in Pontevedra: Adega Eidos and Pazo Baión; or these in Cambados: Don Oligario and Palacio de Fefiñánes, for a do-it-yourself tour.

WINE TOURS

Guiados Pontevedra. You can arrange custom tours of two to three bodegas in the region, including an English-speaking guide, for €90 for four hours (minimum two people). ☎ *654/222081* ⊕ *www.guiadospontevedra.com* ✉ *From €90.*

North West Iberia Wine Tours. One- or three-day wine tours include transport, admissions, gourmet lunch, and wine tasting at two different locations, as well as a visit to a local pazo and camellia garden. ✉ *C. Enrique Marinas Romero 30–5H, A Coruña* ☎ *881/879910* ⊕ *www.northwestiberiawinetours.com* ✉ *From €180.*

GETTING HERE AND AROUND

Cambados is less than an hour from Santiago de Compostela, to the north, and Vigo and Pontevedra, to the south, via the AP9.

EXPLORING

Don Oligario. This award-winning family-run winery offers an intimate guided visit of the winery, followed by a tasting on their terrace, with a view of the vineyards. A 45-minute guided tour costs €6 including two wine tastings (€10 with tapas). ✉ *Refoxos, Corbillón* ☎ *986/520886* ⊕ *www.donolegario.com.*

Palacio de Fefiñánes. Set in a 16th-century stone palace, this illustrious winery has been involved in wine making since the 17th century, and crafts classic albariños, such as the full-bodied and powerful 1583 Albariño de Fefiñánes, a ripe, fruity wine aged one to five years in

Bordeaux barrels. A 30-minute guided tour without a tasting costs €3; a 45-minute guided tour with a tasting of Albariño de Fefiñanes costs €6; and an hour-long tour with two wine tastings costs €10. Reservations advised. ✉ *Pl. de Fefiñanes* ☎ *986/542204* 🌐 *www.fefinanes.com.*

Pazo de Rubianes. The jewel of this property is the camellia garden, one of the largest and most impressive collections of flowers in the world. The camellias bloom November–May, with peak viewing season February–April. The 15th-century manor house is decadently furnished and also worth a visit, as is the attached bodega and chapel. Gourmet picnic baskets with local products can be arranged for those who want to enjoy a leisurely lunch amid the grapevines and flowers. There are also guided tours available, which last about two hours. ✉ *Rúa do Pazo 7* ☎ *986/510534* 🌐 *www.pazoderubianes.com* 🎟 *Free self-guided tour (by appointment); €16 guided visit of the gardens, winery, pazo, and chapel, including a wine tasting.*

WHERE TO EAT AND STAY

$$$$ SPANISH Fodor's Choice ★

🍴 **Yayo Daporta.** The chef, Yayo Daporta, for whom the restaurant is named, is something of a local celebrity, and a true food artist who produces gastronomic masterpieces, such as a cocktail glass filled with cauliflower mousse and fresh-caught local clams with a drizzle of basil-infused olive oil and coffee vinaigrette. Inventive dishes include scallop carpaccio and tempura clam on an algae crisp with clam foam and greens. **Known for:** locally admired chef; inventive dishes; fresh clams. [$] *Average main: €45* ✉ *Rúa Hospital 7* ☎ *986/526062* 🌐 *www.yayodaporta.com* ⏲ *Closed Mon., and Nov. 14–28. No dinner Sun.*

$$$$ HOTEL

🏨 **Parador de Cambados (El Albariño).** This airy mansion's rooms are warmly furnished with wrought-iron lamps, area rugs, and full-length wood shutters over small-pane windows. **Pros:** easily accessible; comfortable rooms; excellent dining. **Cons:** Wi-Fi is patchy in some rooms; old-fashioned room decor; limited parking. [$] *Rooms from: €202* ✉ *Paseo Calzada s/n* ☎ *986/542250* 🌐 *www.parador.es* ⏲ *Closed Jan.* 🛏 *58 rooms* 🍽 *Free Breakfast.*

$$$ HOTEL Fodor's Choice ★

🏨 **Quinta de San Amaro.** This stylish rural hotel is a great base for exploring the surrounding wine region—a stay here includes gorgeous vineyard views as well as a local winery visit and wine tasting. **Pros:** excellent service and great restaurant; good base for exploring local wineries; beautiful views. **Cons:** need a car to get here; somewhat remote at a 15-minute drive from Cambados; small swimming pool. [$] *Rooms from: €130* ✉ *Rúa San Amaro 6* ☎ *630/877590* 🌐 *www.quintadesanamaro.com* 🛏 *14 rooms* 🍽 *Free Breakfast.*

SHOPPING

Cucadas. Head to this crafts shop for its large selection of baskets, copper items, and lace. ✉ *Praza de Fefiñáns 8* ☎ *986/542511.*

SPORTS AND THE OUTDOORS

Piragüilla. For kayak rentals and group kayak tours of the local rivers and islands from the Illa de Arousa, head here. ✉ *Av. da Ponte, nº 174* ☎ *625/336323* 🌐 *www.piraguilla.com.*

O GROVE

31 km (19 miles) northwest of Pontevedra, 75 km (47 miles) south of Santiago de Compostela.

O Grove throws a famous shellfish festival the second week of October, but you can enjoy the day's catch in taverns and restaurants year-round. From O Grove, you can cross a bridge to the island of **A Toxa** (La Toja), famous for its spas—the waters are said to have healing properties. Legend has it that a man abandoned an ailing donkey here and found it up on all fours, fully rejuvenated, upon his return. The island's south side has a palm-filled garden anchored on one side by the **Capilla de San Sebastián,** a tiny church covered in cockleshells. Look out for razor clams on the seashore and then try some freshly caught for lunch in town.

4

VISITOR INFORMATION

Contacts O Grove. ✉ *Praza do Corgo s/n* ☎ *986/731415* 🌐 *www.turismogrove.es.*

WHERE TO EAT

$$$$ SEAFOOD 🍴 **Beiramar Restaurante.** Seafood lovers: look no further. This minimalist but elegant *marisceria* has a view of the port, and only serves fish caught the same day. **Known for:** octopus paella; river crab; cod gratin with alioli and saffron. [$] *Average main: €25* ✉ *Av. Beiramar 30* ☎ *986/731081* 🌐 *www.restaurantebeiramar.com* 🕒 *Closed Mon. No dinner Sun.* 💳 *No credit cards.*

WHERE TO STAY

$$$$ HOTEL 🏨 **Gran Hotel La Toja.** Extravagant and pricey, this classic spa hotel is on the breezy island of A Toxa, just across the bridge from O Grove. **Pros:** glittering sea views; golf course; mineral-rich spa. **Cons:** rooms can be noisy. [$] *Rooms from: €335* ✉ *Isla de La Toja* ☎ *986/730025* 🌐 *www.eurostarshotels.com* 🛏 *199 rooms* 🍽 *No meals.*

SPORTS AND THE OUTDOORS

GOLF

Club de Golf La Toja. Spectacular coastal views and verdant pine forests set the backdrop for players at the 18-hole Club de Golf La Toja. ✉ *Isla de La Toja* ☎ *986/730158, 669/444888* 🌐 *www.latojagolf.com* 🎫 *€75* ⛳ *18 holes, 6695 yards, par 72.*

PONTEVEDRA

135 km (84 miles) southeast of Fisterra, 59 km (37 miles) south of Santiago de Compostela.

At the head of its ría, right where it joins the sea, Pontevedra is a delightful starting point for exploring the Rías Baixas. Its well-preserved old quarter is a dense network of pedestrian-only streets and handsome plazas flanked with elegant stone buildings, many of which are dressed in cascading flowers in spring and summer. The city got its start as a Roman settlement (its name comes from an old Roman bridge over the Río Lérez). As a powerful base for fishing and international trade, Pontevedra was a major presence in the Atlantic in the 16th century.

Nowadays, its streets and plazas are awash with bars and restaurants, and it can get very busy on weekends. It also has the only operating *plaza de toros* (bullring) in Galicia.

GETTING HERE AND AROUND

RENFE and Monbus offer quick, frequent service between Vigo and Pontevedra, a half-hour journey; the same bus and train routes also link Pontevedra to Santiago de Compostela and A Coruña to the north along the AP9.

Contacts Estación de Autobuses Pontevedra. ⊠ *Calle de la Estación s/n* ☎ *986/852408* ⊕ *www.autobusespontevedra.com.*

VISITOR INFORMATION

Contacts Turismo Pontevedra. ⊠ *Casa da Luz, Praza da Verdura s/n* ☎ *986/090890.*

EXPLORING

Adega Eidos. This sleek winery overlooks the beautiful Saxeno harbor, and produces modern takes on traditional albariño harvested from 50-year-old ungrafted vines grown on granite slopes on the westernmost edge of Rías Baixas, and fermented with natural yeasts. A one-hour tour of the bodega with three wine and liquor tastings, plus a snack costs €2, with gourmet preserves €7.50; €8 includes a bottle of wine. ⊠ *Padriñán 65, Sanxenxo, Pontevedra* ☎ *986/690009* ⊕ *www.adegaeidos.com.*

Pazo Baión. Surrounded by lush albariño vineyards, this classic 15th-century stone Galician manor house stands in pleasant contrast to its 100-year-old boutique wine cellar, built in an Art Deco style. Winemaker José Hidalgo produces a silky albariño with notes of citrus and floral aromas. The 60-minute tour costs €10, and includes one wine tasting; a tasting of three wines costs €15. Reservations are required. ⊠ *Pazo Baión, Abelleira, 6, Vilanova de Arousa* ☎ *986/543535* ⊕ *www.pazobaion.com.*

Real Basílica de Santa María la Mayor. The 16th-century seafarers' basilica has lovely, sinuous vaulting and, at the back of the nave, a Romanesque portal. There's also an 18th-century Christ by the Galician sculptor Ferreiro. ⊠ *Av. de Santa María 24* 🎫 *Free.*

WHERE TO EAT AND STAY

$$$$
SPANISH

✕**Casa Solla.** Pepe Solla brings Galicia's bounty to his terrace garden restaurant, 2 km (1 mile) outside of town toward O Grove. Try the *menú de degustación* (tasting menu) to sample a selection of regional favorites, such as *lomo de caballa* (grilled mackerel), *caldo gallego de chorizo* (Galician chorizo sausage soup), *merluza con acelga* (cod with chard), or *jarrete de cordero* (sliced lamb shank). **Known for:** award-winning menu; presentation; tasting menu. $ *Average main: €30* ⊠ *Av. Sineiro 7, San Salvador de Poio* ☎ *986/872884* ☉ *Closed Mon. No dinner Thurs. and Sun.*

$$$
HOTEL

🏨**Parador de Pontevedra (Casa del Barón).** A 16th-century manor house in the heart of the old quarter, this rather dark parador has guest rooms with recessed windows embellished with lace curtains and large wooden shutters; some face a small rose garden. **Pros:** interesting collection of bric-a-brac; tranquil yet central location; free parking. **Cons:** confusing corridors; limited parking; gloomy rooms—a bit haunted house–ish. $ *Rooms from: €164* ✉ *Rúa Barón 19* ☎ *986/855800* ⊕ *www.parador. es* ⇨ *47 rooms* ❍ *Free Breakfast.*

SPORTS AND THE OUTDOORS

Campo de Golf Meis. Set on top of the hilly plateau of Monte Castrove more than 1,640 feet above sea level, Campo de Golf de Meis is a public 18-hole course surrounded by a light pine forest, with a magnificent view of the white sandy beaches and glittering waters of Ría de Arousa below. The wide fairway is framed by stony pines and has six lakes that make for a more challenging game. It's also an excellent value. ✉ *Silván de Armenteira* ☎ *986/680400* ⊕ *www.campodegolfmeis.com* ⌂ *€28 weekdays, €40 weekends* ⌖ *18 holes, 6849 yards, par 72.*

4

VIGO

31 km (19 miles) south of Pontevedra, 90 km (56 miles) south of Santiago de Compostela.

Vigo's formidable port is choked with trawlers and fishing boats and lined with clanging shipbuilding yards. The city's gritty exterior gives way to a compact and lively center that clings to a tiered hill rising over an ancient Roman settlement. A jumbled mass of modernist buildings and granite, red-roof fisherman houses hide the narrow streets of Vigo's appealing *casco vello* (old town). Vigo's highlights can be explored in a few hours.

From 10 to 3:30 daily, on **Rúa Pescadería** in the barrio called **La Piedra,** Vigo's famed *ostreras*—a group of rubber-gloved fisherwomen who have been peddling fresh oysters to passersby for more than 50 years— shuck the bushels of oysters hauled into port that morning. Competition has made them expert hawkers who cheerfully badger all who walk by their pavement stalls. When you buy half a dozen (for about €8), the women plate them and plunk a lemon on top; you can then take your catch into any nearby restaurant and turn it into a meal. A short stroll southwest of the old town brings you to the fishermen's barrio of **El Berbés.** Ribera del Berbés, facing the port, has several seafood restaurants, most with outdoor tables in summer.

GETTING HERE AND AROUND

A small airport connects Vigo to a handful of destinations, like Madrid and Barcelona, but trains and buses are your best bet for transportation within Galicia. Northbound RENFE trains leave on the hour for Pontevedra, Santiago de Compostela, and A Coruña, making stops at the smaller towns in between. Monbus and ALSA also connect Vigo to the same destinations via the AP9, while AUTNA runs a daily shuttle south to Porto and its international airport, a 2½-hour trip.

Contacts Vigo Bus Station. ✉ *Av. de Madrid 57* ☎ *986/373411.* **Vigo Train Station.** ✉ *C. Areal s/n* ☎ *902/320320 RENFE.*

VISITOR INFORMATION

Contacts Vigo. ✉ *Estación Marítima de Ría, Oficina 4, C. Cánovas del Castillo 3* ☎ *986/224757.*

EXPLORING

Islas Cíes. The Cíes Islands, 35 km (21 miles) west of Vigo, are among Spain's best-kept secrets. They form a pristine nature preserve that's one of the last unspoiled refuges on the Spanish coast. Starting on weekends in May and then daily June–late September, **Naviera Mar de Ons** (*986/225272; www.mardeons.com*) runs about eight boats from Vigo's harbor (subject to weather conditions), returning later in the day, for the €18.50 round-trip fare (tickets must be booked in advance on the website). The 45-minute ride brings you to white-sand beaches surrounded by turquoise waters brimming with marine life; there's also great birding. The only way to get around is your own two feet: it takes about an hour to cross the main island. If you want to stay overnight, there's a designated camping area. ⊠ *Estación Marítima* ⊕ *www. campingislascies.com.*

La Lonja (Fish Market). Fishing is central to the livelihood of thousands who live and work in Vigo, and its fish market handles some of the largest quantities of fresh fish in Europe, which is consumed across the continent. At dawn, the market auction does a roaring trade, a chaotic spectacle you can witness firsthand on visits organized by the tourist office. ⊠ *Praza do Porto Pesqueiro* ☎ *986/224757 tourist office.*

WHERE TO EAT

$
SPANISH
✕ **Bar Cocedero La Piedra.** Elegant it may not be, but this jovial tapas bar is a perfect place to devour the freshest catch from the Rúa Pescadería fisherwomen, and it does a roaring lunch trade with Vigo locals. The chefs serve heaping plates of *mariscos* (shellfish) and scallops with roe at market prices; fresh and fruity albariño is the beverage of choice. **Known for:** fresh seafood; front-row seats for oyster hawkers; simple, down-to-earth atmosphere. Ⓢ *Average main: €10* ⊠ *Rúa Pescadería 3* ☎ *986/431204.*

$$$$
SPANISH
✕ **El Mosquito.** Signed photos from the likes of King Juan Carlos and Julio Iglesias cover the walls of this elegant rose- and stone-wall restaurant, open since 1928. Specialties include *lenguado a la plancha* (grilled sole) and *navajas* (razor clams). **Known for:** seafood; caramel flan; extensive wine cellar. Ⓢ *Average main: €25* ⊠ *Praza da Pedra 4* ☎ *986/433570* ⊕ *elmosquitorestaurante.com* ☉ *No dinner Sun.*

$$$
TAPAS
✕ **Tapas Areal.** This ample and lively bar flanked by ancient stone and exposed redbrick walls is a good spot for tapas and beer, as well as albariños and Ribeiros. **Known for:** buzzing atmosphere; albariños; tapas. Ⓢ *Average main: €18* ⊠ *C. México 36* ☎ *986/418643* ☉ *Closed Sun.*

NIGHTLIFE

The streets around Praza de Compostela and the pedestrian-only Rúa Montero Ríos, down toward the waterfront, come alive in the early evening for drinks and tapas. Night owls should check out the snazzier cocktail bars in the Areal district (along Rúa Areal and Rúa de Rosalía de Castro) or the pumping rock and indie scene in the Churruca neighborhood (Rúa Rogelio Abalde, Rúa Churruca) from midnight onward, where you can often stumble across live music.

La Trastienda del Cuatro. Around the corner from Praza de Compostela, this wine bar and restaurant serves fresh and inventive "fusion tapas" and a good selection of wines to a lively, professional crowd. ✉ *Rúa de Pablo Morillo 4* ☎ *986/115881* ⊕ *www.latrastiendadelcuatro.com.*

SHOPPING

There's a large shopping center next to where the cruise ships dock. Close by you'll find A Pedra, the city's main market, where all manner of clothing and electrical goods are for sale. For souvenirs head to the old town, where there is an abundance of artisanal shops selling locally crafted leather, wood, and ceramic goods. On Rúa Cesteiros you can check out Vigo's famous handwoven baskets. Vigo's commercial shopping area is centered on Rúa Principe. At O Progreso market, peruse the freshly caught fish and local produce.

SPORTS AND THE OUTDOORS

There are several horse-riding clubs in the hills around Vigo. The Galician Equestrian Federation is an excellent source of information. And golfers can work on their game at the nearby Ría de Vigo Golf Club.

GOLF

Ría de Vigo Golf Club. The 18-hole Ría de Vigo Golf Club comes with breathtaking views overlooking the estuary and city. ✉ *San Lorenzo Domaio, Moaña, Pontevedra* ☎ *986/327051* ⊕ *www.riadevigogolf.com* 💳 *€70* ⛳ *18 holes, 6683 yards, par 72.*

HORSEBACK RIDING

Granja O Castelo. The Granja O Castelo conducts horseback rides along the pilgrimage routes to Santiago from O Cebreiro and Braga (Portugal). ✉ *Castelo 41, Ponte Caldelas* ☎ *986/425937, 608/381334* ⊕ *www.caminoacaballo.com.*

BAIONA

12 km (8 miles) southwest of Vigo.

At the southern end of the AP9 freeway and the Ría de Vigo, Baiona (Bayona in Castilian) is a summer haunt of affluent gallegos. When Columbus's *Pinta* landed here in 1492, Baiona became the first town to receive the news of the discovery of the New World. Once a castle, **Monte Real** is one of Spain's most popular paradores; walk around the battlements for superb views. Inland from Baiona's waterfront is the jumble of streets that make up Paseo Marítima: head here for seafood restaurants and lively cafés and bars. Calle Ventura Misa is one of the main drags. On your way into or out of town, check out Baiona's **Roman bridge.** The best nearby beach is Praia de América, north of town toward Vigo.

GETTING HERE AND AROUND

ATSA buses leave every half hour from Vigo, bound for Baiona and Nigrán. By car, take the AG57 from Vigo to the north or the PO340 from Tui to the southeast.

WHERE TO STAY

$$$$
HOTEL
Fodor'sChoice
★

🏨 **Parador de Baiona.** This baronial parador, positioned on a hill within the perimeter walls of a medieval castle, has plush rooms, some with balconies and ocean views toward the Islas Cíes. **Pros:** stupendous medieval architecture; views of the ría; luxurious bathrooms. **Cons:** especially pricey for rooms with sea views; occasional plumbing problems; dark rooms. [$] *Rooms from: €290* ⊠ *Monterreal, s/n* ☎ *986/355000* ⊕ *www. parador.es* ⤳ *122 rooms* ⦿❘ *Free Breakfast.*

$$ ⬚ **Pazo de Touza.** This 16th-century stone manor house is surrounded by
HOTEL   manicured gardens, with a terrace that looks out onto a hedge labyrinth. **Pros:** historical manor house; beautiful gardens. **Cons:** 15-minute drive from Baiona; some traffic noise from a nearby road. [$] *Rooms from: €110* ⊠ *Rúa dos Pazos* ☎ *986/383047* ⊕ *www.pazodatouza.info* ⤳ *8 rooms* ⦿❘ *Free Breakfast.*

TUI

14 km (9 miles) southeast of Baiona, 26 km (16 miles) south of Vigo.

The steep, narrow streets of Tui, rich with emblazoned mansions, suggest the town's past as one of the seven capitals of the Galician kingdom. Today it's an important border town; the mountains of Portugal are visible from the cathedral. Across the river in Portugal, the old fortress town of Valença contains reasonably priced shops, bars, restaurants, and a hotel with splendid views of Tui.

GETTING HERE AND AROUND
From Vigo, take the scenic coastal route PO552, which goes up the banks of the Río Miño along the Portuguese border or, if time is short, jump on the inland A55; both routes lead to Tui.

EXPLORING
Cathedral de Santa María de Tuí. A crucial building during the medieval wars between Castile and Portugal, Tui's 13th-century cathedral looks like a fortress. The cathedral's majestic cloisters surround a lush formal garden. ⊠ *Pl. de San Fernando* ☎ *986/600511.*

WHERE TO STAY
$$$ ⬚ **Parador de Tui.** This stately granite-and-chestnut hotel on the bluffs
HOTEL   overlooking the Miño is filled with local art, and the rooms are furnished with antiques. **Pros:** enticing gardens; fine fish cuisine; swimming pool (seasonal). **Cons:** a bit of a walk from Tui proper; somewhat pricey; dark rooms. [$] *Rooms from: €150* ⊠ *Av. Portugal s/n* ☎ *986/600300* ⊕ *www.parador.es* ⊘ *Closed Jan.–mid-Feb.* ⤳ *32 rooms* ⦿❘ *No meals.*

A CORUÑA AND RÍAS ALTAS

Galicia's gusty and rainy northern coast has inspired poets to wax, well, poetic. The sun does shine between bouts of rain, though, suffusing town and country with a golden glow. North of A Coruña, the Rías Altas (Upper Estuaries) notch the coast as you head east toward the Cantabrian Sea.

A CORUÑA

57 km (35 miles) north of Santiago de Compostela.

One of Spain's busiest ports, A Coruña is often (mistakenly) overlooked by travelers. While the weather can be fierce, wet, and windy, it does

The coastline of Baiona is one of the first things the crew of Columbus's ship the *Pinta* saw when they returned from their discovery of America.

give way to bouts of sunshine (it's not uncommon to experience all in one day). This unpredictable weather, along with a thriving commercial center and intriguing historic quarter, gives the city and its people its unique, endearing personality. A Coruña takes pride in its gastronomy and there is a buzzing nightlife scene, as well as a host of interesting sights, including the world's oldest still-functioning lighthouse. Its shining jewel is the city's emblematic row of glass-enclosed, white-paned galleries on the houses that line the harbor—a remarkable sight when the light catches them on a sunny day.

GETTING HERE AND AROUND

The A9 motorway provides excellent access to and from Santiago de Compostela, Pontevedra, Vigo, and Portugal, while Spain's north coast and France are accessible along the N634.

Buses run every hour from A Coruña to Santiago. Trains also operate on an hourly basis to Santiago and Pontevedra from the city's San Cristóbal train station; Madrid can be reached in eight hours on high-speed Talgo trains.

Outside the old town, the city's local buses shuttle back and forth between the Dársena de la Marina seafront and more far-flung attractions, such as the Torre de Hércules lighthouse.

Contacts **A Coruña Bus Station.** ⊠ *Rúa Caballeros 21* ☎ *981/184335.* **A Coruña Train Station.** ⊠ *C. Joaquín Planells Riera s/n* ☎ *902/320320* ⊕ *www. renfe.com.*

A Coruña and Rías Altas

```
0        10 mi
0        10 km
```

Atlantic Ocean

Cabo Ortega
Estaca de Bares
Ortigueira
Cabo Burela
Atios Valdoviño
Viveiro   Burela
Cerámica   Foz   Playa de los   COSTA VERDE
N642   de Sargadelos   Catedrales
Ferrol   A CORUÑA   **LU540**   E70
Fene   Ribadeo   Navia
Pontedeume   Mondoñedo   **AS12**
A Coruña   Sada
N634   SIERRA DE MEIRA
AC552   **Betanzos**   Vilalba   **N640**
AG55   Laracha   **A6**   **AS14**
Carballo   **N550**   **LU541**   Pesoz
AP9   Curtis   Guitiriz   LUGO   Meira
Ordes   Fonte Lanza   **LU530**   ASTURIAS
AC840   Lugo
Santiago de   Arzúa
Compostela   Vilar de
Leboreiro   Donas   **A6**
N550   Narón   Portomarín   Becerreá   SIERRA DE ANCARES
Agolada   **LU633**   Sarriá
Padrón   **AP53**   O Cebreiro   CASTILLA LEÓN
A Estrada   **A6**   Villafranca
PONTEVEDRA   Lalín   del Bierzo
Caldas de Reis   Chantada
Folgoso

VISITOR INFORMATION

Contactse A Coruña. ⊠ *Oficina de Turismo, Pl. de María Pita 6* ☎ *981/923093* ⊕ *www.turismocoruna.com.*

EXPLORING

Paseo Marítimo. To see why sailors once nicknamed A Coruña *la ciudad de cristal* (the glass city), stroll the Paseo Marítimo, said to be the longest seaside promenade in Europe. Although the congregation of boats is charming, the real sight is across the street: a long, gracefully curved row of houses. Built by fishermen in the 18th century, they face *away* from the sea—at the end of a long day, these men were tired of looking at the water. Nets were hung from the porches to dry, and fish was sold on the street below. When Galicia's first glass factory opened nearby, someone thought to enclose these porches in glass, like the latticed stern galleries of oceangoing galleons, to keep wind and rain at bay. The resulting emblematic **glass galleries** spread across the harbor and eventually throughout Galicia. ⊠ *Paseo Marítimo.*

Torre de Hércules. Much of A Coruña sits on a peninsula, on the tip of which sits this city landmark and UNESCO World Heritage Site—the oldest still-functioning lighthouse in the world. First installed during the reign of Trajan, the Roman emperor born in Spain in AD 98, the lighthouse was rebuilt in the 18th century and looks strikingly modern;

all that remains from Roman times are inscribed foundation stones. Scale the 245 steps for superb views of the city and coastline—if you're here on a summer weekend, the tower opens for views of city lights along the Atlantic. Lining the approach to the lighthouse are sculptures depicting figures from Galician and Celtic legends. ✉ *Av. de Navarra s/n* ☎ *981/223730* 🌐 *www.torredeherculesacoruna.es* 🎫 *€3 (free Mon.).*

BEACHES

Playas Orzán and Riazor. A Coruña's sweeping Paseo Marítimo overlooks two excellent, well-maintained beaches, Playa del Orzán and Playa de Riazor. These long curves of fine golden sand tend to be busy in summer with chattering groups of local families and friends enjoying the milder climate. The area of Playa del Orzán in front of Hotel Melía Pita is popular with surfers. Cross the Paseo Marítimo for a choice of cafés and restaurants with animated terraces, while on the seafront, kiosks sell ice cream and snacks. Keep in mind that this is the Atlantic, so test the temperature before taking the plunge. There is no natural shade, but you can rent sun loungers and parasols in summer. **Amenities:** food and drink; lifeguards; showers; toilets. **Best for:** surfing; swimming; walking. ✉ *Paseo Marítimo.*

4

WHERE TO EAT AND STAY

$$ SPANISH 🍴 **Adega O Bebedeiro.** This tiny restaurant is beloved by locals for its authentic food. It feels like an old farmhouse, with stone walls and floors, a fireplace, pine tables and stools, and dusty wine bottles (*adega* is Gallego for bodega, or wine cellar). **Known for:** octopus with clams in garlic sauce; baked scallops; wine cellar. [$] *Average main: €17* ✉ *C. Ángel Rebollo 34* ☎ *981/210609* 🕑 *Closed Mon., and 1st wk in Jan. No dinner Sun.*

$$$ SPANISH 🍴 **El De Alberto.** Steps from the ultramodern Domus, El De Alberto marries the traditional flavors of Galicia with impeccable modern presentation. Alberto, the passionate and friendly owner (and chef), devises repeatedly exciting flavor combinations, such as *pulpo a la brasa con puró de calabaza, salsa kimchi y crujientes de patata* (grilled octopus with pumpkin puree, kimchi sauce, and crispy potatoes) or *zamburiñas en salsa de trufa* (baked scallops with truffle sauce). **Known for:** presentation; grilled octopus; baked scallops. [$] *Average main: €18* ✉ *Rúa Ángel Rebollo 18* ☎ *981/907411* 🕑 *Closed Mon.*

$$$ SEAFOOD 🍴 **La Penela.** This contemporary, bottle-green dining room is the perfect place to feast on fresh fish while sipping albariño—try at least a few crabs or mussels with béchamel, a dish that La Penela is locally famous for. If shellfish isn't your speed, the roast veal is also popular. **Known for:** views of the harbor and Praza María Pita; terrace dining; mussels with béchamel. [$] *Average main: €18* ✉ *Praza María Pita 12* ☎ *981/209200* 🌐 *www.lapenela.com* 🕑 *Closed last 2 wks of Jan. No dinner Sun.*

$$$ HOTEL 🏨 **Hesperia Finisterre.** A favorite with businesspeople and families, the oldest and busiest of A Coruña's top hotels is only a few minutes' walk from the port, and is bursting with on-site amenities. **Pros:** port and city views; heated pool; spa. **Cons:** inconvenient outdoor parking; unimpressive breakfast; additional charge for parking. [$] *Rooms from: €159*

✉ *Paseo del Parrote 2–4* ☎ *981/205400* 🌐 *www.hesperia-finisterre.com* 🛏 *92 rooms* 🍴 *No meals.*

$ B&B/INN 🏨 **Hotel Lois.** Positioned in a quiet part of the street, a few steps from the tapas bars of Calle Estrella, Hotel Lois is an excellent choice for location alone, as well as its clean, contemporary style and excellent value for money. **Pros:** central location; surrounded by restaurants; discount at nearby car park. **Cons:** patchy Wi-Fi in some rooms; no parking on-site; no access to street with car. [$] *Rooms from: €78* ✉ *Estrella 40* ☎ *981/212269* 🌐 *www.loisestrella.com* 🛏 *10 rooms* 🍴 *No meals.*

NIGHTLIFE

Begin your evening in the **Plaza de María Pita**: cafés and tapas bars proliferate off its western corners and inland. **Calles Estrella, Franja, Riego de Agua, Barrera, Galera,** and the **Plaza del Humor** have many tapas bars that get progressively busier as the night develops, some of which serve Ribeiro wine in bowls and free tapas with every drink. Start at the top of Calle Estrella (at the furthest end from Plaza de María Pita) beginning with A Taberna de Cunqueiro (Rúa Estrella 22), and work your way back. Night owls head for the posh and pricey clubs around **Praia del Orzán** (Orzán Beach), particularly along Calle Juan Canalejo. For lower-key entertainment, the old town has cozy taverns and plenty of bars that stay open into the early hours.

A Lagareta. Tucked behind a thick (yet easy-to-miss) wooden door, this vivacious, cozy stone-walled tavern is popular with locals. The bar serves cheese and cold cuts on slate, freshly made tortillas, and modern spins on Galician tapas, accompanied by a good choice of local wines by the glass. ✉ *Rúa Franja 24* ☎ *881/897813.*

Taberna Da Galera. This popular and stylish tapas bar, in the heart of the old town, serves Galician *raciones* to a lively crowd. Prop up at the bar or squeeze into a small wooden table and feast on *tigres* (stuffed mussels) or *pulpo en tempura* (octopus in tempura), and accompany it all with a glass of fresh Ribeiro wine. ✉ *Rúa Galera 32* ☎ *881/923996* 🌐 *www.tabernadagalera.com.*

SHOPPING

Calle Real and **Plaza de Lugo** have boutiques with contemporary fashions. A stroll down **Calle San Andrés,** two blocks inland from Calle Real, or **Avenida Juan Flórez,** leading into the newer town, can yield some sartorial treasures. El Mercado Municipal de San Agustín close to Plaza María Pita is the place to go for local produce.

Alfarería Aparicio. The glazed terra-cotta ceramics from Buño, a town 40 km (25 miles) west of A Coruña on the C552, are prized by aficionados. To see where they're made, drive out to Buño itself, where potters work in private studios all over town; then stop in to this store to see the results. ✉ *Rúa Nova 4* ☎ *981/711136* 🌐 *www.alfareriaaparicio.es.*

Mundo Galego. Stop here for local cheese, wine, liqueur, and other Galician specialties. The shop also organizes tastings. ✉ *Pl. de La Galera 40* ☎ *981/912038* 🌐 *www.mundogalego.com.*

SPORTS AND THE OUTDOORS

In A Coruña and the surrounding area there are sports and leisure activities available year-round, including sailing, golf, and hiking. Swimmers and surfers can take advantage of the 2 km (1 mile) of beach and coastline in the heart of the city.

GOLF

Real Club de Golf de La Coruña. Mackenzie Ross designed this tree-lined course, which has wide fairways and a scattering of lakeside holes. ⊠ *La Zapateira s/n* ☎ *981/285200* ⊕ *www.clubgolfcoruna.com* 🖾 *€100 weekdays, €150 weekends (reservations essential)* ⌖ *18 holes, 6625 yards, par 72.*

BETANZOS

25 km (15 miles) east of A Coruña, 65 km (40 miles) northeast of Santiago de Compostela.

The charming, slightly ramshackle medieval town of Betanzos is still surrounded by parts of its old city wall. An important Galician port in the 13th century, the old town straddles the confluence of the Mendo River and the Mandeo River and is known today for its white galleried houses, stately Gothic monuments, and lively taverns.

GETTING HERE AND AROUND

From Vigo and other destinations to the south, head north up the AP9; from A Coruña, head east for half an hour along the same motorway. The medieval center, with its narrow lanes rising up from the Pont Nova bridge, is best explored on foot.

VISITOR INFORMATOIN

Contacts Betanzos. ⊠ *Praza de Galicia 1* ☎ *981/776666* ⊕ *www.betanzos.es.*

EXPLORING

Iglesia de San Francisco. The 1292 monastery of San Francisco was converted into a church in 1387 by the nobleman Fernán Pérez de Andrade. His magnificent tomb, to the left of the west door, has him lying on the backs of a stone bear and boar, with hunting dogs at his feet and an angel receiving his soul by his head. ⊠ *Pl. de Fernán Pérez Andrade.*

Iglesia de Santa María de Azogue. This 15th-century church, a few steps uphill from the church of San Francisco, is a National Monument. It has Renaissance statues that were stolen in 1981 but subsequently recovered. ⊠ *Pl. de Fernán Pérez Andrade.*

Iglesia de Santiago. The tailors' guild put up the Gothic-style church of Santiago, which includes a Pórtico de la Gloria inspired by the one in Santiago's Cathedral. Above the door is a carving of St. James as the Slayer of the Moors. ⊠ *Pl. de Lanzós.*

VIVEIRO

121 km (75 miles) northeast of Betanzos.

The once-turreted city walls of this popular summer resort are still partially intact. Two festivals are noteworthy here: the **Semana Santa** processions, when penitents follow religious processions on their knees,

A Coruña is a major port town, but fashionistas might know it as where the first Zara clothing shop opened, back in 1975.

and the **Rapa das Bestas,** a colorful roundup of wild horses that occurs the first Sunday in July on nearby Monte Buyo. The beaches in Viveiro Bay are some of the north's finest.

GETTING HERE AND AROUND

Narrow-gauge FEVE trains connect Viveiro to Oviedo, Gijón, and other points eastward. By car, head east on the AP9 from A Coruña and then take the LU540 to Viveiro.

VISITOR INFORMATION

Contacts Viveiro. ⊠ Av. Ramón Canosa 3 ☎ 982/560879 ⊕ www.viveiro.es.

WHERE TO STAY

$$$
HOTEL

🍴 **Hotel Ego.** The view of the ría from this hilltop hotel outside Viveiro is unbeatable, and every room has one. **Pros:** hilltop views; relaxing public areas; excellent restaurant. **Cons:** a little generic; the facade resembles an airport terminal; small spa. $ *Rooms from: €143* ⊠ *Playa de Area 1, off N642, Faro (San Xiao)* ☎ *982/560987* ⊕ *www.hotelego.es* ➴ *45 rooms* ⏸ *No meals.*

OFF THE BEATEN PATH

Cerámica de Sargadelos. Distinctive blue-and-white-glazed contemporary ceramics are made at Cerámica de Sargadelos, 21 km (13 miles) east of Viveiro. In July and August it's usually possible to watch artisans work (weekdays 9–1:15), but call ahead and check. ⊠ *Ctra. Paraño s/n, Cervo* ☎ *982/557841* ⊕ *www.sargadelos.com.*

Playa de las Catedrales (*As Catedrais Beach*). One of Spain's best-kept secrets, this spectacular stretch of sand, also known as Praia de Augas Santas (Beach of the Holy Waters) features vast rock formations, domes, arches, and caves that have been naturally formed over time by the wind and the sea. The arches are accessible for walks when the tide goes out, otherwise the beach can be completely covered. In high season it is mandatory to reserve a ticket to access the actual beach (July–September) **Amenities:** parking. **Best for:** spectacular natural scenery; beach walks; rock formations. ✉ *A8 (516 exit), Ribadeo.*

ASTURIAS

As you cross into the Principality of Asturias, the intensely green countryside continues, belying the fact that this is a major mining region once valued by the Romans for its iron- and gold-rich earth. Asturias is bordered to the southeast by the imposing Picos de Europa, which are best accessed via the scenic coastal towns of Llanes or Ribadesella.

4

LUARCA

105 km (65 miles) east of Luarca, 92 km (57 miles) northeast of Oviedo.

The village of Luarca is tucked into a cove at the end of a final twist of the Río Negro, with a fishing port and, to the west, a sparkling bay. The town is a maze of cobblestone streets, stone stairways, and whitewashed houses, with a harborside decorated with painted flowerpots.

GETTING HERE AND AROUND

To get to Oviedo, Gijón, and other destinations to the east, you can take a FEVE train or an ALSA bus; it's about a two-hour trip. By car, take the A8 west along the coast from Oviedo and Gijón or east up through Luarca from A Coruña.

VISITOR INFORMATION

Contacts Luarca. ✉ *Pl. de Alfonso X El Sabio s/n* ☎ *985/640083* 🌐 *www.turismoluarca.com.*

WHERE TO EAT AND STAY

$$$ SEAFOOD 🍴 **El Barómetro.** Decorated with an ornate barometer to gauge the famously unpredictable local weather, this small, family-run seafood eatery is in a 19th-century building in the middle of the harborfront. In addition to an inexpensive menú del día, there's also a good choice of local fresh fish, including *calamares* (squid) and *espárragos rellenos de erizo de mar* (asparagus stuffed with sea urchins). **Known for:** excellent value prix-fixe lunch; seafood fideo (noodles); popularity with locals. [$] *Average main: €18* ✉ *Paseo del Muelle 5* ☎ *985/470662.*

$$$ SPANISH 🍴 **Restaurante Sport.** This friendly, family-run restaurant has been going since the 1950s. Here you will find large windows overlooking river views, walls adorned with artwork, and a kitchen adept at fabada asturiana and seafood. **Known for:** riverside setting; seafood; rollo de bonito (tuna meatballs in tomato sauce). [$] *Average main: €22* ✉ *Calle Rivero 9* ☎ *985/641078* 🕑 *No dinner Wed. Closed Sun.*

$$ B&B/INN FAMILY Fodor's Choice ★ 🏨 **Hotel Rural 3 Cabos.** Built on a grassy hill with spectacular views of the ocean and Luarca's three famous bays in the distance, this luxurious B&B makes for a charming stay. **Pros:** excellent food; stunning views of green rolling hills and the ocean in the distance; fast Wi-Fi, use of bicycles, and an on-site playground. **Cons:** somewhat out of the

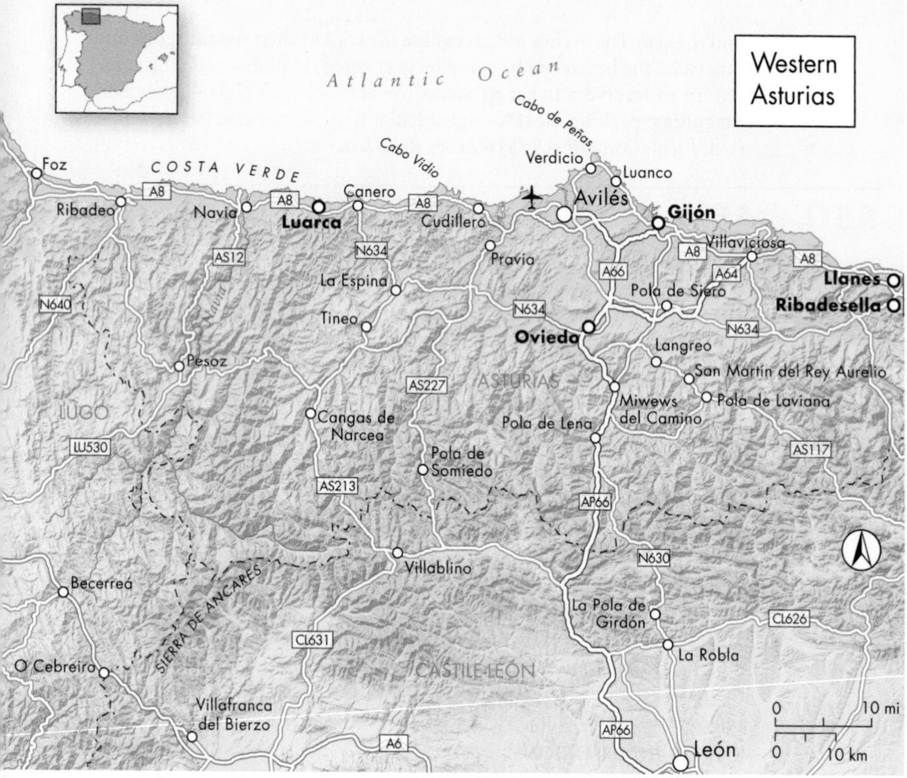

way (15-minute drive to Luarca); car needed. $ *Rooms from: €105* ✉ *Ctra. de El Vallín, Km 4* ☎ *985/924252* 🌐 *www.hotelrural3cabos.com* 🕓 *Closed Jan. (can vary)* 🛏 *6 rooms* 🍴 *Free Breakfast.*

$$ B&B/INN 🏨 **Villa La Argentina.** Built in 1899 by a wealthy *indiano* (a Spaniard who made his fortune in South America), this charming Asturian mansion, on the hill above Luarca, offers modern apartments in the garden or Belle Époque suites in the main building. **Pros:** swimming pool; lovely gardens; peace and quiet. **Cons:** a short uphill walk from town; not central; simple breakfast. $ *Rooms from: €108* ✉ *Villar s/n* ☎ *985/640102* 🌐 *www.villalaargentina.com* 🕓 *Closed Jan. and Feb.* 🛏 *12 rooms* 🍴 *Free Breakfast.*

EN ROUTE

Cudillero. The coastal road leads 35 km (22 miles) east of Luarca to this little fishing village, clustered around its tiny port. The emerald green of the surrounding hills, the bright blue of the water, and the pops of color among the white houses make this village one of the prettiest and most touristic in Asturias. Seafood and cider restaurants line the central street, which turns into a boat ramp at the bottom of town.

OVIEDO

92 km (57 miles) southeast of Luarca, 50 km (31 miles) southeast of Cudillero, 30 km (19 miles) south of Gijón.

Inland, the Asturian countryside starts to look picture-perfect. Gently rolling green hills, and wooden, tile-roof hórreos strung with golden bundles of drying corn replace the stark granite sheds of Galicia. A drive through the hills and valleys brings you to the capital city, Oviedo. Although its surrounds are primarily industrial, Oviedo has three of the most famous pre-Romanesque churches in Spain and a large university, giving it both ancient charm and youthful zest. Start your explorations with the two exquisite 9th-century chapels outside the city, on the slopes of Monte Naranco.

GETTING HERE AND AROUND

Oviedo is served by the A66 tollway, which links to Gijón and Avilés, where you can get on the A8 west to A Coruña or east toward Santander. Madrid is reached on the N630 south.

There are several buses per day to Gijón (30 minutes) and to Santiago and A Coruña (5 hours). Madrid is 5½ hours away by rail from Oviedo's RENFE station, situated on Calle Uría. The FEVE service operates across the north coast, with Gijón easily reached in half an hour and Bilbao just under eight hours away.

Local buses operate along the main arteries of Oviedo, between the train station and shopping areas, but skirt around the rim of the historical center, where Oviedo's oldest buildings are clustered in the labyrinth of streets around the Plaza Alfonso. Considering the short distances, walking is the best option, though taxis are inexpensive.

Contacts Oviedo Bus Station. ⊠ *Calle Pepe Cosmen* ⊕ *www.estaciondeautobusesdeoviedo.com.* **Oviedo Train Station.** ⊠ *Calle Uria, s/n* ☎ *912/320320 RENFE.*

VISITOR INFORMATION

Contacts Oviedo. ⊠ *Pl. de la Constitución 4* ☎ *985/213385* ⊕ *www.turismoviedo.es.*

EXPLORING

Cathedral. Oviedo's Gothic cathedral was built between the 14th and 16th centuries around the city's most cherished monument, the **Cámara Santa** (Holy Chamber). King Ramiro's predecessor, Alfonso the Chaste (792–842), built it to hide the treasures of Christian Spain during the struggle with the Moors. Damaged during the Spanish Civil War, it has since been rebuilt. Inside is the gold-leaf **Cross of the Angels,** commissioned by Alfonso in 808 and encrusted with pearls and jewels. On the left is the more elegant **Victory Cross,** actually a jeweled sheath crafted in 908 to cover the oak cross used by Pelayo in the battle of Covadonga. ⊠ *Pl. Alfonso II El Casto* ☎ *985/219642* ⊕ *www.catedraldeoviedo.es* 🎫 *Cathedral free; from €5 combined ticket for Cámara Santa, cloister, and museum.*

San Julián de los Prados (Santullano). Older than its more famous pre-Romanesque counterparts on Monte Naranco, the 9th-century church of Santullano has surprisingly well-preserved frescoes inside. Geometric patterns, rather than representations of humans or animals, cover almost every surface, along with a cross containing Greek letters. ✉ *C. Selgas 1* ☎ *687/052826* 🎟 *€2 (free 1st Mon. of each month)* ⏲ *Closed Sun.*

Santa María del Naranco and San Miguel de Lillo. These two churches—the first with superb views and its plainer sister 300 yards uphill—are the jewels of an early architectural style called Asturian pre-Romanesque, a more primitive, hulking, defensive line that preceded Romanesque architecture by nearly three centuries. Commissioned as part of a summer palace by King Ramiro I when Oviedo was the capital of Christian Spain, these masterpieces have survived for more than 1,000 years. Tickets for both sites are available in the church of Santa María del Naranco. ✉ *Ctra. de los Monumentos, 2 km (1 mile) north of Oviedo* ☎ *638/260163* 🌐 *www.santamariadelnaranco.es* 🎟 *€3, includes guided tour (free Mon., without guide).*

WHERE TO EAT AND STAY

$$$ SPANISH 🍴 **Casa Chema.** With a sun-dappled terrace overlooking rolling green hills and a sparkling river, this restaurant, 11 km (7 miles) outside Oviedo, is an inviting—and peaceful—spot to savor some of Asturias' best traditional cooking. The fabada, with its buttery soft beans and slow-simmered rich broth, served in earthenware pots, has won the restaurant awards. **Known for:** award-winning fabada; terrace with views; laid-back lunch. [$] *Average main: €20* ✉ *La Arquera 184 (Puerto)* ☎ *985/798200* 🌐 *www.casachema.com* ⏲ *No dinner Sun.–Fri.*

$$$$ SPANISH 🍴 **Casa Fermín.** Skylights, plants, and an air of modernity belie the age of this sophisticated restaurant, which opened in 1924 and is now in its fourth generation. The creative menu changes seasonally and there is also a tasting menu (€70). **Known for:** langoustines with cream of leek; roasted sea bass; elegant setting. [$] *Average main: €26* ✉ *C. San Francisco 8* ☎ *985/216452* 🌐 *www.casafermin.com* ⏲ *Closed Sun.*

$$$ SPANISH 🍴 **La Corte de Pelayo.** Head to this renowned restaurant and meeting spot on one of Oviedo's main thoroughfares for a famous Asturian dish called *cachopo* (a heart-stopping combination of veal, ham, and Asturian cheese wrapped in bread crumbs and deep-fried). If you prefer something a bit lighter, the menu also includes salads, fresh fish, and meat dishes. **Known for:** cachopo; lively atmosphere; central location. [$] *Average main: €20* ✉ *Calle San Francisco 21* ☎ *985/213145* 🌐 *www.lacortedepelayo.com* ⏲ *No dinner Sun. Closed Mon.*

$$ SPANISH 🍴 **Tierra Astur.** This bustling *sidrería* (cider bar) is a popular and classic destination for locals and tourists alike, who come to enjoy the lively atmosphere, a cup of cider poured from a great height, and the traditional, family-style Asturian fare. Try the fabada, or sample from an array of traditional *tablas* (boards) with choice selections from more than 40 artisanal cheeses and local cold cuts, preserved seafood, and fresh fish and meat dishes. **Known for:** cider; cheese platters; succulent chuleton (rib-eye steak). [$] *Average main: €15* ✉ *Calle Gascona 1* ☎ *985/202502* 🌐 *www.tierra-astur.com.*

$$
HOTEL

⚏ **Barceló Oviedo Cervantes.** A playful revamp of this town house in the city center added a neo-Moorish portico to the original latticed facade and indulgent amenities like entertainment systems in some of the bathrooms. **Pros:** fun '70s design; central location close to train station; on-site bar and restaurant. **Cons:** uninteresting views; confusing light switches; below par lighting in rooms. $ *Rooms from:* €90 ⊠ *C. Cervantes 13* ☎ *985/255000* ⊕ *www.barcelo.com* ⇆ *72 rooms* ⓘ *No meals.*

$$$
HOTEL
Fodor's Choice
★

⚏ **Eurostars Hotel de la Reconquista.** Occupying an 18th-century hospice emblazoned with a huge stone coat of arms, the luxurious Reconquista is by far the most distinguished hotel in Oviedo. **Pros:** great location; spacious rooms; good breakfast buffet. **Cons:** some rooms have uninteresting views; poorly lighted rooms; tired room decor. $ *Rooms from:* €180 ⊠ *C. Gil de Jaz 16* ☎ *913/342196* ⊕ *www.hoteldelareconquista. com* ⇆ *142 rooms* ⓘ *Free Breakfast.*

NIGHTLIFE AND PERFORMING ARTS

Calle de Mon. Oviedo gets a little rowdy after dark on weekends, and there's plenty in the way of loud live music. Most of the bars are concentrated on Calle de Mon and its continuation, Calle Oscura. Calle Canóniga, off Calle de Mon, is another street with a number of bars. Calle Gascona is the place to try local Asturian cider in one of the popular sidrerías that line the street. Poured from a great height into the glass by the bartender, they impressively hit the mark each time—which also aerates the naturally still cider. ⊠ *Oviedo.*

SHOPPING

Shops throughout the city carry **azabache jewelry** made of jet.

Joyería Santirso. This family-run shop has been selling silver jewelry, including Asturia's world-famous azabache, for five generations. ⊠ *Calle de la Rúa 7* ☎ *985/225304.*

Mercado El Fontan. Shop for fish, vegetables, and local products at Mercado El Fontan, a market that has been in this spot since the 13th century (although the current property was built in the 19th century). The narrow streets surrounding the market are lined with colorful flower stalls and small shops selling Asturian goods, such as vacuum-packed fava beans and cheeses. ⊠ *Pl. 19 de Octubre* ☎ *985/204394* ⊕ *www. mercadofontan.es.*

SPORTS AND THE OUTDOORS

SKIING

Fuentes de Invierno. An hour's drive from Oviedo in the heart of the Cantabrian Mountains, Fuentes de Invierno has five chairlifts and 15 trails of varying difficulty. ⊠ *Ctra. del Puerto de San Isidro* ☎ *985/481439* ⊕ *www.fuentesdeinvierno.com* ⓘ *€26.*

Valgrande Pajares. This resort has two chairlifts, eight slopes, and cross-country trails. ⊠ *Estación Invernal y de Montaña Valgrande-Pajares, Brañillín, 60 km (37 miles) south of Oviedo, Pajares* ☎ *985/957097* ⊕ *www.valgrande-pajares.com.*

GIJÓN

30 km (19 miles) north of Oviedo.

The Campo Valdés baths, dating back to the 1st century AD, and other reminders of Gijón's time as an ancient Roman port remain visible downtown. Gijón was almost destroyed in a 14th-century struggle over the Castilian throne, but by the 19th century it was a thriving port and industrial city. The lively modern-day city is part fishing port, part summer resort, and part university town, packed with cafés, restaurants, and sidrerías.

GETTING HERE AND AROUND
Oviedo is only 30 minutes away by ALSA bus or FEVE train, both of which run every half hour throughout the day. The A8 coastal highway runs east from Gijón to Santander, and west to Luarca, and eventually A Coruña.

Contacts Gijón Bus Station. ⊠ *C. Magnus Blikstad 1* ☎ *902/422242.* **Gijón Train Station.** ⊠ *C. Sanz Crespo s/n* ☎ *902/100818.*

VISITOR INFORMATION
Contacts Gijón. ⊠ *Escalera 4, Paseo Maritimo de la Playa de San Lorenzo* ☎ *985/341771* ⊕ *www.gijon.info.*

EXPLORING
Cimadevilla. This steep peninsula, the old fishermen's quarter, is now the hub of Gijón's nightlife. At sunset, the sidewalk in front of bar El Planeta (Tránsito de las Ballenas 4), overlooking the harbor, is a prime spot to join in with the locals and drink Asturian cider. From the park at the highest point on the headland, beside Basque artist Eduardo Chillida's massive sculpture *Elogio del Horizonte* (*In Praise of the Horizon*), there's a panoramic view of the coast and city. ⊠ *Gijón.*

Muséu del Pueblu d'Asturies (*Museum of the People of Asturias*). Across the river on the eastern edge of town, past Parque Isabel la Católica, this rustic museum contains traditional Asturian houses, cider presses, a mill, and an exquisitely painted granary. Also here is the **Museo de la Gaita** (Bagpipe Museum). This collection of wind instruments explains their evolution both around the world and within Asturias. ⊠ *Paseo del Doctor Fleming 877, La Güelga s/n* ☎ *985/182960* 🎫 *€3 (free Sun.)* 🕙 *Closed Mon.*

Termas Romanas de Campo Valdés (*Roman baths*). Dating back to the time of Augustus, Gijón's baths are under the plaza at the end of the beach. ⊠ *Campo Valdés s/n* ☎ *985/185151* 🎫 *€3 (free Sun.)* 🕙 *Closed Mon.*

BEACHES
The capital of the Costa Verde, Gijón, overlooks two attractive sandy beaches that are large enough to avoid overcrowding in summer.

Playa de Poniente (*Sunset Beach*). Tucked into the city's harbor, this horseshoe-shape curve of fine artificial sand and calm waters is wonderful for a stroll as the evening draws in. **Amenities:** lifeguards; showers; toilets. **Best for:** sunset; swimming; walking. ⊠ *C. Rodriguez San Pedro.*

Playa de San Lorenzo. Gijón's second popular beach, on the other side of the headland from Playa de Poniente, is a large stretch of golden sand

DID YOU KNOW?

Gijón is a popular stop for travelers in Asturias: it's a large port city with a bit of everything, including a popular summer beach and lots of cafés.

backed by a promenade that extends from one end of town to the other. Across the narrow peninsula and the Plaza Mayor is the harbor, where the fishing fleet comes in with the day's catch. As long as the tide is out, you can sunbathe. The waves are generally moderate, although the weather and sea currents can be unpredictable along the northern coast. **Amenities:** food and drink; lifeguards; showers; toilets; water sports. **Best for:** sunset; swimming; walking. ✉ *Av. Rufo García Rendueles.*

WHERE TO EAT AND STAY

$$$ SPANISH 🍴 **La Galana.** La Galana has all the ingredients of a typical Asturian sidrería, with colossal barrels lining the walls, thick wooden tables, and plenty of standing room at the bar, where locals munch on Cabrales cheese. The kitchen serves classic cider-house fare, but the portions are smaller and the presentation more refined. **Known for:** cider; seafood; refined, creative dishes. [$] *Average main: €18* ✉ *Pl. Mayor 10* ☎ *985/172429* 🌐 *www.restauranteasturianolagalana.es.*

$$$$ SPANISH 🍴 **Restaurante Auga.** This glass-enclosed dining room, housed in what was once Gijón's fish market, overlooks the harbor and serves fine, imaginative seafood and meat dishes. The renowned restaurant's emphasis is on its Cantabrian catch, with specialties like *langostinos frescos en su jugo y tocino ibérico* (fresh prawns in their juice with Iberian bacon) and *merluza de pino "Puerto de Celeiro" con sopa de patata, citricos y cardamomo* (Port of Celeiro line-caught hake, served with potato soup seasoned with citrus and cardamom). **Known for:** harbor and sea views; contemporary seafood dishes; alfresco dining. [$] *Average main: €26* ✉ *C. Claudio Alvargonzález s/n* ☎ *985/168186* 🌐 *www.restauranteauga.com* 🕒 *Closed Mon. No dinner Sun.*

$ B&B/INN 🏨 **Hostel Gijón Centro.** Brilliantly located a few steps from the harbor and Plaza Mayor, this tiny guesthouse offers rooms with large windows affording plenty of natural light, plus simple, modern decor and comfortable beds. **Pros:** excellent value; central location; quiet. **Cons:** tiny bathrooms; no on-site facilities; simple lodging. [$] *Rooms from: €60* ✉ *Flat 1, Calle San Antonio 12* ☎ *657/029242* 🌐 *hostel-centro.gijonhotelspage.com/en* 🛏 *6 rooms* 🍽 *No meals.*

$ B&B/INN 🏨 **Mirador de Ordiales.** Built on the top of a hill, this cozy B&B offers an exquisite view of the valley below and the snowcapped Picos de Europa in the distance. **Pros:** stunning views; good base for hiking; spacious rooms. **Cons:** remote—need a car; 25-minute drive from Gijón city center; breakfast is extra. [$] *Rooms from: €85* ✉ *Ordiales 11B, Siero* ☎ *653/938156, 985/721020* 🌐 *www.elmiradordeordiales.com* 🛏 *3 rooms* 🍽 *No meals.*

$$$$ HOTEL 🏨 **Parador de Gijón.** This is one of the simplest and friendliest paradores in Spain, and most of the rooms in the new wing have wonderful views over the lake or the park. **Pros:** park views; welcoming, down-to-earth staff; great food. **Cons:** austere guest rooms; fairly expensive; some distance from the old town. [$] *Rooms from: €205* ✉ *Av. Torcuato Fernández Miranda 15* ☎ *985/370511* 🌐 *www.parador.es* 🛏 *40 rooms* 🍽 *Free Breakfast.*

SHOPPING

Coalla Gourmet. Stop by this shop selling Asturian specialties, including renowned cheeses, wines, honey, and other local delicacies. In the back, there's a wine bar, which stays open well into the evening, so you can try before you buy. ⊠ *Calle San Antonio 8* ☎ *985/348400.*

RIBADESELLA

67 km (40 miles) east of Gijón, 84 km (50 miles) northeast of Oviedo.

The N632 twists around green hills dappled with eucalyptus groves, allowing glimpses of the sea and sandy beaches below and the snow-capped Picos de Europa looming inland. This fishing village and beach resort is famous for its seafood, its cave, and the canoe races held on the Río Sella the first Saturday in August.

GETTING HERE AND AROUND

FEVE and ALSA connect Ribadesella to Gijón and Oviedo by train and bus, a journey of 1½–2 hours. By car, you can take the A8 from Gijón and Oviedo past Villaviciosa to Ribadesella.

VISITOR INFORMATION

Contacts Ribadesella. ⊠ *Paseo Princesa Letizia s/n* ☎ *985/860038* ⊕ *www. ribadesella.es.*

EXPLORING

Centro de Arte Rupestre Tito Bustillo. Discovered in 1968, the cave here has 20,000-year-old paintings on a par with those in Lascaux, France, and Altamira. Giant horses and deer prance about the walls. To protect the paintings, no more than 375 visitors are allowed inside each day, so reservations are essential. The guided tour is in Spanish. Audio guides are available in English. There's also a **museum** of Asturian cave finds, open year-round. ⊠ *Av. de Tito Bustillo s/n* ☎ *902/306600* ⊕ *www. centrotitobustillo.com* ⊠ *From €6* ☉ *Closed Mon. and Tues., and Jan.*

BEACHES

Playa Santa Marina. To the west of the Río Sella estuary, which divides the town, this gentle curve of golden sand is one of the prettiest beaches in Asturias, tucked neatly beneath the town's seafront promenade, which is lined with elegant 20th-century mansions. Moderate waves provide safe swimming conditions, although, as with all of Spain's Atlantic-facing beaches, currents and weather can be unpredictable. In high season (particularly in August) the beach can get very busy. This part of the coast is not called the "dinosaur coast" for nothing; over by the Punta'l Pozu Viewpoint, you can see footprints embedded in the rocks and cliff faces where they left their mark millions of years ago. Amenities listed are only available June–September. **Amenities:** food and drink; lifeguards; showers; toilets. **Best for:** surfing; swimming. ⊠ *Paseo Agustin de Argüelles Marina.*

WHERE TO EAT

$$$$
SPANISH
✕ **Arbidel.** This one-Michelin-starred restaurant, tucked into the narrow streets of Ribadesella's old town, is adorned with rustic stone walls and a hand-painted mural. It serves traditional Asturian fare with a modern twist, as well as gourmet tapas and a tasting menu

(€49.50–€79.50). **Known for:** Michelin star; good-value tasting menu; apple gazpacho with sardine. [$] *Average main: €28* ✉ *Calle Oscuro 1* ☎ *985/861440* 🌐 *www.arbidel.com.*

LLANES

40 km (25 miles) east of Ribadesella.

This beach town is on a pristine stretch of the Costa Verde. The shores in both directions outside town have vistas of cliffs looming over white-sand beaches and isolated caves. A long canal connected to a small harbor cuts through the heart of Llanes, and along its banks rise colorful houses with glass galleries against a backdrop of the Picos de Europa. At the daily port-side fish market, usually held around 1 pm, vendors display heaping mounds of freshly caught seafood.

GETTING HERE AND AROUND

The scenic A8 coastal route from Gijón continues past Villaviciosa and Ribadesella and then winds through Llanes before heading east towards Santander. FEVE trains and ALSA buses make the trip in 2–3½ hours.

VISITOR INFORMATION

Contacts Llanes. ✉ *Antigua Lonja de Pescado, C/ Marqués de Canillejas 1* ☎ *985/400164* 🌐 *www.llanes.es.*

EXPLORING

Basílica de Santa María del Conceyu. This 13th-century church, which rises over the main square here, is an excellent example of Romantic Gothic architecture. ✉ *Pl. Christo Rey.*

Mirador Panorámico La Boriza. Dotting the Asturian coast east and west of Llanes are *bufones* (blowholes), cavelike cavities that expel water when waves are sucked in. Active blowholes shoot streams of water as high as 100 feet into the air, although it's hard to predict when this will happen, as it depends on the tide and the size of the surf. They are clearly marked so you can find them, and there are barriers to protect you when they expel water. There's a blowhole east of Playa Ballota; try to watch it in action from this mirador east of Llanes, between the villages of Cué and Andrin, near the entrance to Campo de Golf Municipal de Llanes. If you miss it, the view is still worth a stop—on a clear day you can see the coastline all the way east to Santander. ✉ *Llanes.*

Plaza Cristo Rey. Peaceful and well conserved, this plaza marks the center of the old town, which is partially surrounded by the remains of its medieval walls. ✉ *Llanes.*

BEACHES

Playa Ballota. Just 1 km (½ mile) east of Llanes is one of the area's most secluded beaches, the pristine Playa Ballota, with private coves and one of the few stretches of nudist sand in Asturias. **Amenities:** beach bar (seasonal). **Best for:** nudists; swimming; walking. ✉ *Camino Ballota.*

Playa de Torimbia. Farther west of Llanes is the partially nudist Playa de Torimbia, a wild, virgin beach as yet untouched by development. It can be reached only via a footpath—roughly a 15-minute walk. This secluded crescent of fine, white sand and crystal clear waters is backed by Asturias's green hills, making it one of the region's most picturesque beaches. Winds can be strong, and there is no real infrastructure. **Amenities:** none. **Best for:** nudists; solitude; swimming; walking. ✉ *Off C. Niembru, 8 km (5 miles) west of Llanes.*

Playa de Toró. On the eastern edge of town is the Playa de Toró, where fine white sands are peppered with unique rock formations. This pristine beach is ideal for sunbathing and families. **Amenities:** lifeguards; showers; toilets. **Best for:** swimming. ✉ *Av. de Toró.*

Playa del Sablón. Steps from the old town is the protected Playa del Sablón (whose name derives from the Asturian word for "sand"), a little swath of beach that gets crowded on weekends. **Amenities:** food and drink; lifeguards; showers; toilets. **Best for:** swimming. ✉ *C. Sablón.*

4

WHERE TO STAY

$$ HOTEL **Hotel CAEaCLAVELES.** This sleek, modern-design hotel is architecturally captivating, with organic curves, full-length windows, polished cement ceilings, and a grass-covered roof that gently slopes down to ground on either side of the building, allowing guests to walk up and enjoy the views. **Pros:** award-winning architecture; plenty of natural light; quiet and scenic. **Cons:** bathrooms lack privacy; somewhat remote, car needed. [$] *Rooms from: €115* ✉ *La Pereda* ☎ *985/925981* 🌐 *www.caeaclaveles.com* 🕓 *Closed mid-Dec.–mid-Jan.* 🛏 *5 rooms* 🍴 *No meals.*

$$ B&B/INN **La Posada de Babel.** This family-run inn just outside Llanes stands among oak, chestnut, and birch trees on the edge of the Sierra de Cuera. **Pros:** extremely amiable staff; comfy base for hiking; beautiful grounds. **Cons:** slippery stairs to certain rooms; closed in winter. [$] *Rooms from: €99* ✉ *La Pereda s/n, 4 km (2½ miles) southwest of Llanes* ☎ *985/402525* 🌐 *www.laposadadebabel.com* 🕓 *Closed Dec.–Easter* 🛏 *12 rooms* 🍴 *No meals.*

SPORTS AND THE OUTDOORS

GOLF

Club de Golf La Cuesta. This picturesque 18-hole course lies between the Picos de Europa and Cantabrian Sea; its location, 325 feet above sea level, comes with excellent views. ✉ *C. Las Barqueras s/n, 3 km (2 miles) east of Llanes, between Cue and Andrin* ☎ *985/403319* 🌐 *www.golflacuesta.com* 🎫 *€36* ☞ *18 holes, 6407 yards, par 71.*

THE PICOS DE EUROPA

With craggy peaks soaring up to the 8,688-foot Torre Cerredo, the northern skyline of the Picos de Europa has helped seafarers and fishermen navigate the Bay of Biscay for ages. To the south, pilgrims on their way to Santiago enjoy distant but inspiring views of the snowcapped range from the plains of Castile between Burgos and León. Over the years, rain and snow have created canyons plunging 3,000 feet, natural arches, caves, and sinkholes (one of which is 5,213 feet deep).

The Picos de Europa National Park, covering 647½ square km (250 square miles), is perfect for climbers and trekkers: you can explore the main trails, hang glide, ride horses, cycle, or canoe. There are two adventure-sports centers in Cangas de Onís, near the Roman Bridge.

Hiking in the Picos de Europa

CANGAS DE ONÍS

25 km (16 miles) south of Ribadesella, 70 km (43 miles) east of Oviedo.

The first capital of Christian Spain, Cangas de Onís is also the unofficial capital of the Picos de Europa National Park. Partly in the narrow valley carved by the Sella River, it has the feel of a mountain village.

VISITOR INFORMATION

Contacts Cangas de Onís. ✉ *Av. Covadonga 21* ☎ *985/848043* ⊕ *www. cangasdeonis.com/turismo.*

EXPLORING

Picos de Europa Visitor Center. To help plan your rambles, consult the scale model of the park outside the visitor center; staff inside can advise you on suitable routes. There are various stores on the same street that sell maps and guidebooks, a few in English. ✉ *Casa Dago, Av. Covadonga 43* ☎ *985/848614* ⊕ *www.cangasdeonis.com.*

Puente Romano de Congas de Onís sobre el Sella. A high, humpback medieval bridge (also known as the Puente Romano, or Roman Bridge, because of its style) spans the Río Sella gorge with a reproduction of Pelayo's Victory Cross, or La Cruz de la Victoria, dangling underneath. ✉ *Cangas de Onís.*

WHERE TO EAT AND STAY

$$$
SPANISH

✕ **Restaurante Los Arcos.** Situated on one of the town's main squares, this busy tavern serves local cider, fine Spanish wines, and honest regional dishes. The well-priced lunchtime menu features mouthwatering fare such as *revuelto de morcilla* (scrambled eggs with blood sausage), and *pulpo de pedreu sobre crema fina de patata, oricios y germinados eco-logicos* (octopus with creamed potato, sea urchins, and bean sprouts). **Known for:** local cider; lunch menu; scrambled eggs with blood sausage. $ *Average main: €20* ⊠ *Pl. del Ayuntamiento 3* ☎ *985/849277* ⊕ *www. restaurantelosarcos.es.*

$ ☷ **Hotel Posada del Valle.** British couple Nigel and Joanne Burch con-
B&B/INN verted a rustic, 19th-century, stone-wall farmhouse into an idyllic guesthouse; built near the side of a hill, it faces out over spectacular panoramas of the Picos. **Pros:** surrounded by nature; views of the Picos; wealth of local knowledge at your fingertips. **Cons:** remote and difficult to find; breakfast costs extra; restaurant does not serve lunch. $ *Rooms from: €86* ⊠ *Collía, Arriondas* ☎ *985/841157* ⊕ *www.posadadelvalle. com* ▭ *No credit cards* ☉ *Closed Nov.–Mar.* ⇆ *12 rooms* †⊙† *No meals.*

$$$$ ☷ **Parador de Cangas de Onís.** On the banks of the Río Sella just west of
HOTEL Cangas, this friendly parador is made up of an 8th-century Benedictine
Fodor'sChoice monastery and a modern wing: the older building has 11 period-style
★ rooms. **Pros:** gorgeous riverside location and mountain views; excellent food; oodles of history. **Cons:** limited menu; chilly corridors; rooms on lower floor can be noisy. $ *Rooms from: €185* ⊠ *Monasterio de San Pedro de Villanueva, Villanueva s/n, Ctra. N625* ⊹ *From N634 take right turn for Villanueva* ☎ *985/849402* ⊕ *www.parador.es* ⇆ *64 rooms* †⊙† *Free Breakfast.*

SPORTS AND THE OUTDOORS

The tourist office in Cangas de Onís can help you organize a Picos de Europa trek. The Picos visitor center in Cangas has general information, route maps, and a useful scale model of the range.

HIKING

AsturSellaAdventure. Part of the Hotel Montevedro, AsturSellaAdventure specializes in canoeing and canyon rappelling. ⊠ *Ramón Prada Vicente 5* ☎ *985/848079* ⊕ *www.astursellaaventura.com.*

Cangas Aventura Turismo Activo. Rafting, canoeing, Jet Skiing, climbing, trekking, horseback riding, paintballing, and snowshoeing packages are all available here. ⊠ *Av. Covadonga 17 Bajo* ☎ *985/849261* ⊕ *www. cangasaventura.com.*

POTES

51 km (31 miles) southwest of San Vicente de la Barquera, 115 km (69 miles) southwest of Santander, 173 km (104 miles) north of Palencia, 81 km (50 miles) southeast of Cangas de Onís.

Known for its fine cheeses, the region of La Liébana is a highland domain also worth exploring for other reasons. Potes, the area's main city, is named for its ancient bridges and surrounded by the stunning 9th-century **monasteries** of Santo Toribio de Liébana, Lebeña, and Piasca. The gorges of the Desfiladero de la Hermida pass are 13 km (8 miles) north, and the rustic town of Mogrovejo is on the way to the vertiginous cable car at Fuente Dé, 10 km (6 miles) west of Potes.

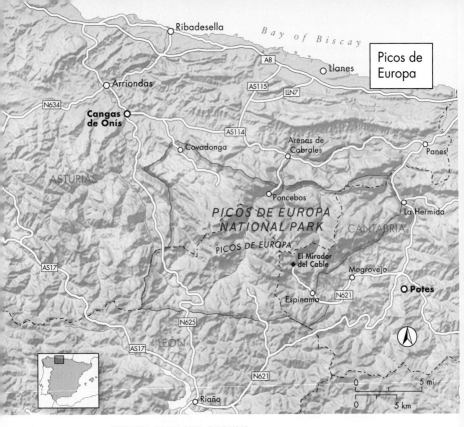

GETTING HERE AND AROUND

Potes is just over two hours from Gijón and Oviedo via the A8, and 1½ hours from Santander via the A8 and N621.

VISITOR INFORMATION

Contacts Potes. ⊠ *Pl. de la Serna s/n* ☎ *942/730078.*

EXPLORING

El Mirador del Cable. As you approach the parador of Fuente Dé, at the head of the valley northwest of the hamlet of Espinama, you'll see a wall of gray rock rising 6,560 feet straight into the air. Visible at the top is the tiniest of huts: El Mirador del Cable (the cable-car lookout point). Get there via a 2,625-foot funicular (€17 round-trip). At the top, you can hike along the Ávila Mountain pasturelands, rich in wildlife, between the central and eastern massifs of the Picos. There's an official entrance to Picos de Europa National Park here. ⊠ *Potes* ☎ *942/736610* ⊕ *www.cantur.com.*

WHERE TO EAT AND STAY

$$ × **El Bodegón.** A simple, friendly, and cozy space awaits behind the ancient
SPANISH stone facade of this restaurant, 200 meters from the main plaza. Part of the house is original, but much has been renovated, providing an attractive combination of traditional mountain design and modern construction.

Known for: great wine; popular spot; highland comfort food. [$] *Average main: €15* ✉ *C. San Roque 4* ☎ *942/730247* 🕒 *Closed Wed.*

$ HOTEL FAMILY 🏨 **Hotel de Oso.** Offering a great value, this cozy lodge is the perfect base for exploring the surrounding Picos de Europa. **Pros:** great base for hiking; decent restaurant; swimming pool and tennis court. **Cons:** decor is a bit outdated; lower floor rooms can be noisy; some rooms are on the small side. [$] *Rooms from: €89* ✉ *Cosgaya* ☎ *942/733018* 🌐 *www.hoteldeloso.es* 🕒 *Closed Dec. 15–Feb. 15* 🛏 *49 rooms* 🍴 *No meals* 💳 *No credit cards.*

CANTABRIA

Historically part of Old Castile, the province of Cantabria was called Santander until 1984, when it became an autonomous community. The most scenic route from Madrid via Burgos to Santander is the slow but spectacular N62, past the Ebro reservoir. Faster and safer is the N627 from Burgos to Aguilar de Campóo connecting to the A67 freeway down to Santander.

SANTANDER

390 km (242 miles) north of Madrid, 154 km (96 miles) north of Burgos, 116 km (72 miles) west of Bilbao, 194 km (120 miles) northeast of Oviedo.

One of the great ports on the Bay of Biscay, Santander is surrounded by beaches that can often be busy, but it still manages to avoid the package-tour feel of so many Mediterranean resorts. A fire destroyed most of the old town in 1941, so the rebuilt city looks relatively modern. The town gets especially fun and busy in summer, when its summer-university community and music-and-dance festival fill the city with students and performers.

From the 1st to the 4th century, under the Romans, Santander—then called Portus Victoriae—was a major port. Commercial life accelerated between the 13th and 16th centuries, but the waning of Spain's naval power and a series of plagues during the reign of Felipe II caused Santander's fortunes to plummet in the late 16th century. Its economy revived after 1778, when Seville's monopoly on trade with the Americas was revoked and Santander entered fully into commerce with the New World. In 1910 the Palacio de la Magdalena was built by popular subscription as a gift to Alfonso XIII and his queen, Victoria Eugenia, lending Santander prestige as one of Spain's royal watering holes.

Modern-day Santander benefits from several promenades and gardens, most of which face the bay. Walk east along the Paseo de Pereda, the main boulevard, to the Puerto Chico, a small yacht harbor. Then follow Avenida Reina Victoria to find the tree-lined park paths above the first of the city's beaches, Playa de la Magdalena. Walk onto the Península de la Magdalena to the Palacio de la Magdalena, today the summer seat of the University of Menéndez y Pelayo. Beyond the Magdalena Peninsula, wealthy locals have built mansions facing the long stretch of shoreline known as El Sardinero, Santander's best beach.

GETTING HERE AND AROUND

Santander itself is easily navigated on foot, but if you're looking to get to El Sardinero beach, take the bus from the central urban transport hub at Jardines de Pereda.

Contacts Santander Bus Station. ⊠ *C. Navas de Tolosa s/n* ☎ *942/211995.* **Santander Train Station.** ⊠ *Pl. de las Estaciones s/n* ☎ *912/320320 RENFE* ⊕ *www.renfe.com.*

VISITOR INFORMATION

Contacts Santander. ⊠ *Jardines de Pereda s/n* ☎ *942/203000* ⊕ *www. turismo.santander.es.*

EXPLORING

Catedral de Santander. The blocky cathedral marks the transition between Romanesque and Gothic. Though largely rebuilt in the neo-Gothic style after serious damage in the town's 1941 fire, the cathedral retained its 12th-century crypt. The chief attraction here is the tomb of Marcelino Menéndez y Pelayo (1856–1912), Santander's most famous literary figure. The cathedral is across Avenida de Calvo Sotelo from the Plaza Porticada. ⊠ *Calle de Somorrostro s/n* ☎ *942/226024* 🎫 *Free.*

Palacio de la Magdalena. Built on the highest point of the Peninsula de Magdalena and surrounded by 62 acres of manicured gardens and rocky beaches, this elegant palace is the most distinctive building in Santander. Built between 1908 and 1912 as a summer home for King Alfonso XIII and Queen Victoria Eugenia, the building has architectural influences from France and England. Today, the palace is used as a venue for meetings, weddings, and college language classes (summer only). There are also daily guided visits—call in advance to schedule a tour in English. ⊠ *Av. Magdalena s/n* ☎ *942/203084* ⊕ *www.palacio-magdalena.com* 🎫 *€3.*

BEACHES

Playa El Sardinero. Gently curving round the bay from the Magdalena Peninsula, Santander's longest and most popular beach has a full range of amenities and fine, golden sand. Although this northeast-facing stretch is exposed, moderate waves in summer make it generally fine for bathing, but its location on the Cantabrian coast keeps the water very cold. In winter months it is a favorite of surfers, particularly the part of the beach in front of Hotel Cuiqui. Be sure to arrive at the beach via the sun-dappled Piquío Gardens, where terraces filled with flowers and trees lead the way down to the beach. **Amenities:** food and drink; lifeguards; showers; toilets; water sports. **Best for:** surfing; swimming; walking. ⊠ *Santander.*

WHERE TO EAT AND STAY

$$$$
SPANISH
✕ **Bodega del Riojano.** The paintings on wine-barrel ends that decorate this classic restaurant have given it the nickname "Museo Redondo" (Round Museum). The building dates back to the 16th century, when it was a wine cellar, which you can see in the heavy wooden beams overhead and the rough and rustic tables. **Known for:** fish of the day; historic setting; specialties from La Rioja. Ⓢ *Average main: €25* ⊠ *C. Río de la Pila 5* ☎ *942/216750* ⊕ *www.bodegadelriojano.com* ☾ *No dinner Sun.*

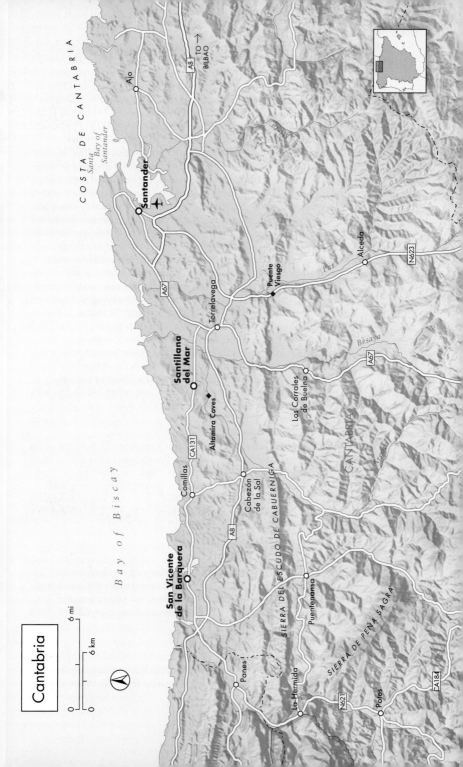

$$$$
SPANISH

✕ **El Serbal.** Five blocks from Santander's marina, this elegant dining room maintains an impressive attention to detail: order the tasting menu, for instance, and you'll be served no fewer than five varieties of olive oil to accompany a delicious assortment of breads. Only the freshest ingredients are used, and the chef makes tasty use of Santander's famed seafood. **Known for:** seafood; tasting menu; cod al pil pil. $ *Average main: €24* ⊠ *Calle de Andrés del Rio 7* ☎ *942/222515* ⊕ *www. elserbal.com* ▭ *No credit cards* ⊘ *Closed Mon. No dinner Sun.*

$$$
SPANISH
Fodor's Choice
★

✕ **La Casona del Judío.** While the à la carte menu at this tasteful, fine-dining establishment is exquisite, and includes a delectable variety of traditional Cantabrian seafood and meat dishes, the real draw is the tasting menus (€39, €49, and €59). This private culinary experience occurs in the romantically lit brick wine cellar below the main restaurant. **Known for:** tasting menus; interaction with the chef; cannelloni stuffed with morcilla sausage. $ *Average main: €20* ⊠ *Calle de Repuente 20* ☎ *942/342726* ⊕ *www.lacasonadeljudio.com* ▭ *No credit cards.*

$$$
HOTEL

🛏 **Abba Santander.** Occupying the building of the historic Hotel México, Abba Santander has gradually been transformed from a family-run inn into a chain hotel with contemporary interiors and modern conveniences. **Pros:** cheerful service; central location; charming architectural details. **Cons:** slippery bathroom floors; busy part of town. $ *Rooms from: €130* ⊠ *C. Calderón de la Barca 3* ☎ *942/212450, 902/153163* ⊕ *www.abbasantanderhotel.com* ⤳ *37 rooms* �’⦿❘ *No meals.*

$$$$
HOTEL

🛏 **Bahía.** Classical style combined with state-of-the-art technology and contemporary furnishings make this Santander's finest hotel—a grand and comfortable perch overlooking the water. **Pros:** in the center of town; great for watching maritime traffic. **Cons:** nearby cathedral bells can be noisy if you're not on the sea side of the hotel; not right on the beach. $ *Rooms from: €197* ⊠ *Calle Cádiz, 22* ☎ *942/205000* ⊕ *www. hotelbahiasantander.com* ⤳ *188 rooms* ❘⦿❘ *No meals.*

$$$
B&B/INN

🛏 **Las Brisas.** Jesús García runs his family's century-old mansion as an upscale, cottage-style hotel by the sea. **Pros:** close to the shore; fresh and briny Atlantic air; cozy basement bar and breakfast room. **Cons:** mildly disorganized; some rooms are a bit cramped; a long walk to the city center. $ *Rooms from: €139* ⊠ *C. la Braña 14, El Sardinero* ☎ *942/270111* ⊕ *www.hotellasbrisas.net* ⊘ *Closed Dec. 15–Feb. 15* ⤳ *13 rooms* ❘⦿❘ *Free Breakfast.*

SPORTS AND THE OUTDOORS

GOLF

Campo Municipal de Golf Mataleñas. On a peninsula overlooking the Cantabrian Bay, this 18-hole golf course has views of rocky cliffs and sandy beaches. It is also equipped with a modern, two-story practice area. ⊠ *Av. Faro* ☎ *942/203075* ⊕ *www.golfmatalenas.com* 🗾 *€45* ⛳ *18 holes, 5005 yards, par 68.*

NIGHTLIFE

Most people start their evening drinking in the bars and taverns in Plaza de Cañadío, on Calle Hernán Cortés and the surrounding streets, while grazing on tapas that can be plucked straight from the top of the bar.

The Altamira Museum's replica of a Paleolithic cave displays paintings of bison.

Night owls can head to Calle del Sol and Calle de Santa Lucía, which have cozy spots for late-night drinking, some with live music.

Cañadio. An after work favorite, Cañadio draws a lively evening crowd for tempting tapas and chilled beer on tap. ⊠ *Calle de Gómez Oreña 15* ☎ *942/314149* ⊕ *www.restaurantecanadio.com.*

SHOPPING

For most items head to the center: the streets around the ayuntamiento are good for clothing, shoes, and sportswear. At the bustling Mercado de la Esperanza, just behind the ayuntamiento, you can find fish and shellfish that have been freshly plucked from the sea of Cantabria, as well as locally produced cheeses and meat. Open-air fruit and vegetable stalls mark the entrance.

Mantequerías Cántabras. Fine foods, including the santanderino specialty *dulces paseigos* (light and sugary cakes), can be sampled and bought here. ⊠ *Pl. de Italia s/n* ☎ *942/272899.*

SANTILLANA DEL MAR

29 km (18 miles) west of Santander.

Fodor'sChoice
★

Santillana del Mar has developed a thriving tourism industry based on the famed cave art discovered 2 km (1 mile) north of town—and the town itself is worth a visit of at least a day. Just as the Altamira Caves have captured the essence of prehistoric life, the streets, plazas, taverns, and manor houses of Santillana del Mar paint a vivid portrait of medieval and Renaissance village life in northern Spain. Its stunning ensemble of 15th- to 17th-century stone houses is one of Spain's greatest architectural collections.

VISITOR INFORMATION

Contacts Santillana del Mar. ✉ *C. Jesús Otero 20* ☎ *942/818812* 🌐 *www.santillanadelmarturismo.com.*

EXPLORING

Altamira Caves. These world-famous caves, 3 km (2 miles) southwest of Santillana del Mar, have been called the Sistine Chapel of prehistoric art for the beauty of their drawings, believed to be some 20,000 years old. First uncovered in 1875, the caves are a testament to early mankind's admiration of beauty and surprising technical skill in representing it, especially in the use of rock forms to accentuate perspective. There's a lottery system for tickets to enter the caves, and only a small number of visitors are allowed in each month—but the reproduction in the **museum** is open to all. ✉ *Museo de Altamira, Marcelino Sanz de Sautuola s/n* ☎ *942/818005* 🌐 *museodealtamira.mcu.es* 🎫 *€3 (free Sat. afternoon and Sun.)* 🕒 *Closed Mon.*

Colegiata de Santa Juliana. Santillana del Mar is built around the Colegiata, Cantabria's finest Romanesque structure. Highlights include the 12th-century cloister, famed for its sculpted capitals, a 16th-century altarpiece, and the tomb of Santa Juliana, who is the town's patron saint and namesake. ✉ *Pl. Abad Francisco Navarro s/n* ☎ *639/830520* 🎫 *€3.*

Museo Diocesano. Inside the 16th-century Regina Coeli convent is a museum devoted to liturgical art, which includes wooden figures of saints, oil paintings of biblical scenes, altarpieces, and a collection of sacred treasures from the colonial New World. ✉ *C. El Cruce s/n* ☎ *942/840317* 🌐 *www.santillanamuseodiocesano.com* 🎫 *€3* 🕒 *Closed Mon.*

WHERE TO STAY

$$ B&B/INN

🏨 **Casa del Organista.** A typical *casona montañesa* (noble mountain manor) with painstakingly crafted stone and wood details, this intimate hideaway makes a slightly rustic, elegant base for exploring one of Spain's finest Renaissance towns. **Pros:** good base; warm interior design; lovely views of tiled roofs and rolling hills. **Cons:** limited availability and difficult to book in high season; some rooms are very small; no elevator. [$] *Rooms from: €96* ✉ *C. Los Hornos 4* ☎ *942/840352* 🌐 *www.casadelorganista.com* 🕒 *Closed Dec. 21–Jan. 20* 🛏 *14 rooms* 🍴 *No meals.*

$$$$ HOTEL
Fodor's Choice ★

🏨 **Parador de Santillana Gil Blas.** Built in the 16th century, this lovely stone palace comes with baronial rooms, with heavy wood beams overhead and splendid antique furnishings. **Pros:** storybook surroundings; elegant decor; attentive service. **Cons:** expensive; a little breezy and chilly in winter; noise carries from the square into the rooms. [$] *Rooms from: €188* ✉ *Pl. Ramón Pelayo 11* ☎ *942/028028* 🌐 *www.parador.es* 🛏 *28 rooms* 🍴 *No meals.*

OFF THE BEATEN PATH

Puente Viesgo. In 1903, in this 16th-century hamlet in the Pas Valley, four caves were discovered under the 1,150-foot peak of Monte del Castillo, two of which—Cueva del Castillo and Cueva de las Monedas—are open to the public. Bison, deer, bulls, and humanoid stick figures are depicted within the caves; the oldest designs are thought to be 35,000 years old. Most arresting are the paintings of 44 hands (curiously, 35 of

them left), reaching out through time. The painters are thought to have blown red pigment around their hands through a hollow bone, leaving the negative image. Reservations are essential. ⊠ *Mt. del Castillo, Puente Viesgo* ☎ *942/598425* ⊕ *cuevas.culturadecantabria.com* ✉ *€3 per cave* ◷ *Closed Mon.; low season closed Mon. and Tues.*

SAN VICENTE DE LA BARQUERA

64 km (40 miles) west of Santander, 15 km (9 miles) west of Comillas.

This is one of the oldest and most beautiful maritime settlements in northern Spain; it was an important Roman port long before many other shipping centers (such as Santander) had gotten firmly established. The 28 arches of the ancient bridge **Puente de la Maza,** which spans the ría, welcome you to town.

GETTING HERE AND AROUND
To get to San Vicente de la Barquera, take an ALSA bus from Santander or drive down the A67 before turning on to the A8.

VISITOR INFORMATION
Contacts San Vicente de la Barquera. ⊠ *Av. del Generalísimo 20* ☎ *942/710797.*

EXPLORING
Nuestra Señora de los Ángeles (*Our Lady of the Angels*). The Romanesque portals of this 15th-century church are extremely striking. ⊠ *C. Alta 12.*

Plaza Mayor. Make sure you check out the arcaded porticoes here and the view over the town from the Unquera road (N634) just inland. ⊠ *San Vicente de la Barquera.*

THE BASQUE COUNTRY, NAVARRA, AND LA RIOJA

WELCOME TO THE BASQUE COUNTRY, NAVARRA, AND LA RIOJA

TOP REASONS TO GO

★ **Explore the Basque coast:** From colorful fishing villages to tawny beaches, the craggy Basque Coast always delights the eye.

★ **Eat pintxos in San Sebastián:** Nothing matches San Sebastián's Parte Vieja, where tavern-hoppers graze at counters heaped with eye-catching morsels.

★ **Appreciate Bilbao's art and architecture:** The gleaming titanium Guggenheim and the Museo de Bellas Artes (Fine Arts Museum) shimmer where steel mills and shipyards once stood, while verdant pastures can be seen in the distance.

★ **Run with the bulls in Pamplona:** Running with a pack of wild animals (and people) will certainly get your adrenaline pumping, but you might prefer to be a spectator.

★ **Drink in La Rioja wine country:** Spain's premier wine region is filled with wine-tasting opportunities and fine cuisine.

Note: The Basque Country, known as "Euskadi" in the Basque language, spills over the French border with two provinces located outside Spain. For ease of reading, we chose not to use qualfiers like "Spanish" when mentioning Spain's autonomous region as the French Basque Country is not covered in this guide.

1 Bilbao and Inland Basque Country. Starring Frank Gehry's titanium brainchild—the Museo Guggenheim Bilbao—Bilbao has established itself as one of Spain's 21st-century magnets. Medieval Vitoria is the capital of Álava and the whole Basque Country, and is relatively undiscovered by tourists.

2 San Sebastián and the Basque Coast. San Sebastián lures travelers with its sophistication, a wide crescent beach, and endless *pintxos* (tapas). Along the coast are fishing villages, scenic ports, beautiful beaches, and sylvan hillsides.

3 Navarra and Pamplona. Navarra offers much more than Pamplona's running-with-the-bulls blowout party. The green Pyrenean hills to the north contrast with the lunar Bárdenas Reales to the southeast, and the wine country south of Pamplona leads to lovely Camino de Santiago way stations like Estella.

4 La Rioja. La Rioja may be Spain's most renowned wine region, but there are culinary jewels to uncover in the Sierra de la Demanda mountain range and in the charming towns of Logroño, Haro, and Laguardia.

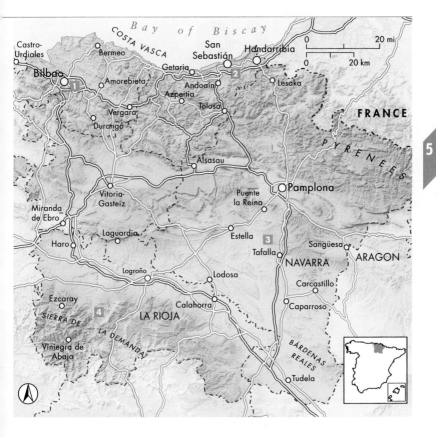

5

EATING AND DRINKING WELL IN THE BASQUE COUNTRY

Basque cuisine, Spain's most prestigious regional gastronomy, draws from the refined French culinary sensibility combined with a rough-and-tumble passion for the camaraderie of the table and for perfectly prepared seafood, meat, and vegetables.

(top left) A nueva cocina interpretation of the classic bacalao al pil pil (top right) A colorful bowl of marmitako (bottom left) An expensive plate of angulas

The so-called *nueva cocina vasca* (new Basque cooking) movement began more than 40 years ago and was originally an echo of the nouvelle cuisine of France. Young chefs like Pedro Subijana and Juan Mari Arzak began deconstructing versions of classic Basque dishes like *marmitako* (tuna and potato stew) and *bacalao al pil pil* (salt cod topped with emulsified garlic sauce) with the aim to redefine and promote Basque cooking on the global stage. Today the region has the world's second-highest concentration of Michelin stars per capita, second only to Kyoto.

Although the core of Basque cooking hinges on the art of preparing fish, there is no dearth of lamb, beef, goat, or pork in the Basque diet or on menus.

CIDER

Don't miss a chance to go to a *sagardotegi*, a boisterous cider house where the cider spurts into your glass straight from the barrel to be quaffed in a single gulp. *Txuletas de buey* (juicy rib eyes grilled over coals) and *tortilla de bacalao* (cod omelet) provide ballast for the rustic apple cider. The cider-cod combination is linked to the Basque fishermen and whalers who carried cider, rather than wine, in their galleys.

BABY EELS

Angulas, known as elvers in English, are a Basque delicacy that has become an expensive treat, with prices reaching €1,000 a kilogram (about 2.2 pounds). The 3- to 4-inch-long eels look like spaghetti with eyes and are typically served in a small earthenware dish sizzling with olive oil, garlic, and a single slice of chili. A special wooden fork is used to eat them, to avoid any metallic taste, and because the wood grips the slippery eels better than metal. Don't be misled by the plethora of "gulas" sold in lower-end tapas bars and groceries across Spain. They look just like angulas, but they're fake—synthetic eels made from processed whitefish.

BACALAO

Cod, a Basque favorite since the Stone Age, comes in various guises. Bacalao al pil pil is a classic Bilbao specialty, simmered—rather than fried—with garlic and olive oil in its own juices. The "pil pil" refers to the sound of the emulsion of cod and olive oil bubbling up from the bottom of the pan. Served with a red chili pepper, this is a beloved Basque delicacy.

BESUGO A LA DONOSTIARRA

Besugo (sea bream) cooked San Sebastián–style is baked in the oven, covered with flakes of garlic that look like scales, and sprinkled with vinegar and parsley before serving.

OX

Oxen in the Basque Country have traditionally been work animals, fed and maintained with great reverence and care. When sacrificed for meat at the age of 12 or 13, their flesh is tender and marbled with streaks of fat rich with grassy aromas. Most of today's ox steaks and chops (*txuleta de buey,* also translated as "beef chop") aren't be from authentic work oxen, but a hulking beefsteak, tender and fragrant, cooked over coals with garlic and a few flakes of sea salt, is almost as beguiling.

TUNA AND POTATO STEW

Marmitako, the Basques' answer to bouillabaisse, is a stick-to-your-ribs potato, yellowfin tuna, and red pepper stew. One bite, and you'll understand why the dish was the preferred restorative for weatherbeaten seafarers. Taken from the French name of the cooking pot (*marmite*), there are marmitako competitions held annually.

WINE

Basque *txakoli,* a simple, zippy white made from tart green indigenous grapes, is refreshing with seafood and pintxos. Those who prefer a red should spring for a wine from Rioja Alavesa, the Basque part of Rioja wine country north of the Ebro.

Updated by Benjamin Kemper

Northern Spain is a misty land of green hills, low russet rooflines, and colorful fishing villages; it's also home to the formerly industrial city of Bilbao, reborn as a center of art and architecture. The semiautonomous Basque Country—with its steady drizzle (onomatopoetically called the *sirimiri*), verdant landscape, and rugged coastline—is a distinct national and cultural entity.

Navarra is considered Basque in the Pyrenees—indeed, Euskera is spoken in much of the region's north—and Navarran in the south, along the Río Ebro. La Rioja, tucked between the Sierra de la Demanda (a mountain range that separates La Rioja from the central Castilian steppe) and the Ebro, is Spain's premier wine country.

Called the País Vasco in Castilian Spanish and Euskadi in the linguistically mysterious, non-Indo-European Basque language, Euskera, the Basque region is essentially a country within a country, or a nation within a state (the semantics are much debated). Though a significant portion of Basques still favor independence from Spain, the separatist terrorist organization ETA (Euskadi Ta Askatasuna, meaning "Basque Homeland and Liberty"), which used to cause some travelers pause, officially disbanded on May 2, 2018. There have been no significant politically motivated acts of violence in the region in years. Basque culture, with its pre-Roman roots, is unlike that of any other region in Spain. In local festivals, you can still watch as locals play such rural sports as chopping mammoth tree trunks and lifting boulders. The Basques' competitive streak carries over into poetry and gastronomy; *bertsolaris* (amateur poets) improvise duels of sharp-witted verse, and gastronomic societies compete in cooking contests to see who can make the best *sopa de ajo* (garlic soup) or marmitako.

PLANNING

WHEN TO GO

Relatively clear skies and warm temperatures last from mid-April to mid-October, making the warm-weather months the best time of year to visit. Some shops and restaurants close in August.

Pamplona in July is bedlam, though for hard-core party animals it's heaven.

The Basque Country is rainy in the winter, but the bracing Atlantic weather can be invigorating if you're in the right mindset. Basque cuisine's heartiest, richest dishes taste their best when it's cold and damp outside.

The September film festival in San Sebastián coincides with the spectacular whaleboat regattas, while the beaches are still ideal and mostly uncrowded.

When looking for a place to stay, remember that the north is an expensive, well-to-do part of Spain, which is reflected in room rates—though some steals can be found in the off-season (and on Airbnb). San Sebastián is particularly pricey, and Pamplona rates triple during San Fermín in July. Be sure to book far ahead for summer travel.

PLANNING YOUR TIME

A road trip through the Basque Country, Navarra, and La Rioja would require at least a week, but you can get a good sense of Bilbao and San Sebastián, the region's most essential cities, in two days each. The Baztán Valley, Pamplona, Laguardia, and La Rioja's capital, Logroño, are other top stops.

If you have a spare day or two, visit Mundaka and the coast of Vizcaya west of Bilbao; Getaria, Pasajes de San Juan, and Hondarribia near San Sebastián; and the wineries of Haro in La Rioja.

La Rioja's Sierra de la Demanda also has some of the finest landscapes in Spain, not to mention culinary pilgrimages to "gastronomical hotel" Echaurren in Ezcaray or Venta de Goyo in Viniegra de Abajo.

FESTIVALS

There's much more to this area's festival scene than the world-famous **San Fermín** and its running of the bulls in Pamplona. From music and dance festivals to colorful religious processions to quirky food fairs, here are a few favorites.

FAMILY **Antxua Eguna** (*Getaria Anchovy Festival*). Join Getaria locals in early May as they ring in anchovy season with gallons of txakoli and mountains of grilled fresh fish. ⊠ *Getaria.*

Aste Nagusia. The "Big Week," a nine-day event celebrating Basque culture, is held in Bilbao in mid-August with a fine series of street concerts, bullfights, and fireworks displays. ⊠ *Bilbao.*

Fodor's Choice **Bilbao BBK Live.** One of Spain's hottest pop and rock music festivals, BBK
★ Live draws over 100,000 fans each year with its lineup of big-name artists. In 2018, headliners included Florence and the Machine, Childish Gambino, The Chemical Brothers, and David Byrne. Those with an

aversion to mud and noisy campgrounds will appreciate the "glamping" accommodation option. ⊠ *Bilbao* ⊕ *www.bilbaobbklive.com.*

Fiesta de la Virgen Blanca (*Festival of the White Virgin*). This weeklong festival (August 4–9) celebrates Vitoria's patron saint with bullfights and street parties. The festivities begin with the arrival of Celedón, a well-dressed dummy that "flies" over the main square holding an umbrella. ⊠ *Vitoria.*

Getaria Festival. Every four years the fishing village of Getaria, near San Sebastián, celebrates Juan Sebastián Elcano's completion of Ferdinand Magellan's voyage around the world. Magellan is usually credited with this achievement, but he died en route, which means Elcano was technically the first explorer to circumnavigate the globe. Events include a solemn procession of weather-beaten, starving "survivors" trudging up from the port along with more lighthearted dances and street parties. The next festival, in 2019, will mark the 500th anniversary of the event. It's always held in August. ⊠ *Getaria.*

Heineken Jazzaldia. Drawing many of the world's top performers, this late-July festival in San Sebastián attracts an international crowd of jazz devotees. ⊠ *San Sebastián* ⊕ *www.heinekenjazzaldia.com.*

Fodor's Choice ★ **La Tamborrada.** Every January 19 and 20, more than 100 platoons of donostiarras (San Sebastián natives) dress up as chefs and Napoleonic soldiers and bang drums as they parade through the streets. The tradition was born out of a mockery of Napoleon's troops, who would march around the city in a similar fashion. Today it's San Sebastián's biggest street party. ⊠ *San Sebastián.*

San Fermín. Pamplona's main event, immortalized by Ernest Hemingway in his 1926 novel *The Sun Also Rises,* is best known for its running of the bulls, a tradition that's dangerous for humans and ultimately lethal for the animals involved. Ethics aside, a huge part of the festival is consumed by nontaurine activities such as processions, live music acts, and fireworks. Held each year July 6–14, every day begins at 8 am with a herd of fighting bulls let loose to run through the narrow streets to the bullring alongside daredevils testing their speed and agility in the face of possible injury or death. The atmosphere is electric and hotel rooms overlooking the course come at a price. ⊠ *Pamplona* ⊕ *www.sanfermin.com.*

San Sebastián Film Festival. Glitterati descend on the city for its international film fest in the second half of September—exact dates vary, so check the website for details. ⊠ *San Sebastián* ⊕ *www.sansebastian-festival.com.*

GETTING HERE AND AROUND

AIR TRAVEL

Bilbao's airport serves much of this area, and there are smaller, notoriously expensive airports at Hondarribia (serving San Sebastián), Logroño, and Pamplona, which are generally only used by domestic carriers in high season.

Airports Aeropuerto de Bilbao. ⊠ *48180 Loiu* ⊕ *www.aena.es.*

DID YOU KNOW?

The French sculptor Louise Bourgeois's (1911–2010) giant spider *Maman,* more than 30 feet tall, stands outside the back entrance to the Guggenheim.

BOAT AND FERRY TRAVEL

Brittany Ferries has routes from Portsmouth (United Kingdom) to Bilbao twice a week. The trip takes between 27 and 34 hours.

BUS TRAVEL

Frequent coach bus service connects the major cities to Madrid, Zaragoza, and Barcelona (with a layover or transfer to Spain's other destinations). The trip between Barcelona and Bilbao takes seven to eight hours. Reserve online at ⊕ *www.alsa.es*.

Bus service between cities and smaller towns is surprisingly comprehensive—and cheap. Consult Google Maps or visit a local tourist office for route information.

CAR TRAVEL

Even the remotest points are an easy one-day drive from Madrid, and northern Spain is superbly covered by freeways.

The drive from Madrid to Bilbao is 397 km (247 miles), about five hours; follow the A1 past Burgos to Miranda del Ebro, where you pick up the AP68. Car rentals are available in the major cities: Bilbao, Pamplona, San Sebastián, Hondarribia, and Vitoria. A note about signage: the Basque word for calle is *kalea*. We have standardized our addresses using "Calle" for ease of Google Mapping, but you will see Kalea on road signs in most Basque locales.

TAXI TRAVEL

In cities, taxis can usually be hailed on the street, and drivers are generally amenable to longer trips (say, from San Sebastián to Astigarraga's cider houses).

TRAIN TRAVEL

For now, standard-speed RENFE trains connect Madrid to Bilbao, San Sebastián, and Logroño, though the much-anticipated AVE (expected to be completed in 2019) will soon make the trip much quicker. Once you've arrived, a car is the most convenient way to get around, but the regional company FEVE runs a delightful narrow-gauge train that winds through stunning landscapes. From San Sebastián, lines west to Bilbao (the Euskotren) and east to Hendaye, France, depart from Estación de Amara; most long-distance trains use RENFE's Estación del Norte. *See the Travel Smart chapter for more information about train travel.*

RIDESHARE TRAVEL

If you don't have a car, the fastest and cheapest way to get from Madrid or Barcelona to major destinations in the Basque Country, Navarra, and La Rioja is via the Blablacar rideshare platform, which boasts more worldwide users than Uber. Simply type your origin and destination into the app, select the itinerary that best suits your schedule, and confirm your booking via credit card. You can then text with the driver to arrange pickup and drop-off locations. Prices remain low because it is a rideshare service as opposed to a taxi-like service and drivers aren't allowed to make a profit (the fee you pay helps offset the cost of gas and tolls). Download the app in your mobile provider's appstore or browse trips on ⊕ *www.blablacar.com*.

RESTAURANTS

Foodies may never want to leave the Basque Country, where the avant-garde and home cooking merge seamlessly. Everywhere you look in the region's cities and towns, there are mom-and-pop taverns, pintxo bars, and *asadores*—restaurants specializing in grilled meats and fish. But this area of Spain is also known for its Michelin-starred destination restaurants, venues sequestered in off-the-beaten-path villages that have become dining meccas, like Asador Etxebarri (Atxondo), Martín Berasategui (Lasarte), and Mugaritz (Errenteria).

HOTELS

Ever since the Guggenheim put Bilbao on the map as a design destination, the city's hotel fleet has expanded and reflected (in the case of the Gran Hotel Domine, literally) the glitter and panache of Gehry's museum. Boutique hotels, chic designer properties, and trusted-brand behemoths have made older hotels look small and quaint by comparison. *Hotel reviews have been shortened. For full information, visit Fodors.com.*

WHAT IT COSTS IN EUROS				
	$	$$	$$$	$$$$
Restaurants	under €12	€12–€17	€18–€22	over €22
Hotels	under €90	€90–€125	€126–€180	over €180

Prices are per person for a main course, or a combination of small plates, at dinner, or, if dinner is not served, at lunch, and for two people in a standard double room in high season, excluding tax.

BILBAO

34 km (21 miles) southeast of Castro-Urdiales, 116 km (72 miles) east of Santander, 397 km (247 miles) north of Madrid.

Time in Bilbao (Bilbo in Euskera) may be recorded as BG or AG (Before Guggenheim or After Guggenheim). Never has a single monument of art and architecture so radically changed a city. Frank Gehry's stunning museum, Norman Foster's sleek subway system, the Santiago Calatrava glass footbridge and airport, the leafy César Pelli Abandoibarra park and commercial complex next to the Guggenheim, and the Philippe Starck Azkuna Zentroa cultural center have contributed to an unprecedented cultural revolution in what was once the industry capital of the Basque Country.

Bilbao's new attractions get more press, but the city's old treasures still quietly line the banks of the rust-color Nervión. The **Casco Viejo** (Old Quarter)—also known as Siete Calles (Seven Streets)—is a charming jumble of shops, bars, and restaurants on the river's right bank, near the Puente del Arenal bridge. This elegant proto-Bilbao nucleus was carefully restored after devastating floods in 1983. Throughout the Casco Viejo are ancient mansions emblazoned with family coats of arms, wooden doors, and fine ironwork balconies. The most interesting square is the 64-arch Plaza Nueva, where an outdoor market is pitched every Sunday morning.

Walking the banks of the Nervión is a satisfying jaunt. After all, this was how—while out on a morning jog—Guggenheim director Thomas Krens first discovered the perfect spot for his project, nearly opposite the right bank's Deusto University. From the Palacio de Euskalduna upstream to the colossal Mercado de la Ribera, parks and green zones line the river. César Pelli's Abandoibarra project fills in the half mile between the Guggenheim and the Euskalduna bridge with a series of parks, the Deusto University library, the Meliá Bilbao Hotel, and a major shopping center.

On the left bank, the wide, late-19th-century boulevards of the **Ensanche** neighborhood, such as Gran Vía (the main shopping artery) and Alameda de Mazarredo, are the city's more formal face. Bilbao's cultural institutions include, along with the Guggenheim, a major museum of fine arts (the Museo de Bellas Artes) and an opera society (Asociación Bilbaína de Amigos de la Ópera, or ABAO) whose program includes 47 performances attended by over 90,000 spectators. In addition, epicureans have long ranked Bilbao's culinary offerings among the best in Spain. Don't miss a chance to ride the trolley line, the Euskotren, for a trip along the river from Atxuri Station to Basurto's San Mamés soccer stadium, reverently dubbed "la Catedral del Fútbol" (the Cathedral of Football).

GETTING HERE AND AROUND

Euskotren's Tranvía Bilbao, running up and down the Ría de Bilbao (aka Nervión Estuary) past the Guggenheim to the Mercado de la Ribera, is an attraction in its own right: silent, swift, and panoramic as it glides up and down its grassy runway. The Euskotren that leaves from Atxuri Station north of the Mercado de la Ribera runs along a spectacular route through Gernika and the Urdaibai Biosphere Preserve to Mundaka and Bermeo, probably the best way short of a boat to see this lovely wetlands preserve.

Bilbobus provides bus service 6:15 am–10:55 pm. Plaza Circular and Plaza Moyua are the principal hubs for all lines. Once the metro and normal bus routes stop service, take a night bus, known as a Gautxori ("night bird"). Six lines run every 30 minutes between Plaza Circular and Plaza Moyúa and the city limits on Friday 11:30 pm–2 am and on Saturday overnight until 7 am.

Metro Bilbao is linear, running down the Nervión estuary from Basauri, above, or east of, the Casco Viejo, all the way to the mouth of the Nervión at Getxo, before continuing to the beach town of Plentzia. The Moyua station is the most central stop and lies in the middle of Bilbao's Ensanche, or modern part. The second subway line runs down the left bank of the Nervión to Santurtzi. The fare is €1.60–€1.90 for a one-way ticket, €3–€3.50 for a return ticket, and just €0.91–€1.19 with the Barik travel card.

The Barik card is good for metro and bus travel and for the Artxanda Furnicular, RENFE, and Euskotren trains and trams, and costs €3 for the card, plus a minimum additional value of €5. Cards can be purchased at Barik vending machines in the Bilbao metro stations and from any of the four Bilbao metro help offices (Attención al Clientes de Metro Bilbao), located in or near four stations: Areeta, San Inazio, Casco Viejo, and Ansio. Hours are weekdays 8:30–7:30, with the San Inazio location also open Saturday 8:30–3. One card can be used by up to 10 people. Transfers cost extra.

For up to 24, 48, or 72 hours, the Bilbao Bizkaia Card allows for unlimited use of the metro, buses, train, tram, and Artxanda funicular railway all around the Bizkaia region; discounts on certain restaurants, bars, and shops; and free entry to a variety of cultural activities including more than 25 sights such as the Guggenheim, Museo de Bellas Artes de Bilbao, and Museo de Reproducciones Artísticas de Bilbao. The card costs €10 for 24 hours, €15 for 48 hours, and €20 for 72 hours.

Bus and Subway Information Bilbobus. ☎ 94/445–3471 ⊕ www.bilbobus. com. **Metro Bilbao.** ☎ 94/425–4025 ⊕ www.metrobilbao.eus.

Stations Bilbao-Abando Railway Station. ✉ Edificio Terminus, Pl. Circular 2, El Ensanche ☎ 94/479–5760 ⊕ www.adif.es. **Euskotren.** ✉ Casco Viejo ☎ 90/254–3210 ⊕ www.euskotren.es. **Termibus Bilbao.** ✉ Gurtubay 1, San Mamés ☎ 94/439–5077 ⊕ www.termibus.es.

VISITOR INFORMATION
Contacts Bilbao Tourism Office. ✉ Pl. Biribila, 1, El Ensanche ☎ 94/479–5760 ⊕ www.bilbaoturismo.net Ⓜ Moyúa.

TOURS
Bilbao Paso a Paso. Bilbao Paso a Paso organizes walking tours, guided visits to the Guggenheim, hot-air-balloon rides, gastronomical tours around the city, and excursions to nearby sites. ✉ Calle Egaña 17, 5th fl., Suite 4, Casco Viejo ☎ 94/415–3892 ⊕ www.bilbaopasoapaso.com ▧ From €175.

Bilbao Turismo. Weekend guided tours, in English and Spanish, are conducted by the tourist office (reservations required). The Casco Viejo tour starts at 10 am at the ground floor of the main tourist office on the Plaza Circular. The Ensanche and Abandoibarra tour begins at noon from the tourist office to the left of the Guggenheim entrance. Both tours last 90 minutes. ✉ Pl. Circular 1, El Ensanche ☎ 94/479–5760 ⊕ www.bilbaoturismo.net ▧ €5.

Bilboats. One- and two-hour boat tours take you downstream from Plaza Pío Baroja the city center, passing some of Bilbao's iconic buildings and bridges. Customized day trips can also be arranged. ✉ Pl. Pío Baroja ☎ 94/642–4157 ⊕ www.bilboats.com ▧ From €13 Ⓜ Moyue.

EXPLORING

Azkuna Zentroa. In the early 20th century this was a municipal wine-storage facility used by Bilbao's Rioja wine barons. Now, the city-block-size, Philippe Starck–designed civic center is filled with shops, cafés, restaurants, movie theaters, swimming pools, fitness centers, and nightlife opportunities at the very heart of the city. Conceived as a hub for entertainment, culture, wellness, and civic coexistence, it added another star to Bilbao's cosmos of architectural and cultural offerings when it opened. The complex regularly hosts film festivals and art exhibitions, and it's a cozy place to take refuge on a rainy afternoon. ✉ *Pl. Arriquibar 4, El Ensanche* ☎ *94/401–4014* ⊕ *www.azkunazentroa.com/az/ingl/home* Ⓜ *Moyúa.*

Fodor's Choice
★
Euskal Museoa Bilbao Museo Vasco (*Basque Museum of Bilbao*). This not-to-miss museum on Basque ethnography and Bilbao's cultural history occupies a 16th-century convent. Highlights include El Mikeldi, a pre-Christian, Iron Age stone animal representation that may be 4,000 years old; the room dedicated to Basque shepherds and the pastoral way of life; and the exhibit *Mar de los Vascos* (*Sea of the Basques*) about whaling, fishing, and maritime activities. ✉ *Pl. Unamuno 4, Casco Viejo* ☎ *94/415–5423* ⊕ *www.euskal-museoa.eus/es* 💶 *€3 (free Thurs.)* 🕓 *Closed Tues.* Ⓜ *Casco Viejo.*

OFF THE BEATEN PATH
Funicular de Artxanda. For an easy and quick excursion, take a five-minute trip on the Artxanda Funicular, a railway that joins downtown Bilbao with the summit of Artxanda Mountain. The panorama from the hillsides of Artxanda is the most comprehensive view of Bilbao, and the summit also includes a park, hotel, sports complex, and several restaurants. The various typical asadores (roasters) here serve delicious beef or fish cooked over coals. ✉ *Pl. de Funicular s/n, Matiko* ☎ *94/445–4966* ⊕ *www.bilbao.net/funicularartxanda* 💶 *€4 round-trip* Ⓜ *Casco Viejo.*

Iglesia de San Nicolás. Honoring the patron saint of mariners, San Nicolás de Bari, the city's early waterfront church, was built over an earlier eponymous hermitage and consecrated in 1756. With a powerful baroque facade over the Arenal, originally a sandy beach, the church weathered significant damage at the hands of French and Carlist troops in the 19th century. Sculptures by Juan Pascual de Mena adorn the interior. Look for the oval plaque to the left of the door marking the high-water mark of the flood of 1983. ✉ *Pl. de San Nicolás 1, Casco Viejo* ☎ *94/416–3424* 💶 *Free* Ⓜ *Casco Viejo.*

Fodor's Choice
★
Mercado de la Ribera. This renovated triple-decker ocean liner, with its prow facing down the estuary toward the open sea, is one of the best markets of its kind in Europe—and one of the biggest with more than 400 retail stands covering 37,950 square feet that run the gamut from fish markets to pintxo bars to wine shops. Like the architects of the Guggenheim and the Palacio de Euskalduna nearly 75 years later, the architect here was playful with this epicurean mecca in the river. From the stained-glass entryway over Calle de la Ribera to the tiny catwalks over the river to the diminutive restaurant on the second floor, the market is an inviting place. ✉ *Calle de la Ribera 22, Casco Viejo* ☎ *94/602–3791* ⊕ *www.mercadodelaribera.net* 🕓 *Closed Sun.* Ⓜ *Casco Viejo.*

Fodor's Choice
★
Museo de Bellas Artes (*Museum of Fine Arts*). Considered one of the top five museums in a country that has a staggering number of museums and great paintings, the Museo de Bellas Artes is like a mini Prado, with representatives from every Spanish school and movement from the 12th through the 20th centuries. The museum's fine collection of Flemish, French, Italian, and Spanish paintings includes works by El Greco, Francisco de Goya y Lucientes, Diego Velázquez, Zurbarán,

José Ribera, Paul Gauguin, and Antoni Tàpies. One large and excellent section traces developments in 20th-century Spanish and Basque art alongside works by better-known European contemporaries, such as Fernand Léger and Francis Bacon. Look especially for Zuloaga's famous portrait of La Condesa Mathieu de Moailles and Joaquín Sorolla's portrait of Basque philosopher Miguel de Unamuno. Three hours might be barely enough to appreciate this international and pan-chronological painting course. ⊠ *Parque de Doña Casilda de Iturrizar, Pl. Museo 2, El Ensanche* ☎ *94/439–6060* ⊕ *www.museobilbao.com* ⊡ *From €9 (free daily 6–8 pm)* ⊙ *Closed Tues.* Ⓜ *Moyúa.*

FodorśChoice **Museo Guggenheim Bilbao.** With its eruption of light in the ruins of Bil-
★ bao's scruffy shipyards and steelworks, the Guggenheim has dramatically reanimated this onetime industrial city. At once suggestive of a silver-scaled fish and a mechanical heart, Frank Gehry's sculpture in titanium, limestone, and glass is the perfect habitat for the 250 contemporary and postmodern artworks it contains. Artists whose names are synonymous with the art of the 20th century (Kandinsky, Picasso, Ernst, Braque, Miró, Pollock, Calder, Malevich) and European artists of the 1950s and 1960s (Eduardo Chillida, Tàpies, Jose Maria Iglesias, Francesco Clemente, and Anselm Kiefer) are joined by contemporary figures (Bruce Nauman, Juan Muñoz, Julian Schnabel, Txomin Badiola, Miquel Barceló, Jean-Michel Basquiat). The ground floor is dedicated to large-format and installation work, some of which—like Richard Serra's *Serpent*—was created specifically for the space. ■**TIP**➜ **Buy tickets in advance online and from Servicaixa ATMs or, in the Basque Country, the BBK bank machines.** ⊠ *Abandoibarra Etorbidea 2, El Ensanche* ☎ *94/435–9080* ⊕ *www.guggenheim-bilbao.es* ⊡ *From €11* ⊙ *Closed Mon. Sept.–June* Ⓜ *Moyúa.*

Parque de Doña Casilda de Iturrizar. Bilbao's main park, stretching east toward the river from the Museo de Bellas Artes, is a lush collection of exotic trees, ducks and geese, fountains, falling water, and great expanses of lawns usually dotted with lovers. It's a sanctuary from the hard-edged Ensanche, Bilbao's modern, post-1876 expansion. Doña Casilda de Iturrizar was a well-to-do 19th-century Bilbao matron who married a powerful banker and used his wealth to support various cultural and beneficent institutions in the city, including this grassy refuge. ⊠ *El Ensanche* Ⓜ *San Mamés.*

Plaza Nueva. This 64-arch neoclassical plaza, built in 1851, is known for its Sunday-morning flea market, December 21 Santo Tomás festivities, and permanent tapas and restaurant offerings. Note the size of the houses' balconies (the bigger the balcony, the richer the original proprietor) and the tiny windows near the top of the facades, where servants' quarters would've been. The building behind the coat of arms at the head of the square was once a government office but is now the **Academia de la Lengua Vasca** (Academy of the Basque Language). The coat of arms shows the tree of Guernica (or Gernika in Basque), symbolic of Basque autonomy, and two wolves, which represent Don Diego López de Haro (López derives from *lupus,* meaning wolf). The bars and shops around the arcades include two **Victor Montes** establishments, one for pintxos at Plaza Nueva 8 and the other for sit-down

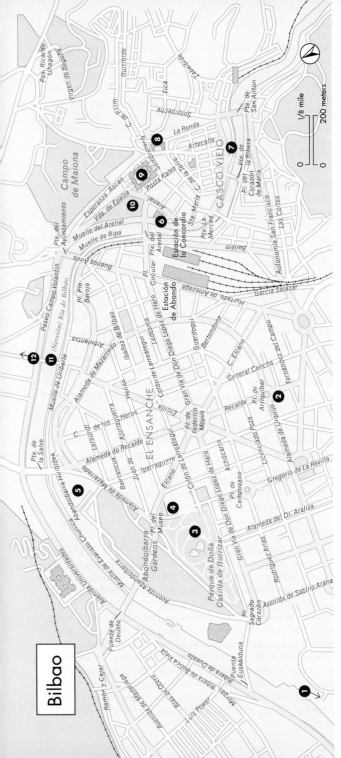

Bilbao

Azkuna Zentroa **2**
Euskal Museo a Bilbao
Museo Vasco **8**
Funicular de Artxanda **12**
Iglesia de San Nicolás ... **10**
Mercado de la Ribera...... **7**
Museo de Bellas Artes **4**

Museo Guggenheim
Bilbao...................... **5**
Parque de Doña Casilda
de Iturrizar................ **3**
Plaza Nueva **9**
Puente de Vizcaya **1**
Puente de Zubi-Zuri **11**
Teatro Arriaga **6**

dining at No. 2. **Café Bar Bilbao** (No. 6), also known as Casa Pedro, has Belle Époque interiors accented by photos of early Bilbao, while **Argoitia** (No. 15), across the square, has a nice angle on the midday sun. ✉ *Casco Viejo* [M] *Casco Viejo.*

Puente de Zubi-Zuri. Santiago Calatrava's seagull-shaped bridge (the name means "white bridge" in Euskera) connects Campo Volantín on the right bank with El Ensanche on the left, and is located just a few minutes from the Guggenheim. Other Calatrava creations in the area include the airport west of Bilbao at Loiu and the bridge at Ondarroa. ✉ *El Ensanche* [M] *Moyúa.*

Teatro Arriaga. This 1,500-seat theater was once as exciting a source of Bilbao pride as the Guggenheim is today. Built between 1886 and 1890, when Bilbao's population was a mere 35,000, the Teatro Arriaga represented a gigantic per-capita cultural investment. The original "Nuevo Teatro" (New Theater) de Bilbao was a lavish Belle Époque, neo-baroque jewel modeled after the Paris Opéra, by architect Joaquín Rucoba (1844–1909); it was renamed in 1902 for the bilbaíno musician considered "the Spanish Mozart," Juan Crisóstomo de Arriaga (1806–26). After a 1914 fire, the new version of the theater opened in 1919. Now largely upstaged by the sprawling, modern Palacio de Euskalduna, the Arriaga still hosts its fair share of opera, theater, concerts, and dance events September–June. ✉ *Pl. Arriaga 1, Casco Viejo* ☎ *94/479–2036* 🌐 *www.teatroarriaga.com* 🕒 *Closed Sun. in July* [M] *Casco Viejo.*

5

OFF THE BEATEN PATH

Puente de Vizcaya (*Hanging Bridge*). One of Bilbao's most extraordinary sights since it was built in 1893, this transporter bridge hung from cables ferries cars and passengers across the Nervión uniting two distinct worlds: the exclusive, bourgeois Arenas and Portugalete, a staid, working-class town. Portugalete is a 15-minute walk from Santurce, where the quayside Hogar del Pescador serves simple fish specialties. Besugo is the traditional choice, but the grilled sardines are equally sublime at a fraction of the price. ✉ *Barria 3, Las Arenas* ✥ *To reach bridge, take subway to Areeta, or drive across Puente de Deusto, turn left on Av. Lehendakari Aguirre, and follow signs for Las Arenas; it's a 10- or 15-min drive from downtown* ☎ *94/480–1012* 🌐 *www.puente-colgante.com* 🎫 *From €1* [M] *Areeta.*

WHERE TO EAT

$$$$ SPANISH

🍴 **Aizian.** Chef José Miguel Olazabalaga's Aizian is anything but a "hotel restaurant," even if it's situated inside the Meliá Bilbao. Sure, his dishes air on the safe side—you won't find tweezed microgreens and dry-ice displays here—but they're dependably delicious: think sautéed wild mushrooms topped with foie gras and a runny egg or seared venison loin with beets and smoked chestnut puree. **Known for:** old-school Basque with a twist; fabulous "torrija," Spanish "French" toast; good value for fine dining. [$] *Average main: €40* ✉ *Meliá Bilbao, Calle Lehendakari Leizaola 29, El Ensanche* ☎ *94/428–0039* 🌐 *www.restaurante-aizian.com* 🕒 *Closed Sun.* [M] *San Mamés.*

$$$ BASQUE
🍴 **Arriaga.** The sagardotegi experience is a must in the Basque Country, but if you can't swing a trip to one of the huge cider houses in the countryside, Arriaga is a fine urban stand-in. Expect unlimited *sidra al txotx* (cider drawn straight from the barrel), sausage stewed in apple cider, codfish omelets, txuletón de buey, and Idiazabal cheese with quince preserves. **Known for:** unlimited cider from the kupela (enormous barrel); char-grilled rib eyes; convivial atmosphere. [$] *Average main: €22* ✉ *Calle Santa Maria 13, Casco Viejo* ☎ *94/416–5670* 🌐 *www.asadorarriaga.com* [M] *Casco Viejo.*

$$$$ BASQUE Fodor's Choice ★
🍴 **Asador Guetaria.** With a wood-paneled dining room decorated with antiques, this family operation is a longtime local favorite for top-quality fish and meats cooked over coals. The kitchen, open to view, cooks *lubina* (sea bass), besugo (sea bream), *dorada* (gilthead bream), txuletas de buey (ox or beef chops), and *chuletas de cordero* (lamb chops) to perfection in a classic asador setting. **Known for:** masterful grilled dishes; familial atmosphere; homey, old-timey dining room. [$] *Average main: €50* ✉ *Colón de Larreátegui 12, El Ensanche* ☎ *94/424–3923, 94/423–2527* 🌐 *www.guetaria.com* [M] *Moyúa.*

$$$$ BASQUE Fodor's Choice ★
🍴 **Azurmendi.** This award-winning restaurant, a 10-minute drive from town, clocks in at number 38 on the "World's 50 Best Restaurants" list, and it's constantly lauded for its envelope-pushing cuisine and industry-leading sustainability practices. The Azurmendi experience begins the moment you enter into its spacious indoor garden. **Known for:** three-Michelin-star dining; most innovative restaurant in Bilbao; aperitivo in the greenhouse before sitting down in the dining room. [$] *Average main: €145* ✉ *Legina Auzoa s/n* ☎ *94/455–8866* 🌐 *www.azurmendi.restaurant* ⏲ *Closed Mon.*

$$ BASQUE
🍴 **Berton Bukoi.** Dinner is served until midnight in this sleek yet casual pintxo spot in the Casco Viejo. The industrial design—think wood tables with a green-tint polyethylene finish and exposed ventilation pipes—belies a comfort-food-heavy menu with star dishes like grilled octopus brochettes and juicy beef tenderloin bites. **Known for:** melt-between-your-fingers jamón; terrific value; pintxos that punch above their weight. [$] *Average main: €15* ✉ *Calle Jardines 8, Casco Viejo* ☎ *94/416–7035* 🌐 *www.berton.eus* [M] *Casco Viejo.*

$$ CAFÉ Fodor's Choice ★
🍴 **Café Iruña.** This is essential Bilbao haunt (est. 1903) on El Ensanche's most popular garden and square, Los Jardines de Albia, is a favorite for its interior design and boisterous ambience. The neo-Mudejar dining room overlooking the square is the place to be (if they try to stuff you in the back dining room, resist or come back another time); chow down on tried-and-true classics like Basque steak frites or bacalao al pil pil. **Known for:** no-nonsense Basque comfort food; always packed with locals; intricate neo-Mudejar dining room. [$] *Average main: €15* ✉ *Calle Berástegui 4, El Ensanche* ☎ *94/423–7021* 🌐 *www.cafeirunabilbao.net* [M] *Moyúa.*

$$$ BASQUE Fodor's Choice ★
🍴 **Casa Rufo.** Charming and cozy, this centenarian Bilbao institution is essentially a series of nooks and crannies tucked into a fine food, wine, olive-oil, cheese, and ham emporium. Leave it to the affable owners to recommend a house specialty such as the oversize txuleton de buey, which pairs wonderfully with the house Rioja *crianza* (two years in oak,

one in bottle) and any number of other bottles from the 1,000-strong wine list. **Known for:** deep wine list with hard-to-find selections; delectable txuleton de buey; homey dining room. $ *Average main: €20* ✉ *Calle Hurtado de Amézaga 5, El Ensanche* ☎ *94/443–2172* ⊕ *www. casarufo.com* ⊙ *Closed Sun.* Ⓜ *Abando.*

$$$$
BASQUE

✕**Etxanobe.** This legendary nueva cocina Basque restaurant relocated to a larger space in early 2018 to accommodate two distinct concepts, La Despensa del Etxanobe and Atelier Etxanobe. La Despensa is sexy and informal with dim lighting, neon signage, and look-at-me plating, while the white-tablecloth Atelier features exquisitely refined, seafood-centric cuisine. **Known for:** two restaurants under one roof—one casual and the other refined; impeccable designer decor; pristine seafood. $ *Average main: €70* ✉ *Calle de Juan de Ajuriaguerra 8, El Ensanche* ☎ *94/442– 1071* ⊕ *www.atelieretxanobe.com* ⊙ *Closed Tues.* Ⓜ *Uribitarte.*

$$$
SPANISH
FAMILY

✕**Gure Kabi.** This family-friendly restaurant off the tourist track serves a wide range of unfussy, lovingly prepared dishes ranging from creamy squid croquetas to griddled European lobster. The best value is the €35 set menu of eight sharable dishes. **Known for:** Basque home cooking; locals-only vibe; efficient service. $ *Average main: €22* ✉ *Calle Particular de Estraunza 4–6, El Ensanche* ☎ *94/600–4843* ⊕ *www.gurekabi. com* ⊙ *Closed Sun.* Ⓜ *Indautxu.*

$$$$
BASQUE
FAMILY

✕**Jolastoki.** If you find yourself in Getxo, the beach town north of Bilbao where the Puente de Vizcaya is located, treat yourself to a meal at this graceful mansion serving mouthwatering dishes like rice with squid and salsa verde and oxtail in Rioja wine sauce. Set menus, ranging in price from €15 to €75 per person, are a good value whether you're looking to save or splurge. **Known for:** location near the Puente de Vizcaya; lots of locally sourced ingredients; wide variety of set menus. $ *Average main: €40* ✉ *Av. Los Chopos 21, Neguri* ☎ *94/491–2031* ⊕ *www.restaurantejolastoki.com* ⊙ *Closed Mon. No dinner Sun. and Tues.* Ⓜ *Gobela, Neguri.*

$$$
BASQUE
FAMILY

✕**La Ribera.** This gastrobar on the ground floor of the eponymous Mercado will satisfy your Basque food cravings after ogling all the shimmering fresh fish, plump jamones, and sweet-smelling fruit. The €14.50 *menú del día* (prix-fixe) is a terrific deal, and the high-brow pintxos are consistently tasty. **Known for:** hip, young vibe; good prix-fixe lunch; wide selection of sweet and savory snacks. $ *Average main: €20* ✉ *Mercado la Ribera, Calle de la Ribera 20, Casco Viejo* ☎ *94/657–5474* ⊕ *www.lariberabilbao.com* ⊙ *Closed Mon.* Ⓜ *Casco Viejo.*

$$$
BASQUE

✕**La Viña del Ensanche.** Littered with used napkins and furnished with simple wood tables beneath jamones ibéricos hanging from the rafters, this lively, deceptively simple bar attracts locals and tourists alike for its exceptional pintxos. Don't pass up the deconstructed Galician-style octopus on a bed of pimentón-laced mashed potatoes or the appetizer of homemade foie gras with three preserves. **Known for:** croquetas made with Joselito jamón ibérico; loud, convivial atmosphere; homemade foie gras. $ *Average main: €20* ✉ *Calle Diputazio 10, El Ensanche* ☎ *94/415–5615* ⊕ *www.lavinadelensanche.com* ⊙ *Closed Sun.* Ⓜ *Moyua.*

5

$$$
BASQUE
Fodor's Choice
★

✕ **Nido Bilbao.** Even the bread is homemade at this wildly popular Basque restaurant on the Left Bank that's renowned for dishes like goose foie gras with raspberry coulis, dry-aged T-bone steaks, and house-made morcilla. A list of small-production and organic wines rounds out the hyperlocal dining experience. **Known for:** homemade everything, from sausages to breads to ice creams; organic and biodynamic wines; market-driven cuisine. $ *Average main: €21* ⊠ *Calle Barroeta Aldamar 3, El Ensanche* ☎ *94/436–0643* ⊕ *www.nidobilbao. com* ☉ *Closed Sun.* Ⓜ *Abando.*

$$
BASQUE
FAMILY
Fodor's Choice
★

✕ **Pentxo.** This is the sort of restaurant bilbaínos like to keep to themselves—it's consistently delicious, shockingly affordable, and unapologetically old-school. Whether you pop in for a pintxo at the bar (the flash-fried *antxoas rellenas*, or stuffed anchovies, are a must) or a €15 prix-fixe lunch (opt for whatever seafood main is listed), you'll leave wishing you could be a regular. **Known for:** local crowd; outstanding pintxos and coffees; unbeatable lunch deal. $ *Average main: €15* ⊠ *Calle Belostikale 20, Casco Viejo* ☎ *94/416–9472* ⊕ *www.restaurantepentxo.com* ☉ *Closed Sun.*

$
TAPAS

✕ **Txiriboga Taberna.** Locals flock to this hole-in-the-wall for what might be the city's best croquetas—choose from jamón, chicken, bacalao, or wild mushroom. The *rabas* (fried calamari) also stand out for their nongreasy, ultracrisp exterior. **Known for:** burst-in-your-mouth croquetas; quintessential Basque taberna; terrific calamari. $ *Average main: €9* ⊠ *Calle Santa Maria 13, Casco Viejo* ☎ *94/415–7874* ☉ *Closed Mon.* Ⓜ *Casco Viejo.*

$$
TAPAS

✕ **Xukela.** This small tavern feels like a professor's study with books and magazines scattered about; there's a sign on the wall that says, "This is an Atheist establishment." But the main draw is the pintxos, imaginative bites ranging from smoked Cantabrian anchovies to mushroom–foie gras toasts. **Known for:** librarylike interiors; nueva cocina tapas at taberna prices; varied wine list. $ *Average main: €14* ⊠ *Calle de El Perro 2, Casco Viejo* ☎ *94/415–9772* Ⓜ *Casco Viejo.*

WHERE TO STAY

$$$
HOTEL
Fodor's Choice
★

▦ **Barceló Bilbao Nervión.** Sandwiched between the Casco Viejo and the industrial area surrounding the Guggenheim, this corporate hotel soars seven stories over the Nervión, and its best rooms boast semicircular windows that make you feel like you're hovering over it. **Pros:** supremely comfortable; great location; stylish modern decor. **Cons:** no river views from interior rooms; not exactly homey; lacks local flavor. $ *Rooms from: €130* ⊠ *Paseo Campo de Volantín 11, Casco Viejo* ☎ *94/445–4700* ⊕ *www.barcelo.com* ⇆ *350 rooms* ⎢◯⎢ *No meals* Ⓜ *Uribitarte.*

$$
B&B/INN
Fodor's Choice
★

▦ **Caravan Cinema.** This cozy, cinema-themed pension is an absolute steal: you'd be hard-pressed to find another €100-a-night hotel in Bilbao with in-room Nespresso machines and huge TVs. **Pros:** excellent value; convenient to main sights; cheerful staff. **Cons:** some rooms overlook a dirty little courtyard; inadequate soundproofing; have to contact proprietor to schedule check-in time. $ *Rooms from: €100* ⊠ *Calle Correo*

11, Casco Viejo ☎ *68/886–0907* 🌐 *www.caravan-cinema.com* 🛏 *11 rooms* 🍴 *No meals* [M] *Arriaga.*

$$$ HOTEL Fodor's Choice ★ 🏨 **El Castillo Arteaga.** Built in the mid-19th century for Empress Eugenia de Montijo, wife of Napoléon III, this neo-Gothic limestone castle with rooms in the watchtowers and defensive walls is one of the most extraordinary lodging options in or around Bilbao. **Pros:** market-driven restaurant worth a trip in itself; views over the wetlands; palatial digs. **Cons:** isolated from the village and 30 minutes from Bilbao; spotty Wi-Fi in some rooms; restaurant is pricey and there aren't many cheap alternatives in the area. [$] *Rooms from: €180* ✉ *Calle Gaztelubide 7, Gautegiz de Arteaga* ✥ *40 km (25 miles) northwest of Bilbao* ☎ *94/627–0440* 🌐 *www.castillodearteaga.com* 🕒 *Closed late Dec.–early Jan.* 🛏 *13 rooms* 🍴 *Free Breakfast.*

$$$ HOTEL 🏨 **Gran Hotel Domine Bilbao.** This Silken-chain art hotel across from the Guggenheim showcases the conceptual wit of Javier Mariscal, creator of Barcelona's 1992 Olympic mascot Cobi, and the structural know-how of Bilbao architect Iñaki Aurrekoetxea. **Pros:** emblematic of Bilbao's architectural renaissance; breakfasts on the rooftop terrace; spacious, updated rooms. **Cons:** hard on the wallet; a little full of its own glamour; soundproofing could be better. [$] *Rooms from: €175* ✉ *Alameda de Mazarredo 61, El Ensanche* ☎ *94/425–3300, 94/425–3301* 🌐 *www.granhoteldominebilbao.com* 🛏 *145 rooms* 🍴 *No meals* [M] *Moyúa.*

$$$$ HOTEL 🏨 **Hotel Carlton.** This grande dame, equidistant from the Casco Viejo and the Abandoibarra neighborhood, exudes old-world grace and charm along with a sense of history—which it has aplenty: Orson Welles, Ava Gardner, Ernest Hemingway, and Lauren Bacall are a just a few luminaries who once posted up here. **Pros:** historic, old-world surroundings; spacious rooms; luxury gym and business center. **Cons:** surrounded by concrete and urban frenzy; "modern" design touches come across as tacky; occasionally grumpy personnel. [$] *Rooms from: €225* ✉ *Pl. Federico Moyúa 2, El Ensanche* ☎ *94/416–2200* 🌐 *www.hotelcarlton.es* 🛏 *142 rooms* 🍴 *Free Breakfast* [M] *Moyúa.*

$$ HOTEL 🏨 **Hotel Ercilla López de Haro.** A converted 19th-century building, the López de Haro has a retro Victorian feel with wallpapered rooms, white-marble floors, and Bergère chairs. **Pros:** minutes from the Casco Viejo; good perks; free parking. **Cons:** hushed atmosphere; underwhelming; maintenance could be improved. [$] *Rooms from: €115* ✉ *Calle Obispo Orueta 2–4, El Ensanche* ☎ *94/423–5500* 🌐 *www.hotellopezdeharo.com* 🛏 *53 rooms* 🍴 *Free Breakfast* [M] *Moyúa.*

$$$$ HOTEL 🏨 **Hotel Miró.** Between the Guggenheim and Bilbao's excellent Museo de Bellas Artes, this boutique hotel refurbished by Barcelona fashion designer Toni Miró competes with the reflecting facade of Javier Mariscal's Domine Bilbao just up the street. **Pros:** tasteful, ultramodern decor; free coffee, tea, and popcorn in the lobby; views of the Guggenheim. **Cons:** blasé staff; dull bagged breakfast included in some rates; uncozy. [$] *Rooms from: €240* ✉ *Alameda de Mazarredo 77, El Ensanche* ☎ *94/661–1880* 🌐 *www.mirohotelbilbao.com* 🛏 *50 rooms* 🍴 *No meals* [M] *Moyúa.*

5

$$$ ⬚ **Hotel Palacio Urgoiti.** This outstanding hotel, occupying a recon-
HOTEL structed 17th-century country palace out toward the airport, is a
FAMILY peaceful retreat with a 9-hole pitch-and-putt in the hotel gardens and
other activities nearby. **Pros:** handy train service into Bilbao; conve-
nient to the airport; elegant environment with easy access to outdoor
activities. **Cons:** 15-minute drive to Bilbao; some flights overhead are
teeth-rattling; indoor pool is freezing. $ *Rooms from: €145* ⊠ *Calle
Arritugane s/n, Mungia* ✛ *13 km (8 miles) west of Bilbao, 2 km (1
mile) from airport* ☎ *94/674–6868* ⊕ *www.palaciourgoiti.com* ⟲ *43
rooms* ⍟ *Free Breakfast.*

$$ ⬚ **Iturrienea Ostatua.** A quirky, cozy hotel, Iturrienea Ostatua occupies
B&B/INN a traditional Basque town house overlooking Bilbao's Casco Viejo.
Fodor'sChoice **Pros:** budget-friendly; attentive personnel; rustic-chic interiors. **Cons:**
★ exterior-facing rooms can be noisy; no on-site parking and the closest
lot is expensive; slow Wi-Fi. $ *Rooms from: €110* ⊠ *Calle Santa María
14, Casco Viejo* ☎ *94/416–1500* ⊕ *www.iturrieneaostatua.com* ⟲ *19
rooms* ⍟ *No meals* Ⓜ *Casco Viejo.*

$$$ ⬚ **Meliá Bilbao Hotel.** Designed by architect Ricardo Legorreta and
HOTEL inspired by the work of Basque sculptor Eduardo Chillida (1920–2002),
this high-rise hotel was built over what was once the nerve center of
Bilbao's shipbuilding industry; fittingly, it recalls a futuristic ocean liner.
Pros: some rooms face the Guggenheim; high levels of comfort; top-
notch dining options. **Cons:** a high-rise colossus; maintenance issues;
inconsistent service. $ *Rooms from: €170* ⊠ *Calle Lehendakari Leiza-
ola 29, El Ensanche* ☎ *94/428–0000* ⊕ *www.melia.com* ⟲ *213 rooms*
⍟ *No meals* Ⓜ *San Mamés.*

$$$ ⬚ **NH Collection Villa de Bilbao.** Although a bit "big-city brisk" (very
HOTEL bilbaíno, not unlike New York City), this four-star is a great value for
money and offers choice extras—morning newspapers at your door,
exceptional breakfasts, well-appointed rooms, and professional service.
Pros: spacious rooms; latest technology and comfort; scenic walk to the
Bellas Artes and Guggenheim museums. **Cons:** disorganized reception
staff; a bit cold and corporate; poor bathroom maintenance. $ *Rooms
from: €150* ⊠ *Gran Vía 87, El Ensanche* ☎ *94/441–6000* ⊕ *www.nh-
hoteles.com* ⟲ *139 rooms* ⍟ *No meals* Ⓜ *San Mamés.*

$ ⬚ **Pensión Méndez I & II.** This may be the best value in the city center
B&B/INN with small but well-maintained rooms, some of which (Nos. 1 and
2) overlook the facade of the Palacio Yohn. **Pros:** excellent value and
location in the middle of the Casco Viejo; prices don't fluctuate in high
season; family-run business. **Cons:** no a/c; rooms with best views are
noisy at night; proprietors don't speak English. $ *Rooms from: €35*
⊠ *Calle Santa María 13, 1st and 4th fls., Casco Viejo* ☎ *94/416–0364*
⊕ *www.pensionmendez.com* ⊟ *No credit cards* ⟲ *24 rooms* ⍟ *No
meals* Ⓜ *Casco Viejo.*

SPORTS AND THE OUTDOORS

SOCCER

Soccer is religion in Bilbao, even if the Athletic de Bilbao soccer team hasn't won a league title in around 30 years. "The Lions" are often in the top half of the league standings and take special pleasure in tormenting powerhouses Madrid and Barcelona. The local rivalry with San Sebastián's Real Sociedad is as bitter as baseball's Yankees–Red Sox feud.

San Mamés Stadium. Athletic de Bilbao got a new home in 2013 with the opening of this €213 million stadium on the Nervión that seats over 53,000. Its retractable roof keeps spectators dry, rain or shine. ⊠ *Rafael Moreno Pitxitxi s/n, San Mamés* ☏ *94/441–3954* ⊕ *www.bilbaostadium.com* Ⓜ *San Mamés.*

SHOPPING

The main stores for clothing are found around Plaza Moyúa in El Ensanche along streets such as Iparraguirre and Rodríguez Arias. The Casco Viejo has dozens of smaller shops, many of them in handsomely restored early houses with gorgeous wooden beams and ancient stones, specializing in an endless variety of products from crafts to antiques. Wool items, gourmet products, and wood carvings from around the Basque Country can be found throughout Bilbao. Basque *txapelas* (berets, or Basque *boinas*) are famous worldwide and make fine gifts.

For international fashion brands, the ubiquitous department store El Corte Inglés is an easy, if unexciting, one-stop shop.

Fodor'sChoice ★ **La Bendita.** This pocket-size gourmet shop tucked beside the cathedral sells the finest sweets, wines, and *conservas* the region has to offer. Slender green txakoli bottles and vintage-label Cantabrian anchovies make wonderful souvenirs. ⊠ *Calle Bidebarrieta 16, Casco Viejo* ☏ *94/652–3623* ⊕ *www.labenditabilbao.com* Ⓜ *Arriaga.*

Malmö. Opened in 2015, this Scandinavian-inflected "concept store" carries art zines, coffee-table books, and designer accessories. Shop wildly patterned Swell thermoses, Cova Orgaz cardboard figurines, and Spanish-made Labobratori notebooks. ⊠ *Calle Dorre 7, Casco Viejo* ☏ *94/646–7014* ⊕ *www.malmogallery.com* Ⓜ *Arriaga.*

SAN SEBASTIÁN, VITORIA, AND THE BASQUE COAST

Heading east along the Bay of Biscay toward Gipuzkoa province and San Sebastián, colorful fishing villages and beach towns appear one after the other on the snaking BI-3438 highway that traces the coastline. Weaving through dewy forests and punctuated with jaw-dropping views of the Atlantic, this is one of the most scenic drives in Spain. After passing the sleepy port of Getaria and a handful of well-to-do resorts, you'll arrive in San Sebastián, Bilbao's aristocratic cousin, a city that invites you to slow down with its elegant boardwalks and leisurely

Basque Culture

The Basques are one of the great mysteries of Europe: nobody knows where they came from or when they arrived in this windswept corner of the Iberian Peninsula. Though the first written records of the Basques are from Roman times, recent studies indicate that this "tribe" of proto-Europeans has inhabited the area for at least 7,000 years. A combination of impenetrable geography and a fierce warrior class kept the Basques somewhat isolated from the rest of the Continent for hundreds, if not thousands, of years—enough time to establish and preserve their distinctive mythology, sports, food, and—perhaps most significantly—the Basque language, which remains alive and well today.

BASQUE LANGUAGE

Although the Basque people speak French north of the border and Spanish south of the border, many consider **Euskera** their first language. The mother tongue is so vital to the Basque identity that the cultural signifier "Basque" in Euskera is is "Euskalduna," literally "Speaker of Basque." As Europe's only non-Indo-European language, Euskera is one of the great enigmas of linguistic scholarship. To the non-speaker, Euskera sounds like rough, consonant-heavy Spanish, though its highly complex grammar has no relation to the Romance languages. About one-quarter of the Basque population speaks Euskera as a first language.

BASQUE CUISINE

Traditional Basque cuisine combines the fresh fish of the Atlantic and upland vegetables, beef, and lamb with a love of sauces that is rare south of the Pyrenees. Today the *nueva cocina vasca* (new Basque cooking) movement has painted Basque food as highly innovative and slightly precious, even if most everyday Basques still eat as they always have. With the sudden trendiness of pintxos (the Basque equivalent of tapas), Basque cuisine is now a part of the culinary zeitgeist in cities from New York to Tokyo.

BASQUE SPORTS

A Basque village without a *frontón* (pelota court) is as unimaginable as an American town without a baseball diamond. Pelota, or **jai alai** in Euskera, is the fastest-moving ball sport, according to Guinness World Records, with ball speeds reaching 150 mph. The game is played on a three-walled court 175 feet long and 56 feet wide with 40-foot side walls, and the object is to angle the ball along or off of the side wall so that it cannot be returned. Betting is popular.

Herrikirolak (rural sports) are based on farming and seafaring. Stone lifters (*harrijasotzaileak* in Euskera) heft weights up to 700 pounds. *Aizkolari* (axe men) chop wood in various contests, and the *Gizon proba* (man trial) pits three-man teams moving weighted sleds. Then there are the *estropadak*, whaleboat rowers who compete in spectacular regattas (culminating in the September competition off La Concha beach in San Sebastián).

When it comes to **soccer,** Basque goaltenders have developed special fame in Spain, where Bilbao's Athletic Club and San Sebastian's Real Sociedad have won national championships with budgets far inferior to those of Real Madrid or FC Barcelona.

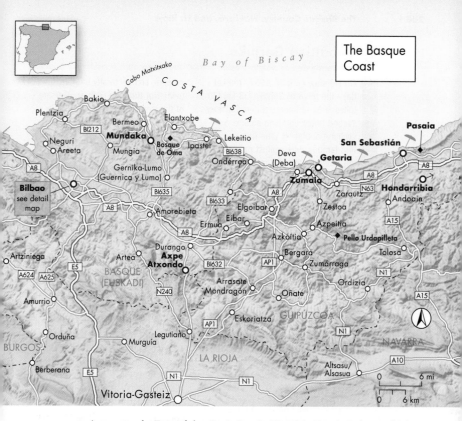

pintxo crawls. East of the city is Pasaia (Spanish: Pasajes), from which the Marquis de Lafayette set off to help the rebel forces in the American Revolution and where Victor Hugo spent a winter writing. Just shy of the French border is Hondarribia, a brightly painted, flower-festooned port town.

MUNDAKA

37 km (23 miles) northeast of Bilbao.

Tiny Mundaka, famous among surfers all over the world for its left-breaking roller at the mouth of the Ría de Gernika, has much to offer nonsurfers as well. The town's elegant summer homes and stately houses bearing family coats of arms compete for pride of place with the hermitage on the Santa Catalina peninsula and the parish church's Renaissance doorway.

VISITOR INFORMATION

Contacts Mundaka. ✉ *Calle Josepa Deuna s/n* ☎ *94/617–7201* ⊕ *www.mundakaturismo.com.*

Embattled Gernika

On Monday, April 26, 1937—market day—the town of Gernika, 33 km (20 miles) east of Bilbao, suffered history's second terror bombing against a civilian population. (The first, much less famous, was against neighboring Durango, about a month earlier.) Gernika, a rural market town, had been one of the symbols of Basque identity since the 14th century: since the Middle Ages, Spanish sovereigns had sworn under the ancient oak tree of Gernika to respect Basque *fueros* (local courts with the sort of autonomy that was anathema to the *generalísimo* Francisco Franco's Madrid-centered "National Movement," which promoted Spanish unity over local identity). The planes of the Nazi Luftwaffe were sent with the blessings of Franco to experiment with saturation bombing of civilian targets and to decimate the traditional seat of Basque autonomy.

When the raid ended, more than 250 civilians lay dead or dying in the ruins, and today Gernika remains a symbol of the atrocities of war, largely thanks to Picasso's famous canvas *Guernica*. The city was destroyed—although the oak tree miraculously emerged unscathed—and has been rebuilt as a

modern, architecturally uninteresting town. Not until the 60th anniversary of the event did Germany officially apologize for the bombing.

When Spain's Second Republic commissioned Picasso to create a work for the Paris 1937 International Exposition, little did he imagine that his grim canvas protesting the bombing of a Basque village would become one of the most famous paintings in history.

Picasso's painting had its own struggle. The Spanish Pavilion in the 1937 International Exposition in Paris nearly substituted a more upbeat work, using *Guernica* as a backdrop. In 1939, Picasso ceded *Guernica* to New York's Museum of Modern Art, stipulating that the painting should return only to a democratic Spain. Over the next 30 years, as Picasso's fame grew, so did *Guernica*'s—as a work of art and symbol of Spain's captivity.

When Franco died in 1975, two years after Picasso, negotiations with Picasso's heirs for the painting's return to Spain were already under way. Now on display at Madrid's Centro de Arte Reina Sofía, *Guernica* is home for good.

BEACHES

Mundaka Beach. This beach is said to have the longest surf break in Europe and among the best in the world, making it a magnet for surfers from around the world. In summer and fall this beach is off-limits to families who just want to splash around. Just inland from the beach is the Urdaibai Natural Preserve, a UNESCO-designated biosphere. **Amenities:** lifeguards; water sports. **Best for:** surfing. ⊠ *Calle Matadero*.

WHERE TO EAT AND STAY

$$$$ ✕ **Baserri Maitea.** In the village of Forua, about 11 km (7 miles) south
BASQUE   of Mundaka and 1 km (½ mile) northwest of Gernika, this restaurant is in a stunning 18th-century *caserío* (Basque farmhouse). Strings of red peppers and garlic hang from wooden beams in the cathedral-like interior, and the kitchen is famous for its hearty yet refined fish and

meat dishes prepared over a wood-fired grill. **Known for:** spectacular ambience in a Basque farmhouse; bacalao dishes; personable waitstaff. $ *Average main: €25* ✉ *Calle Atxondoa s/n* ☎ *94/625–3408* ⊕ *www.baserrimaitea.com* ⊗ *No dinner Sun.–Thurs.*

$$$$ ⤫ **Restaurante Asador Portuondo.** Sweeping beach views, aromas of fresh
BASQUE fish cooking over hot coals, a comfortable country dining room—these are just a few of the reasons Portuondo, a 15-minute walk outside town, is a stalwart Mundaka restaurant. If you're in the mood for something informal, post up at the downstairs pintxo bar. **Known for:** bucolic atmosphere; meats and fish grilled to perfection; buzzy tapas area. $ *Average main: €30* ✉ *Portuondo Auzoa 1, Ctra. Gernika–Bermeo BI2235, Km 47* ☎ *94/687–6050* ⊕ *www.restauranteportuondo.com* ⊗ *Closed Mon.*

$$ 🏨 **Atalaya.** Tastefully converted from a private house, this 1911 land-
HOTEL mark has become a favorite for quick overnight rail getaways from Bilbao—scenery along the 37-km (23-mile) train ride is spectacular. **Pros:** intimate retreat from Bilbao's sprawl and bustle; well-maintained sauna; free parking. **Cons:** tight quarters in some rooms; limited menu in the restaurant; can be lonely in the off-season. $ *Rooms from: €110* ✉ *Calle Itxaropen 1* ☎ *94/687–6899* ⇨ *13 rooms* ⊙| *No meals.*

OFF THE BEATEN PATH

Bosque de Oma (*Painted Forest*). On the road to Kortezubi, 5 km (3 miles) from Gernika, stop off at the Urdaibai Natural Reserve for a stroll through the Bosque de Oma with rows of trees vividly painted by Basque artist Agustín Ibarrola. It's a striking and successful marriage of art and nature. The nearby **Cuevas de Santimamiñe** have important prehistoric cave paintings that can be accessed virtually at a visitor center. ✉ *Barrio Basondo, Kortezubi* ☎ *94/465–1657* ⊕ *www.bosquedeoma.com* ⬚ *Free.*

AXPE ATXONDO

47 km (29 miles) east of Bilbao, 6 km (4 miles) south of Mundaka.

The village of Axpe, in the valley of Atxondo, sits in the shadow of 4,777-foot Mt. Anboto—one of the highest peaks in the Basque Country outside the Pyrenees. According to local lore, the Basque nature goddess Mari lives in a cave close to the summit. Amboto, with its spectral gray rock face, is a sharp contrast to the soft green meadows running up to the very foot of the mountain. In his *Mitología Vasca* (*Basque Mythology*), ethnologist José María de Barandiarán describes the goddess as "a beautiful woman, well constructed in all ways except for one foot, which was like that of a goat."

GETTING HERE AND AROUND

To reach Axpe from Bilbao, drive east on the A8/E70 freeway toward San Sebastián. Get off at the Durango exit, 40 km (24 miles) from Bilbao, and take the BI632 toward Elorrio. At Apatamonasterio turn right onto the BI3313 and continue to Axpe.

WHERE TO EAT AND STAY

$$$$ ⤫ **Etxebarri.** Of all the three-Michelin-star outposts in the Basque Coun-
BASQUE try, Victor Arguinzoniz's Etxebarri may be the most exclusive, since it
Fodor's Choice only opens for lunch (except for Saturday) and reservations are lim-
★ ited. Here, grilling is elevated to an art form, with various types of woods, coals, and tools carefully selected for the preparation of each

dish. **Known for:** No. 6 restaurant on "World's 50 Best" list; temple of open-hearth cuisine; surprisingly unpretentious, laid-back atmosphere. $ *Average main: €60* ⊠ *Pl. San Juan 1* ☎ *94/658–3042* ⊕ *www.asadoretxebarri.com* ⊗ *Closed Mon., all Aug. No dinner Tues.–Fri.*

$ **Mendi Goikoa.** This handsome collection of hillside farmhouses is

HOTEL among the province of Vizcaya's most exquisite hideaways. **Pros:** gor-

Fodor's Choice geous setting; smart and attentive service; sweet, sweet silence. **Cons:**

★ need a car to get here; not open year-round; rooms on the smaller side. $ *Rooms from: €80* ⊠ *Barrio San Juan 33* ☎ *94/682–0833* ⊗ *Closed Nov.–Easter* ⇤ *11 rooms* ⦿ *Free Breakfast.*

GETARIA AND ZUMAIA

80 km (50 miles) east of Bilbao, 22 km (14 miles) west of San Sebastián.

Getaria (Guetaria in Castilian) is known as *la cocina de Guipúzcoa* (the kitchen of the Guipúzcoa province) for its many restaurants and taverns. It was also the birthplace of Juan Sebastián Elcano (1487–1526), the first circumnavigator of the globe and Spain's most emblematic naval hero. Elcano took over and completed Magellan's voyage after Magellan was killed in the Philippines in 1521. The town's galleonlike church has sloping wooden floors resembling a ship's deck. Zarautz, the next town over, has a wide beach and many taverns and cafés.

Zumaia is a snug little port and summer resort with the estuary of the Urola River flowing—back and forth, according to the tide—through town. Zumaia and Getaria are connected along the coast road and by several good footpaths.

VISITOR INFORMATION

Contacts Getaria Tourist Office. ⊠ *Parque Aldamar 2, Getaria* ☎ *94/314–0957* ⊕ *www.getariaturismo.eus.* **Zumaia Tourist Office.** ⊠ *Pl. de Kantauri 13, Zumaia* ☎ *94/314–3396* ⊕ *www.zumaia.eus.*

EXPLORING

Cristóbal Balenciaga Museoa. The haute-couture maestro Cristóbal Balenciaga (1895–1972) was born in Getaria, and the impressive museum created in his honor is a must-see, regardless of your fashion sensibilities. The collection and interactive exhibits are distributed between two buildings, the mansion where Balenciaga was born and a starkly geometric monolith inaugurated in 2011. Feast your eyes on couture specimens from the foundation's 1,200-item collection, from suits to gowns to accessories that represent his life's work. "Balenciaga is a couturier in the truest sense of the word," said Coco Chanel of her rival. "The others are simply fashion designers." ⊠ *Aldamar Parkea 6, Getaria* ☎ *94/300–8840* ⊕ *www.cristobalbalenciagamuseoa.com* ⊠ *€10* ⊗ *Closed Mon. in Sept.–June.*

Espacio Cultural Ignacio Zuloaga. On the N634 at the eastern edge of town, this museum has an extraordinary collection of paintings by Goya, El Greco, Zurbarán, and others, in addition to works by the Basque impressionist Ignacio Zuloaga. The collection is housed in an ancient stone convent surrounded by gardens. The museum opens between 3 and 11 times a month; check the website for a complete schedule. ✉ *Santiago Auzoa 3, Zumaia* 🕾 *67/707–8445* ⊕ *www.espaciozuloaga.com* 🖾 *€5.*

WHERE TO EAT AND STAY

$$$
BASQUE
FAMILY
Fodor's Choice
★

✕**Agroturismo Segore Etxeberri.** Hidden in the lush, hilly countryside southwest of Tolosa—and many miles off the tourist track—is Agroturismo Segore Etxeberri, a restaurant (and five-room B&B) housed in a traditional caserío perched on a hilltop. After snapping a few pics of the jaw-dropping views, tuck into a soul-satisfying Basque feast of roast chicken (raised on the property), stewed game meats, or freshly caught fish. **Known for:** culinary gem in the middle of nowhere; spectacular views; meats and vegetables from the estate. Ⓢ *Average main: €18* ✉ *Calle Valle Santa Marina s/n* 🕾 *94/358–0976* ⊕ *www.segore.com* ⊗ *Closed Tues. No dinner Mon., Wed., and Thurs.*

$$
BASQUE

✕**Bedua.** This rustic (if slightly overpriced) asador draws the crowds for its excellent tortilla de bacalao, txuleta de buey, and fish of all kinds, especially the classic besugo cooked *a la donostiarra* (roasted and covered with a sauce of garlic and vinegar). Txakoli from nearby Getaria is the beverage of choice. **Known for:** pristine seafood and home-grown vegetables; top-quality txuleton; farmhouse-chic ambience. Ⓢ *Average main: €15* ✉ *Cestona, Barrio Bedua, Zumaia* ⊕ *Up Urola, 3 km (2 miles) from Zumaia* 🕾 *94/386–0551* ⊕ *www.bedua.es.*

$$$$
SEAFOOD
Fodor's Choice
★

✕**Elkano.** Ever since Anthony Bourdain waxed poetic about award-winning Elkano's grilled turbot on *Parts Unknown,* the dish has become something of a holy grail among in-the-know foodies. Order the famous flat fish (at its fatty prime in May and June), and you'll receive what Bourdain called an "anatomy lesson" as the maître d' extolls the virtues of each separate cut culminating with the gelatinous fins, which you're encouraged to suck between your fingers, caveman style. **Known for:** grilled turbot; Anthony Bourdain favorite; rare, quirky wines. Ⓢ *Average main: €45* ✉ *Calle Herrieta 2, Getaria* 🕾 *94/314–0024* ⊕ *www.restauranteelkano.com* ⊗ *Closed Tues.*

$
B&B/INN
FAMILY

🛏 **Landarte.** For a taste of country life in a Basque caserío, stay at this restored 16th-century country manor house 1 km (½ mile) from Zumaia and an hour's walk from Getaria. **Pros:** warm, family-friendly atmosphere; traditional cuisine on request; unusual wall art. **Cons:** some top-floor rooms under the low eaves could be tricky for taller guests; €9 breakfast; can't go far without a car. Ⓢ *Rooms from: €88* ✉ *Ctra. Artadi Anzoa 1, Zumaia* 🕾 *94/386–5358* ⊕ *www.landarte.net* ⊗ *Closed mid-Dec.–Feb.* 🛏 *6 rooms* ⭘│ *No meals.*

$$
HOTEL
Fodor's Choice
★

🛏 **Saiaz Getaria.** For panoramic views over the Bay of Biscay, this 15th-century house on Getaria's uppermost street is a perfect choice. **Pros:** historic property; waves lull you to sleep; discounts at nearby spa and gym. **Cons:** soundproofing could be better; spotty Wi-Fi; only two (first-come-first-served) parking spaces. Ⓢ *Rooms from: €109* ✉ *Roke Deuna 25, Getaria* 🕾 *94/314–0143* ⊕ *www.saiazgetaria.com* ⊗ *Closed Dec. 20–Jan. 6* 🛏 *17 rooms* ⭘│ *No meals.*

OFF THE BEATEN PATH

Pello Urdapilleta. For a look at a working Basque farmhouse, or caserío, where the Urdapilleta family farms pigs, sheep, cattle, goats, chickens, and ducks, take a detour up to the village of Bidegoian, on the Azpeitia–Tolosa road. Pello Urdapilleta (which means "pile of pigs" in Euskera) sells artisanal cheeses and Basque heritage-breed pork sausages. ⊠ *Elola Azpikoa Baserria, Bidegoian* ☎ *60/570–1204* ⊕ *www.urdapilleta.eu.*

SHOPPING

Getaria, Zumaia, and the surrounding villages are great places to pick up locally canned anchovies, tuna, and sardines as well as bottles of txakoli and *sagardoa*, Basque cider.

Salanort. This highly regarded conservas company might be most famous for its anchovies, which are always plump and expertly packed, but you can also stock up on local wines and liqueurs here such as patxaran, a digestif made with sloe berries. ⊠ *Nagusia 22, Getaria* ☎ *94/314–0036* ⊕ *www.salanort.com.*

SAN SEBASTIÁN

100 km (62 miles) northeast of Bilbao.

Fodor's Choice ★ San Sebastián (Donostia in Euskera) is a sophisticated city arched around one of the finest urban beaches in the world, **La Kontxa** (The Shell), so named for its resemblance to the shape of a scallop shell, with Ondarreta and Zurriola beaches at the southwestern and northeastern ends. The promontories of Monte Urgull and Monte Igueldo serve as bookends for La Concha, while Zurriola has Monte Ulía rising over its far end. The best way to take in San Sebastián is on foot: promenades and pathways twist up the hills that surround the city and afford postcard-perfect views. The first records of San Sebastián date to the 11th century. A backwater for centuries, the city had the good fortune in 1845 to attract Queen Isabella II, who was seeking relief from a skin ailment in the icy Atlantic waters. Isabella was followed by much of the aristocracy of the time, and San Sebastián became—and remains—a favored summer retreat for Madrid's well-to-do.

The city is bisected by the **Urumea River,** which is crossed by three ornate bridges inspired by late-19th-century French architecture. At the mouth of the Urumea, the incoming surf smashes the rocks with such force that white foam erupts, and the sound is wild and Wagnerian. The city is laid out with wide streets on a grid pattern, thanks mainly to the dozen times it has been all but destroyed by fire. The last conflagration came after the French were expelled in 1813; English and Portuguese forces occupied the city, abused the population, and torched the place. Today, San Sebastián is a seaside resort on par with Nice and Monte Carlo. It becomes one of Spain's most expensive cities in the summer, when French vacationers descend in droves. It is also, like Bilbao, a center of Basque nationalism.

Neighborhoods include the scenic, touristy La Parte Vieja, tucked under Monte Urgull north of the mouth of the Urumea River; hip-and-happening Gros (so named for a corpulent Napoleonic general), across the Urumea to the north; commercial Centro, the main city nucleus around the cathedral; residential Amara, farther east toward the Anoeta sports complex; glitzy La Concha, at center stage around the beach; and stately El Antiguo, at the western end of La Concha. Igueldo is the high promontory over the city at the southwestern side of the bay. Alto de

Miracruz is the high ground to the northeast toward France; Errenteria is inland east of Pasaia; Oiartzun is a village farther north; Astigarraga is in apple-cider country to the east of Anoeta.

GETTING HERE AND AROUND

San Sebastián is a very walkable city, though local buses (€1.75) are also convenient. Buses for Pasajes (Pasaia), Errenteria, Astigarraga, and Oiartzun originate in Calle Okendo, one block west of the Urumea River behind the Hotel Maria Cristina. Bus A-1 goes to Astigarraga; A-2 is the bus to Pasajes.

The Euskotren's Metro Donostialdea, the city train, is popularly known as El Topo (The Mole) for the amount of time it spends underground. It originates at the Amara Viejo station in Paseo Easo and tunnels its way to Hendaye, France, every 30 minutes (€5.80; 45 minutes). Euskotren also serves Bilbao by way of Lasarte–Oria, but buses and Blablacar rideshares will get you there in about half the time. It recently opened new stations that connect the neighboring towns of Lasarte-Oria (€1.19; 12 minutes), Pasaia (€1.19; 12 minutes) and Irun (€1.73; 30 minutes) to San Sebastián.

For the funicular up to Monte Igueldo (☎ 943/213525 ⊕ www.monteigueldo.es; €3.15), the station is just behind Ondarreta beach at the western end of La Concha.

Bus Contacts Estación de autobuses. ✉ Paseo de Federico García Lorca 1 ☎ 94/347–5150 ⊕ www.estaciondonostia.com.

Car Rental Europcar. ✉ Aeropuerto de San Sebastián, Calle Gabarrari 22, Hondarribia ☎ 94/366–8530 ⊕ www.europcar.com.

Train Contacts Estación de Amara (Estación de Easo). ✉ Pl. Easo 9 ☎ 90/254–3210 ⊕ www.renfe.com ✉ Paseo de Francia 22 ☎ 90/224–3402 ⊕ www.renfe.es.

VISITOR INFORMATION

Contacts San Sebastián–Donostia Tourist Office. ✉ Erregina Erregentearen 3, Blvd. 8 ☎ 94/348–1166 ⊕ www.sansebastianturismo.com.

EXPLORING

Every corner of Spain champions its culinary identity, but San Sebastián's refined fare is in a league of its own. Many of the city's restaurants and pintxos spots are in the **Parte Vieja** (Old Quarter), on the east end of the bay beyond the elegant **Casa Consistorial** (City Hall) and formal **Alderdi Eder** gardens. The building that now houses city hall opened as a casino in 1887; after gambling was outlawed early in the 20th century, the town council moved here from the Plaza de la Constitución, the Parte Vieja's main square.

Catedral Buen Pastor (*Cathedral of the Good Shepherd*). You can see the facade of this 19th-century cathedral from the river, across town. With the tallest church spire in the province, the Catedral del Buen Pastor was constructed in the neo-Gothic style. It's worth a glimpse inside at beautiful stained-glass windows. ✉ Pl. del Buen Pastor, Calle Urdaneta 12, Centro ☎ 94/346–4516 ✉ Free ⊗ Closed weekends.

San Sebastián's famed, curving beach La Concha

Iglesia de Santa María del Coro. Just in from the harbor, in the shadow of Monte Urgull, is this baroque church with a stunning carved facade of an arrow-riddled St. Sebastian flanked by two towers. The interior is strikingly restful considering the bustling area. Note the sculptures *The Harmony of Sound,* by Maximilian Peizmann, to the right of the entrance, and *By the Cross to the Light,* by Eduardo Chillida, in the baptistery. ⊠ *Calle Mayor 12, Parte Vieja* ☎ *94/342–3124* ⌖ *€3.*

Fodor'sChoice
★ **Monte Igueldo.** On the western side of the bay, this promontory is a must-visit. You can walk or drive up or take the funicular (€3.15 round-trip), with departures every 15 minutes. From the top, you get a bird's-eye view of San Sebastián's gardens, beaches, parks, wide tree-lined boulevards, and Belle Époque buildings. ⊠ *Igueldo* ☎ *94/321–3525 for funicular* ⊕ *www.monteigueldo.es* ☉ *Closed most of Jan., Wed. Nov.–Feb.*

Tabakalera. Occupying a century-old tobacco factory, this vibrant cultural center, inaugurated in 2015, epitomizes the creative, forward-thinking verve of San Sebastián. Check the website to see what performances, exhibitions, and screenings are planned ahead of your visit, and drop by to steep yourself in the city's here-and-now. ⊠ *Pl. Andre Zigarrogileak 1, Amara* ☎ *94/311–8855* ⊕ *www.tabakalera.eu.*

OFF THE
BEATEN
PATH
Chillida–Leku Museum. In the Jáuregui section of Hernani, 10 minutes south of San Sebastián (close to both Martín Berasategui's restaurant in nearby Lasarte *and* the cider houses of the Astigarraga neighborhood, like Sidrería Petritegi), the Eduardo Chillida Sculpture Garden and Museum, in a 16th-century farmhouse, is a treat for anyone interested in contemporary art. Visits are by appointment only via email: *info@ eduardochillida.com.* ⊠ *Caserío Zabalaga, Barrio Jáuregui 66, Lasarte*

☏ 94/333–6006 ⊕ *www.museochillidaleku.com* ✉ *€15 (recommended donation)* ⊘ *Closed Tues. (except July and Aug.) and Dec. 25–Jan. 1.*

BEACHES

FAMILY **La Kontxa.** San Sebastián's shell-shaped main beach is one of the most famous urban beaches in the world. Night and day, rain or shine, it's filled with locals and tourists alike, strolling and taking in the city's skyline and the uninhabited Isla de Santa Clara just offshore. Several hotels line its curved expanse including the grande dame **Hotel de Londres y de Inglaterra.** The beach has clean, pale sand and few rocks or seaweed, but only a bit of shade, near the promenade wall. Lounge chairs are available for rent. La Concha is safe night and day and is especially popular with families. **Amenities:** lifeguards; showers; toilets. **Best for:** sunrise; sunset; walking. ✉ *Calle de la Concha Ibilbidea.*

Zurriola. Just across the Urumea River from La Kontxa lies this sprawling, less touristy beach. Exposed to the open Atlantic, the beach boasts waves that are big enough to surf—and sometimes too dangerous for kids. **Amenities:** lifeguards; water sports. **Best for:** surfing. ✉ *Zurriola Ibilbidea, Gros.*

WHERE TO EAT

$$$ ✕ **A Fuego Negro.** Sample experimental pintxos here like Kobe beef sliders (the house specialty), bechamel-stuffed mussels, and Basque-style pad Thai. The dim lighting, industrial decor, and rock posters attract a young, hip crowd. **Known for:** "MakCobe" beef slider; innovative pintxos; cool crowd. Ⓢ *Average main: €20* ✉ *Calle 31 de Agosto 31, Parte Vieja* ☏ ⊕ *www.afuegonegro.com* ⊘ *Closed Mon.*
TAPAS

$$$$ ✕ **Arzak.** One of the world's great culinary meccas, award-winning Arzak embodies the prestige, novelty, and science-driven creativity of the Basque culinary zeitgeist. The restaurant and its high-tech food lab—both helmed by founder Juan Mari Arzak's daughter Elena these days—are situated in the family's 19th-century home on the outskirts of San Sebastián, and though the space might not be much to look at, the ever-changing dishes are downright thrilling for their trompe-l'oeil presentations, unexpected flavor combinations, and rare ingredients. **Known for:** thrilling culinary experience; old-school hospitality; on "The World's 50 Best Restaurants" list. Ⓢ *Average main: €210* ✉ *Av. Alcalde Jose Elosegui 273, Alto de Miracruz* ☏ *94/327–8465, 94/328–5593* ⊕ *www.arzak.es* ⊘ *Closed Sun. and Mon., June 15–July 2, and 3 wks in early Nov.*
BASQUE
Fodor'sChoice
★

$ ✕ **Bar Gorriti.** Next to the open-air Brecha Market, this traditional little pintxos bar is a well-priced neighborhood standby filled with good cheer and delicious tapas. **Known for:** fabulous tortilla de bacalao; casual local crowd; simple, well-prepared Basque bites. Ⓢ *Average main: €11* ✉ *Calle San Juan 3, Parte Vieja* ☏ *94/342–8353* ⊕ *www. bargorriti.com* ⊘ *Closed Sun.*
TAPAS

$$$ ✕ **Bergara Bar.** Winner of many a miniature cuisine award, this Gros neighborhood standby offers a stylish take on traditional tapas and pintxos and also serves entrée-sized meals. **Known for:** variety of new-fangled and traditional pintxos; heavenly foie gras; trendy atmosphere. Ⓢ *Average main: €20* ✉ *Calle General Arteche 8, Gros* ☏ *94/327–5026* ⊕ *www.pinchosbergara.es.*
TAPAS

5

$$$$ ✕**Bodegón Alejandro.** Hiding in the basement of a timber building in the
BASQUE heart of the Parte Vieja, this restaurant—where Martín Berasategui cut
his teeth—toes the line between traditional and contemporary Basque
cuisine with dishes like hake in citrus sauce, filet mignon with soufflé
potatoes, and (for dessert) cheese ice cream. **Known for:** affordable and
delectable tasting menus; top-quality beef; seasonal vegetable delicacies like de lágrima peas and white asparagus. Ⓢ *Average main: €24*
✉ *Calle de Fermín Calbetón 4, Parte Vieja* ☎ *94/342–7158* ⊕ *www.
bodegonalejandro.com.*

$$$$ ✕**Casa Urola.** Don't be put off by the slightly outdated decor of this
BASQUE Parte Vieja stalwart—the kitchen at Casa Urola is easily one of the
FAMILY city's most skilled. Savor appetizers made with hard-to-find regional
Fodor'sChoice vegetables like cardoon, borage, and de lágrima peas before moving
★ onto entrées like seared squab presented with a pâté of its own liver
and roasted hake loin with white wine and clams; save room for the
signature torrija (Spanish "French" toast), crisped in brown butter
and dusted with cinnamon sugar. **Known for:** flawless Basque cuisine;
restaurant industry favorite; signature torrija. Ⓢ *Average main: €28*
✉ *Calle Fermin Calbeton 20, Parte Vieja* ☎ *94/344–1371* ⊕ *www.casau-
rolajatetxea.es* ⊘ *Closed Tues.*

$$ ✕**Ganbara.** This busy bar and restaurant near Plaza de la Constitución
TAPAS is now run by the third generation of the same family. Specialty mor-
sels range from shrimp and asparagus to acorn-fed Iberian ham on
croissants to anchovies, sea urchins, and—the house specialty—wild
mushrooms topped with an egg yolk. **Known for:** to-die-for wild mush-
rooms; traditional Basque pintxos; lively and loud atmosphere. Ⓢ *Aver-
age main: €12* ✉ *Calle San Jerónimo 21, Parte Vieja* ☎ *94/342–2575*
⊕ *www.ganbarajatetxea.com* ⊘ *Closed Mon. No dinner Sun.*

$ ✕**Goiz Argi.** The specialty of this tiny bar—and the reason locals flock
TAPAS here on weekends—is the garlicky seared shrimp brochette. **Known for:**
juicy shrimp skewers; good value; cheerful bartenders. Ⓢ *Average main:*
€8 ✉ *Fermín Calbetón 4, Parte Vieja* ☎ *94/342–5204.*

$$$$ ✕**Kokotxa Restaurante.** This simply decorated award-winning restaurant
INTERNATIONAL in the heart of the Parte Vieja hinges on chef Daniel López's clean, inno-
vative cuisine, which plays on traditional Basque and Spanish flavors
and often adds an Asian twist. Opt for a market-driven degustación
or López's classic tasting menu including signature dishes like whole
langoustine with beet rice and sweetbreads with Jerusalem artichokes
and truffles. **Known for:** award-winning dining in the city center; Asian-
inflected Basque cuisine; surprisingly casual atmosphere. Ⓢ *Average
main: €85* ✉ *Calle del Campanario 11, Parte Vieja* ☎ *94/342–1904*
⊕ *www.restaurantekokotxa.com* ⊘ *Closed Mon. No dinner Sun.*

$$$$ ✕**La Cepa.** This boisterous tavern (est. 1948) has ceilings lined with
TAPAS dangling jamones, walls covered with old photos of San Sebastián,
and a dining room packed with locals and tourists in equal measure.
Everything from the Iberian ham to the little olive-pepper-and-anchovy
combos called *penaltis* will whet your appetite; those who opt to stick
around for a full meal should order the dry-aged txuleton. **Known
for:** hand-cut Iberian ham; melt-in-your-mouth steak; amicable staff.

$ *Average main: €25* ✉ *Calle 31 de Agosto 7, Parte Vieja* ☎ *94/342–6394* ⊕ *www.barlacepa.com* ⊘ *Closed Tues. and last 2 wks in Nov.*

$$
TAPAS
Fodor'sChoice
★

✕ **La Cuchara de San Telmo.** You may have to throw an elbow or two to get into this teeming bar, but it's worth braving the sardine-can digs for outstanding pintxos like mushroom-and-Idiazabal risotto and seared foie with Basque cider compote. **Known for:** internationally inflected pintxos; constant crowds; fabulous foie. $ *Average main: €12* ✉ *Calle 31 de Agosto 28, Parte Vieja* ☎ *94/343–5446.*

$$$$
CONTEMPORARY
Fodor'sChoice
★

✕ **Martín Berasategui.** Basque chef Martín Berasategui has more Michelin stars than any other chef in Spain, and at his flagship in the dewy village of Lasarte–Oria, you'll see exactly why. Dishes are Basque at heart but prepared with exacting, French-inflected technique that comes through in dishes like artfully composed salads, elegant caviar preparations, and eel-and-foie-gras millefeuille—a Berasategui signature. **Known for:** once-in-a-lifetime dining experience; idyllic, white-tablecloth outdoor terrace; artful mix of classic and avant-garde. $ *Average main: €79* ✉ *Calle Loidi 4, 8 km (5 miles) south of San Sebastián, Lasarte* ☎ *94/336–6471, 94/336–1599* ⊕ *www.martinberasategui.com* ⊘ *Closed Mon. and Tues., and mid-Dec.–mid-Jan. No dinner Sun.*

$$$$
SPANISH

✕ **Mugaritz.** This bucolic farmhouse in the hills above Errenteria, 8 km (5 miles) northeast of San Sebastián, is a veritable laboratory of modern cooking techniques helmed by (arguably) the most experimental chef in Spain today, Andoni Aduriz. The obligatory three-hour, 20-course experience—which might be too abstract for some—includes dishes like "a sip of flowers and warm water" and "memories of a rabbit" complemented by zany wildcard wines. **Known for:** No. 9 on "The World's 50 Best" restaurant awards; abstract dishes; three-hour immersive dining experience. $ *Average main: €210* ✉ *Otzazulueta Baserria, Aldura Aldea 20, Errenteria* ☎ *94/352–2455, 94/351–8343* ⊕ *www.mugaritz.com* ⊘ *Closed Mon. and mid-Dec.–mid-Apr. No lunch Tues. No dinner Sun.*

$$$
CONTEMPORARY

✕ **Ni Neu.** Chef Mikel Gallo's Ni Neu ("Me, Myself" in Euskera), defined by its experimental comfort-food cuisine, occupies a bright corner of Rafael Moneo's dazzling Kursaal complex at the mouth of the Urumea. The eggs fried at low temperature with potatoes and codfish broth and roast monkfish with mustard seeds and tapenade are two of the most popular dishes, though lighter tapas fare is also available in the bar area. **Known for:** steal €38 tasting menu; riverside dining; traditional Basque fare with a modern twist. $ *Average main: €20* ✉ *Av. Zurriola 1, Gros* ☎ *94/300–3162* ⊕ *www.restaurantenineu.com* ⊘ *Closed Mon. No dinner Tues., Wed., and Sun.*

$$
TAPAS

✕ **Ormazabal.** You'd be hard-pressed to find a homier pintxo bar in San Sebastián: Ormazabal has been luring patrons for decades with its juicy tortillas de bacalao and burst-in-your-mouth croquetas. **Known for:** entertaining waitstaff; hole-in-the-wall local vibe; old-school dishes like spinach croquetas. $ *Average main: €15* ✉ *Calle 31 de Agosto 22, Parte Vieja* ☎ *68/663–3025.*

$$$
BASQUE

✕ **Restaurante Astelena 1997.** Chef Ander González has transformed the narrow stone rooms of a defunct banana warehouse into one of the finest spots for modern Basque dining—at a great price. The €28 weekday menú del día and €42 weekend menú de degustación hinge on what's in season, though dishes like seared txuleton and hake in white wine sauce with clams never come off the menu for a reason. **Known for:** unpretentious yet elegant Basque cuisine; fantastic seafood dishes; surprisingly good value for this part of town. [$] *Average main: €18* ✉ *Euskal Herria 3, Parte Vieja* ☎ *94/342–5867* 🌐 *www.restauranteastelena.com* ⏲ *Closed Mon. No dinner Sun. and Wed.*

$$ TAPAS FAMILY 🍴 **Restaurante La Viña.** This classic, centrally located bar is almost always crowded, drawing busloads of tour groups as well as locals, who come to try the renowned cheesecake. Enjoy a slice of this silky, creamy dessert with a cup of coffee at the wood-paneled bar, or if you're not in the mood for sweets, have one of the sumptuous pintxos—red peppers stuffed with bacalao, croquetas, or veal meatballs—with a glass of Rioja. **Known for:** cheesecake with a cult following; old-timey ambience; wide variety of classic pintxos. [$] *Average main: €15* ✉ *Calle 31 de Agosto 3, Parte Vieja* ☎ *94/342–7495* 🌐 *www.lavinarestaurante.com* ⏲ *Closed Mon.*

$$ TAPAS 🍴 **San Marcial.** Nearly a secret, downstairs in the center of town, this is a quintessentially Basque spot with big wooden tables and a monumental bar filled with *cazuelitas* (small earthenware dishes) and tapas of all kinds. **Known for:** oversize ham-and-cheese croquettes called gavillas; unfussy Basque pintxos and sandwiches; "hidden" location in the old town off the tourist track. [$] *Average main: €13* ✉ *Calle San Marcial 50, Centro* ☎ *94/343–1720* ⏲ *Closed Tues.*

$$ LATIN AMERICAN FAMILY 🍴 **Topa Sukalderia.** This buzzy Latin–Spanish fusion restaurant, opened in 2017, is the brainchild of Andoni Luis Aduriz of two-Michelin-star Mugaritz. A breath of fresh air on the local dining scene serving colorful cocktails and saucy dishes to the backdrop of Cuban jazz, Topa prides itself on making everything from scratch, from its nixtamalized tortillas to its "thousand-day" mole (originally a gift of Enrique Olvera of Pujol). **Known for:** Basque–Latin fusion cuisine; latest project by Mugaritz chef; buzziest restaurant in town. [$] *Average main: €15* ✉ *Calle Agirre Miramon 7, Gros* ☎ *94/356–9143* 🌐 *www.topasukalderia.com* ⏲ *Closed Tues.*

$$$$ BASQUE Fodor's Choice ★ 🍴 **Zelaia.** This traditional sagardotegia (Basque cider house), located 7 km (4 miles) south of San Sebastián, is where the region's top chefs—Juan Mari Arzak, Martín Berasategui, and Pedro Subijana, to name a few—ring in every cider season with a resounding *¡txotx!* ("cheers" in Basque). Removed from the tourist track and open from mid-January to late April, Zelaia invites guests into its barrel-lined warehouses to chow down on a set menu of bacalao-centric dishes, thick-cut steaks, and—for dessert—local sheep's milk cheese with quince preserves and walnuts. **Known for:** authentic cider house; food that's an echelon above other sagardotegias; unlimited cider drinking. [$] *Average main: €30* ✉ *BO Martindegi 29* ☎ *94/355–5851* 🌐 *www.zelaia.es* ⏲ *Closed late Apr.–mid-Jan. and Sun.*

$$$$ BASQUE 🍴 **Zuberoa.** Zuberoa is the kind of restaurant where the chef greets every table and meals start with an amuse-bouche of foie gras—in other words, it's an old-world slice of heaven. Market-driven meals (think roasted wild game, Basque de lágrima peas, and strawberry gazpacho) unfold to the backdrop of a 15th-century farmhouse that empties out

onto an ivy-lined patio in the summer. **Known for:** Michelin-starred old-world Basque cuisine; wonderfully hospitable chef; dining room in a 15th-century caserío. $ *Average main: €40* ⌧ *Araneder Bidea, Barrio Iturriotz, Oiartzun* ☎ *94/349–1228* ⊕ *www.zuberoa.com* ⊘ *Closed Wed., and Sun. June–Oct. No dinner Sun., and Tues. Nov.–May.*

WHERE TO STAY

$$$$ **Arrizul Congress Hotel.** This clean-cut urban hotel, located steps from
HOTEL the river and Zurriola Beach, opened in early 2017 and is has become a dependable option for families and business travelers alike. **Pros:** feels fresh and modern; triples are available; within walking distance of all the main sights. **Cons:** bad soundproofing means noisy mornings; architectural foibles make some rooms awkward; occasionally unprofessional front-desk staff. $ *Rooms from: €259* ⌧ *Calle Ronda 3, Gros* ☎ *94/332–7026* ⊕ *www.hotelarrizulcongress.com* ⟿ *46 rooms* ⋈ *No meals.*

$$$$ **Astoria7 Hotel.** Set in the renovated Astoria Cinema, some of the high-
HOTEL lights of this movie-themed hotel include an ample DVD library featuring classics like *Breakfast at Tiffany's* and Hitchcock's *The Birds,* and a spacious lobby adorned with autographed photos of the many movie stars who have attended the famous San Sebastián Film Festival over the years. **Pros:** spacious rooms; fun and campy cinematographic decor; varied, good-quality breakfast. **Cons:** 20-minute walk (or short bus ride) to beach and La Parte Vieja; not for non-cinephiles; tad overpriced. $ *Rooms from: €250* ⌧ *Calle de la Sagrada Família 1, Centro* ☎ *94/344–5000* ⊕ *www.astoria7hotel.com/en* ⟿ *102 rooms* ⋈ *No meals.*

$$$$ **Hotel de Londres y de Inglaterra.** On the main beachfront promenade
HOTEL overlooking La Kontxa, this stately hotel has a regal, old-world feel and
Fodor's Choice Belle Époque aesthetic that starts in the elegant marble lobby, with its
★ shimmering chandeliers, and continues throughout the hotel. **Pros:** hotel with best views in town; cozy and comfortable rooms; professional service. **Cons:** street side can be noisy on weekends; unremarkable and unkempt breakfast area; noticeable wear and tear. $ *Rooms from: €290* ⌧ *Zubieta 2, La Concha* ☎ *94/344–0770* ⊕ *www.hlondres.com* ⟿ *148 rooms* ⋈ *No meals.*

$$$$ **Hotel María Cristina.** The graceful beauty of the Belle Époque is embod-
HOTEL ied here, in San Sebastián's most luxurious hotel on the west bank of the Urumea, which has played hosts to countless movie stars and dignitaries since opening in 1912. **Pros:** elaborate breakfasts; old-world elegance with new-world amenities; grand historic building. **Cons:** staff can be a bit starchy; some aspects of recent renovations lack taste; drinks at the bar are expensive. $ *Rooms from: €350* ⌧ *Paseo República Argentina 4, Centro* ☎ *94/343–7600* ⊕ *www.hotel-mariacristina.com* ⟿ *136 rooms* ⋈ *No meals.*

$$$ **One Shot Tabakalera House.** Locals call this four-star newcomer a
HOTEL "hotel within a museum" because of its location inside the Tabakalera
Fodor's Choice cultural center, a hotbed of art and innovation inaugurated in 2015.
★ **Pros:** avant-garde design; located within the city's cultural center; close to the RENFE train station. **Cons:** 10-minute walk into town; no room service; no coffeemakers in most rooms. $ *Rooms from: €180* ⌧ *Paseo Duque de Mandas 52, Amara* ☎ *94/393–0028* ⊕ *www.hoteloneshot-tabakalerahouse.com* ⟿ *33 rooms* ⋈ *No meals.*

5

NIGHTLIFE AND PERFORMING ARTS

NIGHTLIFE

BARS AND PUBS **Gu.** The renovated Gu, with its floor-to-ceiling windows overlooking La Kontxa, is a glitzy indoor-outdoor cocktail bar and nightclub. ⊠ *Ijentea 9, Centro* ☎ *84/398–0775* ⊕ *www.gusansebastian.com.*

DANCE CLUBS **Bataplán.** San Sebastián's top dance club is near the western end of La Kontxa. Guest DJs and events determine the vibe, although you can count on high-energy dance music and enthusiastic drinking. ⊠ *Paseo de la Concha 10, Centro* ☎ *94/346–0439* ⊕ *www.bataplandisco.com.*

Disco Friends. Ever since this club opened in 2016, it's attracted a stylish twenty- and thirtysomething crowd with electro-pop music and strong drinks. ⊠ *Blvd. Zumardia 27, Parte Vieja* ☎ *66/393–0598* ⊕ *www. friendsdisco.com.*

MUSIC CLUBS **Akerbeltz.** This feel-good dive bar is a perfect late-night refuge for music and drinks. ⊠ *Calle Mari 19, Parte Vieja* ☎ *94/346–0934, 94/345–1452.*

Fodor'sChoice ★ **BE Club.** Formerly known as Bebop, this San Sebastián classic—which eschews the usual Top 40 in favor of Latin, jazz, and unconventional dance tunes—got a major face-lift in 2018 and is all the better for it. ⊠ *Paseo de Salamanca 3, Parte Vieja* ☎ *94/347–8505.*

PERFORMING ARTS

Kursaal. Home of the Orquesta Sinfónica (Symphony Orchestra) de Euskadi, this venue is also a favorite for ballet, opera, theater, and jazz. ⊠ *Av. de la Zurriola 1, Gros* ☎ *94/300–3000* ⊕ *www.kursaal.eus.*

Teatro Victoria Eugenia. In a stunning 19th-century building, this elegant venue offers varied programs of theater, dance, and more. ⊠ *Paseo de la República Argentina 2, Centro* ☎ *94/348–1160* ⊕ *www.victoriaeugenia.eus.*

SHOPPING

San Sebastián is a busy shopping town. Wander Calle San Martín and the surrounding pedestrian-only streets to see what's in the windows.

Alboka Artesanía. This is the best city-center shop for Basque-made artisanry such as patterned tablecloths and linens, jai-alai balls, ceramics, and traditional dress. ⊠ *Pl. Constitución 8, Parte Vieja* ☎ *94/342–6300* ⊕ *www.albokaartesania.com.*

Casa Ponsol. The best place to buy Basque berets—the Leclerq family has been hatting (and clothing) the local male population for four generations, since 1838. ⊠ *Calle Narrica 4 at Calle Sarriegui 3, Parte Vieja* ☎ *94/342–0876* ⊕ *www.casaponsol.com.*

Elkar. This bookstore is one of the city's best. There's a decent selection of English-language books as well as CDs, games, and stationery. ⊠ *Calle Fermin Calbeton 21, Parte Vieja* ☎ *94/342–0080* ⊕ *www.elkar. com.*

Kado. Pop into this Nordic-inspired boutique for furniture, kitchenware, and splashy artwork. ⊠ *Calle Alfonso VIII 3, Centro* ☎ *94/305–0393* ⊕ *www.kadodecoracion.com.*

The Plaza de la Virgen Blanca is surrounded by impressive buildings.

Mimo. This posh gourmet food and wine shop also hosts Basque cooking classes and food tours in English. ✉ *Calle Okendo 1, Centro* ☎ *94/342–1143* ⊕ *www.mimofood.com.*

VITORIA-GASTEIZ

62 km (39 miles) south of Bilbao, 100 km (62 miles) west of Pamplona.

The capital of the Basque Country, and the region's second-largest city after Bilbao, Vitoria-Gasteiz might be Euskadi's least "Basque" city, at least to the naked eye, since it's neither a seafaring port nor a mountain enclave. It sprawls, instead, over the steppelike *meseta de Álava* (Álava plain) and functions as a modern industrial center with plentiful cultural events, fine restaurants, and museums. The city also boasts a strikingly well-preserved Casco Medieval (Medieval Quarter). Founded by Sancho el Sabio (the Wise) in 1181, the urban center was built largely of granite, so Vitoria's oldest streets and squares seem especially weathered and ancient.

GETTING AROUND

Take the A1 and the PA34 from Pamplona, which takes one hour by car; buses also run regularly between the two cities. From Bilbao, you should take the AP68 and N622, which takes just 44 minutes. Vitoria is a spread-out city, but the area you'll spend your time in is small, only about 1 km (½ mile) square, and easily walked.

Bus Station Estación de Autobuses de Vitoria–Gasteiz. ✉ *Pl. de Euskaltzaindia s/n* ☎ *94/516–1666* ⊕ *www.vitoria-gasteiz.org.*

VISITOR INFORMATION

Contacts Vitoria–Gasteiz. ⊠ *Pl. España 1* ☏ *94/516–1598* ⊕ *www.vitoria-gasteiz.org.*

EXPLORING

Fodor'sChoice
★
Artium. Officially named the Centro-Museo Vasco de Arte Contemporáneo, this former bus station was reopened as a museum in 2002 by former king Juan Carlos, who called it "the third leg of the Basque art triangle, along with the Bilbao Guggenheim and San Sebastián's Chillida Leku." The museum's permanent collection—including 20th- and 21st-century paintings and sculptures by Jorge Oteiza, Chillida, Agustín Ibarrola, and Nestor Basterretxea, among many others—makes it one of Spain's finest treasuries of contemporary art. ⊠ *Calle Francia 24* ☏ *94/520–9020* ⊕ *www.artium.org* ⊡ *€5 (by donation Wed. and weekends following exhibition openings)* ⊘ *Closed Mon.*

Bibat. The 1525 Palacio de Bendaña and adjoining bronze-plated building are home to one of Vitoria's main attractions, the Bibat, which combines the Museo Fournier de Naipes (Playing-Card Museum) with the Museo de Arqueología. The project, by Navarran architect Patxi Mangado, is a daring combination of old and new architecture dubbed "the chest" because of its dark facade. The palacio houses the playing-card collection of Don Heraclio Fournier, who, in 1868, founded a playing-card factory, started amassing cards, and eventually found himself with 15,000 sets, the largest and finest such collection in the world. As you survey rooms of hand-painted cards, the distinction between artwork and game piece is quickly scrambled. The oldest sets date to the 12th century, making them older than the building, and the story parallels the history of printing. The most unusual and finely painted sets come from Japan, India (the Indian cards are round), and the international practice of tarot. The Museo de la Arqueología, in the newest building, has paleolithic dolmens, Roman art and artifacts, medieval objects, and the famous Stele del Jinete (Stele of the Horseback Rider), an early Basque tombstone. ⊠ *Calle Cuchillería 54* ☏ *94/520–3707* ⊡ *Free.*

Fodor'sChoice
★
Catedral de Santa María. Dating back to the 14th century, the cathedral is currently being restored but is still open to visitors—in fact, that's part of the fun. Tour guides hand out protective hard hats and show you around the restoration site. It's a unique opportunity to study the building's architecture from the foundation up. A prominent and active supporter of the project is British novelist Ken Follett, whose novel *World Without End* is about the construction of the cathedral. A statue of the author has been placed on one side of the cathedral. ⊠ *Pl. Santa Maria s/n* ☏ *94/525–5135* ⊕ *www.catedralvitoria.com* ⊡ *From €9.*

Museo de Bellas Artes (*Museum of Fine Arts*). Paintings by Ribera, Picasso, and the Basque painter Zuloaga are among the collection that hangs in this gorgeous baroque building. ⊠ *Paseo Fray Francisco 8* ☏ *94/518–1918* ⊡ *Free* ⊘ *Closed Mon.*

Plaza de España. Across Virgen Blanca, past the monument and the handsome Victoria café, this is an arcaded neoclassical square with the austere elegance typical of formal 19th-century squares all over Spain.

Fodor'sChoice
★

Street Art. In a city as noble and staid as Vitoria, you don't expect to find world-class street art, but that's precisely what's been drawing more and more tourists and artsy types to the parallel streets of Anorbin and Carnicerías in the old town. Feast your eyes on multistory, thought-provoking murals depicting family scenes, landscapes, and political issues. ⊠ *Cantón Anorbin, Vitoria.*

WHERE TO EAT

$$$
SPANISH
Fodor'sChoice
★

✕ **El Portalón.** With dark, creaky wood floors and staircases, bare brick walls, and ancient beams, pillars, and coats of arms, this 15th-century inn turns out classical Castilian and Basque specialties that reflect Vitoria's geography and social history. Try the *cochinillo lechal asado* (grilled suckling pig) or any of the *rape* (monkfish) preparations. **Known for:** 15th-century dining room; Basque comfort food; deep wine list. ⓢ *Average main: €22* ⊠ *Calle Correría 147, Vitoria* 🕾 *94/514–2755* ⊕ *www.restauranteelportalon.com* ⊗ *No dinner Sun.*

$$$
BASQUE
Fodor'sChoice
★

✕ **La Bodeguilla Lanciego.** This inviting white-tablecloth taberna (est. 1959) serves soul-satisfying cuisine in a rustic-chic dining room decorated with taupe curtains, blond-wood chairs, and original artwork. Steak frites are the go-to here with roast turbot coming in a close second. **Known for:** subtle, tasteful decor; excellent chuleta (steak frites); young, motivated staff. ⓢ *Average main: €19* ⊠ *Calle Olagibel 60, Vitoria* 🕾 *94/525–0073* ⊕ *www.labodeguillalanciego.com* ⊗ *Closed Sun.*

$$
TAPAS

✕ **Sagartoki.** This cathedral-like bar serves eclectic Basque bar food by local celebrity chef Senén González in an industrial, modern space. Don't miss the signature *huevo frito,* not really a "fried egg" but rather a crisp, yolky potato raviolo. **Known for:** swanky modern barroom; fantastic "huevo frito" and potato omelet tapas; solid cocktails. ⓢ *Average main: €17* ⊠ *Calle del Prado 18* 🕾 *94/528–8676* ⊕ *www.sagartoki.com.*

$$
TAPAS

✕ **Toloño.** It would be easy to walk past this deceptively simple-looking bar, which has the look of a minimalist American diner with shiny white plastic chairs and a sleek wood bar top. Don't be fooled—behind this unassuming exterior hides one of Vitoria's culinary jewels, which has won a plethora of awards for its innovative pintxos including signature dishes *txangurro gratinado* (crab gratin), *ravioli de conejo* (rabbit ravioli), and *manitas de cerdo con aceite de trufa blanco* (pigs' trotters in white truffle oil). **Known for:** worth-the-wait creative pintxos; hidden-gem bar; pristine seafood dishes. ⓢ *Average main: €15* ⊠ *Cuesta San Francisco 3* 🕾 *94/523–3336* ⊕ *www.tolonobar.com.*

WHERE TO STAY

$$$
HOTEL

🛏 **Hotel & Spa Etxegana.** On top of a mountain in the heart of Basque country's "little Switzerland" 20 minutes north of Vitoria-Gasteiz and 40 minutes south of Bilbao, this relaxing retreat features breathtaking views of the surrounding mountains and an excellent restaurant and spa. **Pros:** stunning views; surrounded by nature; family run and welcoming. **Cons:** half-hour drive to town; it's used as a wedding venue; Wi-Fi could be better in some rooms. ⓢ *Rooms from: €149* ⊠ *Ipiñaburu 38* 🕾 *94/633–8448* ⊕ *www.etxegana.com* ⮠ *18 rooms* ⅏ *Free Breakfast.*

5

$$ **La Casa de los Arquillos.** Brightly lit, with clean Scandinavian design,
B&B/INN this well-priced, adorable bed-and-breakfast has the best location in
Fodor'sChoice town, just steps from the central Plaza de España de Vitoria. **Pros:**
★ unbeatable location; good breakfast; hygge galore. **Cons:** rooms are
up two flights of stairs; no convenient parking; no 24-hour reception.
$ *Rooms from: €120 ⊠ Paseo los Arquillos 1 ☎ 94/515–1259 ⊕ www.
lacasadelosarquillos.com ⇱ 8 rooms ⦿ Free Breakfast.*

$$ **Parador de Argómaniz.** This 17th-century palace has panoramic views
HOTEL over the Álava plains and retains a powerful sense of mystery and
romance, with long stone hallways punctuated by imposing antiques.
Pros: contemporary rooms and comforts; gorgeous details and surroundings; excellent restaurant. **Cons:** isolated—about a 15-minute
drive from Vitoria; no patio furniture on guest-room balconies; noisy
radiators might wake you up. $ *Rooms from: €120 ⊠ Calle del Parador
14, N1, Km 363, Argómaniz ✛ East of Vitoria off N104 toward Pamplona ☎ 94/529–3200 ⊕ www.parador.es ⇱ 53 rooms ⦿ No meals.*

LAGUARDIA

45 km (28 miles) south of Vitoria

Founded in AD 908 to stand guard—as its name suggests—over
Navarra's southwestern flank, Laguardia is situated on a promontory
overlooking the Río Ebro and the vineyards of La Rioja Alavesa wine
country. The peaceful medieval town is an ideal outpost for vineyard-
hopping travelers.

VISITOR INFORMATION

Contacts Laguardia Tourist Office. ⊠ *Casa Garcetas, Calle Mayor 52*
☎ *94/560–0845 ⊕ www.laguardia-alava.com.*

EXPLORING

Starting from the 15th-century Puerta de Carnicerías, or Puerta Nueva,
the central portal off the parking area on the east side of town, the first
landmark is the 16th-century **Ayuntamiento,** with its imperial shield of
Carlos V. Farther into the square is the current town hall, built in the
19th century. A right turn down Calle Santa Engracia takes you past
impressive facades—the floor inside the portal at No. 25 is a lovely
stone mosaic, and a walk behind the triple-emblazoned 17th-century
facade of No. 19 reveals a stagecoach, floor mosaics, wood beams, and
an inner porch. The Puerta de Santa Engracia, with an image of the
saint in an overhead niche, opens out to the right, and on the left, at
the entrance to Calle Víctor Tapia, No. 17 bears a coat of arms with
the Latin phrase "Laus Tibi" (Praise Be to Thee).

Bodega El Fabulista. This family-run bodega is famed for its down-to-
earth, approachable tours, which take place in the 16th-century cavas
below Laguardia and are followed by a tasting of two wines for €7.
⊠ *Pl. San Juan ☎ 94/562–1192 ⊕ www.bodegaelfabulista.com ⊠ €7
⊘ Closed Sun.*

Bodegas Baigorri. This sleek, modern winery is an architectural wonder of glass and steel with floor-to-ceiling windows that overlook the
vineyards and a state-of-the-art multilevel wine cellar. The two-hour

morning tour ends around 2 pm—the perfect time to book lunch at the upstairs restaurant. The tasting menu pairs the three-course menu with four signature wines for just €50 and is highly recommended. ✉ *Ctra. Vitoria–Logroño, Km 53, Logroño* ☎ *94/560–9420* 🌐 *www.bodegasbaigorri.com.*

Casa de la Primicia. Laguardia's oldest civil structure, the 15th-century Casa de la Primicia is where tithes of fresh fruit were collected in medieval times. Visit the restored underground bodega, where tours include wine tastings. ✉ *Calle Páganos 78* ☎ *94/562–1266, 94/560–0296* 🌐 *www.bodegascasaprimicia.com* 🎫 *€10.*

Eguren Ugarte. The family behind this majestic winery has been in the wine-making business for five generations. Surrounded by vineyards on all sides, the tour showcases traditional wine making at its best, and is followed by a tasting of three–five exceptional wines and a pintxo for €10. ✉ *Ctra. A124, Km 61, Páganos* ☎ *94/560–0766* 🌐 *www.egurenugarte.com/en* 🎫 *€10.*

5

Fodor's Choice ★ **Herederos de Marqués de Riscal.** The village of Elciego, 6 km (4 miles) southeast of Laguardia, is the site of the historic Marqués de Riscal winery. Tours of the vineyards—among the most legendary in La Rioja—as well as the cellars are conducted in various languages, including English. Reservations are required. The estate also includes the stunning Frank Gehry–designed **Hotel Marqués de Riscal,** crafted out of waves of metal reminiscent of his Guggenheim Bilbao. ✉ *Calle Torrea 1, Elciego* ☎ *94/560–6000* 🌐 *www.marquesderiscal.com* 🎫 *€16, includes tour and tasting of 2 wines.*

Juanjo San Pedro. This gallery is filled with colorful paintings of landscapes and rural life by local artist Juanjo San Pedro. ✉ *Calle Mayor 5* ☎ *65/892–8580* 🌐 *www.juanjosanpedro.es* 🎫 *Free.*

Santa María de los Reyes. Laguardia's architectural crown jewel is Spain's only Gothic polychrome portal on this church. Protected by a posterior Renaissance facade, the door centers on a lovely, lifelike effigy of La Virgen de los Reyes (Virgin of the Kings), sculpted in the 14th century and painted in the 17th by Ribera. To see it, ask at the tourist office. ✉ *Calle Mayor 52* ☎ *94/560–0845.*

WHERE TO STAY

$$$$ HOTEL 🏨 **Hospedería de los Parajes.** The crown jewel of this quirky hotel is the 16th-century wine cave, which has been converted into a vinoteca with traditional wooden tables—to which each guest is invited to try a glass of wine upon checking in. **Pros:** charming wine cellar; centrally located; cozy, grandmotherly digs. **Cons:** rooms lack light; Wi-Fi spotty in some rooms; expensive and remote parking. [$] *Rooms from: €195* ✉ *Calle Mayor 46–48* ☎ *94/562–1130* 🌐 *www.hospederiadelosparajes.com* 🛏 *18 rooms* 🍴 *Free Breakfast.*

$$$ HOTEL 🏨 **Hotel Castillo El Collado.** Guests are treated like royalty in this castlelike 18th-century manor house. **Pros:** old-world European feel; close to the heart of town; website features every room so you can ask for a specific one. **Cons:** spotty Wi-Fi in some rooms; underwhelming breakfast; maintenance could be improved. [$] *Rooms from: €138* ✉ *Paseo El Collado 1* ☎ *94/562–1200* 🌐 *www.hotelcollado.com* 🛏 *10 rooms* 🍴 *No meals.*

$$$$ HOTEL Fodor's Choice ★ **Hotel Marqués de Riscal.** Frank Gehry's post-Guggenheim hotel concept looks as if a colony from outer space had taken up residence (or crashed) in the middle of one of La Rioja's oldest vineyards. **Pros:** dazzling architecture; five-star environment; superb dining. **Cons:** wildly expensive; interiors are drab in comparison to the exterior; service isn't always five-star. [$] *Rooms from: €410* ✉ *Calle Torrea 1, 6 km (4 miles) southwest of Laguardia, Elciego* ☎ *94/518–0880* 🌐 *www.hotel-marquesderiscal.com* 🛏 *43 rooms* 🍴 *Free Breakfast.*

$$$ HOTEL **Hotel Viura.** The sharp angles and bright colors of this architecturally avant-garde luxury hotel cut a striking contrast to the traditional pueblo surrounding it, and the location—12 km (7 miles) west of Laguardia in the sleepy village of Villabuena de Álava—makes it an good base for exploring La Rioja Alavesa and neighboring Rioja Alta. **Pros:** quirky, instagrammable architecture; rooftop gym and bar; king-size beds. **Cons:** not much to do or see in the village; no spa; soundproofing could be improved. [$] *Rooms from: €165* ✉ *Calle Mayor s/n* ☎ *94/560–9000* 🌐 *www.hotelviura.com* 🛏 *33 rooms* 🍴 *No meals.*

$$ HOTEL Fodor's Choice ★ **Posada Mayor de Migueloa.** This 17th-century palace transports you back in time with its stone floors and rough-hewn ceiling beams, but don't be fooled—modern comforts, like a terrific on-site tavern (get the Riojana-style potatoes), comfortable beds, and soft white linens abound. **Pros:** rustic-chic rooms; off-season specials; restaurant that's a destination in itself. **Cons:** in a pedestrianized area a long way from your car; rooms on the front side exposed to boisterous racket on weekends; no Wi-Fi in some rooms. [$] *Rooms from: €105* ✉ *Calle Mayor de Migueloa 20* ☎ *94/560–0187* 🌐 *www.mayordemigueloa.com* 🕒 *Closed Jan. 8–Feb. 8* 🛏 *8 rooms* 🍴 *Breakfast.*

PASAIA

7 km (4 miles) east of San Sebastián.

Three towns make up the commercial port of Pasaia (Rentería in Spanish): **Pasai Antxo** (Pasajes Ancho), an industrial port; **Pasai de San Pedro** (Pasajes de San Pedro), a large fishing harbor; and historic **Pasai Donibane** (Pasajes de San Juan), a colorful cluster of 16th- and 17th-century buildings. The most scenic way in is via Pasai de San Pedro, on the San Sebastián side of the strait: Catch a five-minute launch across the mouth of the harbor (€0.70 one way, €1.40 round-trip).

In 1777, at the age of 20, General Lafayette set out from Pasai Donibane to aid the American Revolution. Victor Hugo spent the summer of 1843 here writing his *Voyage aux Pyrénées*. The **Victor Hugo House** is the home of the tourist office; the exhibit *Victor Hugo, Traveling Down the Memory* features drawings and documents that belonged to the writer. **Albaola Factory,** a center of maritime culture, is directed by Xabier Agote, who taught boatbuilding in Rockland, Maine.

GETTING HERE AND AROUND

Pasaia Donibane can be reached via Pasai de San Pedro from San Sebastián by cab or bus. Or, if you prefer to go on foot, follow the red-and-white-blazed GR trail that begins at the east end of the Zurriola beach—you're in for a spectacular three-hour hike along the rocky coast. By car, take N1 toward France and, after passing Juan Mari Arzak's eponymous restaurant, at Alto de Miracruz, look for a marked left turn into "Pasai de San Pedro."

TOURS

FAMILY **Mater Museoa** (*Mater Ship Museum*). A former Basque fishing boat now offers tours of the port, visits to a rowing club, and to the Victor Hugo House in Pasai Donibane, as well as a treasure hunt for young and old alike. You can join a one-hour trip or rent the ship out for the whole day (for groups of 10 or more); book ahead, online or by phone. ⊠ *Muelle Pesquero, Pasai de San Pedro, Pasai Donibane* ☎ *61/981–4225* ⊕ *www.matermuseoa.com* 🎟 *€7.*

VISITOR INFORMATION

Contacts Pasaia Tourist Office. ⊠ *Victor Hugo House, Donibane 63, Pasai Donibane* ☎ *94/334–1556* ⊕ *www.oarsoaldea-turismo.net.*

WHERE TO EAT

$$$$ ✕ **Casa Cámara.** Four generations ago, Pablo Cámara turned this 19th-
SEAFOOD century fishing wharf on the Pasaia narrows into a first-class seafood
Fodor'sChoice restaurant. The low-ceilinged dining room has lovely views over the
★ shipping lane and a central "live" tank that rises and falls with the tide and from which lobsters and crayfish can be hauled up for your inspection. **Known for:** pier-side dining; pristine shellfish; quaint, old-timey ambience. 💲 *Average main: €46* ⊠ *Calle San Juan 79, Pasai Donibane* ☎ *94/352–3699* ⊕ *www.casacamara.com* ☉ *Closed Mon., and Wed. Nov.–Easter wk. No dinner Sun.*

HONDARRIBIA

20 km (13 miles) east of Pasaia.

Hondarribia (Fuenterrabía in Spanish) is the last fishing port before the French border and a wonderful day trip from San Sebastián. Lined with fishermen's homes and small fishing boats, the harbor is a scenic if slightly touristy spot. If you have a taste for history, follow signs up the hill to the medieval bastion and onetime castle of Carlos V, now a parador, and keep your eye out for coats of arms emblazoned on the corners of old buildings (as opposed to above entryways)—an Hondarribia peculiarity

VISITOR INFORMATION

Contacts Hondarribia Tourist Office. ⊠ *Pl. de Armas 9* ☎ *94/364–3677* ⊕ *www.bidasoaturismo.com.*

WHERE TO EAT AND STAY

$$$$ ✕ **Alameda.** The three Txapartegi brothers—Mikel, Kepa, and Gorka—
BASQUE are the star chefs behind this restaurant, which opened in 1997 after the brothers' apprenticeship with, among others, Martín Berasategui. The elegantly restored house (and its sunny terrace) in upper Hondarribia is a delight, as are the seasonally rotated combinations of carefully chosen ingredients, from fish to duck to vegetables. **Known for:** Michelin-starred dining; freshest seafood and meats; scenic seaside environs. 💲 *Average main: €50* ⊠ *Calle Minasoroeta 1* ☎ *94/364–2789* ⊕ *www.restaurantealameda.net* ☉ *No dinner Sun., and Mon. and Tues. late Dec.–early Feb.*

5

$$$ SEAFOOD Fodor's Choice ★ 🍴 **Hermandad de Pescadores.** One of the Basque country's most historic and typical fishermen's guilds, this central restaurant exudes tradition. At simple wooden tables and a handsome mahogany bar, local volunteers serve up simple, hearty fare—think sopa de pescado, *mejillones* (mussels), and the *almejas a la marinera* (clams in a thick, garlicky sauce)—at better than reasonable prices. **Known for:** dayboat fish; affordable top-quality seafood—a rarity in the region; homey, unfussy dining room. [$] *Average main: €20* ✉ *Calle Zuloaga 12* ☎ *94/364–2738* ⏲ *Closed Mon., and Christmas–Jan., 1 wk in May, and 1 wk in Oct. No dinner Sun.*

$ B&B/INN FAMILY 🏨 **Casa Artzu.** Better hosts than this warm, friendly clan are hard to find, and their 13th-century family house and renovated barn offer modern accommodations overlooking the Bidasoa estuary and the Atlantic. **Pros:** good value; friendly-family; free parking. **Cons:** credit cards not accepted; breakfast €3 extra; need a car to get to the beach. [$] *Rooms from: €47* ✉ *Barrio Montaña* ☎ *94/364–0530* 🌐 *www.casa-artzu.com* 💳 *No credit cards* 🛏 *6 rooms* 🍽 *No meals.*

$$$$ HOTEL FAMILY Fodor's Choice ★ 🏨 **Parador de Hondarribia.** You can live like a medieval lord in this 10th-century bastion, home in the 16th century to Spain's founding emperor, Carlos V—hence its alternative name: Parador El Emperador. **Pros:** great sea views; cozy old-fashioned rooms; terrific breakfasts. **Cons:** no restaurant; no AC (but ceiling fans); expensive parking. [$] *Rooms from: €290* ✉ *Pl. de Armas 14* ☎ *94/364–5500* 🌐 *www.parador.es* 🛏 *36 rooms* 🍽 *No meals.*

NAVARRA AND PAMPLONA

Bordering the French Pyrenees and populated largely by Basques, Navarra grows progressively less Basque toward its southern and eastern edges. Pamplona, the ancient Navarran capital, draws crowds with its annual feast of San Fermín, but medieval Vitoria, the Basque capital city in the province of Álava, is largely undiscovered by tourists. Olite, south of Pamplona, has a storybook castle. The towns of Puente la Reina and Estella are visually indelible stops on the Camino de Santiago.

PAMPLONA

79 km (47 miles) southeast of San Sebastián.

Pamplona (Iruña in Euskera) is known worldwide for its running of the bulls, made famous by Ernest Hemingway in his 1926 novel, *The Sun Also Rises*. The occasion is the festival of San Fermín, July 6–14, when Pamplona's population triples (along with its hotel rates), so reserve rooms months in advance. Every morning at 8 sharp a rocket is shot off, and the bulls kept overnight in the corrals at the edge of town are run through a series of closed-off streets leading to the bullring, a nearly 2,800-foot dash. Running among them are Spaniards and foreigners feeling audacious (or foolhardy) enough to risk getting gored. The degree of peril in the thrilling *encierro* (running, literally "enclosing") is difficult to gauge. Serious injuries occur nearly every day during the

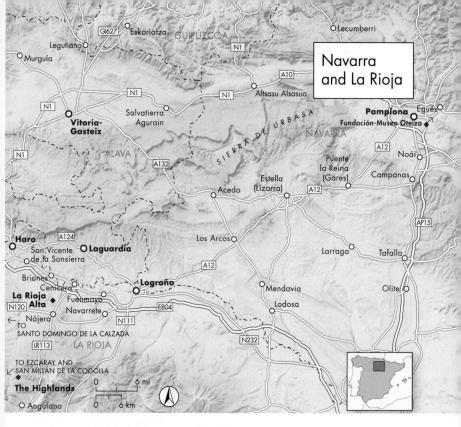

festival; deaths are rare but always a possibility. After the bulls' frantic gallop through town, every one of them is killed in the bullring, a fact that draws ire from many anti-bullfighting Spaniards and animal rights groups. Running is free, but tickets to *corridas* (bullfights) can be difficult to get.

Founded by the Roman emperor Pompey as Pompaelo, or Pampeiopolis, Pamplona was successively taken by the Franks, the Goths, and the Moors. In 750, the Pamplonians put themselves under the protection of Charlemagne and managed to expel the Arabs temporarily. But the foreign commander took advantage of this trust to destroy the city walls; when he was driven out once more by the Moors, the Navarrese took their revenge, ambushing and slaughtering the retreating Frankish army as it fled over the Pyrenees through the mountain pass of Roncesvalles in 778. This is the episode depicted in the 11th-century *Song of Roland*, although its anonymous French poet cast the aggressors as Moors. For centuries after that, Pamplona remained three argumentative towns until they were forcibly incorporated into one city by Carlos III (the Noble, 1387–1425) of Navarra.

GETTING HERE AND AROUND

Bus Station Estación de Autobuses de Pamplona. ⊠ *Av. de Yanguas y Miranda 2* ☎ *90/202–3651* ⊕ *www.estaciondeautobusesdepamplona.com.*

Car Rentals Europcar. ⊠ *Blanca de Navarra Hotel, Av. Pío XII 43* ☎ *94/817–2523* ⊕ *www.europcar.com* ⊠ *Aeropuerto de Pamplona (Noain), Ctra. Bellaterra s/n* ☎ *94/831–2798* ⊕ *www.europcar.com.*

Train Information Estación de Pamplona. ⊠ *Pl. de la Estación 1* ☎ *90/232–0320, 90/243–2343* ⊕ *www.renfe.com.*

VISITOR INFORMATION

Contacts Pamplona Tourist Office. ⊠ *Calle San Saturnino 2* ☎ *94/842–0700* ⊕ *www.turismodepamplona.es.*

EXPLORING

Archivo Real y General de Navarra. This Rafael Moneo–designed structure of glass and stone, ingeniously contained within a Romanesque palace, is Pamplona's architectural treasure. Containing papers and parchments going back to the 9th century, the archive holds more than 75,000 linear feet of documents and has room for more than 55,500 feet more. The library and reading rooms are lined with cherrywood and topped with a gilded ceiling. ⊠ *Calle Dos de Mayo s/n* ☎ *84/842–4667, 84/842–4623* ⊕ *www.cfnavarra.es/agn* ⊠ *Free* ⊙ *Closed weekends.*

QUICK BITES

Café Iruña. Pamplona's gentry has been flocking to this ornate, French-style café since 1888, but Ernest Hemingway made it part of world literary lore in *The Sun Also Rises* in 1926. You can still have a drink with a bronze version of the author in his favorite perch at the far end of the bar, or enjoy views of the plaza from a table on the terrace. **Known for:** Hemingway haunt; chocolate con churros; €16 menú del día. ⊠ *Pl. del Castillo 44* ☎ *94/822–2064* ⊕ *www.cafeiruna.com.*

Cathedral. This is one of the most important religious buildings in northern Spain, thanks to the fragile grace and gabled Gothic arches of its cloister. Inside are the tombs of Carlos III and his wife, marked by an alabaster sculpture. The **Museo Catedralicio Diocesano** (Diocesan Museum) houses religious art from the Middle Ages and the Renaissance. Call in advance for guided tours in English. ⊠ *Calle Curia s/n* ☎ *94/821–2594* ⊕ *www.catedraldepamplona.com* ⊠ *€5* ⊙ *Museum closed Sun.*

Ciudadela. Take an evening *paseo* (stroll) with locals through this central parkland of promenades and pools on the site of an ancient fortress. ⊠ *Pamplona.*

Museo de Navarra. In a 16th-century building once used as a hospital for pilgrims on their way to Santiago de Compostela, this museum has a collection of regional archaeological artifacts and historical costumes. ⊠ *Cuesta de Santo Domingo 47* ☎ *84/842–6493* ⊠ *€2 (free Sat. afternoon and Sun.)* ⊙ *Closed Mon.*

Museo Universidad de Navarra. Designed by local celebrity architect Rafael Moneo, this contemporary art museum opened in 2014 on the University of Navarra Campus. It has an exceptional photograph collection dating to the birth of photography as an art form, and the permanent art collection features classic works by Rothko, Picasso,

Kandinsky, and Tàpies. ✉ *Campus Universitario, Calle Universidad* ☎ *94/842–5700* 🌐 *www.museo.unav.edu* 🎫 *€5.*

Plaza del Castillo. One of Pamplona's greatest charms is the warren of narrow streets near the Plaza del Castillo (especially Calle San Nicolás) filled with restaurants, taverns, and bars. ✉ *Pamplona.*

OFF THE BEATEN PATH

Fundación–Museo Oteiza. East of Pamplona on the road toward France, this museum dedicated to the father of modern Basque art is a must-visit. Jorge Oteiza (1908–2003), in his seminal treatise, *Quosque Tandem,* called for Basque artists to find an aesthetic of their own instead of attempting to become part of the Spanish canon. Rejecting ornamentation in favor of essential form and a noninvasive use of space, Oteiza created a school of artists of which the sculptor Eduardo Chillida (1924–2002) was the most famous. The building itself, Oteiza's home for more than two decades, is a large cube of earth-colored concrete designed by Oteiza's longtime friend, Pamplona architect Francisco Javier Sáenz de Oiza. The sculptor's living quarters, his studio and laboratory, and the workshop used for teaching divide the museum into three sections. ✉ *Calle de la Cuesta 7, Ctra. N150 east for 8 km (5 miles) to Alzuza* ☎ *94/833–2074* 🌐 *www.museooteiza.org* 🎫 *€4 (free Fri.)* 🕒 *Closed Mon.*

5

WHERE TO EAT

$$$$ SPANISH

🍴 **Errejota.** This warm, family-run restaurant (previously called Josetxo) in a stately mansion with a classically elegant interior is one of Pamplona's foremost addresses for refined cuisine. There's something for everyone on the diverse, internationally inflected menu, whose highlights include baby artichokes with langoustine tails and monkfish with black-olive vinaigrette and soy-anchovy mayonnaise. **Known for:** modern Navarrese cuisine; old-world white-tablecloth dining room; standout artichokes. [$] *Average main: €26* ✉ *Pl. Príncipe de Viana 1* ☎ *94/822–2097* 🌐 *www.errejota.es* 🕒 *Closed Sun. (except during San Fermín), and Easter wk and Aug.*

$$$$ SPANISH

🍴 **Europa Restaurante.** The Europa, Pamplona's finest restaurant, in the hotel of the same name, offers refined, Michelin-starred Navarran cooking. The small and light first-floor dining room offers the perfect backdrop to dishes like slow-cooked lamb and pork, or the best bacalao al pil pil you may try on your trip. À la carte dining is reasonably priced, and there are excellent tasting menus available for €42, €62, and €78. **Known for:** seasonal vegetable dishes; nicest restaurant in town; affordable tasting menus. [$] *Average main: €27* ✉ *Calle Espoz y Mina 11* ☎ *94/822–1800* 🌐 *www.hreuropa.com* 🕒 *Closed Sun.*

$ TAPAS Fodor's Choice ★

🍴 **Gaucho.** This legendary tavern, which remains surprisingly calm even during San Fermín, serves some of the best tapas in Pamplona. Opt for classics like garlicky mushroom brochettes and jamón-filled croquetas, or spring for more modern creations such as seared goose liver on toast or almond-encrusted morcilla. **Known for:** delectable foie gras; delicious tapas for all budgets; old-timey atmosphere. [$] *Average main: €8* ✉ *Calle Espoz y Mina 7* ☎ *94/822–5073* 🌐 *www.cafebargaucho.com.*

Running with the Bulls

In *The Sun Also Rises*, Hemingway describes the Pamplona *encierro* (bull running) in anything but romantic terms. Jake Barnes hears the rocket, steps out onto his balcony, and watches the crowd run by: men in white with red sashes and neckerchiefs. "One man fell, rolled to the gutter, and lay quiet." It's a textbook move—an experienced runner who falls remains motionless (bulls respond to movement)—and first-rate observation and reporting. In the next chapter, a man is gored and dies. The waiter at Café Iruña mutters, "You hear? Muerto. Dead. He's dead. With a horn through him. All for morning fun." Despite this risk—and humanitarian concerns—generations of Americans and other internationals have turned this barnyard bull-management maneuver into one of the Western world's most famous rites of passage.

THE RUNNING COURSE
At daybreak, six fighting bulls are guided through the streets by 8–10 *cabestros,* or steers (also known as *mansos,* meaning "tame ones"), to the holding pens at the bullring, from which they will emerge later to fight. The course covers 2,706 feet. The Cuesta de Santo Domingo down to the corrals is the most dangerous part of the run, high in terror and short in distance. The walls are sheer, and the bulls pass quickly. The fear here is of a bull hooking along the wall of the Military Hospital on his way up the hill, forcing runners out in front of the speeding pack in a classic hammer-and-anvil movement. Mercaderes is next, cutting left for about 300 feet by the town hall, then right up Calle Estafeta. The outside of each turn and the centrifugal force of 22,000 pounds of bulls and steers are to be avoided

here. Calle Estafeta is the bread and butter of the run, the longest (about 1,200 feet), straightest, and least complicated part of the course.

THE CLASSIC RUN
The classic run, a perfect blend of form and function, is to remain ahead of the horns for as long as possible, fading to the side when overtaken. The long gallop up Calle Estafeta is the place to try to do it. The trickiest part is splitting your vision so that with one eye you keep track of the bulls behind you and with the other you avoid falling over runners ahead of you.

At the end of Estafeta the course descends left through the *callejón,* or narrow tunnel, into the bullring. The bulls move more slowly here, uncertain of their weak forelegs, allowing runners to stay close and even to touch them as they glide down into the tunnel. The only uncertainty is whether there will be a pileup in the tunnel. The most dramatic photographs of the encierro have been taken here, as the galloping pack slams through what occasionally turns into a solid wall of humanity. If all goes well—no bulls separated from the pack, no mayhem—the bulls will have arrived in the ring in less than three minutes.

LEGAL ISSUES
It is illegal to attempt to attract a bull, thus removing him from the pack and creating a deadly danger. It's also illegal to participate while intoxicated or while taking photos. Sexual assault has become an increasing problem. Every year more women file police reports after being attacked or inappropriately touched in the crowds.

$$ ✕ **La Cocina de Alex Múgica.** In the heart of Pamplona's old town, this
TAPAS   sleek, contemporary bar is famed for its mix of traditional and experi-
mental pintxos, which include *fideuà de callos y hongos* (noodles with
mushrooms and tripe) and pocha (a local bean) and clam "hummus."
Known for: blend of classic and innovative dishes; eye-catching presenta-
tions; good value. $ *Average main: €14* ⊠ *Calle Estafeta 24* ☎ *94/851–*
0125 ⊕ *www.alexmugica.com* ⊘ *Closed Mon. No dinner Sun.*

WHERE TO STAY

$$$$ ⊡ **Gran Hotel La Perla.** The oldest hotel in Pamplona underwent sev-
HOTEL   eral years of refurbishing before it reinvented itself as a luxury lodg-
Fodor's Choice   ing option. **Pros:** staff are well versed in history of the property *The*
★   *Sun Also Rises* in the place where it was first conceived; even entry-
level rooms are spacious; good soundproofing. **Cons:** round-the-clock
mayhem during San Fermín; prices triple during San Fermín; no pool,
gym, or spa. $ *Rooms from: €183* ⊠ *Pl. del Castillo 1* ☎ *94/822–3000*
⊕ *www.granhotellaperla.com* ⇴ *44 rooms* ⦿ *Free Breakfast.*

$ ⊡ **Hotel Maisonnave.** This modern four-star hotel has a nearly perfect
HOTEL   location, tucked away on a relatively quiet pedestrian street, just steps
FAMILY   from all the action on Plaza del Castillo and Calle Estafeta. **Pros:** friendly,
multilingual staff; great location; lively bar and restaurant. **Cons:** mod-
ern interior design lacks local character; more three- than four-star;
corporate feel. $ *Rooms from: €85* ⊠ *Calle Nueva 20* ☎ *94/822–2600*
⊕ *www.hotelmaisonnave.es* ⇴ *138 rooms* ⦿ *No meals.*

$ ⊡ **Hotel Sercotel Europa.** More famous for its world-class Michelin-
HOTEL   starred restaurant on the ground floor, this modestly priced hotel is one
of Pamplona's best-kept secrets, just a block and half from the bullring
and within shouting distance of party central, Plaza del Castillo. **Pros:**
central location; good value; special restaurant offers for hotel guests.
Cons: noisy during the fiesta unless you score an interior room; rooms
on the small side; prices can double during San Fermín. $ *Rooms from:*
€65 ⊠ *Calle Espoz y Mina 11* ☎ *94/822–1800* ⊕ *www.hoteleuropap-*
amplona.com ⇴ *25 rooms* ⦿ *Free Breakfast.*

$$$ ⊡ **Palacio Guendulain.** This 18th-century palace in the center of town has
HOTEL   been restored to its original grandeur with wooden ceilings, Victorian
furniture, and a grand staircase. **Pros:** opportunity to stay in a historical
monument; central location; outstanding service. **Cons:** provides little
refuge from the mayhem during San Fermín; noise from the street is a
problem on weekends; extra charge for parking. $ *Rooms from: €177*
⊠ *Calle Zapatería 53* ☎ *94/822–5522* ⊕ *www.palacioguendulain.com*
⇴ *23 rooms, 2 suites* ⦿ *Free Breakfast.*

NIGHTLIFE AND PERFORMING ARTS

The city has a thumping student life year-round, especially along the
length of Calle San Nicolás, whose daytime bars transform into unpretentious *discotecas* by night. Artsier, more alternative venues line Calle
Navarrería, while slightly starchier nightlife spots geared toward the
40-plus crowd can be found around the Plaza de Toros.

NIGHTLIFE

Canalla. Dress up, or you might flunk the bouncer's inspection at this loungy nightclub, filled until dawn with young singles and couples. Cover charge depends on visiting DJs and events, and Fridays are popular student nights. ⊠ *Av. Bayona 2* ☎ *67/921–9871* ⊕ *www.canalla.es.*

Ozone. This techno-music haven is the most popular dance club in town. Cover charge depends on visiting DJs and events; check the website for lineups and prices. ⊠ *Calle Monasterio de Velate 5* ☎ *94/826–1593* ⊕ *www.ozonepamplona.com.*

PERFORMING ARTS

Edificio Baluarte. The Congress Center and Auditorium, built in 2003 by local architectural star Patxi Mangado, is a sleek assemblage of black Zimbabwean granite. It contains a concert hall of exquisite acoustical perfection utilizing beechwood from upper Navarra's famed Irati *haya* (beech) forest. Performances and concerts, from opera to ballet, are held in this modern venue, built on the remains of one of the five bastions of Pamplona's 16th-century Ciudadela. ⊠ *Pl. del Baluarte* ☎ *94/806–6066* ⊕ *www.baluarte.com.*

Fodor's Choice ★ **Zentral.** A self-proclaimed gastro club, with food and live music offerings, this clubby venue hosts events ranging from Lindy hop dance parties to lectures on food science. It morphs into a DJ-driven discoteca most nights after 1 am. ⊠ *Mercado de Santo Domingo, Calle de Santo Domingo s/n, 1st fl.* ☎ *94/822–0764* ⊕ *www.zentralpamplona.com.*

SHOPPING

Botas are the leather wineskins from which Basques typically drink at bullfights or during fiestas, and the most famous, historic maker, ZZZ, is from Pamplona. The art lies in drinking a stream of wine from a bota held at arm's length without spilling a drop.

Caminoteca Pamplona. Owned by a former pilgrim, this small store stocks everything and anything a veteran pilgrim needs on the Camino de Santiago, from backpacks, proper shoes, hiking socks, and walking sticks to smaller but equally necessary items like blister ointment, rain ponchos, and sporks. ⊠ *Calle de Curia 15* ☎ *94/821–0316* ⊕ *www.caminoteca.com.*

Fodor's Choice ★ **Fragment Store.** This well-curated boutique run by young designers is the city's top spot to buy handmade jewelry and accessories, kitchenware, couture garments, and eye-catching stationery. ⊠ *Calle Nueva 4–6* ☎ *84/841–0430* ⊕ *www.karlotalaspalas.com.*

Gurgur "Delicias de la Estafeta". Come here to buy delicacies from across Navarra, including wines, sweets, cured meats, and cheeses, as well as a variety of bull-themed T-shirts and paraphernalia. ⊠ *Calle Estafeta 21* ☎ *94/820–7992* ⊕ *www.gurgurestafeta.com.*

Kukuxumusu. This chain is famous for colorful pop-art T-shirt prints with San Fermín and Basque themes. There's another outpost at Mercaderes 19. ⊠ *Calle Sanguesa 19* ☎ *90/278–7092* ⊕ *www.kukuxumusu.com.*

Manterola. Here you can buy some toffee called La Cafetera, a local *café con leche* sweet. The shop also sells Navarran wine and other delicacies. ⊠ *Calle Tudela 5* ☎ *94/822–3174* ⊕ *www.manterola.es.*

Olentzero. You can buy botas in most Navarrese towns, but Pamplona's Olentzero gift shop sells the best brand, "The Three Zs," written "ZZZ." ⊠ *Calle de la Estafeta 42* ☎ *94/882–0245* ⊕ *www.olentzeroa.com.*

Torrens Alimentación. Navarran favorites such as piquillo peppers and *chistorra* sausages are sold here. ⊠ *Calle San Miguel 12* ☎ *94/822–4286* ⊕ *www.torrensalimentacion.com.*

OFF THE BEATEN PATH

Olite. An unforgettable glimpse into the Kingdom of Navarra of the Middle Ages is the reward for journeying to this town. The 11th-century church of San Pedro is revered for its finely worked Romanesque cloisters and portal, but it's the town's castle—restored by Carlos III in the French style and brimming with ramparts, crenellated battlements, and watchtowers—that most captures the imagination. You can walk the ramparts, and should you get tired or hungry, part of the castle has been converted into a parador, making a fine place to catch a bite or a few z's. ⊠ *41 km (25 miles) south of Pamplona, Olite* ☎ *94/874–0000.*

LA RIOJA

A rugged compendium of highlands, plains, and vineyards nourished by the Río Ebro, La Rioja (named for the Río Oja) has historically produced Spain's finest wines. Most inhabitants live along the Ebro, in the cities of Logroño and Haro, though the mountains and upper river valleys are arguably the most scenic areas. A mix of Atlantic and Mediterranean climates and cultures with Basque overtones, La Rioja comprises La Rioja Alta (Upper Rioja), the moist and mountainous western end (where most of the region's great wines come from), and La Rioja Baja (Lower Rioja), the dryer eastern extremity with a more Mediterranean climate and less prestigious wines. Logroño, the capital, lies between the two. The wine-making region La Rioja Alavesa *(see Laguardia)* is located in the Basque Country, not the autonomous community of La Rioja.

LOGROÑO

85 km (53 miles) southwest of Pamplona.

A busy industrial city of 153,000, Logroño has a lovely old quarter bordered by the Ebro and medieval walls, with **Breton de los Herreros** and **Muro Francisco de la Mata** being its principal streets. Wine-loving travelers who prefer the bustle of a city to the quietude of the country should hole up here and take day trips to the outlying vineyards.

Near Logroño, the Roman bridge and the *mirador* (lookout) at **Viguera** are the main sights in the lower Iregua Valley. According to legend, Santiago (St. James) helped the Christians defeat the Moors at the **Castillo de Clavijo,** another panoramic spot. The **Leza (Cañon) del Río Leza** is La Rioja's most dramatic canyon.

GETTING HERE AND AROUND

Bus Station Estación de Autobuses de Logroño. ⊠ *Av. España 1* ☎ *94/123–5983.*

Train Station **Estación de Logroño.** ✉ *Av. de Colón 83* ☎ *90/243–2343* 🌐 *www.adif.es.*

VISITOR INFORMATION

Contacts **Oficina de Turismo de Logroño.** ✉ *Calle Portales 50* ☎ *94/127–7000* 🌐 *www.logrono.es.*

EXPLORING

Concatedral de Santa María de La Redonda. Noted for its twin baroque towers, the present-day cathedral was rebuilt in the 16th century in a Gothic style atop ruins of a 12th-century Romanesque church. ✉ *Calle Portales 14* ☎ *94/125–7611* 🌐 *www.laredonda.org* 🎟 *Free.*

Puente de Piedra (*Stone Bridge*). Many of Logroño's monuments, such as this elegant bridge, were built as part of the Camino de Santiago pilgrimage route. ✉ *Av. de Navarra 1.*

5

San Bartolomé. The oldest still-standing church in Logroño, San Bartolomé was built between the 13th and 14th centuries in a French Gothic style. Highlights include the 11th-century Mudejar tower and an elaborate 14th-century Gothic doorway. Some carvings on the stone facade depict scenes from the Bible. This is also a landmark on the Camino de Santiago pilgrimage path. ✉ *Pl. San Bartolomé 2* ☎ *94/125–2254* 🌐 *www.lariojaturismo.com/comunidad/larioja/recurso/iglesia-de-san-bartolome* 🎟 *Free.*

Santa María del Palacio. This 11th-century church is known as La Aguja (the Needle) for its pyramid-shaped 135-foot Romanesque-Gothic tower. ✉ *Calle del Marqués de San Nicolás 30* 🎟 *Free.*

Santiago el Real (*Royal St. James's Church*). Reconstructed in the 16th century, this church is noted for its equestrian statue of the saint (also known as Santiago Matamoros, or St. James the Moorslayer) presiding over the main door. ✉ *Calle Barriocepo 6* ☎ *94/120–9501* 🌐 *www.santiagoelreal.org* 🎟 *Free.*

WHERE TO EAT AND STAY

For tapas, you'll find bars with signature specialties on the connecting streets **Calle del Laurel** and **Travesía de Laurel**, the latter also known as El Sendero de los Elefantes (Path of the Elephants)—an allusion to *trompas* (trunks), Spanish for a snootful. Try Bar Soriano for *champis* (*champiñones,* or mushrooms), Blanco y Negro for *matrimonio* (a green-pepper-and-anchovy sandwich), and La Travesía for tortilla de patata. If you're ordering wine, a young *cosecha* comes in squat *chato* glasses, a *crianza* brings out the crystal, and a *reserva* or *gran reserva* (selected grapes aged over three years in oak and bottle) elicits goblets for proper swirling, nosing, and tasting.

$$$$ **SPANISH**

🍴 **El Cachetero.** A Calle Laurel standby, this refined taberna with wood-paneled walls serves Riojan specialties like roast suckling pig and pimentón-laced potatoes *a la riojana* as well as risottos and excellent seafood dishes. **Known for:** personable waitstaff; refined Riojan cuisine; butter-soft cochinillo asado. [$] *Average main: €25* ✉ *Calle Laurel 3* ☎ *94/122–8463* 🌐 *www.cachetero.com* 🕒 *Closed Tues., and 1st 2 wks in Aug. No dinner Sun.*

The fertile soil and fields of the Ebro River Valley make some of Spain's most colorful landscapes.

$$ SPANISH Fodor's Choice ★ 🍴 **La Taberna de Baco.** This bright, modern bar is a great spot to try seasonal, market-fresh tapas like heirloom tomato salad with chilies and raw onion or cheesy mushroom "carpaccio," but locals flock here for one dish in particular: *oreja a la plancha*, or griddled pig's ear, swimming in punchy *brava* sauce. Shatteringly crisp and unapologetically rich, it's one of the best versions you'll have in Spain. **Known for:** offal even the squeamish can learn to love; wide selection of small-production wines; amiable bartenders. [$] *Average main: €12* ✉ *Calle de San Agustín 10* ☎ *94/121–3544* 🌐 *www.latabernadebaco.com.*

$$ SPANISH Fodor's Choice ★ 🍴 **Tondeluna.** A gastro bar that strives to bring haute cuisine to the masses, Tondeluna has six communal tables (with 10 seats each), and all have views into the kitchen, where cooks plate up dishes both novel and familiar like glazed beef cheeks with apple puree and Getaria-style hake with *panadera* potatoes. **Known for:** good balance of experimental and classic dishes; hip, lively dining room; €20 menú del día. [$] *Average main: €16* ✉ *Calle Muro de la Mata 9* ☎ *94/123–6425* 🌐 *www.tondeluna.com* 🕓 *No dinner Sun.*

$ HOTEL 🏨 **Marqués de Vallejo.** Close to—but not overwhelmed by—the food- and wine-tasting frenzy of nearby Calle del Laurel, this boutique hotel within view of the cathedral is within walking distance of all the major sights. **Pros:** central location; clean, homey rooms; pleasant public areas. **Cons:** street-side rooms can be noisy in summer, when windows are open; furniture looks like it was bought from an early-aughts IKEA catalog; underwhelming breakfast spread. [$] *Rooms from: €80* ✉ *Calle Marqués de Vallejo 8* ☎ *94/124–8333* 🌐 *www.hotelmarquesdevallejo.com* 🛏 *50 rooms* 🍽 *No meals.*

$$ ⌑ **NH Herencia Rioja.** This modern four-star hotel near the old quar-
HOTEL ter has contemporary, comfortable rooms, first-rate facilities, a well-
trained staff, and a businesslike buzz about it. **Pros:** top comfort; two
steps from Calle del Laurel's tapas bonanza; excellent breakfast. **Cons:**
undistinguished modern building; cheerless interiors; tight, white-
knuckle parking. $ *Rooms from: €95* ✉ *Calle Marqués de Murrieta
14* ☎ *94/121–0222* ⊕ *www.nh-hoteles.com* ⇆ *83 rooms* ⍾ *No meals.*

LA RIOJA ALTA

The Upper Rioja, the most prized subregion of La Rioja's wine coun-
try, extends from the Río Ebro to the Sierra de la Demanda. La Rioja
Alta has the most fertile soil, the best vineyards and agriculture, the
most impressive castles and monasteries, a ski resort at Ezcaray, and
the historic economic advantage of being on the Camino de Santiago.

EXPLORING

5

Ezcaray. Enter the Sierra de la Demanda by heading south from Santo
Domingo de la Calzada on LR111. Your first stop is the town of Ezca-
ray, with its aristocratic houses emblazoned with family crests, of which
the **Palacio del Conde de Torremúzquiz** (Palace of the Count of Tor-
remúzquiz) is the most distinguished. Good excursions from here are
the Valdezcaray ski station; the source of the Río Oja at Llano de la
Casa; La Rioja's highest point, the 7,494-foot Pico de San Lorenzo; and
the Romanesque church of Tres Fuentes, at Valgañón. The hamlet is
famous for its wild mushroom–gathering residents—and the resulting
tapas, too. ✉ *Ezcaray.*

Nájera. This town was the capital of Navarra and La Rioja until 1076,
when the latter became part of Castile and the residence of the Cas-
tilian royal family. The monastery of **Santa María la Real** (⊕ *www.
santamarialareal.net*), the "pantheon of kings," is distinguished by its
16th-century Claustro de los Caballeros (Cavaliers' Cloister), a flam-
boyant Gothic structure with 24 lacy, plateresque Renaissance arches
overlooking a grassy patio. The sculpted 12th-century tomb of Doña
Blanca de Navarra is the monastery's best-known sarcophagus, while
the 67 Gothic choir stalls dating from 1495 are among Spain's best.
✉ *Nájera* ☎ *94/136–1083 tourist office.*

Navarrete. From Logroño, drive 14 km (9 miles) west on the A12 to
Navarrete to see its noble houses and 16th-century **Santa María de la
Asunción** church. The village is also famous for ceramics; shop at any
of the artisan shops in the town center.

Fodor'sChoice **San Millán de la Cogolla.** This town, southeast of Santo Domingo de la
★ Calzada, has two jaw-dropping monasteries on the UNESCO World
Heritage sites list. There's **Monasterio de Yuso** (⊕ *www.monasteriodey-
uso.org)*, where a 10th-century manuscript on St. Augustine's *Glosas
Emilianenses* contains handwritten notes in what is considered the earli-
est example of the Spanish language, the vernacular Latin dialect known
as Roman Paladino. And then there's the Visigothic **Monasterio de Suso**
(⊕ *www.monasteriodesanmillan.com/suso*) where Gonzalo de Berceo,
recognized as the first Castilian poet, wrote and recited his 13th-century

verse in the Castilian tongue, now the language of more than 300 million people around the world. ✉ *San Millán de la Cogolla.*

Santo Domingo de la Calzada. This town has always been a key stop on the Camino. Santo Domingo was an 11th-century saint who built roads and bridges for pilgrims and founded the hospital that is now the town's parador. The **cathedral** (✉ *Pl. del Santo 4* ☎ *941/340033*) is a Romanesque-Gothic pile containing the saint's tomb, choir murals, and a walnut altarpiece carved by Damià Forment in 1541. The live hen and rooster in a plateresque stone chicken coop commemorate a legendary local miracle in which a pair of roasted fowl came back to life to protest the innocence of a pilgrim hanged for theft. Be sure to stroll through the town's beautifully preserved medieval quarter. ✉ *N120, 20 km (12 miles) west of Nájera.*

WHERE TO STAY

$$$ HOTEL Fodor's Choice ★ 🏨 **Echaurren.** Rioja's renowned "gastro hotel," Echaurren is a veritable foodie paradise with two envelope-pushing restaurants and Relais & Châteaux–certified digs. **Pros:** Rioja's gastronomical mecca; comfortable beds; highly personal service. **Cons:** loud church bells; entry-level rooms are cramped; no bathtubs in most rooms. [$] *Rooms from: €160* ✉ *Calle Padre José García 19, Ezcaray* ☎ *94/135–4047* 🌐 *www.echaurren.com* 🛏 *25 rooms* 🍴 *Free Breakfast.*

$$ HOTEL 🏨 **Hostería San Millan.** This magnificent inn occupies a wing of the historic Monasterio de Yuso. **Pros:** historic site; graceful building; good breakfasts. **Cons:** somewhat isolated; monastic interiors; popular among the tour-bus set. [$] *Rooms from: €120* ✉ *Monasterio de Yuso, San Millán de la Cogolla* ☎ *94/137–3277* 🌐 *www.hosteriasanmillan.com/hotel* 🛏 *25 rooms* 🍴 *Free Breakfast.*

HARO

49 km (30 miles) west of Logroño.

Haro is the wine capital of La Rioja. Its Casco Viejo (Old Quarter) and best taverns are concentrated along the loop known as La Herradura (the Horseshoe), with the Santo Tomás church at the apex of its curve and Calle San Martín and Calle Santo Tomás leading down to the upper left-hand (northeast) corner of Plaza de la Paz. Up the left side of the horseshoe, Bar La Esquina is the first of many tapas bars. Bar Los Caños, behind a stone archway at San Martín 5, is built into the vaults and arches of the former church of San Martín and serves excellent local crianzas and reservas and a memorable pintxo of quail egg, anchovy, hot pepper, and olive.

VISITOR INFORMATION

Contacts Haro Tourist Office. ✉ *Pl. de la Paz 1* ☎ *94/130–3580* 🌐 *www.haroturismo.org.*

EXPLORING

Bodegas (*wineries*). Haro's century-old bodegas have been headquartered in the *barrio de la estación* (train-station district) ever since the railroad opened in 1863 and are a fantastic place to go winery-hopping since you don't need a car to go between bodegas. Guided tours and tastings, some in English, can be arranged at the facilities themselves or through the tourist office. ✉ *Haro.*

Fodor's Choice ★ **López de Heredia Viña Tondonia winery.** Call or email the historic López de Heredia Viña Tondonia winery to reserve a spot on one of the tours, or drop into the Zaha Hadid–designed tasting room for an informal glass or two. ✉ *Av. Vizcaya 3* ☎ *94/131–0244* 🌐 *www.lopezdeheredia.com* 🎟 *From €10.*

Santo Tomás. The architectural highlight of Haro, this single-nave Renaissance and late-Gothic church was completed in 1564. It has an intricately sculpted plateresque portal on the south side and a gilded baroque organ facade towering over the choir loft. ✉ *Calle Santo Tomás 5* ☎ *94/131–1690* 🌐 *www.haroturismo.org/iglesias/parroquia_de_santo_tomas.*

WHERE TO EAT AND STAY

$$$$ SPANISH Fodor's Choice ★ 🍴 **Terete.** A perennial local favorite, this rustic spot has been roasting lamb in wood ovens since 1877 and serves a hearty *menestra de verduras* (vegetables stewed with bits of ham) that is justly revered as a mandatory sidekick. With rough hand-hewn wooden tables distributed around dark stone and wood-beam dining rooms, the medieval stagecoach-inn environment matches the traditional roasts. **Known for:** 19th-century wood-burning oven; succulent roast lamb and suckling pig; deep, deep Rioja wine list. [$] *Average main: €30* ✉ *Calle Lucrecia Arana 17* ☎ *94/131–0023* 🌐 *www.terete.es* ⏲ *Closed Mon., 1st 2 wks in July, and last 2 wks in Nov. No dinner Sun.*

$$ HOTEL 🏨 **Los Agustinos.** Across the street from the tourist office, Haro's best hotel is built into a 14th-century monastery with a cloister (now a beautiful covered patio) that's considered one of the finest in La Rioja. **Pros:** gorgeous public rooms; convivial hotel bar; close to town center but in a quiet corner. **Cons:** fusty room interiors; €17-per-day breakfast; €17-per-day parking. [$] *Rooms from: €110* ✉ *Calle San Agustín 2* ☎ *94/131–1308* 🌐 *www.hotellosagustinos.com* 🛏 *62 rooms* 🍽 *No meals.*

THE HIGHLANDS

The rivers forming the seven main valleys of the Ebro basin originate in the Sierra de la Demanda, Sierra de Cameros, and Sierra de Alcarama. **Ezcaray** is La Rioja's skiing capital in the **valley of the Río Oja,** just below Valdezcaray in the Sierra de la Demanda. The upper **Najerilla Valley** is La Rioja's mountain sanctuary, an excellent hunting and fishing preserve. The Najerilla River, a rich chalk stream, is one of Spain's best trout rivers. Look for the Puente de Hiedra (Ivy Bridge), its heavy curtain of ivy falling to the surface of the Najerilla. The **Monasterio de Valvanera,** off the C113 near Anguiano, is the sanctuary of La Rioja's patron saint, the Virgen de Valvanera, a 12th-century Romanesque wood carving of the Virgin and Child. **Anguiano** is renowned for its Danza de los Zancos (Dance of the Stilts), held on July 22, when dancers on wooden stilts plummet through the steep streets of the town into the arms of the crowd at the bottom. At the valley's highest point are the Mansilla reservoir and the Romanesque Ermita de San Cristóbal (Hermitage of St. Christopher).

The upper **Iregua Valley,** off N111, has the prehistoric Gruta de la Paz caves at Ortigosa. The artisans of **Villoslada del Cameros** make the region's famous patchwork quilts, called *almazuelas.* Climb to **Pico Cebollera** for a superb view of the valley. Work back toward the Ebro along the Río Leza, through Laguna de Cameros and San Román de Cameros (known for its basket weavers), to complete a tour of the Sierra del Cameros. The upper **Cidacos Valley** leads to the **Parque Jurásico** (Jurassic Park) at Enciso, famous for its dinosaur tracks. The main village in the upper **Alhama Valley** is **Cervera del Rio Alhama,** a center for handmade *alpargatas* (espadrilles).

WHERE TO EAT AND STAY

$$
SPANISH
FAMILY

✕**La Herradura.** Rub shoulders with small-town Riojanos as you tuck into a bowl of *caparrones,* a local stew made with Riojan red beans, sausage, and fatback. The house wine is an acceptable and inexpensive Uruñuela *cosechero* (young wine of the year) from the Najerilla Valley. **Known for:** caparrones, a hearty local stew; down-home village crows; staff with big personalities. $ *Average main: €15* ⊠ *Ctra. de Lerma, Km 42, n14 Anguiano, Anguiano* ☎ *94/137–7151.*

$
HOTEL
FAMILY

▦ **Hospedería Abadía de Valvanera.** Housed in a 16th-century monastery atop a 9th-century hermitage, this rural hotel is an ideal base for hiking, but it's hard to secure a room for October 15, when there's an overnight pilgrimage from Logroño to the monastery's 12th-century carving of the Virgin of Valvanera. **Pros:** cool for the summer; simplicity and silence; rooms of varying sizes for families. **Cons:** spartan accommodations; limited dining choices; decidedly unhip. $ *Rooms from: €65* ⊠ *Monasterio de Valvanera s/n, Carretera LR-435* ☎ *94/137–7044* ⊕ *www. monasteriodevalvanera.es/hospederia* ⤲ *28 rooms* ¶◉¶ *No meals.*

$
B&B/INN

▦ **Venta de Goyo.** A favorite with anglers and hunters, this cheery spot across from the confluence of the Urbión and Najerilla rivers has wood-trimmed bedrooms with red-checker bedspreads and an excellent restaurant specializing in venison, wild boar, partridge, woodcock, and game of all kinds. **Pros:** excellent game and mountain cooking; charming rustic bar; unforgettable homemade jams. **Cons:** next to the road; hot in the summer; a bit isolated. $ *Rooms from: €50* ⊠ *Puente Río Neila 2, Ctra. LR113, Km 24.6, Viniegra de Abajo* ☎ *94/137–8007* ⊕ *www.ventadegoyo.es* ⤲ *22 rooms* ¶◉¶ *No meals.*

THE PYRENEES

WELCOME TO THE PYRENEES

TOP REASONS TO GO

★ **Appreciate the Romanesque:** Stop at Taüll and see the exquisite Romanesque churches and mural paintings of the Noguera de Tor Valley.

★ **Explore Spain's Grand Canyon:** The Parque Nacional de Ordesa y Monte Perdido has stunning scenery, along with marmots and mountain goats.

★ **Hike the highlands:** Explore the verdant Basque highlands of the Baztán Valley and follow the Bidasoa River down to colorful Hondarribia and the Bay of Biscay.

★ **Venture off the highway:** Discover the enchanting medieval town of Alquézar, where the impressive citadel, dating back to the 9th century, keeps watch over the Parque Natural Sierra y Cañones de Guara and its prehistoric cave paintings.

★ **Ride the cogwheel train at Ribes de Freser, near Ripoll:** Ascend the gorge to the sanctuary and ski station at Vall de Núria, then hike to the remote highland valley and refuge of Coma de Vaca.

1 Eastern Catalan Pyrenees. Start from Cap de Creus in the Empordà to get the full experience of the Pyrenean cordillera's rise from the sea; then move west through Camprodón, Setcases, the Ter Valley, and Ripoll.

2 La Cerdanya. The widest and sunniest valley in the Pyrenees, La Cerdanya is an east–west expanse that straddles the French border between two forks of the Pyrenean cordillera. The Río Segre flows down the center of the valley, while snowcapped peaks rise to the north and south.

3 Western Catalan Pyrenees. West of La Seu d'Urgell, the western Catalan Pyrenees include the Vall d'Aran, the Parc Nacional d'Aigüestortes i Estany de Sant Maurici, and the Noguera de Tor Valley with its Romanesque treasures.

4 Aragón and Central Pyrenees. Benasque is the jumping-off point for Aneto, the highest peak in the Pyrenees. The Parque Nacional de Ordesa y Monte Perdido is an unforgettable one- or two-day trek. Jaca, and the Hecho and Ansó valleys, are Upper Aragón at its purest, while the cities, Huesca and Zaragoza, are good lowland alternatives in

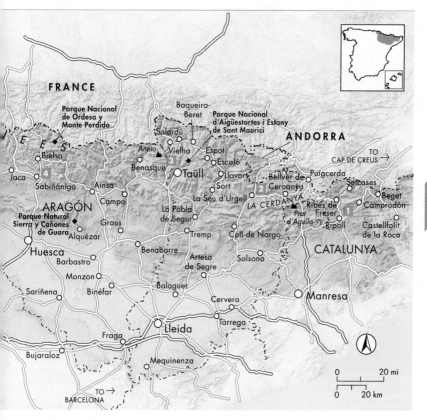

FRANCE

Parque Nacional
de Ordesa y
Monte Perdido

Baqueira-
Beret   Parque Nacional
d'Aigüestortes i Estany
de Sant Maurici

Salardú

ANDORRA

TO →
CAP DE CREUS

Bielsa

Aneto   Vielha   Espot

Escaló

Bellver de

Puigcerda

Sescases

Jaca

Benasque   Taüll

Ollavors

Ceroanya

Beget

Sabiñánigo   Aínsa

Sort

La Seu d'Urgell

LA CERDANYA

Ribes de
Freser

Camprodón

ARAGÓN   Campo

La Pobla
de Segur

Prat
d'Aguilo   Ripoll

Castellfolit
de la Roca

Parque Natural
Sierra y Cañones
de Guara   Alquézar

Graus

Tremp   Coll de Nargo

CATALUNYA

Huesca

Barbastro

Benabarre

Artesa
de Segre   Solsona

Monzon

Balaguer

Sariñena   Binéfar

Cervera   Manresa

Lleida   Tàrrega

Fraga

Bujaraloz

Mequinenza

0   20 mi

0   20 km

TO →
BARCELONA

case bad weather blows you out of the mountains.

5 **The Navarran and Basque Pyrenees.** Beginning in the Roncal Valley, the language you hear may be Euskera, the pre-Indo-European tongue of the Basques. The highlands of Navarra, from Roncesvalles and Burguete down through the Baztán Valley to

Hondarribia, are a magical realm of rolling hillsides, folklore, and emerald pastures.

6

EATING AND DRINKING WELL IN THE PYRENEES

Pyrenean cuisine is hearty mountain fare characterized by thick soups, stews, roasts, and local game. Ingredients are prepared with slightly different techniques and recipes in each valley, village, and kitchen.

(top left) Some typical dishes: grilled T-bone steak, chorizo and longaniza sausages with grilled peppers (top right) Wild black trumpet mushrooms (bottom left) Spring duckling with potatoes

The three main culinary schools across the Pyrenees match the three main cultural identities of the area—from east to west, they are Catalan, Aragonese, and Basque. Within these three principal groups there are further subdivisions corresponding to the valleys or regions of La Garrotxa, La Cerdanya, Ribagorça, Vall d'Aran, Benasque, Alto Aragón, Roncal, and Baztán. Game is common throughout. Trout, mountain goat, deer, boar, partridge, rabbit, duck, and quail are roasted over coals or cooked in aromatic stews called *civets* in Catalonia and *estofadas* in Aragón and the Basque Pyrenees. Fish and meat are often seared on slabs of slate (*a la llosa* in Catalan, *a la piedra* in Castilian Spanish). Sheep, goat, and cow cheeses vary from valley to valley, along with types of sausages and charcuterie.

WILD MUSHROOMS

Valued for their aromatic contribution to the taste process, wild mushrooms come into season in the autumn. They go well with meat or egg dishes. Favorites include *rovellons* (*Lactarius deliciosus,* or saffron milk cap) sautéed with parsley, olive oil, and garlic, and *camagrocs* (*Cantharellus lutescens,* a type of chanterelle) scrambled with eggs.

HIGHLAND SOUPS

As with all mountain soups, *sopa pirenaica* combines restorative animal protein with vegetables and the high-altitude need for liquids. The Spanish version of the French *garbure,* the classic mountain soup from the north side of the Pyrenees, mixes legumes, vegetables, potatoes, pork, chicken, and sometimes lamb or wild boar into a tasty and energizing meal that will help hikers recover energy and be ready to go again the next morning. *Olha aranesa* (Aranese soup) is another Pyrenean power soup, with vegetables, legumes, pork, chicken, and beef in a long-cooked and slowly simmered unctuous stew. Similar to the ubiquitous Catalan *escudella,* another Pyrenean favorite, the olha aranesa combines chickpeas and pasta with a variety of meats and vegetables and is served, like the *cocido madrileño,* in various stages: soup, legumes, vegetables, and meats.

PYRENEAN STEWS

Wild boar stew is known by different names in the various languages of the Pyrenees—*civet de porc senglar* in Catalan, *estofado de jabalí* in Spanish. A dark and gamy treat in cold weather, wild boar is prepared in many different ways between Catalonia, Aragón, and the Basque Country, but most recipes include onions, carrots, mushrooms, bay leaf, oranges, leeks, peppers, dry sherry, brown sugar, and sweet paprika. *Civet*

d'isard (mountain-goat stew), known as *estofado de ixarso* in the Pyrenees of Aragón, is another favorite, prepared in much the same way but with a more delicate taste.

TRINXAT

The Catalan verb *trinxar* means to chop or shred, and *trinxat* is winter cabbage, previously softened by frost, chopped fine, and mixed with mashed potato and fatback or bacon. A quintessential high-altitude comfort food, trinxat plays the acidity of the cabbage against the saltiness of the pork, with the potato as the unifying element.

DUCK WITH TURNIPS

The traditional dish *tiró amb naps* goes back, as do nearly all European recipes that make use of turnips, to pre-Columbian times, before the potato's arrival from the New World. The frequent use of duck (*pato* in Spanish, *anec* in Catalan, *tiró* in La Cerdanya) in the half-French, half-Spanish, all-Catalan Cerdanya Valley two hours north of Barcelona is a taste acquired from French Catalunya, just over the Pyrenees.

Updated by
Elizabeth
Prosser

Separating the Iberian Peninsula from the rest of the European continent, the snowcapped Pyrenees have always been a special realm, a source of legend and superstition. To explore the Pyrenees fully—the flora and fauna, the local cuisine, the remote glacial lakes and streams, the Romanesque art in a thousand hermitages—could take a lifetime.

Each of the three autonomous Pyrenean mountain regions that sit between the Mediterranean and the Atlantic is drained by one or more rivers, forming some three dozen valleys, which were all but completely isolated until around the 10th century. Local languages still abound, with Castilian Spanish and Euskera (Basque) in upper Navarra; Aragonese (and its local varieties) in Aragón; and Catalan at the eastern end of the chain from Ribagorça to the Mediterranean.

Throughout history, the Pyrenees were a strategic barrier and stronghold to be reckoned with. The Romans never completely subdued Los Vascones (as Greek historian Strabo [63–21 BC] called the Basques) in the western Pyrenean highlands. Charlemagne lost Roland and his rear guard at Roncesvalles in 778, and his Frankish heirs lost all of Catalonia in 988. Napoléon Bonaparte never completed his conquest of the peninsula, largely because of communications and supply problems posed by the Pyrenees, and Adolf Hitler, whether for geographical or political reasons, decided not to use post–Civil War Spain to launch his African campaign in 1941. A D-Day option to make a landing on the beaches of northern Spain was scrapped because the Pyrenees looked too easily defendable (you can still see the south-facing German bunkers on the southern flanks of the western Pyrenean foothills). Meanwhile, the mountainous barrier provided a path to freedom for downed pilots, Jewish refugees, and POWs fleeing the Nazis, just as it later meant freedom for political refugees running north from the Franco regime.

PLANNING

WHEN TO GO

If you're a hiker, stick to the summer (June–September, especially July), when the weather is better and there's less chance of a serious snow-fall—not to mention blizzards or lightning storms at high altitudes.

October, with comfortable daytime temperatures and chillier evenings, is ideal for enjoying the still-green Pyrenean meadows and valleys and hillside hunts for wild mushrooms. November brings colorful leaves, the last mushrooms, and the first frosts.

For skiing, come December–March. The green springtime thaw, mid-March–mid-April, is spectacular for skiing on the snowcaps and trout fishing or golfing on the verdant valley floors.

August is the only crowded month, when all of Europe is on summer vacation and the cooler highland air is at its best.

PLANNING YOUR TIME

You could hike all the way from the Atlantic to the Mediterranean in 43 days, but not many have that kind of vacation time. A week is ideal for a single area—La Cerdanya and the Eastern Catalan Pyrenees, easily accessed from Barcelona; the Western Catalan Pyrenees and Vall d'Aran in the Lleida province of Catalonia; Jaca and the central Pyrenees, north of Zaragoza; or the Basque Pyrenees north of Pamplona.

A day's drive up through Figueres (in Catalonia) and Olot will bring you to the town of **Camprodón**. The picturesque villages dotted around this area—in particular **Beget, Sant Joan de les Abadesses**, and **Ripoll**—are all worthy stops, especially for the famous monastery of Santa Maria de Ripoll with its 13th-century Romanesque portal. La Cerdanya's sunny wide plains are popular for walkers and mountain bikers year-round, and skiing in La Molina and Masella in winter. **Puigcerdà, Llívia,** and **Bellver de Cerdanya** are must-visits, too.

To the west, the historic town of **La Seu d'Urgell** is an important stop on the way to the **Parc Nacional d'Aigüestortes i Estany de Sant Maurici**, the **Vall d'Aran,** and the winter-sports center Baqueira-Beret. Stop at **Taüll** and the **Noguera de Tor Valley** for Romanesque churches.

The central Aragonese Pyrenees reveal the most dramatic scenery and Aneto, the highest peak in the Pyrenees. The **Parque Nacional de Ordesa y Monte Perdido** is Spain's most majestic canyon—reminiscent of North America's Grand Canyon. **Alquézar** and **Ainsa** are upper Aragon's best-preserved medieval towns, while **Zaragoza, Huesca,** and **Jaca** are the most important cities.

Farther west, the lower Navarran Pyrenees give way to rolling pasture-lands. **Roncesvalles** is the first stop off for pilgrims on the life-affirming **Camino de Santiago,** and the peaceful **Baztán Valley** guards a land of ancient traditions.

GETTING HERE AND AROUND

AIR TRAVEL

Barcelona's international airport, El Prat de Llobregat (⇨ *Barcelona*), is the largest gateway to the Catalan Pyrenees. Farther west, the Pyr-enees can be reached by international flights going through Madrid

Barajas airport, or Toulouse Blagnac and Biarritz Airport in France. Smaller airports at Zaragoza, Pamplona, and San Sebastián's Hondar-ribia (Fuenterrabía) are useful for domestic flights.

BUS TRAVEL

Bus travel in the Pyrenees is the only way to cross from east to west (or vice versa), other than hiking or driving, but requires some zigzag-ging up and down valleys. In most cases, four buses daily connect the main pre-Pyrenean cities (Barcelona, Zaragoza, Huesca, and Pamplona) and the main highland distributors (Puigcerdà, La Seu d'Urgell, Vielha, Benasque, and Jaca). The time lost waiting for buses makes this option a last resort.

Bus Lines Alosa. ⊠ *Estación Central de Delicias, Av. Navarra, Zaragoza* ☎ *912/722832* ⊕ *alosa.avanzabus.com.* **ALSA.** ⊠ *Estación de Autobuses, Carrer Yanguas y Miranda s/n, Pamplona* ☎ *902/422242* ⊕ *www.conda.es.*

CAR TRAVEL

The easiest way (and in many cases, the *only* way) to tour the Pyrenees is by car—and it comes with the best scenery. The Eje Pirenaico (Pyrenean Axis, or N260) is a carefully engineered, safe cross-Pyrenean route that connects Cap de Creus, the Iberian Peninsula's easternmost point on the Mediterranean Costa Brava (east of Girona and Cadaqués), with Cabo de Higuer, the lighthouse west of Hondarribia at the edge of the Atlantic Bay of Biscay.

The Collada de Toses (Tosses Pass) to Puigcerdà is the most difficult route into the Cerdanya Valley, but it's toll-free, has spectacular scenery, and you get to include Camprodón, Olot, and Ripoll in your itinerary. Safer and faster but more expensive (tolls total more than €22 from Barcelona to Bellver de Cerdanya) is the E9 through the Tuñel del Cadí. Once you're there, most of the Cerdanya Valley's two-lane roads are wide and well paved. As you go west, roads can be more difficult to navigate, winding dramatically through mountain passes.

TRAIN TRAVEL

There are three small train stations deep in the Pyrenees: Ribes de Freser in the eastern Catalan Pyrenees; Puigcerdà, in the Cerdanya Valley; and La Pobla de Segur, in the Noguera Pallaresa Valley. The larger gateways are Zaragoza, Huesca, and Lleida. From Madrid, connect through Barcelona for the eastern Pyrenees, Zaragoza and Huesca for the central Pyrenees, and Pamplona or San Sebastián for the Navarran and Basque Pyrenees. For information on timetables and routes, consult ⊕ *www.renfe.com.*

RESTAURANTS

In the Alta Pyrenees, the cozy stone-wall inns, with their hearty cuisine and comfortable interiors, are a welcome sight after a day's hiking or sightseeing. Often family run and relaxed, they rarely have any kind of dress code and, often, a nourishing meal is brought to a close with a complimentary *chupito* (shot) of local liqueur, finishing the night off with a satisfying thump. Back down in the main cities, restaurants take inspiration from these traditional methods, but offer a more contem-porary style and setting.

HOTELS

Most hotels in the Pyrenees are informal and outdoorsy, with a large fireplace in one of the public rooms. They are usually built of wood, glass, and stone, with steep slate roofs that blend in with the surrounding mountains. Most hotel establishments are family operations passed down from generation to generation. *Hotel reviews have been shortened. For full information, visit Fodors.com.*

WHAT IT COSTS IN EUROS				
	$	$$	$$$	$$$$
Restaurants	under €12	€12–€17	€18–€22	over €22
Hotels	under €90	€90–€125	€126–€180	over €180

Restaurant prices are the average cost of a main course or equivalent combination of smaller dishes at dinner, or, if dinner is not served, at lunch. Hotel prices are the lowest cost of a standard double room in high season.

TOURS

Trekking, horseback riding, adventure sports such as canyoning and ballooning, and more contemplative outings like bird-watching and botanical tours are just a few of the specialties available at the main Pyrenean resorts.

Well populated with trout, the Pyrenees' cold streams provide excellent angling from mid-March to the end of August. Notable places to cast a line are the Segre, Aragón, Gállego, Noguera Pallaresa, Arga, Esera, and Esca rivers. Pyrenean ponds and lakes also tend to be rich in trout.

Pyrenean Experience. British expat Georgina Howard specializes in showcasing Basque-Navarran culture, walking, and gastronomy. The walking tours include accommodations and meals. ⊠ *Iaulin Borda, Ameztia, Ituren* ☎ *650/713759* ⊕ *www.pyreneanexperience.com* ✉ *From €1000.*

EASTERN CATALAN PYRENEES

Catalonia's easternmost Pyrenean valley, the Vall de Camprodón, is still hard enough to reach that, despite pockets of Barcelona summer colonies, it has retained much of its farm culture and mountain wildness. It has several exquisite towns and churches and, above all, mountains like the Sierra de Catllar. Vallter 2000, La Molina, and Núria are ski resorts at either end of the Pyrenean heights on the north side of the valley, but the lowlands in the middle and main body of the valley have remained pasture for sheep, cattle, and horses.

GETTING HERE AND AROUND

To reach the Vall de Camprodón from Barcelona, you can take the C17 through Vic and Ripoll. From Barcelona or the Costa Brava you can also go by way of either Figueres or Girona, through Besalú and Olot on route N260, and then through the C38 Capsacosta tunnel to Camprodón. From France, drive southwest from Céret on the D115 through the Col d'Ares pass, which becomes the C38 as it enters the Camprodón Valley after passing through Prats-de-Molló-La Preste.

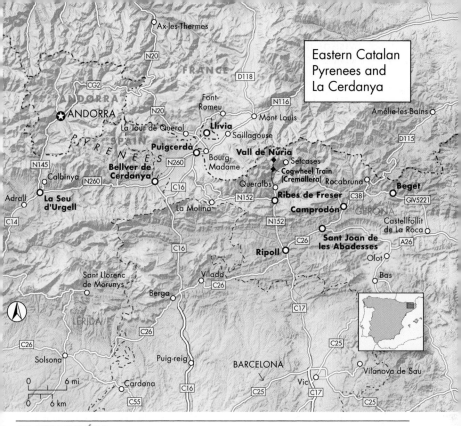

CAMPRODÓN

127 km (79 miles) northwest of Barcelona, 80 km (50 miles) west of Girona.

Camprodón, the capital of its *comarca* (county), lies at the junction of the Ter and Ritort rivers—both excellent trout streams. The rivers flow by, through, and under much of the town, giving it a highland water-front character (as well as a long history of flooding). Its best-known symbol is the elegant 12th-century stone bridge that broadly spans the Ter River in the center of town. The town owes much of its opulence to the summer residents from Barcelona who built mansions along **Passeig Maristany**, the leafy promenade at its northern edge.

GETTING HERE AND AROUND

The C38 runs into the center of town from both north (France) and south (Barcelona, Vic, or Ripoll) directions. If coming from France, the southbound D115 changes into the C38 once over the Spanish border. From either direction, the C38 heads straight toward the center of town. The best way to explore is on foot, as the streets are narrow and can be complicated to navigate by car.

VISITOR INFORMATION

Contacts Camprodón. ✉ *Carrer Sant Roc 22* ☎ *972/740010* 🌐 *www.vallde-camprodon.org.*

FESTIVALS

Festival de Música de Isaac Albéniz. Camprodón's most famous son is composer Isaac Albéniz (1860–1909) who spent more than 20 years in exile in France, where he became friends with musical luminaries such as Pablo Casals, Claude Debussy, and Gabriel Fauré. His celebrated classical guitar piece *Asturias* is one of Spain's best-known works. In July, during the Isaac Albéniz Music Festival, a series of concerts by renowned artists and young talent from the European classical music scene is held in the monastery of Sant Pere. For an up-to-date concert schedule, contact the tourist office. ✉ *Sant Pere de Camprodon, Carrer Monestir, 2* 🌐 *www.albeniz.cat.*

WHERE TO STAY

$$ B&B/INN FAMILY Fodor's Choice ★ 🏨 **Fonda Rigà.** A highland inn with comfortable modern rooms and spectacular views to the sea, this mountain perch is an excellent base for hiking, horseback riding, and viewing Pyrenean flora and fauna. **Pros:** the views and the peace and quiet; well-maintained rooms and facilities; fabulous dining experience. **Cons:** a serious 5-km (3-mile) drive above the valley floor; remote from Camprodón; bookings only by email or phone. [$] *Rooms from: €110* ✉ *Ctra. de Tregurà de Dalt, Km 4.8, at end of Tregurà route, 10 km (6 miles) up Ter Valley from Camprodón* ☎ *972/136000* 🌐 *es.fondariga.com* 🕐 *Closed Nov. 1–15 and June 26–July 12* 🛏 *16 rooms* 🍴 *Free Breakfast.*

$$$ HOTEL 🏨 **Hotel Maristany.** An elegant chalet on Camprodon's grandest promenade, this small but lovely hotel offers a chance to live like the 19th- and 20th-century Barcelona aristocracy who spent summers at this mountain retreat. **Pros:** outside of town center and quiet at night; excellent restaurant; private parking. **Cons:** rooms and baths are somewhat cramped; no children under 10 years; outside the town's historic core. [$] *Rooms from: €132* ✉ *Av. Maristany 20* ☎ *972/130078* 🌐 *www.hotelmaristany.com* 🕐 *Closed Dec. 11–Easter* 🛏 *10 rooms* 🍴 *Free Breakfast.*

$$ HOTEL 🏨 **L'Hotel de Camprodón.** A perfect base for getting a sense of this stylish little mountain hub, this elegant Moderniste building has rooms over the bustling Plaça Dr. Robert on one side and over the river on the other. **Pros:** central location; charming Art Nouveau style and preserved features throughout; wonderful views over the river. **Cons:** no parking; rooms on the square can be noisy in summer; five-night minimum stay in summer. [$] *Rooms from: €92* ✉ *Pl. Dr. Robert 3* ☎ *972/740013* 🌐 *www.hotelcamprodon.com* 🛏 *50 rooms* 🍴 *No meals.*

SHOPPING

Cal Xec. This legendary sausage and cheese store also sells the much-prized, vanilla-flavored Birbas cookies. It's at the end of the Camprodón Bridge. ✉ *Carrer Isaac Albéniz 1* ☎ *972/740084* 🌐 *www.calxec.com.*

Mercat Setmanal. Held every Sunday 9–2, this market sells all manner of artisanal food, crafts, clothing, antiques, and bric-a-brac. ✉ *Pl. del Dr. Robert.*

trains from Barcelona (⊕ *www.renfe.com*), but bus connections must be made through Girona. It's a 10-minute walk from the station to the center, and the small town is easy to explore on foot.

VISITOR INFORMATION

Contacts Ripoll. ⊠ *Pl. de l'Abat Oliva s/n* ☎ *972/702351.*

EXPLORING

Monastery of Santa Maria de Ripoll. Decorated with a pageant of biblical figures, the 12th-century doorway to the church is one of Catalonia's great works of Romanesque art, crafted as a triumphal arch by stone masons and sculptors of the Roussillon school, which was centered around French Catalonia and the Pyrenees. You can pick up a guide to the figures surrounding the portal in the nearby Centro de Interpretación del Monasterio, in Plaça de l'Abat Oliva. The center has an interactive exhibition that explains the historical, cultural, and religious relevence of this cradle of Catalonia. It also provides information about guided tours. ⊠ *Pl. Monasterio s/n* ☎ *972/704203* ⊠ *€6.*

RIBES DE FRESER AND VALL DE NÚRIA

14 km (9 miles) north of Ripoll.

The small town of Ribes de Freser is the starting point of the famous *cremallera* (cogwheel) train, which connects passengers with Núria, a small mountaintop ski resort and pilgrimage site, via a spectacular ascent through the Gorges of Núria.

GETTING HERE AND AROUND

The N260 north of Ripoll heads straight to Ribes de Freser. Continue farther north on the GIV5217 to reach Queralbs by car. Both Queralbs and Ribes de Freser are easily explored on foot.

VISITOR INFORMATION

Contacts Vall de Ribes Tourist Office. ⊠ *Ctra. de Bruguera 2, Ribes de Freser* ☎ *972/727728* ⊕ *www.vallderibes.cat.*

EXPLORING

Camino dels Enginyers. From the ski area of Núria, at an altitude of 6,562 feet, the dramatic, occasionally heart-stopping "engineers' path" is best done in the summer months. The three-hour trek, aided at one point by a cable handrail, leads to the remote highland valley of Coma de Vaca, where a cozy refuge and hearty replenishment await. Phone ahead to make sure there's space and check weather conditions. In the morning you can descend the riverside Gorges de Freser trail, another three-hour walk, to Queralbs, where there are connecting trains to Ribes de Freser. ⊠ *Refugi de Coma de Vaca, Termino Municipal de Queralbs dentro del Espacio protegido Ter Freser, Queralbs* ☎ *649/229012* ⊕ *www.comadevaca.cat/index.php/en* ⊘ *Closed Sept.–May.*

FAMILY
Fodor's Choice
★

Cogwheel train (Cremallera). The 45-minute train ride from the town of Ribes de Freser up to Núria provides one of Catalonia's most unusual excursions—in few other places in Spain does a train make such a precipitous ascent. The cremallera (cogwheel train) was completed in 1931 to connect Ribes with the Santuari de la Mare de Déu de Núria

(Mother of God of Núria) and with mountain hiking and skiing. ✉ *Estación de Ribes-Enllaç, Ribes de Freser* ☎ *972/732020* 🌐 *www.valldenuria.cat/es/invierno/cremallera/presentacion* 🎟 *€22 round-trip* ⏰ *Closed weekdays in Nov.*

Queralbs. The three-hour walk down the mountain from Vall de Núria to the sleepy village of Queralbs follows the course of the cogwheel train on a rather precipitous but fairly easy route, as long as it's not done during the snow season. The path overlooks gorges and waterfalls, overshadowed by sheer peaks, before exiting into the surprisingly charming and tiny village of Queralbs, where houses made of stone and wood cling to the side of the mountain. There is a well-preserved **Romanesque church,** notable for its six-arch portico, marble columns, single nave, and pointed vault. ✉ *Queralbs.*

Santuari de la Mare de Déu de Núria. The legend of this Marian religious retreat is based on the story of Sant Gil of Nîmes, who did penance in the Núria Valley during the 7th century. The saint left behind a wooden statue of the Virgin Mary, a bell he used to summon shepherds to prayer, and a cooking pot; 300 years later, a pilgrim found these treasures in this sanctuary. The bell and the pot came to have special importance to barren women, who, according to local beliefs, were blessed with as many children as they wished after placing their heads in the pot and ringing the bell. ✉ *26 km (16 miles) north of Ripoll, Vall de Núria* 🎟 *Free.*

WHERE TO STAY

$ 🏨 **Hostal Les Roquetes.** A short walk from the cogwheel train station
B&B/INN and the center of the village, this *hostal* has cheerful rooms and some spectacular views. **Pros:** fantastic views; friendly service; good base for walks in the area. **Cons:** limited food options outside of weekends; only accessible by local road or cogwheel train, and those times are limited. [$] *Rooms from: €66* ✉ *Crta. de Ribes 5, Queralbs* ☎ *972/727369* 🌐 *www.hostalroquetes.com* ⏰ *Closed Nov.* 🛏 *8 rooms* 🍴 *No meals.*

LA CERDANYA

The widest, sunniest valley in the Pyrenees is said to be in the shape of the handprint of God. High pastureland bordered north and south by snow-covered peaks, La Cerdanya starts in France, at Col de la Perche (near Mont Louis), and ends in the Spanish province of Lleida, at Martinet. Split between two countries and subdivided into two more provinces on each side, the valley has an identity all of its own. Residents on both sides of the border speak Catalan, a Romance language derived from early Provençal French, and regard the valley's political border with undisguised hilarity. Unlike any other valley in the upper Pyrenees, this one runs east–west and thus has a record annual number of sunlight hours.

PUIGCERDÀ

65 km (40 miles) northwest of Ripoll, 170 km (106 miles) northwest of Barcelona.

Puigcerdà is the largest town in the valley; in Catalan, *puig* means "hill," and *cerdà* derives from "Cerdanya." From the promontory upon which it stands, the views down across the meadows of the valley floor and up into the craggy peaks of the surrounding Pyrenees are dramatic. The 12th-century **Romanesque bell tower**—all that remains of the town church of Santa Maria, destroyed in 1936 at the outset of the Spanish Civil War—and the sunny sidewalk cafés facing it are among Puigcerdà's prettiest spots, as is the Gothic church of **Sant Domènec.** Serving primarily as a base for skiers and hikers from both sides of the border, Puigcerdà has lively restaurants and a bustling shopping promenade. On Sunday, markets sell clothes, cheeses, fruits, vegetables, and wild mushrooms to shoppers.

GETTING HERE AND AROUND

From Ripoll take the northwest-bound N260 for 63 km (39 miles) toward Ribes de Freser. Several trains a day (they are less frequent on weekends) run from Barcelona Sants to Puigcerdà (⊕ *www.renfe.com*). Buses go from Barcelona Estación del Nord (⊕ *www.barcelonanord. com*). Once you reach the center, there is ample parking, and the easiest way to get around town is on foot.

VISITOR INFORMATION

Contacts Puigcerdà Tourist Office. ⊠ *Bell tower, Pl. Santa Maria s/n* ☎ *972/880542* ⊕ *www.puigcerda.cat.*

EXPLORING

FAMILY **Le petit train jaune.** The "little yellow train" has a service that runs from Bourg-Madame and La Tour de Querol, both easy hikes over the border into France from Puigcerdà (Bourg-Madame is the closest). The border at La Tour, a pretty hour-long hike from Puigcerdà, is marked by a stone painted with the Spanish and French flags. It can also be picked up in Villefranche. The *carrilet* (narrow-gauge railway) is the last in the Pyrenees and is used for tours as well as transportation; it winds slowly through La Cerdanya to the medieval walled town of Villefranche de Conflent. The 63-km (39-mile) tour can take most of the day, especially if you stop to browse in Mont Louis or Villefranche. The last section, between La Cabanasse and Villefranche, is the most picturesque. In low season the trains are infrequent and subject to change. Timetables are available at the stations or on⊕ *www.pyrenees-cerdagne.com.* The tourist office for La Cerdanya also has information and timetables. ⊠ *Oficina De Turisme De La Cerdanya, Carretera Cruïlla N-152 N-260 s/n* ☎ *972/140665* ⊕ *www.cerdanya.org.*

Plaça Cabrinetty. Along with its porticoes and covered walks, this square is protected from the wind and ringed by two- and three-story houses of various pastel colors, some with decorative sgraffito designs and all with balconies. ⊠ *Puigcerdà.*

Santa Maria Bell Tower. The 12th-century Santa Maria church in the center of town was largely destroyed in 1936 during the Spanish Civil War.

The only part to have stood the test of time is the bell tower, which is open to visitors. At the top, a 360-degree view of La Cerdanya's towns, bucolic farmlands, and snowy peaks awaits. ✉ *Pl. Santa Maria s/n* ☎ *972/880542* 🎟 *€2.*

> **TIP**
>
> The tourist office on the outskirts of Puigcerdà (*Oficina de Turisme del Consell Comarcal de la Cerdanya, corner of Ctra. N260 and N152* ☎ *972/880542*) has up-to-date information on the best hiking trails in La Cerdanya. If you're planning a long-distance hiking trip, local bus connections will get you to your starting point and retrieve you from the finish line.

WHERE TO EAT AND STAY

$$$ CATALAN 🍴 **Tap de Suró.** Named for the classic bottle stopper (*tap*) made of cork oak bark (*suró*), this wine store, delicatessen, restaurant, and tapas emporium is the perfect place for sunsets, with views down the length of the Cerdanya Valley accompanied by cheeses, duck and goose liver, and other delicacies. Tucked into the western edge of the town ramparts, it has a varied menu and a frequently changing selection of wines—new and old—from all over Spain and southern France. **Known for:** wine and cava; beautiful views; Iberian ham. [$] *Average main: €20* ✉ *Carrer Querol 21* ☎ *678/655928* 🌐 *www.tapdesuro.com* 💳 *No credit cards* 🕒 *Closed Mon. and Tues.*

$$$ HOTEL 🏨 **Hotel del Lago.** A comfortable old favorite near Puigcerdà's emblematic lake, this spa hotel has a graceful series of buildings around a central garden. **Pros:** picturesque location on the iconic lake; friendly treatment and service; short walk to the center. **Cons:** rooms can be hot on summer days; pricey for its services; no restaurant (only breakfast). [$] *Rooms from: €125* ✉ *Av. Dr. Piguillem 7* ☎ *972/881000* 🌐 *www.hotellago.com* 🛏 *24 rooms* 🍽 *No meals.*

$$$$ HOTEL Fodor's Choice ★ 🏨 **La Torre del Remei.** Brilliantly restored by Josep María and Loles Boix, this 1910 Moderniste tower provides luxurious accommodations about 3 km (2 miles) west of Puigcerdà. **Pros:** perfect comfort and sublime cuisine; surrounded by a hiking, skiing, and golfing paradise; beautiful gardens. **Cons:** pricey; a slightly hushed stiffness; far from the town. [$] *Rooms from: €365* ✉ *Camí del Remei, 3, Bolvir de Cerdanya* ☎ *972/140182* 🌐 *www.torredelremei.com* 🛏 *11 rooms* 🍽 *Free Breakfast.*

SHOPPING

Puigcerdà is one big shopping mall—one that's long been a center for contraband clothes, cigarettes, and other items smuggled across the French border.

Carrer Major. This is an uninterrupted row of stores selling books, jewelry, fashion, sports equipment, and lots more. ✉ *Carrer Major.*

Pasteleria Cosp. For the best *margaritas* in town (no, not those—these are crunchy-edged madeleines made with almonds) head for the oldest commercial establishment in Catalonia, founded in 1806. ✉ *Carrer Major 20* ☎ *972/880103.*

Sunday market. On Sunday morning (9–2), head for this weekly market, which, like those in most Cerdanya towns, is a great place to look for local crafts and specialties such as herbs, goat cheese, wild mushrooms, honey, and baskets. ✉ *Paseo 10 de abril.*

LLÍVIA

6 km (4 miles) northeast of Puigcerdà.

A Spanish enclave in French territory, Llívia was marooned by the 1659 Peace of the Pyrenees treaty, which ceded 33 villages to France. Incorporated as a *vila* (town) by royal decree of Carlos V—who spent a night here in 1528 and was impressed by the town's beauty and hospitality—Llívia managed to remain Spanish. In the middle of town, look for the mosaic commemorating Lampègia, *princesa de la paul i de l'amor* (princess of peace and of love), erected in memory of the red-haired daughter of the Duke of Aquitania and lover of Munuza, a Moorish warlord who governed La Cerdanya in the 8th century during the Arab domination.

GETTING HERE AND AROUND

From Puigcerdà you could walk to Llívia, as it is only 6 km (4 miles) northbound through the border of France, but there is a bus, which departs from the Puigcerdà train station. By car, follow the Camí Vell de Llívia onto the N154, which goes directly to Llívia.

VISITOR INFORMATION

Contacts Llívia Tourist Office. ✉ *Carrer dels Forns 10* ☎ *972/896313.*

EXPLORING

Mare de Déu dels Àngels. At the upper edge of town, this fortified church has wonderful acoustics; check to see if any classical music events are on—especially in August, when it hosts an annual classical music festival. Information about the festival's concerts is released in June. ✉ *Carrer dels Forns 13* ☎ *972/896301.*

Museu de la Farmacia. Across from the Mare de Déu dels Àngels church, this ancient pharmacy, housed within the Museo Municipal, was founded in 1415 and has been certified as the oldest in Europe. ✉ *Carrer dels Forns 10* ☎ *972/896313* 🎫 *€4* ☉ *Closed Mon. Sept.–June.*

WHERE TO EAT

$$$ ✕**Can Ventura.** Inside a flower-festooned 17th-century town house made
SPANISH of ancient stones is one of La Cerdanya's best places for both fine cuisine and good value. Beef *a la llosa* (seared on slabs of slate) and duck with orange and spices are house specialties, and the wide selection of *entretenimientos* (hors d'oeuvres or tapas) is the perfect way to begin. **Known for:** beef seared on hot slate; cozy mountain lodge setting; additional bar area for drinks and tapas. 💲*Average main: €18* ✉ *Pl. Major 1* ☎ *972/896178* ⊕ *www.canventura.com* ☉ *Closed Mon. and Tues.*

$$$ ✕**La Formatgeria de Llívia.** Set on Llívia's eastern edge, this restaurant is
SPANISH inside a former cheese factory, and the proprietors continue the tradition
Fodor'sChoice by producing fresh homemade cheese on the premises while you watch. In
★ the restaurant, fine local cuisine and fondues come with panoramic views looking south toward Puigmal and across the valley. **Known for:** fondues and raclettes; homemade cheese; open fire in winter. 💲*Average main: €20* ✉ *Pl. de Ro s/n, Gorguja* ☎ *972/146279* ⊕ *www.laformatgeria.com* ☉ *Closed Tues. and Wed. (except during Aug. and public holidays).*

BELLVER DE CERDANYA

18 km (11 miles) southwest of Puigcerdà, 31 km (19 miles) southwest of Llívia.

Fodor's Choice ★ Bellver de Cerdanya has preserved its slate-roof-and-fieldstone Pyrenean architecture more successfully than many of La Cerdanya's larger towns. Perched on a promontory over the **Río Segre,** which winds around much of the town, Bellver is a mountain version of a fishing village—trout fishing, to be exact. The town's Gothic church of **Sant Jaume** and the arcaded **Plaça Major,** in the upper part of town, are lovely examples of traditional Pyrenean mountain-village design.

GETTING HERE AND AROUND

Take the southwest-bound N260 from Puigcerdà; once here, it's easily explored on foot.

VISITOR INFORMATION

Contacts Bellver de Cerdanya Tourist Office. ✉ *Pl. Major 12* ☎ *973/510016.*

WHERE TO STAY

$$ B&B/INN 🏨 **Aparthotel Bellver.** The warmth of terra-cotta tiles, the great views, and the traditional fireplaces in some of the rooms add to the charm of this mountain lodge and apartment block within the winding streets of central Bellver. **Pros:** central location; open year-round; parking on-site. **Cons:** two-night minimum stay in July and August; no air-conditioning; not many apartments so it books up quickly. [$] *Rooms from: €100* ✉ *Carrer de la Batllia 61–63* ☎ *973/510627* 🌐 *www.aparthotelbellver.com* ⏲ *Sometimes closes 10 days in May or June (check ahead)* 🛏 *12 apartments* 🍴 *No meals.*

LA SEU D'URGELL

20 km (12 miles) south of Andorra la Vella (in Andorra), 45 km (28 miles) west of Puigcerdà, 200 km (120 miles) northwest of Barcelona.

Fodor's Choice ★ La Seu d'Urgell is an ancient town facing the snowy rock wall of the Sierra del Cadí. As the seat (*seu*) of the regional archbishopric since the 6th century, it has a rich legacy of art and architecture. The Pyrenean feel of the streets, with their dark balconies and porticoes, overhanging galleries, and colonnaded porches—particularly **Carrer dels Canonges**—makes Seu mysterious and memorable. Look for the medieval **grain measures** at the corner of Carrer Major and Carrer Capdevila. The tiny food shops on the arcaded Carrer Major are good places to assemble lunch for a hike.

GETTING HERE AND AROUND

Take the N260 southwest from Puigcerdà via Bellver de Cerdanya. From the direction of Lleida, head north on the C13 for 63 km (39 miles), then take the C26 after Balaguer, before joining the C14 for 32 km (20 miles) and then the N260 into the center. There are buses daily from Barcelona. The town is compact and can be explored on foot.

Contacts ALSA. ✉ *Estación de Autobuses* ☎ *902/422242* 🌐 *www.alsa.es.*

VISITOR INFORMATION

Contacts La Seu d'Urgell Tourist Office. ✉ *Calle Mayor 8* ☎ *973/351511* 🌐 *www.turismeseu.com.*

EXPLORING

Fodor's Choice ★ **Catedral de Santa Maria.** This 12th-century cathedral is the finest in the Pyrenees, and the sunlight casting the rich reds and blues of Santa Maria's southeastern rose window into the deep gloom of the transept is a moving sight. The 13th-century cloister is famous for the individually carved, often whimsical capitals on its 50 columns, crafted by the same Roussillon school of masons who carved the doorway on the church of Santa Maria in Ripoll. Don't miss the haunting, 11th-century chapel of **Sant Miquel** or the **Diocesan Museum,** which has a collection of striking medieval murals from various Pyrenean churches and a colorfully illuminated 10th-century Mozarabic manuscript of the monk Beatus de Liébana's commentary on the apocalypse. ✉ *Pl. del Deganat* ☎ *973/353242* 🌐 *www.museudiocesaurgell.org* 🎫 *€3, includes museum* ⏲ *Closed Sun.*

WHERE TO STAY

$ B&B/INN Fodor's Choice ★ 🏨 **Cal Serni.** Ten minutes north of La Seu d'Urgell in the Pyrenean village of Calbinyà, this enchanting 15th-century farmhouse and inn exudes rustic charm and provides inexpensive local gastronomy against a backdrop of panoramic views. **Pros:** mountain authenticity just minutes from La Seu; good value; incredible views. **Cons:** small guest rooms; tight public spaces; simple lodgings. [$] *Rooms from: €60* ✉ *Ctra. de Calbinyà s/n, Valls de Valira, Calbinyà* ☎ *973/352809* 🌐 *www.calserni.com* 🛏 *6 rooms* 🍴 *No meals.*

$$$$ HOTEL 🏨 **El Castell de Ciutat.** Just outside town, the setting of this wood-and-slate structure beneath La Seu's castle makes it one of the finest places to stay in the Pyrenees—rooms on the second floor have balconies overlooking the river and surrounding valley, those on the third have slanted ceilings and dormer windows, and suites include a salon. **Pros:** best restaurant for many miles; magnificent Pyrenean panoramas; onsite spa. **Cons:** standard upper-floor rooms feel slightly cramped; next to a busy highway; misses out on the feel of the town. [$] *Rooms from: €225* ✉ *Ctra. de Lleida (N260), Km 229* ☎ *973/350000* 🌐 *www.hotelelcastell.com* 🛏 *33 rooms, 5 suites* 🍴 *Free Breakfast.*

$$$ HOTEL 🏨 **Parador de la Seu d'Urgell.** These comfortable quarters right in the center of town are built into the 14th-century convent of Sant Domènec. **Pros:** next to the Santa Maria cathedral; handy for wandering through the town; historic building. **Cons:** some rooms are small; mediocre restaurant; no parking. [$] *Rooms from: €160* ✉ *Calle Sant Domènec 6* ☎ *973/352000* 🌐 *www.parador.es* 🛏 *79 rooms* 🍴 *No meals.*

WESTERN CATALAN PYRENEES

"The farther from Barcelona, the wilder" is the rule of thumb, and this is true of the rugged countryside and fauna in the western part of Catalonia. Three of the greatest destinations in the Pyrenees are here: the harmonious, Atlantic-influenced Vall d'Aran; the Noguera de Tor Valley (aka Vall de Boí), with its matching set of gemlike Romanesque

churches; and Parc Nacional d'Aigüestortes i Estany de Sant Maurici, which has a network of pristine lakes and streams. The main geographical units in this section are the valley of the Noguera Pallaresa River, the Vall d'Aran headwaters of the Atlantic-bound Garonne, and the Noguera Ribagorçana River Valley, Catalonia's western limit.

SORT

59 km (37 miles) west of La Seu d'Urgell, 136 km (84 miles) north of Lleida, 259 km (161 miles) northwest of Barcelona.

The capital of the Pallars Sobirà (Upper Pallars Valley) is the area's epicenter for skiing, fishing, and white-water kayaking. The word *sort* is Catalan for "luck," and its local lottery shop, La Bruixa d'Or (The Gold Witch), became a tourist attraction by living up to the town's name and selling more than an average number of winning tickets. Don't be fooled by the town you see from the main road: one block back, Sort is honeycombed with tiny streets and protected corners built to stave off harsh winter weather.

GETTING HERE AND AROUND
Heading westward from La Seu d'Urgell, take the N260 toward Lleida, head west again at Adrall, staying on the N260, and drive 53 km (33 miles) over the Cantó Pass to Sort.

VISITOR INFORMATION
Contacts Pallars Sobirà Tourist Office. ⊠ *Camí de la Cabanera 1* ☏ *973/621002* ⊕ *turisme.pallarssobira.cat.*

WHERE TO EAT

$$$$
SPANISH
Fodor's Choice
★

✕ **Fogony.** Come here for seasonal and contemporary creations from an acclaimed chef and supporter of the slow-food movement, with a prix-fixe menu that may include dishes such as *pollo a la cocotte con trufa* (organic bluefoot chicken with truffle) and *solomillo de ternera de los Pirineos con ligero escabeche de verduras y setas* (fillet of Pyrenean veal with marinated vegetables and mushrooms). This restaurant is one of the best of its kind in the Pyrenees and, if you hit Sort at lunchtime, it makes an excellent reason to stop. **Known for:** part of the "slow food" movement; family run; Michelin star. $ *Average main: €38* ⊠ *Av. Generalitat 45* ☏ *973/621225* ⊕ *www.fogony.com* ☉ *Closed Mon. and Tues. and 2 wks in Jan. No dinner Sun.*

PARC NACIONAL D'AIGÜESTORTES I ESTANY DE SANT MAURICI

33 km (20 miles) north of Sort, 168 km (104 miles) north of Lleida, 292 km (181 miles) northwest of Barcelona.

Catalonia's only national park is a dramatic and unspoiled landscape shaped over 2 million years of glacial activity. Hikers can reach the park from the Noguera Pallaresa and Ribagorçana valleys, from the villages of Espot to the east, and from Taüll and Boí to the west. There are several visitor centers, with maps and information on hiking routes and accommodation, in the villages that border the park, such as Espot and Boí.

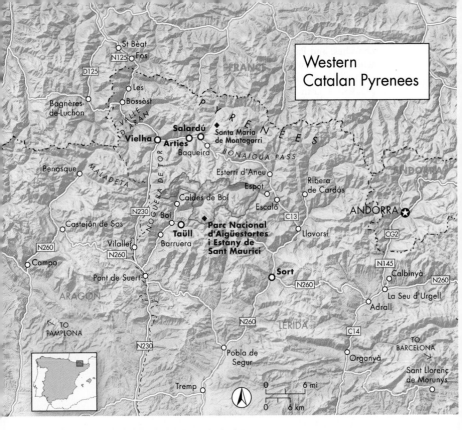

GETTING HERE AND AROUND

The C13 north up the Noguera Pallaresa Valley covers 34 km (21 miles) from Sort to Espot. One of the main entrances to the park is 4 km (2 miles) west of Espot, where there is also a parking lot. No cars are allowed inside the park (except official taxis/transport).

Casa del Parc Nacional de Boí (Park Information Centre - Boí). ⊠ *Ca de Simamet, Carrer de les Graieres, 2, Boí* ☎ *973/696189.*

Casa del Parc Nacional d'Espot (Park Information Centre). ⊠ *Carrer de Sant Maurici, 5, Espot* ☎ *973/624036.*

Fodor's Choice **Parc Nacional d'Aigüestortes i Estany de Sant Maurici.** The breathtaking ★ scenery of this national park is formed by jagged peaks, steep rock walls, and an abundance of high mountain terrain, all of which lie in the shadow of the twin peaks of Els Encantats. More than 300 glacial lakes and lagoons trickle through forests and meadows of wildflowers to the meandering Noguera River watercourses: the Pallaresa to the east and the Ribagorçana to the west. The land range sweeps from soft lower meadows below 5,000 feet to the highest crags at nearly double that height. The twin Encantats measure more than 9,000 feet, and the surrounding peaks of Beciberri, Peguera, Montarto, and Amitges hover between 8,700 feet and a little less than 10,000 feet. The park offers an abundance of walking trails. The most popular is a one-day scenic traverse across the park from east to west, starting at the village of Espot and finishing in Boí.

Between June and September simple mountain lodges (refugios) fill with tired and hungry hikers sharing trail tips and lore; it's essential to make a reservation during this high season.

Park rangers monitor the park, and there are strict rules: no camping, no fires, no swimming, no vehicles beyond certain points, and no off-leash pets. ■TIP→ **Although driving inside the park is not permitted, it is possible to organize taxis to help you on your way from Boí or Espot, and, in summer, buses also provide transportation in and around the park.** For more information on routes, accommodations, and transportation, visit the park's information offices. At any time of year, it is advisable to check weather conditions before setting out. ⊠ *Espot* ⊕ *www.aiguestortes.info* ✉ *Free.*

WHERE TO STAY

There are no hotels in the park, but the nine refugios have staff who provide basic dormitory-style accommodations, as well as dinner and breakfast for hikers June–October and during shorter periods at Christmas and Easter. When these are not open or staffed, shelter is still available in parts of the park, and fireplaces can be used for cooking, but hikers must supply the food and the utensils. Bookings can be made on the website (⊕ *www.lacentralderefugis.com*). If you plan on only day hikes, there are several hotels and restaurants in the villages of Taüll and Boí, on the western side of the park, or Espot to the east.

TAÜLL

58 km (35 miles) south of Vielha.

Taüll is a town of narrow streets and tight mountain design—wooden balconies and steep, slate roofs—that makes an attractive base for exploring the Parc Nacional d'Aigüestortes. The high-sided valley also has one of the greatest concentrations of Romanesque architecture in Europe, and the famous Taüll churches of **Sant Climent** and **Santa María** are among the best examples of Romanesque architecture in the Pyrenees. Other important churches near Taüll include Sant Feliu, at Barruera; Sant Joan Baptista, at Boí; Santa Maria, at Cardet; Santa Maria, at Col; Santa Eulàlia, at Erill la Vall; La Nativitat de la Mare de Deu and Sant Quirze, at Durro.

GETTING HERE AND AROUND

Take the N230 northbound from Lleida for 138 km (86 miles), passing through El Pont de Suert. At Erill la Vall, go east for 4 km (2½ miles) toward Boí and Taüll. Taüll is small enough to walk around unless you are headed to the ski resort, in which case a car is needed. Four-wheel-drive taxis into the Parc Nacional d'Aigüestortes can be organized from Espot (☎ 973/624036 *for tourist office*).

VISITOR INFORMATION

Contacts Centre del Romànic de la Vall de Boí. ⊠ *Carrer del Batalló 5, Erill la Vall* ☎ *973/696715* ⊕ *www.centreromanic.com.* **Taüll Tourist Office.** ⊠ *Passeig de St. Feliu 43, Barruera* ☎ *973/694000* ⊕ *www.vallboi.com.*

EXPLORING

Fodor's Choice ★ **Sant Climent.** At the edge of town, this exquisite three-nave Romanesque church was built in 1123. The six-story belfry has perfect proportions, with Pyrenean stone that changes hues with the light, and a sense of intimacy and balance. In 1922 Barcelona's Museu Nacional d'Art de Catalunya removed the murals for safekeeping, including the famous *Pantocrator,* the work of the "Master of Taüll." The murals presently in the church are reproductions. ✉ *Ctra. de Taüll s/n* 🌐 *www.centreromanic.com* 🎟 *€5.*

WHERE TO EAT

$$ ECLECTIC FAMILY 🍴 **L'Era.** The owners of this rustic restaurant raise their farm animals in ecologically friendly fashion and the menu focuses on the highest quality cuts of organic beef and veal, including grilled steaks and hamburgers, accompanied by sides that include fresh salads. There's also locally cured meat and cheese platters, and the chocolate coulant should not be missed. **Known for:** organic cuts of beef; hamburgers and steak; bar and terrace. [$] *Average main: €15* ✉ *Carrer Major 7* ☎ *973/694192.*

VIELHA

79 km (49 miles) northwest of Sort, 297 km (185 miles) northwest of Barcelona, 160 km (99 miles) north of Lleida.

Vielha (Viella in Spanish), capital of the Vall d'Aran, is a lively crossroads vitally involved in the Aranese movement to defend and reconstruct the valley's architectural, institutional, and linguistic heritage. At first glance, the town looks like a typical ski-resort base, but the compact and bustling old quarter has a Romanesque church and narrow streets filled with a good selection of restaurants, shops, and a couple of late-night bars. Hiking and climbing are popular around Vielha; guides are available year-round and can be arranged through the tourist office.

GETTING HERE AND AROUND

From the direction of Taüll, head south on the L500 for 15 km (9 miles) toward El Pont de Suerte. At Campament de Tor turn right onto the Carretera Lleida–Vielha (N230) northbound to Vielha. Vielha's town center is fairly compact and everything can be reached on foot, but you'll need a car to get to Salardú, Arties, and the ski station of Baqueira-Beret.

VISITOR INFORMATION

Contacts Vielha Tourist Office. ✉ *Carrer Sarriulera 10* ☎ *973/640110* 🌐 *www.visitvaldaran.com.*

EXPLORING

Sant Miquel. Vielha's octagonal, 14th-century bell tower on the Romanesque parish church of Sant Miquel is one of the town's trademarks, as is its 15th-century Gothic altar. The partly damaged 12th-century wood carving *Cristo de Mig Aran,* displayed under glass, evokes a sense of mortality and humanity with a power unusual in medieval sculpture. ✉ *Pl. de la Iglesia.*

Hiking in the Pyrenees

Walking the Pyrenees, with one foot in France and the other in Spain, is an exhilarating experience.

In fall and winter, the Alberes Mountains between Cap de Creus, the Iberian Peninsula's easternmost point, and the border with France at Le Perthus are a grassy runway between the Côte Vermeille's curving beaches to the north and the green patchwork of the Empordá to the south. The well-marked GR (Gran Recorrido) 11 is a favorite two-day spring or autumn hike, with an overnight stay at the Refugi de la Tanyareda, just below and east of Puig Neulós, the highest point in the Alberes.

The eight-hour walk from Coll de Núria to Ulldeter over the Sierra Catllar, above Setcases, is another grassy corridor in good weather April–October. The luminous Cerdanya Valley is a hiker's paradise year-round, while the summertime round-Andorra hike is a memorably scenic 360-degree tour of the tiny country.

The Parc Nacional d'Aigüestortes i Estany de Sant Maurici is superb for trekking from spring through fall. The ascent of the highest peak in the Pyrenees, the 11,168-foot Aneto peak above Benasque, is a long day's round-trip best approached in summer and only by fit and experienced hikers. Much of the hike is over the Maladeta Glacier, from the base camp at the Refugio de La Renclusa.

In the Parque Nacional de Ordesa y Monte Perdido you can take day trips up to the Cola de Caballo waterfall and back around the southern rim of the canyon or, for true mountain goats, longer hikes via the Refugio de Góriz to La Brèche de Roland and Gavarnie or to Monte Perdido, the parador at La Pineta, and the village of Bielsa. Another prized walk involves bed and dinner in the base-camp town of Torla or a night up at the Refugio de Góriz at the head of the valley.

The section of the Camino de Santiago walk from Saint-Jean-Pied-de-Port to Roncesvalles is a marvelous 8- to 10-hour trek any time of year, though check weather reports carefully October–June.

Local *excursionista* (outing) clubs can help you get started; local tourist offices may also have brochures and rudimentary trail maps. Note that the higher reaches are safely navigable only in summer.

Some useful contacts for hiking are **Cercle d'Aventura** (☎ 972/881017 ⊕ www.cercleaventura.com), **Giroguies** (☎ 636/490830 ⊕ www.giroguies.com), **Guies de Meranges** (☎ 616/855535 ⊕ www.guiesmeranges.com), and **Guies de Muntanya** (☎ 629/591614 ⊕ www.guiesdemuntanya.com).

WHERE TO EAT

$$$ ✕ **El Molí.** A picturesque riverside location, knotty pine walls, wood
SPANISH beams, and a rustic menu that highlights regional specialties make this a lovely spot for a meal. The restaurant includes a ground-floor dining room with large windows that frame a broad sweep of the river and a second, smaller dining room tucked away in the attic. **Known for:** chuleton de vaca vieja del Pirineo (aged beef, cooked over hot coals); river

views; calçots (Catalan green onions). $ *Average main: €20* ✉ *Carrèr Sarriulèra 26* ☎ *973/641718* ⊕ *www.hotelelmoli.es/en* ⊗ *No dinner Tues. Closed Wed. and Dec. 18–Jan. 18.*

$$ ✕ **Era Mola** (*Restaurante Gustavo y María José*). This rustic former sta-
SPANISH ble with whitewashed walls serves Aranese dishes with a modern, often French twist. Duck, either stewed with apples or served with *carreretes* (wild mushrooms from the valley), and roast lamb are favorites, as are *foie-gras de pato con pistachos con caramelo de Pedro Ximenez* (duck foie gras with pistachios and Pedro Ximenez syrup). **Known for:** excel-lent service; specialty of pigs' trotters stuffed with mushrooms and truffle sauce; traditional cuisine from Vall d'Aran. $ *Average main: €17* ✉ *Car-rer Marrec 14* ☎ *973/642419* ⊗ *Closed Wed., and May, June, and Oct. No lunch weekdays Dec.–Apr. (except during Christmas and Easter wks).*

WHERE TO STAY

$$$ ⌂ **Hotel El Ciervo.** In Vielha's old quarter, and next to one of the town's
B&B/INN attractive pedestrian-only streets, this family-run inn resembles an idyllic winter cottage, and the personal service includes breakfast, available for a small additional charge, which former guests have touted as the best in Spain. **Pros:** quirky and inviting; excellent breakfast; pleasant furnish-ings. **Cons:** rooms are a little cramped; the feminine, chintz style may not appeal to everyone; breakfast costs extra. $ *Rooms from: €130* ✉ *Pl. de San Orencio 3* ☎ *973/640165* ⊕ *www.hotelelciervo.net* ⊗ *Closed Apr.–mid-June and last 2 wks Oct. and Nov.* ⇆ *20 rooms* ⊙*No meals.*

$$$$ ⌂ **Parador de Vielha.** The shining star at this modern granite parador
HOTEL is a semicircular salon with huge windows and spectacular views over the Maladeta peaks of the Vall d'Aran. **Pros:** terrific observation post; comfortable and relaxed; on-site spa and swimming pool. **Cons:** over-modern and somewhat lacking in character; beside a busy road; 2 km (1 mile) from Vielha old town. $ *Rooms from: €190* ✉ *Ctra. del Túnel s/n* ☎ *973/640100* ⊕ *www.parador.es* ⊗ *Closed mid-Oct.–mid-Nov. (dates vary; check ahead)* ⇆ *118 rooms* ⊙*No meals.*

NIGHTLIFE

DeVins. This popular wine bar has a prime location overlooking the river, and gets busy in the early evening serving tapas, cheese boards, and wine. Later in the evening it becomes a bar dedicated mainly to gin and tonics, but other spirits and a decent wine list are also available. ✉ *Carrèr Major 23* ☎ *647/511146.*

Eth Saxo. This is the most popular late-night bar for all ages in down-town Vielha. ✉ *Carrer Marrec 6.*

SHOPPING

Eth Galin Reiau. This shop, on the same square as the church, has its own brand of products, which range from locally produced pâté foie gras and cheese to liqueurs, marmalades, and honey. ✉ *Pl. de la Gleisa 2* ☎ *973/641941* ⊕ *www.tiendagalinreiau.com.*

SPORTS AND THE OUTDOORS

Skiing, white-water rafting, hiking, climbing, horseback riding, and fly-fishing are just some of the sports available throughout the Vall d'Aran.

Baqueira-Beret Estación de Esquí (*Baqueira-Beret Ski Station*). This ski center offers Catalonia's most varied and reliable skiing. Its 87 km (54 miles) of *pistas* (slopes), spread over 53 runs, range from the gentle Beret slopes to the vertical chutes of Baqueira. The Bonaigua area is a mixture of steep and gently undulating trails, with some of the longest, most varied runs in the Pyrenees. A dozen restaurants and four children's areas are scattered about the facilities, and the thermal baths at Tredós are 4 km (2½ miles) away. ⊠ *Calle Baqueira Beret* ☎ *973/639025* ⊕ *www.baqueira.es.*

ARTIES

7 km (4 miles) east of Vielha, 3½ km (2 miles) west of Salardú.

The village of Arties makes a good stop; here you'll find a lively village of Romanesque, Gothic, and Renaissance styles, straddling a clear river that's presided over by the Montarto Peak.

GETTING HERE AND AROUND
The C28 east out of Vielha heads straight to Arties in 7 km (4 miles). The village is small and best explored on foot. Cross over the bridge over the river to hit the main square.

WHERE TO EAT AND STAY

$$
TAPAS ✕ **Tauèrnes Urtau.** The area's most happening tapas chain is friendly, fun, and always busy. Customers can help themselves at the bar to an assortment of 40 mouthwatering *pinchos* (creative toppings on bread, held together with a toothpick, such as mini hamburger, king prawn with mushrooms, or ravioli with foie gras), or go for the tapas menu and table service. **Known for:** Basque-style "help yourself at the bar" pinchos; cider and local products; rollicking atmosphere. Ⓢ *Average main: €16* ⊠ *Pl. Urtau 12, Artiés* ☎ *973/640926* ⊕ *www.urtau.com* ⊗ *Closed 2 wks in Oct. or Nov.*

$$$$
B&B/INN ⬚ **Casa Irene.** A rustic haven, Casa Irene's style and spacious, elegant rooms make it a desirable place to stay. **Pros:** small and personalized; aesthetically impeccable; free shuttle service to the slopes. **Cons:** streetside rooms can be noisy on summer nights; restaurant closed Monday; often booked up. Ⓢ *Rooms from: €200* ⊠ *Carrer Major 22, 6 km (4 miles) east of Vielha, Artiés* ☎ *973/644364* ⊕ *www.hotelcasairene.com* ⊗ *Closed May, June, Oct., and Nov.* ⬧ *Reservations essential* ⇥ *22 rooms* ⧖ *Free Breakfast.*

$$$
HOTEL ⬚ **Parador de Arties.** Built around the Casa de Don Gaspar de Portolà, once home to the founder of the colony of California, this modern parador with friendly staff has views of the Pyrenees and is handy for exploring the Romanesque sights in nearby villages. **Pros:** marvelous panoramas; quiet and personal for a parador; mountain-lodge style. **Cons:** neither at the foot of the slopes nor in the thick of the Vielha après-ski vibe; requires driving; feels old-fashioned. Ⓢ *Rooms from: €163* ⊠ *Calle San Juan 1, Artiés* ☎ *973/640801* ⊕ *www.parador.es* ⊗ *Closed 40 days after Easter wk (dates can vary)* ⇥ *54 rooms, 3 suites* ⧖ *No meals.*

6

SALARDÚ

9 km (6 miles) east of Vielha.

Salardú is a pivotal point in the Vall d'Aran, convenient to Baqueira-Beret, the Montarto peak, the lakes and Circ de Colomers, Parc Nacional d'Aigüestortes, and the villages of Tredós, Unha, and Montgarri. The town itself, with a little more than 700 inhabitants, is known for its steep streets and its octagonal fortified bell tower.

GETTING HERE AND AROUND

The C28 east out of Vielha goes straight to Salardú and Tredós in 9 km (6 miles) and on to Baqueira-Beret in 13 km (8 miles).

EXPLORING

OFF THE BEATEN PATH

Santa Maria de Montgarri. Partly in ruins, this 11th-century chapel was once an important way station on the route into the Vall d'Aran from France. The beveled, hexagonal bell tower and the rounded stones, which look as if they came from a brook bottom, give the structure a stippled appearance that's a bit like a Pyrenean trout. The Romería de Nuestra Señora de Montgarri (Feast of Our Lady of Montgarri), on July 2, is a country fair with feasting, games, music, and dance. The sanctuary can be reached by following the C142 road until Beret and then walking 6 km (4 miles) along a dirt track that can also be accessed by off-road vehicles. It is difficult to get there during the winter snow season. ✉ *Salardú.*

6

WHERE TO EAT AND STAY

$$$ SPANISH

🍴 **Casa Rufus.** Fresh pine on the walls and the floor, red-and-white-check curtains, and snowy-white tablecloths cozily furnish this restaurant in the tiny, gray-stone village of Gessa, between Vielha and Salardú. Try the *conejo relleno de ternera y cerdo* (rabbit stuffed with veal and pork). **Known for:** said to be one of the best restaurants in the area; wide selection of local meat dishes; good stop off on way to or from the Baqueira ski slopes. [$] *Average main: €18* ✉ *Carrer Sant Jaume 8, Gessa* ☎ *973/645246* 🕓 *Closed May and June, weekdays in Oct. and Nov., and Sun. Oct.–Apr.*

$$$$ SPANISH

🍴 **Taberna Eth Bot.** You can feast where the farm animals once grazed in this converted 16th-century stable, where the fixed-price menu features local Aranese dishes such as *Aranese Olla* (a hearty stew from the Aran Valley), *patatas rellenas* (potato stewed with a choice of meat or vegetables), or *estofado de jabalí y arroz* (wild boar stew served with rice). A bottle of wine, water, and bread—and a shot of local liqueur at the end—are thrown in for good measure. **Known for:** atmospheric building; local Aranese cuisine; no frills, but plenty of atmosphere. [$] *Average main: €35* ✉ *Pl. Mayor 1* ☎ *973/644212.*

$$$$ HOTEL

🏨 **Val de Ruda.** For rustic surroundings—light on luxury but long on comfort—only a two-minute walk from the ski lift, this modern-traditional construction of glass, wood, and stone is a good choice. **Pros:** pleasant and outdoorsy; warm and welcoming after a day in the mountains; friendly family service. **Cons:** some of the upstairs rooms are cozy but tiny; only open during ski season; not cheap. [$] *Rooms from: €255* ✉ *Ctra. Baqueira-Beret Cota 1500* ☎ *973/645258* 🌐 *www.hotelvalderudabaqueira.com* 🕓 *Closed after Easter wk–end Nov.* 🛏 *35 rooms* 🍽 *Free Breakfast.*

ARAGÓN AND CENTRAL PYRENEES

The highest, wildest, and most spectacular range of the Pyrenees is the middle section, farthest from sea level. From Benasque on Aragón's eastern side to Jaca at the western edge are the great heights and most dramatic landscapes of Alto Aragón (Upper Aragón), including the Maladeta (11,165 feet), Posets (11,070 feet), and Monte Perdido (11,004 feet) peaks, the three highest points in the Pyrenean chain.

Communications between the high valleys of the Pyrenees were all but nonexistent until the 19th century: four-fifths of the region had never seen a motor vehicle of any kind until well into the 20th century, and the 150-km (93-mile) border with France between Portalet de Aneu and Vall d'Aran had never had an international crossing. This combination of high peaks, deep defiles (mountain passages), and isolation has produced some of the Iberian Peninsula's best-preserved towns and valleys. Each valley has its own variations on everything from the typical Aragonese folk dance, the *jota,* to cuisine and traditional costume.

ZARAGOZA

138 km (86 miles) west of Lleida, 307 km (191 miles) northwest of Barcelona, 164 km (102 miles) southeast of Pamplona, 322 km (200 miles) northeast of Madrid.

Despite its hefty size (population 680,000), this sprawling provincial capital midway between Barcelona, Madrid, Bilbao, and Valencia is a detour from the tourist track, yet still accessible via the AVE, Spain's high-speed railroad, with both Madrid and Barcelona only 90 minutes away. The first decade of this century were major boom years here, and it's been rated one of Spain's most desirable places to live because of its good air quality, low cost of living, and low population density.

Straddling Spain's greatest river, the Ebro, Zaragoza was originally named Caesaraugusta, for the Roman emperor Augustus, and established as a thriving river port by 25 BC. Its legacy contains everything from Roman ruins and Jewish baths to Moorish, Romanesque, Gothic-Mudejar, Renaissance, Baroque, neoclassical, and Art Nouveau architecture. Parts of the **Roman walls** are visible near the city's landmark **Basílica de Nuestra Señora del Pilar.** Nearby, the medieval **Puente de Piedra** (Stone Bridge) spans the Ebro. Checking out the **Lonja** (Stock Exchange), **La Seo cathedral,** the Moorish **Aljafería** (Fortified Palace and Jewel Treasury), the **Mercado de Lanuza** (Produce Market), and the many **Mudejar churches** in the old town is a good way to navigate Zaragoza's jumble of backstreets.

Worthwhile excursions from Zaragoza include the birthplace of Francisco José de Goya y Lucientes in **Fuendetodos,** 44 km (27 miles) to the southeast, and the **Monasterio de Piedra,** an hour's drive southwest of Zaragoza. Founded in 1195 by Alfonso II of Aragón, this lush oasis of caves, waterfalls, and suspended walkways surround a Cistercian monastery that dates back to the 12th century, and a 16th-century Renaissance section that is now a private hotel (⊕ *www.monasteriopiedra.com*).

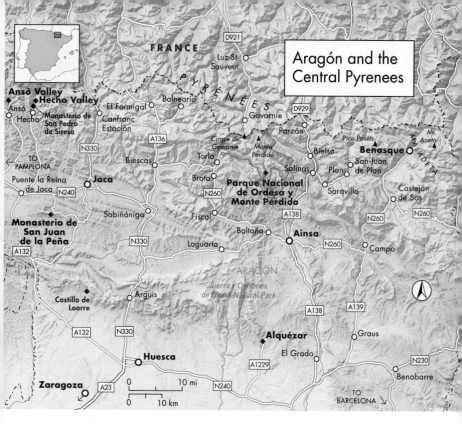

Aragón and the Central Pyrenees

GETTING HERE AND AROUND

There are several trains per day between Zaragoza and Barcelona, Lleida, and Huesca (⊕ *www.renfe.com*). The bus company Alosa (⊕ *www.alosa.es*) runs buses between Zaragoza, Huesca, and Jaca. By car, travel west from Barcelona on the E90 motorway. All of Zaragoza's main sights are accessible on foot, as the center is compact and much of it is traffic-free.

Bus Station Estación Central de Autobuses. ✉ *Calle Miguel Roca i Junyent 7* ☎ *976/700599* ⊕ *www.estacion-zaragoza.es.*

VISITOR INFORMATION

Contacts Zaragoza Tourist Office. ✉ *Pl. de Nuestra Señora del Pilar* ☎ *902/142008* ⊕ *www.zaragozaturismo.es.*

EXPLORING

Fodor'sChoice ★ **Basílica de Nuestra Señora del Pilar** (*Basilica of Our Lady of the Pillar*). Hulking on the banks of the Ebro, the basilica, often known simply as La Pilarica or El Pilar, is Zaragoza's symbol and pride. An immense baroque structure with no fewer than 11 tile cupolas, La Pilarica is the home of the Virgen del Pilar, the patron saint not only of peninsular Spain but of the entire Hispanic world. The fiestas honoring this most Spanish of saints, held the week of October 12, are events of

Mountain trekking in the Huesca province

extraordinary pride and Spanish fervor, with processions, street concerts, bullfights, and traditional jota dancing. The cathedral was built in the 18th century to commemorate the appearance of the Virgin on a pillar (*pilar* , or pedestal) to St. James, Spain's other patron saint, during his legendary appearance as Santiago Matamoros (St. James the Moorslayer) in the 9th century. La Pilarica herself resides in a side chapel that dates to 1754. Among the basilica's treasures are two frescoes by Goya—one of them, *El Coreto de la Vírgen,* painted when he was young and the other, the famous *Regina Martirum*, after his studies in Italy. The bombs displayed to the right of the altar of La Pilarica chapel fell through the roof of the church in 1936 and miraculously failed to explode. You can still see both of the holes, one in the corner of the earlier Goya fresco and the other by the top of the column overhead to the left. Behind La Pilarica's altar is the tiny opening where the devout line up to kiss the rough marble pillar where La Pilarica is believed to have been discovered. There is an elevator in one of the towers for easy access to great views of the city. ⊠ *Pl. del Pilar s/n* 🕾 *Basilica free, tower €3, museum €2* 🕑 *Museum closed Sun.; tower closed Mon. in winter.*

Iglesia de San Pablo. After the basilica and La Seo, this church, with examples of Mudejar architecture in its brickwork, is considered by zaragozanos to be the "third cathedral."⊠ *Carrer San Pablo 42* 🕾 *976/446296* 🕾 *From 2€* 🕑 *Closed Sun.*

La Seo (*Catedral de San Salvador*). Zaragoza's cathedral, at the eastern end of the Plaza del Pilar, is the city's bishopric, or diocesan *seo* (seat). An amalgam of architectural styles, ranging from the Mudejar brick-and-tile exterior to the Gothic altarpiece to exuberant churrigueresque doorways,

La Seo nonetheless has an 18th-century baroque facade that seems to echo those of La Pilarica. The **Museo de Tapices** within contains medieval tapestries. The nearby medieval **Casa y Arco del Deán** form one of the city's favorite corners. ⊠ *Pl. de la Seo* 🖃 *€4, includes museum.*

Museo del Foro. Remains of the Roman forum and the Roman sewage system can be seen here. Two more Roman sites, the **thermal baths** at Calle de San Juan y San Pedro and the **river port** at Plaza San Bruno, are also open to the public. You can organize in advance to see the presentation videos in English through the Museo del Teatro Romano (☎ 976/726075), and English-language audio guides are also available. ⊠ *Pl. de la Seo 2* ☎ *976/721221* 🖃 *€3* ⊘ *Closed Mon.*

Museo del Teatro Romano. In addition to the restored Roman amphitheater here, you can also see objects recovered during the excavation process, including theatrical masks, platters, and even Roman hairpins. ⊠ *Calle San Jorge 12* ☎ *976/726075* 🖃 *€4* ⊘ *Closed Mon.*

Museo Goya Colección Ibercaja. A fine collection of Goya's works, particularly engravings, are on view here. ⊠ *Carrer Espoz y Mina 23* ☎ *976/397328* ⊕ *museogoya.ibercaja.es* 🖃 *4€.*

Palacio de La Aljafería. This is one of Spain's three greatest Moorish palaces. If Córdoba's Mezquita shows the energy of the 10th-century Caliphate and Granada's Alhambra is the crowning 14th-century glory of Al-Andalus (the 789-year Moorish empire on the Iberian Peninsula), then the late-11th-century Aljafería can be seen as the intermediate step. Originally a fortress and royal residence, and later a seat of the Spanish Inquisition, the Aljafería is now the home of the Cortes (Parliament) de Aragón. The 9th-century Torre del Trovador (Tower of the Troubadour) appears in Giuseppe Verdi's opera *Il Trovatore.* ⊠ *Diputados s/n* ☎ *976/289683* ⊕ *www.cortesaragon.es* 🖃 *€5* ⊘ *Closed Thurs. and Fri. if parliament is in session.*

WHERE TO EAT

$$
SPANISH
Fodor's Choice
★

✕ **El Tubo.** Zaragoza's famous El Tubo area, around the intersection of Calle Estébanes and Calle Libertad, offers the chance to eat your way through a diverse array of bite-size sharing plates that are meant to be enjoyed standing up or leaning against a bar stool. Limit yourself to one tapa per bar so you can sample as much as possible. **El Champi** may not be much to look at, but this tiny establishment serves wonderful mushrooms grilled with garlic and olive oil, stacked on bread to soak up the garlic-infused oil. **Known for:** variety of tapas bars; lively atmosphere; narrow, pedestrianized streets. 🟊 *Average main: €15* ⊠ *Calle Estébanes.*

$$$
SPANISH

✕ **Gran Taberna Tragantua.** This rollicking spot serves surprisingly great food, including *solomillicos con salsa de trufa* (little beef fillets with truffle sauce), *albóndigas de solomillicos* (meatballs of beef fillet), and a mouthwatering array of seafood. The beer is fresh and cold, and the house wines, usually from Upper Aragón's own Somontano D.O., are of top value and quality. **Known for:** excellent house wines; seafood dishes; nice lunch location. 🟊 *Average main: €19* ⊠ *Pl. Santa Marta s/n* ☎ *976/299174* ⊕ *www.grupoloscabezudos.es* ⊘ *Closed 2nd wk in June.*

$$
TAPAS

✕ **Los Victorinos.** Named after a much-feared and respected breed of fighting bull, this rustic tavern, located behind La Seo, is heavily adorned

Overlooking the Río Ebro and Zaragoza's Basílica de Nuestra Señora del Pilar

with bullfight-related paraphernalia. It offers an elaborate and inventive selection of pinchos and original tapas of all kinds. *Jamón ibérico de bellota* (acorn-fed Iberian ham), Spain's best-known luxury food, is always a natural choice, though quail eggs or the classic *gilda*—olives, green peppers, and anchovies on a toothpick—are also on the bar and hard to resist. **Known for:** Iberian ham; gilda (olives, green peppers, and anchovies); lively atmosphere. [$] *Average main: €15* ✉ *Calle José de la Hera 6* ☎ *976/394213* 💳 *No credit cards* 🕒 *Closed 2 wks in May. No lunch. No dinner Sun.*

$$$ TAPAS 🍴 **Palomeque.** For upscale tapas, larger portions, and a sit-down restaurant atmosphere, Palomeque is a great choice. Using fresh market produce, dishes are based on traditional recipes and finished off with a clean modern look. **Known for:** duck foie gras shavings on bread; selection of mixed tapas; hidden gem. [$] *Average main: €20* ✉ *Calle Agustín Palomeque 11* ☎ *976/214082* 🌐 *www.restaurantepalomeque.es* 💳 *No credit cards* 🕒 *Closed Sun.*

WHERE TO STAY

$$ HOTEL 🏨 **Catalonia El Pilar.** Overlooking the lovely Plaza Justicia and the baroque Santa Isabel church, this early-20th-century Art Nouveau building is a tourist sight in its own right, featuring an original Modernista wooden elevator and a facade with wrought-iron decorations. **Pros:** quiet location on one of the city's prettiest squares; five-minute walk from the Basílica de Nuestra Señora del Pilar; spotless and efficient. **Cons:** rooms are immaculate but somewhat characterless; some rooms are on the small side; no on-site parking. [$] *Rooms from: €120*

✉ *Calle Manifestación 16* ☎ *976/205858* ⊕ *www.cataloniahotels.com*
🛏 *66 rooms* ⵏⵔ *Free Breakfast.*

$ 🏨 **Hotel Sauce.** When it comes to value for money Hotel Sauce couldn't
HOTEL be better, plus it's located right in the center of Zaragoza, a stone's
throw from El Pilar and a short walk from El Tubo. **Pros:** central location; modern facilities and café on-site; excellent value. **Cons:** reception
service can be erratic; small rooms; not many rooms. **$** *Rooms from:*
€49 ✉ *Espoz y Mina 33* ☎ *976/205050* ⊕ *www.hotelsauce.com* 🛏 *40*
rooms ⵏⵔ *No meals.*

$$$$ 🏨 **Palafox.** One of Zaragoza's top hotels, Palafox combines contem-
HOTEL porary design with traditional urban service and elegance. **Pros:** top
comfort and service; private parking for guests; good restaurant. **Cons:**
modern and somewhat antiseptic; rooms not as impressive as the public spaces; tired decor. **$** *Rooms from: €185* ✉ *Calle Marqués Casa*
Jiménez s/n ☎ *976/237700* ⊕ *www.palafoxhoteles.com* 🛏 *179 rooms*
ⵏⵔ *Free Breakfast.*

HUESCA

68 km (42 miles) northeast of Zaragoza, 123 km (76 miles) northwest
of Lleida.

Once a Roman colony, Huesca would later become the capital of Aragón,
until the royal court moved to Zaragoza in 1118. The town's university
was founded in 1354 and now specializes in Aragonese studies.

GETTING HERE AND AROUND

From Zaragoza there are several trains a day (⊕ *www.renfe.com*). Alosa
(⊕ *www.alosa.es*) runs buses between Huesca and Zaragoza, Lleida,
and Jaca. By car from Zaragoza, head northwest toward Huesca on the
A23. The center is quite small and it's easier to go on foot to the sights,
because the traffic and one-way system can be tricky.

Contacts Bus Station. ✉ *C/ José Gil Cávez 10.*

VISITOR INFORMATION

Contacts Huesca Tourist Office. ✉ *Pl. Luis López Allué s/n* ☎ *974/292170*
⊕ *www.huescaturismo.com.*

EXPLORING

Cathedral. An intricately carved gallery tops the eroded facade of Huesca's 13th-century Gothic cathedral. Damián Forment, a protégé of the
15th-century Italian master sculptor Donatello, created the alabaster
altarpiece, which has scenes from the Crucifixion. ✉ *Pl. de la Catedral*
s/n ☎ *974/231099* 🎟 *€4* ☉ *Museum closed Sun.*

Museo de Huesca. This museum occupies parts of the former royal palace
of the kings of Aragón and holds paintings by Aragonese primitives,
including *La Virgen del Rosario* by Miguel Jiménez, and several works
by the 16th-century Maestro de Sigena. The eight chambers of the
gallery, set around an octagonal patio, include the **Sala de la Campana**
(Hall of the Bell), where, in the 12th century, the beheadings of errant
nobles took place. ✉ *Pl. de la Universidad* ☎ *974/220586* ⊕ *www.*
museodehuesca.es 🎟 *Free* ☉ *Closed Mon.*

San Pedro el Viejo. This church has an 11th-century cloister. Ramiro II and his father, Alfonso I, the only Aragonese kings not entombed at San Juan de la Peña, rest in a side chapel. ✉ *Pl. de San Pedro s/n* 🌐 *www.sanpedroelviejo.com* 🎟 *€3.*

OFF THE BEATEN PATH

Castillo de Loarre. This massively walled 11th-century monastery is nearly indistinguishable from the rock outcroppings that surround it. Inside the walls are a church, a tower, a dungeon, and even a medieval toilet with views of the almond and olive groves in the Ebro basin. ✉ *C. Fuente 2, 36 km (22 miles) west of Huesca off Rte. A132 on A1206, Loarre* ☎ *974/342161* 🌐 *www.castillodeloarre.es* 🎟 *€5* 🕒 *Closed Mon. in winter.*

WHERE TO EAT AND STAY

$$$$ SPANISH

🍴 **Las Torres.** Creating a taste of pure upper Aragón, Huesca's top restaurant makes inventive use of first-rate local ingredients like wild mushrooms, wild boar, venison, and lamb. The glass-walled kitchen is as original as the cooking that emerges from it, and the wine list is strong in Somontanos, Huesca's own D.O. **Known for:** showcasing traditional Aragonese dishes with a modern twist; Michelin star; excellent value. [$] *Average main: €25* ✉ *Calle María Auxiliadora 3* ☎ *974/228213* 🌐 *www.lastorres-restaurante.com* 🕒 *Closed Sun., 15 days over Easter, and Aug. 16–31.*

$$ HOTEL

🏨 **Hotel Abba Huesca.** This modern hotel in Huesca has comfortable rooms and a buzzing contemporary bar where guests and locals mingle. **Pros:** excellent value; upscale feel; on-site bar and restaurant. **Cons:** slightly outside the center of town; area surrounding the hotel is quiet; functional business hotel decor. [$] *Rooms from: €90* ✉ *Calle de Tarbes 14* ☎ *974/292900* 🌐 *www.abbahuescahotel.com* 🛏 *84 rooms* 🍽 *No meals.*

SHOPPING

Ultramarinos La Confianza. Founded in 1871, La Confianza has been declared the oldest grocery store in Spain. It's in the porticoed Plaza Mayor in the old town, and worth popping into to see the tiled floors and hand-painted ceiling, and to browse the shelves stacked high with local products, from dried goods to specialty chocolates and salted cod. ✉ *Pl. Mayor (Pl. López Allué)* ☎ *974/222632* 🌐 *www.ultramarinoslaconfianza.com.*

ALQUÉZAR

51 km (32 miles) northeast of Huesca, 123 km (76 miles) northeast of Zaragoza.

Fodor's Choice ★

As though carved from the rock itself, Alquézar overlooks the Parque Natural Sierra y Cañones de Guara and is one of Aragón's most attractive old towns. A labyrinth of cobbled, winding streets and low archways coil around the town's central square, and many of the buildings' facades bear coat-of-arms motifs dating back to the 16th century. The uniquely shaped town square, formed with no cohesive plan or architectural style, has a porched area that was built to provide shelter from the sun and rain.

GETTING HERE AND AROUND

From Huesca, travel eastward on the A22 or N240 for 29 km (18 miles) before joining the A1229 toward Alquézar. Cars cannot enter the old quarter, so the only way to see the town is on foot.

VISITOR INFORMATION

Contacts Alquézar Tourist Office. ✉ *Calle Arrabal 14* ☎ *974/318940* 🌐 *www.alquezar.es.*

A PAMPLONA ALTERNATIVE

For an unspoiled Pamplona-like fiesta in another pre-Pyrenean capital, with bullfights, *encierros* (running of the bulls through the streets), and all-night revelry, try Huesca's San Lorenzo celebration (August 9–15). Spain's top bullfighters are the main attraction, along with concerts, street dances, and liberal tastings of the excellent Somontano wines of upper Huesca. *Albahaca* (basil) is the official symbol of Huesca, and the ubiquitous green sashes and bandanas will remind you that this is Huesca, not Pamplona (where red is the trimming).

EXPLORING

Colegiata de Santa María. Keeping watch over the Sierra de Guara, the Colegiata, originally a 9th-century Moorish citadel, was conquered by the Christians in 1067. An interesting mix of Gothic, Mudejar, and Renaissance details are found in the shaded cloister, and there are biblical murals that date back to the Romanesque era. The church, built in the 16th century, contains an almost life-size Romanesque figure of Christ, but restoration has taken away some of the building's charm—its interior brickwork is now only a painted representation. ✉ *Diseminado Afueras, off Calle la Iglesia* 🎫 *Free.*

River Vero Cultural Park. Declared a UNESCO World Heritage Site in 1998, this park within the Sierra de Guara contains more than 60 limestone caves with prehistoric cave paintings. Some date back to around 22,000 BC, although the majority are between 12,000 BC and 4000 BC. Information and guided tours are available through the interpretation center in Colungo. Hours vary, so call ahead. ✉ *Calle Las Braules 2, 9½ km (6 miles) east of Alquézar, Colunga* ☎ *974/318185, 974/306006* 🌐 *www.turismosomontano.es* 🎫 *Free.*

WHERE TO EAT AND STAY

$$$$ SPANISH 🍴 **Casa Pardina.** Elegant, romantic dining at a reasonable price is the draw here, with a choice of two fixed-price menus. Locally sourced ingredients come together to create a traditional Aragonese menu, adapted for contemporary tastes, and the wine is from the nearby Somontano region. **Known for:** terrace with views of the church and Sierra de Guara; no à la carte; locally sourced ingredients and local olive oil. [$] *Average main: €29* ✉ *Calle Medio s/n* ☎ *974/318425* 🌐 *www.casapardina.com* 🕒 *Closed Tues. No lunch weekdays Oct.–Easter.*

$ B&B/INN 🏨 **Hotel Santa María de Alquézar.** Just outside the old town walls, this hotel has the best views around—overlooking the Río Vero canyon and the Colegiata de Santa María. **Pros:** breathtaking views; bright rooms; relaxed ambience. **Cons:** noise from the street can be heard in some rooms; outside the walls of the old town; in high season parking is hard to find. [$] *Rooms from: €89* ✉ *Paseo San Hipolito s/n* ☎ *974/318436*

6

🌐 *www.hotel-santamaria.com* ⏲ *Closed Jan.–mid-Feb. Call ahead for other seasonal closures* 🛏 *21 rooms* 🍴 *Free Breakfast.*

SPORTS AND THE OUTDOORS

The Sierra de Guara is one of Europe's best places for canyoning (descending mountain gorges, usually in or near streams and other water sources).

Avalancha. There are several agencies in Alquézar that specialize in guided private or group trips for all levels and ages. Avalancha is one of the best for canyoning equipment, including wet suits and helmets. ✉ *Paseo San Hipolito s/n* ☎ *974/318299* 🌐 *www.avalancha.org.*

AÍNSA

66 km (41 miles) southwest of Benasque, 113 km (70 miles) northeast of Huesca, 214 km (133 miles) northeast of Zaragoza.

Wander through the uninspiring outskirts of Aínsa's new town until the road turns sharply upward toward one of Aragón's most impressive walled medieval towns, where houses are jammed together along narrow cobbled streets, offering sweeping views of the surrounding mountains and Parque Nacional de Odesa.

GETTING HERE AND AROUND

Head north out of Huesca on the E7 and then the N260 for a total of 98 km (61 miles), then take the A2205 for 15 km (9 miles). Aínsa can only be explored on foot once you're through the old city walls.

VISITOR INFORMATION

Contacts Aínsa Tourist Office. ✉ *Av. Ordesa 5* ☎ *974/500767* 🌐 *www.villadeainsa.com.*

EXPLORING

Citadel. The citadel and castle, originally built by the Muslims in the 11th century, was conquered by the Christians and reconstructed in the 16th century. ✉ *Old Quarter.*

Santa María. This 12th-century Romanesque church, with its quadruple-vaulted door and 13th-century cloister, is in the corner of the attractive, porticoed Plaza Mayor. ✉ *Calle Santa Cruz* 🎟 *Free.*

WHERE TO STAY

$$ B&B/INN 🏨 **Hotel Los Siete Reyes.** One of two boutique hotels in Aínsa's Plaza Mayor, Los Siete Reyes occupies a handsome restored historic house with good-size and artistically decorated bedrooms overlooking the square. **Pros:** charming and atmospheric; central location; good views of the mountain or village. **Cons:** noise from the square; interior design makes rooms dark; patchy Wi-Fi in rooms. [$] *Rooms from: €120* ✉ *Pl. Mayor s/n* ☎ *974/500681* 🌐 *www.lossietereyes.com* 🛏 *6 rooms* 🍴 *No meals.*

PARQUE NACIONAL DE ORDESA Y MONTE PERDIDO

79 km (49 miles) west of Bielsa, 45 km (30 miles) west of Aínsa, 92 km (57 miles) north of Huesca.

This great but often overlooked park was founded by royal decree in 1918 to protect the natural integrity of the central Pyrenees. It has expanded from 4,940 to 56,810 acres as provincial and national authorities have added the Monte Perdido massif, the head of the Pineta Valley, and the Escuain and Añisclo canyons.

VISITOR INFORMATION

Contacts Centro Visitantes de Torla. ⊠ *Av. Ordesa s/n, Torla* ☏ 974/486472 ⊕ *www.ordesa.net.*

EXPLORING

Fodor'sChoice
★
Ordesa and Monte Perdido National Park. The entrance to this natural wonder is under the vertical walls of Monte Mondarruego, the source of the Ara River and its tributary, the Arazas, which forms the famous Ordesa Valley. Defined by the Ara and Arazas rivers, the Ordesa Valley is endowed with lakes, waterfalls, high mountain meadows, and forests of pine, fir, larch, beech, and poplar. Protected wildlife includes trout, boar, chamois, and the sarrio or isard (*Rupicapra pyrenaica*) mountain goat.

Well-marked mountain trails lead to waterfalls, caves, and spectacular observation points. The standard tour, a full day's hike (eight hours), runs from the parking area in the Pradera de Ordesa, 8 km (5 miles) northeast of Torla, up the Arazas River, past the Gradas de Soaso (Soaso Risers), a natural stairway of waterfalls) to the Cola de Caballo (Horse's Tail), a lovely fan of falling water at the head of the Cirque de Cotatuero, a sort of natural amphitheater. There is one refuge, Refugio Gorez, north of the Cola de Caballo. A return walk on the south side of the valley, past the Cabaña de los Cazadores (Hunters' Hut), offers a breathtaking view followed by a two-hour descent back to the parking area. A few spots, though not technically difficult, may seem precarious. Information and guidebooks are available at the booth on your way into the park at Pradera de Ordesa. The best time to come is May–mid-November, but check conditions with the tourist office, Centro de Visitantes de Torla, before risking driving into a blizzard in May or missing out on *el veranillo de San Martín* ("Indian summer") in fall. ⊠ *Torla* ☏ *974/486472* ⊕ *www.ordesa.net* ⌦ *Free.*

EN ROUTE
Broto is a typical Aragonese mountain town with an excellent 16th-century Gothic church. Nearby villages, such as **Oto,** have stately manor houses with classic local features: baronial entryways, conical chimneys, and wooden galleries. **Torla** is Parque Nacional de Ordesa y Monte Perdido's main entry point, with regular buses that go up to the park entrance during summer, and is a popular base camp for hikers.

WHERE TO EAT AND STAY

$$
SPANISH
✕ **El Rebeco.** In this graceful, rustic building in the upper part of town, the dining rooms are lined with historic photographs of Torla during the 19th and 20th centuries, and in late fall, civets of deer, boar, and mountain goat are the order of the day. In summer, lighter fare and hearty mountain soups restore hikers between treks. **Known for:** traditional Pyrenean

DID YOU KNOW?

The Parque Nacional de Ordesa y Monte Perdido is sometimes called a junior version of the Grand Canyon. The region was designated a national park partly to protect the Pyrenean ibex, which nevertheless became extinct in 2000.

architecture; inviting terrace; service can be slow. [$] *Average main: €14* ✉ *Calle Fatás 55, Torla* ☎ *974/486068* 🕒 *Closed Nov.–Easter.*

$ B&B/INN 🏨 **Villa de Torla.** This classic mountain refuge, with sundecks, terraces, and a private dining room, has rooms of various shapes and sizes. **Pros:** in the middle of a postcard-perfect Pyrenean village; helpful staff. **Cons:** rooms on the street side can be noisy on weekends and summer nights; not all rooms have a private bathroom. [$] *Rooms from: €75* ✉ *Pl. Aragón 1, Torla* ☎ *974/486156* 🌐 *www.hotelvilladetorla.com* 🕒 *Closed Dec. 10–Mar.* 🛏 *38 rooms* 🍴 *No meals.*

JACA

24 km (15 miles) southwest of Biescas, 164 km (102 miles) north of Zaragoza.

Jaca, the most important municipal center in Alto Aragón, is anything but sleepy. Bursting with ambition and blessed with the natural resources, jacetanos are determined to make their city the site of a Winter Olympics someday. Founded in 1035 as the kingdom of Jacetania, Jaca was an important stronghold during the Christian Reconquest of the Iberian Peninsula and proudly claims never to have bowed to the Moorish invaders. Indeed, on the first Friday of May the town still commemorates the decisive battle in which the appearance of a battalion of women, their hair and jewelry flashing in the sun, intimidated the Moorish cavalry into beating a headlong retreat. Avoid the industrial-looking outskirts and head straight to the atmospheric *casco antiguo* (old town) where there's a splendid 11th-century cathedral and fortress, and where bustling eateries abound.

GETTING HERE AND AROUND

Alosa (🌐 *www.alosa.es*) runs daily buses between Jaca and Zaragoza. There is also a train between Jaca and Huesca or Zaragoza (🌐 *www.renfe.com*). By car, take the E7/N330 northbound from Huesca via Sabiñánigo for 73 km (45 miles). Town sights are easily accessible on foot.

VISITOR INFORMATION

Contacts Jaca Tourist Office. ✉ *Pl. San Pedro 11–13* ☎ *974/360098* 🌐 *www.jaca.es.*

EXPLORING

Canfranc. In July and August a guided train tour departs from the Jaca RENFE station, heading to the valley and Canfranc's magnificent Belle Époque train station, now abandoned. Surely the largest and most ornate building in the Pyrenees, the station has a bewitching history and was used as a location in the 1965 film *Doctor Zhivago*. Ask at the tourist office for schedules—it's a good idea to book ahead of time. In addition, a nontourist train runs year-round between Jaca and Canfranc. ✉ *Canfranc Estación* 🌐 *www.elcanfranero.com, www.renfe.com* 🎟 *€35.*

Catedral de San Pedro. An important stop on the pilgrimage to Santiago de Compostela, Jaca's 11th-century Romanesque Catedral de San Pedro has lovely carved capitals and was the first French-Romanesque cathedral in Spain, paving the way for later Spanish Romanesque architecture. Inside the cathedral and near the cloisters, the **Museo Diocesano** is filled with an excellent collection of Romanesque and Gothic frescoes and artifacts. ⊠ *Pl. de San Pedro 1* 🕾 *Cathedral free, museum €6.*

Ciudadela. The massive pentagonal Ciudadela is an impressive example of 17th-century military architecture. It has a display of more than 35,000 military miniatures, arranged to represent different periods of history. Check the website to confirm hours. ⊠ *Av. del Primer Viernes de Mayo s/n* 🕾 *974/361124, 974/357157* ⊕ *www.ciudadeladejaca.es* 🕾 *From €6* ⊘ *Closed Mon. Oct.–June.*

WHERE TO EAT AND STAY

$$$
SPANISH

×**La Cocina Aragonesa.** This Jaca mainstay is an elegant, rustic space decorated with local farming and mountaineering objects, with a mammoth fireplace at its center. The Aragonese-Basque cuisine is justly famous around town and beyond for fresh and innovative creations, especially game in season, including venison, wild boar, partridge, and duck. **Known for:** redleg partridge stuffed with foie gras; baby onions with black truffles; creative Aragonese-Basque cuisine. 🟲 *Average main: €20* ⊠ *Hotel Conde Aznar, Calle Cervantes 5* 🕾 *974/361000* ⊕ *www.condeaznar.com* ⊘ *Closed Mon., and 10 days in June and Nov. No dinner Sun.*

$$$
TAPAS

×**La Tasca de Ana.** For a taste of Spanish tapas in the Pyrenees, this cozy and fun tavern is one of Jaca's finest. With only a handful of tables and standing room by the bar, it's not the setting for a quiet romantic dinner, but it is recommended for anyone spending an evening in Jaca. **Known for:** quick bite; rodolfito langoustine tapa; lively atmosphere. 🟲 *Average main: €20* ⊠ *Calle Ramiro I 3* 🕾 *974/363621* ⊕ *www.latascadeana.com* ⊘ *Closed 2 wks in May and 2 wks in Sept. No lunch weekdays.*

$
HOTEL

🏨 **Gran Hotel.** This rambling hotel—Jaca's traditional official clubhouse—has seen better days, but its central location makes it a practical base. **Pros:** quiet location just west of the town center; professional and polished service; easy walking distance to the sights. **Cons:** modern and functional construction with no special charm or Pyrenean features; neo–motel room style; no frills. 🟲 *Rooms from: €89* ⊠ *Paseo de la Constitución 1* 🕾 *974/360900* ⊕ *www.granhoteljaca.com* ➭ *165 rooms* ⦿⦶ *Free Breakfast.*

$$$
B&B/INN
Fodor's Choice
★

🏨 **Hotel Barosse.** In a small village on the outskirts of Jaca, this intimate, adults-only bed-and-breakfast is worth sacrificing the central-city location to gain sweeping mountain views and helpful, personalized service. **Pros:** peaceful rural setting; boutique-style accommodations; friendly service. **Cons:** a car is necessary; not in the center of Jaca; adults only. 🟲 *Rooms from: €138* ⊠ *Calle de Estirás 4* 🕾 *974/360582, 638/845992* ⊕ *www.barosse.com* ⊘ *Closed Nov.* ➭ *5 rooms* ⦿⦶ *Free Breakfast.*

NIGHTLIFE

Jaca's music bars are concentrated in the casco antiguo, on Calle Ramiro I and along Calle Gil Bergés and Calle Bellido. In the porticoed Plaza de la Catedral, there are a number of bars with terraces, in the shade of the cathedral, to be enjoyed day or evening.

Bar Casa Fau. This busy bar serves coffee and soft drinks, a good selection of wine by the glass, and beer on tap—all of which can be accompanied

The Monasterio de San Juan de la Peña near Jaca

by tapas and light snacks, and front-row views of the cathedral. ⊠ *Pl. de la Catedral 3* ☎ *974/361594.*

SHOPPING

Bodegas Langa. Sample and shop for regional wine and local artisanal products in this charming local bar-meets-bodega. Be sure to allow time for the tapas menu and a delicious coffee cake while you sip and shop for local wines. ⊠ *Pl. San Pedro 5* ☎ *974/360494* ⊕ *www.bodegaslanga.es.*

MONASTERIO DE SAN JUAN DE LA PEÑA

23 km (14 miles) southwest of Jaca, 185 km (115 miles) north of Zaragoza, 90 km (56 miles) east of Pamplona.

South of the Aragonese valleys of Hecho and Ansó is the Monastery of San Juan de la Peña, a site connected to the legend of the Holy Grail and one of the centers of Christian resistance during the 700-year Moorish occupation of Spain.

GETTING HERE AND AROUND

From Jaca, drive 11 km (7 miles) west on the N240 toward Pamplona to a left turn clearly signposted for San Juan de la Peña. From there it's another 11 km (7 miles) on the A1603 to the monastery.

EXPLORING

Fodor's Choice ★ **Monasterio de San Juan de la Peña.** The origins of this arresting religious sanctuary can be traced to the 9th century, when a hermit monk named Juan settled here on the *peña* (cliff). A monastery was founded on the spot in 920, and in 1071 Sancho Ramirez, son of King Ramiro I, made use of the structure, which was built into the mountain's rock wall, to found this Benedictine monastery. The **cloister,** tucked under the cliff, dates to the 12th century and contains intricately carved capitals depicting biblical scenes. The church of the New Monastery contains the **Kingdom of Aragon Interpretation Centre,** where audio guides in English are available. ✉ *Off N240 on A1603, Jaca* ☎ *974/355119* 🌐 *www.monasteriosanjuan.com* 🎫 *€12 (full ticket).*

HECHO AND ANSÓ VALLEYS

The Hecho Valley is 49 km (30 miles) northwest of Jaca. The Ansó Valley is 25 km (15 miles) west of Hecho, 118 km (73 miles) east of Pamplona.

The Valle de Ansó is Aragón's western limit. Rich in fauna (mountain goats, wild boar, and even a bear or two), it follows the Veral River up to Zuriza. Towering over the head of the valley is Navarra's highest point, the 7,989-foot **Mesa de los Tres Reyes** (Plateau of the Three Kings), named not for the Magi but for the kings of Aragón, Navarra, and Castile, whose 11th-century kingdoms bordered one another here, allowing them to meet without leaving their respective realms. The **Selva de Oza** (Oza Forest), at the head of the Hecho Valley, is above the **Boca del Infierno** (Mouth of Hell), a tight draw that road and river barely squeeze through.

It's worth stopping at the pretty villages of **Ansó** and **Hecho,** where a preserved collection of stone houses are tightly bunched together along narrow cobbled streets overlooking the valley. In Ansó on the last Sunday in August, residents dress in traditional medieval costumes and perform ancestral dances of great grace and dignity.

GETTING HERE AND AROUND

You can reach the Valle de Hecho from Jaca by heading west on the N240 and then north on the A176.

VISITOR INFORMATION

Contacts Hecho Tourist Office. ✉ *Pallar d'Agustín s/n, Hecho* ☎ *974/375505* 🌐 *www.hecho.es.*

EXPLORING

Monasterio de San Pedro de Siresa. The area's most important monument, the 9th-century retreat Monasterio de San Pedro de Siresa, presides over the village of Siresa, just 2 km (1 mile) north of Hecho. Although now only the 11th-century church remains, it is a marvelous example of Romanesque architecture. Cheso, a medieval Aragonese dialect descended from the Latin spoken by the Siresa monks, is thought to be the closest to Latin of all Romance languages and dialects. It has been kept alive in the Hecho Valley, especially in the works of the poet Veremundo Méndez Coarasa. ✉ *Calle San Pedro, Siresa* 🎫 €2.

WHERE TO STAY

$ B&B/INN 🏨 **Casa Blasquico.** This cozy inn is a typical mountain chalet with flowered balconies and a plethora of memorabilia inside. **Pros:** two cute dormered rooms; fine mountain cuisine; friendly service. **Cons:** rooms lack space; public rooms cluttered; no elevator. [$] *Rooms from: €60*

✉ *Pl. la Fuente 1, Hecho* ☎ *974/375007, 657/892128* ⊕ *www.casa-blasquico.es* ✆ *Closed weekdays Nov.–Mar.* 🛏 *6 rooms* 🍴 *No meals.*

EN ROUTE From Ansó, head west to Roncal on the narrow and winding but panoramic 17-km (11-mile) road through the Sierra de San Miguel. To enjoy this route fully, count on taking a good 45 minutes to reach the Esca River and the Roncal Valley.

THE NAVARRAN AND BASQUE PYRENEES

Moving west into the Roncal Valley and the Basque Country, you will note smoother, rolling hills and softer meadows as the rocky central Pyrenees of Aragón begin to descend toward the Bay of Biscay. These wet and fertile uplands and verdant beech forests are a melting pot of Basque-Navarran folklore, culture, tradition, and cuisine. The Basque highlands of Navarra from Roncal through the Irati Forest to Roncesvalles and along the Bidasoa River seem like an Arcadian paradise as the jagged Pyrenean peaks give way to sheep-filled pasturelands, 15th-century *caseríos*, and sleepy watermills.

RONCAL VALLEY

17 km (11 miles) west of Ansó Valley, 72 km (45 miles) west of Jaca, 86 km (53 miles) northeast of Pamplona.

The Roncal Valley, the eastern edge of the Basque Pyrenees, is notable for the sheep's-milk cheese of the same name and as the birthplace of Julián Gayarre (1844–90), the leading tenor of his time. The 34-km (21-mile) drive through the towns of **Burgui** and **Roncal** to **Isaba** winds through green hillsides past caseríos, classical Basque farmhouses covered by long, sloping roofs that were designed to house animals on the ground floor and the family up above to take advantage of the body heat of the livestock. Burgui's red-tile roofs backed by rolling pastures contrast with the vertical rock and steep slate roofs of the Aragonese and Catalan Pyrenees; Isaba's wide-arch bridge across the Esca is a graceful reminder of Roman aesthetics and engineering.

GETTING HERE AND AROUND
To get to the valley from Jaca, take the N240 west along the Aragón River; a right turn north on the A137 follows the Esca River from the head of the Yesa Reservoir up the Roncal Valley.

VISITOR INFORMATION
Contacts Roncal Tourist Office. ✉ *Barrio Iriartea s/n, Roncal* ☎ *948/475256* ⊕ *www.vallederoncal.es.*

EXPLORING
El Tributo de las Tres Vacas (*The Tribute of the Three Cows*). Try to be in the Roncal Valley for this event, which has been celebrated every July 13 since 1375. The mayors of the valley's villages, dressed in traditional gowns, gather near the summit of San Martín to receive the symbolic payment of three cows from their French counterparts, in memory of the settlement of ancient border disputes. Feasting and celebrating follow.

6

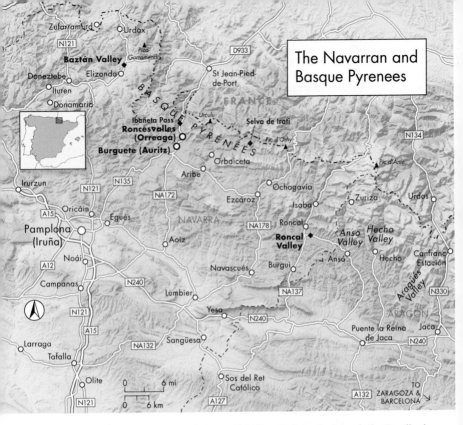

Ochagavía. The road west (NA140) to Ochagavía through the Portillo de Lazar (Lazar Pass) has views of the Anie and Orhi peaks, which tower over the French border. The village itself, with original cobblestone streets and riverside promenade, makes for a pleasant spot to stretch the legs. ✉ *Roncal.*

Selva de Irati (*Irati Forest*). A 15-km (9-mile) detour north through the town of Orbaiceta up to the headwaters of the Irati River, at the Irabia Reservoir, gets you a good look at the Selva de Irati, one of Europe's major beech forests and the source of much of the lumber for the Spanish Armada.

RONCESVALLES (ORREAGA)

64 km (40 miles) northwest of Isaba in the Roncal Valley, 48 km (30 miles) north of Pamplona.

Roncesvalles (often listed as Orreaga, its name in Euskera) is a small village and the site of the Battle of Roncesvalles (or Battle of Roncevaux Pass) when Charlemagne's army, under the command of Roland, was attacked and overcome by Basque soldiers in AD 778. This battle became the inspiration for one of France's most revered literary poems, *Le Chanson de Roland* (*The Song of Roland*), written in the 11th century.

The village's strategic position, 23 km (14 miles) from the original starting line of Saint-Jean-Pied-de-Port in France, has made it the first stop-off point for pilgrims on the Camino de Santiago since the 10th century.

Its Gothic Colegiata (built in the style of the Notre-Dame Cathedral in Paris), hospital, and 12th-century chapel have provided shelter since then. This part of the camino offers some of the best scenery, and many modern-day pilgrims start in Roncesvalles.

GETTING HERE AND AROUND

The N135 northbound out of Pamplona goes straight to Roncesvalles.

VISITOR INFORMATION

Contacts Orreaga-Roncesvalles Tourist Office. ✉ *Antiguo Molino, Calle de Nuestra Señora de Roncesvalles, Orreaga* ☎ *948/760301.*

EXPLORING

Colegiata. Built on the orders of King Sancho VII el Fuerte (the Strong), the Collegiate Church houses the king's tomb, which measures more than 7 feet long. ✉ *Calle de Nuestra Señora de Roncesvalles, Orreaga* 🌐 *www.roncesvalles.es.*

Ibañeta Pass. This 3,468-foot pass, above Roncesvalles, is a gorgeous route into France. A menhir (monolith) marks the traditional site of the legendary battle in *The Song of Roland,* during which Roland fell after calling for help on his ivory battle horn. The well-marked eight-hour walk to or from Saint-Jean-Pied-de-Port (which does *not* follow the road) is the first and one of the most beautiful and dramatic sections of the Santiago pilgrimage. ✉ *Orreaga.*

WHERE TO STAY

$$ HOTEL 🏨 **Casa de Beneficiados.** Whether you're embarking on the pilgrimage, this hotel, in a restored 18th-century building adjoining the Colegiata, provides warm, atmospheric low-lit, stone-walled common areas and modern, comfortable rooms. **Pros:** historic building; friendly service; oozes pilgrim trail ambience. **Cons:** apartments lack the charm of the common areas; simple food; take caution arriving by car in bad weather. [$] *Rooms from: €90* ✉ *Calle Nuestra Señora de Roncesvalles s/n, Orreaga* ☎ *948/760105, 639/754449* 🌐 *www.casadebeneficiados.com* 🕑 *Closed mid-Nov.–mid-Mar.* 🛏 *16 rooms* 🍴 *No meals.*

BURGUETE (AURITZ)

2 km (1 mile) south of Roncesvalles.

Burguete (Auritz, in Euskera) lies between two mountain streams forming the headwaters of the Urobi River and is surrounded by meadows and forests. The town was immortalized in Ernest Hemingway's *The Sun Also Rises,* with its evocative description of trout fishing in an ice-cold stream above a Navarran village. Hemingway himself spent time here doing just that, and he stayed at the Hostal Burguete.

GETTING HERE AND AROUND

The N135 northbound out of Pamplona goes to Burguete in 44 km (27 miles). From Roncesvalles, it's just 2 km (1 mile) south on the N135.

WHERE TO STAY

$ B&B/INN 🏨 **Hotel Loizu.** An inn for pilgrims since the 18th century, the Loizu is now a country-style hotel that makes an excellent base for exploring the Selva de Irati. **Pros:** family-run; friendly service; comfortable, good-size rooms. **Cons:** bathrooms, although adequate, are small and fairly cramped; basic breakfast; can hear noise from other rooms. $ *Rooms from: €60* ✉ *Calle San Nicolás 13, Auritz* ☎ *948/760008* 🌐 *www.loizu.com* ⏲ *Closed mid-Dec.–Mar.* 🛏 *27 rooms* 🍴 *No meals.*

BAZTÁN VALLEY

62 km (38 miles) northwest of Roncesvalles, 80 km (50 miles) north of Pamplona.

Fodor's Choice ★

Tucked neatly above the headwaters of the Bidasoa River, beneath the peak of the 3,545-foot Gorramendi Mountain that looms over the border with France, is the Baztán Valley. These rounded green hills are a scenic halfway stop-off point between the central Pyrenees and the Atlantic. Here the roads of this enchanted Navarran valley meander through picture-perfect villages of geranium-covered, whitewashed, stone-and-mortar houses with red-tile roofs grouped around a central *frontón* (handball court).

This once-isolated pocket of the Basque-Navarran Pyrenees is peppered with smugglers' trails and is the site of the Camino de Baztanas, the oldest stretch of the Camino de Santiago. You can follow the ancient footsteps of pilgrims starting from the historic village of **Urdax.** Nearby, close to the village of **Zugarramurdi,** you can visit a collection of limestone caves, otherwise knowns as Las Cuevas de las Brujas (Witches' Caves), which bore witness to so-called witches' covens and their pagan rituals before their eventual and brutal persecution in the 1600s. In the valley's main town, **Elizondo,** stately homes and ancestral mansions, built by nobles returning with their fortunes from the Americas, straddle the banks of the Baztán River.

Try to be in the village of Ituren in late September for its Carnival, the Day of the Joaldunak, which has been recognized as one of the oldest celebrations in Europe. Here you can see striking costumes hung with clanging cowbells as participants parade from farm to farm and house to house paying homage to their ancestors; some anthropologists argue that the rituals go back to pagan times. Check the exact dates of the event with the tourist office, as each year's schedule depends on the phases of the moon.

VISITOR INFORMATION

Contacts Baztan Valley Tourist Office (*Centro de Turismo Rural de Bértiz*). ✉ *Calle Braulio Iriarte 38, Elizondo* ☎ *948/581517.*

WHERE TO EAT

$$$$ BASQUE FAMILY Fodor's Choice ★

🍴 **Donamariako Benta.** This family-run restaurant and small hotel is notable for its high quality and refined level of service. Created from a former 19th-century residence and stables, the restaurant is cozy in winter, with its crackling fire, and a treat in summer, when you can be seated in the peaceful garden filled with willow trees overlooking the river and watching old salmon leap. **Known for:** pretty outdoor seating in summer; traditional recipes; busy in summer. $ *Average main: €30* ✉ *Barrio de las Ventas 4, Donamaria* ☎ *948/450708* 🌐 *www.donamariako.com* ⏲ *Closed Mon., and Dec. 10–Jan. 5. No dinner Sun.*

7

BARCELONA

WELCOME TO BARCELONA

TOP REASONS TO GO

★ **Explore La Boqueria:** Barcelona's produce market may be the most exciting cornucopia in the world.

★ **Visit Santa Maria del Mar:** The early Mediterranean Gothic elegance, rhythmic columns, and unbroken spaces make this church peerless.

★ **See La Sagrada Família:** Gaudí's unfinished masterpiece is the city's most iconic treasure.

★ **Experience El Palau de la Música Catalana:** This Art Nouveau tour de force is alive with music.

★ **Shop for fashion and design:** How could a city famous for its architecture not offer an abundance of innovative clothing, furniture, and design shops as well?

★ **Watch castellers and sardanas:** Human castles and Catalonia's national dance are two fun ways to appreciate Catalan culture.

1 La Rambla and El Raval. The Ciutat Vella (the Old City) is bisected by La Rambla, the city's all-purpose runway and home of the Boqueria market, the city's heart, soul, and stomach. El Raval is a funky multicultural sprawl, spread out around the MACBA contemporary art museum and the medieval Hospital de la Santa Creu.

2 Barri Gòtic and Born-Ribera. Northeast of La Rambla, Ciutat Vella's Gothic Quarter surrounds the cathedral and a jumble of ancient (mostly pedestrianized) streets filled with shops, cafés, and Gothic architecture. Born-Ribera is across Via Laietana, around Santa Maria del Mar.

3 Barceloneta, La Ciutadella, and Port Olímpic. Barceloneta is a charmingly Naples-like fishermen's village, filled with seafood restaurants and lined with sandy beaches. Port Olímpic, built for the 1992 Olympic Games, is a sprawling succession of restaurants and discos. Ciutadella, just inland, was originally a fortress but is now a park with the city zoo.

4 Eixample. The post-1860 Eixample spreads out above Plaça de Catalunya and contains most of the city's Moderniste architecture, including Gaudí's iconic Sagrada Família church, along with hundreds of shops and places to eat.

5 Upper Barcelona. The village of Gràcia nestles above the Diagonal, with Gaudí's Park Güell at its upper edge. Sarrià and Pedralbes spread out farther west, with two Gaudí buildings, a stunning monastery and cloister, and a rustic village surrounded by upscale residential development.

6 Montjuïc. The promontory over the south side of the city lacks street vibe but the artistic treasures here are not to be missed: Miró, MNAC, the Mies van der Rohe Pavilion, and CaixaForum.

EATING AND DRINKING WELL IN BARCELONA

Barcelona cuisine draws from Catalonia's rustic country cooking and uses ingredients from the Mediterranean, the Pyrenees, and inland farmlands. Cosmopolitan influences and experimental contemporary innovation have combined to make Barcelona, historically linked to France and Italy, an important food destination.

(top left) A stew of broad beans and black and white botifarra sausage (top right) *Esqueixada*, or raw codfish salad (bottom left) A dessert of *mel i mató* (honey with fresh cheese)

The Mediterranean diet of seafood, vegetables, olive oil, and red wine comes naturally to Barcelona. A dish you'll see on many menus is *pa amb tomàquet*: bread rubbed with ripe tomato (garlic optional), then drizzled with olive oil. Fish of all kinds, shrimp, shellfish, and rice dishes combining them are common, as are salads of seafood and Mediterranean vegetables. Vegetable and legume combinations are standard. Seafood and upland combinations, the classic *mar i muntanya* (surf and turf) recipes, join rabbit and prawns or cuttlefish and meatballs, while salty and sweet tastes—a Moorish legacy—are found in recipes such as duck with pears or goose with figs.

CAVA

Order "Champagne" in Barcelona and you'll get anything from French bubbly to dirty looks. Ask, instead, for *cava*, sparkling wine from the Penedès region just southwest of the city. The first cava was produced in 1872 after the phylloxera plague wiped out most of Europe's vineyards. Cava (from the "cave" or wine cellar where it ferments) has a drier, earthier taste than Champagne, and slightly larger bubbles.

SALADS

Esqueixada is a cold salad consisting of strips of raw, shredded, salt-cured cod marinated in oil and vinegar with onions, tomatoes, olives, and red and green bell peppers. Chunks of dried tuna can also be included, as well as chickpeas, roast onions, and potatoes, too. *Escalibada* is another classic Catalan salad of red and green bell peppers and eggplant that have been roasted over coals, cut into strips, and served with onions, garlic, and olive oil.

LEGUMES

Botifarra amb mongetes (sausage with white beans) is the classic Catalan sausage made of pork and seasoned with salt and pepper, grilled and served with stewed white beans and *allioli* (an olive oil and garlic emulsion); botifarra can also be made with truffles, apples, eggs, wild mushrooms, and even chocolate. *Mongetes de Sant Pau amb calamarsets* (tiny white beans from Santa Pau with baby squid) is a favorite mar i muntanya.

VEGETABLES

Espinaques a la catalana (spinach with pine nuts, raisins, and garlic) owes a debt to the Moorish sweet-salt counterpoint and to the rich vegetable-growing littoral along the Mediterranean coast north and south of Barcelona. Bits of bacon, fatback, or *jamón ibérico* may be added; some recipes use fine almond

flakes as well. *Albergínies* (eggplant or aubergine) are a favorite throughout Catalonia, whether roasted, stuffed, or stewed, while *carxofes* (artichokes) fried to a crisp or stewed with rabbit is another staple.

FISH

Llobarro a la sal (sea bass cooked in salt) is baked in a shell of rock salt that hardens and requires a tap from a hammer or heavy knife to break and serve. The salt shell keeps the juices inside the fish and the flesh flakes off in firm chunks, while the skin of the fish prevents excessive saltiness from permeating the meat. *Suquet* is favorite fish stew, with scorpion fish, monkfish, sea bass, or any combination thereof, stewed with potatoes, onions, and tomatoes.

DESSERTS

Crema catalana (Catalan cream) is the most popular dessert in Catalonia, a version of the French crème brûlée, custard dusted with cinnamon and confectioner's sugar and burned with a blowtorch (traditionally, a branding iron was used) before serving. The branding results in a hardened skim of caramelized sugar on the surface. The less sweet and palate-cleansing *mel i mató* (honey and fresh cheese) runs a close second in popularity.

7

BARCELONA'S BEST BEACHES

It's an unusual combination in Europe: a major metropolis fully integrated with the sea. Barcelona's miles of beaches allow for its yin and yang of urban energy and laid-back beach vibe. When you're ready for a slower pace, seek out a sandy refuge.

Since the early 2000s, Barcelona's *platjas* (beaches) have been improved, now stretching some 4 km (2½ miles) from Barceloneta's Platja de Sant Sebastià at the southwestern end, northward via the Platjas de Sant Miquel, Barceloneta, Passeig Marítim, Port Olímpic, Nova Icària, Bogatell, Mar Bella (the last bit of which is a nudist enclave), and La Nova Mar Bella to Llevant. The Barceloneta beach is the most popular stretch, easily accessible by several bus lines, notably the Nos. D20, 39, and the V15, and by the L4 metro at Barceloneta or Ciutadella–Vila Olímpica. The best surfing is at the northeastern end of the Barceloneta beach, while the boardwalk offers miles of runway for walkers, cyclers, and joggers. Topless bathing is common on all beaches in and around Barcelona.

DRESS THE PART

Barcelona is such a free city that in 2011, a law had to be created to prevent people from walking around the city in their birthday suits, as it made tourists feel uncomfortable. Being topless is allowed on any beach in Barcelona but full nudity is reserved to some beaches, like Marbella Beach in Poblenou and Playa San Sebastian in Barceloneta.

PLATJA DE LA BARCELONETA

Just to the left at the end of Passeig Joan de Borbó, this is the easiest beach to get to, hence the most crowded and the most fun from a people-watching standpoint. Along with swimming, there are windsurfing and kitesurfing rentals to be found just up behind the beach at the edge of La Barceloneta. Rebecca Horn's sculpture *L'Estel Ferit,* a rusting stack of cubes, expresses nostalgia for the beach-shack restaurants that lined the beach here until 1992. Surfers trying to catch a wave wait just off the breakwater in front of the excellent beachfront restaurant Agua.

PLATJA DE LA MAR BELLA

Closest to the Poblenou metro stop near the eastern end of the beaches, this is a thriving gay enclave and the unofficial nudist beach of Barcelona (but suited bathers are welcome, too). The watersports center Base Nàutica de la Mar Bella rents equipment for sailing, surfing, and windsurfing. Outfitted with showers, safe drinking fountains, and a children's play area, La Mar Bella also has lifeguards who warn against swimming near the breakwater. The excellent Pescadors restaurant is just inland on Plaça Prim.

PLATJA DE LA NOVA ICÀRIA

One of Barcelona's most popular beaches, this strand is just east of Port Olímpic, with the full range of

entertainment, restaurant, and refreshment venues close at hand. (Xiringuito Escribà, overlooking neighboring Bogatell beach, is one of the most popular restaurants on this stretch.) The beach is directly across from the area developed as the residential Vila Olímpica for the 1992 Games, an interesting housing project that has now become a popular residential neighborhood.

PLATJA DE SANT SEBASTIÀ

The landmark of Barceloneta's southwesternmost beach (at the end of Passeig Joan de Borbó) now is the ultramodern W Barcelona Hotel, but Sant Sebastià is in fact the oldest of the city beaches, where 19th-century barcelonins cavorted in bloomers and bathing costumes. On the west end is the Club Natació de Barcelona, and there is a semiprivate feel that the beaches farther east seem to lack.

PLATJA DE GAVÀ-CASTELLDEFELS

South of Barcelona (take the 45-minute L94 bus from the Estació de Sants or the Plaça de Catalunya) is Gavà Mar, a popular outing for Barcelona families and beach partiers. Gavà Mar extends 4 km (2½ miles) south to join the beach at Castelldefels; returning to Barcelona from Castelldefels allows for a hike down the beach to seaside shacks and restaurants serving calçots and paella.

7

Updated by Steve Tallantyre

The infinite variety and throb of street life, the nooks and crannies of the medieval Barri Gòtic, the ceramic tile and stained glass of Moderniste facades, the art and music, the food (ah, the food!)—one way or another, Barcelona will find a way to get your full attention.

The Catalonian capital greeted the new millennium with a cultural and industrial rebirth comparable only to the late-19th-century Renaixença (Renaissance) that filled the city with its flamboyant Moderniste (Art Nouveau) buildings. An exuberant sense of style—from hip new fashions to cutting-edge interior design, to the extravagant visions of star-status postmodern architects—gives Barcelona a vibe like no other place in the world. Barcelona is Spain's most visited city, and it's no wonder: it's a 2,000-year-old master of the art of perpetual novelty.

Barcelona's present boom began on October 17, 1987, when Juan Antonio Samaranch, president of the International Olympic Committee, announced that his native city had been chosen to host the 1992 Olympics. This single masterstroke allowed Spain's so-called second city to throw off the shadow of Madrid and its 40-year "internal exile" under Franco, and resume its rightful place as one of Europe's most dynamic destinations. The Catalan administration lavished millions in subsidies from the Spanish government for the Olympics, then used the Games as a platform to broadcast the news about Catalonia's cultural and national identity from one end of the planet to the other. More Mediterranean than Spanish, historically closer and more akin to Marseille or Milan than to Madrid, Barcelona has always been ambitious, decidedly modern (even in the 2nd century), and quick to accept the latest innovations. (The city's electric light system, public gas system, and telephone exchange were among the first in the world.) Its democratic form of government is rooted in the so-called Usatges Laws instituted by Ramon Berenguer I in the 11th century, which amounted to a constitution. This code of privileges represented one of the earliest known examples of democratic rule; Barcelona's Consell de Cent (Council of 100), constituted in 1274, was Europe's first parliament and one of the cradles of Western democracy. The center of an important seafaring commercial empire with colonies spread around the Mediterranean as far away as Athens, when Madrid was still a Moorish outpost on the arid Castilian steppe—it was Barcelona that absorbed new ideas and styles first. It borrowed navigation techniques from the Moors. It embraced the ideals of the French Revolution. It nurtured artists like Picasso and Miró, who blossomed in the city's air of freedom and individualism. Barcelona, in short, has always been ahead of the curve.

PLANNING

PLANNING YOUR TIME

The best way to get around Barcelona is on foot; the occasional resort to subway, taxi, or tram will help you make the most of your visit. The comfortable FGC (Ferrocarril de la Generalitat de Catalunya) trains that run up the center of the city from Plaça de Catalunya to Sarrià put you within 20- to 30-minute walks of nearly everything. The metro and the FGC close just short of midnight Monday–Thursday and Sunday, and at 2 am on Friday; on Saturday, the metro runs all night. The main attractions you need a taxi or the metro to reach are Montjuïc (Miró Foundation, MNAC, Mies van der Rohe Pavilion, CaixaFòrum, and Poble Espanyol), most easily accessed from Plaça Espanya; Park Güell above Plaça Lesseps; and the Auditori at Plaça de les Glòries. You can reach Gaudí's Sagrada Família by two metro lines (Nos. 2 and 5), but you may prefer the walk from the FGC's Provença stop, as it's an enjoyable half-hour jaunt that passes by three major Moderniste buildings: Palau Baró de Quadras, Casa Terrades (Casa de les Punxes), and Casa Macaia.

Sarrià and Pedralbes are easily explored on foot. The Torre Bellesguard and the Col.legi de les Teresianes are uphill treks; you might want to take a cab. It's a pleasant stroll from Sarrià down through the Jardins de la Vil.la Cecilia and Vil.la Amèlia to the Cátedra Gaudí (the pavilions of the Finca Güell, with Gaudí's amazing wrought-iron dragon gate); from there, you can get to the Futbol Club Barcelona through the Jardins del Palau Reial de Pedralbes and the university campus, or catch a two-minute taxi.

All of the Ciutat Vella (Barri Gòtic, Born-Ribera, La Rambla, El Raval, and Barceloneta) is best explored on foot. If you stay in Barceloneta for dinner (usually not more than €12), have the restaurant call you a taxi to get back to your hotel.

The city bus system is also a viable option—you get a better look at the city as you go—but the metro is faster and more comfortable. The tramway offers a quiet ride from Plaça Francesc Macià out Diagonal to the Futbol Club Barcelona, or from behind the Parc de la Ciutadella out to Glòries and the Fòrum at the east end of Diagonal.

WHEN TO GO

For optimal weather and marginally fewer tourists, the best times to visit Barcelona and the rest of Catalonia are April–June and mid-September–mid-December. Catalans and Basques vacation in August, causing epic traffic jams at both ends of the month.

FESTIVALS

Festival Ciutat Flamenco. Held annually in May, this lively festival, co-organized by the Taller de Músics (Musicians' Workshop) and the Mercat de les Flors, offers visitors a chance to experience authentic flamenco instrumental, song, and dance performances by both local and international artists. ✉ *Mercat de les Flors, Carrer de Lleida 59, Poble Sec* ☎ *93/329–5667 Taller de Músics, 93/256–2600 Mercat de les Flors* ⊕ *ciutatflamenco.com* Ⓜ *Poble Sec, Plaça Espanya.*

Fodor's Choice ★ **Grec** (*Festival del Grec*). Barcelona's monthlong summer arts festival (late June–July) features acts from the world of dance, performance art, music, and theater. Performances take place in such historic venues as Mercat de les Flors and the Teatre Grec on Montjuïc—an open-air theater built for the 1929 Barcelona International Exposition, which gives the festival its name and serves as the main venue. ✉ *Barcelona* ☎ *93/316–1000* ⊕ *lameva.barcelona.cat/grec.*

Primavera Sound. From its modest beginnings at the architectural miniature museum Poble Espanyol, this event has evolved into one of the biggest and most exciting music festivals in Spain, attracting more than 200,000 visitors each year. Concerts are organized in small venues around the city during the weeks leading up to the event, but the main stint takes place over four days in late May or early June at the Parc del Fòrum. Everybody who's anybody, from Nine Inch Nails to The National, has played here, and you can rest assured that whoever is doing the big summer festival circuit will pass through Primavera. Festival tickets can be bought online. ✉ *Parc del Fòrum, Poblenou* ⊕ *www.primaverasound.com* Ⓜ *El Maresme Fòrum.*

DISCOUNTS AND DEALS

The very worthwhile **Barcelona Card** (⊕ *www.barcelona-card.com*) comes in two-, three-, four-, and five-day versions (€20, €35, €45, and €60). You get unlimited travel on public transport, free admission at numerous museums, and discounts on restaurants, leisure sights, and stores. You can get the card in Turisme de Barcelona offices in Plaça de Catalunya and Plaça Sant Jaume and at the Casa Batlló, the Aquarium, and the Poble Espanyol, among other sites; buy in advance online for a 5% discount.

GETTING HERE AND AROUND

AIR TRAVEL

Most flights arriving in Spain from the United States and Canada pass through Madrid's Barajas (MAD), but the major gateway to Catalonia and other nearby regions is Spain's second-largest airport, Barcelona's spectacular glass, steel, and marble Prat del Llobregat (BCN). The T1 terminal, which opened in 2009, is a sleek, ultramodern facility that uses solar panels for sustainable energy and offers a spa, a fitness center, restaurants and cafés, and VIP lounges. This airport is served by numerous international carriers, but Catalonia also has two other airports that handle passenger traffic, including charter flights. One is just south of Girona, 90 km (56 miles) north of Barcelona and convenient to the resort towns of the Costa Brava. Bus and train connections from Girona to Barcelona work well and cheaply, provided you have the time. The other Catalonia airport is at Reus, 110 km (68 miles) south of Barcelona, a gateway to Tarragona and the beaches of the Costa Daurada. Flights to and from the major cities in Europe and Spain also fly into and out of Bilbao's Loiu (BIL) airport. For information about airports in Spain, consult ⊕ *www.aena.es*.

Airport Information Aeroport de Girona–Costa Brava (GRO). ✉ *17185 Vilobi de Onyar, Girona* ☎ *902/404704 general info on Spanish airports* ⊕ *www. girona-airport.cat*. **Aeropuerto de Madrid (Adolfo Suárez Madrid-Barajas)** (MAD). ✉ *Av. de la Hispanidad s/n, Madrid* ☎ *902/404704 general info on Spanish airports* ⊕ *www.aeropuertomadrid-barajas.com/eng*. **Aeropuerto de Reus** (REU). ✉ *Autovía Tarragona–Reus, Reus* ☎ *902/404704 general info on Spanish airports* ⊕ *www.aena.es/en/reus-airport/reus.html*. **Aeropuerto Internacional de Bilbao** (BIL). ✉ *Loiu 48180, Bilbao* ☎ *902/404704 general info on Spanish airports* ⊕ *www.aeropuertodebilbao.net/en*. **Barcelona El Prat de Llobregat** (BCN). ✉ *C–32B s/n* ☎ *902/404704 general info on Spanish airports* ⊕ *www.aena.es/en/barcelona-airport/index.html*.

GROUND TRANSPORTATION

Check first to see if your hotel in Barcelona provides airport-shuttle service. Few do: visitors normally get into town by train, bus, taxi, or rental car.

The Aerobus service operates two lines from the airport to Plaça de Catalunya: the A1, from Terminal 1, and the A2, from Terminal 2. The A1 departs every 5–10 minutes from 5:35 am to 1:05 am, and the A2 departs every 10 minutes from 5:35 am to 1 am. From Plaça de Catalunya, the A1 leaves for Terminal 1 every 5–10 minutes, 5 am–12:30 am, and the A2 for Terminal 2 departs every 10 minutes, 5 am–12:30 am. The fare is €5.90 one way and €10.20 round-trip. Aerobuses for Terminals 1 and 2 pick up and drop off passengers at the same stops en route, so if you're outward bound make sure that you board the right one (route numbers are clearly posted on the front of the buses).

Cab fare from the airport into town is €30–€35—depending on traffic, the part of town you're heading to, and the amount of baggage you have (there's a €1 surcharge for each suitcase that goes in the trunk). If you're driving your own car, follow signs to the Centre Ciutat, from which you can enter the city along Gran Vía. For the port area, follow signs for the Ronda Litoral. The journey to the center of town can take 25–45 minutes, depending on traffic.

CITY BUS, SUBWAY, AND TRAM TRAVEL

City buses run daily approximately 5:30 am–11:30 pm. Barcelona's 17 night buses generally run until about 5 am. Route maps are displayed at bus stops. Schedules are available at bus and metro stations or at ⊕ *www.tmb.cat*.

Barcelona's tramway system is divided into two subsectors: Trambaix serves the western end of the Diagonal, and Trambesòs serves the eastern end.

In Barcelona the underground metro, or subway, is the fastest, cheapest, and easiest way to get around. Metro lines run Monday–Thursday and Sunday 5 am–midnight, Friday until 2 am, and all night Saturday and holiday evenings. The FGC trains run 5 am until just after midnight on weekdays and 5 am–2 am on weekends and the eves of holidays. Sunday trains run on weekday schedules. Single-fare tickets cost €2.20 (€4.60 to the airport); 10-ride passes cost €10.20.

Contacts Transports Metropolitans de Barcelona (*TMB*). ☎ *93/214–8000, 93/298–7000* ⊕ *www.tmb.cat/en/home.*

TAXI TRAVEL

In Barcelona taxis are black and yellow and show a green rooftop light on the front right corner when available for hire. The meter currently starts at €2.15 and rises in increments of €1.13 every kilometer. These rates apply weekdays 6 am–10 pm. Outside these hours, the rates rise 20%. There is an official supplement of €1 per bag for luggage.

Trips to or from Sants train station entail a supplemental charge of €2.10; to the quay where cruise ships put in, or to the airport, the supplemental charge is €3.10 (there's also a €20 minimum charge from the airport). There are cabstands (*parades*, in Catalan) all over town, and you can also hail cabs on the street, though if you are too close to an official stand they may not stop. You can call for a cab by phone 24 hours a day; the minimum fare is €7. Drivers do not expect a tip, but rounding up the fare is standard.

Contacts Barna Taxi. ☎ *93/322222* ⊕ *barnataxi.com.* **Radio Taxi 033.** ☎ *93/303–3033 to call a cab* ⊕ *radiotaxi033.com.* **Taxi Class Rent.** ☎ *93/307–0707* ⊕ *www.taxiclassrent.com/en.*

TRAIN TRAVEL

International overnight trains to Barcelona arrive from many European cities, including Paris, Grenoble, Geneva, Zurich, and Milan; the route from Paris takes 6½ hours. All long-distance trains currently arrive at and depart from Estació de Sants, although the new station at Sagrera (slated to open in late 2020) will eventually be the city's high-speed train hub. Estació de França, near the port, handles only a few regional trains within Catalonia. Train service connects Barcelona with most other major cities in Spain; in addition a high-speed Euromed route connects Barcelona to Tarragona and Valencia.

Information on local commuter lines (*rodalies* in Catalan, *cercanías* in Castilian) can be found at ⊕ *www.renfe.com/viajeros/cercanias/barcelona/.* Rodalies go, for example, to Sitges from Barcelona, whereas you would take a regular RENFE train to, say, Tarragona. It's important to know whether you are traveling on RENFE or on rodalies (the latter distinguished by a stylized "C"), so you don't end up in the wrong line.

Stations Estació de França. ⊠ *Av. Marquès de l'Argentera 1, Born-Ribera* ☎ *912/320320 RENFE station info* ⊕ *www.renfe.com* Ⓜ *L4 Barceloneta.* **Estació de Passeig de Gràcia.** ⊠ *Passeig de Gràcia/Carrer Aragó, Eixample* ☎ *912/432343 station info, 912/320320 RENFE general info* ⊕ *www.renfe.com* Ⓜ *L2/L3/L4 Passeig de Gràcia.* **Estació de Sants.** ⊠ *Pl. dels Països Catalans s/n, Les Corts* ☎ *912/432343 station info, 902/320320 RENFE general info* ⊕ *www.renfe.com* Ⓜ *L3/L5 Sants Estació.* **Ferrocarrils de la Generalitat de Catalunya (FGC).** ⊠ *Carrer Vergos 44, Sarrià* ☎ *93/366–3000* ⊕ *www.fgc.cat/ eng/index.asp* Ⓜ *Sarrià (FGC).* **RENFE.** ☎ *912/320320* ⊕ *www.renfe.com.*

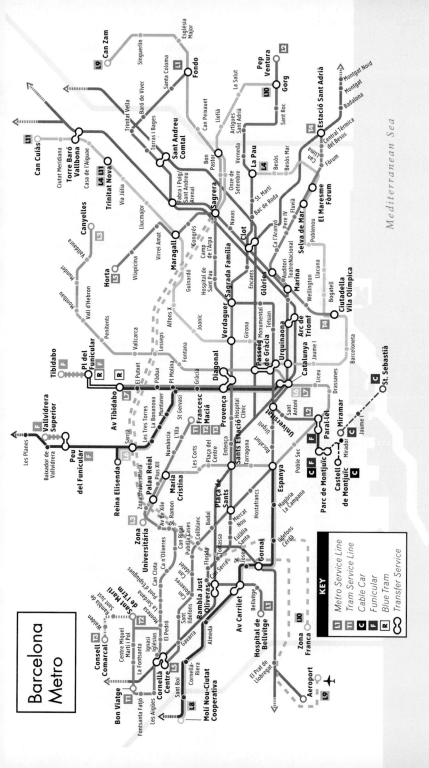

Barcelona Metro

Information and Passes Eurail. ⊕ *www.eurail.com.* **Rail Europe.** ☎ *800/622–8600* ⊕ *www.raileurope.com* ☎ *800/622–8600* ⊕ *www.raileurope.ca.*

TOURS

ART TOURS

The Ruta del Modernisme (Moderniste Route), a self-guided tour, provides an excellent guidebook (available in English) that interprets 120 Moderniste sites from the Sagrada Família and the Palau de la Música Catalana to building facades, lampposts, and paving stones. The €12 guide, sold at the Plaça de Catalunya Tourist Office, Pavellons Güell, and the Recinte Modernista de Sant Pau, comes with a book of vouchers good for discounts up to 50% on admission to most of the Moderniste buildings and sites in the guide in Barcelona and nine other towns and cities in Catalonia. An expanded pack, which includes a guide to the city's Moderniste bars and restaurants and a bag, is available for €18.

Centre del Modernisme, Pavellons Güell. ⊠ *Av. de Pedralbes 7, Pedralbes* ☎ *93/317–7652* ⊕ *www.rutadelmodernisme.com* 🖃 *€5* Ⓜ *L3 Palau Real, Maria Cristina.*

Recinte Modernista de Sant Pau (*Hospital de la Santa Creu i Sant Pau*). ⊠ *Carrer Sant Antoni Maria Claret 167, Eixample* ☎ *93/553–7801* ⊕ *www.santpaubarcelona.org/en* 🖃 *From €14* Ⓜ *L5 Sant Pau/Dos de Maig.*

CULINARY TOURS

Aula Gastronómica. Tapas workshops at this cooking school include visits to the nearby Boqueria or Santa Caterina markets. ⊠ *Carrer Sagristans 5, Entresuelo, Barri Gòtic* ☎ *93/301–1944* ⊕ *www.aulagastronomica. com/cooking-classes* 🖃 *From €35* Ⓜ *L4 Jaume I.*

Epicurean Ways. Jane Gregg, founder of Epicurean Ways, offers gourmet and wine tours of Barcelona and Catalonia. ☎ *434/738–2293 in U.S., 93/802–2688 in Spain* ⊕ *www.epicureanways.com.*

Spanish Journeys. Teresa Parker of Spanish Journeys organizes cooking classes, seasonal specials, custom cultural or culinary tours, corporate cooking retreats, or off-the-beaten-path travel. ⊠ *Wellfleet* ☎ *508/349–9769* ⊕ *www.spanishjourneys.com* 🖃 *From $3895.*

DAY TOURS AND GUIDES

BIKE TOURS **Bike Tours Barcelona.** This company offers a three-hour bike tour (in English) for €25, with a drink included. Just look for the guide with a bike and a blue flag at the northeast corner of the Casa de la Ciutat in Plaça Sant Jaume, outside the Tourist Information Office. Tours depart at 11 am daily; there is an additional tour at 4:30 pm Friday–Monday, April 1–September 15. The company will also organize private guided tours through the Barri Gòtic, parks, the Port Olímpic and Barceloneta, the Ruta Moderniste, and other itineraries on request. Touring on your own? The company also rents bikes by the hour or the day, at its shop in Carrer Esparteria. ⊠ *Carrer Esparteria 3, Barri Gòtic* ☎ *932/682105* ⊕ *biketoursbarcelona.com* Ⓜ *Jaume I.*

BOAT TOURS **Las Golondrinas.** Golondrina harbor boats make short trips from the Portal de la Pau, near the Columbus monument. There's a 40-minute "Barcelona Port" tour of the harbor, an hour-long "Premium" tour that includes a glass of cava, and a 90-minute "Barcelona Sea" ride out past the beaches and up the coast to the Fòrum at the eastern end of Diagonal, plus summer-only tours with live music (usually flamenco or jazz). ⊠ *Pl. Portal de la Pau s/n, Moll de les Drassanes, La Rambla* ☎ *93/442–3106* ⊕ *lasgolondrinas.com/en* 🚇 *From €8* Ⓜ *L3 Drassanes.*

BUS TOURS **Bus Turístic.** The Bus Turístic, sponsored by the tourist office, runs on three circuits that pass all the important sights. The blue route covers upper Barcelona; the red route tours lower Barcelona; and the green route runs from the Port Olímpic along Barcelona's beaches to the Fòrum at the eastern end of Diagonal (April–October only). The cost is €27 with 10% online purchase discount for one day (€36 for two days); onboard or at the ticket booth, cost is €30 (€40 for 2 days). There are audio guides on board, and you receive a booklet with discount vouchers for various attractions. The blue and red routes start at Plaça de Catalunya near Café Zurich. The green route starts at Port Olímpic next to the Hotel Arts. Passengers can jump off and catch a later bus at any stop along the way; some stops are "hubs" where you can switch to a bus on one of the other routes. There's free Wi-Fi on board. ⊠ *Pl. de Catalunya 3, Eixample* ☎ *93/285–3832* ⊕ *www. barcelonabusturistic.cat* 🚇 *From €27* Ⓜ *Catalunya.*

Julià Travel. Julià Travel offers bilingual city walking tours and coach trips to Montserrat, Girona, Sitges, and PortAventura World. ⊠ *Carrer Balmes 5, Eixample* ☎ *93/402–6900* ⊕ *www.juliatravel.com/destinations/barcelona* 🚇 *From €25* Ⓜ *Catalunya, L1/L2 Universitat.*

PRIVATE GUIDES Guides from the organizations listed are generally competent, though the quality of language skills and general showmanship may vary.

Barcelona Guide Bureau. Daily walking tours of the major sites in Barcelona are available, as well as tours to Montserrat and the Dalí Museum in Girona. Some tours offer fast-track entrance to museums and popular venues like the Sagrada Família. ⊠ *Via Laietana 54, 2–2, Born-Ribera* ☎ *93/268–2422, 667/419140 on weekends* ⊕ *www.barcelonaguidebureau.com* 🚇 *From €34* Ⓜ *Urquinaona.*

Heritage Tours. Private custom-designed tours from this company include hotels, private guides, transportation, and cuisine. ⊠ *121 W. 27th St., Suite 1201, New York* ☎ *800/378–4555 toll-free in U.S., 212/206–8400 in U.S.* ⊕ *www.heritagetours.com* 🚇 *Prices vary.*

WALKING TOURS **Urbancultours.** Architect Dominique Tomasov Blinder of Urbancultours specializes in tours about Barcelona's Jewish heritage, and offers explorations of the Barcelona Jewish Quarter and the ancient Jewish cemetery on Montjuïc. ⊕ *www.urbancultours.com.*

VISITOR INFORMATION

Turisme de Barcelona. In addition to being a useful resource for information, tickets, and bookings, Turisme de Barcelona offers daily walking tours of the Barri Gòtic, Picasso's Barcelona, Modernisme, and Gourmet Barcelona, among others; departure times for tours in English depend on which of the tours you choose. Book online for a 10% discount. The Picasso tour, which includes the entry fee for the Museu Picasso, is a great bargain. Tours depart from the Plaça de Catalunya tourist office. ⊠ *Pl. de Catalunya 17, soterrani, Eixample* ☎ *93/285–3834* ⊕ *bcnshop. barcelonaturisme.com/shopv3/* 🚇 *From €14* Ⓜ *Pl. de Catalunya.*

EXPLORING

Barcelona has several main areas to explore. Between Plaça de Catalunya and the port lies the Ciutat Vella, or Old City, including El Barri Gòtic (the Gothic Quarter); the shop-, bar-, and tapas-rich Ribera (the waterfront, also known as Born-Ribera); the populous central promenade of La Rambla; and El Raval, the former slums or outskirts southwest of La Rambla. Above Plaça de Catalunya is the grid-pattern expansion known as the Eixample (literally, the "Expansion"), built after the city's third series of defensive walls were torn down in 1860; this area contains most of Barcelona's Moderniste architecture. Farther north and west, Upper Barcelona includes the former outlying towns of Gràcia and Sarrià, Pedralbes, and, rising up behind the city, Tibidabo and the green hills of the Collserola nature preserve.

Though built in the mid-18th century, Barceloneta is generally considered part of the Ciutat Vella. The Port Olímpic, a series of vast terrace restaurants and discos, is just beyond the Frank Gehry goldfish and the Hotel Arts. The Ciutadella park, once a fortress built not to protect but to dominate Barcelona, is just inland.

Don't overlook the Plaça de les Glòries Catalanes, site of a major urban renewal project that embraces the DHUB design museum complex, the reconfigured Encants Vells flea market, the Auditori music venue, and the Torre Agbar. A few minutes' walk along the Diagonal from here brings you to the top of the Rambla de Poblenou, a former industrial area reborn after the 1992 Olympics as a leafy avenue running down to the ocean, lined with trendy bars and restaurants, quirky shops, and some of the city's most beautiful smaller-scale Moderniste architecture.

CIUTAT VELLA: THE RAMBLA AND THE RAVAL

The promenade in the heart of premodern Barcelona was originally a watercourse, dry for most of the year, that separated the walled Ciutat Vella from the outlying Raval. In the 14th century, the city walls were extended and the arroyo was filled in, so it gradually became a thoroughfare where peddlers, farmers, and tradespeople hawked their wares. (The watercourse is still there, under the pavement. From time to time a torrential rain will fill it, and the water rises up through the drains.) The poet-playwright Federico García Lorca called this the only street in the world he wished would never end—and in a sense, it doesn't.

Fodor's Choice ★ **Antic Hospital de la Santa Creu i Sant Pau.** Founded in the 10th century as one of Europe's earliest medical complexes, the mostly 15th- and 16th-century complex contains some of Barcelona's most impressive Gothic architecture. From the entrance, the first building on the left is the 18th-century **Reial Acadèmia de Cirurgia i Medicina** (Royal Academy of Surgery and Medicine). Across the way on the right is the gateway into the patio of the **Casa de la Convalescència,** where patients were moved for recuperation; it now houses the Institute for Catalan Studies. Through a gate to the left of the Casa de Convalescència is the garden-courtyard of the hospital complex, the **Jardins de Rubió i Lluc,** centered on a baroque cross and lined with orange trees. On

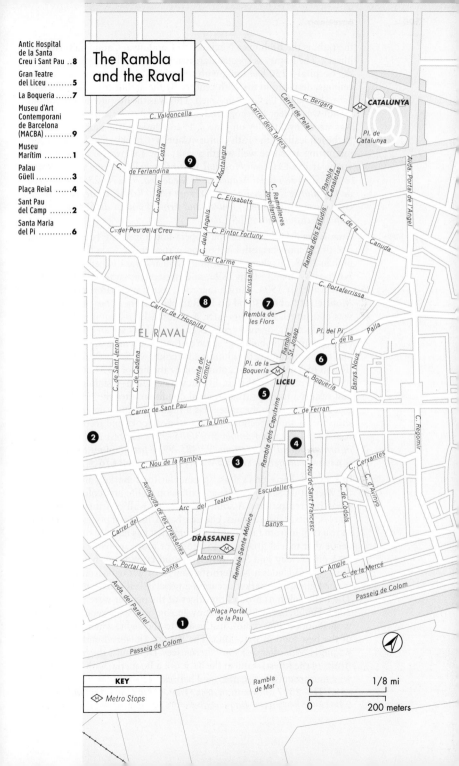

The Rambla and the Raval

CATALUNYA

Pl. de
Catalunya

C. Bergara

Carrer de Pelai

Carrer dels tallers

C. Valdoncella

C. de Ferlandina

C. Montalegre

C. Joaquín

Costa

C. Elisabets

C. Ramelleres
Jovellanos

Rambla
Canaletas

Rambla dels Estudis

C. de la
Canuda

Avda. Portal de l'Angel

C. del Peu de la Creu

C. dels Àngels

C. Pintor Fortuny

Carrer del Carme

C. Jerusalem

C. Portaferrissa

Carrer de l'Hospital

EL RAVAL

Rambla de
les Flors

Rambla St. Josep

Pl. del Pi

Palla

C. de la

Pl. de la
Boqueria

LICEU

C. Boqueria

Banys Nous

C. de Sant Jeroni

C. de Cadena

Junta de
Comerç

Carrer de Sant Pau

C. la Unió

Rambla dels Caputxins

C. de Ferran

C. Regomir

C. Nou de la Rambla

C. Cervantes

C. d'Avinyo

Avinguda de les Drassanes

Arc del Teatre

Escudellers

C. Nou de Sant Francesc

C. de Còdols

Carrer del

Banys

DRASSANES

Madrona

Rambla Santa Mònica

C. Ample

C. de la Mercè

C. Portal de Santa

Avda. del Paral·lel

Passeig de Colom

Plaça Portal
de la Pau

Passeig de Colom

Rambla
de Mar

0 — 1/8 mi
0 — 200 meters

the right is the **Biblioteca Nacional de Catalunya,** Catalonia's national library. The library is spectacular: two parallel halls—once the core of the hospital—230 feet long, with towering Gothic arches and vaulted ceilings, designed in the 15th century by the architect of the church of Santa Maria del Pi, Guillem Abiell. This was the hospital where Antoni Gaudí was taken, unrecognized and assumed to be a pauper, after he was struck by a trolley on June 7, 1926. Outside, the next set of doors to the left leads to the 15th-century **Capella** (Chapel) of the Hospital, an interesting art space well worth a visit, now a showcase for promising young artists. ⊠ *Carrer Hospital 56 (or Carrer del Carme 45), El Raval* ☎ *93/317–1686 Reial Acadèmia de Medecina, 93/270–2300 Biblioteca de Catalunya* ⊕ *www.bnc.cat* ☑ *From €8* ⊙ *Royal Academy of Medicine: closed Sun.–Tues., Thurs., and Fri; Biblioteca de Catalunya and Capella: closed Sun.* Ⓜ *L3 Liceu.*

Fodor'sChoice **Gran Teatre del Liceu.** Barcelona's opera house has long been considered
★ one of the most beautiful in Europe, a rival to La Scala in Milan. First built in 1848, this cherished cultural landmark was torched in 1861, later bombed by anarchists in 1893, and once again gutted by an accidental fire in early 1994. During that most recent fire, Barcelona's soprano Montserrat Caballé stood on La Rambla in tears as her beloved venue was consumed. Five years later, a restored Liceu, equipped for modern productions, opened anew. Even if you don't see an opera, you can take a tour of the building; some of the Liceu's most spectacular halls and rooms, including the glittering foyer known as the Saló dels Miralls (Room of Mirrors), were untouched by the fire of 1994, as were those of Spain's oldest social club, El Círculo del Liceu—established in 1847 and restored to its pristine original condition after the fire. The Espai Liceu downstairs in the annex has a restaurant and cafeteria and a gift shop with a wide selection of opera-related books and recordings. ⊠ *La Rambla 51–59, La Rambla* ☎ *93/485–9914 express and guided tour information and reservations, 93/485–9931 premium visit reservations* ⊕ *www.liceubarcelona.cat* ☑ *Variety of tours from €16* Ⓜ *L4 Liceu.*

Fodor'sChoice **La Boqueria.** Barcelona's most spectacular food market, also known as
★ the Mercat de Sant Josep, is an explosion of life and color with small tapas bar-restaurants. A solid polychrome wall of fruits, herbs, vegetables, nuts, candied fruits, cheeses, hams, fish, and poultry greets you as you turn in from La Rambla. (The market has become such a popular venue that tourist groups of 15 people or more are banned from 8 am to 3 pm, Friday and Saturday. To avoid crowds, go before 8 am or after 5 pm.) Under a Moderniste hangar of wrought-iron girders and stained glass, the market occupies a neoclassical square built in 1840. The Ionic columns around the edges of the market were uncovered in 2001. Highlights include the sunny greengrocer's market outside, along with Pinotxo (Pinocchio), just inside to the right, which serves some of the best food in Barcelona. The Kiosko Universal and Quim de la Boqueria both offer delicious alternatives. Don't miss the *fruits del bosc* (fruits of the forest) stand at the back of La Boqueria, with its display of wild mushrooms, herbs, nuts, and berries. ⊠ *La Rambla 91, La Rambla* ☎ *93/318–2017 information desk, Tues.–Thurs. 8–3, Fri. and Sat. 8–5, 93/318–2584* ⊕ *www.boqueria.info* ⊙ *Closed Sun.* Ⓜ *Liceu.*

The restored pavilions of architect Domènech i Montaner's extraordinary Hospital de Sant Pau (1902–30), now the Recinte Modernista de Sant Pau, make up the world's largest complex of Art Nouveau buildings.

FAMILY
Fodor's Choice
★

Museu d'Art Contemporani de Barcelona (*Barcelona Museum of Contemporary Art, MACBA*). Designed by American architect Richard Meier in 1992, this gleaming explosion of light and geometry in El Raval houses a permanent collection of contemporary art, and regularly mounts special thematic exhibitions of works on loan. Meier gives a nod to Gaudí (with the Pedrera-like wave on one end of the main facade), but his minimalist building otherwise looks unfinished. That said, the MACBA is unarguably an important addition to the cultural capital of this once-shabby neighborhood. The MACBA's 20th-century art collection (Calder, Rauschenberg, Oteiza, Chillida, Tàpies) is excellent, as is the guided tour in English (at 4 pm on Mondays): a useful introduction to the philosophical foundations of contemporary art as well as the pieces themselves. The museum also offers wonderful workshops and activities for kids. ⊠ *Pl. dels Àngels 1, El Raval* ☎ *93/412–0810* ⊕ *www.macba.cat* ✉ *€10 (valid for 1 month)* ☉ *Closed Tues.* Ⓜ *L1/L2 Universitat, L1/L3 Catalunya.*

FAMILY
Fodor's Choice
★

Museu Marítim. The superb Maritime Museum is housed in the 13th-century Drassanes Reials (Royal Shipyards), at the foot of La Rambla adjacent to the harbor front. This vast covered complex launched the ships of Catalonia's powerful Mediterranean fleet directly from its yards into the port. Today these are the world's largest and best-preserved medieval shipyards. On the Avinguda del Paral·lel side of Drassanes is a completely intact section of the 14th- to 15th-century walls—Barcelona's third and final ramparts—that encircled El Raval along the Paral·lel and the Rondas de Sant Pau, Sant Antoni, and Universitat. Though the shipyards seem more like a cathedral than a naval construction site, the Maritime Museum is filled with vessels, including a spectacular collection of ship models. Perhaps the most impressive display is the life-size reconstruction of the galley of Juan de Austria, commander of the Spanish fleet in the Battle of Lepanto. Headphones and infrared pointers provide a first-rate self-guided tour. The cafeteria-restaurant Norai, open daily 9 am to 8 pm, is Barcelona's hands-down winner for dining in a setting of medieval elegance, and has a charming terrace. Admission includes a visit to the schooner *Santa Eulàlia,* a meticulously restored clipper built in 1918, which is moored nearby at the Port Vell. ⊠ *Av. de les Drassanes s/n, La Rambla* 🕾 *93/342–9920* ⊕ *www.mmb.cat* 🖃 *€10 (includes admission to Santa Eulàlia clipper); free Sun. after 3* ☉ *Closed Mon.* Ⓜ *L3 Drassanes.*

Fodor'sChoice   **Palau Güell.** Gaudí built this mansion in 1886–89 for textile baron
★   Count Eusebi de Güell Bacigalupi, his most important patron. The dark facade is a dramatic foil for the brilliance of the inside, where spear-shape Art Nouveau columns frame the windows, rising to support a series of detailed and elaborately carved wood ceilings. The basement stables are famous for the "fungiform" (mushroomlike) columns carrying the weight of the whole building. Don't miss the figures of the faithful hounds, with the rings in their mouths for hitching horses, or the wooden bricks laid down in lieu of cobblestones in the entryway upstairs. The dining room is dominated by a beautiful mahogany banquet table seating 10, an Art Nouveau fireplace in the shape of a deeply curving horseshoe arch, and walls with floral and animal motifs. The passageway built toward La Rambla was all that came of a plan to buy an intervening property and connect three houses into one grand structure, a scheme that never materialized. Gaudí is most himself on the roof, where his playful, polychrome ceramic chimneys seem like preludes to later works like the Park Güell and La Pedrera. ⊠ *Nou de la Rambla 3–5, La Rambla* 🕾 *93/472–5771, 93/472–5775* ⊕ *www. palauguell.cat/en* 🖃 *€12; free 1st Sun. of month, 5–8 pm* ☉ *Closed Mon.* ☞ *Guided tours (1 hr) in English Fri. at 10:30 am and Sat. at 2:30 pm at no additional cost* Ⓜ *L3 Drassanes, Liceu.*

Plaça Reial. Nobel Prize–winning novelist Gabriel García Márquez, architect and urban planner Oriol Bohigas, and Pasqual Maragall, former president of the Catalonian Generalitat, are among the many famous people said to have acquired apartments overlooking this elegant square, a chiaroscuro masterpiece in which neoclassical symmetry clashes with big-city street funk. Plaça Reial is bordered by stately ocher facades with balconies overlooking the wrought-iron **Fountain of the Three Graces,** and an array of lampposts designed by Gaudí in 1879. Cafés and restaurants—several of them excellent—line the square. Plaça Reial is most colorful on Sunday morning, when collectors gather to trade stamps and coins; after dark it's a center of downtown nightlife for the jazz-minded, the young, and the adventurous (it's best to be streetwise touring this area in the late hours). Bar Glaciar, on the uphill corner toward La Rambla, is a booming beer station for young international travelers. Tarantos has top flamenco performances, and Jamboree offers world-class jazz. ⊠ *La Rambla* Ⓜ *L3 Liceu.*

Fodor'sChoice   **Sant Pau del Camp.** Barcelona's oldest church was originally outside the
★   city walls (*del camp* means "in the fields") and was a Roman cemetery as far back as the 2nd century, according to archaeological evidence. What

you see now was built in 1127 and is the earliest Romanesque structure in Barcelona. Elements of the church—the classical marble capitals atop the columns in the main entry—are thought to be from the 6th and 7th centuries. The hulking, mastodonic shape of the church is a reminder of the church's defensive posture in the face of intermittent Roman persecution and later, Moorish invasions and sackings. Check for musical performances here, as the church is an acoustical gem. The tiny stained-glass window high on the facade facing Carrer Sant Pau may be Europe's smallest, a bookend to Santa Maria del Pi's largest. The tiny cloister is Sant Pau del Camp's best feature, and one of Barcelona's semisecret treasures. ⊠ *Carrer de Sant Pau 101, El Raval* ☎ *93/441–0001* 🎫 *Free when Masses are celebrated; guided tour Sun. at 12:45, €3* ⊘ *Cloister closed Sun. during Mass; no tours Sun. in mid-Aug.* Ⓜ *L3 Paral.lel.*

Santa Maria del Pi (*St. Mary of the Pine*). Sister church to Santa Maria del Mar and to Santa Maria de Pedralbes, this early Catalan Gothic structure is perhaps the most fortresslike of all three: hulking, dark, and massive, and perforated only by the main entryway and the mammoth rose window, said to be the world's largest. Try to see the window from inside in the late afternoon to get the best view of the colors. The church was named for the lone *pi* (pine tree) that stood in what was a marshy lowland outside the 4th-century Roman walls. An early church dating back to the 10th century preceded the present Santa Maria del Pi, which was begun in 1322 and finally consecrated in 1453. The interior compares poorly with the clean and lofty lightness of Santa Maria del Mar, but there are two interesting things to see: the original wooden choir loft, and the Ramón Amadeu painting *La Mare de Deu dels Desamparats* (*Our Lady of the Helpless*), in which the artist reportedly used his wife and children as models for the Virgin and children. The church is a regular venue for classical guitar concerts by well-known soloists. Tours of the basilica and bell tower are available in English, by reservation. The adjoining squares, **Plaça del Pi** and **Plaça de Sant Josep Oriol,** are two of the liveliest and most appealing spaces in the Ciutat Vella, filled with much-frequented outdoor cafés and used as a venue for markets selling natural products or paintings, or as an impromptu concert hall for musicians. The handsome entryway and courtyard at No. 4 Plaça de Sant Josep Oriol across from the lateral facade of Santa Maria del Pi is the **Palau Fivaller,** now seat of the Agricultural Institute, an interesting patio to have a look through. Placeta del Pi, tucked in behind the church, has outdoor tables and is convenient for a coffee or tapas. ⊠ *Pl. del Pi 7, Barri Gòtic* ☎ *93/318–4743* ⊕ *basilicadelpi.com* 🎫 *From €4* Ⓜ *L3 Liceu.*

CIUTAT VELLA: BARRI GÒTIC AND BORN-RIBERA

No city in Europe has an ancient quarter to rival Barcelona's Barri Gòtic in its historic atmosphere and the sheer density of its monumental buildings. It's a stroller's delight, where you can expect to hear the strains of a flute or a classical guitar from around the next corner. The Barri Gòtic comprises the area around the Catedral de la Seu and rests squarely atop the first Roman settlement. This high ground the Romans called Mons Taber coincides almost exactly with the early

1st- to 4th-century fortified town of Barcino. Sights to see here include the Plaça del Rei, the remains of Roman Barcino underground beneath the Museu d'Història de Barcelona (Barcelona History Museum), the Plaça Sant Jaume and the area around the onetime Roman Forum, the medieval Jewish Quarter, and the ancient Plaça Sant Just.

Across Via Laietana is the Barri de la Ribera, or Born-Ribera, once the waterfront district around the basilica of Santa Maria del Mar. Born-Ribera includes Carrer Montcada, lined with 14th- to 18th-century Renaissance palaces; Passeig del Born, where medieval jousts were held; Carrer Flassaders and the area around the early mint; the shop- and restaurant-rich Carrer Banys Vells; Plaça de les Olles; and Pla del Palau, where La Llotja, Barcelona's early maritime exchange, housed the fine-arts school where Picasso, Gaudí, and Domènech i Montaner all studied, as did many more of Barcelona's most important artists and architects.

Long a depressed neighborhood, La Ribera began to experience a revival in the 1980s; liberally endowed now with intimate bars, cafés, and trendy boutiques, it continues to enjoy the blessings of gentrification. The Born Centre de Cultura i Memòria, a 19th-century market converted into a cultural center, displays the remains of a an open excavation that offers a fascinating view of pre-1714 Barcelona, destroyed by the victorious troops of Felipe V at the end of the War of the Spanish Succession. The Passeig del Born—"La Rambla" of medieval Barcelona—is once again a pleasant leafy promenade.

Fodor's Choice
★ **Catedral de la Seu.** Barcelona's cathedral is a repository of centuries of the city's history and legend—although as a work of architecture visitors might find it a bit of a disappointment. Don't miss the beautifully carved choir stalls of the Knights of the Golden Fleece; the intricately and elaborately sculpted organ loft over the door out to Plaça Sant Iu (with its celebrated Saracen's Head sculpture); the series of 60-odd wood sculptures of evangelical figures along the exterior lateral walls of the choir; the cloister with its fountain and geese in the pond; and, in the crypt, the tomb of Santa Eulàlia. Among the two dozen ornate and gilded chapels in the basilica, pay due attention to the **Capella de Lepant,** dedicated to Sant Cristo de Lepant. The leafy, palm tree–shaded **cloister** surrounds a tropical garden, and a pool populated by 13 snow-white geese, one for each of the tortures inflicted upon St. Eulàlia in an effort to break her faith. In front of the cathedral is the grand square of **Plaça de la Seu,** where on Saturday from 6 pm to 8 pm, Sunday morning, and occasional evenings, barcelonins gather to dance the *sardana,* the circular folk dance performed for centuries as a symbol-in-motion of Catalan identity and the solidarity of the Catalan people. Also check local listings for the annual series of evening organ concerts held in the cathedral. ⊠ *Pl. de la Seu s/n, Barri Gòtic* ☎ *93/342–8262* ⊕ *www. catedralbcn.org* ⌂ *Free weekdays 8–12:45 and 5:45–7:30, Sat. 8–12:45 and 5:15–8, Sun. 8–1:30 and 5:15–8; €7 donation weekdays 1–5:30, Sat. 1–5, Sun. 2–5; choir €3; rooftop €3* Ⓜ *L4 Jaume I.*

Fodor's Choice
★ **Museu d'Història de Barcelona** (*Museum of the History of Barcelona [MUHBA]*). This fascinating museum just off Plaça del Rei traces Barcelona's evolution from its first Iberian settlement through its Roman

and Visigothic ages and beyond. The Romans took the city during the Punic Wars, and you can tour underground remains of their Colonia Favencia Iulia Augusta Paterna Barcino (Favored Colony of the Father Julius Augustus Barcino) via metal walkways. Some 43,000 square feet of archaeological artifacts, from the walls of houses, to mosaics and fluted columns, workshops (for pressing olive oil and salted fish paste) and street systems, can be found in large part beneath the Plaça. See how the Visgoths and their descendants built the early medieval walls on top of these ruins, recycling chunks of Roman stone and concrete, bits of columns, and even headstones. In the ground floor gallery is a striking collection of marble busts and funerary urns discovered in the course of the excavations. The price of admission to the museum includes entry to the other treasures of the **Plaça del Rei,** including the **Palau Reial Major,** the splendid **Saló del Tinell,** and the chapel of **Santa Àgata.** Also included are visits to other sites maintained by the museum: the most important and central of these are the Temple of Augustus, the Door of the Sea (the largest of the Roman-era city gates) and Dockside Thermal Baths, the Roman Funeral Way in the Plaça de la Vila de Madrid, and the Call (medieval Barcelona's Jewish quarter). The admission ticket also gives visitors a 21% discount on entrance to Park Güell. ⊠ *Palau Padellàs, Pl. del Rei s/n, Barri Gòtic* ☎ *93/256–2100* ⊕ *ajuntament.barcelona.cat/museuhistoria/en/* ⊠ *From €7 (free with Barcelona Card, 1st Sun. of month, and all other Sun. after 3)* ☉ *Closed Mon.* Ⓜ *L4 Jaume I, L3 Liceu.*

Fodor's Choice ★ **Museu Picasso** (*Picasso Museum*). The Picasso Museum is housed in five adjoining palaces on Carrer Montcada, a street known for Barcelona's most elegant medieval palaces. Picasso spent his key formative years in Barcelona (1895–1904), and this collection, while it does not include a significant number of the artist's best paintings, is particularly strong on his early work. Displays include childhood sketches, works from Picasso's Rose and Blue periods, and the many famous 1950s Cubist variations on Velázquez's *Las Meninas* (in Rooms 22–26). The lower-floor sketches, oils, and schoolboy caricatures and drawings from Picasso's early years in A Coruña are perhaps the most fascinating part, showing the facility the artist seemed to possess almost from the cradle. On the second floor are works from his Blue Period in Paris, a time of loneliness, cold, and hunger for the artist. ▰TIP→ **Admission is free the first Sunday of the month and every Thursday 6–9:30 pm. Arrive early to avoid the long lines and crowds.** ⊠ *Carrer Montcada 15–19, Born-Ribera* ☎ *93/256–3000, 93/256–3022 guided tour and group reservations* ⊕ *www.museupicasso.bcn.cat* ⊠ *€12; free Thurs. 6–9:30 pm, and 1st Sun. of month* ☉ *Closed Mon.* ☞ *Guided tours of permanent collection (in English) Wed. at 3 and Sun. at 11 (except Aug.); free with admission* Ⓜ *L4 Jaume I, L1 Arc de Triomf.*

Fodor's Choice ★ **Palau de la Música Catalana.** One of the world's most extraordinary music halls, with facades that are a riot of color and form, the Music Palace is a landmark of Carrer Amadeus Vives, set just across Via Laietana, a 10-minute walk from Plaça de Catalunya. The Palau is a flamboyant tour de force designed in 1908 by Lluís Domènech i Montaner. Originally conceived by the Orfeó Català musical society as a vindication of the

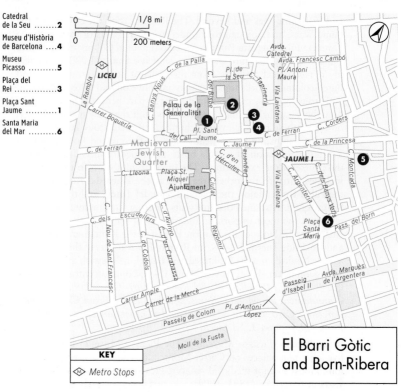

El Barri Gòtic
and Born-Ribera

KEY

◈ Metro Stops

importance of music at a popular level—as opposed to the Liceu opera house's identification with the Catalan aristocracy—the Palau was for many decades an opposing crosstown force with the Liceu. The exterior is remarkable in itself. The Miquel Blay sculptural group is Catalonia's popular music come to life, with everyone included from St. George the dragonslayer to women and children, fishermen, and every strain and strata of popular life and music. The Palau's over-the-top decor overwhelms the senses even before the first note of music is heard. ✉ *Carrer Palau de la Música 4–6, Born-Ribera* ☎ *93/295–7200, 902/442882 box office* ⊕ *www.palaumusica.cat/en* ▣ *Tour €20* Ⓜ *L1/L4 Urquinaona.*

Fodor's Choice **Plaça del Rei.** This little square is as compact a nexus of history as any-
★ thing the Barri Gòtic has to offer. Long held to be the scene of Columbus's triumphal return from his first voyage to the New World—the
precise spot where Ferdinand and Isabella received him is purportedly
on the stairs fanning out from the corner of the square (though evidence
indicates that the Catholic Monarchs were at a summer residence in
the Empordá)—the **Palau Reial Major** (admission included in the €7
entrance fee for the Museu d'Història de Barcelona; closed Mon.) was
the official royal residence in Barcelona. The main room is the **Saló del
Tinell,** a magnificent banquet hall built in 1362. To the left is the **Palau
del Lloctinent** (Lieutenant's Palace); towering overhead in the corner

is the dark 15th-century **Torre Mirador del Rei Martí** (King Martin's Watchtower). The 14th-century **Capella Real de Santa Àgueda** (Royal Chapel of St. Agatha) is on the right side of the stairway, and behind and to the right as you face the stairs is the **Palau Clariana-Padellàs,** moved to this spot stone by stone from Carrer Mercaders in the early 20th century and now the entrance to the **Museu d'Història de Barcelona.** ⊠ *Pl. del Rei s/n, Barri Gòtic* Ⓜ *L3 Liceu, L4 Jaume I.*

Plaça Sant Jaume. Facing each other across this oldest epicenter of Barcelona (and often on politically opposite sides as well) are the seat of Catalonia's regional government, the Generalitat de Catalunya, in the **Palau de La Generalitat,** and the City Hall, the Ajuntament de Barcelona, in the **Casa de la Ciutat.** This square was the site of the Roman forum 2,000 years ago, though subsequent construction filled the space with buildings. The square was cleared in the 1840s, but the two imposing government buildings are actually much older: the Ajuntament dates back to the 14th century, and the Generalitat was built between the 15th- and mid-17th century. ⊠ *Barri Gòtic* ☉ *Closed weekdays* ☞ *Tours of Ajuntament (in Catalan, Spanish, and English) weekends 10–2; tours of Generalitat on 2nd and 4th weekends of month 10:30–1, by reservation only (bring your passport)* Ⓜ *Jaume I.*

Fodor'sChoice
★

Santa Maria del Mar. The most beautiful example of early Catalan Gothic architecture, Santa Maria del Mar is extraordinary for its unbroken lines and elegance, and the lightness of the interior is especially surprising considering the blocky exterior. The site was home to a Christian cult from the late 3rd century. Built by mere stonemasons who chose, fitted, and carved each stone hauled down from a Montjuïc quarry, the church is breathtakingly and nearly hypnotically symmetrical. The medieval numerological symbol for the Virgin Mary, the number eight (or multiples thereof) runs through every element of the basilica: the 16 octagonal pillars are 2 meters in diameter and spread out into rib vaulting arches at a height of 16 meters; the painted keystones at the apex of the arches are 32 meters from the floor; and the central nave is twice as wide as the lateral naves (8 meters each). Although anticlerical anarchists burned the basilica in 1936, it was restored after the end of the Spanish Civil War by Bauhaus-trained architects. Set aside at least a half hour to see Santa Maria del Mar. *La Catedral del Mar* (*The Cathedral of the Sea*) by Ildefonso Falcons chronicles the construction of the basilica and 14th-century life in Barcelona. Check the schedule for concerts. ⊠ *Pl. de Santa Maria 1, Born-Ribera* ☎ *93/310–2390* ⊕ *www. santamariadelmarbarcelona.org* ⊠ *Tour from €10* Ⓜ *L4 Jaume I.*

BARCELONETA AND LA CIUTADELLA

Barceloneta and La Ciutadella make a historical fit. In the early 18th century, some 1,000 houses in the Barri de la Ribera, then the waterfront neighborhood around Plaça del Born, were ordered torn down, to create fields of fire for the cannon of La Ciutadella, the newly built fortress that kept watch over the rebellious Catalans. Barceloneta, then a wetland, was developed almost four decades later, in 1753, to house families who had lost homes in La Ribera.

Open water in Roman times and gradually silted in only after the 15th-century construction of the port, it became Barcelona's fishermen's and stevedores' quarter. With its tiny original apartment blocks, and its history of seafarers, Barceloneta even now maintains its carefree flavor.

Barceloneta. Once Barcelona's pungent fishing port, Barceloneta retains much of its salty maritime flavor, even as it undergoes a long-overdue gentrification. Stop in Plaça de la Barceloneta to see the baroque church of **Sant Miquel del Port,** with its oversize sculpture of the winged archangel. Look for the splendidly remodeled Barceloneta market and its two restaurants. The original two-story houses and the restaurant Can Solé on Carrer Sant Carles are historic landmarks. Barceloneta's surprisingly clean and sandy **beach,** though overcrowded in midsummer, offers swimming, surfing, and a lively social scene late May–September.

El Transbordador Aeri del Port (*port cable car*). This hair-raising cable-car ride over the Barcelona harbor from Barceloneta to Montjuïc (with a midway stop in the port) is an adrenaline rush with a view. The rush comes from being packed in with 18 other people (standing-room only) in a tiny gondola swaying a hundred feet or so above the Mediterranean. The cable car leaves from the tower at the end of Passeig Joan de Borbó and connects the Torre de San Sebastián on the Moll de Barceloneta, the tower of Jaume I in the port boat terminal, and the Torre de Miramar on Montjuïc. Critics maintain, not without reason, that the ride is expensive, the maintenance is so-so, and the queues can seem interminable. On the positive side, this is undoubtedly the slickest way to connect Barceloneta and Montjuïc. The Torre de Altamar restaurant in the tower at the Barceloneta end serves excellent food and wine. ⊠ *Passeig Joan de Borbó 88, Barceloneta* ☎ *93/441–4820* ⊕ *www.telefericodebarcelona.com* ⊡ *From €11* Ⓜ *L4 Barceloneta.*

> **WATCH YOUR STUFF**
>
> While muggings are practically unheard of in Barcelona, petty thievery is common. Handbags, backpacks, camera cases, and wallets are favorite targets, so tuck those away. Should you carry a purse, use one with a short strap that tucks tightly under your arm.

EIXAMPLE

Barcelona's most famous neighborhood, this late-19th-century urban development is known for its dazzling Art Nouveau architecture. Called the "Expansion" in Catalan, the Eixample (ay-*shom*-pla) is an open-air Moderniste museum. Designed as a grid, in the best Cartesian tradition, the Eixample is oddly difficult to navigate; the builders neglected to number the buildings or alphabetize the streets, and even barcelonins can get lost. The grid was the work of engineer Ildefons Cerdà, and much of the construction was done in the peak years of Modernisme by a who's who of the movement's architects, starring Gaudí, Domènech i

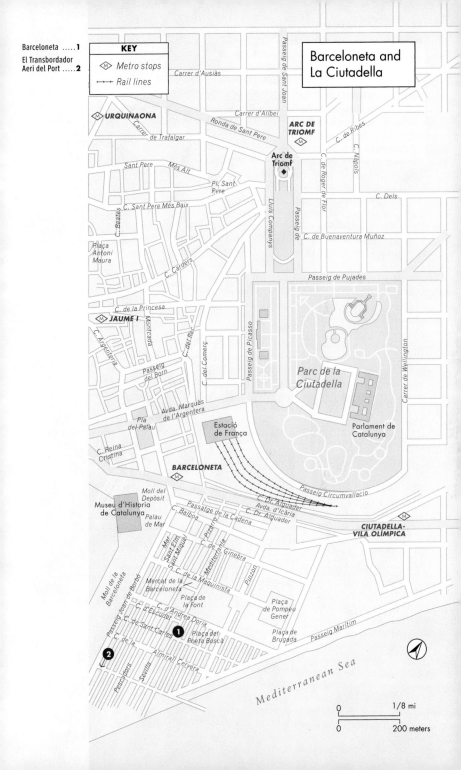

Barceloneta 1
El Transbordador
Aeri del Port 2

KEY

◈ Metro stops

┼──┼ Rail lines

Barceloneta and La Ciutadella

Carrer d'Ausiàs

◈ URQUINAONA

Carrer de Trafalgar

Carrer d'Alibei

Ronda de Sant Pere

ARC DE TRIOMF ◈

C. de Ribes

Arc de Triomf

C. de Roger de Flor

C. de Nàpols

Sant Pere   Més Alt

Pl. Sant Pere

Beates

C. Sant Pere Més Baix

C. Dels

Passeig de Sant Joan

Lluís Companys

Passeig de

C. de Buenaventura Muñoz

Plaça Antoni Maura

C. Carders

C. de la Princesa

◈ JAUME I

Montcada

C. Argenteria

C. del Rec

Passeig del Born

C. del Comerç

Passeig de Picasso

Passeig de Pujades

Parc de la Ciutadella

Carrer de Wellington

Pla del Palau

Avda. Marquès de l'Argentera

Estació de França

Parlament de Catalunya

C. Reina Cristina

BARCELONETA ◈

Passeig Circumvallació

Moll del Dipòsit

C. Dr. Aiguader

Avda. d'Icària

Museu d'Història de Catalunya

Palau de Mar

C. Balboa

Passatge de la Cadena

C. Dr. Aiguader

Mar

Sant Elm

Sant Miquel

C. Pizarro

C. de Ginebra

Mediterrània

Pinzón

CIUTADELLA-VILA OLÍMPICA ◈

Moll de la Barceloneta

Passeig Joan de Borbó

C. de la Maquinista

Mercat de la Barceloneta

Plaça de la Font

Plaça de Pompeu Gener

C. d'Andrea Doria

C. d'Escuder

❶

C. de Sant Carles

Plaça del Poeta Boscà

Plaça de Brugada

Passeig Marítim

C. de la

❷

Pescadors

Sevilla

Almirall Cervera

Mediterranean Sea

⊘

0   1/8 mi

0   200 meters

DID YOU KNOW?

The imposing Gothic church of Santa Maria del Mar stands out in Barcelona as a dramatic counterpoint to the city's exuberant Moderniste architecture.

Montaner, and Puig i Cadafalch. Works by each of this stellar trio are lined up (almost) next to each other along a single block of the Eixample, which has given rise to the nickname the *manzana de la discordia* ("apple of discord"), a play on the Spanish word *manzana*, meaning both "apple" and "block." Rising above it all is Gaudí's Sagrada Família church.

Casa Amatller. The neo-Gothic Casa Amatller was built by Josep Puig i Cadafalch in 1900, when the architect was 33 years old. Eighteen years younger than Domènech i Montaner and 15 years younger than Gaudí, Puig i Cadafalch was one of the leading statesmen of his generation. Puig i Cadafalch's architectural historicism sought to recover Catalonia's proud past, in combination with eclectic elements from Flemish and Dutch architectural motifs. Note the Eusebi Arnau sculptures—especially his St. George and the Dragon, and the figures of a drummer with his dancing bear. The first-floor apartment, where the Amatller family lived, is a museum, with the original furniture and decor (guided tours are offered in English daily at 11 am). ⊠ *Passeig de Gràcia 41, Eixample* ☎ *93/461–7460 tour info and ticket sales* ⊕ *amatller.org/en/* 🎫 *Tours from €19* Ⓜ *L2/L3/L5 Passeig de Gràcia, FGC Provença.*

FAMILY **Casa Batlló.** Gaudí at his most spectacular, the Casa Batlló is actually a makeover: it was originally built in 1877 by one of Gaudí's teachers, Emili Sala Cortés, and acquired by the Batlló family in 1900. Batlló wanted to tear down the undistinguished Sala building and start over, but Gaudí persuaded him to remodel the facade and the interior, and the result is astonishing. The facade—with its rainbow of colored glass and *trencadís* (polychromatic tile fragments) and the toothy masks of the wrought-iron balconies projecting outward toward the street—is an irresistible photo op. Nationalist symbolism is at work here: the scaly roof line represents the Dragon of Evil impaled on St. George's cross, and the skulls and bones on the balconies are the dragon's victims, allusions to medieval Catalonia's code of chivalry and religious piety. Gaudí is said to have directed the composition of the facade from the middle of Passeig de Gràcia, calling instructions to workmen on the scaffolding. Inside, the translucent windows on the landings of the central staircase light up the maritime motif and the details of the building; as everywhere in his oeuvre, Gaudí opted for natural shapes and rejected straight lines. On summer evenings, you can listen to a concert (starts at 8 pm) and enjoy a drink on the terrace, as part of the "Magic Night" program.

Budget-conscious visitors can take in the view from outside the Casa Batlló; the admission fee is ridiculously high (there are discounts for booking in advance online), and you won't see much inside that you can't also see in the Casa Milà, up the Passeig de Gràcia on the opposite side. ⊠ *Passeig de Gràcia 43, Eixample* ☎ *93/216–0306* ⊕ *www.casabatllo.es* 🎫 *From €25* Ⓜ *L2/L3/L4 Passeig de Gràcia, FGC Provença.*

Fodor'sChoice **Casa Milà.** Usually referred to as *La Pedrera* (The Stone Quarry), with
★ a wavy, curving stone facade that undulates around the corner of the block, this building, unveiled in 1910, is one of Gaudí's most celebrated yet initially reviled designs. Seemingly defying the laws of gravity, the

Rebecca Horn's sculpture on Barceloneta's beach is reminiscent of the little shack restaurants that once crowded this sandy spot.

exterior has no straight lines, and is adorned with winding balconies covered with wrought-iron foliage sculpted by Josep Maria Jujol. Gaudí's rooftop chimney park, alternately interpreted as veiled Saharan women or helmeted warriors, is as spectacular as anything in Barcelona, especially in late afternoon when the sunlight slants over the city into the Mediterranean. Inside, the handsome **Espai Gaudí** (Gaudí Space) in the attic has excellent critical displays of Gaudí's works from all over Spain. The Pis de la Pedrera apartment is an interesting look into the life of a family that lived in La Pedrera in the early 20th century. Entrance lines can be long; book ahead for tours. On Nits d'Estiu (aka weekend summer nights mid-June–early September, Friday and Saturday) the Espai Gaudí and the roof terrace are open for drinks and jazz concerts. ⊠ *Passeig de Gràcia 92, Eixample* ☎ *93/214–2576* ⊕ *www.lapedrera. com/en/home* ⌚ *From €22* Ⓜ *L2/L3/L5 Diagonal, FGC Provença.*

Fodor'sChoice **Recinte Modernista de Sant Pau.** Set in what was one of the most beauti-
★ ful public projects in the world—the Hospital de Sant Pau—the Recinte Modernista (Modernist Complex) is a UNESCO World Heritage Site that's extraordinary in its setting, style, and the idea that inspired it. Architect Lluís Domènech i Montaner believed that trees, flowers, and fresh air were likely to help people recover from what ailed them more than anything doctors could do in emotionally sterile surroundings. The hospital wards were set among gardens, their brick facades topped with polychrome ceramic tile roofs in extravagant shapes and details. Domènech also believed in the therapeutic properties of form and color, and decorated the hospital with Pau Gargallo sculptures and colorful mosaics, replete with motifs of hope

The Eixample

KEY

◈ Metro Stops

and healing and healthy growth. Begun in 1900, this monumental production won Domènech i Montaner his third Barcelona "Best Building" award in 1912. No longer a functioning hospital, many of the buildings have been taken over for other purposes.Tours are offered in English daily at 10:30 am. ✉ *Carrer Sant Antoni Maria Claret 167, Eixample* ☎ *93/553–7801* ⊕ *www.santpaubarcelona.org/en* ⊡ *From €14; free 1st Sun. of month* Ⓜ *L5 Sant Pau/Dos de Maig.*

Temple Expiatori de la Sagrada Família. See feature in this chapter. ✉ *P. de la Sagrada Família, Carrer Mallorca 401 Barcelona, Eixample* Ⓜ *L2/ L5 Sagrada Família* ☎ *93/207–3031, 93/208–0414 visitor info* ⊕ *www. sagradafamilia.cat* ⊡ *From €15.*

UPPER BARCELONA: SARRIÀ AND PEDRALBES

Sarrià was originally a country village, overlooking Barcelona from the foothills of the Collserola. Eventually absorbed by the westward-expanding city, the village, 15 minutes by FGC commuter train from Plaça de Catalunya, has become a unique neighborhood with at least four distinct populations: the old-timers, who speak only Catalan among themselves, and talk of "going down to Barcelona" to shop; writers, artists and designers, and people in publishing and advertising, drawn here in the 1970s and 1980s by the creative vibe; yuppie starter families, who largely support Sarrià's gourmet shops and upscale restaurants; and a cadre of expats, who prize the neighborhood for its proximity to international schools.

Did we mention gourmet shops? J. V. Foix, the famous Catalan poet, was a native son of Sarrià; his father founded what is arguably the best patisserie in Barcelona, and his descendants still run the quintessential Sarrià family business. On Sunday, barcelonins come to the village from all over town—Sunday just wouldn't be Sunday without a cake from Foix. Cross Avinguda Foix from Sarrià and you're in Pedralbes, the wealthiest residential neighborhood in the city. (Fútbol superstar Lionel Messi has his multimillion-euro home here; the exclusive Real Club de Tenis de Barcelona is not far off.) The centerpiece of this district is the 14th-century Monestir de Pedralbes; other points of interest include Gaudí's Pavellons de la Finca Güell on Avinguda de Pedralbes, and the gardens of the Palau Reial de Pedralbes, a 20-minute walk downhill from the monastery. The Futbol Club Barcelona's 99,354-seat Camp Nou stadium and museum are another 20 minutes' walk, down below the Diagonal.

Fodor's Choice   **Monestir de Pedralbes.** This marvel of a monastery, named for its original
★   white stones (*pedres albes*), is really a convent, founded in 1326 for the Franciscan order of Poor Clares by Reina (Queen) Elisenda. The three-story Gothic cloister, one of the finest in Europe, surrounds a lush garden. The day cells, where the nuns spend their mornings praying, sewing, and studying, circle the arcaded courtyard. The queen's own cell, the Capella de Sant Miquel, just to the right of the entrance, has murals painted in 1346 by Catalan master Ferrer Bassa. Look for the letters spelling out *Joan no m'oblides* ("John, do not forget me") scratched between the figures of St. Francis and St. Clare (with book and quill), written by a brokenhearted novice. The nuns' upstairs dormitory

contains the convent's treasures: paintings, liturgical objects, and seven centuries of artistic and cultural patrimony. Temporary exhibits are displayed in this space. The refectory where the Poor Clares dined in silence has a pulpit used for readings, while wall inscriptions exhort *Silentium* ("Silence"), *Audi tacens* ("Listening makes you wise"), and *Considera morientem* ("Consider, we are dying"). Notice the fading mural in the corner, and the paving tiles broken by heavy cannon positioned here during the 1809 Napoleonic occupation. ⊠ *Baixada del Monestir 9, Pedralbes* ☎ *93/256–3434* ⊕ *monestirpedralbes.bcn.cat/en* ⊡ *€5; free Sun. after 3 pm, and 1st Sun. of every month* ☾ *Closed Mon.* Ⓜ *Reina Elisenda (FGC).*

FAMILY
Fodor's Choice
★

Park Güell. Alternately shady, green, floral, or sunny, this park is one of Gaudí's, and Barcelona's, most visited venues. Named for and commissioned by Gaudí's main patron, Count Eusebi Güell, it was originally intended as a gated residential community based on the English Garden City model, with a covered marketplace. The pillars of the market support the main public square above it, where impromptu dances and plays were performed. Only two of the houses were ever built (one of which, designed by Gaudí assistant Francesc Berenguer, became Gaudí's home from 1906 to 1926 and now houses the park's Gaudí museum), and the Güell family eventually turned the area over to the city as a public park. Gaudí highlights include the gingerbread gatehouses; the **Casa-Museu Gaudí,** where the architect lived; the Room of a Hundred Columns; and the fabulous serpentine polychrome bench that snakes along the main square by Gaudí assistant Josep Maria. Visitors must pay an entrance fee to the "monumental area," where the main attractions are located; the rest of the park remains free to enter. Tickets can be booked online up to three months in advance. ⊠ *Carrer d'Olot s/n, Gràcia* ☎ *93/409–1831* ⊕ *www.parkguell.cat/en* ⊡ *From €9* Ⓜ *L3 Lesseps, Vallcarca.*

Pavellons de la Finca Güell–Càtedra Gaudí. Work on the Finca began in 1883 as an extension of Count Eusebi Güell's family estate. Gaudí, the count's architect of choice, was commissioned to do the gardens and the two entrance pavilions (1884–87); the rest of the project was never finished. The Pavellons (pavilions) now belong to the University of Barcelona; the one on the right houses the Càtedra Gaudí, a Gaudí library and study center. The fierce wrought-iron dragon gate is Gaudí's reference to the Garden of the Hesperides, as described by national poet Jacint Verdaguer's epic poem *L'Atlàntida* (1877)—the *Iliad* of Catalonia's historic-mythic origins. The property is open for guided tours in English on weekends at 10:15 and 12:15. Admission is limited to 25 visitors: call ahead, or book on the Ruta del Modernisme website. The Ruta is a walking tour covering 120 masterworks of the Moderniste period, including those by Gaudí, Domènech i Montaner, and Puig i Cadafalch. Pick up a guide—which includes a map, suggested short and longer itineraries, and a book of discount vouchers for admission to many of the sites—here at the Pavellons. ⊠ *Av. Pedralbes 7, Pedralbes* ☎ *93/256–2504 guided tours* ⊕ *www.rutadelmodernisme.com* ⊡ *Tours €5* Ⓜ *L3 Palau Reial.*

Continued on page 411

TEMPLE EXPIATORI DE LA
SAGRADA FAMÍLIA

Antoni Gaudí's striking and surreal masterpiece was conceived as nothing short of a Bible in stone, an arresting representation of the history of Christianity. Today this Roman Catholic church is Barcelona's most emblematic architectural icon. Looming over Barcelona like a mid-city massif of grottoes and peaks, the Sagrada Família strains skyward in piles of stalagmites. Construction is ongoing and continues to stretch toward the heavens.

CONSTRUCTION, PAST AND PRESENT

"My client is not in a hurry," was Gaudí's reply to anyone curious about his project's timetable . . . good thing, too, because the Sagrada Família was begun in 1882 under architect Francesc Villar, passed on in 1891 to Gaudí, and is still thought to be more than a decade from completion. Gaudí added Art Nouveau touches to the crypt and in 1893 started the Nativity facade. Conceived as a symbolic construct encompassing the complete story and scope of the Christian faith, the church was intended by Gaudí to impress the viewer with the full sweep and force of the Gospel. At the time of his death in 1926 only one tower of the Nativity facade had been completed.

By 2026, the 100th anniversary of Gaudí's death, after 144 years of construction in the tradition of the great medieval and Renaissance cathedrals of Europe, the Sagrada Família may well be complete enough to call finished. Architect Jordi Bonet continues in the footsteps of his father, architect Lluís Bonet, to make Gaudí's vision complete as he has since the 1980s.

(left) Sagrada Família interior. (top) Shepherds gather to witness the birth of Christ in the Nativity facade.

DETAILS TO DISCOVER:
THE EXTERIOR

GAUDÍ IN THE PASSION FACADE

Subirachs pays double homage to the great Modern-iste master in the Passion facade: Gaudí himself appears over the left side of the main entry making notes or drawings, the evangelist in stone, while the Roman soldiers are modeled on Gaudí's helmeted, Star Wars–like warriors from the roof of La Pedrera.

Gaudí in the Passion facade

TOWER TOPS

Break out the binoculars and have a close look at the pinnacles and peaks of the Sagrada Família's towers. Sculpted by Japanese artist Etsuro Sotoo, these clusters of grapes and different kinds of fruit are symbols of fertility, of rebirth, and of the Resurrection of Christ.

SUBIRACHS IN THE PASSION FACADE

At Christ's feet in the entombment sculpture is a blocky figure with a furrowed brow, thought to be a portrayal of the agnostic's anguished search for certainty. This figure is generally taken as a self-portrait of Subirachs, characterized by the sculptor's giant hand and an "S" on his massive right arm.

Sotoo's ornamental fruit

DONKEY ON THE NATIVITY FACADE

On the left side of the Nativity facade over the Portal of Hope is a *burro*, a small donkey, known to have been modeled from a donkey that Gaudí saw near the work site. The *ruc català* (Catalan donkey) is a beloved and iconic symbol of Catalonia, often displayed on Catalonian bumpers as a response to the Spanish fighting bull.

The donkey in the Nativity facade

THE ROSE TREE DOOR

The richly sculpted Rose Tree Door, between the Nativity facade and the cloisters, portrays Our Lady of the Rose Tree with the infant Jesus in her arms, St. Dominic and St. Catherine of Siena in prayer, with three angels dancing overhead. The sculptural group on the wall known as "The Death of the Just" portrays the Virgin and child comforting a moribund old man, the Spanish prayer "Jesús, José, y María, asistidme en mi última agonía" (Jesus, Joseph, and María, help me in my final agony). The accompanying inscriptions in English, "Pray for us sinners now and at the hour of our death, Amen" are the final words of the Ave María prayer.

The heavily embelished Rose door

COLUMN FROM THE PORTAL OF CHARITY

The column, dead center in the Portal of Charity, is covered with the genealogy of Christ going back through the House of David to Abraham. At the bottom of the column is the snake of evil, complete with the apple of temptation in his mouth, closed in behind an iron grate, symbolic of Christianity's mission of neutralizing the sin of selfishness.

FACELESS ST. VERONICA

Because her story is considered legendary, not historical fact, St. Veronica appears faceless in the Passion facade. Also shown is the veil she gave Christ to wipe his face with on the way to Calvary that was said to be miraculously imprinted with his likeness. The veil is torn in two overhead and covers a mosaic that Subirachs allegedly disliked and elected to conceal.

STAINED-GLASS WINDOWS

The stained-glass windows of the Sagrada Família are work of Joan Vila-Grau. The windows in the west central part of the nave represent the light of Jesus and a bubbling fountain in a bright chromatic patchwork of shades of blue with green and yellow reflections. The main window on the Passion facade represents the Resurrection. Gaudí left express instructions that the windows of the central nave have no color, so as not to alter the colors of the tiles and trencadís (mosaics of broken tile) in green and gold representing palm leaves. These windows will be clear or translucent, as a symbol of purity and to admit as much light as possible.

TORTOISES AND TURTLES

Nature lover Gaudí used as many elements of the natural world as he could in his stone Bible. The sea tortoise beneath the column on the Mediterranean side of the Portal of Hope and the land turtle supporting the inland Portal of Faith symbolize the slow and steady stability of the cosmos and of the church.

SAINT THOMAS IN THE BELL TOWER

Above the Passion facade, St. Thomas demanding proof of Christ's resurrection (thus the expression "doubting Thomas") and perched on the bell tower is pointing to the palm of his hand asking to inspect Christ's wounds.

CHRIST RESURRECTED ABOVE PASSION FACADE

High above the Passion facade, a gilded Christ sits resurrected, perched between two towers.

The column in the Portal of Charity

St. Veronica with the veil

Stained-glass windows

Christ resurrected

MAKING THE MOST OF YOUR TRIP

The Nativity facade

WHEN TO VISIT

To avoid crowds, come first thing in the morning. Save your trip for a sunny day so you can admire the facades at length.

WHAT TO WEAR AND BRING

Visitors are encouraged not to wear shors and to cover bare shoulders. It's a good idea to bring binoculars to absorb details all the way up.

TIMING

If you're just walking around the exterior, an hour or two is plenty of time. If you'd like to go inside to the crypt, visit the museum, visit the towers, and walk down the spiraling stairway, you'll need three to four hours.

HIGHLIGHTS

The Passion facade, the Nativity facade, the Portal of Faith, the Portal of Hope, and the main altar.

BONUS FEATURES

The **museum** displays Gaudí's scale models and shows photographs of the construction. The **crypt** holds Gaudí's remains. For €2 (and a 45-minute wait in line), you can take an elevator to the top of the **bell towers** for spectacular views.

TOURS

English-language tours are given daily at 11 AM, 1 PM, 3 PM, and 5 PM and cost €4.

VISITOR INFORMATION

✉ Pl. de la Sagrada Família, Eixample
☎ 93/207–3031 ⊕ www.sagradafamilia.org
🎟 €11, bell tower elevator €2, audio guides €4
🕐 Oct.–Mar., daily 9–6; Apr.–Sept., daily 9–8
Ⓜ Sagrada Família.

TOWERS

Climbing the towers is no longer permitted, and lines for the elevator are long. Only the Passion Facade may be descended on foot, which is highly recommended for a close look at some of the figures, including that of Gaudí himself.

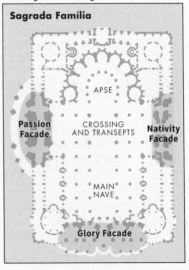

Sagrada Família

APSE

Passion Facade

CROSSING AND TRANSEPTS

Nativity Facade

MAIN NAVE

Glory Facade

Sarrià. The village of Sarrià was originally a cluster of farms and country houses overlooking Barcelona from the hills. Once dismissively described as nothing but "winds, brooks, and convents," this quiet enclave is now a prime residential neighborhood at the upper edge of the city. Start an exploration at the square—the locus, at various times, of antique and bric-a-brac markets, book fairs, artisanal food and wine fairs, sardana dances (Sunday morning), concerts, and Christmas pageants. The 10th-century Romanesque **Church of Sant Vicenç** dominates the main square, the Plaça de Sarrià; the bell tower, illuminated on weekend nights, is truly impressive. Across Passeig de la Reina Elisenda from the church (50 yards to the left) is the 100-year-old Moderniste **Mercat de Sarrià.**

From the square, cut through the Placeta del Roser to the left of the church to the elegant **Town Hall** (1896) in the Plaça de la Vila; note the buxom bronze sculpture of **Pomona,** goddess of fruit, by famed Sarrià sculptor Josep Clarà (1878–1958). Follow the tiny Carrer dels Paletes, to the left of the Town Hall (the saint enshrined in the niche is Sant Antoni, patron saint of *paletes,* or bricklayers), and right on Major de Sarrià, the High Street of the village. For lunch, try Casa Raphael, on the right as you walk down—in business (and virtually unchanged) since 1873. Farther on, turn left into **Carrer Canet.** The two-story row houses on the right were first built for workers on the village estates, now converted to other uses (including a preschool); these, and the houses opposite at Nos. 15, 21, and 23, are among the few remaining original village homes in Sarrià. Turn right at the first corner on Carrer Cornet i Mas and walk two blocks down to Carrer Jaume Piquet.

On the left is No. 30, Barcelona's most perfect small-format **Moderniste house,** thought to be the work of architect Domènech i Montaner, complete with faux-medieval upper windows, wrought-iron grillwork, floral and fruited ornamentation, and organically curved and carved wooden doors either by or inspired by Gaudí himself. The next stop down Cornet i Mas is Sarrià's prettiest square, **Plaça Sant Vicens,** a leafy space ringed by old Sarrià houses and centered on a statue of Sarrià's patron St. Vicenç, portrayed (as always) beside the millstone used to sink him to the bottom of the Mediterranean after he was martyred in Valencia in AD 302. **Can Pau,** the café on the lower corner with Carrer Mañé i Flaquer, is the local hangout, once a haven for authors Gabriel García Marquez and Mario Vargas Llosa, who lived in Sarrià in the late 1960s and early 1970s.

Other Sarrià landmarks to look for include the two **Foix** pastry shops, one at Plaça Sarrià 9–10 and the other at Major de Sarrià 57, above Bar Tomás. The late J. V. Foix (1893–1987), son of the shop's founder, was one of the great Catalan poets of the 20th century, a key player in keeping the Catalan language alive during the 40-year Franco regime. The shop on Major de Sarrià has a bronze plaque identifying the house as the poet's birthplace and inscribed with one of his most memorable verses, translated as, "Every love is latent in the other love / every language is the juice of a common tongue / every country touches the fatherland of all / every faith will be the lifeblood of a higher faith." ⊠ *Sarrià* Ⓜ *Sarrià* (*FGC Line L6*).

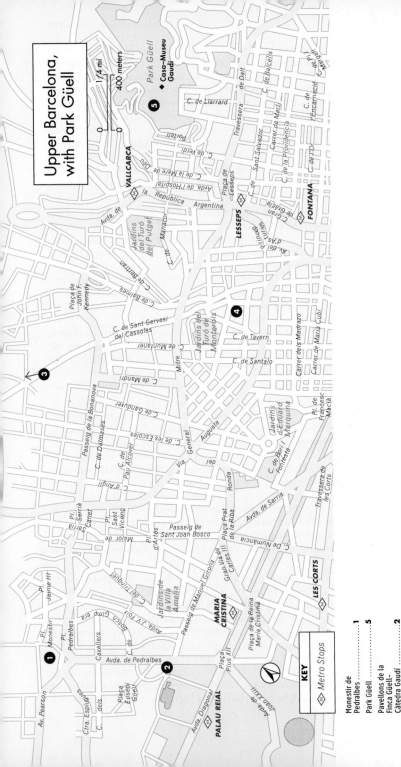

Upper Barcelona, with Park Güell

● Park Güell
◆ Casa–Museu
Gaudí

1/4 mi
400 meters

VALLCARCA

C. de Llarrard
C. del Portell
C. de Verdi

Avda. de la Mare de Déu
la República

Avda. de l'Hospital
Plaça de l'Hospital
Argentina

C. de Manacor
Jardins del Turó
del Putget

C. de Bertran

Avda. de

Plaça de
John F.
Kennedy

C. de Balmes

C. de Sant Gervasi
del Cassoles

Mitre

C. de Muntaner

C. de Mandri

C. de Ganduxer

Passeig de la Bonanova

C. de Dalmases

C. de les Escoles

Pg. Sant
Vicenç

Pl.
Sarrià
Camet

Pl.
Sarrià

C. d'Anglí

C. de
Pau Alcover

Mitre

Jardins del Turó de
Monterols

C. de Tavern

C. de Santaló

Carrer dels Madrazo

Carrer de Marià Cubí

Augusta

Via   Augusta
General   del
Mitre

Ronda

Avda. de Sarrià

C. De Numància

Travessera de
les Corts

Jardins
d'Eduard
Marquina

Pl. de
Frederic
Macià

C. de Bori i
Fontestà

LES CORTS

Avda. Diagonal

PALAU REIAL

Avda. de Pedralbes

Plaça
Pius XII

Pl. de la Reina
Maria Cristina

MARIA
CRISTINA

Passeig de Manuel Girona

Gran Via de
Carles III

Plaça Prat
de la Riba

Passeig de
Sant Joan Bosco

Avda. de
la Villa
Amèlia

Jardins de

Avda. J.V. Foix

C. del Tinquet

C. de Bosch i Gimpera

Cavallers

C. dels
Pl. Eusebi
Güell

Av. Pearson

Cfra. Esplugues

Pl.
Jaume Hª

Pl.
Monestir

Pl.
Pedralbes

Mª Major de

de
Ctra.

LESSEPS

Av. del Piblon

Gran
de Gràcia

C. de Lesseps

FONTANA

C. de l'Encarnació

C. de Pi i
Margall

C. de Balcells

C. de Matí

C. de la Providència

C. de Tiló

C. de Sant Salvador

Travessera de Dalt

C. del
Verdi

Gaudí
Travessera

KEY

◇ Metro Stops

Monestir de
Pedralbes 1

Park Güell 5

Pavellons de la
Finca Güell–
Càtedra Gaudí 2

Sarrià 4

Torre Bellesguard ... 3

FodorśChoice **Torre Bellesguard.** For an extraordinary Gaudí experience, climb up
★ above Plaça de la Bonanova to this private residence built between
1900 and 1909 over the ruins of the summer palace of the last of the
sovereign count-kings of the Catalan-Aragonese realm, Martí I l'Humà
(Martin I the Humane), whose reign ended in 1410. In homage to this
medieval history, Gaudí endowed the house with a tower, gargoyles,
and crenellated battlements; the rest—the catenary arches, the trencadís
in the facade, the stained-glass windows—are pure Art Nouveau. Look
for the red and gold Catalan senyera (banner) on the tower, topped by
the four-armed Greek cross Gaudí often used. Over the front door is
the inscription "*Sens pecat fou concebuda*" ("Without sin was she conceived"), referring to the Immaculate Conception of the Virgin Mary; on
either side of the front door are benches with trencadís of playful fish
bearing the crimson *quatre barres* (four bars) of the Catalan flag as well
as the Corona d'Aragó (Crown of Aragón). The visit includes access to
the roof, which Gaudí designed to resemble a dragon, along with the
gardens, patio, and stables. ■TIP➜ Reservations required for the highly
recommended guided tour (reserva@bellesguardgaudi.com). ⊠ *Calle
Bellesguard 16–20, Sant Gervasi* ☎ *93/250–4093* ⊕ *www.belles-
guardgaudi.com* ⊑ *From €9* ☉ *Closed Mon.* Ⓜ *Av. Tibidabo (FGC).*

MONTJUÏC

This hill overlooking the south side of the port is said to have originally been named Mont Juif for the Jewish cemetery once on its slopes.
Montjuïc is now Barcelona's largest and lushest public space, a vast
complex of museums and exhibition halls, gardens and picnic grounds,
sports facilities—and even a Greek-style amphitheater.

A bit remote from the bustle of Barcelona street life, Montjuïc more
than justifies a day or two of exploring. The Miró Foundation, the
Museu Nacional d'Art de Catalunya, the minimalist Mies van der Rohe
Pavilion, the lush Jardins de Mossèn Cinto Verdaguer, and the gallery
and auditorium of the CaixaFòrum (the former Casaramona textile factory) are all among Barcelona's must-see sights. There are buses within
Montjuïc that visitors can take from sight to sight.

FodorśChoice **Fundació Joan Miró.** The Miró Foundation, a gift from the artist Joan
★ Miró to his native city, is one of Barcelona's most exciting showcases of
modern and contemporary art. The airy white building, with panoramic
views north over Barcelona, was designed by the artist's close friend
and collaborator Josep Lluís Sert and opened in 1975; an extension was
added by Sert's pupil Jaume Freixa in 1988. Miró's playful and colorful
style, filled with Mediterranean light and humor, seems a perfect match
for its surroundings, and the exhibits and retrospectives that open here
tend to be progressive and provocative—look for Alexander Calder's
fountain of moving mercury. Miró himself rests in the cemetery on
Montjuïc's southern slopes. ⊠ *Av. Miramar 71–75, Parc de Montjuïc,
Montjuïc* ☎ *93/443–9470* ⊕ *www.fmirobcn.org* ⊑ *€12* ☉ *Closed Mon.*
Ⓜ *L1/L3 Pl. Espanya; L3 Paral.lel, then Funicular de Montjuïc.*

Mies van der Rohe Pavilion. One of the masterpieces of the Bauhaus School,
the legendary Pavelló Mies van der Rohe—the German contribution to the

1929 International Exhibition, reassembled between 1983 and 1986—remains a stunning "less is more" study in interlocking planes of white marble, green onyx, and glass. In effect, it is Barcelona's aesthetic antonym (in company with Richard Meier's Museu d'Art Contemporani and Rafael Moneo's Auditori) to the flamboyant Art Nouveau—the city's signature Modernisme—of Gaudí and his contemporaries. Note the mirror play of the black carpet inside the pavilion with the reflecting pool outside, or the iconic Barcelona chair designed by Ludwig Mies van der Rohe (1886–1969); reproductions have graced modern interiors around the world for decades. ⊠ *Av. Francesc Ferrer i Guàrdia 7, Montjuïc* ☎ *93/423–4016, 93/215–1011* ⊕ *miesbcn.com* ⊡ *€5* Ⓜ *L1/L3 Pl. Espanya.*

Fodor'sChoice   **Museu Nacional d'Art de Catalunya** (*Catalonian National Museum of Art,*
★   *MNAC*). Housed in the imposingly domed, towered, frescoed, and columned **Palau Nacional,** built in 1929 as the centerpiece of the International Exposition, this superb museum was renovated in 1995 by Gae Aulenti, architect of the Musée d'Orsay in Paris. In 2004 the museum's three holdings (Romanesque, Gothic, and the Cambó Collection—an eclectic trove, including a Goya, donated by Francesc Cambó) were joined by the 19th- and 20th-century collection of Catalan impressionist and Moderniste painters. Also now on display is the Thyssen-Bornemisza collection of early masters, with works by Zurbarán, Rubens, Tintoretto, Velázquez, and others. Pride of place goes to the Romanesque exhibition, the world's finest collection of Romanesque frescoes, altarpieces, and wood carvings, most of them rescued from chapels in the Pyrenees during the 1920s. The central hall of the museum, with its enormous pillared and frescoed cupola, is stunning. ⊠ *Palau Nacional, Parc de Montjuïc s/n, Montjuïc* ☎ *93/622–0360* ⊕ *www.museunacional.cat* ⊡ *From €12 (valid for day of purchase and 1 other day in same month); free Sat. after 3 pm and 1st Sun. of month* ⊗ *Closed Mon.* Ⓜ *L1/L3 Pl. Espanya.*

WHERE TO EAT

Barcelona's restaurant scene is an ongoing adventure. Between avant-garde culinary innovation and the more rustic dishes of traditional Catalan fare, there is a fleet of brilliant classical chefs producing some of Europe's finest Mediterranean cuisine.

Catalans are legendary lovers of fish, vegetables, rabbit, duck, lamb, game, and natural ingredients from the Pyrenees or the Mediterranean. The *mar i muntanya* (literally "sea and mountain," or "surf and turf") is a standard. Combining salty and sweet tastes—a Moorish legacy—is another common theme.

The Mediterranean diet—based on olive oil, seafood, vegetables, onions, garlic, and red wine—is at home in Barcelona, embellished by Catalonia's four basic sauces: *allioli* (whipped garlic and olive oil), *romesco* (almonds, nyora peppers, hazelnuts, tomato, garlic, and olive oil), *sofregit* (fried onion, tomato, and garlic), and *samfaina* (a ratatouille-like vegetable mixture).

Use the coordinate (✛ B2) at the end of each listing to locate a site on the corresponding map.

DID YOU KNOW?

Park Güell was originally designed as an exclusive gated garden community, but failed to attract enough would-be residents. One of the only two houses built here became Gaudí's residence from 1906 to 1926.

MEALTIMES
Barcelona dines late: lunch is served 1:30–4 and dinner 9–11.

RESERVATIONS
Nearly all of Barcelona's best restaurants require reservations.

PRICES
Whereas low-end fixed-price lunch menus can be found for as little as €10, most good restaurants cost closer to €30–€40 ordering à la carte. For serious evening dining, plan on spending €55–€80 per person. *Prices in the restaurant reviews are the average cost of a main course at dinner or, if dinner is not served, at lunch; for tapas bars, the price reflects the cost of a light meal of four to five selections.*

TIPPING AND TAXES
Tipping is not required, as gratuity is included. If you do tip, 5%–10% is acceptable.

WHAT IT COSTS IN EUROS			
	$	$$	$$$	$$$$
Restaurants	under €16	€16–€22	€23–€29	over €29

CIUTAT VELLA: BARRI GÒTIC, BORN-RIBERA, LA RAMBLA, AND EL RAVAL

Chic new restaurants come and go, but the top places in the Ciutat Vella endure.

BARRI GÒTIC

$$
CATALAN
✕ **Agut.** Wainscoting and 1950s canvases are the background for the mostly Catalan crowd in this homey restaurant in the lower reaches of the Barri Gòtic. Agut was founded in 1924, and its popularity has never waned—after all, hearty Catalan fare at a fantastic value is always in demand. **Known for:** must-try civet of wild boar; local wines; local favorite. $ *Average main: €16* ⊠ *Gignàs 16, Barri Gòtic* ☎ *93/315–1709* ⊙ *Closed Mon., and 2 wks in Aug. No dinner Sun.* Ⓜ *Jaume I* ✛ *D5.*

$$
CATALAN
✕ **Cafè de l'Acadèmia.** With wicker chairs, stone walls, and classical music, this place is sophisticated-rustic in style; contemporary Mediterranean cuisine specialties such as *timbal d'escalibada amb formatge de cabra* (roast vegetable salad with goat cheese) make it more than just a café. Politicians and functionaries from the nearby Generalitat frequent this dining room, which is always boiling with life. **Known for:** lively terrace; great set lunch; private wine cellar for larger groups. $ *Average main: €16* ⊠ *Lledó 1, Barri Gòtic* ☎ *93/319–8253* ⊙ *Closed weekends, and 2 wks in Aug.* Ⓜ *Jaume I* ✛ *D5.*

$$
BASQUE
✕ **Irati Taverna Basca.** There's only one drawback to this lively Basque bar between Plaça del Pi and La Rambla: it's narrow at the street end, and harder to squeeze into than the Barcelona metro at rush hour. Skip the tapas on the bar and opt for the plates brought out piping-hot

Architect Arata Isozaki designed the futuristic Palau Sant Jordi Sports Palace.

from the kitchen. **Known for:** quick bites; Basque specialties; txakoli sparkling wine. $ *Average main: €17* ✉ *Cardenal Casañas 17, Barri Gòtic* ☎ *93/302–3084* ⊕ *www.iratitavernabasca.com* Ⓜ *Liceu* ✛ *D4*.

$$ ✕ **Pla.** Filled with couples night after night, this combination music,

CATALAN drinking, and dining place is candlelit and sleekly designed in glass over ancient stone, brick, and wood. The cuisine is light and contemporary, featuring inventive salads and fresh seafood, as well as options for vegetarians and vegans. **Known for:** romantic ambience; extensive wine list; vegetarian options. $ *Average main: €20* ✉ *Bellafila 5, Barri Gòtic* ☎ *93/412–6552* ⊕ *www.restaurantpla.cat* ☾ *No lunch* Ⓜ *Jaume I* ✛ *D5*.

BORN-RIBERA

$$ ✕ **Cal Pep.** A two-minute walk east of Santa Maria del Mar, Cal Pep has

TAPAS been in a permanent feeding frenzy for more than 30 years, intensified even further by the hordes of tourists who now flock here. Pep serves a selection of tapas, cooked and served hot over the counter. **Known for:** excellent fish fry; delicious potato omelet; lively counter scene. $ *Average main: €20* ✉ *Pl. de les Olles 8, Born-Ribera* ☎ *93/310–7961* ⊕ *www.calpep.com* ☾ *Closed Sun., and 3 wks in Aug. No lunch Mon.* Ⓜ *Jaume I, Barceloneta* ✛ *E5*.

$ ✕ **Cuines Santa Caterina.** A lovingly restored market designed by the late

ECLECTIC Enric Miralles and completed by his widow Benedetta Tagliabue provides a spectacular setting for one of the city's most original dining operations. Under the undulating wooden superstructure of the market, the breakfast and tapas bar offers a variety of international culinary specialties. **Known for:** open all day; vegetarian options; Mediterranean fare. $ *Average*

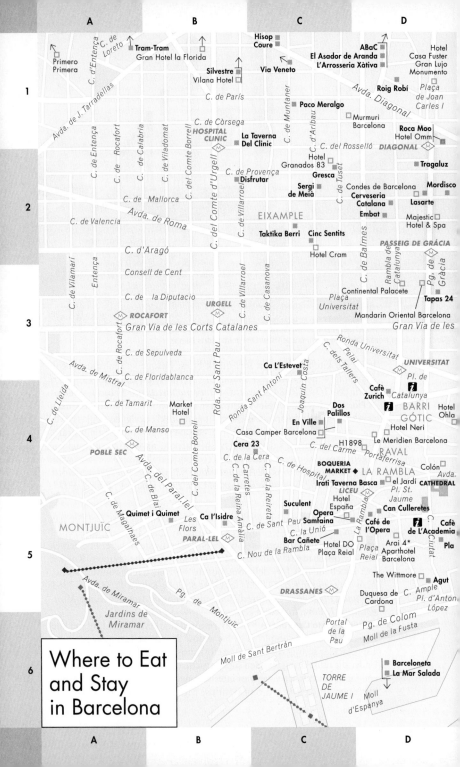

Where to Eat and Stay in Barcelona

A **B** **C** **D**

1

Primero Primera
C. de Loreto
C. d'Entença
Tram-Tram
Gran Hotel la Florida
Hisop
Coure
ABaC
Hotel Casa Fuster Gran Lujo Monumento
Silvestre
Vilana Hotel
Via Veneto
El Asador de Aranda
L'Arrosseria Xàtiva
Roig Robí
Plaça de Joan Carles I
Avda. de J. Tarradellas
C. de París
C. de Muntaner
Paco Meralgo
Avda. Diagonal

2

C. de Còrsega
HOSPITAL CLINIC
La Taverna Del Clinic
C. d'Aribau
Murmuri Barcelona
Roca Moo Hotel Omm
C. de Entença
C. de Rocafort
C. de Calabria
C. de Viladomat
C. del Comte Borrell
C. de Provença
Disfrutar
Gresca
C. del Rosselló
DIAGONAL
Hotel Granados 83
Sergi de Meià
C. de Tuset
Tragaluz
C. de Mallorca
Avda. de Roma
EIXAMPLE
Condes de Barcelona
Cerveseria Catalana
Lasarte
Mordisco
C. de Valencia
C. de Villarroel
Embat
Majestic Hotel & Spa
C. d'Aragó
Taktika Berri
Cinc Sentits
PASSEIG DE GRÀCIA
C. de Vilamarí
Entença
Consell de Cent
C. de Casanova
Hotel Cram
C. de Balmes
Rambla de Catalunya
Pg. de Gràcia

3

C. de la Diputacio
URGELL
Continental Palacete
Tapas 24
ROCAFORT
Plaça Universitat
Mandarin Oriental Barcelona
Gran Via de les Corts Catalanes
Gran Via de les
C. de Sepulveda
Ronda Universitat
Pelai
C. dels Tallers
UNIVERSITAT

4

Avda. de Mistral
C. de Rocafort
C. de Floridablanca
Ca L'Estevet
Joaquin Costa
Pl. de Catalunya
Cafè Zurich
BARRI GÒTIC
Hotel Ohla
C. de Tamarit
Rda. de Sant Pau
Ronda Sant Antoni
Dos Palillos
C. de Lleida
Market Hotel
En Ville
Casa Camper Barcelona
Hotel Neri
C. de Manso
Cera 23
C. de la Cera
C. del Carme
H1898
Portaferrisa
Le Meridien Barcelona
POBLE SEC
Avda. del Paral.lel
C. del Comte Borrell
Carretes
C. de la Reina Amàlia
C. de la Reireta
C. de Hospital
BOQUERIA MARKET
LA RAMBLA
RAVAL
Colón
Avda.
CATHEDRAL

5

C. de Magalhaes
C. de Blai
Quimet i Quimet
Les Flors
Ca l'Isidre
PARAL-LEL
Suculent
Opera
Samfaina
C. de Sant Pau
C. la Unió
LICEU
Irati Taverna Basca
Hotel España
el Jardí
Pl. St. Jaume
Can Culleretes
Cafè de L'Academia
Pla
MONTJUÏC
Bar Cañete
Hotel DO Plaça Reial
La Rambla
Café de l'Opera
Plaça Reial
Arai 4* Aparthotel Barcelona
C. Ciutat.
The Wittmore
Agut
Avda. de Miramar
Pg. de Montjuïc
DRASSANES
Duquesa de Cardona
C. Ample
Pl. d'Anton López
Jardins de Miramar
Portal de la Pau
Pg. de Colom
Moll de la Fusta

6

Moll de Sant Bertrán
Moll de Sant Bertrán
TORRE DE JAUME I
Moll d'Espanya
Barceloneta
La Mar Salada

A **B** **C** **D**

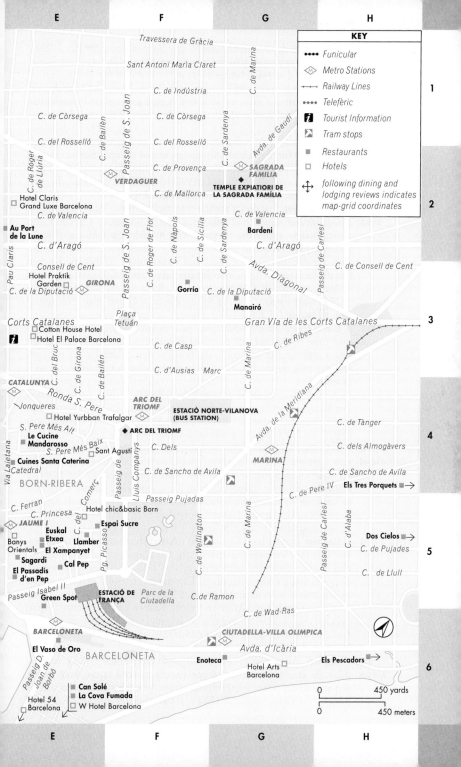

main: €14 ✉ Av. Francesc Cambó 16, Born-Ribera ☎ 93/268–9918 🌐 www.grupotragaluz.com [M] Urquinaona, Jaume I ✢ E4.

$$$$ SEAFOOD 🍴 **El Passadís d'en Pep.** Hidden away at the end of a narrow unmarked passageway off the Pla del Palau, near the Santa Maria del Mar church, this restaurant is a favorite with well-heeled and well-fed gourmands who tuck in their napkins before devouring some of the city's best traditional seafood dishes. Sit down and waiters will begin serving delicious starters of whatever's freshest that day in the market in rapid-fire succession. **Known for:** fresh seafood; starters served in rapid-fire succession; no menu, but you can prebook a set menu online. [$] *Average main: €30 ✉ Pl. del Palau 2, Born-Ribera ☎ 93/310–1021 🌐 www.passadis.com ⏲ Closed Sun., and 3 wks in Aug. [M] Jaume I ✢ E5.*

$ TAPAS 🍴 **El Xampanyet.** Just down the street from the Museu Picasso, dangling *botas* (leather wineskins) announce one of Barcelona's liveliest and most visually appealing taverns, with marble-top tables and walls decorated with colorful ceramic tiles. It's usually packed to the rafters with a rollicking mob of local and out-of-town celebrants. **Known for:** perfect Iberian ham; mouthwatering pa amb tomàquet; real cava. [$] *Average main: €10 ✉ Montcada 22, Born-Ribera ☎ 93/319–7003 💳 No credit cards ⏲ Closed Mon., Easter wk, and Aug. No dinner Sun. [M] Jaume I ✢ E5.*

$$$ BASQUE 🍴 **Euskal Etxea.** An elbow-shaped, pine-paneled space, this bar-restaurant (one of the Sagardi group of Basque restaurants) is one of the better grazing destinations in the Born, with a colorful array of tapas and canapés on the bar, ranging from the olive-pepper-anchovy on a toothpick to chunks of tortilla. Other good bets include the *pimientos de piquillo* (red piquillo peppers) stuffed with codfish paste. **Known for:** Basque pintxos; art gallery on-site; excellent Euskal Txerria confit. [$] *Average main: €23 ✉ Placeta de Montcada 1–3, Born-Ribera ☎ 93/310–2185 🌐 www.gruposagardi.com [M] Jaume I ✢ E5.*

$ ITALIAN 🍴 **Le Cucine Mandarosso.** This no-frills, big-flavor southern Italian restaurant near the Via Laietana is a favorite with locals. Like Naples itself, it's cheap, charming, and over-full, with a generous €12 lunch menu featuring authentic ingredients from the in-store deli. **Known for:** great-value lunch menu; southern Italian specialties; local favorite. [$] *Average main: €9 ✉ Verdaguer i Callis 4, Born-Ribera ☎ 93/319–6250 🌐 www.lecucinemandarosso.com [M] Jaume I ✢ E4.*

$$ TAPAS 🍴 **Llamber.** It may look like one of the stylish, tourist-trap tapas restaurants that have sprung up recently, but Llamber's culinary pedigree sets it apart from the competition; chef Francisco Heras earned his chops in Spain's top restaurants. This dapper, friendly space attracts a mixed crowd with its excellent wine list and well-crafted tapas based on classic Catalan and Asturian recipes. **Known for:** well-crafted tapas; delicious eggplant with honey; good late-night option. [$] *Average main: €17 ✉ Fusina 5, Born-Ribera ☎ 93/319–6250 🌐 www.llamber.com [M] Jaume 1 ✢ E5.*

$$$ BASQUE 🍴 **Sagardi.** An attractive wood-and-stone cider-house replica, Sagardi piles the counter with a dazzling variety of cold tapas; even better, though, are the hot offerings straight from the kitchen. The restaurant in back serves Basque delicacies like veal sweetbreads with artichokes and

txuletas de buey (beef steaks) grilled over coals. **Known for:** multiple locations, all equally good; veal sweetbreads; charcoal grill. $ *Average main: €24* ✉ *Argenteria 62, Born-Ribera* ☎ *93/319–9993* ⊕ *www. gruposagardi.com* Ⓜ *Jaume I* ✛ *E5.*

LA RAMBLA

$ ✕ **Cafè de l'Òpera.** Directly across from the Liceu opera house, this high-
CAFÉ ceiling Art Nouveau café has welcomed operagoers and performers for more than 100 years. It's a central point on the Rambla tourist traffic pattern, so locals are increasingly hard to find, but the café has hung onto its atmosphere of faded glory nonetheless. **Known for:** Art Nouveau decor; good for a drink; late-night hours. $ *Average main: €14* ✉ *La Rambla 74, La Rambla* ☎ *93/317–7585* ⊕ *www.cafeoperabcn. com* Ⓜ *Liceu* ✛ *D5.*

$ ✕ **Cafè Zurich.** This traditional café at the top of La Rambla and directly
CAFÉ astride the main metro and transport hub remains the city's prime meeting point. Forget the food and enjoy a beer or coffee at a table on the terrace, perhaps the best spot in the city to observe street life. **Known for:** people-watching far better than the food; sunny terrace; watch for pickpockets. $ *Average main: €5* ✉ *Pl. de Catalunya 1, La Rambla* ☎ *93/317–9153* Ⓜ *Catalunya* ✛ *D4.*

$ ✕ **Can Culleretes.** Just off La Rambla in the Barri Gòtic, this family-
CATALAN run restaurant founded in 1786 displays tradition in both decor and culinary offerings. Generations of the Manubens and Agut families have kept this unpretentious spot—Barcelona's oldest restaurant, listed in the *Guinness Book of Records*—popular for more than two centuries. **Known for:** Barcelona's oldest restaurant; traditional Catalan cuisine; large portions. $ *Average main: €10* ✉ *Quintana 5, La Rambla* ☎ *93/317–3022* ⊕ *www.culleretes.com* ☾ *Closed Mon., and 4 wks in July and Aug. No dinner Sun.* Ⓜ *Liceu* ✛ *D5.*

$ ✕ **Opera Samfaina.** This gastronomic fantasyland below the Liceu opera
TAPAS house should be terrible, but it smashes right through the kitsch and into
FAMILY pure fun. A multisensory mash-up of movie watching, food, wine, and mind-bending design from the multistarred Roca brothers, it merges tapas bar with total madness to create a unique take on Catalan food traditions. **Known for:** watch a movie while you eat; multiple tapas bars; excellent local wines. $ *Average main: €13* ✉ *La Rambla 51, La Rambla* ☎ *93/481–7871* ⊕ *www.operasamfaina.com* ☾ *Closed Mon., Tues., and Thurs.* Ⓜ *Liceu* ✛ *D5.*

EL RAVAL

$$ ✕ **Bar Cañete.** A superb tapas and *platillos* (small plates) emporium,
TAPAS this spot is just around the corner from the Liceu opera house. The long bar overlooking the burners and part of the kitchen leads down to the 20-seat communal tasting table at the end of the room. **Known for:** Spanish ham specialists; superb tapas; secreto ibérico (a tender cut of pork). $ *Average main: €20* ✉ *Unió 17, El Raval* ☎ *93/270–3458* ☾ *Closed Sun.* Ⓜ *Liceu* ✛ *C5.*

$$ ✕ **Ca l'Estevet.** This restaurant has been serving up old-school Catalan cui-
CATALAN sine to local and loyal customers since 1940 (and under a different name for 50 years before that). The practice has been made perfect; tuck into the likes

of grilled botifarra sausages or roasted kid. **Known for:** Catalan specialties; large portions of escudella i carn d'olla (meat stew); historic location. *[$] Average main: €16 ✉ Valldonzella 46, El Raval ☎ 93/301–2939 🌐 www.restaurantestevet.com 🕘 No dinner Sun. [M] Universitat ✥ C3.*

$$$ CATALAN Fodor's Choice ★ 🍴 **Ca l'Isidre.** A throwback to an age before foams and food science took over the gastronomic world, this restaurant has elevated simplicity to the level of the spectacular since the early 1970s. Isidre and Montserrat share their encyclopedic knowledge of local cuisine with guests, while their daughter Núria cooks traditional Catalan dishes. **Known for:** once frequented by Miró and Dalí; locally sourced produce; art collection. *[$] Average main: €29 ✉ Les Flors 12, El Raval ☎ 93/441–1139 🌐 www.calisidre.com 🕘 Closed Sun., and 1st 2 wks of Aug. [M] Paral.lel ✥ B5.*

$$ SPANISH 🍴 **Cera 23.** Top pick among a crop of modern restaurants putting the razzle back into the run-down Raval, Cera 23 offers a winning combination of great service and robust cooking in a fun, friendly setting; stand at the bar and enjoy a blackberry mojito while you wait for your table. The open kitchen is in the dining area, so guests can watch the cooks create contemporary presentations of traditional Spanish dishes. **Known for:** volcano black rice; open kitchen viewable to diners; exceptional service. *[$] Average main: €16 ✉ Cera 23, El Raval ☎ 93/442–0808 🌐 www.cera23.com 🕘 No lunch weekdays [M] Sant Antoni ✥ C4.*

$$$ ECLECTIC 🍴 **Dos Palillos.** After 10 years as the chief cook and favored disciple of pioneering chef Ferran Adrià, Albert Raurich opened this outstanding Asian-fusion restaurant with an eclectic assortment of tastes and textures. Past the typical Spanish bar in the front room, the Japanese dining room inside is a canvas of rich black surfaces bordered with red chairs. **Known for:** creative pan-Asian cooking with interesting wine pairings; gin- and chocolate-filled doughnuts; tasting and fixed-price menu options. *[$] Average main: €29 ✉ Elisabets 9, El Raval ☎ 93/304–0513 🌐 www.dospalillos.com 🕘 Closed Sun. and Mon., and Aug. No lunch Tues. and Wed. [M] Catalunya, Universitat ✥ C4.*

$ BISTRO 🍴 **En Ville.** With pan-Mediterranean cuisine and reasonable prices, this attractive bistro 100 yards west of the Rambla in the MACBA section of El Raval is a keeper. The inexpensive lunch menu attracts in-the-know locals, and à la carte choices like scallops with pea foam are tempting and economical. **Known for:** value lunch menu; romantic setting; gluten-free cuisine. *[$] Average main: €14 ✉ Doctor Dou 14, El Raval ☎ 93/302–8467 🌐 www.envillebarcelona.es/en 🕘 Closed Sun., and 1 wk in Aug. [M] Catalunya, Liceu, Universitat ✥ C4.*

POBLENOU

$$ TAPAS 🍴 **Els Tres Porquets.** Somewhat off the beaten path (though just a 15-minute stroll from the Auditori and the Teatre Nacional de Catalunya), Els Tres Porquets (The Three Little Pigs) packs in foodies and bon vivants with a wide range of tapas and small dishes. The interesting wine list includes lesser-known but noteworthy selections from Spain and around the world. **Known for:** Iberian specialties; delicious cheeses; interesting wine list. *[$] Average main: €16 ✉ Rambla del Poblenou 165, Poblenou ☎ 93/300–8750 🌐 www.elstresporquets.es 🕘 Closed Sun. [M] Glòries, Clot ✥ H4.*

POBLE SEC

$ | TAPAS | × **Quimet i Quimet.** A foodie haunt, this tiny tapas place is hugely popular with locals and in-the-know visitors alike; if you show up too late, you might not be able to get in—come before 1:30 pm and 7:30 pm, however, and you might snag a stand-up table. Fourth-generation chef-owner Quim and his family improvise ingenious canapés. **Known for:** local wines; family-run; intimate space (long wait times). $ *Average main: €15* ⊠ *Poeta Cabanyes 25, Poble Sec* ☎ *93/442–3142* ⊘ *Closed Sun. and Aug. No dinner Sat.* Ⓜ *Paral.lel* ✛ *B5.*

$$ | CATALAN | Fodor'sChoice | ★ | × **Suculent.** This is a strong contender for the crown of Barcelona's best bistro, as young chef Antonio Romero continues to turn out Catalan tapas and dishes that have roots in rustic classics but reach high modern standards of execution. The name is a twist on the Catalan *sucar lent* (to dip slowly), and excellent bread is duly provided to soak up the sauces. **Known for:** obligatory set menus, except at the bar; must-try steak tartare on marrow bone; cocktail bar next door. $ *Average main: €20* ⊠ *Rambla del Raval 43, El Raval* ☎ *93/443–6579* ⊕ *www.suculent. com* ⊘ *Closed Mon. and Tues.* Ⓜ *Liceu* ✛ *C5.*

BARCELONETA AND THE PORT OLÍMPIC

Barceloneta and the Port Olímpic have little in common beyond their seaside location: the former is a traditional fishermen's quarter; the latter is a frenzied disco strip with thousand-seat restaurants.

$$$ | SEAFOOD | × **Barceloneta.** This restaurant in an enormous riverboat-like building at the end of the yacht marina in Barceloneta is definitely geared up for high-volume business. The food—rice and fish dishes are the specialty—is delicious, the service impeccable, and the hundreds of fellow diners make the place feel like a cheerful New Year's Eve celebration. **Known for:** lively waterside spot; excellent salads, rice, and fish dishes; free valet parking. $ *Average main: €27* ⊠ *L'Escar 22, Barceloneta* ☎ *93/221–2111* ⊕ *www.restaurantbarceloneta.com* Ⓜ *Barceloneta* ✛ *D6.*

$$$ | SPANISH | Fodor'sChoice | ★ | × **Can Solé.** With no sea views or touts outside to draw in diners, Can Solé has to rely on its reputation as one of Barceloneta's best options for seafood for more than a century. Faded photos of half-forgotten local celebrities lines its walls, but there's nothing out-of-date about the well-prepared traditional food. **Known for:** open kitchen; fresh fish daily; traditional Spanish rice dishes. $ *Average main: €28* ⊠ *Sant Carles 4, Barceloneta* ☎ *93/221–5012* ⊕ *restaurantcansole.com/en/* ⊘ *Closed Mon., and 2 wks in Aug. No dinner Sun.* Ⓜ *Barceloneta* ✛ *E6.*

$ | TAPAS | Fodor'sChoice | ★ | × **El Vaso de Oro.** A favorite with gourmands, this often overcrowded little counter serves some of the best beer and tapas in town. The house-brewed artisanal draft beer—named after the Fort family who own and run the bar—is drawn and served with loving care by veteran epauletted waiters who have it down to a fine art. **Known for:** old-school service; stand-up dining; beef fillet is a favorite. $ *Average main: €15* ⊠ *Balboa 6, Barceloneta* ☎ *93/319–3098* ⊕ *www.vasodeoro.com* ⊘ *Closed 1st 3 wks of Sept.* Ⓜ *Barceloneta* ✛ *E6.*

$$$ ✕ **Els Pescadors.** Northeast of the Port Olímpic, in the interesting Poble-
SEAFOOD   nou neighborhood, this handsome late-19th-century dining room has
FAMILY   a lovely terrace on a little square shaded by immense ficus trees. Kids
can play safely in the traffic-free square while their parents feast on
well-prepared seafood specialties such as paella, fresh fish, *fideuà* (a
paella-like noodle dish), and the succulent suquet. **Known for:** village-
square atmosphere; standard-setting rice and fish dishes; pretty terrace.
Ⓢ *Average main: €29* ⊠ *Pl. de Prim 1, Port Olímpic* ☎ *93/225–2018*
⊕ *www.elspescadors.com* Ⓜ *Poblenou* ✛ *H6.*

$$$$ ✕ **Enoteca.** Located in the Hotel Arts, Enoteca is the Barcelona outlet for
CATALAN   the talents of five-Michelin star chef Paco P-rez, two of which he has earned
here. His creative and technically accomplished cooking uses peerless
Mediterranean and Pyrenean products, transforming them into astonish-
ing dishes that are both surprising and satisfying. **Known for:** superstar
chef; extensive wine list; tasting menu. Ⓢ *Average main: €40* ⊠ *Hotel Arts,
Marina 19, Port Olímpic* ☎ *93/483–8108* ⊕ *enotecapacoperez.com/en/*
☉ *Closed Sun. and Mon.* Ⓜ *Ciutadella–Vila Olímpica* ✛ *G6.*

$ ✕ **Green Spot.** To call someplace one of Barcelona's best vegetarian
VEGETARIAN   and vegan restaurants may seem to damn it with faint praise—this is
very much a city of carnivores. But Green Spot's pale oak paneling
elegantly frames an open kitchen and airy dining room that serves
fun, fresh fusion food that everyone will like. **Known for:** delicious
black pizza with activated charcoal; craft beer; contemporary design.
Ⓢ *Average main: €14* ⊠ *Reina Cristina 12, main door is in pedestrian-
ized Porxos de Xifré between Passeig Colom and Port Vell, Barcelo-
neta* ☎ *93/802–5565* ⊕ *www.encompaniadelobos.com/the-green-spot*
Ⓜ *Barceloneta* ✛ *E5.*

$ ✕ **La Cova Fumada.** There's no glitz, no glamour, and not even a sign
TAPAS   on the wall, but the battered wooden doors of this old, family-owned
Fodor'sChoice   tavern hide a tapas bar to be treasured. Loyal customers queue for the
★   market-fresh seafood, served hot from the furiously busy kitchen. **Known
for:** impromptu live music; the original "bomba" fried potato croquette;
erratic opening times. Ⓢ *Average main: €10* ⊠ *Del Baluard 56, in cor-
ner of Barceloneta's main market square, Barceloneta* ☎ *93/221–4061*
☉ *Closed Sun. No dinner Mon.–Wed. and Sat.* Ⓜ *Barceloneta* ✛ *E6.*

$$ ✕ **La Mar Salada.** This restaurant stands out on a street of seafood spe-
SEAFOOD   cialists by offering creative twists on classic dishes at rock-bottom prices.
Fodor'sChoice   Traditional favorites such as paella, black rice, and fideuà (a paella-like
★   pasta dish) are reinvigorated, and freshness is assured as ingredients come
directly from the lonja fish quay across the street, a lively auction where
Barcelona's small fishing fleet sells its wares. **Known for:** fresh in-season
ingredients; excellent-value seafood; creative desserts. Ⓢ *Average main:
€20* ⊠ *Passeig Joan de Borbó 58, Barceloneta* ☎ *93/221–2127* ⊕ *www.
lamarsalada.cat* ☉ *Closed Tues.* Ⓜ *Barceloneta* ✛ *D6.*

EIXAMPLE

Eixample dining, invariably upscale and elegant, ranges from traditional
cuisine to designer fare in sleek minimalist spaces.

$ ✕ **Au Port de la Lune.** The stereotypical decor of this French bistro (think
FRENCH   Serge Gainsbourg photos) verges on parody, but the authentic food is no
Fodor'sChoice   joke. "There's no ketchup. There's no Coca-Cola. And there never will
★   be," reads Guy Monrepos's sign that sets the tone for a no-compromise
showcase of Gallic gastronomy. **Known for:** classic French bistro food
including cassoulet; no substitutions; outrageously boozy sorbet. $ *Average main: €12* ⊠ *Pau Claris 103, Eixample* ☎ *93/412–2224* ⊕ *www.
auportdelalune.net* ⊘ *No dinner Sun.* Ⓜ *Passeig de Gràcia* ✛ *E2.*

$$$ ✕ **Bardeni.** This "meat bar" doesn't take reservations; instead they offer
TAPAS   a walk-in-and-graze tapas menu of items like steak tartare and aged
Fodor'sChoice   filet mignon. Former Catalan Chef of the Year Dani Lechuga throws
★   in the occasional fine-dining dish to lighten things up. **Known for:**
mouthwatering steak tartare; great aged filet mignon; award-winning
chef. $ *Average main: €23* ⊠ *València 454, Eixample* ☎ *93/232–5811*
⊕ *www.caldeni.com/bardeni/* ⊘ *Closed Sun. and Mon.* Ⓜ *Sagrada
Família* ✛ *G2.*

$$ ✕ **Cervecería Catalana.** A bright and booming tapas bar with a few tables
TAPAS   outside, this spot is always packed for a reason: good food at reasonable
FAMILY   prices. Try the small *solomillos* (filets mignons), mini-morsels that will
take the edge off your carnivorous appetite without undue damage to
your wallet, or the jumbo shrimp brochettes. **Known for:** affordable
tapas; perfect jumbo shrimp brochettes; lively atmosphere. $ *Average
main: €16* ⊠ *Mallorca 236, Eixample* ☎ *93/216–0368* Ⓜ *Diagonal,
Provença (FGC)* ✛ *D2.*

$$$$ ✕ **Cinc Sentits.** Obsessively local, scrupulously sourced, and masterfully
CATALAN   cooked, the dishes of Catalan-Canadian chef Jordi Artal put the spot-
Fodor'sChoice   light on the region's finest ingredients in an intimate, sophisticated set-
★   ting. It's hard to believe that this Michelin-starred restaurant is Jordi's
first, but there's no arguing with the evidence of your *cinc sentits* (five
senses). **Known for:** excellent chef; cutting-edge techniques; tasting
menu only. $ *Average main: €100* ⊠ *Aribau 58, Eixample* ☎ *93/323–
9490* ⊕ *cincsentits.com* ⊘ *Closed Sun. and Mon.* Ⓜ *Provença* ✛ *C2.*

$$$$ ✕ **Disfrutar.** Three former head chefs from the now-closed "World's
ECLECTIC   Best Restaurant" elBulli have combined their considerable talents to
Fodor'sChoice   create this roller-coaster ride of culinary fun. Sun streams into the gor-
★   geous interior through skylights, spotlighting tasting menus of dazzling
inventiveness and good taste. **Known for:** otherwordly desserts; tasting
menus only; excellent beetroot meringues. $ *Average main: €120* ⊠ *De
Villarroel 163, Eixample* ☎ *93/348–6896* ⊕ *en.disfrutarbarcelona.com*
⊘ *Closed Sun. and Mon.* Ⓜ *Hospital Clínic* ✛ *B2.*

$$ ✕ **Embat.** An *embat* is a puff of wind in Catalan, and this little bistro
CATALAN   is a breath of fresh air in the sometimes stuffy Eixample. The highly
affordable market cuisine is always impeccably fresh and freshly con-
ceived, from flavorful brunches to a bargain lunch selection and a more
elaborate evening menu. **Known for:** modern, unfussy fare; stylish mini-
malist interior; delicious cod. $ *Average main: €18* ⊠ *Mallorca 304,
Eixample* ☎ *93/458–0855* ⊕ *embatrestaurant.com/* ⊘ *Closed Sun. No
dinner Mon.–Wed.* Ⓜ *Verdaguer* ✛ *D2.*

$$$ ✕ **Gorría.** Named for founder Fermín Gorría, this is quite simply
BASQUE   the best straightforward Basque-Navarran cooking in Barcelona.

7

Everything from the stewed *pochas* (white beans) to the heroic *chuletón* (steak) is as clear and pure in flavor as the Navarran Pyrenees. **Known for:** classic Basque cuisine; excellent wine pairings; valet parking. [$] *Average main: €26* ✉ *Diputació 421, Eixample* ☎ *93/245–1164* 🌐 *www.restaurantegorria.com* 🕓 *Closed Sun. and Aug. No dinner Mon.* [M] *Monumental* ✥ *F3.*

$$ CATALAN Fodor's Choice ★ 🍴 **Gresca.** Chef-owner Rafa Peña applies the skills he honed in the world's most celebrated kitchens in this phenomenally good-value restaurant and its adjacent wine-tapas bar. He cranks out inventive dishes based on humble ingredients to a fervently loyal customer base of local foodies. **Known for:** tapas of the day; adjacent wine-tapas bar; great, affordable cuisine. [$] *Average main: €20* ✉ *Provença 230, Eixample* ☎ *93/451–6193* 🕓 *Closed Sun. and last wk in Aug.–1st wk in Sept.* [M] *Provença (FGC)* ✥ *C2.*

$$$ SPANISH 🍴 **La Taverna Del Clínic.** The Simoes brothers have earned a solid reputation with discerning and deep-pocketed locals for serving creative and contemporary tapas. Their bar spills out onto a sunny street-side terrace where customers can enjoy truffle cannelloni and an award-winning variation on patatas bravas, paired with selections from the excellent wine list. **Known for:** contemporary tapas; award-winning patatas bravas; superb cheese selection. [$] *Average main: €28* ✉ *Roselló 155, Eixample* ☎ *93/410–4221* 🌐 *www.latavernadelclinic.com* 💳 *No credit cards* 🕓 *Closed Sun.* [M] *Hospital Clinic* ✥ *B1.*

$$$$ BASQUE Fodor's Choice ★ 🍴 **Lasarte.** Martin Berasategui, one of San Sebastián's corps of master chefs, placed his Barcelona kitchen in the capable hands of Paolo Casagrande in 2006, and it has been a culinary triumph ever since. Expect an eclectic selection of Basque, Mediterranean, and off-the-map creations, a hefty bill, and fierce perfectionism apparent in every dish. **Known for:** inventive cuisine at one of best restaurants in Barcelona; magnificent tasting menu; heavenly grilled pigeon. [$] *Average main: €50* ✉ *Mallorca 259, Eixample* ☎ *93/445–3242* 🌐 *www.restaurantlasarte.com* 🕓 *Closed Sun., Mon., and 3 wks in Aug.* [M] *Diagonal, Passeig de Gràcia, Provença (FGC)* ✥ *D2.*

$$$ CATALAN Fodor's Choice ★ 🍴 **Manairó.** A *manairó* is a mysterious Pyrenean elf, and Jordi Herrera may be the culinary version; his ingenious meat-cooking methods—such as filet mignon *al faquir* (heated from within on red-hot spikes) or blowtorched on a homemade centrifuge—may seem eccentric but produce diabolically good results. Melt-in-your-mouth meat dishes form the centerpiece of Manairó's menus, but they are ably supported by a bonanza of bold and confident creations that aren't frightened of big flavors. **Known for:** innovative contemporary cuisine; delicious meat dishes; sculptures and artworks by the chef. [$] *Average main: €28* ✉ *Diputació 424, Eixample* ☎ *93/231–0057* 🌐 *www.jordiherrera.es/manairo* 🕓 *Closed Sun., and 1st wk of Jan.* [M] *Monumental* ✥ *G3.*

$$ MEDITERRANEAN 🍴 **Mordisco.** The columns and skylights of this former high-class jewelers now frame a Mediterranean restaurant that emphasizes wholesome and flavorsome fare. Market-fresh produce is available to buy in the deli-like

entrance and makes its way into dishes such as artichoke hearts and hot veal carpaccios that come sizzling from the charcoal grill. **Known for:** enclosed patio; late-night cocktails at upstairs bar Thursday–Sunday; minimalist interior by Sandra Tarruella. $ *Average main: €17* ⊠ *Passatge de la Concepció 10, Eixample* 🕾 *93/487–9656* ⊕ *grupotragaluz. com/restaurante/mordisco/* Ⓜ *Diagonal* ⊹ *D2.*

$$ ✕ **Paco Meralgo.** The name, a pun on *para comer algo* ("to eat some-
TAPAS thing" with an Andalusian accent), may be only marginally amusing, but the tapas here are no joke at all, from the classical *calamares fritos* (fried cuttlefish rings) to the *pimientos de Padrón* (green peppers, some fiery, from the Galician town of Padrón). Whether *à table*, at the counter, or in the private dining room upstairs, this modern space does traditional tapas that reliably hit the spot. **Known for:** traditional tapas; excellent wine list; montaditos (baguette slices with varied toppings). $ *Average main: €18* ⊠ *Muntaner 171, Eixample* 🕾 *93/430–9027* ⊕ *www. restaurantpacomeralgo.com* Ⓜ *Hospital Clínic, Provença (FGC)* ⊹ *C1.*

$$$ ✕ **Roca Moo.** In any space as stylish as Roca Moo, located in the Hotel
CATALAN Omm, there's a real risk of the food playing second fiddle to the sur-
Fodor's Choice roundings. Fortunately, the spotlight is fixed firmly on dishes designed
★ by the Roca brothers, whose Celler de Can Roca restaurant has been rated as the world's best. **Known for:** fashionable haunt; Joan Roca tasting menu; exciting flavors and contemporary cooking techniques. $ *Average main: €29* ⊠ *Hotel Omm, Roselló 265, Eixample* 🕾 *93/445– 4000* ⊕ *www.hotelomm.com* ⊙ *Closed Sun. and Mon., and 3 wks in Jan.* Ⓜ *Diagonal* ⊹ *D1.*

$$ ✕ **Sergi de Meià.** Sergi takes sourcing seriously, serving only ingredi-
SPANISH ents foraged, caught, reared, or grown by people he knows personally.
Fodor's Choice The result is a menu full of wild game, free-range and organic meat,
★ seasonal vegetables, and sustainable fish, raised a notch by the skilled chef. **Known for:** family-run restaurant; breakfast and brunch; always packed. $ *Average main: €16* ⊠ *Aribau 106, Eixample* 🕾 *93/125–5710* ⊕ *www.restaurantsergidemeia.cat/* ⊙ *Closed Sun. and Mon.* Ⓜ *Universitat* ⊹ *C2.*

$$ ✕ **Taktika Berri.** Specializing in San Sebasti n's favorite dishes, this Basque
BASQUE restaurant has only one drawback: a table is hard to score unless you call weeks in advance (an idea to consider before you travel). Your backup plan? The tapas served over the first-come, first-served bar. **Known for:** Basque pintxos; convivial tavern atmosphere; hospitable service. $ *Average main: €20* ⊠ *València 169, Eixample* 🕾 *93/453–4759* ⊙ *Closed Sun. No dinner Sat.* Ⓜ *Hospital Clinic, Provença (FGC)* ⊹ *C2.*

$$ ✕ **Tapas 24.** The tapas emporium of celebrity chef Carles Abellán shows
TAPAS us how much he admires traditional Catalan and Spanish bar food, from patatas bravas to *croquetes de pollastre rostit* (roast chicken croquettes). The counter and terrace are constantly crowded, but the slightly pricey food is worth elbowing your way through the crowd for. **Known for:** traditional tapas with a twist; all-day kitchen; bikini Carles Abellán (ham-and-cheese toastie with truffle oil). $ *Average main: €20* ⊠ *Diputació 269, Eixample* 🕾 *93/488–0977* ⊕ *www.carlesabellan.com/ mis-restaurantes/tapas-24* Ⓜ *Passeig de Gràcia* ⊹ *D3.*

$$$ MEDITERRANEAN 🍴 **Tragaluz.** *Tragaluz* means "skylight" (the sliding roof opens to the stars in good weather), and this is an excellent choice if you're still on a design high from shopping on Passeig de Gràcia or visiting Gaudí's Pedrera. The Mediterranean cuisine is traditional yet light and will please most palates, and it's a popular lunch spot. **Known for:** open-air dining; coffee or postdinner drink upstairs; entrance is through Japanese tavern. [$] *Average main: €25* ✉ *Passatge de la Concepció 5, Eixample* ☎ *93/487–0621* 🌐 *grupotragaluz.com* [M] *Diagonal* ✥ *D2.*

GRÀCIA

This exciting yet intimate neighborhood has everything from the most sophisticated cuisine in town to lively Basque taverns.

$$ SPANISH 🍴 **L'Arrosseria Xàtiva.** This rustic dining room in Gràcia, a spin-off from the original in Les Corts, evokes the rice paddies and lowlands of Valencia. Low lighting imparts a warm glow over exposed brick walls, wood-beam ceilings, and bentwood chairs, and it's a great spot to savor some of Barcelona's finest paellas and rice dishes. **Known for:** traditional paella; lovingly prepared food; all-day kitchen on weekends. [$] *Average main: €22* ✉ *Torrent d'en Vidalet 26, Gràcia* ☎ *93/284–8502* 🌐 *www.grupxativa.com* [M] *Joanic* ✥ *D1.*

$$ CATALAN 🍴 **Roig Robí.** Rattan chairs and a garden terrace characterize this polished dining spot in the bottom corner of Gràcia just above the Diagonal (near Vía Augusta). Rustic and relaxed, Roig Robí (ruby red in Catalan, as in the color of certain wines) maintains a high level of culinary excellence, serving traditional Catalan market cuisine with original touches directed by chef Mercé Navarro. **Known for:** top-notch guinea-fowl canelón; seasonal specials; helmed by excellent chef. [$] *Average main: €21* ✉ *Sèneca 20, Gràcia* ☎ *93/218–9222* 🌐 *www.roigrobi.com* ⏲ *Closed Sun., and 2 wks in Aug. No lunch Sat.* [M] *Diagonal, Gràcia (FGC)* ✥ *D1.*

SARRIÀ, PEDRALBES, AND SANT GERVASI

An excursion to the upper reaches of town offers an excellent selection of restaurants, little-known Gaudí sites, shops, cool evening breezes, and a sense of village life in Sarrià.

$$ CATALAN Fodor's Choice ★ 🍴 **Coure.** *Cuina d'autor* is Catalan for creative or original cooking, and that is exactly what you get in this smart, subterranean space on the restaurant-centric Passeig Marimón, just above the Diagonal thoroughfare. The upstairs bar gets busy with a postwork crowd of food-loving locals, but downstairs is a cool, minimalist restaurant. **Known for:** interesting wine list; great local fish; seasonal mushrooms. [$] *Average main: €22* ✉ *Passatge Marimón 20, Sant Gervasi* ☎ *93/200–7532* 🌐 *www.restaurantcoure.es* ⏲ *Closed Sun. and Mon., and Aug.* [M] *Diagonal* ✥ *C1.*

$$$ CATALAN Fodor's Choice ★ 🍴 **Hisop.** The minimalist interior design of Oriol Ivern's small restaurant is undistinguished, but his cooking is stellar. This is budget-conscious fine dining that avoids exotic ingredients but lifts local dishes to exciting new heights. **Known for:** great-value cuisine; minimalist interior; delicious cod with morel sauce. [$] *Average main: €27* ✉ *Passatge de*

Marimón 9, Sant Gervasi ☎ *93/241–3233* ⊕ *www.hisop.com* ⊘ *Closed Sun., and 1st wk of Jan. No lunch Sat.* Ⓜ *Diagonal* ✛ *C1.*

$$ ╳ **Silvestre.** A graceful and easygoing mainstay in Barcelona's culinary
CATALAN landscape, this restaurant serves modern market cuisine to discerning diners. Look for fresh produce lovingly prepared in dishes such as tuna tartare, noodles and shrimp, or wood pigeon with duck liver. **Known for:** semisecret house wines; cozy setting; half portions available. Ⓢ *Average main: €22* ✉ *Santaló 101, Sant Gervasi* ☎ *93/241–4031* ⊕ *www. restaurante-silvestre.com* ⊘ *Closed Sun., and 3 wks in Aug. No lunch Sat.* Ⓜ *Muntaner* ✛ *B1.*

$$$ ╳ **Tram-Tram.** At the end of the old tram line above the village of Sarrià,
CATALAN this restaurant offers one of Barcelona's finest culinary stops, with Isidre
Fodor'sChoice Soler and his wife, Reyes, at the helm. Perfectly sized portions and an
★ airy white space within this traditional Sarrià house add to the experience. **Known for:** menú de degustació (tasting menu); pleasant interior garden patio; refined Catalan cuisine. Ⓢ *Average main: €24* ✉ *Major de Sarrià 121, Sarrià* ☎ *93/204–8518* ⊕ *tram-tram.com* ⊘ *Closed Mon., and 2 wks in Aug. No dinner Sun. and Tues.* Ⓜ *Sarrià* ✛ *A1.*

$$$$ ╳ **Via Veneto.** Open since 1967, this family-owned temple of fine Cata-
CATALAN lan dining offers a contemporary menu punctuated by old-school clas-
Fodor'sChoice sics. Service from the veteran waiters is impeccable, and diners can
★ safely place themselves in the hands of the expert sommelier to guide them through a daunting 10,000-bottle-strong wine list. **Known for:** favorite of Salvador Dalí and now sports stars; incredible roast duck; smoking room for postprandial cigars. Ⓢ *Average main: €40* ✉ *Ganduxer 10, Sant Gervasi* ☎ *93/200–7244* ⊕ *www.viavenetobarcelona. com* ⊘ *Closed Sun. and Aug. No lunch Sat.* Ⓜ *La Bonanova (FGC), Maria Cristina* ✛ *C1.*

TIBIDABO

$$$$ ╳ **ABaC.** Jordi Cruz is a culinary phenomenon in Spain. The only choice
CATALAN here is between the two tasting menus, and you can trust this chef to give you the best he has; the hypercreative sampling varies wildly from season to season, but no expense or effort is ever spared. **Known for:** celebrity chef; creative in-season dishes; elegant setting in elegant boutique hotel. Ⓢ *Average main: €155* ✉ *Av. del Tibidabo 1–7, Tibidabo* ☎ *93/319–6600* ⊕ *www.abacbarcelona.com* Ⓜ *Tibidabo* ✛ *D1.*

$$ ╳ **El Asador de Aranda.** It's a hike to get to this immense palace a few min-
SPANISH utes' walk above the Avenida Tibidabo metro station—but it's worth it.
FAMILY The kitchen, featuring a vast, wood-fired clay oven, specializes in Castil-
Fodor'sChoice ian cooking, with *cordero lechal* (roast suckling lamb), *morcilla* (black
★ sausage), and pimientos de piquillo as star players. **Known for:** beautiful Art Nouveau setting; excellent roasted lamb; spectacular city views from terrace. Ⓢ *Average main: €22* ✉ *Av. del Tibidabo 31, Tibidabo* ☎ *93/417–0115* ⊕ *www.asadordearanda.net* Ⓜ *Tibidabo (FGC)* ✛ *D1.*

WHERE TO STAY

Barcelona's hotel trade may be centuries removed from Miguel de Cervantes's 17th-century description of it as a "repository of courtesy, travelers' shelter," but in the 400 years or so since *Don Quixote,* the city has never lost its talent for pampering visitors.

Barcelona's pre-Olympics hotel surge in the early 1990s was matched only by its post-Olympics hotel surge in the early 2000s. Barcelona is the premier tourist destination in Spain and a major cruise port in the Mediterranean. Starchitects like Ricardo Bofill and Rafael Moneo have changed the skyline with skyscraper hotels of eye-popping luxury. The real heroes of this story, however, are the architect-designer teams that take one after another of the city's historic properties and restore them with an astonishing tour de force of taste. Hotel restaurants, too—from the Hotel Arts' Enoteca to the Mandarin's Moments—are among the superstar attractions in the city's gastronomic scene.

Use the coordinate (⊕ B2) at the end of each listing to locate a site on the corresponding map.

Hotel reviews have been shortened. For full information, visit Fodors.com.

	WHAT IT COSTS IN EUROS			
	$	$$	$$$	$$$$
Hotels	under €125	€125–€174	€175–€225	over €225

Prices are for two people in a standard double room in high season, excluding tax.

CIUTAT VELLA

The Ciutat Vella includes La Rambla, Barri Gòtic, Born-Ribera, and El Raval districts between Plaça de Catalunya and the port.

BARRI GÒTIC

$$$$ HOTEL FAMILY Fodor's Choice ★ 🏨 **Arai 4* Aparthotel Barcelona** (*Arai-Palau Dels Quatre Rius Monument*). You couldn't ask for a better location from which to explore Barcelona's Barri Gòtic—or for a bivouac more elegant—than one of the Aparthotel suites in this stunning restoration. **Pros:** warm and attentive service; historic character retained in former palace; welcome set with a bottle of wine. **Cons:** somewhat seedy area; on busy street; rooms on the top floor lack historic charm. [$] *Rooms from: €370* ✉ *Avinyó 30, Barri Gòtic* ☎ *93/320–3950* 🌐 *www.hotelarai.com* 🛏 *31 rooms* 🍴 *No meals* [M] *L3 Liceu* ⊕ *D5.*

$$$$ HOTEL 🏨 **Colón.** Around since 1951, the quiet and conservative Colón feels like it's been around forever, and is reasonably priced for the location: near the Catedral de la Seu, which is spectacular when illuminated at night. **Pros:** central location; some rooms have balconies overlooking square; rooftop terrace with heated Jacuzzi. **Cons:** can feel a bit stodgy; narrow bathrooms. [$] *Rooms from: €240* ✉ *Av. Catedral 7, Barri Gòtic*

WHERE TO STAY?

	Neighborhood Vibe	Pros	Cons
Ciutat Vella	Busy. La Rambla never sleeps, El Raval is exciting and exotic, the Barri Gòtic is quiet and medieval, and Born-Ribera hums with restaurants and taverns.	The pulse of the metropolis beats strongest here; the Boqueria and Santa Caterina markets throng with shoppers, while must-see sites are only steps away.	The incessant crush of humanity along La Rambla can be overwhelming, though the Barri Gòtic and Born-Ribera are quieter. El Raval is rough and seedy.
Eixample	Some of Gaudí's best buildings take pride of place here, and many of the city's finest hotels and restaurants are right around the corner. And then there's the shopping ...	The Eixample remains the world's only Art Nouveau neighborhood, constantly rewarding to the eye. Gaudí's unfinished masterpiece, La Sagrada Família, is within walking distance.	A bewildering grid without numbers or alphabetization, the Eixample can seem hard-edged compared to the older, quirkier parts of Barcelona.
Barceloneta and Port Olímpic	The onetime fisherman's quarter, Barceloneta retains its informal, working-class ambience, with laundry flapping over the streets and sidewalk restaurants lining Passeig Joan de Borbó.	Near the beach, this part of town has a laid-back feel. The Port Olímpic is a world apart, but Barceloneta is brimming with the best seafood dining spots in town.	Barceloneta offers few hotel opportunities, while the Port Olímpic's principal offering, the monolithic Hotel Arts, can feel like a tourist colony away from the rest of town.
Pedralbes, Sarrià, and Upper Barcelona	Upper Barcelona is leafy and residential, and the air is always a few degrees cooler. Pedralbes holds Barcelona's finest mansions; Sarrià is a rustic village suspended in the urban sprawl.	Getting above the fray and into better air has distinct advantages, and the upper reaches of Barcelona offers them. A 15-minute train ride connects Sarrià with La Rambla.	The only drawback to staying in Upper Barcelona is the 15-minute commute to the most important monuments and attractions. After midnight on weeknights this will require a taxi.

7

☎ *93/301–1404* 🌐 *www.hotelcolon.es* 🛏 *141 rooms* 🍴 *No meals* [M] *L4 Jaume I* ✥ *D4.*

$$ HOTEL Fodor's Choice ★ **Duquesa de Cardona.** A refurbished 17th-century town house, built when the Passeig de Colom in front was lined with the summer homes of the nobility, this hotel on the waterfront is a five-minute walk from everything in the Barri Gòtic and Barceloneta, and no more than a 30-minute walk to the Eixample. **Pros:** 24-hour room service; menu of fragrances to order for your room; glass of cava on check-in. **Cons:** rooms on the small side; no spa; no parking. [$] *Rooms from: €147* ✉ *Passeig de Colom 12, Barri Gòtic* ☎ *93/268–9090* 🌐 *www.hduquesadecardona.com* 🛏 *51 rooms* 🍴 *No meals* [M] *L4 Barceloneta, L3 Drassanes* ✥ *D5.*

$ HOTEL FAMILY Fodor's Choice ★ **el Jardí.** Facing charming Plaça del Pi and Plaça Sant Josep Oriol, in a pair of conjoined buildings that date to 1860, this family-friendly little budget hotel couldn't be better situated for exploring La Rambla and the Barri Gòtic. **Pros:** central location; friendly English-speaking staff; some rooms have balconies overlooking the square. **Cons:** no room service; no pool, gym, or spa; no place for suitcases in small rooms. $ *Rooms from: €100* ⊠ *Pl. Sant Josep Oriol 1, Barri Gòtic* ☎ *93/301–5900* ⊕ *www.eljardi-barcelona.com* ⇗ *40 rooms* ⊖ *No meals* Ⓜ *L3 Liceu, L4 Jaume I, Catalunya* ✛ *D4.*

$$$$ ⛉ **Hotel Neri.** Just steps from the cathedral, in the heart of the city's
HOTEL old Jewish Quarter, this elegant, upscale, boutique hotel, part of the
Fodor's Choice prestigious Relais & Chateaux hotel group, marries ancient and avant-
★ garde designs. **Pros:** central location (close to Barri Gòtic); barbecue
and occasional live music on the rooftop terrace; 24-hour room ser-
vice. **Cons:** noisy on summer nights and school days; pets allowed only
in deluxe rooms with terraces (pricey surcharge); lighting over beds
could improve. $ *Rooms from: €350* ⊠ *Carrer Sant Sever 5, Barri Gòtic*
☎ *93/304–0655* ⊕ *www.hotelneri.com/en* ⇗ *22 rooms* ⊖ *No meals*
Ⓜ *L3 Liceu, L4 Jaume I* ✛ *D4.*

$$$$ ⛉ **Hotel Ohla.** One of Barcelona's top design hotels (also with incredible
HOTEL food), the Ohla has a neoclassical exterior (not counting the playful eye-
balls stuck to the facade) that belies its avant-garde interior, full of witty,
design-conscious touches. **Pros:** rooftop terrace and pool; remarkable
restaurant Caelis on-site; high-end wines at Vistro 49. **Cons:** adjacent to
noisy Via Laietana; uncomfortable furniture in lobby. $ *Rooms from:*
€280 ⊠ *Via Laietana 49, Barri Gòtic* ☎ *93/341–5050* ⊕ *www.ohlabar-*
celona.com ⇗ *74 rooms* ⊖ *Free Breakfast* Ⓜ *L4 Urquinaona* ✛ *D4.*

$$$$ ⛉ **The Wittmore.** Opened in 2016, the Wittmore is the adults-only roman-
HOTEL tic hideaway par excellence, tucked away in a tiny cul-de-sac in the maze
Fodor's Choice of streets just north of the marina, a short walk to Plaça Colon. **Pros:**
★ rooms include robes and slippers; cocktail bar with fireplace; plunge
pool and bar on rooftop terrace. **Cons:** no children permitted; budget-
busting rates for smallish roofs; overpriced restaurant. $ *Rooms from:*
€350 ⊠ *Riudarenes 7, Barri Gòtic* ☎ *93/550–0885* ⊕ *www.thewitt-*
more.com ⇗ *21 rooms* ⊖ *No meals* Ⓜ *Barceloneta* ✛ *D5.*

BORN-RIBERA

$$ ⛉ **Banys Orientals.** Despite its name, the "Oriental Baths" has no spa,
HOTEL but it does have chic high-contrast design, with dark stained wood and
crisp white bedding, and is reasonably priced for the location. **Pros:**
Rituals toiletries; tasteful design; steps from the port, Picasso Museum,
and the Born area. **Cons:** rooms are on the small side; no room service; no terrace. $ *Rooms from: €150* ⊠ *Argenteria 37, Born-Ribera*
☎ *93/268–8460* ⊕ *www.hotelbanysorientals.com* ⇗ *43 rooms* ⊖ *No*
meals Ⓜ *L4 Jaume I* ✛ *E5.*

$ ⛉ **Hotel chic&basic Born.** The lobby of this hip little boutique hotel in the
HOTEL Born with its leather sofa and banquettes might remind you of a Star-
bucks, but the rooms tell a different story: the concept for chic&basic
was whimsical, edgy accommodations at affordable prices, and designer
Xavier Claramunt rose to the occasion. **Pros:** near upbeat Born-Ribera
scene; bicycle rentals for guests; remote lets you change color of lights
in room. **Cons:** no room service or minibars; no children under 12;
clothing storage limited, on open racks. $ *Rooms from: €120* ⊠ *Carrer*
Princesa 50, Born-Ribera ☎ *93/295–4652* ⊕ *www.chicandbasic.com*
⇗ *31 rooms* ⊖ *No meals* Ⓜ *L4 Jaume I* ✛ *E5.*

$$ ⊞ **Hotel Yurbban Trafalgar.** Guests and locals alike rave about the rooftop
HOTEL terrace at the Yurbban Trafalgar, and with good reason: the panoramic
Fodor'sChoice view is hands down one of the best in the city at this hip yet sophisti-
★ cated hotel. **Pros:** free cheese and wine tasting nightly (8–9 pm); bicycles
free for guests; minutes from Palau de la Música. **Cons:** small rooms;
room service ends at 11 pm; small shower stalls. Ⓢ *Rooms from: €160*
✉ *Carrer Trafalgar 30, Born-Ribera* ☎ *93/268–0727* ⊕ *yurbban.com/
en* ⇆ *56 rooms* ❚❘ *No meals* Ⓜ *L1/L3 Urquinaona* ♣ *E4.*

LA RAMBLA

$$$$ ⊞ **H1898.** Overlooking La Rambla, this imposing mansion (once the
HOTEL headquarters of the Compañiá General de Tabacos de Filipinas) couldn't
Fodor'sChoice be better located—especially for opera fans, with the Liceu just around
★ the corner. **Pros:** impeccable service; ideal location for exploring the
Barri Gòtic; historic spaces plus modern amenities like a spa and roof
deck. **Cons:** subway rumble discernible in lower rooms on the Ram-
bla side; no pets; some street noise from the Rambla in lower rooms.
Ⓢ *Rooms from: €238* ✉ *La Rambla 109, La Rambla* ☎ *93/552–9552*
⊕ *www.hotel1898.com* ⇆ *169 rooms* ❚❘ *No meals* Ⓜ *Catalunya, Liceu*
♣ *D4.*

$$$$ ⊞ **Hotel DO Plaça Reial.** Just at the entrance to the neoclassical Plaça
HOTEL Reial, this charming addition to Barcelona's growing collection of bou-
tique hotels—with its three restaurants, La Terraza (under the arcades
on the square), El Terrat, and La Cuina (downstairs under graceful brick
vaulting)—is a find for foodies and lovers of tasteful design. **Pros:** walk-
ing distance from old city center; helpful multilingual staff; 24-hour
room service. **Cons:** neighborhood can be rowdy at night; no pets; street
noise discernible in lower rooms. Ⓢ *Rooms from: €340* ✉ *Pl. Reial 1, La
Rambla* ☎ *93/481–3666* ⊕ *www.hoteldoreial.com* ⇆ *18 rooms* ❚❘ *Free
Breakfast* Ⓜ *L3 Liceu* ♣ *D5.*

$$$$ ⊞ **Le Méridien Barcelona.** There's no dearth of hotels along La Rambla in
HOTEL the heart of the city, but few rival the upscale Le Méridien, popular with
Fodor'sChoice businesspeople and visiting celebrities alike for its suites overlooking the
★ promenade and cozy amenities. **Pros:** central location; soaker tubs in
deluxe rooms; Mediterranean suites have large private terraces. **Cons:**
no pool; rooms small for the price; €60-per-day surcharge for pets.
Ⓢ *Rooms from: €249* ✉ *La Rambla 111, La Rambla* ☎ *93/318–6200*
⊕ *www.lemeridien.com/barcelona* ⇆ *231 rooms* ❚❘ *No meals* Ⓜ *Cata-
lunya L3 Liceu* ♣ *D4.*

EL RAVAL

$$$ ⊞ **Casa Camper Barcelona.** A marriage between the Camper footwear
HOTEL empire and the (now defunct) Vinçon design store produced this 21st-
FAMILY century hotel halfway between La Rambla and the MACBA (Museum
Fodor'sChoice of Contemporary Art), with a focus on sustainability (think solar panels
★ and water recycling) and a unique "one big family" feel. **Pros:** great
buffet breakfast with dishes cooked to order; just steps from MACBA
and the Boqueria; complimentary 24-hour snack bar. **Cons:** expensive
for what you get; extra per person charge for children over three years
old; no in-room minibar. Ⓢ *Rooms from: €220* ✉ *Carrer Elisabets 11,*

7

Lodging Alternatives

APARTMENT RENTALS

If you want a home base that's roomy enough for a family and comes with cooking facilities, consider a furnished rental. These can save you money, especially if you're traveling with a group. Prices run €90–€300 per day, depending on the quality of the accommodations. Apartment accommodations can be arranged through a number of local agencies.

LOCAL APARTMENT AGENCIES

AB Apartment Barcelona. ⊠ *Gran Vía 558, bajos, Eixample* ☎ *93/481–3577* ⊕ *www.apartmentbarcelona.com* Ⓜ *L1 Universitat, Urgell.*

Aparthotel Bonanova. ⊠ *Carrer Bisbe Sivilla 7, Sant Gervasi* ☎ *93/253–1563* ⊕ *www.bonanova-suite.com* ⌁ *22 apartments, 1 suite* Ⓜ *El Putxet (FGC).*

Aparthotel Nàpols. ⊠ *Carrer Nàpols 116, Eixample* ☎ *93/246–4573* ⊕ *www.abapart.com* ⌁ *33 apartments* Ⓜ *L2 Tetuan, Monumental; L1 Arc de Triomf.*

Barcelona Apartment. ⊠ *Eixample* ☎ *93/451–0402 reservations* ⊕ *www.barcelona-apartment.com.*

Barcelona for Rent. ⊠ *Carrer Bailén 120, Eixample* ☎ *93/458–6340* ⊕ *www.barcelonaforrent.com* Ⓜ *L4/L5 Verdaguer.*

Barceloneta Suites. ⊠ *Carrer Grau i Torras 17, Barceloneta* ☎ *93/221–4225* ⊕ *www.barcelonetasuites.com* ⌁ *16 suites* Ⓜ *L4 Barceloneta.*

Friendly Rentals. ⊠ *Carrer Trafalgar 42, Eixample* ☎ *93/268–8051* ⊕ *www.friendlyrentals.com* Ⓜ *L1/L4 Urquinaona.*

Gobcn Apartments. ⊠ *Av. Paral.lel 91, Poble Sec* ☎ *93/278–1156* ⊕ *www.gobcn.com* Ⓜ *Paral.lel, Poble Sec.*

Oh-Barcelona. ⊠ *Eixample* ☎ *93/467–3779* ⊕ *www.oh-barcelona.com.*

Only-Apartments. ⊠ *Edifici Colón 15F, Av. de les Drassanes 6, La Rambla* ☎ *93/301–7678* ⊕ *www.only-apartments.com* Ⓜ *L3 Drassanes.*

El Raval ☎ *93/342–6280* ⊕ *www.casacamper.com* ⌁ *40 rooms* ⦿ *Free Breakfast* Ⓜ *Catalunya, L3 Liceu* ✛ *C4.*

$$$$
HOTEL
Fodor's Choice
★

☒ **Hotel España.** This beautifully renovated Art Nouveau gem is the second oldest (after the nearby Sant Agustí) and among the best of Barcelona's smaller hotels. **Pros:** near Liceu opera house and La Rambla; alabaster fireplace in the bar lounge; lavish breakfast buffet. **Cons:** lower rooms facing Carrer Sant Pau get some street noise; bed lighting could be improved; no views. ⓢ *Rooms from: €250* ⊠ *Carrer Sant Pau 9–11, El Raval* ☎ *93/550–0000* ⊕ *www.hotelespanya.com* ⌁ *83 rooms* ⦿ *No meals* Ⓜ *L4 Liceu* ✛ *C5.*

$
HOTEL

☒ **Market Hotel.** Wallet-friendly and design conscious, this boutique hotel named for the Mercat de Sant Antoni (a block away) is one of Barcelona's best bargains and walking distance from all of El Raval and the Gothic Quarter sites and attractions. **Pros:** excellent-value Catalan cuisine at on-site restaurant; friendly staff; great showers. **Cons:**

standard rooms on lower floors are a little cramped; soundproofing needs upgrade; some rooms have no views. $ *Rooms from: €100* ✉ *Carrer del Comte Borrell 68, El Raval* ☎ *93/325–1205* ⊕ *www.hotelmarketbarcelona.com* ⇆ *68 rooms* ⊙| *No meals* Ⓜ *L2 Sant Antoni, L1 Urgell* ✛ *B4.*

$$ 🔲 **Sant Agustí.** In a leafy square just off La Rambla, the Sant Agustí
HOTEL bills itself as the oldest billet in Barcelona—it was built in the 1720s
FAMILY for the library of the adjacent convent and reborn as a hotel in 1840.
Pros: steps from the Boqueria market, La Rambla, and the Liceu opera house; intimate breakfast room; very good value for price. **Cons:** Plaça Sant Agusti can be a homeless hangout; not enough closet space; safe boxes too small for laptops. $ *Rooms from: €150* ✉ *Pl. Sant Agustí 3, El Raval* ☎ *93/318–1658* ⊕ *www.hotelsa.com* ⇆ *80 rooms* ⊙| *Free Breakfast* Ⓜ *L3 Liceu* ✛ *E4.*

BARCELONETA AND PORT OLÍMPIC

$$$$ 🔲 **Hotel Arts Barcelona.** This luxurious Ritz-Carlton-owned, 44-story
HOTEL skyscraper overlooks Barcelona from the Port Olímpic, providing stun-
Fodor'sChoice ning views of the Mediterranean, the city, the Sagrada Família, and
★ the mountains beyond. **Pros:** excellent tapas restaurant on-site; fine art throughout hotel; free cava served on club floors daily. **Cons:** a 20-minute hike or more from central Barcelona; very pricey. $ *Rooms from: €355* ✉ *Carrer de la Marina 19–21, Port Olímpic* ☎ *93/221–1000* ⊕ *www.hotelartsbarcelona.com* ⇆ *483 rooms* ⊙| *No meals* Ⓜ *L4 Ciutadella–Vila Olímpica* ✛ *G6.*

$ 🔲 **Hotel 54 Barceloneta.** Just a few minutes' walk from the beach, this
HOTEL modern addition to the Barcelona hotel scene has much to offer in location, comfort, and economy. **Pros:** rooftop terrace overlooks the marina and the Old Port; competent multilingual staff; pleasant, rustic breakfast room. **Cons:** noisy around the clock on Passeig Joan de Borbó; bathrooms lack space and privacy; poor sound insulation between some rooms. $ *Rooms from: €110* ✉ *Passeig de Joan de Borbó 54, Barceloneta* ☎ *93/225–0054* ⊕ *www.hotel54barceloneta.es* ⇆ *28 rooms* ⊙| *No meals* Ⓜ *Barceloneta* ✛ *E6.*

$$$$ 🔲 **W Barcelona.** This towering sail-shaped monolith dominates the sky-
HOTEL line on the Barcelona waterfront; architect Ricardo Bofill's W, now part
Fodor'sChoice of the Marriott International chain, is a stunner inside and out, from the
★ six-story atrium lobby with black ceramic tile floors, suspended basket chairs, and glitter walls, to the adjacent bar-lounge with direct access to the "WET" lounge deck, chill-out divans, and pool. **Pros:** unrivaled views; excellent restaurants on-site; transfer service to/from airport and cruise dock. **Cons:** extra amenities can get pricey; far from public transportation (20-minute hike); loud music in public areas. $ *Rooms from: €280* ✉ *Pl. de la Rosa del Vents 1, Moll de Llevant, Barceloneta* ☎ *93/295–2800* ⊕ *www.w-barcelona.com* ⇆ *473 rooms* ⊙| *No meals* Ⓜ *L4 Barceloneta* ✛ *E6.*

7

EIXAMPLE

$$$ HOTEL
Condes de Barcelona. One of Barcelona's most popular hotels, the Condes de Barcelona is perfectly placed for exploring the sights (and shops) of the city's most fashionable quarter, and—for the privileged location—offers exceptional value. **Pros:** elegant building with subdued contemporary furnishings; prime spot in the middle of the Eixample; excellent value. **Cons:** no spa; no pets; rooftop plunge pool is small. [$] *Rooms from: €190* ✉ *Passeig de Gràcia 73, Eixample* ☎ *93/467–4780* 🌐 *www.condesdebarcelona.com* 🛏 *126 rooms* 🍴 *No meals* [M] *L3/L5 Diagonal, Provença (FGC)* ✣ *D2.*

$$ HOTEL FAMILY Fodor's Choice ★
Continental Palacete. This former palatial family home, or *palacete,* provides a splendid drawing room, a location nearly dead-center for Barcelona's main attractions, views over leafy Rambla de Catalunya, and a 24-hour free buffet. **Pros:** ornate design; attentive staff; ideal location. **Cons:** room decor is relentlessly pink and overdraped; bathrooms are a bit cramped; some street noise. [$] *Rooms from: €153* ✉ *Rambla de Calatunya 30, at Diputació, Eixample* ☎ *93/445–7657* 🌐 *www.hotel-continental.com* 🛏 *22 rooms* 🍴 *Free Breakfast* [M] *L2/L3/L4 Passeig de Gràcia, Plaça Catalunya* ✣ *D3.*

$$$$ HOTEL Fodor's Choice ★
Cotton House Hotel. First a sumptuous family home, this 1879 property was bought in 1961 by the city's Cotton Producers Guild and then became a hotel in 2015; it's now part of Marriott's boutique Autograph Collection and has been redesigned by Lázaro Rosa-Violán with scrupulous respect for the original features of the building: coffered ceilings, geometric parquet floors, and Frank Lloyd Wright–like touches of modernism. **Pros:** spot-on professional, friendly service; restaurant Batuar (€25) open 7 am–midnight; huge terrace off the bar with original fountains. **Cons:** bed size leaves little room to maneuver in basic rooms; some rooms with vanities outside the shower room; fairly pricey. [$] *Rooms from: €320* ✉ *Gran Vía de les Corts Catalanes 670, Eixample* ☎ *93/450–5045* 🌐 *www.hotelcottonhouse.com* 🛏 *88 rooms* 🍴 *No meals* 💳 *No credit cards* [M] *L2/L3/L4 Passeig de Gràcia* ✣ *E3.*

$$$$ HOTEL Fodor's Choice ★
Hotel Claris Grand Luxe Barcelona. Acclaimed as one of Barcelona's best hotels, the Claris is an icon of design, tradition, and connoisseurship. **Pros:** first-rate restaurant La Terraza; Mayan Secret Spa with temazcal and pure chocolate skin treatment; rooms in a variety of styles. **Cons:** basic ("Superior") rooms small for the price; rooftop terrace noise at night can reach down into sixth-floor rooms; capacity bookings can sometimes overwhelm the staff. [$] *Rooms from: €270* ✉ *Carrer Pau Claris 150, Eixample* ☎ *93/487–6262* 🌐 *www.hotelclaris.com* 🛏 *124 rooms* 🍴 *No meals* [M] *L2/L3/L4 Passeig de Gràcia* ✣ *E2.*

$$ HOTEL Fodor's Choice ★
Hotel Cram. A short walk from La Rambla, this Eixample design hotel offers impeccable midcity accommodations with cheerful avant-garde decor and luxurious details. **Pros:** Jordi Cruz's Angle restaurant on-site; great location; dolly slides under the bed for suitcase storage. **Cons:** Aribau is a major uptown artery, noisy at all hours; rooms are a bit small, with quirky shapes; no gym or spa. [$] *Rooms from: €160* ✉ *Carrer Aribau 54, Eixample* ☎ *93/216–7700* 🌐 *www.hotelcram.com* 🛏 *67 rooms* 🍴 *No meals* [M] *L1/L2 Universitat, Provença (FGC)* ✣ *C2.*

$$$$ | HOTEL | Fodor's Choice ★

🏨 **Hotel El Palace Barcelona.** Founded in 1919 by Caesar Ritz, the original Ritz (the grande dame of Barcelona hotels) was renamed in 2005 but kept its lavish Old European style intact, from the liveried doorman in top hat and tails to the lobby's ormolu clocks and massive crystal chandelier. **Pros:** equidistant from Barri Gòtic and central Eixample; L'Éclair features live jazz and more; Mayan-style sauna in the award-winning spa. **Cons:** €30-per-night surcharge for small pets; painfully pricey; formal atmosphere. [$] *Rooms from: €360* ✉ *Gran Vía de les Corts Catalanes 668, Eixample* ☎ *93/510–1130* 🌐 *www.hotelpalacebarcelona.com* 🛏 *120 rooms* 🍴 *No meals* [M] *L2/L3/L4 Passeig de Gràcia* ⊕ *E3.*

$$$ | HOTEL | Fodor's Choice ★

🏨 **Hotel Granados 83.** Designed in the style of a New York City loft and seated on a tree-shaded street in the heart of the Eixample, this hotel blends exposed brick, steel, and glass with Greek and Italian marble and Indonesian tamarind wood to achieve downtown cool. **Pros:** luxurious duplexes with private terraces and semiprivate pools; wide variety of good casual restaurants nearby; free entrance to the Egypian Museum of Barcelona. **Cons:** rooftop terrace pool quite small; standard rooms need more storage space; Wi-Fi can be patchy. [$] *Rooms from: €195* ✉ *Carrer Enric Granados 83, Eixample* ☎ *93/492–9670* 🌐 *www.hotelgranados83.com* 🛏 *84 rooms* 🍴 *No meals* [M] *Provença (FGC)* ⊕ *C2.*

$$$$ | HOTEL | FAMILY | Fodor's Choice ★

🏨 **Hotel Omm.** The lobby of this postmodern architectural stunner tells you what to expect throughout: perfect comfort, cutting-edge design, and meticulous attention to every detail. **Pros:** perfect location for the upper Eixample; fireplace in lounge; superb spa. **Cons:** small plunge pools; restaurant is pricey and a little precious; parking is expensive. [$] *Rooms from: €275* ✉ *Roselló 265, Eixample* ☎ *93/445–4000* 🌐 *www.hotelomm.com* 🛏 *91 rooms* 🍴 *No meals* [M] *L3/L5 Diagonal, Provença (FGC)* ⊕ *D2.*

$$ | HOTEL

🏨 **Hotel Praktik Garden.** If you've ever dreamed about running away with the circus, this quirky little boutique hotel, where the walls are covered with gaily colored circus posters, is just for you. **Pros:** free coffee service in the garden; close to Passeig de Gràcia; pleasant terrace/lounge. **Cons:** pipe racks instead of closets; minimal amenities; no breakfast room. [$] *Rooms from: €140* ✉ *Diputació 325, Eixample* ☎ *93/467–5279* 🌐 *www.hotelpraktikgarden.com* 🛏 *59 rooms* 🍴 *No meals* [M] *Girona* ⊕ *E3.*

$$$$ | HOTEL | Fodor's Choice ★

🏨 **Majestic Hotel & Spa.** With an unbeatable location on Barcelona's most stylish boulevard, steps from Gaudí's La Pedrera and near the area's swankiest shops, this hotel—part town house and part modern extension—is a near-perfect place to stay. **Pros:** rooftop terrace with views of the Mediterranean, Montjuïc, and the Sagrada Família; 24-hour room service; art (including Miró prints) from owner's private collection. **Cons:** some standard rooms a bit small for the price; very pricey buffet breakfast. [$] *Rooms from: €325* ✉ *Passeig de Gràcia 68, Eixample* ☎ *93/488–1717* 🌐 *www.hotelmajestic.es* 🛏 *275 rooms* 🍴 *No meals* [M] *L2/L3/L4 Passeig de Gràcia, Provença (FGC)* ⊕ *D2.*

$$$$ | HOTEL | FAMILY

🏨 **Mandarin Oriental Barcelona.** A carpeted ramp leading from the elegant Passeig de Gràcia (flanked by Tiffany and Brioni boutiques) lends this hotel the air of a privileged—and pricey—inner sanctum. **Pros:** outstanding Moments restaurant; babysitters and parties for the kids, on request; Mimosa interior garden great for drinks. **Cons:** rooms relatively small for a 5-star accommodation; Wi-Fi free in rooms only if booked online; lighting a bit dim. [$] *Rooms from: €575* ✉ *Passeig de Gràcia 38–40, Eixample* ☎ *93/151–8888* 🌐 *www.mandarinoriental.com/barcelona* 🛏 *120 rooms* 🍴 *No meals* [M] *L2/L3/L4 Passeig de Gràcia, L3/L5 Diagonal, Provença (FGC)* ✥ *D3.*

$$$ HOTEL FAMILY Fodor's Choice ★ 🏨 **Murmuri Barcelona.** British designer Kelly Hoppen took this 19th-century town house on La Rambla de Catalunya and transformed it into a chic, intimate urban retreat, with room decor in velvety brown, beige, and black, with big mirrors, dramatic bed lighting, and arresting photography. **Pros:** private terraces in Privilege doubles; strategic Eixample location; exclusive rooftop terrace open year-round. **Cons:** no pool, gym, or spa (though guest privileges at the nearby affiliated Majestic hotel); no pets, except in the apartments; Design doubles a bit small. [$] *Rooms from: €185* ✉ *Rambla de Catalunya 104, Eixample* ☎ *93/550–0600* 🌐 *www.murmuri.com* 💳 *No credit cards* 🛏 *61 rooms* 🍴 *No meals* [M] *L3/L5 Diagonal, Provença (FGC)* ✥ *C1.*

GRÀCIA

$$$$ HOTEL Fodor's Choice ★ 🏨 **Hotel Casa Fuster Gran Lujo Monumento.** This hotel offers one of two chances (the other is the Hotel España) to stay in an Art Nouveau building designed by Lluís Domènech i Montaner, architect of the sumptuous Palau de la Música Catalana. **Pros:** well situated for exploring both Gràcia and the Eixample; ample rooms with luxury-level amenities; all the Moderniste details you could want. **Cons:** rooms facing Passeig de Gràcia could use better soundproofing; no pets; service can be a bit stiff. [$] *Rooms from: €290* ✉ *Passeig de Gràcia 132, Gràcia* ☎ *93/255–3000* 🌐 *www.hotelcasafuster.com* 🛏 *105 rooms* 🍴 *No meals* [M] *L3/L5 Diagonal* ✥ *D1.*

SARRIÀ, SANT GERVASI, AND PEDRALBES

$$$$ HOTEL FAMILY Fodor's Choice ★ 🏨 **Primero Primera.** The Perez family converted their apartment building on a leafy side street in the quiet, upscale, residential neighborhood of Tres Torres and opened it as an exquisitely designed, homey boutique hotel in 2011. **Pros:** retro-modern ambience; 24-hour free snack bar; electric bicycle rentals for guests. **Cons:** bit of a distance from downtown; very small pool; service can be uneven. [$] *Rooms from: €230* ✉ *Doctor Carulla 25–29, Sant Gervasi* ☎ *93/417–5600* 🌐 *www.primeroprimera.com* 💳 *No credit cards* 🛏 *30 rooms* 🍴 *Free Breakfast* [M] *Tres Torres (FGC)* ✥ *A1.*

$$ HOTEL 🏨 **Vilana Hotel.** In an upscale residential neighborhood above Passeig de la Bonanova, this boutique accommodation can ease some of the budgetary strains of coming to a prime tourist destination. **Pros:** quiet surroundings; large, sunlit rooms; pleasant, attentive English-speaking staff. **Cons:** 30 minutes to center of town; no pool or spa; room service closes at 10:30. [$] *Rooms from: €135* ✉ *Vilana 7, Sant Gervasi* ☎ *93/434–0363* 🌐 *vilanahotel.com* 🛏 *22 rooms* 🍴 *No meals* [M] *Sarrià (FGC)* ✥ *B1.*

TIBIDABO

$$$$ HOTEL FAMILY 🏨 **Gran Hotel la Florida.** Peace, privacy, and a stunning panoramic view set this luxurious mountaintop retreat apart. **Pros:** first-rate spa, fitness center, and sauna; friendly and attentive front staff; decor by celebrity designers. **Cons:** pricey food and beverage add-ons; pets accepted with an €80 surcharge; isolated location, with infrequent shuttle service to city center. [$] *Rooms from: €240* ✉ *Ctra. Vallvidrera al Tibidabo 83–93, Tibidabo* ☎ *93/259–3000* 🌐 *www.hotellaflorida.com* 🛏 *70 rooms* 🍴 *No meals* [M] *Tibidabo (FGC)* ✣ *B1.*

NIGHTLIFE AND PERFORMING ARTS

Barcelona's art and nightlife scenes start early and never quite stop. To find out what's on, check "*agenda*" listings in Barcelona's leading daily newspapers *El País, La Vanguardia,* and *El Periódico de Catalunya.* The weekly *Time Out,* published on Wednesday, is a free listings magazine, available from metro stations, cafés, shops, and bars around the city. Weekly online magazine *Le Cool* (🌐 *barcelona.lecool.com*) preselects noteworthy events and activities; it's in Spanish only. Look also for the free monthly English-language *Barcelona Metropolitan* magazine in English-language bookstores and hotel lobbies, or read it online at 🌐 *www.barcelona-metropolitan.com.* Barcelona city hall's website (🌐 *lameva.barcelona.cat/barcelonacultura*) also publishes complete listings and highlights, and has an English edition. *Activitats,* available at the Palau de la Virreina (La Rambla 99) or the Centre Santa Mònica (La Rambla 7), lists cultural events.

NIGHTLIFE

BARRI GÒTIC

BARS

Ocaña. Located in a trio of ancient mansions on buzzy Plaça Reial's southern flank, this venue is dedicated to José Pérez Ocaña, a cross-dressing artist and proud bohemian, and a dominating figure of Barcelona's decadent post-Franco explosion of alternative culture. With an adjoining Mexican restaurant, as well as a sizable café bar, club, and cocktail lounge, Ocaña also has the fiercest drag queen hostesses on the square. It's a wonderful place for people-watching on the terrace, followed by dinner in one of the two distinctive spaces and cocktails at the chic Apotheke bar downstairs. ✉ *Pl. Reial 13–15, Barri Gòtic* ☎ *93/676–4814* 🌐 *www.ocana.cat* [M] *Liceu.*

MUSIC CLUBS

Harlem Jazz Club. Located on a rare tree-lined street in Barri Gòtic, this club attracts patrons of all ages and musical tastes. Listen to live Cuban salsa, swing, and reggae while enjoying killer cocktails in a relaxed and friendly atmosphere. Most concerts start at 10 pm and finish around 1 am, and many people linger until closing time. ✉ *Comtessa de Sobradiel 8, Barri Gòtic* ☎ *93/310–0755* 🌐 *www.harlemjazzclub.es* [M] *Jaume I, Liceu.*

LA RAMBLA

BARS

Bar Pastis. On a tiny street off the bottom of La Rambla, this dusty hole-in-the-wall is a city treasure. For six decades, Bar Pastis has provided patrons with a nostalgic, elbow-to-elbow glimpse at bohemian back-alley Paris circa the 1940s. The nicotine-stained walls, grimy shelves filled with ancient bottles, and the faded portraits of long-ago performers are all genuine. The bar holds acoustic gigs nightly for a hard-to-beat €2 supplement on drinks. Concerts generally start around 10 pm and feature tango, flamenco, soft jazz, blues, or anything that fits the bar's speakeasy groove. ⊠ *Santa Mònica 4, La Rambla* ☎ *93/318–7980* ⊕ *www.barpastis.es* Ⓜ *Drassanes.*

Jamboree-Jazz and Dance-Club. This legendary nightspot has hosted some of the world's most influential jazz musicians since its opening in 1960. Decades later, the club continues to offer two nightly shows and remains a notable haven for new generations of jazz and blues aficionados. After the last performance, the spot transforms into a late-night dance club playing soul, hip-hop, and R&B. ⊠ *Pl. Reial 17, La Rambla* ☎ *93/319–1789* ⊕ *www.masimas.com/en/jamboree* Ⓜ *Liceu.*

BORN-RIBERA

BARS

La Vinya del Senyor. Ambitiously named "The Lord's Vineyard," this romantic wine bar directly across from the entrance to the emblematic church of Santa Maria del Mar is etched into the ground floor of an ancient building. There's an extensive wine list and bite-size edibles, and ardent aficionados order by the bottle and favor tables found up a rickety ladder on the pint-size mezzanine or, when the weather cooperates, outside on the people-watching terrace. ⊠ *Pl. de Santa Maria 5, Born-Ribera* ☎ *93/310–3379* Ⓜ *Jaume I.*

Fodor'sChoice ★ **Rubi Bar.** The whimsical apothecary-like spirits cabinet, exposed-stone wall, and dramatic red lighting will be the first things to catch your eye at this cozy hidden gem, tucked away in the mazelike backstreets of El Born. However, it's the friendly service, relaxed atmosphere, and inventive selection of cocktails—most notably a choice of home-brewed flavored gins tantalizingly displayed on the bar shelves in hand-labeled bottles—that brings patrons back time and again. Add to the mix an eclectic playlist of funk, soul, rock, and pop classics, tasty snacks, and inexpensive mojitos that attracts locals, expats, and the curious, ages 25–50 and beyond. ⊠ *Banys Vells 6, Born-Ribera* ☎ *671/441888* Ⓜ *Jaume I.*

EL RAVAL

BARS

Casa Almirall. The twisted wooden fronds framing the bar's mirror, an 1888 vintage bar-top iron statue of a muse, and Art Nouveau touches such as curvy door handles make this one of the most authentic bars in Barcelona. It's also the second oldest, dating to 1860. (The oldest is the Marsella, another Raval favorite.) It's a good spot for evening drinks after hitting the nearby MACBA (Museu d'Art Contemporani de Barcelona) or for a prelunch *vermut* (vermouth) on weekends.

✉ *Joaquín Costa 33, El Raval* ☎ *93/318–9917* ⊕ *www.casaalmirall. com/en* Ⓜ *Universitat.*

MUSIC CLUBS

Jazz Sí Club. Run by the Barcelona contemporary music school next door, this workshop and (during the day) café is a forum for musicians, teachers, and fans to listen to and debate their art. There is jazz on Monday; pop, blues, and rock jam sessions on Tuesday; jazz Wednesday; Cuban salsa on Thursday; flamenco on Friday; and rock and pop on weekends. The small cover charge (€6–€10, depending on which night you visit) includes a drink; Wednesday has no cover charge. Gigs start between 6:30 and 8:45 pm. ✉ *Requesens 2, El Raval* ☎ *93/329–0020* ⊕ *tallerdemusics.com/en/jazzsi-club/* Ⓜ *Sant Antoni.*

BARCELONETA AND PORT OLÍMPIC

BARS

Fodor's Choice ★ **Eclipse Bar.** The sensational shoreline views from the 26th floor of the seaside W Hotel are undoubtedly a major part of Eclipse's attraction. Add to the mix an ultraslick interior design, an impressive roster of international DJs spinning themed parties every day of the week, and deluxe cocktails decadently paired with sushi, and it's little wonder that this is a favorite spot for glitterati to be seen and heard. ✉ *Pl. de la Rosa dels Vents 1, Barceloneta* ☎ *93/295–2800* ⊕ *www.eclipse-barcelona. com* Ⓜ *Drassanes.*

CASINOS

Casino de Barcelona. Situated on the shore underneath the Hotel Arts, Barcelona's modern casino has everything from slot machines to roulette, plus restaurants, a bar, and a dance club. The casino regularly hosts Texas Hold'em poker tournaments, which add an air of Vegas-style excitement. ✉ *Marina 19–21, Port Olímpic* ☎ *900/354354* ⊕ *www.casinobarcelona.com/en* Ⓜ *Ciutadella–Vila Olímpica.*

DANCE CLUBS

CDLC. Among the glitziest of Barcelona's waterfront clubs, the CDLC (Carpe Diem Lounge Club) embraces all the clichés of Ibizan over-the-top decor. The music is electronic; cocktails are exotic—and pricey. If there are celebrities in town, sooner or later they show up here. ✉ *Passeig Maritim 32, Marina Beach, Port Olímpic* ☎ *93/224–0470, 647/779999 VIP services* ⊕ *www.cdlcbarcelona.com* Ⓜ *Ciutadella–Vila Olímpica.*

Shôko. With tony design touches and Eastern fusion cuisine, Shoko brings its own particular brand of cool to the Barcelona seaside. Located just below Frank Gehry's famous fish sculpture, the swanky restaurant and lounge morphs into a party paradise featuring theme nights with international DJs ready to spin until dawn. ✉ *Passeig Marítim de la Barceloneta 36, Port Olímpic* ☎ *93/225–9200* ⊕ *www.shoko.biz/en* Ⓜ *Ciutadella–Vila Olímpica.*

EIXAMPLE

BARS

Fodor's Choice ★ **Dry Martini Bar.** An homage to the traditional English martini bar of decades past, this stately spot is paradise for cocktail aficionados seeking the most expertly mixed drinks in town (martinis even have their

7

own prep section). From the wood-paneled fixtures of the mirrored bar featuring a vintage brass register, to the knowledgeable barmen dressed in impeccable white coats and ties, to the wall of vintage spirit bottles overlooking plush and regal turquoise and red leather seating, each detail aims to transport the loyal clientele back to an era of inspired excellence. ⊠ *Aribau 162, Eixample* ☎ *93/205–8070* ⊕ *www.drymartiniorg.com* Ⓜ *Provença.*

La Vinoteca Torres. In a space ideally located on Barcelona's exclusive shopping avenue, Passeig de Gràcia, the acclaimed Torres wine dynasty offers an ample selection of their international wines and spirits to accompany delectable Mediterranean fish or meat dishes such as the signature oxtail in Sangre de Toro red wine sauce. The dark, ultramodern space is adorned with walls of stacked wine bottles, and strategic lighting illuminates the natural wood tables. For an extra-special treat, book the private back room that seats up to 14. When the weather is nice, stop by for a quick glass of wine and tapas on the parasol-covered terrace. ⊠ *Passeig de Gràcia 78, Eixample* ☎ *93/272–6625* ⊕ *www. lavinotecatorres.com* Ⓜ *Passeig de Gràcia, Diagonal.*

Milano. For more than a decade, this "secret" basement bar, located in an area otherwise dominated by student pubs and tourist traps, has had a rotating lineup of international acts including blues, soul, jazz, flamenco, swing, and pop. In a space resembling a 1940s cabaret, you'll find paneled oak, a brass bar, spotlit photo prints of previous acts, and red banquette-style seating alongside matching armchairs and tables. The stage is complete with moody lighting and a curtain backdrop. Milano is open from noon for tapas lunch with cocktails (classic and creative), and shows run nightly at 9 pm and 11 pm. ⊠ *Ronda Universitat 35, Eixample* ☎ *93/112–7150* ⊕ *www.camparimilano.com/en* Ⓜ *Catalunya, Universitat.*

Fodor'sChoice ★ **Monvínic.** Conceptualized to celebrate wine culture at its finest, this spectacular space, aptly called "Wineworld" in Catalan, features a ritzy wine bar complete with tablet wine lists, a cavernous culinary space, a reference library, a vertical garden, and the pièce de résistance: a vast cellar housing a mind-blowing 3,500 vintages from around the world. Small plates of regional jamón and inventive riffs on classical Catalan cuisine complement the vino. Wine tastings, both traditional and creative, are held regularly for groups or individuals looking to become oenophiles. ⊠ *Diputació 249, Eixample* ☎ *93/272–6187* ⊕ *www.monvinic.com* Ⓜ *Passeig de Gràcia.*

Fodor'sChoice ★ **Solange Cocktails and Luxury Spirits.** The latest venture from the Pernia brothers—the trio whose Tandem Cocktail Bar (Aribau 86) pioneered Barcelona's emerging cocktail scene back in the '80s—is a sleek, golden-hued, luxurious lounge space aptly named after Solange Dimitrios, 007's original Bond girl. Smartly dressed mixologists cater to well-heeled 30-plus professionals at the stunning long bar or on posh lounge divans so extravagant in look and feel that one expects the debonair spy to walk in at any moment. The homage continues with signature cocktails that reference Bond films, characters, and even a "secret mission" concoction for the more daring. ⊠ *Carrer Aribau 143, Eixample* ☎ *93/164–3625* Ⓜ *Hospital Clínic, Diagonal.*

DANCE CLUBS

Antilla Salsa Barcelona (*Antilla Salsa Barcelona*). You'll find this exuberant Caribbean spot sizzling with salsa, son cubano, and merengue from the moment you step in the door. From 10 to 11 on Wednesday, enthusiastic dance instructors teach bachata for free. After that, the dancing begins and the dancers rarely stop to draw breath. This self-proclaimed "Caribbean cultural center" cranks out every variation of salsa ever invented. There are regular live concerts, and on Friday and Saturday, the mike gives way to animated Latin DJs. ⊠ *Aragó 141, Eixample* ☎ *610/900588 (between 4 pm and 11 pm)* ⊕ *www.antillasalsa. com* Ⓜ *Urgell, Hospital Clínic.*

Bikini Barcelona. This sleek megaclub, which was reborn as part of L'Illa shopping center, boasts the best sound system in Barcelona. A smaller space puts on concerts of emerging and cult artists—the Nigerian singer-songwriter Asa, local soulsters The Pepper Pots, and Gil Scott-Heron in one of his final performances are just some of the noteworthy events here. When gigs finish around midnight, the walls roll back and the space ingeniously turns into a sweaty nightclub. ⊠ *Diagonal 547, Eixample* ☎ *93/322–0800* ⊕ *www.bikinibcn.com* Ⓜ *Maria Cristina.*

Luz de Gas. Luz de Gas, an ornate 19th-century theater, offers everything from live performances (mostly world music and Latin) to wild late-night dancing (expect soul and standards). ⊠ *Muntaner 246, Eixample* ☎ *93/209–7711* ⊕ *www.luzdegas.com* Ⓜ *Muntaner, Diagonal.*

Otto Zutz. Just off Vía Augusta above Diagonal, this nightclub and disco (dating back to 1985) is a perennial Barcelona favorite that keeps attracting a glitzy mix of Barcelona movers and shakers, models, ex-models, wannabe models, and the hoping-to-get-lucky mob that predictably follows this sort of pulchritude. Hip-hop, house, and Latin make up the standard soundtrack on the dance floor, with more mellow notes upstairs and in the coveted Altos Club Privé (or "VIP section," to the rest of us). ⊠ *Lincoln 15, Eixample* ☎ *93/238–0722 office* ⊕ *www. ottozutz.com* Ⓜ *Sant Gervasi, Gràcia.*

GRÀCIA

BARS

Fodor's Choice ★

Elephanta. Diminutive in size but huge in personality and warmth, Elephanta is that rare neighborhood spot that offers a little something for everyone. Patrons enjoy an extensive menu (printed on authentic vinyl covers) of quality gins and seasonal fruity cocktails in a dimly lighted retro space peppered with comfy mismatched furnishings and India-inspired decor. Music varies though the ambience is always chill; perfect for laptop lounging or hosted cultural screenings. ⊠ *Torrent d'en Vidalet 37, Gràcia* ☎ *93/237–6906* ⊕ *elephanta.cat* Ⓜ *Joanic.*

Ítaca. This contemporary cervecería resembles many of the cool offerings routinely sprouting up in Gràcia, one of the city's most popular neighborhoods. Patrons can top off drinks with self-service pours from local brewer Estrella Damm. Local craft favorites such as Brew Dog Punk IPA and classic cocktails are also on offer. Enjoy a drink with nachos, burgers, and tapas while listening to local tunes around the tiny, natural-wood bar. ⊠ *Santa Rosa 14, Gràcia* ☎ *93/013–1047* ⊕ *www. grupitaca.cat* Ⓜ *Fontana.*

Fodor'sChoice
★
Old Fashioned. Reminiscent of a '50s-style gin joint—black and white with red quilted booths and framed prints—this small-but-swanky bar regularly draws in the crowds due in large part to entertaining master mixologists (nattily dressed in suspenders and ties) and their out-of-this-world experimental takes on cocktail classics. Try a Fashionista, the house special prepared with bourbon, sherry, and hazelnuts, among other ingredients, and flambéed with a blowtorch. Other playfully named concoctions include Anything Goes and Run to Your Mama. ⊠ *Carrer de Santa Teresa 1, Gràcia* ☎ *93/368–5277* Ⓜ *Diagonal.*

Fodor'sChoice
★
Viblioteca. Adding a little uptown pizzazz to boho-chic enclave Gràcia, this diminutive, minimalist, white-walled wine bar and eatery is the local "it" vintage. Wines sourced and served with engaging backstories can be sampled at the seven-seater bar or at a table, accompanied by a large assortment of cured meats, cheeses, and salads or with a few choice liquors. Advance booking is highly recommended. ⊠ *Vallfogona 12, Gràcia* ☎ *93/284–4202* ⊕ *www.viblioteca.com* Ⓜ *Fontana.*

POBLENOU

BARS

Fodor'sChoice
★
Balius Bar. Named after the historic hardware store that once stood here, Balius Bar has retro-chic decor, a snazzy playlist (don't miss the live jazz sessions on Sunday), and a puckish "no standing" policy that attract hepcats aged 30 and above looking to kick back with a good cocktail and a side of nostalgia. Afternoons are reserved for vermouth and all the fixings or a chilled cava cocktail paired with fresh, often eco-conscious, bites. In the evenings, creative cocktails are the main draw; try a Cusco Maki, a tangy mixture of pisco, elderflower, and red berries with a splash of lemon. If you're lucky, you might also get a Lindy lesson or two. ⊠ *Carrer de Pujades 196, Poblenou* ☎ *93/315–8650* ⊕ *baliusbar. com* Ⓜ *Poblenou.*

MUSIC CLUBS

Sala Razzmatazz. This mega industrial warehouse turned dance club and concert hall features five distinct clubs in one: Razz Club plays indie rock; The Loft and Lo·li·ta are all about techno and electronica; and smaller, more relaxed venues Pop Bar and Rex Bar focus on experimental electro pop and indie electro, respectively. Resident DJs play nightly though entrance tickets (including one drink) will set you back €12–€20 (cheaper if you buy online), depending on the live act selected. Despite a casual dress code and a party scene seldom pumping before 3 am, expect long lines to get in on the weekends. ⊠ *Almogàvers 122, Poblenou* ☎ *93/320–8200* ⊕ *www.salarazzmatazz.com* Ⓜ *Marina, Bogatell.*

POBLE SEC

BARS

Fodor'sChoice
★
Jonny Aldana. This cheery technicolor bar-resto, featuring a tiled facade and open-window bar with stools inside and out, is bursting with 1950s iconography and blackboards that demand your attention. Wines are sold by the glass, beer is served from the tap, but it's the superb

vermouths and cocktails combined with veggie and vegan tapas that reel in patrons. Local DJs spin on certain nights. ⊠ *Carrer d'Aldana 9, Poble Sec* ☎ *93/174–2083* ⊕ *www.jonnyaldana.com* Ⓜ *Paral.lel.*

Fodor'sChoice **Xix Bar and Gin Corner.** The interior of this Alice in Wonderland–like
★ venue of checkered half-walls, a marble bar, and contempo objets d'art rarely seen on ceilings is the first clue that you've landed somewhere special. Beyond that, with 50-plus flavors of gins and infusions on offer—ranging from spicy ginger to tarty chocolate—an ultra-knowledgeable bar staff, and a lounge-friendly 3 am curfew on weekends, Xix turns conventional cocktail drinkers into card-carrying gin lovers. ⊠ *Carrer de Rocafort 19, Poble Sec* ☎ *93/423–4314* ⊕ *www.xixbar. com* Ⓜ *Poble Sec.*

PERFORMING ARTS

CASTELLERS AND SARDANAS

The Sunday-morning papers carry announcements for local neighborhood celebrations, flea markets and produce fairs, puppet shows, storytelling sessions for children, sardana folk dancing, bell-ringing concerts, and, best of all, *castellers* (⊕ *www.bcn.es* has listings in English). These complex human pyramids, sometimes reaching as high as 10 stories, are a quintessentially Catalan phenomenon that originated in the 17th century, in the Penedès region west of Barcelona. Castellers perform regularly at neighborhood fiestas and key holidays: in Plaça Sant Jaume during the Festes de la Mercé on Sunday in late September, in Sarrià during the Festes de Sarrià in early October, in Plaça Sant Jaume during the Festes de Santa Eulàlia in February, and during other big feast days during the year. Sardanas are performed in front of the Catedral de la Seu at 1 pm on weekends.

CONCERTS

The basílica of Santa Maria del Mar, the church of Santa Maria del Pi, the Monestir de Pedralbes, Drassanes Reials, and the Saló del Tinell, among other ancient and intimate spaces, all hold concerts.

EIXAMPLE

L'Auditori de Barcelona. Functional, sleek, and minimalist, the Rafael Moneo–designed Auditori has a full calendar of classical music performances—with regular forays into jazz, flamenco, and pop—near Plaça de les Glòries. Orchestras that perform here include the Orquestra Simfònica de Barcelona i Nacional de Catalunya (OBC) and the Orquestra Nacional de Cambra de Andorra. The excellent Museu de la Música is on the first floor. ⊠ *Lepant 150, Eixample* ☎ *93/247–9300* ⊕ *www. auditori.cat* Ⓜ *Marina, Monumental, Glòries.*

DANCE

Ballet troupes, both local and from abroad, perform at the Liceu opera house with some regularity; contemporary dance troupes perform in a variety of theaters around town. The Mercat de les Flors theater is the city's main dance center.

POBLE SEC

El Mercat de les Flors. An old flower market converted into a modern performance space, theater, and dance school, the Mercat de Les Flors forms part of the Institut de Teatre and is set on lovely, expansive grounds at the foot of verdant Montjuïc. Modern dance is the mercat's raison d'être, and it remains one of the few theaters in Spain that is exclusively dedicated to contemporary dance. The on-site café has a terrace out on the square, ideal for pre- or post-performance drinks. ✉ *Lleida 59, Poble Sec* ☎ *93/426–1875* ⊕ *mercatflors.cat* Ⓜ *Poble Sec, Espanya.*

FILM

Though many foreign films are dubbed, Barcelona has a full complement of original-language cinema; look for listings marked *v.o.* (*versión original*).

EIXAMPLE

Renoir Floridablanca. A five-minute walk from the Plaça de la Universitat, this cinema is a good choice for current English-language features, primarily of the indie ilk. ✉ *Floridablanca 135, Eixample* ☎ *93/228–9393* ⊕ *www.cinesrenoir.com* Ⓜ *Universitat, Sant Antoni.*

GRÀCIA

Cines Verdi. Gràcia's movie center, with bars and restaurants in the immediate vicinity, unfailingly screens recent releases (with a preference for serious-minded cinema) in their original-language versions. Sister cinema Verdi Park is just around the corner, and also shows films in VOS (original version with Spanish subs). ✉ *Verdi 32, Gràcia* ☎ *93/238–7990* ⊕ *www.cines-verdi.com/barcelona* Ⓜ *Gràcia, Fontana.*

PORT OLÍMPIC

Icaria Yelmo. On the lower level of a small neighborhood shopping mall, the Icaria Yelmo offers a solid mix of blockbusters, 3-D specials, and the latest releases in in their original language, though sometimes weeks after their general premieres. ✉ *Salvador Espriu 61, Port Olímpic* ☎ *902/220922* ⊕ *www.yelmocines.es* Ⓜ *Ciutadella–Vila Olímpica.*

FLAMENCO

In Catalonia, flamenco, like bullfighting, is regarded as an import from Andalusia. However, unlike bullfighting, there is a strong interest in and market for flamenco in Barcelona.

BARRI GÒTIC

Los Tarantos. This small basement boîte spotlights some of Andalusia's best flamenco in 30-minute shows of dance, percussion, and song. At only €15 per ticket, these shows are a good intro to the art and feel much less touristy than most standard flamenco fare. Shows are daily at 7:30, 8:30, and 9:30 pm, with an additional 10:30 pm show June–September. ✉ *Pl. Reial 17, Barri Gòtic* ☎ *93/319–1789* ⊕ *www.masimas.com/en/tarantos* Ⓜ *Liceu.*

MONTJUÏC

El Tablao de Carmen. Large tour groups come to this venerable flamenco dinner-theater venue in the Poble Espanyol named after, and dedicated to, the legendary dancer Carmen Amaya. Die-hard flamenco aficionados might dismiss the ensembles that perform here as a tad touristy, but the dancers, singers, and guitarists are pros. Visitors can enjoy one of the two nightly performances over a drink or over their choice of a full-course, prix-fixe meal. Reservations are recommended. Dinner shows are held daily at 6 pm and 8:30 pm. ⊠ *Poble Espanyol, Av. Francesc Ferrer i Guàrdia 13, Montjuïc* 🕾 *93/325–6895* ⊕ *www.tablaodecarmen. com* Ⓜ *Espanya.*

THEATER
EIXAMPLE
Teatre Nacional de Catalunya. Near Glòries, the area with the highest concentration of development in recent years at the eastern end of the Diagonal, this grandiose glass-enclosed classical temple was designed by Ricardo Bofill, architect of Barcelona's airport. Programs cover everything from Shakespeare to avant-garde theater. Most productions, as the name suggests, are in Catalan but beautiful to witness all the same. ⊠ *Pl. de les Arts 1, Eixample* 🕾 *93/306–5700* ⊕ *www.tnc.cat* Ⓜ *Glòries, Monumental.*

POBLE SEC
El Molino. For most of the 20th century, this venue was the most legendary of all the cabaret theaters on Avinguda Paral·lel. Modeled after Paris's Moulin Rouge, it closed in the late 1990s as the building was becoming dangerously run-down. After an ambitious refurbishment in 2010, El Molino reopened as one of the most stunning state-of-the-art cabaret theaters in Europe. The building now has five—instead of the original two—stories, with a bar and terrace on the third. What has remained the same, however, is its essence—a contemporary version of burlesque, but bump-and-grind all the same. You can purchase tickets online or before performances (which usually start at 9:30 pm). ⊠ *Vilà i Vilà 99, Poble Sec* 🕾 *93/205–5111* ⊕ *www.elmolinobcn.com* Ⓜ *Paral.lel.*

SHOPPING

Between the surging fashion scene, a host of young clothing designers, clever home furnishings, rare and delicious foodstuffs, and art and antiques, Barcelona might just be the best place in Spain to unload extra ballast from your wallet.

SHOPPING DISTRICTS
Barcelona's prime shopping districts are the Passeig de Gràcia, Rambla de Catalunya, Plaça de Catalunya, Porta de l'Àngel, and Avinguda Diagonal up to Carrer Ganduxer.

For high fashion, browse along **Passeig de Gràcia** and **Rambla de Catalunya** and along the **Diagonal** between Plaça Joan Carles I and Plaça Francesc Macià. **Bulevard Rosa** is a fashion and shopping mall off Passeig de Gràcia. For old-fashioned Spanish shops, prowl the Barri Gòtic, especially **Carrer Ferran.** The area surrounding **Plaça del Pi,** from the Boqueria to Carrer Portaferrissa and Carrer de la Canuda, is thick with boutiques, jewelers, and design shops. The **Barri de la Ribera,** around Santa Maria del Mar, especially the Born area, has a cluster of design, fashion, and food shops. Design, jewelry, and knickknacks shops cluster on Carrer Banys Vells and Carrer Flassaders, near Carrer Montcada. The place to go for antiques is the Barri Gòtic, where **Carrer de la Palla** and **Carrer Banys Nous** are lined with shops full of prints, maps, books, paintings, and furniture. An antiques market is held in front of the Catedral de la Seu every Thursday 10–8. **Carrer Tuset**, north of the Diagonal, has lots of small boutiques. The **Maremagnum** mall, in Port Vell, is convenient to downtown. **Diagonal Mar**, at the eastern end of the Diagonal, and the **Fòrum** complex offer many shopping options in a mega–shopping mall environment. **Les Arenes**, the former bullring at Plaça Espanya, has reopened as a shopping mall with FNAC, Mango, Desigual, and Sephora among other stores, as well as 12 movie theaters, restaurants, and the Museu del Rock. **Carrer Lledó**, just off Plaça Sant Just, in the Barri Gòtic behind Plaça Sant Jaume, is a lovely little street lined with shops selling clothes, gifts, and design items. For art, browse the cluster of galleries on **Carrer Consell de Cent** between Passeig de Gràcia and Carrer Balmes and around the corner on La Rambla de Catalunya. The Santa Maria del Mar quarter is another art destination, along Carrer Montcada and the parallel Carrer Banys Vells.

Not to be overlooked are Barcelona's many street markets and fairs. On Thursday, a natural-produce market (honey, cheese) fills Plaça del Pi with interesting tastes and aromas. On Sunday morning, Plaça Reial hosts a stamp and coin market, Plaça Sant Josep Oriol holds a painter's market, and there is a general crafts and flea market near the Columbus Monument at the port end of La Rambla. Sarrià holds a farmers' market with excellent cheeses, sausages, cavas, and vegetables from the Catalonian hinterlands in Plaça de Sarrià on the second and fourth Sunday of every month.

BARRI GÒTIC

ART GALLERIES

Sala Parès. The dean of Barcelona's art galleries, this place opened in 1840 as an art-supplies shop; as a gallery, it dates to 1877 and has shown every Barcelona artist of note since then. Picasso and Miró exhibited their work here, as did Casas and Rossinyol before them. Nowadays, Catalan artists like Perico Pastor and Carlos Morago get pride of place. ⊠ *Petritxol 5, Barri Gòtic* ☎ *93/318–7020* ⊕ *salapares. com* Ⓜ *Liceu, Catalunya.*

BOOKS AND STATIONERY

Papirvm. Exquisite hand-printed papers, marbleized blank books, and writing implements await you at this tiny, medieval-tone shop. ⊠ *Baixada de la Llibreteria 2, Barri Gòtic* ☎ *93/310–5242* ⊕ *papirumbcn.com* Ⓜ *Jaume I.*

CERAMICS

Fodor's Choice ★ **Art Escudellers.** Ceramic pieces from all over Spain are on display at this large store across the street from the restaurant Los Caracoles; more than 140 different artisans are represented, with maps showing what part of Spain the work is from. Wine, cheese, and ham tastings are held downstairs, and you can even throw a pot yourself in the workshop. There are four other branches of Art Escudellers in the old city, including one on the Carrer Avinyó. ⊠ *Escudellers 23–25, Barri Gòtic* ☎ *93/412–6801* ⊕ *www.artescudellers.com* Ⓜ *Liceu, Drassanes.*

CLOTHING

L'Arca. This store sells vintage clothing, fabrics, and accessories, with a focus on wedding dresses, veils, and lace. Despite the found-object attitude and ambience of the place, they're not giving away these vintage baubles, so don't be surprised at the hefty price tags. You'll also find a collection of their own bridal gowns, newly made but in romantic, old-fashioned styles. ⊠ *Banys Nous 20, Barri Gòtic* ☎ *93/302–1598* ⊕ *www.larca.es* Ⓜ *Liceu.*

FOOD

Caelum. At the corner of Carrer de la Palla and Banys Nous, this café and shop sells wines and foodstuffs such as honey, biscuits, chocolates, and preserves made in convents and monasteries all over Spain. You can pop in to pick up an exquisitely packaged pot of jam, or linger longer in the tearoom, part of which is housed in an old medieval bathhouse. ⊠ *De la Palla 8, Barri Gòtic* ☎ *93/302–6993* ⊕ *www.caelumbarcelona. com* Ⓜ *Liceu, Jaume I.*

Formatgeria La Seu. Scotswoman Katherine McLaughlin has put together the Gothic Quarter's most delightful cheese-tasting sanctuary on the site of an ancient buttery. (A 19th-century butter churn is visible in the back room.) A dozen artisanal cow, goat, and sheep cheeses from all over Spain, and olive oils, can be tasted and taken home. La Seu is named for both La Seu cathedral, as the "seat" of cheeses, and for cheese-rich La Seu d'Urgell in the Pyrenees. Katherine's wrapping paper, imaginatively chosen sheets of newspaper, gives a final flourish to purchases. ⊠ *Dagueria 16, Barri Gòtic* ☎ *93/412–6548* ⊕ *www.formatgerialaseu.com* Ⓜ *Jaume I.*

MARKETS

Mercat Gòtic. A browser's bonanza, this interesting if somewhat pricey Thursday market for antique clothing, jewelry, and art objects occupies the plaza in front of the cathedral. ⊠ *Pl. Nova, Barri Gòtic* Ⓜ *Jaume I, Urquinaona.*

SHOES

Fodor'sChoice
★

La Manual Alpargatera. If you appreciate old-school craftsmanship in footwear and reasonable prices, visit this boutique just off Carrer Ferran. Handmade rope-sole sandals and espadrilles are the specialty, and this shop has sold them to everyone—including the Pope. The flat, beribboned espadrilles model used for dancing the sardana is available, as are fashionable wedge heels with peep toes and comfy slippers. The cost of a pair of espadrilles here might put you back about $35, which is far less than the same quality shoes in the United States. ⊠ *Avinyó 7, Barri Gòtic* ☎ *93/301–0172* ⊕ *www.lamanualalpargatera.es* Ⓜ *Liceu, Jaume I.*

BORN-RIBERA

CLOTHING AND JEWELRY

Coquette. Coquette specializes in understated feminine beauty. The now three shops (two in the Born, one uptown) present a small, careful selection of mainly French designers, like Sueur, Des Petits Hauts, and Spain's own Hoss Intrópia. Whether it's a romantic or a seductive look you're after, Coquette makes sure you'll feel both comfortable and irresistible. With an industrial-chic decor, Coquette's boutique in Carrer Bonaire (which also has men's fashion) presents the largest selection. There is another one around the corner at Carrer Rec 65, and the uptown branch is at Carrer dels Madrazo 153 (Sant Gervasi). ⊠ *Bonaire 5, Born-Ribera* ☎ *93/310–3535* ⊕ *coquettebcn.com* Ⓜ *Jaume I.*

Custo Barcelona. Ever since Custido Dalmau and his brother David returned from a round-the-world motorcycle tour with visions of California surfing styles dancing in their heads, Custo Barcelona has been a runaway success with its clingy cotton tops in bright and cheery hues. Now with three branches in Barcelona (including an outlet shop at Plaça del Pi 2, in the Barri Gòtic) and many more across the globe, Custo is scoring even more acclaim by expanding into coats, dresses, and kids' wear. ⊠ *Pl. de les Olles 7, Born-Ribera* ☎ *93/268–7893* ⊕ *www.custo.com* Ⓜ *Jaume I.*

FOOD AND WINE

Fodor'sChoice
★
Casa Gispert. On the inland side of Santa Maria del Mar, this shop is one of the most aromatic and picturesque in Barcelona, bursting with teas, coffees, spices, saffron, chocolates, and nuts. The star element in this olfactory and picturesque feast is an almond-roasting stove in the back of the store—purportedly the oldest in Europe, dating from 1851 like the store itself. Don't miss the acid engravings on the office windows or the ancient wooden back door before picking up a bag of freshly roasted nuts to take with you. ⊠ *Sombrerers 23, Born-Ribera* ☎ *93/319–7535* ⊕ *www.casagispert.com* Ⓜ *Jaume I.*

El Magnífico. Just up the street from Santa Maria del Mar, this coffee emporium is famous for its sacks of coffee beans from all over the globe. Coffee to go is also available—enjoy it on the little bench outside. ⊠ *Carrer Argenteria 64, Born-Ribera* ☎ *93/319–3975* ⊕ *www. cafeselmagnifico.com* Ⓜ *Jaume I.*

La Botifarreria de Santa Maria. This busy emporium next to the church of Santa Maria del Mar stocks excellent cheeses, hams, pâtés, and home-made *sobrassadas* (pork pâté with paprika). Botifarra is the main item here, with a wide range of varieties, including egg sausage for meatless Lent and sausage stuffed with spinach, asparagus, cider, cinnamon, and Cabrales cheese. ⊠ *Santa Maria 4, Born-Ribera* ☎ *93/319–9123* ⊕ *www.labotifarreria.com* Ⓜ *Jaume I.*

Pastelería Hofmann. The late Mey Hofmann, a constellation in Barcelona's gourmet galaxy for the last three decades through her restaurant and cooking courses, established this sideline dedicated exclusively to pastry. Everything from the lightest, flakiest croissants to the cakes, tarts, and ice creams are about as good they get in this sweets emporium just off the Passeig del Born. ⊠ *Flassaders 44, Born-Ribera* ☎ *93/268–8221* ⊕ *www.hofmann-bcn.com* Ⓜ *Jaume I.*

Fodor'sChoice
★
Vila Viniteca. Near Santa Maria del Mar, this is perhaps the best wine treasury in Barcelona, with a truly massive catalogue, tastings, courses, and a panoply of events, including a hugely popular street party to welcome in new-harvest wines (usually late October or early November). Under the same ownership, the tiny grocery store next door offers exquisite artisanal cheeses ranging from French goat cheese to Extremadura's famous Torta del Casar. There are a few tables inside, and, for a corkage fee, you can

enjoy a bottle of wine together with a tasting platter. ⊠ *Agullers 7, Born-Ribera* ☎ *93/777–7017* ⊕ *www.vilaviniteca.es* Ⓜ *Jaume I.*

EL RAVAL

BOOKS

La Central del Raval. This luscious bookstore in the former chapel of the Casa de la Misericòrdia sells books amid stunning architecture and holds regular cultural events. ⊠ *Elisabets 6, El Raval* ☎ *900/802109* ⊕ *www.lacentral.com* Ⓜ *Catalunya.*

EIXAMPLE

ANTIQUES

Bulevard dels Antiquaris. Look carefully for the stairway leading one flight up to this 73-store antiques arcade off Passeig de Gràcia. You never know what you might find: dolls, icons, Roman or Visigothic objects, paintings, furniture, cricket kits, fly rods, or toys from a century ago. Haggling is common practice—but Catalan antiques dealers are tough nuts to crack. ⊠ *Passeig de Gràcia 55, Eixample* ☎ *93/215–4499* ⊕ *www.bulevarddelsantiquaris.com* Ⓜ *Passeig de Gràcia.*

ART GALLERIES

Galeria Joan Prats. "La Prats" has been one of the city's top galleries since the 1920s, showing international painters and sculptors from Henry Moore to Antoni Tàpies. Barcelona painter Joan Miró was a prime force in the founding of the gallery when he became friends with Joan Prats. The motifs of bonnets and derbies on the gallery's facade are callbacks to the trade of Prats's father. José Maria Sicilia and Juan Ugalde have shown here, while Erick Beltrán, Hannah Collins, and Eulàlia Valldosera are among the regular artists on display. ⊠ *Balmes 54, Eixample* ☎ *93/216–0290* ⊕ *www.galeriajoanprats.com* Ⓜ *Passeig de Gràcia.*

Joan Gaspar. One of Barcelona's most prestigious galleries, Joan Gaspar and his father before him brought Picasso and Miró back to Catalonia during the '50s and '60s, along with other artists considered politically taboo during the Franco regime. These days you'll find leading contemporary lights such as Joan Pere Viladecans, Rafols Casamada, or Susana Solano here. ⊠ *Pl. Dr. Letamendi 1, Eixample* ☎ *93/323–0748* ⊕ *www.galeriajoangaspar.com* Ⓜ *Universitat, Provença.*

Sala Dalmau. An old-timer in the established Consell de Cent gallery scene, Sala Dalmau shows an interesting and heterodox range of Catalan and international artists. ⊠ *Consell de Cent 349, Eixample* ☎ *93/215–4592* ⊕ *www.saladalmau.com* Ⓜ *Passeig de Gràcia.*

BOOKS

Casa del Llibre. On Barcelona's most important shopping street, Casa del Llibre is a major book feast with a wide variety of English titles. ⊠ *Passeig de Gràcia 62, Eixample* ☎ *902/026407* ⊕ *www.casadellibro. com* Ⓜ *Passeig de Gràcia.*

CERAMICS

Fodor's Choice ★ **Lladró.** This Valencia company is famed worldwide for the beauty and quality of its figures. Barcelona's only Lladró factory store, this location has exclusive pieces of work, custom-designed luxury items of gold and porcelain, and classic and original works. Look for the cheeky figurines by Jaime Hayon, a Spanish designer, and the spectacular chandeliers by Bodo Sperlein. ⊠ *Passeig de Gràcia 101, Eixample* ☎ *93/270–1253* ⊕ *www.lladro.com* Ⓜ *Diagonal.*

CLOTHING

Adolfo Domínguez. One of Barcelona's longtime fashion giants, this is one of Spain's leading clothing designers, with many locations around town. Famed as the creator of the Iberia Airlines uniforms, Adolfo Domínguez has been in the not-too-radical mainstream of Spanish couture for the past quarter century. ⊠ *Passeig de Gràcia 32, Eixample* ☎ *93/487–4170* ⊕ *www.adolfodominguez.com* Ⓜ *Passeig de Gràcia.*

Fodor's Choice ★ **Cortana.** A sleek and breezy Balearic Islands look for women is what this designer from Mallorca brings to the fashion scene of urban Barcelona in a whitewashed shop reminiscent of an art gallery. Her dresses transmit a casual, minimalistic elegance and have graced many a red carpet all over Spain. ⊠ *Provença 290, Eixample* ☎ *93/487–2070* ⊕ *www. cortana.es* Ⓜ *Provença.*

Loewe. Occupying the ground floor of Lluís Domènech i Montaner's Casa Lleó Morera, Loewe is Spain's answer to Hermès, a classical clothing and leather emporium for men's and women's fashions and luxurious handbags that whisper status (at eye-popping prices). ⊠ *Passeig de Gràcia 35, Eixample* ☎ *93/216–0400* ⊕ *www.loewe.com* Ⓜ *Passeig de Gràcia.*

Fodor's Choice ★ **The Outpost.** A shop dedicated exclusively to men's accessories of the finest kind, the Outpost was created by a former Prada buyer who considers it his mission to bring stylishness to Barcelona men with this oasis of avant-garde fashion. The constantly changing window displays are works of art, providing a first taste of what's to be found inside: Robert Clegerie shoes, Albert Thurston suspenders, Roland Pineau belts, Yves Andrieux hats, Balenciaga ties. You enter the Outpost as a mere mortal, but leave it as a gentleman—provided you carry the necessary cash. ⊠ *Rosselló 281, bis, Eixample* ☎ *93/457–7137* ⊕ *www.theoutpostbcn. com* Ⓜ *Diagonal, Verdaguer.*

Purificación García. Known as a gifted fabric expert whose creations are invariably based on the qualities and characteristics of her raw materials, Galicia-born Purificación García enjoys solid prestige in Barcelona. Understated hues and subtle combinations of colors and shapes place this contemporary designer squarely in the camp of the less-is-more school, and, although her women's range is larger and more diverse, she understands men's tailoring. ⊠ *Provença 292, Eixample* ☎ *93/496–1336* ⊕ *www.purificaciongarcia.com* Ⓜ *Diagonal.*

Sita Murt. The local Catalan designer Sita Murt produces smart, grown-up women's wear under her own label in this minimalist space in the Eixample. Colorful chiffon dresses and light, gauzy tops and knits characterize this line of clothing popular with professional women and wedding goers. ✉ *Mallorca 242, Eixample* ☎ *93/215–2231* ⊕ *www. sitamurt.com* Ⓜ *Passeig de Gràcia, Diagonal.*

DEPARTMENT STORES

El Corte Inglés. Iconic and ubiquitous, this Spanish department store has its main Barcelona branch on Plaça de Catalunya, with two annexes close by: one directly opposite selling midpriced ladies' fashion and another in Porta de l'Àngel for younger fashion and sporting goods. You can find just about anything here—clothing, shoes, perfumes, electronics—and there is a wonderful supermarket and food mall on the lower-ground floor. With branches in all major cities, El Corte Inglés is Spain's only large department store and has leagues of heritage fans. Service is inconsistent, but the sale season in August is worth fighting the crowds for. ✉ *Pl. de Catalunya 14, Eixample* ☎ *93/306–3800* ⊕ *www. elcorteingles.es* Ⓜ *Catalunya* ✉ *Av. Diagonal 617, Diagonal Mar* ☎ *93/366–7100* Ⓜ *Maria Cristina* ✉ *Av. Diagonal 471, Pl. Francesc Macia, Eixample* ☎ *93/493–4800* Ⓜ *Hospital Clinic* ✉ *Portal de l'Àngel 19–21, Barri Gòtic* ☎ *93/306–3800* ⊕ *elcorteingles.es* Ⓜ *Catalunya.*

GIFTS AND SOUVENIRS

Jaime Beriestain Concept Store. The concept store of one of the city's hottest interior designers provides mere mortals the chance to appreciate the Beriestain groove. Reflecting his hotel and restaurant projects, the shop offers an exciting mixture of midcentury modern classics and new design pieces, peppered with freshly cut flowers (also for sale), French candles, handmade stationery, and the latest international design and architecture magazines to dress up your coffee table. The in-store café is worth a visit. ✉ *Pau Claris 167, Eixample* ☎ *93/515–0779* ⊕ *www. beriestain.com* Ⓜ *Diagonal.*

MARKETS

Els Encants Vells. One of Europe's oldest flea markets, Els Encants has a new home—a stunning, glittering metal canopy that protects the rag-and-bone merchants (and their keen customers) from the elements. Stalls, and a handful of stand-up bars, have become a bit more upmarket, too, although you'll still find plenty of oddities to barter over in the central plaza. Saturday is the busiest day—try going on the weekdays that it's open for a more relaxed rummage around this fascinating slice of urban history. ✉ *Av. Meridiana 69, Pl. de Les Glóries Catalans, Eixample* ☎ *93/246–3030* ⊕ *encantsbcn.com/en* Ⓜ *Glòries.*

POBLENOU

HOUSEHOLD ITEMS AND FURNITURE

BD. Barcelona Design, a spare, cutting-edge furniture and home-accessories store, has moved into a former industrial building near the sea. BD cofounder Oscar Tusquets, master designer and architect, gives contemporary-design star Jaime Hayon plenty of space here. The works of past giants, such as Gaudí's Casa Calvet chair, or Salvador Dalí's Gala loveseat, are also available—if your pockets are deep enough. It's not open on weekends. ✉ *Ramón Turró 126, Poblenou* ☎ *93/458–6909* ⊕ *bdbarcelona.com* Ⓜ *Llacuna, Bogatell.*

CATALONIA, VALENCIA, AND THE COSTA BLANCA

WELCOME TO CATALONIA, VALENCIA, AND THE COSTA BLANCA

TOP REASONS TO GO

★ **Girona:** Explore a city where the monuments of Christian, Jewish, and Islamic cultures that coexisted for centuries are just steps apart.

★ **Valencia reborn:** The city has seen a transformation of the Turia River into a treasure trove of museums, concert halls, parks, and architectural wonders.

★ **Great restaurants:** Foodies argue that the fountainhead of creative gastronomy has moved from France to Spain—and in particular to the great restaurants of the Empordà and Costa Brava.

★ **Dalí's home and museum:** "Surreal" doesn't begin to describe the Teatre-Museu Dalí in Figueres or the wild coast of the artist's home at Cap de Creus.

★ **Las Fallas festival:** Valencia's Las Fallas in mid-March, a week of fireworks and solemn processions with a finale of spectacular bonfires, is one of the best festivals in Europe.

Year-round, Catalonia is the most visited of Spain's autonomous communities. The Pyrenees, which separate it from France, provide some of the country's best skiing, and the rugged Costa Brava in the north and the Costa Daurada to the south are havens for sunseekers. Excellent rail, air, and highway connections link Catalonia to the beach resorts of Valencia, its neighbor to the south.

1 Northern Catalonia. Inland and westward from the towns of Girona and Figueres is perhaps the most dramatic and beautiful part of old Catalonia; it's a land of medieval villages and hilltop monasteries, volcanic landscapes, and lush green valleys. The ancient city of Girona is an easy day trip from Barcelona. The upland towns of Besalú and Vic are Catalonia at its most authentic.

2 The Costa Brava. Native son Salvador Dalí put his mark on the northeastern-most corner of Catalonia, where the Costa Brava begins, especially in the fishing village of Cadaqués and the coast of Cap de Creus. From here, south and west toward Barcelona, lie beaches, historical

settlements, and picturesque towns like Sant Feliu de Guixols.

3 Southern Catalonia and Around Valencia. Spain's third-largest city, rich in history and tradition, Valencia is now a cultural magnet for its modern art museum and its space-age City of Arts and Sciences complex. The Albufera Nature Park to the south is an important wetland and wildlife sanctuary. North of Valencia, the monastery of Montserrat is a popular pilgrimage; Sitges has a lovely beach, and Santes Creus and Poblet are beautiful Cistercian monasteries. Roman ruins, chief among them the Circus Maximus, are the reason to go to Tarragona.

4 The Costa Blanca. Culturally and geographically diverse, the Costa Blanca's most populated coastal resorts stretch north from the provincial capital of Alicante to Dénia. Dénia, capital of the Marina Alta region and a port for ferries to the Balearic Islands, has a well-deserved reputation for gastronomy, while Alicante's historic center and vibrant night-owl scene occupy the hub of a rich agricultural area.

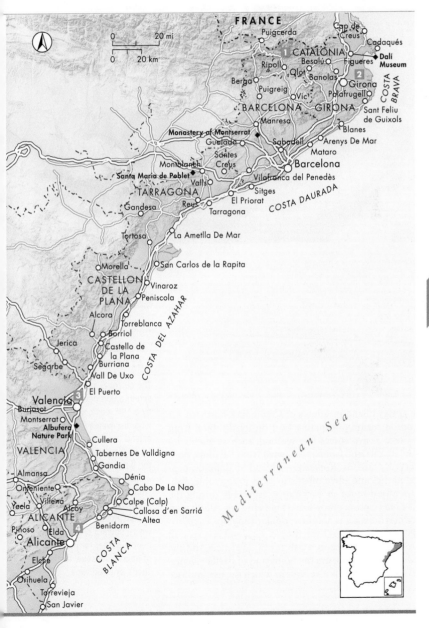

8

EATING AND DRINKING WELL IN CATALONIA, VALENCIA, AND THE COSTA BLANCA

Cuisine in both Catalonia and Valencia includes classic Mediterranean dishes, and Catalans feel right at home with *paella valenciana* (Valencian paella). Fish preparations are similar along the coast, though inland favorites vary from place to place.

Top left: Paella valenciana in a classic paella pan; Top right: Fresh calçots; Bottom right: Suquet of fish, potatoes, onions, and tomatoes

The grassy inland meadows of Catalonia's northern Alt Empordà region put quality beef on local tables; from the Costa Brava comes fine seafood, such as anchovies from L'Escala and *gambas* (prawns) from Palamós, both deservedly famous. *Romesco*—a blend of almonds, peppers, garlic, and olive oil—is used as a vegetable, fish, and seafood sauce in Tarragona, especially during the *calçotadas* (spring onion feasts) in February. *Allioli*, garlicky mayonnaise, is another popular topping. The Ebro Delta is renowned for fresh fish, oysters, and eels, as well as *rossejat* (fried rice in a fish broth). Valencia and the Mediterranean coast are the homeland of paella valenciana. *Arròs a banda* is a variant in which the fish and rice are cooked separately.

CALÇOTS

The *calçot* is a sweet spring onion developed by a 19th-century farmer who discovered how to extend the edible portion by packing soil around the base. It is grilled on a barbecue, then peeled and dipped into romesco sauce. In January, the town of Valls holds a *calçotada* where upward of 30,000 people gather for meals of onions, sausage, lamb chops, and red wine.

RICE

Paella valenciana is one of Spain's most famous gastronomic contributions. A simple country dish dating to the early 18th century, "paella" refers to the wide frying pan with short, sturdy handles that's used to cook the rice. Anything fresh from the fields that day, along with rice and olive oil, traditionally went into the pan, but paella valenciana has particular ingredients: short-grain rice, chicken, rabbit, *garrofó* (a local legume), tomatoes, green beans, sweet peppers, olive oil, and saffron. Artichokes and peas are also included in season. *Paella marinera* (seafood paella) is a different story: rice, cuttlefish, squid, mussels, shrimp, prawns, lobster, clams, garlic, olive oil, sweet paprika, and saffron, all stewed in fish broth. Many other paella variations are possible, including *paella negra*, a black rice dish made with squid ink; *arròs a banda* made with peeled seafood; and *fideuà*, paella made with noodles and usually served with allioli.

fowl, cod, tripe, cuttlefish, pork, and rabbit is another Costa Brava favorite. Stewed for a good five hours until the darkness of the onions and the ink of the cuttlefish have combined to impart a rich chocolate color to the stew, this is a much-celebrated wintertime classic. You'll also find *suquet de peix,* the Catalan fish stew, at restaurants along the Costa Brava.

SEAFOOD STEWS

Sèpia amb pèsols is a vegetable and seafood *mar i muntanya* ("surf and turf") beloved on the Costa Brava: cuttlefish and peas are stewed with potatoes, garlic, onions, tomatoes, and a splash of wine. The *picadillo*—the finishing touches of flavors and textures—includes parsley, black pepper, fried bread, pine nuts, olive oil, and salt. *Es niu* ("the nest") of game

FRUITS AND VEGETABLES

Valencia and the eastern Levante region have long been famous as Spain's *huerta,* or garden. The alluvial soil of the littoral produces an abundance of everything from tomatoes to asparagus, peppers, chard, spinach, onions, artichokes, cucumbers, and the whole range of Mediterranean bounty. Catalonia's Maresme and Empordà regions are also fruit and vegetable bowls, making this coastline a true cornucopia of fresh produce.

WINES

The Penedès wine region west of Barcelona has been joined by new wine Denominations of Origin from all over Catalonia. Alt Camp, Tarragona, Priorat, Montsant, Costers del Segre, Pla de Bages, Alella, and Empordà all produce excellent reds and whites to join Catalonia's sparkling *cava* on local wine lists. The rich, full-bodied reds of Montsant and Priorat, especially, are among the best in Spain.

Updated by
Elizabeth
Prosser

The long curve of the Mediterranean from the French border to Cabo Cervera below Alicante encompasses the two autonomous communities of Catalonia and Valencia, with the country's second- and third-largest cities (Barcelona and Valencia, respectively). Rivals in many respects, the two communities share a language, history, and culture that set them apart from the rest of Spain.

Girona is the gateway to Northern Catalonia's attractions—the Pyrenees, the volcanic region of La Garrotxa, and the beaches of rugged Costa Brava. Northern Catalonia is memorable for the soft, green hills of the Empordà farm country and the Alberes mountain range at the eastern end of the Pyrenees. Across the landscape are *masías* (farmhouses) with staggered-stone roofs and square towers that make them look like fortresses. Even the tiniest village has its church, arcaded square, and *rambla,* where villagers take their evening *paseo* (stroll).

Salvador Dalí's deep connection to the Costa Brava is enshrined in the Teatre-Museu Dalí in Figueres: he's buried in the crypt beneath it. His wife Gala is buried in his former home, a castle in Púbol. His summer home in Port Lligat Bay, north of Cadaqués, is now a museum of his life and work.

The province of Valencia was incorporated into the Kingdom of Aragón, Catalonia's medieval Mediterranean empire, when it was conquered by Jaume I in the 13th century. Along with Catalonia, Valencia became part of the united Spanish state in the 15th century, but defenders of its separate cultural and linguistic identity still resent the centuries of Catalan domination. The Catalan language prevails in Tarragona, a city and province of Catalonia, but Valenciano—a dialect of Catalan—is spoken and used on street signs in the Valencian provinces.

The *huerta* (a fertile, irrigated coastal plain) is devoted mainly to citrus and vegetable farming, which lends color to the landscape and fragrance to the air. Arid mountains form a stark backdrop to the lush coast. Over the years these shores have entertained Phoenician, Greek,

Carthaginian, and Roman visitors; the Romans stayed several centuries and left archaeological remains all the way down the coast, particularly in Tarragona, the capital of Rome's Spanish empire by 218 BC. Rome's dominion did not go uncontested, however; the most serious challenge came from the Carthaginians of North Africa. The three Punic Wars, fought over this territory between 264 and 146 BC, established the reputation of the Carthaginian general Hannibal.

The coastal farmland and beaches that attracted the ancients now call to modern-day tourists, though in parts, a number of "mass-tourism" resorts have marred the shore. Inland, however, local culture survives intact. The rugged and beautiful territory is dotted with small fortified towns, several of which bear the name of Spain's 11th-century national hero, El Cid, commemorating the battles he fought here against the Moors some 900 years ago.

PLANNING

WHEN TO GO

Come for the beaches in the hot summer months, but expect crowds and serious heat—in some places up to 40°C (104°F). The Mediterranean coast is more comfortable in May and September.

February and March are the peak months for skiing in the Pyrenees. Winter travel in the region has other advantages: Valencia still has plenty of sunshine, and if you're visiting villages and wineries in the countryside, you might have the place all to yourself. Note that many restaurants outside the major towns may close on weekdays in winter, so call ahead. Many museums and sites close early in winter (6 pm).

The Costa Brava and Costa Blanca beach areas get hot and crowded in summer, and accommodations are at a premium. In contrast, spring is mild and an excellent time to tour the region, particularly the rural areas, where blossoms infuse the air with pleasant fragrances and wildflowers dazzle the landscape.

PLANNING YOUR TIME

Not far from Barcelona, the beautiful towns of Vic, Girona, and Cadaqués are easily reachable from the city by bus or train in a couple of hours. Figueres is a must if you want to see the Teatre-Museu Dalí. Girona makes an excellent base from which to explore La Garrotxa—for that, you'll need to rent a car. Allot a few days to explore Tarragona, easily reached from Barcelona by train or a 1½-hour drive. If you're driving, take a detour to the wineries in the Penedès region; most of Spain's cava comes from here. Explore Tarragona's Roman wonders on foot, and stop for a meal at any of the fine seafood restaurants in the Serallo fishing quarter.

Valencia is three hours by express train from Barcelona; stop in Tarragona on your way if you have time. From Tarragona, it's a comfortable hour-long train ride to Valencia; if driving, stop off for a meal or stroll in one of the coastal towns like Castellon. Historic Valencia and the Santiago Calatrava–designed City of Arts and Sciences complex can be covered in two days, but stay longer and indulge in the city's food and explore the nightlife in the Barrio del Carmen.

Travel agencies in Alicante can arrange tours of the city and bus and train tours to Guadalest, the Algar waterfalls, the Peñón de Ifach (Calpe) on the Costa Blanca, and inland to Elche.

FESTIVALS

In Valencia, **Las Fallas** fiestas begin March 1 and reach a climax between March 15 and El Día de San José (St. Joseph's Day) on March 19, Father's Day in Spain. Las Fallas originated from St. Joseph's role as patron saint of carpenters; in medieval times, carpenters' guilds celebrated the arrival of spring by cleaning out their shops and making bonfires with scraps of wood. These days it's a 19-day celebration ending with fireworks, floats, carnival processions, and bullfights. On March 19, huge wood and papier-mâché effigies of political figures and other personalities (the result of a year's work by local community groups) are torched to end the fiestas.

GETTING HERE AND AROUND

AIR TRAVEL

El Prat de Llobregat in Barcelona is the main international airport for the Costa Brava; Girona is the closest airport to the region, with bus connections directly into the city and to Barcelona. Valencia has an international airport with direct flights to London, Paris, Brussels, Lisbon, Zurich, and Milan as well as regional flights from Barcelona, Madrid, Málaga, and other cities in Spain. There is a regional airport in Alicante serving the Valencian region and Murcia.

BOAT AND FERRY TRAVEL

Many short-cruise lines along the coast offer the chance to view the Costa Brava from the sea. Visit the port areas in the main towns and you'll quickly spot several tourist cruise lines. Plan to spend around €15–€27, depending on the length of the cruise. Many longer cruises include a stop en route for a swim. The glass-keel Nautilus boats for observation of the Medes Islands underwater park cost around €20 and run daily April–October and weekends November–March.

The shortest ferry connections to the Balearic Islands originate in Dénia. Balearia sails from there to Ibiza, Formentera, and Mallorca.

Boat and Ferry Information Balearia. ☎ *902/160180, 912/660214 from abroad* ⊕ *www.balearia.com.* **Nautilus.** ✉ *Passeig Marítim 23, L'Estartit* ☎ *972/751489* ⊕ *www.english.nautilus.es.*

BUS TRAVEL

Private companies run buses down the coast and from Madrid to Valencia, and to Alicante. ALSA is the main bus line in this region; check local tourist offices for schedules. Sarfa operate buses from Barcelona to Blanes, Lloret, Sant Feliu de Guixols, Platja d'Aro, Palamos, Begur, Roses, L'Escala, and Cadaqués.

Contacts ALSA. ☎ *902/422242* ⊕ *www.alsa.es.* **Moventis Sarfa.** ✉ *Estació del Nord, Alí Bei 80, Barcelona* ☎ *902/302025* ⊕ *compras.moventis.es/en-GB* Ⓜ *Arc de Triomf.* **Sagalés.** ✉ *Estació del Nord , Alí Bei 80, Barcelona*

☎ *902/130014 tickets* ⊕ *www.sagales.com* Ⓜ *Arc de Triomf.* **Sagalés Airport-Line.** ☎ *902/130014* ⊕ *www.sagalesairportline.com.*

CAR TRAVEL

A car is necessary for explorations inland and convenient for reaching locations on the coast, where drives are smooth and scenic. Catalonia and Valencia have excellent roads; the only drawbacks are the high cost of fuel and the high tolls on the *autopistas* (highways, usually designated by the letters "AP"). The national roads (starting with the letter N) can get clogged, however, so you're often better off on toll roads if your time is limited.

TRAIN TRAVEL

Most of the Costa Brava is not served directly by railroad. A local line runs up the coast from Barcelona to Blanes, then turns inland and connects at Maçanet-Massanes with the main line up to France. Direct trains stop only at major connections, such as Girona, Flaçà, and Figueres. To visit one of the smaller towns in between, you can take a fast direct train from Barcelona to Girona, for instance, then get off and wait for a local to come by. The stop on the main line for the middle section of the Costa Brava is Flaçà, where you can take a bus or taxi to your final destination. Girona and Figueres are two other towns with major bus stations that feed out to the towns of the Costa Brava. The train serves the last three towns on the north end of the Costa Brava: Llançà, Colera, and Portbou.

Express intercity trains reach Valencia from all over Spain, arriving at the new Joaquin Sorolla station; from there, a shuttle bus takes you to the Estación del Norte, the terminus in the center of town, for local connections. From Barcelona there are 15 trains a day, including the fast train TALGO, which takes 3½ hours. There are 22 daily trains to Valencia from Madrid; the high-speed train takes about 1 hour 40 minutes.

For the Costa Blanca, the rail hub is Alicante; for southern Catalonia, make direct train connections to Tarragona from either Barcelona or Valencia.

Contacts RENFE. ☎ *902/320320* ⊕ *www.renfe.com.*

TOURS

Hiking, cycling, and walking tours are available around Valencia and the Costa Blanca.

Riding schools in a number of towns in the region provide classes and trekking opportunities. Pick up brochures at local tourist offices.

Learn to sail in most of the major resorts. For kitesurfing or windsurfing, gear is available for rent at many of the beaches. Many companies offer scuba-diving excursions; in the smaller coastal towns it's possible to dive in the protected waters of offshore nature reserves if you book ahead.

This region is a bird-watcher's paradise, especially in the salt pans of Santa Pola and Albufera Lake. The main coastal plain is a migratory highway for thousands of birds winging their way between Europe and Africa.

8

CONTACTS

Abdet. The Sierra Mariola and Sierra Aitana regions are both easily accessible from the Costa Blanca resorts. Abdet, near Guadalest, offers itineraries and traditional self-catering guesthouses amid breathtaking scenery. ⊕ *www.abdet.com* ⌦ *From €380.*

Association of Diving Centers Costa Brava Sub. For comprehensive information on diving, equipment hire, and courses in the Costa Brava region, contact the association, which includes upward of 34 associated and accredited diving centers. ☎ 972/600017 ⊕ *www.submarinismocosta-brava.com/en.*

Ciclo Costa Blanca. If pedal power is your thing, Ciclo Costa Blanca is a good place to start, with both guided and self-guided tours. ✉ *Meta Bike Cafe Comercio Enara 2, Calle Vell de Altea 24, Alicante* ☎ 966/868104 ⊕ *www.ciclocostablanca.com* ⌦ *From €499.*

Mountain Walks. Self-guided or guided bird-watching, mountain-walking, and cycling tours are customized to suit your requirements, with picturesque cottage accommodations, meals, and transportation included in the price. ✉ *San Gregorio 4, Quatretondeta, Alicante* ☎ 965/511044 ⊕ *www.mountainwalks.com* ⌦ *From €120.*

FARMHOUSE STAYS IN CATALONIA

Dotted throughout Catalonia are farmhouses (*casas rurales* in Spanish, and *cases de pagès* or *masíes* in Catalan), where you can spend a weekend or longer. Accommodations vary from small rustic homes to spacious luxurious farmhouses with fireplaces and pools. Stay in a guest room at a bed-and-breakfast, or rent an entire house and do your own cooking. Most tourist offices, including the main Catalonia Tourist Office, have information and listings. Several organizations in Spain have detailed listings and descriptions of Catalonia's farmhouses.

Contacts Agroturisme.org. ☎ 932/680900 ⊕ www.agroturisme.cat. **CatalunyaRural.info.** ⊕ www.catalunyarural.info.

RESTAURANTS

Catalonia's eateries are deservedly famous. Girona's Celler de Can Roca was voted Best Restaurant in the World multiple times in recent years in the annual critics' poll conducted by British magazine *Restaurant,*and a host of other first-rate establishments continue to offer inspiring fine dining in Catalonia, which began in the hinterlands at the legendary Hotel Empordà. Yet you needn't go to an internationally acclaimed restaurant to dine well. Superstar chef Ferran Adrià of the former foodie paradise elBulli dines regularly at dives in Roses, where straight-up fresh fish is the attraction. Northern Catalonia's Empordà region is known for seafood and rich assortment of inland and upland products. Beef from Girona's verdant pastureland is prized throughout Catalonia, while wild mushrooms from the Pyrenees and game from the Alberes range offer seasonal depth to menus across the region. From a simple beachside paella or *llobarro* (sea bass) at a *chiringuito* (beach shack) with tables on the sand, to the splendor of a meal at El Celler de Can Roca, playing culinary hopscotch through Catalonia is a good way to get to know the region.

CLOSE UP

Beaches of the Costa Brava and Costa Blanca

COSTA BRAVA BEACHES

The beaches on the Costa Brava range from stretches of fine white sand to rocky coves and inlets; summer vacationers flock to **Tossa de Mar, Roses,** and **Calella de Palafrugell;** in all but the busiest weeks of July and August, the tucked-away coves of **Cap de Creus National Park** are oases of peace and privacy. **Valencia** has a long beach that's wonderful for sunning and a promenade lined with paella restaurants; for quieter surroundings, head farther south to **El Saler.**

COSTA BLANCA BEACHES

The southeastern coastline of the Costa Blanca varies from the long stretches of sand dunes north of **Dénia** and south of **Alicante** to the coves and crescents in between. The benign climate permits lounging on the beach at least eight months of the year. **Altea,** popular with families, is busy and pebbly, but the old town has retained a traditional pueblo feel with narrow cobbled streets and attractive squares. **Calpe's** beaches have the scenic advantage of the sheer outcrop Peñón de Ifach (Cliff of Ifach), which stands guard over stretches of sand to either side. Dénia has family-friendly beaches to the north, where children paddle in relatively shallow waters, and rocky inlets to the south.

HOTELS

Lodgings on the Costa Brava range from the finest hotels to spartan pensions. The better accommodations have splendid views of the seascape. If you plan to visit during the high season (July and August), be sure to book reservations well in advance at almost any hotel in the area; the Costa Brava remains one of the most popular summer resort areas in Spain. Many Costa Brava hotels close down in the winter season (November–March).

Hotel reviews have been shortened. For full information, visit Fodors. com.

WHAT IT COSTS IN EUROS				
	$	**$$**	**$$$**	**$$$$**
Restaurants	under €12	€12–€17	€18–€22	over €22
Hotels	under €90	€90–€125	€126–€180	over €180

Prices are per person for a main course, or a combination of small plates, at dinner, and for two people in a standard double room in high season, excluding tax.

8

NORTHERN CATALONIA

For many, Northern Catalonia is one of the top reasons reason to visit Spain. The historic center of Girona, its principal city, is a labyrinth of climbing cobblestone streets and staircases, with remarkable Gothic and Romanesque buildings at every turn. El Call, the Jewish Quarter, is one of the best-preserved areas of its kind in Europe, and the Gothic cathedral is an architectural masterpiece. Streets in the modern part of the city are lined with smart shops and boutiques, and the overall quality of life in Girona is considered among the best in Spain.

Nearby towns Besalú and Figueres are vastly different. Figueres is an unremarkable town made exceptional by the Dalí Museum. Besalú is a picture-perfect Romanesque village on a bluff overlooking the Riu Fluvià, with one of the most prestigious restaurants in Catalonia. Lesser known are the medieval towns in and around the volcanic (now extinct) area of La Garrotxa: Vic, Rupit, and Olot boast the best produce in the region.

GIRONA

97 km (60 miles) northeast of Barcelona.

At the confluence of four rivers, Girona (population: 97,000) keeps intact the magic of its historic past; with its brooding hilltop castle, soaring cathedral, and dreamy riverside setting, it resembles a vision from the Middle Ages. Today, as a university center, Girona combines past and vibrant present: art galleries, chic cafés, and trendy boutiques have set up shop in many of the restored buildings of the old quarter, known as the Força Vella (Old Fortress), which is on the east side of the Riu Onyar. Built on the side of the mountain, it presents a tightly packed labyrinth of medieval buildings and monuments on narrow cobblestone streets with connecting stairways. You can still see vestiges of the Iberian and Roman walls in the cathedral square and in the patio of the old university. In the central quarter is El Call, one of Europe's best-preserved medieval (12th- to 15th-century) Jewish communities and an important center of Kabbalistic studies.

The main street of the Força Vella is Carrer de la Força, which follows the old Via Augusta, the Roman road that connected Rome with its provinces.

Explore Girona on foot. As you wander through the old quarter, you will be surprised by new discoveries. One of Girona's treasures is its setting, high above where the Onyar merges with the Ter; the latter flows from a mountain waterfall that can be glimpsed in a gorge above the town. Walk first along the west bank of the Onyar, between the train trestle and the Plaça de la Independència, to admire the classic view of the old town, with its pastel waterfront facades. Many of the windows and balconies are adorned with fretwork grilles of embossed wood or delicate iron tracery. Cross Pont de Sant Agustí over to the old quarter from under the arcades in the corner of Plaça de la Independència and find your way to the Punt de Benvinguda tourist office, to the right at Rambla Llibertat 1. Work your way up through the labyrinth of steep

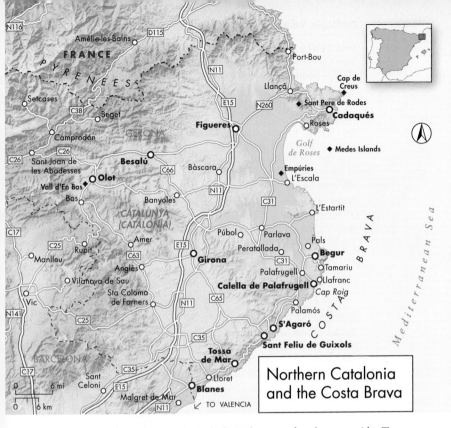

streets, using the cathedral's huge baroque facade as a guide. Try to be in Girona during the second week of May, when the streets of the old quarter are festooned with the flowers of spring during the Girona Festival of Flowers.

GETTING HERE AND AROUND

There are more than 20 daily trains from Barcelona to Girona (continuing on to the French border). Regional trains can take between one and two hours, and can be picked up from a number of stations in Barcelona, while the high-speed AVE train service is a convenient option, running from Barcelona Sants station to Girona in under 40 minutes (it's advisable to prebook the AVE). The train station is about a 20-minute walk from the old quarter; alternatively, taxis can be picked up in front of the train station on arrival. There are frequent Sagalés buses to Girona Airport; they take an average of 75 minutes and cost €16 one-way, €25 round-trip. The Sagales 602 and 603 buses run from Barcelona's El Prat de Llobregat airport and Estació del Nord, in the city center of Barcelona, to Girona city bus station. Getting around the city is easiest on foot or by taxi; several bridges connect the historic old quarter with the more modern town across the river.

Contacts Sagalés. ☎ 902/130014 ⊕ www.sagales.com.

DISCOUNTS AND DEALS

The GironaMuseus discounts admission to all the city's museums. ■TIP→ **Some are free on the first Sunday of every month.** Check the tourist office or at the Punt de Benvinguda welcome center, which can also arrange guided tours.

TOURS

Bike Breaks. In recent times, Girona has developed a passion for all things bike related. Bike Breaks provides bike rentals and tours so that you can get to know the city and its surroundings on two wheels. ⊠ *Carrer Mercaders 14* ☎ *972/205465* ⊕ *www.gironacyclecentre.com* ☞ *From €25.*

Game of Thrones Experience. The success of the TV series *Game of Thrones* has showcased Girona's beauty to the world. The Punt de Benvinguda visitors center provides up-to-date information on local guides who will take you to some locations that defined some of its most famous moments. Prices vary. ⊠ *Berenguer Carnicer 3* ☎ *972/211678.*

Visitor Information Girona Office of Tourism. ⊠ *Rambla de la Llibertat 1* ☎ *972/226575* ⊕ *www.girona.cat/turisme.* **Punt de Benvinguda.** ⊠ *Berenguer Carnicer 3* ☎ *972/211678, 674/955805* ⊕ *www.gironawalks.com.*

EXPLORING

Basílica of Sant Feliu. One of Girona's most beloved churches and its first cathedral until the 10th century, Sant Feliu was repeatedly rebuilt and altered over four centuries and stands today as an amalgam of Romanesque columns, a Gothic nave, and a baroque facade. The vast bulk of this structure is landmarked by one of Girona's most distinctive belfries, topped by eight pinnacles. The basilica was founded over the tomb of St. Felix of Africa, a martyr under the Roman emperor Diocletian. ⊠ *Pujada de Sant Feliu 29* ☎ *972/201407* ☞ *From €7.*

Fodor'sChoice ★ **Cathedral.** At the heart of the Força Vella, the cathedral looms above 90 steps and is famous for its nave—at 75 feet, the widest in the world and the epitome of the spatial ideal of Catalan Gothic architects. Since Charlemagne founded the original church in the 8th century, it has been through many fires and renovations. Take in the rococo-era facade, "eloquent as organ music" and impressive flight of 17th-century stairs, which rises from its own *plaça.* Inside, three smaller naves were compressed into one gigantic hall by the famed architect Guillermo Bofill in 1416. The change was typical of Catalan Gothic "hall" churches, and it was done to facilitate preaching to crowds. Note the famous silver canopy, or *baldaquí* (baldachin). The oldest part of the cathedral is the 11th-century Romanesque **Torre de Carlemany** (Charlemagne Tower).

The cathedral's exquisite 12th-century cloister has an obvious affinity with the cloisters in the Roussillon area of France. Inside the Treasury there's a variety of precious objects. They include a 10th-century copy of Beatus's manuscript *Commentary on the Apocalypse* (illuminated in the dramatically primitive Mozarabic style), the Bible of Emperor Charles V, and the celebrated *Tapís de la Creació* (*Tapestry of the Creation*), considered by most experts to be the finest tapestry surviving from the Romanesque era (and, in fact, thought to be the needlework of Saxons working in England). Made of wool, with predominant colors of green,

There's more to Girona's cathedral than the 90 steps to get to it; inside there's much to see, including the Treasury.

brown, and ocher, the tapestry once hung behind the main altar as a pictorial Bible lesson. Representations of time and nature circle around a central figure, likening paradise to the eternal cosmos presided over by Christ. The bottom band (which appears to have been added at a later date) contains two *iudeis*, or Jews, dressed in the round cloaks they were compelled to wear to set them apart from Christians. This scene is thought to be the earliest portrayal of a Jew (other than biblical figures) in Christian art. ⊠ *Pl. de la Catedral s/n* ☎ *972/427189* ⊕ *www. catedraldegirona.cat* 🖾 *From €7.*

Fodor's Choice
★

El Call. Girona is especially noted for its 13th-century Jewish Quarter, El Call, which branches off Carrer de la Força, south of the Plaça Catedral. The quarter is a network of lanes that crisscross above one another, and houses built atop each other in disorderly fashion along narrow stone medieval streets. With boutique shopping, artsy cafés, and lots of atmospheric eateries and bars, there is plenty to explore.

The word *call* (pronounced "kyle" in Catalan) may come from an old Catalan word meaning "narrow way" or "passage." Others suggest that it comes from the Hebrew word *qahal,* meaning "assembly" or "meeting of the community." The earliest presence of Jews in Girona is uncertain, but the first historical mention dates from 982, when a group of 25 Jewish families moved to Girona from nearby Juïgues. Owing allegiance to the Spanish king (who exacted tribute for this distinction) and not to the city government, this once-prosperous Jewish community—one of the most flourishing in Europe during the Middle Ages—was, at its height, a leading center of learning. ⊠ *Girona.*

WHERE TO EAT

$$$$ CATALAN 🍴 **Bubbles Gastrobar.** Excellent Catalan tapas with Mediterranean-fusion touches are served here in a simple setting just across the river from the Força Vella. Choose from a range of innovative tapas, or go for the dinner tasting menu for €55. **Known for:** tasting menu; innovative tapas; great lunch spot. [$] *Average main: €25* ✉ *Passeig José Canalejas 6* ☎ *972/226002* 🌐 *www.gastrobubbles.com* ⏲ *Closed Sun. and Mon.*

$$$ CATALAN 🍴 **Cal Ros.** Tucked under the arcades just behind the north end of Plaça de la Llibertat, this restaurant combines ancient stone arches with crisp, contemporary furnishings and cheerful lighting. The menu changes regularly, featuring organically raised local produce in season, and fresh fish in updated versions of traditional Catalan cuisine. **Known for:** rice dishes; tucked under the arches of the old quarter; updated traditional cuisine. [$] *Average main: €20* ✉ *Carrer Cort Reial 9* ☎ *972/219176* ⏲ *Closed Mon. and Tues. No dinner Sun.*

$$$$ CONTEMPORARY Fodor'sChoice ★ 🍴 **El Celler de Can Roca.** Annointed twice (in 2013 and 2015) by an international panel of food critics and chefs as the best restaurant in the world, El Celler de Can Roca is a life-changing culinary experience. The Roca brothers—Joan, Josep, and Jordi—showcase their masterful creations in two tasting menus, at €180 and €205. **Known for:** extensive wine selection; one of the best restaurants in the world; reservations required many months or a year ahead. [$] *Average main: €180* ✉ *Can Sunyer 48* ☎ *972/222157* 🌐 *cellercanroca.com* ⏲ *Closed Sun. and Mon. No lunch Tues. Also closed 1 wk in Aug.; Easter wk; Dec. 23–Jan. 16.*

$ CAFÉ **La Fabrica.** Christian, a professional cyclist, and his wife, Amber, opened this inviting space, serving brunch and superb coffee, in an old carpentry factory (La Fabrica means "the factory" in Spanish). There are raw concrete floors, exposed brick walls, high ceilings, and an abundance of bike memorabilia. **Known for:** bike-friendly stop; excellent coffee; setting in converted factory. [$] *Average main: €9* ✉ *Carrer de la Llebre 3* ☎ *972/296622* 🌐 *www.lafabricagirona.com* ⏲ *No dinner.*

$$ CATALAN 🍴 **Restaurante La Carnisseria.** Craftsmanship, family traditions, and a lot of love combine at this restaurant dedicated to providing the best cuts of meat in town. Tucked down a slender street in Girona's ancient Call (Jewish Quarter) and habitually packed with diners on the three nights it is open, La Carnisseria is run by a family of butchers with a shared passion for meat that goes back generations. **Known for:** best cuts of meat in town; warm and professional service in cozy setting; dedicated family business. [$] *Average main: €15* ✉ *Puja Sant Domènec 9* ☎ *697/479784* ⏲ *No lunch. Closed Sun.–Wed.*

WHERE TO STAY

$$$$ RENTAL FAMILY Fodor'sChoice ★ 🏨 **Alemanys 5.** Award-winning architect Anna Noguera and partner Juan-Manuel Ribera transformed a 16th-century house steps from the cathedral into two extraordinary apartments: one for up to five people, the other for six. **Pros:** perfect for families or small groups; ideal location; superb architectural design. **Cons:** difficult to navigate the small streets by car (hotel provides instructions); minimum stay required; needs booking in advance. [$] *Rooms from: €300* ✉ *Carrer Alemanys 5* ☎ *649/885136* 🌐 *www.alemanys5.com* 🛏 *2 apartments* 🍽 *No meals.*

With its picturesque rivers, Girona is often called the Spanish Venice.

$
B&B/INN

Bellmirall. This pretty little *hostal* (guesthouse) in the old city, on the edge of El Call, makes up in value and location what it lacks in amenities and services; when there's no staff on call, you come and go with your own key. **Pros:** steps from the important sites; charming sitting room; good value. **Cons:** bedrooms are small; some rooms have shared bathrooms; no elevator. $ *Rooms from: €88 ⊠ Carrer de Bellmirall 3 ☏ 972/204009 ⊕ www. bellmirall.eu ☉ Closed Jan. ➫ 7 rooms* ⬩⊙⬩ *Free Breakfast.*

$$
HOTEL

Hotel Peninsular. In a handsomely restored early-20th-century building across the Riu Onyar, with views into Girona's historic Força Vella, this modest but useful hotel occupies a strategic spot at the end of the Pont de Pedra (Stone Bridge), a Girona landmark in the center of the shopping district. **Pros:** good location at the hub of Girona life; near the stop for the bus from Girona airport; friendly staff. **Cons:** smallish rooms; basic decor; no frills. $ *Rooms from: €90 ⊠ Carrer Nou 3, Av. Sant Francesc 6 ☏ 972/203800 ⊕ www.hotelpeninsulargirona.com ➫ 48 rooms* ⬩⊙⬩ *No meals.*

NIGHTLIFE

Girona is a university town, so the night scene is especially lively during the school year. In the labyrinth of small streets throughout the pedestrianized Barri Vell (Old Town), several *vermuterias* (vermouth-focused bars), wine bars, and affable taverns provide entertainment as night falls.

Destí Ví Wine Bar. Locals and visitors alike kick-start their evenings at this small, candlelit wine bar close to Plaça del Vi. ⊠ *Plaça Bell Lloc 4 ☏ 972/664827.*

Nou Platea. This nightspot, popular with students and visitors alike, has both disco and live bands in concert, depending on the day of the week. ⊠ *Carrer Jeroni Real de Fontclara 4* ☏ *972/227288.*

Sunset Jazz Club. As the evening develops, drop into the Sunset Jazz Club to catch some live jazz by national and international artists in a softly lit, buzzing venue with exposed brick walls and dark furnishings. ⊠ *Calle Jaume Pons i Martí* ☏ *872/080145* ⊕ *www.sunsetjazz-club.com.*

SHOPPING

BOOKS

Llibreria 22. Girona's best bookstore has a large travel-guide section and a small selection of English fiction. ⊠ *Carrer Hortes 22* ☏ *972/212395* ⊕ *www.llibreria22.net.*

CRAFTS

Dolors Turró. Painter, sculptor, and restorer Dolors Turró knows her angels: making them—in all sorts of shapes and sizes, media, and styles—is what she does best. Drop in to her quirkly little shop-atelier in the old city and put a little putti in your life. ⊠ *Carrer de les Ballesteries 19* ☏ *972/410193.*

FOOD, CANDY, AND WINE

Gluki. This chocolatier and confectioner has been in business since 1870. ⊠ *Carrer Nou 9* ☏ *972/201989* ⊕ *www.gluki.cat.*

La Simfonia. At this relaxed wine shop and bar, you can be guided through a stellar range of regional wines (and cheeses)—and sample before you buy. ⊠ *Pl. de l'Oli 6* ☏ *972/411253* ⊕ *www.lasimfonia.com.*

Rocambolesc. Couldn't get a table at El Celler de Can Roca? Keep trying, but in the meantime there's Rocambolesc, the latest of the Roca family culinary undertakings. This ice-cream kiosk in the heart of the city serves up master confectioner Jordi Roca's exquisite *helados* and takeaway desserts. Expect long lines. There are no seats, so enjoy your treat on the go. ⊠ *Carrer Santa Clara 50* ☏ *972/416667* ⊕ *www.rocambolesc.com.*

Torrons Victoria Candela. Tasty nougat is the specialty here. ⊠ *Carrer Anselm Clavé 3* ☏ *972/211103.*

JEWELRY

Baobab. A lot of designer Anna Casal's original jewelry seems at first sight to be rough-hewn; it takes a second careful look to realize how sophisticated it really is. This shop doubles as her studio. ⊠ *Carrer de les Hortes 18* ☏ *972/410227.*

FIGUERES

37 km (23 miles) north of Girona.

Figueres is the capital of the *comarca* (county) of the Alt Empordà, the bustling county seat of this predominantly agricultural region. Local people come from the surrounding area to shop at its many stores and stock up on farm equipment and supplies. Thursday is market day, and farmers gather at the top of La Rambla to do business and gossip, taking refreshments at cafés and discreetly pulling out and pocketing large rolls

CLOSE UP

Figueres's Famous Son

With a painterly technique that rivaled that of Jan van Eyck, a flair for publicity so aggressive it would have put P. T. Barnum to shame, and a penchant for the shocking (he loved telling people Barcelona's historic Barri Gòtic should be knocked down), artist Salvador Dalí, whose most lasting image may be the melting watches in his iconic 1931 painting *The Persistence of Memory*, enters art history as one of the foremost proponents of surrealism, the movement launched in the 1920s by André Breton. The artist, who was born in Figueres and died there in 1989, decided to create a museum-monument to himself during the last two decades of his life. Dalí often frequented the Cafeteria Astòria at the top of La Rambla (still the center of social life in Figueres), signing autographs for tourists or just being Dalí: he once walked down the street with a French omelet in his breast pocket instead of a handkerchief.

of bills, the result of their morning transactions. What brings the tourists to Figueres in droves, however, has little to do with agriculture and everything to do with Salvador Dalí's jaw-droppingly surreal "theater-museum"—one of the most visited museums in Spain.

GETTING HERE AND AROUND

Figueres is one of the stops on the regular train service from Barcelona to the French border. Local buses are also frequent, especially from nearby Cadaqués, with more than eight scheduled daily. If you're driving, take the AP7 north from Girona. The town is small enough to explore on foot.

VISITOR INFORMATION

Contacts Figueres. ⊠ *Pl. de l'Escorxador 2* ☎ *972/503155* ⊕ *en.visitfigueres.cat.*

EXPLORING

Castell de Sant Ferran. Just a minute's drive northwest of Figueres is this imposing 18th-century fortified castle, one of the largest in Europe—only when you start exploring can you appreciate how immense it is. The parade grounds extend for acres, and the arcaded stables can hold more than 500 horses; the perimeter is roughly 4 km (2½ miles around). This castle was the site of the last official meeting of the Republican parliament (on February 1, 1939) before it surrendered to Franco's forces. Ironically, it was here that Lieutenant Colonel Antonio Tejero was imprisoned after his failed 1981 coup d'état in Madrid. ■ TIP→ **Call ahead and arrange for the two-hour Catedral de l'Aiguas guided tour in English (€15), which includes a trip through the castle's subterranean water system by Zodiac pontoon boat.** ⊠ *Pujada del Castell s/n* ☎ *972/506094* ⊕ *www.lesfortalesescatalanes.info* ☎ *€3* ⊙ *Closed Mon. (except public holidays).*

FAMILY **Museu del Joguet de Catalunya.** Hundreds of antique dolls and toys are on display here—including collections owned by, among others, Salvador Dalí, Federico García Lorca, and Joan Miró. It also hosts Catalonia's only *caganer* exhibit (mid-December–mid-January, in odd-numbered

8

The Dalí Museum in Figueres is itself a work of art. Note the eggs on the exterior: they're a common image in the artist's work.

years). These playful little figures answering nature's call have long had a special spot in the Catalan *pessebre* (Nativity scene). Farmers are the most traditional figures, squatting discreetly behind the animals, but these days you'll find Barça soccer players and politicians, too. Check with the museum for exact dates. ⊠ *Carrer de Sant Pere 1* ☎ *972/504585* ⊕ *www.mjc.cat* ✉ *€7* ⊘ *Closed Mon., and last 2 wks Jan. and 1st 2 wks Feb.*

Fodor's Choice
★

Teatre-Museu Dalí. "Museum" was not a big enough word for Dalí, so he christened his monument a theater. In fact, the building was once the Força Vella theater, reduced to a ruin in the Spanish Civil War. Now topped with a glass geodesic dome and studded with Dalí's iconic egg shapes, the multilevel museum pays homage to his fertile imagination and artistic creativity. It includes gardens, ramps, and a spectacular drop cloth Dalí painted for Les Ballets de Monte Carlo. Don't look for his greatest paintings here, although there are some memorable images, including *Gala at the Mediterranean,* which takes the body of Gala (Dalí's wife) and morphs it into the image of Abraham Lincoln once you look through coin-operated viewfinders. The sideshow theme continues with other coin-operated pieces, including *Taxi Plujós (Rainy Taxi),* in which water gushes over the snail-covered occupants sitting in a Cadillac once owned by Al Capone, or *Sala de Mae West,* a trompe-l'oeil vision in which a pink sofa, two fireplaces, and two paintings morph into the face of the onetime Hollywood sex symbol. Fittingly, another "exhibit" on view is Dalí's own crypt. When his friends considered what flag to lay over his coffin, they decided to cover it with an embroidered heirloom tablecloth instead. Dalí would have liked this unconventional touch if not the actual site: he wanted to be buried at his castle of Púbol next to his wife, but the then-mayor of Figueres took matters into his own hands. The summer night session (check online) is a perfect time to browse through the world's largest surrealist museum. Entrance tickets can be purchased in advance online, or bought in person at the museum ticket office. ✉ *Pl. Gala-Salvador Dalí 5* ☎ *972/677500* 🌐 *www.salvador-dali.org* 🎟 *€14* ⏲ *Closed Mon. Oct.–May (except public holidays).*

OFF THE BEATEN PATH

Casa-Museu Gala Dalí. The third point of the Dalí triangle is the medieval castle of Púbol, where the artist's wife and perennial model, Gala, is buried in the crypt. During the 1970s this was Gala's residence, though Dalí also lived here in the early 1980s. It contains paintings and drawings, Gala's haute-couture dresses, and other objects chosen by the couple. It's also a chance to wander through another Daliesque landscape, with lush gardens, fountains decorated with masks of Richard Wagner (the couple's favorite composer), and distinctive elephants with giraffe's legs and claw feet. Púbol, a small village roughly between Girona and Figueres, is near the C66. If you are traveling by train, get off at the Flaçà station on RENFE's Barcelona–Portbou line; walk or take a taxi 4 km (2½ miles) to Púbol. The Sarfa bus company also has a stop in Flaçà and on the C66 road, some 2 km (1¼ miles) from Púbol. ✉ *Pl. Gala-Dalí s/n, Púbol* ☎ *972/488655* 🌐 *www.salvador-dali.org* 🎟 *€8* ⏲ *Closed Mon. (except mid-June–mid-Sept. and public holidays), and early Jan.–mid-Mar.*

WHERE TO STAY

$ HOTEL

🏨 **Hotel Duràn.** Dalí had his own private dining room in this former stagecoach relay station, though the guest rooms, refurbished in bland pale-wood tones and standard contemporary furnishings, offset the hotel's historic 19th-century exterior. **Pros:** good central location; dining room has pictures of Dalí; family-friendly. **Cons:** rooms lack character; parking inconvenient and an extra charge; no pets. [$] *Rooms from: €80* ✉ *Carrer Lasauca 5* ☎ *972/501250* 🌐 *www.hotelduran.com* 🛏 *65 rooms* 🍴 *No meals.*

$$ HOTEL Fodor's Choice ★

🏨 **Hotel Empordà.** Just 1½ km (1 mile) north of town, this hotel houses the elegant restaurant run by Jaume Subirós that has been hailed as the birthplace of modern Catalan cuisine and has become a beacon for gourmands. **Pros:** historic culinary destination; some rooms have a Jacuzzi; free parking. **Cons:** on an unprepossessing roadside lot beside the busy N11 highway; 15–20 minute walk from Teatre-Museu Dalí; dated decor. [$] *Rooms from: €113* ✉ *Av. Salvador Dalí i Domènech 170* ☎ *972/500562* 🌐 *www.hotelemporda.com* 🛏 *42 rooms* 🍴 *No meals.*

BESALÚ

34 km (21 miles) northwest of Girona, 25 km (15 miles) west of Figueres.

Besalú, the capital of a feudal county until power was transferred to Barcelona at the beginning of the 12th century, remains one of the best-preserved medieval towns in Catalonia. Among its main sights are the 12th-century Romanesque fortified bridge over the Riu Fluvià; two churches—Sant Vicenç (set on an attractive, café-lined plaza) and Sant Pere; and the ruins of the convent of Santa Maria on the hill above town.

GETTING HERE AND AROUND

With a population of less than 2,500, the village is easily small enough to stroll through—restaurants and sights are within walking distance of each other. There is bus service to Besalú from Figueres and the surrounding Costa Brava resorts.

VISITOR INFORMATION

Contacts Besalú Tourist Office. ✉ *Carrer del Pont 1* ☎ *972/591240* 🌐 *www.besalu.cat.*

EXPLORING

Església de Sant Pere. This 12th-century Romanesque church is part of a 10th-century monastery, still in an excellent state of preservation. ✉ *Pl. de Sant Pere s/n.*

Jewish ritual baths. The remains of this 13th-century *mikvah,* or Jewish ritual bath, were discovered in the 1960s; it's one of the few surviving in Spain. A stone stairway leads down into the chamber where the water was drawn from the river, but little else indicates the role that the baths played in the medieval Jewish community. Access is by guided tour only (organized through the tourist office). ✉ *Calle de Pont Vell 1* ☎ *972/591240 tourist office* 🎫 *€3* 🕒 *Admission by guided tour only.*

Pont Fortificat. The town's most emblematic feature is this Romanesque 11th-century fortified bridge with crenellated battlements spanning the Riu Fluvià. ✉ *Carrer del Pont.*

WHERE TO EAT

$$$$ CATALAN Fodor's Choice ★

🍴 **Els Fogons de Can Llaudes.** A faithfully restored 10th-century Romanesque chapel holds proprietor Jaume Soler's outstanding restaurant—one of Catalonia's best. A typical dish could be *confitat de bou i raïm glacejat amb el seu suc* (beef confit au jus with glacé grapes), but the menu changes weekly. **Known for:** rotating fixed-price menu only; excellent decor; Romanesque chapel. [$] *Average main: €80* ✉ *Pl. de Prat de Sant Pere 6* ☎ *972/590858* 🕒 *Closed Tues., and last 2 wks of Nov.*

Besalú contains astonishingly well-preserved medieval buildings.

OLOT

21 km (13 miles) west of Besalú, 55 km (34 miles) northwest of Girona.

Capital of the comarca (administrative region) of La Garrotxa, Olot is famous for its 19th-century school of landscape painters and has several excellent Art Nouveau buildings, including the Casa Solà-Morales, which has a facade by Lluís Domènech i Montaner, architect of Barcelona's Palau de la Música Catalana. The Sant Esteve church at the southeastern end of Passeig d'en Blay is famous for its El Greco painting *Christ Carrying the Cross* (1605).

WHERE TO EAT

$$$$ ✕ **Ca l'Enric.** Chefs Jordi and Isabel Juncà have become legends in the
CATALAN town of La Vall de Bianya, just north of Olot, with exquisite cuisine that's firmly rooted in local products. Dishes star game of all sorts, truffles, and wild mushrooms, and are served in a historic stone-walled 19th-century inn. **Known for:** local ingredients; rotating menu; fixed-price menus. $ *Average main: €85* ⊠ *Ctra. de Camprodon s/n, La Vall de Bianya* ✚ *Nacional 260, Km 91* ☎ *972/290015* ⊕ *www.restaurant-calenric.cat* ⊘ *Closed Mon.; also Dec. 27–Jan. 17 and 1st 2 wks of July (can vary). No dinner Sun.–Wed.*

$$$$ ✕ **Les Cols.** Chef Fina Puigdevall has made this sprawling 18th-century
CATALAN *masia* (Catalan farmhouse) a triumph. In the restaurant, the cuisine on the prix-fixe menu (no à la carte option) is seasonal and based on locally grown products, from wild mushrooms to the extraordinarily flavorful legumes and vegetables produced by the rich, volcanic soil of La Garrotxa. **Known for:** local ingredients; seasonal fixed-price menu; incredible decor. $ *Average main: €60* ⊠ *Mas les Cols, Ctra. de la Canya s/n*

☎972/269209 ⊕ *www.lescols.com* ⊙ *Closed Mon., and 1st 3 wks of Jan. No dinner Sun. and Tues.*

EN
ROUTE

Vall d'En Bas. The villages of Vall d'En Bas lie south of Olot, off the C153. A freeway cuts across this countryside to Vic, but you'll miss a lot by taking it. The twisting old road leads you through rich farmland past farmhouses with dark wooden balconies bedecked with bright flowers. Turn off for Sant Privat d'En Bas and Els Hostalets d'En Bas. Farther on, the picturesque medieval village of **Rupit** has excellent restaurants serving the famous *patata de Rupit*, potato stuffed with duck and beef, while the rugged Collsacabra mountains offer some of Catalonia's most pristine landscapes.

THE COSTA BRAVA

The Costa Brava (Wild Coast) is a nearly unbroken series of sheer rock cliffs dropping down to clear blue-green waters, punctuated by innumerable coves and tiny beaches on narrow inlets, called *calas*. It basically begins at Blanes and continues north along 135 km (84 miles) of coastline to the French border at Portbou. Although the area does have spots of real-estate excess, the rocky terrain of many pockets (Tossa, Cap de Begur, and Cadaqués) has discouraged overbuilding. On a good day here, the luminous blue of the sea contrasts with red-brown headlands and cliffs, and the distant lights of fishing boats reflect on wine-color waters at dusk. Small stands of umbrella pine veil the footpaths to many of the secluded coves and little patches of white sand—often, the only access is by boat.

GETTING HERE AND AROUND

From Barcelona, the fastest way to the Costa Brava by car is to start up the inland AP7 tollway toward Girona, then take Sortida 10 (Exit 10) for Blanes, Lloret de Mar, Tossa de Mar, Sant Feliu de Guíxols, S'Agaró, Platja d'Aro, Palamós, Calella de Palafrugell, and Palafrugell. From Palafrugell, you can head inland for La Bisbal and from there on to Girona, in the heart of Northern Catalonia. To head to the middle section of the Costa Brava, get off at Sortida 6, the first exit after Girona; this will point you directly to the Iberian ruins of Ullastret. To reach the northern part of the Costa Brava, get off the AP7 before Figueres at Sortida 4 for L'Estartit, L'Escala, Empúries, Castelló d'Empúries, Aïguamolls de l'Empordà, Roses, Cadaqués, Sant Pere de Rodes, and Portbou. Sortida 4 will also take you directly to Figueres, Peralada, and the Alberes mountains. The old national route, N11, is slow, heavily traveled, and more dangerous, especially in summer.

TOSSA DE MAR

80 km (50 miles) northeast of Barcelona, 41 km (25 miles) south of Girona.

Christened "Blue Paradise" by painter Marc Chagall, who summered here for four decades, Tossa's pristine beaches are among Catalonia's best. Set around a blue buckle of a bay, Tossa de Mar is a symphony in two parts: the Vila Vella (Old Town) and the Vila Nova (New Town), the latter a lovely district open to the sea and threaded by 18th-century lanes. The Vila Vella is a knotted warren of steep cobblestone streets with many restored buildings. It sits on the Cap de Tossa promontory that juts out into the sea.

Ava Gardner filmed the 1951 British drama *Pandora and the Flying Dutchman* here (a statue dedicated to her stands on a terrace on the medieval walls). Things may have changed since those days, but this beautiful village retains much of the unspoiled magic of its past. The primary beach at Tossa de Mar is the Platja Gran (Big Beach) in front of the town beneath the walls, and just next to it is Mar Menuda (Little Sea), where the small, colorfully painted fishing boats—maybe the same ones that caught your dinner—pull up onto the beach.

The beaches and town act as a magnet for many vacationers in July and August. Out of season, it's far more sedate, but the mild temperatures make it an ideal stop for coastal strolls.

GETTING HERE AND AROUND

The main bus station (the local tourist office is here) is on Plaça de les Nacions Sense Estat. Take Avinguda Ferran and Avinguda Costa Brava to head down the slope to the waterfront and the Vila Vella, which you enter via the Torre de les Hores, and head to the Vila Vella's heart—the Gothic church of Sant Vicenç—for a journey back in time to the Middle Ages.

EXPLORING

Museu Municipal. In a lovingly restored 14th-century house, this museum is said to be Catalonia's first dedicated to modern art. It is home to one of the only three Chagall paintings in Spain, *Celestial Violinist.* ⊠ *Pl. Pintor Roig i Soler 1* 🕾 *972/340709* 💷 *€3* ⊗ *Closed Mon.*

Vila Vella and Castillo de Tossa de Mar. Listed as a national artistic-historic monument in 1931, Tossa de Mar's **Vila Vella** (Old Town) is the only remaining example of a fortified medieval town in Catalonia. Set high above the town on a promontory, the Old Town is presided over by the ramparts and towers of the 13th-century **Castillo de Tossa de Mar,** and is situated on a steep yet worthy climb up from the main town, accessed from the western side of Platja Gran Tossa de Mar (Playa Grande). The cliff-top views, particularly at sunset, are remarkable, and the labyrinth of narrow, cobblestone lanes lined with ancient houses (some dating back to the 14th century) is a delight to explore at a leisurely pace. ◾TIP→ **At Bar del Far del Tossa (Carrer del Far 14), near the lighthouse, you can enjoy the best views in town. Reviving post-climb drinks, snacks, and light meals are available.** ⊠ *Passeig de Vila Vella, 1.*

BEACHES

Mar Menuda (*Little Sea*). Just north of the town center, this gentle 460-foot sandy crescent is a pleasant Blue Flag beach that's popular with local families. The sand is coarse, but the sparkling, calm, shallow waters make it ideal for children. Fishing boats bob peacefully in the water nearby after completing their morning's work. At the top of the beach there is a second cove called La Banyera de Ses Dones (the women's bathtub), which provides ideal conditions for diving, though if the sea is not calm, it is dangerous for swimmers. By day there is little natural shade, so bring adequate sunblock and an umbrella if you plan a long beach session. It gets extremely busy in high season. **Amenities:** none. **Best for:** snorkeling; sunset; swimming. ✉ *Av. Mar Menuda.*

Platja Gran (*Big Beach*). Sweeping past the Vila Vella, this well-maintained, soft-sand beach runs along the front of town to meet the base of the Cap de Tossa. One of the most photographed coastlines in this area of Spain, it is also, at the height of summer, one of the busiest. Conditions are normally fine for swimming (any warnings are announced via loudspeaker). A rising number of motorboats is impacting on the water quality, but for now it retains its Blue Flag status. Running behind the beach, there is no shortage of cafés and kiosks selling ice cream and snacks. There is no natural shade, but you can rent deck chairs and umbrellas. **Amenities:** food and drink; lifeguards; showers; toilets; water sports. **Best for:** snorkeling; sunset; swimming. ✉ *Av. Palma 1.*

WHERE TO EAT AND STAY

$$$$ CATALAN 🍴 **La Cuina de Can Simon.** Elegantly rustic, this restaurant right beside Tossa de Mar's medieval walls serves a combination of classical Catalan cuisine with up-to-date, innovative touches. The menu changes with the season; two tasting menus (€68 and €135) provide more than enough to sample, and you can also order à la carte. **Known for:** top-notch service; seasonal menu; welcoming tapa and cava upon entrance. [$] *Average main: €30* ✉ *Carrer del Portal 24* ☎ *972/341269* 🌐 *www.restaurant-cansimon.com* 🕒 *Closed Mon. and Tues.*

$$ HOTEL FAMILY 🏨 **Hotel Capri.** Located on the beach, this hotel is in hailing distance of the old quarter in the medieval fortress; rooms are simple, and those with sea views have private terraces. **Pros:** family-friendly option; perfect location; good value. **Cons:** rooms are small; minimal amenities; no private parking. [$] *Rooms from: €101* ✉ *Passeig del Mar 17* ☎ *972/340358* 🌐 *www.hotelcapritossa.com* 🕒 *Closed Nov.–Feb.* 🛏 *22 rooms* 🍽 *Free Breakfast.*

$$$$ HOTEL Fodor's Choice ★ 🏨 **Hotel Diana.** Built in 1906 by architect Antoni Falguera i Sivilla, disciple of Antoni Gaudí, this Moderniste gem sits on the square in the heart of the Vila Vella, steps from the beach. **Pros:** attentive service; ideal location, with sea views; Moderniste touches. **Cons:** minimal amenities; room rates unpredictable; some rooms are small. [$] *Rooms from: €250* ✉ *Pl. de Espanya 6* ☎ *972/341886* 🌐 *www.hotelesdante.com* 🕒 *Closed Nov.–Mar.* 🛏 *21 rooms* 🍽 *Free Breakfast.*

$$ HOTEL FAMILY 🏨 **Hotel Sant March.** This family hotel in the center of town is two minutes from the beach, with guest rooms that open onto a pleasant interior garden that serve as an oasis of tranquility in a sometimes hectic town. **Pros:** warm personal touch; good value; central location. **Cons:** no elevator; rooms a bit small; few exterior views. [$] *Rooms from: €110* ✉ *Av. Pelegrí 2* ☎ *972/340078* 🌐 *www.hotelsantmarch.com* 🕒 *Closed Oct. 15–Mar.* 🛏 *29 rooms* 🍽 *Free Breakfast.*

SANT FELIU DE GUIXOLS

23 km (14 miles) northeast of Tossa de Mar.

The little fishing port of Sant Feliu de Guixols is set on a small bay; Moderniste mansions line the seafront promenade, recalling a time when the cork industry made this one of the wealthier towns on the coast. In front of them, a long crescent beach of fine white sand leads around to the fishing harbor at its north end. Behind the promenade, a well-preserved old quarter of narrow streets and squares leads to a 10th-century gateway with horseshoe arches (all that remains of a pre-Romanesque monastery); also here is a church that combines Romanesque, Gothic, and baroque styles. Nearby, the iron-structured indoor market, which dates back to the 1930s, sells the freshest and finest local produce, with colorful stalls often overflowing onto the Plaça del Mercat in front.

GETTING HERE AND AROUND

To get here, take the C65 from Tossa de Mar—though adventurous souls might prefer the harrowing hairpin curves of the G1682 coastal corniche.

EXPLORING

Museu d'Història de la Ciutat. The Romanesque Benedictine monastery houses this museum, which contains interesting exhibits about the town's cork and fishing trades, and displays local archaeological finds. ✉ *Pl. del Monestir s/n* ☎ *972/821575* 🌐 *www.museu.guixols.cat* 🎫 *€2.*

WHERE TO EAT AND STAY

$$ CATALAN 🍴 **Can Segura.** Half a block in from the beach at Sant Feliu de Guixols, this restaurant serves home-cooked seafood and upland specialties. The dining room is always full, with customers waiting their turn in the street, but the staff is good at finding spots at the jovially long communal tables. **Known for:** first-rate seafood specialties; communal dining; excellent rice dishes. [$] *Average main: €13* ✉ *Carrer de Sant Pere 11* ☎ *972/321009.*

$$ SEAFOOD FAMILY 🍴 **El Dorado Mar.** Around the southern end of the beach at Sant Feliu de Guixols, perched over the entrance to the harbor, this superb family seafood restaurant offers sea views as well as fine fare at unbeatable prices. Whether straight seafood such as *lubina* (sea bass) or *dorada* (gilt-head bream) or *revuelto de setas* (eggs scrambled with wild mushrooms), everything served here is fresh and flavorful. **Known for:** affordable cuisine; knockout egg scramble; fresh seafood. [$] *Average main: €17* ✉ *Passeig Irla 15* ☎ *972/321818* 🌐 *www.grupeldorado.com* ⏲ *Closed Wed. Oct.–May.*

$$$$ CATALAN 🍴 **Villa Mas.** This Moderniste villa on the coast road from Sant Feliu to S'Agaró, with a lovely turn-of-the-20th-century zinc bar, serves up typical Catalan and seasonal Mediterranean dishes like *arròs a la cassola* (deep-dish rice) with shrimp brought fresh off the boats in Palamos, just up the coast. The terrace is a popular and shady spot just across the road from the beach. **Known for:** dining on terrace; across from beach; fresh seafood catches. [$] *Average main: €28* ✉ *Passeig de Sant Pol 95* ☎ *972/822526* 🌐 *www.restaurantvillamas.com* ⏲ *Closed Mon. Sept.–May, and mid-Dec.–mid-Jan. No dinner Tues.–Thurs. and Sun. Oct.–Mar.*

$$ **⌂ Hostal del Sol.** Once the summer home of a wealthy family, this Mod-
HOTEL erniste hotel has a grand stone stairway and medieval-style tower, as
FAMILY well as a garden and a lawn where you can relax by the pool. **Pros:**
family-friendly option; good value; good breakfast. **Cons:** bathrooms a
bit claustrophobic; far from the beach; on a busy road. [$] *Rooms from:*
€120 ⌂ Ctra. a Palamós 194 ☎ 972/320193 ⊕ www.hostaldelsol.cat/en
☽ Closed mid-Oct.–Easter ⇆ 41 rooms ⍟ Free Breakfast.

S'AGARÓ

3 km (2 miles) north of Sant Feliu.

S'Agaró is an elegant gated community on a rocky point at the north
end of the cove. The 30-minute walk along the **sea wall** from Hostal de
La Gavina to Sa Conca Beach is a delight, and the one-hour hike from
Sant Pol Beach over to Sant Feliu de Guixols offers views of the Costa
Brava at its best.

WHERE TO STAY

$$$$ **⌂ L'Hostal de la Gavina.** Opened in 1932 by farmer-turned-entrepreneur
HOTEL Josep Ensesa, the original hotel grew from a cluster of country villas
Fodor's Choice into a sprawling complex of buildings of extraordinary splendor that
★ have attracted celebrity guests from Orson Welles and Ava Gardner
to Sean Connery. **Pros:** in a gated community; impeccable service and
amenities; sea views, including from pool and terrace. **Cons:** hard on the
budget; walls are thin; expensive restaurant. [$] *Rooms from: €530 ⌂ Pl.
Roserar s/n, S'Agaró ☎ 972/321100 ⊕ www.lagavina.com ☽ Closed
Nov.–Easter ⇆ 74 rooms ⍟ Free Breakfast.*

CALELLA DE PALAFRUGELL AND AROUND

25 km (15½ miles) north of S'Agaró.

Up the coast from S'Agaró, the C31 brings you to Palafrugell and
Begur; to the east are some of the prettiest, least developed inlets of the
Costa Brava. One road leads to **Llafranc,** a small port with waterfront
hotels and restaurants, and forks right to the fishing village of **Calella
de Palafrugell,** known for its July habaneras festival. (The *habanera* is
a form of Cuban dance music brought to Europe by Catalan sailors in
the late 19th century; it still enjoys a nostalgic cachet here.) Just south
is the panoramic promontory of **Cap Roig,** with views of the barren
Formigues Isles.

North along the coast lie **Tamariu, Aiguablava, Fornell, Platja Fonda,** and
(around the point at Cap de Begur) **Sa Tuna** and **Aiguafreda.** There's
not much to do in any of these hideaways, but you can luxuriate in
wonderful views, some of the Costa Brava's best beaches and coves,
and the soothing quiet. Tamariu, a largely unspoiled former fishing
village backed by simple whitewashed houses and a small strip of sea-
food restaurants that hug the shoreline, is reached by descending a
vertiginous road set between mountains and pine forests. Farther north,
toward Begur, the small, sheltered Aiguablava beach sets the stage for
memorable sunsets. Its restaurant, Toc Al Mar, is a firm favorite with
barcelonins (Barcelona residents) on weekend coastal jaunts.

WHERE TO EAT AND STAY

$$$ CATALAN Fodor's Choice ★ 🍴 **Pa i Raïm.** "Bread and Grapes" in Catalan, this excellent restaurant in writer Josep Pla's ancestral family home in Palafrugell has one rustic dining room as well as another in a glassed-in winter garden. In summer the leafy terrace is the place to be. **Known for:** traditional country cuisine; contemporary fare; standout prawns tempura. [$] *Average main: €20* ✉ *Torres i Jonama 56, Palafrugell* ☎ *972/304572* 🌐 *www.pairaim.com* ⏲ *Closed Mon., and late Mar.–early Apr. (dates can vary). No dinner Sun.–Thurs.*

$$$$ B&B/INN FAMILY 🏨 **El Far Hotel-Restaurant.** Rooms in this 17th-century hermitage attached to a 15th-century watchtower have original vaulted ceilings, hardwood floors, and interiors accented with floral prints; the larger doubles and the suite can accommodate extra beds for children. **Pros:** friendly service; graceful architecture; spectacular views of bay. **Cons:** distance from the beach; pricey for the value; need car. [$] *Rooms from: €235* ✉ *Muntanya de Sant Sebastia, Carrer Uruguai s/n, Llafranc* ☎ *972/301639* 🌐 *www.elfar.net* ⏲ *Closed Jan.-early Feb.* 🛏 *9 rooms* 🍽 *Free Breakfast.*

BEGUR AND AROUND

11 km (7 miles) north of Calella de Palafrugell.

From Begur, go east through the calas or take the inland route past the rose-color stone houses and ramparts of the restored medieval town of **Pals.** Nearby **Peratallada** is another medieval fortified town with an 11th-century castle, tower, and palace. The name is derived from *pedra tallada,* meaning "carved stone," and behind the town's well-preserved walls is a maze of narrow streets and ivy-covered houses built from stone that was carved from the moat, which still encircles the town. In the center, the arcaded Plaça de les Voltes is alive with restaurants, shops, and cafés. North of Pals there are signs for **Ullastret,** an Iberian village dating to the 5th century BC. **L'Estartit** is the jumping-off point for the spectacular natural park surrounding the Medes Islands, famous for its protected marine life and consequently for diving and underwater photography.

EXPLORING

Empúries. The Greco-Roman ruins here are Catalonia's most important archaeological site, and this port is one of the most monumental ancient engineering feats on the Iberian Peninsula. As the Greeks' original point of arrival in Spain, Empúries was also where the Olympic Flame entered Spain for Barcelona's 1992 Olympic Games. ✉ *Calle Puig i Cadafalch s/n* ☎ *972/770208* 🌐 *www.mac.cat* 🎟 *€6* ⏲ *Closed Mon. mid-Nov. mid-Feb.*

Medes Islands (*Underwater Natural Park*). The marine reserve around the Medes Islands, an archipelago of several small islands, is just off the coastline of L'Estartit, and is touted as one of the best places in Spain to scuba dive. Thanks to its protected status, the marine life—eels, octopus, starfish, and grouper—is tame, and you can expect high visibility unless the weather is bad. If diving doesn't appeal, you can take one of the glass-bottomed boats that frequent the islands from the mainland and view from above. ✉ *L'Estartit.*

8

WHERE TO EAT AND STAY

$$$ CATALAN — 🍴 **Restaurant Ibèric.** This excellent pocket of authentic Costa Brava cuisine serves everything from snails to wild boar in season. The terrace is ideal for leisurely dining. **Known for:** eclectic cuisine; high-quality seasonal fare; traditional setting. [$] *Average main: €20* ✉ *Carrer Valls 11, Ullastret* ☎ *972/757108* 🌐 *www.restaurantiberic.com* ⏲ *Closed Mon. No dinner Tues.–Thurs. and Sun.*

$$$$ HOTEL — 🏨 **El Convent Hotel and Restaurant.** Built in 1730, this elegant former convent is a 10-minute walk to the beach at the Cala Sa Riera—the quietest and prettiest inlet north of Begur. **Pros:** outstanding architecture; quiet and private; terrace for dining. **Cons:** minimum three-night stay in summer; rooms are not soundproofed; need car. [$] *Rooms from: €240* ✉ *Ctra. de la Platja del Racó 2, Begur* ☎ *972/623091* 🌐 *www.hotelconventbegur.com* 🛏 *25 rooms* 🍽 *Free Breakfast.*

$$$$ HOTEL FAMILY Fodor's Choice ★ — 🏨 **Hotel Aigua Blava.** What began as a small hostal in the 1920s is now a sprawling luxury hotel, run by the fourth generation of the same family. **Pros:** impeccable service; gardens and pleasant patios at every turn; private playground. **Cons:** no elevator; no beach in the inlet; expensive restaurant. [$] *Rooms from: €330* ✉ *Platja de Fornells s/n, Begur* ☎ *972/622058* 🌐 *www.aiguablava.com* ⏲ *Closed Nov.–Mar.* 🛏 *85 rooms* 🍽 *Free Breakfast.*

CADAQUÉS AND AROUND

70 km (43 miles) north of Begur.

Spain's easternmost town, Cadaqués, still has the whitewashed charm that transformed this fishing village into an international artists' haunt in the early 20th century. Salvador Dalí's house, now a museum, is at Port Lligat, a 15-minute walk north of town.

EXPLORING

Fodor's Choice ★ **Cap de Creus.** North of Cadaqués, Spain's easternmost point is a fundamental pilgrimage, if only for the symbolic geographical rush. The hike out to the lighthouse—through rosemary, thyme, and the salt air of the Mediterranean—is unforgettable. The Pyrenees officially end (or rise) here. New Year's Day finds mobs of revelers awaiting the first emergence of the "new" sun from the Mediterranean. Gaze down at heart-pounding views of the craggy coast and crashing waves with a warm mug of coffee in hand or fine fare on the table at **Bar Restaurant Cap de Creus,** which sits on a rocky crag above the Cap de Creus. On a summer evening, you may be lucky and stumble upon some live music on the terrace. ✉ *Carrer de Cadaqués al Cap de Creus.*

Casa Museu Salvador Dalí. This was Dalí's summerhouse and a site long associated with the artist's notorious frolics with everyone from poets Federico García Lorca and Paul Eluard to filmmaker Luis Buñuel. Filled with bits of the surrealist's daily life, it's an important point in the "Dalí triangle," completed by the castle at Púbol and the Teatre-Museu Dalí in Figueres. You can get here by a 3-km (2-mile) walk north along the beach from Cadaqués. Only small groups of visitors are admitted at any given time, and reservations are required. ✉ *Portlligat s/n, Cadaqués*

The popular harbor of Cadaqués

☎ 972/251015 ⊕ *www.salvador-dali.org* 🖃 €11; *advance reservation required* ⊙ *Closed Mon. and Jan. 9–Feb. 10.*

Fodor's Choice
★

Sant Pere de Rodes. The monastery of Sant Pere de Rodes, 7 km (4½ miles) by car (plus a 20-minute walk) above the pretty fishing village of El Port de la Selva, is a spectacular site. Built in the 10th and 11th centuries by Benedictine monks—and sacked and plundered repeatedly since—this restored Romanesque monolith commands a breathtaking panorama of the Pyrenees, the Empordà plain, the sweeping curve of the Bay of Roses, and Cap de Creus. (Topping off the grand trek across the Pyrenees, Cap de Creus is a spectacular six-hour walk from here on the well-marked GR11 trail.) ■**TIP→ In July and August, the monastery is the setting for the annual Festival Sant Pere (www.festivalsantpere. com), drawing top-tier classical musicians from all over the world.** Find event listings online (in Catalan); phone for reservations or to book a postconcert dinner in the monastery's refectory-style restaurant: ☎ 972/194233 or 610/310073. ⊠ *Camí del Monestir s/n, El Porte de la Selva* ☎ 972/387559 ⊕ *www.mhcat.cat* 🖃 *€5* ⊙ *Closed Mon.*

WHERE TO EAT AND STAY

$$$$
SEAFOOD
Fodor's Choice
★

✕ **Casa Anita.** Simple, fresh, and generous dishes are the draw at this informal little eatery, an institution in Cadaqués. It sits on the street that leads to Port Lligat and Dalí's house. **Known for:** no menu; communal dining; famous clientele. $ *Average main: €25* ⊠ *Carrer Miquel Rosset 16, Cadaqués* ☎ 972/258471 ⊙ *Closed Mon., and mid-Oct.–1st wk in Dec.*

$$$$
CATALAN

✕ **Compartir.** The concept may be similar, but Compartir ("to share") is no tapas restaurant. This award-winning restaurant bases its menu on a small-plate sharing approach that has been taken to another level by the culinary team of Mateu Casañas, Oriol Castro, and Eduard Xatruch (all former elBulli chefs), who transform traditional recipes into an outstanding gourmet experience. **Known for:** sharing plates; creative gastronomy; beautiful courtyard setting. $ *Average main: €24 ⊠ Riera Sant Vicenç s/n, Cadaqués* 🕾 *972/258482* ⊕ *www.compartircadaques. com* ☉ *Closed Mon., and Jan.–early Feb.*

$$$$　🏨 **Hotel Playa Sol.** On the cove of Es Pianc, just a five-minute walk from
HOTEL　the village center, this hotel, in business for more than 50 years, has light
FAMILY　and airy rooms with modern furnishings; all but two have a balcony or terrace, and some have wonderful views of the sea. **Pros:** attentive, friendly service; family-friendly; great views. **Cons:** decor could be more colorful; rooms with balcony and sea views are harder to book; small rooms. $ *Rooms from: €247 ⊠ Riba Es Pianc 3, Cadaqués* 🕾 *972/258100* ⊕ *www.playasol.com* ☉ *Closed Nov.–mid-Feb.* 🛏 *48 rooms* ⫶◯⫶ *No meals.*

$$$　🏨 **Llané Petit.** This intimate, typically Mediterranean bay-side hotel
HOTEL　caters to people who want to make the most of their stay in the village and don't want to spend too much time in their hotel. **Pros:** semiprivate beach next to hotel; free Wi-Fi; good breakfast. **Cons:** small rooms; somewhat lightweight beds and furnishings; some soundproofing issues. $ *Rooms from: €142 ⊠ Pl. Llane Petit s/n, Cadaqués* 🕾 *972/251020* ⊕ *www.llanepetit.com* ☉ *Closed Nov.–Mar.* 🛏 *37 rooms* ⫶◯⫶ *Free Breakfast.*

SOUTHERN CATALONIA AND AROUND VALENCIA

Popular day trips from Barcelona include a visit to the jagged peaks of Montserrat, where the shrine of La Moreneta (the Black Virgin of Montserrat) sits. Farther south, the lively coastal town of Sitges makes a good day out or overnight stop that can be tied in with a side trip to the Cistercian monasteries of Santes Creus and Santa Maria de Poblet, both treasures of Catalan religious heritage. Tarragona, the principal town of southern Catalonia, was in Roman times one of the finest and most important outposts of the empire. Its wine was already famous and its population was the first *gens togata* (literally, the toga-clad people) in Spain, which conferred on them equality with the citizens of Rome. Roman remains, chief among them the Circus Maximus, bear witness to Tarragona's grandeur, and to this the Middle Ages added wonderful city walls and citadels.

Farther south lies Valencia, Spain's third-largest city and the capital of its region and province, equidistant from Barcelona and Madrid. If you have time for a day trip (or you decide to stay in the beach town of El Saler), make your way to the Albufera, a scenic coastal wetland teeming with native wildlife, especially migratory birds.

MONTSERRAT

50 km (31 miles) west of Barcelona.

A popular side trip from Barcelona is a visit to the shrine of La Moreneta (the Black Virgin of Montserrat) and the dramatic sawtooth peaks of Montserrat, as memorable for its strange topography as it is for its religious treasures. The views over the mountains that stretch all the way to the Mediterranean and, on a clear day, to the Pyrenees, are breathtaking. The rugged, boulder-strewn terrain makes for exhilarating walks and hikes.

GETTING HERE AND AROUND

By car from Barcelona, follow the A2/A7 autopista on the upper ring road (Ronda de Dalt), or from the western end of the Diagonal as far as Salida 25 to Martorell. Bypass this industrial center and follow signs to Montserrat. You can also take the FGC train from the Plaça d'Espanya metro station (hourly 7:36 am–5:41 pm, connecting with either the cable car at Aeri Montserrat or with the rack railway (Cremallera) at Monistrol Montserrat. Both the cable car and rack railway take 15 minutes and depart every 20 minutes and 15 minutes, respectively. Once you arrive at the monastery, several funiculars can take you farther up the mountain.

EXPLORING

Fodor'sChoice ★ **La Moreneta.** The shrine of La Moreneta, one of Catalonia's patron saints, resides in a Benedictine monastery high in the Serra de Montserrat, surrounded by jagged peaks that have given rise to countless legends: here St. Peter left a statue of the Virgin Mary carved by St. Luke, Parsifal found the Holy Grail, and Wagner sought musical inspiration. The monastic complex is dwarfed by the grandeur of sheer peaks, and the crests above bristle with chapels and hermitages. The hermitage of Sant Joan can be reached by funicular. Although a monastery has stood on the same site in Montserrat since the early Middle Ages, the present 19th-century building replaced the rubble left by Napoléon's troops in 1812. The shrine is world famous and one of Catalonia's spiritual sanctuaries—honeymooning couples flock here by the thousands seeking La Moreneta's blessing on their marriages, and twice a year, on April 27 and September 8, the diminutive statue of Montserrat's Black Virgin becomes the object of one of Spain's greatest pilgrimages. Only the basilica and museum are regularly open to the public. The basilica is dark and ornate, its blackness pierced by the glow of hundreds of votive lamps. Above the high altar stands the polychrome statue of the Virgin and Child, to which the faithful can pay their respects by way of a separate door. ■ TIP→ **The famous Escolania de Montserrat boys' choir sing the Salve and Virulai from the liturgy weekdays at 1 pm and Sunday at noon.** ✉ *Montserrat* ☎ *No phone* ⊕ *www.montserratvisita.com* 💶 *€16 sanctuary, audio guide, museum, and audiovisual presentation.*

SITGES, SANTES CREUS, AND SANTA MARIA DE POBLET

This trio of attractions south and west of Barcelona can be seen in a day. Sitges is the prettiest and most popular resort in Barcelona's immediate environs, with an excellent beach and a whitewashed and flowery old quarter. It's also one of Europe's premier gay resorts. Monolithic Romanesque architecture and beautiful cloisters characterize the Cistercian monasteries west of here, at Santes Creus and Poblet.

GETTING HERE AND AROUND

By car from Barcelona, head southwest along Gran Vía or Passeig Colom to the freeway that passes the airport on its way to Castelldefels. From here, the freeway and tunnels will get you to Sitges in 20–30 minutes. En route, the small village of Garraf is a worthwhile pit stop, with narrow lanes flanked by whitewashed houses that cling to a promonory looking out to sea. It has a small beach backed by colorful beach huts, providing a quieter refuge from the crowds in Sitges (although it too gets busy in high season). From Sitges, drive inland toward Vilafranca del Penedès and the A7 freeway. The A2 (Lleida) leads to the monasteries. Regular trains leave Sants and Passeig de Gràcia stations for Sitges, Garraf, and Vilafranca del Penedès; the ride takes a half hour to an hour. To get to Santes Creus or Poblet from Sitges, take a Lleida-bound train to L'Espluga de Francolí, 4 km (2½ miles) from Poblet; there's one direct train in the morning at 7:37 and four more during the day with transfers at Sant Vicenç de Calders. From L'Espluga, take a cab to the monastery.

SITGES

43 km (27 miles) southwest of Barcelona.

The fine white sand of the Sitges beach is elbow-to-elbow with sun worshippers April–September. On the eastern end of the strand is an alabaster statue of the 16th-century painter El Greco, usually associated with Toledo, where he spent most of his professional career. The artist Santiago Rusiñol is responsible for this surprise; he was such a Greco fan that he not only installed two of his paintings in his Museu del Cau Ferrat but also had this sculpture planted on the beach.

Just over 30 minutes by train (€3.80 each way), there's regular service from all three Barcelona stations. Buses, roughly the same price, run at least hourly from Plaza Espanya and take about 45 minutes, depending how many stops they make. If you're driving head south on the C32.

EXPLORING

Bodegas Torres. After leaving Sitges, make straight for the A2 autopista by way of Vilafranca del Penedès. Wine buffs may want to stop here for a tour or to taste some excellent Penedès wines. ⊠ *Finca "El Maset", Ctra. BP2121 (direction Sant Martí Sarroca), Vilafranca del Penedès* ☎ *938/177400* ⊕ *www.torres.es* ⊠ *From €12; includes tour and wine tasting.*

Museu del Cau Ferrat. This is the most interesting museum in Sitges, established by the bohemian artist and cofounder of the Quatre Gats café in Barcelona, Santiago Rusiñol (1861–1931), and containing some of his own paintings together with two by El Greco. Connoisseurs of wrought iron will love the beautiful collection of *cruces terminales,*

Whitewashed buildings dominate the landscape in Sitges.

crosses that once marked town boundaries. Next door is the **Museu Maricel de Mar,** with more artistic treasures. ⊠ *Carrer Fonollar 6, Sitges* ☎ *938/940364* ⊕ *www.museusdesitges.com* 🖂 *€10, includes Museu Maricel de Mar* ♥ *Closed Mon.*

Passeig Maritim. A focal point of Sitges life, this long esplanade is an iconic pedestrianized promenade that sweeps past the bay of Sitges. It's backed by upmarket villas, mountain vistas, and ocean views. ⊠ *Sitges.*

**OFF THE
BEATEN
PATH**

Museu Pau Casals. The family house of renowned cellist Pau (Pablo) Casals (1876–1973) is on the beach at Sant Salvador, just east of the town of El Vendrell. Casals, who left Spain in self-imposed exile after Franco seized power in 1939, left a museum of his possessions here, including several of his cellos, original music manuscripts, paintings, and sculptures. Other exhibits describe the Casals campaign for world peace ("Pau," in Catalan, means both Paul and peace), his speech at the United Nations in 1971 (at the age of 95), and his haunting interpretation of *El Cant dels Ocells* (*The Song of the Birds*), his homage to his native Catalonia. Across the street, the Auditori Pau Casals holds frequent concerts and, in July and August, a classical music festival. The museum is about 32 km (20 miles) south of Sitges, en route to Tarragona, ⊠ *Av. Palfuriana 67, Sant Salvador, Tarragona* ☎ *977/684276* ⊕ *www.paucasals.org* 🖂 *€7* ♥ *Closed Mon.*

WHERE TO EAT

$$$
SEAFOOD

✕ **Vivero.** Perched on a rocky point above the bay at Playa San Sebastián, Vivero specializes in paellas and seafood; try their *mariscada,* a meal-in-itself ensemble of lobster, mussels, and prawns. Weather permitting, the best seats in the house are on the terraces, with their wonderful views of the water. **Known for:** outdoor dining; excellent mariscada; wonderful water views. $ *Average main: €22* ✉ *Passeig Balmins s/n, Playa San Sebastián, Sitges* ☎ *938/942149* ⊕ *www.elviverositges.com.*

SANTES CREUS
95 km (59 miles) west of Barcelona.

Sitges, with its beach and its summer festivals of dance and music, film and fireworks, is anything but solemn. Head inland, however, some 45 minutes' drive west, and you discover how much the art and architecture—the very tone of Catalan culture—owes to its medieval religious heritage.

It takes about 45 minutes to drive to Santes Creus from Sitges. Take the C32 west, then get onto the C51 and TP2002.

EXPLORING

Montblanc. The ancient gates are too narrow for cars, and a walk through its tiny streets reveals Gothic churches with stained-glass windows, a 16th-century hospital, and medieval mansions. ✉ *Off A2, Salida 9.*

Santes Creus. Founded in 1157, Santes Creus is the first of the monasteries you'll come upon as the A2 branches west toward Lleida; take Exit 11 off the highway. Three austere aisles and an unusual 14th-century apse combine with the restored cloisters and the courtyard of the royal palace. ✉ *Pl. Jaume el Just s/n, Santes Creus* ☎ *977/638329* 🎫 *€6* ☾ *Closed Mon.*

SANTA MARIA DE POBLET
8 km (5 miles) west of Santes Creus.

This splendid Cistercian monastery, located at the foot of the Prades Mountains, is one of the great masterpieces of Spanish monastic architecture. Declared a UNESCO World Heritage Site, the cloister is a stunning combination of lightness and size, and on sunny days the shadows on the yellow sandstone are extraordinary.

The Barcelona–Lleida train can drop you at L'Espluga de Francolí, from where it's a 4-km (2½-mile) walk to the monastery. Buses from Tarragona or Lleida will get you a little closer, with a 2¾-km (1½-mile) walk. The drive from Sitges takes about an hour, via the C32 and AP2.

EXPLORING

Fodor's Choice
★

Santa Maria de Poblet. Founded in 1150 by Ramón Berenguer IV in gratitude for the Christian Reconquest, the monastery first housed a dozen Cistercians from Narbonne. Later, the Crown of Aragón used Santa Maria de Poblet for religious retreats and burials. The building was damaged in an 1836 anticlerical revolt, and monks of the reformed Cistercian Order have managed the difficult task of restoration since 1940. Today, a community of monks and novices still pray before the splendid retable over the tombs of Aragonese rulers, restored to their former glory by sculptor Frederic Marès; they also sleep in the cold, barren dormitory and eat frugal meals in the stark refectory. ✉ *Off A2 (Salida 9 from Barcelona, Salida 8 from Lleida)* ☎ *977/870089* ⊕ *www.poblet.cat* 🎫 *€9.*

Valls. This town, famous for its early spring calçotada (onion feast) held on the last Sunday of January, is 10 km (6 miles) from Santes Creus and 15 km (9 miles) from Poblet. Even if you miss the big day, calçots are served November–April at rustic and rambling farmhouses such as **Cal Ganxo** in nearby Masmolets (*Carrer Església 13* ☎ *977/605960*). Also, the **Xiquets de Valls,** Catalonia's most famous *castellers* (human castlers), might be putting up a living skyscraper.

TARRAGONA

98 km (61 miles) southwest of Barcelona, 251 km (156 miles) northeast of Valencia.

With its vast Roman remains and medieval Christian monuments, Tarragona has been designated a UNESCO World Heritage Site. The city today is a vibrant center of culture and art, a busy fishing and shipping port, and a natural jumping-off point for the towns and pristine beaches of the Costa Daurada, 216 km (134 miles) of coastline north of the Costa del Azahar.

Though modern Tarragona is very much an industrial and commercial city, it has preserved its heritage superbly. Stroll along the town's cliffside perimeter and you'll see why the Romans set up shop here: Tarragona is strategically positioned at the center of a broad, open bay, with an unobstructed view of the sea. As capital of the Roman province of Hispania Tarraconensis (from 218 BC), Tarraco (as it was then called) formed the empire's principal stronghold in Spain. St. Paul preached here in AD 58, and Tarragona became the seat of the Christian church in Spain until it was superseded by Toledo in the 11th century.

If you're entering the city en route from Barcelona, you'll pass the **Triumphal Arch of Berà,** dating from the 3rd century BC, 19 km (12 miles) north of Tarragona; and from the Lleida (Lérida) autopista, you can see the 1st-century **Roman aqueduct** that helped carry fresh water 32 km (20 miles) from the Gaià River. Tarragona is divided clearly into old and new by Rambla Vella; the old town and most of the Roman remains are to the north, while modern Tarragona spreads out to the south. Start your visit at acacia-lined Rambla Nova, at the end of which is a balcony overlooking the sea, the **Balcó del Mediterràni.** Then walk uphill along Passeig de les Palmeres; below it is the ancient amphitheater, the curve of which is echoed in the modern, semicircular Imperial Tarraco hotel on the promenade.

GETTING HERE AND AROUND

Tarragona is well connected by train: there are half-hourly express trains from Barcelona (1 hour 20 minutes; prices from €8.05) and regular train service from other major cities, including Madrid.

Seven to 10 buses leave Barcelona's Estació del Nord for Tarragona every day. Connections between Tarragona and Valencia are frequent too. There are also bus connections with the main Andalusian cities, plus Alicante and Madrid.

The €18 Tarragona Card, valid for two days, gives free entry to all the city's museums and historical sites, free rides on municipal buses, and discounts at more than 100 shops, restaurants, and bars. It's sold at the main tourist office and at most hotels.

Tours of the cathedral and archaeological sites are conducted by the tourist office, located just below the cathedral.

VISITOR INFORMATION

Contacts Visitor Information Tarragona. ✉ *Carrer Major 37* ☎ *977/250795* 🌐 *www.tarragonaturisme.cat/en.*

EXPLORING

Amphitheater. Tarragona, the Emperor Augustus's favorite winter resort, had arguably the finest amphitheater in Roman Iberia, built in the 2nd century AD for gladiatorial and other contests. The remains have a spectacular view of the sea. You're free to wander through the access tunnels and along the tiers of seats. In the center of the theater are the remains of two superimposed churches, the earlier of which was a Visigothic basilica built to mark the bloody martyrdom of St. Fructuós and his deacons in AD 259. ■ **TIP→ €7.40 buys a combination ticket valid for all Tarragona's Roman sites and is valid for one year.** ✉ *Parc de l'Amphiteatre Roma s/n* ☎ *977/242579* 🎫 *€4* 🕒 *Closed Mon.*

Catedral. Built between the 12th and 14th century on the site of a Roman temple and a mosque, this cathedral shows the transition from Romanesque to Gothic style. The initial rounded placidity of the Romanesque apse gave way to the spiky restlessness of the Gothic—the result is somewhat confusing. If no Mass is in progress, enter the cathedral through the cloister, where the Diocesan Museum houses a collection of artistic and religious treasures. The main attraction here is the 15th-century Gothic alabaster altarpiece of Sant Tecla by Pere Joan, a richly detailed depiction of the life of Tarragona's patron saint. Converted by Sant Paul and subsequently persecuted by local pagans, Sant Tecla was repeatedly saved from demise through divine intervention. ✉ *Pl. Pla de la Seu s/n* ☎ *977/226935* 🌐 *www.catedraldetarragona.com* 🎫 *€5 (cathedral and museum)* 🕒 *Closed Sun. in winter.*

Praetorium. This towering building was Augustus's town house, and is reputed to be the birthplace of Pontius Pilate. Its Gothic appearance is the result of extensive alterations in the Middle Ages, when it housed the kings of Catalonia and Aragón during their visits to Tarragona. ✉ *Pl. del Rei* ☎ *977/221736, 977/242220* 🎫 *From €4* 🕒 *Closed Mon.*

Roman Circus. Students have excavated the vaults of the 1st-century AD Roman arena, near the amphitheater. The plans just inside the gate show that the vaults now visible formed only a small corner of a vast space (350 yards long), where 23,000 spectators gathered to watch chariot races. As medieval Tarragona grew, the city gradually engulfed the circus. ✉ *Pl. del Rei, Rambla Vella s/n* ☎ *977/221736* 🎫 *From €4* 🕒 *Closed Mon.*

WHERE TO EAT AND STAY

$$$$ CATALAN 🍴 **Les Coques.** If you have time for only one meal in the city, take it at this elegant little restaurant in the heart of historic Tarragona. The menu is bursting with both mountain and Mediterranean fare, and the prix-fixe lunch is a bargain at €18. **Known for:** mountain fare; good-value prix-fixe lunch; good wine list. [$] *Average main: €24* ✉ *Carrer Sant Llorenç 15* ☎ *977/228300* 🌐 *www.les-coques.com* 🕒 *Closed Sun.*

Tarragona's cathedral is a mix of Romanesque and Gothic styles.

$$ CATALAN 🍴 **Les Voltes.** Built into the vaults of the Roman Circus, this unique spot serves a hearty cuisine within one of the oldest sites in Europe. You'll find Tarragona specialties, mainly fish dishes, as well as international recipes, with calçots (spring onions, grilled over a charcoal fire) in winter. (For the calçots, you need to reserve a day—preferably two or more—in advance.) **Known for:** reserve calçots a day or more in advance; Tarragona specialties; historic setting. [$] *Average main: €14* ✉ *Carrer Trinquet Vell 12* ☎ *977/230651* 🌐 *www.restaurantlesvoltes.cat* 🕒 *Closed Mon. No dinner Sun.*

8

$ HOTEL 🏨 **Plaça de la Font.** The central location and the cute rooms at this budget choice just off the Rambla Vella in the Plaça de la Font make for a practical base in downtown Tarragona. **Pros:** easy on the budget; comfortable, charming rooms; nearby public parking lot. **Cons:** rooms are on the small side; rooms with balconies can be noisy on weekends; basic facilities. [$] *Rooms from: €78* ✉ *Pl. de la Font 26* ☎ *977/240882* 🌐 *www.hotelpdelafont.com* 🛏 *20 rooms* 🍽 *No meals.*

NIGHTLIFE AND PERFORMING ARTS

Nightlife in Tarragona takes two forms: older and quieter in the upper city, younger and more raucous down below. There are some lovely rustic bars and wine bars in the Casco Antiguo, the upper section of Old Tarragona, around Plaça del Forum and Carrer de Santa Anna. Port Esportiu, a pleasure-boat harbor separate from the working port, has another row of dining and dancing establishments; young people flock here on weekends and summer nights.

El Korxo. This popular wine bar, with chunky wooden tables, subdued lighting, and quirky creative details, offers its clientele a taste of different wines from around Spain, as well as craft beers, charcuterie and cheeses, and other light snacks. ⊠ *Santa Anna 6* ☏ *692/460018.*

Teatre Metropol. Tarragona's center for music, dance, theater, and cultural events stages performances ranging from castellers (human-castle formations, usually performed in August and September) to folk dances. ⊠ *Rambla Nova 46* ☏ *977/244795.*

SHOPPING

Carrer Major. You have to haggle for bargains, but Carrer Major has some exciting antiques stores. They're worth a thorough rummage, as the gems tend to be hidden. ⊠ *Tarragona.*

VALENCIA

351 km (218 miles) southwest of Barcelona, 357 km (222 miles) southeast of Madrid.

Valencia, Spain's third-largest municipality, is a proud city with a thriving nightlife and restaurant scene, quality museums, and spectacular contemporary architecture, juxtaposed with a thoroughly charming historic quarter, making it a popular destination year in and year out. During the civil war, it was the last seat of the Republican Loyalist government (1935–36), holding out against Franco's National forces until the country fell to 40 years of dictatorship. Today it represents the essence of contemporary Spain—daring design and architecture along with experimental cuisine—but remains deeply conservative and proud of its traditions. Although it faces the Mediterranean, Valencia's history and geography have been defined most significantly by the Turia River and the fertile huerta that surrounds it.

The city has been fiercely contested ever since it was founded by the Greeks. El Cid captured Valencia from the Moors in 1094 and won his strangest victory here in 1099: he died in the battle, but his corpse was strapped into his saddle and so frightened the besieging Moors that it caused their complete defeat. In 1102 El Cid's widow, Jimena, was forced to return the city to Moorish rule; Jaume I finally drove them out in 1238. Modern Valencia was best known for its frequent disastrous floods until the Turia River was diverted to the south in the late 1950s. Since then the city has been on a steady course of urban beautification. The lovely bridges that once spanned the Turia look equally graceful spanning a wandering municipal park, and the spectacularly futuristic Ciutat de les Arts i les Ciències (City of Arts and Sciences), most of it designed by Valencia-born architect Santiago Calatrava, has at last created an exciting architectural link between this river town and the Mediterranean. If you're in Valencia, an excursion to Albufera Nature Park (which is in the area said to be the birthplace of paella) is a worthwhile day trip.

GETTING HERE AND AROUND

By car, Valencia is about 3½ hours from Madrid via the A3 motorway, and about the same from Barcelona on the AP7 toll road. Valencia is well connected by bus and train, with regular service to and from cities throughout the country, including nine daily AVE high-speed express trains from Madrid, making the trip in 1 hour 40 minutes, and six Euromed express trains daily from Barcelona, taking about 3½ hours. Valencia's bus station is across the river from the old town; take Bus No. 8 from the Plaza del Ayuntamiento. Frequent buses make the four-hour trip from Madrid and the five-hour trip from Barcelona. Dozens of airlines, large and small, serve Valencia airport, connecting the city with dozens of cities throughout Spain and the rest of Europe.

Once you're here, the city has an efficient network of bus, tram, and metro service. For timetables and more information, stop by the local tourist office. The double-decker Valencia Bus Turístic runs daily 9:45–7:45 (until 9:15 in summer) and departs every 20–30 minutes from the Plaza de la Reina. It travels through the city, stopping at most of the main sights: 24- and 48-hour tickets (€17 and €19, respectively) let you get on and off at eight main boarding points, including the Institut Valencià d'Art Modern, the Museo de Bellas Artes, and the Ciutat de les Arts i les Ciències. The same company also offers a two-hour guided trip (€16) to Albufera Nature Park, including an excursion by boat through the wetlands, departing from the Plaza de la Reina. In summer (and sometimes during the rest of the year) Valencia's tourist office organizes tours of Albufera. You see the port area before continuing south to the lagoon itself, where you can visit a traditional *barraca* (thatch-roof farmhouse).

Bus Contact Valencia Bus Station. ⊠ *Carrer de Menendez Pidal 11* ☎ *963/466266.*

FESTIVALS
Gran Fira de València (Great Valencia Fair). Valencia's monthlong festival, in July, celebrates theater, film, dance, and music. ⊠ *Valencia* ⊕ *www.granfiravalencia.com.*

Fodor's Choice ★ **Las Fallas.** If you want nonstop nightlife at its frenzied best, come during the climactic days of this festival, March 15–19 (it begins March 1), when revelers throng the streets to see the gargantuan *ninots,* effigies made of wood, paper, and plaster depicting satirical scenes and famous people. Last call at many bars and clubs isn't until the wee hours, if at all. On the last night, all but one (the winner is spared) are burned to the ground during La Crema, and it seems as though the entire city is ablaze. ⊠ *Valencia* ⊕ *www.visitvalencia.com/en/whats-on-offer-valencia/festivities/the-fallas.*

TOURS
Valencia Bus Turístic. Valencia's tourist bus allows you to hop on and hop off as you please, while audio commentary introduces the city's history and highlights. ⊠ *Pl. de la Reina s/n* ☎ *699/982514* ⊕ *www.valenciabusturistic.com* 🎫 *From €17.*

VISITOR INFORMATION
Contacts Valencia Tourist Office. ⊠ *Pl. del Ayuntamiento 1* ☎ *963/524908* ⊕ *www.visitvalencia.com/en.*

EXPLORING
Fodor's Choice ★ **Cathedral.** Valencia's 13th- to 15th-century cathedral is the heart of the city. The building has three portals—Romanesque, Gothic, and rococo. Inside, Renaissance and baroque marble was removed to restore the

8

original Gothic style, as is now the trend in Spanish churches. The Capilla del Santo Cáliz (Chapel of the Holy Chalice) displays a purple agate vessel purported to be the Holy Grail (Christ's cup at the Last Supper) and thought to have been brought to Spain in the 4th century. Behind the altar is the left arm of **St. Vincent**, martyred in Valencia in 304. Stars of the cathedral **museum** are Goya's two famous paintings of St. Francis de Borja, Duke of Gandia. Left of the entrance is the octagonal tower **El Miguelete**, which you can climb (207 steps) to the top: the roofs of the old town create a kaleidoscope of orange and brown terra-cotta, with the sea in the background. It's said that you can see 300 belfries from here, many with bright-blue cupolas made of ceramic tiles from nearby Manises. The tower was built in 1381 and the final spire added in 1736. ■TIP→ **The Portal de los Apostoles, on the west side of the cathedral, is the scene every Thursday at noon of the 1,000-year-old ceremony of the Water Tribunal: the judges of this ancient court assemble here, in traditional costume, to hand down their decisions on local irrigation-rights disputes.** ⊠ *Pl. de l'Almoina, s/n, Ciutat Vella* ☎ *963/918127* ⊕ *www.catedraldevalencia.es* ☑ *€7, includes audio guide* ⊙ *Closed Sun. Nov.–Mar.*

FAMILY
Fodor's Choice
★
Ciutat de les Arts i les Ciències. Designed mainly by native son Santiago Calatrava, this sprawling futuristic complex is the home of Valencia's **Museu de les Ciències Príncipe Felipe** (Prince Philip Science Museum), **L'Hemisfèric** (Hemispheric Planetarium), **L'Oceanogràfic** (Oceanographic Park), and **Palau de les Arts** (Palace of the Arts, an opera house and cultural center). With resplendent buildings resembling combs and crustaceans, the Ciutat is a favorite of architecture buffs and curious kids. The Science Museum has soaring platforms filled with lasers, holograms, simulators, hands-on experiments, and a swell "zero gravity" exhibition on space exploration. The eye-shape planetarium projects 3-D virtual voyages on its huge IMAX screen. At l'Oceanogràfic (the work of architect Felix Candela), the largest marine park in Europe, you can take a submarine ride through a coastal marine habitat. Other attractions include an amphitheater, an indoor theater, and a chamber-music hall. ⊠ *Av. del Profesor López Piñero 7* ☎ *961/974686* ⊕ *www. cac.es* ☑ *Museu de les Ciències from €8, L'Oceanogràfic from €30, L'Hemisfèric from €9.*

Fodor's Choice
★
Lonja de la Seda (*Silk Exchange*). On the Plaza del Mercado, this 15th-century building is a product of Valencia's golden age, when the city's prosperity as one of the capitals of the Corona de Aragón made it a leading European commercial and artistic center. The Lonja was constructed as an expression of this splendor and is widely regarded as one of Spain's finest civil Gothic buildings. Its facade is decorated with ghoulish gargoyles, complemented inside by high vaulting and slender helicoidal (twisted) columns. Opposite the Lonja stands the **Iglesia de los Santos Juanes** (Church of the St. Johns), gutted during the 1936–39 Spanish Civil War, and, next door, the Moderniste **Mercado Central** (Central Market, ⇨ *see Shopping*), with its wrought-iron girders and stained-glass windows. ⊠ *Lonja 2, Ciutat Vella* ☎ *962/084153* ☑ *€2* ⊙ *Closed Mon.*

Valencia

Valencia's L'Oceanogràfic (Ciutat de les Arts i les Ciènces) has amazing exhibits, as well as an underwater restaurant.

Fodor'sChoice ★ **Museo de Bellas Artes** (*Museum of Fine Arts*). Valencia was a thriving center of artistic activity in the 15th century—one reason that the city's Museum of Fine Arts, with its lovely palm-shaded cloister, is among the best in Spain. To get here, cross the old riverbed by the Puente de la Trinidad (Trinity Bridge) to the north bank; the museum is at the edge of the **Jardines del Real** (Royal Gardens; open daily 8–dusk), with its fountains, rose gardens, tree-lined avenues, and small zoo. The permanent collection of the museum includes many of the finest paintings by Jacomart and Juan Reixach, members of the group known as the Valencian Primitives, as well as work by Hieronymus Bosch—or El Bosco, as they call him here. The ground floor has a number of brooding, 17th-century Tenebrist masterpieces by Francisco Ribalta and his pupil José Ribera, a Diego Velázquez self-portrait, and a room devoted to Goya. Upstairs, look for Joaquín Sorolla (Gallery 66), the Valencian painter of everyday Spanish life in the 19th century. ⊠ *Calle San Pío V 9, Trinitat* ☎ *963/870300* ⊕ *www.museobellasartesvalencia.gva.es* ⊠ *Free* ⊘ *Closed Mon.*

Palacio del Marqués de Dos Aguas (*Ceramics Museum*). Since 1954, this palace has housed the **Museo Nacional de Cerámica**, with a magnificent collection of local and artisanal ceramics. Look for the Valencian kitchen on the second floor. The building itself, near Plaza Patriarca, has gone through many changes over the years and now has elements of several architectural styles, including a fascinating baroque alabaster facade. Embellished with carvings of fruits and vegetables, the facade was designed in 1740 by Ignacio Vergara. It centers on the two voluptuous male figures representing the Dos Aguas (Two Waters), a reference to Valencia's two main rivers and the origin of the noble title of the Marqués de Dos Aguas. ✉ *Rinconada Federico García Sanchiz 6* ☎ *963/516392* 🎫 *Palace and museum €3; free Sat. 4–8 and Sun.* 🕓 *Closed Mon.*

BEACHES

Playa las Arenas. This wide (nearly 450 feet) and popular grand municipal beach stretches north from the port and the America's Cup marina more than a kilometer (½ mile), before it gives way to the even busier and livelier Platja de Malvarossa. The Paseo Marítimo promenade runs the length of the beach and is lined with restaurants and small hotels, including the **Neptuno** and the upscale **Las Arenas Balneario** resort. There's no shade anywhere, but the fine golden sand is kept pristine and the water is calm and shallow. There are three lifeguard posts and first-aid stations. Brisk off-shore winds can make this ideal for windsurfing and small-craft sailing; there's a sailing school on the beach to meet the demand. Valencia can be mild and sunny year-round, and there are excellent lunch options along the seafront even out of season. **Amenities:** food and drink; lifeguards; showers; toilets; water sports. **Best for:** sunset; swimming; walking; windsurfing. ✉ *Valencia* 🌐 *www.playadelasarenas.com/en.*

WHERE TO EAT

$$$ TAPAS 🍴 **La Casa Montaña.** The walls are lined with rotund wine barrels at this welcoming bodega with a Moderniste facade, tucked down a side street in the city's old fishermen's quarter. Established in 1836, the restaurant serves a large and varied selection of tapas, from melt-in-your-mouth jamón to rustic stews and grilled seafood, all well accompanied by a superlative, regularly updated selection of wines. **Known for:** good tapas and shared plates; loads of character; quality wine list. [$] *Average main: €21* ✉ *Carrer de Josep Benlliure 69* ☎ *963/672314* 🌐 *www.emilianobodega.com* 🕓 *No dinner Sun.*

$$$ SPANISH 🍴 **La Pepica.** Locals regard this bustling, informal restaurant, on the promenade at El Cabanyal beach, as the best in town for seafood paella. Founded in 1898, the walls of the establishment are covered with signed pictures of appreciative visitors, from Ernest Hemingway to King Juan Carlos and the royal family. **Known for:** locally revered seafood paella; fruit tarts; historic locale. [$] *Average main: €20* ✉ *Paseo Neptuno 6* ☎ *963/710366* 🌐 *www.lapepica.com* 🕓 *Closed last 2 wks in Nov. and last 2 wks in Jan. No dinner Sun.–Thurs.*

$$ SPANISH 🍴 **La Riuà.** A favorite of Valencia's well connected and well-to-do since 1982, this family-run restaurant a few steps from the Plaza de la Reina specializes in seafood dishes like *anguilas* (eels) prepared with *all i pebre* (garlic and pepper), *parrillada de pescado* (selection of freshly grilled fish), and traditional paellas. Lunch begins at 2 and not a moment before. **Known for:** specialty eel dish; award-winning dining; longtime family-run establishment. [$] *Average main: €16* ✉ *Calle del Mar 27, bajo* ☎ *963/914571* 🌐 *www.lariua.com* 🕓 *Closed Sun. June–Nov. and Mon. Dec.–May. No dinner Mon. June–Nov. and Sun. Dec.–May.*

$$$ BASQUE 🍴 **Sagardi.** The upstairs dining room at this popular Basque restaurant is dominated by two huge wooden cider barrels, long rustic tables for 10—they're geared to groups and big families, but tables can pull

8

apart as needed—and half-moon windows overlooking San Vicente Mártir, the busy street between the plazas of the City Hall and the cathedral. Indulge here in market-fresh fish, charcoal-grilled *a la donostiarra* (oven-baked, San Sebastian–style, with garlic, cayenne pepper, and apple cider vinegar); or *mollejas* (sweetbreads) of beef with artichokes. **Known for:** market-fresh fish; good for groups; downstairs tapas bar. [$] *Average main: €22* ✉ *Calle San Vicente Mártir 6, Ciutat Vella* ☎ *963/910668* 🌐 *www.sagardi.com.*

WHERE TO STAY

$$ HOTEL **Ad Hoc Monumental.** This nicely designed 19th-century town house sits on a quiet street at the edge of the old city, a minute's walk from the Plaza Almoina and the cathedral in one direction, and steps from the Turia gardens in the other. **Pros:** close to sights but quiet; courteous, helpful staff; great value. **Cons:** parking can be a nightmare; not especially family-oriented; small rooms. [$] *Rooms from: €90* ✉ *Carrer Boix 4, Ciutat Vella* ☎ *963/919140* 🌐 *www.adhochoteles.com* 🛏 *28 rooms* 🍴 *No meals.*

$ B&B/INN Fodor's Choice ★ **Antigua Morellana.** Run by four convivial sisters, this 18th-century town house provides the ultimate no-frills accommodation in the heart of the old city. **Pros:** friendly service; excellent location; complimentary tea in the lounge. **Cons:** no parking; rooms overlooking street can be noisy; small rooms. [$] *Rooms from: €60* ✉ *Carrer d'En Bou 2, Ciutat Vella* ☎ *963/915773* 🌐 *www.hostalam.com* 🛏 *18 rooms* 🍴 *No meals.*

$$$$ HOTEL Fodor's Choice ★ **Caro Hotel.** A triumph of design, opened in 2012, this elegant modern hotel is seamlessly wedded to an important historical property: a 14th-century Gothic palace, built on the 12th-century Arabic wall and over the Roman Circus, fragments of which are on show. **Pros:** good location, a few minutes' walk from the cathedral; spot-on, attentive service; oasis of quiet. **Cons:** the two top-floor rooms have low, slanted ceilings; valet parking is rather pricey; decidedly not family-friendly. [$] *Rooms from: €195* ✉ *Carrer Almirante 14* ☎ *963/059000* 🌐 *www.carohotel.com* 🛏 *26 rooms* 🍴 *No meals.*

$$$$ HOTEL **Palau de la Mar.** In a restored 19th-century palace, this boutique hotel looks out at the Porta de La Mar, which marked the entry to the old walled quarter of Valencia. **Pros:** big bathrooms with double sinks; great location near the sights and shops; courtyard and garden. **Cons:** top-floor rooms have low, slanted ceilings; rooms overlooking road can be noisy; small gym. [$] *Rooms from: €240* ✉ *Av. Navarro Reverter 14, Ciutat Vella* ☎ *963/162884, 902/254255* 🌐 *www.hospes.com* 🛏 *66 rooms* 🍴 *Free Breakfast.*

$$$$ HOTEL **Westin Valencia.** Built in 1917 as a cotton mill, with successive recyclings as a fire station and a stable for the mounted National Police Corps, this classic property was transformed in 2006 into a luxury hotel. **Pros:** attentive, professional, multilingual staff; location steps from the metro that connects directly to the airport; pet-friendly. **Cons:** rates rise to astronomical during special events; some rooms could use refreshing. [$] *Rooms from: €200* ✉ *Av. Amadeo de Saboya 16, Pl. del Reial* ☎ *963/625900* 🌐 *www.westinvalencia.com* 🛏 *135 rooms* 🍴 *No meals.*

NIGHTLIFE AND PERFORMING ARTS

Valencianos have perfected the art of doing without sleep. Nightlife in the old town centers on Barrio del Carmen, a lively web of streets that unfolds north of Plaza del Mercado. Popular bars and pubs dot Calle Caballeros, starting at Plaza de la Virgen; the Plaza del Tossal also has some popular cafés, as does Calle Alta, off Plaza San Jaime.

Some of the funkier, newer places are in and around Plaza del Carmen. Across the river, look for appealing hangouts along Avenida Blasco Ibáñez and on Plaza de Cánovas del Castillo. Out by the sea, Paseo Neptuno and Calle de Eugenia Viñes are lined with clubs and bars, lively in summer. The monthly English-language nightlife and culture magazine *24/7 Valencia* (⊕ *www.247valencia.com*) is free at tourist offices and various bars and clubs; leisure guides in Spanish include *Hello Valencia* (⊕ *www.hellovalencia.es*) and *La Guía Go* (⊕ *www. laguiago.com*).

NIGHTLIFE

BARS AND CAFÉS **Café de las Horas.** This surreal bordello-style bar is an institution for Valencia's signature cocktail, Agua de Valencia (a syrupy blend of cava or champagne, orange juice, vodka, and gin). The bar's warm atmosphere and convivial vibe are perfect for whiling away the hours at the start (or end) of the night. ⊠ *Calle del Conde de Almodóvar 1* ☎ *963/917336* ⊕ *www.cafedelashoras.com.*

Café del Duende. For a taste of *el ambiente andaluz* (Andalusian atmosphere), stop by this flamenco club in the heart of the Barrio del Carmen. It's open Thursday–Saturday from 10 pm (performances start at 10:30 pm on Thursday and at 11 pm on Friday and Saturday). On Sunday performances start at 8 pm. Get there early to secure a seat. ⊠ *Carrer Túria 62, El Carmen* ☎ *630/455289* ⊕ *www.cafedelduende.com.*

Tyris On Tap. Valencia's first craft-beer brewery, Cerveza Tyris, has an animated bar opposite the Mercado Central. Visitors can sample a smorgasbord of locally brewed beers on tap and fill up on chili dogs and burgers to a background of well-selected music. ⊠ *Carrer de la Taula de Canvis 6, El Carmen* ☎ *961/132873* ⊕ *www.cervezatyris.com.*

DANCE CLUBS **Calcatta.** Need tangible proof that Valencia never sleeps? Find it at this Barrio del Carmen disco (Friday and Saturday only, from midnight), where a younger crowd parties to pop, R&B, and house music in a restored 17th-century palacio. Even if you drop by at 6 am, Calcutta will still be open. ⊠ *Calle Reloj Viejo 6, La Seu* ☎ *637/488505.*

Las Ánimas. This is the center-city location of Las Ánimas discos and pubs scattered around Valencia. ⊠ *Pizarro 31* ☎ *902/108527.*

MUSIC CLUBS **Jimmy Glass Jazz Bar.** Aficionados of modern jazz gather at this bar (open Tuesday–Saturday evening, well into the night), which books an impressive range of local and international combos and soloists. ⊠ *Carrer Baja 28, El Carmen* ⊕ *www.jimmyglassjazz.net.*

Radio City. The airy, perennially popular, bar–club–performance space at Radio City offers eclectic nightly shows featuring music from flamenco to Afro-jazz fusion. ⊠ *Carrer Santa Teresa 19, Ciutat Vella* ☎ *963/914151* ⊕ *www.radiocityvalencia.com.*

PERFORMING ARTS

CINEMA **Filmoteca.** The Filmoteca has changing monthly programs of films in their original language (look for *v.o.* for *versión original*) and an artsy haunt of a café. ⊠ *Pl. del Ayuntamiento 17* ☎ *963/539300* ⊕ *www. ivac.gva.es/la-filmoteca.*

MUSIC **Palau de la Música.** On one of the nicest stretches of the Turia riverbed is this huge glass vault, Valencia's main concert venue. Home of the Orquesta de Valencia, the main hall also hosts touring performers from around the world, including chamber and youth orchestras, opera, and an excellent concert series featuring early, baroque, and classical music. It's worth popping in to see the building even without concert tickets, and there is also an **art gallery,** which hosts free changing exhibitions by renowned modern artists. ⊠ *Passeig de l'Albereda 30* ☎ *963/375020* ⊕ *www.palaudevalencia.com.*

Palau de les Arts Reina Sofía. This visually arresting performing arts venue and concert hall, designed by Santiago Calatrava, hosts a rich calendar of opera and classical music throughout the year. ⊠ *Av. del Professor López Piñero (Historiador de la Medicina) 1* ☎ *961/975800* ⊕ *www. lesarts.com.*

SHOPPING

Mercado Central (Central Market). The bustling food market (at nearly 88,000 square feet, one of the largest in Europe) is open Monday–Saturday 7 am–3 pm. Locals and visitors alike line up at the 1,247 colorful stalls to shop for fruit, vegetables, meat, fish, and confectionery. Hop on a stool at The Central Bar, located in the heart of the throng, and taste award-winning chef Ricard Camarena's casual yet no less tasty take on tapas and *bocadillos* (sandwiches), while enjoying front-row-seat viewing of the action. ⊠ *Pl. Ciudad de Brujas s/n* ☎ *963/829100* ⊕ *www.mercadocentralvalencia.es.*

Nela. Browse here, in the heart of the old city, for *abanicos* (traditional silk folding fans), hand-embroidered *mantillas* (shawls), and parasols. ⊠ *Calle San Vicente Mártir 2, Ciutat Vella* ☎ *963/923023.*

Plaza Redonda. A few steps from the cathedral, off the upper end of Calle San Vicente Mártir, the restored Plaza Redonda ("Round Square") is lined with stalls selling all sorts of souvenirs and traditional crafts. ⊠ *Pl. Redonda, El Carmen.*

ALBUFERA NATURE PARK

11 km (7 miles) south of Valencia.

South of Valencia, Albufera Nature Park is one of Spain's most spectacular wetland areas. Home to the largest freshwater lagoon on the peninsula, this protected area and bird-watcher's paradise is bursting with unusual flora and fauna, such as rare species of wading birds. Encircled by a tranquil backdrop of rice fields, it's no surprise that the villages that dot this picturesque place have some of the best options in the region for trying classic Valencian paella or *arròs a banda* (rice cooked in fish stock).

GETTING HERE AND AROUND

From Valencia, buses depart for the park from the corner of Sueca and Gran Vía de Germanías every hour, and every half hour in summer, 7 am–9 pm daily.

EXPLORING

Albufera Nature Park. This beautiful freshwater lagoon was named by Moorish poets—*albufera* means "the sun's mirror." The park is a nesting site for more than 250 bird species, including herons, terns, egrets, ducks, and gulls. Bird-watching companies offer boat rides all along the Albufera. For maps, guides, and tour arrangements, start your visit at the park's information center, the Centre d'Interpretació Raco de l'Olla in El Palmar. ✉ *Ctra. de El Palmar s/n, El Palmar* ☎ *963/868050* 🌐 *www.albufera.com* 🎫 *Free.*

El Palmar. This is the major village in the area, with streets lined with restaurants specializing in various types of paella. The most traditional kind is made with rabbit or game birds, though seafood is also popular in this region because it's so fresh. ✉ *El Palmar.*

WHERE TO EAT

$$ SPANISH 🍴 **Maribel Arroceria.** So tasty is the paella here that even valencianos regularly travel out of the city to Maribel Arroceria, off the main drag in El Palmar. While you sit surrounded by the rice fields of Albufera Nature Park, during the week you can devour a fixed-price lunchtime *menu del dia* (€20) of four starters to share, a paella, and dessert, served in the contemporary, air-conditioned dining room or outside at pavement tables overlooking the canal. **Known for:** highly prized paellas; reasonable prix-fixe lunch menus, plus à la carte options; authentic setting in area considered the birthplace of paella. [$] *Average main: €17* ✉ *Carrer de Francisco Monleón 5, El Palmar* ☎ *961/620060* 🌐 *www.arroceriamaribel.com* ⏲ *Closed Wed. No dinner.*

THE COSTA BLANCA

The stretch of coastline known as the Costa Blanca (White Coast) begins at Dénia, south of Valencia, and stretches down roughly to Torrevieja, below Alicante. It's best known for its magical vacation combo of sand, sea, and sun, with popular beaches and more secluded coves and stretches of sand. Alicante itself has two long beaches, a charming old quarter, and mild weather most of the year.

DÉNIA

Dénia is the port of departure on the Costa Blanca for the ferries to Ibiza, Formentera, and Mallorca—but if you're on your way to or from the islands, stay a night in the lovely little town in the shadow of a dramatic cliff-top fortress. Or, spend a few hours wandering in the Baix la Mar, the old fishermen's quarter with its brightly painted houses, and exploring the historic town center. The town has become something of a culinary hot spot and is home to award-winning restaurants, which for its compact size is something of an achievement.

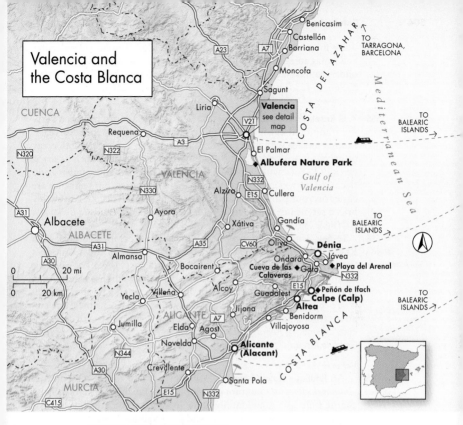

Valencia and
the Costa Blanca

GETTING HERE AND AROUND

Dénia is linked to other Costa Blanca destinations via Line 1 of the Alicante–Benidorm narrow-gauge TRAM train. There's also regular bus service from major towns and cities, including Madrid (7¼–9 hours) and Valencia (1¾–2½ hours). Local buses can get you around all of the Costa Blanca communities.

VISITOR INFORMATION

Contacts Visitor Information Dénia. ✉ Pl. Oculista Buigues 9 ☏ 966/422367 ⊕ www.denia.net.

EXPLORING

Castillo de Dénia. The most interesting architectural attraction here is the castle overlooking the town, and the **Palau del Governador** (Governor's Palace) inside. On the site of an 11th-century Moorish fortress, the Renaissance-era palace was built in the 17th century and was later demolished. A major restoration project is under way. The fortress has an interesting archaeological **museum** as well as the remains of a Renaissance bastion and a Moorish portal with a lovely horseshoe arch. ✉ Av. del Cid–Calle San Francisco s/n ☏ 966/422367 ⊠ €3 (includes entrance to archaeological museum).

FAMILY **Cueva de las Calaveras** (Cave of the Skulls). About 15 km (9 miles) inland from Dénia, this 400-yard-long cave was named for the 12 Moorish skulls found here when it was discovered in 1768. The cave of stalactites and stalagmites has a dome rising to more than 60 feet and leads to an underground lake. ✉ *Ctra. Benidoleig–Pedreguera, Km 1.5, Benidoleig* ☎ *966/404235* 🌐 *www.cuevadelascalaveras.com* 🎟 *€4.*

WHERE TO EAT

$$$ SEAFOOD 🍴 **El Raset.** Across the harbor, this Valencian favorite has been serving traditional cuisine with a modern twist for more than 30 years. From a terrace with views of the water you can choose from an array of excellent seafood dishes, including house specialties such as *arroz en caldero* (rice with monkfish, lobster, or prawns) and *gambas rojas* (local red prawns). À la carte dining can be expensive, but set menus are easier on your wallet. **Known for:** excellent seafood dishes; reasonably priced set menus; tasty paella. [$] *Average main: €20* ✉ *Calle Bellavista 7* ☎ *965/785040* 🌐 *www.grupoelraset.com.*

$$$ SPANISH Fodor's Choice ★ 🍴 **La Seu.** Under co-owners Fede and Diana Cervera and chef Xicu Ramón, this distinguished restaurant in the center of town continues to reinvent and deconstruct traditional Valencian cuisine. The setting is an architectural tour de force: a 16th-century town house transformed into a sunlit modern space with an open kitchen and a three-story-high wall sculpted to resemble a billowing white curtain. **Known for:** creative tapas; unbeatable midweek menu prices; inventive take on Valencian cuisine. [$] *Average main: €20* ✉ *Calle Loreto 59* ☎ *966/424478* 🌐 *www.laseu.es* ⏲ *Closed early Jan.–early Feb. No lunch Mon.*

WHERE TO STAY

$$ B&B/INN Fodor's Choice ★ 🏨 **Art Boutique Hotel Chamarel.** Ask the staff and they'll tell you that *chamarel* means a "mixture of colors," and this hotel brimming with charm, built as a grand family home in 1840, is certainly an eccentric blend of styles, cultures, periods, and personalities. **Pros:** friendly, helpful staff; individual attention; pet-friendly. **Cons:** no pool; not on the beach; rooms over the street are noisy. [$] *Rooms from: €90* ✉ *Calle Cavallers 13* ☎ *966/435007* 🌐 *www.hotelchamarel.com* 🛏 *15 rooms* 🍽 *Free Breakfast.*

$ HOTEL Fodor's Choice ★ 🏨 **Hostal Loreto.** Travelers on tight budgets will appreciate this basic yet impeccable lodging, on a central pedestrian street in the historic quarter just steps from the Town Hall. **Pros:** great central location in former nunnery; good value; broad, comfy roof terrace. **Cons:** no elevator; no amenities; rooms can be dark. [$] *Rooms from: €82* ✉ *Calle Loreto 12* ☎ *966/435419* 🌐 *www.hostalloreto.com* 🛏 *43 rooms* 🍽 *Free Breakfast.*

$$$ B&B/INN Fodor's Choice ★ 🏨 **Hotel El Raset.** Just across the esplanade from the port, where the Balearia ferries depart for Mallorca and Ibiza, this upscale boutique hotel has amenities that few lodgings in Dénia offer. **Pros:** staff is friendly, attentive, and multilingual; good location; good restaurant from same owners down the street. **Cons:** no pool; dim overhead lighting in rooms; pricey private parking. [$] *Rooms from: €156* ✉ *Calle Bellavista 1, Port* ☎ *965/786564* 🌐 *www.hotelelraset.com* 🛏 *20 rooms* 🍽 *Free Breakfast.*

$$$$ HOTEL Fodor's Choice ★ 🏨 **La Posada del Mar.** A few steps across from the harbor, this hotel in the 13th-century customs house has inviting rooms with seafront views; there's a subtle nautical theme, most evident in the sailor's-knot ironwork along the staircase. **Pros:** serene environment; close to center

Dénia's massive fort overlooks the harbor and provides a dramatic element to the skyline, with the Montgü mountains in the background.

of town; lovely sea views. **Cons:** pricey parking; no pool; rooms overlooking the main road can be noisy. [$] *Rooms from: €198* ✉ *Pl. de les Drassanes 2, Port* ☎ *966/432966* 🌐 *www.laposadadelmar.com* 🛏 *31 rooms* 🍴 *Free Breakfast.*

EN ROUTE

The Playa del Arenal, a tiny bay cut into the larger one, is worth a visit in summer. You can reach it via the coastal road (CV736) between Dénia and Jávea.

CALPE (CALP)

35 km (22 miles) south of Dénia.

Calpe has an ancient history, as it was chosen by the Phoenicians, Greeks, Romans, and Moors as a strategic point from which to plant their Iberian settlements. The real-estate developers were the latest to descend upon it: much of Calpe today is overbuilt with high-rise resorts and *urbanizaciónes*. But the old town is a delightful maze of narrow streets and small squares, archways and cul-de-sacs, with houses painted in Mediterranean blue, red, ocher, and sandstone; wherever there's a broad expanse of building wall, you'll likely discover a mural. Calpe is a delightful place to wander.

GETTING HERE AND AROUND

The narrow-gauge TRAM railway from Dénia to Alicante also serves Calpe, as do local buses.

VISITOR INFORMATION

Contacts Visitor Information Calpe. ✉ *Av. Ejércitos Españoles 44, Calp* ☎ *965/836920* 🌐 *www.calpe.es.*

EXPLORING

Fish Market. The fishing industry is still very important in Calpe, and every evening the fishing boats return to port with their catch. The subsequent auction at the fish market can be watched from the walkway of La Lonja de Calpe. ⊠ *Port, Calp* ⊗ *Closed weekends.*

Mundo Marino. Choose from a wide range of sailing trips, including cruises up and down the coast. Glass-bottom boats make it easy to observe the abundant marine life. ⊠ *Puerto Pesquero, Calp* ☎ *966/423066* ⊕ *www. mundomarino.es* ⊠ *From €15.*

Peñón d'Ifach Natural Park. The landscape of Calpe is dominated by this huge calcareous rock more than 1,100 yards long, 1,090 feet high, and joined to the mainland by a narrow isthmus. The area is rich in flora and fauna, with more than 300 species of plants and 80 species of land and marine birds. A visit to the top is not for the fainthearted; wear shoes with traction for the hike, which includes a trip through a tunnel to the summit. The views are spectacular, reaching to the island of Ibiza on a clear day. Check with the local visitor information center about guided tours for groups. ⊠ *Calp.*

WHERE TO EAT AND STAY

$$$

MEDITERRANEAN

✕ **Patio de la Fuente.** In an intimate little space with wicker chairs and pale mauve walls, this restaurant in the old town serves a bargain Mediterranean three-course prix-fixe dinner, wine included; you can also order à la carte. In summer, dine on the comfortable patio out back. **Known for:** outdoor dining; good-value three-course dinner; divine Scotch egg. $ *Average main: €18* ⊠ *Carrer Dos de Mayo 16, Calp* ☎ *965/831695* ⊕ *www.patiodelafuente.com* ⊗ *Closed Sun. and Mon. No lunch.*

$

B&B/INN

🏨 **Pensión el Hidalgo.** This family-run pension near the beach has small but cozy rooms with a friendly, easygoing feel, and several have private balconies overlooking the Mediterranean. **Pros:** beachfront location; reasonable prices; breakfast terrace with sea views. **Cons:** basic design; you must book far ahead in summer; weak Wi-Fi connection in some rooms. $ *Rooms from: €70* ⊠ *Av. Rosa de los Vientos 19, Calp* ☎ *965/839862* ⊕ *www.pensionelhidalgo.com* ⊠ *9 rooms* ⊙ *No meals.*

ALTEA

11 km (7 miles) southwest of Calpe.

Perched on a hill overlooking a bustling beachfront, Altea (unlike some of its neighboring towns) has retained much of its original charm, with an atmospheric old quarter laced with narrow cobblestone streets and stairways, and gleaming white houses. At the center is the striking church of Nuestra Señora del Consuelo, with its blue ceramic-tile dome, and the Plaza de la Iglesia in front.

GETTING HERE AND AROUND

Also on the Dénia–Alicante narrow-gauge TRAM train route, Altea is served by local buses, with connections to major towns and cities. The old quarter is mainly pedestrianized.

DID YOU KNOW?

The town of Altea (from the Moorish name Althaya, which means "health to all") has a popular seafront promenade. The church is easily recognized by its blue-tile domes.

VISITOR INFORMATION

Contacts Visitor Information Altea. ✉ *Calle Sant Pere 14* ☎ *965/844114* 🌐 *www.visitaltea.es.*

WHERE TO EAT

$$$ FRENCH 🍴 **La Costera.** This popular restaurant focuses on fine French fare, with such specialties as house-made foie gras, roasted lubina (sea bass), and beef entrecôte. There's also a variety of game in season, including venison and partridge. Book a table on the small and leafy terrace for a particularly romantic dinner. **Known for:** bucolic outdoor terrace; in-season game; French specialties. [$] *Average main: €20* ✉ *Costera Mestre de Música 8* ☎ *965/840230* 🌐 *www.lacosteradealtea.es* 🕓 *Closed Mon. No lunch Tues.–Thurs. No dinner Sun.*

$$ EUROPEAN 🍴 **Oustau de Altea.** In one of the prettiest corners of Altea's old town, this eatery was formerly a cloister and a school. Today the dining room and terrace combine contemporary design gracefully juxtaposed with a rustic setting, and the restaurant is known for serving polished international cuisine with French flair. **Known for:** cuisine with French style; dishes named after classic films; contemporary artwork. [$] *Average main: €15* ✉ *Calle Mayor 5, Casco Antiguo* ☎ *965/842078* 🌐 *www.oustau.com* 🕓 *Closed Mon. and Feb. No lunch.*

WHERE TO STAY

$ HOTEL 🏨 **Hostal Fornet.** The pièce de résistance at this simple, pleasant hotel, at the highest point of Altea's historic center, is the roof terrace with its stunning view; from here, you look out over the church's distinctive blue-tiled cupola and the surrounding tangle of streets, with a Mediterranean backdrop. **Pros:** lovely views; top value; multilingual owners. **Cons:** no pool or beach; small rooms; door is locked when reception is not staffed, and you have to call to be let in. [$] *Rooms from: €49* ✉ *Calle Beniardá 1, Casco Antiguo* ☎ *965/843005* 🌐 *www.hostalfornetaltea.com* 🛏 *23 rooms* 🍽 *No meals.*

ALICANTE (ALACANT)

82 km (51 miles) northeast of Murcia, 183 km (114 miles) south of Valencia, 52 km (32 miles) south of Altea.

The Greeks called it Akra Leuka (White Summit) and the Romans named it Lucentum (City of Light). A crossroads for inland and coastal routes since ancient times, Alicante has always been known for its luminous skies. The city is dominated by the 16th-century grande dame castle, **Castillo de Santa Bárbara,** a top attraction. The best approach is via the elevator cut deep into the mountainside. Also memorable is Alicante's grand **Esplanada,** lined with date palms. Directly under the castle is the city beach, the Playa del Postiguet, but the city's pride is the long, curved Playa de San Juan, which runs north from the Cap de l'Horta to El Campello.

GETTING HERE AND AROUND

Alicante has two train stations: the main Estación de Madrid and the local Estación de la Marina, from which the local FGV line runs along the Costa Blanca from Alicante to Dénia. The Estación de la Marina is at the far end of Playa Postiguet and can be reached by Buses C1 and C2 from downtown.

The slower narrow-gauge TRAM train goes from the city center on the beach to El Campello. From the same open-air station in Alicante, the Line 1 train departs to Benidorm, with connections on to Altea, Calpe, and Dénia.

VISITOR INFORMATION

Contacts Tourist Information Alicante. ⊠ *Rambla Méndez Núñez 41, Alicante* ☎ *965/200000* ⊕ *www.alicanteturismo.com.* **TRAM.** ⊠ *Alicante-Luceros, Alicante* ☎ *900/720472* ⊕ *www.tramalicante.es.*

EXPLORING

OLD TOWN

Ayuntamiento. Constructed between 1696 and 1780, the town hall is a beautiful example of baroque civic architecture. Inside, a gold sculpture by Salvador Dalí of San Juan Bautista holding the famous cross and shell rises to the second floor in the stairwell. Ask gate officials for permission to explore the ornate halls and rococo chapel on the first floor. Look for the plaque on the first step of the staircase that indicates the exact sea level, used to define the rest of Spain's altitudes "above sea level." ⊠ *Pl. de Ayuntamiento, Alicante* ☎ *965/149100* ⊗ *Closed weekends.*

Basílica de Santa María. Constructed in a Gothic style over the city's main mosque between the 14th and 16th century, this is Alicante's oldest house of worship. The main door is flanked by beautiful baroque stonework by Juan Bautista Borja, and the interior highlights are the golden rococo high altar, a Gothic image in stone of St. Mary, and a sculpture of Sts. Juanes by Rodrigo de Osona. ⊠ *Pl. de Santa María s/n, Alicante* ☎ *965/200000 tourist office (for information)* ⊗ *Closing times can vary due to religious services.*

Concatedral of San Nicolás de Bari. Built between 1616 and 1662 on the site of a former mosque, this church (called a *con*catedral because it shares the seat of the bishopric with the Concatedral de Orihuela) has an austere facade designed by Agustín Bernardino, a disciple of the great Spanish architect Juan de Herrera. Inside, it's dominated by a dome nearly 150 feet high, a pretty cloister, and a lavish baroque side chapel, the Santísima Sacramento, with an elaborate sculptured stone dome of its own. Its name comes from the day that Alicante was reconquered (December 6, 1248) from the Moors, the feast day of St. Nicolás. ⊠ *Pl. Abad Penalva 2, Alicante* ☎ *965/212662* 🎫 *Free* ⊗ *Closed Sun. except services.*

Museo de Bellas Artes Gravina. Inside the beautiful 18th-century Palacio del Conde de Lumiares, MUBAG—as it's best known—has some 500 works of art ranging from the 16th to the early 20th century. MUBAG is within a short walk of the Museo de Arte Contemporaneo de Alicante (MACA), also free entry, which features 20th-century works by Miró, Dalí, and Picasso, among others. ⊠ *Calle de Gravina 13–15, Alicante* ☎ *965/146780* ⊕ *www.mubag.org* 🎫 *Free* ⊗ *Closed Mon.*

8

Alicante's Esplanada de España, lined with date palms, is the perfect place for a stroll. The municipal brass band offers concerts on the bandstand of the Esplanada on Sunday evenings in July and August.

OUTSIDE OLD TOWN

Fodor'sChoice
★
Castillo de Santa Bárbara (*Saint Barbara's Castle*). One of the largest existing medieval fortresses in Europe, Castillo de Santa Bárbara sits atop 545-foot-tall Monte Benacantil. From this strategic position you can gaze out over the city, the sea, and the whole Alicante plain for many miles. Remains from civilizations dating from the Bronze Age onward have been found here; the oldest parts of the castle, at the highest level, are from the 9th through 13th century. The castle is most easily reached by taking the elevator from Avenida Juan Bautista Lafora. The castle also houses the Museo de la Ciudad de Alicante (MUSA) which uses audiovisual presentations and archaeological finds to tell the story of Alicante, its people, and the city's enduring relationship with the sea. ⊠ *Monte Benacantil s/n, Alicante* ☎ *965/152969* ⊕ *www.castillodesantabarbara.com* ⊠ *Castle and museum free, elevator €3.*

Museo Arqueológico Provincial. Inside the old hospital of San Juan de Dios, the MARQ has a collection of artifacts from the Alicante region dating from the Paleolithic era to modern times, with a particular emphasis on Iberian art. ⊠ *Pl. Dr. Gómez Ulla s/n, Alicante* ☎ *965/149000* ⊕ *www.marqalicante.com* ⊠ *€3* ⊘ *Closed Mon.*

Museo de Hogueres. Bonfire festivities are popular in this part of Spain, and the ninots, or effigies, can be elaborate and funny, including satirized political figures and celebrities. Every year the best effigies are saved from the flames and placed in this museum, which also has an audiovisual presentation of the festivities, scale models, photos, and costumes. ⊠ *Rambla de Méndez Nuñez 29, Alicante* ☎ *965/146828* ⊕ *www.hogueras.org* ⊠ *Free* ⊘ *Closed Mon. and Aug.*

WHERE TO EAT

$$ ✕ **El Buen Comer.** On the edge of the old town, this relaxed two-tier res-
SPANISH taurant serves enticing dishes in plentiful portions. Downstairs, indulge
in tapas and simpler dishes, or head to the fancier dining space upstairs
for specialties like roast suckling pig, lamb chops, and sea bass baked
in a carapace of salt. **Known for:** delicious rice dishes; great value for
price; specialty meat and seafood dishes. $ *Average main: €12 ⊠ Calle
Mayor 8, Alicante* ☎ *965/213103* ⊕ *www.elbuencomer.es.*

$$$ ✕ **El Portal.** Blending tradition with novelty is not always an easy task,
SPANISH but it is what draws people back to El Portal in droves. Chef Sergio
Sierra runs a slick operation, from the restaurant's extravagant decor
(think modern interpretation of Roaring '20s) to a menu that is commit-
ted to offering the best flavors of the region—from the freshest seafood
to premium cuts of meat to seasonal produce. **Known for:** montadito de
solomillo de vacuno con trufa (steak sandwich with truffle oil); unique
decor and DJ soundtrack; cocktails, wine, and dinner all in one place.
$ *Average main: €22 ⊠ C. Bilbao 2, Alicante* ☎ *965/143269* ⊕ *www.
elportaltabernawines.com.*

$$$ ✕ **La Taberna del Gourmet.** This wine bar and restaurant in the heart of the
TAPAS *casco antiguo* (old town) earns high marks from locals and international
Fodor'sChoice visitors alike. A bar with stools and counters offers a selection of fresh
★ seafood tapas—oysters, mussels, razor clams—to complement a well-
chosen list of wines from La Rioja, Ribera del Duero, and Priorat, and
the two dining rooms are furnished with thick butcher-block tables and
dark brown leather chairs. **Known for:** excellent wine list; fresh seafood
tapas; reservations essential. $ *Average main: €20 ⊠ Calle San Fer-
nando 10, Alicante* ☎ *965/204233* ⊕ *www.latabernadelgourmet.com.*

$$$ ✕ **Nou Manolín.** An Alicante institution, this inviting exposed-brick and
SPANISH wood-lined restaurant is generally packed with locals, here for the
excellent-value tapas and daily menu. It's a superb place to tuck into
fish freshly caught that afternoon and served up for dinner, a tribute to
the city's enduring relationship with the sea. **Known for:** market-fresh
produce; authentic local vibe; a favorite of culinary superstar Ferran
Adrià. $ *Average main: €20 ⊠ Calle Villegas 3, Alicante* ☎ *965/200368*
⊕ *www.grupogastronou.com.*

WHERE TO STAY

$ ⊡ **Hostal Les Monges Palace.** In a restored 1912 building, this family-run
HOTEL hostal in Alicante's central casco antiguo features lovingly preserved
exposed stone walls, ceramic tile floors, and rooms furnished with
eccentric artwork and quirky charm. **Pros:** personalized service; ideal
location with rooftop terrace; lots of character. **Cons:** the newer, modern
part is not as atmospheric; must book well in advance; bathrooms in
standard rooms are small. $ *Rooms from: €75 ⊠ Calle San Agustín
4, Alicante* ☎ *965/215046* ⊕ *www.lesmonges.es* ⇆ *24 rooms* ❢❍❢ *Free
Breakfast.*

8

NIGHTLIFE

El Barrio, the old quarter west of Rambla de Méndez Núñez, is the prime nightlife area of Alicante, with music bars and discos every couple of steps. In summer, or after 3 am, the liveliest places are along the water, on Ruta del Puerto and Ruta de la Madera.

El Coscorrón. It's an Alicante tradition to start an evening out here, with El Coscorrón's generous mojitos. ⊠ *Calle Tarifa 5, Alicante* ☎ *965/212727.*

SHOPPING

Mercado Central. Bulging with fish, vegetables, and other local items, this is the place to stop by and discover Alicante's fresh produce, traded from this Moderniste-inspired building since 1921. ⊠ *Av. Alfonso el Sabio 10, Alicante.*

IBIZA AND THE
BALEARIC ISLANDS

WELCOME TO
IBIZA AND THE BALEARIC ISLANDS

TOP REASONS TO GO

★ **Pamper yourself:**
Luxurious boutique hotels on restored and rede-signed rural estates are *the* hip places to stay in the Balearics. Many have their own holistic spas: restore and redesign yourself at one of them.

★ **Enjoy seafood delica-cies:** Seafood specialties come straight from the boat to portside restau-rants all over the islands.

★ **Party hard:** Ibiza's summer club scene is the biggest, wildest, and glitziest in the world.

★ **Take in the gorgeous views:** The miradores of Mallorca's Tramuntana, along the road from Valldemossa to Sóller, highlight the most spec-tacular seacoast in the Mediterranean.

★ **Discover Palma:**
Capital of the Balearics, Palma is one of the great unsung cities of the Mediterranean—a showcase of medieval and modern architec-ture, a venue for art and music, a mecca for sail-ors, and a killer place to shop for shoes.

The Balearic Islands lie 80–305 km (50–190 miles) off the Spanish mainland, roughly between Valencia and Barcelona. In the center, Mallorca, with its roll-ing eastern plains and mountainous northwest, is the largest of the group. Menorca, its clos-est neighbor, is virtually flat; but like Ibiza and tiny Formentera to the west, it has a rugged coastline of small inlets and sandy beaches.

1 Ibiza. Sleepy from November to May, the island is Party Central in midsum-mer for retro hippies and nonstop clubbers. Dalt Vila, the medieval quarter of Eivissa, the capital, on the hill overlooking the town, is a UNESCO World Heritage Site.

2 Formentera.
Day-trippers from Ibiza chill out on this (comparatively) quiet little island with long stretches of protected beach.

3 Mallorca. Palma, the island's capital, is a trove of art and architectural gems. The Tramuntana, in the northwest, is a region of forested peaks and steep sea cliffs that few landscapes in the world can match.

4 Menorca. Mahón, the capital city, commands the largest and deepest harbor in the Mediterranean. Many of the houses above the port date to the 18th-century occupation by the British Navy.

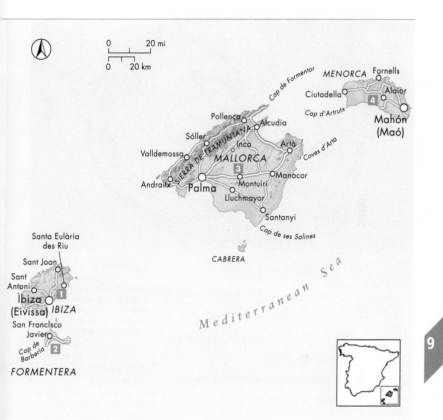

0   20 mi
0   20 km

Cap de Formentor   MENORCA   Fornells

Ciutadella   Alaior

Cap d'Artrutx   **4**

Pollença   Mahón
Alcudia   (Maó)

Sóller   *SIERRA DE TRAMUNTANA*   Inca   Artà

Valldemossa   **MALLORCA**   *Coves d'Arta*

Andraitx   **3**   Manacor

Palma   Montuiri

Lluchmayor

Santanyi

Cap de ses Salines

Santa Eulària
des Riu

Sant Joan   **CABRERA**

Sant
Antoni   *Mediterranean Sea*

Ibiza
(Eivissa)   *IBIZA*

San Francisco
Javier   **1**

*Cap de
Barberia*   **2**

FORMENTERA

9

EATING AND DRINKING WELL IN THE BALEARIC ISLANDS

Mediterranean islands should guarantee great seafood—and the Balearics deliver, with superb products from the crystalline waters surrounding the archipelago. Inland farms supply free-range beef, lamb, goat, and cheese.

(top left) Tumbet is a traditional vegetable dish, served in a clay pot. (top right) Clams are one of the many seafood options you'll find in the Balearics. (bottom left) Local cheese from Menorca

Ibiza's fishermen head out into the tiny inlets for sea bass and bream, which are served in beach shacks celebrated for *bullit de peix* (fish casserole), *guisat* (fish and shellfish stew), and *burrida de ratjada* (ray with almonds). Beyond the great seafood, there are traditional farm dishes that include *sofrit pagès* (lamb or chicken with potatoes and red peppers), *botifarron* (blood sausage), and *rostit* (oven-roasted pork). Mallorcans love their *sopas de peix* (fish soup) and their *panades de peix* (fish-filled pastries), while Menorca's harbor restaurants are famous for *llagosta* (spiny lobster), grilled or served as part of a *caldereta*—a soupy stew. Interestingly, mayonnaise is widely believed to have been invented by the French in Mahón, Menorca, after they took the port from the British in 1756.

BALEARIC ALMONDS

Almonds are omnipresent in the Balearics, used in sweets as well as seafood recipes. Typically used in the *picada*—the ground nuts, spices, and herbs on the surface of a dish—almonds are essential to the Balearic economy. After a 19th-century phylloxera plague decimated Balearic vineyards, almond trees replaced vines and the almond crop became a staple.

VEGETABLES

The *tumbet mallorquin* is a classic Balearic dish made of layers of fried zucchini, bell peppers, potatoes, and eggplant with tomato sauce between each layer. It's served piping hot in individual earthenware casseroles.

SEAFOOD

There are several seafood dishes to look out for in the Balearics. *Burrida de ratjada* is boiled ray baked between layers of potato with almonds. The picada covering the ray during the baking includes almonds, garlic, egg, a slice of fried bread, parsley, salt, pepper, and olive oil. *Caldereta de llagosta* (spiny lobster soup) is a quintessential Menorcan staple sometimes said to be authentic only if the Menorcan spiny lobster is used. *Guisat de marisc* (shellfish stew) is an Ibiza stew of fish and shellfish cooked with a base of onions, potatoes, peppers, and olive oil. Nearly any seafood from the waters around Ibiza may well end up in this staple.

PORK

Rostit (roast pork) is baked in the oven with liver, eggs, bread, apples, and plums. *Sobrasada* (finely ground pork seasoned with sweet red paprika and stuffed in a sausage skin) is one of Mallorca's two most iconic food products (the other is the *ensaimada,* a sweet spiral pastry made with *saim,* or lard). Sobrasada originated in Italy but

became popular in Mallorca during the 16th century.

MENORCAN CHEESE

Mahón cheese is a Balearic trademark, and Menorca has a Denominación de Origen (D.O.), one of the 12 officially designated cheese-producing regions in Spain. The *curado* (fully cured) cheese is the tastiest.

WINE

With just 2,500 acres of vineyards (down from 75,000 in 1891), Mallorca's two D.O. wine regions—Binissalem, near Palma, and Pla i Llevant on the eastern side of the island—will likely remain under the radar to the rest of the world. While you're here, though, treat yourself to a Torre des Canonge white, a fresh, full, fruity wine, or a red Ribas de Cabrera from the oldest vineyard on the island, Hereus de Ribas in Binissalem, founded in 1711. Viticulture on Menorca went virtually extinct with the reversion of the island to Spain after its 18th-century British occupation, but since the last half of the 20th century, a handful of ambitious, serious winemakers—mainly in the area of Sant Lluís—have emerged to put the local product back on the map.

9

BEST BEACHES OF THE BALEARICS

When it comes to oceanfront property, the Balearic Islands have vast and varied resources: everything from long sweeps of beach on sheltered bays to tiny crescents of sand in rocky inlets and coves called *calas*—some so isolated you can reach them only by boat.

(top left) Ibiza is "Party Island," and its beaches get crowded. (top right) The benefits of the popular beaches are their ample amenities. (bottom left) For peace and quiet, head to Macarella on Mallorca.

Not a few of the Balearic beaches, like their counterparts on the mainland coasts, have become destinations for communities of holiday chalets and retirement homes, usually called *urbanizaciónes,* their waterfronts lined with the inevitable shopping centers and pizza joints—skip these and head to the simpler and smaller beaches in or adjoining the Balearics' admirable number of nature reserves. Granted you'll find few or no services, and be warned that smaller beaches mean crowds in July and August, but these are the Balearics' best destinations for sun and sand. The local authorities protect these areas more rigorously, as a rule, than they do those on the mainland, and the beaches are gems.

BEACH AMENITIES

Be prepared: services at many of the smaller Balearic beaches are minimal or nonexistent. If you want a deck chair or something to eat or drink, bring it with you or make sure to ask around to see if your chosen secluded inlet has at least a *chiringuito*: a waterfront shack where the food is likely to feature what the fisherman pulled in that morning.

SES SALINES, IBIZA

Easy to reach from Eivissa, Ibiza's capital, this is one of the most popular beaches on the island, but the setting—in a protected natural park area—has been spared overdevelopment. The beach is relatively narrow, but the fine golden sand stretches more than a kilometer (nearly a mile) along the curve of Ibiza's southernmost bay. Two other great choices, on the east coast, are Cala Mastella, a tiny cove tucked away in a pine woods where a kiosk on the wharf serves the fresh catch of the day, and Cala Llenya, a family-friendly beach in a protected bay with shallow water.

BENIRRÁS, IBIZA

Benirrás is a small cove tucked away on Ibiza's northern coast backed by pine-clad hills. Known for its sunsets and laid-back vibe, it's popular with artists and hippies. Every Sunday at sunset, drummers descend onto the beach to form ritualistic drum circles, one of the island's most popular events. On other days, it's a peaceful stretch of soft sand with calm water to while away a few hours.

PLATJES DE SES ILLETES, FORMENTERA

The closest beach to the port at La Sabina, where the ferries come in from Ibiza, Ses Illetes is Formentera's preeminent party scene: some 3 km (2 miles) of fine white sand with beach bars and

snack shacks, and Jet Skis and windsurfing gear for rent.

ES TRENC, MALLORCA

One of the few long beaches on the island that's been spared the development of resort hotels, this pristine 3-km (2-mile) stretch of soft, white sand southeast of Palma, near Colònia Sant Jordi, is a favorite with nude bathers—who stay mainly at the west end—and day-trippers who arrive by boat. The water is crystal clear blue and shallow for some distance out. The 10-km (6-mile) walk along the beach from Colònia Sant Jordi to the Cap Salines lighthouse is one of Mallorca's treasures.

CALA MACARELLA/CALA MACARETTA, MENORCA

This pair of beautiful, secluded coves edged with pines is about a 20-minute walk through the woods from the more developed beach at Santa Galdana, on Menorca's south coast. Macarella is the larger and busier of the two; Macaretta, a few minutes farther west along the path, is popular with nude bathers and boating parties. Cala Pregonda, on the north coast of Menorca, is a splendid and secluded beach with walk-in access only: it's a lovely crescent cove with pine and tamarisk trees behind and dramatic rock formations at both ends, though it's more difficult to get to.

Updated by
Elizabeth
Prosser

Could anything go wrong in a destination that gets, on average, 300 days of sunshine a year? True, the water is only warm enough for a dip May–October, but the climate does seem to give the residents of the Balearics a sunny disposition year-round. They are a remarkably hospitable people, not merely because tourism accounts for such a large chunk of their economy, but because history and geography have combined to put them in the crossroads of so much Mediterranean trade and traffic.

The Balearic Islands were outposts, successively, of the Phoenician, Carthaginian, and Roman empires before the Moors invaded in 902 and took possession for some 300 years. In 1235, Jaume I of Aragón ousted the Moors, and the islands became part of the independent kingdom of Mallorca until 1343, when they returned to the Crown of Aragón under Pedro IV. With the marriage of Isabella of Castile to Ferdinand of Aragón in 1469, the Balearics were joined to a united Spain. Great Britain occupied Menorca in 1704, during the War of the Spanish Succession, to secure the superb natural harbor of Mahón as a naval base, but returned it to Spain in 1802 under the Treaty of Amiens.

During the Spanish Civil War, Menorca remained loyal to Spain's democratically elected Republican government, while Mallorca and Ibiza sided with Francisco Franco's insurgents. Mallorca then became a base for Italian air strikes against the Republican holdouts in Barcelona. This topic is still broached delicately on the islands; they remain fiercely independent of one another in many ways. Even Mahón and Ciutadella, at opposite ends of Menorca—all of 44 km (27 miles) apart—remain estranged over differences dating to that war.

The tourist boom, which began during Franco's regime (1939–75), turned great stretches of Mallorca's and Ibiza's coastlines into strips of high-rise hotels, fast-food restaurants, and discos.

PLANNING

WHEN TO GO

July and August are peak season in the Balearics; it's hot, and even the most secluded beaches are crowded. Weatherwise, May and October are ideal, with June and September just behind. Winter is quiet; it's too cold for the beach but fine for hiking, golfing, and exploring—though on Menorca the winter winds are notoriously fierce. The clubbing season on Ibiza begins in June.

Note: between November and March or April many hotels and restaurants are closed for their own vacations or seasonal repairs.

PLANNING YOUR TIME

Most European visitors to the Balearics pick one island and stick with it, but you could easily see all three. Start in Mallorca with **Palma.** Begin early at the cathedral and explore the Llotja, the Almudaina palace, and the Plaça Major. The churches of Santa Eulàlia and Sant Francesc and the Arab Baths are a must. Staying overnight in Palma means you can sample the nightlife and have time to visit the museums.

Take the old train to **Sóller** and rent a car for a trip over the Sierra de Tramuntana to **Deiq, Son Marroig,** and **Valldemossa.** The roads are twisty, so give yourself a full day. Spend the night in Sóller, and you can drive from there in less than an hour via **Lluc** and **Pollentia** to the Roman and Moorish ruins at **Alcúdia.**

By fast ferry it's just over three hours from Port d'Alcúdia to **Ciutadella,** on Menorca; the port, the **cathedral,** and the narrow streets of the old city can be explored in half a day. Make your way across the island to **Mahón,** and devote an afternoon to the highlights there. From Mahón, you can take a 30-minute interisland flight to **Eivissa.** On Ibiza, plan a full day for the UNESCO World Heritage Site **Dalt Vila** and the shops of **Sa Penya,** and the better part of another for **Santa Gertrudis** and the north coast. If you've come to Ibiza to party, of course, time has no meaning.

FESTIVALS

In addition to the major public holidays, towns and villages on each of the islands celebrate a panoply of patron saints' days, fairs, and festivals all their own. Highlights include the following:

Eivissa Medieval. Held in Ibiza's capital on the second weekend in May (Thursday–Sunday evenings), this event celebrates the designation of the Dalt Villa as a UNESCO World Heritage Site, with street stalls selling "medieval" fare, craft markets, performances, and processions in costume. ⊠ *Eivissa* ⊕ *medieval-festival-ibiza.ibiza4all.org.*

Festa de Nostra Senyora de la Victoria. On the second Sunday and Monday in May in Sóller, mock battles are staged to commemorate an attack by Turkish pirates in 1561. ⊠ *Sóller* ⊕ *www.sollerweb.com/firo.html.*

Festa de Sant Antoni d'Abat. Celebrated in towns and villages all over Ibiza and Mallorca, this festival, held January 16–17, includes bonfires, costume parades, and a ceremonial blessing of the animals. ⊠ *Eivissa.*

Festa de Sant Bartolomé. Spectacular fireworks mark this festival, which takes place in Sant Antoni on August 24. ⊠ *San Antoni.*

Festa del Mar. Honoring Our Lady of Carmen, patron saint of seafarers, this festival is celebrated on July 16 in the Ibizan towns of Eivissa, Santa Eulàlia, Sant Antoni, and Sant Josep, and also on Formentera. A statue of Our Lady is carried in solemn procession through the streets to the port, where it is put aboard a ship for a ceremonial outing on the ocean. ⊠ *Eivissa.*

Festa des Vermar. The grape harvest festival, complete with processional floats and concerts, is held in Binissalem on the last Sunday in September. ⊠ *Binissalem.*

Festa Major de Sant Joan (*Feast of St. John the Baptist*). Held June 23–24, this festival is celebrated throughout the island of Ibiza. ⊠ *Eivissa.*

Festes de Sant Joan. At this event June 23–24, riders in costume parade through the streets of Ciutadella on horseback, urging the horses up to dance on their hind legs while spectators pass dangerously under their hooves. ⊠ *Ciutadella.*

Festes de Santa Eularia. Ibiza's boisterous winter carnival, held on February 12, includes folk dancing and music. ⊠ *Eivissa.*

Fiestas de la Mare de Déu de Gràcia. Held September 6–9 in Mahón, this celebration is Menorca's final blowout of the season. ⊠ *Maó.*

Processo dels Tres Tocs (*Procession of the Three Knocks*). This festival, held in Ciutadella on January 17, celebrates the 1287 victory of King Alfonso III of Aragón over the Moors. ⊠ *Ciutadella.*

Romería de Sant Marçal (*Pilgrimage of St. Mark*). On June 30 in Sa Cabaneta, a procession of costumed townspeople heads to the church of their patron saint, to draw water from a consecrated cistern thought to give health and strength of heart. ⊠ *Sa Cabaneta.*

Sant Ciriac. Capped with a spectacular fireworks display over the walls of Eivissa's old city, this festival (on August 8) celebrates the Reconquest of Ibiza from the Moors. ⊠ *Eivissa.*

Sant Josep. This festival on March 19, in honor of the patron saint of Sant Josep de sa Talaia on Ibiza, is known for folk dancing, which you can also see in Sant Joan every Thursday evening. ⊠ *Sant Josep de sa Talaia* ⊕ *www.santjosep.net/en.*

Sant Lluís. Celebrations of this saint's day, which are held during the last weekend of August in the town of Sant Lluís, on Menorca, center on an equestrian cavalcade called *la Qualcada.* ⊠ *Sant Lluís.*

Virgen del Carmen. The patron saint of sailors (Our Lady of Mount Carmel) is honored July 15–16 in Formentera with a blessing of the boats in the harbor. The holiday is also celebrated on Ibiza.

GETTING HERE AND AROUND
AIR TRAVEL

The easiest way to reach Mallorca, Menorca, and Ibiza is to fly. Each of the three islands is served by an international airport, all of them within 15–20 minutes by car or bus from their respective capital cities. There are daily domestic connections to each from Barcelona (about 50 minutes), Madrid, and Valencia: no-frills and charter operators fly to Eivissa, Palma, and Mahón from many European cities, especially during the summer. There are also flights between the islands. Book early in high season.

BIKE TRAVEL

The Balearic Islands—especially Ibiza and Formentera—are ideal for exploration by bicycle. Ibiza is relatively flat and easy to negotiate, though side roads can be in poor repair. Formentera is level, too, with bicycle lanes on all connecting roads. Parts of Mallorca are quite mountainous, with challenging climbs through spectacular scenery; along some country roads, there are designated bike lanes. Bicycles are easy to rent, and tourist offices have details of recommended routes. Menorca is relatively flat, with lots of roads that wander through pastureland and olive groves to small coves and inlets.

BOAT AND FERRY TRAVEL

From Barcelona: The Acciona Trasmediterránea and Balearia car ferries serve Ibiza, Mallorca, and Menorca from Barcelona. The most romantic way to get to the Balearic Islands is by overnight ferry from Barcelona to Palma, sailing (depending on the line and the season) between 11 and 11:30 pm; you can watch the lights of Barcelona sinking into the horizon for hours—and when you arrive in Palma, around 7 am, see the spires of the cathedral bathed in the morning sun. Overnight ferries have lounges and private cabins. Round-trip fares vary with the line, the season, and points of departure and destination, but from Barcelona are from around €110 for lounge seats or €270 per person for a double cabin (tax included).

Faster ferries operated by Balearia, with passenger lounges only, speed from Barcelona to Eivissa (Ibiza), to Palma and Alcúdia (Mallorca), and to Mahón (Menorca). Depending on the destination, the trip takes between three and six hours.

From Valencia: Acciona Trasmediterránea ferries leave Valencia late at night for Ibiza, arriving early in the morning. Balearia fast ferries (no vehicles) leave Valencia for Sant Antoni on Ibiza in the late afternoon, making the crossing in about 2½ hours. Acciona Trasmediterránea and Balearia have services from Valencia to Mallorca, and Trasmediterránea also runs a service to Mahón (Menorca). Departure days and times vary with the season, with service more frequent in summer.

From Dénia: Balearia runs a daily three-hour fast ferry service for passengers and cars between Dénia and Ibiza, another between Dénia and Formentera, and a similar eight-hour service between Dénia and Palma on weekends.

Interisland: Daily fast ferries connect Ibiza and Palma; one-way fares run €66–€81, depending on the type of accommodations. The Pitiusa and Trasmapi lines offer frequent fast ferry and hydrofoil service between Ibiza and Formentera (€27 one-way, €40–€44 round-trip). Daily ferries connect Alcúdia (Mallorca) and Ciutadella (Menorca) in three to four hours, depending on the weather; a hydrofoil makes the journey in about an hour.

Boat and Ferry Contacts Acciona Trasmediterránea. ☎ 902/454645 ⊕ *www.trasmediterranea.es/en.* **Balearia.** ☎ 902/160180 ⊕ *www.balearia.com.* **Mediterranea Pitiusa.** ☎ *609/741067 reservations, 971/314461 for Eivissa* *ticket office ⊕ www.mediterraneapitiusa.com.* **Trasmapi.** ☎ *971/314433 information, 971/310711 for Eivissa ticket office ⊕ www.trasmapi.com.*

BUS TRAVEL

There is bus service on all the islands, though it's not extensive, especially on Formentera. ⇨ *Check each island's Getting Here and Around section for details.*

CAR TRAVEL

Ibiza is best explored by car or motor scooter: many of the beaches lie at the end of rough, unpaved roads. Tiny Formentera can almost be covered on foot, but renting a car or a scooter at La Sabina is a time saver. A car is essential if you want to beach-hop on Mallorca or Menorca and explore beyond the main cities and resorts.

TAXI TRAVEL

On Ibiza, taxis are available at the airport and in Eivissa, Figueretas, Santa Eulàlia, and Sant Antoni. On Formentera, there are taxis in La Sabina and Es Pujols. Legal taxis on Ibiza and Formentera are metered, but it's a good idea to get a rough estimate of the fare from the driver before you climb aboard. Taxis in Palma are metered. For trips beyond the city, charges are posted at the taxi stands. On Menorca, you can pick up a taxi at the airport or in Mahón or Ciutadella.

TRAIN TRAVEL

The public Ferrocarriles de Mallorca railroad track connects Palma and Inca, with stops at about half a dozen villages en route.

A journey on the privately owned Palma–Sóller railroad is a must: completed in 1912, it still uses the carriages from that era. The train trundles across the plain to Bunyola, then winds through tremendous mountain scenery to emerge high above Sóller. An ancient tram connects the Sóller terminus to Port de Sóller, leaving every hour on the hour 8–7; the Palma terminal is near the corner of the Plaça d'Espanya, on Calle Eusebio Estada next to the Inca train station.

RESTAURANTS

On the Balearic Islands many restaurants tend to have short business seasons. This is less true of Mallorca, but on Menorca, Ibiza, and especially on Formentera, it might be May (or later) before the shutters are removed from that great seafood shack you've heard so much about. Really fine dining experiences are in short supply on the islands; in the popular beach resorts, the promenades can seem overrun with paella and pizza joints. Away from the water, however, there are exceptional meals to be had—and the seafood couldn't be any fresher.

HOTELS

Many hotels on the islands include a continental or full buffet breakfast in the room rate.

IBIZA

Ibiza's high-rise resort hotels and holiday apartments are mainly in Sant Antoni, Talamanca, Ses Figueretes, and Playa d'en Bossa. Overbuilt Sant Antoni has little but its beach to recommend it. Playa d'en Bossa, close to Eivissa, is prettier but lies under a flight path. To get off the beaten track and into the island's largely pristine interior, look for *agroturismo* lodgings in Els Amunts (the Uplands) and in villages such as Santa Gertrudis or Sant Miquel de Balanzat.

FORMENTERA

If July and August are the only months you can visit, reserve well in advance. Accommodations on Formentera, the best of them on the south Platja de Mitjorn coast, tend to be small private properties converted to studio apartment complexes, rather than megahotels.

MALLORCA

Mallorca's large-scale resorts—more than 1,500 of them—are concentrated mainly on the southern coast and primarily serve the package-tour industry. Perhaps the best accommodations on the island are the number of grand old country estates and town houses that have been converted into boutique hotels, ranging from simple and relatively inexpensive agroturismos to stunning outposts of luxury.

MENORCA

Aside from a few hotels and hostals in Mahón and Ciutadella, almost all of Menorca's tourist lodgings are in beach resorts. As on the other islands, many of these are fully reserved by travel operators in the high season and often require a week's minimum stay, so it's generally most economical to book a package that combines airfare and accommodations. Or inquire at the tourist office about boutique and country hotels, especially in and around Sant Lluís.

Hotel reviews have been shortened. For full information, visit Fodors. com.

WHAT IT COSTS IN EUROS				
	$	**$$**	**$$$**	**$$$$**
Restaurants	under €12	€12–€17	€18–€22	over €22
Hotels	under €90	€90–€125	€126–€180	over €180

Prices in the reviews are the average cost of a main course or equivalent combination of smaller dishes at dinner, or if dinner is not served, at lunch. Hotel prices are the lowest cost of a standard double room in high season.

TOURS

Ibiza resorts run trips to neighboring beaches and to smaller islands. Trips from Ibiza to Formentera include an escorted bus tour. In Sant Antoni, there are a number of tour organizers to choose from.

Most Mallorca hotels and resorts offer guided tours. Typical itineraries are the Caves of Artà or Drac, on the east coast, including the nearby Auto Safari Park and an artificial-pearl factory in Manacor; the Chopin museum in the old monastery at Valldemossa, returning through the writers' and artists' village of Deià; the port of Sóller and the Arab gardens at Alfàbia; the Thursday market and leather factories in Inca; Port de Pollença; Cap de Formentor; and the northern beaches.

Excursions a Cabrera. Several options are available for visits to Cabrera, from a 1½-hour sunset swim, including sparkling wine and dessert, to a daylong tour, with time to explore independently. One option for this is to take a self-guided tour of the island's underwater ecosystem—using a mask and snorkel with their own sound system; the recording explains the main points of interest as you swim. Boats generally depart from Colònia Sant Jordi, 47 km (29 miles) southeast of Palma. You can buy tickets on the dock at Carrer Babriel Roca or online. ⊠ *Colònia de Sant Jordi* ☎ *971/649034* ⊕ *www.excursionsacabrera.es* ⌨ *From €30.*

Yellow Catamarans. On Menorca, sightseeing trips on glass-bottom catamarans leave Mahón's harbor from the quayside near the Xoriguer gin factory. Departure times vary; check with the tourist information office on the Moll de Ponent, at the foot of the winding stairs from the old city to the harbor. ⊠ *Moll de Llevant 12, Maó* ☎ *971/352307, 639/676351 for reservations* ⊕ *www.yellowcatamarans.com* ⌨ *€13.*

IBIZA

Tranquil countryside, secluded coves, and intimate luxury lodging to the north; sandy beaches and party venues by the score to the south; a capital crowned with a historic UNESCO World Heritage Site, and laidback (and English-speaking) hospitality islandwide—Ibiza is a vacation destination not to be missed. Settled by the Carthaginians in the 5th century BC, Ibiza has seen successive waves of invasion and occupation, the latest of which began in the 1960s, when it became a tourist destination. With a full-time population of barely 140,000, it now gets some 2 million visitors a year. It's blessed with beaches—56 of them, by one count—and also has the world's largest nightclub. About a quarter of the people who live on Ibiza year-round are expats.

October through April, the pace of life here is decidedly slow, and many of the island's hotels and restaurants are closed. In the 1960s and early 1970s, Ibiza was discovered by sun-seeking hippies and eventually emerged as an icon of counterculture chic. Ibizans were—and still are—friendly and tolerant of their eccentric visitors. In the late 1980s and 1990s, club culture took over. Young ravers flocked here from all over the world to dance all night and pack the sands of built-up beach resorts like Sant Antoni. That party-hearty Ibiza is still alive and well, but a new wave of luxury rural hotels, offering oases of peace and privacy, with spas and high-end restaurants, marks the most recent transformation of the island into a venue for more upscale tourism. In fact, it is entirely feasible to spend time on Ibiza and not see any evidence of the clubbing and nightlife scene it is so famous for.

GETTING HERE AND AROUND

Ibiza is a 55-minute flight or a nine-hour ferry ride from Barcelona.

Ibizabus serves the island. Buses run to Sant Antoni every 15–30 minutes 7:30 am–midnight (until 10:30 pm November–May) from the bus station on Avenida d'Isidor Macabich in Eivissa, and to Santa Eulàlia every half hour 6:50 am–11:30 pm Monday–Saturday (until 10:30 November–April), with late buses on Saturday in the summer party season at midnight, 1, and 2 am; Sunday service is hourly 7:30 am–11:30 pm (until 10:30 pm November–April). Buses to other parts

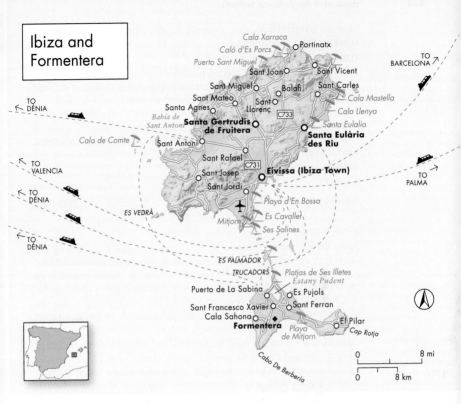

Ibiza and Formentera

Cala Xarraca
Caló d'Es Porcs
Portinatx
Puerto Sant Miguel
Sant Joan
Sant Vicent

TO BARCELONA

Sant Miguel
Balafi
Sant Carles
Cala Mastella
Sant Mateo
Sant Cala Llenya
Santa Agnes
Llorenç
C733
Santa Eulalia
Bahía de Sant Antoni
Santa Gertrudis de Fruitera
Santa Eulària des Riu

TO DÉNIA

Cala de Comte
Sant Antoni
Sant Rafael

TO VALENCIA
Sant Josep
C731
Eivissa (Ibiza Town)

TO PALMA

TO DÉNIA
Sant Jordi
Playa d'En Bossa
ES VEDRÀ
Es Cavallet
Mitjorn
Ses Salines

TO DÉNIA

ES PALMADOR
TRUCADORS
Platjas de Ses Illetes
Estany Pudent
Puerto de La Sabina
Es Pujols
Sant Francesco Xavier
Sant Ferran
Cala Sahona
Formentera
El Pilar
Playa de Mitjorn
Cap Rotja
Cabo De Berbería

0   8 mi
0   8 km

of the island are less frequent, as is the cross-island bus between Sant Antoni and Santa Eulàlia.

On Ibiza, a six-lane divided highway connects the capital with the airport and Sant Antoni. Traffic circles and one-way streets make it a bit confusing to get in and out of Eivissa, but out in the countryside driving is easy and in most cases is the only way of getting to some of the island's smaller coves and beaches.

Bus Contact Ibizabus. ☎ 971/340382, 600/482972 for Discobus ⊕ www. ibizabus.com.

Taxi Contacts Cooperativa Limitada de Taxis de Sant Antoni. ✉ Carrer del Progrés, San Antoní ☎ 971/343764. **Radio-Taxi.** ☎ 971/398483 ⊕ www.taxi-eivissa.com.

EIVISSA (IBIZA TOWN)

Hedonistic and historic, Eivissa (Ibiza, in Castilian) is a city jam-packed with cafés, nightspots, and trendy shops; looming over it are the massive stone walls of **Dalt Vila**—the medieval city declared a UNESCO World Heritage Site in 1999—and its Gothic cathedral. Squeezed between the north walls of the old city and the harbor is **Sa Penya,** a long labyrinth of stone-paved streets with some of the city's best offbeat shopping, snacking, and exploring.

TOURS

FAMILY **Dalt Vila tours.** On nearly every Saturday evening, a 75-minute drama- tized tour of Dalt Vila departs from the Portal de Ses Taules, at the foot of the walls. Three performers in period costume enact a legendary 15th-century love story as they move through the medieval scenes. Res- ervations are essential. The tour is in Spanish, though English-speakers can be accommodated for groups of 10 or more. ⊠ *Portal de Ses Taules, Dalt Vila* ☎ *971/399232* 🎫 *From €10.*

VISITOR INFORMATION

Contacts

Ibiza Tourist Office. ⊠ *La Cúria, Plaça de la Catedral, s/n, Dalt Vila* ☎ *971/399232.*

EXPLORING

Bastió de Sant Bernat (*Bastion of St. Bernard*). From here, behind the cathedral, a promenade with sea views runs west to the bastions of Sant Jordi and Sant Jaume, past the **Castell**—a fortress formerly used as an army barracks. In 2007 work began to transform it into a luxury para- dor, but archaeological discoveries under the work site have delayed the reconstruction indefinitely. The promenade ends at the steps to the **Portal Nou** (New Gate). ⊠ *Eivissa.*

Catedral. Built on a site used for temples and other religious buildings since the time of the Phoenicians, Ibiza's cathedral has a Gothic tower and a baroque nave, and a small museum of religious art and artifacts. It was built in the 13th and 14th centuries and renovated in the 18th cen- tury. ⊠ *Pl. de la Catedral s/n, Dalt Vila* ☎ *971/312773* 🎫 *Museum €1.*

Centre d'Interpretació Madina Yabisa. A few steps from the cathedral, this small center has a fascinating collection of audiovisual materials and exhibits on the period when the Moors ruled the island. ⊠ *Carreró de la Soledat, 2, Dalt Vila* ☎ *971/392390* 🎫 *€2* ⊘ *Closed Mon.*

Museu d'Art Contemporani. Just inside the old city portal arch, this museum houses a collection of paintings, sculpture, and photography from 1959 to the present. The scope of the collection is international, but the empha- sis is on artists who were born or lived in Ibiza during their careers. There isn't much explanatory material in English, however. There is also an underground archaeological site in the basement, some of which dates back as far as the 6th century BC. ⊠ *Ronda Narcís Puget, s/n, Dalt Vila* ☎ *971/302723* ⊕ *www.mace.eivissa.es* 🎫 *Free* ⊘ *Closed Mon.*

Sant Domingo. The roof of this 16th-century church is an irregular arrangement of tile domes. The nearby *ajuntament* (town hall) is housed in the church's former monastery. ⊠ *Carrer General Balanzat 6, Dalt Vila* ☎ *971/399232* ⊘ *Closed Mon.*

BEACHES

Es Cavellet Beach. This wild stretch of white sand hugged by turquoise waves is popular with nudist sunbathers, and can be reached on foot from Ses Salines beach (20-minute walk) or by car (10 km from Ibiza Town, through the salt flats). Parts are backed by sand dunes, and on a clear day it serves up views of Ibiza Town and Formentera. El Chiringuito bar and restaurant, one of Ibiza's favorite waterfront beach bars, is known for its relaxed vibe, good food and cocktails, and its lively season-opening and -closing parties. **Amenities:** food and drink; parking (fee); showers. **Best for:** nudists; swimming. ✉ *Es Cavallet Beach, Sant Josep de sa Talaia.*

Ses Salines. Very much a place to see and be seen, the beach at Ses Salines is a mile-long narrow crescent of golden sand about 10 minutes' drive from Eivissa, in a wildlife conservation area. Trendy restaurants and bars, like the Jockey Club and Malibu, bring drinks to you on the sand and have DJs for the season, keeping the beat in the air all day long. The beach has different areas: glitterati in one zone, naturists in another, gay couples in another. There are no nearby shops, but the commercial vacuum is filled by vendors of bags, sunglasses, fruit drinks, and so on, who can be irritating. The sea is shallow, with a gradual drop-off, but on a windy day breakers are good enough to surf. **Amenities:** food and drink; lifeguards; parking (fee); showers; toilets; water sports. **Best for:** nudists; partiers; swimming; windsurfing. ✉ *Eivissa* ✣ *10 km (6 miles) west on E20 ring road from Eivassa toward airport, then south on PM802 local road to beach.*

WHERE TO EAT AND STAY

$$$$ MEDITERRANEAN

🍴 **Restaurante Jardín La Brasa.** A perennial favorite, La Brasa is tucked down a side street close to the walls of the Dalt Vila. Here you can dine on traditional Ibizan cuisine, such as barbecued entrecôte steak, lamb chops, or grilled squid within a tree-filled courtyard lit by fairy lights and candles—a haven from the bustling surroundings. **Known for:** grilled meat; courtyard setting; reservations needed in high season. [$] *Average main: €25* ✉ *Carrer de Pere Sala 3, Eivissa* ☎ *971/301202* 🌐 *www.labrasaibiza.com.*

$$$ CONTEMPORARY
Fodor's Choice ★

🍴 **Sa Brisa Gastro Bar.** Time was, you could search in vain for innovative cuisine in Eivissa, but that changed with the opening of this stylish place. Enjoy a menu of tapas, salads, seafood, and meat dishes with imaginative Latin touches including delicious homemade *croquetas* (croquettes), shrimp quesadillas with guacamole, and Iberian pork. **Known for:** innovative dishes; stylish, modern interior; great location on the main promenade. [$] *Average main: €18* ✉ *Passeig Vara de Rey 15, Ibiza Nueva* ☎ *971/090649* 🌐 *www.sabrisagastrobar.com.*

$$$$ BASQUE

🍴 **S'Oficina.** Some of the best Basque cuisine on Ibiza is served at this restaurant, just 2 km (1 mile) outside town in Sant Jordi. Marine prints hang on the white walls and ships' lanterns from the ceiling; the bar is adorned with ships' wheels. *Lomo de merluza con almejas* (hake with clams) and *kokotxas* (cod cheeks) are among the specialties. [$] *Average main: €23* ✉ *Carrer de les Begònies 17, Playa d'en Bossa* ✣ *Take highway toward airport and turn off for Playa d'en Bossa; S'Oficina is on left in 1st block past traffic circle on road to beach* ☎ *971/390081* ⏲ *No dinner Sun.–Tues. Oct.–Mar.*

$$$ HOTEL

🏨 **Hostal Parque.** This is the top contender for a budget-friendly billet in the heart of town, and its location at the foot of Dalt Vila couldn't be better. **Pros:** good value; strategic location; views over the square. **Cons:** not much closet space; square in front of the hotel is noisy until the wee hours in high season; no pets. [$] *Rooms from: €160* ✉ *Pl. del*

An evening stroll among the shops in Eivissa

Parque 4, Dalt Vila ☎ *971/301358* ⊕ *www.hostalparque.com* ⤳ *30 rooms* ⦿*No meals.*

$$$
HOTEL

🏨 **Hotel Montesol.** The island's first hotel, the Montesol, opened in 1934 and retains its grand exterior—fashion photographers love the balconies facing the promenade. **Pros:** value for price; convenient; good for meeting people. **Cons:** noisy; small rooms; minimal amenities. $ *Rooms from: €127* ⊠ *Paseo Vara de Rey 2, Eivissa* ☎ *971/931493* ⊕ *www.hotelmontesol.com* ⤳ *55 rooms* ⦿*No meals.*

NIGHTLIFE

Fodor's Choice
★

Ibiza's discos are famous throughout Europe. Keep your eyes open during the day for free invitations handed out on the street—these can save you expensive entry fees. Between June and September, an all-night "Discobus" service (☎ *600/482972* ⊕ *www.discobus.es*) runs between Eivissa, Sant Antoni, Santa Eulàlia/Es Canar, Playa d'En Bossa, and the major party venues. The cost is €3 for one ride, €12 for a five-trip ticket.

BARS AND GATHERING PLACES

FAMILY

Calle Santa Creu. Hidden behind the walls of the Dalt Vila, this narrow lane is lined with bustling eateries. It's at its most atmospheric in the evening, when you can enjoy a candlelit dinner on the cobblestones as the world slowly saunters past. ⊠ *Calle Santa Creu, Dalt Vila.*

Carrer de la Verge (*Carrer de la Mare de Déu*). Gay nightlife converges on this street in Sa Penya. ⊠ *Eivissa.*

Sunset Ashram. There are many places to take in a spectacular sunset in Ibiza, but this one ranks as one of the White Isle's top spots. Set above a beautiful stretch of unspoiled coastline, boho Sunset Ashram mixes beach casual with ambient music, tasty cocktails, and unobstructed panoramic views of the golden hour. Dinner is also served here (reservations essential). ⊠ *Cala Conta, s/n, San Agustin des Vedra* ☎ 661/347222 ⊕ *www.sunsetashram.com/en/.*

CASINO

Casino de Ibiza. This is a small gaming club with roulette tables, blackjack, slots, and poker. You need your passport or other picture ID to enter. There are Texas Hold 'Em tables nightly from 10 pm; the minimum buy-in is €150. ⊠ *Paseo de Juan Carlos I 17, Ibiza Nueva* ☎ 971/806806 ⊕ *www.casinoibiza.com.*

DANCE CLUBS

Amnesia. This popular club in San Rafael opened in 1980 and it's still going strong, with several ample dance floors that throb to house and funk. Like most of the clubs on the island, it opens for the season at the end of May, with a gala bash. ⊠ *Ctra. Eivissa–Sant Antoni, Km 5, Sant Rafel* ☎ 971/198041 ⊕ *www.amnesia.es.*

Keeper. Clubbers start the evening here, where there's no cover and the action starts at 11 pm. The indoor space at Keeper can get a bit cramped, but out on the terrace freedom reigns. ⊠ *Marina Botafoch, Paseo Juan Carlos I s/n, Ibiza Nueva* ☎ 971/310509.

Pacha. A young, international crowd gathers after 2 am at the flagship venue of this club empire, where each of the five rooms offers a different style, including techno, house music, R&B, and hip-hop. ⊠ *Av. 8 de Agosto s/n, Eivissa* ☎ 971/313600, 971/313612 *tickets* ⊕ *www.pachaibiza.com/en.*

Privilege. Billing itself as the largest club in the world, the long-running center of Ibiza's nightlife has a giant dance floor, a swimming pool, and more than a dozen bars. ⊠ *Urbanización San Rafael s/n, Sant Rafel* ☎ 971/198160.

SPORTS AND THE OUTDOORS

BICYCLING

Extra Rent. You can rent cars, Vespas, and scooters here. ⊠ *Av. Santa Eulária des Riu 25–27, Eivissa* ☎ 971/191717, 900/506013 *for info and booking* ⊕ *www.extrarent.com.*

BOATING

Coral Yachting. You can charter all sorts of power craft, sailboats (small and large), and catamarans here, by the day or by the week, with or without a skipper. ⊠ *Marina Botafoc, Local 323–324, Eivissa* ☎ 971/313926 ⊕ *www.coralyachting.com.*

IbizAzul Charters. A variety of motorized craft and sailboats are available for rent here, and 40-foot live-aboard "Goleta" yachts are available for weekend or weeklong charters. ⊠ *Ctra. Ibiza–Portinatx, Km 16.5, Sant Joan* ☎ 971/325264 ⊕ *www.ibizazul.com.*

GOLF

Club de Golf Ibiza. Ibiza's only golf club combines the 9 holes at the Club Roca Llisa resort complex (Course II) with the newer and more challenging 18-hole Course I nearby. Fairway maintenance on Course II leaves a bit to be desired. ⊠ *Ctra. Jesús–Cala Llonga s/n, Santa Eulària* *des Riu* ☎ *971/196052* ⊕ *www.golfibiza.com* ✉ *Course I €98, Course II €65* ⌇. *Course I: 18 holes, 6561 yards, par 72; Course II: 9 holes, 6265 yards (2 rounds), par 71.*

HORSEBACK RIDING

Can Mayans. Hire horses here for rides along the coast and inland. Can Mayans has a riding school, and has a gentle touch with beginners. It's closed on Monday. ⊠ *Ctra. Santa Gertrudis–Sant Lorenç, Km 3, San Lorenzo de Balafia* ☎ *971/187388, 690/922144* ⊕ *www.can-mayans.com.*

SCUBA DIVING

Active Dive. Instruction and guided dives, as well as kayaking, parasailing, and boat rentals are available here. ⊠ *Surf Lounge Ibiza, C/ des Molí 10, San Antoní* ☎ *679/333782* ⊕ *www.active-dive.com.*

Arenal Diving. Book lessons and dives here, from beginner level to advanced, with PADI-trained instructors and guides. ⊠ *Av. Doctor Fleming 16, San Antoní* ☎ *617/280055* ⊕ *www.arenaldiving.com/en/.*

Sea Horse Sub-Aqua Centre. A short distance from Sant Antoni, this aquatic center offers basic scuba training as well as excursions to spectacular nearby dive sites, especially the Cala d'Hort Marine Nature Reserve and the Pillars of Hercules underwater caves. ⊠ *Edificio Yais 5, Calle Vizcaya 8, Playa Port des Torrent s/n, Sant Josep de sa Talaia* ☎ *629/349499, 678/717211* ⊕ *www.seahorsedivingibiza.com.*

TENNIS

Ibiza Club de Campo. With six clay courts, seven paddle tennis courts, a 25-meter pool, and a gym, this is the best-equipped club on the island. Nonmembers can play tennis here for €6 per hour per person. ⊠ *Ctra. Ibiza–Sant Josep, Km 2.5, Sant Josep de sa Talaia* ☎ *971/300088* ⊕ *www.ibizaclubdecampo.es.*

SHOPPING

Although the Sa Penya area of Eivissa still has a few designer boutiques, much of the area is now given over to the so-called hippie market, with stalls selling clothing and crafts of all sorts May–October. Browse Avenida Bartolomeu Rosselló, and the main square of Dalt Vila, for casual clothes and accessories.

Divina. With no shortage of shops in Eivissa selling clothing in the classic white Ibiza style, Divina stands out for its range of clothes for kids, and its modest selection of real Panama hats. ⊠ *Pl. de la Vila 17, Dalt Vila* ☎ *971/300815.*

SANTA EULÀRIA DES RIU

15 km (9 miles) northeast of Eivissa.

At the edge of this town on the island's eastern coast, to the right below the road, a Roman bridge crosses what some claim is the only permanent river in the Balearics (hence *des Riu,* or "of the river"). The town itself follows the curve of a long sandy beach, a few blocks deep with restaurants, shops, and vacation apartments. From here it's a 10-minute drive to Sant Carles and the open-air hippie market, Las Dalias, held there every Saturday morning. ■ TIP→ **The popular Las**

Dalias night market offers shopping with live music, food, and drinks and runs from June to September, every Monday and Tuesday (and on Sunday in August)

GETTING HERE AND AROUND

By car, take the C733 from Eivissa. From May to October, buses run from Eivissa every half hour Monday–Saturday, every hour on Sunday. Service is less frequent the rest of the year.

VISITOR INFORMATION

Contacts Santa Eularia des Riu. ✉ *Carrer Mariano Riquer Wallis 4* ☎ *971/330728* 🌐 *www.visitsantaeulalia.com.*

WHERE TO EAT

$$ ITALIAN 🍴 **Mezzanotte.** This charming little portside Italian restaurant has just 12 tables inside, softly lit with candles and track lighting. The kitchen prides itself on hard-to-find fresh ingredients flown in from Italy. **Known for:** fresh Italian cuisine; sidewalk seating in summer; dried and salted mullet roe from Sardinia. [$] *Average main: €15* ✉ *Paseo de s'Alamera 22* ☎ *627/593940* 🕒 *Closed Jan., Feb., and Mon.*

$$ MEDITERRANEAN 🍴 **Oleoteca Ses Escoles.** Chef-owner Miguel Llabres honed his craft at starred restaurants in Mallorca, and opened here in 2014, to local acclaim. He keeps the menu short, and focuses on garden-fresh seasonal vegetables and free-range local meats. **Known for:** free-range local meats; gourmet shop; Ibizan potato salad. [$] *Average main: €17* ✉ *Ctra. Ibiza-Portinatx, Km 9.8, Sant Joan de Labritja* ☎ *871/870229* 🌐 *www.canmiquelguasch.com* 🕒 *Closed Jan., and Mon. Oct.–Apr.*

WHERE TO STAY

$$$$ B&B/INN 🏨 **Can Curreu.** The traditional architecture here, reminiscent of a Greek island village, features a cluster of low buildings with thick whitewashed walls, the edges and corners gently rounded off—and each room has one of these buildings to itself, with a private patio artfully separated from its neighbors. **Pros:** friendly, efficient staff; horseback riding stables; luxurious spa. **Cons:** pricey; bit of a drive to the nearest beaches; patchy Wi-Fi. [$] *Rooms from: €295* ✉ *Ctra. de Sant Carles, Km 12* ☎ *971/335280* 🌐 *www.cancurreu.com* 🛏 *18 rooms* 🍽 *Free Breakfast.*

$$$$ B&B/INN Fodor's Choice ★ 🏨 **Can Gall.** Santi Marí Ferrer remade his family's *finca* (farmhouse), with its massive stone walls and native *savina* wood beams, into one of the island's friendliest and most comfortable country inns. **Pros:** family-friendly; oasis of quiet; poolside pergola for events and yoga sessions. **Cons:** 15-minute drive to beaches; some private terraces a bit small; often booked out for weddings. [$] *Rooms from: €235* ✉ *Ctra. Sant Joan, Km 17.2, San Lorenzo de Balafia* ☎ *971/337031, 670/876054* 🌐 *www.agrocangall.com* 🕒 *Closed Nov.–Mar.* 🛏 *2 rooms, 9 suites* 🍽 *Free Breakfast.*

$ HOTEL 🏨 **Hostal Yebisah.** The longtime residents and civic boosters Toni and Tanya Molio, who are credited with the idea of dredging sand from the bay to create the beach at Santa Eulària, run this simple lodging on the little promenade in the heart of town. **Pros:** friendly service; ideal location; good value. **Cons:** bathrooms a bit cramped; minimal amenities; best rates only for minimum booking of four nights. [$] *Rooms from: €86* ✉ *Paseo S'Alamera 13* ☎ *971/330160* 🌐 *www.hostalyebisah.com* 🕒 *Closed Nov.–Apr.* 🛏 *26 rooms* 🍽 *No meals.*

SPORTS AND THE OUTDOORS

BICYCLING

Kandani. Bicycle rentals start at €15 for one day or €10 per day for week-long rentals, and accessories are also available, as are guided cycling tours. ✉ *Carrer César Puget Riquer 27* ☎ *971/339264* 🌐 *www.kandani.es.*

DIVING

Punta Dive Ibiza. With three separate locations, this is one of the best-equipped and best-staffed diving centers on the island, for beginners and experienced PADI-qualified divers alike. ✉ *Playa Cala Martina s/n* ☎ *971/336726* 🌐 *www.puntadive.com.*

Subfari. This is one of the best places to come for diving off the north coast of the island. ✉ *Puerto de Portinatx s/n, 22 km (14 miles) north via C733, Sant Joan de Labritja* ☎ *971/337558, 677/466040* 🌐 *www.subfari.es.*

SANTA GERTRUDIS DE FRUITERA

15 km (9 miles) north of Eivissa.

Blink and you miss it: that's true of most of the small towns in the island's interior and especially so of Santa Gertrudis. It's not much more than a bend in the road, but worth a look. The brick-paved town square is closed to vehicle traffic—perfect for the sidewalk cafés and boutique stores. From here, you are only a few minutes' drive from some of the island's flat-out best resort hotels and spas and the most beautiful secluded northern coves and beaches: **S'Illa des Bosc, Benirrás** (where they have drum circles to salute the setting sun), **S'Illot des Renclí, Portinatx,** and **Caló d'En Serra.** Artists and expats like it here: they've given the town an appeal that now makes for listings of half a million dollars or more for a modest two-bedroom house.

GETTING HERE AND AROUND

By car, take the C733 from Eivissa. From May to October, buses run from Eivissa every 90 minutes on weekdays, less frequently on weekends and the rest of the year.

WHERE TO EAT AND STAY

$$ SPANISH 🍴 **Can Caus.** Ibiza might pride itself on its seafood, but there comes a time for meat and potatoes. When that time comes, take the 20-minute drive to the outskirts of Santa Gertrudis to this family-style roadside restaurant where you can feast on skewers of barbecued sobrasada, goat chops, and lamb kebabs. **Known for:** grilled meats; local vibe; Ibizan home cooking. [$] *Average main: €16* ✉ *Ctra. Sant Miquel, Km 3.5, Santa Gertrudis* ☎ *971/197516* 🌐 *www.cancaus-ibiza.com* ⏲ *Closed Mon. Oct.–May.*

$$ MEDITERRANEAN 🍴 **La Paloma.** Channeling that Ibiza-boho vibe, La Paloma feels like a refuge for artists and hippies, nestled amid the shady overhang of orange and lemon trees. The eclectic and concise menu uses freshly prepared seasonal produce, often featuring crunchy salads, Middle Eastern and North African–inspired dishes, fish, and homemade pasta (the chef is Italian and many of the ingredients come directly from there). [$] *Average main: €16* ✉ *C/ Can Pou 4, San Lorenzo de Balafia* ✥ *7 km*

(4½ miles) from Sant Gertrudis de Fruitera ☎ 971/325543 🌐 www.palomaibiza.com ⊗ Closed Nov. and Mon. Oct.–May.

$$$$ B&B/INN Fodor's Choice ★ **Cas Gasí.** A countyside setting on a hillside overlooking a valley makes this lovely late-19th-century manor house a quiet escape in a lively destination, with photo-ready views of Ibiza's only mountain (1,567-foot Sa Talaiassa). **Pros:** great views; attentive personal service; peace and quiet; free yoga classes in the morning. **Cons:** minimum stay required in July and August; not geared to families; very expensive. [$] *Rooms from: €525 ✉ Cami Vell a Sant Mateu s/n, Santa Gertrudis ☎ 971/197700 🌐 www.casgasi.com 🛏 9 rooms, 1 suite 🍴 Free Breakfast.*

FORMENTERA

Environmental protection laws shield much of Formentera, making it a calm respite from neighboring Ibiza's dance-until-you-drop madness. Though it does get crowded in the summer, the island's long white-sand beaches are among the finest in the Mediterranean; inland, you can explore quiet country roads by bicycle in relative solitude.

From the port at La Sabina, it's only 3 km (2 miles) to Formentera's capital, **Sant Francesc Xavier,** a few yards off the main road. There's an active hippie market in the small plaza in front of the church. At the main road, turn right toward Sant Ferran, 2 km (1 mile) away. Beyond Sant Ferran the road continues for 7 km (4 miles) along a narrow isthmus, staying slightly closer to the rougher northern side, where the waves and rocks keep yachts—and thus much of the tourist trade—away.

The plateau on the island's east side ends at the lighthouse **Faro de la Mola.** Nearby is a **monument to Jules Verne,** who set part of his 1877 novel *Hector Servadac* (published in English as *Off on a Comet*), in Formentera. The rocks around the lighthouse are carpeted with purple thyme and sea holly in spring and fall.

Back on the main road, turn right at Sant Ferran toward Es Pujols. The few hotels here are the closest Formentera comes to beach resorts, even if the beach is not the best. Beyond Es Pujols the road skirts **Estany Pudent,** one of two lagoons that almost enclose La Sabina. Salt was once extracted from Pudent, hence its name, which means "stinking pond," although the pond now smells fine. At the northern tip of Pudent, a road to the right leads to a footpath that runs the length of **Trucadors,** a narrow sand spit. The long, windswept beaches here are excellent.

GETTING HERE AND AROUND

Formentera is a one-hour ferry ride from Ibiza or 25 minutes on the jet ferry. Balearia operates ferry services to Formentera from Ibiza and Dénia, the nearest landfall on the Spanish mainland.

On Ibiza, you can also take ferries from Santa Eulària and Sant Antoni to La Sabina (1 hour, €23) as well as numerous ferries to the coves and calas on the east and west coasts of the island. Day-trippers can travel to Formentera for a few hours in the sun before heading back to Ibiza to plug into the nightlife.

A very limited bus service connects Formentera's villages, shrinking to one bus each way between San Francisco and Pilar on Saturday and disappearing altogether on Sunday and holidays.

Ferry Contacts Balearia. 🌐 *www.balearia.com.*

Taxi Contacts Parada de Taxis La Sabina. ☎ *971/322002.*

VISITOR INFORMATION

Contacts Formentera Tourist Office. ✉ *Estación Maritima s/n, La Savina* ☎ *971/322057.*

BEACHES

Fodor'sChoice ★ **Platjas de Ses Illetes.** The closest beach to the port at La Sabina is an exquisitely beautiful string of dunes stretching to the tip of the Trucador Peninsula at Es Pau. Collectively called Ses Illetes, they form part of a national park and are consistently voted by travel site contributors as among the five best beaches in the world. Ibiza clubbers like to take the fast ferry over from Eivissa after a long night and chill out here, tapping the sun for the energy to party again; this sort of photosynthesis is especially popular with young Italian tourists. The water is fairly shallow and the meadows of seagrass in it shelter colorful varieties of small fish; the fairly constant breezes are good for windsurfing. Nude and topless sunbathing raises no eyebrows anywhere along the dunes. Be warned: there's no shade here at all, and rented umbrellas fetch premium prices. **Amenities:** food and drink; lifeguards; showers; toilets; water sports. **Best for:** nudists; snorkeling; swimming; windsurfing. ✉ *4 km (2½ miles) north of La Sabina, La Savina.*

WHERE TO STAY

$$$$ B&B/INN 🏨 **Can Aisha.** With only five apartments, this converted stone farmhouse can feel like a family compound, especially when everyone is gathered on the sundeck or around the communal barbecue. **Pros:** all apartments have private terraces; shops and restaurants nearby; kitchenettes with basic equipment. **Cons:** no kids and no pets; short season. [$] *Rooms from: €252* ✉ *Venda de Sa Punta 3205, Es Pujols* ☎ *618/721427* 🌐 *www.canaisha.com* 🕒 *Closed roughly Oct.–May* 🛏 *5 apartments* 🍴 *Free Breakfast.*

SHOPPING

El Pilar is the chief crafts village here. Stores and workshops sell handmade items, including ceramics, jewelry, and leather goods. El Pilar's crafts market draws shoppers on Sunday and Wednesday from May–mid-Oct. May through mid-October, crafts are sold in the morning at the San Françesc Xavier market and in the evening in Es Pujols.

SPORTS AND THE OUTDOORS

DIVING

Vell Marí. You can take diving courses Monday–Saturday here. ⊠ *Puerto de la Savina, Marina de Formentera, Local 14–16, La Savina* ☎ *971/322105.*

MALLORCA

Saddle-shape Mallorca is more than five times the size of Menorca or Ibiza. The Sierra de Tramuntana, a dramatic mountain range soaring to nearly 5,000 feet, runs the length of its northwest coast, and a ridge of hills borders the southeast shores; between the two lies a flat plain that in early spring becomes a sea of almond blossoms, the so-called snow of Mallorca. The island draws more than 10 million visitors a year, many of them bound for summer vacation packages in the coastal resorts. The beaches are beautiful, but save time for the charms of the northwest and the interior: caves, bird sanctuaries, monasteries and medieval towns, local museums, outdoor cafés, and village markets.

GETTING HERE AND AROUND

From Barcelona, Palma de Mallorca is a 50-minute flight, an 8-hour overnight ferry, or a 4½-hour catamaran journey.

If you're traveling by car, Mallorca's main roads are well surfaced, and a four-lane, 25-km (15-mile) motorway penetrates deep into the island between Palma and Inca. The Vía Cintura, an efficient beltway, rings Palma. For destinations in the north and west, follow the "Andratx" and "Oeste" signs on the beltway; for the south and east, follow the "Este" signs. Driving in the mountains that parallel the northwest coast and descend to a corniche (cliff-side road) is a different matter; you'll be slowed not only by the narrow winding roads but also by tremendous views, tourist traffic, and groups of cyclists.

VISITOR INFORMATION

Contacts Oficina de Turismo de Mallorca. ⊠ *Aeropuerto de Mallorca, Son Sant Joan s/n, Palma* ☎ *971/789556* ⊕ *www.infomallorca.net.*

PALMA DE MALLORCA

If you look north of the cathedral (La Seu, or the seat of the bishopric, to Mallorcans) on a map of the city of Palma, you can see around the Plaça Santa Eulàlia a jumble of tiny streets that made up the earliest settlement. Farther out, a ring of wide boulevards traces the fortifications built by the Moors to defend the larger city that emerged by the 12th century. The zigzags mark the bastions that jutted out at regular intervals. By the end of the 19th century, most of the walls had been demolished; the only place where you can still see the massive defenses is at Ses Voltes, along the seafront west of the cathedral.

A *torrent* (streambed) used to run through the middle of the old city, dry for most of the year but often a raging flood in the rainy season. In the 17th century it was diverted to the east, along the moat that ran outside the city walls. Two of Palma's main arteries, La Rambla and the Passeig d'es Born, now follow the stream's natural course. The traditional evening *paseo* (promenade) takes place on the bustling Born.

If you come to Palma by car, park in the garage beneath the Parc de la Mar (the ramp is just off the highway from the airport, as you reach the cathedral) and stroll along the park. Beside it run the huge bastions guarding the Palau Reial de l'Almudaina; the cathedral, golden and massive, rises beyond. Where you exit the garage, there's a **ceramic mural** by the late Catalan artist and Mallorca resident Joan Miró, facing the cathedral across the pool that runs the length of the park.

If you begin early enough, a walk along the ramparts at Ses Voltes from the mirador beside the cathedral is spectacular. The first rays of the sun turn the upper pinnacles of La Seu bright gold and then begin to work their way down the sandstone walls. From the Parc de la Mar, follow Avinguda Antoni Maura past the steps to the palace. Just below the Plaça de la Reina, where the **Passeig d'es Born** begins, turn left on Carrer de la Boteria into the Plaça de la Llotja. (If the Llotja itself is open, don't miss a chance to visit—it's the Mediterranean's finest Gothic-style civic building.) From there stroll through the Plaça Drassana to the **Museu d'Es Baluard,** at the end of Carrer Sant Pere. Retrace your steps to Avinguda Antoni Maura. Walk up the Passeig d'es Born to Plaça Joan Carles I, then right on Avenida de La Unió.

GETTING HERE AND AROUND

Palma's Empresa Municipal de Transports (EMT) runs 65 bus lines and a tourist train in and around the Mallorcan capital. Most buses leave from the Intermodal station, next to the Inca railroad terminus on the Plaça d'Espanya; city buses leave from the ground floor, while intercity buses leave from the underground level. The tourist office on the Plaça d'Espanya has schedules. Bus No. 1 connects the airport with the city center and the port; No. 2 circumnavigates the historic city center; Nos. 3 and 20 connect the city center with the Porto Pi commercial center; No. 46 goes to the Fundació Pilar i Joan Miró, and No. 21 connects S'Arenal with the airport. The fare for a single local ride is €1.50; to the airport it's €3.

You can hire a horse-drawn carriage with driver at the bottom of the Born, and also on Avinguda Antonio Maura, in the nearby cathedral square, and on the Plaça d'Espanya, at the side farthest from the train station. A tour of the city costs €30 for a half hour, €50 for an hour. ■TIP→ **Haggle firmly, and the driver might come down a bit off the posted fare.**

Boats from Palma to neighboring beach resorts leave from the jetty opposite the Auditorium, on the Passeig Marítim. The tourist office has a schedule.

Bus Information Empresa Municipal de Transports. ✉ *C/ Josep Anselm Clavé 5* ☎ *971/214444* ⊕ *www.emtpalma.es.*

Bus Station Estació Intermodal. ✉ *Estació Intermodal, Pl. d'Espanya s/n* ☎ *971/177777* ⊕ *www.tib.org.*

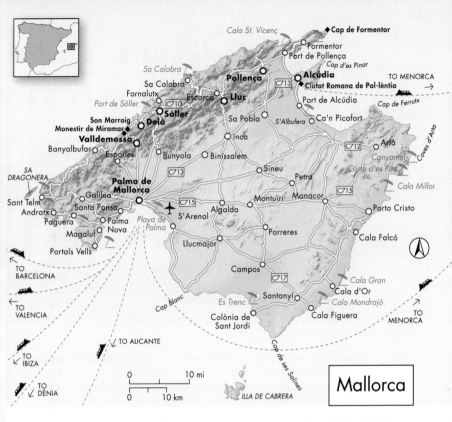

Mallorca

Taxi Information Radio-Taxi Ciutat. ✉ *Francesc Sancho 7* ☎ *971/201212* ⊕ *www.radiotaxiciutat.com.*

Train Station Estació Intermodal. ✉ *Pl. Espanya s/n* ☎ *971/752051, 971/177777* ⊕ *www.tib.org/portal/en/web/ctm/inici.*

VISITOR INFORMATION
Contacts Oficine d'Informació Turística. ✉ *Pl. de la Reina 2* ☎ *971/173990* ⊕ *www.infomallorca.net.*

TOURS
City Sightseeing. The open-top City Sightseeing bus leaves from behind the Palau de la Aludaina every 20–25 minutes starting at 9:30 am and makes 16 stops throughout the town, including Plaça de la Reina, the Passeig Marítim, and the Castell de Bellver. Tickets are valid for 24 or 48 hours, and you can get on and off as many times as you wish. All Palma tourist offices have details. ✉ *Av. Antoni Maura 24* ⊕ *www. city-sightseeing.com/tours/spain/palma-de-mallorca.htm* 🎟 *From €18.*

EXPLORING
Banys Arabs (*Arab Baths*). One of Palma's oldest monuments, the 10th-century public bathhouse has a wonderful walled garden of palms and lemon trees. In its day, it was not merely a place to bathe but a social

Cathedral of Palma de Mallorca

institution where you could soak, relax, and gossip with your neighbors. ⊠ *Carrer Can Serra 7, Centro* ☎ *637/046534* ⊡ *€3.*

Castell de Bellver (*Bellver Castle*). Overlooking the city and the bay from a hillside, the castle was built at the beginning of the 14th century, in Gothic style but with a circular design—the only one of its kind in Spain. It houses an archaeological museum of the history of Mallorca, and a small collection of classical sculpture. The Bus Turistic 50 and the EMT municipal buses Nos. 3, 20, and 46 all stop a 20-minute walk from the entrance. On Thursday evenings in July, from 9:30, there are classical music concerts in the courtyard, performed by the Ciutat de Palma Symphony Orchestra. ⊠ *Carrer de Camilo José Cela s/n* ☎ *971/735065, 971/225900 concerts box office* ⊕ *castelldebellver. palmademallorca.es* ⊡ *€4, free Sun.* ☉ *Closed Mon.*

Fodor'sChoice ★ **Catedral de Majorca** (*La Seu*). Palma's cathedral is an architectural wonder that took almost 400 years to build. Begun in 1230, the wide expanse of the nave is supported by 14 70-foot-tall columns that fan out at the top like palm trees. The nave is dominated by an immense rose window, 40 feet in diameter, dating to 1370. Over the main altar (conse-crated in 1346) is the surrealistic *baldoquí* (baldachin) by Antoni Gaudí, completed in 1912. This enormous canopy, with lamps suspended from it like elements of a mobile, rises to a Crucifixion scene at the top. To the right, in the Chapel of the Santísimo, is an equally remarkable 2007 work by the sculptor Miquel Barceló: a painted ceramic tableau covering the walls like a skin. Based on the New Testament account of the miracle of the loaves and fishes, it's a bizarre composition of rolling waves, gaping cracks, protruding fish heads, and human skulls. The **bell**

tower above the cathedral's Plaça Almoina door holds nine bells, the largest of which is called N'Eloi, meaning "Praise." The 5-ton N'Eloi, cast in 1389, requires six men to ring it and has shattered stained-glass windows with its sound. ■TIP→ **From April through October you can take a guided tour of the bell tower and the cathedral's terraces overlooking panoramic views of the city. Reservations must be made in advance on the website.** ⊠ *Pl. Almoina s/n, Centro* ☎ *971/723130, 902/022445* ⊕ *www.catedraldemallorca.org* ☎ *€7.*

Fodor's Choice ★ **Museu d'Es Baluard** (*Museum of Modern and Contemporary Art of Palma*). West of the city center, this museum rises on a long-neglected archaeological site, parts of which date back to the 12th century. The building itself is an outstanding convergence of old and new: the exhibition space uses the surviving 16th-century perimeter walls of the fortified city, including a stone courtyard facing the sea and a promenade along the ramparts. There are three floors of galleries, and the collection includes work by Miró, Picasso, and Antoni Tàpies, among other major artists. The courtyard café–terrace Restaurant del Museu (closed Monday October–mid-June) affords a fine view of the marina. To get here, take the narrow Carrer de Sant Pere through the old fishermen's quarter, from Plaça de la Drassana. ⊠ *Pl. Porta de Santa Catalina 10, Santa Catalina* ☎ *971/908200* ⊕ *www.esbaluard.org/en* ☎ *€6 (€5 Tues.)* ☼ *Closed Mon.*

Museu Fundació Pilar y Joan Miró (*Pilar and Joan Miró Foundation Museum*). The permanent collection here includes a great many drawings and studies by the Catalan artist, who spent his last years on Mallorca, but it exhibits far fewer finished paintings and sculptures than the Fundació Miró in Barcelona. While the exhibits are fairly limited, the setting and views of Palma alone are worth taking the detour. ⊠ *Carrer Saridakis 29* ☎ *971/701420* ⊕ *www.miromallorca.com* ☎ *€8 (free Sat. after 3)* ☼ *Closed Mon.*

Museu Fundación Juan March. A few steps from the north archway of the Plaça Major is the Museu Fundación Juan March. This fine little museum was established to display what had been a private collection of modern Spanish art. The building itself was a sumptuous private home built in the 18th century. The second and third floors were redesigned to accommodate a series of small galleries, with one or two works at most—by Pablo Picasso, Joan Miró, Juan Gris, Salvador Dalí, Antoni Tàpies, and Miquel Barceló, among others—on each wall. ⊠ *Sant Miquel 11, Centro* ☎ *971/713515* ⊕ *www.march.es/museupalma* ☎ *Free* ☼ *Closed Sun.*

Passeig des Born. While it's known as one of the best streets in Palma to hit the shops, this tree-lined promenade is also a favored place to *pasear* (stroll), lined with palatial-style stone residences (most of which have now been converted into hotels and shops) and busy café-terraces. Bar Bosch, straddling Passeig des Born and Plaza Rei Joan Carles I, has been a key gathering point for locals since 1936. ⊠ *Passeig des Born.*

Plaça Major. A crafts market fills this elegant neoclassical space 10–2 on Friday and Saturday (Monday–Saturday in July and August). Until 1823, this was the local headquarters of the Inquisition. A flight of steps on the east side of the Plaça Major leads down to **Las Ramblas,** a pleasant promenade lined with flower stalls. ⊠ *Centro.*

Sant Francesc. The 13th-century monastery church of Sant Francesc was established by Jaume II when his eldest son took monastic orders and gave up rights to the throne. Fra Junípero Serra, the missionary who founded San Francisco, California, was later educated here; his statue stands to the left of the main entrance. The basilica houses the tomb of eminent 13th-century scholar Ramón Llull. The cloisters (enter via the side door, on the right) are especially beautiful and peaceful. The €5 entrance fee includes entrance to five other churches and is valid for one year. ⊠ *Pl. Sant Francesc 7, Centro* ☎ *971/712695* 🎫 *€5* ⊘ *Closed Sun.*

Santa Eulàlia. Carrer de la Cadena leads to this imposing Gothic church, where, in 1435, 200 Jews were forced to convert to Christianity after their rabbis were threatened with being burned at the stake. ⊠ *Pl. Santa Eulalia 2, Centro* ☎ *971/714625* 🎫 *Free.*

BEACHES

FAMILY **Es Trenc.** Even though it's nearly an hour's drive from Palma, this pristine 2-km (1-mile) stretch of fine white sand on Mallorca's southern coast, much longer than it is wide, is one of the most popular beaches on the island— arrive late on a Saturday or Sunday in summer, and you'll be hard-pressed to fine a space to stretch out. At times the water can be a bit choppy, and there are occasional patches of seaweed—but otherwise the clear, clean water slopes off gently from the shore for some 30 feet, making it ideal for families with younger kids. Es Trenc is in a protected natural area free of hotels and other developments, which makes for good bird-watching. Naturists lay their claim to part of the beach's eastern end. **Amenities:** food and drink; lifeguards; parking (fee); toilets. **Best for:** nudists; partiers; swimming; walking. ⊠ *MA6040 s/n, 10 km (6 miles) south of Campos, 6½ km (4 miles) east of Colònia Sant Jordi, Colònia de Sant Jordi.*

WHERE TO EAT

$ ✕ **Café la Lonja** (*Sa Llotja*). A great spot for hot chocolate or a unique
TAPAS tea or coffee, this classic establishment in the old fishermen's neighborhood has a young vibe that goes well with the style of the place. Both the sunny terrace in front of the Llotja and the bar inside are excellent places for drinks and sandwiches. **Known for:** quick pit stop; terrace with views of the Llotja; coffee and snacks. $ *Average main: €9* ⊠ *Carrer Sa Lonja del Mar 2* ☎ *971/722799* ⊕ *www.cafelalonja.es/en.*

$$$$ ✕ **Forn de Sant Joan.** This former bakery turned restaurant ("forn" means
MEDITERRANEAN "bakery" or "oven" in Mallorquin) dates back to the 19th century, and features exposed brick walls, colorful floor tiles, modern art on the walls and picture-perfect Mediterranean-style tapas. There's a cocktail bar on the ground floor that overlooks the street, and one of the three distinct dining areas is the area where bread dough was once prepared. **Known for:** former 19th-century bakery; elevated tapas and Mediterranean dishes; cocktail bar. $ *Average main: €25* ⊠ *Carrer de Sant Joan 4* ☎ *971/728422* ⊕ *www.forndesantjoan.com.*

$$ ✕ **La Bóveda.** This popular restaurant serves huge, tasty portions of tapas
TAPAS and inexpensive platters such as chicken or ham croquetas, grilled cod, garlic shrimp, and *revueltos de ajos con morcilla* (scrambled eggs with

garlic and black sausage). Within hailing distance of the Llotja, the tables in the back are always at a premium (they're cooler on summer days), but there's additional seating at the counter or on stools around upended wine barrels. **Known for:** down-to-earth portions of traditional tapas; ham croquettes; local vibe. [$] *Average main: €14* ✉ *Carrer de la Botería 3* ☎ *971/714863* ⏲ *Closed Sun.*

$$$$ CONTEMPORARY Fodor's Choice ★ 🍴 **Simply Fosh.** While Palma suffers no dearth of rough-and-ready eateries, Simply Fosh has little or no competition in the fine-dining category. The renowned chef Marc Fosh offers several tasting menus, which are executed superbly, with the best local seasonal produce transformed into remarkable dishes with surprising twists. **Known for:** award winning; tasting menus based on local produce; good value weekday lunch menu. [$] *Average main: €89* ✉ *Carrer de la Missió 7A* ☎ *971/720114* 🌐 *www.simplyfosh.com/en.*

WHERE TO STAY

$$$$ HOTEL Fodor's Choice ★ 🏨 **Cap Rocat.** What was once a 19th-century military fortress on the southern flank of the Bay of Palma has been converted into one of Mallorca's—and arguably Europe's—most distinctive hotels. **Pros:** stunning backdrop; superb cuisine; impeccable service. **Cons:** isolated from the bustle—and nightlife; lacks a sandy beach; sky-high prices. [$] *Rooms from: €500* ✉ *Ctra. de Enderrocat s/n, Cala Blava* ☎ *971/747878* 🌐 *www.caprocat.com* ⏲ *Closed Nov.–mid-Mar.* 🛏 *30 rooms* 🍽 *Free Breakfast.*

$$$ B&B/INN 🏨 **Dalt Murada.** In an ideal location in the old part of Palma, a minute's walk to the cathedral, this town house, dating back to the 15th century, was the Sancho Moragues home until 2001, when the family opened it as a hotel. **Pros:** rooftop terrace with views; modern touches in historic home; steps from the cathedral. **Cons:** thin walls; no parking; erratic service. [$] *Rooms from: €140* ✉ *Carrer Almudaina 6A, Centro* ☎ *971/425300* 🌐 *www.daltmurada.com* ⏲ *Closed Nov.–Apr.* 🛏 *23 rooms* 🍽 *No meals.*

$ HOTEL 🏨 **Hostal Apuntadores.** A favorite among budget travelers, this lodging in the heart of the old town, within strolling distance of the bustling Passeig d'es Born, has a rooftop terrace with what is arguably the city's best view—overlooking the cathedral and the sea. **Pros:** good value; rooms have a/c and heat; some rooms have balconies. **Cons:** can be noisy; the cheapest rooms share bathrooms; basic decor. [$] *Rooms from: €72* ✉ *Carrer Apuntadores 8, Centro* ☎ *971/713491* 🌐 *www.palmahostal.com* ⏲ *Closed mid-Dec.–mid-Feb.* 🛏 *28 rooms* 🍽 *No meals.*

$$$ HOTEL 🏨 **Hotel Almudaina.** Business travelers from the mainland favor this comfortable, central hotel, and it's an excellent choice for vacationers as well. **Pros:** steps from Palma's upscale shopping; courteous, efficient service; rooftop terrace and bar. **Cons:** public spaces are small; limited parking; rooms directly below the Sky Bar can be noisy. [$] *Rooms from: €150* ✉ *Av. Jaume III 9, Centro* ☎ *971/727340* 🌐 *www.hotelalmudaina.com* 🛏 *70 rooms* 🍽 *Free Breakfast.*

$$$ HOTEL Fodor's Choice ★ 🏨 **Hotel Born.** Romanesque arches and a giant palm tree spectacularly cover the central courtyard and reception area of this shabby-chic hotel, which occupies the former mansion of a noble Mallorcan family. **Pros:** convenient for sightseeing; romantic courtyard floodlit at night; good value. **Cons:** small rooms on the street side; poor soundproofing;

mediocre breakfast. $ *Rooms from: €150* ⊠ *Carrer Sant Jaume 3* ☎ *971/712942* ⊕ *www.hotelborn.com* ⇴ *30 rooms* ⦿| *Free Breakfast.*

$$$$
B&B/INN
⬜ **Palau Sa Font.** Warm Mediterranean tones and crisp, clean lines give this boutique hotel in the center of the shopping district an atmosphere very different from anything else in the city. **Pros:** buffet breakfast until 11; helpful English-speaking staff; 16th-century former Episcopal palace. **Cons:** pool is small; good soundproofing, but area can be noisy in summer; rooms a bit small for the price. $ *Rooms from: €189* ⊠ *Carrer Apuntadores 38* ☎ *971/712277* ⊕ *www.palausafont.com* ☽ *Closed mid-Jan.–mid-Feb.* ⇴ *19 rooms* ⦿| *Free Breakfast.*

NIGHTLIFE

Mallorca's nightlife is never hard to find. Many of the hot spots are concentrated 6 km (4 miles) west of Palma at **Punta Portals,** in Portals Nous, where the royal yacht is moored when former king Juan Carlos I comes to Mallorca in early August for the Copa del Rey international regatta. Another major area is **Avinguda Gabriel Roca.** This section of the Passeig Marítim holds many taverns, pubs, and clubs. The network of streets in the old town, around Carrer Apuntadores, is also prime barhopping territory.

BARS AND CAFÉS

Fodor's Choice
★
Bar Abaco. The over-the-top baroque exuberance of this bar sets it far apart from its setting in an otherwise unfunky, old neighborhood. There are urns and baskets of fresh flowers and fruit tumbling out on to the floor, stone pillars and vaulted ceilings, tall candles, and ambient opera music. Be warned: Abaco's signature cocktails are pricey. It's open 8 pm–1 am Monday–Thursday, and until 3 am on Friday and Saturday. ⊠ *Carrer de Sant Joan 1* ☎ *971/714939* ⊕ *www.bar-abaco.es.*

Carrer Apuntadores. On the west side of Passeig d'es Born in the old town, this street is lined with casual bars and cafés that appeal to night owls in their twenties and thirties. On the weekend, you can often come across impromptu live rock and pop acts performed on small stages. ⊠ *Palma.*

Plaça de la Llotja. This square, along with the surrounding streets, is the place to go for *copas* (drinking, tapas sampling, and general carousing). ⊠ *Palma.*

Wineing. Tucked down Calle Apuntadores, the Wineing offers a unique way to try wines from across the island and beyond. Sample wines via a card-operated system that dispenses small tastings (or larger glasses, if you feel inclined). There is also a menu of tapas, cheese platters, and grilled meats to share. ⊠ *Calle Apuntadores 24* ☎ *971/214011* ⊕ *www.wineing.es.*

DANCE CLUBS

Tito's. Outdoor elevators transport you from the street to the dance floor at the sleek and futuristic Tito's. ⊠ *Passeig Marítim, Av. Gabriel Roca 31* ☎ *971/730017* ⊕ *www.titosmallorca.com.*

MUSIC CLUBS

Jazz Voyeur Club. Some of Palma's best jazz combos—and the occasional rock group—play this small, smoky club in the old portside neighborhood. There's music every night, and it keeps going until 3 am on Friday and Saturday. ⊠ *Carrera Apuntadores 5* ☎ *971/720780* ⊕ *www.jazzvoyeurclub.com.*

SPORTS AND THE OUTDOORS

BALLOONING

Majorca Balloons. For spectacular views of the island, float up in a hot-air balloon, which lifts off daily April–October, weather permitting, at sunrise and sunset. Call for a reservation: the office is open 10–1 and 5–8. Feeling romantic? The company offers moonlight flights for two, for a mere €600. ⊠ *C/Farallo 4, Manacor* ☎ *971/596969* ⊕ *www.mallorcaballoons.com* ▨ *1-hr flights €160 per person.*

BICYCLING

With long, flat stretches and heart-pounding climbs, Mallorca's 675 km (420 miles) of rural roads adapted for cycling make the sport the most popular on the island; many European professional teams train here. Tourist-board offices have excellent leaflets on bike routes with maps, details about the terrain, sights, and distances. The companies below can rent you bikes for exploring Palma and environs.

Embat Ciclos. Some 10 km (6 miles) from the city center, on the beach in Platja de Palma, Embat has both standard touring and electric bikes for rent, and will happily assist with organizing tours of the island. ⊠ *Bartolomé Riutort 27, Can Pastilla* ☎ *971/492358* ⊕ *www.embatciclos.com.*

Palma on Bike. This bike-rental shop, just below the Plaça de la Reina in Palma, is open daily 9:30–3 and 4–8. You can also organize a tour from here. ⊠ *Av. Antoni Maura 10, Centro* ☎ *647/103996, 971/718062* ⊕ *www.palmaonbike.com.*

BIRD-WATCHING

Mallorca has two notable nature reserves.

Sa Dragonera. This island and its large colony of sea falcons are accessible by boat from Sant Elm, at the western tip of Mallorca. The boats, run by the operator Cruceros Margarita, leave from in front of El Pescador restaurant at the port of Sant Elm daily every 30 minutes. ⊠ *Sant Elm* ☎ *629/606614, 639/617545 for Cruceros Margarita* ⊕ *www.crucerosmargarita.com* ▨ *Boat €12.*

S'Albufera de Majorca. This is the largest wetlands zone in Mallorca. ⊠ *Ctra. Port d'Alcúdia–Ca'n Picafort, Alcúdia* ☎ *971/892250* ⊕ *www.mallorcaweb.net/salbufera* ☞ *Stop at Centre de Recepció (Reception Center) sa Roca for permission to enter park.*

GOLF

Mallorca has more than 20 18-hole golf courses, among them PGA championship venues of fiendish difficulty. The Federación Balear de Golf (Balearic Golf Federation) can provide more information.

Federación Balear de Golf (*Balearic Golf Federation*). ⊠ *Cami de Son Vida 38* ☎ *971/722753* ⊕ *www.fbgolf.com.*

Fodor's Choice ★ **Golf Alcanada.** This 18-hole course, designed by Robert Trent Jones Jr., is widely regarded as the best club on the island, with spectacular views of the bay and lighthouse. ⊠ *Ctra. del Faro s/n, Alcúdia* ☎ *971/549560* ⊕ *www.golf-alcanada.com/en* ▨ *€105–€150 for 18 holes, €62–€75 for 9 holes (depending on season)* ⚑ *18 holes, 7107 yards, par 72.*

9

Mallorca is a popular place for cyclists, and many European professionals train here.

HIKING

Mallorca is excellent for hiking. In the Sierra de Tramuntana, you can easily arrange to trek one way and take a boat, bus, or train back. Ask the tourist office for the free booklet *20 Hiking Excursions on the Island of Mallorca,* with detailed maps and itineraries.

Grup Excursionista de Majorca (*Majorcan Hiking Association*). This associaton can provide hiking information. ⊠ *Carrer dels Horts 1* ☎ *971/718823* ⊕ *www.gemweb.org.*

SAILING

Cruesa Majorca Yacht Charter. A wide range of yachts, cruisers, and catamarans are available for rent here, by the day or the week. ⊠ *Av. Antonio Maura 18, entlo 2 izq* ☎ *971/282821* ⊕ *www.cruesa.com/en.*

Federación Balear de Vela (*Balearic Sailing Federation*). For information on sailing, contact the federation. ⊠ *Edificio Palma Arena, Av. Uruguay s/n* ☎ *971/402412* ⊕ *www.federacionbalearvela.org.*

SCUBA DIVING

Big Blue. This dive center, next to the Hotel Hawaii on the beach boardwalk in Palmanova, offers PADI-certified courses for beginners (€269), including two dives with full equipment: tanks, wet suits, regulators, masks, and fins. ⊠ *Carrer Martin Ros Garcia 6, Palmanova* ☎ *971/681686* ⊕ *www.bigbluediving.net.*

TENNIS

Tennis is very popular here—the more so for world champion Rafael Nadal being a Mallorcan. There are courts at many hotels and private clubs, and tennis schools as well. The Federació de Tennis de les Illes

Balears (Balearics Tennis Federation) can provide information about playing in the area.

Federació de Tennis de les Illes Balears (*Balearic Tennis Federation*). ⊠ *Edificio Palma Arena, C/ Uruguay s/n* ☎ *971/720956* ⊕ *www.ftib.es/es/ welcome.*

SHOPPING

Mallorca's specialties are shoes and leather clothing, utensils carved from olive wood, porcelain and handblown glass, and artificial pearls. Look for designer fashions on the **Passeig d'es Born** and for antiques on **Costa de la Pols,** a narrow little street near the Plaça Riera. The **Plaça Major** has a modest crafts market Friday and Saturday 10–2 (in summer the market is also open on weekdays). During summer, there's a crafts market on the seafront at Sa Llotja. Palma has a range of food markets, including Mercat Oliva, where you can browse stalls piled high with local produce, meat, and fish. At the recently opened San Juan Gastronomic Market (⊕ *www.mercadosanjuanpalma.es*) sample street-style food, cocktails, and wine in an impressive Moderniste building, constructed in the 1900s.

Many of Palma's best shoe shops are on Avenida Rei Jaime III, between the Plaça Juan Carles I and the Passeig Mallorca.

FOOD

Colmado Santo Domingo. This is a wonderful little shop for the artisanal food specialties of Mallorca: sobresada of black pork, sausages of all sorts, cheeses, jams, and honeys and preserves. ⊠ *Carrer Santo Domingo 1, Centro* ☎ *971/714887* ⊕ *www.colmadosantodomingo.com.*

GLASS AND CERAMICS

Gordiola. Glassmakers since 1719, Gordiola has a factory showroom in Alguida, on the Palma–Manacor road, where you can watch the glass being blown and even try your hand at making a piece. ⊠ *Ctra. Palma–Manacor, Km 19, Algaida* ☎ *971/665046* ⊕ *www.gordiola.com.*

SHOES AND LEATHER GOODS

Alpargatería La Concepción. Mallorca's most popular footwear is the simple, comfortable slip-on espadrille (usually with a leather front over the first half of the foot and a strap across the back of the ankle). Look for a pair here. ⊠ *Carrer de la Concepción 17* ☎ *971/710709* ⊕ *www. zapateriamallorca.com.*

Lottusse. Shop here for high-end shoes, leather coats, and accessories. ⊠ *Av. Jaume III 2* ☎ *971/710203* ⊕ *www.lottusse.com.*

OFF THE BEATEN PATH

Mercat de Sineu. The island's biggest market takes place every Wednesday, 8 am to 1 pm, in the town of Sineu, 34 km (21 miles) east of Palma. The market, among the island's oldest, dates back to the 14th century, when livestock was auctioned—a practice that continues to this day. Come early if you want to see the auction, which takes place in and around the main square. Local crafts and produce, plants and flowers, clothing and leather goods are traded throughout the village along the labyrinth of narrow streets, which can get very busy. In the 14th century, King Jaime II chose Sineu as the new capital of Mallorca, connecting Palma with Sineu via a long, straight road that can still be traced today. The remains of the ancient palace and former residence of King Jaime II, as well as other important monuments, can be visited across the town. ✉ *Pl. Es Fossar.*

VALLDEMOSSA

18 km (11 miles) north of Palma.

The jumping-off point for a drive up the spectacular coast of the Tramuntana, this pretty little town, north of Palma, is famous for the vast complex of the Reial Cartuja monastery. Surrounded by natural beauty and stunning views, it was also here where Chopin spent the winter of 1838 with George Sand. As most tourists tend to bus in during the day for a few hours and leave, it is worth spending an evening in Valldemossa to soak up the true atmosphere of this beautiful village. At sundown, the quiet streets and plaças are a delight to wander through, flanked by sandy stone houses with green shutters and overflowing plant pots. A classical music festival paying tribute to Chopin (among other composers) is held every August, with most performances taking place in the Reial Cartuja monastery.

GETTING HERE AND AROUND

Valldemossa is a 20-minute drive from Palma on the MA1130. Regular bus service from the Plaça d'Espanya in Palma gets you to Valldemossa in about a half hour.

VISITOR INFORMATION

Contacts Valldemossa Tourist Office. ✉ *Av. de Palma 7* ☎ *971/612019.*

EXPLORING

Fodor'sChoice ★ **Cartoixa de Valldemossa (monastery)** (*Royal Carthusian Monastery*). The monastery was founded in 1339, but after the monks were expelled in 1835, it acquired a new lease on life by offering apartments to travelers. The most famous lodgers were Frédéric Chopin and his lover, the Baroness Amandine Dupin, the French novelist better known by her pseudonym, George Sand. The two spent three difficult months here in the cold, damp winter of 1838–39.

In the **church,** note the frescoes above the nave—the monk who painted them was Goya's brother-in-law. The **pharmacy,** made by the monks in 1723, is almost completely preserved. A long corridor leads to the apartments, furnished in period style, occupied by Chopin and Sand (the piano is original). Nearby, another set of apartments houses the local **museum,** with mementos of Archduke Luis Salvador and a collection of old printing blocks. From here you return to the ornately furnished **King Sancho's palace,** a group of rooms originally built by King Jaume II for his son. The tourist office, in Valldemossa's main plaza, sells a ticket good for all of the monastery's attractions. ✉ *Pl. de la Cartuja s/n* ☎ *971/612986* 🌐 *www.cartujadevalldemossa.com* 🎟 *€10* 🕒 *Closed Mar. and Sun. Nov.–Feb.*

WHERE TO STAY

$$$$ HOTEL Fodor'sChoice ★ 🏨 **Gran Hotel Son Net.** About equidistant from Palma and Valldemossa, this restored estate house—parts of which date back to 1672—is one of Mallorca's most luxurious hotels. **Pros:** attentive staff; family-friendly; convenient to Palma. **Cons:** a bit far from the beaches; all this luxury comes at a high price; need car. [$] *Rooms from: €500* ✉ *Carrer Castillo de Son Net s/n, Puigpunyent* ☎ *971/147000* 🌐 *www.sonnet.es* 🛏 *26 rooms* 🍴 *Free Breakfast.*

$$$$ B&B/INN Fodor's Choice ★ **Mirabó de Valldemossa.** At the far end of a winding dirt road in the hills overlooking the Reial Cartuja, across the valley of Valldemossa, this luxurious little agroturismo is a romantic hideaway that's hard to reach and even harder to tear yourself away from. **Pros:** friendly personal service; peace and quiet. **Cons:** no restaurants nearby; no gym or spa; those low stone doorways can be a headache. [$] *Rooms from: €260* ✉ *Ctra. Valldemossa, Km 16* ☎ *661/285215* *9 rooms* 🍴 *Free Breakfast.*

DEIÀ

9 km (5½ miles) southwest of Sóller.

Deià is perhaps best known as the adopted home of the English poet and writer Robert Graves, who lived here off and on from 1929 until his death in 1985. His grave can be found in the small cemetery at the top of the village. Deià is still a favorite haunt of writers and artists, including Graves's son Tomás, author of *Pa amb Oli* (*Bread and Olive Oil*), a guide to Mallorcan cooking, and British painter David Templeton. Ava Gardner lived here for a time; so, briefly, did Picasso. The setting is unbeatable—all around Deià rise the steep cliffs of the Sierra de Tramuntana. There's live jazz on summer evenings, and on warm afternoons literati gather at the beach bar in the rocky cove at Cala de Deià, 2 km (1 mile) downhill from the village. Walk up the narrow street to the village church; the small **cemetery** behind it affords views of mountains terraced with olive trees and of the coves below. It's a fitting spot for Graves's final resting place, in a quiet corner.

About 4 km (2½ miles) west of Deià is **Son Marroig,** a former estate of Austrian archduke Luis Salvador (1847–1915), which is now preserved as a museum, with a lovely garden and stunning coastal views. If you're driving, the best way to reach Son Marroig is the twisty MA10.

GETTING HERE AND AROUND

The Palma–Port de Sóller bus (€4.35) passes through Deià six times daily in each direction Monday–Saturday, five times on Sunday. Taxis to Deià from Palma cost €45 by day, €50 at night; from the airport the fares are €50/€55, and from Sóller €22/€24. Intrepid hikers can walk from Deià through the mountains to Sóller, on a trail of moderate difficulty, in about 2½ hours.

EXPLORING

Ca N'Alluny (*La Casa de Robert Graves*). The Fundació Robert Graves opened this museum dedicated to Deià's most famous resident in the house he built in 1932. The seaside house is something of a shrine: Graves's furniture and books, personal effects, and the press he used to print many of his works are all preserved. ✉ *Ctra. Deià-Sóller s/n* ☎ *971/636185* 🌐 *www.lacasaderobertgraves.com* *€7* ⏲ *Closed Sun.*

Cala Deia. Encircled by high pine-topped cliffs, this rocky cove connects to various coastal walking paths as well as a narrow road that twists its way down from the village. Year-round, clear turquoise water makes it great for snorkeling and swims. The popular Ca's Patro March restaurant, hewn into the rocks, overhangs the sea and stirring views; it's often booked out days in advance. There is also a simple beach bar. ✉ *Cala Deia.*

Monestir de Miramar. On the road south from Deià to Valldemossa, this monastery was founded in 1276 by Ramón Llull, who established a school of Asian languages here. It was bought in 1872 by the Archduke Luis Salvador and restored as a mirador. Explore the garden and the tiny cloister, then walk below through the olive groves to a spectacular lookout. ⊠ *Ctra. Deià–Valldemossa (MA10), Km 67* ☎ *971/616073* 🎫 *€4* ⊘ *Closed Sun.*

Son Marroig. This estate belonged to Austrian archduke Luis Salvador, who arrived here as a young man and fell in love with the place. He acquired huge tracts of land along the northwestern coast, building miradors at the most spectacular points, but otherwise leaving the pristine beauty intact. Below the mirador, you can see **Sa Foradada**, a rock peninsula pierced by a huge archway, where the archduke moored his yacht. Now a museum, the estate house contains the archduke's collections of Mediterranean pottery and ceramics, Mallorcan furniture, and paintings. The garden is especially fine. From April through early October, the Deià International Festival holds classical concerts here. ⊠ *Ctra. Deià–Valldemossa (MA10), Km 65* ☎ *971/639158* ⊕ *www.sonmarroig.com* 🎫 *€4.*

WHERE TO STAY

$$$$
HOTEL
FAMILY
Fodor's Choice
★

🏨 **Belmond La Residencia.** Two 16th- and 17th-century manor houses, on a hill facing the village of Deià, have been artfully combined to make this exceptional hotel, superbly furnished with Mallorcan antiques, modern canvases, and canopied four-poster beds. **Pros:** some rooms have private plunge pools; private shuttle to the sea; tennis coach, pro shop, and clinic. **Cons:** expensive; narrow stairs to the Tower Suite. $ *Rooms from: €630* ⊠ *Son Canals s/n* ☎ *971/639011* ⊕ *www.belmond.com/la-residencia-mallorca* 🛏 *67 rooms, 1 villa* ⦿ *Free Breakfast.*

$$$$
HOTEL
Fodor's Choice
★

🏨 **Hotel Es Molí.** A converted 17th-century manor house in the hills above the valley of Deià, this peaceful hotel is known for its traditional sense of luxury. **Pros:** attentive service; heated pool with spacious terrace; chamber music concerts twice a week during the summer. **Cons:** steep climb to annex rooms; short season; three-night minimum for some stays in high season. $ *Rooms from: €365* ⊠ *Ctra. Valldemossa–Deià s/n* ☎ *971/639000* ⊕ *www.esmoli.com* ⊘ *Closed Nov.–Mar.* 🛏 *87 rooms* ⦿ *Free Breakfast.*

$$$
B&B/INN
FAMILY

🏨 **s'Hotel D'es Puig.** This family-run "hotel on the hill" has a back terrace with a lemon-tree garden and a wonderful view of the mountains. **Pros:** peaceful setting; two pools (one heated); private parking for guests. **Cons:** public spaces can feel a bit cramped; no pets; books out quickly. $ *Rooms from: €170* ⊠ *Carrer d'es Puig 4* ☎ *971/639409, 637/820805* ⊕ *www.hoteldespuig.com* ⊘ *Closed Dec. and Jan.* 🛏 *14 rooms* ⦿ *Free Breakfast.*

SÓLLER

13 km (8 miles) north of Jardins d'Alfàbia, 30 km (19 miles) north of Palma.

All but the briefest visits to Mallorca should include at least an overnight stay in Sóller, one of the most beautiful towns on the island, with palatial homes built in the 19th and early 20th centuries by the landowners and merchants who thrived on the export of the region's oranges, lemons, and almonds. Many of the buildings here, like the **Church of Sant Bartomeu** and the **Bank of Sóller**, on the Plaça Constitució, and the nearby **Can Prunera**, are gems of the Moderniste style, designed by contemporaries of Antoni Gaudí. The tourist information office in the **town hall**, next to Sant Bartomeu, has a walking-tour map of the important sites.

GETTING HERE AND AROUND

You can travel in retro style from Palma to Sóller on one of the six daily trains (four daily in February, March, November, and December; €25 round-trip) operated by Ferrocarril de Sóller, which depart from Plaça d'Espanya. With a string of wooden rail cars with leather-covered seats dating to 1912, the train trundles along for about an hour, making six stops along the 27-km (17-mile) route; the scenery gets lovely—especially at Bunyola and the Mirador Pujol—as you approach the peaks of the Tramuntana. From the train station in Sóller, a charming old trolley car, called the Tranvía de Sóller, threads its way down through town to the Port de Sóller. The fare is €7 each way. You can also buy a combination round-trip ticket for the train and the trolley for €32. The mountain road between Palma and Sóller is spectacular—lemon and olive trees on stone-walled terraces, farmhouses perched on the edges of forested cliffs—but demanding. ■TIP➜ **If you're driving to Sóller, take the tunnel (€5.05) at Alfabía instead. Save your strength for even better mountain roads ahead.**

Train and Trolley Contact Ferrocarril de Sóller. ✉ *Pl. d'Espanya 6, Palma* ☎ *971/752051 in Palma, 971/752028 in Palma, 971/630130 in Sóller* ⊕ *www. trendesoller.com.*

VISITOR INFORMATION

Contacts Sóller Tourist Office. ✉ *Pl. Espanya 15* ☎ *971/638008.*

EXPLORING

Can Prunera. A minute's walk or so from the Plaça de la Constitució, along Sóller's main shopping arcade, brings you to this charming museum, where Moderniste style comes to life. In the lovingly restored family rooms on the first floor of this imposing town house you can see how Sóller's well-to-do embraced the Art Deco style: the ornate furniture and furnishings, the stained glass and ceramic tile, and the carved and painted ceilings all helped announce their status in turn-of-the-century Mallorcan society. Upstairs, Can Prunera also houses a small collection of paintings by early modern masters, among them Man Ray, Santiago Rusiñol, Paul Klee, and Joan Miró; the garden is an open-air museum in its own right, with sculptures by José Siguiri, Josep Sirvent, and other Mallorcan artists. ✉ *Carrer de la Lluna 86–90* ☎ *971/638973* ⊕ *www.canprunera.com* 🎫 *€5* ⊗ *Closed Mon. Nov.–Feb.*

Station Building Galleries. Maintained by the Fundació Tren de l'Art, these galleries have two small but remarkable collections—one of engravings by Miró, the other of ceramics by Picasso. ✉ *Pl. Espanya 6* 🎫 *Free* ⊗ *Closed Sun.*

WHERE TO EAT AND STAY

$$

CATALAN

✕ **Sa Cova.** On Sóller's busy central square, this friendly and informal restaurant specializes in traditional local cooking, with a nod to touristic expectations. Skip the inevitable paella, and opt instead for the *sopas mallorquines,* a thick vegetable soup served over thin slices of bread, or the Mallorcan pork loin, stuffed with nuts and raisins. **Known for:** sopas mallorquines; outdoor seating; great people-watching. [$] *Average main: €16* ✉ *Pl. Constitució 7* ☎ *971/633222.*

$$ B&B/INN **Can Isabel.** Just across the tram tracks from the train station, this former home still feels much like a family hideaway. **Pros:** convenient location; good value; pretty gardens. **Cons:** rooms on the small side; no elevator; no private parking. [$] *Rooms from: €132* ✉ *Carrer Isabel II 13* ☎ *971/638097* 🌐 *www.canisabel.com* ⏲ *Closed Nov.–end-Feb.* 🛏 *6 rooms* 🍴 *Free Breakfast.*

$$$$ HOTEL **Gran Hotel Sóller.** A former private estate with an imposing Moderniste facade, this is the biggest hotel in town. **Pros:** friendly and efficient service in at least five languages; short walk from town center; convenient to trams. **Cons:** pricey for what you get; small pools; functional decor. [$] *Rooms from: €220* ✉ *Carrer Romaguera 18* ☎ *971/638686* 🌐 *www.granhotelsoller.com* 🛏 *40 rooms* 🍴 *Free Breakfast.*

$$ B&B/INN **Hotel Ca'n Abril Tramuntana.** About a minute's walk from the main square, this family-friendly boutique hotel is an oasis of quiet in summer, when Sóller gets most of its tourist traffic. **Pros:** friendly service; honesty bar; excellent value. **Cons:** no elevator; no pets; parking off-site (€10 per day). [$] *Rooms from: €125* ✉ *Carrer Pastor 26* ☎ *971/633579, 672/360507* 🌐 *www.hotel-can-abril-soller.com* ⏲ *Closed Nov.–mid-Mar.* 🛏 *10 rooms* 🍴 *Free Breakfast.*

$$$ B&B/INN **La Vila Hotel & Restaurant.** Owner Toni Oliver obviously put a lot of work into this lovingly restored town house on Sóller's central square. **Pros:** friendly service; good location; lovely Art Nouveau features. **Cons:** rooms on the square can be noisy; no elevator; no pets. [$] *Rooms from: €152* ✉ *Pl. de la Constitució 14* ☎ *971/634641* 🌐 *www.lavilahotel.com* 🛏 *8 rooms* 🍴 *Free Breakfast.*

SPORTS AND THE OUTDOORS

Ten minutes or so from the center of Sóller on the trolley, the beachfront at Port de Sóller offers all sorts of water-based fun.

Nautic Soller. On the northwest coast at Port de Sóller, this place has sea kayaks and motorboats available for rent May–October. ✉ *C/ de la Marina 4, Port de Sóller* ☎ *609/354132* 🌐 *www.nauticsoller.com.*

SHOPPING

Eugenio. For three generations, the craftsmen of the Eugenio family—originally sculptors and furniture makers—have been making bowls, cutting boards, and all sorts of kitchen utensils by hand, from old olive wood. The wood can only be cut between September and April; it's soaked in water for five weeks and then cured for a year before the carver turns his hand to it, and the resulting shapes and textures are lovely. The shop, across the street from the train station, is always packed. Eugenio is happy to ship purchases abroad. ✉ *Carrer Jerónimo Estades 11* ☎ *971/630984.*

EN ROUTE

Fornalutx. This pretty little mountain village nestled amid lemon and orange groves, 4 km (2½ miles) north of Sóller, is a worthy scenic detour. Much of its appeal emanates from the narrow pedestrianized streets, blond-stone houses speckled with bougainvillea and topped with red-tiled roofs, and the views over the Sóller valley.

Mallorca's Sierra de Tramuntana provides excellent views for hikers.

ALCÚDIA

54 km (34 miles) northeast of Palma.

Nothing if not strategic, Alcúdia is the ideal base for exploring Mallorca's north coast, with the 13-km-long (8-mile-long) beach from Port d'Alcúdia to C'an Picafort and the adjacent Playa de Muro, the birdwatchers' paradise in the S'Albufera wetlands, and the spectacular drive along the corniche to Cap de Formentor. The charming little walled town itself is a capsule version of Mallorcan history: the first city here was a Roman settlement, in 123 BC. The Moors reestablished a town here, and after the Reconquest it became a feudal possession of the Knights Templar; the first ring of city walls dates to the early 14th century. Begin your visit at the **Church of Sant Jaume** and walk through the maze of narrow streets inside to the **Porta de Xara,** with its twin crenellated towers.

GETTING HERE AND AROUND

Porta de Alcúdia, where the ferry arrives from Ciutadella, is a 3-km (2-mile) taxi ride from the center of Alcúdia. There is also direct bus service from Palma.

VISITOR INFORMATION

Contacts Alcúdia Tourist Office. ✉ *Pg. de Pere Ventayol, s/n* ☎ *971/549022* ⊕ *www.alcudiamallorca.com.*

EXPLORING

Ciutat Romana de Pol·lèntia. Archaeological remains of the ancient city of Pollentia, which dates to about 70 BC, include La Portella residential area, the Forum, and the 1st-century-AD Roman theater. The Museu Monogràfic de Pollentia has a small collection of statuary and artifacts from the nearby excavations of the Roman capital of the island. ✉ *Av. dels Prínceps d'Espanya s/n* ☎ *971/547004, 971/897102* 🌐 *www.pollentia.net* 🎟 *€3, includes museum and archaeological site* 🕒 *Closed Mon.*

POLLENÇA

8 km (5 miles) from Alcúdia, 50 km (31 miles) from Palma.

This is a pretty little town, with a history that goes back at least as far as the Roman occupation of the island; the only trace of that period is the stone **Roman Bridge** at the edge of town. In the 13th century, Pollença and much of the land around it was owned by the Knights Templar, who built the imposing church of **Nuestra Senyora de Los Ángeles** on the west side of the present-day Plaça Major. The church looks east to the 1,082-foot peak of the Puig de Maria, with the 15th-century sanctuary at the top. The **Calvari** of Pollença is a flight of 365 stone steps to a tiny chapel, and a panoramic view as far as Cap de Formentor. There's a colorful weekly market at the foot of the steps on Sunday mornings.

GETTING HERE AND AROUND

Pollença is a fairly easy drive from Palma on the MA013. A few buses each day connect Pollença with Palma and Alcúdia.

VISITOR INFORMATION

Contacts Pollença Tourist Office. ✉ *Guillen Cifre de Colonya s/n* ☎ *971/535077.*

FESTIVALS

Festival Pollença. An acclaimed international music event, this festival is held each July and August. Since its inception, in 1961, it has attracted such performers as Mstislav Rostropovich, Jessye Norman, the St. Petersburg Philharmonic, the Camerata Köln, and the Alban Berg Quartet. Concerts are held in the cloister of the Convent of Sant Domingo. ✉ *Pollença* ☎ *971/534011* 🌐 *www.festivalpollenca.com.*

EXPLORING

OFF THE BEATEN PATH

Cap de Formentor. The winding road north from Port de Pollença to the tip of the island is spectacular. Stop at the Mirador de la Cruete, where the rocks form deep, narrow inlets of multishaded blue. A stone tower called the Talaia d'Albercuix marks the highest point on the peninsula. Continue on, around hairpin bends—and past superb coastal views—to reach Cala Formentor beach. The drive is certainly not for the faint-hearted, but the beach at the end is one of Mallorca's best, with fine white sand and calm turquoise water, backed by a forest of pine trees that offer shade. ✉ *Formentor.*

WHERE TO STAY

$$ B&B/INN 🏨 **Hotel Juma.** This little hotel, which opened in 1907, is on Pollença's main square, making it a good choice for a weekend stay because of the Sunday market that takes place there. **Pros:** great location; tasty breakfast in the bar; good value. **Cons:** parking can be a problem; rooms overlooking square can be noisy; basic decor and amenities. [$] *Rooms from: €125* ✉ *Pl. Major 9* ☎ *971/535002* 🌐 *www.pollensahotels.com* 🕒 *Closed mid-Nov.–mid-Mar.* 🛏 *7 rooms* 🍴 *Free Breakfast.*

DID YOU KNOW?

The town of Pollença was built 6 km (4 miles) from the coast and the city's port to avoid pirate attacks.

$$$$ B&B/INN Fodor's Choice ★ **Hotel Son Sant Jordi.** A favorite way station for groups of cyclists touring the island, the Son Sant Jordi is a small, family-friendly gem of a boutique hotel, formerly the convent of the adjacent Church of Sant Jordi. **Pros:** pleasant patio garden; lots of character and charm; great location. **Cons:** a tad pricey; three-night minimum stay June–September; no parking on-site. [$] *Rooms from: €182* ✉ *Carrer Sant Jordi 29* ☎ *971/530389* 🌐 *www.hotelsonsantjordi.com/en* 🛏 *12 rooms* 🍴 *Free Breakfast.*

$$$$ RESORT Fodor's Choice ★ **Son Brull Hotel & Spa.** "Oasis" is what springs to mind when driving up through family vineyards to this brilliantly restored medieval monastery, reborn as a deluxe resort hotel. **Pros:** charm and sophistication; strategic location for exploring Pollença, Alcúdia, and the S'Albufereta wildlife reserve; free daily yoga and Pilates sessions. **Cons:** pricey; minimum booking for some arrivals in high season; no sea view might disappoint some. [$] *Rooms from: €700* ✉ *Ctra. Palma–Pollença, Km 50* ☎ *971/535353* 🌐 *www.sonbrull.com* 🕒 *Closed Dec. and Jan.* 🛏 *13 rooms, 10 suites* 🍴 *Free Breakfast.*

LLUC

20 km (12 miles) southwest of Pollença.

The Santuari de Lluc, which holds the Black Virgin and is a major pilgrimage site, is widely considered Mallorca's spiritual heart.

GETTING HERE AND AROUND

The Santuari is about midway between Sóller and Pollença on the hairpin route over the mountains (MA10). Two buses daily connect these towns, stopping in Lluc. Taxi fare from either town is about €35.

EXPLORING

Santuari de Lluc. La Moreneta, also known as La Virgen Negra de Lluc (the Black Virgin of Lluc), is a votary statue of the Virgin Mary that's held in a 17th-century **church,** the center of this sanctuary complex. The **museum** has an eclectic collection of prehistoric and Roman artifacts, ceramics, paintings, textiles, folk costumes, votive offerings, Nativity scenes, and work by local artists. Between September and June, a children's choir sings psalms in the chapel at morning and evening services, Monday–Saturday, and at 11 am for Sunday Mass. The Christmas Eve performance of the "Cant de la Sibila" ("Song of the Sybil"), based on a medieval prophecy of the end of the world, is an annual choral highlight. ✉ *Pl. dels Peregrins 1* ☎ *971/871525* 🌐 *www.lluc.net/eng* 🎟 *Free, museum €4.*

MENORCA

Menorca, the northernmost of the Balearics, is a knobby, cliff-bound plateau with some 193 km (120 miles) of coastline and a central hill called El Toro, from the 1,100-foot summit of which you can see the whole island. Prehistoric monuments—*taulas* (huge stone T-shapes), *talayots* (spiral stone cones), and *navetes* (stone structures shaped like overturned boats)—left by the first Neolithic settlers are all over the island.

Tourism came late to Menorca, which aligned with the Republic in the Spanish Civil War; Franco punished the island by discouraging the investment in infrastructure that fueled the Balearic boom on Mallorca and Ibiza. Menorca has avoided many of the problems of overdevelopment: there are still very few high-rise hotels, and the herringbone road system, with a single central highway, means that each resort is small and separate. There's less to see and do on Menorca, and more unspoiled countryside than on the other Balearics. The island, home to some 220 species of birds and more than 1,000 species of plants, was designated a Biosphere Reserve in 1993. Menorca is where Spaniards and Catalans tend to take their families on vacation.

GETTING HERE AND AROUND

To get to Menorca from Barcelona take the overnight ferry, fast hydrofoil (about 3 hours), or a 40-minute flight. It's a six-hour ferry ride from Palma.

Several buses a day run the length of Menorca between Mahón and Ciutadella, stopping en route at Alaior, Mercadal, and Ferreries. The bus line Autos Fornells serves the northeast; Transportes Menorca connects Mahón with Ciutadella and with the major beaches and calas around the island. From smaller towns there are daily buses to Mahón and connections to Ciutadella. In summer, regular buses shuttle beachgoers from the west end of Ciutadella's Plaça Explanada to the resorts to the south and west; from Mahón, excursions to Menorca's most remote beaches leave daily from the jetty next to the Nuevo Muelle Comercial.

If you want to beach-hop in Menorca, it's best to have your own transportation, but most of the island's historic sights are in Mahón or Ciutadella, and once you're in town everything is within walking distance. You can see the island's archaeological remains in a day's drive, so you may want to rent a car for just that part of your visit.

Bus Contacts Autocares Torres. ☎ 902/075066 ⊕ www.bus.e-torres.net/en. **Autos Fornells.** ☎ 971/154390 ⊕ www.autosfornells.com. **Transportes Menorca.** ☎ 971/360475 ⊕ www.tmsa.es.

MAHÓN (MAÓ)

Established as the island's capital in 1722, when the British began their nearly 80-year occupation, Mahón still bears the stamp of its former rulers. The streets nearest the port are lined with four-story Georgian town houses; the Mahónese drink gin and admire Chippendale furniture; English is widely spoken. The city is quiet for much of the year, but between June and September the waterfront pubs and restaurants swell with foreigners.

GETTING HERE AND AROUND

There's ferry service here from Mallorca, but it's much less frequent than to Ciutadella. Within Mahón, Autocares Torres has three bus routes around the city and to the airport.

Bus Station Estació Autobuses. ✉ Carrer Josep Anselm Clavé s/n, Maó ☎ 971/360475.

Taxi Contact Radio-Taxi. ☎ 971/367111, 971/482222 ⊕ www.taximenorca.es.

VISITOR INFORMATION

Contacts Aeropuerto de Menorca Tourist Office. ✉ *Arrivals terminal, Maó* ☎ *971/356944* 🌐 *www.menorca.es.* **Mahón Tourist Office (Port).** ✉ *Moll de Llevant 2, Maó* ☎ *971/355952* 🌐 *www.menorca.es.*

EXPLORING

TOP ATTRACTIONS

La Verge del Carme. This church has a fine painted and gilded altarpiece. Adjoining the church are the cloisters, now a **market,** with stalls selling fresh produce and a variety of local cheeses and sausages. The central courtyard is a venue for a number of cultural events throughout the year. ✉ *Pl. del Carme, Maó* ☎ *971/362402.*

Santa María. Dating to the 13th century, this church was rebuilt in the 18th century, during the British occupation, and then restored again after being sacked during the Spanish Civil War. The church's pride is its 3,006-pipe baroque organ, imported from Austria in 1810. Organ concerts are given here at 7:30 on Saturday evening, and at 11 am and 7 pm on Sunday. The altar, and the half-domed chapels on either side, have exceptional frescoes. ✉ *Pl. de la Constitució s/n, Maó* ☎ *971/362278.*

BEACHES

FAMILY **Cala Galdana.** A smallish horseshoe curve of fine white sand, framed by almost vertical pine-covered cliffs, is where Menorca's only river, the Agendar, reaches the sea through a long limestone gorge. The surrounding area is under environmental protection—the handful of resort hotels and chalets above the beach (usually booked solid June–September by package-tour operators) were grandfathered in. Cala Galdana is family-friendly in the extreme, with calm, shallow waters, and a nearby water park–playground for the kids. A favorite with Menorcans and visitors alike, it gets really crowded in high season, but a 20-minute walk through the pine forest leads to the otherwise inaccessible little coves of Macarella and Macaretta, remote beaches popular with naturists and boating parties. **Amenities:** food and drink; lifeguards; showers; water sports. **Best for:** swimming; walking. ✉ *35 km (21 miles) from Mahón, Ferreries* ✥ *Take ME1 to Ferreries, then head south from there on local ME22.*

WHERE TO EAT

$$$$ SEAFOOD 🍴 **El Jàgaro.** This simple waterfront restaurant, at the east end of the harbor promenade, is a local favorite. The lunchtime crowd comes for the platter of lightly fried mixed fish with potatoes; knowledgeable clients home in on local specialties like *cap-roig* (scorpionfish) with garlic and wine sauce, or paella *bogavante* (with clawed lobster). **Known for:** spiny lobster stew (caldereta); harbor-front setting; local flavor. [$] *Average main: €27* ✉ *Moll de Llevant 334, Maó* ☎ *971/362390, 659/462467* ⏲ *Closed Mon. No dinner Sun. Nov.–Mar.*

$$$$ SPANISH Fodor's Choice ★ 🍴 **Es Moli de Foc.** Originally a flour mill, this is the oldest building in the village of Sant Climent, and the food is exceptional. Taste seasonal dishes, which can include prawn carpaccio with cured Mahón cheese and artichoke oil, black paella with monkfish and squid, and *carrilleras de ternera* (beef cheeks) with potato. **Known for:** historic building; brewery on-site; rustic local food with style. [$] *Average main: €24* ✉ *Carrer Sant Llorenç 65, 4 km (2½ miles) southwest of town,*

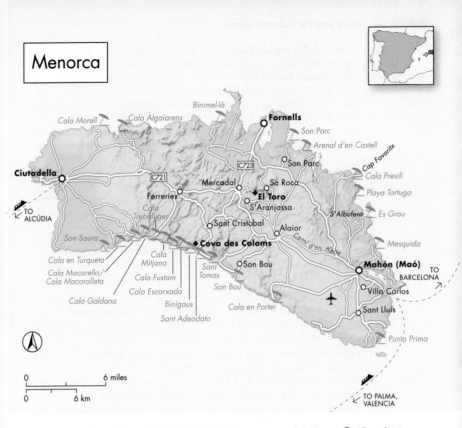

Menorca

Cala Morell • Cala Algaiarens • Binimel-là

Fornells
Son Parc
Arenal d'en Castell
Cap Favoritx

Ciutadella

C723
Son Parc
Cala Presili
Playa Tortuga

C721
Mercadal
Sa Roca
El Toro
S'Aranjassa
S'Albufera
Es Grau

TO ALCÚDIA

Ferreries
Cala Trebalúger
Sant Cristobal
Alaior
Camí d'en Kane
Mesquida

Cova des Coloms

Son Saura

Cala en Turqueta
Cala Mitjana
Sant Tomas
Son Bou
Mahón (Maó)
TO BARCELONA

Cala Macarella/
Cala Macaralleta
Cala Fustam
Son Bou
Villa Carlos

Cala Galdana
Cala Escorxada
Binigaus
Cala en Porter
Sant Lluís

Sant Adeodato
Punta Prima

0 — 6 miles
0 — 6 km

TO PALMA,
VALENCIA

Sant Climent ☎ 971/153222 ⊕ *www.esmolidefoc.es* ☉ *Closed Mon. Oct.–June. No lunch Mon. in July and Aug., and Tues.–Sun. Oct.–June.*

WHERE TO STAY

$$$$
HOTEL

🏨 **Hotel Port Mahón.** This standby may not win many prizes for imaginative design, but it's a solid choice, with rooms with hardwood floors, generic but comfortable furniture, and plenty of closet space. **Pros:** decent value; good buffet breakfast; some rooms have private terraces with impressive views. **Cons:** pool and garden front on the Passeig Marítim; no air-conditioning; uninspired design. $ *Rooms from: €200* ⊠ *Av. Fort de l'Eau s/n, Maó* ☎ *971/362600* ⊕ *www.sethotels.com/en/ port-mahon-hotel-en.html* 🛏 *82 rooms* ⍾ *Free Breakfast.*

$$$$
B&B/INN
Fodor'sChoice
★

🏨 **Hotel Rural y Restaurante Biniarroca.** Antique embroidered bed linens, shelves with knickknacks, and comfy chairs—this is an English vision of a peaceful and secluded rural retreat, and its glory is the garden of irises, lavender, and flowering trees. **Pros:** excellent food on-site; some suites have private terraces; peaceful surroundings. **Cons:** bit of a drive to the beach; some low ceilings; adults only. $ *Rooms from: €200* ⊠ *Cami Vell 57, Sant Lluís* ☎ *971/150059* ⊕ *www.biniarroca.com* ☉ *Closed Nov.–Easter* 🛏 *17 rooms, 1 suite* ⍾ *Free Breakfast.*

$$$$ B&B/INN Fodor's Choice ★ **Jardi de Ses Bruixes Boutique Hotel.** Built in 1811 by a Spanish ship captain, this *casa señorial* (town house) in the heart of Mahón was lovingly restored by architect and co-owner Fernando Pons and opened in 2014 as a boutique hotel. **Pros:** amiable, eager-to-please staff; strategic location; at-home atmosphere. **Cons:** difficult to reach by car, though there is free public parking a few minutes' walk away; bathtubs in the bedrooms sacrifice privacy to design; thin walls. [$] *Rooms from: €250* ✉ *Calle de San Fernando 26, Maó* ☎ *971/363166* 🌐 *www.hotelsesbruixes.com* 🛏 *16 rooms* 🍴 *Free Breakfast.*

$$$$ B&B/INN **Sant Joan de Binissaida.** An avenue lined with chinaberry and fig trees leads to this lovely restored farmhouse with environmental credentials, including some solar power and organic produce from the farm. **Pros:** vistas clear to the port of Mahón; huge pool; excellent restaurant. **Cons:** bit of a drive to the nearest beach; rooms in the annex lack privacy; short season, with three-night minimum stay in summer. [$] *Rooms from: €340* ✉ *Camí de Binissaida 108, Es Castell* ☎ *971/355598* 🌐 *www.binissaida.com* 🕒 *Closed Nov.–Apr.* 🛏 *12 rooms* 🍴 *Free Breakfast.*

NIGHTLIFE

Akelarre Jazz & Dance Club. This stylish bar near the port has a café-terrace downstairs and live jazz and blues on Thursday and Friday night. It's open year-round 10:30 am–4 am, and serves tapas and snacks to share in the evening. ✉ *Moll de Ponent 41–43, Maó* ☎ *971/368520.*

Casino Sant Climent. From May to September, catch live jazz on Tuesday evening at the Casino bar and restaurant. Book ahead for tables on the terrace. ✉ *Sant Jaume 4, 4 km (2½ miles) southwest of Mahón, Sant Climent* ☎ *971/153418* 🌐 *www.casinosantcliment.com.*

Cova d'en Xoroi. The hottest spot in Menorca is *the* place to catch the sun going down, drink in hand, a 20-minute drive from Mahón in the beach resort of Cala en Porter. This dance-until-dawn club is in a series of caves in a cliff high above the sea, which, according to local legend, was once the refuge of a castaway Moorish pirate. In addition to the nighttime DJs, there are afternoon–evening chill-out events with live music. ✉ *Carrer de Sa Cova s/n, Cala en Porter* ☎ *971/377236* 🌐 *www.covadenxoroi.com.*

Es Cau. Dug like a cave into the bluff of the little cove of Cala Corb, this is where locals gather (Thursday–Saturday 10 pm–3 am) to sing and play guitar: *habañeras,* love songs, songs of exile and return—everyone knows the songs and they all join in. It's hard to find, but anybody in Es Castell can point the way. ✉ *Cala Corb s/n, Es Castell.*

SPORTS AND THE OUTDOORS

BICYCLING

Asociación Cicloturista de Menorca. Ask here about organized bike tours of the island. ✉ *Moll de Llevant 173, Maó* ☎ *971/364816, 610/464816* 🌐 *www.menorcacicloturista.com/en.*

Bike Menorca. Rent a road bike or mountain bike by the day (from €15) from this full-service outfitter. ✉ *Av. Francesc Femenías 44, Maó* ☎ *971/353798* 🌐 *www.bikemenorca.com.*

DIVING

The clear Mediterranean waters here are ideal for diving. Equipment and lessons are available at Cala En Bosc, Son Parc, Fornells, Ciutadella, and Cala Tirant, among others.

Blue Islands Diving. ⊠ *Passatge Riu 7, Serpentona, Cala Galdana* ⊕ *www. blueislandsdiving.com.*

GOLF

Golf Son Parc. Menorca's sole golf course, designed by Dave Thomas, is 9 km (6 miles) east of Mercadal, about a 20-minute drive from Mahón. Rocky bunkers, and the occasional stray peacock on the fairways, make this an interesting and challenging course. The club, open year-round, also has two composition tennis courts and a restaurant ⊠ *Urb. Son Parc s/n, Mercadal* ☎ *971/188875* ⊕ *www.golfsonparc.com/en* 🖥 *€35–€50 for 9 holes, €45–€75 for 18 holes, depending on season* 🏌 *18 holes, 5653 yards, par 69.*

WALKING

In the south, each cove is approached by a *barranca* (ravine or gully), often from several miles inland. The head of **Barranca Algendar** is down a small, unmarked road immediately on the right of the Ferreries–Cala Galdana road; the barranca ends at the local beach resort, and from there you have a lovely walk north along the sea to an unspoiled half moon of sand at **Cala Macarella**. Extend your walk north, if time allows, through the forest along the riding trail to **Cala Turqueta**, where you'll find some of the island's most impressive grottoes.

SHOPPING

Menorca is known for shoes and leather goods, as well as cheese, gin, and wine. Wine was an important part of the Menorcan economy as long ago as the 18th century: the British, who knew a good place to grow grapes when they saw one, planted the island thick with vines. Viticulture was abandoned when Menorca returned to the embrace of Spain, and it has reemerged only in the past few years.

Boba's. Duck into the little alley between Carrer Nou and Carrer de l'Angel, and discover the atelier where Llorenç Pons makes his *espardenyes d'autor* (traditional rope-sole sandals) in original and surprising designs. ⊠ *Pont de l'Angel 4, Maó* ☎ *647/587456.*

Fodor's Choice ★ **Bodegas Binifadet.** This is the most promising of the handful of the local wineries, with robust young reds and whites on store shelves all over Menorca. The owners have expanded their product line into sparkling Chardonnay (sold only on the premises), olive oil, jams and conserves, and wine-based soaps and cosmetics. It's well worth a visit, not merely for tastings and guided tours (the website has details), but—weather permitting—for a meal on the terrace (Easter–October, noon–4; mid-May–September, noon–midnight). The kitchen puts an international touch on traditional Menorcan recipes and products; the local red prawns in sea salt (€22) are great. In midsummer, reservations are a must. You can also simply drop by for a glass of wine on the terrace; the surroundings are picturesque and peaceful. ⊠ *Ses Barraques s/n, Sant Lluís* ☎ *971/150715* ⊕ *www.binifadet.com.*

Pons Quintana. This showroom has a full-length window overlooking the factory where its very chic women's shoes are made. ⊠ *Carrer Sant*

Antoni 120, 13 km (8 miles) northeast of Mahón, Alaior ☎ *971/371050* ⊕ *www.ponsquintana.com/en.*

Xoriguer. One gastronomic legacy of the British occupation was gin. Visit this distillery on Mahón's quayside near the ferry terminal, where you can sample various types of gin, and buy some to take home. ✉ *Moll de Ponent, Maó* ☎ *971/362197* ⊕ *www.xoriguer.es.*

CIUTADELLA

44 km (27 miles) west of Mahón.

Ciutadella was Menorca's capital before the British settled in Mahón, and its history is richer. Settled successively by the Phoenicians, Greeks, Carthaginians, and Romans, Ciutadella fell to the Moors in 903 and became a part of the Caliphate of Córdoba until 1287, when Alfonso III of Aragón reconquered it. He gave estates in Ciutadella to nobles who aided him in the battle, and to this day the old historic center of town has a distinctly aristocratic tone. In 1558 a Turkish armada laid siege to Ciutadella, burning the city and enslaving its inhabitants. It was later rebuilt, but never quite regained its former stature.

As you arrive via the ME1, the main artery across the island from Mahón, turn left at the second traffic circle and follow the ring road to the Passeig Marítim; at the end, near the **Castell de Sant Nicolau** is a **monument to David Glasgow Farragut,** the first admiral of the U.S. Navy, whose father emigrated from Ciutadella to the United States. From here, take Passeig de Sant Nicolau to the **Plaēa de s'Esplanada** and park near the Plaça d'es Born.

GETTING HERE AND AROUND

Autocares Torres has a single bus line running between Ciutadella and the beaches and calas near the city.

Bus Contact Autocares Torres. ☎ *902/075066* ⊕ *www.bus.e-torres.net/en.*

Bus Station Estación de Autobuses de Ciutadella. ✉ *Pl. de S'Esplanada s/n.*

Taxi Contact Radio Taxi Menorca. ☎ *971/367111, 971/482222* ⊕ *www. taximenorca.es.*

VISITOR INFORMATION

Contacts Ciutadella Tourist Office. ✉ *Edifici Ajuntament, Pl. d'es Born 15* ☎ *971/484155* ⊕ *www.menorca.es.*

EXPLORING

TOP ATTRACTIONS

Catedral. Carrer Major leads to this Gothic edifice, which has some beautifully carved choir stalls. The side chapel has round Moorish arches, remnants of the mosque that once stood on this site; the bell tower is a converted minaret. ✉ *Pl. de la Catedral* ☎ *971/380739* 🔁 *€3.*

Port. Ciutadella's port is accessible from steps that lead down from Carrer Sant Sebastià. The waterfront here is lined with seafood restaurants, some of which burrow into caverns far under the Born. ✉ *Ciutadella.*

BEACHES

Cala Macarella and Cala Macaralleta. What just might be the two most beautiful of Menorca's small beaches are reachable three ways: by boat, by car from the Mahón–Ciutadella highway (ME1), or, if you're feeling robust and ambitious, on foot from the little resort town of Cala Galdana. Cala Macarella is a little crescent of white sand lapped by breathtakingly turquoise and blue waters that are calm and shallow, and sheltered by rocks on both sides. Remote as it is, it's popular with locals as well as vacationers. A 10-minute walk along the cliffs brings you to the even smaller and more tranquil Cala Macaralleta, where there are no amenities and fewer sunseekers. **Amenities:** food and drink; lifeguards; parking (no fee); toilets. **Best for:** swimming; walking. ✉ *Urb. Serpentona.*

WHERE TO EAT AND STAY

$$$ SEAFOOD 🍴 **Cafe Balear.** Seafood doesn't get much fresher than here, as the owners' boat docks nearby every day except Sunday. The relaxed atmosphere welcomes either a quick bite or a full dining experience. **Known for:** lobster caldreta; portside location; fresh-off-the-boat catches. [$] *Average main: €20* ✉ *Pl. de San Juan 15* ☎ *971/380005* ⏲ *Closed Nov. and Mon.*

$$$ SEAFOOD 🍴 **S'Amarador.** At the foot of the steps that lead down to the port, this restaurant has a café-terrace out front that's perfect for people-watching, drinks, and tapas. Fresh seafood in any form is a sure bet here: try the John Dory, baked, grilled, or fried with garlic—or splurge on the caldereta (€65). **Known for:** bustling terrace; flavorsome lobster stew; good value fixed-price lunch menu. [$] *Average main: €20* ✉ *Pere Capllonch 42* ☎ *971/383524, 619/421518* 🌐 *www.samarador.com.*

$$$$ B&B/INN FAMILY 🏨 **Hotel Rural Sant Ignasi.** About 10 minutes by car from the central square, and set in a centuries-old oak forest, this comfortable manor house dates to 1777 and is a favorite with young Spanish families. **Pros:** good value; friendly staff; tennis and paddle tennis courts. **Cons:** kids in the pool all day; short season; three-night minimum stay in summer. [$] *Rooms from: €260* ✉ *Ronda Norte s/n* ✣ *Take Ronda Norte to 2nd traffic circle at Polígono Industrial; just past traffic circle turn left on Son Juaneda and follow signs* ☎ *971/385575* 🌐 *www.santignasi.com* ⏲ *Closed mid-Oct.–Apr.* 🛏 *17 rooms, 8 suites* 🍽 *Free Breakfast.*

$$$$ B&B/INN Fodor's Choice ★ 🏨 **Hotel Tres Sants.** This chic boutique hotel is in the heart of Ciutadella, on a narrow cobblestone street behind the cathedral, and has killer views from the rooftop terrace, extending over the old city and (in good weather) across the ocean as far as Mallorca. **Pros:** suites for families; ideal location for exploring the city; on-site spa access 24 hours. **Cons:** no parking; no elevator; communal breakfasts don't suit everyone. [$] *Rooms from: €245* ✉ *Carrer Sant Cristofol 2* ☎ *626/053536* 🌐 *www.grupelcarme.com/en/tres-sants* 🛏 *6 rooms, 2 suites* 🍽 *Free Breakfast.*

SPORTS AND THE OUTDOORS

HORSEBACK RIDING

Horseback riding, breeding, and dressage have been traditions on the island for hundreds of years, and the magnificent black Menorcan horses play an important role, not only as work animals and for sport, but also in shows and colorful local festivals. There are 17 riding clubs on the island, a number of which offer excursions on the rural lanes of the unspoiled countryside. The Camí de Cavalls is a riding route in 20

Ciutadella's harbor, just below the main square and lined with restaurants, is perfect for a summer evening stroll.

stages that completely circumnavigates the island. Cavalls Son Angel in Ciutadella, Centre Equestre Equimar in Es Castell, and Menorca a Cavall in Ferreries organize excursions for adults and children. Son Martorellet, on the road to the beach at Cala Galdana, is a ranch where you can visit the stables and watch dressage training exhibitions every Wednesday and Thursday afternoon at 3:30; there's an equestrian show in traditional costume every Saturday at 4:30, February–November.

FAMILY **Cavalls Son Àngel.** This equestrian center specializes in excursions along the Cami de Cavalls, the horseback route that circumnavigates the island, with rides that range from one to two hours for beginners (€22–€40) to three- or five-day trips (September–June only) with lunches en route. Riders on the longer excursions need to arrange their own overnight accommodations. ⊠ *Camí d'Algaiarens s/n* ☎ *609/833902, 649/488098* ⊕ *www.cavallssonangel.com.*

FAMILY **Centre Ecuestre Equimar** (*Menorca Horse Riding*). Excursions on horseback through the countryside or to the beach are €25–€85, depending on the length of the ride and the destination; there are also 30-minute pony rides for €15. Hour-long classes for all levels from beginners to experts start at €20, private lessons at €30. ⊠ *Club Hipic Haras Del Mar, Sant Climent* ☎ *669/255487, 646/459734* ⊕ *www.menorcahorseriding.com.*

FAMILY **Menorca a Cavall.** Hour-and-a-half-long excursions, along portions of the Camí de Cavalls, are €30 in autumn and winter, €35 in spring and summer. Longer rides run €50–€75, depending on the season. Single- and two-day routes along the south coast of Menorca can also be organized autumn through spring. ⊠ *Finca Es Calafat, Ctra. Ferreries–Cala*

Galdana (ME22), Km 4.3, Ferreries ☎ *971/374637, 685/990545* 🌐 *www.menorcaacavall.com.*

FAMILY **Son Martorellet.** The equestrian performances at the Son Martorellet stables, featuring demonstrations of dressage with the famed Menorcan horses, are offered Wednesday and Thursday afternoons. ✉ *Ctra. Ferreries–Cala Galdana, Km 1.7, Ferreries* ☎ *971/373406, 639/156851* 🌐 *www.sonmartorellet.com.*

SHOPPING

The *polígono industrial* (industrial complex) on the right as you enter Ciutadella has a number of shoe factories, each with a shop. Prices may be the same as in stores, but the selection is wider. In Plaça d'es Born, a market is held on Friday and Saturday.

For the best shopping, try the Ses Voltes area, the Es Rodol zone near Plaça Artrutx, and along the Camí de Maó between Plaça Palmeras and Plaça d'es Born.

Hort Sant Patrici. This is a good place to buy the tangy, Parmesan-like Mahón cheese. There's a shop, beautiful grounds with a small vineyard, a sculpture garden and botanical garden, and a display of traditional cheese-making techniques and tools. On Monday, Tuesday, Thursday, and Saturday from 9–11 am you can watch the cheese being made. Guided tours (by reservation; €8) are available on Tuesday, Thursday, and Saturday at 10 am. Hort Sant Patrici has its own vineyards and olive trees, and nestled among them is a bed-and-breakfast, the **Ca Na Xini** (*www.canaxini.com/en/rural-boutique-hotel-menorca*), with eight rooms done in dazzling minimalist white. ✉ *Camí Sant Patrici s/n, Ferreries* ✣ *18 km (11 miles) east of Ciutadella; exit ME1 at 2nd traffic circle after Ferreries onto Cami Sant Patrici* ☎ *971/373702* 🌐 *www.santpatrici.com.*

Maria Juanico. Interesting plated and anodized silver jewelry and accessories are created by Maria at a workshop in the back of her store. ✉ *Carrer Seminari 38* ☎ *971/480879* 🌐 *www.mariajuanico.com/en/tienda.*

Nadia Rabosio. This inventive designer has created an original selection of jewelry and hand-painted silks. ✉ *Carrer Santissim 4* ☎ *971/384080.*

EL TORO

24 km (15 miles) northwest of Mahón.

The peak of El Toro is Menorca's highest point, at all of 1,555 feet. From the monastery on top you can see the whole island and across the sea to Mallorca.

GETTING HERE AND AROUND

Follow signs in Es Mercadal, the crossroads at the island's center.

WHERE TO EAT

$$ CATALAN 🍴 **Molí d'es Recon.** A great place to stop for a lunch of typical local cuisine, this restaurant is in an old windmill at the west end of Es Mercadal, on the ME1 about halfway between Mahón and Ciutadella and about 4 km (2½ miles) from El Toro. It has fortress-grade, whitewashed stone walls and low vaulted ceilings, and a constant air of cheerful bustle. [$] *Average main: €15* ✉ *Carrer Major 53, Mercadal* ☎ *971/375392.*

FORNELLS

35 km (22 miles) northwest of Mahón.

A little village (full-time population: 500) of whitewashed houses with red-tile roofs, Fornells comes alive in the summer high season, when Spanish and Catalan families arrive in droves to open their holiday chalets at the edge of town and in the nearby beach resorts. The bay—Menorca's second largest and deepest—is good for windsurfing, sailing, and scuba diving. The first fortifications built here to defend the Bay of Fornells from pirates date to 1625.

SPORTS AND THE OUTDOORS
SAILING
Several miles long and a mile wide but with a narrow entrance to the sea and virtually no waves, the Bay of Fornells gives the beginner a feeling of security and the expert plenty of excitement.

Wind Fornells. Here, on the beach just off Carrer del Rosari, you can rent windsurfing boards and dinghies, and take lessons, individually or in groups. It's open May–October. ⊠ *Ctra. Es Mercadal–Fornells s/n, Mercadal* ☎ *664/335801* ⊕ *www.windfornells.com.*

COVA DES COLOMS

35 km (22 miles) northwest of Mahón.

There are caverns and grottoes all over the Balearics, some of them justly famous because of their size, spectacular formations, and subterranean pools. This one is well worth a visit.

GETTING HERE AND AROUND
Take the road from Ferreries to Es Migjorn Gran, park by the cemetery, and follow the signs on the footpath, about 30 minutes' walk toward the beach at Binigaus. Signs direct you to the gully, where you descend to the cave.

Cova des Coloms (*Cave of Pigeons*). This massive cave is the most spectacular on Menorca, with eerie rock formations rising up to a 77-foot-high ceiling. When planning your visit, bear in mind that it's a 30-minute walk each way from the nearest parking. ⊠ *On eastern side of ravine from Es Migjorn Gran to beach, Ciutadella.*

ANDALUSIA

WELCOME TO ANDALUSIA

TOP REASONS TO GO

★ **Appreciate exquisite architecture:** Granada's Alhambra and Córdoba's Mezquita are two of Spain's—if not the world's—most impressive sites.

★ **Dance the flamenco:** "Olé" deep into the night at a heel-clicking flamenco performance in Jerez de la Frontera, the "cradle of flamenco."

★ **Admire priceless paintings:** Bask in the golden age of Spanish art at Seville's Museo de Bellas Artes.

★ **Explore ancient glory:** Cádiz, believed to be the oldest port in Europe, is resplendent with its sumptuous architecture and a magnificent cathedral.

★ **Visit the white villages:** Enjoy the simple beauty of a bygone age by exploring the gleaming *pueblos blancos*.

Andalusia is infinitely varied and diverse within its apparent unity. Seville and Granada are like feuding sisters, one vivaciously flirting, the other darkly brooding; Córdoba and Cádiz are estranged cousins, one landlocked, the other virtually under sail; Huelva is a verdant Atlantic Arcadia; and Jaén is an upland country bumpkin—albeit one with Renaissance palaces—compared with the steamy cosmopolitan seaport of Málaga which, along with the southern Andalusian cities and towns of Marbella and Tarifa, is covered in the Costas chapter.

1 Seville. Long Spain's chief riverine port, the captivating city of Seville sits astride the Guadalquivir River, which launched Christopher Columbus to the New World and Ferdinand Magellan around the globe. South of the capital is fertile farmland; in the north are highland villages. Don't miss stunning, mountaintop Ronda, which has plenty of atmosphere and memorable sights.

2 Huelva. Famed as oak-forested grazing grounds for the treasured *cerdo ibérico* (Iberian pig), Huelva's Sierra de Aracena is a fresh and leafy mountain getaway on the border of Portugal. The province's Doñana National Park is one of Spain's greatest national treasures.

3 Cádiz Province and Jerez de la Frontera. Almost completely surrounded by water, the city of Cádiz is Western Europe's oldest continually inhabited city, a dazzling bastion at the edge of the Atlantic. Jerez de la Frontera is known for its sherry, flamenco, and equestrian culture.

4 Córdoba. A center of world science and philosophy in the 9th and 10th centuries, Córdoba is a living monument to its past glory. Its prized building is the Mezquita (mosque). In the countryside, acorns and olives thrive.

5 Jaén Province. Andalusia's northeasternmost province is a striking contrast of olive groves, pristine wilderness, and Renaissance towns with elegant palaces and churches.

6 Granada. Christian and Moorish cultures are dramatically counterposed in Granada, especially in the graceful enclave of the Alhambra.

10

EATING AND DRINKING WELL IN ANDALUSIA

Andalusian cuisine, as diverse as the geography of seacoast, farmland, and mountains, is held together by its Moorish aromas. Cumin seed and other Arabian spices, along with salty-sweet combinations, are ubiquitous.

(top left) A cool bowl of gazpacho, with accompaniments to be added as desired (top right) Crispy fried fish are an Andalusian delicacy. (bottom right) Fried calamari with lemon

The eight Andalusian provinces cover a wide geographical and culinary spectrum. Superb seafood is at center stage in Cádiz, Puerto de Santa María, and Sanlúcar de Barrameda. *Jamón ibérico de bellota* (Iberian acorn-fed ham) and other Iberian pork products rule from the Sierra de Aracena in Huelva to the Pedroches Mountains north of Córdoba. In Seville look for products from the Guadalquivir estuary, the Sierra, and the rich Campiña farmland all prepared with great creativity. In Córdoba try *salmorejo cordobés* (a thick gazpacho), *rabo de toro* (oxtail stew), or representatives of the salty-sweet legacy from Córdoba's Moorish heritage such as *cordero con miel* (lamb with honey). Spicy *crema de almendras* (almond soup) is a Granada favorite along with *habas con jamón* (broad beans with ham) from the Alpujarran village of Trevélez.

SHERRY

Dry sherry from Jerez de la Frontera (fino) and from Sanlúcar de Barrameda (manzanilla), share honors as favorite tapas accompaniments. Manzanilla, the more popular choice, is fresher and more delicate, with a slight marine tang. Both are the preferred drinks at Andalusian ferias (fairs), particularly in Seville in April and Jerez de la Frontera in May.

COLD VEGETABLE SOUPS

Spain's most popular contribution to world gastronomy after paella may well be gazpacho, a simple peasant soup served cold and filled with scraps and garden ingredients. Tomatoes, cucumber, garlic, oil, bread, and chopped peppers are the ingredients, and side plates of chopped onion, peppers, garlic, tomatoes, and croutons accompany, to be added to taste. Salmorejo cordobés, a thicker cold vegetable soup with the same ingredients but a different consistency, is used to accompany tapas.

MOORISH FLAVORS

Andalusia's 781-year sojourn at the heart of Al-Andalus, the Moorish empire on the Iberian Peninsula, left as many tastes and aromas as mosques and fortresses. Cumin-laced *boquerones en adobo* (marinated anchovies) or the salty-sweet *cordero a la miel* (lamb with honey) are two examples, along with coriander-spiked *espinacas con garbanzos* (spinach with garbanzo beans) and *perdiz con dátiles y almendras* (partridge stewed with dates and almonds). Desserts especially reflect the Moorish legacy in morsels such as *pestiños,* cylinders or twists of fried dough in anise-honey syrup.

FRIED FISH

Andalusia is famous for its fried fish, from *pescaito frito* (fried whitebait) to *calamares fritos* (fried squid rings).

Andalusians are masters of deep-frying techniques using very hot olive and vegetable oils that produce peerlessly crisp, dry *frituras* (fried seafood); much of Andalusia's finest tapas repertory is known for being served up piping hot and crunchy. Look for *tortilla de camarones,* a delicate lacework of tiny fried shrimp.

STEWS

Guisos are combinations of vegetables, with or without meat, cooked slowly over low heat. Rabo de toro is a favorite throughout Andalusia, though Córdoba claims the origin of this dark and delicious stew made from the tail of a fighting bull. The segments of tail are cleaned, browned, and set aside before leeks, onions, carrots, garlic, and bay leaves are stewed in the same pan. Cloves, salt, pepper, a liter of wine, and a half liter of beef broth are added to the stew with the meat, and they're all simmered for two to three hours until the meat is falling off the bone and thoroughly tenderized. *Alboronía,* also known as *pisto andaluz,* is a traditional stew of eggplant, bell peppers, and zucchini, a recipe traced back to 9th-century Baghdad and brought to Córdoba by the Umayyad dynasty.

10

FLAMENCO

Rule one about flamenco: You don't see it. You feel it. The pain and yearning on the dancers' faces and the eerie voices are real. If the dancers manage to summon the *duende* and allow this soulful state of emotion to take over, then they have done their jobs well.

FLAMENCO 101

Origins: The music is largely Arabic in its beginnings, but you'll detect echoes of Greek dirges and Jewish chants, with healthy doses of Flemish and traditional Castillian thrown in. Hindu sways, Roman mimes, and other movement informs the dance, but we may never know the specific origins of flamenco. The dance, along with the nomadic Gypsies, spread throughout Andalusia and within a few centuries had developed into many variations and styles, some of them named after the city where they were born (such as malagueñas, sevillanas) and others taking on the names after people, emotions, or bands. In all, there are more than 50 different styles

(or *palos*) of flamenco, four of which are the stylistic pillars others branch off from—differing mainly in rhythm and mood: Toná, Soleá, Fandango, and Seguidilla.

Clapping and Castanets: The sum of its parts are awe-inspiring, but if you boil it down, flamenco is a combination of music, singing, and dance. Staccato hand-clapping almost sneaks in as a fourth part—the sounds made from all the participants' palms, or *palmas* is part of the duende—but this element remains more of a connector that all in the performance take part in when their hands are free. Hand-clapping was likely flamenco's original key instrument before the guitar, *cajón* (wooden box used for percussion), and other instruments arrived on the scene. Perhaps the simplest way to augment the clapping is to add a uniquely designed six-string guitar, in which case you've got yourself a *tablao,* or people seated around a singer and clapping. Dance undoubtedly augments the experience, but isn't necessary for a tablao. These exist all throughout Andalusia and are usually private affairs with people who love flamenco. One needn't be a Gypsy in order to take part in it. But it doesn't hurt. *Castanets* (or *palillos*) were absorbed by the Phoenician culture and adopted by the Spanish, now part of their own folklore. They accompany other traditional folk dances in Spain and are used pervasively throughout flamenco (though not always present in some forms of dance).

Flamenco Now: Flamenco's enormous international resurgence has been building for the past few decades. Much of this revival can be attributed to pioneers like legendary singer Camarón de la Isla, guitarist Paco de Lucía, or even outsiders like Miles Davis fusing flamenco with other genres like jazz and rock. This melding brought forth flamenco pop—which flourished in the '80s and continues today—as well as disparate fusions with almost every genre imaginable, including heavy metal and hip-hop. Today the most popular flamenco

fusion artists include Ojos de Brujo and Demarco Flamenco.

FLAMENCO HEAD TO TOE

Wrists rotate while hands move, articulating each finger individually, curling in and out. The trick is to have it appear like an effortless flourish. Facial expression is considered another tool for the dancer, and it's never plastered on but projected from some deeper place. For women, the hair is usually pulled back in touring flamenco performances in order to give the back row a chance to see more clearly the passionate expressions. In smaller settings like tablaos, hair is usually let down and is supposed to better reveal the beauty of the female form overall. The dancer carries their body in an upright and proud manner: the chest is out. shoulders back. Despite this position, the body should never carry tension—it needs to remain pliable and fluid. With professional dancers, the feet can move so quickly, they blur like humming bird wings in action. When they move slowly, you can watch the different ways a foot can strike the floor. A *planta* is when the whole foot strikes the floor, as opposed to when the ball of the foot or the heel (*taco*) hits. Each one must be a "clean" strike or the sound will be off.

10

Updated by
Joanna Styles

Gypsies, flamenco, horses, bulls—Andalusia is the Spain of story and song, simultaneously the least and most surprising part of the country: least surprising because it lives up to the hype and stereotype that long confused all of Spain with the Andalusian version, and most surprising because it is, at the same time, so much more.

To begin with, five of the eight Andalusian provinces are maritime, with colorful fishing fleets and a wealth of seafood usually associated with the north. Second, there are snowcapped mountains and ski resorts in Andalusia, the kind of high sierra resources normally associated with the Alps, or even the Pyrenees, yet the Sierra Nevada—with Granada at the foothills—is within sight of North Africa. Third, there are wildlife-filled wetlands and highland pine and oak forests rich with game and trout streams, not to mention free-range Iberian pigs. And last, there are cities like Seville that somehow manage to combine all of this with the creativity and cosmopolitanism of London or Barcelona.

Andalusia—for 781 years (711–1492) a Moorish empire and named for Al-Andalus (Arabic for "Land of the West")—is where the authentic history and character of the Iberian Peninsula and Spanish culture are most palpably, visibly, audibly, and aromatically apparent.

An exploration of Andalusia must begin with the cities of Seville, Córdoba, and Granada as the fundamental triangle of interest and identity. All the romantic images of Andalusia, and Spain in general, spring vividly to life in Seville: Spain's fourth-largest city is a cliché of matadors, flamenco, tapas bars, Gypsies, geraniums, and strolling guitarists, but there's so much more than these urban treasures. A more thorough Andalusian experience includes such unforgettable natural settings as Huelva's Sierra de Aracena and Doñana wetlands, Jaén's Parque Natural de Cazorla, Cádiz's pueblos blancos, and Granada's Alpujarras mountains.

PLANNING

WHEN TO GO

The best months to go to Andalusia are October and November and April and May. It's blisteringly hot in the summer; if that's your only chance to come, plan time in the Pedroches of northern Córdoba province, Granada's Sierra Nevada and Alpujarras highlands, or the Sierra de Cazorla in Jaén to beat the heat. Autumn catches the cities going about their business, the temperatures are moderate, and you will rarely see a line form.

December through March tends to be cool, uncrowded, and quiet, but come spring, it's fiesta time, with Seville's Semana Santa (Holy Week, between Palm Sunday and Easter) the most moving and multitudinous. April showcases whitewashed Andalusia at its floral best, every patio and facade covered with flowers from bougainvillea to honeysuckle.

PLANNING YOUR TIME

A week in Andalusia should include visits to Córdoba, Seville, and Granada to see, respectively, the Mezquita, the cathedral and its Giralda minaret, and the Alhambra. Two days in each city nearly fills the week, though the extra day would be best spent in Seville, Andalusia's most vibrant concentration of art, architecture, culture, and excitement.

Indeed, a week or more in Seville alone would be ideal, especially during the Semana Santa celebration, when the city becomes a giant street party. With more time on your hands, Cádiz, Jerez de la Frontera, and Sanlúcar de Barrameda form a three- or four-day jaunt through flamenco, sherry, Andalusian equestrian culture, and tapas emporiums.

A three-day trip through the Sierra de Aracena will introduce you to a lovely Atlantic upland, filled with Mediterranean black pigs deliciously fattened on acorns, while the Alpujarras, the mountain range east of Granada, is famed for its pueblos blancos. In this region you can find anywhere from three days to a week of hiking and trekking opportunities in some of the highest and wildest reaches in Spain. For nature enthusiasts, the highland Cazorla National Park and the wetland Doñana National Park are Andalusia's highest and lowest outdoor treasures.

FESTIVALS

Andalusia has some of Spain's most important and most colorful festivals, and highlights include **Carnival,** on the days leading up to Ash Wednesday (which can fall late January–early March), and **Semana Santa** (Holy Week, between Palm Sunday and Easter). Both are big celebrations, especially in Cádiz, Córdoba, and Seville. Other events range from international music festivals to more localized celebrations, such as the early August horse races on the beaches of Sanlúcar de Barrameda and the mid-October olive harvest in Jaén.

Concurso de Arte de Flamenco (*National Flamenco Competition*). Devotees of Spain's unique style of music and dance flock to the city for this event, held every third year—the next is in 2019—in November. ✉ *Córdoba.*

Cruces de Mayo (*Festival of Crosses*). Celebrated throughout the Spanish-speaking world, this ancient festival is a highlight of Córdoba's calendar of events, with lots of flower-decked crosses and other floral displays, processions, and music in early May. ⊠ *Córdoba.*

Encuentros Flamencos. Some of the country's best performers are featured in this early-December event in Granada. ⊠ *Granada.*

Feria de Abril (*April Fair*). Held two weeks after Easter, this secular celebration focuses on horses, pageantry, and bullfights. ⊠ *Seville.*

Feria de Mayo. The city's foremost street party is held during the last week of May. ⊠ *Córdoba.*

Feria del Caballo (*Horse Fair*). In early May, carriages and riders fill the streets of Jerez and purebreds from the School of Equestrian Art compete in races and dressage displays. ⊠ *Jerez de la Frontera.*

Festival de los Patios (*Patio Festival*). This celebration, awarded UNESCO World Heritage status in 2012, is held during the second week of May, a fun time to be in the city, when owners throw open their flower-decked patios to visitors (and to judges, who nominate the best), and the city celebrates with food, drink, and flamenco. ⊠ *Córdoba.*

Festival Internacional de Jazz de Granada. Established in 1980, this November festival attracts big names from the world of jazz—no less than Oscar Peterson, Dizzie Gillespie, Miles Davis, and Herbie Hancock, among many others, have delighted fans. ⊠ *Granada* ⊕ *www.jazzgranada.es.*

Festival Internacional de Música y Danza de Granada. With some events in the Alhambra itself, this international music and dance festival runs mid-June–mid-July. Tickets go on sale in mid-April. ⊠ *Granada* ⊕ *www.granadafestival.org.*

Fiesta de Otoño (*Autumn Festival*). In September, this festival in Jerez celebrates the grape harvest and includes a procession, the blessing of the harvest on the steps of the cathedral, and traditional-style grape treading. ⊠ *Jerez de la Frontera.*

International Guitar Festival. During the first two weeks of July, an array of major international artists perform at this celebration of guitar music, including classical, jazz, rock, folk, and—of course—flamenco. In addition to a full schedule of concerts, there are exhibitions, workshops, and conferences. ⊠ *Córdoba* ⊕ *www.guitarracordoba.org.*

La Bienal de Flamencol. Celebrating the best talents in flamenco, this festival is held every two years, the next being in 2020. ⊠ *Seville* ⊕ *www.labienal.com.*

Romería del Rocío. Pentecost weekend (seven Sundays after Easter) brings this Gypsy favorite—a pilgrimage on horseback and by carriage to the hermitage of La Virgen del Rocío (Our Lady of the Dew). ⊠ *Huelva.*

GETTING HERE AND AROUND
AIR TRAVEL

Andalusia's regional airports can be reached via Spanish domestic flights or from major European hubs. Málaga Airport (*see Costa del Sol and Costa de Almería*) is one of Spain's major hubs and a good access point for exploring this part of Andalusia.

The region's second-largest airport, after Málaga, is in Seville. The smaller Aeropuerto de Jerez is 7 km (4 miles) northeast of Jerez on the road to Seville. Buses run from the airport to Jerez and Cádiz. Flying into Granada's airport from Madrid or Barcelona is also a good option if you want to start your trip in Andalusia. It's easy to get into Granada from the airport.

BUS TRAVEL

The best way to get around Andalusia, if you're not driving, is by bus. Buses serve most small towns and villages and are faster and more frequent than trains. ALSA is the major bus company; tickets can be booked online, but be aware that non-Spanish credit cards occasionally cause problems with the system. Payment via PayPal is usually problem-free.

Bus Contacts ALSA. ☎ *902/422242* ⊕ *www.alsa.es.*

CAR TRAVEL

If you're planning to explore beyond Seville, Granada, and Córdoba, a car makes travel convenient.

The main road from Madrid is the A4 through Córdoba to Seville, a four-lane *autovía* (highway). From Granada or Málaga, head for Antequera, then take the A92 autovía by way of Osuna to Seville. Road trips from Seville to the Costa del Sol (by way of Ronda) are slow but scenic. Driving in western Andalusia is easy—the terrain is mostly flat land or slightly hilly, and the roads are straight and in good condition. From Seville to Jerez and Cádiz, the A4 toll road gets you to Cádiz in under an hour. The only way to access Doñana National Park by road is to take the A49 Seville–Huelva highway, exit for Almonte/Bollullos Par del Condado, then follow the signs for El Rocío and Matalascañas. The A49 west of Seville will also lead you to the freeway to Portugal and the Algarve. There are some beautiful scenic drives here, about which the respective tourist offices can advise you. The A369, heading southwest from Ronda to Gaucín, passes through stunning whitewashed villages.

With the exception of parts of the Alpujarras, most roads in this region are smooth, and touring by car is one of the most enjoyable ways to see the countryside. Local tourist offices can advise about scenic drives. One good route heads northwest from Seville on the A66 passing through stunning scenery; turn northeast on the A461 to Santa Olalla de Cala to the village of Zufre, dramatically set at the edge of a gorge. Backtrack and continue on to Aracena. Return via the Minas de Riotinto (signposted from Aracena), which will bring you back to the A66 heading east to Seville.

Rental Contact Autopro. ☎ *952/176545* ⊕ *www.autopro.es.*

10

FERRY TRAVEL

From Cádiz, Trasmediterránea operates ferry services to the Canary Islands with stops at Las Palmas de Gran Canaria (39 hours) and connecting ferries on to Fuerteventura, Lanzarote, La Palma, and Santa Cruz de Tenerife. There are no direct ferries from Seville.

Contact Acciona Trasmediterránea. ⊠ *Estación Marítima, Cádiz* ☎ *902/454645* ⊕ *www.trasmediterranea.es.*

TAXI TRAVEL

Taxis are plentiful throughout Andalusia and may be hailed on the street or from specified taxi stands. Fares are reasonable, and meters are strictly used; the minimum fare is about €4. You are not required to tip taxi drivers, although rounding off the amount is appreciated.

In Seville or Granada, expect to pay around €20–€25 for cab fare from the airport to the city center.

TRAIN TRAVEL

From Madrid, the best approach to Andalusia is via the high-speed AVE. In just 2½ hours, the spectacular ride winds through olive groves and rolling fields of Castile to Córdoba and on to Seville.

Seville, Córdoba, Jerez, and Cádiz all lie on the main rail line from Madrid to southern Spain. Trains leave Madrid for Seville (via Córdoba), and two of the non-AVE trains continue to Jerez and Cádiz. Travel time from Seville to Cádiz is 1½ hours. Trains also depart regularly for Barcelona (4 daily, 5½ hours), and Huelva (3 daily, 1½ hours). From Granada, Málaga, Ronda, and Algeciras, trains go to Seville via Bobadilla.

RESTAURANTS

Eating out is an intrinsic part of the Andalusian lifestyle. Whether it's sharing some tapas with friends over a prelunch drink or a three-course à la carte meal, many Andalusians eat out at some point during the day. Unsurprisingly, there are literally thousands of bars and restaurants throughout the region catering to all budgets and tastes.

At lunchtime, check out the daily menus (*menús del día*) offered by many restaurants, usually three courses and excellent value (expect to pay €8–€15, depending on the type of restaurant and location). Roadside restaurants, known as *ventas,*usually provide good food in generous portions and at reasonable prices. Be aware that many restaurants add a service charge (*cubierto*), which can be as much as €3 per person, and some restaurant prices don't include value-added tax (*impuesto sobre el valor añadido/I.V.A.*) at 10%.

Andalusians tend to eat later than their fellow Spaniards: lunch is 2–4 pm, and dinner starts at 9 pm (10 pm in the summer). In cities, many restaurants are closed Sunday night (fish restaurants tend to close on Monday) and in inland towns and cities, some close for all of August.

HOTELS

Seville has grand old hotels, such as the Alfonso XIII, and a number of former palaces converted into sumptuous hostelries.

The Parador de Granada, next to the Alhambra, is a magnificent way to enjoy Granada. Hotels on the Alhambra hill, especially the parador, must be reserved far in advance. Lodging establishments in Granada's city center, around the Puerta Real and Acera del Darro, can be unbelievably noisy, so if you're staying there, ask for a room toward the back. Though Granada has plenty of hotels, it can be difficult to find lodging during peak tourist season (Easter–late October).

In Córdoba, several pleasant hotels occupy houses in the old quarter, close to the mosque. Other than during Holy Week and the Festival de los Patios in May, it's easy to find a room in Córdoba, even without a reservation.

Rental accommodations bookable on portals such as Airbnb are popular in large towns and cities, although quality varies so double-check reviews before you book

Not all hotel prices include value-added tax (I.V.A.) and the 10% surcharge may be added to your final bill. Check when you book. *Hotel reviews have been shortened. For full information, visit Fodors.com.*

WHAT IT COSTS IN EUROS				
	$	**$$**	**$$$**	**$$$$**
Restaurants	under €12	€12–€17	€18–€22	over €22
Hotels	under €90	€90–€125	€126–€180	over €180

Restaurant prices are the average cost of a main course or equivalent combination of smaller dishes at dinner. Hotel prices are the lowest cost of a standard double room in high season.

TOURS

Alúa. For help with planning and getting the equipment for hiking, rock climbing, mountain biking, caving, and other active sports throughout Andalusia, this is a good place to start. ⊠ *Calle Concejal Francisco Ruiz Librero, Bormujos* ☎ *955/110776* ⊕ *www.alua.es* ✉ *From €20.*

Cabalgar Rutas Alternativas. This is an established Alpujarras equestrian agency that organizes horseback riding in the Sierra Nevada. ⊠ *C. Ermita, Bubión* ☎ *958/763135* ⊕ *www.ridingandalucia.com* ✉ *From €25.*

Faro del Sur. Activities such as trekking, cycling, sailing, and kayaking in western Andalusia are available, and tours include kayaking along the Guadalquivir River and sailing along the Huelva coastline. ⊠ *Puerto Deportivo L-1, Isla Cristina* ☎ *959/344490* ⊕ *www.farodelsur.com* ✉ *From €300.*

Glovento Sur. Up to five people at a time are taken in balloon trips above Granada, Ronda, Seville, Córdoba, or other parts of the region. ⊠ *Placeta Nevot 4, #1A, Granada* ☎ *958/290316* ⊕ *www.gloventosur. com* ✉ *From €165.*

Guías de Cazorla. Guided hikes, horseback riding, canyoning, and four-wheel-drive tours in the Sierra de Cazorla are offered. ⊠ *Calle Pósteles 18, Cazorla* ☎ *953/720112* ⊕ *guiasdecazorla.es* ✉ *From €25.*

10

Nevadensis. Based in the Alpujarras, Nevadensis leads guided hiking, climbing, and skiing tours of the Sierra Nevada. Note that prices are per group. ⊠ *Pl. de la Libertad, Pampaneira* ☎ *958/763127* ⊕ *www. nevadensis.com* ✉ *From €150.*

Sierra eXtreme. Choose from a wide range of adventure sports such as walking, climbing, caving, and canyoning in the Andalusian mountains with this company. ☎ *637/727365* ⊕ *www.sierraextreme.net* ✉ *From €25.*

Sierra Trails. Trail rides in the Alpujarras, lasting up to a week, can be organized through this company. The price includes airport transfers, overnight stays, and most meals. ⊠ *Ctra. de la Sierra, Bubión* ☎ *608/453802* ⊕ *www.spain-horse-riding.com* ✉ *From €575.*

SEVILLE

550 km (340 miles) southwest of Madrid.

Seville's whitewashed houses bright with bougainvillea, ocher-color palaces, and baroque facades have long enchanted both sevillanos and travelers. It's a city for the senses—the fragrance of orange blossom (orange trees line many streets) suffuses the air in spring, the sound of flamenco echoes through the alleyways in Triana and Santa Cruz, and views of the great Guadalquivir River accompany you at every turn. This is also a fine city in its architecture and people—stroll down the swankier pedestrian shopping streets and you can't fail to notice just how good-looking everyone is. Aside from being blessed with even features and flashing dark eyes, sevillanos exude a cool sophistication that seems more Catalan than Andalusian.

This bustling city of more than 700,000 does have some downsides: traffic-choked streets, high unemployment, a notorious petty-crime rate, and at times the kind of impersonal treatment you won't find in the smaller cities of Granada and Córdoba.

The layout of the historic center of Seville makes exploring easy. The central zone—**Centro**—around the cathedral, the Alcázar, Calle Sierpes, and Plaza Nueva, is splendid and monumental, but it's not where you'll find Seville's greatest charm. **El Arenal,** home of the Maestranza bullring, the Teatro de la Maestranza concert hall, and a concentration of picturesque taverns, still buzzes the way it must have when stevedores loaded and unloaded ships from the New World. Just southeast of Centro, the medieval Jewish quarter, **Barrio de Santa Cruz,** is a lovely, whitewashed tangle of alleys. The **Barrio de la Macarena** to the northeast is rich in sights and authentic Seville atmosphere. The fifth and final neighborhood to explore, on the far side of the Río Guadalquivir, is in many ways the best of all—**Triana,** the traditional habitat for sailors, bullfighters, and flamenco artists, as well as the main workshop for Seville's renowned ceramicists.

GETTING HERE AND AROUND

AIR TRAVEL

Seville's airport is about 7 km (4½ miles) east of the city. There's a bus from the airport to the center of town every half hour daily (5:20 am–1:15 am; €4 one-way). Taxi fare from the airport to the city center is around €22 during the day, and €25 at night and on Sunday. A number of private companies operate private airport-shuttle services.

BIKE TRAVEL

As an almost completely flat city, Seville is perfect for bike travel, and there are several bike rental companies within the city, including Bici4City and Oh my bikes!

Contacts Bici4City. ✉ Calle Peral 6, Centro ☎ 954/229883 ⊕ www.bici4city.com. **Oh my bikes!** ✉ Av. Menéndez y Pelayo 11, Barrio de Santa Cruz ☎ 954/536017 ⊕ www.ohmybikes.com.

BUS TRAVEL

Seville has two intercity bus stations: Estación Plaza de Armas, the main one, with buses serving Córdoba, Granada, Huelva, and Málaga in Andalusia, plus Madrid and Portugal, and other international destinations; and the smaller Estación del Prado de San Sebastián, serving Cádiz and nearby towns and villages.

Certain routes operate limited night service midnight–2 am Monday–Thursday, with services until 5 am Friday–Sunday. Single rides cost €1.40, but if you're going to be busing a lot, it's more economical to buy a rechargeable multitravel pass, which works out to €0.69 per ride. Special Tarjetas Turísticas (tourist passes) valid for one or three days of unlimited bus travel cost (respectively) €5 and €10. Tickets are sold at newsstands and at the main bus station, Prado de San Sebastián.

Contacts Estación del Prado de San Sebastián. ✉ Calle Vázquez Sagastizábal, El Arenal ☎ 955/479290. **Estación Plaza de Armas.** ✉ Puente Cristo de la Expiración, Centro ☎ 955/038665 ⊕ www.autobusesplazadearmas.es.

CAR TRAVEL

Getting in and out of Seville by car isn't difficult, thanks to the SE30 ring road, but getting around in the city by car is problematic. We advise leaving your car at your hotel or in a lot while you're here.

TAXI TRAVEL

Contacts Radio Taxi Sevilla. ☎ 954/580000.

TRAIN TRAVEL

Train connections include the high-speed AVE service from Madrid, with a journey time of less than 2½ hours.

Contacts Estación Santa Justa. ✉ Av. Kansas City, El Arenal ☎ 912/320320.

TOURS

In Seville, the tourist office (*see Visitor Information*) has information on various organized tours.

Azahar Sevilla Tapas Tours. Local food and wine expert Shawn Hennessey leads guided tours round Seville's best tapas bars (traditional and gourmet). Choose from several different tours, lunch or evening. ⊕ sevillatapastours.com ⌑ *From €65.*

Seville's grand Alcázar is a UNESCO World Heritage Site and an absolute must-see.

History and Tapas Tour. Glean local, historical, and culinary knowledge on a variety of tours around sights and tapas bars. ⊕ *www.sevilleconcierge. com* ✉ *From €60.*

Sevilla Bike Tour. Guided tours, leaving from the Makinline Shop on Calle Arjona at 10:30 am, take in the major sights of the city and offer interesting stories and insider information along the way. You'll cover about 10 km (6 miles) in three hours. Reservations are required on weekends and recommended on weekdays. ⊠ *Calle Arjona 8, Centro* ☎ *954/562625* ⊕ *www.sevillabiketour.com* ✉ *From €25.*

Sevilla Walking Tours. A choice of three walking tours are conducted in English: the City Walking Tour, leaving Plaza Nueva from the statue of San Fernando; the Alcázar Tour, leaving Plaza del Triunfo from the central statue; and the Cathedral Tour, also leaving from the Plaza del Triunfo central statue. ☎ *902/158226, 616/501100* ⊕ *www.sevillawalk-ingtours.com* ✉ *From €12.*

Your First Flamenco Experience. Local dancer Eva Izquierdo from Triana teaches you how to clap in time, stand, and take your first dance steps, in authentic costume. ⊠ *Seville* ☎ *626/007868* ⊕ *www.ishowusevilla. com* ✉ *From €36.*

VISITOR INFORMATION

Contacts Ciy & Province of Seville. ⊠ *Pl. de Triunfo 1, by cathedral, Barrio de Santa Cruz* ☎ *954/210005* ⊕ *www.turismosevilla.org.*

EXPLORING

CENTRO

Fodor'sChoice **Alcázar.** The Plaza del Triunfo forms the entrance to the Mudejar palace
★ built by Pedro I (1350–69) on the site of Seville's former Moorish *alcázar* (fortress). Though the Alcázar was designed and built by Moorish workers brought in from Granada, it was commissioned and paid for by a Christian king more than 100 years after the Reconquest of Seville. Highlights include the oldest parts of the building, the 14th-century Sala de Justicia (Hall of Justice) and, next to it, the intimate Patio del Yeso (Courtyard of Plaster); Pedro's Mudejar palace, arranged around the beautiful Patio de las Doncellas (Court of the Damsels); the Salón de Embajadores (Hall of the Ambassadors), the most sumptuous hall in the palace; the Renaissance Palacio de Carlos V (Palace of Carlos V), endowed with a rich collection of Flemish tapestries; and the Estancias Reales (Royal Chambers), with rare clocks, antique furniture, paintings, and tapestries. ⊠ *Pl. del Triunfo, Santa Cruz* ☎ 954/502323 ⊕ *www.alcazarsevilla.org* ☑ *€12 (free Mon. 6–7 Apr.–Sept. and Mon. 4–5 Oct.–Mar.).*

Fodor'sChoice **Cathedral.** Seville's cathedral can be described only in superlatives: it's
★ the largest and highest cathedral in Spain, the largest Gothic building in the world, and the world's third-largest church, after St. Peter's in Rome and St. Paul's in London. After Ferdinand III captured Seville from the Moors in 1248, the great mosque begun by Yusuf II in 1171 was used as a Christian cathedral. In 1401 Seville pulled down the old mosque, leaving only its minaret and outer courtyard, and built a new cathedral in just over a century. The magnificent *retablo* (altarpiece) in the Capilla Mayor (Main Chapel) is the largest in Christendom. The Capilla Real (Royal Chapel) is concealed behind a curtain, but duck in if you're quick, quiet, and properly dressed (no shorts or sleeveless tops). Don't forget the Patio de los Naranjos (Courtyard of Orange Trees), where the fountain in the center was used for ablutions before people entered the original mosque. ⊠ *Pl. Virgen de los Reyes, Centro* ☎ *954/214971* ⊕ *www.catedraldesevilla.es* ☑ *€9 (free Mon. 4:30–6).*

Fodor'sChoice **Palacio de la Condesa de Lebrija.** This lovely palace has three ornate
★ patios, including a spectacular courtyard graced by a Roman mosaic taken from the ruins in Itálica, surrounded by Moorish arches and fine *azulejos* (painted tiles). The side rooms house a collection of archaeological items. The second floor contains the family apartments and visits are by guided tour only. ■TIP➡ **It's well worth paying the extra for the second-floor tour, which gives an interesting insight into the collections and the family.** ⊠ *Calle Cuna 8, Centro* ☎ *954/227802* ☑ *From €6 (free Mon. 6–7).*

BARRIO DE SANTA CRUZ

Fodor'sChoice **Casa de Pilatos.** With its fine patio and superb azulejo decorations, this
★ palace is a beautiful blend of Spanish Mudejar and Renaissance architecture, and is considered a prototype of an Andalusian mansion. It was built in the first half of the 16th century by the dukes of Tarifa, ancestors

10

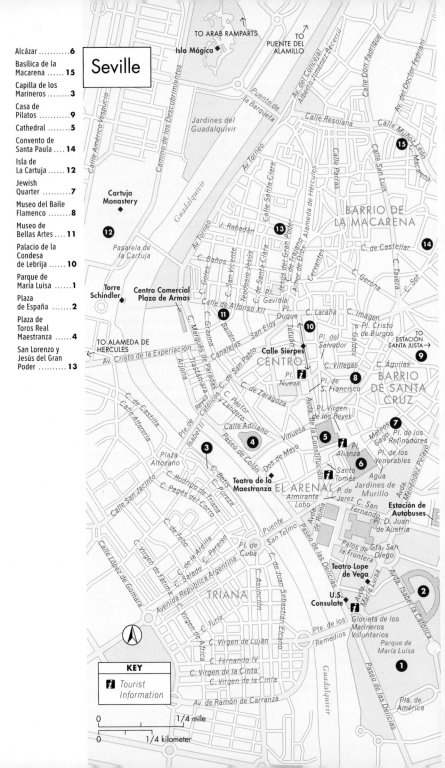

Seville

TO ARAB RAMPARTS

TO
PUENTE DEL
ALAMILLO

Isla Mágica ◆

Jardines del
Guadalquivir

Cartuja
Monastery ◆

Pasarela de
la Cartuja

Torre
Schindler ◆

Centro Comercial
Plaza de Armas

TO ALAMEDA DE
HÉRCULES

BARRIO DE
LA MACARENA

CENTRO

BARRIO
DE SANTA
CRUZ

EL ARENAL

Teatro de la
Maestranza ◆

Plaza
Altozano

Teatro Lope
de Vega ◆

U.S.
Consulate

Estación de
Autobuses

TRIANA

Glorieta de los
Marineros
Voluntarios

Parque de
María Luisa

Pta. de
América

KEY

i Tourist
Information

0   1/4 mile

0   1/4 kilometer

of the present owner, the Duke of Medinaceli. It's known as Pilate's House because Don Fadrique, first marquis of Tarifa, allegedly modeled it on Pontius Pilate's house in Jerusalem, where he had gone on a pilgrimage in 1518. The upstairs apartments, which you can see on a guided tour, have frescoes, paintings, and antique furniture. Admission includes an audio guide in English. ⊠ *Pl. de Pilatos 1, Barrio de Santa Cruz* 🕾 *954/225298* 🖳 *From €8.*

> ### WHERE'S COLUMBUS?
>
> Christopher Columbus knew both triumph and disgrace, yet he found no repose—he died, bitterly disillusioned, in Valladolid in 1506. No one knows for certain where he's buried; he was reportedly laid to rest for the first time in the Dominican Republic and then moved over the years to other locations. A portion of his remains can be found in Seville's cathedral.

Fodor's Choice ★ **Jewish Quarter.** The twisting alleyways and traditional whitewashed houses add to the tourist charm of this *barrio*. On some streets, bars alternate with antiques and souvenir shops, but most of the quarter is quiet and residential. On the Plaza Alianza, pause to enjoy the antiques shops and outdoor cafés. In the Plaza de Doña Elvira, with its fountain and azulejo benches, young sevillanos gather to play guitars. Just around the corner from the hospital, at Callejón del Agua and Jope de Rueda, Gioacchino Rossini's Figaro serenaded Rosina on her Plaza Alfaro balcony. Adjoining the Plaza Alfaro, in the Plaza Santa Cruz, flowers and orange trees surround a 17th-century filigree iron cross, which marks the site of the erstwhile church of Santa Cruz, destroyed by Napoléon's General Jean-de-Dieu Soult. ⊠ *Barrio de Santa Cruz.*

Museo del Baile Flamenco. This private museum in the heart of Santa Cruz (follow the signs) was opened in 2007 by the legendary flamenco dancer Cristina Hoyos and includes audiovisual and multimedia displays explaining the history, culture, and soul of Spanish flamenco. There are also regular classes and shows. ⊠ *Calle Manuel Rojas Marcos 3, Barrio de Santa Cruz* 🕾 *954/340311* ⊕ *www.museoflamenco.com* 🖳 *€10.*

EL ARENAL AND PARQUE MARÍA LUISA

Parque María Luisa is part shady, midcity forestland and part monumental esplanade. El Arenal, named for its sandy riverbank soil, was originally a neighborhood of shipbuilders, stevedores, and warehouses. The heart of El Arenal lies between the Puente de San Telmo, just upstream from the Torre de Oro, and the Puente de Isabel II (Puente de Triana). El Arenal extends as far north as Avenida Alfonso XII to include the Museo de Bellas Artes. Between the park and El Arenal is the university.

Fodor's Choice ★ **Museo de Bellas Artes** (*Museum of Fine Arts*). This museum—one of Spain's finest for Spanish art—is in the former convent of La Merced Calzada, most of which dates from the 17th century. The collection includes works by Murillo (the city celebrated the 400th anniversary of his birth in 2018) and the 17th-century Seville school, as well as by

Zurbarán, Diego Velázquez, Alonso Cano, Valdés Leal, and El Greco. You will also see outstanding examples of Sevillian Gothic art and baroque religious sculptures in wood (a quintessentially Andalusian art form). In the rooms dedicated to Sevillian art of the 19th and 20th centuries, look for Gonzalo Bilbao's *Las Cigarreras,* a group portrait of Seville's famous cigar makers. An arts and crafts market is held outside the museum on Sunday. ⊠ *Pl. del Museo 9, El Arenal* ☎ *954/542942* ⊕ *www.museosdeandalucia.es* 🖼 *€2* ⊘ *Closed Mon.*

Fodor's Choice **Parque de María Luisa.** Formerly the garden of the Palacio de San Telmo,
★ this park blends formal design and wild vegetation. In the burst of development that gripped Seville in the 1920s, it was redesigned for the 1929 World's Fair, and the impressive villas you see now are the fair's remaining pavilions, many of them consulates or schools; the old Casino holds the Teatro Lope de Vega, which puts on mainly musicals. Note the Anna Huntington **statue of El Cid** (Rodrigo Díaz de Vivar, 1043–99), who fought both for and against the Muslim rulers during the Reconquest. The statue was presented to Seville by the Massachusetts-born sculptor for the 1929 World's Fair. ⊠ *Main entrance, Glorieta San Diego, Parque Maria Luisa.*

FAMILY **Plaza de España.** This grandiose half-moon of buildings on the eastern edge of the Parque de María Luisa was Spain's centerpiece pavilion at the 1929 World's Fair. The brightly colored azulejo pictures represent the provinces of Spain, while the four bridges symbolize the medieval kingdoms of the Iberian Peninsula. In fine weather you can rent small boats to row along the arc-shape canal. To escape the crowds and enjoy views of the square from above, pop upstairs. ⊠ *Parque Maria Luisa.*

Plaza de Toros Real Maestranza (*Royal Maestranza Bullring*). Sevillanos have spent many a thrilling evening in this bullring, one of the oldest and loveliest *plazas de toros* in Spain, built between 1760 and 1763. The 20-minute tour (in English) takes in the empty arena, a museum with elaborate costumes and prints, and the chapel where matadors pray before the fight. Bullfights take place in the evening Thursday–Sunday, April–July and in September. Tickets can be booked online or by phone; book well in advance to be sure of a seat. ⊠ *Paseo de Colón 12, El Arenal* ☎ *954/210315 for visits, 954/560759 for bullfights* ⊕ *www. realmaestranza.es for tours, www.plazadetorosdelamaestranza.com for tickets* 🖼 *Tours €8 (free Mon. 3–7).*

BARRIO DE LA MACARENA

This immense neighborhood covers the entire northern half of historic Seville and deserves to be walked many times. Most of the best churches, convents, markets, and squares are concentrated around the center in an area delimited by the Arab ramparts to the north, the Alameda de Hercules to the west, the Santa Catalina church to the south, and the Convento de Santa Paula to the east. The area between the Alameda de Hercules and the Guadalquivir is known to locals as the Barrio de San Lorenzo, a section that's ideal for an evening of tapas grazing.

Basílica de la Macarena. This church holds Seville's most revered image, the Virgin of Hope—better known as La Macarena. Bedecked with candles and carnations, her cheeks streaming with glass tears, the Macarena steals the show at the procession on Holy Thursday, the highlight of Seville's Semana Santa pageant. The patron of Gypsies and the protector of the matador, her charms are so great that young sevillano bullfighter Joselito spent half his personal fortune buying her emeralds. When he was killed in the ring in 1920, La Macarena was dressed in widow's weeds for a month. The adjacent museum tells the history of Semana Santa traditions through processional and liturgical artifacts amassed by the Brotherhood of La Macarena over four centuries. ⊠ *Calle Bécquer 1, La Macarena* 🕾 *954/901800* 🔖 *Basilica free, museum €5.*

> ### FIESTA TIME!
>
> Seville's color and vivacity are most intense during Semana Santa, when lacerated Christs and bejeweled, weeping Mary statues are paraded through town on floats borne by often-barefoot penitents. Two weeks later, sevillanos throw Feria de Abril, featuring midday horse parades with men in broad-brim hats and Andalusian riding gear astride prancing steeds, and women in ruffled dresses riding sidesaddle behind them. Bullfights, fireworks, and all-night singing and dancing complete the spectacle.

Fodor's Choice ★ **Convento de Santa Paula.** This 15th-century Gothic convent has a fine facade and portico, with ceramic decoration by Nicolaso Pisano. The chapel has some beautiful azulejos and sculptures by Martínez Montañés. It also contains a small museum and a shop selling delicious cakes and jams made by the nuns. ⊠ *Calle Santa Paula 11, La Macarena* 🕾 *954/536330* 🔖 *€4* ☉ *Closed Mon.*

San Lorenzo y Jesús del Gran Poder. This 17th-century church has many fine works by such artists as Martínez Montañés and Francisco Pacheco, but its outstanding piece is Juan de Mesa y Velasco's *Jesús del Gran Poder (Christ Omnipotent).* ⊠ *Pl. San Lorenzo 13, La Macarena* 🕾 *954/915672* 🔖 *Free.*

TRIANA

Triana used to be Seville's Gypsy quarter. Today, it has a tranquil, neighborly feel by day and a distinctly flamenco feel at night. Cross over to Triana via the **Puente de Isabel II,** an iron bridge built in 1852 and the first to connect the city's two sections. Start your walk in the **Plaza del Altozano,** the center of the Triana district and traditionally the meeting point for travelers from the south crossing the river to Seville. Admire the facade of the Murillo pharmacy here before walking up **Calle Jacinto.** Look out for the fine **Casa de los Mensaque** (now the district's administrative office and usually open on weekday mornings), home to some of Triana's finest potters and housing some stunning examples of Seville ceramics. Turn right into **Calle Alfarería** (Pottery Street) and admire some of the ceramic facades—Fábrica Montalván at No. 23 is particularly fine. Return via Calle Betis along the riverside. To reach attractions in La Cartuja, take Bus C1.

10

Capilla de los Marineros. This seamen's chapel is one of Triana's most important monuments and home to the Brotherhood of Triana, whose Semana Santa processions are among the most revered in the city. There's also a small museum dedicated to the Brotherhood. ⊠ *Calle Pureza 2, Triana* ☎ *954/332645* 🖾 *Free, museum €4.*

Isla de La Cartuja. Named after its 14th-century Carthusian monastery, this island in the Guadalquivir River across from northern Seville was the site of the decennial Universal Exposition (Expo) in 1992. The island has the Teatro Central, used for concerts and plays; Parque del Alamillo, Seville's largest and least-known park; and the Estadio Olímpico, a 60,000-seat covered stadium. The best way to get to La Cartuja is by walking across one or both (one each way) of the superb Santiago Calatrava bridges spanning the river. The Puente de la Barqueta crosses to La Cartuja, and downstream the Puente del Alamillo connects the island with Seville. Buses C1 and C2 also serve La Cartuja. ⊠ *Triana.*

Isla Mágica. The eastern shore of Isla de la Cartuja holds this theme park with more than 20 attractions, including the hair-raising Jaguar roller coaster. ⊠ *Isla de la Cartuja, Av. de los Descubrimiento s/n, Triana* ☎ *902/161716* ⊕ *www.islamagica.es* 🖾 *€30* ⊗ *Closed Nov.–Apr. and weekdays in May and Oct.*

Monasterio de Santa María de las Cuevas (*Monasterio de La Cartuja*). The 14th-century monastery was regularly visited by Christopher Columbus, who was also buried here for a few years. Part of the building houses the **Centro Andaluz de Arte Contemporáneo,** which has an absorbing collection of contemporary art. ⊠ *Av. Américo Vespucio, La Cartuja* ☎ *955/037070* 🖾 *€3* ⊗ *Closed Mon.*

WHERE TO EAT

Use the coordinate (✛ B2) at the end of each listing to locate a site on the corresponding map.

CENTRO

$ | ✕ **Casa Morales.** Down a side street off the Avenida de la Constitución,
TAPAS | this historic bar takes you back to 19th-century Seville with wooden shelving stacked with wine bottles, a wood-beam ceiling, and tiled walls. It was established in 1850 as a wine store and is still run by the same family. **Known for:** local atmosphere; wine list; tripe with chickpeas. $ *Average main: €8* ⊠ *Calle García de Vinuesa 11, Centro* ☎ *954/221242* ⊟ *No credit cards* ⊗ *Closed Sun.* ✛ *B3.*

$ | ✕ **Espacio Eslava.** The crowds gathered outside this local favorite off
TAPAS | the Alameda de Hercules may be off-putting at first, but the creative,
Fodor'sChoice | inexpensive tapas (from €2.60) are well worth the wait. Try delicacies
★ | like the *solomillo de pato con pan de queso y salsa de peras al vino* (duck fillet with cheesy bread and pears in wine sauce). **Known for:** tapas; sokoa, a Basque dessert; vegetable strudel. $ *Average main: €10* ⊠ *Calle Eslava 3, Centro* ☎ *954/906568* ⊟ *No credit cards* ⊗ *Closed Mon. No dinner Sun.* ✛ *B1.*

The half moon of Plaza de España

$$ SPANISH 🍴 **La Azotea.** With a young vibe and a vast and inventive menu, this tiny restaurant offers a welcome change from Seville's typical fried fare. The owners' haute-cuisine ambitions are reflected in excellent service and lovingly prepared food—but not in the prices. **Known for:** creative tapas; seasonal menu; local vibe. [$] *Average main: €15* ✉ *Calle Jesus del Gran Poder 31, Centro* ☎ *955/116748* 💳 *No credit cards* 🕒 *Closed Sun. and Mon.* ✥ *B1.*

BARRIO DE SANTA CRUZ

$$$$ SPANISH 🍴 **Abantal.** Slightly off the beaten path but well worth seeking out, Chef Julio Fernández's tasting menu takes you on a journey of the senses featuring seemingly ordinary local produce and traditional recipes elevated with unusual textures and preparations. The menu changes with the seasons, but always has 10 dishes (€75) or 13 (€90) as well as extra-virgin olive oil–and-cheese menus. **Known for:** fine dining; innovative take on dishes; excellent service. [$] *Average main: €70* ✉ *Calle Alcalde José de la Bandera 7, Barrio de Santa Cruz* ☎ *954/540000* 🌐 *www.abantalrestaurante.es* 🕒 *Closed Sun., Mon., and Aug.* ✥ *D3.*

$$$$ SPANISH 🍴 **Ispal.** At this new fine-dining venue near the Prado de San Sebastián bus station, chef Antonio Rodríguez Bort (the winner of several prestigious national tapas awards) has created one of the city's most exciting and innovative menus, using ingredients only from the province of Seville. The two tapas tasting menus (€39 and €59) include dishes such as *cochinillo de la sierra con vainilla, jugo de zanahoria y ajo asado* (suckling pig with vanilla, carrot, and roast garlic) and *calentito de bacalao con chocolate especiado* (cod "doughnut" with spicy chocolate). **Known for:** exceptional tapas; regional wine list; suckling

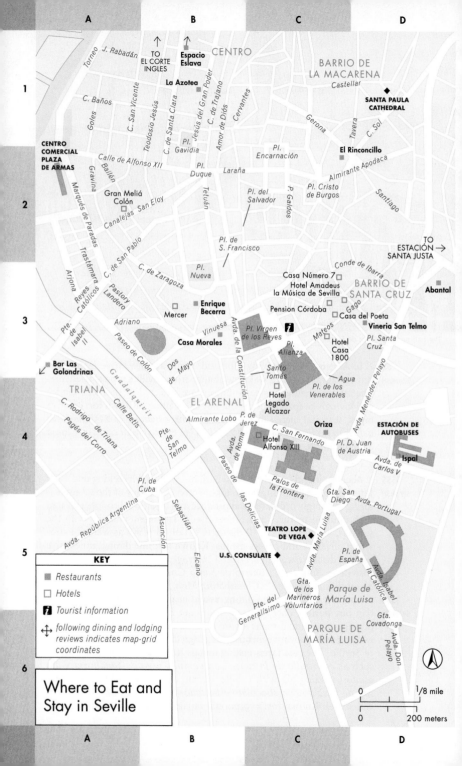

Where to Eat and Stay in Seville

KEY

- ■ Restaurants
- □ Hotels
- 🚹 Tourist information
- ✛ following dining and lodging reviews indicates map-grid coordinates

CENTRO

BARRIO DE LA MACARENA

BARRIO DE SANTA CRUZ

TRIANA

EL ARENAL

PARQUE DE MARÍA LUISA

TO EL CORTE INGLES

Espacio Eslava

La Azotea

CENTRO COMERCIAL PLAZA DE ARMAS

Gran Meliá Colón

Castellar

SANTA PAULA CATHEDRAL

El Rinconcillo

Pl. Encarnación

Pl. del Salvador

Pl. Cristo de Burgos

TO ESTACIÓN SANTA JUSTA

Pl. de S. Francisco

Conde de Ibarra

Casa Número 7
Hotel Amadeus
la Música de Sevilla

Abantal

Pl. Nueva

Pension Córdoba

Casa del Poeta

Vineria San Telmo

Mercer

Enrique Becerra

Casa Morales

Vinuesa

Pl. Virgen de los Reyes

Gago

Mateos

Hotel Casa 1800

Pl. Santa Cruz

Bar Las Golondrinas

Pl. Alianza

Santo Tomás

Agua

Pl. de los Venerables

Hotel Legado Alcazar

Oriza

ESTACIÓN DE AUTOBUSES

Almirante Lobo

Hotel Alfonso XIII

Pl. D. Juan de Austria

Ispal

Palos de la Frontera

Gta. San Diego

TEATRO LOPE DE VEGA

U.S. CONSULATE

Pl. de España

Gta. de los Marineros Voluntarios

Parque de María Luisa

Gta. Covadonga

0   1/8 mile

0   200 meters

pig. $ *Average main: €39* ⊠ *Pl. de San Sebastián 1, Barrio de Santa Cruz* ☎ *954/547127* ⊕ *restauranteispal.com* ☾ *Closed Mon. No dinner Sun.* ✛ *D4.*

$$$$
SPANISH
✕**Oriza.** On the edge of the Murillo Gardens opposite the university, Oriza has an atrium-style dining room with high ceilings and wall-to-wall stained-glass windows; in warm weather, you can eat on the terrace under the orange trees. The menu combines traditional Andalusian dishes with a modern touch and includes red tuna, octopus salad, and meat dishes. **Known for:** traditional tapas at the bar; tuna steak; outside terrace. $ *Average main: €30* ⊠ *Calle San Fernando 41, Santa Cruz* ☎ *954/227254* ☾ *Closed Sun.* ✛ *C4.*

$$
SPANISH
Fodor's Choice
★
✕**Vineria San Telmo.** Whether you eat in the dimly lit dining room or on the street-level terrace, prepare to spend some time perusing a menu full of surprises. All dishes are superb and sophisticated, especially the eggplant stew with tomato, goat cheese, and smoked salmon; the Iberian pork with potato; and the oxtail in phyllo pastry. **Known for:** creative tapas; wine cellar; Iberian pork with potato. $ *Average main: €12* ⊠ *Paseo Catalina de Ribera 4, Santa Cruz* ☎ *954/410600* ✛ *D3.*

EL ARENAL AND PARQUE MARÍA LUISA

$$$
SPANISH
Fodor's Choice
★
✕**Enrique Becerra.** Excellent tapas (try the lamb kebab with dates and couscous), a lively bar, and an extensive wine list await at this restaurant run by the fifth generation of a family of celebrated restaurateurs (Enrique's brother Jesús owns Becerrita). The menu focuses on traditional, home-cooked Andalusian dishes, such as cod in a green sauce, pork fillet in whisky, and *cola de toro guisado con salsa de vino tinto* (stewed oxtail in red wine sauce). **Known for:** traditional Andalusian dishes; fried eggplant stuffed with prawns. $ *Average main: €20* ⊠ *Calle Gamazo 2, El Arenal* ☎ *954/213049* ⊕ *enriquebecerra.com* ✛ *B3.*

BARRIO DE LA MACARENA

$
SPANISH
✕**El Rinconcillo.** Founded in 1670, this lovely spot serves a classic selection of dishes, such as the *pavía de bacalao* (fried breaded cod), a superb salmorejo, and espinacas con garbanzos (creamed spinach with chickpeas) all in generous portions. The views of the Iglesia de Santa Catalina out the front window upstairs are unbeatable, and your bill is chalked up on the wooden counters as you go (tapas are attractively priced from €2). **Known for:** tapas; crowds of locals; views of Iglesia de Santa Catalina. $ *Average main: €10* ⊠ *Calle Gerona 40, La Macarena* ☎ *954/223183* ⊕ *www.elrinconcillo.es* ✛ *C2.*

TRIANA

$$
SPANISH
✕**Bar Las Golondrinas.** Run by the same family for more than 50 years and lavishly decorated in the colorful tiles that pay tribute to the neighborhood's potters, Las Golondrinas is a fixture of Triana life. The staff never change, and neither does the menu: the recipes for the *punta de solomillo* (sliced sirloin), *chipirones* (fried baby squid) and *caballito de jamón* (ham on bread) have been honed to perfection, and they're served as tapas (€2) or *raciones* that keep everyone happy. **Known for:** vibrant atmosphere; traditional tapas; value. $ *Average main: €12* ⊠ *Calle Antillano Campos 26, Triana* ☎ *954/332616* ✛ *A3.*

10

WHERE TO STAY

Use the coordinate (⊕ B2) at the end of each listing to locate a site on the corresponding map.

CENTRO

$$$$ HOTEL Fodor's Choice ★ 🏨 **Mercer.** Housed in a 19th-century mansion, Mercer is one of the city's top boutique hotels, featuring a lofty patio with a fountain, a stunning marble staircase, and a striking geometric chandelier atop a glass gallery. **Pros:** luxury lodging; spacious rooms; rooftop terrace with plunge pool. **Cons:** pricey; a little too prim; patio rooms have no views. [$] *Rooms from: €430* ✉ *Calle Castelar 26, Centro* ☎ *954/223004* 🌐 *www.mercersevilla.com* 🛏 *10 rooms* 🍴 *Free Breakfast* ⊕ *B3.*

BARRIO DE SANTA CRUZ

$$$$ HOTEL 🏨 **Casa del Poeta.** Up a narrow alleyway, behind an ordinary facade, a 17th-century palace is a cool oasis of calm just a heartbeat from some bustling Santa Cruz streets. **Pros:** peaceful, central location; authentic palatial atmosphere; rooftop with a view. **Cons:** difficult to reach by car (call shortly before arrival for staff to meet you); could be too traditional for some; service can be a little slow. [$] *Rooms from: €225* ✉ *Calle Don Carlos Alonso Chaparro 3, Santa Cruz* ☎ *954/213868* 🌐 *www.casadelpoeta.es* 🛏 *17 rooms* 🍴 *No meals* ⊕ *C3.*

$$$ B&B/INN Fodor's Choice ★ 🏨 **Casa Número 7.** Dating to 1850, this converted town house retains an elegant but lived-in feel, with family photographs, original oil paintings, and plush furnishings throughout. **Pros:** the personal touch of a B&B; great location; delightfully different. **Cons:** uninteresting breakfast; faces onto noisy street; interior is a little dark. [$] *Rooms from: €177* ✉ *Calle Virgenes 7, Santa Cruz* ☎ *954/221581* 🌐 *www.casanumero7.com* 🛏 *6 rooms* 🍴 *Free Breakfast* ⊕ *C3.*

$$$ HOTEL Fodor's Choice ★ 🏨 **Hotel Amadeus La Música de Sevilla.** With pianos in some of the soundproofed rooms, other instruments for guests to use, a music room off the central patio, and regular classical concerts, this acoustic oasis is ideal for touring professional musicians and music fans in general. **Pros:** small but charming rooms; roof terrace; friendly service. **Cons:** no direct car access; ground-floor rooms can be dark; layout slightly confusing. [$] *Rooms from: €150* ✉ *Calle Farnesio 6, Santa Cruz* ☎ *954/501443* 🌐 *www.hotelamadeussevilla.com* 🛏 *30 rooms* 🍴 *No meals* ⊕ *C3.*

$$$$ B&B/INN Fodor's Choice ★ 🏨 **Hotel Casa 1800.** This classy boutique hotel, in a refurbished 19th-century mansion, is an oasis in bustling Santa Cruz. **Pros:** top-notch amenities; great service; central location. **Cons:** rooms facing the patio can be noisy; no restaurant; on noisy side street. [$] *Rooms from: €280* ✉ *Calle Rodrigo Caro 6, Santa Cruz* ☎ *954/561800* 🌐 *www.hotelcasa1800sevilla.com* 🛏 *33 rooms* 🍴 *No meals* ⊕ *C3.*

$$$ HOTEL 🏨 **Hotel Legado Alcázar.** Nestling next to the Alcázar—the monument and hotel share walls—this 17th-century noble house offers a tasteful boutique experience in a very quiet corner. **Pros:** very quiet but central location; historic features; views of the Alcázar. **Cons:** no restaurant on-site; room size varies; could be too traditional for some. [$] *Rooms from: €174* ✉ *Calle Mariana de Pineda 18, Barrio de Santa Cruz* ☎ *954/091818* 🌐 *www.legadohoteles.com* 🛏 *18 rooms* 🍴 *No meals* ⊕ *C4.*

$ **Pensión Córdoba.** Just a few blocks from the cathedral, nestled in the
HOTEL heart of Santa Cruz, this small, family-run inn is an excellent value.
Pros: quiet, central location; friendly staff; rooms have a/c. **Cons:** no
entry after 3 am; no breakfast; no elevator to second floor. $ *Rooms
from: €65* ⊠ *Calle Farnesio 12, Santa Cruz* ☎ *954/227498* ⊕ *www.pen-
sioncordoba.com* ▬ *No credit cards* ↩ *12 rooms* ❄ *No meals* ✢ *C3.*

EL ARENAL AND PARQUE MARÍA LUISA

$$$$ **Gran Meliá Colón.** Originally opened for 1929's Ibero-American
HOTEL Exposition, this classic hotel retains many original features, including a
marble staircase leading up to a central lobby crowned by a magnificent
stained-glass dome and crystal chandelier. **Pros:** good central location;
excellent restaurant; some great views. **Cons:** some rooms overlook air
shaft; on a busy and noisy street; pricey. $ *Rooms from: €350* ⊠ *Calle
Canalejas 1, El Arenal* ☎ *954/505599* ⊕ *www.melia.com* ↩ *189 rooms*
❄ *No meals* ✢ *A2.*

$$$$ **Hotel Alfonso XIII.** Inaugurated by King Alfonso XIII in 1929 and gra-
HOTEL ciously restored over the years, this grand hotel is a splendid, historic,
Fodor'sChoice Mudejar-style palace, built around a central patio and surrounded by
★ ornate brick arches. **Pros:** both stately and hip; impeccable service;
historic surroundings. **Cons:** a tourist colony; expensive; could be too
sophisticated for some. $ *Rooms from: €350* ⊠ *Calle San Fernando 2,
El Arenal* ☎ *954/917000* ⊕ *www.hotel-alfonsoxiii-seville.com* ↩ *148
rooms* ❄ *Free Breakfast* ✢ *C4.*

NIGHTLIFE AND PERFORMING ARTS

Seville has a lively nightlife and plenty of cultural activity. The free
monthly magazine *El Giraldillo* (⊕ *www.elgiraldillo.es*) lists classical
and jazz concerts, plays, dance performances, art exhibits, and films in
Seville and all major Andalusian cities. (For American films in English,
look for the designation *v.o.*, or *versión original.*)

NIGHTLIFE

One of the highlights of venturing out on the town in Seville is sipping
a cocktail while you take in the views of the old quarter from a rooftop
terrace. Or you can make for one of the bars offering live music.

10

BARS

EME Catedral Hotel. This rooftop terrace has some of the best views of
the cathedral in town. Sip your cocktail to the sound of resident DJs
most nights. The terrace is open daily from noon. ⊠ *Calle Alemanes
27, Barrio de Santa Cruz* ☎ *954/560000* ⊕ *www.emecatedralhotel.com*
Ⓜ *Puerta de Jerez.*

Naima Café Jazz. This tiny venue off Alameda de Hércules features jazz,
blues, or jam sessions every night. It's open from 8 pm till late. ⊠ *Calle
Trajano 47, Centro* ☎ *954/382485* Ⓜ *Sevilla–Santa Justa.*

PERFORMING ARTS

FLAMENCO CLUBS

Seville has a handful of commercial *tablaos* (flamenco clubs), patronized
more by tourists than locals. They generally offer somewhat mechanical
flamenco at high prices, with mediocre cuisine. Check local listings and

Outdoor restaurants in Seville's Barrio de Santa Cruz

ask at your hotel for performances by top artists. Spontaneous flamenco is often found for free in *peñas flamencas* (flamenco clubs) and flamenco bars in Triana. Note that most are closed from July to September.

La Casa del Flamenco. Catch an authentic professional performance in the heart of Santa Cruz on the atmospheric patio of a 15th-century house where the excellent acoustics mean there's no need for microphones or amplifiers. Shows start daily at 7 pm and 8:30 pm. ⊠ *Calle Ximénez de Enciso 28* ☎ *954/500595* ⊕ *www.lacasadelflamencosevilla.com* ☞ *€18.*

Lola de los Reyes. This venue in Triana presents reasonably authentic shows and hosts "flamenco afternoons" on Friday and Saturday—check the website for details. Entrance is free but there's a one-drink minimum. ⊠ *Calle Pureza 107, Triana* ☎ *667/631163* ⊕ *www.loladelosreyes.es* Ⓜ *Blas Infante/Parque de los Príncipes.*

Los Gallos. This intimate club in the heart of Santa Cruz attracts mainly tourists. Performances are entertaining and reasonably authentic. ⊠ *Pl. Santa Cruz 11, Santa Cruz* ☎ *954/216981* ⊕ *www.tablaolosgallos.com* ☞ *€35, includes one drink.*

Teatro Central. This modern venue on the Isla de la Cartuja stages theater, dance (including flamenco), and classical and contemporary music. Tickets can be bought at El Corte Inglés stores or via ⊕ *www.elcorteingles.es.* ⊠ *Calle José de Gálvez 6, Triana* ☎ *955/542155 (information), 902/400222 (tickets)* ⊕ *www.teatrocentral.es.*

Teatro de la Maestranza. Long prominent in the opera world, Seville is proud of its opera house. Tickets go quickly, so book well in advance (online is best). ⊠ *Paseo de Colón 22, El Arenal* ☎ *954/223344 for info,* *954/226573 for tickets* ⊕ *www.teatrodelamaestranza.es.*

Teatro Lope de Vega. Classical music, ballet, and musicals are performed here. Tickets are best booked online. ⊠ *Av. María Luisa s/n, Parque Maria Luisa* ☎ *954/472828 for info, 600/950746 for tickets* ⊕ *www. teatrolopedevega.org.*

SHOPPING

Seville is the region's main shopping area and the place for archetypal Andalusian souvenirs, most of which are sold in the Barrio de Santa Cruz and around the cathedral and La Giralda, especially on Calle Alemanes. The shopping street for locals is Calle Sierpes, along with neighboring Cuna, Tetuan, Velázquez, Plaza Magdalena, and Plaza Duque—boutiques abound here. For antiques, try Mateos Gago, opposite La Giralda, and in the Barrio de Santa Cruz on Jamerdana and Rodrigo Caro, off Plaza Alianza. For ceramics in the Barrio de Santa Cruz, browse along Mateos Gago; on Romero Murube, between Plaza Triunfo and Plaza Alianza, on the edge of the barrio; and between Plaza Doña Elvira and Plaza de los Venerables. Flamenco wear can be expensive; local women will gladly spend the equivalent of a month's grocery money (or more) on their frills, with dresses running €150–€600 and up.

CENTRO

Ángela y Adela Taller de Diseño. Come here for privately fitted and custommade flamenco dresses. ⊠ *Calle Luchana 6, Centro* ☎ *954/227186.*

Calle Sierpes. This is Seville's classy main shopping street. Near the southern end, at No. 85, a plaque marks the spot where the Cárcel Real (Royal Prison) once stood. Miguel de Cervantes began writing *Don Quixote* in one of its cells. ⊠ *Centro.*

La Campana. Under the gilt-edged ceiling at Seville's most celebrated pastry outlet (founded in 1885), you can enjoy the flanlike *tocino de cielo,* or "heavenly bacon." ⊠ *Calle Sierpes 1, Centro* ☎ *954/223570.*

Lola Azahares. For flamenco wear, this is one of Seville's most highly regarded stores. ⊠ *Calle Cuna 31, Centro* ☎ *954/222912.*

Luisa Perez y Riu. Flamenco dresses and all the accessories, designed with a modern touch, are sold at this shop between Calles Sierpes and Cuna. ⊠ *Calle Rivero 9, Centro* ☎ *607/817624* Ⓜ *Puerta de Jerez.*

Martian Ceramics. In central Seville, Martian has high-quality dishes, especially the finely painted flowers-on-white patterns native to Seville. ⊠ *Calle Sierpes 74, Centro* ☎ *954/213413.*

Plaza del Duque. A few blocks north of Plaza Nueva, Plaza del Duque has a crafts market Thursday–Saturday. ⊠ *Centro.*

BARRIO DE SANTA CRUZ

Extraverde. Taste a selection of olive oils at this shop-restaurant in the heart of Santa Cruz. ⊠ *Pl. Doña Elvira 8, Santa Cruz* ☎ *954/218417.*

10

EL ARENAL AND PARQUE MARÍA LUISA

Artesanía Textil. You can find blankets, shawls, and embroidered table-cloths woven by local artisans at this textile shop. ⊠ *Calle García de Vinuesa 33, El Arenal* ☎ *954/215088.*

El Postigo. This permanent arts-and-crafts market opposite El Corte Inglés is open every day except Sunday. ⊠ *Pl. de la Concordia, El Arenal.*

BARRIO DE LA MACARENA

El Jueves. This antiques and flea market is held in the Barrio de la Macarena on Thursday morning. ⊠ *Calle Feria, La Macarena.*

TRIANA

Librería Vértice. A large assortment of books in English, Spanish, French, and Italian can be found at this American-owned store just over the river in Triana. ⊠ *Av. Adolfo Suárez 4, Triana* ☎ *954/450100* ⊕ *libreriavertice.mycomandia.com.*

Mercado de Triana. The Triana market, which began as an improvised fish market on the banks of the Guadalquivir in the 1830s, is housed in a shiny building next to the bridge and has been given the stamp "Traditional Shopping Center." The vendors, however, sell a colorful mix of food, flowers, cheap fashion, and costume jewelry. It closes at 3 pm and stalls are not open on Sunday, although the building is. ⊠ *Pl. del Alzotano, Triana.*

Potters' district. Look for traditional azulejo tiles and other ceramics in the Triana potters' district, on Calle Alfarería and Calle Antillano Campos. ⊠ *Triana.*

AROUND SEVILLE

CARMONA

32 km (20 miles) east of Seville off A4.

Wander the ancient, narrow streets here and you'll feel as if you've been transported back in time. Claiming to be one of the oldest inhabited places in Spain (both Phoenicians and Carthaginians had settlements here), Carmona, on a steep, fortified hill, became an important town under the Romans and the Moors. There are many Mudejar and Renaissance churches and convents (several open weekend mornings only), medieval gateways, and simple whitewashed houses of clear Moorish influence, punctuated here and there by a baroque palace. Local fiestas are held in mid-September.

GETTING HERE AND AROUND

There's excellent bus service between Seville and Carmona—the journey takes under 40 minutes, making it an easy day trip. Within Carmona itself, it's easy to get around on foot.

VISITOR INFORMATION

Contacts Carmona. ⊠ *Alcázar de la Puerta de Sevilla* ☎ *954/190955* ⊕ *www.turismo.carmona.org.*

EXPLORING

Alcázar del Rey Don Pedro (*King Pedro's Fortress*). The Moorish Alcázar was built on Roman foundations and converted by King Pedro the Cruel into a Mudejar palace. Pedro's summer residence was destroyed by a 1504 earthquake, and all that remains are ruins that can be viewed but not visited. However, the parador within the complex has a breathtaking view, and the café and restaurant are lovely spots to have a refreshment or meal. ✉ *Calle Los Alcázares s/n.*

FAMILY **Museo de la Ciudad.** This interesting museum behind Santa María has exhibits on Carmona's history with particular emphasis on Roman finds. There's plenty for children, and the interactive exhibits are labeled in English and Spanish. ✉ *Calle San Ildefonso 1* ☎ *954/140128* 🌐 *www.museociudad.carmona.org* 🎫 *€3.*

Roman Necropolis. At the western edge of town 900 tombs were placed in underground chambers between the 4th and 2nd centuries BC. The necropolis walls, decorated with leaf and bird motifs, have niches for burial urns and tombs such as the **Elephant Vault** and the **Servilia Tomb,** a complete Roman villa with colonnaded arches and vaulted side galleries. ✉ *Calle Enmedio* ☎ *600/143632* 🎫 *€2* 🕒 *Closed Mon.*

Santa María. This Gothic church was built between 1424 and 1518 on the site of Carmona's former Great Mosque and retains its beautiful Moorish courtyard, studded with orange trees. ✉ *Calle Martín* 🎫 *€3* 🕒 *Closed Sun. and Mon.*

WHERE TO STAY

$$$ HOTEL 🏨 **Parador Alcázar del Rey Don Pedro.** This parador has superb views from its hilltop position among the ruins of Pedro the Cruel's summer palace. **Pros:** unbeatable views over the fields; great sense of history; restaurant serves local specialties. **Cons:** feels slightly lifeless after Seville. [$] *Rooms from: €150* ✉ *Calle del Alcázar* ☎ *954/141010* 🌐 *www.parador.es* 🛏 *63 rooms* 🍴 *No meals.*

ITÁLICA

10

12 km (7 miles) north of Seville, 1 km (½ mile) beyond Santiponce.

Neighboring the small town of Santiponce, Itálica is Spain's oldest Roman site and one of its greatest, and is well worth a visit when you're in Seville. If you're here during July, try to get tickets for the International Dance Festival held in the ruins (🌐 *www.festivalitalica.es*).

GETTING HERE AND AROUND

The M170A bus route runs frequently (daily 8 am–3:30 pm) between the Plaza de Armas bus station in Seville and Itálica. Journey time is 20 minutes. If you have a rental car, you could include a visit to the ruins on your way to Huelva. Allow at least two hours for your visit.

EXPLORING

Fodor's Choice ★ **Itálica.** One of Roman Iberia's most important cities in the 2nd century, with a population of more than 10,000, Itálica today is a monument of Roman ruins. Founded by Scipio Africanus in 205 BC as a home for veteran soldiers, Itálica gave the Roman world two great emperors: Trajan

(AD 52–117) and Hadrian (AD 76–138). You can find traces of city streets, cisterns, and the floor plans of several villas, some with mosaic floors, though all the best mosaics and statues have been removed to Seville's Museum of Archaeology. Itálica was abandoned and plundered as a quarry by the Visigoths, who preferred Seville. It fell into decay around AD 700. The remains include the huge, elliptical **amphitheater,** which held 40,000 spectators, a **Roman theater,** and **Roman baths.** Part of the last season of *Game of Thrones* was filmed here in 2018. The small visitor center offers information on daily life in the city. ⊠ *Av. Extremadura 2, Santiponce* ☎ *600/141767* ⊕ *www.juntadeandalucia. es/cultura/museos* ☑ *€2* ⊙ *Closed Mon.*

RONDA

147 km (91 miles) southeast of Seville, 61 km (38 miles) northwest of Marbella.

Fodor'sChoice ★ Ronda, one of the oldest towns in Spain, is known for its spectacular position and views. Secure in its mountain fastness on a rock high over the Río Guadalevín, the town was a stronghold for the legendary Andalusian bandits who held court here from the 18th to the early 20th century. Ronda's most dramatic element is its ravine (360 feet deep and 210 feet across)—known as **El Tajo**—which divides La Ciudad, the old Moorish town, from El Mercadillo, the "new town" which sprang up after the Christian Reconquest of 1485. Tour buses roll in daily with sightseers from the coast 49 km (30 miles) away, and on weekends affluent sevillanos flock to their second homes here. Stay overnight midweek to see this noble town's true colors.

In the lowest part of town, known as El Barrio, you can see parts of the old walls, including the 13th-century Puerta de Almocabar and the 16th-century Puerta de Carlos V gates. From here, the main road climbs past the Iglesia del Espíritu Santo (Church of the Holy Spirit) and up into the heart of town.

GETTING HERE AND AROUND

By road, the most attractive approach is from the south. The winding but well-maintained A376 from San Pedro de Alcántara, on the Costa del Sol, travels north up through the mountains of the Serranía de Ronda. But you can also drive here from Seville via Utrera—it's a pleasant drive of a little under two hours. At least four daily buses run here from Marbella, two from Málaga, and six from Seville. The Ronda tourist office publishes an updated list (available on the visitor information website).

VISITOR INFORMATION

Contacts Ronda. ⊠ *Paseo de Blas Infante s/n* ☎ *952/187119* ⊕ *www.turismo-deronda.es.*

EXPLORING

Juan Peña El Lebrijano. Immediately south of the Plaza de España, this is Ronda's most famous bridge (also known as the Puente Nuevo, or New Bridge), an architectural marvel built between 1755 and 1793. The bridge's lantern-lit parapet offers dizzying views of the awesome gorge. Just how many people have met their ends here nobody knows, but the architect of the Puente Nuevo fell to his death while inspecting work on the bridge. During the civil war, hundreds of victims were hurled from it. ⊠ *Ronda.*

La Ciudad. Cross the Puente Nuevo to enter the old Moorish town, with twisting streets and white houses with birdcage balconies. ⊠ *Ronda.*

Palacio de Mondragón (*Palace of Mondragón*). This stone palace with twin Mudejar towers was probably the residence of Ronda's Moorish kings. Ferdinand and Isabella appropriated it after their victory in 1485. Today, it's the museum of Ronda and you can wander through the patios, with their brick arches and delicate Mudejar-stucco tracery, and admire the mosaics and *artesonado* (coffered) ceiling. The second floor holds a small museum with archaeological items found near Ronda, plus the reproduction of a dolmen, a prehistoric stone monument. ⊠ *Pl. Mondragón* ☎ *952/870818* ⊡ *€4.*

Plaza de Toros. The main sight in Ronda's commercial center, El Mercadillo, is the bullring. Pedro Romero (1754–1839), the father of modern bullfighting and Ronda's most famous native son, is said to have killed 5,600 bulls here during his long career. In the museum beneath the plaza you can see posters for Ronda's very first bullfights, held here in 1785. The plaza was once owned by the late bullfighter Antonio Ordóñez, on whose nearby ranch Orson Welles's ashes were scattered (as directed in his will)—indeed, the ring has become a favorite of filmmakers. Every September, the bullring is the scene of Ronda's *corridas goyescas,* named after Francisco Goya, whose *tauromaquias* (bullfighting sketches) were inspired by Romero's skill and art. The participants and the dignitaries in the audience don the costumes of Goya's time for the occasion. Seats for these fights cost a small fortune and are booked far in advance. Other than that, the plaza is rarely used for fights except during Ronda's May festival. ⊠ *Calle Virgen de la Paz* ☎ *952/871539* ⊕ *www.rmcr.org* ⊡ *€7.*

WHERE TO EAT

$
TAPAS

✕ **Entre Vinos.** Just off the main road opposite the Hotel Colón, this small and cozy bar has established itself as one of Ronda's best for tapas and wine. Local Ronda wines are a specialty here—in fact, they're the only ones available, although with over 100 on the wine list, you'll be spoiled for choice; ask the waiter for recommendations and which tapas to pair them with. **Known for:** Ronda wines; gourmet tapas; bodega atmosphere. $ *Average main: €5* ⊠ *Calle Pozo 2* ☎ *658/582976* ▭ *No credit cards* ⊙ *Closed Sun. and Mon.*

$$$
SPANISH

✕ **Pedro Romero.** Named for the father of modern bullfighting, this restaurant opposite the bullring is packed with bullfight paraphernalia and photos of previous diners who include Ernest Hemingway and Orson Welles. Mounted bulls' heads peer down at you as you tuck into *choricitos al vino blanco de Ronda* (small sausages in Ronda white wine), *rabo de toro Pedro Romero* (slow-cooked oxtail stew with herbs) or *magret de pato con pera asada* (duck breast with baked pear). **Known for:** traditional Ronda cooking; bullfighting decor; friendly service. $ *Average*

10

The stunningly perched hilltop town of Ronda

main: €18 ✉ *Calle Virgen de la Paz 18* ☎ *952/871110* 🌐 *www.rpedro-romero.com.*

$$$$ SPANISH Fodor's Choice ★ 🍴 **Restaurante Bardal.** Awarded a Michelin star in 2017, Bardal has quickly gained a reputation for very fine dining. In fresh white interiors with striking brick and tile features, chef Benito Gómez prepares two tasting menus from fresh produce available that day, combining traditional Andalusian cooking with innovative techniques and top-class presentation. **Known for:** simple but tasty food; wine list; tableside service. [$] *Average main: €75* ✉ *Calle José Aparacio 1* ☎ *951/489828* 🌐 *www.restaurantebardal.com* 🕒 *Closed Mon. and Jan.*

WHERE TO STAY

$$ B&B/INN 🏨 **Alavera de los Baños.** Fittingly, given its location next to the Moorish baths, there's an Arab theme throughout this small, German-run hotel (which was used as a backdrop for the film classic *Carmen*). **Pros:** atmospheric and historic; owners speak several languages; first-floor rooms have their own terraces. **Cons:** rooms vary in size; steep climb into town. [$] *Rooms from: €100* ✉ *Calle San Miguel s/n* ☎ *952/879143* 🌐 *www.alaveradelosbanos.com* 🕒 *Closed Dec.–mid-Feb.* 🛏 *11 rooms* 🍽 *Free Breakfast.*

$$ HOTEL Fodor's Choice ★ 🏨 **Hotel Reina Victoria.** Something of a grande dame among Ronda hotels, this Swiss-chalet-style hotel was built in 1906 on a gorge cliff top at the north end of town; the north-facing rooms have some of the best views of the surrounding plains and mountains of any Ronda hotel. **Pros:** historic atmosphere; commanding views; attentive service. **Cons:** Wi-Fi can be unstable; slightly out of town; limited parking. [$] *Rooms*

from: €120 ⊠ *Calle Jerez 25* ☎ *952/871240* ⊕ *www.cataloniahotels. com* ⌁ *95 rooms* ⧖ *No meals.*

$$
B&B/INN
⧉ **La Perla Blanca.** Located to the northwest of Ronda just off the road to Seville, this couples-only boutique hotel sits in the midst of its own vineyards and winery. **Pros:** peace and quiet; personalized service; King Suite has its own hot tub and garden. **Cons:** need a car to get to Ronda; not for families. ⓈⓈ *Rooms from: €100* ⊠ *Fuente la Higuera II* ☎ *657/148673* ⊕ *www.la-perlablanca.com* ⌁ *7 rooms* ⧖ *Free Breakfast.*

$$$
B&B/INN
⧉ **Montelirio.** The 18th-century mansion of the Count of Montelirio, perched over the deep plunge to El Tajo, has been carefully refurbished, maintaining some original features, but the highlight is the breathtaking view over the valley. **Pros:** valley views; historic building; Turkish bath and open fireplace make it great for winter. **Cons:** some rooms have windows to the street; parking limited; could be too stuffy for some. Ⓢ *Rooms from: €140* ⊠ *Calle Tenorio 8* ☎ *952/873855* ⊕ *www. hotelmontelirio.com* ⌁ *15 rooms* ⧖ *No meals.*

$
B&B/INN
⧉ **San Gabriel.** In the oldest part of Ronda, this hotel is run by a family who converted their 18th-century home into an enchanting, informal hotel. **Pros:** traditional Andalusian house; some rooms have Jacuzzi bathtubs; wine cellar includes local vintages. **Cons:** some rooms are rather dark; no panoramic views; could be too antique for some. Ⓢ *Rooms from: €75* ⊠ *Calle Marqués de Moctezuma 19* ☎ *952/190392* ⊕ *www.hotelsangabriel.com* ⌁ *22 rooms* ⧖ *No meals.*

AROUND RONDA: CAVES, ROMANS, AND PUEBLOS BLANCOS

This area of spectacular gorges, remote mountain villages, and ancient caves is fascinating to explore and a dramatic contrast to the clamor and crowds of the coast.

GETTING HERE AND AROUND

Public transportation is very poor in these parts. Your best bet is to visit by car—the area is a short drive from Ronda.

EXPLORING

Fodor's Choice ★
Acinipo. Old Ronda, 20 km (12 miles) north of Ronda, is the site of this old Roman settlement, a thriving town in the 1st century AD that was abandoned for reasons that still baffle historians. Today it's a windswept hillside with piles of stones, the foundations of a few Roman houses, and what remains of a theater. Views across the Ronda plains and to the surrounding mountains are spectacular. The site's opening hours vary depending on staff availability and excavations—check with the Ronda tourist office by phone before visiting. ⊠ *Ronda* ⌖ *Take A376 toward Algodonales; turnoff for ruins is 9 km (5 miles) from Ronda on MA449* ☎ *951/041452* ▦ *Free.*

Cueva de la Pileta (*Pileta Cave*). At this prehistoric site, 20 km (12 miles) west of Ronda, a Spanish guide (who speaks some English) will hand you a paraffin lamp and lead you on a roughly 60-minute walk that reveals prehistoric wall paintings of bison, deer, and horses outlined in black, red, and ocher. One highlight is the Cámara del Pescado (Chamber of the Fish), whose drawing of a huge fish is thought to

10

Andalusia's classic *pueblos blancos* (white villages) look like Picasso paintings come to life.

be 15,000 years old. Tours take place on the hour and last around an hour. ⊠ *Benaoján* ✛ *Drive west from Ronda on A374 and take left exit for village of Benaoján from where caves are well signposted* ☎ *687/133338* 🖅 *€8.*

Olvera. Here, 13 km (8 miles) north of Setenil, two imposing silhouettes dominate the crest of the hill: the 11th-century castle Vallehermoso, a legacy of the Moors, and the neoclassical church of La Encarnación, reconstructed in the 19th century on the foundations of the old mosque.

Setenil de las Bodegas. This small city, in a cleft in the rock cut by the Río Guadalporcín, is 8 km (5 miles) north of Acinipo. The streets resemble long, narrow caves, and on many houses the roof is formed by a projecting ledge of heavy rock.

Zahara de la Sierra. A solitary watchtower dominates a crag above this village, its outline visible for miles around. The tower is all that remains of a Moorish castle where King Alfonso X once fought the emir of Morocco; the building remained a Moorish stronghold until it fell to the Christians in 1470. Along the streets you can see door knockers fashioned like the hand of Fatima: the fingers represent the five laws of the Koran and are meant to ward off evil. ✛ *From Olvera, drive 21 km (13 miles) southwest to the village of Algodonales, then south on A376 for 5 km (3 miles).*

GRAZALEMA AND THE SIERRA DE GRAZALEMA

Grazalema: 28 km (17 miles) northwest of Ronda.

The village of Grazalema is the prettiest of the pueblos blancos. Its cobblestone streets of houses with pink-and-ocher roofs wind up the hillside, red geraniums splash white walls, and black wrought-iron lanterns and grilles cling to the house fronts.

The Sierra de Grazalema Natural Park encompasses a series of mountain ranges known as the Sierra de Grazalema, which straddle the provinces of Málaga and Cádiz. These mountains trap the rain clouds that roll in from the Atlantic, and the area has the distinction of being the wettest place in Spain, with an average annual rainfall of 88 inches. Because of the park's altitude and prevailing humidity, it's one of the last habitats for the rare fir tree *Abies pinsapo*; it's also home to ibex, vultures, and birds of prey. Parts of the park are restricted, accessible only on foot and when accompanied by an official guide.

GETTING HERE AND AROUND

The village of Grazalema itself is quite small and is best reached by private car as there's little public transport.

VISITOR INFORMATION

Contacts Grazalema. ✉ *Pl. de los Asomaderos 7, Grazalema* ☎ *956/132052.*

EXPLORING

El Bosque. An excursion from Grazalema takes you through the heart of this protected reserve, home to a trout stream and information center. Follow the A344 west through dramatic mountain scenery, past Benamahoma. ✉ *Grazalema.*

Ubrique. From Grazalema, the A374 takes you to this town on the slopes of the Saltadero Mountains, known for its leather tanning and embossing industry. Look for the **Convento de los Capuchinos** (Capuchin Convent), the church of **San Pedro,** and, 4 km (2½ miles) away, the ruins of the Moorish castle **El Castillo de Fátima.**

WHERE TO STAY

$ B&B/INN Fodor's Choice ★ 🏨 **La Mejorana.** An ideal base for exploring the area, this is the spot to find rural simplicity and stunning mountain views. **Pros:** in the center of the village; tastefully furnished; home-away-from-home atmosphere. **Cons:** no TV in rooms; rustic feel not for everyone. [$] *Rooms from: €64* ✉ *Calle Santa Clara 6, Grazalema* ☎ *956/132327* 🌐 *www.lamejorana.net* 🛏 *6 rooms* 🍴 *Free Breakfast.*

10

HUELVA

When you've had enough of Seville's urban bustle, nature awaits in Huelva. From the Parque Nacional de Doñana to the oak forests of the Sierra de Aracena, nothing in this area is much more than an hour's drive from Seville. If you prefer history, hop on the miners' train at Riotinto or visit Aracena's spectacular caves. Columbus's voyage to the New World was sparked near here, at the monastery of La Rábida and in Palos de la Frontera. The visitor center at La Rocina has Doñana

Andalusia's White Villages

Andalusia's pueblos blancos (white villages) are usually found nestled on densely wooded hills, clinging to the edges of deep gorges, or perched on hilltops. The picturesque locations of the pueblos blancos usually have more to do with defense than anything else, and many have crumbling fortifications that show their use as defensive structures along the frontier between the Christian and Moorish realms. In a few, the remains of magnificent Moorish castles can be spied. The suffix *de la frontera,* literally meaning "on the frontier," tacked onto a town's name reflects this historical border position.

VEJER DE LA FRONTERA

This dazzling white town is perched high on a hill, perfectly positioned to protect its citizens from the threat of marauding pirates. Today it is one of the most charming pueblos blancos on the Cádiz coast, known for its meandering cobbled lanes, narrow arches, and large number of atmospheric bars and restaurants. Vejer is popular with an artsy crowd that has brought art galleries, crafts shops, and sophisticated restaurants.

FRIGILIANA

This impossibly pretty whitewashed village is 7 km (4½ miles) north of the well-known resort of Nerja. Despite the encroachment of modern apartment buildings, the old center has remained relatively unchanged. Pots of crimson geraniums decorate the narrow streets, while the bars proudly serve the local sweet wine. Frigiliana is a good place for seeking out ceramics made by the town's

craftspeople. Hikers can enjoy the 3-km (2-mile) hike from the old town to El Fuerte, the hilltop site of a 1569 skirmish between the Moors and the Christians (⇨ *see Chapter 11*).

GAUCÍN

The countryside surrounding Ronda is stunning, especially in the spring when the ground is carpeted with wildflowers, including exquisite purple orchids. Not surprisingly, the Serranía de Ronda (as this area is known) is famous for its superb walking. Gaucín is a lovely village crowned by a ruined Moorish castle. It is popular with artists who open their studios to the public each year in late spring (visit ⊕ *www.artgaucin.com* for dates). The town also has several excellent restaurants and sophisticated boutique hotels.

PITRES AND LA TAHA

Granada's Alpujarras mountains are home to some of Andalusia's most unspoiled white villages. Two of the best known are Bubión and Capileira, while the Pitres and La Taha villages of Mecina, Mecinilla, Fondales, Ferreirola, and Atalbéitar are lovely hamlets separated by rough tracks that wind through orchards and woodland, set in a valley that attracts few visitors.

GRAZALEMA

About a half hour from Ronda, Grazalema is the prettiest—and the whitest—of the white towns. It's a small town, worth some time wandering, and well situated for a visit to the mountains of the Sierra de Grazalema Natural Park.

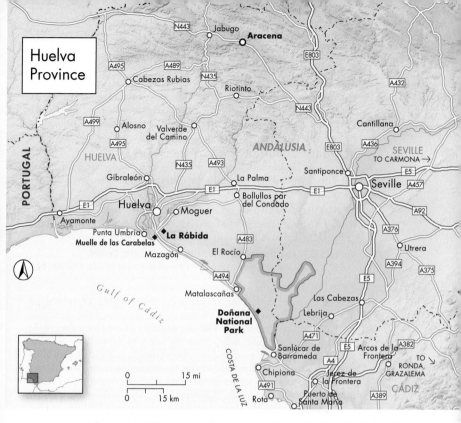

Huelva
Province

PORTUGAL

ANDALUSIA

HUELVA

SEVILLE
TO CARMONA →

Gulf of Cádiz

COSTA DE LA LUZ

CÁDIZ

Doñana
National
Park

| 0 | 15 mi |
| 0 | 15 km |

information. The province is also something of a foodie destination, named Spain's Gastronomic Capital for 2017.

Once a thriving Roman port, the city of Huelva, an hour east of Faro, Portugal, was largely destroyed by the 1755 Lisbon earthquake. As a result, it claims the dubious honor of being the least distinguished city in Andalusia—it's the attractions nearby that most merit a visit to this part of Spain. If you do end up visiting the city, **Taberna el Condado**, **La Mirta**, or **El Chiringuito de Antonio** are the places to go for shellfish tapas and rice.

10

GETTING HERE AND AROUND

Huelva has good bus connections from Seville, but traveling to the main sights in the province is difficult by public transportation so you're better off renting a car.

Bus Station Huelva. ⊠ *Av. Doctor Rubio s/n* ☎ *959/256900.*

Taxi Contact Tele Taxi. ☎ *959/250022.*

Train Station Huelva. ⊠ *Av. de Italia* ☎ *912/320320.*

DOÑANA NATIONAL PARK

100 km (62 miles) southwest of Seville.

The jewel in Spain's crown when it comes to national parks, and one of Europe's most important wetlands, Doñana is a paradise for wildlife in their natural habitat. Most of the park is heavily protected and closed to visitors, although you can visit with one of the authorized tour companies who organize visits by jeep, foot, or horseback.

GETTING HERE AND AROUND

To explore Doñana and its surroundings you need your own transportation, particularly to get to the different visitor centers, all some distance apart.

VISITOR INFORMATION

In addition to the centers listed here, there is a visitor center for the park at Sanlúcar de Barrameda called La Fábrica de Hielo.

Contcts El Acebuche. ☎ *959/439629*. **La Rocina Visitor Center.** ☎ *959/439569*. **Palacio de Acebrón.** ✉ *Ctra. de la Rocina* ☎ *671/593138*.

EXPLORING

FAMILY **Doñana National Park.** One of Europe's most important swaths of
Fodor's Choice unspoiled wilderness, these wetlands spread out along the west side
★ of the Guadalquivir estuary. The site was named for Doña Ana, wife of a 16th-century duke, who, prone to bouts of depression, one day crossed the river and wandered into the wetlands, never to be seen alive again. The 188,000-acre park sits on the migratory route from Africa to Europe and is the winter home and breeding ground for as many as 150 rare species of birds. Habitats range from beaches and shifting sand dunes to marshes, dense brushwood, and sandy hillsides of pine and cork oak. Two of Europe's most endangered species, the imperial eagle and the lynx, make their homes here, and kestrels, kites, buzzards, egrets, storks, and spoonbills breed among the cork oaks.

WHERE TO STAY

$ ⬚ **Toruño.** Despite its location behind the famous Rocío shrine, the
HOTEL theme at this simple, friendly hotel is nature—it's run by the same cooperative that leads official park tours, and has become a favorite of birders. **Pros:** views over the wetlands; bird-watching opportunities; restaurant serving reasonably priced traditional food. **Cons:** not great for extended stays; basic accommodation; busy during pilgrimage week. $ *Rooms from: €80* ✉ *Pl. del Acebuchal 22, El Rocío* ☎ *959/442323* ⊕ *www.toruno.es* ⬗ *30 rooms* ⅋ *Free Breakfast*.

LA RÁBIDA

8 km (5 miles) northwest of Mazagón.

La Rábida's monastery is worth a stop if you're a history buff: it's nicknamed "the birthplace of America" because in 1485 Columbus came from Portugal with his son Diego to stay in the Mudejar-style Franciscan monastery, where he discussed his theories with friars Antonio de Marchena and Juan Pérez. They interceded on his behalf with Queen Isabella, who had originally rejected his planned expedition.

Wild Andalusian horses near the village of El Rocío, in Doñana National Park

EXPLORING

Muelle de las Carabelas (*Caravel's Wharf*). Two kilometers (1 mile) from La Rábida's monastery, on the seashore, this is a reproduction of a 15th-century port. The star exhibits here are the full-size models of Columbus's flotilla, the *Niña, Pinta,* and *Santa María,* built using the same techniques as in Columbus's day. You can go aboard each and learn more about the discovery of the New World in the adjoining museum. ⊠ *Paraje de la Rábida* ☎ *959/530597* 📧 *€4* ⊗ *Closed Mon.*

Santa María de La Rábida. The Mudejar-style Franciscan monastery of this church has a much-venerated 14th-century statue of the **Virgen de los Milagros** (Virgin of Miracles). There are relics from the discovery of America displayed in the museum and the **frescoes** in the gatehouse were painted by Daniel Vázquez Díaz in 1930. ⊠ *Camino del Monasterio, Ctra. de Huelva* ☎ *959/350411* ⊕ *www.monasteriodelarabida. com* 📧 *€4* ⊗ *Closed Mon.*

ARACENA

105 km (65 miles) northeast of Huelva, 100 km (62 miles) northwest of Seville.

Stretching north of the provinces of Huelva and Seville is the 460,000-acre Sierra de Aracena nature park, an expanse of hills cloaked in cork and holm oak. This region is known for its cured Iberian hams, which come from the prized free-ranging Iberian pigs that gorge on acorns in the autumn months before slaughter; the hams are buried in salt and then hung in cellars to dry-cure for at least two years. The best Iberian hams have traditionally come from the village of **Jabugo.**

GETTING HERE AND AROUND

Because this area is remote, it's best to get around by car.

VISITOR INFORMATION

Contacts Aracena. ✉ *Calle Pozo de la Nieve, at cave entrance* ☎ *663/937877.*

> **COLUMBUS SETS SAIL**
>
> On August 2, 1492, the *Niña,* the *Pinta,* and the *Santa María* set sail from the town of Palos de la Frontera. At the door of the church of **San Jorge** (1473), the royal letter ordering the levy of the ships' crew and equipment was read aloud, and the voyagers took their water supplies from the fountain known as La Fontanilla at the town's entrance.

EXPLORING

FAMILY **Gruta de las Maravillas** (*Cave of Marvels*). In the town of Aracena, the capital of the region, the main attraction is this spectacular cave. Its 12 caverns contain long corridors, stalactites and stalagmites arranged in wonderful patterns, and stunning underground lagoons. Only 1,000 people may visit per day, so go early if visiting in high season. ✉ *Calle Pozo de la Nieve, Pedraza de la Sierra* ☎ *663/937876* 🎟 *€9.*

WHERE TO EAT AND STAY

$$ SPANISH 🍴 **Montecruz.** The downstairs bar here serves simple tapas, but it's the upstairs restaurant that makes it worth a visit. The rustic dining room is decorated with wall paintings and hunting trophies, and the kitchen serves only regional produce and dishes. **Known for:** tapas; lomo de jabalí (boar tenderloin); gurumelos salteados con jamón y gambas (mushroom stir-fried with ham and shrimp). [$] *Average main: €14* ✉ *Pl. de San Pedro* ☎ *959/126013* 🌐 *www.restaurantemontecruz.com.*

$$$ B&B/INN Fodor's Choice ★ 🏨 **Finca Buenvino.** This lovely country house, 6 km (4 miles) from Aracena, is nestled in 150 acres of woods and is run by a charming British couple, Sam and Jeannie Chesterton, who include big breakfasts in the room price and offer dinner for €35. **Pros:** intimate and personal; friendly hosts; heated infinity pool. **Cons:** somewhat removed from village life; you need a car to get here. [$] *Rooms from: €140* ✉ *N433, Km 95, Los Marines* ☎ *959/124034* 🌐 *www.fincabuenvino.com* 🛏 *7 rooms* 🍽 *Free Breakfast.*

CÁDIZ PROVINCE AND JEREZ DE LA FRONTERA

A trip through this province is a journey into the past. Winding roads take you through scenes ranging from flat and barren plains to seemingly endless vineyards, and the rolling countryside is carpeted with blindingly white soil known as *albariza*—unique to this area and the secret to the grapes used in sherry production. In Jerez de La Frontera, you can savor the town's internationally known sherry and delight in the skills and forms of purebred Carthusian horses.

Throughout the province, the pueblos blancos provide striking contrasts with the terrain, especially at Arcos de la Frontera, where the village sits dramatically on a crag overlooking the gorge of the Río Guadalete.

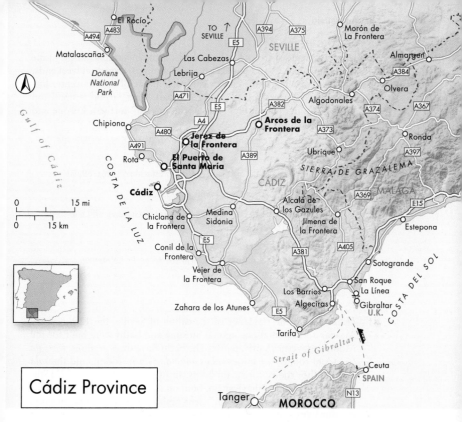

In the city of Cádiz you can absorb about 3,000 years of history in what is generally considered the oldest continuously inhabited city in the Western world.

JEREZ DE LA FRONTERA

97 km (60 miles) south of Seville.

Jerez, world headquarters for sherry, is surrounded by vineyards of chalky soil, producing palomino grapes that have funded a host of churches and noble mansions. Names such as González Byass, Domecq, Harvey, and Sandeman are inextricably linked with Jerez. The word "sherry," first used in Great Britain in 1608, is an English corruption of the town's old Moorish name, Xeres. Both sherry and thoroughbred horses (the city was European Capital of Horses in 2018) are the domain of Jerez's Anglo-Spanish aristocracy, whose Catholic ancestors came here from England centuries ago. At any given time, more than half a million barrels of sherry are maturing in Jerez's vast aboveground cellars.

GETTING HERE AND AROUND

Jerez is a short way from Seville with frequent daily trains (journey time is around an hour) and buses (1 hour 15 minutes), fewer on weekends. If you're traveling to the city by car, park in one of the city-center lots or at your hotel as street parking is difficult. Jerez Airport is small and served by a number of flights to destinations in northern Europe and within Spain.

Airport Jerez de la Frontera Airport. ⊠ *Ctra. N-IV, Km 628.5* ☏ *902/404704* ⊕ *www.aena.es.*

Bus Station Jerez de la Frontera. ⊠ *Pl. de la Estación* ☏ *956/149990.*

Taxi Contact Tele Taxi. ☏ *956/344860, 956/350537.*

Train Station Jerez de la Frontera. ⊠ *Pl. de la Estación s/n, off Calle Diego Fernández Herrera* ☏ *912/320320.*

VISITOR INFORMATION

Contacts Jerez de la Frontera. ⊠ *Edificio Los Arcos, Pl. del Arenal* ☏ *956/338874* ⊕ *www.turismojerez.com.*

EXPLORING

TOP ATTRACTIONS

Alcázar. Once the residence of the caliph of Seville, the 12th-century Alcázar and its small, octagonal **mosque** and **baths** were built for the Moorish governor's private use. The baths have three sections: the *sala fría* (cold room), the larger *sala templada* (warm room), and the *sala caliente* (hot room) for steam baths. In the midst of it all is the 17th-century **Palacio de Villavicencio,** built on the site of the original Moorish palace. A camera obscura, a lens-and-mirrors device that projects the outdoors onto a large indoor screen, offers a 360-degree view of Jerez. ⊠ *Calle Alameda Vieja* ☏ *956/149955* ⊠ *From €5.*

Catedral de Jerez. Across from the Alcázar and around the corner from the González Byass winery, the cathedral has an octagonal cupola and a separate bell tower, as well as Zurbarán's canvas *La Virgen Niña* (*The Virgin as a Young Girl*). ⊠ *Pl. de la Encarnación* ☏ *956/169059* ⊠ *€5* ☉ *Closed Sun.*

Fodor's Choice ★ **Plaza de la Asunción.** Here on one of Jerez's most intimate squares you can find the Mudejar church of **San Dionisio,** patron saint of the city (Monday–Thursday 10–noon, free), and the ornate **cabildo municipal** (city hall), with a lovely plateresque facade dating to 1575. ⊠ *Jerez de la Frontera.*

FAMILY
Fodor's Choice ★ **Real Escuela Andaluza del Arte Ecuestre** (*Royal Andalusian School of Equestrian Art*). This prestigious school operates on the grounds of the Recreo de las Cadenas, a 19th-century palace. The school was masterminded by Alvaro Domecq in the 1970s, and every Tuesday and Thursday (Thursday only in January and February) the Cartujana horses—a cross between the native Andalusian workhorse and the Arabian—and skilled riders in 18th-century riding costume demonstrate intricate dressage techniques and jumping in the spectacular show *Cómo Bailan los Caballos Andaluces* (roughly, *The Dancing Horses of Andalusia*). ■TIP→ **Reservations are essential.** The price of admission depends on

Riders fill the streets during Jerez's Feria del Caballo (Horse Fair) in early May.

how close to the arena you sit; the first two rows are the priciest. At certain other times you can visit the museum, stables, and tack room, and watch the horses being schooled. ⊠ *Av. Duque de Abrantes* ☎ *956/318008 for info* ⊕ *www.realescuela.org* ✉ *From €11.*

WHERE TO EAT

$$ ╳ **Albores.** Opposite the city hall, this restaurant, with pleasant out-
SPANISH door seating under orange trees and a sleek interior with low lighting,
Fodor's Choice serves modern dishes with a traditional base. The menu is extensive
★ and changes often, although must-try staples include *buñuelos de langostinos con muselina de perejil* (king prawn fritters with parsley cream) and tuna tartare. **Known for:** innovative dishes; swift service; tuna cooked any which way. $ *Average main: €15* ⊠ *Calle Consistorio 12* ☎ *956/320266* ⊕ *www.restaurantealbores.com* ⊟ *No credit cards.*

$ ╳ **Bar Juanito.** Traditional bars don't come more authentic than Bar
SPANISH Juanito, which has been serving local dishes for over 40 years. You're spoiled for choice with more than 52 tapas on the menu, but house specials are artichoke dishes (in season in early spring) and *berza jerezana* (stew made with Swiss chard, chickpeas, and pork). **Known for:** tapas; artichoke dishes; live music on Saturday. $ *Average main: €10* ⊠ *Calle Pescadería Vieja 8–10* ☎ *956/342986.*

$$$ ╳ **La Carboná.** In a former bodega, this eatery has a rustic atmosphere
SPANISH with arches, wooden beams, and a fireplace for winter nights, and in
Fodor's Choice summer you can often enjoy live music and sometimes flamenco danc-
★ ing while you dine. The chef has worked at several top restaurants, and his menu includes traditional grilled meats as well as innovative twists on classic dishes, such as foie gras terrine with pear and cardamom,

and *mero con curry de palo cortado* (grouper fish with sherry curry). **Known for:** sherry tasting menu; bodega setting; innovative dishes. Ⓢ *Average main: €20* ✉ *Calle San Francisco de Paula 2* ☏ *956/347475* ✆ *Closed Tues.*

$ ✕**Mesón del Asador.** Just off the Plaza del Arenal, this rustic meat res-
SPANISH   taurant is always packed with young locals who crowd around the bar for cheap and generous tapas (from €3). Oxtail stew, fried chorizo, black pudding, and pig's-cheek stew come in huge portions, resulting in an incredibly inexpensive meal. **Known for:** grilled meats; generous portions; inexpensive tapas. Ⓢ *Average main: €11* ✉ *Calle Remedios 2–4* ☏ *952/322658* ▭ *No credit cards.*

$$ ✕**Venta Esteban.** This restaurant is slightly off the beaten track, but well
SPANISH   worth seeking out for traditional Jerez cuisine in a pleasant setting.
FAMILY   Choose tapas in the bar or à la carte in the spacious and airy din-
ing rooms. **Known for:** seafood; traditional stews; homemade custard. Ⓢ *Average main: €15* ✉ *Colonia de Caulina C.11–03* ⊹ *Just off Seville highway exit* ☏ *956/316067* ⊕ *www.restauranteventaesteban.es.*

WHERE TO STAY

$$ ▥ **Hotel Casa Grande.** This cozy hotel, bang in the city center with all
HOTEL   the main attractions on its doorstep, comes complete with its original 1920s Art Nouveau design and period antiques. **Pros:** central loca-tion; personalized service; roof terrace. **Cons:** no pool; decor might not appeal to everyone; some rooms have street noise. Ⓢ *Rooms from: €100* ✉ *Pl. de las Angustias 3* ☏ *956/345070* ⊕ *www.hotelcasagrande. eu* ⇥ *15 rooms* �’⍤❘ *No meals.*

$ ▥ **Hotel Doña Blanca.** Slightly off the main tourist route but still within
HOTEL   easy walking distance to attractions, this traditional town-house hotel offers spacious accommodations with some of the best prices in the city. **Pros:** private terrace in some rooms; great value; generously sized rooms. **Cons:** cold breakfast choices only; not right in the city center; might be too basic for some. Ⓢ *Rooms from: €50* ✉ *Calle Bodegas 11* ☏ *956/348761* ⊕ *www.hoteldonablanca.com* ⇥ *30 rooms* ❘⍤❘ *No meals.*

$ ▥ **Hotel Palacio Garvey.** Dating from 1850, this luxurious boutique hotel
B&B/INN   was once the home of the prestigious Garvey family, and the original neoclassical architecture and interior decoration have been tastefully restored. **Pros:** in the center of town; fashionable and contemporary feel; sense of history. **Cons:** breakfast offers few choices; elevator does not reach all floors; some rooms face the street, which can be noisy. Ⓢ *Rooms from: €70* ✉ *Calle Tornería 24* ☏ *956/326700* ⊕ *www.hotel-palaciogarvey.es* ⇥ *16 rooms* ❘⍤❘ *Free Breakfast.*

$$$ ▥ **Hotel Villa Jerez.** Tastefully furnished, this hacienda-style hotel offers
B&B/INN   luxury on the outskirts of town. **Pros:** elegant gardens; Italian restau-rant on-site; saltwater swimming pool. **Cons:** outside of town center. Ⓢ *Rooms from: €130* ✉ *Av. de la Cruz Roja 7* ☏ *956/153100* ⊕ *www. hace.es/hotelvillajerez* ⇥ *15 rooms* ❘⍤❘ *No meals.*

$ ▥ **La Fonda Barranco.** A block away from the cathedral and behind the
HOTEL   police station, this typical Jerez town house has been restored to its full bourgeois glory, preserving original tiled floors, beamed ceilings, and a light central patio. **Pros:** personalized attention; central location;

good value. **Cons:** some rooms are dark; no elevator; basic breakfast. [$] *Rooms from: €75* ✉ *Calle Barranco 12* ☎ *956/332141* 🌐 *www.lafondabarranco.com* 💳 *No credit cards* 🛏 *8 rooms, 2 apartments* 🍴 *Free Breakfast.*

SPORTS AND THE OUTDOORS

Circuito Permanente de Velocidad. Formula One Grand Prix races—including the Spanish motorcycle Grand Prix on the first weekend in May—are held at Jerez's racetrack. ✉ *Ctra. Arcos, Km 10* ☎ *956/151100* 🌐 *www.circuitodejerez.com.*

SHOPPING

Calle Corredera and **Calle Bodegas** are the places to go if you want to browse for wicker and ceramics.

ARCOS DE LA FRONTERA

31 km (19 miles) east of Jerez.

Fodor's Choice ★ Its narrow and steep cobblestone streets, whitewashed houses, and finely crafted wrought-iron window grilles make Arcos the quintessential Andalusian pueblo blanco. Make your way to the main square, the Plaza de España, the highest point in the village; one side of the square is open, and a balcony at the edge of the cliff offers views of the Guadalete Valley. On the opposite end is the church of **Santa María de la Asunción,** a fascinating blend of architectural styles—Romanesque, Gothic, and Mudejar—with a plateresque doorway, a Renaissance retablo, and a 17th-century baroque choir. The Ayuntamiento stands at the foot of the old castle walls on the northern side of the square; across is the Casa del Corregidor, onetime residence of the governor and now a parador. Arcos is the westernmost of the 19 pueblos blancos dotted around the Sierra de Cádiz.

GETTING HERE AND AROUND

Arcos is best reached by private car, but there are frequent bus services here from Cádiz, Jerez, and Seville on weekdays. Weekend services are less frequent.

VISITOR INFORMATION

Contacts Arcos de la Frontera. ✉ *Cuesta de Belén 5* ☎ *956/702264* 🌐 *www.arcosdelafrontera.es.*

WHERE TO EAT

$ TAPAS 🍴 **El Paquetito.** At the bottom of the climb up to the old town, this small restaurant serves—according to many—the best tapas (from €2.50) in Arcos. Signature tapas are *paquetitos* (little parcels) of phyllo pastry with seven different fillings; the most requested are the goat cheese with spinach and pine nuts, and the salmon with herbed cheese. **Known for:** good-value tapas; goat cheese paquetitos; fried eggplant with honey. [$] *Average main: €10* ✉ *Av. Miguel Mancheño 1* ☎ *956/704937* 💳 *No credit cards* ⏲ *Closed Tues.*

$$ SPANISH 🍴 **Restaurante Tamizia.** The old town has only one real restaurant—within the parador hotel—and it boasts perhaps the best views ever from a table. Wherever you choose to sit (bar, terrace, or restaurant),

10

Just about the whole city turns out for Jerez's Feria del Caballo, and traditional Andalusian costumes are a common sight.

you'll dine looking over the cliff top over miles of green countryside beyond. **Known for:** views from your dinner table; dishes using local produce; rabo de toro. $ *Average main: €14* ⊠ *Parador Casa del Corregidor, Pl. del Cabildo* ☎ *956/700500.*

WHERE TO STAY

$
B&B/INN
Fodor'sChoice
★

El Convento. Perched atop the cliff behind the town parador, this tiny hotel in a former 17th-century convent shares the amazing view of another hotel in town, its swish neighbor (La Casa Grande). **Pros:** location; intimacy; value. **Cons:** small spaces; lots of stairs; no restaurant. $ *Rooms from: €85* ⊠ *Calle Maldonado 2* ☎ *956/702333* ⊕ *www. hotelelconvento.es* ⊘ *Closed Nov.–Feb.* ⇴ *13 rooms* ⦿ *No meals.*

$$
B&B/INN
Fodor'sChoice
★

La Casa Grande. Built in 1729, this extraordinary 18th-century mansion encircles a central patio with lush vegetation and is perched on the edge of the 400-foot cliff to which Arcos de la Frontera clings. **Pros:** attentive owner; impeccable aesthetics; amazing views. **Cons:** inconvenient parking; long climb to the top floor; interior is a little dark. $ *Rooms from: €100* ⊠ *Calle Maldonado 10* ☎ *956/703930* ⊕ *www. lacasagrande.net* ⇴ *7 rooms* ⦿ *No meals.*

$$$
HOTEL

Parador Casa del Corregidor. Expect a spectacular view from the terrace, as this parador clings to the cliff side, overlooking the rolling valley of the Río Guadalete. **Pros:** gorgeous views from certain rooms; elegant interiors; good restaurant. **Cons:** public areas a little tired; expensive bar and cafeteria; not all rooms have views. $ *Rooms from: €150* ⊠ *Pl. del Cabildo* ☎ *956/700500* ⊕ *www.parador.es* ⇴ *24 rooms* ⦿ *No meals.*

EL PUERTO DE SANTA MARÍA

12 km (7 miles) southwest of Jerez, 17 km (11 miles) north of C diz.

This attractive if somewhat dilapidated little fishing port on the northern shores of the Bay of Cádiz, with lovely beaches nearby, has white houses with peeling facades and vast green grilles covering the doors and windows. The town is dominated by the Terry and Osborne sherry and brandy bodegas. Columbus once lived in a house on the square that bears his name (Cristobal Colón), and Washington Irving spent the autumn of 1828 at Calle Palacios 57. The marisco bars along the Ribera del Marisco (Seafood Way) are El Puerto de Santa María's main claim to fame. La Dorada, Romerijo, and Casa Paco Ceballos are among the most popular, along with El Beti, at Misericordia 7. The tourist office organizes several tours around the port, and some include visits to the more than 70 (!) tapas bars in the town.

> **NOTABLE RESIDENTS**
>
> Christopher Columbus and author Washington Irving once lived in the small fishing village of Puerto de Santa María.

GETTING HERE AND AROUND

The local train between Cádiz and Jerez stops here, and there are regular buses from Cádiz and Seville. If you're visiting El Puerto de Santa María en route, a car is your best option.

VISITOR INFORMATION

Contacts El Puerto de Santa María. ⊠ *Pl. del Castillo, El Puerto de Santa María* ☎ *956/483715* ⊕ *www.turismoelpuerto.com.*

EXPLORING

Castillo de San Marcos. This castle was built in the 13th century on the site of a mosque. Created by Alfonso X, it was later home to the Duke of Medinaceli. Among the guests were Christopher Columbus, who tried unsuccessfully to persuade the duke to finance his voyage west, and Juan de la Cosa, who, within these walls, drew up the first map ever to include the Americas. The red lettering on the walls is a 19th-century addition. Visits are by tour only (in English at 11:30) which must be booked by phone or email; Thursday and Saturday visits include the next-door bodega. ⊠ *Pl. de Alfonso X, El Puerto de Santa María* ☎ *627/569335* ✎ *servicios.turisticos@caballero.es* ☒ *Castle visit only free; €8 castle visit and bodega* ☉ *Closed Sun., Mon., Wed., and Fri.*

Plaza de Toros. The stunning neo-Mudejar bullring was built in 1880 thanks to a donation from the winemaker Thomas Osborne. It originally had seating for exactly 12,816 people, the entire population of Puerto at that time. ⊠ *Los Moros, El Puerto de Santa María* ☒ *Free* ☉ *Closed Tues., Thurs., and weekends.*

WHERE TO EAT AND STAY

$$$$
SPANISH
Fodor'sChoice
★

✕ **Aponiente.** The recipient of a Michelin star annually since 2013, Ángel León showcases his creative seafood dishes in this unusual restaurant housed in an 18th-century tidal mill whose decor takes you under the sea with fishtail-back chairs and mermaids. Aponiente serves two menús de degustación (€190 for 13 dishes, €220 for 17). **Known for:** seafood;

10

Puerto de Santa María is a wonderful tapas- and sherry-tasting destination.

creative use of everyday ingredients; tasting menus. $ *Average main:* *€190 ⊠ Calle Puerto Escondido 6, El Puerto de Santa María ⊕ www.* *aponiente.com.*

$$$ ✕**El Faro del Puerto.** In a villa outside town, the "Lighthouse in the
SPANISH Port" is run by the same family that established the classic El Faro in
Cádiz. Like its predecessor, it serves excellent seafood, most of which
is freshly caught locally. **Known for:** fresh seafood; impressive wine list;
alfresco dining. $ *Average main: €22 ⊠ Ctra. Fuentebravia–Rota, Km* *0.5, El Puerto de Santa María ☎ 956/870952 ⊕ www.elfarodelpuerto.* *com ☉ No dinner Sun. Sept.–July.*

$$ 🏨 **Monasterio San Miguel.** Dating from 1733, this former monastery is a
HOTEL few blocks from the harbor; there's nothing spartan about the former
cells, which are now plush suites with all the trappings. **Pros:** supremely
elegant; efficient service; restaurant on-site. **Cons:** tired furnishings in
common areas and some rooms; breakfast has little variety; could be
too formal for some. $ *Rooms from: €120 ⊠ Calle Virgen de los Mila-* *gros 27, El Puerto de Santa María ☎ 956/540440 ⊕ www.sanmiguel-* *hotelmonasterio.com ⇆ 165 rooms ⦿No meals.*

CÁDIZ

32 km (20 miles) southwest of Jerez, 149 km (93 miles) southwest of *Seville.*

Fodor's Choice With the Atlantic Ocean on three sides, Cádiz is a bustling town that's
★ been shaped by a variety of cultures, and has the varied architecture to
prove it. Founded as Gadir by Phoenician traders in 1100 BC, Cádiz
claims to be the oldest continuously inhabited city in the Western world.

Hannibal lived in Cádiz for a time, Julius Caesar first held public office here, and Columbus set out from here on his second voyage, after which the city became the home base of the Spanish fleet. In the 18th century, when the Guadalquivir silted up, Cádiz monopolized New World trade and became the wealthiest port in Western Europe. Most of its buildings—including the cathedral, built in part with wealth generated by gold and silver from the New World—date from this period. The old city is African in appearance and immensely intriguing—a cluster of narrow streets opening onto charming small squares. The golden cupola of the cathedral looms above low white houses, and the whole place has a slightly dilapidated air. Spaniards flock here in February to revel in the carnival celebrations, and occasional cruise ships visit the harbor, but in general it's not very touristy.

GETTING HERE AND AROUND
Every day, around 15 local trains connect Cádiz with Seville, Puerto de Santa María, and Jerez. The city has two bus stations. The main one, run by Comes, serves most destinations in Andalusia and farther afield; the other, run by Socibus, serves Córdoba and Madrid. There are buses to and from Sanlúcar de Barrameda (13 on weekdays), Arcos de la Frontera (4 daily), and the Costa del Sol (via Seville, 4 daily). Cádiz is easy to get to and navigate by car. Once there, the old city is easily explored by foot.

Bus Station Cádiz–Estación de Autobuses Comes. ⊠ *Pl. de Sevilla* ☎ *956/807059.* **Cádiz-Estación de Autobuses Socibus.** ⊠ *Av. Astilleros s/n* ☎ *956/257415.*

Taxi Contact Radiotaxi. ☎ *956/212121.*

Train Station Cádiz. ⊠ *Pl. de Sevilla s/n* ☎ *912/320320.*

VISITOR INFORMATION
Contacts Local Tourist Office. ⊠ *Paseo de Canalejas* ☎ *956/241001* ⊕ *www. turismo.cadiz.es.* **Regional Tourist Office.** ⊠ *Av. Ramón de Carranza s/n* ☎ *956/203191* ⊕ *www.cadizturismo.com.*

EXPLORING
Begin your explorations in the Plaza de Mina, a large, leafy square with palm trees and plenty of benches. Look out for the ornamental facade on the Colegio de Arquitectos (College of Architects), on the west side of the square.

Cádiz Cathedral. Five blocks southeast of the Torre Tavira are the gold dome and baroque facade of Cádiz's cathedral, begun in 1722, when the city was at the height of its power. The Cádiz-born composer Manuel de Falla, who died in 1946 at the age of 70, is buried in the **crypt**. The **museum,** on Calle Acero, displays gold, silver, and jewels from the New World, as well as Enrique de Arfe's processional cross, which is carried in the annual Corpus Christi parades. The cathedral is known as the New Cathedral because it supplanted the original 13th-century structure next door, which was destroyed by the British in 1592, rebuilt, and rechristened the church of **Santa Cruz** when the New Cathedral came along. The climb up to the Clock Tower (Torre del Reloj) is worth it for

Cádiz's majestic cathedral, as seen from the Plaza de la Catedral

the views. ⊠ *Pl. Catedral* ☎ *956/286154* 🎟 *€5, includes crypt, museum, tower, and church of Santa Cruz.*

Museo de Cádiz (*Provincial Museum*). On the east side of the Plaza de Mina is Cádiz's provincial museum. Notable pieces include works by Murillo and Alonso Cano as well as the *Four Evangelists* and a set of saints by Zurbarán. The archaeological section contains Phoenician sarcophagi from the time of this ancient city's birth. ⊠ *Pl. de Mina* ☎ *856/105023* 🎟 *€2* ⏱ *Closed Mon.*

Oratorio de San Felipe Neri. A walk up Calle San José from the Plaza de la Mina will bring you to this church, where Spain's first liberal constitution (known affectionately as *La Pepa*) was declared in 1812. It was here, too, that the Cortes (Parliament) of Cádiz met when the rest of Spain was subjected to the rule of Napoléon's brother, Joseph Bonaparte (more popularly known as Pepe Botella, for his love of the bottle). On the main altar is an *Immaculate Conception* by Murillo, the great sevillano artist who in 1682 fell to his death from a scaffold while working on his *Mystic Marriage of St. Catherine* in Cádiz's Chapel of Santa Catalina. ⊠ *Calle Santa Inés 38* ☎ *662/642233* 🎟 *€3 (free Sun.)* ⏱ *Closed Mon.*

FAMILY
Fodor's Choice
★

Torre Tavira. At 150 feet, this is the highest point in the old city. More than a hundred such watchtowers were used by Cádiz ship owners to spot their arriving fleets. A camera obscura gives a good overview of the city and its monuments; the last show is a half hour before closing time. ⊠ *Calle Marqués del Real Tesoro 10* ☎ *956/212910* 🎟 *€6.*

WHERE TO EAT AND STAY

$ ✕ **Casa Manteca.** Cádiz's most quintessentially Andalusian tavern is in
SPANISH the neighborhood of La Viña, named for the vineyard that once grew
Fodor's Choice here. *Chacina* (Iberian ham or sausage) and *chicharrones de Cádiz* (cold
★ pork) served on waxed paper and washed down with manzanilla (sherry
from Sanlúcar de Barrameda) are standard fare at the low wooden
counter that has served bullfighters and flamenco singers, as well as
dignitaries from around the world, since 1953. The walls are covered
with colorful posters and other memorabilia from the annual carnival,
flamenco shows, and ferias. **Known for:** atmospheric interior; delicious
cold cuts; manzanilla. $ *Average main: €9* ⊠ *Corralón de los Carros
66* 🕿 *956/213603* ⊗ *No dinner Sun. and Mon.*

$$$ ✕ **El Faro.** This famous fishing-quarter restaurant near Playa de la Caleta
SPANISH is deservedly known as one of the best in the province. From the outside,
Fodor's Choice it's one of many whitewashed houses with ocher details and shiny black
★ lanterns; inside it's warm and inviting, with half-tile walls, glass lan-
terns, oil paintings, and photos of old Cádiz. **Known for:** fresh fish; rice
dishes; tapas. $ *Average main: €22* ⊠ *Calle San Felix 15* 🕿 *956/211068*
⊕ *www.elfarodecadiz.com.*

$$ ✕ **La Candela.** A block north of Plaza Candelaria and on one of Cádiz's
SPANISH narrow pedestrian streets, La Candela is a good place to try local fare
with a modern twist. Chicharrones de Cádiz come with cheese and sun-
dried tomatoes, the seasonal artichokes come in a variety of ways, and
several dishes have Asian touches, served tempura style or with wasabi
sauce. **Known for:** tapas; homemade cheesecake; Spanish-Asian fusion
food. $ *Average main: €13* ⊠ *Calle Feduchy 1* 🕿 *956/221822* ⊕ *www.
lacandelatapasbar.com* ▬ *No credit cards.*

$$ ⌂ **Argantonia.** This small, family-run hotel in the historic center of town
HOTEL combines traditional style and modern amenities; each of the three
floors in the 19th-century mansion has been decorated in a different
style: Andalusian (first), French colonial (second), and simple rustic
colonial (third). **Pros:** friendly and helpful staff; great location; good-
size bathrooms. **Cons:** rooms in the original building on the small side;
street-facing rooms can be noisy; small breakfast area. $ *Rooms from:
€120* ⊠ *Calle Argantonio 3* 🕿 *956/211640* ⊕ *www.hotelargantonio.
com* ▬ *No credit cards* ⌘ *17 rooms* ⦿ *Free Breakfast.*

$$ ⌂ **Hotel Patagonia Sur.** With a handy central location just two blocks
HOTEL from the cathedral, this modern hotel offers functional and inexpen-
sive lodging, especially during low season. **Pros:** central location; good
value; top-floor rooms have a private terrace. **Cons:** small rooms; street
noise can be intrusive; might be too basic for some. $ *Rooms from:
€100* ⊠ *Calle Cobos 11* 🕿 *856/174647* ⊕ *www.hotelpatagoniasur.es*
⌘ *16 rooms* ⦿ *No meals.*

$$$$ ⌂ **Parador de Cádiz.** With a privileged position overlooking the bay, this
HOTEL parador has large modern rooms, most with balconies facing the sea.
Pros: great views of the bay; pool; bright and cheerful. **Cons:** expensive
parking; very quiet out of season. $ *Rooms from: €250* ⊠ *Av. Duque
de Nájera 9* 🕿 *956/226905* ⊕ *www.parador.es/en/paradores/parador-
de-cadiz* ⌘ *124 rooms* ⦿ *No meals.*

10

CÓRDOBA'S HISTORY

The Romans invaded Córdoba in 206 BC, later making it the capital of Rome's section of Spain. Nearly 800 years later, the Visigoth king Leovigildus took control, but the tribe was soon supplanted by the Moors, whose emirs and caliphs held court here from the 8th to the early 11th century. At that point Córdoba was one of the greatest centers of art, culture, and learning in the Western world; one of its libraries had a staggering 400,000 volumes. Moors, Christians, and Jews lived together in harmony within Córdoba's walls. In that era, it was considered second in importance only to Constantinople; but in 1009, Prince Muhammad II and Omeyan led a rebellion that broke up the caliphate, leading to power flowing to separate Moorish kingdoms.

Córdoba remained in Moorish hands until it was conquered by King Ferdinand in 1236 and repopulated from the north of Spain. Later, the Catholic Monarchs used the city as a base from which to plan the conquest of Granada. In Columbus's time, the Guadalquivir was navigable as far upstream as Córdoba, and great galleons sailed its waters. Today, the river's muddy water and marshy banks evoke little of Córdoba's glorious past, but an old Arab waterfall and the city's bridge—of Roman origin, though much restored by the Arabs and successive generations, most recently in 2012—recall a far grander era.

CÓRDOBA

166 km (103 miles) northwest of Granada, 407 km (250 miles) southwest of Madrid, 239 km (143 miles) northeast of Cádiz, 143 km (86 miles) northeast of Seville.

Strategically located on the north bank of the Guadalquivir River, Córdoba was the Roman and Moorish capital of Spain, and its old quarter, clustered around its famous Mezquita, remains one of the country's grandest and yet most intimate examples of its Moorish heritage. Once a medieval city famed for the peaceful and prosperous coexistence of its three religious cultures—Islamic, Jewish, and Christian—Córdoba is also a perfect analogue for the cultural history of the Iberian Peninsula.

Córdoba today, with its modest population of a little more than 330,000, offers a cultural depth and intensity—a direct legacy from the great emirs, caliphs, philosophers, physicians, poets, and engineers of the days of the caliphate—that far outstrips the city's current commercial and political power. Its artistic and historical treasures begin with the Mezquita-Catedral (mosque-cathedral), as it is generally called, and continue through the winding, whitewashed streets of the Judería (the medieval Jewish quarter); the jasmine-, geranium-, and orange-blossom-filled patios; the Renaissance palaces; and the two dozen churches, convents, and hermitages, built by Moorish artisans directly over former mosques.

GETTING HERE AND AROUND

BIKE TRAVEL

Never designed to support cars, Córdoba's medieval layout is ideal for bicycles, and there's a good network of designated bicycle tracks.

Duribaik. Bicycle rental is available here at reasonable rates (€5 for 3 hours and €7 for 6 hours). English is spoken. ⊠ *Calle Sevilla 13* ☎ *957/788470* ⊕ *www.duribaik.com.*

BUS TRAVEL

Córdoba is easily reached by bus from Granada, Málaga, and Seville. The city has an extensive public bus network with frequent service. Buses usually start running at 6:30 or 7 am and stop around midnight. You can buy 10-trip passes at newsstands and the bus office in Plaza de Colón. A single-trip fare is €1.30.

Córdoba has organized open-top bus tours of the city that can be booked via the tourist office.

Contacts Córdoba. ⊠ *Glorieta de las Tres Culturas* ☎ *957/404040* ⊕ *www. estacionautobusescordoba.es.*

CAR TRAVEL

The city's one-way system can be something of a nightmare to navigate, and it's best to park in one of the signposted lots outside the old quarter.

TAXI TRAVEL

Contacts Radio Taxi. ☎ *957/764444.*

TRAIN TRAVEL

The city's modern train station is the hub for a comprehensive network of regional trains, with regular service to Seville, Málaga, Madrid, and Barcelona. Trains for Granada change at Bobadilla.

Contacts Train Station. ⊠ *Glorieta de las Tres Culturas* ☎ *912/320320.*

VISITOR INFORMATION

Contacts Tourist Office. ⊠ *Pl. de las Tendillas 5, Centro* ☎ *902/201774* ⊕ *www.turismodecordoba.org.*

10

EXPLORING

Córdoba is an easily navigable city, with twisting alleyways that hold surprises around every corner. The main city subdivisions used in this book are the **Judería** (which includes the Mezquita); **Sector Sur,** around the **Torre de la Calahorra** across the river; the area around the **Plaza de la Corredera,** a historic gathering place for everything from horse races to bullfights; and the **Centro Comercial,** from the area around Plaza de las Tendillas to the Iglesia de Santa Marina and the Torre de la Malmuerta. Incidentally, the last neighborhood is much more than a succession of shops and stores. The town's real life, the everyday hustle and bustle, takes place here, and the general atmosphere is very different from that of the tourist center around the Mezquita, with its plethora of souvenir shops. Some of the city's finest Mudejar churches and best taverns, as well as the Palacio de los Marqueses de Viana, are in this pivotal part of town well back from the Guadalquivir waterfront.

Some of the most characteristic and rewarding places to explore in Córdoba are the parish churches and the taverns that inevitably accompany them, where you can taste *fino de Moriles,* a dry, sherrylike wine from the Montilla-Moriles D.O., and *tentempiés* (tapas—literally, "keep you on your feet"). The *iglesias fernandinas* (so called for their construction after Fernando III's conquest of Córdoba) are nearly always built over mosques with stunning horseshoe-arch doorways and Mudejar towers, and taverns tended to spring up around these populous hubs of city life. Examples are the Taberna de San Miguel (aka Casa el Pisto) next to the church of the same name, and the Bar Santa Marina (aka Casa Obispo) next to the Santa Marina Church.

■TIP→ Córdoba's officials frequently change the hours of the city's sights; before visiting an attraction, confirm hours with the tourist office or the sight itself.

Alcázar de los Reyes Cristianos (*Fortress of the Christian Monarchs*). Built by Alfonso XI in 1328, the Alcázar is a Mudejar-style palace with splendid gardens. (The original Moorish Alcázar stood beside the Mezquita, on the site of the present Bishop's Palace.) This is where, in the 15th century, the Catholic Monarchs held court and launched their conquest of Granada. Boabdil was imprisoned here in 1483, and for nearly 300 years the Alcázar served as the Inquisition's base. The most important sights here are the Hall of the Mosaics and a Roman stone sarcophagus from the 2nd or 3rd century. ⊠ *Pl. Campo Santo de los Mártires, Judería* ☎ *957/201716* ☞ *€5* ☉ *Closed Mon.*

Calleja de las Flores. You'd be hard-pressed to find prettier patios than those along this tiny street, a few yards off the northeastern corner of the Mezquita. Patios, many with ceramics, foliage, and iron grilles, are key to Córdoba's architecture, at least in the old quarter, where life is lived behind sturdy white walls—a legacy of the Moors, who honored both the sanctity of the home and the need to shut out the fierce summer sun. Between the first and second week of May—right after the early-May **Cruces de Mayo** (Crosses of May) competition, when neighborhoods compete at setting up elaborate crosses decorated with flowers and plants—Córdoba throws a **Patio Festival,** during which private patios are filled with flowers, opened to the public, and judged in a municipal competition. Córdoba's tourist office publishes an itinerary of the best patios in town (downloadable from *www.turismodecordoba.org*)—note that most are open only in the late afternoon on weekdays but all day on weekends. ⊠ *Córdoba.*

Fodor'sChoice **Madinat Al-Zahra** (*Medina Azahara*). Built in the foothills of the Sierra ★ Morena by Abd ar-Rahman III for his favorite concubine, az-Zahra (the Flower), this once-splendid summer pleasure palace was begun in 936. Historians say it took 10,000 men, 2,600 mules, and 400 camels 25 years to erect this fantasy of 4,300 columns in dazzling pink, green, and white marble and jasper brought from Carthage. A palace, a mosque, luxurious baths, fragrant gardens, fish ponds, an aviary, and a zoo stood on three terraces here, until, in 1013, it was sacked and destroyed by Berber mercenaries. In 1944 the Royal Apartments

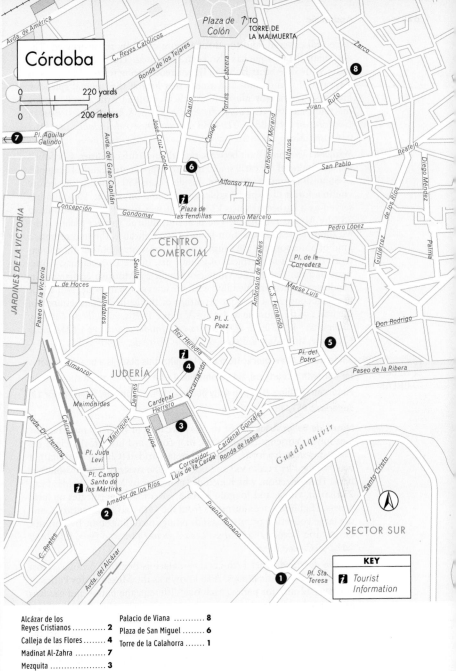

Córdoba

0   220 yards

0   200 meters

KEY

i   Tourist Information

were rediscovered, and the throne room carefully reconstructed. The outline of the mosque has also been excavated. The only covered part is the Salon de Abd ar-Rahman III (currently being restored); the rest is a sprawl of foundations and arches that hint at the original splendor. First visit the nearby museum and then continue with a walk among the ruins. ☒ *Ctra. de Palma del Río, Km 5.5, 8 km (5 miles) west of Córdoba on C431* ☎ *957/104933* ⊕ *www.museosdeandalucia.es* ☜ *€2* ☾ *Closed Mon.*

Fodor'sChoice
★
Mezquita (*Mosque*). Built between the 8th and 10th centuries, Córdoba's mosque is one of the earliest and most transportingly beautiful examples of Spanish Islamic architecture. Inside, some 850 columns rise before you in a forest of jasper, marble, granite, and onyx. The Mezquita has served as a cathedral since 1236, but it was founded as a mosque in 785 by Abd ar-Rahman I. The beautiful **mihrab** (prayer niche) is the Mezquita's greatest jewel. In front of the mihrab is the **maksoureh**, a kind of anteroom for the caliph and his court; its mosaics and plaster-work make it a masterpiece of Islamic art. In the 13th century, Christians had the **Capilla de Villaviciosa** built by Moorish craftsmen, its Mudejar architecture blending with the lines of the mosque. Not so the heavy, incongruous baroque structure of the cathedral, sanctioned in the heart of the mosque by Carlos V in the 1520s. ☒ *Calle de Torrijos, Judería* ☎ *957/470512* ⊕ *mezquita-catedraldecordoba.es* ☜ *Mezquita €10, free Mon.–Sat. 8:30 am–9:30 am; Torre del Alminar €2.*

▌**NEED A BREAK**
Salón de Té. A few blocks from the Mezquita, this place is a beautiful spot for tea, with a courtyard, side rooms filled with cushions, and a shop selling Moroccan clothing. It's open daily noon–10 pm. ☒ *Calle del Buen Pastor 13, Judería* ☎ *957/487984.*

Fodor'sChoice
★
Museo de Bellas Artes. Hard to miss because of its deep-pink facade, Córdoba's Museum of Fine Arts, in a courtyard just off the Plaza del Potro, belongs to a former Hospital de la Caridad (Charity Hospital). It was founded by Ferdinand and Isabella, who twice received Columbus here. The collection, which includes paintings by Murillo, Valdés Leal, Zurbarán, Goya, and Joaquín Sorolla y Bastida, concentrates on local artists. Highlights are altarpieces from the 14th and 15th centuries, and the large collection of prints and drawings including some by Fortuny, Goya, and Sorolla. ☒ *Pl. del Potro 1, San Francisco* ☎ *957/103659* ☜ *€2* ☾ *Closed Mon.*

Palacio de Viana. This 17th-century palace is one of Córdoba's most splendid aristocratic homes. Also known as the **Museo de los Patios**, it contains 12 interior patios, each one different; the patios and gardens are planted with cypresses, orange trees, and myrtles. Inside the building are a carriage museum, a library, embossed leather wall hangings, fili-gree silver, and grand galleries and staircases. As you enter, note that the corner column of the first patio has been removed to allow the entrance of horse-drawn carriages. ☒ *Pl. Don Gomé 2, Centro* ☎ *957/496741* ☜ *From €5* ☾ *Closed Mon.*

Plaza de San Miguel. The square and café terraces around it, and its excel-lent tavern, Taberna San Miguel–Casa El Pisto, form one of the city's finest combinations of art, history, and gastronomy. The San Miguel church has an interesting facade with Romanesque doors built around Mudejar horseshoe arches, and a Mudejar dome inside. ✉ *Centro.*

Torre de la Calahorra. The tower on the far side of the Puente Romano (Roman Bridge), which was restored in 2008, was built in 1369 to guard the entrance to Córdoba. It now houses the **Museo Vivo de Al-Andalus** (Al-Andalus is Arabic for "Land of the West"), with films and audiovisual guides (in English) on Córdoba's history. Climb the narrow staircase to the top of the tower for the view of the Roman bridge and city on the other side of the Guadalquivir. ✉ *Av. de la Confederación, Sector Sur* ☎ *957/293929* 🌐 *www.torrecalahorra.es* 🎫 *€5, includes audio guide.*

WHERE TO EAT

$$ INTERNATIONAL

🍴 **Amaltea.** Satisfying both vegetarians and their meat-eating friends, this organic restaurant includes some meat and fish on the menu. There's a healthy mix of Mexican, Asian, Spanish, and Italian-influenced dishes, including pasta with artichokes, chicken curry with mango and apricots, and couscous. **Known for:** vegetarian food; inviting interior with relaxed vibe; pasta with artichokes. [$] *Average main: €14* ✉ *Ronda de Isasa 10, Centro* ☎ *957/491968* ⏲ *No dinner Sun.; no lunch in Aug.*

$ TAPAS

🍴 **Bar Santos.** This very small, quintessentially Spanish bar, with no seats and numerous photos of matadors and flamenco dancers, seems out of place surrounded by the tourist shops and overshadowed by the Mezquita, but its appearance—and its prices—are part of its charm. Tapas (from €2.50) such as *albóndigas en salsa de almendras* (meatballs in almond sauce) and *bocadillos* (sandwiches that are literally "little mouthfuls") are excellent in quality and value, while the *tortilla de patata* (potato omelet) is renowned and celebrated both for its taste and its heroic thickness. **Known for:** tortilla de patata; inexpensive tapas. [$] *Average main: €6* ✉ *Calle Magistral González Francés 3, Judería* ☎ *957/488975.*

$$$ SPANISH Fodor's Choice ★

🍴 **Bodegas Campos.** A block east of the Plaza del Potro, this traditional old bodega with high-quality service is the epitome of all that's great about Andalusian cuisine. The dining rooms are in barrel-heavy rustic rooms and leafy traditional patios (take a look at some of the signed barrels—you may recognize a name or two, such as the former U.K. prime minister Tony Blair). **Known for:** bodega setting; regional dishes. [$] *Average main: €20* ✉ *Calle Los Lineros 32, San Pedro* ☎ *957/497500* 🌐 *www.bodegascampos.com* ⏲ *No dinner Sun.*

$$ ECLECTIC

🍴 **Casa Mazal.** In the heart of the Judería, this pretty little restaurant serves a modern interpretation of Sephardic cuisine, with organic dishes that are more exotic than the usual Andalusian fare. The many vegetarian options include *berenjena timbal* (eggplant and tomato "pie"), and the *costillas de cordero con pasas al aroma de la miel* (lamb chops with raisins and honey) and *bacalao confitado a la naranja* (cod with orange) are delicious. **Known for:** traditional Sephardic cuisine; romantic ambience; vegetarian dishes. [$] *Average main: €15* ✉ *Calle Tomás Conde 3, Judería* ☎ *957/941888* 💳 *No credit cards.*

$$$

SPANISH

✕ **Casa Pepe de la Judería.** Geared toward a tourist clientele, this place is always packed, noisy, and fun. Antiques and some wonderful old oil paintings fill this three-floor labyrinth of rooms just around the corner from the mosque, near the Judería. **Known for:** traditional Andalusian food; croquetas de jamón; live music on the roof terrace in summer. $ *Average main: €20* ⊠ *Calle Romero 1, off Deanes, Judería* ☎ *957/200744.*

$$$

SPANISH

Fodor'sChoice

★

✕ **El Caballo Rojo.** This is one of the most famous traditional restaurants in Andalusia, frequented by royalty and society folk. The interior resembles a cool, leafy Andalusian patio, and the dining room is furnished with stained glass and dark wood; the upstairs terrace overlooks the Mezquita. **Known for:** fine traditional dining; rabo de toro; excellent service. $ *Average main: €22* ⊠ *Calle Cardenal Herrero 28, Judería* ☎ *957/475375* ⊕ *www.elcaballorojo.com.*

$$$$

SPANISH

Fodor'sChoice

★

✕ **El Choco.** The city's most exciting restaurant, which has renewed its Michelin star annually since 2012, El Choco has renowned chef Kisko Garcia at the helm whipping up innovative dishes with a twist on traditional favorites, including *guiso con choco en amarillo* (cuttlefish stew) and *pato asado lentamente* (slow-cooked duck). Two tasting menus are available (€90 for 14 dishes and €120 for 17 dishes), both containing plenty of creative surprises. **Known for:** creative Andalusian cooking; good value Michelin-star tasting menu; cuttlefish stew. $ *Average main: €90* ⊠ *Compositor Serrano Lucena 14, Centro* ☎ *957/264863* ⊕ *www.restaurantechoco.es* ☾ *Closed Mon. and mid-July–mid-Sept.*

$$$

SPANISH

✕ **El Churrasco.** The name suggests grilled meat, but this restaurant in the heart of the Judería serves much more than that. In the colorful bar try tapas (from €3) such as the *berenjenas crujientes con salmorejo* (crispy fried eggplant slices with thick gazpacho). **Known for:** grilled meat; tapas; alfresco dining. $ *Average main: €20* ⊠ *Calle Romero 16, Judería* ☎ *957/290819* ☾ *Closed Aug.*

$$

SPANISH

✕ **La Regadera.** It feels as if you could be outside at this bright venue on the river whose fresh interior comes with miniature wall gardens and lots of watering cans (*regaderas*)—there's even a fresh herb garden in the middle. Local produce takes center stage on the menu where you'll find a mix of traditional and modern dishes including house specials such as slow-cooked lamb, *tartar de atún rojo* (red tuna tartare), and violet ice cream with strawberries. **Known for:** fresh, innovative cuisine; gardenlike interior; tuna tartare. $ *Average main: €13* ⊠ *Ronda de Isasa 10, Judería* ☎ *957/101400* ⊕ *www.regadera.es* ☾ *Closed Mon.*

$$

SPANISH

✕ **La Tinaja.** On the river to the east of the city, this bodega-bar has kept its original 18th-century-house layout, which means that you can eat in different rooms as well as outside on the pleasant terrace. The food is traditional, with an emphasis on local produce and Córdoba staples such as *mazamorra con atún rojo ahumado* (traditional almond soup with smoked tuna) and *cardos con gambas y almejas* (giant artichokes with shrimp and clams) as well as oxtail and salmorejo. **Known for:** grilled meat; riverside terrace; homemade foie gras. $ *Average main: €13* ⊠ *Paseo de la Ribera 12, Centro* ☎ *957/047998* ⊕ *latinajadecordoba.com.*

A typical Córdoba patio, filled with flowers

$ TAPAS 🍴 **Taberna de San Miguel.** Just a few minutes' walk from the Plaza de las Tendillas and opposite the lovely San Miguel Church, this popular tapas spot—also known as the Casa el Pisto (Ratatouille House)—was established in 1880. You can choose to squeeze in at the bar and dine on tapas (€2.50) or spread out a little more on the patio decked with ceramics and bullfighting memorabilia, where half and full portions are served. **Known for:** tapas, including pisto; historic ambience; patio with bullfighting memorabilia. [$] *Average main: €10* ✉ *Pl. San Miguel 1, Centro* ☎ *957/470166* 🌐 *www.casaelpisto.com* 💳 *No credit cards* 🕒 *Closed Sun., Aug.*

10

$ TAPAS 🍴 **Taberna Sociedad de Plateros.** On a narrow side street just steps away from the Plaza del Potro, this delightful spot dates to the 17th century. One of the city's most historic inns, it has a large patio that adjoins a traditional marble bar where locals meet. **Known for:** tapas; home-style cooking; local haunt. [$] *Average main: €8* ✉ *Calle San Francisco 6, Plaza de la Corredera* ☎ *957/470042* 🕒 *Closed Mon. Sept.–June, and Sun. in July and Aug.*

WHERE TO STAY

$$ B&B/INN 🏨 **Casa de los Azulejos.** This 17th-century house still has original details like the majestic vaulted ceilings and, with the use of stunning azulejos—hence the name—it mixes Andalusian and Latin American influences. **Pros:** interesting architecture; generous breakfast buffet; tropical central patio. **Cons:** hyperbusy interior design; limited privacy; plunge pool is only open in summer. [$] *Rooms from: €90* ✉ *Calle Fernando*

Colón 5, Centro ☎ 957/470000 🌐 www.casadelosazulejos.com 🛏 9 rooms 🍴 Free Breakfast.

$$$$ HOTEL Fodor's Choice ★ 🏨 **Hospes Palacio del Bailío.** One of the city's top lodging options, this tastefully renovated 17th-century mansion is built over the ruins of a Roman house (visible beneath glass floors) in the historic center of town. **Pros:** dazzling interiors; impeccable comforts; central location. **Cons:** not easy to access by car; pricey. [$] *Rooms from: €285 ✉ Calle Ramírez de las Casas Deza 10–12, Plaza de la Corredera ☎ 957/498993 🌐 www.hospes.es 🛏 53 rooms 🍴 No meals.*

$$$$ HOTEL Fodor's Choice ★ 🏨 **Hotel Balcón de Córdoba.** Located in a tastefully restored 17th-century convent, this boutique hotel has spacious, quiet rooms, and the Mezquita is almost within arm's reach from the rooftop terrace. **Pros:** central location; historic building; rooftop views of the Mezquita. **Cons:** difficult to access by car; very quiet; small breakfast area. [$] *Rooms from: €240 ✉ Calle Encarnación 8 ☎ 957/498478 🌐 www.balcondecordoba.com 🛏 10 rooms 🍴 Free Breakfast.*

$ HOTEL 🏨 **Hotel Maestre.** Around the corner from the Plaza del Potro, this is an affordable hotel in which Castilian-style furniture, gleaming marble, and high-quality oil paintings add elegance to excellent value. **Pros:** good location; great value; helpful reception staff. **Cons:** no elevator and lots of steps; ancient plumbing; could be too basic for some. [$] *Rooms from: €58 ✉ Calle Romero Barros 4–6, San Pedro ☎ 957/472410 🌐 www.hotelmaestre.com 🛏 26 rooms 🍴 No meals.*

$$$ B&B/INN Fodor's Choice ★ 🏨 **La Llave de la Judería.** This small hotel, occupying a collection of houses just a stone's throw from the Mezquita, combines enchanting antique furnishings with modern amenities, but its greatest asset is its exceptionally helpful staff. **Pros:** beautiful interiors; rooms are equipped with computers; close to the Mezquita. **Cons:** rooms facing street can be noisy; direct car access is difficult; dark reception area. [$] *Rooms from: €150 ✉ Calle Romero 38, Judería ☎ 957/294808 🌐 www.lallavedelajuderia.es 💳 No credit cards 🛏 9 rooms 🍴 Free Breakfast.*

$$$ HOTEL 🏨 **NH Collection Amistad Córdoba.** Two 18th-century mansions overlooking Plaza de Maimónides in the heart of the Judería have been melded into a modern business hotel with a cobblestone Mudejar courtyard, carved-wood ceilings, and a plush lounge. **Pros:** pleasant and efficient service; large rooms; central location. **Cons:** parking is difficult; main access via steep steps with no ramp; a little impersonal. [$] *Rooms from: €150 ✉ Pl. de Maimónides 3, Judería ☎ 957/420335 🌐 www.nh-hoteles.com 🛏 108 rooms 🍴 No meals.*

$$ HOTEL 🏨 **Viento 10.** Tucked away to the east of the old quarter, but within just 10 minutes' walk of the Mezquita is a quiet, romantic haven, once part of the 17th-century Sacred Martyrs Hospital. **Pros:** quiet location; pillow menu; Jacuzzi and sauna. **Cons:** some walking distance to the main monuments; a little plain; not easy to find. [$] *Rooms from: €100 ✉ Calle Ronquillo Briceño 10, San Pedro ☎ 957/764960 🌐 www.hotelviento10.es 💳 No credit cards ⏲ Closed Jan, and 2 wks in Aug. 🛏 8 rooms 🍴 No meals.*

NIGHTLIFE AND PERFORMING ARTS

NIGHTLIFE

Córdoba locals hang out mostly in the areas of Ciudad Jardín (the old university area), Plaza de las Tendillas, and the Avenida Gran Capitán.

Bodega Guzman. For some traditional tipple, check out this atmospheric bodega near the old synagogue. Its sherries are served straight from the barrel in a room that doubles as a bullfighting museum. ⊠ *Calle de los Judios 6, Judería.*

Café Málaga. A block from Plaza de las Tendillas, this is a laid-back hangout for jazz and blues aficionados. There's live music most days and occasional flamenco nights. ⊠ *Calle Málaga 3, Centro* ☎ *957/474107.*

PERFORMING ARTS

FLAMENCO

Tablao Cardenal. Córdoba's most famous flamenco club offers performances by established artists on a pleasant open-air patio. Admission is €23 (including a drink) and the 90-minute shows take place Monday–Thursday at 10 pm and on Friday and Saturday at 10:30 pm. ⊠ *Calle Buen Pastor 2, Judería* ☎ *619/217922.*

SHOPPING

Córdoba's main shopping district is around Avenida Gran Capitán, Ronda de los Tejares, and the streets leading away from Plaza Tendillas.

Meryan. This is one of Córdoba's best workshops for embossed leather. ⊠ *Calleja de las Flores 2* ☎ *957/475902* ⊕ *www.meryancor.com.*

Fodor'sChoice ★ **Zoco.** Córdoba's artisans have workshops and sell their crafts in the Zoco, open daily 10–8 (workshops weekdays 10–2 and 5–8, weekends 11–2). ⊠ *Calle Judíos, opposite synagogue, Judería* ☎ *957/290575.*

SIDE TRIPS FROM CÓRDOBA

10

If you have time to go beyond Córdoba and have already seen the Medina Azahara palace ruins, head south to the wine country around Montilla and the Subbética mountain range, a cluster of small towns virtually unknown to travelers.

The entire Subbética region is protected as a natural park, and the mountains, canyons, and wooded valleys are stunning. You'll need a car to explore, though, and in some parts, the roads are rather rough. To reach these enticing towns in *la campiña* (the countryside), take the low road (A318) through Montilla, cutting north to Baena via Zuheros, or take the high road (A307) through Espejo and Baena, cutting south through Cabra.

For park information or hiking advice, contact the **Mancomunidad de la Subbética** (⊠ *Ctra. Carcabuey–Zagrilla, Km 5.75, Carcabuey* ☎ *957/704106* ⊕ *www.turismodelasubbetica.es*).

You can also pick up information, including a pack of maps titled *Rutas Senderistas de la Subbética,* from any local tourist office. The handy cards detail 12 walks with sketched maps.

Southern Córdoba is also the province's main olive-producing region, with the town of **Lucena** at its center. If you follow the Ruta del Aceite (Olive Oil Route), you'll pass some of the province's most picturesque villages. In Lucena is the Torre del Moral, where Granada's last Nasrid ruler, Boabdil, was imprisoned in 1483 after launching an unsuccessful attack on the Christians;

> **SWEET WINE**
>
> Montilla's grapes contain so much sugar (transformed into alcohol during fermentation) that they are not fortified with the addition of extra alcohol. For this reason, the locals claim that Montilla wines do not give you a hangover.

and the Parroquia de San Mateo, a small but remarkable Renaissance-Gothic cathedral. Furniture and brass and copper pots are made in the town. Southeast of Lucena, the C334 crosses the **Embalse de Iznájar** (Iznájar Reservoir) amid spectacular scenery. On the C334, halfway between Lucena and the reservoir, in **Rute,** you can sample the potent *anís* (anise) liqueur for which this small, whitewashed town is famous.

MONTILLA

46 km (28 miles) south of Córdoba.

Heading south from Córdoba toward Málaga, you'll pass through hills ablaze with sunflowers in early summer before you reach the vineyards of the Montilla-Moriles D.O. Every fall, 47,000 acres' worth of Pedro Ximénez grapes are crushed here to produce the region's rich Montilla wines, which are similar to sherry. Montilla-Moriles has also developed a young white wine similar to Portugal's Vinho Verde.

GETTING HERE AND AROUND

Regular buses connect Montilla with Córdoba and Granada, but to make the most of your time, visit Montilla en route by car to either city. Montilla's small size makes it an easy pedestrian destination. Allow half a day to visit.

VISITOR INFORMATION

Contacts Montilla. ⊠ *Calle Castillo s/n* ☎ *957/652354* ⊕ *www.montillaturismo.es.*

EXPLORING

Bodegas Alvear. Founded in 1729, this bodega in the center of town is Montilla's oldest. Besides being informative, the fun tour and wine tasting give you the chance to buy a bottle or two of Alvear's tasty version of the sweet Pedro Ximénez aged wine. ■TIP➔ **Phone ahead to book a tour in English.** ⊠ *Calle María Auxiliadora 1* ☎ *957/652939* ⊕ *www.alvear.es* 🎟 *From €9* ☉ *Closed Sun.*

WHERE TO EAT

$$
SPANISH
✕ **Las Camachas.** The best-known restaurant in southern Córdoba Province is in an Andalusian-style hacienda outside Montilla—near the main road toward Málaga. Start with tapas in the attractive bar, then move on to one of the six dining rooms, where regional specialties include *alcachofas al Montilla* (artichokes braised in Montilla wine), salmorejo, *perdiz a la campiña* (country-style partridge), and *pierna de cordero*

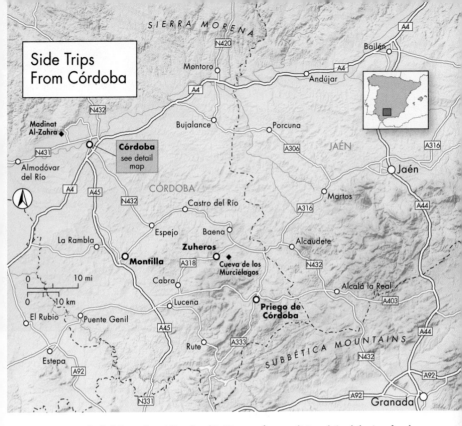

Side Trips
From Córdoba

lechal (leg of suckling lamb). **Known for:** traditional Andalusian food; use of Montilla wine; tapas bar. $ *Average main: €15* ⊠ *Av. Europa 3* ☎ *957/650004.*

10

SHOPPING

On the outskirts of town, coopers' shops produce barrels of various sizes, some small enough to serve as creative souvenirs.

Tonelería J. L. Rodríguez. On Montilla's main road, it is worth stopping here not just to buy barrels and local wines, but also to pop in the back and see the barrels being made. ⊠ *Ctra. Córdoba–Málaga (N331), Km 43.3* ☎ *957/650563* ⊕ *www.toneleriajlrodriguez.com.*

ZUHEROS

80 km (50 miles) southeast of Córdoba.

Zuheros, at the northern edge of the Subbética mountain range and at an altitude of 2,040 feet, is one of the most attractive villages in the province of Córdoba. From the road up, it's hidden behind a dominating rock face topped by the dramatic ruins of a castle built by the Moors over a Roman castle. There's an expansive view back over the valley from here. Next to the castle is the Iglesia de Santa María, built over a mosque. The base of the minaret is the foundation for the bell tower.

Olive groves near Priego de Córdoba

GETTING HERE AND AROUND
Several daily buses connect Zuheros with Seville and Córdoba, although the schedule isn't ideal for sightseeing. Driving is the best option for exploring the surrounding area, including the Cueva de los Murciélagos (Cave of the Bats). Zuheros is compact and easy to get around, although there's a steep climb from the car park to the village.

EXPLORING
Cueva de los Murciélagos (*Cave of the Bats*). Some 4 km (2½ miles) above Zuheros along a winding road, the Cueva de los Murciélagos runs for about 2 km (1 mile), although only about half of that expanse is open to the public. The main attractions are the wall paintings dating to the Neolithic Age (6000–3000 BC) and Chalcolithic Age (3000–2000 BC), but excavations have indicated that the cave was inhabited as far back as 35,000 years ago. Items from the Copper and Bronze ages, as well as from the Roman period and the Middle Ages, have also been found here. Visits are by guided tour only and must be booked in advance, by phone or email (*turismo@zuheros.es*). ✉ *CV247, off Calle Santo* ☎ *957/694545 Tues.–Fri. 10–1:30* 🎟 *€6* ⏱ *Closed Mon.*

Museo Histórico-Arqueológico Municipal. This museum displays archaeological remains found in local caves and elsewhere; some date back to the Middle Paleolithic period some 35,000 years ago. You can also visit the remains of the Renaissance rooms in the castle, across the road, included in the admission. Visits to the museum and castle are by guided tour only. ✉ *Pl. de la Paz 2* ☎ *957/694545* 🎟 *€2* ⏱ *Closed Mon.*

WHERE TO STAY

$
B&B/INN
⊞ **Zuhayra.** Fresh from a refurbishment in 2017, this small hotel on a narrow street has comfortable rooms painted a sunny yellow with views over the village rooftops to the valley below. **Pros:** cozy public spaces; stunning vistas; best dining in the village. **Cons:** plain decor; pool is small. $ *Rooms from: €60* ⊠ *Calle Mirador 10* ☎ *957/694693* ⊕ *www.zercahoteles.com* ⇆ *18 rooms* ⏍ *Free Breakfast.*

PRIEGO DE CÓRDOBA

103 km (64 miles) southeast of Córdoba, 25 km (15 miles) southeast of Zuheros.

Fodor'sChoice
★
The jewel of Córdoba's countryside is Priego de Córdoba, a town of 23,500 inhabitants at the foot of Mt. Tinosa. Wander down Calle del Río, opposite the town hall, to see 18th-century mansions, once the homes of silk merchants. At the end of the street is the Fuente del Rey (King's Fountain), with some 130 water jets, built in 1803. Don't miss the lavish baroque churches of La Asunción and La Aurora or the Barrio de la Villa, an old Moorish quarter with a maze of narrow streets of white-walled buildings.

GETTING HERE AND AROUND

Priego has reasonable bus service from Córdoba (2½ hours) and Granada (1½ hours), although your best bet is to visit by car en route to either of these cities. Once there, it's perfect for pedestrian exploration.

VISITOR INFORMATION

Contacts Priego de Córdoba. ⊠ *Pl. de la Constitución 3* ☎ *957/700625* ⊕ *www.turismodepriego.com.*

WHERE TO EAT AND STAY

$$
SPANISH
⨯ **Balcón del Adarve.** This local favorite sits at the end of the town's Paseo and enjoys commanding views from the terrace of the river ravine and surrounding countryside. The interior dining room has a cozy townhouse ambience with heavy wood furniture, and there's outdoor dining as well. **Known for:** countryside views; rabo de toro; grilled meat. $ *Average main: €16* ⊠ *Paseo de Colombia 36* ☎ *957/547075* ⊕ *www.balcondeladarve.com* ⊙ *Closed Mon.*

$$
HOTEL
⊞ **Hotel Museo La Patria Chica.** This charming hotel opened in 2017, housed in a fully restored 19th-century mansion, and is complete with a pretty interior patio and peaceful private garden. **Pros:** central location; period furnishings; pool and restaurant on-site. **Cons:** quiet; slightly out of the town center; some rooms face the street. $ *Rooms from: €100* ⊠ *Carrera de las Monjas 47* ☎ *957/058383* ⊕ *www.hotelpatriachica.com* ⇆ *15 rooms* ⏍ *Free Breakfast.*

$
B&B/INN
⊞ **La Posada Real.** In the heart of Priego's Barrio de la Villa, this restored town house has two sections, each with geranium-decked balconies and typical Andalusian touches. **Pros:** friendly owner; traditional town house; center of town. **Cons:** rooms on the small side; car access difficult; a little basic. $ *Rooms from: €50* ⊠ *Calle Real 14* ☎ *957/541910* ⊕ *www.laposadareal.com* ⇆ *7 rooms* ⏍ *No meals.*

10

JAÉN PROVINCE

Jaén is dominated by its Alcázar. To the northeast are the olive-producing towns of Baeza and Úbeda. Cazorla, the gateway to the Parque Natural Sierra de Cazorla Segura y Las Villas, lies beyond.

JAÉN

107 km (64 miles) southeast of Córdoba, 93 km (58 miles) north of Granada.

Nestled in the foothills of the Sierra de Jabalcuz, Jaén is surrounded by towering peaks and olive-clad hills. The modern part of town holds little interest for travelers these days, but the old town is an atmospheric jumble of narrow cobblestone streets hugging the mountainside. Jaén's grand parador, in the city's hilltop castle, is a great reason to stop here.

The Arabs called this land Geen (Route of the Caravans) because it formed a crossroad between Castile and Andalusia. Captured from the Moors by Ferdinand III in 1246, Jaén became a frontier province, the site of many a skirmish and battle over the following 200 years between the Moors of Granada and Christians from the north and west.

GETTING HERE AND AROUND

You can reach Jaén by bus from Granada, Madrid, and Málaga (*ALSA* ☎ *902/422242* ⊕ *www.alsa.es*), and also by train from Granada. Jaén is compact and all sights are easy to visit on foot, with the exception of the castle, 3 km (2 miles) from the center and a steep climb—if you can't face the ascent, take a taxi.

VISITOR INFORMATION

Contacts Jaén. ⊠ *Calle Maestra 8* ☎ *953/190455* ⊕ *www.turjaen.org.*

EXPLORING

Fodor's Choice ★ **Baños Árabes.** Explore the narrow alleys of old Jaén as you walk from the cathedral to the Baños Árabes (Arab Baths), which once belonged to Ali, a Moorish king of Jaén, and probably date to the 11th century. In 1592, a viceroy of Peru named Fernando de Torres y Portugal built himself a mansion, the **Palacio de Villardompardo,** right over the baths, so it took years of painstaking excavation to restore them to their original form. The palace contains a fascinating, albeit small, museum of folk crafts and a larger museum devoted to native art. ⊠ *Palacio de Villardompardo, Pl. Luisa de Marillac* ☎ *953/248068* ⊠ *Free* ☺ *Closed Mon.*

Basílica Menor de San Ildefonso (*Smaller Basilica of Saint Ildefonso*). Set on the square and in the district of the same name, this large church is one of Jaén's treasures. Built mainly in the Gothic style with baroque details, the magnificent gilded altar is the highlight. ⊠ *Pl. de San Ildefonso* ☎ *953/190346* ⊠ *Free.*

Fodor's Choice ★ **Castillo de Santa Catalina.** This castle, perched on a rocky crag 400 yards above the center of town, is Jaén's star monument. It may have originated as a tower built by Hannibal, but whatever its origins, the site was fortified continuously over the centuries. The Nasrid king Alhamar, builder of Granada's Alhambra, constructed an alcázar here, but Ferdinand III captured it from him in 1246 on the feast day of Santa Catalina

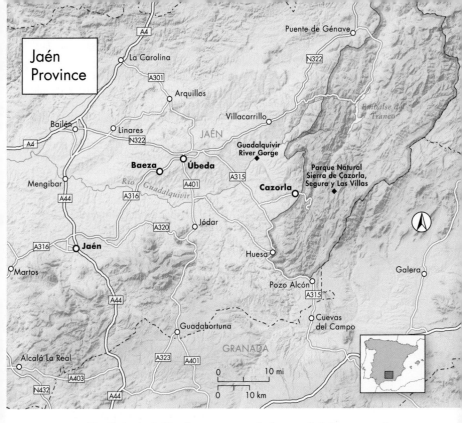

Jaén
Province

(St. Catherine). Catalina consequently became Jaén's patron saint, so when the Christians built a castle and chapel here, they dedicated both to her. ⊠ *Ctra. del Castillo de Santa Catalina* ☎ 953/120733 💌 €4.

Jaén Cathedral. Looming above the modest buildings around it, the cathedral was begun in 1492 on the site of a former mosque and took almost 300 years to build. Its chief architect was Andrés de Vandelvira (1509–75)—many more of his buildings can be seen in Úbeda and Baeza. The ornate facade was sculpted by Pedro Roldán, and the figures on top of the columns include San Fernando (Ferdinand III) and the four evangelists. The cathedral's most treasured relic is the **Santo Rostro** (Holy Face), the cloth with which, according to tradition, St. Veronica cleansed Christ's face on the way to Calvary, leaving his image imprinted on the fabric. The *rostro* (face) is displayed every Friday 10:30–noon and 5–6. In the underground **museum,** look for the paintings *San Lorenzo,* by Martínez Montañés; the *Immaculate Conception,* by Alonso Cano; and a Calvary scene by Jácobo Florentino. ⊠ *Pl. Santa María* ☎ 953/241448 💌 €5.

Museo de Jaén. This museum is divided into two sections within the rooms of a 1547 mansion: archaeological finds and fine art. The Bronze Age and Roman era are particularly well represented and the patio showcases the facade of the erstwhile Church of San Miguel. The fine-arts section has a room full of Goya lithographs. ✉ *Paseo de la Estación 29* ☎ *953/101366* 🎫 *€2* 🕒 *Closed Mon.*

Museo Íbero. The long-awaited Iberian Museum opened in late 2017 to much acclaim in a striking modern building on the site of the old prison that once housed Franco's political prisoners. It has one of the best collections of Iberian (pre-Roman, from the 6th to 1st century BC) artifacts in Spain including 20 life-size Iberian sculptures discovered by chance near the village of Porcuna in 1975. The wolf's head is particularly striking. Exhibitions portray the Iberian lifestyle and culture and showcase some of the 3,500 pieces in the immense collection. ✉ *Paseo de la Estación 41* ☎ *953/001692* 🎫 *€2* 🕒 *Closed Mon.*

WHERE TO EAT AND STAY

$$$ SPANISH

🍴 **Casa Antonio.** Exquisite Andalusian food with a contemporary twist is served at this somber yet elegant restaurant with three small dining rooms, all with cherrywood-paneled walls and dramatic contemporary artwork. Try the *alcachofas con vieira* (artichokes with scallops) or *cochinillo lechal con compota de manzana y romero* (suckling pig with apple and rosemary sauce). **Known for:** fresh local produce; suckling pig; artichokes with scallops. [$] *Average main: €18* ✉ *Calle Fermín Palma 3* ☎ *953/270262* 🕒 *Closed Mon., and Aug.*

$$$ SPANISH

🍴 **Taberna El Zurito.** Locals and visitors rave about this tiny bar less than 10 minutes' walk north of the cathedral. It's one of the oldest bars in the city (established in 1912), has just two tables plus bar space, and is crammed with Jaén memorabilia—but the homemade dishes more than make up for the lack of elbow room. **Known for:** authentic Jaén experience; cozy space; rabo de toro. [$] *Average main: €18* ✉ *Calle Correa Weglison 6* ☎ *605/988016* 💳 *No credit cards* 🕒 *Closed Sun.*

$$$ HOTEL Fodor's Choice ★

🏨 **Parador de Jaén.** Built amid the mountaintop towers of the Castillo de Santa Catalina, this 13th-century castle is one of the showpieces of the parador chain and a good reason to visit Jaén. **Pros:** architectural grandeur; panoramic views; historic and atmospheric building. **Cons:** outside Jaén; long walk down to sights (and steep climb up again); could be too grandiose for some. [$] *Rooms from: €170* ✉ *Calle Castillo de Santa Catalina* ☎ *953/230000* 🌐 *www.parador.es* 🛏 *45 rooms* 🍽 *No meals.*

BAEZA

48 km (30 miles) northeast of Jaén on N321.

Fodor's Choice ★

The historic town of Baeza, nestled between hills and olive groves, is one of the best-preserved old towns in Spain. Founded by the Romans, it later housed the Visigoths and became the capital of a Moorish *taifa,* one of some two dozen mini-kingdoms formed after the Ummayad Caliphate was subdivided in 1031. Ferdinand III captured Baeza in 1227, and for the next 200 years it stood on the frontier of the Moorish kingdom of Granada. In the 16th and 17th centuries, local nobles gave the city a wealth of Renaissance palaces.

GETTING HERE AND AROUND

Frequent buses (16 per day on weekdays, 12 per day on weekends; *ALSA* ☎ *902/422242* ⊕ *www.alsa.es*) connect Baeza with Jaén and Úbeda, although a private car is the best option given the remoteness of the town and that you may want to explore nearby Úbeda on the same day. Baeza is small and flat, and with its sights clustered round the very center it's very easy to explore on foot.

TOURS

Semer Guided Tours. Two-hour guided tours around Baeza (in English, minimum two people, Tuesday–Sunday) recount the history, culture, and traditions of the town. Tours of Úbeda are also available, with a discount for combined tours of both towns. ⊠ *Calle Rastro de la Carniceria 3* ☎ *953/757916* ⊕ *www.semerturismo.com* ☞ *From €9.*

VISITOR INFORMATION

Contacts Baeza. ⊠ *Pl. del Pópulo* ☎ *953/779982* ⊕ *www.ubedaybaezaturismo.com.*

EXPLORING

Ayuntamiento (*Town Hall*). Baeza's Ayuntamiento was designed by cathedral master Andrés de Vandelvira. The facade is ornately decorated with a mix of religious and pagan imagery; look between the balconies for the coats of arms of Felipe II, the city of Baeza, and the magistrate Juan de Borja. Ask at the tourist office about visits to the *salón de plenos,* a meeting hall with painted, carved woodwork. ⊠ *Pl. Cardenal Benavides.*

Baeza Cathedral. Originally begun by Ferdinand III on the site of a former mosque, the cathedral was largely rebuilt by Andrés de Vandelvira, architect of Jaén's cathedral, between 1570 and 1593, though the west front has architectural influences from an earlier period. A fine 14th-century rose window crowns the 13th-century Puerta de la Luna (Moon Door). Don't miss the baroque silver monstrance (a vessel in which the consecrated Host is exposed for the adoration of the faithful), which is carried in Baeza's Corpus Christi processions—the piece is kept in a concealed niche behind a painting, but you can see it in all its splendor by putting a coin in a slot to reveal the hiding place. Next to the monstrance is the entrance to the clock tower, where a small donation and a narrow spiral staircase take you to one of the best views of Baeza. The remains of the original mosque are in the cathedral's Gothic cloisters. ⊠ *Pl. de Santa María* ☎ *953/744157* 🎫 *€4.*

Museo de Baeza. Tucked away behind the tourist office, the Baeza Museum is in itself a museum piece. Housed in a 15th-century noble palace, the facade and interiors are home to an interesting display of Baeza's history, from Roman remains to more recent religious paintings. ⊠ *Calle Casas Nuevas* ☎ *953/741582* 🎫 *€2* ☽ *Closed Mon.*

WHERE TO EAT AND STAY

$$$ ✕ **Palacio de Gallego.** With a very special location next to the cathedral,
SPANISH this is one of the best restaurants in town, known most of all for its barbecue dishes. Red tuna steak stars on the *asados* menu (roasted dishes) but you can also try meat, including game, as well as *almejas* (clams).

10

Known for: barbecue; tuna steak; outdoor terrace. $ *Average main: €20* ⊠ *Calle Santa Catalina* ☎ *667/760184* ⊘ *Closed Mon. and Tues.*

$$$ ⚟ **Hotel Puerta de la Luna.** This beautifully restored 17th-century pal-
HOTEL ace, one of Baeza's finest accommodation options, is centered on two
Fodor'sChoice patios—one with a pond and views of the cathedral tower and the other
★ with a small pool. **Pros:** stunning architecture; central location; good
food on-site. **Cons:** difficult to find; basic breakfast; quiet. $ *Rooms
from: €170* ⊠ *Calle Canónigo Melgares Raya 7* ☎ *953/747019* ⊕ *www.
hotelpuertadelaluna.com* ⤳ *44 rooms* ⦿ *No meals.*

ÚBEDA

9 km (5½ miles) northeast of Baeza on N321.

Fodor'sChoice Úbeda's *casco antiguo* (old town) is one of the most outstanding
★ enclaves of 16th-century architecture in Spain. It's a stunning surprise
in the heart of Jaén's olive groves, set in the shadow of the wild Sierra
de Cazorla mountain range. For crafts enthusiasts, this is Andalusia's
capital for many kinds of artisan goods. Follow signs to the Zona
Monumental, where there are countless Renaissance palaces and stately
mansions, though most are closed to the public.

GETTING HERE AND AROUND
Frequent buses (16 weekdays, 12 weekends; *ALSA* ☎ *902/422242*
⊕ *www.alsa.es*) connect Úbeda with Jaén and Baeza, although a private
car is the best option given the remoteness of the town and that you
may want to explore nearby Baeza in the same day. Úbeda's sights are
all within easy reach of the center so exploring on foot is easy.

TOURS
Semer Guided Tours. Two-hour guided tours around Úbeda (in English,
minimum two people, Tuesday–Sunday) recount the history, culture,
and traditions of the town. Tours of Baeza are also available, with a
discount on combined tours of both towns. ⊠ *Calle Juan Montilla 3*
☎ *953/757916* ⊕ *www.semerturismo.com* ↝ *From €11.*

VISITOR INFORMATION
Contacts Úbeda. ⊠ *Pl. de Andalucía 5* ☎ *953/779204* ⊕ *www.turismodeubeda.
com.*

EXPLORING
Ayuntamiento Antiguo (*Old Town Hall*). Begun in the early 16th century
but restored as a beautiful arcaded baroque palace in 1680, the for-
mer town hall is now a conservatory of music. From the hall's upper
balcony, the town council watched celebrations and autos-da-fé ("acts
of faith"—executions of heretics sentenced by the Inquisition) in the
square below. You can't enter the town hall, but on the north side
you can visit the 13th-century church of San Pablo, with an Isabel-
line south portal. ⊠ *Pl. Primero de Mayo, off Calle María de Molina*
☎ *953/750637* ▱ *Church free* ⊘ *Closed Mon.*

Hospital de Santiago. Sometimes jokingly called the Escorial of Anda-
lusia (in allusion to Felipe II's monolithic palace and monastery out-
side Madrid), this is a huge, angular building in the modern section of

town, and yet another one of Vandelvira's masterpieces in Úbeda. The plain facade is adorned with ceramic medallions, and over the main entrance is a carving of Santiago Matamoros (St. James the Moorslayer) in his traditional horseback pose. Inside are an arcaded patio and a grand staircase. Now a cultural center, it holds some of the events at the International Spring Dance and Music Festival. ✉ *Av. Cristo Rey* ☎ *953/750842* 🎟 *Free* 🕒 *Closed Sun. in July, and weekends in Aug.*

Sacra Capilla de El Salvador. The Plaza Vázquez de Molina, in the heart of the casco antiguo, is the site of this building, which is photographed so often that it's become the city's unofficial symbol. It was built by Vandelvira, but he based his design on some 1536 plans by Diego de Siloé, architect of Granada's cathedral. Considered one of the masterpieces of Spanish Renaissance religious art, the chapel was sacked in the frenzy of church burnings at the outbreak of the civil war, but it retains its ornate western facade and altarpiece, which has a rare Berruguete sculpture. ✉ *Pl. Vázquez de Molina* ☎ *609/279905* 🎟 *€5 (free Mon.–Sat. 9:30–10, Sun. 6–7).*

Fodor's Choice ★ **Sinagoga del Agua.** This 13th-century synagogue counts among Úbeda's most amazing discoveries. Entirely underground and known as the Water Synagogue for the wells and natural spring under the Mikveh, it comprises seven areas open to visitors, including the main area of worship, Mikvah, Women's Gallery, and rabbi's quarters. During summer solstice the sun's rays illuminate the stairway, providing the only natural light in the synagogue. ✉ *Calle Roque Rosas* ☎ *953/758150* 🌐 *www.sinagogadelagua.com* 🎟 *€5.*

WHERE TO EAT

$$$ SPANISH 🍴 **Asador de Santiago.** At this adventurous restaurant just off the main street, the chef prepares both Spanish classics, like white shrimp from Huelva or suckling pig from Segovia, and innovative dishes like *ajoblanco de piñones con granizado de mango* (cream of garlic and almond soup with pine nuts and mango sorbet). There's a delicious menú de degustación Monday–Thursday and plenty of roast meats. **Known for:** fine dining; Spanish classics; tasting menu. [$] *Average main: €20* ✉ *Av. Cristo Rey 4* ☎ *953/750463* 🕒 *No dinner Sun.*

$$ SPANISH 🍴 **Cantina La Estación.** Meals at one of Úbeda's top restaurants are served in a train-carriage interior decorated with railway memorabilia. Highly rated by locals who flock here on weekends, this distinctive eatery serves creative dishes like *presa ibérica en salsa de mostaza* (Iberian pork in mustard sauce) and *bacalao confitado* (caramelized cod), plus a tempting menú de degustación (€42). **Known for:** innovative dishes; value tasting menu; fun interior. [$] *Average main: €17* ✉ *Cuesta de la Rodadera 1* ☎ *687/777230* 🕒 *Closed Wed. No dinner Tues.*

$$$ SPANISH 🍴 **Taberna Misa de 12.** This small bar has the best position on the leafy square, one block from the Plaza del Ayuntamiento, and the pleasant outside terrace is the best place to enjoy the tapas. Despite the tiny kitchen, the menu stretches long and includes homemade croquettes and roasted peppers, red tuna tartare, and Iberian pork cuts. **Known for:** tapas; wine list; outdoor dining. [$] *Average main: €18* ✉ *Pl. Primero de Mayo 7* ☎ *953/828197* 🌐 *www.misade12.com* 🕒 *Closed Mon. and Tues.*

WHERE TO STAY

$ ⚏ **Hotel El Postigo.** Tucked away in the center of town, this is a modern
HOTEL surprise among Úbeda's historical buildings and an oasis of peace and
quiet. **Pros:** central location; tasty breakfast; patio has a pool. **Cons:**
difficult to access by car; lacks character; mediocre breakfast. $ *Rooms
from: €60* ⊠ *Calle Postigo 5* ☎ *953/795550* ⊕ *www.hotelelpostigo.com*
⊐ *26 rooms* ⦿ *Free Breakfast.*

$$$ ⚏ **Palacio de la Rambla.** In old Úbeda, this stunning 16th-century man-
B&B/INN sion has been in the same family since it was built—it still hosts the
Fodor'sChoice Marquesa de la Rambla when she's in town—and eight of the rooms
★ are available for overnighters. **Pros:** central location; elegant style; all
rooms have access to the garden. **Cons:** little parking; grandiosity not
for everyone; some areas a little tired. $ *Rooms from: €132* ⊠ *Pl. del
Marqués 1* ☎ *953/750196* ⊕ *www.palaciodelarambla.com* ☽ *Closed
July and Aug.* ⊐ *8 rooms* ⦿ *Free Breakfast.*

$$$ ⚏ **Parador de Úbeda.** Designed by Andrés de Vandelvira, this splendid
HOTEL parador is in a 16th-century ducal palace in a prime location on the
Fodor'sChoice Plaza Vázquez de Molina, next to the Capilla del Salvador. **Pros:** elegant
★ surroundings; perfect location; excellent restaurant. **Cons:** parking is
difficult; church bells in the morning; could be too formal for some.
$ *Rooms from: €160* ⊠ *Pl. Vázquez de Molina s/n* ☎ *953/750345*
⊕ *www.parador.es* ⊐ *36 rooms* ⦿ *No meals.*

SHOPPING

Little Úbeda is the crafts capital of Andalusia, with workshops devoted
to carpentry, basket weaving, stone carving, wrought iron, stained glass,
and, above all, the city's distinctive green-glaze pottery. Calle Valencia
is the traditional potters' row, running from the bottom of town to
Úbeda's general crafts center, northwest of the casco antiguo (follow
signs to Calle Valencia or Barrio de Alfareros).

Úbeda's most famous potter was Paco Tito, whose craft is carried on
at three different workshops run by two of his sons, Pablo and Juan,
and a son-in-law, Melchor, each of whom claims to be the sole true
heir to his father's art.

Alfarería Góngora. All kinds of ceramics are sold here. ⊠ *Calle Cuesta
de la Merced 32* ☎ *953/754605.*

Juan Tito. The extrovert Juan Tito can often be found at the potter's
wheel in his rambling shop, which is packed with ceramics of every
size and shape. You can also shop online. ⊠ *Pl. del Ayuntamiento 12*
☎ *953/751302* ⊕ *www.alfareriatito.com.*

Melchor Tito. You can see classic green-glazed items—the focus of
Melchor Tito's work—being made in his workshops in Calle Valencia
and Calle Fuenteseca 17, which are both also shops. ⊠ *Calle Valencia
44* ☎ *953/753692.*

Pablo Tito. Clay sculptures of characters from *Don Quixote,* fired by
Pablo Tito in an old Moorish-style kiln, are the specialty of this studio
and shop. There is also a museum (Monday–Saturday 8–2 and 4–8,
Sunday 10–2) on the premises. ⊠ *Calle Valencia 22* ☎ *953/751496.*

The picturesque town of Cazorla

CAZORLA

48 km (35 miles) southeast of Úbeda.

Unspoiled and remote, the village of Cazorla is at the east end of Jaén province. The pine-clad slopes and towering peaks of the Cazorla and Segura sierras rise above the village, and below it stretch endless miles of olive groves. In spring, purple jacaranda trees blossom in the plazas.

GETTING HERE AND AROUND

The remoteness and size of the Parque Natural Cazorla plus the lack of frequent public transportation make this somewhere to explore by car.

VISITOR INFORMATION

Contacts Cazorla Tourist Office. ⊠ *Paseo Santo Cristo 19* ☎ *953/710102* ⊕ *www.cazorla.es.*

EXPLORING

FAMILY

Fodor's Choice

★

Parque Natural Sierra de Cazorla, Segura y Las Villas (*Cazorla, Segura and Las Villas Nature Park*). For a break from man-made sights, drink in the scenery or watch for wildlife in this park, a carefully protected patch of mountain wilderness 80 km (50 miles) long and 30 km (19 miles) wide. Deer, wild boar, and mountain goats roam its slopes and hawks, eagles, and vultures soar over the 6,000-foot peaks. Early spring is the ideal time to visit; try to avoid the summer and late-spring months, when the park teems with tourists and locals. It's often difficult, though by no means impossible, to find accommodations in fall, especially on weekends during hunting season (September–February). Between June and October, the park maintains seven well-equipped campgrounds. For information on hiking, camping, canoeing, horseback riding, or guided excursions, contact the **Agencia de Medio Ambiente** (*Calle Martínez Falero 11, Cazorla* ☎ *953/711534*), or the park visitor center. ✉ *Cazorla* 🌐 *www.sierrasdecazorlaseguraylasvillas.es/en.*

Centro de Interpretación Torre del Vinagre. A short film shown in the interpretive center introduces the park's main sights. Displays explain the plants and geology, and there's a small hunting museum. Staff can advise on camping, fishing, and hiking trails. ✉ *Ctra. del Tranco (A319), Km 48, Torre del Vinagre* ☎ *953/713017* 🌐 *www.sierrasdecazorlaseguraylasvillas.es* 🕒 *Closed Mon. and Nov.–mid-Mar.*

EN ROUTE

Guadalquivir River Gorge. Leave the Parque Natural by an alternative route—drive along the spectacular gorge carved by the Guadalquivir River, a rushing torrent beloved by kayaking enthusiasts. At the Tranco Dam, follow signs to Villanueva del Arzobispo, where the N322 takes you back to Úbeda, Baeza, and Jaén. ✉ *Cazorla.*

WHERE TO EAT AND STAY

$$ SPANISH

🍴 **Leandro.** One of the best places to eat in the village, this atmospheric restaurant decorated in traditional local style serves up mountain game such as venison, goat, and wild boar, cooked on the barbecue or on hot stones. Other house specialties include homemade burgers, local trout, and partridge pâté. **Known for:** barbecue game meat; cheese millefeuille pastry; good value. [$] *Average main: €14* ✉ *Calle Hoz 3* ☎ *953/720632* 🌐 *www.mesonleandro.com* 🕒 *Closed Tues.*

$ B&B/INN

🏨 **Casa Rural Plaza de Santa Maria.** In the heart of the village with lovely views of the castle, this restored 17th-century mansion offers some of the best value lodging in the area. **Pros:** quiet, central location; stunning castle views; large terraces with loungers. **Cons:** a little basic; inconsistent decor; difficult car access. [$] *Rooms from: €50* ✉ *Callejón de la Pza. de Santa María* ☎ *953/722087* 🌐 *www.plazadesantamaria.com* 🛏 *9 rooms* 🍽 *Free Breakfast.*

$$$ HOTEL

🏨 **Parador de Cazorla.** You'll find this modern parador isolated in a valley at the edge of the nature reserve, 26 km (16 miles) north of Cazorla, in a quiet place that's popular with hunters and anglers. **Pros:** lovely views from the pool; restaurant serves excellent mountain game; bucolic setting. **Cons:** not all rooms have views; access is difficult; uninspiring exterior. [$] *Rooms from: €160* ✉ *Sierra de Cazorla, s/n* ☎ *953/727075* 🌐 *www.parador.es* 🛏 *34 rooms* 🍽 *No meals.*

GRANADA

430 km (265 miles) south of Madrid, 261 km (162 miles) east of Seville, 160 km (100 miles) southeast of Córdoba.

The Alhambra and the tomb of the Catholic Monarchs are the pride of Granada. The city rises majestically from a plain onto three hills, dwarfed—on a clear day—by the Sierra Nevada. Atop one of these hills perches the reddish-gold Alhambra palace, whose stunning view takes in the sprawling medieval Moorish quarter, the caves of the Sacromonte, and, in the distance, the fertile *vega* (plain), rich in orchards, tobacco fields, and poplar groves. In 2013, Granada celebrated its 1,000th anniversary as a kingdom.

Split by internal squabbles, Granada's Moorish Nasrid dynasty gave Ferdinand of Aragón his opportunity in 1491. Spurred by Isabella's religious fanaticism, he laid siege to the city for seven months, and on January 2, 1492, Boabdil, the "Rey Chico" (Boy King), was forced to surrender the keys of the city. As Boabdil fled the Alhambra via the Puerta de los Siete Suelos (Gate of the Seven Floors), he asked that the gate be sealed forever.

GETTING HERE AND AROUND

AIR TRAVEL

Four daily flights connect Granada with Madrid and four with Barcelona.

Contacts Aeropuerto de Granada (*Aeropurto Federico García Lorca*). ☎ *902/404704.*

BUS TRAVEL

Granada's main bus station is at Carretera de Jaén, 3 km (2 miles) northwest of the center of town beyond the end of Avenida de Madrid. Most buses operate from here, except for buses to nearby destinations such as Fuentevaqueros, Viznar, and some buses to Sierra Nevada, which leave from the city center's Plaza del Triunfo near the RENFE station. Luggage lockers (*la consigna*) are available at the main bus and train stations, and you can also leave your luggage at City Locker (Placeta de las Descalzas 3) and Lock & Be Free (Calle Salamanca 13).

Autocares Bonal operates buses between Granada and the Sierra Nevada. **ALSA** buses run to and from Las Alpujarras (8 times daily), Córdoba (10 times daily), Seville (9 times daily), Málaga (16 times daily), and Jaén, Baeza, Úbeda, Cazorla, Almería, Almuñécar, and Nerja (several times daily).

In Granada, **airport** buses (€2.90) run between the center of town and the airport, leaving every hour 5 am–9:45 pm from the Palacio de Congresos and making a few other stops along the way to the airport. Times are listed at the bus stop.

Granada has an extensive public bus network within the city. You can buy 5-, 10-, and 20-trip discount passes on the buses and at newsstands. The single-trip fare is €1.40. Granada Cards include bus trips plus guaranteed tickets for the Alhambra and other main monuments (without having to wait in lines). The three-day card costs €37 and the five-day card €40, saving at least a third on regular prices. You can purchase the cards at the municipal tourist office, but it's best to buy them online via (⊕ *granadatur.com/granada.card*) in advance of your visit (you can print them at the tourist office).

Contacts Granada. ✉ *Ctra. Jaén, Granada* ☎ *902/422242.*

TAXI TRAVEL

Contacts Taxi Genil. ☎ *958/132323.* **Tele Radio Taxi.** ☎ *958/280654.*

TRAIN TRAVEL

There are regular trains from Seville and Almería, but service from Málaga and Córdoba is less convenient, necessitating a change at Bobadilla. A new fast track is planned for completion in early 2019;

10

it will reduce journey times considerably (50 minutes to Málaga and 90 minutes to Seville). There are a couple of daily trains from Madrid, Valencia, and Barcelona.

Contacts Station. ⊠ *Av. de los Andaluces* ☎ *912/320320.*

TOURS

Cycling Country. For information about cycling tours around Granada (Andalusia and Spain), 1–10 days long, contact this company, run by husband-and-wife team Geoff Norris and Maggi Jones in a town about 55 km (33 miles) away. ⊠ *Calle Salmerones 18, Alhama de Granada* ☎ *958/360655* ⊕ *www.cyclingcountry.com* 🖃 *From €30.*

Granada Tapas Tours. Long-time British resident Gayle Mackie offers a range of tapas tours lasting up to three hours. ⊠ *Granada* ☎ *619/444984* ⊕ *www.granadatapastours.com* 🖃 *From €40, including 6 tapas.*

VISITOR INFORMATION

Contacts Municipal Tourist Office. ⊠ *Pl. del Carmen 9, Centro* ☎ *958/248280* ⊕ *www.granadatur.com.* **Provincial Tourist Office.** ⊠ *Calle Cárcel Baja 3, Centro* ☎ *958/247128* ⊕ *www.turgranada.es.*

EXPLORING

Granada can be characterized by its major neighborhoods: East of the Río Darro and up the hill is **La Alhambra.** South of it and around a square and a popular hangout area, Campo del Príncipe, is **Realejo.** To the west of the Darro and going from north to south are the two popular neighborhoods **Sacromonte** and **Albayzín** (also spelled Albaicín). The latter is the young and trendy part of Granada, full of color, flavor, charming old architecture, and narrow, hilly streets. On either side of Gran Vía de Colón and the streets that border the cathedral (Reyes Católicos and Recogidas—the major shopping areas) is the area generally referred to as **Centro,** the city center. These days much of the Alhambra and Albayzín areas are closed to cars, but starting from the Plaza Nueva there are minibuses—Nos. C1, C2, C3, and C4—that run frequently to these areas.

LA ALHAMBRA

Fodor's Choice
★

Alhambra. With more than 2.5 million visitors a year, the Alhambra is Spain's most popular attraction. This sprawling palace-fortress was the last bastion of the 800-year Moorish presence on the Iberian Peninsula. Composed of royal residential quarters, court chambers, baths, and gardens, surrounded by defense towers and massive walls, the Alhambra is an architectural gem. The courtyards, patios, and halls offer an ethereal maze of Moorish arches, columns, and domes containing intricate stucco carvings and patterned ceramic tiling. The heart of the Alhambra, the **Palacios Nazaríes** contain delicate apartments, lazy fountains, and tranquil pools, and are divided into three sections: the *mexuar,* where business, government, and palace administration were headquartered; the *serrallo,* state rooms where the sultans held court; and the *harem.* The beautiful **Sala de los Abencerrajes** (Hall of the Moors) has a fabulous, ornate ceiling and star-shaped cupola reflected in the pool below. ⊠ *Cuesta de Gomérez, Alhambra* ☎ *858/953616*

Granada

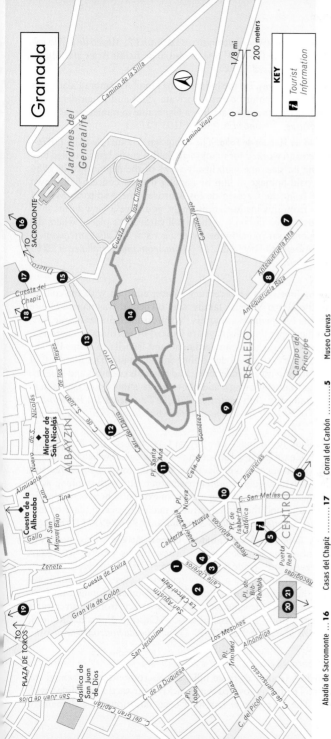

Jardines del Generalife

Camino de la Silla

Camino Viejo

KEY

🅸 Tourist
   Information

0 ——— 1/8 mi

0 ——— 200 meters

TO SACROMONTE

Cuesta del Chapiz

Cuesta de los Chinos

Cuesta de los Reyes

Camino del Sacromonte

REALEJO

Campo del Príncipe

Antequeruela Alta

Antequeruela Baja

ALBAYZÍN

Mirador de San Nicolás

Cuesta de la Alhacaba

Cta. del Darro

Pl. Santa Ana

Cta. de Gomérez

C. San Matías

C. Pavaneras

CENTRO

Pl. de Isabela Católica

Puerta Real

Reyes Católicos

Calle Nueva

Calderería

Calle Libreros

Cuesta de Elvira

Gran Vía de Colón

San Agustín

La Cárcel Baja

Pl. de Bib-Rambla

Los Mesones

San Jerónimo

Basílica de San Juan de Dios

C. de la Duquesa

Pl. Trinidad

Tablas

Alhóndiga

C. de Benavascaso

C. del Picón

TO PLAZA DE TOROS

⊕ *www.tickets.alhambra-patronato.es* ✉ *From €2, Museo de la Alhambra and Palacio de Carlos V free* ⊙ *Museo de Bellas Artes and Museo de la Alhambra closed Mon.*

Carmen de los Mártires. Up the hill from the Hotel Alhambra Palace, this turn-of-the-20th-century *carmen* (private villa) and its gardens—the only area open to tourists—are like a Generalife in miniature. ✉ *Paseo de los Mártires, Alhambra* ☎ *958/849103* ✉ *Free.*

Casa-Museo de Manuel de Falla. The composer Manuel de Falla (1876–1946) lived and worked for many years in this rustic house tucked into a charming hillside lane with lovely views of the Alpujarras. In 1986 Granada paid homage to him by naming its new concert hall (down the street from the Carmen de los Mártires) the Auditorio Manuel de Falla—from this institution, fittingly, you have a view of his little white house. Note the bust in the small garden: it's placed where the composer once sat to enjoy the sweeping vista. ✉ *Calle Antequeruela Alta 11, Alhambra* ☎ *958/222189* ⊕ *museomanueldefalla.com* ✉ *€3* ⊙ *Closed Mon.*

REALEJO

Casa de los Tiros. This 16th-century palace, adorned with the coat of arms of the Grana Venegas family who owned it, was named House of the Shots for the musket barrels that protrude from its facade. The stairs to the upper-floor displays are flanked by portraits of miserable-looking Spanish royals, from Ferdinand and Isabella to Felipe IV. The highlight is the carved wooden ceiling in the Cuadra Dorada (Hall of Gold), adorned with gilded lettering and portraits of royals and knights. Old lithographs, engravings, and photographs show life in Granada in the 19th and early 20th centuries. ✉ *Calle Pavaneras 19, Realejo-San Matías* ☎ *600/143175* ⊕ *www.juntadeandalucia.es/cultura/museos/MCTGR* ✉ *€2* ⊙ *Closed Mon.*

El Cuarto Real. Just a block away from Casa de los Tiros is the newly restored El Cuarto Real, a 13th-century Nasrid palace which has decorations almost identical to the Alhambra. Only the fortified tower remains standing with its exquisite *qubba* (reception room) with stunning walls and ceiling motifs. The adjoining modern extension houses temporary art exhibitions and the formal gardens make a peaceful place to rest. ✉ *Pl. de los Campos 6, Realejo-San Matías* ☎ *958/849111* ✉ *Free.*

Fundación Rodríguez-Acosta/Instituto Gómez Moreno. This nonprofit organization was founded at the behest of the painter José Marí Rodríguez-Acosta. Inside a typical carmen, it houses works of art, archaeological finds, and a library (currently closed to visitors) collected by the Granada-born scholar Manuel Gómez-Moreno Martínez. Other exhibits include valuable and unique objects from Asian cultures and the prehistoric and classical eras. ✉ *Callejón Niños del Rollo 8, Realejo-San Matías* ☎ *958/227497* ⊕ *www.fundacionrodriguezacosta.com* ✉ *€5.*

SACROMONTE

The third of Granada's three hills, the Sacromonte rises behind the Albayzín. The hill is covered with prickly pear cacti and riddled with caverns. The Sacromonte has long been notorious as a domain of

Continued on page 656

ALHAMBRA: PALACE-FORTRESS

 Floating mirage-like on its promontory overlooking Granada, the mighty and mysterious Alhambra shimmers vermilion in the clear mountain air, with the white peaks of the Sierra Nevada rising behind it. This sprawling palace-fortress, named from the Arabic for "red citadel" *(al-Qal'ah al-Hamra)*, was the last bastion of the 800-year Moorish presence on the Iberian Peninsula. Composed of royal residential quarters, court chambers, baths, and gardens, surrounded by defense towers and massive walls, the Alhambra is an architectual gem where Moorish kings worked and played—and murdered their enemies.

LOOK UP

Among the stylistic
elements you can see
in the Alhambra are
Arabesque geometrical
designs, and elaborate
Mocárabe arches.

Built of perishable materials, the Alhambra was meant to be forever replenished and replaced by succeeding generations. The Patio de los Leones' (above) has recently been restored to its original appearance.

INSIDE THE FORTRESS

More than 3 million annual visitors come to the Alhambra today, making it Spain's top attraction. Vistors revel in the palace's architectural wonders, most of which had to be restored after the alterations made after the Christian reconquest of southern Spain in 1492 and the damage from an 1821 earthquake. Incidentally, Napoléon's troops commandeered the site in 1812 with intent to level it but their attempts were foiled.

The courtyards, patios, and halls offer an ethereal maze of Moorish arches, columns, and domes containing intricate stucco carvings and patterned ceramic tiling. The intimate arcades, fountains, and light-reflecting pools throughout are identified in the ornamental inscriptions as physical renderings of paradise taken from the Koran and Islamic poetry. The contemporary visitor to this dreamlike space feels the fleeting embrace of a culture that brought its light to a world emerging from medieval darkness.

ARCHITECTURAL TERMS

Arabesque: An ornament or decorative style that employs flower, foliage, or fruit, and sometimes geometrical, animal, and figural outlines to produce an intricate pattern of interlaced lines.

Mocárabe: A decorative element of carved wood or plaster based on juxtaposed and hanging prisms resembling stalactites. Sometimes called *muquarna* (honeycomb vaulting), the impression is similar to a beehive and the "honey" has been described as light.

Mozárabe: Sometimes confused with Mocárabe, the term Mozárabe refers to Christians living in Moorish Spain. Thus, Christian artistic styles or recourses in Moorish architecture (such as the paintings in the Sala de los Reyes) are also identified as *mozárabe,* or, in English, mozarabic.

Mudéjar: This word refers to Moors living in Christian Spain. Moorish artistic elements in Christian architecture, such as horseshoe arches in a church, also are referred to as Mudéjar.

ALHAMBRA'S ARCHITECTURAL HIGHLIGHTS

The columns used in the construction of the Alhambra are unique, with extraordinarily slender cylindrical shafts, concave base moldings, and carved rings decorating the upper extremities. The capitals have simple cylindrical bases under prism-shaped heads decorated in a variety of vegetal motifs. Nearly all of these columns support false arches constructed purely for decorative purposes. The 124 columns surrounding the Patio de los Leones (Court of the Lions) are the best examples.

Cursive epigraphy is used to quote the Koran and Arabic poems. Considered the finest example of this are the Ibn-Zamrak verses that decorate the walls of the Sala de las Dos Hermanas.

Glazed ceramic tiles covered with geometrical patterns in primary colors cover the walls of the Alhambra with a profusion of styles and shapes. Red, blue, and yellow are the colors of magic in Sufi tradition, while green is the life-giving color of Islam.

The horseshoe arch, widening before rounding off with lower ends extending around the circle until they begin to converge, was the quintessential Moorish architectural innovation, used not only for aesthetic and decorative purposes but because it allowed greater height than the classical, semicircular arch inherited from the Greeks and Romans. The horseshoe arch also had a mystical significance in recalling the shape of the *mihrab*, the prayer niche in the *qibla* wall of a mosque indicating the direction of prayer and suggesting a door to Mecca or to paradise. Horseshoe arches and arcades are found throughout the Alhambra.

The Koran describes paradise as "gardens underneath which rivers flow," and water is used as a practical and ornamental architectural element throughout the Alhambra. Whether used musically, as in the canals in the Patio de los Leones or visually, as in the reflecting pool of the Patio de los Arrayanes, water is used to enhance light, enlarge spaces, or provide musical background for a desert culture in love with the beauty and oasis-like properties of hydraulics in all its forms.

Court of the Lions

Cursive epigraphy

Ceramic tiles

Gate of Justice

Alhambra fountains

The Alcazaba was built chiefly by Nasrid kings in the 1300s.

PALACIO NAZARÍES

ALCAZABA

TO GENERALIFE →

Jardines del Partal

PALACIO DE CARLOS V

LAY OF THE LAND

The complex has three main parts: the Alcazaba, the Palacio Nazaríes (Nasrid Royal Palace), and the Generalife. Across from the main entrance is the original fortress, the Alcazaba. Here, the watchtower's great bell was once used to announce the opening and closing of the irrigation system on Granada's great plain.

A wisteria-covered walkway leads to the heart of the Alhambra, the Palacios Nazaríes. Here, delicate apartments, lazy fountains, and tranquil pools contrast vividly with the hulking fortifications outside. It is divided into three sections: the *mexuar,* where business, government, and palace administration were headquartered; the *serrallo,* a series of state rooms where the sultans held court and entertained their ambassadors; and the *harem,* which in its time was entered only by the sultan, his family, and their most trusted servants, most of them eunuchs. Nearby is the Renaissance Palacio de Carlos V (Palace of Charles V), featuring a perfectly square exterior but a circular interior courtyard. Designed by Pedro Machuca, a pupil of Michelangelo, it is where the sultan's private apartments once stood. Part of the building houses the free Museo de la Alhambra, devoted to Islamic art. Upstairs is the more modest Museo de Bellas Artes.

Over on Cerro del Sol (Hill of the Sun) is Generalife, the ancient summer palace of the Nasrid kings.

TIMELINE

1238 First Nasrid king, Ibn el-Ahmar, begins Alhambra.

1391 Nasrid Palaces is completed.

1492 Boabdil surrenders Granada to Ferdinand and Isabella, parents of King Henry VIII's first wife, Catherine of Aragon.

1524 Carlos V begins Renaissance Palace.

1812 Napoléonic troops arrive with plans to destroy Alhambra.

1814 The Duke of Wellington sojourns here to escape the pressures of the Peninsular War.

1829 Washington Irving lives on the premises and writes *Tales of the Alhambra,* reviving interest in the crumbling palace.

1862 Granada municipality begins Alhambra restoration that continues to this day.

ALHAMBRA'S PASSAGES OF TIME

From Columbus's commissioning to a bloody murder, historic events as well as everyday affairs happened between these walls.

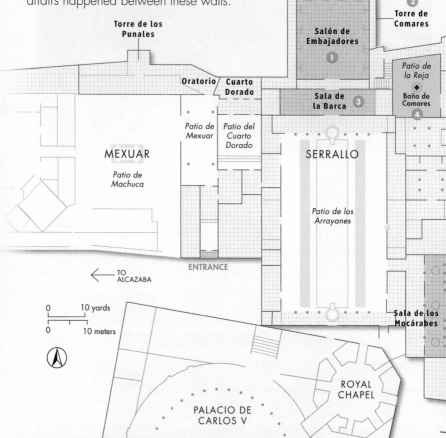

PALACIOS NAZARIÁES (NASRID ROYAL PALACE)

Torre de los Punales

Torre de Comares

Salón de Embajadores ❶

Patio de la Reja

Oratorio / Cuarto Dorado

Sala de la Barca ❸

Baño de Comares ❹

Patio de Mexuar / Patio del Cuarto Dorado

MEXUAR

SERRALLO

Patio de Machuca

Patio de los Arrayanes

ENTRANCE

← TO ALCAZABA

Sala de los Mocárabes

0   10 yards
0   10 meters

PALACIO DE CARLOS V

ROYAL CHAPEL

Tower of Comares and Patio de los Arrayanes

❶ In El Salón de Embajadores, Boabdil drew up his terms of surrender, and Christopher Columbus secured royal support for his historic voyage in 1492. The carved wooden ceiling is a portrayal of the seven Islamic heavens, with six rows of stars topped by a seventh-heaven cupulino or micro-cupola.

❷ Torre de Comares, a lookout in the corner of this hall is where Carlos V uttered his famous line, "Ill-fated the man who lost all this."

❸ Mistakenly named from the Arabic word *baraka* (divine blessing), Sala de la Barca has a carved wooden ceiling often described as an inverted boat.

Sala de los Reyes

6 Sultana Zoraya often found refuge in this charming little balcony (Mirador de Daraxa) overlooking the Lindaraja garden.

7 Shhh, don't tell a secret here. In the Sala de los Ajimeces, a whisper in one corner can be clearly heard from the opposite corner.

8 In the Sala de las Dos Hermanas, twin slabs of marble embedded in the floor are the "sisters," though Washington Irving preferred the story of a pair of captive Moorish beauties.

9 In the Patio de los Leones (Court of the Lions), a dozen crudely crafted lions (restored to their former glory in 2012) support the fountain at the center of this elegant courtyard, representing the signs of the zodiac sending water to the four corners.

10 In the Sala de los Abencerrajes, Muley Hacen (father of Boabdil) murdered the male members of the Abencerraje family in revenge for their chief's seduction of his daughter Zoraya. The rusty stains in the fountain are said to be bloodstains left by the pile of Abencerraje heads.

The star-shaped cupola, reflected in the pool, is considered the Alhambra's most beautiful example of stalactite or honeycomb vaulting.

The octagonal dome over the room is best viewed at sunset when the 16 small windows atop the dome admit sharp, low sunlight that refracts kaleidoscopically through the beehive-like prisms.

11 In the Sala de los Reyes, the ceiling painting depicts the first 10 Nasrid rulers. It was painted by a Christian artist since Islamic artists were not allowed to usurp divine power by creating human or animal figures.

The overhead painting of the knight rescuing his lady from a savage man portrays chivalry, a concept introduced to Europe by Arabic poets.

12 The terraces of Generalife grant incomparable views of the city.

Generalife gardens

Peinador de la Reina **5**

Apartamientos de Carlos V

Patio de Lindaraja

HAREM

Mirador de Daraxa **6**

Sala de los Ajimeces **7**

Sala de las Dos Hermanas **8**

Patio de los Leones **9**

Sala de los Reyes **11**

Cistern

Sala de los Abencerrajes **10**

TO JARDINES DEL PARTAL, GENERALIFE **12**

4 The Baño de Comares is where the sultan's favorites luxuriated in brightly tiled pools beneath star-shape pinpoints of light from the ceiling above.

5 El Peinador de la Reina, a nine-foot-square room atop a small tower was the Sultana's boudoir. The perforated marble slab was used to infiltrate perfumes while the queen performed her toilette. Washington Irving wrote his *Tales of the Alhambra* in this romantic tree-house-like perch.

Granada's Gypsies and thus a den of thieves and scam artists, but its reputation is largely undeserved. The quarter is more like a quiet Andalusian *pueblo* (village) than a rough neighborhood. Many of the quarter's colorful *cuevas* (caves) have been restored as middle-class homes, and some of the old spirit lives on in a handful of *zambras* (flamenco performances in caves, which are garishly decorated with brass plates and cooking utensils). These shows differ from formal flamenco shows in that the performers

mingle with you, usually dragging one or two onlookers onto the floor for an improvised dance lesson. Ask your hotel to book you a spot on a cueva tour, which usually includes a walk through the neighboring Albayzín and a drink at a tapas bar in addition to the zambra.

Abadía de Sacromonte. The caverns on Sacromonte are thought to have sheltered early Christians; 15th-century treasure hunters found bones inside and assumed they belonged to San Cecilio, the city's patron saint. Thus, the hill was sanctified—*sacro monte* (holy mountain)—and an abbey built on its summit, the Abadía de Sacromonte. ⊠ *C. del Sacromonte, Sacromonte* ☎ *958/221445* ⊠ *€4.*

Museo Cuevas del Sacromonte. The Museo Etnográfico shows how people lived here, and other areas in this interesting complex show the flora and fauna of the area as well as cultural activities. There are live flamenco concerts during the summer months. ⚠ **Even if you take Bus No. C2 (from Plaza Nueva) or the city sightseeing bus to get here, you will still be left with a steep walk of more than 650 feet to reach the center.** ⊠ *Barranco de los Negros, Sacromonte* ☎ *958/215120* ⊕ *www.sacromontegranada.com* ⊠ *€5.*

ALBAYZÍN

Fodor's Choice ★ Covering a hill of its own, across the Darro ravine from the Alhambra, this ancient Moorish neighborhood is a mix of dilapidated white houses and immaculate carmenes. It was founded in 1228 by Moors who had fled Baeza after Ferdinand III captured the city. Full of cobblestone alleyways and secret corners, the Albayzín guards its old Moorish roots jealously, though its 30 mosques were converted to baroque churches long ago. A stretch of the Moors' original city wall runs beside the ridge called the **Cuesta de la Alhacaba.** If you're walking—the best way to explore—you can enter the Albayzín from either the Cuesta de Elvira or the Plaza Nueva. Alternatively, on foot or by taxi (parking is impossible), begin in the Plaza Santa Ana and follow the Carrera del Darro, Paseo Padre Manjón, and Cuesta del Chapíz. One of the highest points in the quarter, the plaza in front of the church of San Nicolás (€2; *open mornings only*)—the **Mirador de San Nicolás**—has one of the finest views in all of Granada: on the hill opposite, the turrets and towers of the Alhambra form a dramatic silhouette against the snowy peaks of the

Sierra Nevada. The sight is most magical at dawn, dusk, and on nights when the Alhambra is floodlighted. Take note of the mosque just next to the church—views of the Alhambra from the mosque gardens are just as good as those from the Mirador de San Nicolás and a lot less crowded. Interestingly, given the area's Moorish history, the two sloping, narrow streets of Calderería Nueva and Calderería Vieja that meet at the top by the Iglesia San Gregorio have developed into something of a North African bazaar, full of shops and vendors selling clothes, bags, crafts, and trinkets. The numerous little teahouses and restaurants here have a decidedly Moroccan flavor. Be warned that there have been some thefts in the area, so keep your money and valuables out of sight. Many of the streets are cobbled so wear sturdy footwear with thick soles.

Casa de los Pisa. Originally built in 1494 for the Pisa family, the claim to fame of this house is its relationship to San Juan de Dios, who came to Granada in 1538 and founded a charity hospital to take care of the poor. Befriended by the Pisa family, he was taken into their home when he fell ill in February 1550. A month later, he died there, at the age of 55. Since that time, devotees of the saint have traveled from around the world to this house with a stone Gothic facade, now run by the Hospital Order of St. John. Inside are numerous pieces of jewelry, furniture, priceless religious works of art, and an extensive collection of paintings and sculptures depicting St. John. ⊠ *Calle Convalecencia 1, Albaicín* ☎ *958/222144* 🖾 *€3* ⊙ *Closed Sun.*

Casas del Chapíz. There's a delightful garden in this fine 16th-century Morisco house (built by Moorish craftsmen under Christian rule). It houses the School of Arabic Studies. ⊠ *Cuesta del Chapíz 22, Albaicín* ☎ *958/222290* 🖾 *€2.*

El Bañuelo (*Little Bath House*). These 11th-century Arab steam baths might be a little dark and dank now, but try to imagine them some 900 years ago, filled with Moorish beauties. Back then, the dull brick walls were backed by bright ceramic tiles, tapestries, and rugs. Light comes in through star-shape vents in the ceiling, à la bathhouse in the Alhambra. ⊠ *Carrera del Darro 31, Albaicín* ☎ *958/229738* 🖾 *€5.*

OFF THE BEATEN PATH
Paseo Padre Manjón. Along the Río Darro, this *paseo* is also known as the Paseo de los Tristes (Promenade of the Sad Ones) because funeral processions once passed this way. The cafés and bars here are a good place for a coffee break. The park, dappled with wisteria-covered pergolas, fountains, and stone walkways, has a stunning view of the Alhambra's northern side. ⊠ *Albaicín.*

Palacio de los Córdova. At the end of the Paseo Padre Manjón, this 17th-century noble house today holds Granada's municipal archives and is used for municipal functions and art exhibits. You're free to wander about the large garden, the only area open to visitors. ⊠ *Cuesta del Chapiz 4, Albaicín* ☎ *958/180021* 🖾 *Free.*

CENTRO

Capilla Real (*Royal Chapel*). Catholic Monarchs Isabella of Castile and Ferdinand of Aragón are buried at this shrine. When Isabella died in 1504, her body was first laid to rest in the Convent of San Francisco. The architect Enrique Egas began work on the Royal Chapel in 1506

10

and completed it 15 years later, creating a masterpiece of the ornate Gothic style now known in Spain as Isabelline. In 1521 Isabella's body was transferred to the Royal Chapel crypt, joined by that of her husband, Ferdinand, and later her daughter, Juana la Loca (Joanna the Mad), son-in-law, Felipe el Hermoso (Philip the Handsome), and Prince Felipe of Asturias. The **crypt** containing the coffins is simple, but it's topped by elaborate marble tombs showing Ferdinand and Isabella lying side by side. The **altarpiece** comprises 34 carved panels depicting religious and historical scenes. The **sacristy** holds Ferdinand's sword, Isabella's crown and scepter, and a fine collection of Flemish paintings once owned by Isabella. ⊠ *Calle Oficios, Centro* ☏ *958/227848* ⊕ *www.capillarealgranada.com* ⊠ *€5.*

Cathedral. Carlos V commissioned the cathedral in 1521 because he considered the Capilla Real "too small for so much glory" and wanted to house his illustrious late grandparents someplace more worthy. Carlos undoubtedly had great intentions, as the cathedral was created by some of the finest architects of its time: Enrique Egas, Diego de Siloé, Alonso Cano, and sculptor Juan de Mena. Alas, his ambitions came to little, for the cathedral is a grand and gloomy monument, not completed until 1714 and never used as the crypt for his grandparents (or parents). Enter through a small door at the back, off the Gran Vía. Old hymnals are displayed throughout, and there's a museum, which includes a 14th-century gold-and-silver monstrance given to the city by Queen Isabella. ⊠ *Gran Vía, Centro* ☏ *958/222959* ⊠ *€5 (including audio guide).*

Centro José Guerrero. Just across a lane from the cathedral and Capilla Real, this building houses colorful modern paintings by José Guerrero. Born in Granada in 1914, Guerrero traveled throughout Europe and lived in New York in the 1950s before returning to Spain. The center also runs excellent temporary contemporary art shows. ⊠ *Calle Oficios 8, Centro* ☏ *958/225185* ⊕ *www.centroguerrero.org* ⊠ *Free* ☾ *Closed Mon.*

Corral del Carbón (*Coal House*). This building was used to store coal in the 19th century, but its history is much longer. Dating to the 14th century, it was used by Moorish merchants as a lodging house, and then by Christians as a theater. It's one of the oldest Moorish buildings in the city and the only Arab structure of its kind in Spain. ⊠ *Pl. Mariana Pineda, Centro* ⊠ *Free.*

Palacio Madraza. This building conceals the Islamic seminary built in 1349 by Yusuf I. The intriguing baroque facade is elaborate; inside, across from the entrance, an octagonal room is crowned by a Moorish dome. It hosts occasional free art and cultural exhibitions. ⊠ *Calle Zacatín, Centro* ☏ *958/241299* ⊠ *€2.*

OUTSKIRTS OF TOWN

Casa-Museo Federico García Lorca. Granada's most famous native son, the poet Federico García Lorca, gets his due here, in the middle of a park devoted to him on the southern fringe of the city. Lorca's onetime summer home, **La Huerta de San Vicente,** is now a museum (guided tours only)—run by his niece Laura García Lorca—with such artifacts as his beloved piano and changing exhibits on specific aspects of his life.

⊠ Parque García Lorca, Virgen Blanca, Arabial ☎ 958/258466 ⊕ www. huertadesanvicente.com ▣ €3 (free Wed.) ⊘ Closed Mon.

Monasterio de La Cartuja. This Carthusian monastery in northern Granada (2 km [1 mile] from the center of town and reached by Bus No. N7) was begun in 1506 and moved to its present site in 1516, though construction continued for the next 300 years. The exterior is sober and monolithic, but inside are twisted, multicolor marble columns; a profusion of gold, silver, tortoiseshell, and ivory; intricate stucco; and the extravagant sacristy—it's easy to see why it has been called the Christian answer to the Alhambra. Among its wonders are the trompe-l'oeil spikes, shadows and all, in the Sanchez Cotan cross over the *Last Supper* painting at the west end of the refectory. If you're lucky, you may see small birds attempting to land on these faux perches. ⊠ *Camino de Alfacar, Cartuja* ☎ *958/161932* ▣ *€5.*

FAMILY **Parque de las Ciencias** (*Science Park*). Across from Granada's convention center and easily reached on Bus No. C4, this museum (one of the most visited in Andalusia) has a planetarium and interactive demonstrations of scientific experiments. The 165-foot observation tower has views to the south and west. ⊠ *Av. del Mediterráneo, Zaidín* ☎ *958/131900* ⊕ *www.parqueciencias.com* ▣ *From €7* ⊘ *Closed Mon.*

WHERE TO EAT

One of the great things about Granada tapas bars is that you receive a free tapa (often very generous) with every drink. You can't choose your tapa, but you'll rarely be disappointed. Poke around the streets between the Carrera del Darro and the Mirador de San Nicolás, particularly around the bustling Plaza San Miguel Bajo, for Granada's most colorful twilight hangouts. Also try the bars and restaurants in the arches underneath the Plaza de Toros (Bullfighting Ring), on the west side of the city, a bit farther from the city center.

For a change, check out some Moroccan-style tea shops, known as *teterías*—these first emerged in Granada and are now also popular in most Spanish cities. Tea at such places can be expensive, so be sure to check the price of your brew before you order. The highest concentration of teterías is in the Albayzín, particularly around Calle Calderería Nueva where, within a few doors from each other, you find Al Faguara, Dar Ziryab, and As Sirat. Tetería Ábaco, up the steep Cuesta del Perro Alto side street, is worth the climb for the Alhambra views from its roof terrace.

10

REALEJO

$$$$ ✕ **Damasqueros.** The modern, wood-paneled dining room and warm
SPANISH lighting form the perfect setting for the creative Andalusian cuisine
Fodor's Choice cooked here by local chef Lola Marín, who learned her trade with some
★ of Spain's top chefs, such as Martín Berasategui. The tasting menu changes weekly and always includes in-season produce in its five courses (cold and hot starters, fish, meat, and dessert), which for another €20 can each be paired with wine from the list that runs to more than 120 choices, including several Granada wines. **Known for:** fresh local

produce; innovative tasting menu; wine pairing. $ *Average main: €40* ⊠ *Calle Damasqueros 3, Realejo-San Matías* ☎ *958/210550* ⊕ *www. damasqueros.com* ⊗ *Closed Mon. No dinner Sun.*

$$$ × **La Alacena de las Monjas.** Just as popular with locals as visitors, this
SPANISH restaurant in the heart of the Realejo district sits on the first floor and basement of a 14th-century convent—you can see the original clay vats that supplied the water downstairs. You can also dine outside in the lovely, quiet square. **Known for:** historic setting; red tuna; steak. $ *Average main: €20* ⊠ *Pl. del Padre Suarez 5, Realejo-San Matías* ☎ *958/229519* ⊕ *www.alacenadelasmonjas.com.*

ALBAYZÍN

$$ × **El Pilar del Toro.** This bar and restaurant, just off Plaza Nueva, is in
SPANISH a 17th-century palace with a stunning patio (complete with original marble columns) and peaceful garden. The menu emphasizes meat dishes such as *chuletas de cordero* (lamb chops) and the house specialty, braised rabo de toro. **Known for:** atmospheric patio; oxtail; elegant upstairs restaurant. $ *Average main: €15* ⊠ *Calle Hospital de Santa Ana 12, Albaicín* ☎ *958/225470* ⊕ *pilardeltoro.es.*

$$$ × **El Trillo.** Tucked away in the warren of alleyways in a restored
SPANISH Albayzín villa, this lovely small restaurant offers perhaps the best food
Fodor's Choice in the area. There's a formal dining room, outside garden with pear and
★ quince trees, plus a roof terrace with Alhambra views. **Known for:** fine dining; views of the Alhambra; rice with wild boar. $ *Average main: €18* ⊠ *Callejón del Aljibe del Trillo 3, Albaicín* ☎ *958/225182* ⊕ *www. restaurante-eltrillo.com.*

$$$ × **Mirador de Morayma.** Buried in the Albayzín, this hard-to-find restau-
SPANISH rant might appear to be closed—but ring the doorbell, and once inside, you'll have unbeatable views across the gorge to the Alhambra, particularly from the wisteria-laden outdoor terrace. In colder weather you can enjoy the open fireplace and attractive dining space inside. **Known for:** views of the Alhambra; tasting and à la carte menus; red tuna with tomato compote and garlic sauce. $ *Average main: €19* ⊠ *Calle Pianista García Carrillo 2, Albaicín* ☎ *958/228290* ⊕ *miradordemorayma.com/ en* ⊗ *No dinner Sun.*

$$ × **Paprika.** Inside a pretty brick building and with an informal terrace
VEGETARIAN sprawling over the wide steps of the Cuesta de Abarqueros, Paprika offer unpretentious vegan food. Most ingredients and wines are organic, and dishes include salads, stir-fries, and curries, such as Thai curry with tofu, coconut, and green curry sauce. **Known for:** choice of vegan food; value plate of the day; organic ingredients. $ *Average main: €12* ⊠ *Cuesta de Abarqueros 3, Albaicín* ☎ *958/804785* ⊕ *www.paprika-granada.com* ⊟ *No credit cards.*

$$ × **Ruta del Azafrán.** A charming surprise nestled at the foot of the
SPANISH Albayzín by the Darro—this sleek contemporary space in the shadow of the Alhambra offers a selection of specialties. The menu is interesting and diverse and includes dishes like chicken *pastela* (sweet-savory pie), lamb couscous, and several different risottos. **Known for:** wide choice of dishes; views of the Alhambra, especially at night; chicken pastela. $ *Average main: €16* ⊠ *Paseo de los Tristes 1, Albaicín* ☎ *958/226882* ⊕ *rutadelazafran.com.*

Part of the Holy Week procession in Granada

CENTRO

$$$ ✕ **Bodegas Castañeda.** A block from the cathedral across Gran Vía, this is
SPANISH a delightfully typical Granada bodega with low ceilings and dark wood
furniture. In addition to the wines, specialties here are plates of cheese,
pâté, and *embutidos* (cold meats). **Known for:** tapas; atmospheric bar;
Spanish tortilla with creamy alioli. $ *Average main: €18* ✉ *Calle Almi-
receros 1–3, Centro* ☎ *958/215464.*

$$ ✕ **Café Botánico.** Southeast of Granada's cathedral, this is a modern hot
TAPAS spot, a world apart from Granada's usual traditional tapas bar. Here
Fodor's Choice you'll find a bright-orange-and-beige interior and an eclectic crowd
★ of students, families, and businesspeople. **Known for:** international
menu; good value lunch deal; homemade desserts. $ *Average main:
€13* ✉ *Calle Málaga 3, Centro* ☎ *958/271598.*

$$$ ✕ **Cunini.** Around the corner from the cathedral, this is one of Granada's
SPANISH best fish restaurants. Catch-of-the-day fish and shellfish, fresh from the
boats at Motril, are displayed in the window at the front of the tapas
bar, adjacent to the cozy wood-paneled dining room. **Known for:** fresh
seafood; the only place in town serving angulas (glass eels); outdoor din-
ing. $ *Average main: €21* ✉ *Pl. Pescadería 14, Centro* ☎ *958/250777*
⊘ *Closed Mon. No dinner Sun.*

$$ ✕ **La Bodega de Antonio.** Just off Calle Puentezuelas, this authentic patio
SPANISH complete with original pillars provides a cozy vibe. Specials include the
house cod (with prawns and clams) and Galician-style octopus, best
enjoyed with a *cerdito* (a "little pig" ceramic jug of sweet white wine,
so named for its snout pourer). **Known for:** generous portions; tapas;
Galician-style octopus. $ *Average main: €12* ✉ *Calle Jardines 4, Centro*
☎ *958/252275* ⊘ *Closed Wed., and Aug.*

$$ TAPAS Fodor's Choice ★ 🍴 **La Brujidera.** Also known simply as Casa de Vinos (wine house), this place, up a pedestrian street just behind Plaza Nueva, is a must for Spanish wine lovers. The cozy interior is reminiscent of a ship's cabin, with wood paneling lining the walls, along with bottles of more than 150 Spanish wines. **Known for:** long wine list; meat and cheese boards; vermouth and sherries on tap. [$] *Average main: €12* ✉ *Monjas del Carmen 2, Centro* ☎ *958/222595* 🌐 *labrujidera.ga* 💳 *No credit cards* 🕓 *Closed 1 wk in Feb.*

$$ TAPAS 🍴 **Los Diamantes.** This cheap and cheerful bar is a big favorite with locals and draws crowds whatever the time of year. Specialties include fried fish and seafood—try the *surtido de pescado* (assortment of fried fish) to sample the best—as well as *mollejas fritas* (fried lambs' brains). **Known for:** fried fish; no seating; busy atmosphere. [$] *Average main: €12* ✉ *Calle Navas 28, Centro* ☎ *958/222572* 🌐 *www.barlosdiamantes.com* 💳 *No credit cards.*

$$ SPANISH 🍴 **Oliver.** The interior may look a bit bare, but whatever this fish restaurant lacks in warmth it makes up for with the food. Less pricey than its neighbor Cunini, it serves simple but high-quality dishes like grilled mullet, dorado baked in salt, prawns with garlic, and monkfish in saffron sauce. **Known for:** tapas bar; fresh fish; migas (fried bread crumbs). [$] *Average main: €16* ✉ *Pl. Pescadería 12, Centro* ☎ *958/262200* 🌐 *restauranteoliver.com* 🕓 *Closed Sun.*

$$$ SPANISH 🍴 **Tinta Fina.** Underneath the arches just off Puerta Real, this modern bar and restaurant has a reputation for being one of Granada's most chic venues. This trendy spot is especially known for fresh seafood, including oysters and red shrimp, tuna tartare, and grilled octopus. **Known for:** seafood; cocktail and G&T menus; chic atmosphere. [$] *Average main: €20* ✉ *Calle Angel Ganivet 5, Centro* ☎ *958/100041* 🌐 *www.tintafinarestaurante.com.*

OUTSKIRTS OF TOWN

$$$$ BASQUE 🍴 **Restaurante Arriaga.** Run by Basque chef Álvaro Arriaga, this restaurant sits on the top floor of the Museo de la Memoria de Andalucía just outside the city (it's well worth the taxi drive) and enjoys panoramic views of Granada with the Sierra Nevada behind. Choose from two tasting menus (€50 for six dishes and €65 for nine dishes), both with one surprise after another. À la carte specialties include Basque cod in garlic sauce and hake cheeks in traditional green sauce. **Known for:** tasting menus; culinary surprises (the menu starts with dessert!); panoramic views of Granada. [$] *Average main: €25* ✉ *Av. de las Ciencias 2, Armilla* ☎ *958/132619* 🌐 *www.restaurantearriaga.com* 🕓 *No dinner Sun.*

WHERE TO STAY

Staying in the immediate vicinity of the Alhambra tends to be pricier than the city center. The latter is a good choice if you want to combine your Alhambra trip with visits to the vibrant commercial center with its excellent shops, restaurants, and magnificent cathedral. The Albayzín is also a good place to stay for sheer character: this historic Arab quarter still has a tangible Moorish feel with its pint-size plazas and winding pedestrian streets.

LA ALHAMBRA

$$$
B&B/INN
Fodor'sChoice
★

Carmen de la Alcubilla del Caracol. In a traditional *granadino* villa on the slopes of the Alhambra, this privately run lodging is one of Granada's most stylish hotels. **Pros:** great views; bright, airy rooms; walking distance to the Alhambra. **Cons:** tough climb in hot weather. *$ Rooms from: €140* ⊠ *Calle Aire Alta 12, Alhambra* ☎ *958/215551* ⊕ *www.alcubilladelcaracol.com* ⊘ *Closed mid-July–Aug.* ➷ *7 rooms* ⦿ *No meals.*

$$$$
HOTEL

Hotel Alhambra Palace. Built by a local duke in 1910, this neo-Moorish hotel is on leafy grounds at the back of the Alhambra hill, and has a very *Arabian Nights* interior (think orange-and-brown overtones, multicolor tiles, and Moorish-style arches and pillars). **Pros:** bird's-eye views; location near the Alhambra; large, warmly decorated rooms. **Cons:** steep climb up from Granada; often packed with business people (it doubles as a convention center); might be too grandiose for some. *$ Rooms from: €250* ⊠ *Pl. Arquitecto García de Paredes 1, Alhambra* ☎ *958/221468* ⊕ *www.h-alhambrapalace.es* ➷ *126 rooms* ⦿ *Free Breakfast.*

$$$$
HOTEL
Fodor'sChoice
★

Parador de Granada. This is Spain's most expensive and most popular parador, right within the walls of the Alhambra. **Pros:** good location; lovely interiors; garden restaurant. **Cons:** no views in some rooms; removed from city life; very expensive. *$ Rooms from: €400* ⊠ *Calle Real de la Alhambra, Alhambra* ☎ *958/221440* ⊕ *www.parador.es/en/paradores/parador-de-granada* ➷ *40 rooms* ⦿ *No meals.*

ALBAYZÍN

$$$
B&B/INN
Fodor'sChoice
★

Casa Morisca. The architect who owns this 15th-century building transformed it into a hotel so distinctive that he received Spain's National Restoration Award for his preservation of original architectural elements, including barrel-vaulted brickwork, wooden ceilings, and the original pool. **Pros:** historic location; award-winning design; easy parking. **Cons:** stuffy interior rooms; no full restaurant on-site; slightly out of the town center. *$ Rooms from: €130* ⊠ *Cuesta de la Victoria 9, Albaicín* ☎ *958/221100* ⊕ *www.hotelcasamorisca.com* ➷ *14 rooms* ⦿ *Free Breakfast.*

$$$$
HOTEL

Hotel Casa 1800. A stone's throw from the Paseo de los Tristes, this restored 17th-century mansion has a fine, tiered patio. **Pros:** historic building; deluxe suite has balcony with views of the Alhambra; walking distance to most sights. **Cons:** on a street that doesn't permit cars. *$ Rooms from: €200* ⊠ *Calle Benalua 11, Albaicín* ☎ *958/210700* ⊕ *www.hotelcasa1800granada.com* ➷ *25 rooms* ⦿ *No meals.*

CENTRO

$$$$
HOTEL

Hospes Palacio de los Patos. This beautifully restored palace is unmissable, sitting proudly on its own in the middle of one of Granada's busiest shopping streets. **Pros:** central location; historic setting; great spa and restaurant. **Cons:** expensive parking; some street noise. *$ Rooms from: €270* ⊠ *Calle Solarillo de Gracia 1, Centro* ☎ *958/535790* ⊕ *www.hospes.es* ➷ *42 rooms* ⦿ *No meals.*

$
HOTEL

Hostal Rodri. This very comfortable and quiet hostel lies conveniently off Plaza de la Trinidad near the cathedral and is a good option for

10

cheaper lodging in a city with so many upscale accommodations. **Pros:** central location; clean, comfortable rooms; value. **Cons:** some rooms on small side; no direct car access; could be too basic for some. $ *Rooms from: €48* ⊠ *Calle Laurel de las Tablas 9, Centro* ☎ *958/288043* ⊕ *www.hostalrodri.com* ↝ *10 rooms* ⏐◯⏐ *No meals.*

$$$
HOTEL

☷ **Hotel Párraga Siete.** This family-run hotel in the heart of the old quarter within easy walking distance of sights and restaurants offers excellent value and amenities superior to its official two-star rating. **Pros:** central, quiet location; good on-site restaurant; easy nearby parking. **Cons:** difficult to access by car; interiors might be too sparse for some; no historic character. $ *Rooms from: €150* ⊠ *Calle Párraga 7, Centro* ☎ *958/264227* ⊕ *www.hotelparragasiete.com* ↝ *20 rooms* ⏐◯⏐ *No meals.*

$$$
B&B/INN

☷ **Palacio de los Navas.** In the center of the city, this palace was built by aristocrat Francisco Navas in the 16th century and it later became the Casa de Moneda (the Mint); its original architectural features blend well with modern ones. **Pros:** great location; peaceful oasis during the day; rooms are set around a beautiful interior patio. **Cons:** can be noisy at night; breakfast uninspiring. $ *Rooms from: €140* ⊠ *Calle Navas 1, Centro* ☎ *958/215760* ⊕ *www.hotelpalaciodelosnavas.com* ↝ *19 rooms* ⏐◯⏐ *Free Breakfast.*

NIGHTLIFE AND PERFORMING ARTS

NIGHTLIFE

Granada's ample student population makes for a lively bar scene. Some of the trendiest bars are in converted houses in the Albayzín and Sacromonte and in the area between Plaza Nueva and Paseo de los Tristes. Calle Elvira, Calderería Vieja, and Calderería Nueva are crowded with laid-back coffee and pastry shops. In the modern part of town, Pedro Antonio de Alarcón and Martinez de la Rosa have larger but less glamorous offerings. Another nighttime gathering place is the Campo del Príncipe, a large plaza surrounded by typical Andalusian taverns.

Bohemia Jazz Café. This atmospheric jazz bar has piano performances and occasional live bands. ⊠ *Pl. de los Lobos 11, Centro.*

El Tabanco. In the heart of the Albayzín, this small venue is an art gallery by day and live music venue (mostly flamenco and jazz) by night. Book in advance to be sure of a seat. ⊠ *Cuesta de San Gregorio 24, Albaicín* ☎ *662/137046* ⊕ *www.eltabanco.com.*

Eshavira Club. At this dimly lighted club you can hear sultry jazz (Wednesday and Thursday) and flamenco (Friday and Saturday) at 11 pm. Admission fee includes a drink. ⊠ *Calle Postigo de la Cuna 2, Albaicín* ☎ *958/290829.*

PERFORMING ARTS
FLAMENCO

Flamenco can be enjoyed throughout the city, especially in the Gypsy cuevas of the Albayzín and Sacromonte, where zambra shows—informal performances by Gypsies—take place almost daily year-round. The most popular cuevas are along the Camino de Sacromonte, the major street in the neighborhood of the same name. Be warned that this area has become very tourist oriented, and prepare to part with lots of money (at least €25 is average) for any show. Some shows include the price of round-trip transportation to the venue from your hotel, usually cheaper than two taxi journeys. In early September, an annual flamenco festival takes place in the delightful Corral del Carbón square (⊕ *www.losveranosdelcorral.es*). A program of flamenco events in the city is available from the tourist office.

Cueva La Rocío. This is a good spot for authentic flamenco shows, staged nightly at 10 and—when there's sufficient demand—at 11. ⊠ *C. del Sacromonte 70, Albaicín* ☎ *958/227129* ⊕ *cuevalarocio.es.*

El Templo del Flamenco. Slightly off the beaten track (take a taxi to get here) and less touristy because of it, this venue has shows at 10 daily. ⊠ *Calle Parnaleros Alto 41, Albaicín* ☎ *622/500052* ⊕ *templodelflamenco.com.*

Jardines de Zoraya. This show doesn't take place in a cave, but the music and dance are some of the most authentic you'll find. Daily shows are at 8 and 10:30 pm. ⊠ *Calle Panaderos 32, Albaicín* ☎ *958/206266* ⊕ *www.jardinesdezoraya.com.*

Peña Platería. This private club in the Albayzín is devoted to flamenco. Performances are usually on Thursday and Saturday evenings—check the club's Facebook page for details. ⊠ *Calle Plazoleta de Toqueros 7, Albaicín* ☎ *958/210650* ⊕ *www.facebook.com/plateriaflamenco.*

SHOPPING

A Moorish aesthetic pervades Granada's ceramics, marquetry (especially the *taraceas,* wooden boxes with inlaid tiles on their lids), woven textiles, and silver-, brass-, and copper-ware. The main shopping streets, centering on the Puerta Real, are the Gran Vía de Colón, Reyes Católicos, Zacatín, and Recogidas. Most antiques shops are on Cuesta de Elvira and Alcaicería—off Reyes Católicos. Cuesta de Gomérez, on the way up to the Alhambra, also has several handicrafts shops and guitar workshops.

Espartería San José. For wicker baskets and esparto-grass mats and rugs, head to this shop off the Plaza Pescadería. ⊠ *Calle Jáudenes 3, Centro* ☎ *958/267415.*

La Oliva. Tucked away off Plaza Marina Pineda in the city center, this tiny shop specializes in locally sourced produce (wine, cheese and cold cuts), but its star attraction is the selection of olive oils from different areas of Andalusia. You can try before you buy and tasting sessions are also available. ⊠ *Calle Virgen del Rosario 9, Centro* ☎ *958/225754* ⊕ *www.laoliva.eu.*

10

SIDE TRIPS FROM GRANADA

The fabled province of Granada spans the Sierra Nevada, with the beautifully rugged Alpujarras and the highest peaks on mainland Spain—Mulhacén at 11,407 feet and Veleta at 11,125 feet. This is where you can find some of the prettiest, most ancient villages, and it's one of the foremost destinations for Andalusia's increasingly popular rural tourism. Granada's vega, covered with orchards, tobacco plantations, and poplar groves, stretches for miles around.

EN ROUTE   Twelve kilometers (8 miles) south of Granada on A44, the road reaches a spot known as the **Suspiro del Moro** (Moor's Sigh). Pause here a moment and look back at the city, just as Granada's departing "Boy King" Boabdil did 500 years ago. As he wept over the city he'd surrendered to the Catholic Monarchs, his scornful mother pronounced her now legendary rebuke: "You weep like a woman for the city you could not defend as a man."

FUENTEVAQUEROS

19½ km (12 miles) northwest of Granada.

Museo Casa Natal Federico García Lorca. Born in the village of Fuentevaqueros on June 5, 1898, the poet lived here until age six. His childhood home opened as a museum in 1986, when Spain commemorated the 50th anniversary of his assassination (he was shot without trial by Nationalists at the start of the civil war in August 1936) and celebrated his reinstatement as a national figure after 40 years of nonrecognition during the Francisco Franco regime. The house has been restored with original furnishings, and the former granary, barn, and stables have been converted into exhibition spaces, with temporary art shows and a permanent display of photographs, clippings, and other memorabilia. A two-minute video shows the only existing footage of Lorca. Visits are by guided tour only. ✉ *C. del Poeta García Lorca 4* ☎ *958/516453* ⊕ *www.patronatogarcialorca.org/casamuseo.php* 💲 *€2* ☉ *Closed Mon.*

THE SIERRA NEVADA

The drive southeast from Granada to Pradollano along the A395—Europe's highest road, by way of Cenes de la Vega—takes about 45 minutes. It's wise to carry snow chains from mid-November to as late as April or even May. The mountains here make for an easy and worthwhile excursion, especially for those keen on trekking.

EXPLORING

Mulhacén. To the east of Granada, the mighty Mulhacén, the highest peak in mainland Spain, soars to 11,427 feet. Legend has it that it came by its name when Boabdil, the last Moorish king of Granada, deposed his father, Abul Hassan Ali, and had the body buried at the summit of the mountain so that it couldn't be desecrated. For more information on trails to the two summits, check the National Park Service's site (⊕ *www.nevadensis.com*).

Pico de Veleta. Peninsular Spain's second-highest mountain is 11,125 feet high. The view from its summit across the Alpujarras to the sea at distant Motril is stunning, and on a very clear day you can see the coast of North Africa. When the snow melts (July and August) you can drive or take a minibus from the Albergue Universitario (Universitario mountain refuge) to within around 400 yards of the summit—a trail takes you to the top in around 45 minutes. ■TIP➔ **It's cold up there, so take a warm jacket and scarf, even if Granada is sizzling hot.**

SPORTS AND THE OUTDOORS

SKIING

FAMILY **Estación de Esquí Sierra Nevada.** Europe's southernmost ski resort is one of its best equipped. At the Pradollano and Borreguiles stations, there's good skiing from December through April or May; each has a special snowboarding circuit, floodlighted night slopes, a children's ski school, and après-ski sun and swimming in the Mediterranean less than an hour away. In winter, buses to Pradollano leave Granada's bus station three times a day on weekdays and four times on weekends and holidays. Tickets are €9 round-trip. As for Borreguiles, you can get there only on skis. There's an information center (⊕ *www.sierranevada.es)* at Plaza de Andalucía 4.

THE ALPUJARRAS

Village of Lanjarón: 46 km (29 miles) south of Granada.

Fodor'sChoice A trip to the Alpujarras, on the southern slopes of the Sierra Nevada, ★ takes you to one of Andalusia's highest, most remote, and most scenic areas, home for decades to painters, writers, and a considerable foreign population. The Alpujarras region was originally populated by Moors fleeing the Christian Reconquest (from Seville after its fall in 1248, then from Granada after 1492). It was also the final fiefdom of the unfortunate Boabdil, conceded to him by the Catholic Monarchs after he surrendered Granada. In 1568 rebellious Moors made their last stand against the Christian overlords, a revolt ruthlessly suppressed by Felipe II and followed by the forced conversion of all Moors to Christianity and their resettlement farther inland and up Spain's eastern coast. The villages were then repopulated with Christian soldiers from Galicia, who were granted land in return for their service. To this day, the Galicians' descendants continue the Moorish custom of weaving rugs and blankets in the traditional Alpujarran colors of red, green, black, and white, and they sell their crafts in many of the villages. Be on the lookout for handmade basketry and pottery as well.

Houses here are squat and square; they spill down the southern slopes of the Sierra Nevada, bearing a strong resemblance to the Berber homes in the Rif Mountains, just across the Mediterranean in Morocco. If you're driving, the road as far as Lanjarón and Orgiva is smooth sailing; after that come steep, twisting mountain roads with few gas stations. Beyond sightseeing, the area is a haven for outdoor activities such as hiking and horseback riding. Inquire at the **Information Point** at Plaza de la Libertad, at Pampaneira.

10

EN ROUTE

Lanjarón and Nearby Villages. The western entrance to the Alpujarras is some 46 km (29 miles) from Granada at Lanjarón. This spa town is famous for its mineral water, collected from the melting snows of the Sierra Nevada and drunk throughout Spain. **Orgiva,** the next and largest town in the Alpujarras, has a 17th-century castle. Here you can leave the A348 and follow signs for the villages of the Alpujarras Altas (High Alpujarras), including **Pampaneira, Capileira,** and especially **Trevélez,** which lies on the slopes of the Mulhacén at 4,840 feet above sea level. Reward yourself with a plate of the local jamón serrano. Trevélez has three levels—the Barrio Alto, Barrio Medio, and Barrio Bajo—and the butchers are concentrated in the lowest section (Bajo). The higher levels have narrow cobblestone streets, whitewashed houses, and shops.

WHERE TO STAY

$ HOTEL FAMILY 🏨 **Hotel Alcadima.** One of the best-value hotels in the area, this pleasant if unfancy hotel in the rustic spa town of Lanjarón makes a good base for exploring the lower part of the Alpujarras. **Pros:** swimming pool; excellent restaurant; two-bedroom suites are ideal for families. **Cons:** Lanjarón isn't the prettiest village in the area; could be too plain for some; down an unattractive side street. [$] *Rooms from: €70* ✉ *Calle Francisco Tarrega 3* ☎ *958/770809* 🌐 *www.alcadima.com* 🛏 *45 rooms* 🍴 *No meals.*

$ RENTAL 🏨 **Los Tinaos.** Located on the way to Trevélez in the pretty whitewashed village of Bubión that almost clings to the mountainside, these comfortable apartments (for two or four people) come squeaky-clean, with open log fires as well as central heating, and sweeping views across the valley. **Pros:** valley views; a short walk from Pitres; bar serving locally produced wine. **Cons:** steep walk down. [$] *Rooms from: €55* ✉ *Calle Parras 2, Bubión* ☎ *958/763217* 🌐 *www.lostinaos.com* 🛏 *10 rooms* 🍴 *No meals.*

$ B&B/INN 🏨 **Sierra y Mar.** Near Pitres and the Río Trevélez in the tiny hamlet of Ferreirola, famous for its streams and natural springs, lies this cozy village house with mountain views at every turn. **Pros:** quiet retreat; mountain views; pretty garden terrace. **Cons:** off the beaten tourist track. [$] *Rooms from: €69* ✉ *Calle Albaizín 3* ☎ *958/766171* 🌐 *www.sierraymar.com* 🛏 *9 rooms* 🍴 *Free Breakfast.*

COSTA DEL SOL AND COSTA DE ALMERÍA

WELCOME TO COSTA DEL SOL AND COSTA DE ALMERÍA

TOP REASONS TO GO

★ **Enjoy the sun and sand:** Relax at any of the beaches; they're all free, though in summer there isn't much towel space.

★ **Soak up the atmosphere:** Spend a day in Málaga, Picasso's birthplace, visiting the museums, exploring the old town, and strolling the Palm Walkway in the port.

★ **Check out Puerto Banús:** Wine, dine, and celebrity-watch at the Costa del Sol's most luxurious and sophisticated port town.

★ **Visit Cabo de Gata:** This protected natural reserve is one of the wildest and most beautiful stretches of coast in Spain.

★ **Shop for souvenirs:** Check out the weekly market in one of the Costa resorts to pick up bargain-price souvenirs, including ceramics.

The towns and resorts along the southeastern Spanish coastline vary considerably according to whether they lie to the east or to the west of Málaga. To the east are the Costa de Almería and the Costa Tropical, less developed stretches of coastline. Towns like Nerja act as a gateway to the dramatic mountainous region of La Axarquía. West from Málaga along the Costa del Sol proper, the strip between Torremolinos and Marbella is the most densely populated. Seamless though it may appear, as one resort merges into the next, each town has a distinctive character, with its own sights, charms, and activities.

1 The Costa de Almería. This Costa region is hot and sunny virtually year-round and is notable for its spectacular beaches, unspoiled countryside, and (less appealingly) plastic greenhouse agriculture. Right on the coast is Almería, a handsome, under-rated city with a fascinating historic center with narrow pedestrian streets flanked by sunbaked ocher buildings and tapas bars.

2 The Costa Tropical. Less developed than the Costa del Sol, this stretch of coastline is distinctive for its attractive seaside towns, rocky coves, excellent water sports, and mountainous interior.

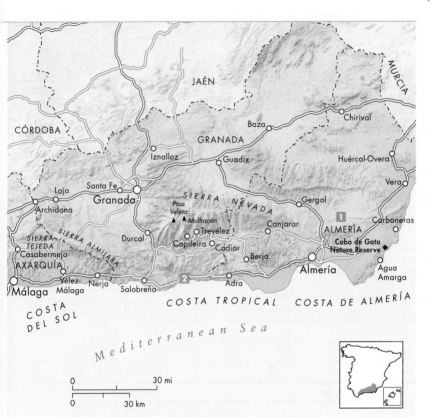

3 **Málaga Province.** Don't miss the capital of the province: this up-and-coming cruise port retains a traditional Andalusian feel; better known are the coastal resorts due west with their sweeping beaches and excellent tourist facilities.

4 **Gibraltar.** "The Rock" is an extraordinary combination of Spain and Great Britain, with a fascinating history. There are also some fine restaurants here, as well as traditional Olde English pubs.

EATING AND DRINKING WELL ALONG SPAIN'S SOUTHERN COAST

Spain's southern coast is known for fresh fish and seafood, grilled or quickly fried in olive oil. Sardines roasted on spits are popular along the Málaga coast, while upland towns offer more robust mountain fare, especially in Almería.

(top left) Beachside dining on the Costa del Sol *(top right)* Sardines being roasted over glowing logs *(bottom left)* A classic potato-based stew

Chiringuitos, small shanties along the beaches, are summer-only Costa del Sol restaurants that serve fish fresh off the boats. Málaga is known for seafood restaurants serving *fritura malagueña de pescaíto* (fried fish). In mountain towns, you'll find superb *rabo de toro* (oxtail), goat and sheep cheeses, wild mushrooms, and game dishes. Almería shares Moorish aromas of cumin and cardamom with its Andalusian sisters to the west, but also turns the corner toward its northern neighbor, Murcia, where delicacies such as *mojama* (salt-dried tuna) and *hueva de maruca* (ling roe) have been favorites since Phoenician times. Almería's wealth of vegetables and legumes combine with pork and game products for a rougher, more powerful culinary canon of thick stews and soups.

TO DRINK

Málaga has long been famous for the sweet *muscatel* wine that Russian empress Catherine the Great loved so much she imported it to Saint Petersburg duty-free in 1792. In the 18th century, muscatel was sold medicinally in pharmacies for its curative powers and is still widely produced and often served as accompaniment to dessert or tapas.

COLD ALMOND AND GARLIC SOUP

Ajoblanco, a summer staple in Andalusia, is a refreshing salty-sweet combination served cold. Exquisitely light and sharp, the almond and garlic soup has a surprisingly creamy and fresh taste. Almonds, garlic, hard white bread, olive oil, water, sherry vinegar, and a topping of muscat grapes are standard ingredients.

FRIED FISH MÁLAGA-STYLE

A popular dish along the Costa del Sol and the Costa de Almería, *fritura malagueña de pescaíto* is basically any sort of very small fish—such as anchovies, cuttlefish, baby squid, whitebait, and red mullet—fried in oil so hot that the fish end up crisp and light as a feather. The fish are lightly dusted in white flour, crisped quickly, and drained briefly before arriving piping hot and bone-dry on your plate. For an additional Moorish aroma, fritura masters add powdered cumin to the flour.

ALMERÍA STEWS

Almería is known for heartier fare than neighboring Málaga. *Puchero de trigo* (wheat and pork stew) is a fortifying winter comfort stew of boiled whole grains of wheat cooked with chickpeas, pork, black sausage, fatback, potatoes, saffron, cumin, and fennel. *Ajo colorao* (also known as *atascaburras*) is another popular stew, which consists of potatoes, dried peppers, vegetables,

and fish that are simmered into a thick red-orange stew *de cuchara* (eaten with a spoon). Laced with cumin and garlic and served with thick country bread, it's a stick-to-your-ribs mariner's soup.

ROASTED SARDINES

Known as *moraga de sardinas*, or *espeto de sardinas*, this method of cooking sardines is popular in the summer along the Pedregalejo and Carihuela beaches east and west of Málaga: the sardines are skewered and extended over logs at an angle so that the fish oils run back down the skewers instead of falling into the coals and causing a conflagration. Fresh fish and cold white wine or beer make this a beautiful and relaxing sunset beach dinner.

A THOUSAND AND ONE EGGS

Something about the spontaneous nature of Spain's southern latitudes seems to lend itself to the widespread use of eggs to bind ingredients together. In Andalusia and especially along the Costa del Sol, *huevos a la flamenca* (eggs flamenco-style) is a time-tested dish combining peppers, potatoes, ham, and peas with an egg broken over the top and baked sizzling hot in the oven. *Revuelto de setas y gambas* (scrambled eggs with wild mushrooms and shrimp) is a tasty combination and a common entrée. And, of course, there is the universal Iberian potato omelet, the *tortilla de patatas*.

BEST BEACHES OF THE SOUTHERN COAST

Tourists have been coming to the Costa del Sol since the 1950s, attracted by its magical combination of brochure-blue sea, miles of beaches, and reliably sunny weather.

(top left) One of the many resorts in Torremolinos (top right) Tarifa is known for its wind: great for windsurfing, kiteboarding, and kite flying. (bottom left) Crashing waves at Cabo de Gata

The beaches here range from the gravel-like shingle in Almuñécar, Nerja, and Málaga to fine, gritty sand from Torremolinos westward. The best (and most crowded) beaches are east of Málaga and those flanking the most popular resorts of Nerja, Torremolinos, Fuengirola, and Marbella. For more secluded beaches, head west of Estepona and past Gibraltar to Tarifa and the Cádiz coast. The beaches change when you hit the Atlantic, becoming appealingly wide with fine golden sand. The winds are usually quite strong here, which means that although you can't read a newspaper while lying out, the conditions for windsurfing and kiteboarding are near perfect.

Beaches are free, and busiest in July, August, and on Sundays May–October when malagueño families arrive for a full day on the beach and lunch at a chiringuito.

OVER THE TOPLESS

In Spain, as in many parts of Europe, it is perfectly acceptable for women to go topless on the beach, although covering up is the norm at beach bars. There are several nude beaches on the Costas; look for the *playa naturista* sign. The most popular are in Maro (near Nerja), Benalnatura (Benalmádena Costa), Cabo Pino (Marbella), and near Tarifa.

BEST BEACHES

11

LA CARIHUELA, TORREMOLINOS

This former fishing district of Torremolinos has a wide stretch of beach. The chiringuitos here are some of the best on the Costa, and the promenade, which continues until Benalmádena port, with its striking Asian-inspired architecture and great choice of restaurants and bars, is delightful for strolling.

CARVAJAL, FUENGIROLA

Backed by low-rise buildings and greenery, the beach here is unspoiled and refreshingly low-key. East of Fuengirola center, the Carvajal beach bars have young crowds, with regular live music in summer. It's also an easily accessible beach on the Málaga–Fuengirola train, with a stop within walking distance of the sand.

PLAYA LOS LANCES, TARIFA

This white sandy beach is one of the least spoiled in Andalusia. Near lush vegetation, lagoons, and the occasional campground and boho-chic hotel (*see listing for the Hurricane Hotel*), Tarifa's main beach is famed throughout Europe for its windsurfing and kiteboarding, so expect some real winds: *levante* from the east and *poniente* from the west.

CABO DE GATA, ALMERÍA

Backed by natural parkland, with volcanic rock formations creating dramatic cliffs and secluded bays,

Almería's stunning Cabo de Gata coastline includes superb beaches and coves within the protected UNESCO Biosphere Reserve. The fact that most of the beaches here are only accessible via marked footpaths adds to their off-the-beaten-track appeal.

PUERTO BANÚS, MARBELLA

Looking for action? Some great beach scenes flank the world-famous luxurious port. Pedro's Beach is known for its excellent, laid-back Caribbean-style seafood restaurants, good music, and hip, good-looking crowd. Another superb sandy choice are the coves west of the marina, so-called boutique beaches, with club areas and massages available, as well as attractive beaches and tempting shallow waters.

EL SALADILLO, ESTEPONA

Between Marbella and Estepona (take the Cancelada exit off the A7), this relaxed and inviting beach is not as well known as its glitzier neighbors. It's harder to find, so mainly locals in the know frequent it. There are two popular seafood restaurants here, plus a volleyball net, showers, and sun beds and parasols for rent.

Updated by
Joanna Styles

With roughly 320 days of sunshine a year, the Costa del Sol well deserves its nickname, "the Sunshine Coast." It's no wonder much of the coast has been built up with resorts and high-rises. Don't despair, though; you can still find some classic Spanish experiences, whether in the old city of Marbella or one of the smaller villages like Casares. And despite the hubbub of high season, visitors can always unwind here, basking or strolling on mile after mile of sandy beach.

Technically, the stretch of Andalusian shore known as the Costa del Sol runs west from the Costa Tropical, near Granada, to the tip of Tarifa, the southernmost point in Europe, just beyond Gibraltar. For most of the Europeans who have flocked here over the past 50 years, though, the Sunshine Coast has been largely restricted to the 70-km (43-mile) sprawl of hotels, vacation villas, golf courses, marinas, and nightclubs between Torremolinos, just west of Málaga, and Estepona, down toward Gibraltar. Since the late 1950s this area has mushroomed from a group of impoverished fishing villages into an overdeveloped seaside playground and retirement haven. The city of Almería and its coastline, the Costa de Almería, is southwest of Granada's Alpujarras region, and due east of the Costa Tropical (around 147 km [93 miles] from Almuñécar).

PLANNING

WHEN TO GO

May, June, and September are the best times to visit this coastal area, when there's plenty of sunshine but fewer tourists than in the hottest season of July and August. Winter can have bright sunny days, but you may feel the chill, and many hotels in the lower price bracket have heat for only a few hours a day; you can also expect several days of rain. Holy Week, the week before Easter Sunday, is a fun time to visit to see the religious processions.

PLANNING YOUR TIME

Travelers with their own wheels who want a real taste of the area in just a few days could start by exploring the relatively unspoiled villages of the Costa Tropical: wander around quaint Salobreña, then hit the larger coastal resort of Nerja and head inland for a look around pretty Frigiliana.

Move on to Málaga next; it has lots to offer, including several top art museums, excellent restaurants, and some of the best tapas bars in the province. It's also easy to get to stunning, mountaintop Ronda (⇨ see Chapter 10), which is also on a bus route.

Hit the coast at Marbella, the Costa del Sol's swankiest resort, and then take a leisurely stroll around Puerto Banús. Next, head west to Gibraltar for a day of shopping and sightseeing before returning to the coast and Torremolinos for a night on the town.

Choose your base carefully, as the various areas here make for very different experiences. Málaga is a vibrant Spanish city, virtually untainted by mass tourism, while Torremolinos is a budget destination catering mostly to the mass market. Fuengirola is quieter, with a large population of middle-aged expatriates; farther west, the Marbella–San Pedro de Alcántara area is more exclusive and expensive.

GETTING HERE AND AROUND

AIR TRAVEL

Delta Airlines runs direct flights from JFK (New York) to Málaga late May–September and via Charles de Gaulle (Paris) the rest of the year. All other flights from the United States connect in Madrid. British Airways flies several times daily from London (City, Gatwick, and Heathrow) to Málaga, and several budget airlines, such as easyJet, Norwegian Air, and Ryanair also link the two cities. There are direct flights to Málaga from most other major European cities on Iberia or other airlines. Iberia Express/Vueling has four flights daily from Madrid (1 hour 15 minutes), four flights daily from Barcelona (1½ hours), and regular flights from other Spanish cities.

Málaga's Costa del Sol airport is 10 km (6 miles) west of town and is one of Spain's most modern. Trains from the airport into town run every 20 minutes 6:44 am–12:54 am (12 minutes, €1.80) and from the airport to Fuengirola every 20 minutes 5:32 am–11:42 pm (34 minutes, €2.70), stopping at several resorts en route, including Torremolinos and Benalmádena.

From the airport there's also bus service to Málaga every half hour 7 am–midnight (€3). At least 10 daily buses (more frequently July–September) run between the airport and Marbella (45 minutes, €6.15–€8.20). Taxi fares from the airport to Málaga, Torremolinos, and other resorts are posted inside the terminal: from the airport to Marbella is about €65, to Torremolinos €15, and to Fuengirola €35. Many of the better hotels and all tour companies will arrange for pickup at the airport.

Airport Contact Aeropuerto Costa del Sol (AGP) (*Aeropuerto de Málaga*). ✉ *Av. Comandante García Morato s/n, Málaga* ☎ *952/048804* ⊕ *www.aena.es*.

BIKE TRAVEL

The Costa del Sol is famous for its sun and sand, but many people supplement their beach time with mountain-bike forays into the hilly interior, particularly around Ojén, near Marbella, and along the mountain roads around Ronda. One popular route, which affords sweeping vistas, follows the mountain road from Ojén west to Istán. The Costa del Sol's temperate climate is ideal for biking, though it's best not to exert yourself on the trails in July and August, when temperatures soar. There are numerous bike-rental shops in the area, particularly in Marbella, Ronda, and Ojén; many shops also arrange bike excursions. The cost to rent a mountain bike for the day is around €20. Guided bike excursions, which include bikes, support staff, and cars, generally start at about €50 a day.

Bike Rental Contact Bike Tours Malaga. ✉ *Calle Vendeja 6, Málaga* ☎ *951/252264* ⊕ *www.biketoursmalaga.com.* **Marbella Rent a Bike.** ☎ *952/811062* ⊕ *www.marbellarentabike.com.*

BUS TRAVEL

Until the high-speed AVE train line opens between Antequera and Granada in 2019, buses are the best way to reach the Costa del Sol from Granada, and, aside from the train service from Málaga to Fuengirola, the best way to get around once you're here. During holidays it's wise to reserve your seat in advance for long-distance travel.

On the Costa del Sol, bus services connect Málaga with Cádiz (4 daily), Córdoba (4 daily), Granada (16 daily), and Seville (6 daily). In Fuengirola you can catch buses for Mijas, Marbella, Estepona, and Algeciras. The Avanzabus bus company serves most of the Costa del Sol and Cádiz. ALSA serves Granada, Córdoba, Seville, and Nerja. Los Amarillos serves Jerez and Ronda. There are also daily buses between Málaga airport and Granada and Seville.

Bus Contacts ALSA. ☎ *902/422242* ⊕ *www.alsa.es.* **Avanzabus.** ☎ *912/722832* ⊕ *www.avanzabus.com.* **Los Amarillos.** ☎ *902/210317* ⊕ *www. losamarillos.es.*

CAR TRAVEL

A car allows you to explore Andalusia's mountain villages. Mountain driving can be hair-raising but is getting better as highways are improved.

Málaga is 536 km (333 miles) from Madrid, taking the A4 to Córdoba, then the A44 to Granada, the A92 to Antequera, and the A45; 162 km (101 miles) from Córdoba via Antequera; 220 km (137 miles) from Seville; and 131 km (81 miles) from Granada by the shortest route of the A92 to Loja, then the A45 to Málaga.

To take a car into Gibraltar you need, in theory, an insurance certificate and a logbook (a certificate of vehicle ownership). In practice, all you need is your passport. Head for the well-signposted multistory parking garage, as street parking on the Rock is scarce.

National Car-Rental Agencies Helle Hollis. ☎ *952/245544* ⊕ *www.hellehollis.com.*

TAXI TRAVEL

Taxis are plentiful throughout the Costa del Sol and may be hailed on the street or from specified taxi ranks marked "Taxi." Restaurants are usually happy to call a taxi for you, too. Fares are reasonable, and meters are strictly used. You are not required to tip taxi drivers, though rounding up the amount will be appreciated.

TRAIN TRAVEL

Málaga is the main rail terminus in the area, with 12 high-speed trains per day from Madrid (2 hours 25 minutes–2 hours 50 minutes, depending on the train). Málaga is also linked by high-speed train with Barcelona (6 daily, 5 hours 45 minutes–6 hours 35 minutes, depending on the train). Six daily trains also link Seville with Málaga in just under two hours.

From Granada to Málaga (3–3½ hours), you must change at Bobadilla, making buses more efficient from here (the high-speed AVE line due for completion in 2019 will reduce the journey time to 50 minutes). Málaga's train station is a 15-minute walk from the city center, across the river.

RENFE connects Málaga, Torremolinos, and Fuengirola, stopping at the airport and all resorts along the way. The train leaves Málaga every 20 minutes 5:20 am–11:30 pm, and Fuengirola every 20 minutes 6:10 am–12:20 am. For the city center, get off at the last stop. A daily train connects Málaga and Ronda via the dramatic Chorro gorge (1 hour 50 minutes).

RESTAURANTS

Málaga is best for traditional Spanish cooking, with a wealth of bars and seafood restaurants serving fritura malagueña, the city's famous fried seafood. Torremolinos's Carihuela district is also a good destination for lovers of Spanish seafood. The area's resorts serve every conceivable foreign cuisine, from Thai to the Scandinavian smorgasbord. For delicious cheap eats, try the chiringuitos. Strung out along the beaches, these summer-only restaurants serve seafood fresh off the boats. Because there are so many foreigners here, meals on the coast are served earlier than elsewhere in Andalusia; most restaurants open at 1 or 1:30 for lunch and 7 or 8 for dinner.

HOTELS

Most hotels on the developed stretch between Torremolinos and Fuengirola offer large, functional rooms near the sea at competitive rates, but the area's popularity as a budget destination means that most such hotels are booked in high season by package-tour operators. Finding a room at Easter, in July and August, or over holiday weekends can be difficult if you haven't reserved in advance. In July and August many hotels require a stay of at least three days. Málaga is an increasingly attractive base for visitors to this corner of Andalusia and has some good hotels. Marbella, meanwhile, has more than its fair share of grand lodgings, including some of Spain's most expensive rooms. Gibraltar's handful of hotels tends to be more expensive than most comparable lodgings in Spain.

There are also apartments and villas for short- or long-term stays, ranging from traditional Andalusian farmhouses to luxury villas. One excellent source for apartment and villa rentals is **Spain Holiday** (☎ 951/204601 ⊕ *www.spain-holiday.com*). For Marbella, you can also try **Nordica Rentals** (☎ 952/811552 ⊕ *www.nordicarentals.com*), and, for high-end rentals, **The Luxury Villa Collection** (☎ 656/668710 ⊕ *www. theluxuryvillacollection.com*). Our local writers vet every hotel to recommend the best overnights in each price category, from budget to expensive. Unless otherwise specified, you can expect a private bath, phone, and TV in your room. *Hotel reviews have been shortened. For full information, visit Fodors.com.*

WHAT IT COSTS IN EUROS				
	$	$$	$$$	$$$$
Restaurants	under €12	€12–€17	€18–€22	over €22
Hotels	under €90	€90–€125	€126–€180	over €180

Restaurant prices are the average cost of a main course or equivalent combination of smaller dishes at dinner, or, if dinner is not served, at lunch. Hotel prices are the lowest cost of a standard double room in high season.

GOLF IN THE SUN
Nicknamed the "Costa del Golf," the Sun Coast has some 45 golf courses within putting distance of the Mediterranean. Most of the courses are between Rincón de la Victoria (east of Málaga) and Gibraltar. The best time for golfing is October–June; greens fees are lower in high summer. Check out the comprehensive website ⊕ *www.golfinspain. com* for up-to-date information.

TOURS
Several companies run one- and two-day excursions from Costa del Sol resorts. You can book with local travel agents and hotels; excursions leave from Málaga, Torremolinos, Fuengirola, Marbella, and Estepona, with prices varying by departure point. Most tours last half a day, and in most cases you can be picked up at your hotel. Popular tours include Málaga, Gibraltar, the Cuevas de Nerja, Mijas, Tangier, and Ronda. The Costa del Sol's varied landscape is also wonderful for hiking and walking, and several companies offer walking or cycling tours.

TOUR OPERATORS
John Keo Walking Tours. This company provides guided walks and hikes around the eastern Costa del Sol, weekdays only. Reservations are essential. ☎ 647/273502 ⊕ *www.hikingwalkingspain.com* 🚶 *From €25.*

Julia Travel. One of the largest tour operators in Spain offers a good selection of excursions on the Costa del Sol. ☎ 934/026900 ⊕ *www. juliatravel.com* 🚶 *From €32.*

Sierra MTB. A good range of rural and urban guided cycling tours suit all levels. Weekend and weeklong packages, including accommodations and a different bike ride every day, are available in addition to day trips. ☎ 616/295251 ⊕ *www.sierracycling.com* 🚶 *From €85.*

Viajes Rusadir. This local firm specializes in Costa del Sol excursions and private tours. ☎ *952/463458* ⊕ *www.viajesrusadir.com* ✉ *From €25.*

VISITOR INFORMATION

The official website for the Costa del Sol is ⊕ *www.visitacostadelsol. com*; it has good information on sightseeing and events, guides to towns and villages, and contact details for the regional and local tourist offices, which are listed under their respective towns and cities. Tourist offices are generally open Monday–Saturday 10–7 (until 8 in summer) and Sunday 10–2.

THE COSTA DE ALMERÍA

South of Spain's Murcia Coast lie the shores of Andalusia, beginning with the Costa de Almería. Several of the coastal towns here, including Agua Amarga, have a laid-back charm, with miles of sandy beaches and a refreshing lack of high-rise developments. The mineral riches of the surrounding mountains gave rise to Iberia's first true civilization, whose capital can still be glimpsed in the 4,700-year-old ruins of Los Millares, near the village of Santa Fe de Mondújar. The small towns of Níjar and Sorbas maintain an age-old tradition of pottery making and other crafts, and the western coast of Almería has tapped unexpected wealth from a parched land, thanks to modern techniques of growing produce in plastic greenhouses. In contrast to the inhospitable landscape of the mountain-fringed Andarax Valley, the area east of Granada's Alpujarras, near Alhama, has a cool climate and gentle landscape, both conducive to making fine wines.

THE CABO DE GATA NATURE RESERVE

40 km (25 miles) east of Almería, 86 km (53 miles) south of Mojácar.

The southeast corner of Spain is one of the country's last unspoiled wildernesses, and much of the coastline is part of a highly protected nature reserve. San José, the largest village, has a pleasant bay, though these days the village has rather outgrown itself and can be very busy in summer. Those preferring smaller, quieter destinations should look farther north, at places such as Agua Amarga and the often-deserted beaches nearby.

GETTING HERE AND AROUND

You need your own wheels to explore the nature reserve and surrounding villages, including San José. When it's time to hit the beach, Playa de los Genoveses and Playa Monsul, to the south of San José, are some of the best. A rough road follows the coast around the spectacular cape, eventually linking up with the N332 to Almería. Alternatively, follow the signs north for the towns of Níjar (approximately 20 km [12 miles] north) and Sorbas (32 km [20 miles] northeast of Níjar); both towns are famed for their distinctive green-glazed pottery, which you can buy directly from workshops.

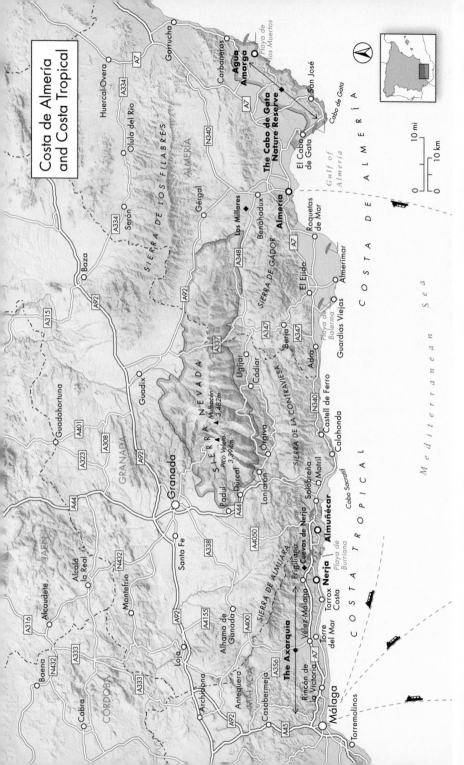

Costa de Almería and Costa Tropical

Playa de los Muertos

Agua Amarga

Carboneras

San José

The Cabo de Gata Nature Reserve

El Cabo de Gata

Cabo de Gata

Gorrucha

Huércal-Overa

A7

A334

Olula del Rio

Serón

A334

Baza

A92

A315

Gérgal

N340

ALMERÍA

SIERRA DE LOS FILABRES

Guadahortuna

A401

A323

A308

Guadix

A92

Los Millares

Benahadux

Almería

Roquetas de Mar

Gulf of Almería

C O S T A   D E   A L M E R Í A

SIERRA DE GADOR

El Ejido

Almerimar

Guardias Viejas

Playa de Balerma

Berja

A348

Ugíjar

A347

Cádiar

A347

Adra

N340

Castell de Ferro

Calahonda

SIERRA DE LA CONTRAVIESA

Cabo Sacratif

Motril

Salobreña

Cuevas de Nerja

Almuñécar

C O S T A   T R O P I C A L

M e d i t e r r a n e a n   S e a

GRANADA

Granada

S I E R R A   N E V A D A

Mulhacén 3,482m

Pico Veleta 3,394m

A44

A337

Padul

Dúrcal

Lanjarón

Órgiva

A44

A4050

Santa Fe

A338

Alhama de Granada

A4155

A400

Nerja

Frigiliana

SIERRA DE ALMIJARA

Playa de Burriana

Nerja

Torrox Costa

Torrox

Vélez-Málaga

Torre del Mar

The Axarquía

A356

Rincón de la Victoria

A7

Málaga

MÁLAGA

Torremolinos

A45

Casabermeja

Antequera

Archidona

A92

Loja

A333

Montefrío

Alhama de Granada

JAÉN

Alcalá la Real

Alcaudete

A316

CÓRDOBA

Baena

Cabra

N432

A333

A92

A44

10 mi

10 km

Dramatic views of the coastline from the Cabo de Gata natural park

EXPLORING

Parque Natural Marítimo y Terrestre Cabo de Gata–Níjar. Birds are the main attraction at this nature reserve just south of San José; it's home to several species native to Africa, including the *camachuelo trompetero* (large-beaked bullfinch), which is not found anywhere else outside Africa. Check out the Centro Las Amoladeras visitor center at the park entrance, which has an exhibit and information on the region and organizes guided walks and tours of the area. ⊠ *Road from Almería to Cabo de Gata, Km 6, San José* ☎ *950/160435* ⊘ *Closed Mon. and Tues.*

BEACHES

El Playazo. *Playazo* literally means "one great beach," and this sandy cove is certainly one of the gems in the Cabo de Gata nature reserve. Just a few minutes' drive from the village of Rodalquilar (once home to Spain's only gold mine), the yellow-sand beach is surrounded by ocher-color volcanic rock; an 18th-century fortress stands at one end. These are sheltered waters, so bathing is safe and warm, and the offshore rocks make for great snorkeling. This beach is deserted during most of the year, and its isolation and lack of amenities mean that even in the summer months you won't come across too many other beachgoers. Although nude bathing isn't officially allowed here, it is tolerated. **Amenities:** none. **Best for:** snorkeling; solitude; sunrise. ⊠ *Rodalquilar, San José.*

Playa de los Genoveses. Named after the Genovese sailors who landed here in 1127 to aid King Alfonso VII, this beach is one of the area's best known and most beautiful. The long, sandy expanse is backed by pines, eucalyptus trees, and low-rising dunes. The sea is shallow, warm, and crystal clear here—snorkeling is popular around the rocks at either end of the cove. Free parking is available mid-September–mid-June; in July and August, you must park in nearby San José and take a minibus to the beach (€1.50). The beach can also be reached via an easy coastal walk from San José, a 7-km (4½-mile) round-trip. The beach has no amenities to speak of, so take plenty of water if it's hot. **Amenities:** parking. **Best for:** snorkeling; solitude; sunset; walking. ✉ *San José.*

WHERE TO STAY

$ B&B/INN 🏨 **Hostal La Isleta.** This low-rise, white, blocky building with blue trim is nothing fancy—what you're paying for is the location, within a stone's throw of the beach on a charming bay, with superb, relaxing sea views. **Pros:** waterfront location; excellent seafood restaurant. **Cons:** no frills; can be noisy with families in summer; basic breakfast. [$] *Rooms from: €60* ✉ *Calle Isleta del Moro, San José* ☎ *950/389713* 🛏 *10 rooms* 🍴 *No meals.*

AGUA AMARGA

22 km (14 miles) north of San José, 55 km (34 miles) east of Almería.

Like other coastal hamlets, Agua Amarga started out in the 18th century as a tuna-fishing port. These days, as perhaps the most pleasant village on the Cabo de Gata coast, it attracts lots of visitors, although it remains much less developed than San José. One of the coast's best beaches is just to the north: the dramatically named **Playa de los Muertos** (Beach of the Dead), a long stretch of fine gravel bookended with volcanic outcrops.

GETTING HERE AND AROUND

If you're driving here from Almería, follow signs to the airport, then continue north on the A7; Agua Amarga is signposted just north of the Parque Natural Cabo de Gata. The village itself is small enough to explore easily on foot.

WHERE TO EAT AND STAY

$$ SPANISH ✕ **Hostal Restaurante La Palmera.** At the far eastern end of the beach, the terrace at this hotel restaurant sits right on the sand; get a table here rather than inside the less impressive dining room. Fresh fish, locally caught and grilled, is the highlight of the menu, which also includes simple salads and plates of fried fish. **Known for:** locally caught fish; beachfront dining; arroz a banda (rice with fish and aioli). [$] *Average main: €15* ✉ *Calle Aguada 4* ☎ *950/138208* 🌐 *hostalrestaurantela-palmera.net/en* 🕒 *Closed mid-Jan.–Mar.*

$$$ HOTEL 🏨 **Boutique Hotel El Tio Kiko.** On a hill to the west of the village, this modern luxury hotel has commanding sea views and is close enough to the main beach to walk (but far enough to enjoy peace and quiet). **Pros:** sea views; rooms have balconies, some with hot tubs; varied breakfast. **Cons:** up a hill; could be too quiet for some; adults-only from mid-June-mid September. [$] *Rooms from: €180* ✉ *Calle Embarque 12* ☎ *950/138080* 🌐 *www.eltiokiko.com* 🛏 *27 rooms* 🍴 *Free Breakfast.*

ALMERÍA

183 km (114 miles) east of Málaga.

Warmed by the sunniest climate in Andalusia, Almería is a youthful Mediterranean city, basking in sweeping views of the sea from its coastal perch and close to several excellent beaches. It's also a capital of the grape industry, thanks to its wonderfully mild climate in spring and fall. Rimmed by tree-lined boulevards and some landscaped squares, the city's core is a maze of narrow, winding alleys formed by flat-roofed, distinctly Mudejar houses. Now surrounded by modern apartment blocks, these dazzlingly white older homes continue to give Almería an Andalusian flavor. Barely touched by tourism, this compact city is well worth a visit—allow an overnight stay to take in the main sights en route to or from Cabo de Gata or Málaga. Be sure to try the tapas bars, where you'll be offered a free (and usually elaborate) tapa with your drink.

GETTING HERE AND AROUND

Bus No. 30 (€1.05) runs roughly every 35 minutes 7 am–11 pm from Almería airport to the center of town (Calle del Doctor Gregorio Marañón).

The city center is compact, and most of the main sights are within easy strolling distance of each other.

VISITOR INFORMATION

Contacts **Almería Visitor Information.** ⊠ *Pl. de la Constitución* ☎ *950/210538* ⊕ *www.almeriatourism.com.*

EXPLORING

Alcazaba. Dominating the city is this fortress, built by Caliph Abd ar-Rahman I and given a bell tower by Carlos III. From here you have sweeping views of the port and city. Among the ruins of the fortress, which was damaged by earthquakes in 1522 and 1560, are landscaped gardens of rock flowers and cacti. ⊠ *Calle Almanzor* ☎ *950/801008* 🎫 *€2* ⊙ *Closed Mon.*

Cathedral. Below the Alcazaba is the local cathedral, with buttressed towers that give it the appearance of a castle. It's in Gothic style, but with some classical touches around the doors. Guided tours are available, and admission includes a visit to the ecclesiastical museum. ⊠ *Pl. de la Catedral* ☎ *950/234848* 🎫 *€5.*

Fodor'sChoice ★ **Refugios de la Guerra Civil** (*Civil War Shelters*). Almería, the last bastion of the Republican government during the Spanish Civil War, was hit by 754 bombs launched via air and sea by Nationalist forces. To protect civilians, 4½ km (2¾ miles) of tunnels were built under the city to provide shelter for more than 34,000 people. About 1 km (½ mile) can now be visited on a guided tour that covers the food stores, sleeping quarters, and an operating theater for the wounded, with its original medical equipment. ⊠ *Pl. Manuel Pérez García s/n* ☎ *950/268696* 🎫 *€3* ⊙ *Closed Mon.*

OFF THE BEATEN PATH

Los Millares. This important archaeological site is nearly 2½ km (1½ miles) southwest from the village of Santa Fe de Mondújar and 19 km (12 miles) from Almería. This collection of ruins scattered on a windswept hilltop was the birthplace of civilization in Spain nearly 5,000 years ago. Large, dome-shape tombs show that the community had an advanced society, and the existence of formidable defense walls indicates it had something to protect. A series of concentric fortifications shows that the settlement increased in size, eventually holding some 2,000 people. The town was inhabited from 2700 to 1800 BC and came to dominate the entire region. Guided tours are available: call in advance to book. Allow two hours for your visit. ✉ *Santa Fe de Mondújar* ☎ *677/903404* 🎟 *Free* 🕘 *Closed Mon. and Tues.*

WHERE TO EAT AND STAY

$$$ SPANISH 🍴 **La Encina.** This justly popular restaurant is housed in an 1860s building that also incorporates an 11th-century Moorish well. Time may have stood still with the setting, but the cuisine reflects a modern twist on traditional dishes, including seafood mains like *bacalao con cebolla, miel y pasas con cruijiente de espinacas* (cod with onion, honey, and raisins) or *rabo de novillo con almendras* (oxtail stew with almonds). **Known for:** creative tapas; wine list; bacalao. [$] *Average main: €18* ✉ *Calle Marín 3* ☎ *950/273429* 🌐 *www.restaurantelaencina.net* 🕘 *Closed Mon.*

$$$ SPANISH 🍴 **Valentín.** This popular, central spot serves fine regional specialties, such as *arroz de marisco* (rice with seafood), *cazuela de rape en salsa de almendras* (monkfish stew with almond sauce), and the delicious *kokotxas de bacalao en salsa de ostras* (cod cheeks in oyster sauce). The surroundings are rustic-yet-elegant Andalusian: whitewashed walls, dark wood, and exposed brick. **Known for:** rice dishes; seafood. [$] *Average main: €20* ✉ *Calle Tenor Iribarne 10* ☎ *950/264475.*

$$ HOTEL 🏨 **Aire Hotel.** In the heart of the old quarter, early-19th-century architecture is paired with comfortable and up-to-date amenities in this boutique hotel with strong design features. **Pros:** central location; terrace with great views; underground Arab baths are included in the rate. **Cons:** bathrooms are in view from the guest rooms; street noise in some rooms. [$] *Rooms from: €110* ✉ *Pl. de la Constitución 4* ☎ *950/282096* 🌐 *www.airehotelalmeria.com* 🛏 *10 rooms* 🍽 *No meals.*

$ HOTEL 🏨 **Hotel Catedral.** In full view of the cathedral, this small hotel combines traditional charm (it has kept many of its original mid-19th-century features, including a stunning arched entryway) with modern elegance. **Pros:** cathedral views; rooftop terrace with plunge pool; good breakfast. **Cons:** reception staff could be friendlier; hotel events can be noisy. [$] *Rooms from: €62* ✉ *Pl. de la Catedral 8* ☎ *950/234011* 🌐 *www.hotelcatedral.net* 🛏 *20 rooms* 🍽 *No meals.*

$ HOTEL 🏨 **Nuevo Torreluz.** Value is the overriding attraction at this comfortable and elegant modern hotel, which has slick, bright rooms and the kind of amenities you'd expect to come at a higher price. **Pros:** great central location; large rooms; good value. **Cons:** no pool; breakfast served in hotel next door; rooms in the main building are more expensive. [$] *Rooms from: €70* ✉ *Pl. Flores 10* ☎ *950/234399* 🌐 *www.torreluz.com* 🛏 *98 rooms* 🍽 *No meals.*

NIGHTLIFE AND THE ARTS

In Almería, the action's on **Plaza Flores,** moving down to the beach in summer.

Fodor's Choice ★ **Peña El Taranto.** For more than 55 years, this excellent venue (home to the city's Arab water deposits) has been one of the main centers for flamenco in Andalusia, and foot-stomping live flamenco and concerts are performed every two weeks. Check in advance for exact times and dates. ✉ *Calle Tenor Iribame 20* ☎ *950/235057* ⊕ *www.eltaranto.com.*

THE COSTA TROPICAL

East of Málaga and west of Almería lies the Costa Tropical. Housing developments resemble buildings in Andalusian villages rather than the bland high-rises elsewhere, and its tourist onslaught has been mild. A flourishing farming center, the area earns its keep from tropical fruit, including avocados, mangoes, and pawpaws (also known as custard apples). You may find packed beaches and traffic-choked roads at the height of the season, but for most of the year the Costa Tropical is relatively free of other tourists, if not also devoid of expatriates.

ALMUÑÉCAR

85 km (53 miles) east of Málaga.

This small-time resort with a shingle beach is popular with Spanish and Northern European vacationers. It's been a fishing village since Phoenician times, 3,000 years ago, when it was called Sexi; later, the Moors built a castle here for the treasures of Granada's kings. The road west from Motril and Salobreña passes through what was the empire of the sugar barons, who brought prosperity to Málaga's province in the 19th century: the cane fields now give way to lychees, limes, mangoes, pawpaws, and olives.

The village is actually two, separated by the dramatic rocky headland of Punta de la Mona. To the east is Almuñécar proper, and to the west is **La Herradura,** a quiet fishing community. Between the two is the Marina del Este yacht harbor, which, along with La Herradura, is a popular diving center. A renowned jazz festival takes place annually in July, often showcasing big names.

GETTING HERE AND AROUND

The A7 runs north of town. There is an efficient bus service to surrounding towns and cities, including Málaga, Granada, Nerja, and, closer afield, La Herradura. Almuñécar's town center is well laid out for strolling, and the local tourist office has information on bicycle and scooter rental.

VISITOR INFORMATION

Contacts Almuñécar. ✉ *Palacete de la Najarra, Av. de Europa* ☎ *958/631125* ⊕ *www.turismoalmunecar.es.*

EXPLORING

Castillo de San Miguel (*St. Michael's Castle*). A Roman fortress once stood here, later enlarged by the Moors, but the castle's present aspect, crowning the city, owes more to 16th-century additions. The building

A religious procession in Almuñécar

was bombed during the Peninsular War in the 19th century, and what was left was used as a cemetery until the 1990s. You can wander the ramparts and peer into the dungeon; the skeleton at the bottom is a reproduction of human remains discovered on the spot. ✉ *Calle San Miguel Bajo* ☎ *958/838623* 🎟 *€3, includes admission to Cueva de Siete Palacios* 🕓 *Closed Mon.*

Cueva de Siete Palacios (*Cave of Seven Palaces*). Beneath the Castillo de San Miguel is this large, vaulted stone cellar of Roman origin, now Almuñécar's archaeological museum. The collection is small but interesting, with Phoenician, Roman, and Moorish artifacts. ✉ *Calle San Miguel Bajo* ☎ *958/838623* 🎟 *€3, includes admission to Castillo de San Miguel* 🕓 *Closed Mon.*

WHERE TO EAT AND STAY

$$ INTERNATIONAL Fodor's Choice ★ 🍴 **El Arbol Blanco Playa.** Now located on the seafront (it was once a hike to get to the former hilltop location), this superb restaurant has a light and airy dining room, an outside terrace, and stunning sea views. The dishes, all creatively presented, include traditional options like oven-baked lamb as well as more innovative choices such as skate in Champagne sauce, a perfect pair for the excellent local white wine, Calvente blanco. The desserts are sublime, particularly the cheesecake. [$] *Average main: €15* ✉ *Paseo Marítimo Reina Sofía* ✥ *Next to Aquatrópic* ☎ *958/634038* 💳 *No credit cards* 🕓 *Closed Wed.*

$$ HOTEL 🏨 **Casablanca.** This quaint, family-run hotel comes with a pink-and-white neo-Moorish facade, a choice location next to the beach and near the botanical park, and comfortable rooms that are all different. **Pros:** great location; intimate, family-run atmosphere; all rooms have private

balconies or views. **Cons:** rooms vary, and some are small; parking can be difficult. $ *Rooms from: €95* ✉ *Pl. San Cristóbal 4* ☎ *958/635575* ⊕ *www.hotelcasablancaalmunecar.com* ⤴ *39 rooms* ⦿ *No meals.*

NERJA

52 km (32 miles) east of Málaga, 22 km (14 miles) west of Almuñécar.

Nerja—the name comes from the Moorish word *narixa*, meaning "abundant springs"—has a large community of expats, who live mainly outside town in *urbanizaciones* ("village" developments). The old village is on a headland above small beaches and rocky coves, which offer reasonable swimming despite the gray, gritty sand. In July and August, Nerja is packed with tourists, but the rest of the year it's a pleasure to wander the old town's narrow streets.

GETTING HERE AND AROUND

Nerja is a speedy hour's drive east from Málaga on the A7. If you're driving, park in the underground lot just west of the Balcón de Europa (it's signposted) off Calle La Cruz. The town is small enough to explore on foot.

VISITOR INFORMATION

Contacts Nerja. ✉ *Calle Carmen 1* ☎ *952/521531* ⊕ *www.nerja.es.*

EXPLORING

FAMILY

Fodor'sChoice

★

Balcón de Europa. The highlight of Nerja, this tree-lined promenade is on a promontory just off the central square, with magnificent views of the mountains and sea. You can gaze far off into the horizon using the strategically placed telescopes, or use this as a starting point for a horse-and-carriage clip-clop ride around town. Open-air concerts are held here in July and August. ✉ *Nerja.*

Cuevas de Nerja (*Nerja Caves*). Between Almuñécar and Nerja, these caves are on a road surrounded by giant cliffs and dramatic seascapes. Signs point to the cave entrance above the village of Maro, 4 km (2½ miles) east of Nerja. Its spires and turrets, created by millennia of dripping water, are now floodlit for better views. One suspended pinnacle, 200 feet long, is the world's largest known stalactite. The cave painting of seals discovered here may be the oldest example of art in existence—and the only one known to have been painted by Neanderthals. The awesome subterranean chambers create an evocative setting for concerts and ballets during the Nerja Festival of Music and Dance, held annually during late June to early July. There is also a bar-restaurant near the entrance with a spacious dining room that has superb views. ■ TIP→ **Afternoon visits are by guided tour only, September–June. They take around 45 minutes so arrive at least an hour before closing time. Private tours in English are available (€15, bookable online).** ✉ *Maro* ☎ *952/529520* ⊕ *www.cuevadenerja.com* 🎫 *€10.*

OFF THE
BEATEN
PATH

Frigiliana. On an inland mountain ridge overlooking the sea, this pretty village has spectacular views and an old quarter of narrow, cobbled streets and dazzling white houses decorated with pots of geraniums. It was the site of one of the last battles between the Christians and the Moors. Frigiliana is a short drive from the highway to the village; if you don't have a car, you can take a bus here from Nerja, which is 8 km (5 miles) away. ✉ *Frigiliana* ☎ *952/534261 for tourist information office.*

BEACHES

Las Alberquillas. One of the string of coves on the coastline west of Nerja, this beach of gray sand mixed with shingle is backed by pine trees and scrub that perfume the air. Reachable only via a stony track down the cliffs, this protected beach is one of the few on the Costa del Sol to be almost completely untouched by tourism. Its moderate waves mean you need to take care when bathing. The snorkeling around the rocks at either end of the beach is among the best in the area. This spot's seclusion makes the beach a favorite with couples and nudists—it's reasonably quiet even at the height of summer. Limited parking is available off the N340 highway, but there are no amenities, so take plenty of water. **Amenities:** none. **Best for:** nudists; snorkeling; solitude. ✉ *N340, Km 299.*

WHERE TO EAT AND STAY

$$$$ MEDITERRANEAN Fodor's Choice ★

🍴 **Oliva.** Mediterranean cuisine based on fresh, local produce takes center stage at this restaurant, which has both a minimalist, intimate dining room and a pleasant patio that's heated in winter. Highlights include the sole millefeuille, baby garlic, and ginger mayo, and *pluma ibérica* (Iberian pork) with *ras el hanout* (Moroccan spice mix) and eggplant puree. **Known for:** the best innovative cuisine in town; wine list; Iberian pork. [$] *Average main: €24* ✉ *Calle La Pintada 7* ☎ *952/522988* 🌐 *www.restauranteoliva.com.*

$$ B&B/INN Fodor's Choice ★

🏨 **Hotel Carabeo.** Down a side street near the center of town but still near the sea, this British-owned boutique hotel combines a great location and views with comfortable, pleasant rooms. **Pros:** sea views; great location; excellent restaurant. **Cons:** not open out of season; difficult to get a room in high season. [$] *Rooms from: €90* ✉ *Calle Hernando de Carabeo 34* ☎ *952/525444* 🌐 *www.hotelcarabeo.com* ⏲ *Closed late Oct.–late Mar.* 🛏 *7 rooms* 🍽 *Free Breakfast.*

NIGHTLIFE AND PERFORMING ARTS

El Colono. Although the flamenco show is undeniably touristy, this club has an authentic *olé* atmosphere. The food is good, and local specialties, including paella and seafood soup, are served. Dinner shows (€38), with a three-course meal, begin at 7:30 pm on Wednesday. ✉ *Calle Granada 6* ☎ *678/672350* ⏲ *Closed Jan.–Easter.*

THE AXARQUÍA

Vélez-Málaga: 36 km (22 miles) east of Málaga.

The Axarquía region stretches from Nerja to Málaga, and the area's charm lies in its mountainous interior, peppered with pueblos, vineyards, and tiny farms. Its coast consists of narrow, pebbly beaches and drab fishing villages on either side of the high-rise resort town of Torre del Mar.

GETTING HERE AND AROUND

Although bus routes are fairly comprehensive throughout the Axarquía, reaching the smaller villages may involve long delays; renting a car is convenient and lets you get off the beaten track and experience some of the beautiful unspoiled hinterland in this little-known area. The

Views of the Mediterranean Sea, with the mountains in the background

four-lane A7 highway cuts across the region a few miles in from the coast; traffic on the old coastal road (N340) is slower.

VISITOR INFORMATION

Contacts Cómpeta. ⊠ *Av. de la Constitución, Vélez-Málaga* ☎ *952/553685* ⊕ *www.competa.es.*

Cooking and Culture Days. Experience local food and culture at a traditional *finca* in the heart of the Axarquía. ⊕ *larosilla-catering.com/ cooking-culture* ✉ *From €65.*

EXPLORING

Ruta del Sol y del Vino and Ruta de la Pasa. The Axarquía has a number of tourist trails that take in the best of local scenery, history, and culture. Two of the best are the Ruta del Sol y del Vino (Sunshine and Wine Trail), through Algarrobo, Cómpeta (the main wine center), and Nerja; and the Ruta de la Pasa (Raisin Trail), which goes through Moclinejo, El Borge, and Comares. The trails are especially spectacular during the late-summer grape harvest or in late autumn, when the leaves of the vines turn gold.

Vélez-Málaga. The capital of the Axarquía is a pleasant agricultural town of white houses, strawberry fields, and vineyards. It's worth a half-day trip to see the **Thursday market,** Contemporary Art Centre (CAC), the ruins of a **Moorish castle,** and the church of **Santa María la Mayor,** built in the Mudejar style on the site of a mosque that was destroyed when the town fell to the Christians in 1487. The town also has a thriving flamenco scene with regular events (⊕ *www.flamencoabierto. com).* ⊠ *Vélez-Málaga.*

WHERE TO EAT AND STAY

$$ SPANISH 🍴 **El Convento.** Housed in a restored convent, this cozy restaurant offers atmospheric dining inside and a pleasant terrace outside. Excellent tapas and *tostas* (toppings on toasted bread) are available at the bar in addition to an extensive menu of local and international dishes in the restaurant. **Known for:** good value dining; tostas; croquettes. [$] *Average main: €12 ✉ Calle de los Moros 5, Vélez-Málaga ☎ 951/250100.*

$$ HOTEL 🏨 **Hotel Palacio Blanco.** This light and airy boutique hotel is housed in a charmingly restored 18th-century mansion just a short distance from the castle. **Pros:** spacious rooms; rooftop terrace with pool; central location. **Cons:** no on-site parking; first-floor rooms are a little dark. [$] *Rooms from: €95 ✉ Calle Felix Lomas 4, Vélez-Málaga ☎ 952/549174 🌐 www.palacioblanco.com 🛏 9 rooms 🍽 Free Breakfast.*

MÁLAGA PROVINCE

The city of Málaga and the provincial towns of the upland hills and valleys to the north create the kind of contrast that makes travel in Spain so tantalizing. The region's Moorish legacy—tiny streets honeycombing the steamy depths of Málaga, the layout of the farms, and the crops themselves, including olives, grapes, oranges, and lemons—is a unifying visual theme. Ronda and the whitewashed villages of Andalusia behind the Costa del Sol make for one of Spain's most scenic and emblematic driving routes.

To the west of Málaga, along the coast, the sprawling outskirts of Torremolinos signal that you're entering the Costa del Sol, with its beaches, high-rise hotels, and serious number of tourists. On the far west, you can still discern Estepona's fishing village and Moorish old quarter amid its booming coastal development. Just inland, Casares piles whitewashed houses over the bright-blue Mediterranean below.

MÁLAGA

175 km (109 miles) southeast of Córdoba.

Málaga is one of southern Spain's most welcoming and happening cities, and it more than justifies a visit. Visitor figures soared after the Museo Picasso opened in 2003 and again after a new cruise-ship terminal opened in 2011, and the city has had a well-earned face-lift, with many of its historic buildings restored or undergoing restoration. The area between the river and the port has been transformed into the Soho art district, and since the arrival of three new art museums in 2015, the city has become one of southern Europe's centers for art. Alongside all this rejuvenation, some great shops, and lively bars and restaurants have sprung up all over the center.

True, the approach from the airport certainly isn't that pretty, and you'll be greeted by huge 1970s high-rises that march determinedly toward Torremolinos. But don't give up: in its center and eastern suburbs, this city of about 550,000 people is a pleasant port, with ancient streets and lovely villas amid exotic foliage. Blessed with a subtropical climate, it's covered in lush vegetation and averages some 324 days of sunshine a year.

Central Málaga lies between the Río Guadalmedina and the port, and the city's main attractions are all here. The Centro de Arte Contemporáneo (CAC) sits next to the river; to the east lies the Soho district, hoisted from its former seedy red-light reputation to a vibrant cultural hub with galleries and up-and-coming restaurants. Around La Alameda boulevard, with its giant weeping fig trees, is old-town Málaga: elegant squares, pedestrian shopping streets such as Calle Marqués de Larios, and the major monuments, which are often tucked away in labyrinthine alleys.

Eastern Málaga starts with the pleasant suburbs of El Palo and Pedregalejo, once traditional fishing villages. Here you can eat fresh fish in the numerous chiringuitos and stroll Pedregalejo's seafront promenade or the tree-lined streets of El Limonar. A few blocks west is Málaga's bullring, **La Malagueta,** built in 1874, and Muelle Uno (port-front commercial center), whose striking glass cube is now home to the Centre Pompidou. It's great for a drink and for soaking up views of the old quarter.

GETTING HERE AND AROUND
If you're staying at one of the coastal resorts between Málaga and Fuengirola, the easiest way to reach Málaga is via the train (every 20 minutes). If you're driving, there are several well-signposted underground

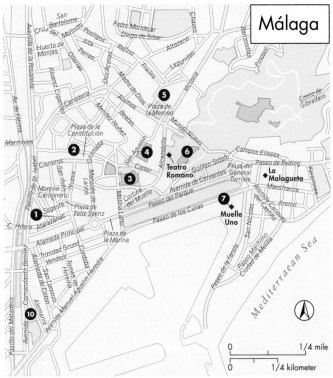

parking lots, and it's not that daunting to negotiate by car. Malaga has two metro lines from the west, and both reach central train and bus stations; extension to the center is due in late 2019.

Málaga is mostly flat, so the best way to explore it is on foot or by bike via the good network of designated bike paths. To get an overview of the city in a day, hop on the Málaga Tour City Sightseeing Bus. There is a comprehensive bus network, too, and the tourist office can advise on routes and schedules.

Pick up a free audio guide to Málaga at the visitor information center in Plaza de la Marina. Guides talk you through the history and local anecdotes along five different walking routes. They are available for 48 hours' use, and you need to show your passport and a credit card.

Bike Rental Contact Málaga Bike Tours. ✉ *Calle Trinidad Grund 5* ☎ *606/978513* ⊕ *www.malagabiketours.eu.*

Bus Contact Málaga bus station. ✉ *Paseo de los Tilos* ☎ *952/350061* ⊕ *www.estabus.emtsam.es.*

Car Rental Contacts Europcar. ✉ *Málaga Costa del Sol Airport* ☎ *902/503010* ⊕ *www.europcar.es.* **Niza Cars.** ✉ *Málaga Costa del Sol Airport* ☎ *951/013520* ⊕ *www.nizacars.es.*

Taxi Company Unitaxi. ☎ *952/320000* ⊕ *www.unitaxi.es.*

Train Information Málaga train station. ✉ *Esplanada de la Estación* ☎ *912/320320* ⊕ *www.renfe.com.*

TOURS

Málaga Tour City Sightseeing Bus. This open-top, hop-on hop-off tour bus gives you an overview of Málaga's main sites in a day, including the Gibralfaro. Buy tickets online ahead of your trip or when you board the bus. ✉ *Málaga* ⊕ *www.city-sightseeing.com* ✉ *€18.*

VISITOR INFORMATION

Contacts Málaga. ✉ *Pl. de la Marina, Paseo del Parque* ☎ *951/926620* ⊕ *www.malagaturismo.com.*

Spain Food Sherpas. Eat your way around Málaga with the Taste of Tapas Tour or the evening Wine and Tapas Tour with local guides who know their stuff when it comes to the city's culinary culture. ✉ *Málaga* ☎ *644/329806* ⊕ *www.spainfoodsherpas.com* ✉ *From €58.*

EXPLORING

Alcazaba. Just beyond the ruins of a Roman theater on Calle Alcazabilla stands Málaga's greatest monument. This fortress was begun in the 8th century, when Málaga was the principal port of the Moorish kingdom, although most of the present structure dates to the 11th century. The inner palace was built between 1057 and 1063, when the Moorish emirs took up residence; Ferdinand and Isabella lived here for a while after conquering the city in 1487. The ruins are dappled with orange trees and bougainvillea and include a small museum; from the highest point you can see over the park and port. ✉ *Entrance on Calle Alcazabilla* ✉ *From €3 (free Sun. from 2 pm).*

Centre Pompidou Málaga. The only branch outside France of the Centre Pompidou in Paris opened in March 2015 in the striking glass cube designed by Daniel Buren at Muelle Uno on Málaga port. Housing more than 80 paintings and photographs, the museum showcases 20th- and 21st-century modern art, with works by Kandinsky, Chagall, Scurti, Miró, and Picasso on permanent display. There are also regular temporary exhibitions each year. ✉ *Pasaje Doctor Carrillo Casaux s/n* ☎ *951/926200* ⊕ *www.centrepompidou-malaga.eu* ✉ *From €7, free Sun. from 5 pm* ☉ *Closed Tues.*

Málaga Cathedral. Built between 1528 and 1782, the cathedral is a triumph, although a generally unappreciated one, having been left unfinished when funds ran out. Because it lacks one of its two towers, the building is nicknamed "La Manquita" (the One-Armed Lady). The enclosed choir, which miraculously survived the burnings of the civil war, is the work of 17th-century artist Pedro de Mena, who carved the wood wafer-thin in some places to express the fold of a robe or shape of a finger. The choir also has a pair of massive 18th-century pipe organs, one of which is still used for the occasional concert. Adjoining the cathedral is a small museum of religious art and artifacts. A walk around the cathedral on Calle Cister will take you to the magnificent Gothic Puerta del Sagrario. A rooftop walkway (guided tours only) gives you

DID YOU KNOW?

As seems appropriate for the city of Picasso's birth, the works on view at Málaga's Museo Picasso are mainly those that the master kept for himself or gave to family members.

stunning views of the ocher domes and the city. ⊠ *Calle Molina Lario* ☎ *640/871711* ✉ *From €6 (free 9–10 am Mon.–Thurs.).*

Mercado de Atarazanas. From the Plaza Felix Saenz, at the southern end of Calle Nueva, turn onto Sagasta to reach the Mercado de Atarazanas. The typical 19th-century iron structure incorporates the original **Puerta de Atarazanas,** the exquisitely crafted 14th-century Moorish gate that once connected the city with the port. Don't miss the magnificent stained-glass window depicting highlights of this historic port city as you stroll round the stalls, filled with local produce. The bars at the entrance offer good-value tapas, open at lunchtime only. ⊠ *Calle Atarazanas* ⊘ *Closed Sun.*

Museo Carmen Thyssen Málaga. Like Madrid, Málaga has its own branch of this museum, with more than 200 works from Baroness Thyssen's private collection. Shown in a renovated 16th-century palace, the collection features mainly Spanish paintings from the 19th century, but also has work from two great 20th-century artists, Joaquín Sorolla y Bastida and Romero de Torres. The museum also hosts regular exhibitions, talks, and art workshops. ⊠ *Calle Compañia 10* ☎ *902/303131* ⊕ *www.carmenthyssenmalaga.org* ✉ *From €6, free Sun. from 5 pm* ⊘ *Closed Mon.*

Fodor'sChoice ★ **Museo Picasso.** Part of the charm of this art gallery, one of the city's most prestigious museums, is that its small collection is such a family affair. These are the works that Pablo Picasso kept for himself or gave to his family, including the exquisite *Portrait of Lola*, the artist's sister, which he painted when he was 13, and the stunning *Three Graces*. The holdings were largely donated by two family members—Christine and Bernard Ruiz-Picasso, the artist's daughter-in-law and her son. The works are displayed in chronological order according to the periods that marked Picasso's 73-year development as an artist. The museum is housed in a former palace where, during restoration work, Roman and Moorish remains were discovered. These are now on display, together with the permanent collection of Picassos and temporary exhibitions. ∎TIP➔ **Guided tours in English are available; book at least five days ahead.** ⊠ *Calle San Agustín* ☎ *952/127600* ⊕ *www.museopicassomalaga.org* ✉ *€9 (free last 2 hrs on Sun.).*

WHERE TO EAT

$$ SPANISH ✕ **Eboka.** Tucked behind the Picasso Museum, Eboka has quickly established a reputation as an excellent gastro bar serving Mediterranean dishes made from local produce. Inside, the restaurant is contemporary with low lighting and plant motifs on the walls, and outside there's a pleasant terrace. **Known for:** sharing plates; wine list; outdoor terrace. Ⓢ *Average main: €15* ⊠ *Calle Pedro de Toledo 4* ☎ *952/124671* ⊕ *www.ebokarestaurante.com.*

$$ MEDITERRANEAN ✕ **El Ambigu de la Coracha.** Located beneath the Gibralfaro, this modern restaurant with a lovely terrace offers sweeping views of Málaga below—more than worth the climb to get here—and local cuisine with an international influence. Starters, like king prawn ceviche with local avocado, make ideal sharing plates. **Known for:** views of Málaga; local wines and produce; olive oil tasting. Ⓢ *Average main: €14* ⊠ *Calle Campo Eliseos* ☎ *951/900046* ⊕ *elambigudelacoracha.com* ⊘ *Closed Mon.*

$$$
MEDITERRANEAN

✕ **El Palmeral.** Set among the Palm Walk near the cruise-ship terminal and with first-class views of the harbor, this restaurant has become a firm favorite with locals and visitors. Sit inside the modern glass cube for elegant dining or outside for a more informal meal (or just coffee). **Known for:** harbor views; paella; croquetas. $ *Average main: €18* ✉ *Muelle 2* ☎ *674/277645* ⊕ *www.palmeralmalaga.com.*

> **SOMETHING SWEET**
>
> For coffee and cakes, malagueños favor Lepanto, the classy shop at Calle Marqués de Larios 7, where uniform-clad staff serve a variety of pastries, cakes, and other sweets. Just next door at Casa Mira is delicious homemade ice cream.

$$$
SPANISH
Fodor's Choice
★

✕ **Los Patios de Beatas.** Sandwiched between the Museo Picasso and Fundación Picasso is one of Málaga's largest wine collections (there are over 500 on the list). The two historic mansions that make up this restaurant include an original patio and 17th-century stone wine vats; you can sit on bar stools in the beamed tapas section, where the walls are lined with dozens of wine bottles, or dine on the airy patio, which is covered with stained glass. **Known for:** wine list; innovative tapas; stunning interior. $ *Average main: €20* ✉ *Calle Beatas 43* ☎ *952/210350* ⊕ *www.lospatiosdebeatas.com* ▭ *No credit cards.*

$$$
INTERNATIONAL

✕ **Óleo Restaurante.** Attached to the Centro de Arte Contemporáneo, this small restaurant offers a range of Mediterranean dishes and sushi best enjoyed on the riverside terrace. Sharing plates include hummus or Vietnamese rolls with Málaga kid goat; highlights on the main menu are *carrillada ibérica con couscous* (stewed Iberian pork), tuna steak, and a long list of sushi. **Known for:** sushi; stewed Iberian pork; riverside dining. $ *Average main: €18* ✉ *Calle Alemania* ✛ *Next to CAC* ☎ *952/219062* ⊕ *www.oleorestaurante.es* ⊘ *Closed Mon.*

WHERE TO STAY

$
HOTEL

▭ **Castilla.** This centrally located and gracious hotel has well-priced rooms that are small but functional, with double glazing to block out any late-night street revelry—those facing the side street or the interior patio are the quietest. **Pros:** great location between the city center and the port; parking. **Cons:** rooms are small; friendly owners don't speak much English. $ *Rooms from: €85* ✉ *Calle Córdoba 7* ☎ *952/218635* ⊕ *www.hotelcastillaguerrero.com* ⬏ *51 rooms* ⦿ *No meals.*

$$$$
HOTEL

▭ **Gran Hotel Miramar.** Málaga's giant "wedding-cake" palace was opened by King Alfonso XIII in 1926 as one of the city's first hotels and fully restored to its former glory in 2017; if you can't splurge on a room, at least treat yourself to a coffee or cocktail here. **Pros:** most luxurious accommodations in town; personal butler service; stunning interior patio. **Cons:** faces a busy road; short walk from city center; pricey. $ *Rooms from: €340* ✉ *Paseo de Reding 22* ☎ *952/603000* ⊕ *www.granhotelmiramarmalaga.com* ⬏ *190 rooms* ⦿ *No meals.*

$$$$
HOTEL
Fodor's Choice
★

▭ **Parador de Málaga–Gibralfaro.** The attractive rooms at this cozy, gray-stone parador are some of the best in Málaga, with spectacular views of the city and the bay, so reserve well in advance. **Pros:** some of the best views on the Costa; good restaurant; rooftop pool. **Cons:** some distance from town; tired communal areas. $ *Rooms from: €190* ✉ *Monte de*

Gibralfaro s/n, Monte ☎ *952/221902* 🌐 *www.parador.es* 🛏 *38 rooms* 🍴 *No meals.*

$$$ HOTEL 🏨 **Room Mate Larios.** On the central Plaza de la Constitución, in the middle of a sophisticated shopping area, this elegantly restored 19th-century building holds luxuriously furnished rooms. **Pros:** stylish; king-size beds; rooftop bar with cathedral views. **Cons:** daytime noise from shopping street; interior rooms are dark. [$] *Rooms from: €175* ✉ *Marqués de Larios 2* ☎ *952/222200* 🌐 *www.room-matehotels.com* 🛏 *45 rooms* 🍴 *No meals.*

NIGHTLIFE AND PERFORMING ARTS

Málaga's main nightlife districts are Maestranza, between the bullring and the Paseo Marítimo, and the beachfront in the suburb of Pedregalejo. Central Málaga also has a lively bar scene around the Plaza Uncibay and Plaza de la Merced. Malaga holds a biennial flamenco festival with events throughout the year; the next one is in 2019.

Kelipé Centro de Arte Flamenco. Flamenco shows are held here Thursday–Saturday night at 9 pm. ✉ *Calle Muro de Puerta Nueva 10* 🌐 *www.kelipe.net* 🎟 *€25.*

ANTEQUERA

64 km (40 miles) north of Málaga, 87 km (54 miles) northeast of Ronda.

The town of Antequera holds a surprising number of magnificent baroque monuments (including some 30 churches)—it provides a unique snapshot of a historic Andalusian town, one a world away from the resorts on the Costa del Sol. It became a stronghold of the Moors after their defeat at Córdoba and Seville in the 13th century. Its fall to the Christians in 1410 paved the way for the Reconquest of Granada; the Moors' retreat left a fortress on the town heights.

Next to the town fortress is the former church of **Santa María la Mayor.** Built of sandstone in the 16th century, it has a ribbed vault and is now used as a concert hall. The church of **San Sebastián** has a brick baroque Mudejar tower topped by a winged figure called the Angelote (Big Angel), the symbol of Antequera. The church of **Nuestra Señora del Carmen** (Our Lady of Carmen) has an extraordinary baroque altarpiece that towers to the ceiling. On Thursday, Friday, and Saturday evening, mid-June–mid-September, many monuments are floodlit and open until late.

GETTING HERE AND AROUND

There are several daily buses from Málaga and Ronda to Antequera. Drivers will arrive via the A367 and A384, and should head for the underground parking lot on Calle Diego Ponce in the center of town, which is well signposted. Antequera is small and compact, and most monuments are within easy walking distance, although the castle is up a fairly steep hill. You need a car to visit the Dolmens.

VISITOR INFORMATION

Contacts Municipal Tourist Office. ✉ *Calle Encarnación 4* ☎ *952/702505* 🌐 *turismo.antequera.es.*

EXPLORING

Archidona. About 8 km (5 miles) from Antequera's Lovers' Rock, the village of Archidona winds its way up a steep mountain slope beneath the ruins of a Moorish castle. This unspoiled village is worth a detour for its **Plaza Ochavada,** a magnificent 17th-century octagon resplendent with contrasting red and ocher stone. ⊠ *A45, Archidona.*

Fodor'sChoice **Dolmens.** These mysterious prehistoric megalithic burial chambers, just
★ outside Antequera, were built some 4,000 years ago out of massive slabs of stone weighing more than 100 tons each. The best-preserved dolmen is La Menga. Declared UNESCO World Heritage sites in 2016, the Dolmens offer an interesting insight into the area's first inhabitants and their burial customs, well explained at the visitor center. Note that gates close 30 minutes before closing time. ⊠ *Signposted off Málaga exit rd.* ☎ *952/712206* ⬛ *Free* ☾ *Closed Mon.*

Fuente de Piedra. Europe's major nesting area for the greater flamingo is a shallow saltwater lagoon. In February and March, these birds arrive from Africa by the thousands to breed, returning to Africa in August when the water dries up. The visitor center has information on wildlife. Bring binoculars if you have them. On weekends and public holidays in April through June—flamingo hatching time—the visitor center suspends its usual lunchtime closure. Guided tours are available in English (€8 per person; book ahead online). ⊠ *Antequera ✛ 10 km (6 miles) northwest of Antequera, off A92 to Seville* ☎ *952/712554* ⊕ *www.reservatuvisita.es* ⬛ *Free* ☾ *Closed lunchtime.*

Museo de la Ciudad de Antequera. The town's pride and joy is *Efebo,* a beautiful bronze statue of a boy that dates back to Roman times. Standing almost 5 feet high, it's on display along with other ancient, medieval, and Renaissance art and artifacts in this impressive museum. ⊠ *Pl. Coso Viejo* ☎ *952/708300* ⊕ *turismo.antequera.es* ⬛ *€3 (free Sun.)* ☾ *Closed Mon.*

Fodor'sChoice **Parque Natural del Torcal de Antequera** (*El Torcal Nature Park*). Well-
★ marked walking trails (stay on them) guide you at this park, where you can walk among eerie pillars of pink limestone sculpted by aeons of wind and rain. Guided hikes (in Spanish only) can be arranged, as well as stargazing in July and August. The visitor center has a small museum. ⊠ *Centro de Visitantes, 10 km (6 miles) south on Ctra. C3310* ☎ *952/243324* ⬛ *Free.*

Peña de los Enamorados. The dramatic silhouette of the Peña de los Enamorados (Lovers' Rock) is an Andalusian landmark. Legend has it that a Moorish princess and a Christian shepherd boy eloped here one night and cast themselves to their deaths from the peak the next morning. The rock's outline is often likened to the profile of the cordobés bullfighter Manolete. ⊠ *East on A45.*

WHERE TO EAT AND STAY

$$ ✕ **El Mesón Ibérico Dehesa Las Hazuelas.** Down the road from the tourist
SPANISH office, this ordinary-looking restaurant serves excellent and abundant Spanish cooking for some of the best prices in the area. Inside, traditional wine barrels share space with modern leather stools, pine furniture, and a flat-screen television, and there's also a pleasant outside

terrace. **Known for:** tapas; generous portions; gin list. [$] *Average main: €12* ✉ *Calle Encarnación 9* ☎ *661/563658.*

$$ SPANISH 🍴 **Restaurante Arte de Cozina.** As the name suggests, this cozy restaurant offers art in cooking, and its take on typical local dishes is one of the best in the area. The menu is seasonal with an emphasis on local produce; it might include *porrilla de espinacas con huevo* (spinach stew with egg) and the *choto malagueño* (kid goat in spicy sauce). **Known for:** traditional dishes; kid goat; bienmesabe dessert. [$] *Average main: €13* ✉ *Calle Calzada 25* ☎ *952/840014* 🌐 *artedecozina.com.*

$$$ HOTEL 🏨 **Parador de Antequera.** Within a few minutes' walk of the historic center, this parador provides a welcome oasis of calm for relaxing after sightseeing, and panoramic vistas of the Peña de los Enamorados can be seen from the gardens, restaurant, and some rooms. **Pros:** quiet, romantic setting; views; pool with loungers. **Cons:** slightly out of town; interior design could be too impersonal for some; not all rooms have views. [$] *Rooms from: €140* ✉ *Pl. García del Olmo 2* ☎ *952/840261* 🌐 *www.parador.es* 🛏 *58 rooms* 🍽 *No meals.*

THE GUADALHORCE VALLEY

About 34 km (21 miles) from Antequera, 66 km (41 miles) from Málaga.

The awe-inspiring **Garganta del Chorro** (Gorge of the Stream) is a deep limestone chasm where the Río Guadalhorce churns and snakes its way some 600 feet below the road. The railroad track that worms in and out of tunnels in the cleft was, amazingly, the main line heading north from Málaga for Bobadilla junction and, eventually, Madrid until the AVE track was built.

North of the gorge, the Guadalhorce has been dammed to form a series of scenic reservoirs surrounded by piney hills, which constitute the **Parque de Ardales** nature area. Informal, open-air restaurants overlook the lakes and a number of picnic spots. Driving along the southern shore of the lake, you reach Ardales and, turning onto the A357, the old spa town of **Carratraca.** Once a favorite watering hole for both Spanish and foreign aristocracy, it has a Moorish-style Ayuntamiento and an unusual polygonal bullring. Today the 1830 guesthouse has been renovated into the luxury Villa Padierna spa hotel. The splendid Roman-style marble-and-tile bathhouse has benefited from extensive restoration.

PLANNING

GETTING HERE AND AROUND

Coming from Antequera, take the "El Torcal" exit, turning right onto the A343, then from the village of Alora, follow the minor road north. From Málaga go west on the A357 through Cártama, Pizarra, Carratraca, and Ardales. Once you're in the Garganta del Chorro valley, Diputación, which manages the walk, runs a shuttle bus (€1.55) to take you from one end to the other. Buses run Tuesday–Sunday 12:30–6 (or 8, depending on the season), hourly during the week and every 30 minutes on weekends.

EXPLORING

Fodor's Choice ★ **Caminito del Rey.** Clinging to the cliff side in the valley, the "King's Walk" is a suspended catwalk built for a visit by King Alfonso XIII at the beginning of the 19th century. It reopened in March 2015 after many years and a €9 million restoration and is now one of the province's main tourist attractions—as well as one of the world's dizziest. No more than 400 visitors are admitted daily for the walk, which includes nearly 3 km (2 miles) on the boardwalk itself and nearly 5 km (3 miles) on the access paths. It takes four to five hours to complete, and it's a one-way walk, so you need to make your own way back to the start point at the visitor center at the Ardales end (shuttle buses offer regular service; check when the last bus leaves and time your walk accordingly). A certain level of fitness is required and the walk is not recommended for young children or anyone who suffers from vertigo. ■ TIP➡ This is one of the Costa del Sol's busiest attractions; book ahead. ⊠ *Valle del Guadalhorce* ⊕ *www.caminitodelrey.info* 🎫 *From €10* ⟳ *Closed Mon.*

TORREMOLINOS

11 km (7 miles) west of Málaga, 16 km (10 miles) northeast of Fuengirola, 43 km (27 miles) east of Marbella.

Torremolinos is all about fun in the sun. It may be more subdued than it was in the action-packed 1960s and '70s, but it remains the gay capital of the Costa del Sol. Scantily attired Northern Europeans of all ages still jam the streets in season, shopping for bargains on Calle San Miguel, downing sangria in the bars of La Nogalera, and congregating in the bars and English pubs. By day, the sunseekers flock to El Bajondillo and La Carihuela beaches, where, in high summer, it's hard to find towel space on the sand.

Torremolinos has two sections. The first, Central Torremolinos, is built around the Plaza Costa del Sol; Calle San Miguel, the main shopping street; and the brash Plaza de la Nogalera, which is full of overpriced bars and restaurants. The Pueblo Blanco area, off Calle Casablanca, is more pleasant; and the Cuesta del Tajo, at the far end of Calle San Miguel, winds down a steep slope to El Bajondillo beach. Here, crumbling walls, bougainvillea-clad patios, and old cottages hint at the quiet fishing village of bygone years.

The second, much nicer, section of Torremolinos is La Carihuela. To get here, head west out of town on Avenida Carlota Alessandri and turn left following the signs. This more authentically Spanish area still has a few fishermen's cottages and excellent seafood restaurants. The traffic-free esplanade is pleasant for strolling, especially on a summer evening or Sunday at lunchtime, when it's packed with Spanish families. Just 10 minutes' walk north from the beach is the Parque de la Batería, a very pleasant park with fountains, ornamental gardens, and good views of the sea.

GETTING HERE AND AROUND

Torremolinos is a short train or bus journey from Málaga. The town itself is mostly flat, except for the steep slope to El Bajondillo—if you don't want to walk, take the free elevator.

Beach umbrellas at the edge of the surf in Torremolinos

Bus Contact Bus Station. ✉ *Calle Hoyo* ☎ *No phone.*

Taxi Contact Radio Taxi Torremolinos. ☎ *952/380600.*

VISITOR INFORMATION
Contacts La Carihuela. ✉ *Paseo Marítimo, next to Hotel Tropicana on seafront* ☎ *952/372956* ⊕ *www.turismotorremolinos.es.* **Torremolinos.** ✉ *Pl. Comunidades Autónomas* ☎ *952/371909.*

BEACHES
FAMILY **La Carihuela.** This 2-km (1-mile) stretch of sand running from the Torremolinos headland to Puerto Marina in Benalmádena is a perennial favorite with Málaga residents as well as visitors. Several hotels, including the Tropicana, flank a beach promenade that's perfect for a stroll, and there are plenty of beach bars where you can rent a lounger and parasol—and also enjoy some of the best pescaíto on the coast. The gray sand is cleaned regularly, and the moderate waves make for safe bathing. Towel space (and street parking) is in short supply during the summer months, but outside high season this is a perfect spot for soaking up some winter sunshine. **Amenities:** food and drink; lifeguards (mid-June–mid-September); showers; toilets; water sports. **Best for:** swimming; walking. ✉ *West end of town, between center and Puerto Marina.*

WHERE TO EAT
$$ ✕ **Casa Juan.** Thanks to the malagueño families who flock here on week-
SEAFOOD ends for the legendary fresh seafood, this restaurant seats 170 inside and 150 outside in an attractive square, one block back from the seafront. Try for a table overlooking the mermaid fountain. **Known for:** zarzuela

de marisco (seafood stew); fried fish; rice dishes. $ *Average main: €12* ✉ *Pl. San Ginés, La Carihuela* ☎ *952/373512.*

$$ ✕**Yate El Cordobes.** Ask the locals which beachfront chiringuito they pre-
SPANISH   fer and El Yate will probably be the answer. Run and owned by an affable
cordobés family, the menu holds few surprises, but the seafood is freshly
caught, and meat and vegetables are top quality. **Known for:** fresh sea-
food; grilled dorada (sea bream); beachside dining. $ *Average main: €12*
✉ *Paseo Marítimo Playamar s/n* ☎ *952/384956* ☉ *Closed Jan.–mid-Feb.*

WHERE TO STAY

$$$$ 🏠 **Hotel Fénix.** One of the handful of adults-only hotels here, Hotel Fénix
HOTEL   offers easy access to both the city center via the main entrance and El
Bajondillo beach (one block away) via the first floor. **Pros:** handy loca-
tion; good breakfast; sea views. **Cons:** some rooms have limited view;
not on the beachfront; no kids allowed. $ *Rooms from: €205* ✉ *Av. de
las Mercedes 22* ☎ *952/051994* ⊕ *www.thepalmexperiencehotels.com*
🛏 *126 rooms* ⦿❙ *No meals.*

$$$ 🏠 **Hotel La Luna Blanca.** A touch of Asia comes to Torremolinos at Spain's
HOTEL   only Japanese hotel, tucked away at the western end of the resort and a
few minutes' walk from La Carihuela. **Pros:** peaceful; close to La Carihuela; free parking. **Cons:** can be difficult to find; steep walk back from
the beach. $ *Rooms from: €130* ✉ *Pasaje del Cerrillo 2* ☎ *952/053711*
⊕ *www.hotellalunablanca.com* 🛏 *11 rooms* ⦿❙ *Free Breakfast.*

$$$ 🏠 **Hotel MS Tropicana.** On the beach at the far end of La Carihuela, in
HOTEL   one of the most pleasant parts of Torremolinos, this low-rise resort
FAMILY   hotel has a loyal following for its friendly and homey style and com-
fortable, bright rooms. **Pros:** great for families; surrounded by bars
and restaurants; has its own beach club. **Cons:** can be noisy; a half-
hour walk to the center of Torremolinos; minimum four-night stay
in July and August. $ *Rooms from: €140* ✉ *Trópico 6, La Carihuela*
☎ *952/386600* ⊕ *www.hotelmstropicana.com* ☉ *Closed Jan. and Feb.*
🛏 *84 rooms* ⦿❙ *Free Breakfast.*

NIGHTLIFE AND PERFORMING ARTS

Most nocturnal action is in the center of Torremolinos, and most of its
gay bars are in or around the Plaza de la Nogalera, in the center, just
off the Calle San Miguel.

Parthenon. One of the longest-established gay bars in Torremolinos has
live music and drag shows most nights. Check the club's Facebook page
for details. ✉ *La Nogalera 716* ☎ *678/479381.*

Taberna Flamenca Pepe López. Many of the better hotels stage flamenco
shows, but you may also want to check out this venue, which has shows
throughout the year (call or check the website to confirm times). ✉ *Pl.
de la Gamba Alegre* ☎ *952/381284* ⊕ *www.tabernaflamencapepelopez.
com* ▦ *€30.*

FUENGIROLA

16 km (10 miles) west of Torremolinos, 27 km (17 miles) east of Marbella.

Fuengirola is less frenetic than Torremolinos. Many of its waterfront
high-rises are vacation apartments that cater to budget-minded sun

seekers from Northern Europe and, in summer, a large contingent from Córdoba and other parts of Spain. The town is also a haven for British retirees (with plenty of English and Irish pubs to serve them) and a shopping and business center for the rest of the Costa del Sol. The Tuesday market here is the largest on the coast and a major tourist attraction.

GETTING HERE AND AROUND

Fuengirola is the last stop on the train line from Málaga. There are also regular buses that leave from Málaga's and Marbella's main bus stations.

Bike Rental Contact Route Electric Bike. ⊠ *Paseo Marítimo Rey de España 10* 🕾 *951/405150* ⊕ *www.route-electricbike.com.*

Bus Contact Bus Station. ⊠ *Av. Alfonso X 111* 🕾 *No phone.*

Taxi Contact Radio Taxi Fuengirola. 🕾 *952/471000.*

VISITOR INFORMATION

Contacts Fuengirola Tourist Office. ⊠ *Av. Jesús Santos Rein 6* 🕾 *952/467457.*

EXPLORING

FAMILY **Bioparc Fuengirola.** In this modern zoo, wildlife live in a cageless environment as close as possible to their natural habitats. The Bioparc is involved in almost 50 international breeding programs for species in danger of extinction and also supports conservation projects in Africa and several prominent ecological initiatives. Four different habitats have been created, and chimpanzees, big cats, and crocodiles may be viewed, together with other mammals such as white tigers and pygmy hippos, as well as reptiles and birds. There are also daily shows and exhibitions, and various places to get refreshments. In July and August, the zoo stays open until midnight to allow visitors to see the nocturnal animals. ⊠ *Av. José Cela 6* 🕾 *952/666301* ⊕ *www.bioparcfuengirola.es* 🖭 *€20.*

Castillo de Sohail. On the hill at the far west of town is the impressive Castillo de Sohail, built as a fortress against pirate attacks in the 10th century and named for the Moorish term for Fuengirola. Don't miss the views of the valley, sea, and coast from the battlements. Concerts are held here during the summer months. ⊠ *Calle Tartessos* ✛ *15-min walk west from center* 🕾 *952/589349* 🖭 *Free* ⊗ *Closed Mon. and July–mid-Sept.*

BEACHES

FAMILY **Carvajal.** Lined with low-rises and plenty of greenery, this typically urban beach is between Benalmádena and Fuengirola. One of the Costa del Sol's Blue Flag holders (awarded to the cleanest beaches with the best facilities), the 1¼-km (¾-mile) beach has yellow sand and safe swimming conditions, which make it very popular with families. Beach bars rent lounge chairs and umbrellas, and there's regular live music in the summer. Like most beaches in the area, Playa Carvajal is packed throughout July and August, and most summer weekends, but at any other time this beach is quite quiet. The Benalmádena end has a seafront promenade and street parking, and the Carvajal train station (on the Fuengirola–Málaga line) is just a few yards from the beach. **Amenities:** food and drink; lifeguards (mid-June–mid-September); parking (no fee); showers; toilets; water sports. **Best for:** sunrise; swimming. ⊠ *N340, Km 214–216.*

WHERE TO EAT AND STAY

$$ INTERNATIONAL

🍴 **Moochers Jazz Cafe.** Inside an old fisherman's cottage, this classic restaurant lies in the heart of Fuengirola's "Fish Alley," just off the seafront promenade. It's popular with expats as well as tourists—there's live music every evening, and tables are surrounded by jazz and other music memorabilia. **Known for:** live music; pancakes; rooftop dining in summer. [$] *Average main: €12* ✉ *Calle de la Cruz* ☎ *952/477154* 🌐 *www.moochersjazzcafe.com* 🕓 *No lunch.*

$$ SPANISH

🍴 **Restaurante Bodega La Solera.** Tucked into the elbow of a narrow street near the main church square, this restaurant serves up superb Spanish dishes, including *albóndigas de ibérico en salsa de almendras* (Iberian pork meatballs in almond sauce), and *bacalao frito sobre pisto de verduras* (fried cod on ratatouille). The three-course daily menu with a half bottle of wine (€16.50) offers a wide range of choices. **Known for:** Iberian pork meatballs; good-value daily menu; wine selection. [$] *Average main: €15* ✉ *Calle Capitán 13* ☎ *952/467708* 🌐 *www.restaurantelasolera.es* 🕓 *Closed Tues.*

$ VEGETARIAN

Fodor's Choice ★

🍴 **Vegetalia.** This attractive, long-established vegetarian restaurant has a large, pleasant dining space decorated with vibrant artwork. It's best known for its excellent, and vast, lunchtime buffet (€8.95), which includes salads and hot dishes like red-lentil croquettes, vegetable paella, and soy "meatballs." Leave room for the house-made desserts, especially the peach-mousse cheesecake. **Known for:** vegetable dishes; lunch buffet; soy meatballs. [$] *Average main: €9* ✉ *Calle Santa Isabel 8, Santa Fe de los Boliches* ☎ *952/586031* 🌐 *www.restaurantevegetalia.com* 🕓 *No dinner. Closed July, Aug., and Sun.*

$$$ HOTEL

🏨 **Florida Hotel & Spa.** This glossy spa hotel has a sophisticated edge on its high-rise neighbors, with light and airy rooms and private terraces overlooking the port and surrounding beach. **Pros:** great location; in-house spa. **Cons:** can be an overload of tour groups; very small pool; three-night minimum stay in July and August. [$] *Rooms from: €170* ✉ *Calle Doctor Galvez Ginachero* ☎ *952/922700* 🌐 *www.hotel-florida.es* 🛏 *184 rooms* 🍽 *No meals.*

$ B&B/INN

🏨 **Hostal Italia.** Right off the main plaza and near the beach, this deservedly popular family-run hotel has bright and comfortable but small rooms; guests return year after year, particularly during the October feria. **Pros:** friendly owners; most rooms have balconies; surrounded by restaurants and bars. **Cons:** some street noise; rooms are small. [$] *Rooms from: €70* ✉ *Calle de la Cruz 1* ☎ *952/474193* 🌐 *www.hostal-italia.com* 🛏 *40 rooms* 🍽 *No meals.*

NIGHTLIFE AND PERFORMING ARTS

Salón de Variétés Theater. From October through June, amateur local troupes stage plays and musicals in English here. The venue also hosts occasional touring tribute acts. ✉ *Calle Emancipación 30* ☎ *952/474542* 🌐 *www.salonvarietestheatre.com.*

Horsewomen in Fuengirola's El Real de la Feria

MIJAS

8 km (5 miles) north of Fuengirola, 18 km (11 miles) west of Torremolinos.

Mijas is in the foothills of the sierra just north of the coast. Long ago foreign retirees discovered the pretty, whitewashed town, and though the large, touristy square may look like an extension of the Costa, beyond it are hilly residential streets with timeworn homes. Try to visit late in the afternoon, after the tour buses have left.

Mijas extends down to the coast, and the coastal strip between Fuengirola and Marbella is officially called **Mijas-Costa.** This area has several hotels, restaurants, and golf courses.

GETTING HERE AND AROUND

Buses leave Fuengirola every half hour for the 25-minute drive through hills peppered with large houses. If you have a car and don't mind a mildly hair-raising drive, take the more dramatic approach from Benalmádena-Pueblo, a winding mountain road with splendid views. You can park in the underground parking garage signposted on the approach to the village.

VISITOR INFORMATION

Contacts Mijas Tourist Office. ☒ *Av. Virgen de la Peña* ☏ *952/589034* ⊕ *turismo.mijas.es.*

EXPLORING

Centro de Arte Contemporáneo. This modern art center contains more than 400 works from the Remedios Medina Collection, including the second largest collection of Picasso ceramics in the world. A total of

130 works by Picasso are on display along side paintings, etchings, and other pieces by artists such as Dalí, Braque, and Foujita. ⊠ *Calle Málaga 28* ☎ *952/590442* ⊕ *www.cacmijas.info* 🕮 *€3* ⊙ *Closed Mon.*

Iglesia Parroquial de la Inmaculada Concepción (*Immaculate Conception*). This delightful village church, up the hill from the bullring, is worth a visit. It's impeccably decorated, especially at Easter, and the terrace and spacious gardens have a splendid panoramic view. ⊠ *Pl. de la Constitución* 🕮 *Free.*

Museo Mijas. This charming museum occupies the former Ayuntamiento. Its themed rooms, including an old-fashioned bakery and bodega, surround a patio, and regular art exhibitions are mounted in the upstairs gallery. ⊠ *Pl. de la Libertad* ☎ *952/590380* 🕮 *€1.*

WHERE TO EAT

$$$
MEDITERRANEAN
✕ **Casa 5.** Just a five-minute walk from the contemporary art museum, this welcoming restaurant offers a seasonal menu with nods to Mediterranean and Asian cuisine. Staples include the *pulpo ahumado lima y limón* (smoked octopus with lemon and lime) and *arroz a la dehesa con pimientos caramelizados y secreto ibérico* (country-style rice with caramelized peppers and Iberian pork belly). **Known for:** Mediterranean-Asian fusion; smoked octopus; alfresco dining. $ *Average main: €19* ⊠ *Calle Málaga 5* ☎ *952/591152* ⊙ *Closed Mon.*

$
SPANISH
✕ **El Cañuelo.** A major appeal of this restaurant is that it is slightly off the well-trodden tourist route and has a strong local following, especially at tapas time (the first is free, others from €1.50). The intimate, rustic-style dining room provides a welcoming setting for enjoying a wide range of dishes, including surprisingly good pizzas as well as generous portions of heartwarming local specialties like braised oxtail, *bacalao al pisto* (cod with ratatouille), and prawns in a spicy chili sauce. **Known for:** tapas; strong local following; bacalao. $ *Average main: €10* ⊠ *Calle Málaga 38* ☎ *952/486581* ⊙ *Closed Mon.*

$$$
SPANISH
✕ **Mirlo Blanco.** In an old house on the pleasant Plaza de la Constitución, this restaurant is run by a Basque family that's been in the Costa del Sol restaurant business for decades. The cozy indoor dining room, with log fire for cooler days, is welcoming and intimate, with original and noteworthy artwork interspersed among the arches, hanging plants, and traditional white paintwork. **Known for:** Basque specialties; local institution; Grand Marnier soufflé. $ *Average main: €22* ⊠ *Calle Cuesta de la Villa 13* ☎ *952/485700* ⊕ *www.mirlo-blanco.es* ⊙ *Closed Jan.*

$$$
EUROPEAN
✕ **Valparaíso.** Halfway up the road from Fuengirola on the way to Mijas, this sprawling house is in its own garden, complete with swimming pool. This is a favorite among local (mainly British) expatriates, some of whom come in full evening dress to celebrate birthdays or other events. **Known for:** duck in orange sauce; live music; lovely gardens. $ *Average main: €18* ⊠ *Ctra. de Mijas–Fuengirola, Km 4* ☎ *952/485975* ⊕ *www. valparaisomijas.com* ⊙ *No lunch June–Oct., and Mon.–Sat. Nov.–May; no dinner Sun. Nov.–late Apr.*

MARBELLA

27 km (17 miles) west of Fuengirola, 28 km (17 miles) east of Estepona, 50 km (31 miles) southeast of Ronda.

Fodor's Choice ★ Thanks to its year-round mild climate and a spectacular natural backdrop, Marbella has been a playground for the rich and famous since the 1950s, when wealthy Europeans first put it on the map as a high-end tourist destination. Grand hotels, luxury restaurants, and multimillion-euro mansions line the waterfront. The town is a mixture of a charming Casco Antiguo (Old Quarter), where visitors can get a taste of the real Andalusia; an ordinary, tree-lined main thoroughfare (Avenida Ricardo Soriano) flanked by high-rises; and a buzzing Paseo Marítimo (Seafront Promenade), which now stretches some 10 km (6 miles) to San Pedro in the west. The best beaches are to the east of the town between El Rosario and the Don Carlos Hotel. Puerto Banús, the place to see and be seen during the summer, is Spain's most luxurious marina, home to some of the most expensive yachts you will see anywhere. A bevy of restaurants, bars, and designer boutiques are nearby.

TAKE A BOAT

A 30-minute ferry trip runs between Marbella and Puerto Banús (€8.50 one-way March–November ⊕ www.fly-blue.com), giving you the chance to admire the Marbella mountain backdrop and maybe catch a glimpse of the local dolphins. If you're feeling energetic, walk back the 7 km (4½ miles) along the beachfront promenade stopping at one of the many beach bars for a welcome refreshment or ice cream.

GETTING HERE AND AROUND

There are regular buses from and to the surrounding resorts and towns, including Fuengirola, Estepona (both every 30 minutes), and Málaga (hourly).

Bus Contact Bus Station. ⊠ *Av. Trapiche* ☎ *No phone.*

VISITOR INFORMATION

Contacts Marbella Tourist Office. ⊠ *Pl. de los Naranjos 1* ☎ *952/768707* ⊕ *www.marbellaexclusive.com.*

EXPLORING

Museo del Grabado Español Contemporáneo. In a restored 16th-century palace in the Casco Antiguo, this museum shows some of the best in contemporary Spanish prints. Some of Spain's most famous 20th-century artists, including Picasso, Miró, and Tàpies, are on show. Temporary exhibitions are also mounted here. ⊠ *Calle Hospital Bazán* ☎ *952/765741* ⊕ *www.mgec.es* ☎ *€3* ⊗ *Closed Sun.*

Plaza de los Naranjos. Marbella's appeal lies in the heart of its Casco Antiguo, which remains surprisingly intact. Here, a block or two back from the main highway, narrow alleys of whitewashed houses cluster around the central Plaza de los Naranjos (Orange Tree Square), where colorful, albeit pricey, restaurants vie for space under the orange trees. Climb onto what remains of the old fortifications and stroll along the Calle Virgen de los Dolores to the Plaza de Santo Cristo. ⊠ *Marbella.*

Puerto Banús. Marbella's wealth glitters most brightly along the Golden Mile, a tiara of star-studded clubs, restaurants, and hotels west of town and stretching from Marbella to Puerto Banús. A mosque and the former residence of Saudi Arabia's late King Fahd reveal the influence of Middle Eastern oil money in this wealthy enclave. About 7 km (4½ miles) west of central Marbella (between Km 175 and Km 174), a sign indicates the turnoff leading down to Puerto Banús. Though now hemmed in by a belt of high-rises, Marbella's plush marina, with 915 berths, is a gem of ostentatious wealth, a Spanish answer to St. Tropez. Huge yachts and countless expensive stores and restaurants make for a glittering parade of beautiful people that continues long into the night. The backdrop is an Andalusian pueblo—built in the 1960s to resemble the fishing villages that once lined this coast. ✉ *Marbella.*

BEACHES

FAMILY **Marbella East Side Beaches.** Marbella's best beaches are to the east of town, between the Monteros and Don Carlos hotels, and include Costa Bella and El Alicate beaches. The 6-km (4-mile) stretch of yellow sand is lined with residential complexes and sand dunes (some of the last remaining on the Costa del Sol). The sea remains shallow for some distance, so bathing is safe. Beach bars catering to all tastes and budgets dot the sands, as do several exclusive beach clubs (look for Nikki Beach, for instance, where luxury yachts are anchored offshore). Tourists and locals flock to these beaches in the summer, but take a short walk away from the beach bars and parking lots, and you'll find a less crowded spot for your towel. **Amenities:** food and drink; lifeguards (mid-June–mid-September); parking (fee in summer); showers; toilets; water sports. **Best for:** swimming; walking. ✉ *A7, Km 187–193.*

Playas de Puerto Banús. These small sandy coves are packed almost to bursting in the summer, when they're crowded with young, bronzed, perfect bodies: topless sunbathing is almost de rigueur. The sea is shallow along the entire stretch, which is practically wave free and seems warmer than other beaches nearby. In the area are excellent Caribbean-style beach bars with good seafood and fish, as well as lots of options for sundown drinks. This is also home to the famous Ocean and Sala Beach clubs with their oversize sun beds, Champagne, and nightlong parties. **Amenities:** food and drink; lifeguards (mid-June–mid-September); showers; toilets; water sports. **Best for:** partiers; sunset; swimming. ✉ *Puerto Banús.*

WHERE TO EAT

$$ SEAFOOD 🍴 **Altamirano.** The modest, old-fashioned exterior of this local favorite is a bit deceiving: inside you'll be greeted not with stodgy decor but rather with three spacious dining rooms with Spanish soccer memorabilia, photos of famous patrons, and tanks of fish. Seafood choices run long and include fried or grilled squid, spider crab, lobster, sole, red snapper, and sea bass. **Known for:** seafood; homemade rice pudding; outdoor dining. [$] *Average main: €13* ✉ *Pl. Altamirano* ☎ *952/824932* 🌐 *www.baraltamirano.es.*

$$$ INTERNATIONAL Fodor's Choice ★ 🍴 **Cappuccino.** Just under the Don Pepe Hotel and right on the promenade, this is the perfect spot for some refreshment before or after you tackle a long stroll along the seafront. Done in navy and white with wicker chairs, this outdoor café-restaurant has a fitting nautical theme,

and if the temperature drops, blankets and gas heaters are at the ready. **Known for:** ocean views; brunch; stylish terrace. $ *Average main: €18* ✉ *Calle de José Meliá* ☎ *952/868790.*

$$$$ MEDITERRANEAN 🍴 **Dani García Restaurante.** Avant-garde celebrity chef Dani Garcia's Marbella restaurant was conceived as an outdoor space with white furnishings and linens, surrounded by lush vertical gardens, and in view of the open kitchen, which is abuzz with activity. Using food science–inspired methods, he transforms traditional ingredients into innovatively textured, flavored, and visually stunning dishes. **Known for:** prestigious chef; food science; wine list. $ *Average main: €55* ✉ *Puente Romano Hotel, Bulevar Hohenlohe s/n* ☎ *952/764252* 🌐 *www.grupodanigarcia.com* ⏲ *Closed Sun. and Mon. Sept.–June.*

$ SPANISH 🍴 **La Niña del Pisto.** Tucked away in the Casco Antiguo, this small venue with upstairs and downstairs dining offers a taste of Córdoba tapas and Montilla wine in Marbella. There is a good choice of tapas and sharing plates, including homemade croquettes, cold cuts, fried fish (the squid is particularly good), and the house pisto (ratatouille) served with a fried egg or pork. **Known for:** tapas; pisto; Montilla wine. $ *Average main: €10* ✉ *Calle Lázaro 2* ☎ *633/320022* ⏲ *Closed Sun. and Mon.*

$$$$ MEDITERRANEAN 🍴 **Messina.** Between the Casco Antiguo and the seafront, this innovative restaurant has an unpromising plain exterior, but forge ahead: the interior's chocolate browns and deep reds make for cozy surroundings for a quiet dinner from chef Mauricio Giovanni, who renewed his Michelin star in 2017. The menu has an Italian slant, with more than a sprinkling of Spanish cuisine in its unusual fusion dishes. **Known for:** innovative dining; good-value tasting menus; cozy atmosphere. $ *Average main: €25* ✉ *Av. Severo Ochoa 12* ☎ *952/864895* 🌐 *www.restaurantemessina.com* 💳 *No credit cards* ⏲ *Closed Sun. No lunch Sat., and weekdays in July and Aug.*

$$$ SPANISH 🍴 **Paellas y Más.** Located on the west side of town, about a 10-minute walk from the center, this modern restaurant specializes in rice dishes; there are 14 on the menu, including the signature baked rice with pork and the squid rice with prawns and chickpeas. Sit inside in the elegant dining room or outside on the shady terrace on the plaza. *Fideuá* (similar to paella but made with noodles instead of rice) also features on the menu. **Known for:** rice dishes; fideuá (a noodle version of paella); baked rice with pork. $ *Average main: €18* ✉ *Calle Hermanos Salom 3* ☎ *952/822511* 🌐 *www.restaurantepaellasymas.com.*

WHERE TO STAY

$$$ HOTEL 🏨 **La Morada Mas Hermosa.** On one of Marbella's prettiest plant-filled pedestrian streets (on the right just up Calle Ancha), this small hotel has a warm, homey feel, and the rooms are lovely. **Pros:** real character; quiet street, yet near the action; short walk from the beach. **Cons:** some rooms accessed by steep stairs; no parking. $ *Rooms from: €145* ✉ *Calle Montenebros 16A* ☎ *952/924467* 🌐 *www.lamoradamashermosa.com* ⏲ *Closed Jan.–mid-Feb.* 🛏 *7 rooms* 🍽 *Free Breakfast.*

$$$ HOTEL 🏨 **La Villa Marbella.** Just a short walk from the Plaza de los Naranjos, these private rooms and apartments, decorated in Asian style with Thai screens, offer a quiet hideaway. **Pros:** central but quiet location; rooftop terrace and pool; good breakfast. **Cons:** multiple buildings; no on-site parking; some rooms are a little dark. $ *Rooms from:*

€130 ✉ Calle Príncipe 10 ☎ 952/766220 🌐 www.lavillamarbella.com 🛏 12 rooms 🍴 Free Breakfast.

$$ HOTEL **Lima.** Two blocks from the beach and a short walk from the Casco Antiguo stands this midrange option which has appealing though slightly generic rooms. **Pros:** downtown location is good for town and beach; beach towels are provided; open all year. **Cons:** room size varies considerably; street noise in some rooms; lacks character of other properties. [$] *Rooms from: €120 ✉ Av. Antonio Belón 2 ☎ 952/770500 🌐 www.hotellimamarbella.com 🛏 64 rooms 🍴 No meals.*

$$$$ HOTEL Fodor's Choice ★ **Marbella Club.** The grande dame of Marbella hotels offers luxurious rooms, tropical grounds, and sky-high rates; the sense of seclusion is emphasized by its lofty palm trees, dazzling flower beds, and a beachside tropical pool area. **Pros:** luxurious, classic hotel; superb facilities; some bungalow rooms have private pools. **Cons:** a drive from Marbella's restaurants and nightlife; extremely expensive. [$] *Rooms from: €900 ✉ Blvd. Principe Alfonso von Hohenlohe at Ctra. de Cádiz, Km 178, 3 km (2 miles) west of Marbella ☎ 952/822211 🌐 www.marbellaclub.com 🛏 130 rooms 🍴 No meals.*

$$ HOTEL Fodor's Choice ★ **The Town House.** In a choice location on one of old Marbella's prettiest squares, this former family home is now a luxurious boutique hotel. **Pros:** upbeat design; great central location; rooftop terrace and bar. **Cons:** no parking; street-facing rooms are noisy on weekends. [$] *Rooms from: €120 ✉ Calle Alderete 7, Pl. Tetuan ☎ 952/901791 🌐 www.townhouse.nu 🛏 9 rooms 🍴 Free Breakfast.*

NIGHTLIFE

Much of the nighttime action in Marbella revolves around Puerto Banús—the main marina—in bars like Sinatra's and Joys Bar, but there are cosmopolitan nightspots elsewhere in the town, too, centered on the small marina and the old quarter, along with a sophisticated casino.

Casino Marbella. This chic gambling spot is in the Hotel Andalucía Plaza, just west of Puerto Banús. Shorts and sports shoes are not allowed, and passports are required. It's open daily 8 pm–4 am (9 pm–5 am in August). *✉ Hotel Andalucía Plaza, N340 ☎ 952/814000 🌐 www.casinomarbella.com.*

La Sala. This is one of Marbella's most popular nightspots for "older" clubbers (those out or nearly out of their twenties). Dine in before you dance to the live music. *✉ Calle Belmonte, near bullring, Puerto Banús ☎ 952/814145.*

Olivia Valére. Marbella's most famous nightspot, with an impressive celebrity guest list, attracts a sophisticated crowd with its roster of big-name DJs and stylish surroundings that resemble a Moorish palace. To get here, head inland from the town's mosque (it's easy to spot). Doors open at midnight (daily in July and August; Friday and Saturday only, September–June) and close at 7 am. *✉ Ctra. de Istán, Km 0.8 ☎ 952/828861.*

DID YOU KNOW?

Tourists and locals make the most of Málaga's temperate off-season climate, lingering over coffee at outdoor cafés.

OJÉN

10 km (6 miles) north of Marbella.

For a contrast to the glamour of the coast, drive up to Ojén, in the hills above Marbella. Take note of the beautiful pottery and, if you're here the first week in August, don't miss the **Festival de Flamenco** (August), which attracts some of Spain's most respected flamenco names, including Juan Peña Fernández (aka El Lebrijano), Miguel Póveda, and Marina Heredia. Four kilometers (2½ miles) from Ojén is the **Refugio del Juanar,** a former hunting lodge in the heart of the Sierra Blanca, at the southern edge of the Serranía de Ronda, a mountainous wilderness. A walking trail takes you a mile from the Refugio to the **Mirador** (lookout), with a sweeping view of the Costa del Sol and the coast of North Africa.

GETTING HERE AND AROUND

Approximately eight buses leave from the Marbella main bus station for Ojén on weekdays and Saturday with just four on Sunday.

WHERE TO STAY

$$ B&B/INN 🏨 **La Posada del Angel.** With friendly Dutch owners and rooms with lots of traditional Andalusian features and even a few Moroccan touches, this hotel makes a perfect rural retreat. **Pros:** chance to sample Andalusian village life; heated pool; some rooms have terraces with a view. **Cons:** could be too quiet for some; slightly off the beaten track. [$] *Rooms from: €98* ✉ *Calle Mesones 21* ☎ *952/881808* 🌐 *www.laposadadelangel.net* 🛏 *16 rooms* 🍴 *Free Breakfast.*

$ HOTEL 🏨 **Refugio del Juanar.** Once an aristocratic hunting lodge (King Alfonso XIII came here), this secluded hotel and restaurant was sold to its staff in 1984 for the symbolic sum of 1 peseta and is a world apart from the glamour of Marbella, just 30 minutes' drive away. **Pros:** superb for hikers; traditional Andalusian looks. **Cons:** can seem very cut off; some areas are a little tired. [$] *Rooms from: €80* ✉ *Sierra Blanca s/n* ☎ *952/881000* 🌐 *www.juanar.com* 🛏 *25 rooms* 🍴 *Free Breakfast.*

ESTEPONA

17 km (11 miles) west of San Pedro de Alcántara, 22 km (14 miles) west of Marbella.

Estepona is a pleasant and relatively tranquil seaside resort, despite being surrounded by lots of urban developments. The beach, more than 1 km (½ mile) long, has better-quality sand than the Costa norm, and the promenade is lined with well-kept, aromatic flower gardens. The gleaming white **Puerto Deportivo** is packed with bars and restaurants, serving everything from fresh fish to Chinese food. Back from the main Avenida de España, the old quarter of cobbled narrow streets and squares is surprisingly unspoiled, and decorated with flower pots. Keep your eyes open for the many modern sculptures in the squares and 30-odd giant murals that cover entire facades throughout the town. The tourist office provides a guide to the artists and a mural map.

GETTING HERE AND AROUND

Buses run every half hour 6:30 am–11 pm from Marbella to Estepona. The town is compact enough to make most places accessible via foot.

Bus Contact Bus Station. ✉ *Av. de España.*

VISITOR INFORMATION

Contacts Estepona Tourist Office. ✉ *Pl. de las Flores s/n* ☎ *952/802002* 🌐 *www.estepona.es/turismo.*

EXPLORING

Museo de Arte de la Diputación. Housed in the historic 18th-century Casa de las Tejerinas palace, this art museum, which opened in 2018 and is known as MAD, showcases contemporary Andalusian and Spanish artists. Focusing on work produced this century, the museum has 50 pieces from artists including Málaga-born Dadi Dreucol and Chema Lumbreras, Santiago Idáñez from Seville, and Judas Arrieta from the Basque Country. Also worthy of note are the central patio and ornate facade. ✉ *Casa de las Tejerinas, Pl. de las Flores* ☎ *952/069695* 🌐 *www.madantequera.com* 🎟 *Free* 🕓 *Closed Sun. and Mon.*

Parque Botánico (*Botanical Gardens*). This lush green space in the middle of Estepona houses Europe's largest orchidarium. More than 1,600 species, from South America and Asia, are exhibited under a futuristic 100-foot glass dome containing a giant cascade. Guided tours are available. ✉ *Calle Terraza 86* ☎ *951/517074* 🌐 *www.orchidariumestepona.com* 🎟 *€3* 🕓 *Closed Mon.*

BEACHES

El Saladillo. Something of a Costa del Sol secret, this quiet 4-km (2½-mile) beach of gray sand has long, empty stretches with plenty of room for towels, even in high summer, making it a great place to relax, walk, or swim. The water's safe for swimming when waves are low, but watch out for the undertow when it's windy. Between San Pedro and Estepona, and flanked by residential developments, El Saladillo has the occasional beach bar. **Amenities:** food and drink; lifeguards (mid-June–mid-September); showers; toilets; water sports. **Best for:** solitude; sunset; walking. ✉ *A7, Km 166–172.*

WHERE TO EAT AND STAY

$$$ INTERNATIONAL Fodor's Choice ★

🍴 **Alcaría de Ramos.** Originally founded by José Ramos (a winner of Spain's National Gastronomy Prize) in 1978, this restaurant in El Paraíso complex still has an enthusiastic and loyal following. The menu features Mediterranean dishes with an emphasis on local ingredients, such as Iberian pork or the catch of the day in Estepona port. **Known for:** Iberian pork; chocolate soufflé; generous portions. [$] *Average main: €18* ✉ *Urbanización El Paraíso, N340, Km 167* ☎ *952/886178* 🌐 *www.laalcariaderamos.es* 🕓 *Closed Sun. No lunch.*

$$$ SPANISH

🍴 **La Casa del Rey.** Just a block from Plaza de las Flores, a 200-year-old building hides this sleek, modern wine bar, serving some of the best tapas in town. Choose from a long list of hot and cold *pinchos* (from €2)—the rabo de toro en hojaldre (oxtail in pastry) and *graten de bacalao* (cod gratin) are perennial favorites—tostas (hot open sandwiches), and miniburgers, or from the à la carte menu, where meat dishes star. **Known for:** tapas; wine list; rabo de toro (oxtail). [$] *Average main: €18* ✉ *Calle Raphael 7* ☎ *951/965414* 🌐 *lacasadelreyestepona.com.*

$$$$ HOTEL

🏨 **Hotel Fuerte Estepona.** The hotel, part of the local Fuerte chain, sits to the west of Estepona right on a tranquil beach, which you have almost

DID YOU KNOW?

Casares is one of the most atmospheric of the pueblos blancos and is becoming increasingly more of a tourist destination.

to yourself outside high season. **Pros:** tranquil location; spacious rooms with mountain or ocean views; both family and adults-only areas. **Cons:** out of town; may be too quiet for some; three-night minimum stay in July and August. *$ Rooms from: €200 ⊠ Ctra. A7, Km 150, Arroyo Vaquero ☎ 900/828210 ⊕ www.fuertehoteles.com ⊗ Closed Nov.–Mar. ➦ 210 rooms ⏐◉⏐ Free Breakfast.*

$$$$ 🛏 **Kempinski Hotel Bahía.** Entirely refurbished in 2018, this luxury resort,
RESORT between the coastal highway and the sea, looks like a cross between a Moroccan casbah and a take on the Hanging Gardens of Babylon, with tropical gardens and a succession of large swimming pools meandering down to the beach. **Pros:** great location; excellent amenities; all rooms have balconies with sea views. **Cons:** so-so beach; some distance from Estepona; expensive. *$ Rooms from: €400 ⊠ Playa El Padrón, Ctra. A7, Km 159 ☎ 952/809500 ⊕ www.kempinski.com ➦ 144 rooms ⏐◉⏐ Free Breakfast.*

CASARES

20 km (12 miles) northwest of Estepona.

Fodor'sChoice The mountain village of Casares lies high above Estepona in the Sierra
★ Bermeja, with streets of ancient white houses piled one on top of the other, perched on the slopes beneath a ruined but impressive Moorish castle. The heights afford stunning views over orchards, olive groves, and woods to the Mediterranean sparkling in the distance.

GETTING HERE AND AROUND
Buses are few and far between to Casares and the best way to visit the village is by your own means. Be prepared for some steep slopes when you sightsee.

WHERE TO EAT AND STAY
$$$ ✕ **Arroyo Hondo.** Tucked in one of the many bends on the road from
ECLECTIC Estepona, this local favorite fuses Mediterranean, Japanese, and Thai cuisines. The rustic interior, in ocher tones with a log fire, makes for cozy meals, and the terrace and poolside tables are perfect for alfresco dining with panoramic vistas. **Known for:** lovely setting; chicken kara-age (deep-fried Japanese-style); pork belly roast on Sunday. *$ Average main: €18 ⊠ Ctra. de Casares, Km 10, Málaga ☎ 952/895152 ⊗ Closed Mon. No dinner Sun., and Tues. and Wed. Oct.–May.*

$$$$ 🛏 **Finca Cortesín.** If you're looking for a luxury option on this side of the
RESORT coast, then this suites-only hotel, on a 532-acre estate adjacent to an 18-hole Cabell Robinson golf course, will probably exceed your expectations. **Pros:** luxury standards and service; Michelin-starred restaurant; spa with a snow cabin. **Cons:** very pricey; some distance from resorts; four-night minimum stay in July and August. *$ Rooms from: €900 ⊠ Ctra. de Casares, Km 2, Málaga ☎ 952/937800 ⊕ www.fincacortesin. com ➦ 67 rooms ⏐◉⏐ Free Breakfast.*

TARIFA

74 km (46 miles) southwest of San Roque.

Fodor'sChoice Tarifa's strong winds helped keep it off the tourist maps for years, but
★ now it is Europe's biggest center for windsurfing and kiteboarding,

Windsurfing at Tarifa

and the wide, white-sand beaches stretching north of the town have become a huge attraction. Those winds have proven a source of wealth in more direct ways, also, via the electricity created by vast wind farms on the surrounding hills. This town at the southernmost tip of mainland Europe—where the Mediterranean and the Atlantic meet—has continued to prosper. Downtown cafés, which not that long ago were filled with men playing dominoes and drinking *anís,* now serve croissants with their café con leche and make fancy tapas for a cosmopolitan crowd. The lovely hilltop village of Vejer de la Frontera, 51 km (32 miles) west of Tarifa, is an easy side trip and its coastline offers stunning beaches and the historic Cape Trafalgar, where the English Armada beat Napoléon in an epic naval battle in 1805.

GETTING HERE AND AROUND
Buses connect Tarifa and Vejer de la Frontera with Algeciras, but this is an area best visited by car, especially if you want to explore the coastline. There's no public transportation to Baelo Claudia.

VISITOR INFORMATION
Contacts Tarifa Tourist Office. ⊠ *Paseo de la Alameda s/n* ☎ *956/680993* ⊕ *turismodetarifa.com.*

EXPLORING

Fodor'sChoice
★
Baelo Claudia. On the Atlantic coast, 24 km (15 miles) north of Tarifa, stand the impressive Roman ruins of Baelo Claudia, once a thriving production center of garum, a salty, pungent fish paste appreciated in Rome. The visitor center includes a museum. Concerts are regularly held at the restored amphitheater during the summer months. ⊠ *Tarifa*

✣ *Take N340 toward Cádiz 16 km (10 miles), then turn left for Bolonia on CA8202* ☎ *956/106797* 🎟 *€2* 🕓 *Closed Mon.*

Castle. Tarifa's 10th-century castle is famous for the siege of 1292, when the defender Guzmán el Bueno refused to surrender even though the attacking Moors threatened to kill his captive son. In defiance, he flung his own dagger down to them, shouting, "Here, use this," or something to that effect (they did indeed kill his son). The Spanish military turned the castle over to the town in the mid-1990s, and it now has a **museum** about Guzmán and the sacrifice of his son. There are impressive views of the African coast from the battlements and towers. ✉ *Av. Fuerza Armadas* 🎟 €2.

BEACHES

Playa Los Lances. This part of the Atlantic coast consists of miles of white and mostly unspoiled beaches and this, to the north of Tarifa and the town's main beach, is one of the longest. Backed by low-lying scrub and lagoons, the beach is also close to the odd campground, boho-chic hotel, and kitesurfing school. Its windswept sands make for perfect kitesurfing: together with Punta Paloma (just up the coast) it's where you'll see most sails surfing the waves and wind. Amenities are concentrated at the Tarifa end of the beach, where there are a few bars and cafés, usually open mid-June–mid-September, and this is naturally where the crowds congregate in the summer. Otherwise, most of the beach is deserted year-round. Swimming is safe here, except in high winds, when there's a strong undertow. **Amenities:** food and drink (mid-June–mid-September); lifeguards; showers; toilets. **Best for:** solitude; sunset; walking; windsurfing. ✉ *Tarifa.*

WHERE TO STAY

$$$$ B&B/INN 🏨 **Casa La Siesta.** Slightly off the beaten track, in the midst of Vejer's rolling countryside, this oasis of tranquillity offers fine lodging and dining for adults only. **Pros:** stunning setting; luxurious fittings and furnishings; excellent breakfast. **Cons:** could be too quiet for some; no kids allowed. [$] *Rooms from: €340* ✉ *Los Parralejos s/n, Vejer de la Frontera* ☎ *956/232003* 🌐 *www.casalasiesta.com* 🕓 *Closed Nov.–Jan.* 🛏 *7 rooms, 1 house* 🍴 *Free Breakfast.*

$$$ HOTEL 🏨 **Hurricane Hotel.** Surrounded by lush subtropical gardens and fronting the beach, the Hurricane is one of the best-loved hip hotels on this stretch of coastline, famous for its Club Mistral wind- and kitesurfing school, and its horseback-riding center. **Pros:** fun and sophisticated; excellent restaurant; lovely gardens with beach access. **Cons:** 6 km (3½ miles) from Tarifa proper; rooms are plain; some noise from the highway. [$] *Rooms from: €164* ✉ *N340, Km 78* ☎ *956/684919* 🌐 *www.hotelhurricane.com* 🛏 *21 rooms* 🍴 *Free Breakfast.*

GIBRALTAR

20 km (12 miles) east of Algeciras, 77 km (48 miles) southwest of Marbella.

The Rock of today is a bizarre anomaly of Moorish, Spanish, and—especially—British influences. There are double-decker buses, "bobbies" in helmets, and red mailboxes. Millions of pounds have been spent in developing its tourist potential, and a steady flow of expat Brits comes here from Spain to shop at Morrisons supermarket and other stores. This tiny

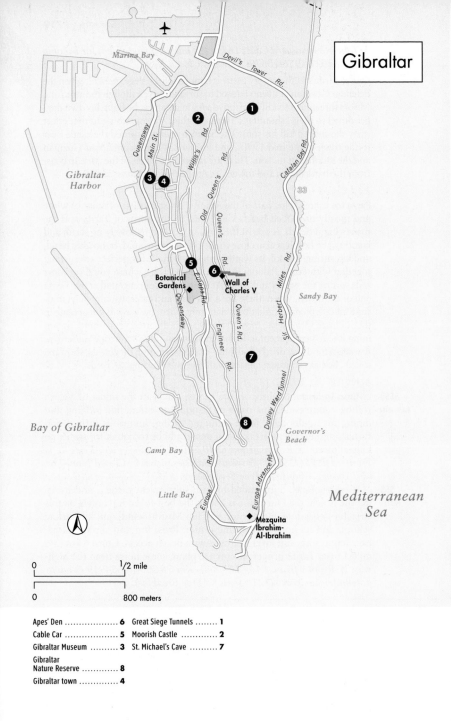

Gibraltar

Marina Bay

Devil's Tower Rd.

①

②

Queensway

Main St.

Willis's Rd.

③ ④

Gibraltar
Harbor

Old Queen's Rd.

Queen's Rd.

Catalan Bay Rd.

33

⑤

⑥ ◆ Wall of
Charles V

Botanical
Gardens ◆

Europa Rd.

Queensway

Queen's Rd.

Queen's Rd.

Engineer Rd.

Sir Herbert Miles Rd.

Sandy Bay

⑦

Dudley Ward Tunnel

⑧

Bay of Gibraltar

Camp Bay

Governor's
Beach

Little Bay

Europa Rd.

Europa Advance Rd.

Mediterranean
Sea

◆ Mezquita
Ibrahim-
Al-Ibrahim

| 0 | | 1/2 mile |
| 0 | | 800 meters |

British colony—nicknamed "Gib" or simply "the Rock"—whose impressive silhouette dominates the strait between Spain and Morocco, was one of the two Pillars of Hercules in ancient times, marking the western limits of the known world and commanding the narrow pathway between the Mediterranean Sea and the Atlantic Ocean. The Moors, headed by Tariq ibn Ziyad, seized the peninsula in 711, preliminary to the conquest of Spain. The Spaniards recaptured Tariq's Rock in 1462. The English, heading an Anglo-Dutch fleet in the War of the Spanish Succession, gained control in 1704, and, after several years of local skirmishes, Gibraltar was finally ceded to Great Britain in 1713 by the Treaty of Utrecht. Spain has been trying to get it back ever since. In 1779 a combined French and Spanish force laid siege to the Rock for three years, to no avail. During the Napoleonic Wars, Gibraltar served as Admiral Horatio Nelson's base for the decisive naval Battle of Trafalgar, and during the two world wars, it served the Allies well as a naval and air base. In 1967 Franco closed the land border with Spain to strengthen his claims over the colony, and it remained closed until 1985.

There are likely few places in the world that you enter by walking or driving across an airport runway, but that's what happens in Gibraltar. First you show your passport; then you make your way out onto the narrow strip of land linking Spain's Línea with Britain's Rock. Unless you have a good reason to take your car—such as loading up on cheap gas or duty-free goodies—you're best off leaving it in a guarded parking area in La Línea, the Spanish border town. Don't bother hanging around here; it's a seedy place. In Gibraltar you can hop on buses and take taxis that expertly maneuver the narrow, congested streets. The Official Rock Tour—conducted either by minibus or, at a greater cost, taxi—takes about 90 minutes and includes all the major sights, allowing you to choose where to come back and linger later.

In 2018, tensions between Gibraltar and Spain continued to be high, and as a result, lines for leaving the colony, both via car and on foot, are long—it can take up to three hours to cross the border into Spain. This situation is unlikely to change, as there's little sign of any progress on any sort of joint Anglo-Spanish sovereignty, which the majority of Gibraltarians fiercely oppose.

When you call Gibraltar from Spain or another country, prefix the seven-digit telephone number with 00–350. Gibraltar's currency is the Gibraltar pound (£), whose exchange rate is the same as the British pound. Euros are accepted everywhere, although you will get a better exchange rate if you use pounds.

GETTING HERE AND AROUND

There are frequent day tours organized from the Costa del Sol resorts, either via your hotel or any reputable travel agency.

VISITOR INFORMATION

Contacts Gibraltar. ⊠ *Grand Casemates Sq.* ☎ *200/45000* ⊕ *www.visitgibraltar.gi.*

EXPLORING

Apes' Den. The famous Barbary Apes are a breed of cinnamon-color, tailless macaques (not apes, despite their name) native to Morocco's Atlas Mountains. Legend holds that as long as they remain in Gibraltar, the British will keep the Rock; Winston Churchill went so far as to issue an order for their preservation when their numbers began to dwindle during World War II. They are publicly fed twice daily, at 8 and 4, at Apes' Den, a rocky area down Old Queens Road near the Wall of Carlos V. Among the macaques' talents are their grabbing of food, purses, cell phones, and cameras, so be on guard.

Fodor'sChoice **Cable Car.** You can reach St. Michael's Cave—or ride all the way to the
★   top of Gibraltar—on a cable car. The car doesn't go high off the ground, but the views of Spain and Africa from the Rock's pinnacle are superb. It leaves from a station at the southern end of Main Street, which is known as the Grand Parade. ⊠ *Grand Parade* 🖭 *£16 round-trip.*

Gibraltar Museum. Often overlooked by visitors heading to the Upper Rock Reserve, this museum houses a beautiful 14th-century Moorish bathhouse and an 1865 model of the Rock; the displays evoke the Great Siege and the Battle of Trafalgar. There's also a reproduction of the "Gibraltar Woman," the Neanderthal skull discovered here in 1848. The museum also serves as an interpretation hub for the prehistoric remains found in the limestone caves of Gorham's Cave Complex, which received UNESCO heritage status in 2016. ⊠ *Bomb House La.* ☎ *200/74289* ⊕ *www.gibmuseum.gi* 🖭 *£5* ⊘ *Closed Sun.*

Gibraltar Nature Reserve. The reserve, accessible from Jews' Gate, includes St. Michael's Cave, the Apes' Den, the Great Siege Tunnels, the Moorish Castle, and the Military Heritage Center, which chronicles the British regiments that have served on the Rock. The Skywalk, a glass viewing platform opened (appropriately) by Mark Hamill, aka Luke Skywalker, in 2018, offers 360-degree views of the Rock and ocean from 370 yards up. You can drive up to the reserve or access via the cable car. ⟊ *From Rosia Bay, drive along Queensway and Europa Rd. as far as Casino, above Alameda Gardens. Make a sharp right here, up Engineer Rd. to Jews' Gate, a lookout over docks and Bay of Gibraltar toward Algeciras* 🖭 *£12 for all attractions.*

Gibraltar town. The dignified Regency architecture of Great Britain blends well with the shutters, balconies, and patios of southern Spain in colorful, congested Gibraltar town, where shops, restaurants, and pubs beckon on Main Street. At the Governor's Residence, the ceremonial Changing of the Guard takes place six times a year, and the Ceremony of the Keys takes place twice a year. Make sure you see the Anglican Cathedral of the Holy Trinity; the Catholic Cathedral of St. Mary; and the Crowned Law Courts, where the famous case of the sailing ship *Mary Celeste* was heard in 1872.

Great Siege Tunnels. Formerly known as the Upper Galleries, these tunnels were carved out during the Great Siege of 1779–82. At the northern end of Old Queen's Road, you can plainly see the openings from which the guns were pointed at the Spanish invaders. They form part of what is arguably

The Rock of Gibraltar

the most impressive defense system anywhere in the world. The privately managed World War II Tunnels nearby are also open to the public but are less dramatic. ⊠ *Old Queen's Rd.* 🎟 *WWII tunnel tour £8, weekdays only.*

Moorish Castle. The castle was built by the descendants of the Moorish general Tariq ibn Ziyad (670–720), who conquered the Rock in 711. The present Tower of Homage dates to 1333, and its besieged walls bear the scars of stones from medieval catapults (and later, cannonballs). Admiral George Rooke hoisted the British flag from its summit when he captured the Rock in 1704, and it has flown here ever since. The castle may be viewed from the outside only. ⊠ *Willis's Rd.*

St. Michael's Cave. This is the largest of Gibraltar's 150 caves; a visit here is part of the tour of the Upper Rock Nature Preserve. This series of underground chambers full of stalactites and stalagmites is sometimes used for very atmospheric (albeit damp) concerts and other events. The skull of a Neanderthal woman (now in the British Museum) was found at the nearby Forbes Quarry eight years before the world-famous discovery in Germany's Neander Valley in 1856; nobody paid much attention to it at the time, which is why the prehistoric species is called Neanderthal rather than *Homo calpensis* (literally, "Gibraltar Man," after the Romans' name for the Rock: Calpe). ⊠ *Queen's Rd.*

WHERE TO EAT AND STAY

$$
STEAKHOUSE
✕ **Charlie's Steak House.** Don't let the brash neon exterior put you off: inside is one of the best steak houses in the region. Hugely popular among locals for its long list of juicy steaks, this diner-style venue also

serves lamb, fried fish, and Indian curries. **Known for:** steak; Indian curries; English desserts. $ *Average main: £16* ✉ *Marina Bay , 4/5 Britannia House* ☎ *200/69993* ⊕ *www.charliessteakandgrill.com.*

$ ✕ **La Bodeguiya.** After nearly two decades on the Spanish side of the Rock,
SPANISH the owners of La Bodeguiya decided to open a sister Spanish tapas bar at this location in Gibraltar. Packed to the brim at lunchtime, the restaurant serves tapas of Iberian pork and seafood (shrimp and king prawn are specialties), plus Spanish staples such as croquettes and potato salad. **Known for:** tapas; loyal following; Iberian pork and seafood. $ *Average main: £10* ✉ *10 Chatham Courterguard* ☎ *200/64211* ⊙ *Closed Sun. and Mon.*

$ ✕ **Sacarello's.** Right off Main Street, this busy restaurant is as well
BRITISH known for its excellent coffee and cakes as it is for the rest of its food. There's a varied salad and quiche buffet, as well as stuffed baked potatoes and daily specials, which could include beef curry, or baked lamb with honey mustard. **Known for:** coffee and cakes; lunch menu; cozy, old-fashioned English setting. $ *Average main: £10* ✉ *57 Irish Town* ☎ *200/70625* ⊕ *www.sacarellosgibraltar.com* ⊙ *Closed Sun. No dinner.*

$$$ ▦ **The Rock.** This hotel overlooking the straits first opened in 1932,
HOTEL and although furnishings in the rooms and restaurants are elegant and colorful, they still preserve something of the English colonial style, with bamboo, ceiling fans, and a terrace bar covered with wisteria. **Pros:** old-world atmosphere; magnificent bay views; good breakfast. **Cons:** inconvenient for shopping; up a steep hill. $ *Rooms from: £180* ✉ *3 Europa Rd.* ☎ *200/73000* ⊕ *www.rockhotelgibraltar.com* ⇆ *84 rooms* ⦿ *Free Breakfast.*

$$$$ ▦ **Sunborn.** This giant yacht hotel (it's seven floors high and 155 yards
HOTEL long) has a permanent home in Gibraltar's marina and offers luxury accommodations complete with ocean views, a casino, a spa, and a restaurant on the top deck, plus lots of luxury extras. **Pros:** unusual place to stay; luxury extras; central, waterfront location. **Cons:** some may find it claustrophobic; not all cabins have views; noise from airport and nearby bars. $ *Rooms from: £210* ✉ *35 Ocean Village Promenade* ☎ *200/16000* ⊕ *www.sunborngibraltar.com* ⇆ *189 rooms* ⦿ *No meals.*

NIGHTLIFE

Lord Nelson. A restaurant during the day and a lively bar at night, the Lord Nelson has karaoke on Saturday night and jam sessions and live music during the week. Many ales are on tap. ✉ *Grand Casemates Sq.* ☎ *200/50009* ⊕ *www.lordnelson.gi.*

SPORTS AND THE OUTDOORS

Bird- and dolphin-watching, diving, and fishing are popular activities on the Rock. For details on tours and outfitters, visit the Gibraltar government tourism website (⊕ *www.visitgibraltar.gi*) or call the local tourist office (☎ *200/45000*).

TRAVEL SMART
SPAIN

GETTING HERE AND AROUND

▌ AIR TRAVEL

Flying time from New York to Madrid is about seven hours; from London, it's just over two hours.

Regular nonstop flights serve Spain from many major cities in the eastern United States; flying from other North American cities usually involves a stop. If you're coming from North America and want to land in a city other than Madrid or Barcelona, consider flying a European carrier.

The Visit Europe Pass from Oneworld (which includes American Airlines, Iberia, and British Airways among others) is the most useful aviation pass for Spain. It is available only to residents of countries outside Europe, and must be booked before departure with a Oneworld member airline. The pass gives you access to 220 destinations in 53 countries in Europe and North Africa. It's available as an add-on to an international flight to Europe booked with any of the airlines in the Oneworld alliance, and is accepted for as long as the international ticket is valid. You must buy a minimum of two coupons for flights within Europe, but there's no maximum.

A number of low-cost carriers operate from the United Kingdom to Spain such as Vueling (⊕ *www.vueling.com*), Jet2 (⊕ *www.jet2.com*), and flybe (⊕ *www.flybe.com*). They provide competition to the market's main players, easy-Jet (⊕ *www.easyjet.com*) and Ryanair (⊕ *www.ryanair.com*). All these carriers offer frequent flights, cover small cities as well as large ones, and have very competitive fares. Skyscanner (⊕ *www.skyscanner.net*), and Momondo (⊕ *www.momondo.com*) are comprehensive search sites for cheap flights worldwide.

Contacts Air Europa. ☎ 844/415–3955 in U.S., 902/401501 in Spain ⊕ www.aireuropa.com. **Iberia.** ☎ 800/772–4642 in U.S.,

901/111500 in Spain ⊕ www.iberia.com. **Transportation Security Administration.** ⊕ www.tsa.gov. **Visit Europe Pass.** ⊕ www.oneworld.com.

AIRPORTS

Most flights from North America land in, or pass through, Madrid's Barajas Airport (MAD). The other major gateway is Barcelona's Prat de Llobregat (BCN). From the United Kingdom and elsewhere in Europe, regular flights also touch down in Málaga (AGP), Alicante (ALC), Palma de Mallorca (PMI), and many other smaller cities.

Airport Information AENA. ☎ 902/404704, 91/321–1000 when calling from outside Spain ⊕ www.aena.es.

FLIGHTS

From North America, Air Europa flies to Madrid; American Airlines, part of the Oneworld Alliance, Iberia, and US Airways fly to Madrid and Barcelona; Delta flies direct to Barcelona, Madrid, and Málaga (June–September). Note that some of these airlines use shared facilities and do not operate their own flights. Within Spain, Iberia is the main domestic airline and also operates low-cost flights through its budget airlines Iberia Express and Vueling. Air Europa and Ryanair both offer inexpensive flights on most domestic routes. The earlier before your travel date you purchase the ticket, the more bargains you're likely to find. Air Europa, Iberia Express, Vueling, and Ryanair also have flights from Spain to other destinations in Europe.

Iberia runs a shuttle, the Puente Áereo, offering flights just over an hour long between Madrid and Barcelona, every 30 minutes (more often during peak travel times) 6:45 am–9:45 pm. You don't need to reserve; you can buy your tickets at the airport ticket counter upon arriving or book online at ⊕ *www.iberia.com.* Passengers can also use the self-service check-in counters to avoid the line. Puente Áereo departs from Terminal T1 in Barcelona; in Madrid, the shuttle departs from Terminal 4.

Airline Contacts Air Europa. ☎ 844/415–3955 in U.S., 902/401501 in Spain ⊕ www.aireuropa.com. **American Airlines.** ☎ 800/433–7300 in U.S., 902/054654 in Spain ⊕ www.aa.com. **Delta Airlines.** ☎ 800/221–1212 for U.S. reservations, 800/241–4141 for international reservations, 800/000142 in Spain ⊕ www.delta.com. **Iberia.** ☎ 800/772–4642 in U.S. and Canada ⊕ www.iberia.com. **Iberia Express.** ☎ 901/111500 ⊕ www.iberiaexpress.com. **United.** ☎ 800/864–8331 ⊕ www.united.com.

Within Spain Air Europa. ☎ 902/401501 ⊕ www.aireuropa.com. **Iberia.** ☎ 901/111500 ⊕ www.iberia.com. **Vueling.** ☎ 902/808022 ⊕ www.vueling.com.

▌ BOAT TRAVEL

Regular car ferries connect the United Kingdom with northern Spain. Brittany Ferries sails from Plymouth to Santander, and from Portsmouth to Santander and Bilbao. Trasmediterranea and Baleària connect mainland Spain to the Balearic and Canary islands.

Direct ferries from Spain to Tangier leave daily from Tarifa and Algeciras on FRS, International Shipping, and Trasmediterranea. Otherwise, you can take your car either to Ceuta (via Algeciras, on Baleària) or Melilla (via Málaga, on Trasmediterranea)—two Spanish enclaves on the North African coast—and then move on to Morocco.

Contacts Baleària. ☎ 902/160180 ⊕ www.balearia.com. **Brittany Ferries.** ☎ 01752/648000 in U.K., 902/108147 in Spain ⊕ www.brittany-ferries.com. **FRS.** ☎ 956/681830 ⊕ www.frs.es. **Trasmediterranea.** ☎ 902/454645 ⊕ www.trasmediterranea.es.

▌ BUS TRAVEL

Within Spain, a number of private companies provides bus service, ranging from knee-crunchingly basic to luxurious. Fares are almost always lower than the corresponding train fares, and service covers more towns, though buses are less frequent on weekends. Smaller towns don't usually have a central bus depot, so ask the tourist office where to wait for the bus. Spain's major national long-haul bus line is ALSA.

ALSA has four luxury classes in addition to its regular seating. Premium, available on limited routes from Madrid, includes a number of services such as à la carte meals and a private waiting room while Supra+ and Supra Economy include roomy leather seats and onboard meals. You also have the option of *asientos individuales*, individual seats (with no other seat on either side) that line one side of the bus. The last class is Eurobus, with a private waiting room, comfortable seats, and plenty of legroom. The Supra+ and Eurobus usually cost, respectively, up to one-third and one-fourth more than the regular seats.

At bus station ticket counters, most major credit cards (except American Express) are accepted. If you buy your ticket on the bus, it's cash only.

During peak travel times (Easter, August, and Christmas), it's a good idea to make a reservation at least a week in advance.

Contacts ALSA. ☎ 902/422242 ⊕ www.alsa.es. **Eurolines Spain.** ☎ 902/405040, 933/674400 ⊕ www.eurolines.es.

▌ CAR TRAVEL

Your own driver's license is valid in Spain, but U.S. citizens are highly encouraged to obtain an International Driving Permit (IDP). The IDP may facilitate car rental and help you avoid traffic fines—it translates your state-issued driver's license into 10 languages so officials can easily interpret the information on it. Permits are available from the American Automobile Association.

Driving is the best way to see Spain's rural areas. The main cities are connected by a network of excellent four-lane divided highways (*autovías* and *autopistas*), which are designated by the letter *A* and have speed limits—depending on the area—of 80 kph (50 mph)–120 kph (75 mph). If the artery is a toll highway (*peaje*), it is designated *AP*. The letter *N* indicates a *carretera nacional*: a national or intercity route, with local traffic, which may have four or two lanes. Smaller towns and villages are connected by a network of secondary roads maintained by regional, provincial, and local governments, with an alphabet soup of different letter designations.

RENTAL CARS

Alamo, Avis, Budget, Europcar, Hertz, and Enterprise have branches at major Spanish airports and in large cities. Smaller, regional companies and wholesalers offer lower rates. The online outfit Pepe Car has been a big hit with travelers; in general, the earlier you book, the less you pay. Rates run as low as €15 per day, taxes included—but note that pickups at its center-city locations are considerably cheaper than at the airports. All agencies have a range of models, but virtually all cars in Spain have manual transmission. ■TIP→ **If you don't want a stick shift, reserve weeks in advance and specify automatic transmission, then call to reconfirm your automatic car before you leave for Spain.** Rates in Madrid begin at the equivalents of $60 per day and $190 per week for an economy car with air-conditioning, manual transmission, and unlimited mileage, including 21% tax. A small car is cheaper and prudent for the tiny roads and parking spaces in many parts of Spain.

Anyone age 18 or older with a valid license can drive in Spain, but most rental agencies will not rent cars to drivers under 23.

Major Agencies Avis. ☎ *800/633–3469, 902/180854 in Spain* ⊕ *www.avis.com.* **Budget.** ☎ *800/214–6094, 902/112585 in Spain* ⊕ *www.budget.com.* **Enterprise.** ☎ *902/111902 in Spain* ⊕ *www.enterprise. es.* **Europcar.** ☎ *902/503010 in Spain* ⊕ *www.europcar.es.* **Hertz.** ☎ *800/654–3001, 902/027659 in Spain* ⊕ *www.hertz.com.* **Pepe Car.** ☎ *902/996666 in Spain* ⊕ *www.pepecar. com.*

ROAD CONDITIONS

Spain's highway system includes some 6,000 km (3,600 miles) of well-maintained superhighways. Still, you'll find some stretches of major national highways that are only two lanes wide, where traffic often backs up behind trucks. Autopista tolls are steep, but as a result these highways are often less crowded than the free ones. If you're driving down through Catalonia, be aware that there are more tolls here than anywhere else in Spain. This can result in a quicker journey but at a sizable cost. If you spring for the autopistas, you'll find that many of the rest stops are nicely landscaped and have cafeterias with decent but overpriced food.

Most Spanish cities have notoriously long morning and evening rush hours. Traffic jams are especially bad in and around Barcelona, Madrid, and Seville. If possible, avoid the morning rush, which can last until noon, and the evening rush, which lasts 7–9. Also be aware that at the beginning, middle, and end of July and August, the country suffers its worst traffic jams (delays of six–eight hours are common) as millions of Spaniards embark on, or return from, their annual vacations.

ROADSIDE EMERGENCIES

Rental agencies Hertz and Avis have (optional) 24-hour breakdown service. If you belong to AAA, you can get emergency assistance from the Spanish counterpart, RACE.

Emergency Service RACE. ☎ 900/100992 for info, 900/112222 for assistance ⊕ www. race.es.

RULES OF THE ROAD

Spaniards drive on the right and pass on the left, so stay in the right-hand lane when not passing. Children under 12 may not ride in the front seat, and seat belts are compulsory for both front- and backseat riders. Speed limits are 30 kph (19 mph) or 50 kph (31 mph) in cities, depending on the type of street, 100 kph (62 mph) on national highways, 120 kph (75 mph) on the autopista or autovía. The use of cell phones by drivers, even on the side of the road, is illegal, except with completely hands-free devices.

Severe fines are enforced throughout Spain for driving under the influence of alcohol. Spot Breathalyzer checks are often carried out, and you will be cited if the level of alcohol in your bloodstream is found to be 0.05% or above.

Spanish highway police are increasingly vigilant about speeding and illegal passing. Police are empowered to demand payment on the spot from non-Spanish drivers. Police disproportionately target rental-car drivers for speeding and illegal passing, so play it safe.

▌ TRAIN TRAVEL

The chart here has information about popular train routes. See Experience Spain for a map of the country, with train routes. Prices are for one-way fares (depending on seating and where purchased) and subject to change.

TRAIN TRAVEL TIMES	
Madrid to Barcelona: €50–€180	High-speed AVE trains make the trip in 2 hours 30 minutes
Madrid to Bilbao: €15–€50	Semi-express Alvia train time is 5 hours 4 minutes
Madrid to Málaga: €48.20–€135.40	Fastest AVE trains take 2 hours 25 minutes
Madrid to Seville: €23–€127.50	Fastest AVE trains take 2 hours 20 minutes
Madrid to Santander: €15.50–€67.10	Semi-express Alvia is 4 hours 5 minutes
Madrid to Valencia: €27.40–€125	Fastest AVE trains take 1 hour 42 minutes
Madrid to Santiago de Compostela: €16.90–€73.30	Fastest time about 5 hours
Barcelona to Bilbao: €19.85–€85.90	Running time about 6 hours 36 minutes
Barcelona to Valencia: €12.20–€73.60	Fastest time 3 hours 35 minutes
Seville to Granada: €18.10–€30.15	Running time about 3 hours 22 minutes

International trains run from Madrid to Lisbon (10 hours 30 minutes, overnight) and Barcelona to Paris (6 hours 20 minutes).

Spain's wonderful high-speed train, the 290-kph (180-mph) AVE, travels between Madrid and Seville (with a stop in Córdoba) in 2½ hours; prices start at about €50 each way. It also serves the Madrid–Barcelona route, cutting travel time to just under three hours. From Madrid you can also reach Lleida, Huesca (one AVE train daily), Valencia, Málaga, Toledo, and Valladolid.

The fast Talgo service is also efficient, but other elements of the state-run rail system (RENFE) are still a bit subpar by European standards, and some long-distance trips with multiple stops can be tediously slow. Although some overnight trains have comfortable sleeper cars, first-class fares that include a sleeping compartment are comparable to, or more expensive than, airfares.

The easiest way to make reservations is to go to the English version of the RENFE website (⊕ *www.renfe.com*—click "Welcome" on the top line) or use the RenfeTicket smartphone app (to buy tickets using the app, you need to register and to have bought a RENFE ticket with your credit card). Book early if you're traveling during Holy Week, on long holiday weekends, or in July and August. (The site allows you to make reservations up to 62 days in advance, which is important in qualifying for online purchase discounts.)

Caveats: You cannot buy tickets online for certain regional lines or for commuter lines (*cercanías*). Station agents cannot alter your reservations; you must do this yourself online. The RENFE website may not work with all browsers, but it does accept all major credit cards, including American Express.

DISCOUNTS

If you purchase a ticket on the RENFE website for the AVE or any of the Grandes Líneas (the faster, long-distance trains, including the Talgo) you can get a discount of 20%–60%, depending on how far ahead you book and how you travel: discounts on one-way tickets tend to be higher than on round-trips. Discount availabilities disappear fast: the earliest opportunity is 62 days in advance of travel. If you have a domestic or an international airline ticket and want to take the AVE within 48 hours of your arrival but haven't booked online, you can still get a 10% discount on the AVE one-way ticket and 25% for a round-trip ticket with a dated return. On regional trains, you get a 10% discount on round-trip tickets (15% on AVE medium-distance trains).

■ TIP➔ If there are more than two of you traveling on the AVE, look for the word "mesa" in the fare column, quoting the price per person for four people traveling together and sitting at the same table. If you select the price, it tells you how much the deal is for one, two, and three people. You have to buy all the tickets at the same time, but they're between 20% and 60% cheaper than regular tickets.

RAIL PASSES

Spain is one of 28 European countries in which you can use the Eurail Global Pass, which buys you unlimited rail travel in all participating countries for the duration of the pass. Choose from passes which allow a set number of days to travel during a one-, two- or three-month period, or passes offering continuous travel within the chosen period. Prices range from $482 (for passengers 26 or older) for five days' travel with one-month period to $1,677 (for passengers 26 or older) for continuous travel during a three-month period. There are discounts for children (ages 4–11) and youths (ages 12–27).

If Spain is your only destination, a Eurail Spain Pass allows between three and eight days of unlimited train travel in Spain within a one-month period for $291–$480 (first class) and $235–$386 (second class). There are also combination passes for those visiting Spain and Portugal, Spain and France, and Spain and Italy.

Many travelers assume that rail passes guarantee them seats on the trains they wish to ride: not so. Reserve seats even if you're using a rail pass.

Contacts Eurail. ⊕ *www.eurail.com.* **Rail Europe.** ☎ *800/622–8600 in U.S. and Canada* ⊕ *www.raileurope.com.* **RENFE.** ☎ *912/320320 for tickets and info* ⊕ *www.renfe.es.*

ESSENTIALS

▌ACCOMMODATIONS

By law, hotel prices in Spain must be posted at the reception desk and should indicate whether the value-added tax (I.V.A. 10%) is included. Note that high-season rates prevail not only in summer but also during Holy Week and local fiestas. In much of Spain, breakfast is normally *not* included. *Prices in the reviews are the lowest cost of a standard double room in high season.*

Be sure you understand the hotel's cancellation policy. Some places allow you to cancel without any kind of penalty—even if you prepaid to secure a discounted rate—if you cancel at least 24 hours in advance. Others require you to cancel a week in advance or penalize you the cost of one night. Small inns and bed-and-breakfasts are most likely to require you to cancel far in advance.

APARTMENT AND HOUSE RENTALS

If you are interested in a single-destination vacation, or are staying in one place and using it as a base for exploring the local area, renting an apartment or a house can be a good idea. However, it is not always possible to ensure the quality beforehand, and you may be responsible for supplying your own bed linens, towels, etc.

Contacts **Holiday Lettings.** ⊕ *www.holiday-lettings.co.uk.* **Home Away.** ⊕ *www.homeaway. com.* **Interhome.** ☎ *800/882–6864* ⊕ *www. interhomeusa.com.* **Villas and Apartments Abroad.** ☎ *212/213–6435* ⊕ *www.vaanyc. com.* **Villas International.** ☎ *415/499–9490, 800/221–2260* ⊕ *www.villasintl.com.*

HOSTELS

Youth hostels (*albergues juveniles*) in Spain are usually large and impersonal (but clean) with dorm-style beds. Most are geared to students, though many have a few private rooms suitable for families and couples. These rooms fill up quickly, so book at least a month in advance.

Other budget options are the university student dorms (*residencia estudiantil*), some of which offer accommodations in summer, when students are away.

▌TIP→ **Note that in Spain hostales are not the same as the dorm-style youth hostels common elsewhere in Europe—they are inexpensive hotels with individual rooms, not communal quarters.**

Contacts **Hostelling International—USA.** ☎ *240/650–2100* ⊕ *www.hiusa.org.*

HOTELS AND BED-AND-BREAKFASTS

The Spanish government classifies hotels with one to five stars, with an additional rating of five-star GL (Gran Lujo) indicating the highest quality. Although quality is a factor, the rating is technically only an indication of how many facilities the hotel offers. For example, a three-star hotel may be just as comfortable as a four-star hotel but lack a swimming pool.

All hotel entrances are marked with a blue plaque bearing the letter *H* and the number of stars. The letter *R* (for *residencia*) after the letter *H* indicates an establishment with no meal service, with the possible exception of breakfast. The designations *fonda* (F), *pensión* (P), *casa de huéspedes* (CH), and *hostal* (Hs) indicate budget accommodations: these are no longer official categories, but you'll still find them across the country. In most cases, especially in smaller villages, rooms in such buildings will be basic but clean; in large cities, these rooms can be downright dreary.

When inquiring in Spanish about whether a hotel has a private bath, ask if it's an *habitación con baño*. Although a single room (*habitación sencilla*) is usually available, singles are often on the small side. Solo travelers might prefer to pay a bit extra for single occupancy of a double room (*habitación doble uso individual*). Make sure you request a double bed (*cama de matrimonio*) if you want one—if you don't ask, you will usually end up with two singles.

The Spanish love small country hotels and agritourism. Rusticae (⊕ *www.rusticae.es*) is an association of more than 170 independently owned hotels in restored palaces, monasteries, mills, and estates, generally in rural Spain. Similar associations serve individual regions, and tourist offices also provide lists of establishments. In Galicia, *pazos* are beautiful, old, often stately homes converted into small luxury hotels; Pazos de Galicia (⊕ *www.pazosdegalicia.com*) is the main organization for them. In Cantabria, *casonas* are small to large country houses, but they may not have individual websites, so check the regional tourist office websites for booking and contact information. If you're headed for Andalusia, the Asociación de Hoteles Rurales Andalucia (AHRA ⊕ *www.ahra.es*) is a useful resource.

A number of *casas rurales* (country houses similar to B&Bs) offer pastoral lodging either in guest rooms or in self-catering cottages. You may also come across the term *finca*, for country estate house. Many *agroturismo* accommodations are fincas converted to upscale B&Bs.

PARADORES

The Spanish government operates nearly 100 *paradores*—upscale hotels often in historic buildings or near significant sites. Rates are reasonable, considering that most paradores have four- or five-star amenities, and the premises are invariably immaculate and tastefully furnished, often with antiques or reproductions. Each parador has a restaurant serving regional specialties, and you can stop in for a meal without spending the night. Paradores are popular with foreigners and Spaniards alike, so make reservations well in advance.

Contact Paradores de España.
☎ *902/547979 in Spain, 818/884–1984 in U.S.*
⊕ *www.parador.es.*

■ COMMUNICATIONS

PHONES

The country code for Spain is 34. The country code is 1 for the United States and Canada.

If you're going to be traveling in Spain for an extended period, buy a local SIM card (ensure your phone is unlocked), use Skype or FaceTime, or install a free messager app on your smartphone, such as Viber or WhatsApp.

CALLING WITHIN SPAIN

Most area codes begin with a 9 (some begin with 8). To call within Spain—even locally—dial the area code first. Numbers preceded by a 900 code are toll-free in Spain; however, 90x numbers are not (e.g., 901, 902). Phone numbers starting with a 6 or 7 belong to mobile phones. Note that when calling a mobile phone, you do not need to dial the area code first.

■ ELECTRICITY

Spain's electrical current is 220–240 volts, 50 cycles alternating current (AC); wall outlets take Continental-type plugs, with two round prongs.

■ EMERGENCIES

The pan-European emergency phone number (☎ *112*) is operative in all of Spain, or you can dial the emergency numbers here for the national police, local police, fire department, or medical services. On the road, there are emergency phones marked "SOS" at regular intervals on autovías and autopistas. If your documents are stolen, contact both the local police and your embassy.

Foreign Embassies and Consulates

U.S. Embassy. ✉ *Calle Serrano 75, Madrid* ☎ *91/587–2200 for U.S.-citizen emergencies* ⊕ *es.usembassy.gov* ✉ *Paseo Reina Elisenda 23, Barcelona* ☎ *932/802227* ⊕ *es.usembassy.gov/embassy-consulates/barcelona.*

General Emergency Contacts Emergency telephone number. ☎ *112.* **Fire department.** ☎ *080.* **Local police.** ☎ *092.* **Medical service.** ☎ *061.* **National police.** ☎ *091.*

▌ HOURS OF OPERATION

The ritual of a long afternoon siesta is no longer as ubiquitous as it once was. However, the tradition does remain, and many people take a postlunch nap before returning to work or continuing on with their day. The two- to three-hour lunch break makes it possible to eat and then snooze. Midday breaks generally begin at 1 or 2 and end between 4 and 5, depending on the city and the sort of business. The midafternoon siesta—often a half-hour power nap in front of the TV—fits naturally into the workday cycle, since Spaniards tend to work until 7 or 8 pm.

Banks are generally open weekdays from 8:30 or 9 until 2 or 2:30. From October to May the major banks and savings banks open on Thursday until 6:30 or 7:30. Currency exchanges at airports, train stations, and in the city center stay open later; you can also cash traveler's checks at El Corte Inglés department stores until 10 pm (some branches close at 9 or 9:30). Most government offices are open weekdays 9–2.

Most museums are open from 9:30 to 2 and 4 to 7 or 8, every day but Monday. Schedules are subject to change, particularly between the high and low seasons, so confirm opening hours before you make plans. A few large museums, such as Madrid's Prado and Reina Sofía and Barcelona's Picasso Museum, stay open all day, without a siesta.

Pharmacies keep normal business hours (9–1:30 and 5–8), but every midsize town (or city neighborhood) has a duty pharmacy that stays open 24 hours. The location of the nearest on-duty pharmacy is usually posted on the front door of all pharmacies.

When planning a shopping trip, remember that almost all shops in Spain close from 1 or 2 pm for at least two hours. The only exceptions are large supermarkets and major chains, such as the department store El Corte Inglés. Most shops are closed on Sunday, and in Madrid and several other places they're also closed Saturday afternoon. Larger shops in tourist areas may stay open Sunday in summer and during the Christmas holiday.

HOLIDAYS

Spain's national holidays, observed countrywide, are New Year's Day on January 1 (*Año Nuevo*), Three Kings Day on January 6 (*Día de los Tres Reyes*), Good Friday (*Viernes Santo*), Labor Day on May 1 (*Día del Trabajo*), Assumption on August 15 (*Asunción*), Columbus Day on October 12 (*Día de la Hispanidad*), All Saints Day on November 1 (*Todos los Santos*), Constitution Day on December 6 (*Día de la Constitución*), Immaculate Conception on December 8 (*Immaculada Concepción*), and Christmas Day on December 25 (*Navidad*). Holidays observed in many parts of Spain, but not all, include Father's Day on March 19 (*San José,* observed in Madrid and some regional communities), Maundy Thursday (*Jueves Santo,*observed in most of Spain except Catalonia, Valencia, and the Balearic Islands), Easter Monday (*Día de Pascua,* observed in Catalonia, Valencia, and the Balearic Islands), St. John's Day on June 24, with bonfire celebrations the night before (*San Juan,* observed in Catalonia, Valencia, and the Balearic Islands), *Corpus Christi* (June), St. Peter and St. Paul Day on June 29 (*San Pedro y San Pablo*), and St. James Day on July 25 (*Santiago*). In addition, each region, city, and town has its own holidays honoring political events and patron saints.

Many stores close during *Semana Santa* (Holy Week—also sometimes translated as Easter Week), the week that precedes Easter.

▌ MAIL

Spain's postal system, or *correos*, does work, but delivery times vary widely. An airmail letter to the United States may take from four days to two weeks; delivery to other destinations is equally unpredictable. Sending your letters by priority mail (*urgente*) or the cheaper registered mail (*certificado*) ensures speedier and safer arrival.

Airmail letters to the United States cost €1.85 for up to 20 grams (¾ ounce). Letters within Spain are €0.65. Postcards carry the same rates as letters. You can buy stamps at licensed tobacco shops; post offices no longer sell stamps, but stamp mail with the correct amount.

Because mail delivery in Spain can often be slow and unreliable, it's best to have your mail held at a Spanish post office; have it addressed to "Lista de Correos" (the equivalent of *poste restante*) in a town you'll be visiting. Postal addresses should include the name of the province in parentheses, for example, Marbella (Málaga).

SHIPPING PACKAGES

When time is of the essence, or when you're sending valuable items or documents overseas, you can use a courier (*mensajero*). The major international agencies, such as FedEx, UPS, and DHL, have representatives in Spain; the biggest Spanish courier service is Seur. MRW is another local courier that provides express delivery worldwide.

Express Services Correos. ☎ *902/197197* ⊕ *www.correos.es.* **MRW.** ☎ *902/300400* ⊕ *www.mrw.es.* **Seur.** ☎ *902/101010* ⊕ *www. seur.com.*

▌ MONEY

ATMS AND BANKS

Your bank will probably charge a fee for using ATMs abroad; the foreign bank you use may also charge a fee. Nevertheless, you'll usually get a better rate of exchange at an ATM than you will at a currency-exchange office or even when changing money in a bank, and extracting funds as you need them is a safer option than carrying around a large amount of cash.

▌TIP➔ **PINs with more than four digits are not recognized at ATMs in Spain. If yours has five or more, remember to change it before you leave.**

You'll find ATMs in every major city in Spain, as well as in most smaller towns. ATMs will be part of the Cirrus and/or Plus networks and will allow you to withdraw euros with your credit or debit card, provided you have a valid PIN.

CURRENCY AND EXCHANGE

Since 2002, Spain has used the European monetary unit, the euro (€). Euro bills come in denominations of 5, 10, 20, 50, 100, 200, and 500; coins are worth 1 cent of a euro, 2 cents, 5 cents, 10 cents, 20 cents, 50 cents, 1 euro, and 2 euros. Forgery is quite commonplace in parts of Spain, especially with 50-euro notes. You can generally tell a forgery by the feel of the paper: counterfeits tend to be smoother than the legal notes, and the metallic line down the middle is darker than those in real bills. Local merchants (even those with counterfeit-spotting equipment) may refuse to accept €200 and €500 bills.

▌TIP➔ **Even if a currency-exchange booth has a sign promising no commission, rest assured that there's some kind of huge, hidden fee. (Oh ... that's right. The sign didn't say no fee.) And as for rates, you're almost always better off getting foreign currency at an ATM or exchanging money at a bank.**

■ PASSPORTS AND VISAS

Visitors from the United States need a passport valid for a minimum of six months to enter Spain.

■ TIP➔ Before your trip, make two copies of your passport's data page (one for someone at home and another for you to carry separately). Or scan the page and email it to someone at home and yourself.

VISAS

Visas are not necessary for those with U.S. passports valid for a minimum of six months and who plan to stay in Spain for tourist or business purposes for up to 90 days. Should you need a visa to stay longer than this, contact the Spanish consulate office nearest to you in the United States to apply for the appropriate documents.

■ TAXES

Value-added tax, similar to sales tax, is called I.V.A. in Spain (pronounced "*ee-vah*," for *impuesto sobre el valor añadido*). It's levied on both products and services, such as hotel rooms and restaurant meals. When in doubt about whether tax is included, ask, "*¿Está incluido el I.V.A.?*" The I.V.A. rate for hotels and restaurants is currently 10%, regardless of their number of stars. A special tax law for the Canary Islands allows hotels and restaurants there to charge 7% I.V.A. Menus will generally note at the bottom whether tax is included ("*I.V.A. incluido*") or not ("*más 10% I.V.A.*").

Although food, pharmaceuticals, and household items are taxed at the lowest rate (4%), most consumer goods are now taxed at 21%. A number of shops participate in Global Refund (formerly Europe Tax-Free Shopping), a V.A.T. refund service that makes getting your money back relatively hassle-free. You cannot get a refund on the V.A.T. for such items as meals or services such as hotel accommodations or taxi fares.

Global Blue is a Europewide service with 300,000 affiliated stores and more than 700 refund counters at major airports and border crossings. The refund form, called a Tax Free Check or Refund Cheque, is the most common across the European continent. The service issues refunds in the form of cash, check, or credit-card adjustment.

V.A.T. Refunds Global Blue. ☎ *866/706–6090 in U.S., 00800/3211–1111 in Spain (toll-free), weekdays 8–6* ⊕ *www.globalblue.com.*

■ TIME

Spain is on Central European Time, six hours ahead of Eastern Standard Time. Like the rest of the European Union, Spain switches to daylight saving time on the last weekend in March and switches back on the last weekend in October.

Time Zones Timeanddate.com. ⊕ *www.timeanddate.com/worldclock.*

■ TIPPING

Aside from tipping waiters and taxi drivers, Spaniards tend not to leave extra in addition to the bill. Restaurant checks do not list a service charge on the bill but consider the tip included. If you want to leave a small tip in addition to the bill, tip 5%–10% of the bill (and only if you think the service was worth it), and leave less if you eat tapas or sandwiches at a bar—just enough to round out the bill to the nearest €1.

Tip taxi drivers about 10% of the total fare, plus a supplement to help with luggage. Note that rides from airports carry an official surcharge plus a small handling fee for each piece of luggage.

Tip hotel porters €1 per bag and the bearer of room service €1. A doorman who calls a taxi for you gets €1. If you stay in a hotel for more than two nights, you can tip the maid about €1 per night, although it isn't generally expected.

Tour guides should be tipped about €2, barbers €0.50–€1, and women's hairdressers at least €1 for a wash and style. Restroom attendants are tipped €0.50.

■ TOURS

SPECIAL-INTEREST TOURS

Madrid and Beyond. An array of customized private luxury tours (no two are the same) are offered by this company, focusing on culinary, cultural, and sports-related themes. ☏ *91/758–0063 in Spain, 917/470–9460 in U.S.* ⊕ *www.madridandbeyond.com* ✉ *Prices available on application.*

Toma Tours. This company provides personalized and small-group tours with the focus on discovering Andalusia's culture, landscape, and gastronomy beyond the guidebook. ☏ *650/733116* ⊕ *tomaandcoe.com* ✉ *From €1690.*

ART

Atlas Travel Center/Escorted Spain Tours. Based in the United States, this company offers a range of tours with accents on art, cultural history, and the outdoors. ☏ *888/942–3301* ⊕ *www.escortedspaintours.com* ✉ *From €1030.*

Heritage Tours. Based in New York, this company helps arrange customized cultural tours based on your interests and budget. Guides are drawn from a network of curators, gallery owners, and art critics. ☏ *800/378–4555, 212/206–8400* ⊕ *www.heritagetours.com* ✉ *Prices vary.*

Olé Spain Tours. This guide offers art and historical tours to Spain. ☏ *915/515294* ⊕ *www.olespaintours.com* ✉ *From €310.*

BIRD-WATCHING

Discovering Doñana. In the Coto Doñana National Park in Andalusía, this company offers some of the best guided bird-watching tours and expeditions in Spain. ☏ *620/964369* ⊕ *www.discoveringdonana.com* ✉ *From €35.*

CULINARY AND WINE

Artisans of Leisure. This company offers personalized food-and-wine and cultural tours to Spain. ☏ *800/214–8144, 212/243–3239* ⊕ *www.artisansofleisure.com* ✉ *From €8560.*

Cellar Tours. Based in Madrid, Cellar Tours offers a wide array of wine and cooking tours to Spain's main wine regions. ☏ *911/436553 in Spain, 310/496–8061 in U.S.* ⊕ *www.cellartours.com* ✉ *From €2800.*

HIKING

Spain Adventures. This company offers hiking and biking around Spain, as well as unusual tours such as yoga and cooking. ☏ *772/564–0330* ⊕ *www.spainadventures.com* ✉ *From €3090.*

LANGUAGE PROGRAMS

Go Abroad. This is one of the best resources for language schools in Spain. ☏ *720/570–1702* ⊕ *www.goabroad.com.*

VOLUNTEER PROGRAMS

Go Abroad. This is the best resource for volunteering and finding paid internships in Spain. ☏ *720/570–1702* ⊕ *www.goabroad.com.*

INDEX

PHOTO CREDITS

/ age fotostock (501). Charles Bowman / age fotostock (507). Hidalgo & Lopesino / age fotostock (509). Alan Copson / age fotostock (512). **Chapter 9: Ibiza and the Balearic Islands:** Stuart Pearce / age fotostock (515). Bartomeu Amengual / age fotostock (518). Laurie Geffert Phelps (519). Rafael Campillo / age fotostock (519). Gardel Bertrand / age fotostock (520). Salvador Álvaro Nebot / age fotostock (521). Anibal Trejo/Shutterstock (521). Karolina Ksiazek/Shutterstock (522). Stuart Pearce / age fotostock (532). Skowron/Shutterstock (542). Hubertus Blume / age fotostock (548). Martin Siepmann / age fotostock (555). snap fotodesign / age fotostock (557). Gonzalo Azumendi / age fotostock (566). **Chapter 10: Andalusia:** José Fuste Raga / age fotostock (569). Seiffe / age fotostock (572). Carmen Martínez Banús/iStockphoto (573). ampFotoStudio/Shutterstock (573). Rieger Bertrand / age fotostock (574). Pyroshot I Dreamstime.com (575). Katja Kreder/imagebroker / age fotostock (575). Christine B. Patronick (576). Moirenc Camille / age fotostock (584). Johnny Stockshooter / age fotostock (591). Doug Scott / age fotostock (596). lbuchanan (602). riverside (604). Alessandra Sarti / age fotostock (609). S Tauqueur / age fotostock (613). Travel Pix Collection / age fotostock (616). Francisco Barba / age fotostock (618). Ken Welsh / age fotostock (620). Lucas Vallecillos / age fotostock (629). Thomas Dressler / age fotostock (634). Juergen Richter / age fotostock (643). Vladimir Korostyshevskiy/Shutterstock (649). JLImages / Alamy (649). Peter Horree / Alamy (650). Jerónimo Alba / age fotostock (651). Werner Otto / age fotostock (652). Sylvain Grandadam / age fotostock (652). Tony Wright/earthscapes / Alamy (652). Ken Welsh / age fotostock (652). Javier Larrea / age fotostock (653). Hideo Kurihara / Alamy (654). Javier Larrea / age fotostock (655{2}). Jeronimo Alba / age fotostock (661). **Chapter 11: Costa del Sol and Costa de Almeria:** Shutterstock/Artur Bogacki (669). Jochem Wijnands / age fotostock (672). gildemax/wikipedia.org (673). J.D. Dallet / age fotostock (673). J.D. Dallet / age fotostock (674). Public Domain (675). Claus Mikosch/iStockphoto (675). Freefly/iStockphoto (676). Daniela Sachsenheimer/Shutterstock (683). Herbert Scholpp / age fotostock (688). Judi / Fodors.com member (691). Ken Welsh / age fotostock (696). Renault Philippe / age fotostock (703). Jerónimo Alba / age fotostock (707). J.D. Dallet / age fotostock (713). Taka / age fotostock (716). J.D. Dallet / age fotostock (718). Freefly/iStockphoto (723). **About Our Writers:** All photos are courtesy of the writers.

NOTES

ABOUT OUR WRITERS

Lauren Frayer lived in Madrid for seven years and was the Madrid correspondent for National Public Radio and the *Los Angeles Times*. In summer 2018, Lauren moved to Mumbai to become NPR's India correspondent. She has also been based in Lisbon, Cairo, Jerusalem, Baghdad, and Washington. Her work has appeared on NPR and in the *New York Times* and the *Los Angeles Times*.

Benjamin Kemper followed the siren song of Ibérico ham from New York to Madrid, Spain, where he writes about the places that make him hungriest. The Caucasus, Portugal, France, and—por supuesto—Spain are his main beats. Beyond Benjamin's frequent collaborations with Fodor's, his work has appeared in the *Wall Street Journal*, *Condé Nast Traveler*, *AFAR*, *Smithsonian Magazine*, and *Travel + Leisure*, among other publications.

Originally from the north of England, **Elizabeth Prosser** has lived in Barcelona since 2007. When she is not indulging in her passion for travel, she works as a freelance writer and editor covering a range of topics including travel, lifestyle, property and technology for a range of print and online publications.

Joanna Styles is a freelance writer based in Malaga, Andalusia, just about the perfect place to live. Since she first spotted orange trees in the sunshine and the snow-capped Sierra Nevada, she's been passionate about Andalusia, its people, places, and culture. Thirty years later she's still discovering hidden corners. Joanna is the author of www.guidetomalaga.com.

Steve Tallantyre Steve Tallantyre is a British journalist and copywriter. He moved from Italy to Barcelona in the late 1990s. Married to a Catalan native, with two "Catalangles" children, Steve writes about the region's restaurants, and food culture for leading international publications. He also owns a popular blog about Barcelona cuisine ⊕ *www.foodbarcelona.com* and is the founder of a copywriting agency ⊕ *www.BCNcontent.com*.